U.S. Environmental Policy and Politics

U.S. Environmental Policy and Politics: A Documentary History

Kevin Hillstrom

CQ PRESS

A Division of SAGE
Washington, D.C.

CQ Press
2300 N Street, NW, Suite 800
Washington, DC 20037
Phone: 202-729-1900; toll-free, 1-866-4CQ-PRESS (1-866-427-7737)

Web: www.cqpress.com

Cover design: Naylor Design Inc.
Cover photo: ©iStockphoto.com
Composition: C&M Digitals (P) Ltd.

⊗ The paper used in this publication exceeds the requirements of the American National Standard for Information Sciences—Permanence of Paper for Printed Library Materials, ANSI Z39.48–1992.

Printed and bound in the United States of America

14   13   12   11   10   1   2   3   4   5

Library of Congress Cataloging-in-Publication Data

U.S. environmental policy and politics : a documentary history / [edited by] Kevin Hillstrom.
    p. cm.
  Includes bibliographical references and index.
    ISBN 978-1-60426-475-3 (hardcover : alk. paper) 1. Environmental policy—United States—History—Sources. 2. Environmental policy—United States—History. 3. Environmentalism—United States—History—Sources. 4. Environmentalism—United States—History. I. Hillstrom, Kevin II. Title: United States environmental policy and politics.

  GE180.U185 2010
  333.720973—dc22

                                                2010008570

Contents

6. ENVIRONMENTAL POLICY-MAKING DURING THE NEW DEAL (1920–1940)   272

ENVIRONMENTAL POLICY TRENDS IN POSTWAR AMERICA   272

ENVIRONMENTAL HEALTH IN THE WORKPLACE   274

COMPETING VISIONS AND AGENCY RIVALRIES   276

THE FOREST SERVICE–PARK SERVICE RIVALRY   277

NEW DEAL CONSERVATION AND THE CIVILIAN CONSERVATION CORPS   279

WATER PROJECTS OF THE NEW DEAL ERA   281

RESPONDING TO THE DUST BOWL   283

CHANGING PERSPECTIVES ON WILDLIFE   285

Documents

7. ENVIRONMENTAL POLITICS IN THE AGE OF SUBURBANIZATION (1940–1960)   336

THE ARSENAL OF DEMOCRACY   336

THE POSTWAR SUBURBANIZATION BOOM   338

9. PUBLIC HEALTH AND ENVIRONMENTAL REGULATION (1980–PRESENT)

Documents

11. ENERGY POLICY AND GLOBAL CLIMATE CHANGE   662

Documents

Thematic Table of Contents

Documents

ENERGY SOURCES AND PRODUCTION

FORESTRY

GOVERNANCE AND REGULATION

HAZARDOUS MATERIALS AND WASTE DISPOSAL

HUNTING AND WILDLIFE PRESERVATION

LAND DEVELOPMENT AND CONTINENTAL EXPANSION

MINING

NATIONAL PARKS, MONUMENTS, AND PROTECTED LANDS

NATIVE AMERICANS

Preface

U.S. Environmental Policy and Politics: A Documentary History is part of CQ Press's new retrospective and topical documentary history series. These volumes are based on the same formula that has made CQ Press's acclaimed Historic Documents series a mainstay of public, university, and high school library collections across the country: carefully selected primary sources supplemented with authoritative original writing that provides vital context for featured documents.

But unlike the original Historic Documents series, which uses primary documents to chronicle worldwide events in politics, economics, health, and other areas in a single calendar year, these new volumes are devoted to providing users with detailed information on a single major aspect of American history from the colonial era to the twenty-first century. This inaugural volume focuses on environmental policy and politics.

OVERVIEW OF COVERAGE

CQ Press selected environmental policy as the subject for its inaugural volume of the retrospective series because of the pivotal role that natural resources—and the consumption and stewardship thereof—have played in shaping the society we live in today. As with every volume of the series, *U.S. Environmental Policy and Politics* provides a broad cross-section of essential and illuminating primary source documents from various eras in American history. Many of the 150 primary source documents featured in this book are essential to any meaningful study of America's evolving attitudes and policies toward the environment—and the ways in which environmental concerns have intersected over the years with issues of energy consumption, government regulation, economic growth, and lifestyle choices. These selections are further supplemented with revealing, hard-to-find primary documents that provide fascinating insights into the perspectives of lawmakers, conservation organizations, business interests, and scientists on environmental issues and events of the day.

The book consists of a wide range of document types drawn from both governmental and nongovernmental sources. Legislative acts, presidential speeches, court decisions, and international agreements provide students with documentation of government action and political debate. Examples of these primary sources include the Indian Removal Act (1830), the Yellowstone Act (1872), the Endangered Species Act (1973), and the Kyoto Protocol (1997).

In addition to essential government resources, the volume includes extensive coverage of essays, novels, and investigative works that have shaped the direction and tenor of environmental politics and policy–making in the United States. Excerpts are included from such works as George Perkins Marsh's *Man and Nature* (1864), Upton Sinclair's *The Jungle* (1906), and Rachel Carson's *Silent Spring* (1962).

Finally, *U.S. Environmental Policy and Politics* features numerous lesser-known but fascinating primary documents that illuminate America's historic struggle to balance environmental protection with economic development, private property rights, and other societal considerations. These documents, which provide valuable insights into the evolution of environmental policy and politics in the United States, include a 1739 newspaper column by Ben Franklin urging the passage of municipal legislation to reduce air and water pollution in Philadelphia; an 1893 railroad brochure, "6,000 Miles Through Wonderland," that beckons early American tourists to explore the natural wonders of the West; and congressional testimony from 2007 hearings about uranium poisoning on Navajo lands.

Together, this collection of primary sources constitutes a unique, unparalleled resource for the study of American attitudes and policy–making on environmental and conservation issues from the colonial era to the present day. The wide breadth of coverage enables readers to explore the many ways in which past policy decisions and political attitudes have shaped modern environmental policy–making—and to understand why some political battles over environmental protection and natural resource development have flared up again and again over the generations. By studying America's responses to past environmental crises, readers also will be better equipped to analyze the various solutions being proposed to combat growing manifestations of global warming, potentially catastrophic levels of species extinction, escalating freshwater shortages, and other pressing environmental issues of the twenty-first century. Finally, *U.S. Environmental Policy and Politics* provides users with in-depth coverage of individual environmental issues of high interest to readers, including wilderness preservation, endangered species protection, toxic waste disposal, urban sprawl, air and water pollution, logging and mining practices, global climate change, and environmental justice.

ORGANIZATION OF THE BOOK

One of the chief goals of the topical documentary histories is to show how every featured primary document fits into the larger story of America's historical development. To meet this mandate and explain how each primary source document is a response—in one way or another—to America's ever-evolving political, cultural, environmental, and demographic landscape, the author places great emphasis on providing historical context for understanding in each volume.

To that end, this volume is organized into thematic chapters. Most of the documents featured in these chapters are organized in chronological order, although a few are arranged by subject matter. Each chapter opens with an introductory overview that puts the chapter's featured primary documents in a larger social, political, economic, and scientific context. These informative chapter overviews introduce the main players, events, and themes that will be fleshed out in the documents to come. In addition, each primary document is supplemented with an authoritative headnote that provides readers with additional historical background about the document in question. These introductory notes provide additional details (who, what, where, when, why) about the circumstances under which the featured document was created. Together, these two narrative features provide users with a full understanding of the myriad forces that converged in the making of each document. Many of the documents have been excerpted to provide readers with the essential portions of the documents. In all cases, a full citation to the original can be found at the end of the document. A chronology of major environmental laws and events in U.S. history, a bibliography of sources consulted in the production of the book, and a subject index complete the book.

Acknowledgments

Many librarians, archivists, and researchers assisted me at various junctures in this project. Special thanks go out to Shannon Bowen at the American Heritage Center at the University of Wyoming, Cliff McCarthy of the Connecticut Valley Historical Museum, Andrea Mauck and John Brucksch at the National Park Service's Harpers Ferry Center, and Susan Searcy at the Nevada State Archives. I would also like to extend my appreciation to the entire staff at the Brighton District Library in Brighton, Michigan, for their unfailing professionalism and good humor. I was also greatly aided by Doug Goldenberg-Hart, Andrew Boney, and Emily Bakely at CQ Press, all of whom provided valuable guidance and timely assistance throughout the production of this book.

Introduction

When European colonists first settled in the New World, they brought philosophies of economic development, land ownership, and spiritual betterment predicated on taming the American wilderness and exploiting the spectacular bounty of natural resources contained therein. They placed few restrictions on the consumption of timber, minerals, soil, water, fish and game, and other "limitless" assets found in colonial America or on the disposal of waste materials generated by the sawmills, tanneries, plantations, and farming settlements that sprouted ever deeper in the American interior.

This state of affairs endured long after the establishment of the United States. Deep into the nineteenth century, in fact, the intertwined imperatives of geographic expansion, economic growth, and national pride all worked in tandem to extract, consume, and reshape the riches contained in the continent's forests, prairies, waterways, and mountain ranges. These alterations of the natural environment, carried out without regard for their ecological consequences, proved cataclysmic for Native American tribes and once-prolific species such as bison and the passenger pigeon, all of whom were swept aside by the onslaught of steamboats, railroad locomotives, telegraph lines, surveying stakes, and plows. These losses were mourned only by a relative few; the rest of the young nation hurtled forward across the land at breakneck speed, eager to lay claim to the next timber stand, mineral deposit, or crop-sustaining river over the horizon.

By the early twentieth century, however, the evidence of intensifying environmental degradation—entire states skinned of their forests; plummeting populations of various species of wild game; and rivers strangled by the detritus of mining, farming, and logging operations—became impossible for some policymakers and citizens to ignore. Such giants of American conservation history as President Theodore Roosevelt, Forest Service chief Gifford Pinchot, and Sierra Club founder John Muir emerged during this time. Their passion for their cause, their ability to inspire fellow citizens to appreciate the value of wilderness, and their understanding of the importance of sustainable resource use helped make the Progressive Era the first great age of environmental law in U.S. history. In addition, these environmental pioneers branded on the American consciousness the revolutionary but wholly democratic idea that government policies should ensure that, as Roosevelt put it in his autobiography, "the rights of the public to the natural resources outweigh private rights." These principles were further codified into American thought during the New Deal era of the 1930s, when the federal government implemented ambitious environmental programs to combat the Dust Bowl, deforestation, and other problems.

As these new environmental laws, regulations, and agencies were unfurled across the continent, they enjoyed fairly broad public acceptance. But they also aroused the deep and lasting enmity of a wide array of industrial titans, western politicians, land speculators, states' rights advocates, and other opponents. These detractors assailed the new conservationist policies as an affront to American capitalism and an assault on individual freedoms. And these charges did not subside over time. To the contrary, they were repeated again and again during the ensuing decades, even as the scaffolding of municipal, state, and federal environmental laws steadily grew to address air and water pollution, land loss through development, and other negative consequences of population growth, technological advancement, and economic expansion.

The next momentous era of environmental law and policy took place during the 1960s and 1970s. During this "golden age" of environmentalism, a host of important and politically popular federal agencies and laws came into being, from the Environmental Protection Agency (created in 1970) to the Endangered Species Act (established in 1973). But this surge in federal oversight of both industrial and individual behavior sparked fresh rounds of furious argument between conservative and liberal constituencies about the efficacy and desirability of environmental laws that governed everything from toxic waste disposal and wilderness preservation to economic development of private property.

By the close of the 1990s, these divergent philosophies of governance and environmental stewardship—debated again and again throughout the administrations of Presidents Ronald Reagan, George H. W. Bush, and Bill Clinton—had widened the ideological chasm between the Republican and Democratic parties to an unprecedented level. These partisan tensions further escalated during the 2001 to 2009 administration of George W. Bush. Bush's "smart regulation" policies ignited numerous rhetorical firefights in Congress and various media outlets over the merits of a vast array of environmental laws and regulations—and the impact of those provisions on ecosystem preservation, economic opportunity, energy independence, individual liberty, and the lives of future generations of Americans.

Environmental politics and policy–making in the United States, then, has come a long way in the past four centuries. The first European colonists to arrive on America's shores were loath to institute *any* restrictions on wilderness development and natural resource exploitation and consumption. Today, however, environmental laws are integral and much-debated elements of our society, shaping the ways that we live, work, play, and otherwise relate to the world around us on a daily basis. This book aims to show not only how this evolution took place, but also to explain why these policies have had such a profound impact on the wider arc of American history.

CHAPTER 1

Seizing Land and
Riches in the New World

1600–1800

During the sixteenth and seventeenth centuries, Native American tribes that had lived and prospered for centuries without any inkling of continents beyond their own were confronted with a disorienting infusion of explorers and emigrants from distant lands. These newcomers—settlers and traders and missionaries—were garbed strangely and spoke unfamiliar languages. The Indians who ranged across the North American continent were able to familiarize themselves with these new customs and languages over time. But other European imports proved much more difficult for them to process, understand, and withstand. The European colonists brought strange and baffling philosophies about land ownership, religion, and economic development to the New World—as well as a host of deadly pathogens and invasive species. In addition, the new arrivals carried with them a mindset of ecological conquest that put them at fundamental odds with the worldview of the indigenous peoples of North America. As one environmental historian summarized, "[T]hey brought with them European ideas of what the New World was—and visions of what it should be."[1]

THE WORLD THEY FOUND

The earliest European colonists to land in America found a continent teeming with Native American tribes, each with their own unique culture and relationship to the land and natural resources that sustained them. Historians estimate that the native population of North America at the beginning of the seventeenth century ranged somewhere between four and ten million people. The vast majority of these Indians lived deep in the interior and had little or no contact with Europeans. Some tribes along the North Atlantic seaboard, however, became drawn into the fur trade during the sixteenth century. This system, in which Indians traded the pelts of beaver and other fur-bearing animals to European trading companies in exchange for decorative beads, brass kettles, fishing hooks, iron-bladed tools, and other manufactured goods, marked the first incursion of European-style commerce and concepts of natural resource exploitation into the New World.

Still, the hand of the British crown remained light on the New World until the early 1600s, when the first permanent English colonies established tenuous footholds on the rugged eastern ramparts of Virginia and New England. The Jamestown settlement, established in the Virginia Colony in 1607, and the Plymouth settlement, founded in

PENN'S TREATY WITH THE INDIANS.

European colonists acquired land and resources from Native American tribes by a variety of means, from formal treaty agreements that heavily favored colonial interests to outright seizures of traditional Indian hunting and farming grounds.

modern-day Massachusetts in 1620, heralded the beginning of a new and fateful chapter in Native American–European relations.

The first colonists to arrive in America were overwhelmed by the wild vitality of the natural world that confronted them—and they were dumbstruck by the wealth of game, fish, timber, and tillable land glittering before their eyes. "If I should tell you how some have killed a hundred geese in a week, fifty ducks at a shot, forty teals at another, it may be counted impossible though nothing [is] more certain,"[2] marveled one Englishman in 1634. It did not take long for these intrepid pioneers to make a basic calculation: If they could bend the "vast and empty chaos"[3] looming before them to their will, then they would be positioned to secure the political, religious, and economic freedoms that had eluded them back in the Old World **(see Document 1.1)**.

The colonists recognized that the Indians who already occupied these lands were at the very least a complicating factor in these ambitious plans—and at worst loomed as a serious impediment to their realization. After all, as many as 20,000 Algonquin-speaking natives lived in coastal Virginia at the time of Jamestown's founding.[4] Even greater numbers of Indians—from 70,000 to 144,000—made their homes in the woods of southern New England, where the Plymouth and Massachusetts Bay (founded in 1629) colonies were located.[5]

Still, the picture was not entirely bleak. The English settlers were heartened by the realization that the local Indian tribes had not made many European-style "improvements" to the land. The indigenous peoples of the Eastern Seaboard had cleared some lowland forest areas to plant modest fields of corn, beans, and squash, and they used fire as a forest management tool to create grassy pastures for deer. These land-clearing practices created open parklike expanses in some parts of the eastern forestland and promoted the development of a "mosaic" of New England ecosystems with "forests in many different states of ecological succession."[6] But the Indians' role in shaping these natural landscapes was not widely recognized or adequately appreciated. And in many other respects they did simply live off the land, hunting for meat and animal skins and foraging for nuts and other dietary staples. To the European eye, this sustenance-oriented relationship with the land cast the Indians' "ownership" of the New World into serious doubt.

RATIONALIZING LAND ACQUISITION

The colonists thus went about the process of acquiring the land and resources they needed from the current occupants—and perfecting their rationalizations for the methodologies they employed to do so. Eager to convert the natural resources of the New World into commodities that could be harvested, packaged, and shipped to Europe for financial gain, they decided that the Indians had been so derelict in exploiting the natural bounty around them that they had in essence forfeited their right of ownership. As John Winthrop, governor of the Massachusetts Bay Colony (modern-day Boston), explained, "[T]he Natives in New England . . . inclose noe Land, neither have any settled habitation, nor any tame Cattle to improve the Land by, and soe have noe other but a Naturall Right to those countries, soe as if we leave them sufficient for their use, we may lawfully take the rest."[7]

The early colonial settlers also seized on religious justifications for the taking of Indian land. "Puritans insisted that the Christian God meant for them to enjoy the land, in reward for their godly industry, and to punish the Indians for their pagan indolence," observed historian Alan Taylor. "The colonists appointed themselves to judge how much land the Indians needed, which shrank with every passing year. The resolves of the town of Milford in Connecticut in 1640 were especially blunt: 'voted that the earth is the Lord's and the fulness thereof; voted, that the earth is given to the Saints; voted, we are the Saints.'"[8]

Ultimately, however, the colonists recognized that they needed to find a legal basis for their plans to take New World land and convert its raw resources into profitable farm land and lucrative commodities for trade. They quickly settled on two principles that were widely accepted in Europe at the time. The first principle was that land that had not been "subdued" could be seized by someone who intended to improve it through European-style cultivation or other economic development. English concepts of land tenure thus recognized the Indians' ownership of tilled fields but not of the land they used for foraging or hunting. The second principle was that Christians could legitimately assert sovereignty over non-Christian "savages" and their territories.[9] A few early colonists, most notably Roger Williams of the Massachusetts Bay Colony, objected to this supremely convenient line of thought, but defenses of Native American rights attracted few adherents among the other settlers.

Still, the British colonists proceeded carefully. They were cognizant of the fact that England and other European nations had entered into previous treaties with various tribes, which gave the latter a patina of legal legitimacy. More important, the military superiority of the Indian tribes during the early years of colonization precluded any notions of outright land seizures. With this in mind, the early settlers were instructed to offer "reasonable" compensation to Indians for their lands so "that wee may avoyde the least scruple of intrusion."[10]

In addition, there existed in some colonial quarters a genuine desire to treat the indigenous Americans with a measure of deference and respect. "The Indians . . . are the Bulwark of this Settlement," declared the South Carolina Board of Trade in 1713. "Suffer not the Traders to cheat and use them with insolence."[11] Other early settlers in New England and elsewhere sought to coax the "savages" into Christianity and European-style farming techniques. This was a condescending and paternalistic approach, but it at least conveyed an appreciation of the intrinsic humanity and worth of the Indians.

These attitudes never became ascendant among the European settlements, however. Instead, the early land transfers that took place between settlers and Native Americans in colonial America swiftly ratcheted up tensions between the two camps. These tensions arose because the two sides had fundamentally different understandings of what the agreements meant. When the Indians signed land deeds in exchange for trade goods, they believed that they were simply agreeing to share the land with the colonists. They recognized that the Europeans would build permanent dwellings, clear some of the land in question for farming, and erect fences for livestock, but Native Americans also believed that they would continue to have free rein to hunt and fish and forage on the land.

They were quickly and firmly disabused of this assumption by the colonists, who approached the deals armed with European concepts of private property. The colonists asserted that once the Indians sold a parcel of land and the property came under English jurisdiction, the Indians had no right to set foot on that land again without the permission of the new owner. And that permission was generally not forthcoming from early colonists and settlers who saw every tree and pelt and acre of land as an essential weapon in their ongoing battle for survival (in the early years of colonization) and upward economic mobility (after settlements became well-established). Indeed, harassment and arrest of Indian "trespassers" on newly private lands escalated in both the New England and Virginia colonies from the 1630s forward.

In some cases, land transfers were worded in ways that gave Indians ongoing rights to hunt, fish, and forage. These types of arrangements were most commonplace in the first half of the seventeenth century, when the European presence in the New World was still tenuous. But as the settlements grew in size and strength, these access rights were often stripped away from the Indians, who usually had no recourse but to retreat deeper into the continent interior (**see Document 1.2**).

ESCALATING PRESSURE ON INDIANS AND RESOURCES

By the mid-seventeenth century, Native American tribes from the upper Great Lakes to the Chesapeake Bay were reeling from the changes occurring all across their historical homelands. European incursions seemed to be taking place everywhere they turned. Dutch colonists led by Henry Hudson established permanent settlements in present-day New York, while Dutch traders penetrated southern New England and present-day Pennsylvania. Further west, French trading companies carved out a lucrative fur trade among the Chippewa, Huron, Ottawa, and other Great Lakes tribes.

The English presence along the Eastern Seaboard, meanwhile, continued to inexorably expand, to the growing consternation of the indigenous population. In Virginia, relations between the colonists and the resident Indians, a confederacy of tribes known as the Powhatans or Virginia Algonquins, soured quickly. Settlers pressured Indians to sign over valuable tracts of land—especially land that had already been cleared by the Indians—so that they could expand production of their valuable tobacco crop. In return, the Native Americans received assurances that other lands would remain theirs in perpetuity, but these promises were not kept. Instead, white settlers increasingly encroached on the diminishing acres of fields and game-filled woods still held by the Powhatans. Meanwhile, the colony's population was continually replenished by tall-masted ships that appeared on the horizon with ominous frequency.

The Powhatans ultimately responded to the escalating threat with violence—a pattern that would be repeated by other desperate Indian tribes all across the continent over the next century and a half. These attacks removed any lingering remorse that the colonists might have felt about their land-grabbing tactics. "There is scarce any man amongst us that doth soe much as afforde [the Indians] a good thought in his hart and most men . . . give them nothinge but maledictions and bitter execrations," wrote one Jamestown resident in 1621.[12]

The settlers relentlessly pushed the indigenous population deeper into the interior, taking full advantage of their comparatively advanced weaponry and their growing advantages in numbers. This expanding numerical superiority stemmed in part from dropping mortality rates in the stabilizing colonial settlements and steady infusions of new emigrants from overseas. By 1660, in fact, Virginia and Maryland housed more than 35,000 colonists—the majority of them native-born—and by the close of the seventeenth century more than 100,000 settlers lived in Virginia, Maryland, and the Carolinas.[13] But the single biggest factor in the expanding European domination of the region was the collapse of Indian populations from disease.

The same basic sequence of events unfolded in New England. Settlers moved steadily inland, bolstered by new waves of immigration, the increased vitality of their extraction-based economy, and the ever-weakening negotiating position of the disease-wracked native tribes. By 1660 New England contained more than twice as many European settlers as the thriving Virginia colonies, and it became the epicenter of the New World trade in fish, timber, crops, furs, and other commodities that could be extracted from the retreating wilderness.

Frustrated and desperate Indians attempted to stem the tide of encroachment but to no avail. In many cases, they initially tried to negotiate with the Europeans, appealing to their sense of honor and the Indians' deteriorating circumstances. "You know our fathers had plenty of deer . . . and our coves [were] full of fish and fowl," charged the Narragansett chief Miantonomi in 1642. "But these English have gotten our land, they with scythes cut down the grass, and with axes fell the trees; their cows and horses eat the grass, and their hogs spoil our clam banks, and we shall be starved."[14] When these entreaties failed—sometimes sooner, sometimes later—the Indians took up arms against the white New Englanders, most notably in the Pequot War of 1637–1638 and the gruesome King Philip's War of 1675–1676. These wars took many white lives, but they took a far greater toll on Native American populations across the New England region.

This decline in tribal power forced Native Americans to accede to European principles of law—especially in the realm of land ownership and resource use—which they still did not fully grasp. "The individual Indian became more and more subject to white codes of law and white regulation of his activities," summarized one historian. "The 'Indian Country' came gradually to be delimited by white surveyors rather than by Indian warriors"[15] (**see Document 1.7**).

EXPLOITATION OF LAND AND PEOPLES IN THE SOUTH AND WEST

Similar patterns of steadily diminishing Indian access to land and resources unfurled in other parts of the continent. In the Southwest, the establishment of Spanish missions and presidios brought wrenching changes to the lives of indigenous peoples and the natural resources on which they depended. Horses, cattle, and sheep carried to the New World by the invaders completely exhausted area grasslands, then moved out in ever-widening circles from the Spanish missions and presidios. The Spanish also took control of huge expanses of land that had been used for hunting and farming by countless generations of Indians. With their traditional means of subsistence stripped from them, the region's Native American population was reduced to peasantry. "The Indians of California," wrote one historian, "were driven from a changed countryside into missions where they were forced to seek a subsistence in non-native crops and European methods of agriculture. Within the compass of a single generation, Indians saw the world around them come undone."[16]

Along the Gulf Coast and the Mississippi River, the population of the so-called "Petites Nations"—a French term for the many small tribes in the region—plummeted as a result of exposure to diseases carried by Europeans and warfare sparked by intertribal jockeying for position with Spanish, French, and English traders. The Indians' spiraling dependence on the alcohol, guns, and other commodities offered by traders also led them to adopt a rapacious attitude toward the wild game and other natural resources that had sustained their people for so long. For example, French Louisiana's governor, Jean Baptiste le Moyne, Sieur de Bienville, reported in February 1743 that "the trade in deerskins [exported back to France] amounts at present to more than one hundred thousand pounds" annually. Because the average deerskin pelt averaged two pounds each, this meant that 50,000 deer were harvested for their skins in that year alone.[17]

The Petites Nations also sought to accommodate the new power in their midst in other ways, such as by abandoning their traditional religious beliefs for Christianity. But white encroachment, dwindling resources, and plagues of disease overwhelmed them. As Bienville himself wrote, "It is known that this country . . . was formerly the most densely populated with Indians, but at present of these prodigious quantities of different nations one sees only pitiful remnants."[18]

Even the native Indians who made their homes on Alaska's rugged and remote Aleutian Islands were not immune to the phenomenon of white invasion. During the course of the eighteenth century, Russian hunters known as *promyshlenniki* descended on the islands to harvest the region's large populations of sea otters (for their fur) and Steller's sea cows (for their meat, skin, and fat, which could be converted into a prized fuel for oil lamps). The predations of these market hunters caused Aleutian sea otter populations to crash and resulted in the outright extinction of Steller's sea cows.

The impact of the *promyshlenniki* on native tribes was similarly dire. The Russian hunters frequently stormed entire Aleut villages and held women and children captive. To obtain their freedom, the Aleut men had to hand over huge numbers of sea otter pelts. Acquiring this ransom required months of hunting, during which time the *promyshlenniki* used Aleut women as sex slaves. This ordeal exposed the Aleutians to new sexually transmitted diseases; destroyed community bonds; and ushered in widespread malnutrition and near-starvation because the extortion left Aleutian hunters with little time to harvest the fish, seals, whales, and other dietary staples on which their villages depended. From the 1740s to the end of the century, these outside pressures reduced the Aleut population by 90 percent and depopulated entire islands that had once harbored thriving villages.[19]

Not all tribes that had extensive contact with European traders and settlements suffered such humiliations or near-extirpations. In the upstate region of the New York colony, for example, the Iroquois Confederacy or Six Nations—comprised of the Onondaga, Oneida, Mohawk, Seneca, Cayuga, and Tuscarora tribes—remained formidable well into the eighteenth century, despite serious struggles with smallpox and other imported diseases. Their continued vitality was in large measure a testament to their skill in setting English and French colonial interests against one another. But their stand was in essence a centuries-long rear-guard action against an ever-strengthening foe that placed greater value on fish, timber, and pelts than on the rights and welfare of the indigenous people.

In 1659, for example, one party of Mohawks made a fairly representative complaint when they asserted that Dutch traders "say we are brothers and are joined together with chains, but that lasts only as long as we have beavers. After that, we are no longer thought of."[20]

EPIDEMICS AND CHANGING LAND USE IN AMERICA

In virtually every corner of the continent, the single greatest factor that aided European settlers in their quest to acquire land and natural resources was the debilitating impact of new diseases on indigenous people. Deadly pathogens brought to the New World by European colonists and traders wiped out huge numbers of Indians with stunning speed. The epidemics severely reduced Indians' capacity to defend their hunting grounds and agricultural fields from European incursions. As their numbers diminished, many tribes felt they had no choice but to sign land deeds and treaties that steadily reduced their access to the most desirable woods, rivers, lakes, and fields in their territory. And because the European colonizers exploited these newly acquired lands much more intensively, these transfers had huge ecological consequences.

The epidemics that tore through the New World's indigenous populations after European contact reached nightmarish dimensions for several reasons. First, their distant ancestors' multigenerational passage from Asia into North America kept them in arctic and subarctic environments that were inhospitable to most pathogens. This extended exposure to cold conditions acted as a sort of filter, so that as Indians migrated further south they left many communicable diseases behind. Second, precontact Indians scattered over wide geographical areas and did not establish large, permanent, heavily crowded communities that can serve as breeding grounds for many communicable diseases. These factors did not completely insulate Native Americans from deadly diseases—home-grown diseases such as tuberculosis, hepatitis, and syphilis all took a toll on various peoples—but these threats never metastasized into full-blown annihilation.

When Europeans came to the New World in the sixteenth and seventeenth centuries, however, they brought with them a multitude of deadly diseases—smallpox, measles, typhus, malaria, cholera, diphtheria, yellow fever, and others—that had incubated in crowded, filthy population centers of Europe and Asia *after* the Paleo-Indians had crossed the Bering Land Bridge and disappeared into the Americas. Moreover, these colonists and traders kept domesticated livestock that carried their own microscopic parasites. They thus unknowingly exported all of these pathogens to the New World, where they spread like wildfire among a native population that had no immunological defenses against them. As one historian summarized, "[T]he breath, blood, sweat, and lice of the colonizers (and of their livestock and rats) . . . depopulate[ed] the lands that they wanted for settlement"[21] (**see Document 1.4**).

The first epidemics in the New World occurred in the early sixteenth century during Spain's brutal colonization of the Caribbean, Central America, Mexico, and parts of the American Southwest and Southeast. The next dark wave of death struck the tribes who made their homes along a broad swath of Atlantic coastline from Canada's Gaspé Peninsula to the Virginia Colony in the early seventeenth century. These epidemics of the late 1500s were triggered by native contact with European fur traders and fishermen, and they actually predated the establishment of the Jamestown and Plymouth colonies. In 1616, for instance, the French Jesuit missionary Pierre Biard wrote that native groups in Maine and Nova Scotia "often complain that, since the French mingle with and carry on trade with them, they are dying fast."[22]

The devastation wreaked by these pathogens further escalated in the 1630s and 1640s, as European settlements expanded. One colonist in Massachusetts, for instance, recorded in the early 1630s that "whole towns" of Algonquin Indians "were swept away [by smallpox], in some not so much as one soul escaping Destruction."[23] Plymouth Governor William Bradford, meanwhile, provided an especially chilling assessment of a 1634 outbreak of smallpox among the natives of the upper Connecticut River Valley:

> Usually they that have of this disease have them in abundance, and for want of bedding and linen and other helps, they fall into a lamentable condition as they lie on their hard mats, the pox breaking and mattering and running one into another, their skin cleaving by reason thereof to the mats they lie on. When they turn, a whole side will flay off at once as it were, and they will be all of a gore blood, most fearful to behold. And then, being very sore, what with cold and other distempers, they die like rotten sheep.[24]

To be sure, some of these diseases also took a heavy toll on white settlements in the second half of the seventeenth century. Epidemics swept through towns such as Boston and Charleston periodically, claiming 10 percent or more of the population in individual outbreaks.[25] But the Indians' complete lack of immunity to these pathogens had even more harrowing consequences. By the mid-seventeenth century, Native American groups up and down the Atlantic coast had been broken by these plagues. "The Indians affirm," said one Dutch settler in 1650, "that before the arrival of the Christians, and before the small pox broke out amongst them, they were ten times as numerous as they now are."[26]

As white settlers made inroads deeper into the American continent, this grim tableau played out again and again. The tribes of the South, the Great Lakes, the Great Plains and Intermountain West, and the Pacific Coast all suffered mightily from exposure to European diseases during the eighteenth and nineteenth centuries. And whenever smallpox or diphtheria or some other killer raged through a region, it further reduced the capacity of area tribes to keep a grip on the land and resources that had nurtured them and their way of life for generations. "The American land was more like a widow than a virgin," summarized historian Francis Jennings. "Europeans did not find a wilderness here; rather, however involuntarily, they made one. Jamestown, Plymouth, Salem, Boston, Providence, New Amsterdam, Philadelphia—all grew upon sites previously occupied by Indian communities. . . . The so-called settlement of America was a *re*settlement, a reoccupation of a land made waste by the diseases and demoralization introduced by the newcomers"[27] **(see Document 1.9)**.

LAND DEVELOPMENT POLICIES IN THE COLONIES

As the colonies steadily expanded in size, they disrupted surrounding ecosystems in a host of ways, large and small. But although some of the settlers' efforts to carve new lives for themselves in the New World were environmentally destructive, the context in which these activities took place has to be understood. "The seventeenth-century settler did not look on wilderness with the eyes of a . . . Sierra Club backpacker," wrote Wallace Stegner:

> Our wilderness is safe, theirs was not. Our wilderness is islands in a tamed continent, theirs was one vast wild space, totally unknown, prowled by God-knew-what wild beasts and wild men. In New England

they also feared it as the trysting place of witches and devils. Even without devils, the struggle to survive fully occupied the first generation or two, and survival meant, in man's version of God's word, "subduing" the wild earth. Nobody questioned the value of that effort. Civilization was a good; wilderness was what had to be subdued to create the human habitations that looked like progress and triumph even when they were only huts in a stump field.[28]

The early colonies pursued starkly different policies of land settlement and development in this civilizing quest. These differing strategies stemmed in large part from the fact that the British crown never put together any sort of grand strategy or overall policy for New World land development. Some colonization companies and proprietors had been established through grants from the king (who retained title to the lands). But the various legal and economic restrictions and conditions specified in these charters varied considerably from document to document. And in the case of the Pennsylvania colony, the land that founder William Penn received in the New World was actually a payment for royal debts owed to his father.[29] But even though the terms granted to colonial proprietors and charter companies by the king varied in some respects, all charters were predicated on actual physical possession of the land.

The legal boundaries stipulated in these charters were another major factor in the development of the individual colonies. Colonies that were surrounded by other colonies, such as Maryland, Delaware, and Rhode Island, only had limited space to expand. But colonies such as Virginia and Georgia, which had open borders to the west, were able to claim vast territories for themselves—even though their colonial administrators had virtually no knowledge of what lay beyond the Appalachians.

Individual colonies took different approaches in distributing land for settlement and development. In the Chesapeake region, for example, much of the land was settled under the "headright" system, in which proprietors offered guarantees of land (usually 50 acres) to anyone who paid his own or someone else's passage to the New World. This system enabled wealthy donors who paid for the passage of multiple immigrants to the colonies to acquire large tracts of land in the Chesapeake. These tracts became the foundation for many of the large plantations of the South. The New England colonies, meanwhile, bestowed lands on settlers who banded together as corporate groups, which in turn became the foundations of towns that made extensive use of "commons" for grazing livestock, obtaining timber, and other purposes. In 1681 Pennsylvania became the first colony to sell lands directly to individual buyers. Unlike Pennsylvania, which required buyers to preserve one acre of forest for every five acres they cleared, none of the other colonies imposed any resource conservation stipulations in their bills of sale.

SUBDUING NATURE

Irrespective of the methods by which public land was placed into private hands, colonial land use practices and policies revolved around converting American forests and fields into European-style farms and pastures, or as one scholar put it, "settlers meant to replace a nature that they called wilderness with another nature called pastoral."[30] To this end, they brought an array of domesticated plants and livestock with them to the New World, including wheat, barley, rye, pigs, horses, cattle, sheep, and honeybees. (During the Colonial Era, the sight of the unassuming honeybee evoked a particular dread among Native Americans. As Thomas Jefferson explained in his 1785 *Notes on the State of Virginia*,

"[T]he bees have generally extended themselves into the country, a little in advance of the white settlers. The Indians therefore call them the white man's fly, and consider their approach as indicating the approach of the settlements of the whites."[31])

In addition to these commercially valuable imports, stowaways on European ships bound for America included dozens of insect species, rats, and weeds. In fact, some botanists estimate that fully half of the weed species currently present in the United States originated in Europe. These unwanted invasive species, combined with the aforementioned domesticated livestock and plants, greatly altered regional ecosystems—as did the plowing, grazing, hunting, and logging practices of the colonists. By the close of the seventeenth century, New England forests had not only become the colonists' leading source of building materials and heating and cooking fuel, but also ranked as the primary raw material for England's massive naval fleet (England even imposed so-called "Broad Arrow" laws in the colonies to reserve some timber stands for its fleet, but these laws were widely ignored by settlers). Complex and interdependent ecological links among numerous species of flora and fauna were forever reconfigured—and in some cases rent asunder—by such onslaughts.

By the mid-seventeenth century, the economic vitality of the colonies—which were experiencing steady influxes of arrivals from the Old World by this time—increasingly hinged on relentless expansion into previously undeveloped wilderness areas. In New England, "the livestock of the colonists . . . required more land than all other agricultural activities put together," wrote scholar William Cronon. "Competition for grazing lands acted as a centrifugal force that drove towns and settlements apart."[32] In the Chesapeake region, the shortsighted farming practices of early planters accelerated soil depletion, which in turn set in place a cycle of continual abandonment of played-out fields and clearing of forests for new tobacco production.

Taming the American wilderness, however, involved more than just clearing land or draining swamps and marshlands for planting and grazing. It also required other forms of land alteration, most notably the erection of mills, dams, weirs, and ditches to harness the power of America's rivers for economic gain. These types of projects were carried out almost as soon as the first European colonists set foot on New World soil—in 1623 settlers built a dam on Maine's Piscataqua River to power a sawmill—and proliferated from that point forward. Frequently, these manmade alterations had unintended ecological consequences. In 1789, for instance, the completion of Hadley Falls Dam on the Connecticut River shut the gate on 300 miles of waterways that had been prime spawning grounds for salmon and shad.[33]

Usually, however, wild animals were not just collateral damage in the campaign to reshape the New World in line with market economy ideals. Some animals were regarded as raw material—market commodities—for the accumulation of wealth, such as deer, beaver, mink, and other fauna with commercially valuable body parts. Harvests of these valuable animals increased exponentially in some regions of the New World, with few allowances made for maintaining sustainable populations.

Other animals constituted an economic threat to early settlers, and they were treated accordingly. Bears, cougars, wolves, coyotes, eagles, pigeons, and many other species were targeted for eradication all across colonial America because of their negative impact on settlers' bottom lines. Towns frequently organized collective hunts in which dozens of participants invaded woods believed to house populations of wolves or bear. Bounties were also offered to any hunter—white or Indian—who brought in the head of a wolf. These bounties, which ranged from a few shillings or bushels of corn to allotments of gunpowder and shot, were funded by livestock owners who were legally obligated to contribute. The effect of the bounty, "like that of the fur trade, was to establish a price for wild animals, to create a court-ordered market for them, and so encourage their destruction," observed Cronon.[34]

Determined to protect their livestock, orchards, and crops, colonists waged a ruthless war on any and all creatures that interfered with their operations. As a result, some forests and river valleys were virtually depopulated of predators, which in turn triggered a cascade of other disruptions to those regional ecosystems. These disruptions were further exacerbated by the epic scale of deforestation that was taking place up and down the eastern ramparts of America. By the 1790s, one visitor to the upper Hudson River valley reported that "In this vast tract of country no deer, or other useful animal or next to none exist; and scarce a living creature is to be seen. Thus has a country, once abounding in animated nature, for want of Laws to protect, or sense in the people to kill with moderation and in seasonable times, in the short space of 20 years become still as death."[35]

AMERICA'S FIRST RESOURCE CONSERVATION POLICIES

The zeal with which colonists set out to subjugate the American wilderness reflected admirable qualities of ambition, dedication, and perseverance. But as the decades passed, a growing number of settlers, town fathers, and other observers expressed reservations about the colonists' stewardship of the land and other natural resources in their possession. "The grain fields, the meadows, the forests, the cattle, etc. are treated with equal carelessness," charged Peter Kalm, a Swedish naturalist who traveled extensively through America in the mid-eighteenth century[36] **(see Document 1.8)**.

Some colonists also recognized this problem, and they took steps to address it. Of course, "environmental policies" and "conservation movements" did not exist at this early stage in American history. But the first glimmerings of these forces did reveal themselves in the seventeenth and eighteenth centuries in the form of a smattering of land-use policies and regulations.

Many of these early foundations of modern American environmental policy were local in nature. In the 1630s, for example, Plymouth residents noticed that mill activity was disrupting fish spawning on area rivers. The settlement subsequently passed regulations that limited the harvesting of some fish species and forced mills to suspend operations and let water flow freely during spawning and other designated seasons. In the late seventeenth and early eighteenth centuries, numerous settlements across New England drafted regulations governing the cutting of timber, imposing grazing boundaries for livestock, and putting light restrictions on the hunting of deer and other commercially valuable species **(see Document 1.3)**.

Fisheries management was a particular early focus across New England. Rules designed to reduce the negative impact of dams, mills, and overzealous fishermen on spawning fish species rank among the earliest "environmental" regulations in America. Fishing practices on the Merrimack River, for example, were the subject of fourteen legislative acts in New Hampshire between 1764 and 1820, whereas lawmakers in neighboring Massachusetts passed seventeen such acts between 1783 and 1820.[37]

Some of these early regulations were honored, at least by the majority of the community. But others, such as attempts in Virginia, New York, and other New England and mid-Atlantic colonies to place seasonal restrictions on the hunting of deer, heath hen, and other wild game, were generally ignored. In fact, some of these earliest attempts at crafting what we now recognize as environmental policy were widely ridiculed by settlers who viewed the inexhaustibility of America's natural resources as a bedrock truth of their existence.

PRIVATE PROPERTY RIGHTS IN THE COLONIES

Most of the early regulations governing land and water use were not particularly onerous. To the contrary, most were of limited scope and only fitfully enforced anyway. Nevertheless, they ran afoul of a uniquely "American" concept of private property rights that was emerging across the colonies. Back in England, the traditional hegemony of the state and landed class, and the kingdom's limited supply of natural resources, had made private property rights an esoteric subject for most citizens. In America, however, policies of territorial and commercial expansion, heightened political and economic freedom, and the continent's seemingly limitless natural wealth all contributed to an expansive view of property rights among the colonists.

As a result, many colonists resisted the efforts of British and colonial administrators to maintain their status as the ultimate arbiters of land and resource use. They increasingly asserted that they should be able to do whatever they wished with the land they owned.

These hardening attitudes made it exceedingly difficult for the English crown to impose limits on resource use and land settlement in the colonies. For example, the Crown's "Broad Arrow" policies, which reserved the finest New World timber stands for the Royal Navy, were widely disregarded by the colonists. As one historian pointed out, these disputes between colonists and Parliament were "not unlike twentieth-century controversies over government regulation of wetlands, floodplains, and endangered species habitat"[38] **(see Document 1.5)**.

Some members of Parliament recognized that the Broad Arrow laws and other unenforceable restrictions on natural resource use were actually eroding Crown authority in the colonies. In 1775 Edmund Burke warned that "this hoarding of a royal wilderness" would not be honored in America:

> You can not station garrisons in every part of these deserts. If you drive the people from one place, they will carry on their annual tillage, and remove with their flocks and herds to another. Many of the people in the back settlements are already little attached to particular situations. Already they have topped the Appalachian Mountains. From thence they behold before them an immense plain, one vast, rich, level meadow; a square of five hundred miles. Over this they would wander without a possibility of restraint; they would change their manners with the habits of their life; would soon forget a government by which they were disowned; would become hordes of English Tartars; and, pouring down upon your unfortified frontiers a fierce and irresistible cavalry, become masters of your governors and your counselors, your collectors and comptrollers, and of all the slaves that adhered to them. Such would, and, in no long time, must be, the effect of attempting to forbid as a crime, and to suppress as an evil, the command and blessing of Providence, "Increase and multiply." Such would be the happy result of an endeavor to keep as a lair of wild beasts that earth which God, by an express charter, has given to the children of men.[39]

EARLY PUBLIC HEALTH POLICIES

Regulations of a recognizable environmental character, however, did gain broader acceptance in the realm of public health. Members of the early colonies generally recognized that officials had an obligation and right to impose some rules on the larger community for the sake of public health. Most of these early public health regulations were rooted in a legitimate fear of the carnage that diseases wreaked on communities, both in terms of lives lost and economic disruption.

The New England colonies—and especially the Massachusetts Bay Colony—were the birthplace of most of these early public health regulations. Many of these earliest measures took the form of quarantine policies. In 1647 the General Court of Massachusetts ordered a quarantine of all ships from the West Indies to ward off an outbreak of disease on the islands. Several other maritime quarantines were approved by the colony over the ensuing half-century, and legislation was also passed authorizing local officials to isolate community members diagnosed with smallpox or other deadly diseases.

Colonial Massachusetts also passed and implemented the first public sanitation regulations in the New World. In 1634 authorities in Boston ordered that "no person shall leave any fish or garbage near the said Bridge or common landing place between the two creeks whereby any annoyance may come to the people that pass that way." Legislation to reduce pollution in Boston Harbor; remove animal carcasses from city streets; and reduce air, soil, and water pollution from slaughterhouses also was passed into law in Massachusetts by the close of the seventeenth century.[40]

Additional public health regulations were passed in the eighteenth century, especially in more heavily populated areas. Because the population in the southern colonies was smaller and more widely dispersed, public health regulations were fewer. But Charleston and other fast-growing cities in the region were an exception. As far back as 1704, for example, city officials in Charleston passed laws regulating slaughterhouses and privies out of a concern that "the air is greatly infected and many maladies and other intolerable diseases daily happen."[41]

The fast-growing towns of New York, Boston, and Philadelphia, however, were the leading locales for the introduction of public health regulations in colonial America. As centers of manufacturing and other economic activity, they attracted growing numbers of people with each passing year. During the second half of the seventeenth century, authorities in these and other growing cities passed ordinances that governed the placement and construction of privies; punished citizens for fouling public thoroughfares and water sources; provided for the removal of dead animals (a common occurrence); and established restrictive zones for butchers, slaughterhouse operators, and other high-polluting private businesses. But growth was chaotic and enforcement of zoning restrictions was patchy at best, so anxiety about public sanitation and protection of local waterways and other "commons" continued to grow.

Progress in this regard was slow and halting. Many early attempts to regulate business activity were beaten back by wealthy and politically connected businessmen. In 1739, for example, Benjamin Franklin launched a highly publicized campaign to force Philadelphia's tanners to stop polluting a local tributary of the Delaware River. Franklin's efforts were thwarted by the tanners and their political allies at every turn, to his great disgust **(see Document 1.6)**.

Other efforts were more successful. In 1786, for example, Boston established a department of inspectors to improve street sanitation. Ten years later, the state of New

York passed health legislation that gave city officials new authority to impose local ordinances in the realm of public sanitation. And in 1797 Massachusetts passed the Great Public Health Act, which authorized towns and districts across the state to appoint health committees and health officers to monitor public health and regulate certain municipal sanitation practices (see Document 1.10).

All told, these various public health measures—along with colonial rules governing natural resource use and consumption—were modest in scope. And as the United States entered into its first full century of existence, many of these regulations were swept aside, dashed to pieces, or otherwise overwhelmed by the incoming waves of industrialization and immigration that crashed on American shores in the nineteenth century. Still, these early laws and regulations are now recognized as some of the first manifestations of "environmental policy" in America.

NOTES

1. Philip Shabecoff, *A Fierce Green Fire: The American Environmental Movement* (New York: Hill and Wang, 1993), 9.

2. William Wood, *New England's Prospect* (1634; repr., Amherst: University of Massachusetts Press, 1992), 52.

3. Robert Cushman, "Reasons and Considerations Touching the Lawfulness of Removing out of England into the Parts of America," in *Remarkable Providences 1600–1760*, ed. John Demos (New York: Braziller, 1972), 4.

4. Jay Gitlin, "Empires of Trade, Hinterlands of Settlement," in *The Oxford History of the American West*, eds. Clyde A. Milner II, Carol A. O'Connor, and Martha Sandweiss (New York: Oxford University Press, 1994), 87.

5. Francis Jennings, *The Invasion of America: Indians, Colonialism, and the Cant of Conquest* (Chapel Hill: University of North Carolina Press for the Institute of Early American History and Culture, 1975), 29; Neil Salisbury, *Manitou and Providence: Indians, Europeans, and the Making of New England* (New York: Oxford University Press, 1982), 26–27.

6. William Cronon, *Changes in the Land: Indians, Colonists, and the Ecology of New England* (New York: Hill and Wing, 1983), 51.

7. Quoted in Alan Taylor, *American Colonies* (New York: Viking, 2001), 192.

8. Ibid.

9. James Wilson, *The Earth Shall Weep: A History of Native America* (New York: Atlantic Monthly Press, 1999), 84.

10. Ibid.

11. Quoted in Ronald Wright, *Stolen Continents: The Americas through Indian Eyes Since 1492* (Boston: Houghton Mifflin, 1992), 92.

12. Ibid., 70.

13. Gitlin, "Empires of Trade, Hinterlands of Settlement," 89.

14. Quoted in Taylor, *American Colonies*, 193.

15. Wilcomb E. Washburn, *Red Man's Land/White Man's Law: The Past and Present Status of the American Indian*, (1971; Norman: University of Oklahoma Press, 1995), 242.

16. Steven W. Hackel, "Shifting Patterns of Land Use in Monterey, California, before 1850," in *To Harvest, To Hunt: Stories of Resource Use in the American West*, ed. Judith L. Li (Corvallis: Oregon State University, 2007), 64.

17. Daniel H. Usner Jr., *Indians, Settlers, and Slaves in a Frontier Exchange Economy: The Lower Mississippi Valley before 1783* (Chapel Hill: University of North Carolina Press, 1992), 146.

18. Quoted in Taylor, *American Colonies*, 389.

19. Glynn Barratt, *Russia in Pacific Waters, 1715–1825* (Vancouver: University of British Columbia Press, 1981).

20. Quoted in Matthew Dennis, *Cultivating a Landscape of Peace* (Ithaca, N.Y.: Cornell University Press, 1999), 171.

21. Taylor, *American Colonies,* 42, 43.

22. Quoted in Cronon, *Changes in the Land,* 86.

23. Quoted in John Duffy, "Smallpox and the Indians in the American Colonies," *Bulletin of the History of Medicine* 25 (July–August 1951): 327.

24. William Bradford, *Of Plymouth Plantation,* ed. Samuel Eliot Morison (New York: Knopf, 1952), 271.

25. John Duffy, *The Sanitarians: A History of American Public Health* (Champaign: University of Illinois Press, 1992), 10.

26. Quoted in Jennings, *The Invasion of America,* 24.

27. Jennings, *The Invasion of America,* 30.

28. Wallace Stegner, "A Capsule History of Conservation," in *Where the Bluebird Sings to the Lemonade Springs: Living and Writing in the West* (New York: Penguin, 1993), 118–119.

29. Richard N. L. Andrews, *Managing the Environment, Managing Ourselves: A History of American Environmental Policy* (New Haven, Conn.: Yale University Press, 1999), 34.

30. Alan Taylor, "'Wasty Ways': Stories of American Settlement," in *Environmental History* 3, no. 3 (July 1998), 291–309.

31. Thomas Jefferson, *Notes on the State of Virginia* (1785; New York: Penguin, 1999), 79.

32. Cronon, *Changes in the Land,* 139.

33. Tim Palmer, *Endangered Rivers and the Conservation Movement* (Berkeley: University of California Press, 1986), 16.

34. Cronon, *Changes in the Land,* 132–133.

35. William Strickland, *Journal of a Tour in the United States of America, 1794–1795* (New York: New York Historical Society, 1971), 147.

36. Peter Kalm, *Peter Kalm's Travels in North America,* ed. Adolph B. Benson (1770, repr., New York: Dover, 1966).

37. Theodore Steinberg, *Nature Incorporated: Industrialization and the Waters of New England* (New York: Cambridge University Press, 1991), 171–172.

38. Andrews, *Managing the Environment, Managing Ourselves,* 40.

39. Edmund Burke, *Edmund Burke's Speech on Conciliation with the Colonies Delivered in the House of Commons, March 22, 1775* (New York: Appleton, 1900), 82–83.

40. Wendy E. Parmet, "Health Care and the Constitution: Public Health and the Role of the State in the Framing Era," *Hastings Constitutional Law Quarterly* (Winter 1992), 267–335.

41. Ibid.

DOCUMENT
1.1

A Pilgrim Describes the
Struggle for Survival at Plymouth

"The Whole Countrie . . . Represented a Wild & Savage Heiw"

1620

William Bradford was one of the original pilgrims who crossed the Atlantic to the New World on the Mayflower *in 1620. He was an original member of the Plymouth Colony in Massachusetts, and when Governor John Carver died during that first long winter in America, Bradford succeeded him as governor. He served in that capacity for most of the next thirty-seven years, until his death in 1657.*

The following excerpt is from Bradford's personal journal, which he kept from 1620 to 1647. This journal, which was later published as Of Plimoth Plantation, *is one of the most famous works of the era of European settlement of the New World. In this passage, Bradford recounts the colony's first few months of existence. The excerpt is notable for two reasons. First, his description of the land confronting them as a "hidious & desolate wilderness, full of wild beasts & willd men" reflects the prevailing attitude of the pilgrims: America was a chaotic place that would have to be subjugated if they hoped to prevail in their colonization plans. Second, his account makes it clear that the entire colony might very well have perished were it not for the aid of Indians in the region.*

Being thus arived in a good harbor and brought safe to land, they fell upon their knees & blessed yᵉ God of heaven, who had brought them over yᵉ vast & furious ocean, and delivered them from all yᵉ periles & miseries therof, againe to set their feete on yᵉ firme and stable earth, their proper elemente. And no marvell if they were thus joyefull, seeing wise Seneca was so affected with sailing a few miles on yᵉ coast of his owne Italy; as he affirmed, that he had rather remaine twentie years on his way by land, then pass by sea to any place in a short time; so tedious & dreadfull was yᵉ same unto him.

But hear I cannot but stay and make a pause, and stand half amased at this poore peoples presente condition; and so I thinke will the reader too, when he well considers yᵉ same. Being thus passed yᵉ vast ocean, and a sea of troubles before in their preparation (as may be remembred by yᵗ which wente before), they had now no freinds to wellcome them, nor inns to entertaine or refresh their weatherbeaten bodys, no houses or much less townes to repaire too, to seeke for succoure. It is recorded in scripture as a mercie to yᵉ apostle & his shipwraked company, yᵗ the barbarians shewed them no smale kindnes in refreshing them, but these savage barbarians, when they mette with them (as after will appeare) were readier to fill their sids full of arrows then otherwise. And for yᵉ season it was winter, and they that know yᵉ winters of yᵗ countrie know them to be sharp & violent, & subjecte to cruell & feirce stormes, deangerous to travill to known places, much more to serch an unknown coast. Besids, what could they see but a hidious & desolate wilderness, full of wild beasts & willd men? and what multituds ther might be of them they knew not. Nether could they, as it were, goe up to yᵉ tope of Pisgah, to vew from this willderness a more goodly cuntrie to feed their hops; for which way soever they turnd their eys (save upward to yᵉ heavens) they could have litle solace or content in respecte of any outward objects. For sumer being done, all things stand upon them with a wetherbeaten face; and ye whole countrie, full of woods & thickets, represented a wild & savage heiw. If they looked behind them, ther was ye mighty ocean which they had passed, and was now as a maine barr & goulfe to seperate them from all ye civill parts of ye world. . . . Let it also be considred what weake hopes of supply & succoure they left behinde them, y^t might bear up their minds in this sade condition and trialls they were under; and they could not but be very smale. . . . What could now sustaine them but ye spirite of God & his grace? . . .

Being thus arrived at Cap-Cod ye 11. of November, and necessitie calling them to looke out a place for habitation, (as well as the maisters & mariners importunitie,) they having brought a large shalop with them out of England, stowed in quarters in ye ship, they now gott her out & sett their carpenters to worke to trime her up; but being much brused & shatered in ye shipe wth foule weather, they saw she would be longe in mending. Wherupon a few of them tendered them selves to goe by land and discovere those nearest places, whilst ye shallop was in mending; and ye rather because as they wente into y^t harbor ther seemed to be an opening some 2. or 3 leagues of, which ye maister judged to be a river. It was conceived ther might be some danger in ye attempte, yet seeing them resolute, they were permited to goe, being 16. of them well armed, under ye conduct of Captain Standish, having shuch instructions given them as was thought meete. They sett forth ye 15. of Nove^{br}:

> **Besids, what could they see but a hidious & desolate wildernes, full of wild beasts & willd men? and what multituds ther might be of them they knew not.**
>
> —William Bradford

and when they had marched aboute ye space of a mile by ye sea side, they espied 5. or 6. persons with a dogg coming towards them, who were salvages; but they fled from them, & rañe up into ye woods, and ye English followed them, partly to see if they could speake with them, and partly to discover if ther might not be more of them lying in ambush. But ye Indeans seeing them selves thus followed, they againe forsooke the woods, & rane away on the sands as hard as they could, so as they could not come near them, but followed them by ye tracte of their feet sundrie miles, and saw that they had come the same way. So, night coming on, they made their randevous & set out their sentinels, and rested in quiete y^t *night,* and the next morning followed their tracte till they had headed a great creake, & so left the sands, & turned an other way into ye woods. But they still followed them by geuss, hopeing to find their dwellings; but they soone lost both them & them selves, falling into shuch thickets as were ready to tear their cloaths & armore in peeces, but were most distresed for wante of drinke. But at length they found water & refreshed them selves, being ye first New-England water they drunke of, and was now in thir great thirste as pleasante unto them as wine or bear had been in for-times. Afterwards they directed their course to come to ye other shore, for they knew it was a necke of land they were to crosse over, and so at length gott to ye sea-side, and marched to this supposed river, & by ye way found a pond of clear fresh water, and shortly after a good quantitie of clear ground wher ye Indeans had formerly set corne, and some of their graves. And proceeding furder they saw new-stuble wher corne had been set ye same year, also they found wher latly a house had been, wher some planks and a great ketle was remaining, and heaps of sand newly padled with their hands, which they, digging up, found in them diverce faire Indean baskets filled with corne, and some in eares, faire and good, of diverce collours, which seemed to them a very goodly sight, (haveing never seen any shuch before). . . .

[The settlement begins to take shape, but disease and hunger take a heavy toll on the colony's population.]

All this while yᵉ Indians came skulking about them, and would sometimes show them selves aloofe of, but when any aproached near them, they would rune away. And once they stoale away their tools wher they had been at worke, & were gone to diner. But about yᵉ 16. *of March* a certaine Indian came bouldly amongst them, and spoke to them in broken English, which they could well understand, but marvelled at it. At length they understood by discourse with him, that he was not of these parts, but belonged to yᵉ eastrene parts, wher some English-ships came to fhish, with whom he was aquainted, & could name sundrie of them by their names, amongst whom he had gott his language. He became proftable to them in aquainting them with many things concerning yᵉ state of yᵉ cuntry in yᵉ east-parts wher he lived, which was afterwards profitable unto them; as also of yᵉ people hear, of their names, number, & strength; of their situation & distance from this place, and who was cheefe amongst them. His name was *Samaset*; he tould them also of another Indian whos name was *Squanto,* a native of this place, who had been in England & could speake better English then him selfe. Being, after some time of entertainmente & gifts, dismist, a while after he came againe, & 5. more with him, & they brought againe all yᵉ tooles that were stolen away before, and made way for yᵉ coming of their great Sachem, called *Massasoyt*; who, about 4. or 5. *days after,* came with the cheefe of his freinds & other attendance, with the aforesaid *Squanto.* With whom, after frendly entertainment, & some gifts given him, they made a peace with him (which hath now continued this 24. years) in these terms.

1. That neither he nor any of his, should injurie or doe hurte to any of their people.
2. That if any of his did any hurte to any of theirs, he should send yᵉ offender, that they might punish him.
3. That if any thing were taken away from any of theirs, he should cause it to be restored; and they should doe yᵉ like to his.
4. If any did unjustly warr against him, they would aide him; if any did warr against them, he should aide them.
5. He should send to his neighbours confederats, to certifie them of this, that they might not wrong them, but might be likewise comprised in yᵉ conditions of peace.
6. That when ther men came to them, they should leave their bows & arrows behind them.

After these things he returned to his place caled *Sowams,* some 40. mile from this place, but *Squanto* continūed with them, and was their interpreter, and was a spetiall instrument sent of God for their good beyond their expectation. He directed them how to set their corne, wher to take fish, and to procure other comodities, and was also their pilott to bring them to unknowne places for their profitt, and never left them till he dyed. . . .

Source: Bradford, William. *Of Plimoth Plantation.* Boston: Wright and Potter, 1898, pp. 94–99, 114–116.

Document 1.2

An English Fur Trader Purchases Indian Land in Massachusetts Colony

"They Shal . . . Have Liberty to Take Fish & Deer"

July 15, 1636

After European colonies became established in the New World, one of the first priorities of the settlers was to secure legal control of the surrounding woods and rivers from indigenous tribes of the region. Because European settlers used the land and the natural resources contained therein much more intensively than the Indians, these land transfers had a momentous impact on local ecosystems.

Following is the text of a 1636 land title transfer agreement between representatives of Puritan businessman William Pynchon and local Agawam Indians. The land in question, located around the confluence of the Connecticut and Agawam rivers, was targeted for purchase by Pynchon because of its large population of beaver, the pelts of which were extremely valuable for trade. One of the tracts of land specified in this deed— one of the earliest Indian land deeds in the annals of American history—eventually became the site of the city of Springfield, Massachusetts. The deed also includes guarantees that the Agawam Indians would be accorded rights to hunt, fish, and forage on the land. These rights, however, were gradually abrogated as white population growth crowded them out of the territory.

A Coppy of a Deed Whereby the Indians at Springfield Made Sale of Certain Lands on Both Sides of the Great River at Springfield to William Pynchon Esq. Mr. Henry Smith & Jehu Burr for the Town of Springfield for Ever

SPRINGFIELD TOWNE DEED FRO YE INDIANS

Agaam alias Agawam: This fifteenth day of July 1636.—

It is agreed between Commucke & Matanchan ancient Indians of Agaam for & in the name of al the other Indians, & in particular for & in ye name of Cuttonus the right owner of Agaam & Quana, & in the Name of his mother Kewenusk the Tamasham or wife of Wenawis, & Niarum the wife of Coa. to & with William Pynchon Henry Smith & Jehu Burr their heires & associates for ever to trucke & sel al that ground & muckeo-squittaj or medows, accomsick, viz: on the other side of Quana; & al the ground & muckeosquittaj on the side of Agaam, except Cottinackeesh or ground that in now planted for ten fatham of Wampam, Ten Coates, Ten howes, Ten hatchets, & Ten knifes: and also the said ancient Indians with the Consent of the rest, & in particular wth the Conent of Menis & Wrutherna & Napompenam, do trucke & sel to William Pynchon Henry Smith & Jehu Burr, & their successors for ever, al that ground on the East side of Quinnecticot River called Usquaiok & Nayasset reaching about four or five miles in Length, from the north end of Masaksicke up to Chickuppe River, for four fatham of

Wampam, four coates, four howes, four hatchets, four knifes: Also the Said ancient Indians Doe wth the Consent of the other Indians, & in particular wth the Consent of Machetuhood Wenepawin, & Mohemoos trucke & sel the ground & muckeosquittaj & grounds adjoyning, called Masaksicke, for four fatham of wampam, four Coates, four hatchets, & four howes & four knifes.

And the said Pynchon hath in hand paid the said eighteen fatham of Wampam eighteen coates, 18 hatchets, 18 howes, 18 knifes to the said Commucke & Matanchan, & doth further condition wth the Sd Indians, that they shal have & enjoy all that connackeesh, or ground that is now planted; And have liberty to take Fish & Deer, ground nuts, walnuts akornes & sasachiminesh or a kind of pease, And also if any of our cattle spoile their corne, to pay as it is worth; & that hogs shall not goe on the side of Agaam but in akorne time Also the said Pynchon doth give to Wrutherna two Coates over & above the said Particulars expressed, & In Witness hereof the two said Indians & the Rest, doe set to their hands, this present 15th day of July 1636

The marke of X Menis	The marke of X Macassack
The marke of X Kenix	The marke X of Wineawis
The marke of X Ussessas alias Nepineum	The marke of X Cuttonus
The marke of X Winepawin	The marke X of Matanchan
The marke of X Machetuhood	The marke of X Wrutherna
The marke of X Commuk	The marke X of Coa

The marke X of Keckusnek

Witnesse to all with in expressed that they understood al by Ahaughton an Indian of the Massachusett.

John Allen	The Marke of X John Cownes
The marke of X Richard Everet	
Faithful Thayeler	Thomas Horton
The marke of X Ahaughton	Joseph Parsons

Joseph Parsons a Testimony to this Deed did at the Court at Northampton, March 1661: 62: testify on oath that he was a witness to this bargaine between mr Pynchon &c & the Indians as attests Elizur Holyoke Recorder.

July: 8th 1679 entred the Records for ye County of Hampshire

by me John Holyoke Recorder.

Source: Wright, Harry Andrew, ed. *Indian Deeds of Hampden County.* Springfield, Massachusetts, 1905, pp. 11–12.

DOCUMENT
1.3

Game Hunting Regulations in Rhode Island Colony

"There Shall Be No Shootinge of Deere"

February 4, 1646

Early American colonists hunted the continent's wild animals with tremendous zeal. Wild game such as deer and beaver were hunted for their meat or fur. Meanwhile, predators such as foxes, wolves, and bear were treated as vermin that needed to be extirpated if the colonists hoped to establish a European-style pastoral existence in the New World.

The following text is from a report of a town council meeting in Portsmouth in Rhode Island Colony in 1646. The excerpt shows the town fathers' decision to adopt a formal predator eradication policy in which hunters would receive financial rewards for the slaying of wolves. The council also approved language establishing hunting seasons for deer. This provision—very rare for its time—reflected a dawning realization around the settlement that area deer herds were being harvested by colonists at an unsustainable rate. These game hunting regulations were patterned after ones that had been established in Newport in 1639—the first-ever hunting regulations passed into law in Rhode Island Colony.

At a meeting, February the 4th, 1646.

It is agreed to concur with Newport in an order that there shall be no shooting of deere for the space of two months; and if any shall shoot, he shall forfeit five pounds; half to him that sueth, and the other halfe to the Treasurie. The reason of this order is, that the wolves the more readily come to bayte that they may be catched for the general good of the Island. . . .

It is ordered, that the wolfe catcher shall be payed out of the treasurie, and that he that killeth a wolfe shall come to Mr. Balston and Mr. Sanford for theire pay.

It is further ordered, that Newport shall pay four pounds for the killinge of a wolfe, and Portsmouth twentie shillings. . . .

It is further ordered, that there shall be noe shooting of deere from the first of May till the first of November; and if any shall shoot a deere within that time he shall forfeit five pounds; one halfe to him that sueth, and the other to the Treasury. . . .

Source: Bartlett, John Russell, ed. *Records of the Colony of Rhode Island and Providence Plantations in New England.* Vol. 1, 1636 to 1663. Providence: A. Crawford Greene and Brothers, 1856, pp. 84–85.

DOCUMENT
1.4

A Planter Takes Stock of Indian Tribes in Virginia

"They Have . . . Reason to Lament the Arrival of the Europeans"

1705

By the end of the seventeenth century, indigenous peoples up and down the Atlantic seaboard were in disarray. Many Indian communities and cultures had been shattered by white incursions onto traditional hunting and fishing grounds, deadly epidemics of smallpox and other diseases, and assimilation into the capitalist economic system of the Europeans. In the following excerpt from his 1705 work History and Present State of Virginia, *wealthy planter Robert Beverley delivers a grim status report on the declining fortunes of various tribes in the region.*

The *Indians of Virginia* are almost wasted, but such Townes, or People as retain their Names, and live in Bodies, are here-under set down; all which together can't raise five hundred fighting Men. They live poorly, and much in Fear of the Neighbouring *Indians*. Each Town, by the Articles of Peace, 1677 pays 3 *Indian* Arrows for their Land, and 20 Beaver-Skins for Protection every Year.

In *Accomac* are 8 Towns, *viz.*

Matomkin is much decreased of late by the Small Pox, that was carried thither.

Gingoteque. The few remains of this Town are join'd with a Nation of the *Maryland Indians.*

Kiequotank is reduc'd to very few Men.

Matchopungo has a small number yet living.

Occahanock, has a small number yet living.

Pungoteque. Govern'd by a Queen, but a small Nation.

Oanancock has but four or five Families.

Chiconessex has very few, who just keep the name.

Nanduye. A Seat of the Empress. Not above 20 Families, but she hath all the Nations of this Shore under Tribute.

In *Northampton, Gangascoe,* which is almost as numerous as all the foregoing Nations put together.

In *Prince George, Wyanoke,* is extinct.

In *Charles City, Appamatox* is extinct.

In *Surery. Nottawayes,* which are about a hundred Bow-Men, of late a thriving and increasing People.

By *Nansamond. Meheering* has about thirty Bow-Men, who keep at a stand.

Nansamond. About thirty Bow-men: They have increased much of late.

In *King William's* County, 2. *Pamunkie,* has about forty Bow-men, who decrease.

Chickahomonie, which had about sixteen Bow-men, but lately increas'd.

In *Essex. Rappahannock,* extinct.

In *Richmond. Port-Tabago,* extinct.

In *Northumberland. Wiccocomoco,* has but few Men living, which yet keep up their Kingdom, and retain their Fashion; yet live by themselves, separate from all other *Indians,* and from the *English.*

§.49. Thus I have given a succinct Account of the *Indians;* happy, I think, in their simple State of Nature, and in their Enjoyment of Plenty, without the Curse of Labour. They have on several accounts reason to lament the arrival of the *Europeans,* by whose means they seem to have lost their Felicity, as well as their Innocence. The *English* have taken away great Part of their country, and consequently made every thing less plenty amongst them. They have introduc'd Drunkenness and Luxury amongst them, which have multiplied their Wants, and put them upon desiring a thousand Things, they never dreamed of before. . . .

Source: Beverley, Robert. *The History and Present State of Virginia.* 2nd ed. London: B. and S. Tooke, 1722, pp. 199–200.

D O C U M E N T
1 . 5

England's Broad Arrow Policy in Colonial America

"To Prevent the Destruction . . . of His Majesties Woods"

October 30, 1730

In 1691 England moved decisively to claim white pine forests in the American colonies for the exclusive use of its Royal Navy. This action was prompted by rising Crown concerns about its access to traditional sources of timber for shipbuilding and growing recognition that eastern white pines were ideal for the crafting of ship masts. Over the ensuing four decades England issued a succession of additional regulations that further established their legal stranglehold over all American forests that had not already passed into private ownership—along with woodlands to which private individuals had title.

These Broad Arrow policies—so-called because Royal Surveyors emblazoned three arrow-like marks on all trees they reserved for the King—proved to be an utter failure, however. They aroused greater anger among the colonists, who interpreted them as an outrageous violation of their private property rights. Disregarding the claim that all of New England was "Crown Land" of the British Empire, many colonists—settlers, craftsmen, and shipbuilders—harvested broad arrow trees for their own use. Their rebellious actions heightened tensions between the colonists and British administrators in far-reaching ways. "The Broad Arrow Policy not only failed, but became one of the irritants leading to revolution," wrote historian Richard N. L. Andrews. "Colonial legislatures ignored it, colonial courts refused to convict its violators, and colonists themselves flouted it."[1]

The following is an excerpt from a statement issued by Jonathan Belcher, governor of colonial New Hampshire, in 1730. It reiterates the British Parliament's insistence that colonial forests are part of the king's domain.

A PROCLAMATION TO PREVENT THE DESTRUCTION OR SPOIL OF HIS MAJESTIES WOODS.—

Foreasmuch as the Preservation of His Majesties Woods within this and the neighbouring Provinces is highly necessary for furnishing the Royal Navy, and divers Acts of Parliament have been accordingly from time to time made & pass'd for that end; notwithstanding which and the care of this Governmᵗ to prevent & punish the Destruction and spoil of His Majesties Woods, many evil minded Persons have broke thro' the restraints of the Law in that behalf; and have for their own private gain made great wast of such trees as might be fit for His Majesties service. . . . It is Enacted "That from and after the Twenty first day of September one thousand seven hundred & twenty two, no Person or Persons within the Colonys or plantations of Nova Scotia, New Hampshire, the Massachusetts Bay & Province of Mayne, Rhode Island, & Providence Plantations, the Narraganset Countrey, or Kings province, and Connecticut in New England & New York & New Jersey in America, or within any of them do or shall presume to cut, fell or destroy any white pine trees, not growing within any Township or the bounds, lines, or limits thereof in any of the sᵈ Colonies or plantations without His Majesties Royal Lycense . . .

. . . And whereas their late Majestys King William & Queen Mary for the better providing & furnishing Masts for the Royal Navy . . . Did reserve to themselves their heirs & successors all Trees of the Diameter of twenty four inches & upwards at twelve inches from the ground growing upon any soil of Tract of Land within the sd Province or Territory, not then before granted to any private Person: In order therefore to make the sd Reservation more effectual Be it further Enacted by the Authority aforesd that no Person or Persons whatsoever within the sd Province of the Massachusetts Bay or New England do or shall presume to cut or destroy any white pine trees of the Diameter of twenty four inches, or upwards at twelve inches from the ground, not growing within some soil or Tract of Land within the sd Province granted to some private person or Persons before the seventh day of October which was in the year 1690 without His Majesties Lycense first had and obtained . . .

Dated this thirtieth day of October 1730 . . .

GOD SAVE THE KING—

Source: Belcher, Jonathan. "A Proclamation to Prevent the Destruction or Spoil of His Majesties Woods." In *Miscellaneous Provincial and State Papers, 1725–1890*. Vol. 18, edited by Isaac W. Hammond. Manchester, N.H.: John B. Clark, 1890, pp. 32–35.

NOTE

1. Richard N. L. Andrews, *Managing the Environment, Managing Ourselves: A History of American Environmental Policy* (New Haven, Conn.: Yale University Press, 1999), 40.

Benjamin Franklin Rails against Industrial Pollution in Philadelphia

"The Smoak Arising from the Tan . . . Is Exceedingly Offensive"

August 30, 1739

In the late 1730s Benjamin Franklin and several of his neighbors petitioned the Pennsylvania Assembly to force Philadelphia tanners to stop polluting local waterways (with lime and materials from animal carcasses) and fouling the city's air. They urged the Assembly to relocate the tanners outside the city, where they would not pose a public health threat and lower the value of nearby properties. The tanners promptly mounted a fiery defense, claiming that their private rights were being threatened. Franklin countered by charging that the damage they were doing to the local environment violated the "public rights" of the people of Philadelphia.

The Pennsylvania Assembly essentially declined to act on the petition, which the tanners interpreted as a vindication of their stand. They trumpeted their victory in the August 16 edition of the American Weekly Mercury, *a newspaper that regularly sparred with Franklin's own* Pennsylvania Gazette. *Angered and dismayed by this turn of events, Franklin responded with an anonymous* Gazette *letter addressed to "Mr. Franklin" in which he castigated the tanners as environmental despoilers with no regard for public rights. The text of Franklin's letter is reprinted here.*

The tanners continued to operate with impunity until the early 1760s, despite suspiciously high incidences of death and illness around the riverside district where they were ensconced. In 1763, however, Franklin—by now a member of the Pennsylvania Assembly himself—helped shepherd a new law into being that flatly forbade the city's tanners from dumping chemicals and animal parts into the river, as they had been doing for the previous half-century.

Mr. Franklin,

The Tanners of *Philadelphia,* having in the Mercury of *August* 16, published a partial Account of the Hearing before the Assembly, on the Petition relating to Tan-Yards, magnifying what was said on their own side, and stifling every thing that was urged by the Petitioners in support of their Petition, you are desired to give the Publick the Substance of what they have suppres'd, which is as follows.

The Prayer of the Petition was, that the erecting [of] new Tan-Yards within the Bounds of the City, should be forbidden, and that those already erected should be removed in such Time as might be tho't reasonable; And the Reasons given by the Petitioners were, in fact, that many offensive and unwholesome Smells do arise from Tan-Yards, to the great Annoyance of the Neighborhood, and therefore to the great Injury of all those who have Lots or Tenements near them, as it considerably lessens the Value of such Lots and Tenements. That the *Dock-Street,* upon which the Tanners are seated, was given with the Dock for publick Service, but that the Tanners had taken up and encumber'd the Street with their Pits, and had choaked the Dock (which was formerly navigable as high as *Third Street*) with their Tan [and] Horns. That the said Dock if open might be of great Use in several respects, and particularly in Case of Fires in that Part of the Town: but as it now lies, is a grievous Nuisance. That the Smoak arising from the burning Tan fills all the neighbouring Houses, and is exceedingly offensive. That there are, not very far from the Town, Places which might be as convenient to the Tanners, and not so injurious to the City. That if they were in some reasonable time to remove, their Grounds by the great Improvements that would be made near the Dock, would become more valuable to build on, then to be us'd as Tan-Yards; But however, as the Tanners who own Land on the Dock are very few, and the People whose Interest is affected by their Remaining there, are a very great Number, the Damage they would suffer in removing, would be but a Trifle, in Comparison to the Damage done to others, and to the City, by their Continuing where they are. Notwithstanding which, if the Tanners could be so regulated as to become inoffensive, the Petitioners declar'd that they should be therewith satisfied.

Upon which the Tanners themselves propos'd the following Regulations, *viz*:

A convenient Method for the better regulating of Tan-Yards, submitted by the Tanners to the Honourable House of Representatives of the Freemen of the Province of Pennsylvania.

Let the Tanyards be well paved between all the Pitts, and washed once every Day: Let the Watering-Pools and Masterings (which are the only Parts that afford offensive Smells) be enclosed on every side, and roofed over, within which Enclosure may be a subterranean Passage to receive the Washings and Filth of the Yard into the Dock or River at High Water; Let the whole Yard be likewise inclosed on all Sides with some strong close Fence, at least seven or eight Feet high, and every Tanner be obliged every Week to cart off his Tan, Horns, and such offensive Offals.

William Hudson, Jun. John Ogden
Samuel Morris John Howell
  William Smith

John Snowdon *being out of Town, we the Subscribers declare his Assent to the above Proposal.*

Samuel Morris
John Howell

These are the Proposals of the Tanners themselves to prevent or remove the Nuisance arising from their Tan-Yards; by which 'tis confes'd that they now are, and 'tis certain they have long been, a Nuisance.

What Regard these Gentlemen in the *Mercury* have shown to Truth, may be observ'd from the Account they give of the Assembly's Determination, on the Affair. "Upon the whole the Petition was REJECTED, the Tanners *Right* to follow their Trades within the City, ACCORDING TO THEIR OWN PROPOSALS, asserted, and the Corporation to see that they comply'd with SUCH a Regulation."

Let this be compar'd with the following Extract from the Minutes of the House, *viz.*
"After a full Hearing of both Parties,
Resolved,
That the City of Philadelphia *being the Place where the Tanners, Skinners, etc., have planted their Farms, Lime-Pits, etc. The Inconveniences arising from their Yards and Pits must be best known there; It is therefore referred to the Mayor and Community of Philadelphia, by an Ordinance for that Purpose, to make such Provision for the Relief of the*

Petitioners, against the Tanners, Skinners, Butchers, etc, as they shall find to be necessary and consistent with the Powers of their Corporation: And that if it shall appear to them, that the Aid of the Legislature is wanting to compel Obedience to such necessary Orders or Regulations as they shall make in that Behalf, that they apply to the General Assembly of this Province for the Time being for that Purpose. And the Tanners having proposed to this House certain Regulations for preventing the Inconveniences complained of, arising from the Tan-yards, it is further ordered, That a true Copy of the said Proposals be delivered, with a Copy of this Resolve, to the Mayor of Philadelphia *for the Time being.*

It is hard to imagine what could induce the Tanners to publish a Relation, so partial and so false; Did they imagine the Mayor and Commonalty would never hear of the Resolve of the House? Or that the long-injured Petitioners would forget to prosecute their Petition, according to the Direction of that Resolve?

In Prudence they ought not to have triumph'd before the Victory; and in Justice they should not have call'd that a *Daring Attempt on the Liberties of the Tradesmen of Philadelphia,* which was only a modest Attempt to deliver a *great Number* of Tradesmen from being poisoned by *a few,* and restore to them the *Liberty* of Breathing freely in their own Houses.

But an inclination to stir up Faction, Heats and Animosities among Fellow-Citizens, who should live in Love and Peace, will carry some Men thro' thick and thin. I cannot think, however, that all the Tanners are of that Disposition; and I doubt the Hot-Heads which produc'd that Paper, and call'd it *The Account of the Tanners,* will not be thank'd for it by some of their own brethren.

Source: Franklin, Benjamin. "The Tanners of Philadelphia." *Pennsylvania Gazette,* August 30, 1739.

DOCUMENT 1.7 Indians and Colonists Argue over Land Rights and Deeds

"Your People Daily Settle on These Lands, and Spoil Our Hunting"

1742

Colonists entered the New World armed with rigid concepts of private property ownership that were alien to Native Americans. Indians saw land and the natural resources contained therein—rivers, fish, minerals, game—as the collective property of the tribe, and they were wholly unfamiliar with the European concepts of land as a commodity that could be bought or sold.

These two conflicting views of land ownership and attached rights triggered escalating tensions between Indians and colonists. Again and again the two sides were at loggerheads over the issues of land ownership and access to resources. Even in places like colonial Pennsylvania, where William Penn had diligently sought to establish good relations with area tribes, hostilities over land rights sometimes boiled over into bloodshed. In many instances, these hostilities were triggered by white squatters who felt no compunction about claiming and settling "unimproved" land that the Indians used for hunting, foraging, travel, and refuge.

The fundamental differences between the two parties' philosophies are evident in this 1742 exchange between an Onondaga chief named Canassateego and Lieutenant Governor George Thomas of Pennsylvania. The remarks of Canassateego and Thomas excerpted here were first published in a 1747 book by Cadwallader Colden. The first colonial representative to the Iroquois Confederacy, Colden later became governor of New York province.

CANASSATEEGO:

Brethren, the Governor and Council, and all present,

According to our Promise we now propose to return you an Answer to the several Things mentioned to us Yesterday, and shall beg Leave to speak to publick Affairs first. . . . On this Head you Yesterday put us in Mind, first, "Of *William Penn's* early and constant Care to cultivate Friendship with all the *Indians;* of the Treaty we held with one of his Sons, about ten Years ago; and of the Necessity there is at this Time of keeping the Roads between us clear and free from all Obstructions." We are all very sensible of the kind Regard that good Man *William Penn* had for all the *Indians,* and cannot but be pleased to find that his Children have the same. We well remember the Treaty you mention, held with his Son on his Arrival here, by which we confirmed our League of Friendship, that is to last as long as the Sun and Moon endure. In Consequence of this, we, on our Part, shall preserve the Road free from all Incumbrances; in Confirmation whereof we lay down this String of Wampum.

You in the next Place said you would enlarge the Fire and make it burn brighter, which we are pleased to hear you mention; and assure you, we shall do the same, by adding to it more Fewel, that it may still flame out more strongly than ever: In the last Place, you were pleased to say that we are bound by the strictest Leagues, to watch for each others Preservation; that we should hear with our Ears for you, and you hear with your Ears for us: This is equally agreeable to us; and we shall not fail to give you early Intelligence, whenever any thing of Consequence comes to our Knowledge: And to encourage you to do the same, and to nourish in your Hearts what you have spoke to us with your Tongues, about the Renewal of our Amity and the Brightening of the Chain of Friendship; we confirm what we have said with another Belt of Wampum.

Brethren,

We received from the Proprietors Yesterday, some Goods in Consideration of our Release of the Lands on the West-side of the *Susquehannah*. It is true, we have the full Quantity according to Agreement; but if the Proprietor had been here himself, we think, in Regard of our Numbers and Poverty, he would have made an Addition to them. If the Goods were only to be divided amongst the *Indians* present, a single Person would have but a small Portion; but if you consider what Numbers are left behind, equally entitled with us to a Share, there will be extremely little. We therefore desire, if you have the Keys of the Proprietor's Chest, you will open it, and take out a little more for us.

We know our Lands are now become more valuable. The white People think we do not know their Value; but we are sensible that the Land is everlasting, and the few Goods we receive for it are soon worn out and gone. For the future, we will sell no Lands but when Brother *Onas* [the Proprietor] is in the Country; and we will know beforehand, the Quantity of the Goods we are to receive. Besides, we are not well used with respect to the Lands still unsold by us. Your People daily settle on these Lands, and spoil our

Hunting.—We must insist on your removing them, as you know they have no Right to settle to the Northward of *Kittochtinny-Hills.*—In particular, we renew our Complaints against some People who are settled at *Juniata,* a Branch of the *Susquehannah,* and all the Banks of that River, as far as *Mahaniay;* and desire they may be forthwith made to go off the Land, for they do great Damage to our Cousins the *Delawares.*

We have further to observe, with respect to the Lands lying on the West-side of the *Susquehannah,* that though Brother *Onas* (meaning the Proprietor) has paid us for what his People possess, yet some Parts of the Country have been taken up by Persons, whose Place of Residence is to the South of this Province, from whom we have never received any Consideration. This Affair was recommended to you by our Chiefs at our last Treaty; and you then, at our earnest Desire, promised to write a Letter to that Person who has the Authority over those People, and to procure us his Answer. As we have never heard from you on this Head, we want to know what you have done in it. If you have not done any Thing, we now renew our Request, and desire you will inform the Person whose People are seated on our Lands, that that Country belongs to us, in Right of Conquest—we having bought it with our Blood, and taken it from our Enemies in fair War; and we expect, as Owners of that Land, to receive such a Consideration for it as the Land is worth. We desire you will press him to send a positive Answer. Let him say Yes or No. If he says Yes, we will treat with him; if No, we are able to do ourselves Justice; and we will do it, by going to take Payment ourselves.

It is customary with us to make a Present of Skins, whenever we renew our Treaties. We are ashamed to offer our Brethren so few, but your Horses and Cows have eat the Grass our Deer used to feed on. This has made them scarce, and will, we hope, plead in Excuse for our not bringing a larger Quantity. If we could have spared more, we would have given more, but we are really poor; and desire you'll not consider the Quantity, but few as they are, accept them in Testimony of our Regard. . . .

Lieutenant Governor George Thomas:

Brethren,

We thank you for the many Declarations of Respect you have given us, in this solemn Renewal of our Treaties. We receive, and shall keep your String and Belts of Wampum, as Pledges of your Sincerity, and desire those we gave you may be carefully preserved, as Testimonies of ours.

In answer to what you say about the Proprietaries—they are all absent, and have taken the Keys of their Chest with them; so that we cannot, on their Behalf, enlarge the Quantity of Goods. Were they here, they might perhaps be more generous; but we cannot be liberal for them. The Government will, however, take your Request into Consideration; and in Regard to your Poverty, may perhaps make you a Present. . . .

The Number of Guns, as well as every Thing else, answers exactly with the Particulars specified in your Deed of Conveyance, which is more than was agreed to be given you. It was your own Sentiments, that the Lands on the West-side of the *Susquehannah,* were not so valuable as those on the East; and an Abatement was to be made, proportionable to the Difference in Value. But the Proprietor overlooked this, and ordered the full Quantity to be delivered, which you will look on as a Favour.

It is very true, that Lands are of late becoming more valuable; but what raises their Value? Is it not entirely owing to the Industry and Labour used by the white People, in their Cultivation and Improvement? Had not they come amongst you, these Lands would have been of no Use to you, any further than to maintain you. And is there not, now you have sold so much, enough left for all the Purposes of Living? What you say of the Goods, that they are soon worn out, is applicable to every Thing; but you know very well, that they cost a great deal of Money; and the Value of Land is no more, than it is worth in Money.

On your former complaints against People's settling the Lands on *Juniata,* and from thence all along on the River *Susquahannah* as far as *Mahaniahy,* some Magistrates were sent expressly to remove them, and we thought no Persons would presume to stay after that. . . .

CANASSATEEGO AND OTHER MEMBERS OF THE IROQUOIS DELEGATION:

These Persons who were sent did not do their Duty: so far from removing the People, they made Surveys for themselves, and they are in League with the Trespassers. We desire more effectual Methods may be used, and honester Persons employed.

Source: Colden, Cadwallader. *The History of the Five Indian Nations of Canada.* London: Printed for T. Osborne, 1747, pp. 62–67.

A Naturalist Decries Wasteful Resource Use in America

DOCUMENT 1.8

"Their Eyes Are Fixed upon the Present Gain, and They Are Blind to Futurity"

1753

Peter Kalm was a Swedish naturalist who visited North America from 1748 to 1751 to study the flora and fauna of the New World on behalf of the Swedish Academy. During his travels Kalm was shocked again and again by the colonists' wasteful use of natural resources. Two years after his return to Sweden, Kalm published an account of his adventures titled Peter Kalm's Travels in North America. *In this book, the author excoriated the European settlers as ravenous and heedless consumers of America's natural bounty, and he expressed dismay at their ignorance of sustainable farming practices.*

[Note: The long "s" in the original text has been modernized and presented as a short "s."]

Agriculture was in a very bad state hereabouts. When a person had bought a piece of land, which perhaps had never been ploughed since the creation, he cut down part of the wood, tore up the roots, ploughed the ground, sowed corn on it, and the first time he got a plentiful crop. But the same land being tilled for several years successively, without being manured, it as last must, of course, lose its fertility. Its possessor therefore leaves it fallow, and proceeds to another part of his ground, which he treats in the same manner. Thus he goes on till he has changed a great part of his possessions into corn-fields, and by that means deprives the ground of its fertility. He then returns to the first field, which now is pretty well recovered; this he again tills as long as it will afford him a good crop, but when its fertility is exhausted he leaves it fallow again and proceeds to the rest as before.

It being customary here, to let the cattle go about the fields and in the woods both day and night, the people cannot collect much dung for manure. But by leaving the land fallow for several years a great quantity of weeds spring up in it, and get such strength, that it requires a considerable time to extirpate them. From hence it likewise comes, that the corn is always so much mixed with weeds. The great richness of the soil which the first *European* colonists found here, and which had never been ploughed before, has given rife to this neglect of agriculture, which is still observed by many of the inhabitants. But they do not consider that when the earth is quite exhausted a great space of time, and an infinite deal of labour, is necessary to bring it again into good order, especially in these countries which are almost every summer so scorched by the excessive heat and drought. . . .

All the old *Swedes* and *Englishmen* born in *America,* whom I ever questioned, asserted that there were not nearly so many birds fit for eating at present as there used to be when they were children, and that their decrease was visible. They even said, that they had heard their fathers complain of this, in whose childhood the bays, rivers and brooks were quite covered with all sorts of water fowl, such as wild geese, ducks, and the like. But at present there was sometimes not a single bird upon them; about sixty or seventy years ago, a single person could kill eighty ducks in a morning; but at present you frequently waited in vain for a single one. A *Swede* above ninety years old assured me that he had in his youth killed twenty-three ducks at a shot.

> *Before the arrival of the* **Europeans,** *the country was uncultivated and full of great forests. . . . But since the arrival of great crouds of* **Europeans,** *things are greatly changed; the country is well peopled, and the woods are cut down.*
>
> —Peter Kalm

This good luck no body is likely to have at present, as you are forced to ramble about for a whole day, without getting a fight of more than three or four. *Cranes** at that time came hither by hundreds in the spring: at present there are very few. The *wild Turkeys,* and the birds, which the *Swedes* in this country call *Partridges* and *Hazel-hens,* were seen in large flocks in the woods. But at this time a person gets tired with walking before he can start a single bird.

The cause of this diminution is not difficult to find. Before the arrival of the *Europeans,* the country was uncultivated and full of great forests. The few *Indians* that lived here seldom disturbed the birds. They carried on no trade among themselves, iron and gun powder were unknown to them. One hundredth part of the fowl which at that time were so plentiful here, would have suffised to feed the few inhabitants; and considering that they cultivated their small maize fields, caught fish, hunted stags, beavers, bears, wild cattle, and other animals whose flesh was delicious to them, it will soon appear how little they disturbed the birds. But since the arrival of great crouds of *Europeans,* things are greatly changed: the country is well peopled, and the woods are cut down: the people increasing in this country, they have by hunting and shooting in part extirpated the

---

*WHEN Captain *Amadas,* the first *Englishman* that ever landed in *North America,* set foot on shore (to use his own words) *such a flocke of Cranes (the most part white) arose under us, with such a cry, redoubled by many echoes, as if an armie of men had shouted altogether.*

birds, in part scared them away: in spring the people still take both eggs, mothers, and young indifferently, because no regulations are made to the contrary. And if any had been made, the spirit of freedom which prevails in the country would not suffer them to be obeyed. . . .

The rye grows very ill in most of the fields, which is chiefly owing to the carelessness in agriculture, and to the poorness of the fields, which are seldom or never manured. After the inhabitants have converted a tract of land into fields, which has been a forest for many centuries together, and which consequently had a very fine soil, they use it as such as long as it will bear any corn, and when it ceases to bear any, they turn it into pastures for the cattle, and take new corn-fields in another place, where a fine soil can be met with and where it has never been made use of for this purpose. This kind of agriculture will do for some time; but it will afterwards have bad consequences, as every one may clearly see. A few of the inhabitants, however, treated their fields a little better: the *English* in general have carried agriculture to a higher degree of perfection than any other nation. But the depth and riches of the soil which those found here who came over from *England* (as they were preparing land for ploughing, which had been covered with woods from times immemorial) misled them, and made them careless husbandmen. It is well known that the *Indians* lived in this country for several centuries before the *Europeans* came into it; but it is likewise known, that they lived chiefly by hunting and fishing, and had hardly any fields. . . . [A] farmer's cabbage and turnip ground, taken together, is always as extensive, if not more so, than all the corn-fields and kitchen-gardens of an *Indian* family. Therefore, the *Indians* could hardly subsist for one month upon the produce of their gardens and fields. Commonly, the little villages of *Indians* are about twelve or eighteen miles distant from each other. From hence one may judge how little ground was formerly employed for corn fields; and the rest was overgrown with thick and tall trees. And though they cleared (as is yet usual) new ground, as soon as the old one had lost its fertility, yet such little pieces as they made use of were very inconsiderable, when compared to the vast forests which remained. Thus the upper fertile soil increased considerably, for centuries together; and the *Europeans* coming to *America* found a rich and fine soil before them, lying as loose between the trees as the best bed in a garden. They had nothing to do but to cut down the wood, put it up in heaps, and to clear the dead leaves away. They could then immediately proceed to plowing, which in such loose ground is very easy; and having sown their corn, they got a most plentiful harvest.

This easy method of getting a rich crop has spoiled the *English* and other *European* inhabitants, and induced them to adopt the same method of agriculture which the *Indians* make use of; that is, to sow uncultivated grounds, as long as they will produce a crop without manuring, but to turn them into pastures as soon as they can bear no more, and to take on new spots of ground, covered since time immemorial with woods, which have been spared by the fire or the hatchet ever since the creation. This is likewise the reason why agriculture, and the knowledge of this useful branch is so imperfect here, that one can learn nothing in a great tract of land, neither of the *English,* nor from the *Swedes, Germans, Dutch* and *French;* except that from their gross mistakes and carelessness for futurity, one finds opportunities every day of making all sorts of observations, and of growing wise at the expence of other people. In a word, the corn fields, the meadows, the forests, the cattle, &c. are treated with great carelessness by the inhabitants. We can hardly be more lavish of our woods in *Sweden* and *Finland* than they are here: their eyes are fixed upon the present gain, and they are blind to futurity.

Every day their cattle are harassed by labour, and each generation decreases in goodness and size, by being kept short of food, as I have before mentioned. On my travels in this country I observed several plants, which the horses and cows preferred to all others. They were wild in this country and likewise grew well on the driest and poorest ground, where no other plants would succeed. But the inhabitants did not know how to turn this to their advantage, owing to the little account made of Natural History, that science being here (as in other parts of the world) looked upon as a mere trifle, and the pastime of fools. I am certain, and my certainty is founded upon experience, that by mean of these plants, in the space of a few years, I have been able to turn the poorest ground, which would hardly afford food for a cow, into the richest and most fertile meadow, where great flocks of cattle have found superfluous food, and are grown fat upon. I own that these useful plants were not to be found on the grounds of every planter: but with a small share of natural knowledge, a man would easily collect them in the places where they are to be got. I was astonished when I heard the country people complaining of the badness of the pastures; but I likewise perceived their negligence, and often saw excellent plants growing on their own grounds, which only required a little more attention and assistance from their unexperienced owners. I found every where the wisdom and goodness of the Creator; but too seldom saw any acknowledgment or adequate estimation of it among men. . . .

Source: Kalm, Peter. *Peter Kalm's Travels in North America.* Translated by John Reinhold Forster. 2 vols, 2nd ed. London: T. Lowndes, 1772–1773. Vol. 1, pp. 144–145, 226–228; Vol. 2, pp. 45–49. Available at the American Journeys Web site, www.americanjourneys.org/aj-117/index.asp.

DOCUMENT
1.9

A Petition by Mohegan Indians to the Connecticut State Assembly

"With Hearts Full of Sorrow and Grief"

1789

In 1783 the eight-year Revolutionary War came to a close, freeing the thirteen rebellious colonies in America to go about the business of creating a new nation independent from the dictates of the English crown. This was a time of great pride and hope for the citizenry of the newly minted United States, but the war's outcome did not appreciably improve the prospects of Native Americans in the colonies. To the contrary, most Indian tribes remained in various stages of disintegration as a result of the corrosive impact of disease, land loss, and steady erosion of their religious and cultural traditions.

The following petition reveals the depths of their despair. Written by two Mohegan leaders, Henry Quaquaquid and Robert Ashpo, it pleads with the Connecticut state legislature to help their beleaguered tribespeople. They freely acknowledge that the Mohegans' legendary sense of tribal solidarity has been lost and that some members have turned on each other in their struggle for survival. The petition also serves as a sort of eulogy for a vibrant and independent way of life that no longer exists.

"We beg leave to lay our concerns and burdens at your excellencies' feet. The times are exceedingly altered, yea the times are turned upside down; or rather we have changed the good times, chiefly by the help of the white people. For in times past our forefathers lived in peace, love and great harmony, and had every thing in great plenty. When they wanted meat, they would just run into the bush a little way, with their weapons, and would soon return, bringing home good venison, raccoon, bear and fowl. If they chose to have fish, they would only go to the river, or along the seashore; and they would presently fill their canoes with variety of fish, both scaled and shell-fish. And they had abundance of nuts, wild fruits, ground nuts and ground beans; and they planted but little corn and beans. They had no contention about their lands, for they lay in common; and they had but one large dish, and could all eat together in peace and love. But alas! It is not so now; all our hunting and fowling and fishing is entirely gone. And we have begun to work our land, keep horses and cattle and hogs; and we build houses and fence in lots. And now we plainly see that one dish and one fire will not do any longer for us. Some few there are that are stronger than others; and they will keep off the poor, weak, the halt and blind, and will take the dish to themselves. Yea, they will rather call the white people and the mulattoes to eat out of our dish; and poor widows and orphans must be pushed aside, and there they must sit, crying and starving, and die. And so we are now come to our good brethren of the Assembly, with hearts full of sorrow and grief, for immediate help. And therefore our most humble and earnest request is, that our dish of suckutash may be equally divided amongst us, that every one may have his own little dish by himself, that he may eat quietly and do with his dish as he pleases, that every one may have his own fire."

Source: De Forest, John W. *History of the Indians of Connecticut from the Earliest Known Period to 1850.* Hartford, Conn.: Wm. Jas. Hamersley, 1852, pp. 480–481.

DOCUMENT
1.10

An Act to Prevent the Spreading of Contagious Sickness

" . . . Whose Duty It Shall Be to Remove All Filth of Any Kind Whatever"

June 22, 1797

During the course of the eighteenth century, officials in some American colonies, cities, and towns took halting steps to institute regulations designed to protect the public health. Most of these early policies were crafted to combat the spread of contagious diseases like smallpox, malaria, scarlet fever, and diphtheria, which were carried to the New World by the European settlers. Establishing the parameters for quarantines of individuals and ships believed to be carrying these pathogens was a primary point of emphasis in these early public health rules. Town fathers and state authorities also believed that a hazy but clear linkage existed between sickness and the presence of garbage; human and animal waste; and effluents from the operations of slaughterhouses, tanneries, and other businesses.

These points of recognition led to the passage of laws such as Massachusetts's Public Health Act of 1797, excerpted here. The two major features of this legislation, which was approved on June 22 by the state assembly, were a set of quarantine rules for suspected carriers of disease and language empowering municipalities to create public health departments so as to enforce local sanitation regulations.

An Act to Prevent the Spreading of Contagious Sickness

SECT. 1. *Be it Enacted by the Senate and House of Representatives in General Court assembled, and by the authority of the same,* That for the better preventing the spreading of infection, when it shall happen that any person or persons coming from abroad, or belonging to any town or place within this State, shall be visited, or shall lately before have been visited with the plague, small pox, pestilential or malignant fever, or other contagious sickness, the infection whereof may probably be communicated to others, the selectmen of the town where such person or persons may arrive or be, are hereby empowered to take care and make effectual provision in the best way they can, for the preservation of the inhabitants, by removing such sick or infected person or persons and placing him or them in a separate house or houses, and by providing nurses, attendance, and other assistance and necessaries for them, which nurses, attendance and other assistance and necessaries, shall be at the charge of the parties themselves, their parents or masters (if able) or otherwise at the charge of the town or place whereto they belong; and in case such person or persons are not inhabitants of any town or place within this State, then at the charge of the Commonwealth. . . .

SECT. 3. *And be it further enacted,* That it shall and may be lawful for the Selectmen of any town near to, or bordering upon, either of the neighboring States, to appoint by writing under their hands, some meet person or persons to attend at ferries or other places by or over which passengers may pass from such infected places; which person or persons so appointed, shall have power to examine such passengers as they may suspect to bring infection with them, and, if need be, to hinder and restrain them from traveling, until licensed thereto by a Justice of the Peace within such county, or by the selectmen of the town in which such person or persons may come; and any passenger who coming from such infected place, shall (without license as aforesaid) presume to travel within this State, unless it be to return by the most direct way to the State from whence he came, after he shall be cautioned to depart by the person or persons appointed as aforesaid, shall forfeit and pay the sum of *one hundred dollars;* the several forfeitures aforesaid to be recovered by action of debt in any Court of Record proper to try the same, one moiety to and for the use of the town where the offence shall be committed, the other moiety to the use of the person who may sue for the same.

SECT. 4. *And be it further Enacted,* That if need be, any two Justices of the Peace may make out a warrant directed to the Sheriff of the County, or his deputy, or Constables of the town or place where any such sick person or persons may be, requiring them or any of them, in the name of the Commonwealth, with the advice and direction of the Selectmen of the same, to remove such infected person or persons, or to impress and take up convenient houses, lodging, nurses, attendance and other necessaries, for the accommodation, safety and relief of the sick. And such Sheriff, his Deputy and Constable, are hereby authorized and required to execute such Warrant accordingly. . . .

SECT. 6. *And be it further enacted,* That inquiry shall be made by the officer or other person on duty at the castle in the harbour of *Boston,* of every vessel coming from sea, and passing by the said castle, whether any infectious sickness be on Board, or has been on board, since such vessel left the port from whence she last came; and if any such vessel has any sickness on board, or has had any on board since her leaving such port, in such case, orders shall be given by said officer, or other person on duty, to the master or commander of such vessel, immediately to anchor, and to remain at anchor until a certificate shall be obtained from the major part of the selectmen of the town of *Boston*, that they are of opinion such vessel may come up to the town without danger to the inhabitants, or until the said Master or commander shall receive orders from the said Selectmen to anchor his Vessel near the Hospital on *Rainsford's Island* in the harbour of *Boston*. And in case any master or commander of a vessel, shall by himself or the people on voard, make false answer, when enquired of as aforesaid, by the Officer or other person on duty as aforesaid, or after orders are given as aforesaid, shall neglect or refuse to anchor near the Castle as aforesaid or come on shore, or suffer any passenger or other person belonging to the vessel, to come on shore, or any goods to be taken out before the vessel shall have anchored, or without liberty from the Selectmen as aforesaid; or in case any master or commander of a vessel ordered to anchor near the Hospital aforesaid, shall neglect or refuse so to do; in every such case, every Master or Commander so offending, shall forfeit and pay for each offence the sum of Four hundred Dollars, or suffer six months imprisonment. . . .

SECT. 11. *And be it further enacted* That each town, or district in this Commonwealth, may at their meeting held in March or April, annually, or at any other meeting legally warned for the purpose, when they shall adjudge it to be necessary choose and appoint a health Committee to consist of not less than five nor more than nine suitable persons, or one person to be a Health Officer, whose duty it shall be to remove all filth of any kind whatever, which shall be found in any of the Streets, Lanes, Wharves, Dock, or in any other place whatever within the limits of the yown to which such Committee or Health Officer belongs, whenever such filth shall in their judgment endanger the lives or the health of the inhabitants thereof; all the expenses whereof to be paid by the person or persons who placed it there if known, or if not, by the town by which said committee or Health Officer was appointed. And whenever any filth as aforesaid, shall be found on private property, said Committee or Health Officer shall notify and order the owner or occupier thereof after twenty-four hours notice to remove the same, at their own expense; and in case said owner or occupier shall neglect to remove such filth from his or her property, after the expiration of the time aforesaid he or they so offending shall forfeit and pay a fine of *one hundred dollars,* to be sued for and recovered with costs of suit, by said Committee or Health Officer before any Court proper to try the same, for the use of the Poor of the Town in which such offence is committed. And said owner or occupier as aforesaid shall be liable and obliged to repay to said Town all costs and charges which the said Committee or Health Officer may have incurred in removing the filth from his or her property, and in case of refusal to pay the same, he or they may be sued in the same way as is provided in this Act for the recovery of fines as aforesaid.

Source: *Acts and Resolves of Massachusetts, 1796–97.* Boston: Commonwealth of Massachusetts, 1797, pp. 356–365.

CHAPTER 2

An Emerging Empire

---

1 8 0 0 – 1 8 5 0

This early era of American environmental history was marked by an almost complete *absence* of regulation regarding the use of the continent's timber, game, minerals, water, and other natural resources. Environmental policy remained virtually nonexistent in part because conservation concerns had not yet penetrated the national consciousness and in part because governmental authority was weak in many parts of the nation's interior, where much of the greatest land alteration and natural resource exploitation had shifted. Instead, just as in America's colonial era, the emphasis among lawmaker and citizen alike remained on geographic expansion and economic betterment. And in most areas of the country, both of these goals hinged on the acquisition, commodification, liquidation, alteration, and development of natural resources. This reality gave legislators—from U.S. senators down to town council members—little incentive to turn their faces into those hurricane winds of free enterprise and buck the laissez-faire governing philosophy of the day.

A WHIRLWIND OF TERRITORIAL EXPANSION

In the aftermath of the American Revolution, the amount of territory under the jurisdiction of the federal government of the United States grew at an astounding rate. Between 1780 and 1802 the original thirteen states ceded their frontier holdings west of the Appalachian Mountains to the national government—more than 540 million acres in all—as a condition of the original Articles of Confederation. Meanwhile, national leaders scrambled to establish guidelines for handling the Old Northwest Territory, a vast territory around the Great Lakes that the federal government had acquired from Great Britain at the end of the Revolutionary War. This 266,000-square-mile territory eventually became modern-day Michigan, Ohio, Illinois, Indiana, Wisconsin, and part of Minnesota.

The ultimate disposition of these lands was shaped by two major laws, the first of which was the Land Ordinance of 1785. This law provided a blueprint for the measurement and distribution of the heavily forested territory. It instructed government surveyors to divide the Northwest Territory into townships that were six miles square, a total of thirty-six square miles of territory. These townships were, in turn, divided into thirty-six, one-mile-square (640-acre) sections, one of which was reserved for public schooling and four of which were set aside to disperse to Revolutionary War veterans. The remaining sections would then be sold at public auction at a minimum price of a dollar an acre. This scheme provided an orderly methodology for taking inventory of the natural resources of

Territorial expansion paved the way for massive investments in infrastructure "improvements" across the American interior. One such project was the 325-mile Erie Canal, which became a vital trade artery between eastern ports and the Great Lakes region after its completion in 1825.

the Great Lakes region and an efficient system for the disbursal of those resources into private hands for development. "Thus, not just with rifle, plow, and ax but also with compass and plumb line did the new Americans impose their will on nature," summarized environmental journalist Philip Shabecoff.[1]

The second major federal act regarding the Northwest Territory was the Northwest Ordinance of 1787, which set conditions for future statehood within the territory and formally instituted English common law into the region. Of note, this act also stipulated strong private property rights for individuals, such as guarantees that private landholdings could be passed down from generation to generation. When the national government acquired new territories in the West and Gulf Coast regions in the nineteenth century, these same laws were extended into those areas as well.

Surveying of the Old Northwest Territory began in 1786 at the precise point where the Ohio River spilled across the western border of Pennsylvania. The government surveyors moved steadily westward from there, laying down a grid of townships and sections that eventually spread all the way across the continent to the Pacific Ocean. "That first square inch of the first surveyor's stake was a kind of polestar of national development, the anchored point of reckoning for more than a billion acres," observed scholar Elliott West. "Nowhere else in the world would an area of such size be laid out in a uniform land system."[2]

In 1803 another massive slab of the North American continent was acquired by the United States from France. The Louisiana Purchase engineered by President Thomas Jefferson added 827,000 square miles (523 million acres) to the United States, roughly doubling its size in one fell swoop (**see Document 2.2**).

Opponents of the acquisition derided the territory as "a great waste, a wilderness unpeopled with any beings except wolves and wandering Indians."[3] Jefferson and his allies, however, recognized that as the new territory was settled and developed it would lift the young nation to a new level of economic power. This land eventually became the states of Arkansas; Missouri; Iowa; Nebraska; South Dakota; almost all of Oklahoma and Kansas; and large portions of modern-day Colorado, Louisiana, Minnesota, Montana, North Dakota, and Wyoming.

Exploring the Lands beyond the Mississippi

As adventurous settlers spilled into these newly acquired regions and began carving out new farms and communities, Jefferson cast his gaze across the Mississippi to the mysterious lands that lay beyond that mighty waterway. He was convinced that this region—including Spanish-held territories in the modern-day American Southwest—constituted the next building block in the coalescing quest to build an American empire in the New World. With this in mind, Jefferson secured funding from Congress for four expeditions of western exploration designed to pave the way for future geographic and economic expansion. Future generations of Americans would, according to Jefferson, "fill up the canvas we begin." [4]

In 1804 William Dunbar and George Hunter led a two-year expedition into modern-day Arkansas. Two years later, an ill-fated expedition to chart the length of the Red and Arkansas rivers set forth under the command of Thomas Freeman and Peter Custis. That same year, Zebulon Pike commanded a two-year expedition of discovery that reached the southern Rockies. But all of these undertakings paled in importance to the expedition mounted by Meriwether Lewis and William Clark and their Corps of Discovery. Preparation for the mission began in late 1803, and more than two years later the team returned to St. Louis in September 1806 (see Document 2.1).

The grand purposes of the famed Lewis and Clark expedition were to find an all-water route connecting the Mississippi to the Pacific coast, to identify

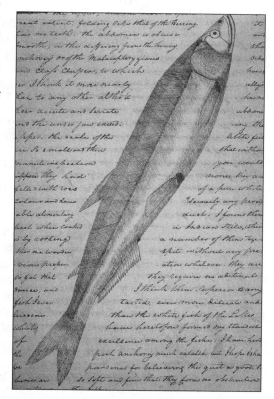

After Thomas Jefferson's purchase of 523 million acres from France in 1803, Meriwether Lewis and William Clark led their famous expedition through the Louisiana Territory. The trip lasted more than two years and covered some 8,000 miles. This page from William Clark's journal depicts the white salmon trout observed during the course of the expedition.

promising regions for farming and other commercial activity, and to lay the groundwork with northwestern Indian tribes for the establishment of profitable new networks of trade in furs and other resources. During their three-year sojourn, Lewis and Clark covered 8,000 miles of American wilderness. They mapped out the courses of the Missouri and Columbia rivers and the locations of ancient forests, mountains, and prairies. In the process, they provided arresting descriptions of the cultures of indigenous tribespeople; related harrowing encounters with grizzly bears and boat-crushing rapids; and provided the first European descriptions of hundreds of previously unknown trees, plants, and animals. "The Lewis and Clark expedition provided a huge store of information about the landscape, the natural history, and the native peoples of the West," summarized Gregory

Nobles. "No other expedition before the first human landing on the moon did as much to ignite interest in the unknown. The West had become the landscape of the nation's imagination."[5]

INDIAN LANDS NO MORE

This era of land acquisition, feverish exploration, and soaring expansionist rhetoric was enormously disquieting to Native American tribes around the Great Lakes, west of the Appalachians, and along the Gulf Coast. They knew that the tribes of the East had been pried loose from their traditional territories during the eighteenth century, and some saw proliferating signs of white encroachment in their own woods and fields as harbingers of their own doom. White lawmakers and negotiators tried to reassure them. The U.S. Congress even declared in the 1787 Northwest Ordinance that "the utmost good faith shall always be observed towards the Indians: their lands and property shall never be taken from them without their consent; and, in their property, rights, and liberty, they shall never be invaded or disturbed, unless in just and lawful wars authorized by Congress; but laws founded in justice and humanity, shall from time to time be made for preventing wrongs being done to them, and for preserving peace and friendship with them."[6]

Some members of Congress may have viewed this declaration as a sincerely meant one, but others regarded such rhetoric as a meaningless sop that could be brushed aside in the future. And as the white demand for new land, new development, and new economic opportunities continued to escalate, the future arrived swiftly. By the close of the first decade of the nineteenth century, the once-dominant Cherokees of the American Southeast had ceded more than half their territory to the U.S. government and reluctantly taken up Christianity, farming, and slavery. All of these wrenching changes were overseen by Cherokee leaders who were convinced that assimilation was essential to the tribe's survival.

Other tribes resisted white settlers and government negotiators with greater force. Indians such as Tecumseh, a leader of the Shawnee people in the Ohio River Valley, organized or took part in violent campaigns against the invaders (see **Document 2.3**). Other tribes, both in the Great Lakes region and the South, flatly refused to sell their land. But defiant Indian leaders, like Tecumseh, were inevitably slain or otherwise neutralized, and many of the tribes eventually succumbed to the relentless pressure and signed their lands over. The few remaining hold-outs, meanwhile, were fleeced in one way or another. Some government negotiators forged the signatures of tribal leaders on documents of cession, whereas others bribed the chieftains or got them intoxicated to secure their cooperation. In other instances, white speculators, settlers, and traders illegally took up residence in Indian territory. When the Indians tried to drive them off, American military forces were quickly sent to eliminate the threat to the citizenry. The United States thus "dispossess[ed] the Indians by force or by punitive treaties that the government imposed on the defeated tribes."[7]

In December 1817 President James Monroe informed Congress of the signing of several of these one-sided treaties, then dispensed with the usual empty rhetorical gestures about Indian rights. Instead, he candidly acknowledged that the steadily expanding American population possessed a great appetite for the land and natural resources still possessed by Native American tribes, and he further intimated that assimilation was the Indians' sole hope for survival in the face of this hunger:

By these acquisitions, and others that may reasonably be expected soon to follow, we shall be enabled to extend our settlements from the inhabited parts of the State of Ohio along Lake Erie into the Michigan Territory, and to connect our settlements by degrees through the State of Indiana and the Illinois Territory to that of Missouri. A similar and equally advantageous effect will soon be produced to the south, through the whole extent of the States and territory which border on the waters emptying into the Mississippi and the Mobile.

In this progress, which the rights of nature demand and nothing can prevent, marking a growth rapid and gigantic, it is our duty to make new efforts for the preservation, improvement, and civilization of the native inhabitants. The hunter state can exist only in the vast uncultivated desert. It yields to the more dense and compact form and greater force of civilized population; and of right it ought to yield, for the earth was given to mankind to support the greatest number of which it is capable, and no tribe or people have a right to withhold from the wants of others more than is necessary for their own support and comfort.[8]

Two years later the United States signed a treaty with Spain giving America the territory that became Florida. This acquisition gave U.S. leaders control over the one piece of southeastern territory that had previously eluded them. It also opened up another front for white settlement, to the dismay of the peninsula's indigenous peoples.

INDIAN REMOVAL IN THE SOUTH

Native American tribes on the eastern side of the Mississippi continued to lose ground—literally—to white settlement and development throughout the early and mid-1820s. But the transfer of land and natural resources from Indian to white hands accelerated greatly after the election of Andrew Jackson to the presidency in 1828.

From the outset, Jackson was determined to remove the remnants of the so-called Five Civilized Tribes (Cherokee, Chickasaw, Choctaw, Creek, and Seminole) from the American Southeast. His single-minded efforts in this regard stemmed in part from his own deeply held prejudices against Indians, but they were also driven by public clamoring for new land for cotton cultivation. Ever since the unveiling of Eli Whitney's revolutionary cotton gin in 1793, production of the crop had soared. But southern planters along the Atlantic Coast quickly worked their lands to exhaustion, so they turned their attention to the so-called "cotton frontier"—uncultivated Indian land in parts of Georgia, Alabama, and Mississippi blessed with rich soil perfect for growing cotton.

State officials in Georgia took the early lead in claiming these remaining Indian lands for white use. Georgia legislators took action to strip Indians in the state of all land ownership rights, a campaign that met with Jackson's approval. "Build a fire under them," he reportedly told one state senator. "When it gets hot enough, they'll move."[9] Cherokee leaders fought back in the only venue open to them—the U.S. legal system. Remarkably, their argument that individual states could not pass laws affecting independent Indian nations was sympathetically received by the U.S. Supreme Court. In *Cherokee Nation v. Georgia* (1831), the court revealed a plainly paternalistic mindset when it described the Cherokee Nation's relationship to the United States as "that of a ward to his guardian." But the Court also held that the Cherokees had an "unquestionable right to the lands they occupy."[10]

One year later, in *Worcester v. Georgia,* the Court ruled that only the federal govern-ment—not individual states—had the power to pass laws or make treaties with indigenous peoples. According to the Court opinion handed down by Chief Justice John Marshall, "[T]he Cherokee nation . . . is a distinct community, occupying its own territory . . . in which the laws of Georgia can have no force, and which the citizens of Georgia have no right to enter but with the assent of the Cherokees themselves, or in conformity with trea-ties and with the acts of Congress. . . . These laws of Georgia are therefore unconstitu-tional, void, and of no effect."[11]

This proved to be a Pyrrhic victory for the Cherokee and other southern tribes, however. Jackson openly mocked the Court's *Worcester v. Georgia* decision. In a possibly apocryphal story, Jackson was even reputed to have declared, "John Marshall has ren-dered his decision. Now let him enforce it." The veracity of this particular anecdote aside, its tone accurately reflected the president's contempt for the legal reasoning underlying the Court's decision.

Indeed, Jackson's dismissive reaction resulted in large part from the fact that by the time the *Worcester v. Georgia* decision came down, he had already implemented draco-nian federal policies against the tribes. In May 1830 Jackson signed the Indian Removal Act, which opened up all remaining Indian territory in the South to white settlement and exploitation. The Act also authorized Jackson to forcibly relocate tribes to lands west of the Mississippi if they did not accept government offers of compensation (**see Document 2.7**).

Jackson wielded this authority ruthlessly, and by the close of the 1830s the southern bayous, forests, and valleys that had once supported dozens of tribes had been wiped clean of their presence. The most notorious example of this government-mandated ejec-tion of Indians from their homelands was the 1838–1839 "Trail of Tears," in which the remnants of the Cherokee Nation were herded together by U.S. troops and forced to march a thousand miles to a reservation in Oklahoma. An estimated 4,000 Indians died along the way. All told, the Indian Removal Act opened about 25 million acres of land to farming, timber cutting, swamp drainage, and other environment-altering activity. Simi-lar events unfolded, albeit on a smaller scale, in the Old Northwest Territory, where Sac, Fox, and other Native tribes were pried loose from their Great Lakes world and forcibly marched to government-created reservations west of the Mississippi.

FROM SEA TO SHINING SEA

America's formal territorial expansion underwent a lull in the 1830s and early 1840s. Thanks to the reports of Lewis and Clark and assorted frontiersmen who followed in their wake, Americans knew that the so-called Great American Desert beyond the Mississippi actually had tantalizing potential for settlement and development. In fact, it became an article of faith among many Americans that the "manifest destiny" of the United States was to someday establish itself as an empire of truly continental reach and breadth (**see Document 2.9**). But despite the tantalizing reports of Lewis and Clark and other intrepid explorers of the far West, Americans of the 1830s remained largely preoccupied with "civilizing" the Great Lakes and the lands contained in the Louisiana Purchase. Other factors kept development of the far West on the back burner as well. The massive wave of European immigration that crashed on American shores in the nineteenth century was only in its early stages at this time, so there was ample land for people—immigrant and native-born alike—in the East. In addition, transportation options and development capital for the West were extremely limited. Finally, proposed strategies of western land settlement had become entangled in the ever more vexing slavery issue, with pro-slavery and anti-slavery forces both angling to shape the political, economic, and social implications of America's territorial expansion to their benefit.

After Democrat James Polk became America's eleventh president in 1845, however, this extended pause in the nation's westward expansion came to an end. A devoted proponent of the Manifest Destiny philosophy, Polk immediately became involved in a tense showdown with Great Britain over possession of the Oregon Territory. The 1844 Democratic platform on which Polk ran had claimed the entire Oregon territory, from California northward to a latitude of 54'40", the southern boundary of Russian Alaska. After being sworn in, Polk resisted the calls of expansionists who cried, "Fifty-four forty or fight!" But his political brinksmanship on the Oregon issue alarmed and angered many members of Her Majesty's government. In the end, the Polk administration and British officials averted possible war in the Pacific Northwest by hammering out an 1846 settlement in which the United States received all disputed territory—about 180 million acres—south of the 49th parallel.

Polk also moved quickly to annex Texas as America's twenty-eighth state, then brazenly approached Mexico with an offer to purchase California. These moves precipitated the Mexican-American War of 1846–1848, which ended very badly for Mexico. American forces crushed their opponent in battle after battle, and by the time the war ended in February 1848 with the Treaty of Guadalupe Hidalgo, the Mexican government had little negotiating leverage. It was forced to cede nearly half of its national territory—today's American Southwest from California to Texas, a sum of about 334 million acres—to the United States in exchange for $15 million. This treaty was made even more painful for Mexico by its timing: It was signed only weeks after the discovery of gold in California, a discovery that helped galvanize America's great westward migration in the second half of the nineteenth century. Another 19 million acres of Mexican territory were acquired by the United States in 1853 in the Gadsden Purchase. This land eventually became the southern section of the state of Arizona.

ARRIVAL OF THE INDUSTRIAL AGE

By the time Polk left office in March 1849 (poor health led him to decide against running for a second term), the United States had finally become transcontinental in scope. The contiguous borders of the modern-day United States had been branded across the continent from sea to shining sea, to the delight of land speculators and intrepid settlers alike. In addition, economic activity based on natural resource exploitation—the California gold rush, fur trading in the Pacific Northwest, harvesting of buffalo on the Great Plains—was already flourishing in some remote pockets of the West.

Nonetheless, most American economic activity and resource development remained concentrated east of the Mississippi during the first half of the nineteenth century because it was here that the cataclysmic societal and environmental changes wrought by the Industrial Revolution first manifested themselves.

America's Industrial Age was launched in the early nineteenth century along the shorelines of New England's rivers. British immigrant Samuel Slater, Massachusetts native Francis Cabot Lowell, and assorted investors used new technological innovations to establish America's first machine-based industrial enterprises—textile mills. And because early textile mill operations were predicated on water power, New England's rivers became the cornerstone of the industry's fortunes. Throughout the first half of the 1800s and beyond, the textile industry maximized those resources to the fullest extent possible through dams, diversions, and other engineering work. These changes, however, came at a steep environmental price. As one historical study notes, "[I]n order to exploit the kinetic energy of New England's rivers the early industrial capitalists had literally to take them apart and extract their power, a process they could not accomplish, given the technology at hand, without nearly killing them as ecosystems"[12]

This environmental toll occurred in large part because during the first decades of the nineteenth century, well-entrenched legal doctrines in New England about water rights were altered to conform to the wishes of the region's emerging industrial corporations. The corporate interests eviscerated English common law rights, codified in a series of colonial "fish acts," that had explicitly prohibited textile mills or other commercial business from obstructing the free passage of migratory fish.

Since the colonial era, laws across the colonies had explicitly protected the public's unfettered right to waterways for fishing and recreation—to the point that citizens had legal authority to remove dams and other obstructions if they posed a significant impediment to that access. This authority stemmed from the belief that navigable watercourses—rivers, lakes, and bays—were open to common use by the public and were not the property of riparian landowners. But mill owners and their legislative allies chipped away at these laws, and in 1848 they came crashing down. That year, Massachusetts legislators passed a statute that gave the textile owners who controlled the Merrimack River's Lawrence Dam—the largest dam in the United States or Europe at the time—the option of doing away with fish ladders or dam breaches that had previously been mandated to help the Merrimack's spawning fish species survive. Instead, the dam operators (who were also the mill owners) could provide financial compensation to upstream fishermen for fish losses. This law was ultimately affirmed by the state Supreme Court, which sided with the corporate interests. Justice Lemuel Shaw explained that in the Court's view, the legislature had the power to decide "whether the public good expected from the fishery . . . or the public advantage . . . from building up a large manufacturing town . . . should preponderate."[13] Environmental considerations received short shrift in this legal jousting.

This absence of concern for ecological health or resource sustainability was the rule rather than the exception all across the industrializing East. Indeed, the advent of the Industrial Revolution and the corresponding growth of the nation's market economy gave new fuel to what environmental historian Theodore Steinberg termed the "commodification of nature"—a belief that natural resources were nothing more than commercial commodities to be liquidated, harvested, or otherwise developed in the name of economic growth and national glory. "The market revolution," charged another environmental historian, "threatened the American environment more than any other development in modern history. . . . It made profit-and-loss the sole criterion for dealing with nature."[14] In light of this attitude, few efforts were made to regulate the activities in textile mills, tanneries, iron ore quarries, sawmills, and other polluting enterprises that were accounting for more and more jobs. From 1820 to 1840, in fact, the number of American workers employed in the manufacturing and construction sectors more than doubled, from 350,000 to almost 800,000.

Regions of the country that failed to recognize the obvious necessity of squeezing profit out of nature came to be viewed with equal parts scorn and pity. In 1846, for example, the Massachusetts textile titan Abbot Lawrence upbraided a Virginian acquaintance for his state's lack of initiative in this regard. "The truth is that nature has been profuse in her gifts in behalf of your people, and you have done but little for yourselves," he admonished. "The waterpower on the James River at Richmond is unrivalled, and it seems a great waste of natural wealth to permit it to run into the sea, having hardly touched a water-wheel."[15]

THE TRANSPORTATION REVOLUTION

Technological advances in the early 1800s also had an enormous impact on the young nation's transportation infrastructure—which in turn opened huge tracts of American wilderness to farming, timber cutting, mining, and other land-altering activities. In 1807 inventor Robert Fulton inaugurated the nation's steamboating era with his legendary voyage up New York's Hudson River. American entrepreneurs, investors, and legislators embraced this new steam-driven technological marvel. By the close of the 1820s steam-powered vessels had become essential elements in the fast-growing domestic trade in timber, cotton, wheat, and other market goods all across the eastern United States. In addition, they became instrumental in rolling back the frontier—first west of the Appalachians and eventually west of the Mississippi. By 1840 hundreds of steamboats were plying the 5,000-mile Ohio–Mississippi river system on a daily basis. A few years later, more than two dozen steam packets could be found huffing up and down the Missouri River, providing the first wave of white settlers and fur traders in the region with an essential link to the wider economic world.

Coastal steamers also contributed to the accelerating environmental exploitation taking place across America. During the 1830s and 1840s, coastal lines based in port cities received ever-escalating volumes of wheat, timber, coal, tobacco, and cotton from the nation's interior, where land clearing for crop cultivation, livestock use, mining, and timber was accelerating in lockstep with the nation's economic and population growth. Regularly scheduled steamship freight and passenger packets plied coastal waters up and down the New England coastline, and by 1852 seventeen steamers had established regular runs between New York City and major southern ports like Charleston, Mobile, Savannah, and Richmond.

This revolution in water-based transportation was greatly aided by government sponsorship and pro-development policies. Construction of the famed Erie Canal, for example, was financed by the state of New York. This massive project was championed by New York politician De Witt Clinton, who vowed that it would "convey more riches on its waters than any other canal in the world," releasing financial resources "to be expanded in great public improvements; in encouraging the arts and sciences; in patronizing the operations of industry; in fostering the inventions of genius, and in diffusing the blessing of knowledge"[16] **(see Document 2.5).**

Clinton was right, as it turned out. When the 363-mile-long canal was completed in 1825, it opened a tremendously lucrative trade link between eastern population centers such as New York City and the territories of the Great Lakes region. It reduced freight costs between New York and the Great Lakes by more than 80 percent and cut shipping time from a month to a little longer than a week. Shipments of Great Lakes timber, minerals, and crops to the East soared. The holds of westbound ships, meanwhile, were crammed with factory-made textiles and farming tools intended for the immigrant families that were pouring into the newly accessible farmlands of the Upper Midwest. Many of these changes were evident within a few months of the canal's opening. "It is an impressive sight to gaze up and down the canal" from one of the numerous bridges that spanned the Erie, declared one admirer. "In either direction, as far as the eye can see, long lines of boats can be observed. By night, their flickering head lamps give the impression of swarms of fireflies."[17] The stunning success of the Erie Canal also triggered an explosion of publicly financed canal building in other parts of the East. By 1850 more than 3,700 miles of publicly funded canals had been carved into the American interior.

Official policies designed to aid water transport also changed American environmental conditions in other significant ways. From the 1820s through the 1840s, for example, the federal government adopted policies of western river "improvement" that involved all manner of river re-engineering. Some of the steps taken, such as removing giant logjams that hindered river navigation and commerce, had limited and temporary environmental repercussions. But others, such as dam and levee building, water diversions, and clearing of forestlands along river corridors (the latter to supply steamers with fuel and ensure that the waterways remained clear of hazards), destroyed ancient spawning runs and clogged streams with soil runoff from exposed riverbanks (see Document 2.8).

Distinctions among these river-altering policies, which varied so enormously in their respective environmental consequences, were virtually nonexistent. All were heartily endorsed by lawmakers, business interests, and government officials as equally valid weapons to be used against nature. The exclusive concern of policymakers was to wrestle America's wild rivers and forests into submission and force them to serve new masters of economic advancement and national empire. "It is difficult to form a just conception of the magnitude of this work or fully to appreciate the important results that are to flow from it," wrote one government engineer who helped clear the Red River in Arkansas for navigation and settlement in the 1830s:

> The river is navigable more than a thousand miles above the raft [logjam to be removed], and through a region not surpassed in fertility by any on the continent. This extensive country is comparatively unsettled; its vast resources and wealth remain to be developed. . . . Hundreds are looking to its removal as the signal for entering the country. The success of the undertaking once involved in doubt, and the permanent advantages that must result from it, are no longer matters of uncertainty.[18]

ARRIVAL OF THE IRON HORSE

At the same time that rivers and harbors were being reshaped across the country to meet commercial navigation needs, another technological marvel of the Industrial Age—the railroad—was also making its presence felt. The first significant U.S. railroad—the Baltimore & Ohio Railroad—did not open for traffic until 1830. By the mid-1830s, however, more than 200 rail lines had been chartered, and tracks were being laid to connect cities and towns all across the eastern United States. This construction was helped along at every stage by federal, state, and local policymakers who saw railroads as even more economically transformational than steamboats and steamships. As Marshall Moore, territorial governor of Washington, declared at mid-century, "[Railroads are] not a mere convenience to local populations, but a vast machinery for the building up of empires. They are the true alchemy of the age, which transmutes the otherwise worthless resources of a country into gold."[19]

This rendering of the railroad as an almost mythological entity became commonplace not only in halls of power, but also in the nation's newspapers and magazines. *Putnam's Monthly Magazine*, for example, lauded the so-called Iron Horse as an earth-shaking, fire-breathing embodiment of Manifest Destiny: "Shall not cities be formed from his vaporous breath, and men spring up from the cinders of his furnace? Imagine, then, the vulcan-wrought engine rushing from sea to sea, dispensing lightning from its sides and thunder from its wheels."[20] Ralph Waldo Emerson, meanwhile, described railroad iron as "a magician's rod, in its power to evoke the sleeping energies of land and water."[21]

This conventional wisdom—that railroads could unlock new horizons of land development and wealth across the continent—led legislators to approve massive donations of federal land for their use. All told, the United States granted 37 million acres of the public domain for railroad rights-of-way over the course of the nineteenth century (even larger grants were made directly to railroad companies in the 1860s and 1870s). The federal government also donated 3.4 million acres to the states for road construction and another 13.9 million acres for canal construction.[22] In addition, Congress passed legislation such as the Swamp and Overflow Act, which authorized states to "reclaim" wetlands rich in biodiversity for agricultural use and flood control. Legislators of all political stripes agreed that these types of "internal improvements" were essential to the young nation's future growth and prosperity (**see Document 2.11**).

Yet even as government policymakers, farmers, mill owners, engineers, and investors hailed each other—and themselves—for their success in reshaping the American landscape into more market-friendly forms, the first stirrings of concern for the natural world also rippled across the land. One early conservationist voice was the famed naturalist and painter John James Audubon. In the 1820s Audubon went on an extended tour of the Ohio River Valley, a region that he had first visited two decades earlier. After concluding his second tour, he expressed utter shock about the ways in which the region had changed:

> [When I] call back to my mind the grandeur and beauty of those almost uninhabited shores; when I picture to myself the dense and lofty summits of the forests, that everywhere spread along the hills and overhung the margins of the stream, unmolested by the axe of the settler; when I know how dearly purchased the safe navigation of that river has been, by the blood of many worthy Virginians; when I see that no longer any aborigines are to be found there, and that the vast herds of Elk, Deer, and Buffaloes which once pastured on these hills, and in these valleys, making for themselves great roads to the several salt-springs, have ceased to exist; when I reflect that all this grand portion of our Union, instead of being in a state of nature, is now more or less covered with villages, farms, and towns, where the din of hammers and machinery is constantly heard; that the woods are fast disappearing under the axe by day, and the fire by night; that hundreds of steamboats are gliding to and fro, over the whole length of the majestic river, forcing commerce to take root and to prosper at every spot; when I see the surplus population of Europe coming to assist in the destruction of the forest, and transplanting civilization into its darkest recesses; when I remember that these extraordinary changes have all taken place in the short period of twenty years, I pause, wonder, and although I know all to be fact, can scarcely believe its reality.[23]

MOVING PUBLIC LANDS INTO PRIVATE HANDS

Regional environmental transformations such as the one documented by Audubon were made possible not only by steamboats, locomotives, and other machines, but also by federal land policies that placed a premium on swiftly transferring public lands into private ownership. This philosophy, which was carried over from the colonial era, had practical underpinnings. Land sales were used to pay off government debts, stimulate economic growth, and attract European immigrants.

But public land disposal policies in the opening decades of the nineteenth century also reflected the enduring political philosophy of Thomas Jefferson, who envisioned America as a fundamentally agrarian society. Laws of this era were designed to encourage private ownership and development of American land for farming purposes. The Harrison Land Act of 1800, for example, gave people the opportunity to buy land in the Old Northwest Territory directly from the federal government—and even extended credit to would-be buyers who could not afford to purchase available parcels outright. A series of Preemption Acts (1830–1841) passed by Congress also promoted privatization by cutting the purchase price of public land in many parts of the country. In these and other cases, small-scale agrarian settlers were among the greatest beneficiaries.

Much of the time, however, these federal land disposal policies amounted to little more than a legislative scramble to impose order on economic and expansionist forces that had metastasized beyond the control of presidents or congressmen. "Land disposal policies largely followed the settlers rather than leading them," explained scholar Richard N. L. Andrews. "The national government simply had neither the administrative capacity nor the political support to restrain the all-out private appropriation and exploitation of the environment that economic opportunities and its own policies promoted."[24]

Land development remained the unquestioned cornerstone of federal natural resource policy until the presidency of John Quincy Adams (1825–1829), who displayed an awareness that the continent's natural resources, although rich and abundant, were finite. This realization did not deter him from supporting a range of pro-development land policies during his presidency, but it also led him to support legislation to develop what we would now call "sustainable" models of natural resource extraction and consumption for forests and other resources in the public domain (see Document 2.6).

Adams also recognized that conservation efforts could be advanced through investments in scientific study of the natural world, as evidenced by his 1828 proposal to establish federal forest reserves dedicated to conservation and research. But these efforts were thwarted by political foes who wanted no limits on exploitation of land and resources in the West and other frontier areas. These setbacks discouraged Adams so much that he glumly reflected that "my own system of administration, which was to make the national domain the inexhaustible fund for progressive and unceasing internal improvement, has failed."[25]

The presidents who followed Adams in the first half of the nineteenth century—Andrew Jackson, Martin Van Buren, William Henry Harrison (who died after only a month in the Oval Office), John Tyler, and James Polk—did not demonstrate similar concern that rampant exploitation of land and resources might be placing America's future economic and environmental health in jeopardy. They endorsed the Manifest Destiny ideal of economic and geographic expansion and put governmental agencies and resources to work in support of that principle. Jackson in particular hewed to a strong "states' rights" political orientation, and he vetoed several federal internal improvement bills that he felt were insufficiently "national" in scope and disproportionately benefited individual states. To Jackson's way of thinking, funding for such projects was the responsibility of states, not the federal government.

Notably, however, Polk did sign legislation creating the U.S. Department of the Interior in March 1849. This cabinet department consolidated the General Land Office, the Indian Affairs Office, and several other offices concerned with the nation's internal affairs. In the second half of the nineteenth century, this agency became the nation's leading administrator of public lands, its most prominent sponsor of western wilderness exploration, and its chief overseer of territorial governments.

VANISHING WILDERNESS AND WILDLIFE

The relentless rollback of the western frontier obscured to some degree the cataclysmic environmental changes that were taking place at the same time in the once-wild lands between the Atlantic shoreline and the mountains of Appalachia. From Maine to Florida, an expanding arsenal of railroads, foundries, mercantile stores, coal mines, steamboats, textile and paper mills, dairy farms, and cotton plantations were all churning away on the shoulders of brawny workmen and the dollars of investors and speculators. Their combined efforts generated explosive growth in eastern cities, new opportunities for inventors and entrepreneurs, shiny promises of a better life for prospective immigrants—and environmental despoilment on an epic scale.

Effective laws to conserve woodlands remained virtually nonexistent in the New England and Middle Atlantic states, so deforestation became a significant problem. River, harbor, and stream conservation continued to receive fitful attention from lawmakers, but these vital ecosystems for waterfowl and spawning fish also attracted city builders, industrialists, and fishermen. Destructive logging, farming, and industrial practices choked more and more waterways with chemicals that poisoned fish, sawdust that smothered spawning beds, and soil from denuded riverbanks. "The destroying angel has visited these once fair forests and limpid streams," lamented one visitor to Virginia's James River corridor in 1850. "Everything everywhere betrays improvident and reckless management."[26] Finally, the handful of environmental laws and regulations that did exist were frequently flouted. In Augusta, Maine, for example, developers in 1838 built a dam—in clear defiance of state laws—that annihilated salmon populations in the entire Kennebec River basin.[27]

Official regulations or science-based guidelines for the encouragement of sustainable cultivation also remained virtually absent in the East (see Document 2.12). As a result, many eastern farmers continued to engage in practices that depleted soil of essential nutrients, then simply moved on to the next tract of land when the overused fields were ruined. "[The American farmer] seldom or never looks forward to the future and progressive improvement of his land," charged one disgusted Englishman after touring eastern farms in 1819. "He uses it as asses are used in this country, worked while they have a spark of life in them, without one care about their support or preservation."[28] A quarter century later, a New Yorker traveling through South Carolina indicated that nothing had changed: "Frequent use of the plow, and the unremitted culture of the soil in corn and cotton, have not only deteriorated the quality of the land, but exposed the surface to be washed away by the heavy rains of these latitudes. . . . The traveler . . . encounters little else than bare hills of red clay, washed into hideous gullies or barren fields."[29]

Wildlife populations east of the Mississippi plummeted in the face of these myriad habitat-shattering trends. And private and market demand for the meat, pelts, and plumage of various wildlife species added additional pressure. Some state and local officials tried to stave off—or at least blunt—these population crashes by passing conservation laws. In 1801, for example, state legislators in New York passed new statutes limiting obstructions to the seasonal migration of native Atlantic salmon. In 1818 Massachusetts lawmakers passed a law to prevent the killing of "useful birds" such as partridges, robins, and larks **(see Document 2.4)**. And several eastern states passed new laws to protect white-tailed deer and other popular game. Authorities never adequately enforced these laws, however, and poaching by ordinary citizens and market hunters increased to epidemic levels. By the 1820s, in fact, market hunters had so depleted eastern forests of game that they turned their attention to the upper Great Lakes. Once they arrived there, the market hunters—with the willing assistance of early settlers—decimated bear, deer, bison, and elk populations in the wildlands of northern Wisconsin and Michigan's Upper Peninsula within a matter of a few decades.

This wastefulness showed that Americans maintained their certitude about the inexhaustibility of the continent's natural resources. It also reflected a bedrock political/philosophical belief that property owners had the right to do whatever they wanted with the resources on their land and a conviction that government's role was to aid—not suppress—economic and geographic expansion.

In a few corners of America, however, citizens watched this wanton destruction of habitat and wildlife with mounting dismay. Observers such as Audubon, Henry David Thoreau, Ralph Waldo Emerson, and George Catlin published meditations on America's vanishing natural world that—generations later—would greatly influence public policy and public attitudes on environmental issues **(see Document 2.10)**. And a small but influential corps of sportsmen began to speak out on the need for stronger conservation laws. Sportsmen like William Elliott, author of the 1846 book *Carolina Sports by Land and Water,* admitted that to many Americans whose ancestors had struggled under European class systems, "the preservation of game is associated in the popular mind with ideas of aristocracy—peculiar privileges to the rich—and oppression towards the poor." But he submitted that the "right to hunt wild animals" without "discretion or limitations" could no longer go unchallenged. Elliott insisted that "conservators" had to defend the nation's besieged forests, rivers, and wildlife from "the throng of destructives who seem bent on . . . extermination."[30]

Other sportsmen added their voices to the nascent conservationist cause. "No other country in the world presents to the sportsman so long a catalogue of the choicest game, whether of fur, fin, or feather, as the United States," declared Henry William Herbert in 1848. But Herbert—writing under the pen name Frank Forrester—warned that if market hunting was not curbed and public awareness of habitat destruction and wildlife loss did not improve, "the game that swarmed of yore in all the fields and forests, in all the lakes, rivers, bays, and creeks of its vast territory are in peril of becoming speedily extinct."[31] These sentiments expressed by Elliott and Herbert became the foundation of the conservationist policies that emerged in America in the second half of the nineteenth century.

NOTES

1. Philip Shabecoff, *A Fierce Green Fire: The American Environmental Movement* (New York: Hill and Wang, 1993), 27.

2. Elliott West, "American Frontier," in *The Oxford History of the American West,* ed. Clyde Milner II, Carol A. O'Connor, and Martha A. Sandweiss (New York: Oxford University Press, 1994), 124.

3. Quoted in Gregory H. Nobles, *American Frontiers: Cultural Encounters and Continental Conquest* (New York: Hill and Wang, 1997), 118.

4. Quoted in *Rivers, Edens, Empires: Lewis and Clark and the Revealing of America*, Library of Congress exhibition, www.loc.gov/exhibits/lewisandclark/lewis-overview.html.

5. Nobles, *American Frontiers*, 120.

6. Quoted in West, "American Frontier," 125.

7. Alvin M. Josephy Jr., *500 Nations: An Illustrated History of North American Indians* (New York: Gramercy, 1994), 281.

8. James Monroe, First Annual Message to Congress, December 12, 1817. Available at The American Presidency Project, www.presidency.ucsb.edu/ws/?pid=29459.

9. Quoted in Josephy, *500 Nations*, 326.

10. *Cherokee Nation v. Georgia*, 30 U.S. 1 (1831). Available at http://supreme.justia.com/us/30/1/case.html.

11. *Worcester v. Georgia*. 31 U.S. 515 (1832). Available at http://supreme.justia.com/us/31/515/case.html.

12. Donald Worster, "The Natural Environment: The North," in *Encyclopedia of American Social History*, ed. Mary Kupiece Cayton, Peter W. Williams, and Elliot J. Gorn (New York: Scribner's, 1993).

13. Quoted in Diana Muir, *Reflections in Bulloughs Pond: Economy and Ecosystem in New England* (Hanover, N.H.: University Press of New England, 2000), 163.

14. Carolyn Merchant, *The Columbia Guide to American Environmental History* (New York: Columbia University Press, 2002), 68.

15. Abbott Lawrence, *Memoir of Abbot Lawrence*, ed. Hamilton Andrews Hill (Boston: Little, Brown, 1883), 138, 140.

16. Quoted in Peter L. Bernstein, *Wedding of the Waters: The Erie Canal and the Making of a Great Nation* (New York: Norton, 2005), 343.

17. Quoted in Page Smith, *The Shaping of America*. Vol. 3 of *A People's History of the Young Republic* (New York: McGraw-Hill, 1980), 774.

18. Quoted in *Reports from the Court of Claims Submitted to the House of Representatives, 1859–1860* (Washington, D.C.: Thomas H. Ford, 1860), 15.

19. Quoted in D. W. Meinig, *The Shaping of America, Vol. 3: Transcontinental America, 1850–1915* (New Haven, Conn.: Yale University Press, 2000), 68.

20. Quoted in James A. Ward, *Railroads and the Character of America, 1820–1887* (Knoxville: University of Tennessee Press, 1986).

21. Ralph Waldo Emerson, "The Young American." Originally published in *Nature: Addresses and Lectures*, 1849. Reprinted in *The Collected Works of Ralph Waldo Emerson* (New York: Oxford University Press, 1884), 296.

22. Richard N. L. Andrews, *Managing the Environment, Managing Ourselves: A History of American Environmental Policy* (New Haven, Conn.: Yale University Press, 1999), 89–90.

23. John James Audubon, *Audubon and His Journals*, vol. 2, ed. Maria R. Audubon (New York: Scribner's, 1897), 206–207.

24. Andrews, *Managing the Environment, Managing Ourselves*, 93.

25. Quoted in Frederick Jackson Turner, *The Frontier in American History* (New York: Holt, 1920), 26.

26. Quoted in Steven Stoll, *Larding the Lean Earth: Soil and Society in Nineteenth Century America* (New York: Hill and Wang, 2002), 137.

27. Tim Palmer, *Endangered Rivers and the Conservation Movement* (Berkeley: University of California Press, 1986), 16.

28. Quoted in Stoll, *Larding the Lean Earth*, 35.

29. "Letter from J.R. Poinsett on the Saluda River near Greensville, SC," in *Transactions of the New York State Agricultural Society*, vol. 4. (Albany: E. Mack, 1845), 340.

30. William Elliott, *Carolina Sports by Land and Water* (1846, repr., Columbia, SC: State Co. Printers, 1918), 260.

31. Quoted in John F. Rieger, *American Sportsmen and the Origins of Conservation*, 3rd ed. (Corvallis: Oregon State University Press, 2001), 36.

Thomas Jefferson Requests Funding for the Lewis and Clark Expedition

"To Enlarge the Boundaries of Knowledge by Undertaking Voyages of Discovery"

January 18, 1803

President Thomas Jefferson was convinced that the future prosperity of the young nation he led hinged on westward expansion—possibly even to the distant shores of the Pacific Ocean. This conviction not only led him to pursue negotiations with France on the Louisiana Purchase, but also to simultaneously lobby Congress for funding for expeditions that would map the great unknown wilderness beyond the Mississippi River. Jefferson believed that such expeditions held the key to America's future geographic and economic expansion. He also asserted that these fact-finding missions would lay the groundwork for the establishment of trading outposts and communities that would eventually lead to assimilation of western Indian tribes into white society.

These beliefs are reflected in this confidential letter that Jefferson wrote to Congress in January 1803 requesting funding for a special mission of exploration into the West via the wild Missouri River. The funding request was approved, and the expedition of which Jefferson speaks would eventually become the famed Lewis and Clark Expedition.

Gentlemen of the Senate, and of the House of Representatives:

As the continuance of the act for establishing trading houses with the Indian tribes will be under the consideration of the Legislature at its present session, I think it my duty to communicate the views which have guided me in the execution of that act, in order that you may decide on the policy of continuing it, in the present or any other form, or discontinue it altogether, if that shall, on the whole, seem most for the public good.

The Indian tribes residing within the limits of the United States, have, for a considerable time, been growing more and more uneasy at the constant diminution of the territory they occupy, although effected by their own voluntary sales: and the policy has long been gaining strength with them, of refusing absolutely all further sale, on any conditions; insomuch that, at this time, it hazards their friendship, and excites dangerous jealousies and perturbations in their minds to make any overture for the purchase of the smallest portions of their land. A very few tribes only are not yet obstinately in these dispositions. In order peaceably to counteract this policy of theirs, and to provide an extension of territory which the rapid increase of our numbers will call for, two measures are deemed expedient. First: to encourage them to abandon hunting, to apply to the raising stock, to agriculture and domestic manufacture, and thereby prove to themselves that less land and labor will maintain them in this, better than in their former mode of living. The extensive forests necessary in the hunting life, will then become useless, and they will see advantage in exchanging them for the means of improving their farms, and of increasing their domestic comforts. Secondly: to multiply trading houses among them, and place within their reach those things which will contribute more to their domestic comfort, than the possession of extensive, but uncultivated wilds. Experience and reflection will develop to them the wisdom of exchanging what they can spare and we want, for what we can spare and they want. In leading them to agriculture, to manufactures, and civilization; in bringing together their and our settlements, and in preparing them ultimately to participate in the benefits of our governments, I trust and believe we are acting for their greatest good. At these trading houses we have pursued the principles of the act of Congress, which directs that the commerce shall be carried on liberally, and requires only that the capital stock shall not be diminished. We consequently undersell private traders, foreign and domestic, drive them from the competition; and thus, with the good will of the Indians, rid ourselves of a description of men who are constantly endeavoring to excite in the Indian mind suspicions, fears, and irritations towards us. A letter now enclosed, shows the effect of our competition on the operations of the traders, while the Indians, perceiving the advantage of purchasing from us, are soliciting generally, our establishment of trading houses among them. In one quarter this is particularly interesting. The Legislature, reflecting on the late occurrences on the Mississippi, must be sensible how desirable it is to possess a respectable breadth of country on that river, from our Southern limit to the Illinois at least; so that we may present as firm a front on that as on our Eastern border. We possess what is below the Yazoo, and can probably acquire a certain breadth from the Illinois and Wabash to the Ohio; but between the Ohio and Yazoo, the country all belongs to the Chickasaws, friendly tribe within our limits, but the most decided against the alienation of lands. The portion of their country most important for us is exactly that which they do not inhabit. Their settlements are not on the Mississippi, but in the interior country. They have lately shown a desire to become agricultural; and this leads to the desire of buying implements and comforts. In the strengthening and gratifying of these wants, I see the only prospect of planting on the Mississippi itself, the means of its own safety. Duty has required me to submit these views to the judgment of the Legislature; but as their disclosure might embarrass and defeat their effect, they are committed to the special confidence of the two Houses.

While the extension of the public commerce among the Indian tribes, may deprive of that source of profit such of our citizens as are engaged in it, it might be worthy the attention of Congress, in their care of individual as well as of the general interest, to point, in another direction, the enterprise of these citizens, as profitably for themselves, and more usefully for the public. The river Missouri, and the Indians inhabiting it, are not as well known as is rendered desirable by their connexion with the Mississippi, and consequently with us. It is, however, understood, that the country on that river is inhabited by numerous tribes, who furnish great supplies of furs and peltry to the trade of another nation, carried on in a high latitude, through an infinite number of portages and lakes, shut up by ice through a long season. The commerce on that line could bear no competition with that of the Missouri, traversing a moderate climate, offering according to the best accounts, a continued navigation from its source, and possibly with a single portage, from the Western Ocean, and finding to the Atlantic a choice of channels through the Illinois or Wabash, the lakes and Hudson, through the Ohio and Susquehanna, or Potomac or James rivers, and through the Tennessee and Savannah, rivers. An intelligent officer, with ten or twelve chosen men, fit for the enterprise, and willing to undertake it, taken from our posts, where they may be spared without inconvenience, might explore the whole line, even to the Western Ocean, have conferences with the natives on the subject of commercial intercourse, get admission among them for our traders, as others are admitted, agree on convenient deposits for an interchange of articles, and return with the information acquired, in the course of two summers. Their arms and accoutrements, some instruments of observation, and light and cheap presents for the Indians, would be all the apparatus they could carry, and with an expectation of a soldier's portion of land on their return, would constitute the whole expense. Their pay would be going on, whether here or there.

While other civilized nations have encountered great expense to enlarge the boundaries of knowledge by undertaking voyages of discovery, and for other literary purposes, in various parts and directions, our nation seems to owe to the same object, as well as to its own interests, to explore this, the only line of easy communication across the continent, and so directly traversing our own part of it. The interests of commerce place the principal object within the constitutional powers and care of Congress, and that it should incidentally advance the geographical knowledge of our own continent, cannot be but an additional gratification. The nation claiming the territory, regarding this as a literary pursuit, which is in the habit of permitting within its dominions, would not be disposed to view it with jealousy, even if the expiring state of its interests there did not render it a matter of indifference. The appropriation of two thousand five hundred dollars, "for the purpose of extending the external commerce of the United States," while understood and considered by the Executive as giving the legislative sanction, would cover the undertaking from notice, and prevent the obstructions which interested individuals might otherwise previously prepare in its way.

TH: JEFFERSON
Jan. 18. 1803

Source: Jefferson, Thomas. "Jefferson's Secret Message to Congress." *Rivers, Edens, and Prairies: Lewis & Clark and the Revealing of America*. Library of Congress exhibit. www.loc.gov/exhibits/lewisandclark/transcript56.html.

DOCUMENT
2.2

The Louisiana Purchase

"You Have Bought Louisiana for a Song"

April 30, 1803

After months of feverish diplomatic haggling, the United States negotiated the purchase of the Louisiana Territory—an 827,000-square-mile tract that included the port city of New Orleans—from France in 1803. The Louisiana Purchase doubled the size of the United States and ushered in a turbulent new era of land and natural resource exploitation in America.

Some Americans balked at the $15 million purchase price for the Louisiana Territory. Others insisted that Jefferson did not have the Constitutional authority to make such a transaction. But many applauded the move, marveling at the vast new reserves of timber, soil, water, and game that could now be fed into the nation's nascent market economy. They insisted that the architects of the Purchase—President Thomas Jefferson, Secretary of State James Monroe, and U.S. Minister to France Robert Livingston—had bestowed on America a bargain for the ages. As Horatio Gates exulted in a July 18, 1803, letter to Jefferson, "Let the Land rejoice, for you have bought Louisiana for a Song."

TREATY BETWEEN THE UNITED STATES OF AMERICA AND THE FRENCH REPUBLIC

The President of the United States of America and the First Consul of the French Republic in the name of the French People desiring to remove all Source of misunderstanding relative to objects of discussion mentioned in the Second and fifth articles of the Convention of the 8th Vendémiaire an 9/30 September 1800 relative to the rights claimed by the United States in virtue of the Treaty concluded at Madrid the 27 of October 1795, between His Catholic Majesty & the Said United States, & willing to Strengthen the union and friendship which at the time of the Said Convention was happily reestablished between the two nations have respectively named their Plenipotentiaries to wit The President of the United States, by and with the advice and consent of the Senate of the Said States; Robert R. Livingston Minister Plenipotentiary of the United States and James Monroe Minister Plenipotentiary and Envoy extraordinary of the Said States near the Government of the French Republic; And the First Consul in the name of the French people, Citizen Francis Barbé Marbois Minister of the public treasury who after having respectively exchanged their full powers have agreed to the following Articles.

Article I

Whereas by the Article the third of the Treaty concluded at St Ildefonso the 9th Vendémiaire an 9 (1st October) 1800 between the First Consul of the French Republic and his Catholic Majesty it was agreed as follows.

"His Catholic Majesty promises and engages on his part to cede to the French Republic six months after the full and entire execution of the conditions and Stipulations herein relative to his Royal Highness the Duke of Parma, the Colony or Province of Louisiana with the Same extent that it now has in the hand of Spain, & that it had when France possessed it; and Such as it Should be after the Treaties subsequently entered into between Spain and other States."

And whereas in pursuance of the Treaty and particularly of the third article the French Republic has an incontestible title to the domain and to the possession of the said Territory—The First Consul of the French Republic desiring to give to the United States a strong proof of his friendship doth hereby cede to the United States in the name of the French Republic for ever and in full Sovereignty the said territory with all its rights and appurtenances as fully and in the Same manner as they have been acquired by the French Republic in virtue of the above mentioned Treaty concluded with his Catholic Majesty.

Art: II

In the cession made by the preceeding article are included the adjacent Islands belonging to Louisiana all public lots and Squares, vacant lands and all public buildings, fortifications, barracks and other edifices which are not private property.—The Archives, papers & documents relative to the domain and Sovereignty of Louisiana and its dependances will be left in the possession of the Commissaries of the United States, and copies will be afterwards given in due form to the Magistrates and Municipal officers of such of the said papers and documents as may be necessary to them.

Art: III

The inhabitants of the ceded territory shall be incorporated in the Union of the United States and admitted as soon as possible according to the principles of the federal Constitution to the enjoyment of all these rights, advantages and immunities of citizens of the United States, and in the mean time they shall be maintained and protected in the free enjoyment of their liberty, property and the Religion which they profess.

Art: IV

There Shall be Sent by the Government of France a Commissary to Louisiana to the end that he do every act necessary as well to receive from the Officers of his Catholic Majesty the Said country and its dependances in the name of the French Republic if it has not been already done as to transmit it in the name of the French Republic to the Commissary or agent of the United States.

Art: V

Immediately after the ratification of the present Treaty by the President of the United States and in case that of the first Consul's shall have been previously obtained, the commissary of the French Republic shall remit all military posts of New Orleans and other parts of the ceded territory to the Commissary or Commissaries named by the President to take possession—the troops whether of France or Spain who may be there shall cease to occupy any military post from the time of taking possession and shall be embarked as soon as possible in the course of three months after the ratification of this treaty.

Art: VI

The United States promise to execute Such treaties and articles as may have been agreed between Spain and the tribes and nations of Indians until by mutual consent of the United States and the said tribes or nations other Suitable articles Shall have been agreed upon.

Art: VII

As it is reciprocally advantageous to the commerce of France and the United States to encourage the communication of both nations for a limited time in the country ceded by the present treaty until general arrangements relative to commerce of both nations may be agreed on; it has been agreed between the contracting parties that the French Ships coming directly from France or any of her colonies loaded only with the produce and manufactures of France or her Said Colonies; and the Ships of Spain coming directly from Spain or any of her colonies loaded only with the produce or manufactures of Spain or her Colonies shall be admitted during the Space of twelve years in the Port of New-Orleans and in all other legal ports-of-entry within the ceded territory in the Same manner as the Ships of the United States coming directly from France or Spain or any of their Colonies without being Subject to any other or greater duty on merchandize or other or greater tonnage than that paid by the citizens of the United States.

During that Space of time above mentioned no other nation Shall have a right to the Same privileges in the Ports of the ceded territory—the twelve years Shall commence three months after the exchange of ratifications if it Shall take place in France or three months after it Shall have been notified at Paris to the French Government if it Shall take place in the United States; It is however well understood that the object of the above article is to favour the manufactures, Commerce, freight and navigation of France and of Spain So far as relates to the importations that the French and Spanish Shall make into the Said Ports of the United States without in any Sort affecting the regulations that the

United States may make concerning the exportation of the produce and merchandize of the United States, or any right they may have to make Such regulations.

Art: VIII

In future and for ever after the expiration of the twelve years, the Ships of France shall be treated upon the footing of the most favoured nations in the ports above mentioned.

Art: IX

The particular Convention Signed this day by the respective Ministers, having for its object to provide for the payment of debts due to the Citizens of the United States by the French Republic prior to the 30th Sept. 1800 (8th Vendé miaire an 9) is approved and to have its execution in the Same manner as if it had been inserted in this present treaty, and it Shall be ratified in the same form and in the Same time So that the one Shall not be ratified distinct from the other.

 Another particular Convention Signed at the Same date as the present treaty relative to a definitive rule between the contracting parties is in the like manner approved and will be ratified in the Same form, and in the Same time and jointly.

Art: X

The present treaty Shall be ratified in good and due form and the ratifications Shall be exchanged in the Space of Six months after the date of the Signature by the Ministers Plenipotentiary or Sooner if possible.

 In faith whereof the respective Plenipotentiaries have Signed these articles in the French and English languages; declaring nevertheless that the present Treaty was originally agreed to in the French language; and have thereunto affixed their Seals.

 Done at Paris the tenth day of Floreal in the eleventh year of the French Republic; and the 30th of April 1803.

  Robt R Livingston [seal]

  Jas. Monroe [seal]

  Barbé Marbois [seal]

Source: Miller, Hunter, ed. *Treaties and Other International Acts of the United States of America.* Vol. 2. Washington, D.C.: Government Printing Office, 1931.

DOCUMENT 2.3

Tecumseh Decries Land Cessions

"White People Have No Right to Take the Land from the Indians"

August 1810

The Shawnee Chief Tecumseh was one of the most formidable Indian leaders to confront land-hungry whites in the early nineteenth century. He emerged as an important historical figure in the aftermath of the 1809 Treaty of Fort Wayne, in which several tribes of the Old Northwest sold large tracts of land along the Wabash River to white interests. Tecumseh had been away when this treaty was signed, and when he returned he responded swiftly. He and his brother Tenskwatawa cobbled together a confederacy of American Indian tribes that explicitly rejected accommodationist approaches to the white interlopers. Instead, Tecumseh demanded the return of all Indian lands, a position that vastly complicated white efforts to colonize and settle the southern Great Lakes region.

In this August 1810 speech, known as the Speech at Vincennes, Tecumseh directly addresses Indiana Territory governor William Henry Harrison, who three decades later became America's ninth president. This speech explains Tecumseh's central premise—that because all the Indian tribes hold the lands of America in common, no single tribe had the right to sell off land and resources without the approval of all the other tribes.

Tecumseh's efforts to rescind land transfer agreements such as the Treaty of Fort Wayne came to naught, and within a matter of months his confederacy was engaged in open warfare against American forces. Tecumseh and his followers joined the side of the British against the Americans in the War of 1812, reasoning that a victorious English crown might return them their homelands in gratitude. But Tecumseh's desperate hope for a British triumph went unfulfilled, and he himself died in battle in Canada in October 1813 at the hands of American forces led by Harrison himself.

It is true I am a Shawnee. My forefathers were warriors. Their son is a warrior. From them I only take my existence; from my tribe I take nothing. I am the maker of my own fortune; and oh! That I could make that of my red people, and of my country, as great as the conceptions of my mind, when I think of the Spirit that rules the universe. I would not then come to Governor Harrison to ask him to tear the treaty, and to obliterate the landmark; but I would say to him, Sir, you have liberty to return to your own country.

The being within, communing with the past ages, tells me, that once, nor until lately, there was no white man on this continent. That it then all belonged to red men, children of the same parents, placed on it by the Great Spirit that made them, to keep it, to traverse it, to enjoy its production, and to fill it with the same race. Once a happy race. Since made miserable by the white people, who are never contented, but always encroaching. The way, and the only way to check and stop this evil, is, for all the red men to unite in claiming a common and equal right in the land, as it was at first, and should be yet; for it never was divided, but belongs to all, for the use of each. That no part has a right to sell, even to each other, much less to strangers; those who want all, and will not do with less. The white people have no right to take the land from the Indians, because they had it first; it is theirs. They may sell, but all must join. Any sale not made by all is not valid. The late sale is bad. It was made by a part only. Part do not know how to sell. It requires all to make a bargain for all. All red men have equal rights to the unoccupied land. The right of occupancy is as good in one place as in another. There cannot be two occupancies in the same place. The first excludes all others. It is not so in hunting or traveling; for there the same ground will serve many, as may follow each other all day; but the camp is stationary, and that is occupancy. It belongs to the first who sits down on his blankets or skins, which he has thrown upon the ground, and till he leaves it no other has a right.

Source: Drake, Samuel Gardner. *Biography and History of the Indians of North America.* Boston: Antiquarian Institute, 1837. 11th ed. 1841, pp. 617–618.

An Act to Protect "Useful" Birds in Massachusetts

"It Is Desirable to Promote the Increase and Preservation of Birds"

February 1818

In February 1818 legislators in Massachusetts approved one of the first significant wildlife protection laws in America. This law, the first bird protection measure introduced in the United States, reflected a dawning awareness that Americans were consuming and exploiting some of America's natural bounty at an unsustainable rate. The 1818 Act, however, also reflected the continued hegemony of economic matters in an era when issues of environmental stewardship and ecosystem integrity were virtually absent as factors in American land use and natural resource policymaking.

The language of the Act, excerpted here, explicitly differentiates between bird species that helped the bottom-line profitability of agricultural operations (by consuming crop-eating insects, for instance) and those that were not useful to farmers or actually hindered their operations. The former birds were deemed worthy of protection by the state; annihilation of the latter could be pursued without restriction.

AN ACT TO PREVENT THE DESTRUCTION OF CERTAIN USEFUL BIRDS AT UNSEASONABLE TIMES OF THE YEAR

Whereas there are within the Commonwealth, many birds which are useful and profitable to the citizens, either as articles of food, or as instruments in the hands of Providence to destroy various noxious insects, grubs and caterpillars, which are prejudicial or destructive to vegetation, fruits and grain; and it is desirable to promote the increase and preservation of birds of the above description, and to prevent the wanton destruction of them at improper seasons:

SEC 1. *Be it enacted by the Senate and House of Representatives, in General Court assembled, and by the authority of the same,* That hereafter it shall not be lawful for any person to take, kill or destroy, any of the birds called partridges and quails, at any time from the first day of March, to the first day of September in every year; and no person shall take, kill or destroy, any of the birds called woodcocks, snipes, larks and robins, at any time from the first day of March to the fourth day of July in each year; and if any person shall take or kill, or shall sell, buy or have in his possession after being killed, or taken, any of the birds aforesaid, within the times limited as aforesaid respectively, he shall forfeit and pay for each and every partridge, quail, or woodcock, so taken, killed or in his possession, two dollars; and for each and every snipe, lark or robin, so killed, taken, or in his possession, one dollar. . . .

SEC. 2. *Be it further enacted,* that if any person shall shoot at or kill any of the birds aforesaid, or any other birds, upon lands not owned or occupied by himself, without license from the owner or occupant of such lands, at any time from the first day of March to the fourth day of July in each year, such persons shall forfeit and pay to the occupant or owner of such lands, where he may shoot at, or kill such birds, ten dollars, as a penalty in addition to all other actual damages, to be recovered by the party injured, by an action of trespass, in any court having jurisdiction of the amount demanded: *Provided however, that nothing in this act shall be construed to prevent the killing of crows, blackbirds, owls, blue jays, and hawks, at any season of the year. . . .*

Source: *Laws of the Commonwealth of Massachusetts,* Vol. 7, chap. 103. Boston: Russell, Cutler, 1818.

DOCUMENT 2.5   De Witt Clinton Heralds the Opening of the Erie Canal

"It Will Create the Greatest Inland Trade Ever Witnessed"

April 26, 1824

During the first half-century of America's existence, rivers were the nation's most important arteries for commerce. In the opening decades of the nineteenth century, however, American legislators and business interests decided to augment this natural transportation system with artificial canals. The greatest of these canal projects was New York State's Erie Canal. Construction of this canal, built in an eight-year period from 1817 to 1825, was authorized by state lawmakers who believed that it would unlock the natural riches of the American interior for a new generation of merchants, steamship owners, farmers, ranchers, and timbermen.

When this state-sponsored 363-mile canal opened for business in 1825, it produced a sustained surge in economic expansion, land settlement, and natural resource exploitation from New England to the Great Lakes territories. It also spawned a frenzy of other canal-building schemes, and by 1850 more than 3,700 miles of canals—most of them publicly financed—had been carved into the flesh of the continent. The greatest of these canal systems connected the Great Lakes with the Ohio and Mississippi Rivers.

The following speech was delivered in Albany in 1824 by De Witt Clinton, the nation's leading champion of the construction of the Erie Canal. In his remarks, Clinton— who served at various times in his long career as a U.S. senator, New York governor, and mayor of New York City—heralds the impending opening of the canal and predicts— accurately—that it will usher in a new era of economic prosperity and commercial growth for New York and the wider nation. Clinton also defends the use of public money to finance the endeavor, and his entire speech is suffused with the conviction that policies that encouraged land "improvements" were essential to America's future. This belief would become an increasingly prevalent one during the first half of the nineteenth century.

To the committee of a meeting of the citizens of New York, of which William Few, Esq. was chairman, and John Rathbone, Esq. secretary.

GENTLEMEN—I know of no event that has a more powerful demand on my gratitude than the proceedings of the citizens of New-York, respecting my agency in the navigable communications between our Mediterranean seas and the Atlantic Ocean. The approbation of a meeting so numerous and respectable, conveyed through a channel so virtuous and enlightened, is a reward that ought to satisfy the most aspiring ambition.

At the commencement of the year 1816, a few individuals held a consultation in the city of New-York, for the purpose of calling the public attention to the contemplated western and northern canals. The difficulties to be surmounted were of the most formidable aspect. The state, in consequence of her patriotic exertions during the war, was considerably embarrassed in her finances; a current of hostility had set in against the project; and the preliminary measures, however well intended, ably devised, or faithfully executed, had unfortunately increased, instead of allaying prejudice; and such was the weight of these, and other considerations, that the plan was generally viewed as abandoned. Experience evinces that it is much easier to originate a measure successfully, than it is to revive one which has been already unfavourably received. Notwithstanding these appalling obstacles, which were duly considered, a public meeting was called of which William Bayard was chairman, and John Pintard secretary; a memorial in favour of the canal policy was read and approved, and a correspondent spirit was excited through the community, which induced the legislature to pass a law authorising surveys and examinations. And let me, on this occasion, discharge a debt of gratitude and of justice to the late Robert Bowne. He is now elevated above human panegyric,

As an organ of communication between the Hudson, the Mississippi, the St. Lawrence, the great lakes of the north and west, and their tributary rivers, it will create the greatest inland trade ever witnessed.

—De Witt Clinton

and reposes, I humbly and fervently believe, in the bosom of his God. He had at an early period, devoted his attention to this subject, and was master of all its important bearings. To his wise counsels, intelligent views, and patriotic exertions, we were under incalculable obligations. I never left the society of this excellent and venerable man without feeling the most powerful inducements for the most animated efforts.

The proceedings under the act of 1816, presented such conclusive testimonials in favour of the proposed canals, that a law was enacted authorising their commencement, but not without the most decided opposition. I am aware that some of the most pure and intelligent men in the community were unfriendly to the prosecution of a measure which appeared to them either impracticable in attainment, or overwhelming in expense; but it must certainly be considered an extraordinary feature in our history, that the representatives of your city, the place most benefited by the canals, should take the lead in hostility. This fact is not mentioned in the way of reproach, but to show the difficulties which environed the measure in every step of its progress.

After my election to the chair of state, I found that the opposition to the canal was mingled with the agitations of the times, and that its destinies were to a certain extent identified with my official position. At this crisis, I was induced to continue in my station as a canal commissioner, from a persuasion that my retirement might be considered an abandonment; and from a conviction that I could render more essential benefit to the undertaking by remaining at my post, and encountering all the obloquy, resentments, and misrepresentations, which at that period were so strongly indicated: And I had finally the satisfaction to see that the successful progress of the work had dispelled the doubts of its well-meaning opponents, and silenced the clamours of its enemies of a different description.

From the extinguishment of open hostility, to the present period, I have not been without serious apprehensions, that events might occur to prevent the consummation of this work; and I have rejoiced at the termination of each year of its progress, and watched over it with indescribable anxiety. Although I have no reason to suspect the fidelity of the agents entrusted with the disbursements of the public monies, yet I was sensible that any loss by accident, or any misapplication by design, might prove fatal. And I was at all times aware, that the intervention of a foreign war might prevent the necessary loans, and that the national government, without any hostile design, might, by repealing and imposing certain duties, inflict an irreparable injury on our financial arrangements.

On the 4th of July, 1817, the work was commenced. The Champlain and the greater part of the Erie Canal are now in a navigable state, and in less than a year the whole, comprising an extent of about four hundred and twenty-five miles, will be finished. Every year's experience will enhance the results in the public estimation, and benefits will be unfolded which we can now hardly venture to anticipate. As a bond of union between the Atlantic and the western states, it may prevent the dismemberment of the American empire. As an organ of communication between the Hudson, the Mississippi, the St. Lawrence, the great lakes of the north and west, and their tributary rivers, it will create the greatest inland trade ever witnessed. The most fertile and extensive regions of America will avail themselves of its facilities for a market. All their surplus productions, whether of the soil, the forest, the mines, or the waters, their fabrics of art and their supplies of foreign commodities, will concentrate in the city of New-York, for transportation abroad or consumption at home. Agriculture, manufactures, commerce, trade, navigation, and the arts will receive a correspondent encouragement. That city will in the course of time become the granary of the world, the emporium of commerce, the seat of manufactures, the focus of great monied operations, and the concentrating point of vast, disposable, and accumulating capitals, which will stimulate, enliven, extend, and reward the exertions of human labour and ingenuity, in all their processes and exhibitions; and, before the revolution of a century, the whole island of Manhattan, covered with habitations and replenished with a dense population, will constitute one vast city. . . .

Any view of the subject, and this view particularly, must elicit our humble and devout thanks to Almighty God, for disposing the minds of the people of this state, at the most propitious period, in favour of this work, and for enabling them to persevere amidst all surrounding impediments. A free state has thus set an illustrious example to the world; has evinced the energies of republican government, and demonstrated that the people of this country have had the heads to conceive, the hearts to undertake, and the hands to execute, the most useful and stupendous work of the age.

But although your city will derive the greatest benefit from the canals, yet it will by no means be exclusive. Like the Nile, they will enrich the whole country through which they pass, and all the adjacent regions will feel their benignant and animating influence. Great market towns will be established in every direction, and the banks of the majestic Hudson will exhibit a line of villages and cities, that will grow with the growth, and flourish with the enlivening and reacting prosperity of our commercial metropolis. The revenue will not only extinguish the debt and defray the expenses of the government, but it will in time realise a vast fund, applicable to all the objects of human improvement. Upon intellectual and moral cultivation we must rely for the conservation of our republican government, and for the protection of the last hopes of freedom and the best destinies of man. When every child in the state shall become the child of the commonwealth, and shall receive the blessings of education at the public expense, then we may be assured that neither fraud nor violence, neither intrigue nor corruption, can destroy the sacred temple of liberty.

Under any aspect of the occurrence which has produced this manifestation of your friendship and confidence, I have no reason to entertain any resentment, or to express any regret, whether we estimate it by the ordinary standard that graduates the character of human actions, or contemplate it in connection with other events still more extraordinary. Indeed I view it as a subject of high felicitation, since it has honoured me with the approbation of the most respectable and the most respected among my fellow-citizens. The venerable chairman of your meeting was one of the illustrious band of sages that formed our national constitution; and on the committee I recognise the names of some of the men of the revolution, whose deeds of patriotism will transmit an inestimable legacy of fame, and a glorious example of heroic virtue, to their posterity. The intellectual and moral worth, and high character of the committee, and of the chairman and secretary of the meeting, and its number and respectability, afford conclusive evidence of the favourable opinion of the citizens of New-York, and I shall certainly rank their expression of it among the highest honours and most auspicious events of my life.

I cannot conclude, without offering my particular acknowledgments to those gentlemen who have presented me in person with the proceedings, for their condescending kindness: and I most respectfully tender my sincere and heartfelt thanks to my fellow-citizens who composed the meeting, and the committee who represent it, for their favourable notice of my efforts to promote the prosperity of our country.

ALBANY, April 26, 1824.

Source: Clinton, De Witt. *Memoir of De Witt Clinton, With an Appendix, Containing Numerous Documents, Illustrative of the Principal Events of His Life.* Vol. 2, edited by David Hosack. New York: J. Seymour, 1829, pp. 476–480.

DOCUMENT 2.6

Congress Establishes Federal Forest Reserves for Naval Use

An Act for "the Collection of Timber for . . . Construction of Vessels of War"

December 4, 1827

America's very first federal purchases of forestland were actually made for military reasons. On February 25, 1799, the Federal Timber Purchasers Act appropriated $200,000 for the fledgling U.S. Navy to buy forestland for shipbuilding materials. The Navy used these funds to buy Blackbeard and Grover Islands, two heavily forested islands off the coast of mainland Georgia. In 1817 Secretary of State John Quincy Adams engineered the purchase of an additional 19,000 acres of forestland on three Gulf Coast islands—Commissioners, Cypress, and Six Islands—off the coast of Louisiana. These tracts provided another guaranteed source of shipbuilding timber to the Navy.

In 1825 Adams ended his eight-year tenure as secretary of state in the Monroe Administration and was sworn in as the sixth president of the United States. Two years later, Adams acted to create the nation's first—albeit very modest—forest reserves. The Federal Timber Reservation Act of March 3, 1827, established the Santa Rosa live oak timber reserve near Pensacola, Florida. Like earlier purchases, the forestlands on this 30,000-acre tract were reserved for the U.S. Navy. But this act also gave Adams the authority to take "proper measures" to protect American live oak timber supplies, and it approved active government cultivation of live oaks.[1] Adams felt that the establishment of these tiny naval forest reserves was important enough to warrant inclusion in his third State of the Union address, which he delivered on December 4, 1827. Following is the pertinent excerpt:

. . . The fortification of the coasts and the gradual increase and improvement of the Navy are parts of a great system of national defense which has been upward of 10 years in progress, and which for a series of years to come will continue to claim the constant and persevering protection and superintendence of the legislative authority. Among the measures which have emanated from these principles the act of the last session of Congress for the gradual improvement of the Navy holds a conspicuous place. The collection of timber for the future construction of vessels of war, the preservation and reproduction of the species of timber peculiarly adapted to that purpose, the construction of dry docks for the use of the Navy, the erection of a marine railway for the repair of the public ships, and the improvement of the navy yards for the preservation of the public property deposited in them have all received from the Executive the attention required by that act, and will continue to receive it, steadily proceeding toward the execution of all its purposes. . . .

Source: Adams, John Quincy. Third Annual Message to Congress, December 4, 1827. Available at The American Presidency Project, www.presidency.ucsb.edu/ws/?pid=29469.

NOTE

1. Jay P. Kinney, *The Development of Forest Law in America* (New York: John Wiley & Sons, 1917), 239.

DOCUMENT 2.7

Andrew Jackson Hails the Benefits of Indian Removal

"What Good Man Would Prefer a Country Covered with Forests and . . . Savages?"

December 6, 1830

In the 1820s white pressure on Indian lands in the eastern United States steadily increased, driven by relentless demand for new farmland, discoveries of new natural resources to be exploited (such as gold on tribal lands in Georgia), and technological advances in transportation and industry.

President Andrew Jackson and the U.S. Congress relieved this mounting pressure in one ruthless stroke by passing the Indian Removal Act of May 28, 1830. This law opened up remaining Indian lands on the "southwestern frontier"—primarily Alabama, Georgia, Kentucky, Mississippi, North Carolina, and Tennessee—to white settlement. It gave Jackson sweeping powers to negotiate agreements with the tribes wherein they would give up all lands east of the Mississippi in exchange for territory in the West, which had not yet completed its transition in the minds of Americans from desolate wasteland to untapped Eden.

Resigned to their weak negotiating position, many Native Americans in the Southeast wearily accepted Jackson's offers and departed. Those that refused to hand over their traditional homelands were forcibly removed. By 1837 the Jackson Administration had virtually depopulated America's southeastern ramparts of Indians. It forcibly removed 46,000 Native American people from their lands and secured the departure of even greater numbers of Indians by pressuring tribal leaders to sign treaties. The Indian Removal Act thus opened about 25 million acres of land to the growing of cotton, tobacco, and other commodities. This massive government-mandated transfer of ownership had major ecological consequences for the entire region.

The following excerpt is from Jackson's 1830 State of the Union address to Congress, which he delivered on December 6, 1830. In this portion of his message, Jackson not only frames Indian removal as a vital element in the nation's march to greatness, but also insists that the "discontented" tribes should view their impending relocation with "gratitude."

. . . It gives me pleasure to announce to Congress that the benevolent policy of the Government, steadily pursued for nearly 30 years, in relation to the removal of the Indians beyond the white settlements is approaching to a happy consummation. Two important tribes have accepted the provision made for their removal at the last session of Congress, and it is believed that their example will induce the remaining tribes also to seek the same obvious advantages.

The consequences of a speedy removal will be important to the United States, to individual States, and to the Indians themselves. The pecuniary advantages which it promises to the Government are the least of its recommendations. It puts an end to all possible danger of collision between the authorities of the General and State Governments on account of the Indians. It will place a dense and civilized population in large tracts of country now occupied by a few savage hunters. By opening the whole territory between Tennessee on the north and Louisiana on the south to the settlement of the whites it will incalculably strengthen the SW frontier and render the adjacent States strong enough to repel future invasions without remote aid. It will relieve the whole State of Mississippi and the western part of Alabama of Indian occupancy, and enable those States to advance rapidly in population, wealth, and power. It will separate the Indians from immediate contact with settlements of whites; free them from the power of the States; enable them to pursue happiness in their own way and under their own rude institutions; will retard the progress of decay, which is lessening their numbers, and perhaps cause them gradually, under the protection of the Government and through the influence of good counsels, to cast off their savage habits and

> *The waves of population and civilization are rolling to the westward, and we now propose to acquire the countries occupied by the red men of the South and West by a fair exchange, and, at the expense of the United States, to send them to a land where their existence may be prolonged and perhaps made perpetual.*
>
> —Andrew Jackson

become an interesting, civilized, and Christian community. These consequences, some of them so certain and the rest so probable, make the complete execution of the plan sanctioned by Congress at their last session an object of much solicitude.

Toward the aborigines of the country no one can indulge a more friendly feeling than myself, or would go further in attempting to reclaim them from their wandering habits and make them a happy, prosperous people. I have endeavored to impress upon them my own solemn convictions of the duties and powers of the General Government in relation to the State authorities. For the justice of the laws passed by the States within the scope of their reserved powers they are not responsible to this Government. As individuals we may entertain and express our opinions of their acts, but as a Government we have as little right to control them as we have to prescribe laws for other nations.

With a full understanding of the subject, the Choctaw and the Chickasaw tribes have with great unanimity determined to avail themselves of the liberal offers presented by the act of Congress, and have agreed to remove beyond the Mississippi River. Treaties have been made with them, which in due season will be submitted for consideration. In negotiating these treaties they were made to understand their true condition, and they have preferred maintaining their independence in the Western forests to submitting to the laws of the States in which they now reside. These treaties, being probably the last which will ever be made with them, are characterized by great liberality on the part of the Government. They give the Indians a liberal sum in consideration of their removal, and comfortable subsistence on their arrival at their new homes. If it be their real interest to maintain a separate existence, they will there be at liberty to do so without the inconveniences and vexations to which they would unavoidably have been subject in Alabama and Mississippi.

Humanity has often wept over the fate of the aborigines of this country, and Philanthropy has been long busily employed in devising means to avert it, but its progress has never for a moment been arrested, and one by one have many powerful tribes disappeared from the earth. To follow to the tomb the last of his race and to tread on the graves of extinct nations excite melancholy reflections. But true philanthropy reconciles the mind to these vicissitudes as it does to the extinction of one generation to make room for another. In the monuments and fortifications of an unknown people, spread over the extensive regions of the West, we behold the memorials of a once powerful race, which was exterminated or has disappeared to make room for the existing savage tribes. Nor is there anything in this which, upon a comprehensive view of the general interests of the human race, is to be regretted. Philanthropy could not wish to see this continent restored to the condition in which it was found by our forefathers. What good man would prefer a country covered with forests and ranged by a few thousand savages to our extensive Republic, studded with cities, towns, and prosperous farms, embellished with all the improvements which art can devise or industry execute, occupied by more than 12,000,000 happy people, and filled with all the blessings of liberty, civilization, and religion?

The present policy of the Government is but a continuation of the same progressive change by a milder process. The tribes which occupied the countries now constituting the Eastern States were annihilated or have melted away to make room for the whites. The waves of population and civilization are rolling to the westward, and we now propose to acquire the countries occupied by the red men of the South and West by a fair exchange, and, at the expense of the United States, to send them to a land where their existence may be prolonged and perhaps made perpetual.

Doubtless it will be painful to leave the graves of their fathers; but what do they more than our ancestors did or than our children are now doing? To better their condition in an unknown land our forefathers left all that was dear in earthly objects. Our children by thousands yearly leave the land of their birth to seek new homes in distant regions. Does Humanity weep at these painful separations from every thing, animate and inanimate, with which the young heart has become entwined? Far from it. It is rather a source of joy that our country affords scope where our young population may range unconstrained in body or in mind, developing the power and faculties of man in their highest perfection.

These remove hundreds and almost thousands of miles at their own expense, purchase the lands they occupy, and support themselves at their new homes from the moment of their arrival. Can it be cruel in this Government when, by events which it can not control, the Indian is made discontented in his ancient home to purchase his lands, to give him a new and extensive territory, to pay the expense of his removal, and support him a year in his new abode? How many thousands of our own people would gladly embrace the opportunity of removing to the West on such conditions! If the offers made to the Indians were extended to them, they would be hailed with gratitude and joy.

And is it supposed that the wandering savage has a stronger attachment to his home than the settled, civilized Christian? Is it more afflicting to him to leave the graves of his fathers than it is to our brothers and children? Rightly considered, the policy of the General Government toward the red man is not only liberal, but generous. He is unwilling to submit to the laws of the States and mingle with their population. To save him from this alternative, or perhaps utter annihilation, the General Government kindly offers him a new home, and proposes to pay the whole expense of his removal and settlement.

In the consummation of a policy originating at an early period, and steadily pursued by every Administration within the present century—so just to the States and so generous to the Indians—the Executive feels it has a right to expect the cooperation of Congress and of all good and disinterested men. The States, moreover, have a right to demand it. It was substantially a part of the compact which made them members of our Confederacy. With Georgia there is an express contract; with the new States an implied one of equal obligation. Why, in authorizing Ohio, Indiana, Illinois, Missouri, Mississippi, and Alabama to form constitutions and become separate States, did Congress include within their limits extensive tracts of Indian lands, and, in some instances, powerful Indian tribes? Was it not understood by both parties that the power of the States was to be coextensive with their limits, and that with all convenient dispatch the General Government should extinguish the Indian title and remove every obstruction to the complete jurisdiction of the State governments over the soil? Probably not one of those States would have accepted a separate existence—certainly it would never have been granted by Congress—had it been understood that they were to be confined for ever to those small portions of their nominal territory the Indian title to which had at the time been extinguished.

It is, therefore, a duty which this Government owes to the new States to extinguish as soon as possible the Indian title to all lands which Congress themselves have included within their limits. When this is done the duties of the General Government in relation to the States and the Indians within their limits are at an end. The Indians may leave the State or not, as they choose. The purchase of their lands does not alter in the least their personal relations with the State government. No act of the General Government has ever been deemed necessary to give the States jurisdiction over the persons of the Indians. That they possess by virtue of their sovereign power within their own limits in as full a manner before as after the purchase of the Indian lands; nor can this Government add to or diminish it.

May we not hope, therefore, that all good citizens, and none more zealously than those who think the Indians oppressed by subjection to the laws of the States, will unite in attempting to open the eyes of those children of the forest to their true condition, and by a speedy removal to relieve them from all the evils, real or imaginary, present or prospective, with which they may be supposed to be threatened. . . .

Source: Jackson, Andrew. "Second Annual Message." *The Statesmanship of Andrew Jackson as Told in His Writings and Speeches.* Edited by Francis Newton Thorpe. New York: Tandy Thomas, 1909, pp. 110–115.

DOCUMENT 2.8

Henry Shreve on Western River Improvements

"For Some Five or Six Years the Trees Have Been Cut from the Falling Banks"

September 30, 1833 and May 1, 1834

During the first half of the nineteenth century, steam technology revolutionized transportation and business in the United States. And as steamboats and steamships proliferated on the nation's large lakes and rivers and in its coastal waters, state and federal governments adopted internal "improvement" policies that dramatically reshaped the character of rivers across the country. These policies took varied forms, from removing natural logjams or "snags" in waterways to neutralizing sandbars and other threats to navigation through dam building, dredging, and other acts of river re-engineering. Another common policy was to cut down huge swaths of forest on either side of riverbanks so as to keep rivers clear of obstacles in the future. All of these government-sanctioned actions had a wrenching impact on riverine ecosystems and the flora and fauna therein.

Henry Shreve was the most famous of the individuals who wrestled American rivers into submission for the steamer trade. A steamboat owner and inventor who first made his mark on the Mississippi, Shreve developed a steam-powered "snag" boat capable of tackling even the most imposing logjams. He touted the usefulness of his design to government officials who wanted to clear deadfall-clogged western rivers for commerce, and in 1827 the Adams Administration appointed Shreve Superintendent of Western River Improvements. During his twelve-year tenure in that position, Shreve cleared huge logjams and other obstructions from the Mississippi, Ohio, Arkansas, and Red rivers. He also supervised the clearing of tens of thousands of trees along river corridors.

The environmental repercussions of his work notwithstanding, Shreve undoubtedly played a significant role in opening the West for commerce and settlement. Shreve was fully aware of this, and he spent many years trying to negotiate better compensation from the government for his yeoman river-clearing efforts. All of these entreaties, however, came to naught.

The following two letters were written by Shreve during his career as "snagboat captain" on many of America's major river systems. The first letter excerpted here, from 1833, is part of a progress report Shreve sent to General Charles Gratiot, the chief engineer in the War Department, and it includes a firm rejection of accusations that Shreve's timber-cutting campaigns constitute an "injury" to rivers. In the second piece of correspondence, from 1834, Shreve summarizes his river-clearing exploits as part of his (unsuccessful) campaign to coax additional compensation from Congress.

Annual Report of Work Done for Improving the Navigation of the Ohio, Mississippi, Red, and Arkansas Rivers, Ending 30th of September, 1833.

September 30, 1833

In the months of October, November, and December, 1832; January, February, and March of this year; the steam snag-boats Heliopolis and Archimedes removed from the bed of the Mississippi 1,293 snags. The same boats in August and September, 1833, removed from the bed of that river 667 snags, in all 1,960 snags during the year. The crews of the same boats have within the year felled from the falling-in banks of the Mississippi, at times when the water was too high to remove snags, and when the engines of the boats were out of repair, about 10,000 trees. During the month of November last, those boats were engaged in removing the Choctaw Indians from Memphis, Tennessee, and Vicksburg, Mississippi, to the mouth of the Arkansas river.

One hundred men were employed in August, September, October, November, and December, 1832, felling timber on the banks of the Mississippi river, and cutting snags from the dry bars and island chutes. They proceeded from St. Louis to the mouth of the St. Francis river, distant 500 miles, where they cleared the timber from the falling banks and dry sand bars. The last named work, (felling timber from the banks of the river,) is thought by many persons to be an injury, and not an improvement to the river. I am, however, of a very different opinion. I believe it to be the only effectual mode of removing obstructions from the shores, and of great importance to the improvement of the channel. This opinion has been formed from actual observation. For some five or six years the trees have been cut from the falling banks of the river, nearly all the distance for the first 300 miles below the mouth of the Ohio, where the shores of the river are comparatively clear of snags, logs, roots, safe to laud at with a flat-boat, and in the stream the accumulation of snags are not more than half so great as in those parts of the river where the timber has not been felled from the banks; nor are the banks safe to land at with any description of boat, in consequence of the bends where the banks fall in being very much obstructed along the shores with the trees, roots, and legs that are falling in with the banks. Many persons object to felling the timber above alluded to, alleging that the stumps roll in as the bank caves in, and lie on the bottom, forming a dangerous obstruction to the navigation. This seems an erroneous opinion. Every man, well acquainted with the character of the Mississippi river, must recollect that the banks that fall in are washed by the deepest and most rapid portion of the stream; consequently, when a stump slides from its foundation, it sinks below the draft of any craft that can navigate the river, as the bends where the banks fall in are universally from ten to fifteen feet deeper than the best channels over the bars that stretch across the river from the foot of one bend to the head of the next at almost every point in the river. Where the timber falls in, the roots sink, and the top either floats and forms a snag, or the top of the tree lies on the bank, and keeps the shores perpetually obstructed to such an extent that the flat-boats are prevented from attempting to land at them, and if caught in a gale of wind they are obliged to pull for the first bend they can make, and are frequently stove and lost; and if they make the land, they are liable to be sunk by the trees falling on them.

That work has, however, been abandoned for the present year, very much against my judgment.

During the last year several steamboats have been lost by striking logs and snags; but none of them were good and substantially built boats. I would here beg leave to observe, that a great many of the boats now navigating the Mississippi river are very light timbered, just sufficient to hold the plank together to bear caulking; consequently, if one of those boats strikes a snag, drift-log, or anything of sufficient weight to fracture the plank, the boat is stove and sunk. The inquiry is then made, what did she strike? the universal reply is, one of Shreve's stumps; but if it was a stump, and a first rate substantial boat were to strike it, she would evidently be stove; for a stump is one of the most dangerous description of obstructions that could be in the river. But I have not known a good substantial steamboat to be stove, excepting one, for the last four years. The heavy boats of 300 tons and upwards, are nearly all stout well built boats and from their greater draft of water are more liable to strike than those of a smaller class, and if they do strike must receive a much heavier shock from their greater weight and greater speed with which they run, for the largest boats are universally the swiftest; yet but one of that class of boats has been stove in the Mississippi river in the last four years. Consequently, I am of the opinion that almost all the losses of steamboats for the last four years from being stove, have occurred from the insufficiency of the boats, and not from the stumps to which nearly all the losses are charged. I am of the opinion that the Mississippi river is at this time as safe to navigate, excepting in extreme low water, as it will ever be. . . .

For a statement of the operations at the Great raft on Red river, I beg leave to refer to my report on that subject, under date of the 30th of July last. A rough sketch of the Red river, the bayous, lakes, and swamps where the raft is situated is herewith forwarded. It was taken from the foot of the raft at Coate's bluff as I passed up; from thence to the head, from the best information I could obtain, it is by no means strictly correct, but will convey a more correct idea of the country than can be otherwise given.

Preparations were made for removing the snags in the Arkansas river in August last. But when the steam snag-boats entered that river, it was found too low to operate with those boats, and but 20 snags were removed. So soon as the water rises in the approaching winter, that work will be begun and executed, to as great an extent as the appropriation for that purpose will admit.

I am, sir, very respectfully, your obedient servant,
HENRY M. SHREVE.
Superintendent.

To the Honorable the Senate and House of Representatives of the United States in Congress Assembled:

May 1, 1834

Your petitioner respectfully represents, that he is the inventor of the steam snag-boats called Heliopolis and Archimedes, the property of the United States, which are now, and have been, in the service of the government, since 1829, under the direction of your petitioner, as superintendent on the Mississippi and its waters. That the invention has been attended with complete success; has answered all the hopes of the inventor, and fully met the anticipations of the government. That the government, in 1824, offered a premium of one thousand dollars, for a model of a machine adapted to the removal of snags and sawyers from the bed of the Mississippi river—the premium to be awarded by the board of engineers, to the proprietor of the best model that might be offered. That the sum of $1,000 was paid to a gentleman for a machine which proved worthless, and that many thousands would probably have been fruitlessly expended in the same way had not the snag-boat of your petitioner been constructed and brought into use. By the use of the snag-boats the obstacles to the navigation of the Ohio, Mississippi, and Arkansas rivers have been overcome, and the improvements effected have saved millions to the industrious and enterprising citizens of the great valley of the Mississippi. By the aid of his invention the Missouri river may be rendered navigable two thousand miles above its junction with the Mississippi; and it will be required in the improvement of the navigation of all the great rivers of the west.

With the aid of Heliopolis and Archimedes, the progress made by your petitioner, in two months and ten days, in the removal or destruction of the great Red river raft, in Louisiana, was matter of general astonishment. About a sixth part of a work which was deemed almost impracticable—which no person believed could be accomplished for a less sum than a million of dollars—has been effected for $21,633. The raft was originally one hundred and forty miles in length. About seventy miles of it has been cut through; and your petitioner feels confident that, with an expenditure of one hundred thousand dollars more, the improvement may be completed before the first of June, 1835.

Your petitioner further states that, with the aid of said snag-boats, thirty-two men can perform as much labor in a day as can be performed by five hundred men without such boats; that when the Red river raft shall be removed, from the foot to the head, the navigation in the original channel will be as good as it has hitherto been below the raft; and that when the bayous running into the river shall be opened, and the outlets be closed, (which will necessarily be effected in the progress of the removal of the raft,) half a million of acres on the line of the raft will be reclaimed; a safe steamboat navigation will be opened six hundred miles up Red river, (above the raft,) through a fertile country of sufficient extent to form two large States, and the speedy gale of at least one hundred millions of acres of the public land (much of which is well adapted to the cultivation of cotton) will be insured.

Your petitioner further states that, had his invention been of a nature to be applied to private interests or to individual pursuits, he could have made it the means of independence and wealth. Had it been of that character, he could, under the Constitution and laws of the country, have secured to himself the exclusive benefit thereof; but its nature is such as to preclude the employment of it in any other than national improvements. He, therefore, appeals to the justice of Congress for reasonable and adequate compensation for his invention, from which he can, under existing circumstances, derive no personal advantage, but which must be beneficial to his country for ages to come. He does not ask for money: he asks only the privilege of locating twenty-five thousand acres of land, which may be reclaimed by the removal of the Red river raft, at the government price, (one dollar and a quarter per acre;) payment for which to be made within one year after the lands referred to shall have been surveyed under the authority of the government.

And your petitioner will ever pray, &c. H. M.
SHREVE.
WASHINGTON CITY, *May* 1, 1834.

Source: Reports from the Court of Claims Submitted to the House of Representatives, 1859–1860. Washington, D.C.: Thomas H. Ford, 1860, pp. 70–71, 82–85.

DOCUMENT 2.9

An American Newspaperman Unfurls His Vision of Continental Conquest

"The Great Nation of Futurity"

November 1839

Throughout the first half of the nineteenth century, America's stewardship of its land, water, and other natural resources was shaped in large measure by the emerging concept of Manifest Destiny. By the latter years of this era in particular, many Americans had become convinced that geographic expansion of national borders all the way to the Pacific Ocean was within the country's grasp—and that taming the western wilderness for profit and glory would in fact be a fulfillment of God's anointment of the United States as a favored nation.

American columnist and Democratic political activist John O'Sullivan was an early and influential spokesman for this viewpoint. In 1845, in fact, O'Sullivan coined the term "manifest destiny" in a newspaper column that sought to stoke public support for the annexation of Texas. "Our manifest destiny," he wrote, "[is] to overspread the continent allotted by Providence for the free development of our yearly multiplying millions." But O'Sullivan had actually articulated the philosophical underpinnings of Manifest Destiny six years earlier, in a column that appeared in the United States Magazine and Democratic Review. *The following is the text of that 1839 column.*

The American people having derived their origin from many other nations, and the Declaration of National Independence being entirely based on the great principle of human equality, these facts demonstrate at once our disconnected position as regards any other nation; that we have, in reality, but little connection with the past history of any of them and still less with all antiquity, its glories, or its crimes. On the contrary, our national birth was the beginning of a new history, the formation and progress of an untried political system, which separates us from the past and connects us with the future only; and so far as regards the entire development of the natural rights of man, in moral, political, and national life, we may confidently assume that our country is destined to be *the great nation* of futurity.

It is so destined, because the principle upon which a nation is organized fixes its destiny, and that of equality is perfect, is universal. It presides in all the operations of the physical world, and it is also the conscious law of the soul—the self-evident dictate of morality, which accurately refines the duty of man to man, and consequently man's rights as man. Besides, the truthful annals of any nation furnish abundant evidence that its happiness, its greatness, its duration, were always proportionate to the democratic equality in its system of government. . . .

What friend of human liberty, civilization, and refinement can cast his view over the past history of the monarchies and aristocracies of antiquity, and not deplore that they ever existed? What philanthropist can contemplate the oppressions, the cruelties, and injustice inflected by them on the masses of mankind and not turn with moral horror from the retrospect?

America is destined for better deeds. It is our unparalleled glory that we have no reminiscences of battlefields, but in defense of humanity, of the oppressed of all nations, of the rights of conscience, the rights of personal enfranchisement. Our annals describe no scenes of horrid carnage, where men were led on by hundreds of thousands to slay one another, dupes and victims to emperors, kings, nobles, demons in the human form called heroes. We have had patriots to defend our homes, our liberties, but no aspirants to crowns or thrones; nor have the American people ever suffered themselves to be led on by wicked ambition to depopulate the land, to spread desolation far and wide, that a human being might be placed on a seat of supremacy.

We have no interest in the scenes of antiquity, only as lessons of avoidance of nearly all their examples. The expansive future is our arena, and for our history. We are entering on its untrodden space, with the truths of God in our minds, beneficent objects in our hearts, and with a clear conscience unsullied by the past. We are the nation of human progress, and who will, what can, set limits to our onward march? Providence is with us, and no earthly power can. We point to the everlasting truth on the first page of our national declaration, and we proclaim to the millions of other lands, that "the gates of hell"—the powers of aristocracy and monarchy—"shall not prevail against it."

The far-reaching, the boundless future will be the era of American greatness. In its magnificent domain of space and time, the nation of many nations is destined to manifest to mankind the excellence of divine principles; to establish on earth the noblest temple ever dedicated to the worship of the Most High—the Sacred and the True. Its floor shall be a hemisphere—its roof the firmament of the star-studded heavens, and its congregation a Union of many Republics, comprising hundreds of happy millions, calling . . . no man master, but governed by God's natural and moral law of equality, the law of brotherhood—of "peace and good will amongst men." . . .

Yes, we are the nation of progress, of individual freedom, of universal enfranchisement. Equality of rights is the cynosure of our union of States, the grand exemplar of the correlative equality of individuals; and while truth sheds its effulgence, we cannot retrograde, without dissolving the one and subverting the other. We must onward to the fulfilment of our mission—to the entire development of the principle of our organization—freedom of conscience, freedom of person, freedom of trade and business pursuits, universality of freedom and equality. This is our high destiny, and in nature's eternal, inevitable decree of cause and effect we must accomplish it. All this will be our future history, to establish on earth the moral dignity and salvation of man—the immutable truth and beneficence of God. For this blessed mission to the nations of the world, which are shut out from the life-giving light of truth, has America been chosen; and her high example shall smite unto death the tyranny of kings, hierarchs, and oligarchs, and carry the glad tidings of peace and good will where myriads now endure an existence scarcely more enviable than that of beasts of the field. Who, then, can doubt that our country is destined to be *the great nation* of futurity?

Source: O'Sullivan, John L. "The Great Nation of Futurity," *United States Magazine and Democratic Review*, November 1839, pp. 2–3, 6–7.

DOCUMENT 2.10

An American Warns of Human and Ecological Disaster on the Great Plains

"Nature's Works Are Always Worthy of Our Preservation and Protection"

1841

Writer and painter George Catlin (1796–1872) was one of the most discerning and sympathetic observers of the cataclysmic changes that washed over the tribes and lands of the Great Plains over the course of the nineteenth century. In his seminal 1841 work Letters and Notes on the Manners, Customs, and Condition of the North American Indian, *Catlin distilled his impressions from eight years of traveling throughout the West. He celebrated the "honourable" character of the Indians, mourned the impact of the white man's alcohol and market economy on tribal cultures, and decried white policies and attitudes that were driving the bison to extinction.*

These trends bothered Catlin so much that he urged American policymakers to establish great public spaces—national parks—where Indians and bison alike could roam unmolested. This was a truly radical proposal in the 1840s, and it was dismissed out of hand by businessmen, lawmakers, and government administrators who viewed any restrictions on land development and natural resource exploitation as anathema to American ideals. A mere three decades later, however, Catlin's visionary call for federal protection of valuable natural areas became a reality with the 1872 establishment of Yellowstone National Park in Wyoming. The following is an excerpt from Catlin's 1841 masterwork.

It is truly a melancholy contemplation for the traveler in this country, to anticipate the period which is not far distant, when the last of these noble animals [the bison], at the hands of white and red men, will fall victims to their cruel and improvident rapacity; leaving these beautiful green fields, a vast and idle waste, unstocked and unpeopled for ages to come, until the bones of the one and the traditions of the other will have vanished, and left scarce an intelligible trace behind. . . .

Thus much I wrote of the buffaloes, and of the accidents that befall them, as well as of the fate that awaits them; and before I closed my book, I strolled out one day to the shade of a plum-tree, where I laid in the grass on a favourite bluff, and wrote thus:—

"It is generally supposed, and familiarly said, that a man '*falls*' into a reverie; but I seated myself in the shade a few minutes since, resolved to *force* myself into one; and for this purpose I laid open a small pocket-map of North America, and excluding my thoughts from every other object in the world, I soon succeeded in producing the desired illusion. This little chart, over which I bent, was seen in all its parts, as nothing but the green and vivid reality. I was lifted up upon an imaginary pair of wings, which easily raised and held me floating in the open air, from whence I could behold beneath me the Pacific and the Atlantic Oceans—the great cities of the East, and the mighty rivers. I could see the blue chain of the great lakes at the North—the Rocky Mountains, and beneath them and near their base, the vast, and almost boundless plains of grass, which were speckled with the bands of grazing buffaloes!

"The world turned gently around, and I examined its surface; continent after continent passed under my eye, and yet amidst them all, I saw not the vast and vivid green, that is spread like a carpet over the Western wilds of my own country. I saw not elsewhere in the world, the myriad herds of buffaloes—my eyes scanned in vain, for they were not. And when I turned again to the wilds of my native land, I beheld them all in motion! For the distance of several hundreds of miles from North to South, they were wheeling about in vast columns and herds—some were scattered, and ran with furious wildness—some lay dead, and others were pawing the earth for a hiding-place—some were sinking down and dying, gushing out their life's blood in deep-drawn sighs—and others were contending in furious battle for the life they possessed, and the ground that they stood upon. They had long since assembled from the thickets, and secret haunts of the deep forest, into the midst of the treeless and bushless plains, as the place for their safety. I could see in a hundred places, amid the wheeling bands, and on their skirts and flanks, the leaping wild horse darting among them. I saw not the arrows, nor heard the twang of the sinewy bows that sent them; but I saw their victims fall!—on other steeds that rushed along their sides, I saw the glistening lances, which seemed to lay across them; their blades were

It is a melancholy contemplation for one who has traveled as I have, through these realms, and seen this noble animal in all its pride and glory, to contemplate it so rapidly wasting from the world.

—George Catlin

blazing in the sun, till dipped in blood, and then I lost them! In other parts (and there were many), the vivid flash of *fire-arms* was seen—*their* victims fell too, and over their dead bodies hung, suspended in air, little clouds of whitened smoke, from under which the flying horsemen had darted forward to mingle again with, and deal death to, the trampling throng.

"So strange were men mixed (both red and white) with the countless herds that wheeled and eddied about, that all below seemed one vast extended field of battle—whole armies, in some places, seemed to blacken the earth's surface;—in other parts, regiments, battalions, wings, platoons, rank and file, and '*Indian-file*'—all were in motion; and death and destruction seemed to be the watch-word amongst them. In their turmoil, they sent up great clouds of dust, and with them came the mingled din of groans and trampling hoofs, that seemed like the rumbling of a dreadful cataract, or the roaring of distant thunder. Alternate pity and admiration harrowed up in my bosom and my brain, many a hidden thought; and amongst them a few of the beautiful notes that were once sung, and exactly in point: '*Quadraupedante putrem sonitu qu tit ungula campum*' [the horses' hooves with four-fold beat shake the crumbling plain]. Even such was the din amidst the quadrupeds of these vast plains. And from the craggy cliffs of the Rocky Mountains also were seen descending into the valley, the myriad Tartars, who had not horses to ride, but before their well-drawn bows the fattest of the herds were falling. Hundreds and thousands were strewed upon the plains—they were flayed, and their red-dened carcasses left; and about them bands of wolves, and dogs, and buzzards were seen devouring them. Contiguous, and in sight, were the distant and feeble smokes of wig-wams and villages, where the skins were dragged, and dressed for white man's luxury! Where they were all sold for *whiskey,* and the poor Indians laid drunk, and were crying. I cast my eyes into the towns and cities of the East, and there I beheld buffalo robes hang-ing at almost every door for traffic; and I saw also the curling smokes of a thousand *Stills*—and I said, 'Oh insatiable man, is thy avarice such! Wouldst thou tear the skin from the back of the last animal of this noble race, *and rob thy fellow-man of his meat, and for it give him poison!*'"

* * *

Many are the rudenesses and wilds in Nature's works, which are destined to fall before the deadly axe and desolating hands of cultivating man; and so amongst her ranks of *living,* of beast and human, we often find noble stamps, or beautiful colours, to which our admiration clings; and even in the overwhelming march of civilized improvements and refinements do we love to cherish their existence, and lend our efforts to preserve them in their primitive rudeness. Such of Nature's works are always worthy of our preservation and protection; and the further we become separated (and the face of the country) from that pristine wildness and beauty, the more pleasure does the mind of enlightened man feel in recurring to those scenes, when he can have them preserved for his eyes and his mind to dwell upon.

Of such "rudeness and wilds," Nature has no where presented more beautiful and lovely scenes, than those of the vast prairies of the West; and of *man* and *beast,* no nobler specimens than those who inhabit them—the *Indian* and the *buffalo*—joint and original tenants of the soil, and fugitives together from the approach of civilized man; they have fled to the great plains of the West, and there, under an equal doom, they have taken up their *last abode,* where their race will expire, and their bones will bleach together.

It may be that *power* is *right,* and *voracity a virtue;* and that these people, and these noble animals, are *righteously* doomed to an issue that *will* not be averted. It can be easily proved—we have a civilized science that can easily do it, or anything else that may be required to cover the iniquities of civilized man in catering for his unholy appetites. It can be proved that the weak and ignorant have no *rights*—that there can be no virtue in darkness—that God's gifts have no meaning or merit until they are appropriated by civilized man—by him brought into the light, and converted to his use and luxury. We have a mode of reasoning (I forget what it is called) by which all this can be proved, and even more. The *word* and the *system* are entirely of *civilized* origin; and latitude is admirably given to them in proportion to the increase of civilized wants, which often require a *judge* to overrule the laws of nature. I say that *we* can prove such things; but an *Indian* cannot. It is a mode of reasoning unknown to him in his nature's simplicity, but admirably adapted to subserve the interests of the enlightened world, who are always their own judges, when dealing with the savage; and who, in the present refined age, have many appetites that can only be lawfully indulged, by proving God's laws defective.

It is not enough in this polished and extravagant age, that we get from the Indian his lands, and the very clothes from his back, but the food from their mouths must be stopped, to add a new and useless article to the fashionable world's luxuries. The ranks must be thinned, and the race exterminated, of this noble animals, and the Indians of the great plains left without the means of supporting life, that white men may figure a few years longer, enveloped in buffalo robes—that they may spread them, for their pleasure and elegance, over the backs of their sleighs, and trail them ostentatiously amidst the busy throng, as a thing of beauty and elegance that had been made for them! . . .

It is a melancholy contemplation for one who has traveled as I have, through these realms, and seen this noble animal in all its pride and glory, to contemplate it so rapidly wasting from the world, drawing the irresistible conclusion too, which one must do, that its species is soon to be extinguished, and with it the peace and happiness (if not the actual existence) of the tribes of Indians who are joint tenants with them, in the occupancy of these vast and idle plains.

And what a splendid contemplation too, when one (who has traveled these realms, and can duly appreciate them) imagines them as they *might* in future be seen, (by some great protecting policy of government) preserved in their pristine beauty and wildness, in a *magnificent park,* where the world could see for ages to come, the native Indian in his classic attire, galloping his wild horse, with sinewy bow, and shield and lance, amid the fleeting herds of elks and buffaloes. What a beautiful and thrilling specimen for America to preserve and hold up to the view of her refined citizens and the world, in future ages! A *nation's Park,* containing man and beast, in all the wild and freshness of their nature's beauty!

I would ask no other monument to my memory, nor any other enrolment of my name amongst the famous dead, than the reputation of having been the founder of such an institution.

Such scenes might easily have been preserved, and still could be cherished on the great plains of the West, without detriment to the country or its borders; for the tracts of country on which the buffaloes have assembled, are uniformly sterile, and of no available use to cultivating man. . . .

Source: Catlin, George. *Letters and Notes of the Manners, Customs, and Condition of the North American Indians.* Vol. 1. 1841. Reprint, Philadelphia: Willis P. Hazard, 1857, pp. 389, 392–401.

DOCUMENT
2.11

The Swamp and Overflow Act

"To Reclaim the . . . Whole of Those Swamp and Overflowed Lands"

1850

In the mid-nineteenth century, states such as Florida, Louisiana, and Michigan with large expanses of federally owned wetlands viewed these ecologically rich tracts of land as useless because they could not be cultivated or otherwise developed for commercial profit. State and federal lawmakers thus hammered out a policy whereby federally owned swamps and marshlands "unfit for cultivation" would be ceded to the states, which could then finance drainage and development of the acreage. The text of this act is reprinted here.

When the Swamp and Overflow Act of 1850, also known as the Arkansas Act or the Swamp Land Act, came into law, it triggered a massive wave of land and ecosystem alteration in Arkansas, Alabama, California, Florida, Illinois, Indiana, Iowa, Michigan, Mississippi, Missouri, Ohio, and Wisconsin. About 64 million acres were ultimately transferred under the act—including 20 million acres in Florida alone. The Act also generated a surge in surveying chicanery, for the act specified that federal wetlands should be transferred to states only when the greater part of a legal subdivision was wet and unfit for cultivation. In California, for instance, unscrupulous speculators bribed surveyors to label valuable forests as swampland. They promptly bought the parcels, then turned around and sold them to timber companies for spectacular profits.

Be it enacted by the Senate and House of Representatives of the United States of America in Congress assembled, That to enable the State of Arkansas to construct the necessary levees and drains to reclaim the swamp and overflowed lands therein, the whole of those swamp and overflowed lands, made unfit thereby for cultivation, which shall remain unsold at the passage of this Act, shall be, and the same are hereby granted to said State.

Sec. 2. *And be it further enacted,* That it shall be the duty of the Secretary of the Interior, as soon as may be practicable after the passage of this act, to make out an accurate list and plats of the lands described as aforesaid and transmit the same to the governor of the State of Arkansas, and, at the request of said governor, cause a patent to be issued to the State therefore; and on that patent, the fee simple to said lands shall vest in the State of Arkansas, subject to the disposal of the Legislature thereof; *Provided, however,* That the proceeds of said lands, whether from sale or by direct appropriation in kind, shall be applied, exclusively, as far as necessary, to the purpose of reclaiming said lands by means of the levees and drains aforesaid.

Sec. 3. *And be it further enacted,* That in making out a list and plats of the land aforesaid, all legal subdivisions, the greater part of which is "wet and unfit for cultivation," shall be included in said list and plats; but when the greater part of a subdivision is not of that character, the whole of it shall be excluded therefrom.

Sec. 4. *And be it further enacted,* That the provisions of this Act be extended to, and their benefits be conferred upon, each of the other States of the Union in which such swamp and overflowed lands, known as designated as aforesaid, may be situated.

Source: *The Statutes at Large and Treaties of the United States of America.* Vol. 9, edited by George Minot. Boston: Little, Brown, 1854, p. 519.

A Blunt Warning about Unsustainable Farming Practices in America

"The Productive Power of Nearly All the Land . . . Is Fearfully Lessening"

September 1851

American agricultural production soared during the first half of the nineteenth century, lifted by steady growth in the nation's population; a culture that placed high value on hard work and economic success; and local, state, and federal policies that encouraged geographic expansion and intensive exploitation of land and natural resources.

But some observers refused to take part in the nation's self-congratulatory representation of these trends as stepping stones on the path of Manifest Destiny. To the contrary, a small but vocal group of critics openly castigated American farmers and policymakers as profligate wasters of soil and resources. They warned that if the United States did not stop treating land as an inexhaustible resource, a grim day of reckoning would ensue. One such critic was writer, botanist, and landscape designer Andrew Jackson Downing. The following is an excerpt from his posthumously published Rural Essays *(1853). Downing errs in this essay in dismissing the idea that the United States might one day become a great industrial power, but many of his criticisms of farming practice and land use proved prescient.*

The National Ignorance of the Agricultural Interest.

September, 1851.

To general observers, the prosperity of the United States in the great interests of trade, commerce, manufactures, and agriculture, is a matter of every-day remark and general assent. The country extends itself from one zone to another, and from one ocean to another. New States are settled, our own population increases, emigration pours its vast tide upon our shores, new soils give abundant harvests, new settlements create a demand for the necessaries and luxuries of life provided by the older cities, and the nation exhibits at every census, so unparalleled a growth, and such magnificent resources, that common sense is startled, and only the imagination can keep pace with the probable destinies of the one hundred millions of Americans that will speak one language, and, we trust, be governed by one constitution, half a century hence.

> *[I]t does not require much scrutiny on the part of a serious inquirer, to discover that we are in some respects like a large and increasing family, running over and devouring a great estate to which they have fallen heirs, with little or no care to preserve or maintain it.*
>
> —Andrew Jackson Downing

As a wise man, who finds his family increasing after the manner of the ancient patriarchs, looks about him somewhat anxiously, to find out if there is likely to be bread enough for their subsistence, so a wise statesman, looking at this extraordinary growth of population, and this prospective wealth of the country, will inquire, narrowly, into its productive powers. He will desire to know whether the national domain is so managed that it will be likely to support the great people that will be ready to live upon it in the next century. He will seek to look into the present and the future sufficiently to ascertain whether our rapid growth and material abundance do not arise almost as much from the migratory habits of our people, and the constant taking-up of rich prairies, yielding their virgin harvests of breadstuffs, as from the institutions peculiar to our favored country.

We regret to say, that it does not require much scrutiny on the part of a serious inquirer, to discover that we are in some respects like a large and increasing family, running over and devouring a great estate to which they have fallen heirs, with little or no care to preserve or maintain it, rather than a wise and prudent one, seeking to maintain that estate in its best and most productive condition.

To be sure, our trade and commerce are pursued with a thrift and sagacity likely to add largely to our substantial wealth, and to develope the collateral resources of the country. But, after all, trade and commerce are not the great interests of the country. That interest is, as every one admits, agriculture. By the latter, the great bulk of the people live, and by it all are fed. It is clear, therefore, if that interest is neglected or misunderstood, the population of the country may steadily increase, but the means of supporting that population (which can never be largely a manufacturing population) must necessarily lessen, proportionately, every year.

Now, there are two undeniable facts at present staring us Americans in the face—amid all this prosperity: the first is, that the productive power of nearly all the land in the United States, which has been ten years in cultivation, is fearfully lessening every season, from the desolating effects of a ruinous system of husbandry; and the second is, that in consequence of this, the rural population of the older States is either at a stand-still, or it is falling off, or it increases very slowly in proportion to the population of those cities and towns largely engaged in commercial pursuits.

Our census returns show, for instance, that in some of the States (such as Rhode Island, Connecticut, Delaware, and Maryland), the only increase of population is in the *towns*—for in the rural population there is no growth at all. In the great agricultural State of New-York, the gain in the fourteen largest towns is sixty-four per cent., while in the rest of the State it is but nineteen per cent. In Pennsylvania, thirty-nine and a quarter per cent, in the large towns, and but twenty-one per cent, in the rural districts. The politicians in this State, finding themselves losing a representative in the ratio, while Pennsylvania gains two, have, in alarm, actually deigned to inquire into the growth of the agricultural class, with some little attention. They have not generally arrived at the truth, however, which is, that Pennsylvania is, as a State, much better farmed than New-York, and hence the agricultural population increases much faster.

It is a painful truth, that both the press and the more active minds of the country at large are strikingly ignorant of the condition of agriculture in all the older States, and one no less painful, that the farmers, who are not ignorant of it, are, as a body, not intelligent enough to know how to remedy the evil.

"And what is that evil?" many of our readers will doubtless inquire. We answer, the miserable system of farming steadily pursued by eight-tenths of all the farmers of this country, since its first settlement; a system which proceeds upon the principle of taking as many crops from the land with as little manure as possible—until its productive powers are exhausted, and then—emigrating to some part of the country where they can apply the same practice to a new soil. It requires far less knowledge and capital to wear out one good soil and abandon it for another, than to cultivate a good soil so as to maintain its productive powers from year to year, unimpaired. Accordingly, the migration is always "to THE WEST." There, is ever the Arcadia of the American farmer; there are the acres which need but to be broken up by the plough, to yield their thirty or forty bushels of wheat to the acre. Hence, the ever full tide of farmers or farmers' sons, always sets westward, and the lands at home are left in a comparatively exhausted and barren state, and hence, too, the slow progress of farming as an honest art, where every body practises it like a highway robber.

There are, doubtless, many superficial thinkers, who consider these western soils *exhaustless*—"prairies where crop after crop can be taken, by generation after generation." There was never a greater fallacy. There are acres and acres of land in the counties bordering the Hudson—such counties as Dutchess and Albany—from which the early settlers reaped their thirty to forty bushels of wheat to the acre, as easily as their great-grandchildren do now in the most fertile fields of the valley of the Mississippi. Yet these very acres now yield only twelve or fourteen bushels each, and the average yield of the county of Dutchess—one of the most fertile and best managed on the Hudson, is at the present moment only six bushels of wheat to the acre! One of our cleverest agricultural writers has made the estimate, that of the twelve millions of acres of cultivated land in the State of New-York, eight millions are in the hands of the "skinners," who take away every thing from the soil, and put nothing back; three millions in the hand of farmers who manage them so as to make the lands barely hold their own, while one million of acres are well fanned, so as to maintain a high and productive state of fertility. And as New-York is confessedly one of the most substantial of all the older States, in point of agriculture, this estimate is too flattering to be applied to the older States. Even Ohio—newly settled as she is, begins to fall off per acre, in her annual wheat crop, and before fifty years will, if the present system continues, be considered a worn out soil.

The evil at the bottom of all this false system of husbandry, is no mystery. A rich soil contains only a given quantity of vegetable and mineral food for plants. Every crop grown upon a fertile soil, takes from it a certain amount of these substances, so essential to the growth of another crop. If these crops, like most of our grain crops, are sent away and consumed in other counties, or other parts of the counties—as in the great cities, and *none of their essential elements* in the way of vegetable matter, lime, potash, etc., *restored to the soil,* it follows as a matter of course, that eventually the soil *must* become barren or miserably unprofitable. And such is, unfortunately, the fact. Instead of maintaining as many animals as possible upon the farm, and carefully restoring to the soil in the shape of animal and mineral manure, all those elements needful to the growth of future vegetables, our farmers send nearly all their crops for sale in cities—and allow all the valuable animal and mineral products of these crops to go to waste in those cities.*

"Oh! but," the farmer upon worn out land will say, "we cannot *afford* to pay for all the labor necessary for the high farming you advocate." Are you quite sure of that assertion? We suspect if you were to enter carefully into the calculation, as your neighbor, the merchant, enters into the calculation of his profit and loss in his system of trade, you would find that the difference in value between one crop of 12 bushels and another of 30 bushels of wheat to the acre, would leave a handsome profit to that farmer who would pursue with method and energy, the practice of never taking an atom of food for plants from the soil in the shape of a crop, without, in some natural way, replacing it again. For, it must be remembered, that needful as the soil is, every plant gathers a large part of its food from the air, and the excrement of animals fed upon crops, will restore to the soil all the needful elements taken from it by those crops.

The principle has been demonstrated over and over again, but the difficulty is to get the farmers to *believe* it. Because they can get crops, such as they are, from a given soil, year after year, without manure, they think it is only necessary for them to *plant*—Providence will take care of the harvest. But it is in the pursuit of this very system, that vast plains of the old world, once as fertile as Michigan or Ohio, have become desert wastes, and it is perfectly certain, that when we reach the goal of a hundred millions of people, we shall reach a famine soon afterwards, if some new and more enlightened system of agriculture than our national "skinning" system, does not beforehand spring up and extend itself over the country.

And such a system can only be extensively disseminated and put in practice by raising the *intelligence* of farmers generally. We have, in common with the Agricultural Journals, again and again pointed out that this is mainly to be hoped for through a *practical* agricultural education. And yet the legislatures of our great agricultural States vote down,

---

*In Belgium—the most productive country in the world,—the urinary excrements of each cow are sold for $10 a year, and are regularly applied to the land, and poudrette is valued as gold itself.

year after year, every bill reported by the friends of agriculture to establish schools. Not one such school, efficient and useful as it might be, if started with sufficient aid from the State, exists in a nation of more than twenty millions of farmers. "What matters it," say the wise men of our State legislatures, "if the lands of the Atlantic States are worn out by bad farming? Is not the GREAT WEST the granary of the world?" And so they build canals and railroads, and bring from the west millions of bushels of grain, and send not one fertilizing atom back to restore the land. And in this way we shall by-and-by make the fertile prairies as barren as some of the worn out farms of Virginia. And thus "the sins of the fathers are visited upon the children, even to the fourth generation!"

Source: Downing, Andrew Jackson. *Rural Essays.* 1853. Reprint, New York: Leavitt & Allen, 1857, pp. 390–395.

CHAPTER 3

Conservation Gains in an Era of Frontier Conquest

1850–1900

Most American land and resource policies of the second half of the nineteenth century were crafted with an eye toward extraction, exploitation, and development. The nation remained determined to fulfill its Manifest Destiny—to become the planet's economic and geographic leviathan—and it used all the weapons in its legislative arsenal to advance this goal. These weapons included enormous land grants to intrepid pioneers and powerful railroad companies that subsequently laid down the markers of Western settlement and laws that threw the timber, minerals, and other natural riches of the public domain into the hungry maw of the nation's ever-expanding market economy. Yet during this same period, growing numbers of politicians, sportsmen, and scientists cautioned that the nation needed to curb its heedless consumption of land and resources. This recognition of limits, which had been virtually absent in American politics and policymaking to this point, gave rise to a conservation ethic that saw the preservation of wildlife, forests, and rivers as both a moral imperative and a matter of long-term economic security.

FROM PUBLIC DOMAIN TO PRIVATE ENTERPRISE

When mid-nineteenth century American lawmakers cast their gaze westward beyond the Mississippi River, they beheld an epic landscape that throbbed with economic potential. But the western half of the continent was only lightly peopled with market hunters, gold prospectors, and a smattering of settlers at that time (the Native American "savages" inhabiting this world did not figure into their calculations), so they determined that the key to unlocking the riches of the region was to prime the pump of settlement. Legislators and government officials did so by launching the greatest land privatization campaign in American history. Tens of millions of acres of land were transferred out of the public domain and into private hands by century's end for the purpose of economic development.

The rollout of these land transfer policies did not always proceed smoothly. Most notably, proposals in the 1850s to distribute western lands into private hands became entangled in the escalating sectional quarrel over slavery. Abolitionist politicians and organizations encouraged swift settlement, in large measure because they felt that the addition of new states that did not incorporate the "peculiar institution" into their way of

American settlement of the western frontier had a cataclysmic impact on the continent's natural resources. For example, nineteenth-century market hunting, predator eradication policies, and habitat loss led to the near extinction of species such as the wolf and bison and the permanent loss of other species such as the passenger pigeon.

life would advance their cause. Slave-owning Southerners reached the same conclusion, so they remained wary of political schemes to settle the West until the passage of the Kansas–Nebraska Act in 1854. This act repealed the 1820 Missouri Compromise and permitted slavery in U.S. territories north of the 36° 30´ latitude. Under the terms of the act, residents of individual territories would decide for themselves—rather than by federal edict—whether to permit slavery within their borders. This legislation triggered an early wave of western settlement, as freesoilers and pro-slavery parties rushed into Kansas and Nebraska and waged furious battles for control of their legislative tillers.

Other land distribution legislation was less fraught with controversy. Laws such as the 1854 Graduation Act, the 1862 Homestead Act, the 1862 Morrill Act (also known as the Land Grant College Act), the 1864 Coal Lands Disposal Act, the 1877 Desert Land Act, and the 1887 Dawes Act (which effectively privatized huge swaths of American Indian reservation land and resources for development) all were passed with broad support. Their popularity stemmed from the fact that they had been at least nominally crafted to benefit small farmers and ordinary citizens who had become increasingly exorcised about the federal government's penchant for bestowing lucrative land grants to railroads and other large corporations during the 1850s.

The Homestead Act was the most momentous of these acts to transfer public land into private hands. It offered virtually free public land to eastern farmers, recent immigrants, and others who wanted to make a new start in the West. Under the terms of the act, western lands were dispersed in 160-acre parcels (half-mile squares), and land titles for these plots would be granted to settlers after five years of cultivation. One to four million acres of western land were homesteaded annually under this law through the close of the century—and land transfers more than doubled after the 1909 passage of the Enlarged Homestead Act, which raised the homestead grant to settlers from 160 to 320 acres and reduced the title transfer wait from five to three years[1] **(see Document 3.1)**.

The act has been credited as the single greatest force in the settlement of the Great Plains after the Civil War and as an integral element of America's tremendous agricultural expansion from 1870 through World War I. But the legislation also contained loopholes that land speculators and corporate interests exploited for their own gain. As a result, the majority of the public land that was distributed via the Homestead Act ultimately ended up in the hands of timber, mining, and railroad titans. And the land that did go to actual homesteaders was all too often cursed with poor soil quality and sparse rainfall. For these unfortunate homesteaders, the romance of a pioneer life made possible through the largess of the federal government curdled quickly.

OPENING THE WEST THROUGH RAILROAD LAND GRANTS

In addition to the public lands that American railroad companies secured through manipulation of the Homestead Act and similar federal programs, the railroads acquired huge swaths of the public domain directly through government land grants. The rationale driving these federal and state land policies was simple. Politicians believed that generous grants of land to railroads along the rail corridors would give the lines an incentive to turn around and sell or lease the land to settlers, who would in turn provide the railroads with a reliable and profitable source of traffic. Broadly speaking, this plan worked well in advancing the causes of western settlement and economic expansion. Lawmakers and other government officials, however, were slow to appreciate the manifold ecological consequences of the grants.

The first major transfer of federal public land took place in 1850, when the U.S. Congress authorized the General Land Office to hand over 3.7 million acres to the state of Illinois to help promote and finance expansion of the Illinois Central Railroad. Fortified by this gift, the Illinois Central boasted the nation's largest rail system by the close of the 1850s. This early success story prompted the approval of other railroad land grants totaling approximately 18 million acres to Michigan, Wisconsin, Florida, and several Mississippi River Valley states by the end of the 1850s. Public land disposal for railroads reached its apex, however, from 1860 to 1871, when the federal government granted more than 94 million acres directly to railroad companies. One particular milestone of this period was the Pacific Railway Act of 1862, which used lucrative land grants as incentive for the construction of the nation's first transcontinental railroad, which was completed in 1869 **(see Document 3.2)**.

These land disposal packages were, without exception, extremely generous. In addition to bestowing strong rights-of-way corridors to railroad lines, federal authorities provided them with alternating parcels of land on either side of these corridors (which they could develop, lease, or sell) and rights to take huge quantities of timber and stone from adjacent lands that remained in the public domain. Thirty-year government loans also were frequently bundled into these allocations, and railroads frequently were given the option of plucking additional valuable lands out of the public domain.

Some lawmakers and newspaper editors denounced the railroad land grants, describing them as a "colossal robbery of the public domain."[2] But influential statesmen such as Thomas Hart Benton, Henry Clay, Jefferson Davis, Stephen A. Douglas, and William Seward joined forces with boosters of western settlement, such as Asa Whitney and William Gilpin, to rebuff these charges **(see Document 3.14)**. They pointed out that similar federal outlays had been made for canals and other internal improvements earlier in the century, with positive economic results. And they imbued rail lines with alchemic powers to transform the wild frontier into a mosaic of civilized towns, farms, and ranches. Constructing these "roads through the prairies," declared Clay, "will bring millions of acres immediately into the market."[3]

In this nineteenth-century allegory, a female figure is shown carrying the telegraph lines that crossed the nation with the completion of the transcontinental railroad in 1869. A symbol of a new era of American progress and expansion, the figure is also leading farmers westward—at the expense of Native Americans and bison shown fleeing to the left.

But once the spigot opened, no one in power showed much interest in turning it off. The grants of public land to railroads poured out of Washington and territorial statehouses year after year. By the close of the nineteenth century more than 180 million acres had been taken out of the public domain and placed in the hands of rail corporations (about 35 million acres were later forfeited back to the federal government when the companies failed to complete lines by specified deadlines). In return, the carriers laid down more than 225,000 total miles of iron track across the nation—and became the backbone of American commerce in the process. Iron rails pumped huge volumes of commodities from wheat farms, timber camps, copper mines, oil refineries, flour mills, canneries, slaughterhouses, and fruit orchards into newly ascendant cities like Los Angeles, San Francisco, Denver, Chicago, Tacoma, and Dallas and into the established cities of the East.

In addition, railroad rights-of-way became the avenues by which another transformative technology—the telegraph—penetrated the hinterlands. Thousands of miles of telegraph wires were festooned along America's railways in the 1860s and 1870s, and this new and virtually instantaneous mode of communication gave a further dose of adrenaline to the nation's industrializing economy. "The information supplied by the telegraph was like a drug to businessmen, who swiftly became addicted," observed historian Tom Standage. "In combination with the railways, which could move goods quickly from one place to another, the rapid supply of information dramatically changed the way business was done."[4]

PROPAGANDA TRUMPS REALITY

Eager to maximize profits from their new lines, railroad carriers launched an impressive propaganda campaign to lure pioneers westward. Railroad agents trolled European cities and the overcrowded metropolises back east, exhorting potential settlers to secure their share of the West's untapped riches and opportunities before it was too late. Regional carriers such as the Northern Pacific and Southern Pacific also published numerous brochures, posters, and books detailing these opportunities. Territorial governors, transatlantic steamship companies, and western newspaper editors also lent their voices. These efforts, combined with heavily publicized federal land dispersal policies such as the Homestead Act, found fertile soil in the crowded, impoverished inner cities of the East and the Old World. Settlers heeded the call of opportunity by the tens of thousands, and before long "the breaking wave of settlement was eating up half a meridian a year; from one season to the next, settlements were thirty miles farther out."[5]

Some western destinations, like California, lived up to their billing. Blessed with large swaths of fertile soil, a temperate climate, and a treasure chest of roaring rivers carrying water that could be used for irrigation, California began its long march toward economic powerhouse status during this era. But settlers who made their stand in more arid regions of the West—lands that had been called the "Great American Desert" in pre-Civil War days—were not so fortunate. These hardy pioneers had embraced a popular theory propounded by western boosters that "rain follows the plow." One champion of this doctrine, which was a sort of hybrid of devout religious faith and deeply flawed science, was Nebraskan Charles Dana Wilbur. "The raindrop never fails to fall and answer to the imploring power or prayer of labor," he stated in 1881. "To those who possess the divine faculty of hope—the optimists of our times—it will always be a source of pleasure to understand that the Creator never imposed a perpetual desert upon the earth, but, on the contrary, has so endowed it that man, by the plow, can transform it, in any country, into farm areas."[6]

The myth that plow-wielding settlers could be agents of climate alteration garnered a brief veneer of legitimacy in the 1870s, when the arid West experienced a cycle of generous rainfall and climatologists endorsed the theory. But observers such as John Wesley Powell, a geologist and veteran explorer of the arid West, knew better. He recognized that "rain follows the plow" was wishful thinking and that limited water availability would greatly constrain economic development in arid parts of the region over the long term. In 1874 testimony before Congress, in fact, Powell declared that "when all the waters running in the streams of this region are conducted on the land, there will be but a small portion of the country redeemed, varying in the different territories perhaps from one to three percent."[7]

Over the ensuing years, Powell made many recommendations for sensible and limited "redemption" of western lands, most notably in his landmark 1879 *Report on the Lands of the Arid Region of the United States* (**see Document 3.7**). But Congress, General Land Office bureaucrats, and developers all turned a deaf ear to his proposed doctrine of limited and communal land and water use in the West. The land rush continued unabated—until the late 1880s, when a multi-year drought crushed agrarian communities across the Great Plains. The populations of Nebraska and Kansas plummeted as disillusioned settlers, who had watched helplessly as their crops and dreams withered and died, retreated eastward or pulled up stakes for one of the boom communities along the Pacific Coast. These grim years brought home the importance of irrigation and reliable water supply in a way that even the most perceptive official report never could.

Natural Resource Management in the Land Rush Era

Another remarkable aspect of the government-sanctioned disposal and transformation of western lands during the nineteenth century was the lack of institutional control over the process. The General Land Office (GLO), which was responsible for public domain lands in the United States from its inception in 1812 (it was placed within the Department of the Interior when that department was formed in 1849), was given resources to survey, plat, and sell public land in the West but had few assets and little authority when it came to planning this development, monitoring its environmental impact, and curbing corporate or individual abuses of the public resources under its charge. "For a full century and a half," pointed out one scholar, "the GLO and its successor, the Bureau of Land Management, had no single overarching law to guide them, but were responsible merely for administering the hundreds of separate, conflicting and often loosely drafted land disposal laws and resulting claims that emerged piecemeal over that period."[8] In many remote parts of the West, in fact, railroads played a pivotal role in the formulation of public land management policies. Their record in this regard was mixed. Carriers that were primarily concerned with filling their coffers in the short term helped institutionalize territorial and state policies of environmental plunder, but other, more farsighted companies actually encouraged efficient irrigation methods, water conservation, and other sustainable land-use practices long before territorial, state, and federal authorities were able—or inclined—to do so.[9]

Gradually, however, public policies and laws for the management of environmental resources crystallized in the foaming wake of the westward-moving frontier of settlement. And as these regulations and guidelines washed first across the Great Lakes region and prairie states, and then the intermountain West, until finally fetching up against the Pacific Coast, an epic battle between competing philosophies of resource stewardship was joined. This clash, between the forces of resource conservation and those of unfettered resource utilization and harvest, is still being waged today.

The stakes in this contest were highlighted by a succession of federally sponsored scientific surveys of America's frontier territories. These expeditions, which began in the 1860s and continued through the end of the century, provided lawmakers, developers and corporate executives alike with a valuable inventory of the rich environmental resources that lay untapped in the West. The work of the U.S. Geological Survey (USGS), which was established by Congress in 1879 for the explicit purpose of carrying out professional surveying of western land and its resources, was of particular value in this regard. But although USGS work greatly aided corporate interests in the short term by filling in the locations of valuable stands of timber, reliable water resources, and other blanks in the map, the agency's efforts would have long-term environmental benefits because it was during this period that the USGS implemented topographic mapping, resource inventories and surveys, and other science-based administrative procedures that gradually became essential elements of federal environmental management.[10]

EARLY MINING LAWS

Mining was one of the early flashpoints in this war to shape resource management policies, and it remains a key environmental battleground in the twenty-first century. In the second half of the nineteenth century, however, the contest was a rout, with pro-development legislators carrying the day. Pro-development forces held sway because mining was a major engine of economic growth in many parts of the country. "Mining had a key role in opening the new country. . . . Gold in California, copper in Montana, coal and oil in Pennsylvania, iron ore in Minnesota, and lead in Illinois attracted fortune hunters and job seekers."[11]

Mining's central role in the industrialization of the Midwest is unquestioned, and Ohio coal, Pennsylvania oil, and Michigan copper all contributed mightily to the nation's economic expansion. But it was the mineral resources of the West that inspired the creation of the nation's most sweeping nineteenth-century mining laws.

Mining in the West essentially began with the 1848 California gold rush, then moved steadily eastward into the intermountain West, where coal fields and gold, silver, and copper strikes breathed economic life into Colorado, Nevada, Montana, and other states and territories. By the time Texas and Oklahoma learned that they were sitting on huge lakes of oil in the 1890s, the primacy of extraction over environmental protection had become entrenched in federal mining laws.

Many of the earliest western mining laws were actually cobbled together in the region's hardscrabble mining camps as codes of conduct. "Though differing in detail, all were based on the principles that the public lands were free to be exploited by American citizens, that claims to the lands could be staked out in the order of first come, first served, and that the miner must develop his discovery in order to maintain his claim," explained Frederick Merk. "As time went on, the codes were incorporated in county, state, and territorial laws."[12]

Federal policymakers, meanwhile, did not make any attempt to regulate mining on public land until the late 1860s and early 1870s. Up to that point the national government had been silent on procedures for establishing mining claims, and it had failed to provide any mechanism for extracting royalties from the profits of private mining activity in the public domain.[13] The three primary federal mining laws that were passed during this period did little but formally sanction mining operations that had been taking place on public land anyway. The first of these was the landmark Mining Law of 1866, which proclaimed that "the mineral lands of the public domain . . . are hereby declared to be free and open to exploration and occupation" in accordance with local mining laws. The law also ratified the "first come, first served" philosophy that underpinned the Homestead Act and other federal land and resource distribution policies of the era. As one western historian explained,

> The miners' precedent was carried into water allocation for irrigation and domestic use. Such disparate resources as wildlife and oil came to be awarded by a similar principle of priority, the rule of capture. . . . In the complexity of American resource law, no one principle was applied with consistency, but "first in time, first in right" had a widespread influence. While prior appropriation sorted out innumerable property disputes, it did so by giving an almost mystical weight to the idea of getting there first.[14]

The Placer Act of 1870 expanded the policies of the 1866 act, which had focused on lode mining, to include hydraulic surface mining (also known as placer mining). In addition, it authorized miners to claim rights on an unlimited number of 160-acre parcels for just $2.50 an acre, even if valuable mineral deposits appeared to be absent. This proved to be a bonanza for speculators who could claim public lands for mining and then use them for agriculture or other purposes. The 1872 General Mining Act, meanwhile, was crafted to provide some long-overdue uniformity to mining claims in such realms as claim sizes, patent applications, and fees, and it stipulated that miners with claims needed to spend $100 annually in development work to keep those claims. But it also further codified the mining industry's virtually unrestricted access to "all lands owned by the United States government." And like the earlier mining laws, it notably made no provision for a royalty program or imposed any financial penalties for environmental damage caused as a result of mining activity (see Document 3.4).

THE FIGHT OVER TIMBER IN THE PUBLIC DOMAIN

Federal, state, and territorial policymakers adopted similarly pro-extraction laws in the realm of timber resources from 1850 to 1900 with predictable results. At mid-century American forestland (public and private) was being cleared at a rate of more than 37,000 square miles annually, and over the next fifty years an estimated 168 million acres of forest were cut down and cleared.[15] The timber industry's assault on the forests during this era, asserted western historian and conservationist Wallace Stegner, "was like a feeding frenzy of sharks."[16]

Most of this lumbering took place west of New England and the mid-Atlantic states for the simple reason that the great forests of these regions were already gone, utilized by the first generations of Americans to build homes, barns, stores, rail ties, and wagons; drive their steam-powered trains and steamboats; and provide warmth and cooking fuel in homestead kitchens. But when America turned its timber-hungry gaze westward, it did so armed with new technologies for cutting, milling, and transporting wood and an immigrant-swollen population that was demanding timber for a multitude of purposes. The consequences for western forests when these two forces met were explosive. "The pattern of the spread of lumbering," according to forest historian Michael Williams, "was one of a continuously expanding wave of exploitation, which, despite local pauses and advances, moved with generally gathering momentum across the continent. . . . The wave seemed to have an ever-increasing height and volume as it reached each new region of exploitation in turn, first the Lake States, then the South, and then the Pacific Northwest."[17] Or as Ralph Waldo Emerson pithily described this phenomenon in 1860 in *Conduct of Life,* "the steam [of American industry] puffs and expands as before, but this time it is dragging all Michigan on its back to hungry New York and hungry England."[18]

The epic scale of timber-cutting activity was made possible by federal and state governments that saw resource extraction as a cornerstone of American economic prosperity—and believed that the nation possessed infinite storehouses of those resources. The few regulations that Congress and state legislatures imposed on cutting and removing timber in the public domain were only weakly enforced from 1800 through the close of the Civil War. Timber enforcement agents stood little chance against frontier communities that deeply resented "outsiders" interfering with their efforts to sustain themselves and their families. When western politicians and their corporate benefactors in the logging, mining, and railroad industries also pushed back, enforcement of illegal logging became virtually nonexistent.

This situation remained unchanged until the 1870s, when Congress took its first steps to cobble together actual federal forest policies. The first milestone in this regard was its passage of the Timber Culture Act of 1873, which offered 160 acres of public land to any individual willing to plant trees on 40 of the acres and nurture their growth for ten years. This stipulation was inserted not out of sustainability concerns, but because it was thought that new trees would increase rainfall on the Great Plains.

The next major legislation passed by Congress was the 1878 Timber and Stone Act. This law focused on forested mountains of the West and other federal lands that were valuable chiefly for their timber stores rather than their agricultural potential. Crafted to encourage further settlement, it permitted individuals to buy designated 160-acre tracts for $2.50 an acre—a fraction of the actual value of the land. Conservation and enforcement provisions of the act, meanwhile, were relatively toothless. For example, the act reaffirmed that harvesting timber from public land was illegal, but it exempted many of the nation's biggest consumers of wood, including miners, ranchers, and farmers, from this restriction. In addition, the penalties it imposed for timber trespass provided little deterrent to lawbreakers. Those caught stealing timber from the public domain were given the option of escaping prosecution simply by paying the minimum land purchase price.[19] Finally, the Timber and Stone Act was vulnerable to easy manipulation by corporate interests. When new tracts opened for sale, timber firms recruited large groups of individuals who bought clusters of parcels, then turned around and sold them to the timber giants. Consequently, the majority of the 14 million acres of federal land that were privatized through this act actually ended up in corporate ownership. Another piece of forest legislation passed by Congress in 1878—the Free Timber Act—provided further evidence of the low regard that policymakers had for calls to rein in America's forest-clearing frenzy. This law, which allowed residents of western states to cut timber freely on public lands for farming, mining, or other "domestic purposes," sparked a fresh onslaught on fast-dwindling forestlands (**see Document 3.6**).

These policies had a cataclysmic environmental impact on forests and watersheds from the Appalachians to the edge of the Pacific. Sawdust from mills and erosion from denuded hillsides choked the life out of many rivers. Some wildlife populations crashed as their forest habitat vanished. Flooding increased in areas where water-retaining woodlands had been claimed by the lumberman's ax. And slash piles left by cutting operations became epic fire hazards. In 1871 one of these tinderboxes of sawdust and branches erupted into the greatest forest fire in recorded history in North America. Wisconsin's Great Peshtigo Fire burned 1.3 million acres and claimed more than 1,500 lives. Other slash-fueled conflagrations that same year set another 3 million acres ablaze in Minnesota and Michigan. By the close of the nineteenth century, some 80 million acres had been scarred by fire across a broad belt of land extending from the Great Lakes to the Deep South.[20]

CONSERVATION VOICES BREAK THROUGH

The breakneck pace at which America was consuming its forests and other natural resources was applauded by most congressmen, businessmen, newspaper editors, and ordinary citizens. They viewed exploitation of the environment as integral to the nation's economic expansion, and many of them felt that their sweeping "improvements" symbolized the nation's fulfillment of its Manifest Destiny. But other observers grew uneasy about what was transpiring. A new generation of writers, poets, and painters, their sensibilities shaped by transcendentalism and romanticism, released works that celebrated the beauty of nature and the spiritual value of wilderness. These influential artists ranged from the painters of the Hudson River School to philosophers such as Ralph Waldo Emerson, Henry David Thoreau, George Perkins Marsh, John Burroughs, and John Muir. These men produced works that both celebrated wild nature and lamented our inability to establish a more harmonious relationship with the natural world. "Man is everywhere a disturbing agent," wrote Marsh in his 1864 work *Man and Nature*, one of the landmark documents of American environmental thought. "Wherever he plants his foot, the harmonies of nature are turned to discord. . . . We are, even now, breaking up the floor and wainscoting and doors and window frames of our dwelling, for fuel to warm our bodies and seethe our pottage"[21] (**see Document 3.3**).

Simultaneously, a small but growing chorus of scientists, government officials, sportsmen, and scholars began calling for changes in the nation's treatment of its natural resources on more utilitarian grounds. Leaving the philosophical arguments for environmental stewardship to the "nature writers," men such as Carl Schurz, who served as secretary of the interior for President Rutherford B. Hayes from 1877 to 1881, issued blunt warnings freighted with scientific data about the unsustainable course that America was charting for itself in the realm of resource use (see Document 3.12). Meanwhile, sportsmen such as Thaddeus Norris, author of *The American Angler's Book* (1864), painted grim scenes of environmental degradation for hunting and fishing enthusiasts:

> Many a fly-fisher who travels a long way to enjoy his favorite sport is shocked at witnessing the willful extermination of [Atlantic] salmon and [brook] trout—the former by spearing, netting, and erecting high dams without providing for their free passage up and down—the latter by snaring them on their spawning beds, catching them in seines and eel weirs, and drawing off millponds. On trout streams there are still other agencies at work: the coal mine poisoning the brook with sulphur; the sawmill filling it with slabs and sawdust; the factory with its dyestuff; and the tannery fouling the clear stream, covering the bottom of the pools and the spawn beds with its bleached bark, and killing the fish by hundreds with the obnoxious discharge of its lime vat. Any law against such vandalism in the United States is seldom or . . . feebly enforced.[22]

These dark heraldings generally emphasized economic or recreational self-interest rather than soliloquies about the intrinsic value of nature, but in the long run they complemented the preachings of Thoreau, Marsh, Muir, and other early nature writers. In some cases, the influence of the nature writers on resource agencies was plain to see. In 1867, for example, a state forestry official named Increase A. Lapham delivered a report called *The Disastrous Effects of the Destruction of Forest Trees Now Going on So Rapidly in the State of Wisconsin* to the Wisconsin legislature. Emblazoned on the cover of this report was a quote from Marsh's *Man and Nature*:

> Man has too long forgotten that the earth was given to him for usufruct alone, not for consumption, still less for profligate waste.

Together, these disparate voices began to mold and change public and political opinion—albeit slowly and with many setbacks—about the moral and commercial importance of environmental resource stewardship. "The extent to which nature writers . . . influenced environmental reform in this country may well be unprecedented in American politics," asserted literary scholar Daniel G. Payne. They "framed the issues of the debate, provided the ethical, ecological, and rhetorical underpinnings of the reformist position, and attracted the mass audience that . . . formed the basis of both the conservation and environmental movements."[23]

America's first pro-conservation organizations and magazines also appeared during this era. Popular periodicals dedicated to hunting and fishing, including *American Sportsman, Forest and Stream, Field and Stream,* and *American Angler,* all appeared in the 1870s and 1880s. Concerned about dwindling wildlife habitats and the plummeting populations of some game animals and birds, the editors of these magazines regularly issued calls for new environmental regulations and wilderness protection to the readers, who tended to be both wealthy and politically connected. The most prominent of these magazines, *Forest and Stream,* stated in its very first issue (August 1873) that it was dedicated to the "preservation of our rapidly diminishing forests" and warned that the interests of sports-men were in dire "jeopardy . . . from the depletion of our timberlands by fire and axe."[24]

These sentiments were echoed by organizations such as John Muir's Sierra Club (founded in 1892); the Boone and Crockett Club, founded by *Forest and Stream* editor George Bird Grinnell and Theodore Roosevelt in 1887; and the Audubon Society, which was also founded by Grinnell (in 1886). These groups believed that wilderness preserva-tion depended on rousing local, state, and federal governments from their regulatory slumber. The Boone and Crockett Club, for example, declared in its founding constitution that it intended to "work for the preservation of the large game of this country, and as far as possible, to further legislation for that purpose, and to assist in enforcing the existing laws."[25] Muir, meanwhile, delivered reams of similar rhetoric from his Sierra Club perch. "Government protection should be thrown around every wild grove and forest on the mountains, as it is around every private orchard, and the trees in public parks," he pro-claimed in 1896. "To say nothing of their value as fountains of timber, they are worth infinitely more than all the gardens and parks of towns."[26] This preservation message, which Muir delivered relentlessly during the 1890s, made him the nation's leading advo-cate for wilderness by the close of the nineteenth century.

RALLYING GOVERNMENT RESOURCES TO THE CONSERVATION CAUSE

The conservation message advanced by this coalition of scientists, administrators, writers, and sportsmen encountered fierce resistance from politicians, corporations, workers, and other constituencies that had prospered under the government's longstanding pro-extraction and pro-land privatization policies. But the calls for sustainable resource use and environmental preservation gradually broke down some of these walls and began infiltrating legislative chambers and government reports alike. And when these walls began to fall in the last quarter of the nineteenth century, America's beleaguered forests and wildlife became the leading focus of conservation-oriented policymaking.

To be sure, a smattering of prescient officials and lawmakers had expressed anxiety about America's heedless use of these natural resources well before the 1870s. In 1850, for example, U.S. Commissioner of Patents Thomas Ewing issued a blistering assessment of the nation's exploitive attitude toward its resources. "The waste of valuable timber in the U.S. . . . will hardly be appreciated until our population reaches 50 million. Then the folly and shortsightedness of this age will meet with a degree of censure and reproach not pleasant to contemplate."[27] Other government reports warning about the negative eco-logical and economic impact of deforestation in the upper Great Lakes, the South, and the West proliferated from mid-century forward. Some of these same reports called for the creation of state and federal forestry commissions, reforestation projects to heal battered watersheds, and adoption of European-style forest management practices that placed a premium on resource sustainability. Schurz and some other officials urged the presidents and congressmen they served to pass laws that would curb the unrelenting exploitation of timber, water, soil, and mineral resources in the public domain.

For many years, Congress not only ignored these recommendations but perversely passed new legislation (such as the 1878 Free Timber Act) that *further* increased develop-ment pressure on forestlands and the wildlife contained therein. The notion that America possessed a limitless storehouse of natural wealth was a difficult one to vanquish from Washington, D.C., and the country's statehouses. A representative example of this attitude could be seen in 1857 in the Ohio state senate, where legislators dismissed a bill that would have provided legal protection to the passenger pigeon with the observation that the birds were so "wonderfully prolific" that "no ordinary destruction can lessen them, or be missed from the myriads that are yearly produced."[28] Fewer than sixty years later, the last known passenger pigeon died in a Cincinnati Zoo.

Nonetheless, signs of progress in advancing the coalescing conservationist agenda could also be seen. In fact, American policymakers passed a handful of laws from 1864 to 1900 that would become springboards for the conservation movement's "golden age" in the early twentieth century. In 1864 Congress passed the Yosemite Act, which designated a spectacular tract of public land in California's Yosemite Valley as parkland, and ceded the park to the state of California for administration. This was an important milestone— the first federal legislation in American history that preserved public land for "public use, resort, and recreation."

In 1872, eight years after Yosemite Park was born, Congress created Yellowstone National Park in Wyoming, the first truly "national" park in American history (Yosemite did not become a national park until 1906, after ownership was transferred back to the federal government) (see Document 3.5). The positive popular response to the creation of the park was not lost on lawmakers. Yellowstone became the regulatory model for a stunning collection of other national parks created to protect wilderness areas of spectacular scenic beauty or ecological significance for the enjoyment of all Americans. By 1900 there were six national parks dotting the landscape of the West. State authorities began to show interest in also establishing "wilderness parks." In 1885, for instance, New York Governor David B. Hill signed a bill establishing the 715,000-acre Adirondack Forest Preserve in his state.

THE FOREST RESERVE ACT

The establishment of what we know today as national forests also began during this period but only after years of fierce legislative brawling. In 1885, 1888, 1889, and 1890 western lawmakers backed by extraction-based industries managed to defeat a succession of congressional bills that would have created public forest reserves. But on March 3, 1891, the landmark General Revision Act of 1891 was passed by Congress at the urging of President Benjamin Harrison. This act reshuffled the deck of public land laws in America by repealing the Timber Culture and Preemption Acts, limiting homestead claims to 160 acres, and limiting all other claims—mineral lands excluded—to 320 acres per individual. It also introduced new monitoring and enforcement mechanisms for the Desert Land Act (see Document 3.13).

The General Revision Act was hardly perfect. Laws that had triggered rampant overcutting of forestlands such as the Free Timber Act and Timber and Stone Act actually became even more vulnerable to abuse as a result of provisions introduced in the General Revision Act. The 1891 legislation also featured a momentous rider that had been tacked on to the bill at the last minute thanks to maneuvering by Harrison's Interior Secretary John W. Noble. This rider—the 1891 Forest Reserve Act—changed America's relationship with its forests forever. It empowered the president to create "national forest reserves" by withdrawing forestlands from the public domain. The act also enshrined new regulations for public access and use of other federally managed forestlands.

Four weeks after the passage of the Forest Reserve Act, on March 30, 1891, Harrison issued a presidential proclamation creating the nation's first federal forest reserve, the 1.24-million-acre Yellowstone Park Timber Land Reservation on the southern border of

Yellowstone National Park. Harrison then withdrew another 12 million acres from the public domain at Noble's urging, shielding them within fifteen distinct national forest reserves. Thus were the first bricks in the foundation of America's national forest system laid.[29]

Western timber and mining interests and their legislative allies denounced these withdrawals of land from unfettered use, but other industries offered a more measured response to the actions of Harrison and pro-conservation lawmakers. Western water companies, for example, had become convinced that their long-term fortunes depended on greater watershed protection.[30] And some powerful western railroads quickly grasped that majestic parklands and forest reserves had the potential to generate profitable new levels of passenger traffic. "Western railroads provided the leverage to transform conservationist visions into actual laws and functioning programs," asserted historian Richard J. Orsi. "If the laying down of tracks blighted some immediate wilderness, the building of rail lines by the Southern Pacific and other companies through spectacular mountains and deserts and along rivers and ocean coasts, along with their advertising of the West and fostering of mass tourism, also encouraged a new conservationist ethic by opening up the region's wild beauties to a wider, influential middle-class public"[31] **(see Document 3.15)**.

When Grover Cleveland became president in 1893, he built on Harrison's work, quickly setting aside two new reserves with a combined area of 4.5 million acres. He did not exercise this authority again, however, until the closing days of his presidency in 1897, when he created another thirteen forest reserves totaling more than 21 million acres. These so-called "Cleveland reserves," which included large tracts of land that were suitable for cultivation, sparked howls of protest from westerners and timber allies in Congress, but legislative efforts to nullify the reserves ultimately failed. Instead, Congress continued its pivot away from forest privatization toward public conservation and resource management with the 1897 Forest Management Act (also known as the Organic Act). This law sanctioned the Cleveland reserves; authorized the federal government to manage grazing, timber harvests, and other natural resource extraction within the forest reserves on a permanent basis; and laid out criteria for the selection and retention of future reserves.

HALTING THE WAR ON WILDLIFE

American policymakers also adopted a slate of conservation-oriented wildlife laws during the second half of the nineteenth century. But these laws were crafted within an economic and social environment that divided wildlife into desirable and undesirable categories. For example, populations of wolves, coyotes, mountain lions, and other predatory animals that fed on cattle, sheep, and wild game favored by hunters plummeted as a result of official territorial, state, and federal policies of extermination **(see Document 3.9)**. These "anti-vermin" laws enjoyed broad public acceptance in western ranching communities, as one North Dakota hunter explained in 1900: "A question of public policy, of justice and of fairness come in and requires the state to protect the general interests of the people and defend them from every public enemy; and what greater enemy can the state have than one that is able to wage war on the state's chief industry both day and night."[32]

In addition, reforms in the realm of harvesting and selling animal parts came about only after species like the buffalo had been driven to the brink of extinction. The nation's deplorable treatment of the buffalo, in fact, became a particular inspiration for wildlife conservation laws. At the beginning of the nineteenth century, millions of buffalo—up to 30 million by some estimates—had covered the continent. One traveler on the Santa Fe Trail in 1839 spent three days passing a single herd, and he estimated that the herd covered 1,350 square miles.[33] But by the 1890s the buffalo had been virtually extinguished from the Great Plains, their ranks wasted by habitat loss, diseases introduced by domestic cattle, and the depredations of white and Indian market hunters whose brutal practices were greatly aided by the introduction of the railroad and telegraph into the heart of buffalo territory. Army Colonel Richard Irving Dodge conservatively estimated that from 1872 to 1874 alone, nearly 1.4 million buffalo hides were shipped on the Santa Fe, Kansas Pacific, and Union Pacific railroads—and that, because of the wastefulness of hide hunters, every hide shipped to market represented five dead bison.[34]

Observers of the slaughter such as George Catlin and William T. Hornaday lamented the demise of the great beast and its crushing impact on Great Plains Indians, for whom the bison had long been an essential source of food, clothing, and shelter (**see Document 3.10**). But many government officials and white settlers actually supported this wildlife annihilation precisely *because* of its debilitating effect on Native American tribes. In 1873 Secretary of the Interior Columbus Delano bluntly reported to President Ulysses S. Grant that "I would not seriously regret the total disappearance of the buffalo from our western prairies" because it would force resident Indians to turn to European-style cultivation.[35] Two years later, General Philip Sheridan cast the market hunters who left millions of bison carcasses to rot on the plains as American heroes. "These men have done more in the last two years, and will do more in the next year, to settle the vexed Indian question than the entire regular army has done in the last thirty years," he stated in an address to the Texas legislature, which was pondering a bill that would have extended protections to the last remnants of the state's buffalo herd. "They are destroying the Indians' commissary. . . . For the sake of a lasting peace, let them kill, skin, and sell until the buffaloes are exterminated. Then your prairies will be covered with speckled cattle and the festive cowboy, who follows the hunter as a second forerunner to an advanced civilization."[36] Sheridan's testimony helped kill the bill. In addition, his counsel also contributed to the decision of his former Civil War commander, President Grant, to ignore a June 1874 bill passed by Congress by wide margins that would have extended federal protection to the bison. The bill languished and eventually expired without Grant's signature.

The disappearance of the bison from the Great Plains and other regions of the country provided a grim parallel to the experience of the Indians, who were shunted by U.S. authorities onto some of the dustiest and darkest corners of the continent over the course of the century. Tribes responded to this inexorable process in a variety of ways, including assimilation, armed rebellion, and desperate pleas for mercy and fairness (**see Document 3.8**). But all of these strategies ultimately failed because they were no match for the white hunger for new soil, timber, mineral, and water resources.

OPPOSITION TO NEW WILDLIFE CONSERVATION LAWS

Whereas American politicians were divided over policies governing the future of the bison—and were downright enthusiastic about state-sanctioned campaigns against wolves and other threats to livestock—they were generally more accepting of efforts to limit and regulate the taking of other wildlife with high commercial or recreational value. In fact, numerous state and federal laws were passed to protect dwindling fisheries and game species during the last three decades of the nineteenth century.

To be sure, the wildlife protection agenda had to surmount numerous obstacles during this era. One challenge was longstanding public indifference or hostility to game laws. "People complain [about diminishing wildlife], and the legislature passes game laws, and nobody pays any attention to them after they are passed," fumed the authors of an 1868 *Report of the Commissioners of Fisheries of Massachusetts*. "Why? Because we insist on considering wild animals as our remote forefathers considered them, when men were scarce and wild animals were plenty."[37] One prominent Michigan sportsman-conservationist, William T. Mershon, experienced this problem firsthand. He spearheaded the filing of poaching charges against two local men who had been caught "shining" deer—using a reflecting lantern at night to mesmerize deer for easy killing—out of season. But despite overwhelming evidence of their guilt, the jury returned a verdict of not guilty. "I am satisfied that no jury can be impaneled in the ordinary way, by the officers now in charge, that will convict any of the violators of the Game Law," Mershon said afterward, "no matter how direct the evidence and positive the testimony."[38]

Another problem confronted by legislators and wildlife officials was making sense of the piecemeal approach to wildlife management that had prevailed in the territories and states during the era of settlement. "Our laws upon the subject of game, and fish, seem to be a heterogeneous mass of special enactments, passed at the suggestion of various members of past legislatures," stated the *First Annual Report of the State Fish Commissioners of Minnesota* in 1875. "They . . . seem to have no coherence or general design; and if carried out it would be difficult to say whether they would be a benefit or harm to the game and fish of the State."[39]

Fault lines of social status and economic class also complicated efforts to enact and enforce laws and regulations conserving wildlife and fisheries. Rural landowners and commercial hunters and fishers ridiculed the notion that policymakers in Washington, D.C., or state legislatures had a better understanding of wildlife issues than themselves. More important, farmers, ranchers, and market hunters and fishers saw wildlife resources as sources of subsistence and profit. They bristled at the contemptuous dismissal of "pothunters"—men who engaged in subsistence hunting to fill the family meal pot—by members of the sporting fraternity who had the luxury of embracing "sporting" methods of fishing and hunting. Subsistence hunters resented the efforts of sportsmen and other wealthy conservationists (and most conservationists of this era *were* relatively well-to-do) to hurt their livelihoods by restricting harvesting on public lands and in public waters, and they described such attempts as anathema to American ideals of liberty and freedom. As the Ohio Fish Commission observed in 1873, "It does not accord with the prevalent ideas of humanity to imprison a person for obtaining food from 'nature's preserve,' especially when that 'preserve' is not private property."[40] A nineteenth-century historian of the Carolinas, meanwhile, mused that the typical southerner believed that "a poor laborer that is master of his gun, etc., hath as good a claim to have continued coarses of delicacies crowded upon his table, as he that is master of a great purse."[41]

Despite all of these impediments, a wave of wildlife conservation laws spread across the United States, moving generally from east to west. Support for these laws gained traction in part because citizens became more accepting of the idea that wildlife regulations actually benefited *them* in the long run. As George Bird Grinnell wrote in *Forest and Stream* in 1882:

> Why shall not we, the people, demand of our representatives at Boston, at Albany, at Lansing and Springfield and . . . [Sacramento] and all other seats of legislation, the due protection of our, the people's interests, by the conservation of our game and fish? Laws prohibiting the destruction of game in its breeding season and of fish on their spawning grounds

are not for the advantage of any narrow class or clique. They are for the good of us, the people. Take this broad, tenable ground: the greatest good to the greatest number.[42]

But new game regulations also came into being for the most basic reason of all: Policymakers belatedly recognized that the nation's great storehouse of wildlife was vanishing as a result of unsustainable patterns of consumption. In the end, this grim reality trumped all other considerations.

STATES TAKE THE LEAD

Some wildlife conservation steps were taken at the federal level. In 1871, for instance, the establishment of the U.S. Fish Commission marked the first time that a federal agency had been created to deal with the conservation of a specific natural resource. Federal wildlife management also benefited during the 1870s and 1880s from an influx of administrators and agents who placed a high value on science-based decision-making in natural resource management (see Document 3.11).

Most of the wildlife conservation laws that came into being during this time, however, were state-level regulations. The wave of new legislation began in New England, the long-settled birthplace of the American republic. This region actually had various long-standing local and state wildlife regulations—some of them even dated back to the colonial era—but by the post–Civil War era, officials worried that if additional measures were not taken, the pressures wrought on regional wildlife by industrialization, urbanization, and unrelenting market demand for wild feathers, furs, and meat would snuff some species out forever. In 1867, for example, the New England Commissioners of River Fisheries mourned that "a half century ago," salmon, shad, alewives, and other species of freshwater fish had "furnished abundant and wholesome food to the people; but, by the erection of impassable dams, and needless pollution of ponds and rivers, and by reckless fishing . . . our streams and lakes have been pretty much depopulated."[43]

These and other stark reports filed by various New England fish, wildlife, and forest commissions—many of which had not even been established until after the conclusion of the Civil War—led state legislatures across the Northeast to pass a bundle of new business regulations and game laws. In Massachusetts and New Hampshire, for example, laws were approved in the late 1860s and early 1870s that required fishways on major rivers and imposed multi-year prohibitions on the harvesting of salmon and other imperiled species.[44] In the realm of deer and game bird hunting, meanwhile, some New England states restricted certain hunting and trapping practices, such as hunting with hounds. In addition, these states became much more serious about punishing violators of seasonal restrictions on hunting and other regulations. But perhaps the most telling sign of all that attitudes about wildlife protection and ecosystem integrity were evolving was the fact that some New England states began extending protection to nongame species.[45]

The wave of state-sponsored wildlife conservation moved on from New England to the West, following earlier patterns of western settlement with remarkable consistency. The Great Lakes states and Great Plains followed New England in passing new hunting and fishing regulations in addition to habitat protection measures. Even western states, which maintained a strong anti-regulatory stance on most natural resource issues, adopted a smattering of conservation-minded game laws—although the region's war on predatory animals continued unabated. In 1871, twenty-two states and territories had imposed some sort of seasonal restrictions on deer hunting. Thirty years later all but two states had such laws on the books.[46]

The only region of the country that showed no meaningful increase in its statutory commitment to wildlife protection was the Deep South. Aside from minor seasonal restrictions on deer hunting that were rarely enforced, southern legislatures refused to reconsider their longstanding laissez-faire attitude toward wildlife management. Regarding Arkansas, for instance, the editors of an 1871 compilation of state game laws called *Fur, Fin and Feather* professed a mix of anger and bewilderment. "We are unable to state whether there are any laws in this state for the protection and preservation of game or not. We have endeavored to obtain the desired information from the State authorities, but have been unsuccessful in getting any light on the subject; and all the Statutes and laws of the State we have had access to are totally silent in regard to the matter. And we are therefore inclined to believe that Arkansas, like Texas, has no game-protecting laws, and that the pot-hunter, who is held in utter detestation by every legitimate sportsman, is here left to pursue his wanton destruction unmolested."[47]

The states' legal authority to impose and enforce game and habitat protection laws was challenged in numerous courts across the country. But the courts sided with the states, upholding the legitimacy of their claim of resource "ownership." As the Supreme Court of Minnesota declared in the 1894 decision *State of Minnesota v. Rodman,* "[T]he correct doctrine in this country [is] that the ownership of wild animals, so far as they are capable of ownership, is in the state, not as proprietor, but in its sovereign capacity as the representative, and for the benefit, of all its people in common."[48] The U.S. Supreme Court also put its stamp of approval on this doctrine in cases such as *Geer v. Connecticut* (1896) and *Ward v. Race Horse* (1896). The latter case was particularly notable because it abrogated Native American hunting rights in national parks and forests and other public lands and forced them to obey state game laws—even in cases where more expansive hunting rights had been previously guaranteed by federal treaty (**see Document 3.16**).

SPORTSMEN CHAMPION THE LACEY ACT

America's early conservation leaders were encouraged by the passage of new wildlife laws and the more serious approach to game law enforcement that many states were displaying. But they recognized that the emerging regulatory infrastructure was fragile and that it needed shoring up in numerous areas. To this end, conservationists of all stripes—legislators, fish and game commissioners, sportsmen, and other private citizens—worked to rouse the public from its general indifference toward poachers and other violators of game laws. They also lobbied to give scientists and knowledgeable wildlife officials greater influence over legislation in state houses and policymaking in agencies entrusted with land and resource management responsibilities.

Another major crusade waged by conservationists was to pass laws and regulations that would choke the life out of market hunting. The operations of commercial hunters, whether they worked for railroads and timber companies or as independent contractors, were entirely focused on maximizing profit by taking as much game as possible. The economic incentive for market hunters in pursuing a ruthless strategy of relentless harvesting was understandable, but their depredations emerged as a major factor in the rapidly declining populations of a variety of prized species. Numerous game bird species were decimated to provide plumage for women's hats (and the once-prolific passenger pigeon was extinguished from the planet altogether), and populations of deer, bison, and other animals plummeted as market hunters scrambled to meet soaring market demand for the meat and skins of "wild game." Conservationists recognized that numerous species were in danger of being extirpated altogether if this threat was not met with force. In this particular fight, sportsmen's organizations and periodicals staked out a position at the tip of the spear.

Prominent sportsmen–politicians ranging from Theodore Roosevelt to John F. Lacey (chief sponsor of the Lacey Act of 1894, which ended hunting in Yellowstone National Park) regularly railed against commercial hunting during the 1890s. They were joined by influential opinion-shapers in the hunting and fishing community, such as Grinnell, who in 1894 used the pages of *Forest and Stream* to deliver to his fellow sportsmen a call-to-arms against market hunting:

> With all the discussion of the subject in the columns of the *Forest and Stream* from 1873 to 1894, there has been and is a general consensus of opinion that the markets are answerable for a larger proportion of game destruction than any other agency or all other agencies combined. The practical annihilation of one species of large game [the bison] from the continent, and the sweeping off of other species from vast regions formerly populated by them, have not been brought about by the settlement of the country, but by unrelenting pursuit for commercial purposes. . . . No plea of necessity, of economy of value as food, demands the marketing of game. If every market stall were to be swept of its game today, there would be no appreciable effect upon the food supply of the country. Well, then, why not recognize this, and direct our efforts . . . toward the utter abolition of the sale of game? Why should we not adopt as a plan in the sportsman's platform a declaration to this end—*That the sale of game should be forbidden at all seasons?*[49]

These various efforts paid off in 1900 with the Lacey Bird Law, another trailblazing piece of conservation legislation penned by John Lacey, a Republican congressman from Iowa **(see Document 3.17)**. The Lacey Bird Law (also known as the Lacey Act of 1900) established federal penalties for interstate and international commerce in wild game. The institution of these penalties had the practical effect of extinguishing in one fell swoop the commercial hunting practices that had caused such widespread carnage over the previous century. But the passage of this act also confirmed that a monumental shift in America's approach to conservation issues was taking place. Up to this point, the "state ownership doctrine" had held sway in land and resource policymaking, but the signing of the Lacey Bird Law, combined with the Forest Reserve Act and other legislative landmarks of the 1890s, signaled that a new era of federal control over wildlife and other natural resources was at hand. And when Theodore Roosevelt took up residence in the White House in September 1901, he seized on this shift to craft a conservation legacy that endures to this day.

NOTES

1. Richard N. L. Andrews, *Managing the Environment, Managing Ourselves: A History of American Environmental Policy* (New Haven, Conn.: Yale University Press, 1999), 87.

2. Quoted in John Graham Brooks, *The Social Unrest: Studies in Labor and Socialist Movements* (New York: Macmillan, 1905), 113–114.

3. Ibid., 113.

4.   Tom Standage, *The Victorian Internet: The Remarkable Story of the Telegraph and the Nineteenth Century's Online Pioneers* (New York: Walker, 1998), 166.

5.   Marc Reisner, *Cadillac Desert: The American West and Its Disappearing Water* (1986, rev. ed. New York: Penguin, 1993), 35.

6.   Charles Dana Wilbur, *The Great Valleys and Prairies of Nebraska and the Northwest* (Omaha: Daily Republican Print, 1881).

7.   Quoted in Peter Beaumont, *Environmental Management and Development in Drylands* (New York: Routledge, 1993), 138.

8.   Andrews, *Managing the Environment, Managing Ourselves,* 94.

9.   Richard J. Orsi, *Sunset Limited: The Southern Pacific Railroad and the Development of the American West 1850–1930* (Berkeley: University of California Press, 2005).

10.   Andrews, *Managing the Environment, Managing Ourselves,* 76–77.

11.   Philip Shabecoff, *A Fierce Green Fire: The American Environmental Movement* (New York: Hill and Wang, 1993), 34.

12.   Frederick Merk, *History of the Westward Movement* (New York: Knopf, 1978), 415.

13.   Patricia Nelson Limerick, *The Legacy of Conquest: The Unbroken Past of the American West* (New York: W.W. Norton, 1988), 65.

14.   Ibid., 66.

15.   Michael Williams, *Americans and Their Forests: A Historical Geography* (Cambridge: Cambridge University Press, 1989).

16.   Wallace Stegner, *Where the Bluebird Sings to the Lemonade Springs: Living and Writing in the West* (New York: Penguin, 1992), 121.

17.   Williams, *Americans and Their Forests,* 193.

18.   Ralph Waldo Emerson, *The Conduct of Life* (1860; Boston: Houghton Mifflin, 1904), 86.

19.   Andrews, *Managing the Environment, Managing Ourselves,* 101.

20.   Stephen J. Pyne, *Fire in America: A Cultural History of Wildland and Rural Fire* (Seattle: University of Washington Press, 1997).

21.   George Marsh, *Man and Nature,* ed. David Lowenthal (1864; repr., Cambridge, Mass.: Harvard University Press, 1965), 36, 52.

22.   Thaddeus Norris, *The American Angler's Book: Embracing the Natural History of Sporting Fish, and the Art of Taking Them* (Philadelphia: E. H. Butler, 1864), 459–460.

23.   Daniel G. Payne, *Voices in the Wilderness: American Nature Writers and Environmental Politics* (Buffalo: State University of New York at Buffalo, 1996), 3–4.

24.   Quoted in John F. Reiger, *American Sportsmen and the Origins of Conservation* 3rd ed. (Corvallis: Oregon State University Press, 2001), 111.

25.   George Bird Grinnell, ed., *American Big Game in Its Haunts: The Book of the Boone and Crockett Club* (New York: Forest and Stream Publishing, 1904), 485.

26.   John Muir, "The National Parks and Forest Reservations" *Sierra Club Bulletin* 1, no. 7 (January 1896): 271–284. Quoted in *The Wilderness World of John Muir,* ed. Edwin Way Teale (New York: Mariner Books, 2001), 321.

27.   Thomas Ewing, *Annual Report of the Secretary of the Interior,* House Executive Document, 31st Cong., 1st Sess., vol. III, no. 5, pt. 2 (serial no. 570), U.S. Congress, House of Representatives, Washington, D.C., 1850.

28.   Quoted in James A. Tober, *Who Owns the Wildlife? The Political Economy of Conservation in Nineteenth-Century America* (Westport, Conn.: Greenwood Press, 1981), 17.

29.   H. K. Steen, *The U.S. Forest Service: A History* (Seattle: University of Washington Press, 1975).

30.   Samuel P. Hays, *Conservation and the Gospel of Efficiency* (New York: Atheneum, 1969), 36.

31.   Richard J. Orsi, *Sunset Limited: The Southern Pacific Railroad and the Development of the American West., 1850–1930* (Berkeley: University of California Press, 2005), 349, 355.

32.   Quoted in *War Against the Wolf: America's Campaign to Exterminate the Wolf,* ed. Rick McIntyre (Stillwater, MN: Voyageur Press, 1995), 127.

33. Andrew C. Isenberg, *The Destruction of the Bison: An Environmental History, 1750–1920* (New York: Cambridge University Press, 2000), 23.

34. Ibid., 136.

35. Quoted in Harold P. Danz, *Of Bison and Man* (Niwot: University Press of Colorado, 1997), 112.

36. Quoted in Valerius Geist, *Buffalo Nation: History and Legend of the North American Bison* (Stillwater, MN: Voyageur Press, 1998), 91.

37. Quoted in Tober, *Who Owns the Wildlife?*, vii.

38. Quoted in Dave Dempsey, *On the Brink: The Great Lakes in the 21st Century* (East Lansing: Michigan State University Press, 2004), 42.

39. Quoted in Tober, *Who Owns the Wildlife?*, 139.

40. Quoted in Dempsey, *On the Brink*, 40.

41. John Lawson, *The History of Carolina* (Raleigh: Strother and Marcom, 1860), 29.

42. Quoted in Reiger, *American Sportsmen and the Origins of Conservation*, 67.

43. Quoted in Theodore Steinberg, *Nature Incorporated: Industrialization and the Waters of New England* (New York: Cambridge University Press, 1991), 167.

44. Ibid., 193.

45. Tober, *Who Owns the Wildlife?*, 140.

46. Tober, *Who Owns the Wildlife?*, 152–153.

47. *Fur, Fin and Feather: A Compilation of the Game Laws of the Different States and Provinces of the United States and Canada: To Which Is Added a List of Hunting and Fishing Localities, and Other Useful Information for Gunners and Anglers* (New York: M.B. Brown and Co., 1871), 116.

48. Quoted in Tobor, *Who Owns the Wildlife?*, 148.

49. George Bird Grinnell, George Bird, and Charles B. Reynolds. "A Plank," *Forest and Stream* (Feb. 3, 1894), 89.

DOCUMENT
3.1

The Homestead Act

"An Act to Secure Homesteads to . . . Settlers on the Public Domain"

May 20, 1862

The Homestead Act was one of the most important pieces of land policy legislation in American history. A landmark in the evolution of American agricultural law, it gave all adult citizens, and immigrants who intended to become citizens, the right to claim 160 acres of surveyed government land in the frontier West. The main stipulation imposed on claimants was that they "improve" the parcels they received from the federal government.

This Act was essential in the settlement of the Great Plains, but loopholes in the legislative language were exploited by wealthy and politically connected cattlemen, railroads, and timber and mining interests. Of the estimated 500 million acres of public domain land that passed into private ownership from 1862 to 1904 as a result of this Act, only 80 million acres went to small farmers and other homesteaders. The remaining 420 million acres ended up in the possession of speculators and corporate interests. Following is the complete text of the Homestead Act.

An Act to Secure Homesteads to Actual Settlers on the Public Domain.

Be it enacted by the Senate and House of Representatives of the United States of America in Congress assembled, That any person who is the head of a family, or who has arrived at the age of twenty-one years, and is a citizen of the United States, or who shall have filed his declaration of intention to become such, as required by the naturalization laws of the United States, and who has never borne arms against the United States Government or given aid and comfort to its enemies, shall, from and after the first January, eighteen hundred and sixty-three, be entitled to enter one quarter section or a less quantity of unappropriated public lands, upon which said person may have filed a preemption claim, or which may, at the time the application is made, be subject to preemption at one dollar and twenty-five cents, or less, per acre; or eighty acres or less of such unappropriated lands, at two dollars and fifty cents per acre, to be located in a body, in conformity to the legal subdivisions of the public lands, and after the same shall have been surveyed: *Provided,* That any person owning and residing on land may, under the provisions of this act, enter other land lying contiguous to his or her said land, which shall not, with the land so already owned and occupied, exceed in the aggregate one hundred and sixty acres.

SEC. 2. *And be it further enacted,* That the person applying for the benefit of this act shall, upon application to the register of the land office in which he or she is about to make such entry, make affidavit before the said register or receiver that he or she is the head of a family, or is twenty-one years or more of age, or shall have performed service in the army or navy of the United States, and that he has never borne arms against the Government of the United States or given aid and comfort to its enemies, and that such application is made for his or her exclusive use and benefit, and that said entry is made for the purpose of actual settlement and cultivation, and not either directly or indirectly for the use or benefit of any other person or persons whomsoever; and upon filing the said affidavit with the register or receiver, and on payment of ten dollars, he or she shall thereupon be permitted to enter the quantity of land specified: *Provided, however,* That no certificate shall be given or patent issued therefor until the expiration of five years from the date of such entry; and if, at the expiration of such time, or at any time within two years thereafter, the person making such entry; or, if he be dead, his widow; or in case of her death, his heirs or devisee; or in case of a widow making such entry, her heirs or devisee, in case of her death; shall prove by two credible witnesses that he, she, or they have resided upon or cultivated the same for the term of five years immediately succeeding the time of filing the affidavit aforesaid, and shall make affidavit that no part of said land has been alienated, and that he has borne rue allegiance to the Government of the United States; then, in such case, he, she, or they, if at that time a citizen of the United States, shall be entitled to a patent, as in other cases provided for by law: *And provided, further,* That in case of the death of both father and mother, leaving an Infant child, or children, under twenty-one years of age, the right and fee shall ensure to the benefit of said infant child or children; and the executor, administrator, or guardian may, at any time within two years after the death of the surviving parent, and in accordance with the laws of the State in which such children for the time being have their domicile, sell said land for the benefit of said infants, but for no other purpose; and the purchaser shall acquire the absolute title by the purchase, and be entitled to a patent from the United States, on payment of the office fees and sum of money herein specified.

SEC. 3. *And be it further enacted,* That the register of the land office shall note all such applications on the tract books and plats of his office, and keep a register of all such entries, and make return thereof to the General Land Office, together with the proof upon which they have been founded.

SEC. 4. *And be it further enacted,* That no lands acquired under the provisions of this act shall in any event become liable to the satisfaction of any debt or debts contracted prior to the issuing of the patent therefor.

SEC. 5. *And be it further enacted,* That if, at any time after the filing of the affidavit, as required in the second section of this act, and before the expiration of the five years aforesaid, it shall be proven, after due notice to the settler, to the satisfaction of the register of the land office, that the person having filed such affidavit shall have actually changed his or her residence, or abandoned the said land for more than six months at any time, then and in that event the land so entered shall revert to the government.

SEC. 6. *And be it further enacted,* That no individual shall be permitted to acquire title to more than one quarter section under the provisions of this act; and that the Commissioner of the General Land Office is hereby required to prepare and issue such rules and regulations, consistent with this act, as shall be necessary and proper to carry its provisions into effect; and that the registers and receivers of the several land offices shall be entitled to receive the same compensation for any lands entered under the provisions of this act that they are now entitled to receive when the same quantity of land is entered with money, one half to be paid by the person making the application at the time of so doing, and the other half on the issue of the certificate by the person to whom it may be issued; but this shall not be construed to enlarge the maximum of compensation now prescribed by law for any register or receiver: *Provided,* That nothing contained in this act shall be so construed as to impair or interfere in any manner whatever with existing preemption rights: *And provided, further,* That all persons who may have filed their applications for a preemption right prior to the passage of this act, shall be entitled to all privileges of this act: *Provided, further,* That no person who has served, or may hereafter serve, for a period of not less than fourteen days in the army or navy of the United States, either regular or volunteer, under the laws thereof, during the existence of an actual war, domestic or foreign, shall be deprived of the benefits of this act on account of not having attained the age of twenty-one years.

SEC. 7. *And be it further enacted,* That the fifth section of the act entitled "An act in addition to an act more effectually to provide for the punishment of certain crimes against the United States, and for other purposes," approved the third of March, in the year eighteen hundred and fifty-seven, shall extend to all oaths, affirmations, and affidavits, required or authorized by this act.

SEC. 8. *And be it further enacted,* That nothing in this act shall be so construed as to prevent any person who has availed him or herself of the benefits of the first section of this act, from paying the minimum price, or the price to which the same may have graduated, for the quantity of land so entered at any time before the expiration of the five years, and obtaining a patent therefor from the government, as in other cases provided by law, on making proof of settlement and cultivation as provided by existing laws granting preemption rights.

APPROVED, May 20, 1862.

Source: The Homestead Act. *Our Documents: 100 Milestone Documents from the National Archives.* National Archives and Records Administration. Available at www.ourdocuments.gov/doc.php?doc=31&page=transcript.

DOCUMENT 3.2

The Pacific Railway Act

"A Railroad and Telegraph Line from the Missouri River to the Pacific Ocean"

July 1, 1862

Even as the Civil War was shaking the foundations of the United States, the U.S. Congress remained intent on settling the western frontier and extracting the region's natural resources in service to national economic expansion. To this end Congress in 1862 passed the Pacific Railway Act, which provided for the construction of the nation's first transcontinental railroad.

This Act authorized two railroad companies—the Central Pacific and the Union Pacific (the latter of which was actually created by the Act)—to construct a railroad line extending from the city of Sacramento, California, to Omaha, Nebraska, on the banks of the Missouri River. The legislation provided generous land grants and other incentives to the railroads, which would begin laying tracks at opposite ends of the designated route, work steadily toward one another, and meet somewhere in the undeveloped interior. But instead of working cooperatively, the two lines tried to eclipse the other in laying down track. They knew that because of the terms delineated in the Pacific Railway Act, each mile of track they laid down represented future wealth in the form of land grants and federal subsidies. By early 1869, the two lines had entered opposite ends of Utah, but neither of the land-hungry companies showed any inclination to establish a site where they could unite their respective lines. "Like two weary but evenly matched armies at the end of a long war, each railway company continued to maneuver for advantages over the other, running their parallel grades for miles past each other, the C.P. stubbornly heading for Ogden [Utah], and the U.P. hellbent for nowhere."[1] The stalemate was brought to an end by the intercession of President Ulysses S. Grant, who strong-armed them into joining their lines together at Promontory Point, Utah, on May 10, 1869. This milestone marked the beginning of a new, railroad-driven era of land development, resource use, and environmental transformation in the West. Following are excerpts from the 1862 Act.

An Act to Aid in the Construction of a Railroad and Telegraph Line from the Missouri River to the Pacific Ocean, and to Secure to the Government the Use of the Same for Postal, Military, and Other Purposes.

Be it enacted by the Senate and House of Representatives of the United States of America in Congress assembled, That [a roster of investors] . . . together with commissioners to be appointed by the secretary of the Interior, and all persons who shall or may be associated with them, and their successors, are hereby created and erected into a body corporate and politic in deed and in law, by the name, style, and title of "The Union Pacific Railroad Company;" and by that name shall have perpetual succession, and shall be able to sue and to be sued, plead and be impleaded, defend and be defended, in all courts of law and equity within the United States, and may make and have a common seal; and the said corporation is hereby authorized and empowered to layout, locate, construct, furnish, maintain, and enjoy a continuous railroad and telegraph, with the appurtenances, from a point on the one hundredth meridian of longitude west from Greenwich, between the south margin of the valley of the Republican River and the north margin of the valley of the Platte River, in the Territory of Nebraska, to the western boundary of Nevada Territory, upon the route and terms hereinafter provided, and is hereby vested with all the powers, privileges, and immunities necessary to carry into effect the purposes of this act as herein set forth. . . .

SEC. 2. *And be it further enacted,* That the right of way through the public lands be, and the same is hereby, granted to said company for the construction of said railroad and telegraph line; and the right, power, and authority is hereby given to said company to take from the public lands adjacent to the line of said road, earth, stone, timber, and other materials for the construction thereof; said right of way is granted to said railroad to the extent of two hundred feet in width on each side of said railroad where it may pass over the public lands, including all necessary grounds for stations, buildings, workshops, and depots, machine shops, switches, side tracks, turntables, and, water stations. The United States shall extinguish as rapidly as may be the Indian titles to all lands falling under the operation of this act and required for the said right of way and; grants hereinafter made.

> *The United States shall extinguish as rapidly as may be the Indian titles to all lands falling under the operation of this act and required for the said right of way.*
> —The Pacific Railway Act

SEC 3. *And be it further enacted,* That there be, and is hereby, granted to the said company, for the purpose of aiding in the construction, of said railroad and telegraph line, and to secure the safe and speedy transportation of the mails, troops, munitions of war, and public stores thereon, every alternate section of public land, designated by odd numbers, to the amount of five alternate sections per mile on each side of said railroad, on the line thereof, and within the limits often miles on each side of said road, not sold, reserved, or otherwise disposed of by the United States, and to which a preemption or homestead claim may not have attached, at the time the line of said road is definitely fixed: *Provided,* That all mineral lands shall be excepted from the operation of this act; but where the same shall contain timber, the timber thereon is hereby granted to said company. And all such lands, so granted by this section, which shall not be sold or disposed of by said company within three years after the entire road shall have been completed, shall be subject to settlement and preemption, like other lands, at a price not exceeding one dollar and twenty-five cents per acre, to be paid to said company.

SEC. 4. *And be it further enacted,* That whenever said company shall have completed forty consecutive miles of any portion of said railroad and telegraph line, ready for the service contemplated by this act, and supplied with all necessary drains, culverts, viaducts, crossings, sidings, bridges, turnouts, watering places, depots, equipments, furniture, and all other appurtenances of a first class railroad, the rails and all the other iron used in the construction and equipment of said road to be American manufacture of the best quality, the President of the United States shall appoint three commissioners to examine the same and report to him in relation thereto; and if it shall appear to him that forty consecutive miles of said railroad and telegraph line have been completed and equipped in all respects as required by this act, then, upon certificate of said commissioners to that effect, patents shall issue conveying the right and title to said lands to said company, on each side of the road as far as the same is completed, to the amount aforesaid; and patents shall in like manner issue as each forty miles of said railroad and telegraph line are completed, upon certificate of said commissioners. . . .

SEC. 7. *And be it further enacted,* That said company shall file their assent to this act, under the seal of said company, in the Department of the Interior, within one year after the passage of this act, and shall complete said railroad and telegraph from the point of beginning, as herein provided, to the western boundary of Nevada Territory before the first day of July, one thousand eight hundred and seventy-four: Provided, That within two years after the passage of this act said company shall designate the general route of said road, as near as may be, and shall file a map of the same in the Department of the Interior, whereupon the Secretary of the Interior shall cause the lands within fifteen miles of said designated route or routes to be withdrawn from preemption, private entry, and sale; and when any portion of said route shall be finally located, the Secretary of the Interior shall cause the said lands herein before granted to be surveyed and set off as fast as may be necessary for the purposes herein named: *Provided,* That in fixing the point of connection of the main trunk with the eastern connections, it shall be fixed at the most practicable point for the construction of the Iowa and Missouri branches, as hereinafter provided.

SEC. 8. *And be it further enacted,* That the line of said railroad and telegraph shall commence at a point on the one hundredth meridian of a longitude west from Greenwich, between the south margin of the valley of the Republican River and the north margin of the valley of the Platte River, in the Territory of Nebraska, at a point to be fixed by the President of the United States, after actual surveys; thence running westerly upon the most direct, central, and practicable route, through the territories of the United States, the western boundary of the Territory of Nevada, there to meet and connect with the line of the Central Pacific Railroad Company of California.

SEC. 9. *And be it further enacted,* That the Leavenworth, Pawnee, and Western Railroad Company of Kansas are hereby authorized to construct a railroad and telegraph line, from the Missouri River, at the mouth of the Kansas River, on the south side thereof, so as to connect with the Pacific railroad of Missouri, to the aforesaid point, on the one hundredth meridian of longitude west from Greenwich, as herein provided, upon the same terms and conditions in all respects as are provided in this act for the construction of the [Union Pacific Railroad]. . . . The Central Pacific Railroad Company of California, a corporation existing under the laws of the State of California, are hereby authorized to construct a railroad and telegraph line from the Pacific coast, at or near San Francisco, or the navigable waters of the Sacramento River, to the eastern boundary of California, upon the same terms and conditions, in all respects, as are contained in this act for the construction of said railroad and telegraph line first mentioned, and to meet and connect with the first mentioned railroad and telegraph line on the eastern boundary of California. Each of said companies shall file their acceptance of the conditions of this act in the Department of the Interior within six months after the passage of this act.

SEC. 10. *And be it further enacted,* That the said company chartered by the State of Kansas shall complete one hundred miles of their said road, commencing at the mouth of the Kansas River as aforesaid, within two years after filing their assent to the conditions of this act, as herein provided, and one hundred miles per year thereafter until the whole is completed; and the said Central Pacific Railroad Company of California shall complete fifty miles of their said road within two years after filing their assent to the provisions of this act, as herein provided, and fifty miles per year thereafter until the whole is completed; and after completing their roads, respectively, said companies, or either of them, may unite upon equal terms with the first-named company in constructing so much of said railroad and telegraph line and branch railroads and telegraph lines in this act hereinafter mentioned, through the Territories from the State of California to the Missouri River, as shall then remain to be constructed, on the same terms and conditions as provided in this act in relation to the said Union Pacific Railroad Company . . . and the Central Pacific Railroad Company of California, after completing its road across said State, is authorized to continue the construction of said railroad and telegraph through the Territories of the United States to the Missouri River, including the branch roads specified in this act, upon the routes hereinbefore and hereinafter indicated, on the terms and conditions provided in this act in relation to the said Union Pacific Railroad Company, until said roads shall meet and connect, and the whole line of said railroad and branches and telegraph is completed.

SEC. 11. *And be it further enacted,* That for three hundred miles of said road most mountainous and difficult of construction, to wit: one hundred and fifty miles westwardly from the eastern base of the Rocky Mountains, and one hundred and fifty miles eastwardly from the western base of the Sierra Nevada mountains, said points to be fixed by the President of the United States, the bonds to be issued to aid in the construction thereof shall be treble the number per mile hereinbefore provided, and the same shall be issued, and the lands herein granted be set apart, upon the construction of every twenty miles thereof, upon the certificate of the commissioners as aforesaid that twenty consecutive miles of the same are completed and between the sections last named of one hundred and fifty miles each, the bonds to be issued to aid in the construction thereof shall be double the number per mile first mentioned, and the same shall be issued, and the lands herein granted be set apart, upon the construction of every twenty miles thereof, upon the certificate of the commissioners as aforesaid that twenty consecutive miles of the same are completed: Provided, That no more than fifty thousand of said bonds shall be issued under this act to aid in constructing the main line of said railroad and telegraph. . . .

SEC. 15. *And be it further enacted,* That any other railroad company now incorporated, or hereafter to be incorporated, shall have the right to connect their road with the road and branches provided for by this act, at such places and upon such just and equitable terms as the President of the United States may prescribe. . . .

SEC. 19. *And be it further enacted,* That the several railroad companies herein named are authorized to enter into an arrangement with the Pacific Telegraph Company, the Overland Telegraph Company, and the California State Telegraph Company, so that the present line of telegraph between the Missouri River and San Francisco may be moved upon or along the line of said railroad and branches as fast as said roads and branches are built; and if said arrangement be entered into and the transfer of said telegraph line be made in accordance therewith to the line of said railroad and branches, such transfer shall, for all purposes of this act, be held and considered a fulfillment on the part of said railroad companies of the provisions of this act in regard to the construction of said line of telegraph. And, in case of disagreement, said telegraph companies are authorized to remove their line of telegraph along and upon the line of railroad herein contemplated without prejudice to the rights of said railroad companies named herein. . . .

APPROVED, July 1, 1862.

Source: *A Century of Lawmaking for a New Nation: U.S. Congressional Documents and Debates, 1774–1875. Statutes at Large. 37th Congress, 2nd Session, 1862.* New York: Little, Brown, 1862, pp. 489–498.

NOTE

1. Dee Brown, *Hear that Lonesome Whistle Blow: The Epic Story of the Transcontinental Railroads* (1977; New York: Henry Holt, 2001), 122.

George Perkins Marsh Discusses *Man and Nature*

"Man Is Everywhere a Disturbing Agent"

1865

During the course of the nineteenth century, several American writers produced influential works that explored themes of environmental stewardship and respect for nature. These books and essays, penned by Henry David Thoreau, John Burroughs, John Muir, George Perkins Marsh, Florence Merriam, Ralph Waldo Emerson, and others, contributed greatly to changing American perceptions of the value of nature—which in turn increased public and political support for resource conservation proposals.

George Perkins Marsh occupies a particularly notable place in this constellation of early "nature" writers. A diplomat, philologist, and scholar, his prodigious intellectual gifts eventually led him to the subject of ecology. His 1865 work Man and Nature *argued that the expanding American empire would—like earlier civilizations in history—doom itself if it did not rein in its present course of rampant environmental degradation. This book became a touchstone of the nineteenth-century conservation movement, and many of its principal arguments are still embraced by environmentalists today. In the following excerpt from this seminal work (footnotes removed), Marsh focuses on the negative impacts of rapacious resource consumption and alien crop and livestock species on fragile ecosystems. He also opines that mankind has displayed little capacity to handle environment-changing technological and industrial developments wisely.*

Man has too long forgotten that the earth was given to him for usufruct alone, not for consumption, still less for profligate waste. Nature has provided against the absolute destruction of any of her elementary matter, the raw material of her works; the thunderbolt and the tornado, the most convulsive throes of even the volcano and the earthquake, being only phenomena of decomposition and recomposition. But she has left it within the power of man irreparably to derange the combinations of inorganic matter and of organic life, which through the night of æons she had been proportioning and balancing, to prepare the earth for his habitation, when, in the fulness of time, his Creator should call him forth to enter into its possession.

Apart from the hostile influence of man, the organic and the inorganic world are, as I have remarked, bound together by such mutual relations and adaptations as secure, if not the absolute permanence and equilibrium of both, a long continuance of the established conditions of each at any given time and place, or at least, a very slow and gradual succession of changes in those conditions. But man is everywhere a disturbing agent. Wherever he plants his foot, the harmonies of nature are turned to discords. The proportions and accommodations which insured the stability of existing arrangements are overthrown. Indigenous vegetable and animal species are extirpated, and supplanted by others of foreign origin, spontaneous production is forbidden or restricted, and the face of the earth is either laid bare or covered with a new and reluctant growth of vegetable forms, and with alien tribes of animal life. These intentional changes and substitutions constitute, indeed, great revolutions; but vast as is their magnitude and importance, they are, as we shall see, insignificant in comparison with the contingent and unsought results which have flowed from them.

The fact that, of all organic beings, man alone is to be regarded as essentially a destructive power, and that he wields energies to resist which, nature—that nature whom all material life and all inorganic substance obey—is wholly impotent, tends to prove that, though living in physical nature, he is not of her, that he is of more exalted parentage, and belongs to a higher order of existences than those born of her womb and submissive to her dictates.

There are, indeed, brute destroyers, beasts and birds and insects of prey—all animal life feeds upon, and, of course, destroys other life,—but this destruction is balanced by compensations. It is, in fact, the very means by which the existence of one tribe of animals or of vegetables is secured against being smothered by the encroachments of another; and the reproductive powers of species, which serve as the food of others, are always proportioned to the demand they are destined to supply. Man pursues his victims with reckless destructiveness; and, while the sacrifice of life by the lower animals is limited by the cravings of appetite, he unsparingly persecutes, even to extirpation, thousands of organic forms which he cannot consume.

The earth was not, in its natural condition, completely adapted to the use of man, but only to the sustenance of wild animals and wild vegetation. These live, multiply their kind in just proportion, and attain their perfect measure of strength and beauty, without producing or requiring any change in the natural arrangements of surface, or in each other's spontaneous tendencies, except such mutual repression of excessive increase as may prevent the extirpation of one species by the encroachments of another. In short, without man, lower animal and spontaneous vegetable life would have been constant in type, distribution, and proportion, and the physical geography of the earth would have remained undisturbed for indefinite periods, and been subject to revolution only from possible, unknown cosmical causes, or from geological action.

But man, the domestic animals that serve him, the field and garden plants the products of which supply him with food and clothing, cannot subsist and rise to the full development of their higher properties, unless brute and unconscious nature be effectually combated, and, in a great degree, vanquished by human art. Hence, a certain measure of transformation of terrestrial surface, of suppression of natural, and stimulation of artificially modified productivity becomes necessary. This measure man has unfortunately exceeded. He has felled the forests whose network of fibrous roots bound the mould to the rocky skeleton of the earth; but had he allowed here and there a belt of woodland to reproduce itself by spontaneous propagation, most of the mischiefs which his reckless destruction of the natural protection of the soil has occasioned would have been averted. He has broken up the mountain reservoirs, the percolation of whose waters through unseen channels supplied the fountains that refreshed his cattle and fertilized his fields; but he has neglected to maintain the cisterns and the canals of irrigation which a wise antiquity had constructed to neutralize the consequences of its own imprudence. While he has torn the thin glebe which confined the light earth of extensive plains, and has destroyed the fringe of semi-aquatic plants which skirted the coast and checked the drifting of the sea sand, he has failed to prevent the spreading of the dunes by clothing them with artificially propagated vegetation. He has ruthlessly warred on all the tribes of animated nature whose spoil he could convert to his own uses, and he has not protected the birds which prey on the insects most destructive to his own harvests.

Purely untutored humanity, it is true, interferes comparatively little with the arrangements of nature, and the destructive agency of man becomes more and more energetic and unsparing as he advances in civilization, until the impoverishment, with which his exhaustion of the natural resources of the soil is threatening him, at last awakens him to the necessity of preserving what is left, if not of restoring what has been wantonly wasted. The wandering savage grows no cultivated vegetable, fells no forest, and extirpates no useful plant, no noxious weed. If his skill in the chase enables him to entrap numbers of the animals on which he feeds, he compensates this loss by destroying also the lion, the tiger, the wolf, the otter, the seal, and the eagle, thus indirectly protecting the feebler quadrupeds and fish and fowls, which would otherwise become the booty of beasts and birds of prey. But with stationary life, or rather with the pastoral state, man at once commences an almost indiscriminate warfare upon, all the forms of animal and vegetable existence around him, and as he advances in civilization, he gradually eradicates or transforms every spontaneous product of the soil he occupies. . . .

The rapid extension of railroads, which now everywhere keeps pace with, and sometimes even precedes, the occupation of new soil for agricultural purposes, furnishes great facilities for enlarging our knowledge of the topography of the territory they traverse, because their cuttings reveal the composition and general structure of surface, and the inclination and elevation of their lines constitute known hypsometrical sections, which give numerous points of departure for the measurement of higher and lower stations, and of course for determining the relief and depression of surface, the slope of the beds of watercourses, and many other not less important questions.

The geological, hydrographical, and topographical surveys, which almost every general and even local government of the civilized world is carrying on, are making yet more important contributions to our stock of geographical and general physical knowledge, and, within a comparatively short space, there will be an accumulation of well established constant and historical facts, from which we can safely reason upon all the relations of action and reaction between man and external nature.

But we are, even now, breaking up the floor and wainscoting and doors and window frames of our dwelling, for fuel to warm our bodies and seethe our pottage, and the world cannot afford to wait till the slow and sure progress of exact science has taught it a better economy. . . .

Source: Marsh, George P. *Man and Nature; or, Physical Geography as Modified by Human Action.* New York: Scribner, 1865, pp. 35–40, 53–55.

DOCUMENT 3.4

The General Mining Act of 1872

"All Valuable Mineral Deposits . . . Are . . . Free and Open to Exploration and Purchase"

M A Y   1 0 ,   1 8 7 2

The General Mining Act of 1872 was one of the most significant land policy laws enacted in the nineteenth century. It formally sanctioned mining as a laudable and appropriate activity on land in the public domain by opening "all lands owned by the United States *government" to "exploration and occupation" by miners and mining companies. In return, the federal government asked for virtually nothing from buyers. The Act demanded no royalties from the wealth that might result from exploitation of natural resources on these lands, nor did it place any limits on the environmental carnage wreaked by mining or other activities carried out on these lands. Eager to see the West settled and developed, Congress gave buyers who could afford the modest financial outlay—$2.50 to $5 an acre— free rein to treat the land however they saw fit.*

The General Mining Act of 1872 is widely recognized as the primary reason that more than 270 million acres of public lands are open to mining across the United States today. The law undoubtedly has greatly aided economic development in the West since its passage, and it has been amended over the years to protect national parks and other public lands deemed worthy of protection. However, it has also been cited by the Environmental Protection Agency as a chief culprit in the despoilment of more than 40 percent of the headwaters of western streams and rivers since its passage and as the root cause of a wide assortment of other environmental problems. Although environmental organizations have launched repeated campaigns to amend or repeal the antiquated law in recent years, none have achieved the necessary level of congressional support for passage. As a result, the controversial General Mining Act of 1872—excerpted here—remains largely intact today.

AN ACT TO PROMOTE THE DEVELOPMENT OF THE MINING RESOURCES OF THE UNITED STATES.

Be it enacted by the Senate and House of Representatives of the United States of America, in Congress assembled,

Sec. 1. That all valuable mineral deposits in lands belonging to the United States, both surveyed and unsurveyed, are hereby declared to be free and open to exploration and purchase, and the lands in which they are found to occupation and purchase, by citizens of the United States and those who have declared their intention to become such, under regulations prescribed by law, and according to the local customs or rules of miners, in the several mining districts, so far as the same are applicable and not inconsistent with the laws of the United States.

Sec. 2. That mining claims upon veins or lodes of quartz or other rock in place bearing gold, silver, cinnabar, lead, tin, copper, or other valuable deposits heretofore located, shall be governed as to length along the vein or lode by the customs, regulations, and laws in force at the date of their location. A mining claim located after the passage of this act, whether located by one or more persons, may equal, but shall not exceed, one thousand five hundred feet in length along the vein or lode; but no location of a mining claim shall be made until the discovery of the vein or lode within the limits of the claim located. No claim shall extend more than three hundred feet on each side of the middle of the vein at the surface, nor shall any claim be limited by any mining regulation to less than twenty-five feet on each side of the middle of the vein at the surface. . . .

Sec. 3. That the locators of all mining locations heretofore made, or which shall hereafter be made, on any mineral vein, lode, or ledge, situated on the public domain, their heirs and assigns . . . shall have the exclusive right of possession and enjoyment of all the surface included within the lines of their locations. . . .

Sec. 5. That the miners of each mining district may make rules and regulations not in conflict with the laws of the United States, or with the laws of the State or Territory in which the district is situated, governing the location, manner or recording, amount of work necessary to hold possession of a mining-claim, subject to the following require-ments: The location must be distinctly marked on the ground so that its boundaries can be readily traced. . . . On each claim located after the passage of this act, and until a patent shall have been issued therefor, not less than one hundred dollars' worth of labor shall be performed or improvements made during each year. On all claims located prior to the passage of this act, ten dollars' worth of labor shall be performed or improvements made each year for each one hundred feet in length along the vein until a patent shall have been issued therefor. . . .

Sec. 6. That a patent for any land claimed and located for valuable deposits may be obtained in the following manner: Any person, association, or corporation authorized to locate a claim under this act, having claimed and located a piece of land for such pur-poses, who has, or have, complied with the terms of this act, may file in the proper land-office an application for a patent . . . and shall thereupon be entitled for said land, in manner following: The register of the land-office, upon the filing of such application, plat, field-notes, notices, and affidavits, shall publish a notice that such application has been made, for the period of sixty days, in a newspaper to be by him designated as published nearest to said claim; and he shall also post such notice in his office for the same period. The claimant at the time of filing this application, or at any time thereafter, within the sixty days of publication, shall file with the register a certificate of the United States surveyor-general that five hundred dollars' worth of labor has been expended or improve-ments made upon the claim by himself or grantors; that the plat is correct. . . . If no adverse claim shall have been filed with the register and the receiver of the proper land-office at the expiration of the sixty days of publication, it shall be assumed that the appli-cant is entitled to a patent, upon the payment to the proper officer of five dollars per acre, and that no adverse claim exists; and thereafter no objection from third parties to the issuance of a patent shall be heard, except it be shown that the applicant has failed to comply with this act. . . .

Source: Lindley, Curtis. "Act of May 10, 1872." In *Commissioner of the General Land Office and the Secretary of the Interior Thereunder; Together with the Circular Instructions from the General Land Office, and Forms for Establishing Proof of Claims; also, the Decisions of the Supreme Court of the United States under the Mining Acts.* San Francisco: A.L. Bancroft and Company, 1881, pp. 22–26.

DOCUMENT
3.5

Yellowstone Becomes America's First National Park

"A Public Park or Pleasuring-Ground for the Benefit and Enjoyment of the People"

March 1, 1872

On March 1, 1872, the U.S. Congress approved the Yellowstone Act, which established the first national park in America. Environmental protection provisions in this legislation were limited, but they were strengthened in later years through a flurry of other laws.

The establishment of Yellowstone National Park was an environmental policy landmark on a number of levels. It paved the way for the creation of other national parks, of course, and eventually for the establishment of a National Park Service. But the Yellowstone Act also signaled a turning point in America's attitude toward land and natural resource management. In passing this Act, lawmakers exhibited a growing awareness of the need for resource conservation policies—and a dawning realization that the value of some of the continent's natural treasures could not be measured in economic terms. Following is the complete text of the Act.

An Act to Set Apart a Certain Tract of Land Lying near the Headwaters of the Yellowstone River as a Public Park, Approved March 1, 1872

Be it enacted by the Senate and House of Representatives of the United States of America in Congress assembled, That the tract of land in the Territories of Montana and Wyoming, lying near the headwaters of the Yellowstone River, and described as follows, to wit, commencing at the junction of Gardiner's river with the Yellowstone river, and running east to the meridian passing ten miles to the eastward of the most eastern point of Yellowstone lake; thence south along said meridian to the parallel of latitude passing ten miles south of the most southern point of Yellowstone lake; thence west along said parallel to the meridian passing fifteen miles west of the most western point of Madison lake; thence north along said meridian to the latitude of the junction of Yellowstone and Gardiner's rivers; thence east to the place of beginning, is hereby reserved and withdrawn from settlement, occupancy, or sale under the laws of the United States, and dedicated and set apart as a public park or pleasuring-ground for the benefit and enjoyment of the people; and all persons who shall locate or settle upon or occupy the same, or any part thereof, except as hereinafter provided, shall be considered trespassers and removed therefrom.

SEC 2. That said public park shall be under the exclusive control of the Secretary of the Interior, whose duty it shall be, as soon as practicable, to make and publish such rules and regulations as he may deem necessary or proper for the care and management of the same. Such regulations shall provide for the preservation, from injury or spoliation, of all timber, mineral deposits, natural curiosities, or wonders within said park, and their retention in their natural condition. The Secretary may in his discretion, grant leases for building purposes for terms not exceeding ten years, of small parcels of ground, at such places in said park as shall require the erection of buildings for the accommodation of visitors; all of the proceeds of said leases, and all other revenues that may be derived from any source connected with said park, to be expended under his direction in the management of the same, and the construction of roads and bridle-paths therein. He shall provide against the wanton destruction of the fish and game found within said park, and against their capture or destruction for the purposes of merchandise or profit. He shall also cause all persons trespassing upon the same after the passage of this act to be removed therefrom, and generally shall be authorized to take all such measures as shall be necessary or proper to fully carry out the objects and purposes of this act.

Source: "Yellowstone Act." *America's National Parks: The Critical Documents.* Edited by Lars N. Dilsaver. National Park Service. www.nps.gov/history/history/online_books/anps/anps_1c.htm.

The Free Timber Act

"To Fell and Remove Timber on the Public Domain for Mining and Domestic Purposes"

June 3, 1878

The Free Timber Act of 1878 was one of a flurry of congressional acts passed during the 1870s that opened western forestlands to exploitation by a wide range of users, from individual homesteaders and miners to timber companies and railroads. This legislation was introduced by western lawmakers eager to liquidate the region's natural resources in the name of economic development and social improvement. But even though the Act "met genuine and reasonable local demands," observed one historian, "it provided scope for the excessive abuse of the forests."[1]

Under the terms of the Act, residents of the eight Rocky Mountain states and territories—Colorado, Nevada, New Mexico, Arizona, Utah, Wyoming, Idaho, and Montana—received broad authority to cut timber on "mineral lands" in the public domain for construction, agriculture, mining, and other undefined "domestic purposes." The vague wording of the Act, combined with the paucity of federal enforcement mechanisms in the West, proved disastrous. Vast tracts of forests were felled without regard for the environmental consequences, and the few timber agents assigned to the region were further stymied in their efforts to punish trespassers by the fact that defining publicly owned "mineral lands" was exceedingly difficult. Conservation efforts were made even more hopeless in 1882, when Congress broadened the act to allow "lumber dealers, mill owners and railroad contractors to cut timber even for commercial purposes, and for sale as well as use." And in 1891, Congress even eliminated the "mineral lands" stipulation, opening the door to a fresh onslaught of timber felling across the public domain. Following is the complete text of the original 1878 Act.

AN ACT AUTHORIZING THE CITIZENS OF COLORADO, NEVADA AND THE TERRITORIES TO FELL AND REMOVE TIMBER ON THE PUBLIC DOMAIN FOR MINING AND DOMESTIC PURPOSES.

Be it enacted by the Senate and House of Representatives of the United States of America in Congress assembled, That all citizens of the United States and other persons, bona fide residents of the State of Colorado, or Nevada, or either of the Territories of New Mexico, Arizona, Utah, Wyoming, Dakota, Idaho, or Montana, and all other mineral districts of the United States, shall be, and are hereby, authorized and permitted to fell and remove, for building, agricultural, mining, or other domestic purposes, any timber or other trees growing or being on the public lands, said lands being mineral, and not subject to entry under existing laws of the United States, except for mineral entry, in either of said States, Territories, or districts of which such citizens or persons may be at the time bona fide residents, subject to such rules and regulations as the Secretary of the Interior may pre-scribe for the protection of the timber and of the undergrowth growing upon such lands, and for other purposes: *Provided,* the provisions of this act shall not extend to railroad corporations.

SEC. 2. That it shall be the duty of the register and the receiver of any local land-office in whose district any mineral land may be situated to ascertain from time to time whether any timber is being cut or used upon any such lands, except for the purposes authorized by this act, within their respective land districts; and, if so, they shall immediately notify the Commissioner of the General Land Office of that fact; and all necessary expenses incurred in making such proper examinations shall be paid and allowed such register and receiver in making up their next quarterly accounts.

SEC. 3. Any person or persons who shall violate the provisions of this act, or any rules and regulations in pursuance thereof made by the Secretary of the Interior, shall be deemed guilty of a misdemeanor, and, upon conviction, shall be fined in any sum not exceeding five hundred dollars, and to which may be added imprisonment for any term not exceeding six months.

Approved, June 3, 1878.

Source: *Statutes of the United States of America.* Washington, D.C.: Government Printing Office, 1878, p. 88. Reprinted in: Clark, Horace, Charles Heltman, and Charles Consaul. *Mineral Law Digest.* Chicago: Callaghan and Company, 1897, pp. 449–451.

NOTE

1. Michael Williams, *Americans and Their Forests: A Historical Geography* (New York: Cambridge University Press, 1989), 398.

DOCUMENT
3.7

John Wesley Powell's Cautionary Report on Settlement of the West

"These Lands Will Maintain but a Scanty Population"

1879

During the second half of the nineteenth century, speculators, settlers, corporations, and lawmakers acted in concert to subdue the American West, the nation's "last frontier." But even as this frenzy of settlement and resource development was unfolding, a few knowledgeable observers were counseling caution. Citing their firsthand experiences in and observations of the West, they stubbornly refused to abandon their "reality-based" impressions and leap aboard the Manifest Destiny bandwagon.

The famed explorer and geologist John Wesley Powell ranked as the foremost of these cautionary figures. In 1879 Powell—who had led the first expedition down the Colorado River through the Grand Canyon a dozen years earlier—issued A Report on the Lands of the Arid Region of the United States in his capacity as head of the U.S. Geological Survey for the Rocky Mountain region. In this report, Powell emphasized that water was the lynchpin of western settlement in the arid regions of the West, and he methodically dismantled the sunny assumptions of speculators and legislators about the land's capacity to support unlimited development. Powell recognized that in the West limited water availability from rainfall and rivers meant that conventional agricultural systems could not be imposed on a large-scale basis. "Powell was advocating cooperation, reason, science, an equitable sharing of the natural wealth, and—implicitly if not explicitly—a return to the Jeffersonian ideal," observed historian Marc Reisner. "He wanted the West settled slowly, cautiously, in a manner that would work."[1]

Powell's report is today regarded as a remarkably cogent and clear-eyed analysis of the water resource issues that have bedeviled the American West for the past century and a half. But when it was first published it was widely ignored or panned by lawmakers, pioneers, and railroad tycoons who viewed its call for limited development as anathema to their vision of American empire. Following are excerpts (with footnotes removed) from Powell's unpopular report.

. . . The Arid Region is somewhat more than four-tenths of the total area of the United States, and as the agricultural interests of so great an area are dependent upon irrigation it will be interesting to consider certain questions relating to the economy and practicability of distributing the waters over the lands to be redeemed. . . .

The diversion of a large stream from its channel into a system of canals demands a large outlay of labor and material. To repay this all the waters so taken out must be used, and large tracts of land thus become dependent upon a single canal. It is manifest that a farmer depending upon his own labor cannot undertake this task. To a great extent the small streams are already employed, and but a comparatively small portion of the irrigable lands can be thus redeemed; hence the chief future development of irrigation must come from the use of the larger streams. Usually the confluence of the brooks and creeks which form a large river takes place within the mountain district which furnishes its source before the stream enters the lowlands where the waters are to be used. The volume of water carried by the small streams that reach the lowlands before uniting with the great rivers, or before they are lost in the sands, is very small when compared with the volume of the streams which emerge from the mountains as rivers. This fact is important. If the streams could be used along their upper ramifications while the several branches are yet small, poor men could occupy the lands, and by their individual enterprise the agriculture of the country would be gradually extended to the limit of the capacity of the region; but when farming is dependent upon larger streams such men are barred from these enterprises until cooperative labor can be organized or capital induced to assist. Before many years all the available smaller streams throughout the entire region will be occupied in serving the lands, and then all future development will depend on the conditions above described. . . .

> *[I]f in the eagerness for present development a land and water system shall grow up in which the practical control of agriculture shall fall into the hands of water companies, evils will result therefrom that generations may not be able to correct.*
>
> —John Wesley Powell

REGULAR DIVISION LINES FOR PASTURAGE FARMS NOT PRACTICABLE.

Many a brook which runs but a short distance will afford sufficient water for a number of pasturage farms; but if the lands are surveyed in regular tracts as square miles or townships, all the water sufficient for a number of pasturage farms may fall entirely within one division. If the lands are thus surveyed, only the divisions having water will be taken, and the farmer obtaining title to such a division or farm could practically occupy all the country adjacent by owning the water necessary to its use. For this reason divisional surveys should conform to the topography, and be so made as to give the greatest number of water fronts. For example, a brook carrying water sufficient for the irrigation of 200 acres of land might be made to serve for the irrigation of 20 acres to each of ten farms, and also supply the water for all the stock that could live on ten pasturage farms, and ten small farmers could have homes. But if the water was owned by one man, nine would be excluded from its benefits and nine-tenths of the land remain in the hands of the government.

FARM RESIDENCES SHOULD BE GROUPED.

These lands will maintain but a scanty population. The homes must necessarily be widely scattered from the fact that the farm unit must be large. That the inhabitants of these districts may have the benefits of the local social organizations of civilization—as schools, churches, etc., and the benefits of cooperation in the construction of roads, bridges, and other local improvements, it is essential that the residences should be grouped to the greatest possible extent. This may be practically accomplished by making the pasturage farms conform to topographic features in such manner as to give the greatest possible number of water fronts.

PASTURAGE LANDS CANNOT BE FENCED.

The great areas over which stock must roam to obtain subsistence usually prevents the practicability of fencing the lands. It will not pay to fence the pasturage fields, hence in many cases the lands must be occupied by herds roaming in common; for poor men cooperative pasturage is necessary, or communal regulations for the occupancy of the ground and for the division of the increase of the herds. Such communal regulations have already been devised in many parts of the country.

RECAPITULATION.

The Arid Region of the United States is more than four-tenths of the area of the entire country excluding Alaska.

In the Arid Region there are three classes of lands, namely, irrigable lands, timber lands, and pasturage lands.

Irrigable Lands.

Within the Arid Region agriculture is dependent upon irrigation.

The amount of irrigable land is but a small percentage of the whole area.

The chief development of irrigation depends upon the use of the large streams.

For the use of large streams cooperative labor or capital is necessary.

The small streams should not be made to serve lands so as to interfere with the use of the large streams.

Sites for reservoirs should be set apart, in order that no hinderance may be placed upon the increase of irrigation by the storage of water.

Timber Lands.

The timber regions are on the elevated plateaus and mountains.

The timber regions constitute from 20 to 25 per cent of the Arid Region.

The area of standing timber is much less than the timber region, as the forests have been partially destroyed by fire.

The timber regions cannot be used as farming lands; they are valuable for forests only.

To preserve the forests they must be protected from fire. This will be largely accomplished by removing the Indians.

The amount of timber used for economic purposes will be more than replaced by the natural growth.

In general the timber is too far from the agricultural lands to be owned and utilized directly by those who carry on farming by irrigation.

A division of labor is necessary, and special timber industries will be developed, and hence the timber lands must be controlled by lumbermen and woodmen.

Pasturage Lands.

The grasses of the pasturage lands are scant, and the lands are of value only in large quantities.

The farm unit should not be less than 2,560 acres.

Pasturage farms need small tracts of irrigable land; hence the small streams of the general drainage system and the lone springs and streams should be reserved for such pasturage farms.

The division of these lands should be controlled by topographic features in such manner as to give the greatest number of water fronts to the pasturage farms.

Residences of the pasturage farms should be grouped, in order to secure the benefits of local social organizations, and cooperation in public improvements.

The pasturage lands will not usually be fenced, and hence herds must roam in common.

As the pasturage lands should have water fronts and irrigable tracts, and as the residences should be grouped, and as the lands cannot be economically fenced and must be kept in common, local communal regulations or cooperation is necessary. . . .

***

The general subject of water rights is one of great importance. In many places in the Arid Region irrigation companies are organized who obtain vested rights in the waters they control, and consequently the rights to such waters do not inhere in any particular tracts of land.

When the area to which it is possible to take the water of any given stream is much greater than the stream is competent to serve, if the land titles and water rights are severed, the owner of any tract of land is at the mercy of the owner of the water right. In general, the lands greatly exceed the capacities of the streams. Thus the lands have no value without water. If the water rights fall into the hands of irrigating companies and the lands into the hands of individual farmers, the farmers then will be dependent upon the stock companies, and eventually the monopoly of water rights will be an intolerable burden to the people.

The magnitude of the interests involved must not be overlooked. All the present and future agriculture of more than four-tenths of the area of the United States is dependent upon irrigation, and practically all values for agricultural industries inhere, not in the lands but in the water. Monopoly of land need not be feared. The question for legislators to solve is to devise some practical means by which water rights may be distributed among individual farmers and water monopolies prevented.

The pioneers in the "new countries" in the United States have invariably been characterized by enterprise and industry and an intense desire for the speedy development of their new homes. These characteristics are no whit less prominent in the Rocky Mountain Region than in the earlier "new countries"; but they are even more apparent. The hardy pioneers engage in a multiplicity of industrial enterprises surprising to the people of long established habits and institutions. Under the impetus of this spirit irrigation companies are organized and capital invested in irrigating canals, and but little heed is given to philosophic considerations of political economy or to the ultimate condition of affairs in which their present enterprises will result. The pioneer is fully engaged in the present with its hopes of immediate remuneration for labor. The present development of the country fully occupies him. For this reason every effort put forth to increase the area of the agricultural land by irrigation is welcomed. Every man who turns his attention to this department of industry is considered a public benefactor. But if in the eagerness for present development a land and water system shall grow up in which the practical control of agriculture shall fall into the hands of water companies, evils will result therefrom that generations may not be able to correct, and the very men who are now lauded as benefactors to the country will, in the ungovernable reaction which is sure to come, be denounced as oppressors of the people.

The right to use water should inhere in the land to be irrigated, and water rights should go with land titles. . . .

***

If there be any doubt of the ultimate legality of the practices of the people in the arid country relating to water and land rights, all such doubts should be speedily quieted through the enactment of appropriate laws by the national legislature. Perhaps an amplification by the courts of what has been designated as the *natural right* to the use of water may be made to cover the practices now obtaining; but it hardly seems wise to imperil interests so great by intrusting them to the possibility of some future court made law.

Source: Powell, John Wesley. *A Report on the Lands of the Arid Region of the United States, with a More Detailed Account of the Lands of Utah.* 2nd ed. Washington, D.C.: Government Printing Office, 1879, pp. 9, 11, 22–24, 40–41, 43.

NOTE

1. Marc Reisner, *Cadillac Desert: The American West and Its Disappearing Water* (1986. rev. ed. New York: Penguin, 1993), 48.

Chief Joseph Asks the U.S. Congress for Justice

"The White Man Would Not Let Us Alone"

January 14, 1879

White hunger for new lands to settle and develop remained unquenchable throughout the nineteenth century, and Indian peoples that had prospered for generations on lands west of the Mississippi River found themselves facing the same implacable foe as their conquered eastern brethren. Native responses to the rising waves of white settlers, miners, hunters, and ranchers ranged from accommodation to violent resistance, but in the end the military might, technological superiority, and numerical advantages enjoyed by the United States and its citizenry were too much to overcome. Tribe after tribe was pushed off the fertile lands they had long used and pushed onto reservations. This loss of land was devastating to Native American livelihoods and cultures, and the shift in land use toward white agriculture, ranching, mining, and other intensive commercial practices had enduring environmental consequences for the entire West.

One of the most famous—and all too representative—stories of Indian dislocation from this era concerned the Nez Percés people of the Pacific Northwest. The Nez Percés, who had developed a thriving society based around the salmon that surged through the rivers of modern-day Washington, Oregon, and Idaho, had historically been great friends to the Americans. They had provided valuable aid to the Lewis and Clark Expedition, welcomed fur traders and missionaries to their lands, and even sided with American military forces in clashes with other tribes. In 1855 the Nez Percés agreed to a treaty that ceded some traditional lands to the Americans but also established a large reservation that included their most treasured fishing grounds and culturally significant ancestral lands. This land was supposed to be theirs in perpetuity, but when white prospectors found gold on the reservation, the U.S. government turned on the Nez Percés. In 1863 government agencies demanded that the tribe's various bands relinquish nearly six million acres of reservation land and resettle on a new reservation that was about one tenth the size of the old one. Some band leaders such as the notorious collaborator Chief Lawyer signed the agreement, but others refused. American officials nonetheless trumpeted the treaty as one that committed the entire Nez Percés nation to its terms.

One of the largest bands to defy the U.S. government was the Wallowa Valley band led by a chieftain named Tuekakas. In 1871 he died and his son, who came to be known to Americans as Chief Joseph, took the reins of leadership. For the next several years he and his followers defied governmental efforts to pry them loose from their ancestral lands. At the same time, however, white settlers poured onto Wallowa lands in ever greater numbers, to the great consternation of Chief Joseph.

When years of intense negotiations failed to gain relief for his people, Joseph began to feel that he had no choice but to accept the U.S. government's demands. But widespread theft of Nez Percés horses and the murder of a few settlers at the hands of another band of Nez Percés triggered violent clashes between the U.S. Army and the Wallowa and other "nontreaty" bands. Joseph then led about 750 Nez Percés on a desperate journey to

Canada, where they hoped to find peace. U.S. military forces gave chase, but Joseph outwitted them again and again. Under Joseph's leadership, they eluded the U.S. Army for four months and traveled nearly 1,400 miles before they were finally captured—almost within sight of the Canadian border. The exhausted Nez Percés refugees were promptly shipped to miserable reservations in modern-day Kansas and Oklahoma, where many eventually perished from sickness and disease.

Seeking relief for his tribespeople, Joseph secured permission to go to Washington, D.C. On January 14, 1879, he spoke before Congress and assorted cabinet members and delivered an eloquent and passionate request for justice and mercy for his people. But despite his emotional testimony, excerpted here, Congress made no effort to redress the many wrongs that had been inflicted on the Nez Percés people over the years. Joseph was kept in custody for several years, then shunted off to a reservation in Washington Territory. He died there in 1904 without ever again seeing the Wallowa Valley lands where his father was buried.

My friends, I have been asked to show you my heart. I am glad to have a chance to do so. I want the white people to understand my people. Some of you think an Indian is like a wild animal. This is a great mistake. I will tell you all about our people, and then you can judge whether an Indian is a man or not. I believe much trouble and blood would be saved if we opened our hearts more. I will tell you in my way how the Indian sees things. The white man has more words to tell you how they look to him, but it does not require many words to speak the truth. What I have to say will come from my heart, and I will speak with a straight tongue. Ah-cum-kin-i-ma-me-hut (The Great Spirit) is looking at me, and will hear me.

My name is In-mut-too-yah-lat-lat (Thunder traveling over the Mountains). I am chief of the Wal-lam-wat-kin band of Chute-pa-lu, or Nez Percés (nose-pierced Indians). I was born in eastern Oregon, thirty-eight winters ago. My father was chief before me. When a young man, he was called Joseph by Mr. Spaulding, a missionary. He died a few years ago. There was no stain on his hands of the blood of a white man. He left a good name on the earth. He advised me well for my people.

Our fathers gave us many laws, which they had learned from their fathers. These laws were good. They told us to treat all men as they treated us; that we should never be the first to break a bargain; that it was a disgrace to tell a lie; that we should speak only the truth; that it was a shame for one man to take from another his wife, or his property without paying for it. We were taught to believe that the Great Spirit sees and hears everything, and that he never forgets; that hereafter he will give every man a spirit-home according to his deserts: if he has been a bad man, he will have a bad home. This I believe, and all my people believe the same.

We did not know there were other people besides the Indian until about one hundred winters ago, when some men with white faces came to our country. They brought many things with them to trade for furs and skins. They brought tobacco, which was new to us. They brought guns with flint stones on them, which frightened our women and children. Our people could not talk with these white-faced men, but they used signs which all people understand. These men were Frenchmen, and they called our people "Nez Percés," because they wore rings in their noses for ornaments. Although very few of our people wear them now, we are still called by the same name. These French trappers said a great many things to our fathers, which have been planted in our hearts. Some were good for us, but some were bad. Our people were divided in opinion about these men.

Some thought they taught more bad than good. An Indian respects a brave man, but he despises a coward. He loves a straight tongue, but he hates a forked tongue. The French trappers told us some truths and some lies.

The first white men of your people who came to our country were named Lewis and Clarke. They also brought many things that our people had never seen. They talked straight, and our people gave them a great feast, as a proof that their hearts were friendly. These men were very kind. They made presents to our chiefs and our people made presents to them. We had a great many horses, of which we gave them what they needed, and they gave us guns and tobacco in return. All the Nez Percés made friends with Lewis and Clarke, and agreed to let them pass through their country, and never to make war on white men. This promise the Nez Percés have never broken. No white man can accuse them of bad faith, and speak with a straight tongue. It has always been the pride of the Nez Percés that they were the friends of the white men. When my father was a young man there came to our country a white man (Rev. Mr. Spaulding) who talked spirit law. He won the affections of our people because he spoke good things to them. At first, he did not say anything about white men wanting to settle on our lands. Nothing was said about that until about twenty winters ago, when a number of white people came into our country and built houses and made farms. At first our people made no complaint. They thought there was room enough for all to live in peace, and they were learning many things from the white men that seemed to be good. But we soon found that the white men were growing rich very fast, and were greedy to possess everything the Indian had. My father was the first to see through the schemes of the white men, and he warned his tribe to be careful about trading with them. He had suspicion of men who seemed so anxious to make money. I was a boy then, but I remember well my father's caution. He had sharper eyes than the rest of our people.

Next there came a white officer (Governor Stevens), who invited all the Nez Percés to a treaty council. After the council was opened he made known his heart. He said there were a great many white people in the country, and many more would come; that he wanted the land marked out so that the Indians and white men could be separated. If they were to live in peace it was necessary, he said, that the Indians should have a country set apart for them, and in that country they must stay. My father, who represented his band, refused to have anything to do with the council, because he wished to be a free man. He claimed that no man owned any part of the earth, and a man could not sell what he did not own.

Mr. Spaulding took hold of my father's arm and said, "Come and sign the treaty." My father pushed him away, and said: "Why do you ask me to sign away my country? It is your business to talk about spirit matters, and not to talk to us about parting with our land." Governor Stevens urged my father to sign his treaty, but he refused. "I will not sign your paper," he said; "you go where you please, so do I; you are not a child, I am no child; I can think for myself. No man can think for me. I have no other home than this. I will not give it up to any man. My people would have no home. Take away your paper. I will not touch it with my hand."

My father left the council. Some of the chiefs of the other bands of the Nez Percés signed the treaty, and then Governor Stevens gave them presents of blankets. My father cautioned his people to take no presents, for "after a while," he said, "they will claim that you have accepted pay for your country." Since that time four bands of the Nez Percés have received annuities from the United States. My father was invited to many councils, and they tried hard to make him sign the treaty, but he was firm as the rock, and would not sign away his home. His refusal caused a difference among the Nez Percés.

Eight years later (1863) was the next treaty council. A chief called Lawyer, because he was a great talker, took the lead in this council, and sold nearly all the Nez Percés country. My father was not there. He said to me: "When you go into council with the white man, always remember your country. Do not give it away. The white man will cheat you out of your home. I have taken no pay from the United States. I have never sold our land." In this treaty Lawyer acted without authority from our band. He had no right to sell the Wallowa (*winding water*) country. That had always belonged to my father's own people, and the other bands had never disputed our right to it. No other Indians ever claimed Wallowa.

In order to have all people understand how much land we owned, my father planted poles around it and said:

"Inside is the home of my people—the white man may take the land outside. Inside this boundary all our people were born. It circles around the graves of our fathers, and we will never give up these graves to any man."

The United States claimed they had bought all the Nez Percés country outside of Lapwai Reservation, from Lawyer and other chiefs, but we continued to live on this land in peace until eight years ago, when white men began to come inside the bounds my father had set. We warned them against this great wrong, but they would not leave our land, and some bad blood was raised. The white men represented that they were going upon the war-path. They reported many things that were false.

The United States Government again asked for a treaty council. My father had become blind and feeble. He could no longer speak for his people. It was then that I took my father's place as chief. In this council I made my first speech to white men. I said to the agent who held the council:

"I did not want to come to this council, but I came hoping that we could save blood. The white man has no right to come here and take our country. We have never accepted any presents from the Government. Neither Lawyer nor any other chief had authority to sell this land. It has always belonged to my people. It came unclouded to them from our fathers, and we will defend this land as long as a drop of Indian blood warms the hearts of our men."

The agent said he had orders, from the Great White Chief at Washington, for us to go upon the Lapwai Reservation, and that if we obeyed he would help us in many ways. "You *must* move to the agency," he said. I answered him: "I will not. I do not need your help; we have plenty, and we are contented and happy if the white man will let us alone. The reservation is too small for so many people with all their stock. You can keep your presents; we can go to your towns and pay for all we need; we have plenty of horses and cattle to sell, and we won't have any help from you; we are free now; we can go where we please. Our fathers were born here. Here they lived, here they died, here are their graves. We will never leave them." The agent went away, and we had peace for a little while.

Soon after this my father sent for me. I saw he was dying. I took his hand in mine. He said: "My son, my body is returning to my mother earth, and my spirit is going very soon to see the Great Spirit Chief. When I am gone, think of your country. You are the chief of these people. They look to you to guide them. Always remember that your father never sold his country. You must stop your ears whenever you are asked to sign a treaty selling your home. A few years more, and white men will be all around you. They have their eyes on this land. My son, never forget my dying words. This country holds your father's body. Never sell the bones of your father and your mother." I pressed my father's hand and told him I would protect his grave with my life. My father smiled and passed away to the spirit-land.

I buried him in that beautiful valley of winding waters. I love that land more than all the rest of the world. A man who would not love his father's grave is worse than a wild animal.

For a short time we lived quietly. But this could not last. White men had found gold in the mountains around the land of the winding water. They stole a great many horses from us, and we could not get them back because we were Indians. The white men told lies for each other. They drove off a great many of our cattle. Some white men branded our young cattle so they could claim them. We had no friend who would plead our cause before the law councils. It seemed to me that some of the white men in Wallowa were doing these things on purpose to get up a war. They knew that we were not strong enough to fight them. I labored hard to avoid trouble and bloodshed. We gave up some of our country to the white men, thinking that then we could have peace. We were mistaken. The white man would not let us alone. We could have avenged our wrongs many times, but we did not. Whenever the Government has asked us to help them against other Indians, we have never refused. When the white men were few and we were strong we could have killed them all off, but the Nez Percés wished to live at peace.

If we have not done so, we have not been to blame. I believe that the old treaty has never been correctly reported. If we ever owned the land we own it still, for we never sold it. In the treaty councils the commissioners have claimed that our country had been sold to the Government. Suppose a white man should come to me and say, "Joseph, I like your horses, and I want to buy them." I say to him, "No my horses suit me, I will not sell them." Then he goes to my neighbor, and says to him: "Joseph has some good horses. I want to buy them, but he refuses to sell." My neighbor answers, "Pay me the money, and I will sell you Joseph's horses." The white man returns to me, and says, "Joseph, I have bought your horse, and you must let me have them." If we sold our lands to the Government, this is the way they were bought. . . .

Source: Joseph, Chief. "An Indian's View of Indian Affairs." *North American Review*, no. 128 (April 1879): 415–420.

DOCUMENT
3.9

A Montana Resident Praises Territorial Policies against "Destructive Wild Animals"

"The Bounty Is . . . One Dollar on a Wolf, Eight Dollars on . . . Panthers, and the Same on Bears"

July 22, 1886

During America's westward expansion, eradication of predatory animals such as wolves, coyotes, mountain lions, and bears was a high priority—just as it had been for earlier generations of settlers in the East. Annihilation of these species was pursued partly for pocketbook reasons: These predators posed a potential threat to livestock and crops. But there also was a philosophical component to the war on wolves and bears and cougars.

These creatures loomed as the embodiment of the savage wilderness that Americans were determined to subdue and make their own. State and territorial governments took an active role in carrying out these eradication campaigns. They offered bounties on a wide assortment of predator species (although wolves and coyotes were the chief targets), dispensed poisons to ranchers and hunters, and pursued resource policies that transformed wild sanctuaries of habitat into mining towns, pasturelands, and clear-cuts. These policies are discussed in considerable depth in the following letter, which appeared in the July 22, 1886, issue of Forest and Stream *magazine. Written by a correspondent identified only as Carl from Fort Keogh, Montana, the letter details a number of the bounty and other eradication policies supported by officials, legislators, and cattlemen in the Montana Territory in the 1880s.*

Montana is simply overrun with destructive wild animals at present. During the year 1884, soon after the last buffalo disappeared across the Canadian border, and when the great herds of domestic cattle succeeded to the stamping grounds of the native bison, there was a remarkable increase in the number of gray wolves on the Montana ranges. To be accurate, this species of wolf, together with his cousin, the prairie coyote, always did hang around the buffalo herds, ever watchful to pounce upon some superannuated bull driven from the band by the younger ones, or to snap up some weak calf or unwise animal that chances to stray too far from the main body. With the disappearance of the buffaloes from Montana, these scavengers of the prairie also disappeared, because, being left without sufficient food supply, they of course followed the wild herds as they retired to more remote pastures. In 1884 the great buffalo herds in the Canadian northwest became pretty well decimated, and so the wolves returned to their old haunts. Not being so particular as to object to beefsteak when buffalo hump was not to be had, they played sad havoc with the cattle herds that year. Cattlemen did not begin to pay much attention to the matter until last year, when it was found that it knocked considerably from their profits to support such immense swarms of these pests. Cattle and especially young and weak calves, dropped during the winter time, have been the food upon which they subsisted.

In 1884 the Territory offered a bounty for the scalps of destructive wild animals brought in to be punched. The bounty is fifty cents on a coyote, one dollar on a wolf, eight dollars on mountains lions or panthers, and the same on bears. This law cost the Territorial Treasurer $12,740.50 that year, besides which nearly every county offered as much, if not more for the scalps of wild animals than did the Territory. Many cowboys entered into the scheme of poisoning wolves, which besides affording them plenty of sport and winter amusement, also yielded a handsome largess for the ear punching, after which the skins were sold. In this way a number of the cowboys more than doubled their summer's pay which they received for rounding up and herding cattle. Some of the counties also offered strychnine to all who would use it, and even some of the cattlemen volunteered to subscribe a beef or two. This latter alternative, however, was not necessary, as there are always sufficient dead animals lying around to be used for bait and even the wolves and coyotes themselves manufactured plenty of material for their own destructions in the animals they killed for food. Such an industrious warfare has been carried on for two years against the coyotes and wolves, that one would suppose the rascally thieves would begin to show a diminution in numbers, but such is not the case.

In 1885 they were on the ranges in greater swarms than ever and the damage they did counted heavily against the profits for the year. On the chestnut range in Northwestern

Montana the stockmen came to the front with a handsome offer to wolf killers, which will make it a paying business for anybody to engage in that occupation alone. It will give the wolfer plenty of poison and not less than $5 for each skin, after which he is at liberty to sell the hides for what he can get.

Mr. Wallace Taylor, of Choteau County, in a recent letter, reported a bad state of affairs in his section of the country, occasioned by the wolves devouring cattle and sheep. He says, "The animals are rapidly increasing and getting bolder every day. They even attack bulls and large cows, and in many instances get away with them. The stockmen are doing everything in their power to exterminate them by the liberal use of poison and the increase of bounty; but thus far the animals have not diminished, and the stockmen fear they will actually be obliged to leave that part of the Territory and secure other quarters." Mr. Taylor is a reliable gentleman, who is not given to exaggeration, so we may receive with the utmost confidence what he says. Mr. Chas. Smith, inspector of the cattle district in and around Helena, in his last report speaks particularly of the great loss of lambs by depredating wolves. "The animals are rapidly increasing," he says, "and getting bolder and more ferocious each day. The sheepmen are becoming frightened over the rapid disappearance of their flocks and are using every means to exterminate the pests." At the last convention of cattlemen, held at Miles City, the question of destroying wolves was one of the principal topics discussed. The discussion developed the fact that the number of calves destroyed by the wolves is simply astounding, and a campaign in earnest was organized against these nuisances. One stockman stated he could show carcasses of fifteen or twenty calves which had been killed by wolves near his ranch. Another stockman had found four in one day near his ranch that the wolves had slain and all agreed that there had been a large increase of wolves in the country this year. One hundred and fifty dollars was in a few minutes paid into the hands of the chairman of the committee to purchase poison to be given to those who wished to kill wolves. In addition to the above, the chairman of the wolf committee informed all that it was expected of each stockman to keep on hand a large supply of poison, and have his employees put it out judiciously and persistently. Mr. Van Buren, a member present, announced his intention of putting out a supply of poison 150 miles in length, and many of the stockmen present offered to furnish him meat to use for bait. . . .

As before remarked, some of the cowboys have gone regularly into the business of wolf killing. J.W. Proctor, of Billings, arrived a day or two ago from the Musselshell, where he spread a string of poisoned meat thirty miles long, for the delectation of the gray wolves and coyotes out there. Unfortunately a heavy snow storm covered up the bait, but nevertheless a great many "varmints" were bagged; certainly sufficient to pay all expenses and leave a handsome margin besides.

In Yellowstone County the boys have struck quite a bonanza. In addition to the territorial bounty the county offers one dollar on a coyote, and two dollars on a wolf. This just doubles the territorial bounty on each animal killed or brought in.

A young fellow named Martin, with not much on his hands except idle time, practiced a week at the business in Yellowstone county, and the result was nine wolf skins and twenty-six coyote skins. To sum up he got $13 and $26 for coyote ears, and $9 and $18 for those of the wolves; after which he sold the hides for an average of about $1.50 each to a fur dealer in Billings. Total profit, $118.50 and lots of fun; cost about $5.00 for strychnine and time. Bait was had in one dead animal picked up on the range.

Source: "Montana Wolves and Panthers." *Forest and Stream* 26 (July 22, 1886): 508–509.

William Hornaday Laments the Extermination of the Bison

DOCUMENT
3.10

"The Wild Creatures Were Gradually Swept Away"

1889

During the course of the nineteenth century, the American buffalo experienced a stunning population crash brought on by habitat loss, disease, and heedless market hunger for hides and other bison parts. The buffalo population plummeted from tens of millions of creatures to near extinction in less than a century. This virtual extinguishment of the great buffalo herds of the plains is almost universally regarded today as one of the most shameful chapters in American environmental history.

Conservationist and zoologist William Temple Hornaday monitored the final decades of this slaughter from Washington, D.C., where he served as chief taxidermist of the United States National Museum at the Smithsonian Institution. He traveled to Montana in 1886 in this official capacity to obtain bison specimens for the museum. He succeeded in this endeavor but was haunted by the sight of vast plains now emptied of bison. Three years later Hornaday published The Extermination of the American Bison, *a mournful elegy for the seemingly doomed creature. His book, however, managed to spark successful conservation efforts on behalf of the buffalo. And Hornaday, who went on to become the first director of the New York Zoological Park, devoted much of his later life to bison protection and conservation.*

In the following excerpts from Hornaday's influential book, the author first attacks the unsustainable slaughter of the bison as an epic example of economic stupidity. Hornaday also notes how depriving Native Americans of the bison has increased their dependence on federal financial assistance. He then goes on to condemn American policymakers for their refusal to take measures to save the bison—and ridicule them for their claims of powerlessness in the matter. Finally, Hornaday issues a demand for new wildlife conservation policies at the local, state, and especially federal levels. He asserts that if lawmakers, administrators, and citizens fail to take action on behalf of other threatened—and economically valuable—species of wildlife, many of those species will be pushed to the same abyss.

It may fairly be supposed that if the people of this country could have been made to realize the immense money value of the great buffalo herds as they existed in 1870, a vigorous and successful effort would have been made to regulate and restrict the slaughter. The fur seal of Alaska, of which about 100,000 are killed annually for their skins, yield an annual revenue to the Government of $100,000 and add $900,000 more to the actual wealth of the United States. It pays to protect those seals, and we mean to protect them against all comers who seek their unrestricted slaughter, no matter whether the poachers be American, English, Russian, or Canadian. It would be folly to do otherwise, and if those who would exterminate the fur seal by shooting them in the water will not desist for the telling, then they must by the compelling.

The fur seal is a good investment for the United States, and their number is not diminishing. As the buffalo herds existed in 1870, 500,000 head of bulls, young and old, could have been killed every year for a score of years without sensibly diminishing the size of the herds. At a low estimate these could easily have been made to yield various products worth $5 each, as follows: Kobe, $2.50; tongue, 20 cents; meat of hindquarters, $2; bones, horns, and hoofs, 25 cents; total, $5. And the amount annually added to the wealth of the United States would have been $2,500,000.

On all the robes taken for the market, say, 200,000, the Government could have collected a tax of 50 cents each, which would have yielded a sum doubly sufficient to have maintained a force of mounted police fully competent to enforce the laws regulating the slaughter. Had a contract for the protection of the buffalo been offered at $50,000 per annum, say, or even half that sum, an army of competent men would have competed for it every year, and it could have been carried out to the letter. But, as yet, the American people have not learned to spend money for the protection of valuable game; and by the time they do learn it, there will be no game to protect.

Even despite the enormous waste of raw material that ensued in the utilization of the buffalo product, the total cash value of all the material derived from this source, if it could only be reckoned up, would certainly amount to many millions of dollars—perhaps twenty millions, all told. This estimate may, to some, seem high, but when we stop to consider that in eight years, from 1876 to 1884, a single firm, that of Messrs. J. & A. Boskowitz, 105 Greene street, New York, paid out the enormous sum of $923,070 (nearly one million) for robes and hides, and that in a single year (1882) another firm, that of Joseph Ullman, 165 Mercer street, New York, paid out $216,250 for robes and hides, it may not seem so incredible. . . .

> *We come now to a history which I would gladly leave unwritten. Its record is a disgrace to the American people in general, and the Territorial, State, and General Government in particular.*
>
> —William Temple Hornaday

The Eskimo has his seal, which yields nearly everything that he requires; the Korak of Siberia depends for his very existence upon his reindeer; the Ceylon native has the cocoa-nut palm, which leaves him little else to desire, and the North American Indian had the American bison. If any animal was ever designed by the hand of nature for the express purpose of supplying, at one stroke, nearly all the wants of an entire race, surely the buffalo was intended for the Indian.

And right well was this gift of the gods utilized by the children of nature to whom it came. Up to the time when the United States Government began to support our Western Indians by the payment of annuities and furnishing quarterly supplies of food, clothing, blankets, cloth, tents, etc., the buffalo had been the main dependence of more than 50,000

Indians who inhabited the buffalo range and its environs. Of the many different uses to which the buffalo and his various parts were, put by the red man, the following were the principal ones:

The body of the buffalo yielded fresh meat, of which thousands of tons were consumed; dried meat, prepared in summer for winter use; pemmican (also prepared in summer), of meat, fat, and berries; tallow, made up into large balls or sacks, and kept in store; marrow, preserved in bladders; and tongues, dried and smoked, and eaten as a delicacy.

The skin of the buffalo yielded a robe, dressed with the hair on, for clothing and bedding; a hide, dressed without the hair, which made a teepee cover, when a number were sewn together; boats, when sewn together in a green state, over a wooden framework. Shields, made from the thickest portions, as rawhide; ropes, made up as rawhide; clothing of many kinds; bags for use in traveling; coffins, or winding sheets for the dead, etc.

Other portions utilized were sinews, which furnished fiber for ropes, thread, bow-strings, snow-shoe webs, etc.; hair, which was sometimes made into belts and ornaments; "buffalo chips," which formed a valuable and highly-prized fuel; bones, from which many articles of use and ornament were made; horns, which were made into spoons, drinking vessels, etc. . . .

The total disappearance of the buffalo has made no perceptible difference in the annual cost of the Indians to the Government. During the years when buffaloes were numerous and robes for the purchase of fire-arms and cartridges were plentiful, Indian wars were frequent, and always costly to the Government. The Indians were then quite independent, because they could take the war path at any time and live on buffalo indefinitely. Now, the case is very different. The last time Sitting Bull went on the war-path and was driven up into Manitoba, he had the doubtful pleasure of living on his ponies and dogs until he became utterly starved out. Since his last escapade, the Sioux have been compelled to admit that the game is up and the war-path is open to them no longer. Should they wish to do otherwise they know that they could survive only by killing cattle, and cattle that are guarded by cowboys and ranchmen are no man's game. Therefore, while we no longer have to pay for an annual campaign in force against hostile Indians, the total absence of the buffalo brings upon the nation the entire support of the Indian, and the cash outlay each year is as great as ever.

The value of the American bison to civilized man can never be calculated, nor even fairly estimated. It may with safety be said, however, that it has been probably tenfold greater than most persons have ever supposed. It would be a work of years to gather statistics of the immense bulk of robes and hides, undoubtedly amounting to millions in the aggregate; the thousands of tons of meat, and the train-loads of bones which have been actually utilized by man. Nor can the effect of the bison's presence upon the general development of the great West ever be calculated. It has sunk into the great sum total of our progress, and well nigh lost to sight forever. . . .

I. Causes of the Extermination.

The causes which led to the practical extinction (in a wild state, at least) of the most economically valuable wild animal that ever inhabited the American continent, are by no means obscure. It is well that we should know precisely what they were, and by the sad fate of the buffalo be warned in time against allowing similar causes to produce the same results with our elk, antelope, deer, moose, caribou, mountain sheep, mountain goat, walrus, and other animals. It will be doubly deplorable if the remorseless slaughter we have witnessed during the last twenty years carries with it no lessons for the future. A continuation of the record we have lately made as wholesale game butchers will justify posterity in dating us back with the mound-builders and cave-dwellers, when man's only known function was to slay and eat.

The primary cause of the buffalo's extermination, and the one which embraced all others, was the descent of civilization, with all its elements of destructiveness, upon the whole of the country inhabited by that animal. From the Great Slave Lake to the Rio

Grande the home of the buffalo was everywhere overrun by the man with a gun; and, as has ever been the case, the wild creatures were gradually swept away, the largest and most conspicuous forms being the first to go.

The secondary causes of the extermination of the buffalo may be catalogued as follows:

1. Man's reckless greed, his wanton destructiveness, and improvidence in not husbanding such resources as come to him from the hand of nature ready made.
2. The total and utterly inexcusable absence of protective measures and agencies on the part of the National Government and of the West States and Territories.
3. The fatal preference on the part of hunters generally, both white and red, for the robe and flesh of the cow over that furnished by the bull.
4. The phenomenal stupidity of the animals themselves, and their indifference to man.
5. The perfection of modern breech-loading rifles and other sporting fire-arms in general.

Each of these causes acted against the buffalo with its fall force, to offset which there was *not even one* restraining or preserving influence, and it is not to be wondered at that the species went down before them. Had any one of these conditions been eliminated the result would have been reached far less quickly. Had the buffalo, for example, possessed one-half the fighting qualities of the grizzly bear he would have fared very differently, but his inoffensiveness and lack of courage almost leads one to doubt the wisdom of the economy of nature so far as it relates to him. . . .

THE PERIOD OF SYSTEMATIC SLAUGHTER . . .

We come now to a history which I would gladly leave unwritten. Its record is a disgrace to the American people in general, and the Territorial, State, and General Government in particular. It will cause succeeding generations to regard us as being possessed of the leading characteristics of the savage and the beast of prey—cruelty and greed. We will be likened to the blood-thirsty tiger of the Indian jungle, who slaughters a dozen bullocks at once when he knows he can eat only one.

In one respect, at least, the white men who engaged in the systematic slaughter of the bison were savages just as much as the Piegan Indians, who would drive a whole herd over a precipice to secure a week's rations of meat for a single village. The men who killed buffaloes for their tongues and those who shot them from the railway trains for sport were murderers. In no way does civilized man so quickly revert to his former state as when he is alone with the beasts of the field. Give him a gun and something which he may kill without getting himself in trouble, and, presto! he is instantly a savage again, finding exquisite delight in bloodshed, slaughter, and death, if not for gain, then solely for the joy and happiness of it. There is no kind of warfare against game animals too unfair, too disreputable, or too mean for white men to engage in if they can only do so with safety to their own precious carcasses. They will shoot buffalo and antelope from running railway trains, drive deer into water with hounds and cut their throats in cold blood, kill does with fawns a week old, kill fawns by the score for their spotted skins, slaughter deer, moose, and caribou in the snow at a pitiful disadvantage, just as the wolves do; exterminate the wild ducks on the whole Atlantic seaboard with punt guns for the metropolitan markets; kill off the Rocky Mountain goats for hides worth only 50 cents apiece, destroy wagon loads of trout with dynamite, and so on to the end of the chapter. . . .

The slaughter of the buffalo down to the very point of extermination has been so very generally condemned, and the general Government has been so unsparingly blamed for allowing such a massacre to take place on the public domain, it is important that the public should know all the facts in the case. To the credit of Congress it must be said that several very determined efforts were made between the years 1871 and 1876 looking toward the protection of the buffalo. The failure of all those well-meant efforts was due to our republican form of Government. Had this Government been a monarchy the buffalo would have been protected; but unfortunately in this case (perhaps the only one on record wherein a king could have accomplished more than the representatives of the people) the necessary act of Congress was so hedged in and beset by obstacles that it never became an accomplished fact. Even when both houses of Congress succeeded in passing a suitable act (June 23, 1874) it went to the President in the last days of the session only to be pigeon-holed, and die a natural death. . . .

At various times the legislatures of a few of the Western States and Territories enacted laws vaguely and feebly intended to provide some sort of protection to the fast disappearing animals. One of the first was the game law of Colorado, passed in 1872, which declared that the killers of game should not leave any flesh to spoil. The western game laws of those days amounted to about as much as they do now; practically nothing at all. I have never been able to learn of a single instance, save in the Yellowstone Park, wherein a western hunter was prevented by so simple and innocuous a thing as a game law from killing game. Laws were enacted, but they were always left to enforce themselves. The idea of the frontiersman (the average, at least) has always been to kill as much game as possible before some other fellow gets a chance at it, *and before it is all killed off!* So he goes at the game, and as a general thing kills all he can while it lasts, and with it feeds himself and family, his dogs, and even his hogs, to repletion. I knew one Montana man north of Miles City who killed for his own use twenty-six black-tail deer in one season, and had so much more venison than he could consume or give away that a great pile of carcasses lay in his yard until spring and spoiled.

During the existence of the buffalo it was declared by many an impossibility to stop or prevent the slaughter. Such an accusation of weakness and imbecility on the part of the General Government is an insult to our strength and resources. The protection of game is now and always has been simply a question of money. A proper code of game laws and a reasonable number of salaried game-wardens, sworn to enforce them and punish all offenses against them, would have afforded the buffalo as much protection as would have been necessary to his continual existence. To be sure, many buffaloes would have been killed on the sly in spite of laws to the contrary, but it was wholesale slaughter that wrought the extermination, and that could easily have been prevented. A tax of 50 cents each on buffalo robes would have maintained a sufficient number of game-wardens to have reasonably regulated the killing, and maintained for an indefinite period a bountiful source of supply of food, and also raiment for both the white man of the plains and the Indian. By judicious management the buffalo could have been made to yield an annual revenue equal to that we now receive from the fur-seals—$100,000 per year. . . .

There is nowhere in this country, nor in any of the waters adjacent to it, a living species of any kind which the United States Government can not fully and perpetually protect from destruction by human agencies if it chooses to do so. The destruction of the buffalo was a loss of wealth perhaps twenty times greater than the sum it would have cost to conserve it, and this stupendous waste of valuable food and other products was committed by one class of the American people and permitted by another with a prodigality and wastefulness which even in the lowest savages would be inexcusable.

Source: Hornaday, William T. *The Extermination of the American Bison.* From *The Report of the National Museum, 1886-'87.* Washington, D.C.: Government Printing Office, 1889, pp. 438–441, 471, 496–497, 523, 529.

DOCUMENT
3.11

An Act to Protect Salmon Runs in Alaska

"To Prevent the . . . Exhaustion of These Valuable Fisheries"

March 2, 1889

During the last quarter of the nineteenth century, wildlife conservation became an increasingly prominent part of the legislative agenda at the local, state, and federal levels. To be sure, resistance to these measures was strong among some lawmakers, corporate interests, and citizens. In addition, enforcement mechanisms for these policies remained poorly funded and indifferently carried out in many instances. Nonetheless, legislative acts crafted to protect economically valuable wildlife species proliferated during this era. One such representative act, a federal measure to protect Alaskan salmon, is reprinted here.

AN ACT TO PROVIDE FOR THE PROTECTION OF THE SALMON FISHERIES OF ALASKA, MARCH 2, 1889.

Be it enacted, &c., That the erection of dams, barricades, or other obstructions in any of the rivers of Alaska, with the purpose or result of preventing or impeding the ascent of salmon or other anadromous species to their spawning grounds, is hereby declared to be unlawful, and the Secretary of the Treasury is hereby authorized and directed to establish such regulations and surveillance as may be necessary to insure that this prohibition is strictly enforced and to otherwise protect the salmon fisheries of Alaska;

And every person who shall be found guilty of a violation of the provisions of this section shall be fined not less than two hundred and fifty dollars for each day of the continuance of such obstruction.

SEC. 2. That the Commissioner of Fish and Fisheries is hereby empowered and directed to institute an investigation into the habits, abundance, and distribution of the salmon of Alaska, as well as the present conditions and methods of the fisheries, with a view of recommending to Congress such additional legislation as may be necessary to prevent the impairment or exhaustion of these valuable fisheries, and placing them under regular and permanent conditions of production.

SEC. 3. That section nineteen hundred and fifty-six of the Revised Statutes of the United States is hereby declared to include and apply to all the dominion of the United States in the waters of Behring Sea;

And it shall be the duty of the President, at a timely season in each year, to issue his proclamation and cause the same to be published for one month in at least one newspaper if any such there be published at each United States port of entry on the Pacific coast, warning all persons against entering said waters for the purpose of violating the provisions of said section; and he shall also cause one or more vessels of the United States to diligently cruise said waters and arrest all persons, and seize all vessels found to be, or to have been, engaged in any violation of the laws of the United States therein.

Source: *Supplement to the Revised Statutes of the United States.* Edited by William A. Richardson. Washington, D.C.: Government Printing Office, 1891, p. 701.

DOCUMENT
3.12

A Former Interior Secretary Calls for a "Rational Forest Policy"

"A Spendthrift People Recklessly Wasting Its Heritage"

October 15, 1889

Carl Schurz was one of the most important voices for environmental conservation of the nineteenth century. During his tenure as secretary of the Department of Interior from 1877 to 1881 in the Hayes Administration, Schurz maneuvered to curb illegal logging, use science in crafting forest policies, educate Americans about the environmental and economic importance of healthy forests, and garner support for the creation of federal forest reserves. He also strongly defended John Wesley Powell's much-criticized but prophetic report on the limitations of settlement in the arid regions of the West.

Many of Schurz's efforts to implement reforms in America's natural resources laws were thwarted by lawmakers who believed that the German-born secretary did not understand the nation's economic needs or appreciate the full scale of its natural wealth. But even after retirement, Schurz continued to press for government reforms, especially in the realm of forest policy. On October 15, 1889, for example, Carl Schurz appeared before a gathering of members of the American Forestry Association and the Pennsylvania Forestry Association in Philadelphia and delivered a manifesto for forest protection that was remarkable for its time. Schurz's "The Need of a Rational Forest Policy" speech acknowledged that some timber harvesting served "legitimate wants," but it castigated congressmen, timber thieves, and careless citizens alike for their "criminally reckless" treatment of the forests. It also emphasized the importance of forests to national water supplies, and it called on lawmakers and bureaucrats at both the state and federal levels to adopt policies for forest conservation and sustainable logging practices. Schurz's speech, excerpted here, has been credited with helping build congressional support for passage of the landmark General Revision Act of 1891, which included vital provisions for the establishment of national forest reserves.

Members of the forestry associations, and ladies and gentlemen:

I cannot refrain from expressing my thanks to the Committee of Arrangements for doing me the honor of inviting me to take part in this meeting. It is true, not until yesterday could I see my way clear to come, and I have not been able to prepare an elaborate address, such as seems to have been expected of me. All I can offer is a few offhand remarks, more in the nature of a conversational talk than of a formal speech. I pray you, therefore, to divest yourselves of all solemnity of expectation.

Let me in the first place assure you of my most earnest sympathy in your efforts. I am heart and soul with you: nor is this to me a new subject. I know the advocates of the cause to which you are devoted are looked upon by many as a set of amiable sentimentalists, who have fallen in love with the greenness of the woods and break out in hysteric wails when a tree is cut down. I assure you I have been led to take an earnest interest in this subject by considerations of an entirely unsentimental, practical nature, and this, no doubt, is the case with most of you. The more study and thought I have given the matter, the firmer has become my conviction that the destruction of the forests of this country will be the murder of its future prosperity and progress. This is no mere figure of speech, no rhetorical exaggeration. It is simply the teaching of the world's history, which no fair-minded man can study without reaching the same conclusion.

I am aware that there are people who turn with a sneer from the expression of any fear that our country may become sterile; who profess to be highly amused when those countries in Asia are pointed out to them which once were called lands "flowing with milk and honey"; whose mountains were covered with forests, whose hills with the vine and the fig-tree and whose plains with waving grainfields, which nourished teeming and prosperous populations, building up mighty cities and great monuments of the civilization of their times; now bare soil, barren and desolate wastes and deserts, roamed over by wild beasts and robbers, the ancient prosperity changed into misery, famine and decay, the people relapsed into barbarism; or when we point to Spain, once covered with a luxuriant vegetation, one of the most fertile countries of antiquity, the granary of the Roman Empire; at the close of the middle ages still the realm in whose dominions the sun never set; now in a great measure stripped bare, the old fertility gone, the people in large districts struggling with poverty and want.

The destruction of our forests is so fearfully rapid that, if we go on at the same rate, men whose hair is already gray will see the day when in the United States from Maine to California and from the Mexican Gulf to Puget Sound there will be no forest left worthy of the name.

—Carl Schurz

Infatuated persons among us turn up their noses at these and similar lessons and superciliously exclaim: What do we in this great and free country of ours care about abroad? Let me say to you that the laws of nature are the same everywhere. Whoever violates them anywhere, must always pay the penalty. No country ever so great and rich, no nation ever so powerful, inventive and enterprising can violate them with impunity. We most grievously delude ourselves if we think that we can form an exception to the rule. And we have made already a most dangerous beginning, and more than a beginning, in the work of desolation. The destruction of our forests is so fearfully rapid that, if we go on at the same rate, men whose hair is already gray will see the day when in the United States from Maine to California and from the Mexican Gulf to Puget Sound there will be no forest left worthy of the name.

Who is guilty of that destruction? It is not merely the lumberman cutting timber on his own land for legitimate use in the pursuit of business gain; it is the lumberman who, in doing so, destroys and wastes as much more without benefit to anybody. It is not merely the settler or the miner taking logs for his cabin and fence-rails and fire-wood, or timber for building a shaft, but it is the settler and the miner laying waste acres or stripping a mountain slope to get a few sticks. It is all these, serving indeed legitimate wants, but doing it with a wastefulness criminally reckless.

But it is not only these. It is the timber thief—making haste to strip the public domain of what he can lay his hands on, lest another timber thief get ahead of him—and, in doing this, destroying sometimes far more than he steals. It is the tourist, the hunter, the mining prospector who, lighting his camp-fire in the woods to boil water for his coffee or to fry his bacon, and leaving that fire un-extinguished when he proceeds, sets the woods in flames and delivers countless square miles of forest to destruction.

It is all these, but it is something more, and, let us confess it, something worse. It is a public opinion looking with indifference on this wanton, barbarous, disgraceful vandalism. It is a spendthrift people recklessly wasting its heritage. It is a Government careless of the future and unmindful of a pressing duty.

I have had some personal experience of this. The gentleman who introduced me did me the honor of mentioning the attention I devoted to this subject years ago as Secretary of the Interior. When I entered upon that important office, having the public lands in charge, I considered it my first duty to look around me and to study the problems I had to deal with. Doing so I observed all the wanton waste and devastation I have described. I observed the notion that the public forests were everybody's property, to be taken and used or wasted as anybody pleased, everywhere in full operation. I observed enterprising timber thieves not merely stealing trees, but stealing whole forests. I observed hundreds of sawmills in full blast, devoted exclusively to the sawing up of timber stolen from the public lands. I observed a most lively export trade going on from Gulf ports as well as Pacific ports, with fleets of vessels employed in carrying timber stolen from the public lands to be sold in foreign countries, immense tracts being devastated that some robbers might fill their pockets.

I thought that this sort of stealing was wrong, in this country no less than elsewhere. Moreover, it was against the spirit and letter of the law. I, therefore, deemed it my duty to arrest that audacious and destructive robbery. Not that I had intended to prevent the settler and the miner from taking from the public lands what they needed for their cabins, their fields or their mining shafts; but I deemed it my duty to stop at least the commercial depredations upon the property of the people. And to that end I used my best endeavors and the means at my disposal, scanty as they were.

What was the result? No sooner did my attempts in that direction become known, than I was pelted with telegraphic despatches from the regions most concerned, indignantly inquiring what it meant that an officer of the Government dared to interfere with the legitimate business of the country! Members of Congress came down upon me, some with wrath in their eyes, others pleading in a milder way, but all solemnly protesting against my disturbing their constituents in this peculiar pursuit of happiness. I persevered in the performance of my plain duty. But when I set forth my doings in my annual report and asked Congress for rational forestry legislation, you should have witnessed the sneers at the outlandish notions of this "foreigner" in the Interior Department. . . .

What the result of my appeals was at the time I am speaking of, you know. We succeeded in limiting somewhat the extent of the depredations upon the public forests, and in bringing some of the guilty parties to justice. A few hundred thousand dollars were recovered for timber stolen, but the recommendations of rational forestry legislation went for nothing. Some laws were indeed passed, but they appeared rather to favor the taking of timber from the public lands than to stop it. Still, I persevered, making appeal after appeal, in public and in private, but I found myself standing almost solitary and alone.

Deaf was Congress, and deaf the people seemed to be. Only a few still voices rose up here and there in the press in favor of the policy I pursued. Thank Heaven, the people appear to be deaf no longer. It is in a great measure owing to your wise and faithful efforts that the people begin to listen, and that in several States practical steps have already been taken in the right direction.

As the chairman very truthfully and pointedly said, the forestry question divides itself into two branches, preservation and restoration. The first appears at present by far the most important. There are forests in this as in all countries, the preservation of which is absolutely necessary, because they perform an office which nothing else can perform.

Whatever differences of opinion there may be as to the influence of the forest on climate in other respects, it is universally conceded that the forest is in an important sense the regulator of the flow of waters. It is a well-known story. Springs and water-courses which flow with steadiness while the forest stands, are, when the forest has disappeared, dried up or at least largely reduced in volume one part of the year, to be transformed into raging and destructive torrents during another part. In the shape in which it would be a blessing, the water fails. It appears in the shape of a curse. Of paramount necessity, therefore, is the preservation of the forest which covers the headwaters of the great rivers and their affluents, especially in the mountain regions with steep and rocky slopes, where the forest once destroyed can never be restored. Once strip the precipitous mountainside, and the rain and melting snow will soon wash down the scanty soil; the naked rock will appear on the surface, and the growth of a protecting vegetation will be impossible forever. The mountain torrents, swelled by rain and melted snow that no longer find any earth to soak, will then periodically rush down with undiminished volume, inundating the valleys below, and in many cases covering them with gravel and loose rock swept down from the steep slopes, gradually rendering them unfit for agriculture and sometimes even for the habitation of men. I have had occasion to observe such results in more than one instance.

The preservation of mountain forests of this kind is therefore of supreme importance, and where they are still in public possession they should be set apart as permanent reservations, either by the several States or by the General Government—or when they are in private hands, they should, if possible, be regained by the Government and reserved.

Steps of that kind have fortunately been taken with regard to the Adirondacks in New York, but those steps have unfortunately been too long delayed, for, as is reported, the destruction of the Adirondack forests has already gone far enough to cause a diminution of the reliable water supply in the Mohawk and Hudson rivers of from thirty to fifty per cent; nor have they proved effective and comprehensive enough, for that destruction is still going on at a distressing rate. As to Pennsylvania, a service of incalculable value would be rendered to her people if the State regained control over the forest lands in the heart of her mountain regions, for the hand of the destroyer is mercilessly active. A few years ago I happened, on a railroad inspection, to penetrate into the mountains of north-western Pennsylvania and beheld a spectacle of direful import. A corporation, a large majority of whose stock was said to be held in Massachusetts, had acquired an area of forest land of, if I remember rightly, 200,000 acres. They not only cut down every tree, but they destroyed even the underbrush, not leaving a stick or a shoot standing. They made the mountainsides as bare as the palm of my hand. And when I asked the superintending officer of the company what was meant by this radical destruction, which would not even leave a chance for the forest to grow up on these slopes in the future, the answer was, that the company did not wish the forest to grow up there again; it was its object first to sell the logs and then to clear the land for the purpose of selling it as pasture. It is not hazard-ous to predict that when those mountainsides have been washed by rain for a few seasons, many, if not most of them, will no longer furnish verdure enough to nourish a goat. Such things are going on in the mountains of Pennsylvania, and unless in some way they be stopped, it will soon be too late.

There is a mountain region in the far Northwest which demands the earliest possi-ble attention of our National authorities. It is the great area of mountain forest covering the headwaters of the Missouri and Columbia. The Government cannot too soon take effective steps to protect these forests, which are among the most important in the United States, against destruction, by making them a permanent reservation and having them carefully guarded.

When speaking of the preservation of forests, we do not . . . mean that they should be kept untouched and unused as the miser keeps his hoard, but that they should be made useful in a way preventing their destruction and even improving their value, as forests are made useful in other civilized countries.

In my first annual report as Secretary of the Interior, twelve years ago, I made some recommendations leading to that end, the main points being in substantial accord with the project of a bill drafted by your committee. Permit me to read them:

All timber lands still belonging to the United States should be withdrawn from the operation of the preemption and homestead laws, as well as the location of the various kinds of scrip.

Timber lands fit for agricultural purposes should be sold, if sold at all, only for cash, and so graded in price as to make the purchaser pay for the value of the timber on the land. This will be apt to make the settler careful and provident in the disposition he makes of the timber.

A sufficient number of Government agents should be provided to protect the tim-ber on public lands from depredation, and to institute to this end the necessary proceed-ings against depredators, by seizures and by criminal as well as civil actions. Such agents should also be authorized and instructed, under the direction of the Department of the Interior or the Department of Agriculture, to sell for the United States, in order to satisfy the current local demand, timber from the public lands under proper regulations, and in doing so especially to see to it that no large areas be entirely stripped of their timber, so as not to prevent the natural renewal of the forest. This would enable the people of the mining States and of the territories to obtain the timber they need in a legal way, at the same time avoiding the dangerous consequences above pointed out.

The extensive as well as wanton destruction of the timber upon the public lands by the wilful or negligent and careless setting of fires calls for earnest attention. While in several, if not all of the States, such acts are made highly penal offenses by statute, no law of the United States provides specifically for their punishment when committed upon the public lands, nor for a recovery of damages thereby sustained. I would therefore recom-mend the passage of a law prescribing a severe penalty for the wilful, negligent or careless setting of fires on the public lands of the United States, principally valuable for the timber thereon, and also for the recovery of all damages thereby sustained.

While such measures might be provided for by law without unnecessary delay, I would also suggest that the President be authorized to appoint a commission, composed of qualified persons, to study the laws and practices adopted in other countries for the preservation and cultivation of forests, and to report to Congress a plan for the same object applicable to our circumstances.

The provisions your project of a forestry bill has added to this plan are certainly appropriate, especially the proposed Forestry Commission to superintend the execution of this policy. It has been objected that the introduction of such a system would involve an addition to the number of public officers, and cost money. Certainly it would, as the Army costs money, as the police costs money, as the building of sewers costs money, as public schools cost money and as so many other things necessary to the safety and well being of the people cost money. But I do not hesitate to say that the money spent for the Army, the police and public schools is not spent to greater public advantage than the money spent for the introduction of a rational forestry system would be. However, a part of the public service already existing might well be used for the purpose of guarding at least the forests belonging to the public domain of the United States. It may well be assumed that although trifling Indian disturbances may still occur here and there, the danger of Indian wars on a large scale is now behind us. If a wise, just and humane Indian policy be followed, we may be sure that it is altogether over. Not a few of our outlying military posts may then be abandoned, and a part of our Army will become disposable for other purposes. Why should not two or three battalions be organized as forest guards or forest rangers, the men, perhaps, also to receive some useful instruction to fit them for their new duties? Surely, no soldier could, in time of peace and there being no prospect of war, be more usefully employed. . . .

We are all agreed also on the necessity of spreading information on this important subject. No respectable university or agricultural college should be without a department in which forestry as a science is taught; and most of us will no doubt see the day when the importance of that science will be recognized by every thinking American. Let us hope that this appreciation will come in time. I regret we cannot forcibly enough impress upon the American people the necessity of speedy measures looking to the preservation of our mountain forests which, when once destroyed, cannot be renewed. Unless this be done in time, our children will curse the almost criminal improvidence of their ancestors; but if it is done in time, those who are instrumental in doing it will deserve and will have the blessings of future generations.

To bring up the public opinion of this country to the point where it will command such measures, a vigorous and unceasing agitation is required. I do not underestimate the difficulties it will have to overcome. It is the shortsighted greed which acts upon the rule to grab all that can be got at the moment, and "let the devil take the hindmost," not stopping to consider that he who does so may be among the hindmost himself, and that in this case his children certainly will be. It is that spirit of levity, so prevalent among our people, which teaches to eat and drink and be merry to-day, unmindful of the reckoning that will come to-morrow. It is the cowardice of the small politician who, instead of studying the best interests of the people, trembles lest doing his full duty may cost him a vote, and who is not seldom apt to fear the resentment of the thieves more than that of honest men. Such influences you will have to overcome, but you will meet them in the future as bravely as you have met them in the past, and may a speedy and complete triumph crown your patriotic efforts.

Source: Schurz, Carl. "The Need for a Rational Forest Policy." *Speeches, Correspondence, and Political Papers of Carl Schurz.* Vol. V, edited by Frederic Bancroft. New York: G. P. Putnam's Sons/Knickerbocker Press, 1913, pp. 23–33.

DOCUMENT 3.13

A Scientific Report Lays the Groundwork for the Forest Reserve Act

"That the Rapid . . . Destruction of Our Great Forest Areas May Be Prevented"

January 20, 1890

In the 1870s the U.S. Congress passed several momentous land policy laws that wreaked havoc on the nation's dwindling public domain forestlands. As evidence of the negative ecological and economic repercussions of this legislation accumulated, early conservationists, struggling farmers, small business owners, and progressive-minded critics united against the Gilded Age "robber barons" who had become the primary beneficiaries of America's timber wealth.

In 1891 Congress responded to the mounting furor with the General Revision Act. This law, passed over the vehement objections of timber companies, railroads, mining companies, and their legislative allies, ushered in a startling revision of the nation's public land laws and policies. It imposed reforms in the areas of homesteading and mining and in general signaled the federal government's intention to be a more active steward of the nation's natural resources. The clearest example of this philosophical shift could be found in the closing paragraphs of the Act, where a rider that came to be known as the Forest Reserve Act had been tacked on at the insistence of John W. Noble, who served as secretary of the interior under President Benjamin Harrison. The Forest Reserve Act gave the president the authority to create "forest reserves"—what we today call national forests—by removing forestlands from the public domain. Harrison made extensive use of this new power, bestowing federal protection on more than fourteen million acres of forestland before his term ended in early 1893. Thus was laid the foundation for America's current national forest system.

The following document from January 1890—fourteen months before the Forest Reserve Act came into law—shows Harrison's keen interest in establishing a system for the "preservation of the forests upon the public domain." It opens with a brief introductory statement from Harrison to Congress, then passes along correspondence from a scientific task force dedicated to the advancement of a "proper forest policy" in the United States.

MESSAGE from the PRESIDENT OF THE UNITED STATES

Transmitting

Report relative to the preservation of the forests on the public domain.

January 20, 1890.—Read, referred to the Committee on Agriculture and Forestry, and ordered to be printed.

To the Senate and House of Representatives:

I transmit herewith a letter of Prof. T.C. Mendenhall, chairman of a committee of the American Association for the Advancement of Science, and president of that association, and also the memorial prepared by said committee relating to the preservation of the forests upon the public domain.

I very earnestly recommend that adequate legislation may be provided to the end that the rapid and needless destruction of our great forest areas may be prevented.

Benj. Harrison
Executive Mansion
January 20, 1890

OFFICE OF THE COAST SURVEY
Washington, D.C., January 11, 1890.
SIR: In accordance with a resolution passed by the American Association for the Advancement of Science at its last annual meeting, calling for the appointment of a committee to urge the importance of immediate action looking to the establishment of a proper administration of the timber lands remaining in the hands of the Government, a copy of which resolution has been sent to you previously, we now beg to submit . . . brief arguments in favor of a change in our present forest policy, and respectfully request that you will transmit this statement to the Senate and House of Representatives of the United States, with such recommendations as you may see proper.

Very respectfully,
T.C. Mendenhall
Chairman of Committee,
President of the American Association for the Advancement of Science

MEMORIAL OF THE AMERICAN ASSOCIATION FOR THE ADVANCEMENT OF SCIENCE IN BEHALF OF A PROPER FOREST POLICY.
To the PRESIDENT OF THE UNITED STATES:
The first national legislation which recognized the necessity of looking after the forestry interests of the country in general grew out of the representations made before Congress fifteen years ago by a committee of the American Association for the Advancement of Science.

These representations led to the appointment in the year 1887 of an agent, and later the establishment of a forestry division in the Department of Agriculture, for the purpose of gathering and making accessible such information as would lead our people to a proper conception of the value and significance of a forest cover in the economic life of our nation.

Twelve years have passed, during which sufficient knowledge of our forest conditions and of the general relations of these to cultural, climatic, and economic conditions have been gathered, to show that further action on the part of the General Government is necessary if we wish to preserve this relation favorable to the future development of the country.

The American Association for the Advancement of Science, actuated alone by a desire to promote a rational development of the country's resources, has therefore appointed the undersigned committee to memorialize the President and Congress of the United States under the following resolution:

> *Resolved,* that it is the sense of the American Association for the Advancement of Science that immediate action should be taken looking to the establishment of a proper administration of the remaining timber lands in the hands of the Governments of the United States and Canada, for the purpose of insuring the perpetuity of the forest cover

on the western mountain ranges, preserving thereby the dependent favorable hydrologic conditions.

Resolved further, that a committee of five be, and is hereby, appointed to present this resolution, and to urge the importance thereof to the President and the Congress of the United States, and to the premier and Parliament of Canada and of the provincial governments, and that such committee be instructed to prepare in proper form any data necessary, and to use every honorable means to accomplish the purpose herein set forth, and that the president of this association be hereby appointed chairman of such committee, together with four others whom he shall appoint.

The committee in presenting this memorial desire not to argue at length any theory as to forest influences or to discuss the present unsatisfactory condition of our forest areas and national timber lands—which has been amply done in the reports of the Secretaries of Agriculture and of the Interior—but they respectfully submit in support of the request of the association such points as will explain and justify the presentation of this memorial.

1. The action which is asked of Congress concerns only a particular part of our forest area, that part which is in possession of the General Government, the property of the nation.
2. It is asked upon the presumption that the present administration of this property, probably from ignorance of its proper value and its real significance, is unsatisfactory, and that a change of policy is immediately urgent if this value is to be retained and the far-reaching injury, which from its present rapid deterioration may be anticipated, is to be avoided.
3. It is asked upon the presumption that the value of this property, situated mainly upon the water-sheds of our Western river systems, lies much more in its significance for the future cultural development of a vast adjoining country than in the material which it now furnishes to the pioneer settler and miner.
4. It is also assumed that the only proper person to administer this property for the benefit of the country at large and the preservation of the dependent cultural conditions is the Government itself, which alone can have an interest in the future of society beyond present and personal gain.

As the reports cited have shown, the administration of the timber lands has been unsatisfactory for lack of proper legislation and of provisions sufficient to protect this property against material loss and deterioration. Timber thieving and destruction by fire have been allowed to unnecessarily waste this national property, while the officers in charge were powerless to protect it. The pioneer legislation, which may have been sufficient twenty-five years ago, has long outlived its usefulness and should make way for such administration as will meet the demands of civilized existence in settled communities.

A vast empire, considered useless not long ago, has been found capable of human occupancy and agricultural production if the means for its development, water, can be brought upon it, and the extent to which this land may be utilized depends upon the amounts of water available.

The opinions of our greatest climatologists have been divided as to the influence of forests on precipitation. But evidence, carefully and scientifically scrutinized, is accumulating which tends to show that, under certain conditions at least, such influence may not be improbable. However this may be, overwhelming evidence can be brought to show that a potent influence upon the distribution of available water supplies from rain and snow is exerted by a forest cover, so that a government having to deal with the problem of cultural development of a part of its domain by irrigation, cannot compass the water question without at the same time giving attention and proper regard to the forestry question.

Removal of the mountain forest means invariably disturbance of the natural "run-off"; favorable sometimes, unfavorable mostly.

It may be difficult to devise at once such a plan for the administration of these forests, with a view to their continuity, as can be put in practice under the present social and political conditions of that part of our country in which this timbered area is situated; and a special investigation of these conditions and careful adjustment between the present needs of the population for wood material and the future needs of a forest cover for hydrologic purposes appears desirable, although various measures for a forest administration which seem capable of practical application have been proposed.

We, therefore, the undersigned committee, in the conservative and scrutinizing spirit that should characterize the proposition of the scientific body which we represent respectfully recommend:

That a joint committee of the Senate and House of Representatives of the United States be appointed to consider the needs of legislation in behalf of the public timber domain with a view of providing for the appointment of a commission of competent men, salaried and employed for this service alone, for the purpose of investigating the necessity of preserving certain parts of the present public forest area as requisite for the maintenance of favorable water conditions, and to devise a practical plan for the permanent administration of such parts of it as shall appear desirable to be retained under government control.

The committee further recommends that, pending such investigation, all timber lands now in the hands of the United States be withdrawn from sale and provision be made to protect the said lands from theft and ravages by fire and to supply in a rational manner the local needs for wood and lumber until a permanent system of forest administration be had.

It is also suggested that inasmuch as the various Departments and Government bureaus, namely, the Department of Agriculture in its Forestry Division, the Department of the Interior in its Land Office and Geological Survey, the Department of War in its Signal Office, the Treasury Department in its Coast and Geodetic Survey, are more or less closely interested in this matter and have collected data useful in the work of such a commission, these Departments should co-operate and act as advisors of said Commission.

All of which is respectfully submitted.

T.C. Mendenhall,
President of the Association and Chairman,
B. E. Fernow, of New York,
Secretary,
E.W. Hilgard, of California,
C.E. Bessey, of Nebraska,
Wm. Saunders, of Canada,
Committee.

Source: "Preservation of the Forests on the Public Domain." Message from the President of the United States Transmitting Report in *The Executive Documents of the Senate of the United States for the First Session of the Fifty-First Congress, 1889–90.* Senate Executive Doc. No. 36. Washington, D.C.: Government Printing Office, 1890.

William Gilpin Describes an American Empire Built on Railroads

DOCUMENT
3.14

"The American Realizes That Progress Is God"

1890

As the United States approached the end of the nineteenth century, conservation efforts on behalf of threatened forest resources, watersheds, and wildlife gained broader acceptance in some quarters of American society, including the halls of Congress and assorted statehouses. But most land and resource development policies continued to be made in service to the goals of territorial expansion and economic development, which remained entrenched in the public consciousness as the twin pillars on which America's fast-emerging greatness rested. And Americans recognized that despite the sometimes ruthless and rapacious ways of their fabulously wealthy owners, the nation's economic well-being in the new industrial age had come to hinge on the railroads that connected the nation's wheat-, beef-, timber-, and mineral-producing hinterlands to the markets of the great cities.

The great boosters of western settlement and development certainly recognized the importance of the Iron Horse to the fortunes of the region. To that end, they ranked among the leading champions of pro-development governmental policies that funneled millions of acres of valuable land out of the public domain and into the hands of railroad owners and executives. Indeed, prominent boosters such as William Gilpin, the first governor of the Colorado Territory, portrayed railroads as divine instruments of Manifest Destiny through which Americans could subjugate and transform the wilderness, plunder its hidden riches, and construct a continental empire. This viewpoint, which had many adherents west of the Mississippi, made it much more difficult for county, state, territorial, and federal politicians and administrators to institute laws and policies that sought to rein in destructive and unsustainable use of western land and natural resources. The following is an excerpt from The Cosmopolitan Railway, *an 1890 work in which Gilpin called for the construction of an international rail system that would connect North America and Russia via the Bering Strait.*

The Railway as a Factor of Progress

To the very existence of civilized communities the railroad has become almost as much a necessity as is the circulation of the blood to the individual. Not only do we depend upon it for the means of locomotion, but for almost everything that we eat or drink or wear. And in no country in the world do people rely so much on their railroads as in the United States, where in the more thinly populated sections coal for fuel and lumber for building are often conveyed by rail hundreds of miles from the place of production. But perhaps their greatest benefit has been in the opening up for settlement of vast and fertile regions, before unpeopled except by savages and wild beasts. It is not indeed too much to say, that but for the advent of the railway, the population of this republic, instead of being spread over its entire surface, would still have been mainly confined to its thirteen original states, and with but a small percentage of that which now exists on the Pacific slope.

Nowhere has the railway wrought such marvellous results as in Colorado and on to the Pacific, converting, as at the touch of a magic wand, what was before little else than a desert, or at best a pasture-ground, into a region abounding with grain and fruit, with all the choicest products of the farm, the orchard, and the vineyard, and giving especially to Colorado and California a commercial and industrial development such as has never before been witnessed in the lifetime of a single generation.

Said General Sherman in one of his reports to the secretary of war: "No person who has not been across the continent can possibly comprehend the change now in progress there. Nearly two thirds of the domain of the United States lies west of the Mississippi, and at the close of the civil war the greater part of it was occupied by wild beasts, buffalo, elk, antelope, and deer, and by wilder Indians. Now, by the indomitable courage, industry, and thrift of our people, this vast region has been reduced to a condition of comparative civilization. Three great railroads now traverse the continent, with branches innumerable, and a fourth is making rapid progress. States, territories, cities, and towns have grown up; neat cattle have already displaced the buffalo; sheep and goats have displaced the elk, deer, and antelope; and crops of wheat, rye, barley, and oats are now grown in regions believed hitherto to be desert or inaccessible. This is the real cause of the prosperity which now blesses our country and swells the coffers of our national treasury."

Railways, multiplied and spanning the continent, are essential domestic institutions; more powerful and more permanent than law or popular consent or political constitutions to thoroughly complete the grand system of fluvial arteries which fraternize us into one people.

—William Gilpin

To the railroad is largely due the fact that in proportion to her area and population California is now the largest wheat and fruit producing region in the world, and that her metropolis already ranks among the leading commercial and manufacturing centres of the union, with a population exceeding 300,000, with a property valuation assessed at more than $1,000,000,000, with exports of over $100,000,000 a year, and with its warehouses filled with the products of every quarter of the earth. Little more than a quarter of a century ago a single train would have contained the entire population for hundreds of miles to the northward of Fort Yuma; but now we have in southern California one of the wealthiest sections of the Pacific coast, with lands before considered worthless, except as cattle-ranges, now selling at from $50 to $300 an acre. Taking, for instance, a belt of ten miles in the San Joaquin valley on either side of the Southern Pacific, containing in all some 3,000,000 acres, it is estimated that the value of these lands has increased since the opening of the road by more than $50,000,000; while towns which never before existed, except perhaps on paper, have now become thriving commercial and agricultural centres.

In other sections of the Pacific coast the benefit of railroads has been no less widely felt. Before their advent but little progress was made in developing the great mining districts of Nevada and Utah, of Colorado and Arizona, for without their aid no thorough development was possible. To the Comstock lode, for instance, it would have been almost impossible to bring, except by rail, the heavy machinery required for the deeper levels from which hundreds of millions have been extracted; nor could the mines of Colorado and other districts have been profitably worked unless the railroad had been there to forward their supplies and carry to market their bullion. . . .

The benefit of railways, steamboats, and telegraphs has been extended to every civilized nation of the earth, with the exception only of China, where, as I have said, a railroad system has recently been inaugurated. In truth, it has been a marvellous development, and one as rapid as marvellous, though still with a gradual progression, for at every step the most difficult problems were encountered in pure and applied science, and in various branches of manufacture. But now has been achieved, through this wondrous combination of science and mechanism, the greatest speed and facility of communication that the human mind has yet conceived, a boon that commerce has sought, and sought in vain, almost from the beginning of the world. To accomplish this task has been the work of little more than half a century, and yet its cost may be counted by thousands of millions. But assuredly these millions have not been expended in vain; they have brought forth fruit a hundred-fold; for while by the demands of commerce these agencies have been created and extended, they have also developed the traffic without which they could never have been sustained.

As to the gold discoveries, their first effect was to produce a vast migration to the countries where they occurred, and thus also to people not only the great continent of the southern hemisphere, but more than one half of the North American continent. Besides giving new direction to commerce, they have filled the coffers of our banks, and given such confidence to banking operations that vast stores of gold and silver were distributed among the channels of trade. They have caused a very considerable advance in prices and in wages, with a largely increased demand for manufactured goods, resulting partly from the transfer of eastern and European labor to new and more productive fields of industry. They have made of California one of the granaries of the world, and of Colorado the centre of a new and unexpected development of the wealth of the mountains, and have planted in the antipodes a group of prosperous colonies which, as the United States of Australia, shall one day surpass the fading glories of the mother country.

It is, of course, in the United States that the discovery of the precious metals in Colorado and the regions to the westward has made itself most widely felt. Without them would have been impossible the marvellous progress which the present generation has witnessed in railroad and commercial development. Without them the financial straits of the civil war would have been much further intensified; nor would the nation's debt have been so rapidly reduced, or the nation's treasure vaults made to overflow with surplus funds. The effect on commerce has been magical. . . .

The American people now reach and cross the threshold, where they emerge from the twilight of the futile world of thought behind. They enter into the full and perpetual light and promise of political and social science.

A glance of the eye thrown across the North American continent, accompanying the course of the sun from ocean to ocean, reveals an extraordinary landscape. It displays immense forces, characterized by order, activity, and progress.

The structure of nature, the march of a vast population, the creations of the people, individually and combined, are seen in infinite varieties of form and in gigantic dimensions.

The pioneer army perpetually advances, reconnoitres, strikes to the front. Empire plants itself upon the trail. Agitation, creative energy, industry, throb throughout and animate this crowding host. Occupation, solidity, and permanence attend every movement and follow every camp.

The American realizes that progress is God. He clearly recognizes and accepts the continental mission of his country and his people. His faith is impregnably fortified by this vision of power, unity, and forward motion. . . .

Behold here the panorama which crowns the middle region of our union, fans the immortal fire of patriotism, and beckons on the energetic host of our people! Here, through the heart of our territory, our population, our states, our cities, our mines, our farms, and habitations, will be on the highway of the condensed commerce of mankind—where passengers and cargoes may, at any time or place, embark upon or leave the vehicles of transportation.

Railways, multiplied and spanning the continent, are essential domestic institutions; more powerful and more permanent than law or popular consent or political constitutions to thoroughly complete the grand system of fluvial arteries which fraternize us into one people; to bind the two seaboards to this one continental union, like ears to the human head; to radicate the rural foundations of the union so broad and deep, and establish its structures so solid, that no possible force or stratagem can shake its permanence; to secure such scope and space to progress, that equality and prosperity shall never be impaired, or chafe for want of room.

To Denver is secured a career into which all these favorable facts of position and circumferent area are now united. The North American people number sixty millions in strength. Two millions annually shift their homes. This force is, par excellence, the pioneer army of the North American people. This movement causes an uninterrupted pressure of the people from east to west, resembling the drift of the ocean which accompanies the great tidal wave.

Diurnally is the surface of the sea lifted up in silence and poured upon the coasts of the continents. Exactly similar to this is the movement, annually gathering force, and seen to impel our people through and through from the eastern to the western limit of the land. The inscrutable force of gravity, which with minute accuracy holds the planets in their orbits, or causes each drop of rain to fall, sways the instinct of society. This gravitation presses from all directions upon the axis, and to the focus of intensity. This regular instinct of movement has been transiently interfered with by the artificial passions and demoralization of civil strife. It rapidly assumes again its temper and its regularity.

Our neighbors from California work up to us with miraculous energy and celerity. They bring with them the open avenue to us from Asia. The Mexican column reaches us from the south. On the north the activity is great, and in close contact. These several columns simultaneously converge upon us. They increase every moment in numbers, weight, and celerity of motion. We no longer march into the blind wilderness, dependent upon and chained exclusively to Europe in the rear. We open up in front the gorgeous arena of the Asiatic ocean. . . .

A large majority of the American people now reside within the Mississippi basin, and in this Asiatic front of our continent, which is born from us. Nascent powers, herculean from the hour of their birth, unveil their forms and demand their rights. States for the pioneers, self-government for the pioneers, untramelled way for the imperial energies of the forces of the Rocky mountains and the Pacific sea, may not long be withheld by covetous, arbitrary, and arrogant jealousy and injustice.

In the conflict for freedom it is not numbers or cunning that conquers; but rather daring, discipline, and judgment, combined and tempered by the condensed fire of faith and intrepid valor. As it is my hope in these pages to contribute what may be valuable, I adhere strictly to severe facts, and reject absolutely all theory and speculation. These facts are as indestructibly established as is the alphabet, and are as worthy of unquestioning faith and credence.

That we may look into the gathering achievements of the near future, without obscurity, and with an accurate prophetic vision, I may without hesitation submit what is within my own personal experience.

It fell to my lot, during the years from 1840 to 1845, alone, and in extreme youth, to seek and chalk out, in the immense solitudes filling the space from Missouri to China, the lines of this dazzling empire of which we now hold the oracular crown; to have stood by its cradle; to have been the witness of its miraculous growth.

It is not for me, in this season of gathering splendor, to speak tamely upon a subject of such intense and engrossing novelty and interest. I may properly here quote the concluding sentences of a report which I was required to make on the 2d of March, 1846, to the United States senate, at that time brimful of illustrious statesmen. What I said then and there, in the first dawning twilight of our glory, I will now repeat:

> "The calm, wise man sets himself to study aright and understand clearly the deep designs of providence, to scan the great volume of nature, to fathom, if possible, the will of the creator, and to receive with respect what may be revealed to him.

> "Two centuries have rolled over our race upon this continent. From nothing we have become 20,000,000. From nothing we are grown to be in agriculture, in commerce, in civilization, and in natural strength, the first among nations existing or in history. So much is our destiny, so far, up to this time, transacted, accomplished, certain, and not to be disputed. From this threshold we read the future.

> "The untransacted destiny of the American people is to subdue the continent, to rush over this vast field to the Pacific ocean, to animate the many hundred millions of its people, and to cheer them upward, to set the principle of self-government at work, to agitate these herculean masses, to establish a new order in human affairs, to set free the enslaved, to regenerate superannuated nations, to change darkness into light, to stir up the sleep of a hundred centuries, to teach old nations a new civilization, to confirm the destiny of the human race, to carry the career of mankind to its culminating point, to cause stagnant people to be reborn, to perfect science, to emblazon history with the conquests of peace, to shed a new and resplendent glory upon mankind, to unite the world in one social family, to dissolve the spell of tyranny and exalt charity, to absolve the curse that weighs down humanity, and to shed blessings round the world.

> "Divine task! immortal mission! Let us tread fast and joyfully the path before us. Let every American heart open wide for patriotism to glow undimmed, and confide with religious faith in the sublime and prodigious destiny of his well-loved country!"

. . . That the Americans are the greatest of nations in a geographical sense, by reason of the geographical position no less than the extent of their domain, will not, I think, be disputed. But they are no less great as a people who hold in their hands the shaping of their own destiny, who are learning, year by year, to govern themselves more wisely, and living, as they do, in perfect security, can devote themselves entirely to the arts of peace. Nowhere in the world is there a country in which the masses live in such comfort, nowhere is labor so well remunerated, and nowhere are there such natural resources, such energy and power to unfold them. Nowhere are there so many schools, so many libraries, where rich and poor may study side by side, so many learned and charitable societies, so little of vice and pauperism, so much of moral and intellectual worth. All this is the work of a single century; what shall another century bring forth?

Source: Gilpin, William. *The Cosmopolitan Railway: Compacting and Fusing Together All the World's Continents*. San Francisco: History Company, 1890, pp. 108–110, 182–183, 199, 226–232.

A Tourist Brochure Beckons Travelers to the Northwest Territories

"A Trip Through This Indian Story Land and White Man's Wonderland"

1893

During the last four decades of the nineteenth century, growing numbers of Americans were introduced to the spectacular natural wonders of the West. The establishment of Yosemite Park (1864) and Yellowstone National Park (1872) beckoned affluent Americans with a taste for adventure, as did the proliferating rail lines that afforded views of red rock canyons, roaring rivers, and richly forested mountainsides. Moreover, these destinations were coming into being at a time when industrial and technological advances were pushing the nation's economy to ever greater heights—thus creating larger numbers of Americans with the financial resources to ponder such trips.

Railroad executives were quick to recognize the economic potential of western tourism, and they crafted a wide array of promotional brochures and other tracts to pump up this lucrative new revenue stream. Their efforts paid big dividends. "As a result of vigorous advertising, the trains brought enormous throngs of visitors to the western lands, including the brand-new national parks," affirmed historian Thurman Wilkins. But the rail-driven tourist trade also had the unintended but beneficial side effect of increasing public support for land conservation policies. "Tourism . . . proved a powerful means of popularizing wilderness during the latter part of the nineteenth century."[1]

The following excerpt is from 6,000 Miles through Wonderland, an 1893 promotional tract sponsored by the Northern Pacific Railway. Northern Pacific took a leading role among railroads in popularizing the West as a tourist destination. In 1883 it began rail service to Yellowstone, where it also constructed luxury hotels to house the nation's first generation of wilderness tourists. Two years later, Northern Pacific rolled out a slick advertising campaign that portrayed Yellowstone as "Wonderland" and the entire Northern Pacific line as "The Wonderland Route." This particular promotional piece was penned by Olin D. Wheeler (1852–1925), who had worked as a topographer for John Wesley Powell before becoming a writer for Northern Pacific.

SEWARD'S PROPHECY.

> Breathes there a man with soul so dead
>
> Who never to himself hath said,
>
> This is my own, my native land ?—
>
> Scott.

The American people are reputed a nation of travelers. The allegation is undoubtedly a true one, and is applicable to no one class alone. Rich and poor, high official and private citizen, the aristocrat and the tramp, each and all exercise the "inalienable right" of an American citizen—and travel. To such an extent is this so that it has been stated, and currently accepted as true, that were it not for the American dollars left in Europe by travelers serious distress would result at many of the points embraced in the continental tour.

In so far as scenery alone is concerned the evidence is beyond dispute that this country can match anything that the old country has to show, and in many cases so far excel it that comparison is out of the question. It is time lost and money thrown away to go from here there to see fine scenery alone. We have more of it than have they.

William H. Seward, prophet, seer, and statesman, pierced the veil far into the future when, standing in 1860 on the platform at the door of the capitol of the State of Minnesota, in St. Paul, he gave utterance in substance to this, at that time, remarkable statement:

> I find myself for the first time upon the high land in the center of the continent of North America, equidistant from the waters of Hudson Bay and the Gulf of Mexico. Here is the place, the central place, where the agricultural products of this region of North America must pour out their tributes to the world. I have cast about for the future and ultimate seat of power of North America. I looked to Quebec, to New Orleans, to Washington, San Francisco, and St. Louis for the future seat of power. But I have corrected that view. I now believe that the ultimate last seat of government on this great continent will be found somewhere not far from the spot on which I stand, at the head of navigation of the Mississippi River.

No one starting from this land of the mystic Hiawatha and whirling westward

> To the doorway of the west wind,

> To the portals of the sunset,

through the enchanting Lake Park region of Minnesota, the waving grain fields and delicately sculptured Bad Lands of North Dakota, the vast cattle ranges and mineral-bearing mountains of Montana and Idaho, and the timbered hills and laughing valleys—the joy of the horticulturist—of Washington and Oregon, can for one moment doubt that here indeed is the nucleus of a coming empire.

From the billowy fields of Minnesota and the Dakotas will go forth the bread to feed the nations. From the plateaus and grazing-grounds of North Dakota and Montana will come the beef and mutton and beasts of burden for our own extended domain. From the womb of the mountains of Montana and Idaho will be extracted the precious metals for use in commerce and the arts. From the mountain-bound valleys and plains of Washington and the Puget Sound country will be sent far and wide fruits as luscious as were those which the spies carried back to Joshua from the Land of Canaan.

Here, in this magnificent domain of lofty mountain, sweeping plain, circling valley, pointed cliff, cañoned river, geysered basin, rolling prairie; here, where mountain peaks touch the clouds, rivers throw themselves from dizzy heights into cañon depths below, valleys smile under the benign touch of the Creator, chimneys smoke to the zenith, turning the crudities of the mountains into the polished productions of art, the cattle graze on the thousand hills, the lakes of emerald shimmer and flash in the sunlight, the green fields bend to the evening breeze over leagues of undulating prairie; here is the beginning of an empire destined to exert a vast influence on future civilization. Well may the patriotic American sing in this year 1893, after a trip through this Indian story land and white man's wonderland:

> My Country, 'tis of thee,

> Sweet Land of Liberty,

Of thee I sing.

I love thy rocks and rills,

Thy woods and templed hills,

My heart with rapture thrills

Like that above. . . .

THROUGH WONDERLAND.

SEEN FROM CAR WINDOWS. ST. PAUL AND MINNEAPOLIS—DULUTH AND THE SUPERIORS—ASHLAND—MINNESOTA PRAIRIES—LAKE PARK REGION, ETC.

A considerable proportion of travelers on American railways have not the time to stop over at the more noted places, nor to make side trips nor excursions to the more interesting points situated a greater or less distance from the immediate line of the railway. What they see must be seen from the windows of the car which for the time being is their home. What they learn of the country through which they ride, its mountains and rivers, plains, valleys, deserts, hamlets, and cities, must be learned from what they see from car windows as they roll onward at thirty and forty miles an hour. This being the case the traveler naturally inquires what he can see in this to some extent limited way as he travels by this or that particular route. Over which line of railway among so many can he, all things considered, see the most, and consequently learn the most, for the expenditure of money he must needs make.

I think I hazard no rash statement when I say that from the time that one takes seat in the cars either at St. Paul or Duluth, the eastern termini of the Northern Pacific, or even at Chicago, the eastern terminus of the Wisconsin Central, its leased line, there is not, with the single exception of a few short hours in the Columbia River Valley, a time that the outlook is not either attractive or interesting.

With the exception noted, the prospect at all times, from a scenic point, varies from the quiet and pleasant pastoral features of the Minnesota and Dakota prairies through the entire category to the grand and uplifting panorama afforded by the passage of the Rocky and Cascade mountains. . . .

[Wheeler goes on to detail the attractions along the Northern Pacific route, including a chapter devoted to the beauty of Yellowstone National Park.]

The Yellowstone Park! The gem of wonderland. The land of mystic splendor. Region of bubbling caldron and boiling pool with fretted rims, rivaling the coral in delicacy of texture and the rainbow in variety of color; of steaming funnels exhaling into the etherine atmosphere in calm, unruffled monotone and paroxysmal ejection vast clouds of fleecy vapor from the underground furnaces of the God of Nature. Sylvan parkland, where amidst the unsullied freshness of flower-strewn valley and bountiful woodland the native fauna of the land browse in fearless joy wander wild and free, unfretted by sound of huntsman's horn, the long-drawn bay of the hound, and the sharp crack of the rifle.

Land of beauteous vale and laughing water, thundering cataract and winding ravine; realm of the Ice King and the Fire King; enchanted spot, where mountain and sea meet and kiss each other; where the murmurs of the river, as it meanders through heaven-blest valleys, become harsh and sullen amid the pine-covered hills which darken and throttle its joyous song, until, uncontrollable, it throws itself, a magnificent sheet of diamond spray and plunging torrent, over precipices, and rolls along an emerald flood betwixt cañon walls such as the eye of mortal hath seldom seen. . . .

The park is intended as a great pleasure ground for the pleasure and instruction of the people. It is under the direct control of the United States Government, and a sufficient number of soldiery are kept there the year through to patrol the park and afford a watchful supervision of it, prevent acts of vandalism, enforce the regulations governing the use of the park, and see that all parties have the protection of the laws of the land.

It is an offense punished by summary ejection to tamper with any of the objects in the park, kill or capture game, be careless in the use of camp fires, etc. Fishing with hook and line is allowable.

Under Government supervision new roads are being opened, and old ones are constantly kept repaired.

The transportation facilities through the park deserve special mention.

The horses used are not the wild, unreliable bronco of the plains and mountains, but good, steady stage horses. Harness and coaches are of the world-renowned Concord pattern, which means that strength, safety, and durability are the prime objects aimed at. The coaches are made specially for tourist travel, and so as to allow the occupant the freest outlook possible. The best drivers to be obtained are used, and are under orders to afford all possible facilities and information to passengers to see, and understand what they see.

The tour of the park at any time during the regular season is a source of pleasure. The writer made it during the last week of August. If, however, one can choose the time, and desires to see it when the hills and valleys and parks are clothed in their freshest green, when the streams are fullest, when the mountain flowers are crowding bud and leaf to their fruition, dressing out the slopes and vales in summer attire, and emitting upon a balmy air odors of delicious fragrance, the early part of the season is to be preferred. June seems to meet all these conditions the best, and those botanically inclined will probably obtain their greatest pleasure at that time.

A word as to the fauna.

The domains of the park are a haven of refuge to all animals for thousands of square miles about. They know this, and frequent the park in large numbers. Bear, deer, elk, antelope, buffalo, mountain sheep, and all the other varieties of wild animals are here, and are very often seen as the stages roll along, or from the hotels. They are very tame, and molest no one. Indeed, the bears are scavengers for the hotels, and the guests flock out at night to see Bruin gorge himself and go rolling away when filled.

There are large herds of deer and elk, and probably 300 buffalo roaming o'er the valleys and hills. The habitat of the latter in summer is usually in the region about Yellowstone Lake.

The fishing to be found here can not be surpassed. Nearly all the waters of the park contain fish of some sort. Mountain trout are everywhere, grayling are found in the Madison and Gallatin rivers, and whitefish in the Yellowstone, Madison, and Gardiner.

The angler, however, will probably find his greatest sport at Yancey's. Here in the Yellowstone, after it has plunged through the Grand Cañon, is afforded a chance for the fisherman seldom, if ever, equaled.

Source: Wheeler, Olin D. *6,000 Miles through Wonderland: Being a Description of the Marvelous Region Traversed by the Northern Pacific Railroad.* Chicago: Rand McNally, 1893, pp. 9–11, 65, 69–70.

NOTE

1. Thurman Wilkins, *John Muir: Apostle of Nature* (Norman: University of Oklahoma Press, 1995), xxvi.

The Case of *Ward v. Race Horse*

"The Wilderness . . . Was Destined to be Occupied and Settled by the White Man"

May 25, 1896

In the years following the creation of Yellowstone National Park in 1872, tensions arose between local Shoshone, Crow, and Bannock people, who were determined to exercise well-established treaty rights to hunt and forage within the park boundaries, and park officials fielding complaints from tourists about the presence of the Indians. When the park imposed new rules denying entry to the Native Americans, the region was rocked by a flurry of violent incidents and mass arrests of Indians for game law violations. In an effort to settle the issue, the various parties agreed to bring a test case before the federal judiciary. A Bannock leader named Race Horse killed seven elk in the Jackson Hole area in violation of park rules, then submitted himself for arrest for violating Wyoming state game laws.

The case of Ward v. Race Horse *(John Ward was the sheriff who made the arrest) was first heard by Circuit Judge John Riner, who concluded that local Indian rights granted in the 1868 Fort Bridger Treaty took precedent over the laws of Wyoming, which had become a state only five years earlier, in 1890. But the state of Wyoming appealed the ruling to the U.S. Supreme Court, and on May 25, 1896, the Court reversed Riner's decision by seizing on a ruthless and convenient rationalization. It asserted that the "unoccupied lands" made available to the Indians in the treaty would sooner or later be incorporated into the United States, at which time state laws had to be honored. In other words, argued one historian, the Court essentially declared that the Fort Bridger Treaty "must be viewed in the context of American assumptions at the time—that is, a temporary expedient that government officials expected neither to honor nor to uphold in light of subsequent events."[1]*

This ruling gave new legal muscle and authority to the increasing number of state laws across the country that sought to conserve wildlife, forests, and other resources. But it was a crushing blow to western tribes. It abrogated native rights in national parks and forests and other reserves, which proliferated across the country over the ensuing half century. From this point forward, any legislation that created a new national park also marked another dark chapter in a two-century-long tale of native dispossession. The ruling also formally obligated state and federal agencies, including the Bureau of Indian Affairs, to keep Native Americans off of public lands during closed hunting seasons and confine them to their reservations. More than a century later, Ward v. Race Horse, *which one scholar has described as "in many respects the Indian equivalent of* Plessy v. Ferguson,*"[2] remains the legal basis for restricting all native hunting in the state of Wyoming. Following are excerpts from the majority decision in the* Ward v. Race Horse *case, written by Associate Justice Edward Douglas White.*

It is wholly immaterial, for the purpose of the legal issue here presented, to consider whether the place where the elk were killed is in the vicinage of white settlements. It is also equally irrelevant to ascertain how far the land was used for a cattle range, since the sole question which the case presents is whether the treaty made by the United States with the Bannock Indians gave them the right to exercise the hunting privilege, therein referred to, within the limits of the state of Wyoming, in violation of its laws. If it gave such right, the mere fact that the state had created school districts or election districts, and had provided for pasturage on the lands, could no more efficaciously operate to destroy the right of the Indian to hunt on the lands than could the passage of the game law. If, on the other hand, the terms of the treaty did not refer to lands within a state, which were subject to the legislative power of the state, then it is equally clear that, although the lands were not in school and election districts, and were not near settlements, the right conferred on the Indians by the treaty would be of no avail to justify a violation of the state law.

The power of a state to control and regulate the taking of game cannot be questioned. (*Geer v. Connecticut.*) The text of article 4 of the treaty, relied on as giving the right to kill game within the state of Wyoming, in violation of its laws, is as follows:

> But they shall have the right to hunt on the unoccupied lands of the United States, so long as game may be found thereon, and so long as peace subsists among the whites and Indians on the borders of the hunting districts.

It may at once be conceded that the words "unoccupied lands of the United States," if they stood alone, and were detached from the other provisions of the treaty on the same subject, would convey the meaning of lands owned by the United States, and the title to or occupancy of which had not been disposed of. But, in interpreting these words in the treaty, they cannot be considered alone, but must be construed with reference to the context in which they are found. Adopting this elementary method, it becomes at once clear that the unoccupied lands contemplated were not all such lands of the United States, wherever situated, but were only lands of that character embraced within what the treaty denominates as "hunting districts." This view follows as a necessary result from the provision which says that the right to hunt on the unoccupied lands shall only be availed of as long as peace subsists on the borders of the hunting districts. Unless the districts thus referred to be taken as controlling the words "unoccupied lands," then the reference to the hunting districts would become wholly meaningless, and the cardinal rule of interpretation would be violated, which ordains that such construction be adopted as gives effect to all the language of the statute. Nor can this consequence be avoided by saying that the words "hunting districts" simply signified places where game was to be found, for this would read out of the treaty the provision as "to peace on the borders" of such districts, which clearly pointed to the fact that the territory referred to was one beyond the borders of the white settlements. The unoccupied lands referred to being therefore contained within the hunting districts, by the ascertainment of the latter the former will be necessarily determined, as the less is contained in the greater. The elucidation of this issue will be made plain by an appreciation of the situation existing at the time of the adoption of the treaty, of the necessities which brought it into being, and of the purposes intended to be by it accomplished.

> *The right to hunt, given by the treaty, clearly contemplated the disappearance of the conditions therein specified. Indeed, it made the right depend on whether the land in the hunting districts was unoccupied public land of the United States.*
>
> —Edward Douglas White

When, in 1868, the treaty was framed, the progress of the white settlements westward had hardly, except in a very scattered way, reached the confines of the place selected for the Indian reservation. While this was true, the march of advancing civilization foreshadowed the fact that the wilderness, which lay on all sides of the point selected for the reservation, was destined to be occupied and settled by the white man, hence interfering with the hitherto untrammeled right of occupancy of the Indian.

For this reason, to protect his rights, and to preserve for him a home where his tribal relations might be enjoyed under the shelter of the authority of the United States, the reservation was created. While confining him to the reservation, and in order to give him the privilege of hunting in the designated districts, so long as the necessities of civilization did not require otherwise, the provision in question was doubtless adopted, care being, however, taken to make the whole enjoyment in this regard dependent absolutely upon the will of congress. To prevent this privilege from becoming dangerous to the peace of the new settlements as they advanced, the provision allowing the Indian to avail himself of it only while peace reigned on the borders was inserted. To suppose that the words of the treaty intended to give to the Indian the right to enter into already established states, and seek out every portion of unoccupied government land, and there exercise the right of hunting, in violation of the municipal law, would be to presume that the treaty was so drawn as to frustrate the very object it had in view. It would also render necessary the assumption that congress, while preparing the way, by the treaty, for new settlements and new states, yet created a provision, not only detrimental to their future well-being, but also irreconcilably in conflict with the powers of the states already existing.

It is undoubted that the place in the state of Wyoming, where the game in question was killed, was, at the time of the treaty, in 1868, embraced within the hunting districts therein referred to. But this fact does not justify the implication that the treaty authorized the continued enjoyment of the right of killing game therein, when the territory ceased to be a part of the hunting districts, and came within the authority and jurisdiction of a state. The right to hunt, given by the treaty, clearly contemplated the disappearance of the conditions therein specified. Indeed, it made the right depend on whether the land in the hunting districts was unoccupied public land of the United States. This, as we have said, left the whole question subject entirely to the will of the United States, since it provided, in effect, that the right to hunt should cease the moment the United States parted with the title to its land in the hunting districts. No restraint was imposed by the treaty on the power of the United States to sell, although such sale, under the settled policy of the government, was a result naturally to come from the advance of the white settlements in the hunting districts to which the treaty referred. And this view of the temporary and precarious nature of the right reserved in the hunting districts is manifest by the act of congress creating the Yellowstone Park reservation, for it was subsequently carved out of what constituted the hunting districts at the time of the adoption of the treaty, and is a clear indication of the sense of congress on the subject. The construction which would affix to the language of the treaty any other meaning than that which we have above indicated would necessarily imply that congress had violated the faith of the government and defrauded the Indians by proceeding immediately to forbid hunting in a large portion of the territory where it is now asserted there was a contract right to kill game created by the treaty in favor of the Indians.

The argument now advanced in favor of the continued existence of the right to hunt over the land mentioned in the treaty, after it had become subject to state authority, admits that the privilege would cease by the mere fact that the United States disposed of its title to any of the land, although such disposition, when made to an individual, would give him no authority over game, and yet that the privilege continued when the United States had called into being a sovereign state, a necessary incident of whose authority was the complete power to regulate the killing of game within its borders. This argument indicates at once the conflict between the right to hunt in the unoccupied lands within the hunting districts and the assertion of the power to continue the exercise of the privilege in question in the state of Wyoming in defiance of its laws. That "a treaty may supersede a prior act of congress, and an act of congress supersede a prior treaty," is elementary. . . .

The act which admitted Wyoming into the Union, as we have said, expressly declared that that state should have all the powers of the other states of the Union, and made no reservation whatever in favor of the Indians. These provisions alone considered would be in conflict with the treaty, if it was so construed as to allow the Indians to seek out every unoccupied piece of government land, and thereon disregard and violate the state law, passed in the undoubted exercise of its municipal authority. But the language of the act admitting Wyoming into the Union, which recognized her co-equal rights, was merely declaratory of the general rule. . . .

Determining . . . the question whether the provision of the treaty giving the right to hunt on unoccupied lands of the United States in the hunting districts is repealed, in so far as the lands in such districts are now embraced within the limits of the state of Wyoming, it becomes plain that the repeal results from the conflict between the treaty and the act admitting that state into the Union. The two facts, the privilege conferred and the act of admission, are irreconcilable, in the sense that the two, under no reasonable hypothesis, can be construed as co-existing.

The power of all the states to regulate the killing of game within their borders will not be gainsaid, yet, if the treaty applies to the unoccupied land of the United States in the state of Wyoming, that state would be bereft of such power, since every isolated piece of land belonging to the United States as a private owner, so long as it continued to be unoccupied land, would be exempt in this regard from the authority of the state.

Wyoming, then, will have been admitted into the Union, not as an equal member, but as one shorn of a legislative power vested in all the other states of the Union, a power resulting from the fact of statehood and incident to its plenary existence. Nor need we stop to consider the argument, advanced at bar, that as the United States, under the authority delegated to it by the constitution in relation to Indian tribes, has a right to deal with that subject, therefore it has the power to exempt from the operation of state game laws each particular piece of land, owned by it in private ownership within a state, for nothing in this case shows that this power has been exerted by congress. The enabling act declares that the state of Wyoming is admitted on equal terms with the other states, and this declaration, which is simply an expression of the general rule, which presupposes that states, when admitted into the Union, are endowed with powers and attributes equal in scope to those enjoyed by the states already admitted, repels any presumption that in this particular case congress intended to admit the state of Wyoming with diminished governmental authority. The silence of the act admitting Wyoming into the Union, as to the reservation of rights in favor of the Indians, is given increased significance by the fact that congress, in creating the territory, expressly reserved such rights. Nor would this case be affected by conceding that congress, during the existence of the territory, had full authority, in the exercise of its treaty-making power, to charge the territory, or the land therein, with such contractual burdens as were deemed best, and that, when they were imposed on a territory, it would be also within the power of congress to continue them in the state, on its admission into the Union. Here the enabling act not only contains no expression of the intention of congress to continue the burdens in question in the state, but, on the contrary, its intention not to do so is conveyed by the express terms of the act of admission. Indeed, it may be further, for the sake of the argument, conceded that, where there are rights created by congress, during the existence of a territory, which are of such a nature as to imply their perpetuity, and the consequent purpose of congress to continue them in the state, after its admission, such continuation will, as a matter of construction, be upheld, although the enabling act does not expressly so direct. Here the nature of the right created gives rise to no such implication of continuance, since, by its terms, it shows that the burden imposed on the territory was essentially perishable, and intended to be of a limited duration. Indeed, the whole argument of the defendant in error rests on the assumption that there was a perpetual right conveyed by the treaty, when, in fact, the privilege given was temporary and precarious. But the argument goes further than this, since it insists that although, by the treaty, the hunting privilege was to cease whenever the United States parted merely with the title to any of its lands, yet that privilege was to continue, although the United States parted with its entire authority over the capture and killing of game. . . .

For these reasons the judgment below was erroneous, and must therefore be reversed, and the case must be remanded to the court below with directions to discharge the writ and remand the prisoner to the custody of the sheriff, and it is so ordered.

Source: *Ward v. Race Horse*, No. 841, 163 U.S. 504 (May 25, 1896). Available at http://caselaw.lp.findlaw .com/scripts/cases/getcase.pl?court=US&vol=163&invol=504.

Notes

1. Mark David Spence, *Dispossessing the Wilderness: Indian Removal and the Making of the National Parks* (New York: Oxford University Press, 2000), 67.
2. Ibid., 68.

DOCUMENT 3.17

The Lacey Bird Law

To Aid in the "Restoration of Game-Birds and Other Wild Birds"

M A Y   1 8 ,   1 9 0 0

On May 18, 1900, the U.S. Congress passed the Lacey Bird Law, the first comprehensive federal legislation designed to protect wildlife. One week later the landmark law was signed into law by President William McKinley. This legislation, named after its chief sponsor, Representative John F. Lacey, outlawed the interstate shipment of any wild birds or animals slain in violation of state laws. It constituted a major blow to market hunters, and it marked an important step forward in expanding federal regulatory authority on natural resource conservation issues. In addition, the passage of the Lacey Bird Law invigorated sportsmen, hunting and fishing organizations, and the sporting press, all of whom had helped stoke Congressional support for the law. In the aftermath of this triumph, conservation-minded sportsmen assumed an even more prominent role in galvanizing public support for local, state, and federal land and resource conservation policies.

AN ACT TO ENLARGE THE POWERS OF THE DEPARTMENT OF AGRICULTURE, PROHIBIT THE TRANSPORTATION BY INTERSTATE COMMERCE OF GAME KILLED IN VIOLATION OF LOCAL LAWS, AND FOR OTHER PURPOSES.

Be it enacted by the Senate and House of Representatives in the United States of America in Congress assembled, That the duties and powers of the Department of Agriculture are hereby enlarged so as to include the preservation, distribution, introduction, and restoration of game-birds and other wild birds. The Secretary of Agriculture is hereby authorized to adopt such measures as may be necessary to carry out the purposes of this act and to purchase such game-birds and other wild birds as may be required therefor, subject, however, to the laws of the various States and Territories. The object and purpose of this act is to aid in the restoration of such birds in those parts of the United States adapted thereto where the same have become scarce or extinct, and also to regulate the introduction of American or foreign birds or animals in localities where they have not heretofore existed.

The Secretary of Agriculture shall from time to time collect and publish useful information as to the propagation, uses, and preservation of such birds. And the Secretary of Agriculture shall make and publish all needful rules and regulations for carrying out the purposes of this act, and shall expend for said purposes such sums as Congress may appropriate therefor.

SEC. 2.—That it shall be unlawful for any person or persons to import into the United States any foreign wild animal or bird except under special permit from the United States Department of Agriculture: *Provided,* That nothing in this section shall restrict the importation of natural history specimens for museums or scientific collections or the importation of certain cage birds, such as domesticated canaries, parrots, or such other species as the Secretary of Agriculture may designate.

The importation of the mongoose, the so-called "flying-foxes" or fruit bats, the English sparrow, the starling, or such other birds or animals as the Secretary of Agriculture may from time to time declare injurious to the interest of agriculture or horticulture is hereby prohibited, and such species upon arrival at any of the ports of the United States shall be destroyed or returned at the expense of the owner. The Secretary of the Treasury is hereby authorized to make regulations for carrying into effect the provisions of this section.

SEC. 3.—That it shall be unlawful for any person or persons to deliver to any common carrier or for any common carrier to transport from one State or Territory to another State or Territory, or from the District of Columbia or Alaska to any State or Territory, or from any State or Territory to the District of Columbia or Alaska, any foreign animals or birds the importation of which is prohibited, or the dead bodies or parts thereof of any wild animals or birds where such animals or birds have been killed in violation of the laws of the State, Territory, or District in which the same were killed: *Provided,* That nothing herein shall prevent the transportation of any dead birds or animals killed during the season when the same may be lawfully captured and the export of which is not prohibited by law in the State, Territory, or District in which the same are killed.

SEC. 4.—That all packages containing such dead animals, birds, or parts thereof, when shipped by interstate commerce, as provided in Section 1 of this act, shall be plainly and clearly marked, so that the name and address of the shipper and the nature of the contents may be readily ascertained on inspection of the outside of such packages. For each evasion or violation of this act the shipper shall, upon conviction, pay a fine of not exceeding two hundred dollars; and the consignee knowingly receiving such articles so shipped and transported in violation of this act shall, upon conviction, pay a fine of not exceeding two hundred dollars; and the carrier knowingly carrying or transporting the same shall, upon conviction, pay a fine of not exceeding two hundred dollars.

SEC. 5.—That all dead bodies, or parts thereof, of any foreign game-animals or game- or song-birds, the importation of which is prohibited, or the dead bodies or parts thereof of any wild game-animals or game- or song-birds transported into any State or Territory, or remaining therein for use, consumption, sale, or storage therein, shall, upon arrival in such State or Territory, be subject to the operation and effect of the laws of such State or Territory enacted in the exercise of its police powers, to the same extent and in the same manner as though such animals and birds had been produced in such State or Territory, and shall not be exempt therefrom by reason of being introduced therein in original packages or otherwise. This act shall not prevent the importation, transportation, or sale of birds or bird plumage manufactured from the feathers of barn-yard fowl.

Source: "The Lacey Bird Law." In *Birds in Their Relations to Man: A Manual of Economic Ornithology for the United States and Canada.* Edited by Clarence M. Weed and Ned Dearborn. Philadelphia: J.B. Lippincott, 1903, pp. 320–322.

CHAPTER 4

Theodore Roosevelt and the Age of Conservation

1900-1920

The broad outlines of modern-day attitudes and policies toward wilderness preservation and sustainable natural resource use came into focus in the opening decades of the twentieth century. The men who breathed life into these programs and ideals—men such as President Theodore Roosevelt, Forest Chief Gifford Pinchot, and wilderness advocate John Muir—remain iconic figures in America's canon of environmental leadership. The pillars on which the country's current systems of national parks, national forests, and wildlife refuges rest were erected by these strong-willed individuals and their allies.

But the stunning conservation advances unfurled during America's Progressive Era were not universally hailed. During this so-called "golden age" of conservation, environmental issues also became hugely contentious subjects of public debate and acrimony. As Roosevelt and others revolutionized the nation's natural resource policies, their methods and priorities sparked opposition from a wide array of constituencies—and even exposed bitter ideological divisions within the conservation movement itself. A century later, the ideological offspring of these camps continue to wage political battle over the shape and substance of environmental policy–making in America.

THEODORE ROOSEVELT AND THE PROGRESSIVE ERA

The United States entered the twentieth century in a state of profound social turmoil and uncertainty about the future. On the one hand, Americans expressed immense pride and satisfaction when they looked back on their handiwork of the previous century. After all, they had tamed much of a wild, sprawling continent during that time—an accomplishment symbolized by the U.S. Bureau of the Census's 1890 announcement that rapid western settlement had brought about the "closing of the frontier." Americans were also heartened by the nation's prodigious economic growth, its industrial ingenuity, and its expanding stores of scientific knowledge.

But the Industrial Revolution had also transformed the country in unsettling ways. The national economy was dominated by corporate trusts that were in turn directed by ruthless titans of business such as John D. Rockefeller, the emperor of Standard Oil, and J. P. Morgan, the banking and railroad magnate. These behemoths controlled entire sectors of the U.S. economy. In 1900, in fact, 1 percent of the nation's companies produced 40 percent of the nation's manufacturing output.[1] In the meantime, Americans were expressing growing resentment about endemic political corruption, mounting labor

Avid hunter and conservationist Theodore Roosevelt used his expansive view of executive authority to push a progressive environmental agenda during his two terms in office. Here, Roosevelt is pictured with conservationist John Muir at Glacier Point overlooking Yosemite Valley in 1903.

unrest over persistently low wages and poor working conditions, general alarm about immigrant-fueled overcrowding and impoverishment in the cities, and increasing trepidation about the country's voracious consumption of natural resources.

In response to these troubling byproducts of industrialization and population growth, political and social reformers known as "progressives" leaped into the breach. Progressive reformers at the turn of the century came from every economic class, but they hailed primarily from middle-class and upper-class backgrounds. Educated, affluent, and politically connected, these reformers waged campaigns of social and economic justice that hinged on expanding the power of government to intervene where necessary and impose new guidelines on the behavior of industry and individual alike, all in service to the progressive vision of a more just, equitable, and sustainable society. And when Theodore Roosevelt became president in 1901, these idealistic reformers gained a vital ally in the White House.

Roosevelt had served as vice president to President William McKinley for less than a year when McKinley was shot by a gunman during a visit to Buffalo on September 10, 1901. McKinley died three days later, and Roosevelt was sworn in as America's twenty-sixth president on September 14. He quickly signaled his intention to pursue the same sorts of progressive public policy reforms that had marked his tenure as governor of New York State in the late 1890s. In his first annual message to Congress, delivered only three months after taking occupancy of the Oval Office, Roosevelt delivered a warning shot across the bow of corporate America. "The captains of industry who have driven the railway systems across this continent, who have built up our commerce, who have developed our manufactures, have on the whole done great good to our people," he acknowledged. "Without them the material development of which we are so justly proud could never have taken place. . . . Yet it is also true that there are real and great evils [in corporate America] . . . and a resolute and practical effort must be made to correct these evils."[2] He also declared his intention to make fundamental changes in America's stewardship of its natural resources (**see Document 4.1**).

As his first term unfolded, Roosevelt displayed again and again his bedrock conviction that government had a legitimate role to play in protecting the public interest from excessive corporate power and the collateral damage wreaked by industrialization. "Roosevelt saw himself as an active mediator representing the public, and an equal to the lords of both labor and industry," explained one scholar.[3] To this end, Roosevelt embraced an expansive interpretation of executive powers. As he later stated in his autobiography, he believed that

> every executive officer, and above all every executive officer in high position, was a steward of the people bound actively and affirmatively to do all he could for the people. . . . I declined to adopt the view that what was imperatively necessary for the Nation could not be done by the President unless he could find some specific authorization to do it. My belief was that it was not only his right but his duty to do anything that the needs of the Nation demanded unless such action was forbidden by the Constitution or by the law . . . I did not usurp power, but I did greatly broaden the use of executive power.[4]

Armed with pent-up public demand for meaningful reform and his own furious intellect and larger-than-life personality, Roosevelt took up the progressive banner with gusto. He implemented initiatives and executive orders designed to address many problems bedeviling the country in the early 1900s, including child labor, squalid urban tenements, rapacious business monopolies, and the "spoils system" of political patronage. He also used the "bully pulpit" of the presidency to flog Congress and corporate interests to fall in line behind his leadership. His boldest use of executive authority, however, came in the realm of natural resource policy.

Roosevelt strode onto the White House stage at a time when Congress was already showing signs of stirring from its longstanding practice of leaving natural resource stewardship to private enterprise. Legislation such as the 1891 Forest Reserve Act and the 1899 Rivers and Harbors Act signaled a growing belief that *some* regulatory limits had to be imposed on private exploitation of the public domain. But Roosevelt was a lifelong hunter and outdoorsman who had seen firsthand the damage that unchecked resource commodification had done to forests, prairies, lakes, and rivers in many parts of the country. He knew that woodlands not only constituted a vital economic resource, but also played an important role in watershed protection and nurturing wildlife. And he had spent countless hours in the wilderness in the company of sportsman–conservationists such as George Bird Grinnell, the longtime editor of *Forest and Stream* and organizer of the first Audubon Society.

So when it came to reworking the ways in which America handled its natural resources, Roosevelt was a man on a mission. "The idea that our natural resources were inexhaustible still obtained [when I took office], and there was as yet no real knowledge of their extent and condition," he later explained in his autobiography. "The relation of the conservation of natural resources to the problems of National welfare and National efficiency had not yet dawned on the public mind. The reclamation of arid public lands in the West was still a matter for private enterprise alone; and our magnificent river system, with its superb possibilities for public usefulness, was dealt with by the National Government not as a unit, but as a disconnected series of pork-barrel problems, whose only real interest was in their effect on the reelection or defeat of a Congressman here and there."[5]

ROOSEVELT AND PINCHOT

Roosevelt's approach to natural resource policy pivoted on his conviction that effective stewardship of America's lands and waterways was impossible without the active involvement of the federal government. To this end, Roosevelt wielded his executive authority like a fishing net, casting it into the deep waters of America's public domain and hauling out forest reserves, national monuments, and wildlife refuges by the score. Simultaneously, he set in motion the creation—or expansion—of federal agencies and departments to manage both old and new classes of public land. The president's right-hand man in the development of this infrastructure and the guiding principles under which it operated was Gifford Pinchot, the nation's chief forester and Roosevelt's unofficial minister of conservation.

An early apostle of science-based forestry, Pinchot had become the head of the Interior Department's Forestry division in 1898, succeeding Bernard Fernow. He was an ardent advocate for systematic forest management who had rejoiced at the passage of the 1891 Forest Reserve Act, calling it "the most important legislation in the history of Forestry in America."[6] But he recognized that the Forest Reserve Act was only a first step in changing the way Americans viewed and used their woodlands. "When the Gay Nineties began, the common word for our forests was 'inexhaustible,'" Pinchot recalled in his autobiography:

> To waste timber was a virtue and not a crime. . . . [Timbermen] regarded forest devastation as normal and second growth as a delusion of fools. . . . And as for sustained yield, no such idea had ever entered their heads. The few friends the forest had were spoken of, when they were spoken of at all, as impractical theorists, fanatics, or "denudatics," more or less touched in the head. What talk there was about forest protection was no more to the average American that the buzzing of a mosquito, and just about as irritating.[7]

Pinchot had become friends with Roosevelt during the latter's tenure as New York's governor. Once Roosevelt entered the Oval Office, the forester enjoyed unprecedented access to the president for a mere division chief. Within a matter of a few months, in fact, Pinchot had become entrenched as Roosevelt's most trusted advisor on natural resource development and conservation issues. The subsequent triumphs of the Roosevelt Administration in the area of conservation have to be understood in that context: They were the product of a remarkable partnership between two men fervently committed to their cause.

THE RECLAMATION ACT OF 1902

The Roosevelt Administration's first landmark in environmental policy–making was the National Reclamation Act of 1902, which dramatically expanded the federal government's role in developing and managing water and power resources in the arid West (see Document 4.2). It came at a time when further western development seemed stymied by the region's limited access to water and the modest financial resources of state governments in the territory. These realities gave the Reclamation Act—and the programs it spawned—a measure of western popularity that later federal resource management measures would lack. "To resist a federal reclamation program," explained historian Marc Reisner, "was to block all further migration to the West and to ensure disaster for those who were already there—or for those who were on the way."[8]

The Reclamation Act thoroughly nationalized the work of irrigation by creating a federal agency within the Interior Department's Geological Survey called the Reclamation Service. This new service was armed with an explicit mandate to capture and develop water resources in the West for irrigation. These ambitious engineering projects, owned and operated by the federal government, would be financed in part from receipts from sales of irrigable public lands and in part from a self-perpetuating funding mechanism: payments from irrigators and other users of the water that would be made available when the dams, canals, and reservoirs were completed. The Act also gave the Department of the Interior broad freedom to allocate Reclamation dollars as it saw fit, thus ushering in what scholar Richard N. L. Andrews called "the first statutory affirmation of the Progressive idea that environmental assets should be managed not by elected representatives, but by technical professionals and politically neutral administrators."[9]

The creation of the service prompted a fresh surge of interest in western settlement. The total number of homestead applications in the eleven arid states of the far West more than tripled between 1900 and 1910,[10] and regional boosters hailed the coming conversion of desert to garden. "It is evident that the [Texas] Panhandle, as it has been and as it is now regarded in the popular mind, will soon be a thing of the past," proclaimed a 1906 magazine published by the Santa Fe and Topeka Railroad. "The great cattle ranches, the wandering masses of cattle, the rounding cowboy, the vast circumference of unpeopled desert. . . . All these, it can be foreseen, will give way perhaps almost entirely in time, as they are now fast giving way to the spreading farm element. To have begun to conquer, by new methods, what has long been considered a repulsive desert, is in itself a monumental tribute to man's patience, ingenuity, and enterprise."[11]

Such optimism ultimately proved well-founded (although ranching operations were revitalized rather than snuffed out by Reclamation projects). In 1907 the Reclamation Service was separated from the Geological Survey, and in 1923 it became the Bureau of Reclamation. During these early years it attracted engineering talent from all over the country because, as Reisner put it, "the prospect of reclaiming a desert seemed infinitely more satisfying than designing a steel mill in Gary, Indiana."[12] By 1930 the Bureau of Reclamation had completed twenty-nine projects serving more than 2.5 million acres of irrigable land.[13] From the 1930s through the 1960s the agency became virtually synonymous with western water development.

PINCHOT AND THE NATION'S FORESTS

Roosevelt watched the Bureau of Reclamation take its first institutional steps with fatherly pride, but his determination to stake out a more prominent federal role in natural resource management did not end there. To the contrary, his efforts were just beginning. By the time his first term came to a close in early 1905, Roosevelt had designated twenty-six new national forest reserves containing about 16.3 million acres, bringing the total amount of "federal reserve" forestland—public lands where logging, hunting, fishing, and other uses were generally still permitted but subject to federally mandated limitations—in the United States to nearly 63 million acres. He then opened his second term by signing the 1905 Transfer Act into law. This measure transferred the responsibility for the management of America's expanding national forest system from the Department of the Interior's General Land Office—which had a long history of sycophancy to the timber barons, mine owners, and railroad magnates of the West—to the Department of Agriculture, where Pinchot's fledgling Forest Service was located.

The Transfer Act did just what Roosevelt (and Pinchot) intended: It put responsibility for all of America's federal forests in the forest chief's lap. "The transfer meant a revolutionary change," Pinchot wrote. "We had the power, as we had the duty, to protect the Reserves for the use of the people, and that meant stepping on the toes of the biggest interests in the West. From that time on, it was fight, fight, fight."[14]

Of note, the act was also part of a larger bundle of 1905 forest legislation that gave Pinchot serious administrative power and autonomy and transformed the national forests from abstractions that existed mostly on paper into lands patrolled and managed by a corps of professional foresters. It included a five-year deal wherein all receipts from the sale of timber, grazing rights, water rights, and other commercial activity within the forest reserves would be diverted to a separate fund for forest reserve management. This was a great gift to Pinchot because it significantly reduced the Forest Service's dependence on appropriations from Congress—some members of which were voicing mounting dismay with the administration's relentlessly pro-conservation policies.

Pinchot moved quickly to consolidate his administrative grip on the nation's forests and to advance the Roosevelt administration's vision of public forestlands as commercial assets suitable for multiple industrial uses, provided that they were managed with an eye toward long-term sustainability and long-term public benefit. This is a detail that has sometimes been lost in the sepia-toned portrait of Roosevelt as America's first great conservationist. The reputation is well-earned, but both Roosevelt and his forest chief viewed resource conservation through the prism of utilitarianism. Pinchot in particular frequently equated wilderness with waste, and he regarded natural resources as the country's "great sources of prosperity."[15] In light of this philosophy, relatively few public lands—even those of significant physical beauty—were spared from some form of commercial use. "Under the Theodore Roosevelt conservation movement," summarized historian Samuel Hays, "The apostles of the gospel of efficiency subordinated the aesthetic to the utilitarian"[16] **(see Document 4.9)**.

Pinchot imposed order and limits on the exploitation of the "great sources of prosperity" under his supervision. He enlisted talented professionals from the fields of forestry, geology, and hydrology in the work of the Forest Service and gave them explicit instructions for making his proposed sustainable or "wise use" regimen a reality. One cornerstone of this management plan, which the Roosevelt Administration also emphasized on other public lands, was market-based fees for the extraction of timber, minerals, and grazing privileges. No longer would timber and mining companies be permitted to reap millions in profits from public lands without compensating the American people. "The Forest Service . . . fought the predatory big man as no government had done before," declared Pinchot. "Big Money was King in the Great Open Spaces, and no mistake. But in the national forests, Big Money was not King."[17]

Another Forest Service priority was stepped-up enforcement of existing laws crafted to address timber trespass and other looting of the public domain. Pinchot even cast his gaze beyond the public forest reserves to the health and sustainability of privately owned forests, lending technical and scientific assistance to their industrial owners. And even as all of this was going on, Pinchot's band of foresters were roaming across the length and breadth of the West, surveying and mapping great expanses of woodlands for inclusion in the national forest system.

By the close of Roosevelt's presidency in 1909, Pinchot was applying his principles of sustainable conservation to 149 national forests encompassing about 194 million acres.

The existence of this expanded tapestry of national forests was a result of Roosevelt's continued enthusiasm for designating new forest reserves; from 1905 to 1909 alone, he set aside a stunning 131 million acres.

ROOSEVELT AND THE PRESERVATIONIST ETHIC

Roosevelt was fully supportive of Pinchot-style "wise use" of America's forests and other natural resources. He not only saw the implementation of such policies as necessary for long-term economic growth, but also as an issue of national security and patriotism. But unlike his hard-driving forest chief, the president also possessed a profound spiritual appreciation for the wonders of nature and the call of wilderness. When he and John Muir went on a famous March 1903 camping trip into the heart of Yosemite, for instance, the president and the Sierra Club founder were of one mind about the priceless majesty of the place.

Roosevelt's emotional connection to the wild was nurtured by his years as a sportsman, but counterintuitively, his affluent background also probably played an important role. As environmental historian William Cronon noted, "[T]he very men who most benefited from urban-industrial capitalism were among those who believed they must escape its debilitating effects. If the frontier was passing, then men who had the means to do so should preserve for themselves some remnant of its wild landscape so that they might enjoy the regeneration and renewal that came from sleeping under the stars, participating in blood sports, and living off the land. The frontier might be gone, but the frontier experience could still be had if only wilderness were preserved."[18]

Roosevelt himself frequently espoused his brand of conservation as one with both practical and aesthetic strains. "Birds should be saved for utilitarian reasons; and, moreover, they should be saved because of reasons unconnected with dollars and cents," he declared after leaving office.

> A grove of giant redwoods or sequoias should be kept just as we keep a great and beautiful cathedral. The extermination of the passenger-pigeon meant that mankind was just so much poorer. . . . And to lose the chance to see frigate-birds soaring in circles above the storm, or a file of pelicans winging their way homeward across the crimson afterglow or the sunset, or a myriad of terns flashing in the bright light of midday as they hover in a shifting maze above the beach—why, the loss is like the loss of a gallery of the masterpieces of the artists of old time.[19]

These convictions led Roosevelt to designate five new national parks during his presidency. He also approved the 1906 transfer of Yosemite from state to federal authority, paving the way for it to also receive full national park protections. And in 1903 he inaugurated the nation's wildlife refuge system by extending federal protection to tiny Pelican Island in Florida's Indian River. Roosevelt designated a total of fifty-five federal bird and game reservations during his administration. These refuges, which were placed under the authority of the Department of Interior, placed greater emphasis on wildlife preservation than the multiple-use management ethos that governed Department of Agriculture policies in the national forests.

Another landmark in American wilderness preservation came in 1906, when Roosevelt signed the Antiquities Act into law. The language of this act gave Roosevelt and successor presidents the authority to preserve from commercial development "historic landmarks, historic and prehistoric structures, and other objects of historic or scientific interest" in the public domain by designating them as national monuments (**see Document 4.3**).

Roosevelt wielded this newfound power exuberantly. He established the first eighteen national monuments in the United States, beginning with Devil's Tower in Wyoming (established September 24, 1906) and ending with Mount Olympus in Washington (March 2, 1909) in only two and a half years. Several of these national monuments ultimately became national parks, most notably the Grand Canyon in Arizona. "Keep this great wonder of nature as it is," declared Roosevelt in announcing national monument protection for the Grand Canyon. "You can not improve it. The ages have been at work on it, and man can only mar it."

Significantly, the agencies and departments charged with stewardship of these refuges, parks, and monuments were professionalized in much the same manner as Pinchot's Forest Service. Indeed, America's entire system of governance underwent substantial change during Roosevelt's presidency. "From a system largely limited to congressional lawmaking it became an elaborate structure which relied heavily on administrative agencies with discretionary authority to translate broad strategy mandates into the technical details of day-to-day implementation," summarized one scholar. "An administrative system largely staffed through political patronage was transformed into one staffed by scientific and technical professionals."[20]

Conservation Rhetoric and Public Policy in the Roosevelt White House

As the Roosevelt Administration rewrote the policies and programs governing public land use in America, it also embarked on a relentless campaign to educate citizens and lawmakers alike about the importance of this course of action. Trusted "Roosevelt conservationists" such as Pinchot, geologist WJ McGee, Reclamation Service engineer F. H. Newell, and Interior Secretary James R. Garfield all took turns spreading the message. Roosevelt, however, took the lead in this effort. He took this role partly because he knew that his personal popularity could help generate crucial public support for his conservation agenda. But Roosevelt also did so out of frustration with the public's continued sluggish response to what he saw as a genuine crisis. "For Roosevelt, rapaciousness regarding the environment may have been contemptible, but indifference was intolerable," observed scholar Leroy Dorsey. "The greedy timber barons, then, were not the only ones that Roosevelt the prophet called to judgment. . . . He maintained that the much larger group that threatened to deprive future generations of God's environmental gifts was the American people themselves; their sin, one of indifference."[21]

Still, Roosevelt's bluntest remarks were usually reserved for Washington lawmakers. In his annual message to Congress in December 1907, for instance, he thundered that

> The conservation of our natural resources and their proper use constitute the fundamental problem which underlies almost every other problem of our National life. . . . The reward of foresight for this Nation is great and easily foretold. But there must be the look ahead, there must be a realization of the fact that to waste, to destroy, our natural resources, to skin and exhaust land instead of using it so as to increase

its usefulness, will result in undermining in the days of our children the very prosperity which we ought by right to hand down to them amplified and developed. For the last few years, the Government has been endeavoring to get our people to look ahead and to substitute a planned and orderly development of our resources in place of a haphazard striving for immediate profit. . . . There has been, of course, opposition to this work; opposition from some interested men who desire to exhaust the land for their own immediate profit without regard to the welfare of the next generation, and opposition from honest and well-meaning men who did not fully understand the subject or who did not look far enough ahead.[22]

Roosevelt's crusade also led him to embrace other public relations efforts. In the spring of 1908, for instance, he and Pinchot organized and presided over the first-ever White House Conference on Conservation (see Document 4.4). At the conclusion of this three-day event, which drew governors, congressmen, and resource experts from all across the country, the conference issued a "Declaration for Conservation of Natural Resources" supporting administration policies. This conference also laid the groundwork for the creation of the National Conservation Commission.

Other natural resource commissions also sprang up during Roosevelt's last months in office, including ones committed to scientific study of the management of inland waterways and public lands. These commissions gathered together many of the finest and most dedicated administrators and scientists in the country. And they approached their work with the same understanding that informed the efforts of other natural resource management agencies and departments created or overhauled during the Roosevelt years: that the resources of the public domain were to be used for the long-term public interest.

THE BACKLASH AGAINST CONSERVATION

Many Americans welcomed the policy changes implemented by the Roosevelt conservationists and accepted the underlying reasoning for them as articulated by the president and his lieutenants. But there were also pockets of fierce resistance to Roosevelt's new conservation paradigm. This unhappiness could be found in all regions, but political opposition was concentrated in the western states, which possessed economies that were heavily dependent on resource-extraction industries and large tracts of public land directly affected by Roosevelt's new land-use policies. Western critics were skeptical of *any* federal limitations on their activities, and they frequently asserted that the administration's resource policies trampled on states' rights, smothered entrepreneurship and economic growth, and deprived development-hungry states of tax revenues that could be generated if the reserved lands were held in private ownership.

This anger spiraled to its greatest heights during the president's 1905–1909 term, when Roosevelt designated most of the federal forest reserves, refuges, parks, and monuments created under his watch. And it manifested itself in myriad different forms. In 1907, for example, western lawmakers used that year's Agricultural Appropriations Act to curb what they saw as forest conservation run amok. They inserted language eliminating the independent funding sources created for Pinchot and the Forest Service by the 1905 Transfer Act. The 1907 act also renamed all federal forest reserves "national forests" to remove "any connotation that these areas were to be locked up as inviolate sanctuaries."[23]

Most telling, the 1907 Agricultural Appropriations Act forbade the creation or enlargement of any additional forest reserves in Washington, Oregon, Idaho, Montana, Colorado, and Wyoming without the explicit approval of Congress. The Roosevelt Administration's high-handed response to this congressional reproach further exacerbated the West's smoldering resentment: Roosevelt hurriedly bestowed federal protection on an additional sixteen million acres of forestland in those six states in the eight days between congressional passage of the appropriations act and his signing of the bill into law on March 4.

Opponents of Roosevelt's conservation policies worked diligently to sway public opinion and lawmakers' votes to their side. In June 1907 Colorado Governor Henry Buchtel hosted a Denver Public Lands Convention that attracted hundreds of western legislators and representatives of the ranching, agricultural, mining, and timber industries. The convention featured numerous speakers who condemned the administration's conservation philosophy and demanded that the federal government cede national forests and other public lands over to the states. "I object to landlordism by the rich and by the government alike," declared one of the featured speakers, U.S. Senator Henry Teller of Colorado.

> And I do not see any difference, except that I believe the individual landlord would be more endurable than a government landlord, and if those of you who have lived in the neighborhood of forest reserves do not support me in that view it is because you have not been observing. . . . I thank God that the trees are gone and that in their place have come men and women, Christian men and Christian women, liberty-loving men and liberty-loving women; and I assert here today that I do not believe there is an acre of public land where the public timber has ever been cut off that has not gone into beneficial use for the people of this country.[24]

Pro-development writers and newspaper editors added their voices to the chorus of complaint. In northern Minnesota a local newspaper responded bitterly on learning of a 1905 decision by Roosevelt to shield more than 140,000 acres of regional forestland from timbering (four years later this tract became the state's Superior National Forest). "Northern Minnesota is much too earnest in her building up an empire out of a wilderness to be patient with silly schemes or forest reserves, parks and hunting grounds that will block her efforts to make something out of herself," charged the *Ely Miner*.[25] Author George L. Knapp issued an anti-conservation broadside in which he sardonically described himself as one of the nation's "exiles in sin who hold that a large part of the 'conservation' movement is unadulterated humbug."[26] As these sorts of condemnations proliferated, conservationists—both within and outside of government—counterattacked with vigor. They defended the wisdom and necessity of resource conservation and denounced some pro-development arguments as transparent rationalizations for greed and gluttony.

These battle lines remained in place after Roosevelt left the White House and his hand-picked successor, William H. Taft, took up residence. In September 1910, for example, a Second National Conservation Congress convened in St. Paul, Minnesota, became stalemated in acrimony (**see Document 4.6**). Republican Governor Bryant Butler Brooks of Wyoming issued a representative soliloquy from the pro-development western delegation: "How can we educate our children, how can we maintain good government and good law, how can we do all those necessary and essential things to maintain a high state of civilization and progress, if over one-half of the State is to be held permanently as a

Federal resource, giving no taxation or revenue whatever to the support of our State governments?"[27] Democratic Governor Edwin L. Norris of Montana, meanwhile, attacked federal conservation policies from the states' rights angle: "You cannot trust the State? Why not? If you cannot trust the people of Montana to conserve its resources, if you cannot trust the State of Wyoming to conserve its resources, can we trust the State of Maine, or the State of Florida to conserve them for us? What reasons have we to assume that the people of the State of Massachusetts or the State of Louisiana are more patriotic in that respect than are our own people?"[28]

These protests were met with stern rebukes from attendees who supported active federal management of natural resources. "I do know that the great syndicates and the great corporations that want to gobble up all these coal lands and control these [water] power sites [in the West], every bloody one of them, want State control," stated Republican Governor Walter R. Stubbs of Kansas. "And the reason they want State control is because the meshes are too small in the national net; the Federal Government has given them genuine supervision and genuine control of national resources, and I thank God for it, too. . . . And I say to you today that the American people ought to build a monument to Theodore Roosevelt and Gifford Pinchot for the work they have done in this line."[29]

The bitterness between these factions continued to flare throughout the 1910s. Opponents of federal management of natural resource commodities and public lands continued to issue indignant calls for expanded state control. And partisans of Roosevelt-style federal management programs, including leading officials of the Forest and Reclamation services, continued to condemn such proposals as irresponsible and disingenuous (**see Document 4.7**).

Conservation Laws Exacerbate Class Divisions

The trend toward increased regulation of timber cutting, grazing, and hunting also opened other schisms in American society. In rural areas from the Great Lakes to the Gulf Coast to the Pacific Northwest, local residents had historically enjoyed almost total freedom to engage in subsistence-level timber felling, hunting, and other activities on public land. And for many such families, these foraging and hunting activities were all that kept hunger and cold at bay, especially during long winter months. As local forests, streams, and wildlife increasingly came under the aegis of federal and state authorities in the late nineteenth and early twentieth centuries, rural Americans protested—and in many cases simply defied—the new restrictions by engaging in poaching and other illegal activities.

Conservationists generally tried to minimize the level of resistance to their policies emanating from this corner. Instead, they continued to train their rhetorical guns on greedy timber barons and water magnates. "Many opponents of conservation were wealthy, but labeling all their critics as plutocrats was also a way for conservationists to deflect attention from their program's tendency to deny freedoms long inherent to local life," explained historian Louis Warren. "Among the people who suffered most were the rural poor. There was no escaping this contradiction: where the 'national commons' secured liberties for some, it also brought a significant degree of coercion."[30]

Resource management professionals and their philosophical allies, most notably affluent sportsmen and fishermen who were at the vanguard of the conservation movement, rarely showed much empathy for the locals' plight. Instead, they responded to local challenges by stepping up enforcement and denigrating the morality of violators. This was especially true in the area of wildlife management, where stamping out market hunting and curbing "pothunting" (subsistence hunting for one's immediate family) had come to be seen within the affluent conservationist fraternity as essential in stabilizing wildlife populations. "Elite recreational hunters began to set standards of behavior for other hunters, cleaning the fields of all who did not abide by the sportsmen's ethic," summarized Warren. "The backbone of the conservationist cause, recreational hunters lobbied lawmakers to pass game laws that effectively wrote their own sporting ideals into legal statutes."[31]

Many sportsmen/conservationists also dropped their historic opposition to hunting and fishing licenses during this period. During the nineteenth century, state attempts to introduce licensing requirements for residents or nonresidents had foundered on the commonly held belief that they were contrary to American ideals of democracy and neighborliness. They had also been dismissed as unnecessary in a nation blessed with a limitless bounty of wild game. But licensing was revisited in the early twentieth century, in large measure because it was seen by state administrators and wealthy sportsmen alike as a good source of funding for rapidly expanding wildlife and resource protection programs. Poor hunting-dependent citizens in rural areas, however, were understandably less supportive of these new demands on their pocketbooks.[32]

Some conservationists took note of the feelings of frustration and powerlessness that state and federal resource control engendered in rural communities. Some even expressed wariness about turning "America's conservation regimes into a copy of Europe's notoriously undemocratic game codes, where landowners owned the wildlife, hunting had become a privilege of the wealthy, and wildlife had practically vanished because the masses took no interest in protecting it."[33] By the 1910s government agents and officials like New Mexico forester Aldo Leopold, who became one of the country's most prominent conservationist voices of the 1930s and 1940s, were emphasizing the importance of crafting "democratic" regulations that would keep national forests and other public lands open to all hunters and recreationists.[34]

The implementation of these measures, however, failed to pacify some critics who wanted a return to the unregulated environment in which Americans had once hunted, fished, mined, and cut timber. In fact, local communities (still poor and rural, and often with extraction-based economies) and conservation agencies and organizations (still educated, affluent, and urban-based) continue to do battle today—more than a century after the schism first opened—over a wide range of natural resource management issues.

IMMIGRATION AND THE CONSERVATION MOVEMENT

The additional economic burdens imposed on rural, subsistence-oriented communities by federal and state conservation programs and policies in the opening decades of the twentieth century were largely unintended—or were at least not imposed with spite. An exception to this general rule, however, could be seen in official attitudes toward immigrant communities. In some regions of the country, immigrants endured nakedly discriminatory hunting and land-use policies and laws.

This officially sanctioned hostility stemmed from a complex mix of socioeconomic factors. By the early 1900s the United States was in the midst of the greatest immigration wave in its history. Each year, millions of Europeans made the arduous voyage across the Atlantic, then disappeared into American cities, towns, and fields in search of a better life. But unlike earlier waves of immigration, these new arrivals did not hail primarily from England, Germany, or Ireland. Instead, they mostly came from impoverished regions of Southern and Eastern Europe. Some native-born Americans and established emigrants from Western Europe welcomed the new immigrants, but others regarded their arrival with undisguised alarm. Some worried that the new immigrants brought unwanted competition for jobs and housing; others thought that they would undermine "American" cultural and religious values. Conservationists, meanwhile, wondered how a nation that was finally coming to terms with its profligate history of resource use could possibly accommodate millions of new people every year and still adhere to a model of sustainable resource use. And of course, all of these economic, cultural, and environmental concerns were heavily garnished with xenophobia.

Most of the anti-immigrant sentiment proffered by conservationists came in the realm of hunting, which was both an important wage supplement to many immigrant families and a respite from the industrial din where breadwinners spent most of their days. "Conservationists and sport hunters increasingly singled out the foreign-born for criticism," reported scholar Adam Rome. "The most reviled were the Italians. But the critics also attacked other groups, especially the 'Slavs,' a designation at the time for people from almost any central or eastern European nation."[35] State wildlife agencies across the country emphasized that "alien hunters" accounted for a disproportionate share of poaching incidents. In 1908, for example, the Pennsylvania Game Commission asserted that "by far the greatest number of cases of violation of our game laws reported to us during the past season, killing of game out of season, hunting on Sunday, killing song and insectivorous birds, is of wrongs done by the unnaturalized foreign born resident of this State, mostly Italians."[36] One year later, the Pennsylvania state legislature passed a sweeping law forbidding immigrants from hunting any wild game in the state (**see Document 4.5**).

Some opinion-makers in the conservation community, meanwhile, described immigrants as a virtual blight upon the land. "It is well known to all those interested in game conservation that one of the worst and most ruthless set of destroyers of our wild life is a class of foreign immigrants from Southern Europe," wrote Henry Chase in *Forest and Stream,* the most influential sportsmen's magazine of the Progressive Era. "They will shoot for their larders any living wild thing that crosses their path, from a deer to a chipmunk—from a wild goose to a sparrow. No living creature can escape them."[37] The famous naturalist William Hornaday was even more scathing. Writing in *Our Vanishing Wildlife,* he raged that "the Italian laborer is a human mongoose [toward wildlife]. Give him power to act, and he will quickly exterminate every wild thing that wears feathers or hair. To our song birds he is literally a 'pestilence that walketh at noonday.'"[38] These and other blanket condemnations of entire ethnic groups remained a persistent facet of the conservationist movement for years.

TAFT AND THE BALLINGER-PINCHOT FEUD

When William H. Taft succeeded Roosevelt as president in March 1909, he inherited all of these simmering political tensions. He also entered the Oval Office with a far different philosophy of governance and executive authority than his colorful predecessor. Unlike Roosevelt, Taft subscribed to a narrow and limited conception of presidential power based on strict interpretation of legal statutes and the Constitution. Taft's constructionist orientation had enormous consequences for U.S. conservation policy.

Taft was sensitive to the need for some resource conservation measures, and he added to the nation's roll of national parks, monuments, and forests during his single term. In 1911, for example, he signed the Weeks Act, which paved the way for extension of the national forest system into the eastern United States (see Document 4.12). Taft also kept Pinchot as his forest chief, partly to reassure skeptical "Roosevelt" Republicans of his loyalty to conservationist principles. But the new president viewed Roosevelt's frequent use of executive orders to secure land for national reserves, parks, and forests with disapproval. Convinced that Roosevelt's actions were both unduly extravagant and of dubious legality, Taft initiated steps to retroactively pass some of these new acquisitions through congressional channels for "proper" legislative approval. He abandoned this course of action only after it became clear that Pinchot and other Roosevelt conservationists were willing to mount a rebellion to stave off the threat.

Taft relented in that case, but elsewhere he maneuvered to make significant modifications to the Roosevelt conservation program that had been left in his care. In essence, Taft wanted to shift the creation and implementation of conservation policies out of the executive office and into the hands of Congress and individual statehouses. To this end, he pushed Congress to take the reins from the White House in identifying and securing future lands to be set aside for federal management and protection. Increased congressional authority over the disposition of public lands ultimately resulted in a greater level of state control over the management of public forests, waterways, and other resources within their borders, which Taft also supported.

In addition, Taft worked to remove or loosen some of the limitations that Roosevelt and members of his inner conservation circle had imposed on coal, oil, hydroelectric, and timber-cutting operations on public lands. The new president wanted to increase corporate access to public lands by relaxing leasing restrictions and other conservation regulations crafted by the Roosevelt Administration. This desire led Taft to appoint former Seattle mayor and well-known privatization advocate Richard Ballinger as his interior secretary.

Ballinger enthusiastically endorsed Taft's plans to open public lands to more extensive private development. "You chaps who are in favor of this conservation program are all wrong," stated Secretary Ballinger in a 1909 interview. "You are hindering the development of the west. In my opinion, the proper course to take with regard to [public lands] is to divide it up among the big corporations and the people who know how to make money out of it and let the people at large get the benefits of the circulation of the money."[39]

As Taft and Ballinger tried to roll back the previous administration's expansion of federal authority over natural resources, conservationists who felt personally betrayed by Taft rushed to defend Roosevelt's legacy. The leader of this crusade was Pinchot, who accused the new interior secretary of fraud and malfeasance in his treatment of public coal lands in Alaska. Republicans quickly took sides in the savage public relations and legal battles that followed, with the Progressives moving to Pinchot's camp and the conservatives standing behind Ballinger. American newspapers, meanwhile, issued numerous reports on the whole sordid spectacle (see Document 4.8).

Taft finally dismissed Pinchot for insubordination in January 1910, but by that time the damage had already been done. The ugly war between Pinchot and Ballinger further polarized the Republicans' conservative and progressive wings—and helped convince Roosevelt to come out of retirement and try to unseat Taft for the 1912 Republican nomination. When he failed in that bid, Roosevelt launched a third-party challenge that in effect delivered the White House to Democratic nominee Woodrow Wilson in the fall 1912 elections.

THE BATTLE FOR HETCH HETCHY

At the same time that the Ballinger-Pinchot feud showcased the philosophical gulf between conservationists and deregulators, another pitched political battle exposed once and for all the fault lines that existed *within* the conservation movement. This clash over the fate of California's Hetch Hetchy Valley pitted utilitarian conservationists of the Pinchot school against preservationists of the Muir camp, and it became one of the most famous disputes in American environmental history.

The clash originated in the opening decade of the twentieth century, when the city fathers of San Francisco identified the Tuolomne River in Yosemite National Park as a resource that could provide needed water and electricity to the growing Bay area. In damming the Tuolomne, however, a beautiful section of the park known as the Hetch Hetchy Valley would have to be flooded. This was completely unacceptable to the leadership of the Sierra Club and other wilderness preservationists who insisted that lands possessed of great beauty or ecological significance were of priceless value (**see Document 4.11**).

An impressive campaign to save Hetch Hetchy was launched by a coalition of preservationists, newspaper editors, and lawmakers who castigated the pro-damming crowd as greedy and shortsighted. "[This] incomparable wonderland," wrote Sierra Club official Edward Taylor Parsons, "is threatened with destructive invasion in order that selfish and local interests may profit in a financial way. . . . If the needless and destructive right to flood the wonderful Hetch-Hetchy Valley is granted to San Francisco, the precedent that would be established would shake to the very foundation the whole National Park policy. Thereafter, no National Park, however great and wonderful, would be safe from despoliation."[40] The *Portland Oregonian,* meanwhile, characterized San Francisco's efforts to dam the Tuolomne and flood Hetch Hetchy as outright theft: "The Hetch Hetchy Valley belongs to the people and they ought to be able to keep it."[41]

Supporters of the damming scheme, however, responded with equal vigor. Oakland Mayor Warren Olney, who had been a stalwart member of the Sierra Club before the Hetch Hetchy controversy erupted, declared that "there have been many objections made to San Francisco and the Other Bay Cities utilizing the waters of Tuolumne River, but these objections have been made mostly by people who do not understand the actual condition that confronts the Bay Cities, or else are lacking in the ability to take a broad, comprehensive view of the situation and the needs of humanity."[42] Pinchot himself also appeared before Congress to defend the utilitarian underpinnings of the dam proposal. "I believe if we had nothing else to consider than the delight of the few men and women who would yearly go into the Hetch Hetchy Valley, then it should be left in its natural condition. But the considerations on the other side of the question to my mind are simply overwhelming, and so much so that I have never been able to see that there was any reasonable argument against the use of this water supply by the city of San Francisco."[43] Roosevelt's interior secretary, James R. Garfield, also offered an earnest defense of the proposed project (**see Document 4.10**).

The fight over Hetch Hetchy eventually became so politically charged, however, that both Roosevelt and Taft temporized on the issue. The impasse lasted until 1913, when Congress finally passed the so-called Raker Bill approving the damming of the Tuolomne in the Hetch Hetchy Valley, and President Woodrow Wilson signed the legislation on December 19. Wilson's decision to go along with the flooding of Hetch Hetchy prompted a fresh outcry from opponents of the development plan. The scheme, lamented *The New York Times,* "converts a beautiful national park into a water tank for the city of

San Francisco."[44] The Hetch Hetchy controversy also marked the beginning of an enduring era of estrangement between dedicated wilderness preservationists and the disciples of multiple-use management that held the reins of the Forest Service and other natural resource agencies.

THE NATIONAL PARK SYSTEM IS BORN

In many other respects, the Wilson years constituted a lull in the evolution of American environmental policy. The Wilson Administration did formally establish the first big wave of national forests east of the Mississippi River, and in 1918 Wilson signed a landmark international conservation treaty—the Migratory Bird Treaty—that placed migratory bird species under the protection of federal authorities. But Wilson was more focused on issues such as economic policy reform and World War I, and his administration was mostly content to maintain the status quo in the realm of land and resource policy. As a result, neither public land advocates nor privatizers made big policy gains during his two terms—with one glaring exception. In 1916 Wilson signed legislation creating the National Park Service, which in turn created the framework for the national park system that remains in place today **(see Document 4.13)**.

The need for such an agency had become increasingly obvious to preservationists and bureaucrats alike during the Progressive Era, when a flurry of new parks had come into being. During this time, Muir and other advocates for wilderness preservation such as Frederick Law Olmsted Jr. and J. Horace McFarland called for the implementation of stringent park regulations that would minimize man's capacity to be a "disturbing agent," in the words of George Perkins Marsh, and save the last remnants of undisturbed nature from exploitation. "The wilderness still exists," declared one preservationist. "Man has ravaged and plundered the earth in large measure, but there are still great tracts of wilderness where bear and deer and cougar wander as in the days of old."[45]

To preservationists, the need for park policies that forbade timber cutting, water diversions, and other industrial practices had been hammered home in distressing fashion by the Hetch Hetchy defeat. But they recognized that as long as management of America's individual national parks and monuments remained scattered among different departments (Interior, Agriculture, and War prior to 1916) with different priorities and rivalries, implementing uniform regulations would be an overwhelming logistical and political task. Preservationists thus determined that the best way to usher preservationist policies into existence was through the creation of a central national parks bureau that could speak up for wilderness protection and aesthetic conservation in the same way that the Reclamation and Forest services carried the torch for utilitarian, multiple-use conservation.[46]

Ironically, one of the lawyers who had represented San Francisco in the war over Hetch Hetchy became a key ally of the preservationists in their quest to create a federal parks bureau. In 1913 Franklin Knight Lane left his private practice to become Wilson's interior secretary. He thought the parks idea was a good one, and he recruited conservationist and industrialist Stephen T. Mather to spearhead a publicity campaign to promote the cause. Mather quickly assembled a formidable coalition of wilderness preservationists, influential congressmen and journalists, and railroad executives who saw park tourism as a way to increase their revenues. Their cumulative political clout enabled Lane and Mather to overcome the opposition of the Forest Service, which wanted the parks transferred to their jurisdiction—in part because of legitimate fears that the new bureau would eventually seek to claim scenic lands held by the Forest Service for its own.

On August 25, 1916, President Wilson signed the National Park Service Act (also known as the Organic Act), which established the National Park Service within the Department of the Interior. The new agency gained immediate control over fourteen national parks and twenty-one national monuments scattered across the country. The act also mandated that park preservation and public enjoyment would be the highest missions of the Service. For park champions like Mather, who went on to become the agency's first director, the creation of the National Park Service ranked as a triumph of the first degree for all Americans. "The Yosemite, the Yellowstone, the Grand Canyon are national properties in which every citizen has a vested interest," he said. "They belong as much to the man of Massachusetts, of Michigan, of Florida, as they do to the people of California, of Wyoming, and of Arizona. . . . Who will gainsay that the parks contain the highest potentialities of national pride, national contentment, and national health? A visit inspires love of country . . . [and] contains the antidote for national restlessness."[47]

NOTES

1. Neil Wynn, *From Progressivism to Prosperity: World War I and American Society* (New York: Holmes and Meier, 1986), 3.

2. Theodore Roosevelt, First Annual Message to Congress, December 3, 1901. Available at The American Presidency Project, www.presidency.ucsb.edu/ws/index.php?pid=29542&st=roosevelt&st1=.

3. David Traxel, *Crusader Nation: The United States in Peace and the Great War 1898–1920* (New York: Alfred A. Knopf, 2006), 16.

4. Theodore Roosevelt, *Theodore Roosevelt: An Autobiography* (New York: Macmillan, 1913), 389.

5. Ibid., 410.

6. Gifford Pinchot, *Breaking New Ground.* (1947. Reprint. Washington, D.C.: Island Press, 1998), 85.

7. Ibid., 27.

8. Marc Reisner, *Cadillac Desert: The American West and Its Disappearing Water* (1986. Rev. ed. New York: Penguin, 1993), 111.

9. Richard N. L. Andrews, *Managing the Environment, Managing Ourselves: A History of American Environmental Policy* (New Haven, Conn.: Yale University Press, 1999), 141–142.

10. Paul W. Gates, *History of Public Land Law Development.* U.S. Public Land Law Review Commission (Washington D.C.: Government Printing Office, 1968), 668.

11. Quoted in Brad D. Lookingbill, *Dust Bowl, USA: Depression America and the Ecological Imagination, 1929–1941* (Athens: Ohio University Press, 2001), 12.

12. Reisner, *Cadillac Desert,* 113.

13. David A. Adams, *Renewable Resource Policy: The Legal-Institutional Foundations* (Washington, D.C.: Island Press, 1993), 73.

14. Gifford Pinchot, *Breaking New Ground* (1947. Washington, D.C.: Island Press, 1998), 258, 259.

15. Gifford Pinchot, *The Fight for Conservation* (Seattle: University of Washington Press, 1910), 81.

16. Samuel Hays, *Conservation and the Gospel of Efficiency* (Cambridge, Mass.: Harvard University Press, 1959), 127.

17. Pinchot, *Breaking New Ground,* 184.

18. William Cronon, *Uncommon Ground: Rethinking the Human Place in Nature* (New York: W.W. Norton, 1996), 78.

19. Theodore Roosevelt, *A Book-Lover's Holidays in the Open* (New York: Charles Scribner's Sons, 1920), 317.

20. Andrews, *Managing the Environment, Managing Ourselves,* 137.

21. Leroy G. Dorsey, "Preaching Conservation: Theodore Roosevelt and the Rhetoric of Civil Religion," in *Green Talk in the White House: The Rhetorical Presidency Encounters Ecology*, ed. Tarla Rai Peterson (College Station: Texas A&M Press, 2004), 48.

22. Theodore Roosevelt, Seventh Annual Message to Congress, December 3, 1907. Available at The American Presidency Project, www.presidency.ucsb.edu/ws/?pid=29548.

23. Adams, *Renewable Resources Policy*, 127.

24. Henry Teller, Remarks at Denver Public Land Convention. *Proceedings of the Public Land Convention. Held in Denver, Colorado, June 18–20, 1907* (Denver, CO: Public Land Convention, 1907), 45–47.

25. Quoted in Benjamin Heber Johnson, "Conservation, Subsistence, and Class at the Birth of Superior National Forest," *Environmental History* 4, no. 1, (January 1999): 80–99.

26. George L. Knapp, "The Other Side of Conservation," *North American Review* 191, (1910): 465–481.

27. Bryant Butler Brooks, Remarks. *Proceedings of the Second National Conservation Congress, at Saint Paul, September 5–8, 1910* (Washington, D.C.: National Conservation Congress, 1911), 73.

28. Ibid., 57.

29. Ibid., 76.

30. Louis Warren, *The Hunter's Game: Poachers and Conservationists in Twentieth-Century America* (New Haven, Conn.: Yale University Press, 1997), 181.

31. Ibid., 14.

32. James A. Tober, *Who Owns the Wildlife? The Political Economy of Conservation in Nineteenth-Century America* (Westport, Conn.: Greenwood Press, 1981).

33. Warren, *The Hunger's Game*, 80.

34. Aldo Leopold, "The National Forests: The Last Free Hunting Grounds of the Nation," *Journal of Forestry* 17, no. 2 (1919), 150–153.

35. Adam Rome, "Nature Wars, Culture Wars: Immigration and Environmental Reform in the Progressive Era," *Environmental History* (July 2008), 432–453.

36. Quoted in Warren, *The Hunger's Game*, 28.

37. Henry Chase, "Important Game Law Decision," *Forest and Stream* (Feb. 28, 1914).

38. William Hornaday, *Our Vanishing Wildlife: Its Extermination and Preservation* (New York: Charles Scribner's Sons, 1913), 100–101.

39. "Mr. Ballinger and the National Grab-Bag," Interview with John L. Mathews. *Hampton's Magazine* (December 1909).

40. Edward Taylor Parsons, "Proposed Destruction of Hetch-Hetchy," *Out West*, July 31, 1909, 607–627.

41. *Hetch Hetchy Reservoir Hearings Held before the Committee on the Public Lands of the House of Representatives, January 9 and 12, 1909*. Washington: Government Printing Office, 1909.

42. Warren Olney, "Water Supply for the Cities about the Bay of San Francisco," *Out West*, July 31, 1909, 599–605.

43. Gifford Pinchot, Testimony. *Hetch Hetchy Reservoir Hearings Held before the Committee on the Public Lands of the House of Representatives, June 25–28, July 7, 1913*. Washington, D.C.: Government Printing Office, 1913.

44. Editorial, *The New York Times*, December 9, 1913.

45. George S. Evans, "The Wilderness," *Overland Monthly*, January 1904, 31.

46. Robert M. Utley and Barry Mackintosh, *The Department of Everything Else: Highlights of Interior History* (Washington, D.C.: Department of Interior, 1989), www.nps.gov/history/history/online_books/utley-mackintosh/interior6.htm.

47. "Famous Quotes Concerning the National Parks: Stephen T. Mather, NPS Director, 1917–1929," *National Park Service History*, www.nps.gov/history/history/hisnps/NPSThinking/famousquotes.htm.

President Roosevelt's First Annual Message to Congress

"Forest and Water Problems Are . . . the Most Vital Internal Questions"

December 3, 1901

When President Theodore Roosevelt delivered his first annual message to Congress on December 3, 1901, he signaled his clear intention to leave an indelible stamp on the nation's natural resource policies. Roosevelt was determined to implement major new federal conservation measures to address decades of improvident exploitation of water, mineral, and timber resources. And because Roosevelt also was armed with an expansive view of executive authority—and a seemingly bottomless well of self-confidence and energy—he also intimated to Congress that he intended to act swiftly and decisively on his conservation beliefs. The president was true to his word. During the course of his presidency, Roosevelt weaved a formidable tapestry of conservation laws and pro-wilderness policies that endure to this day.

In the following excerpt from his first message to Congress, Roosevelt discusses some of his plans to institute new federal policies for the commercial development and environmental protection of America's rivers and forests.

Public opinion throughout the United States has moved steadily toward a just appreciation of the value of forests, whether planted or of natural growth. The great part played by them in the creation and maintenance of the national wealth is now more fully realized than ever before.

Wise forest protection does not mean the withdrawal of forest resources, whether of wood, water, or grass, from contributing their full share to the welfare of the people, but, on the contrary, gives the assurance of larger and more certain supplies. The fundamental idea of forestry is the perpetuation of forests by use. Forest protection is not an end of itself; it is a means to increase and sustain the resources of our country and the industries which depend upon them. The preservation of our forests is an imperative business necessity. We have come to see clearly that whatever destroys the forest, except to make way for agriculture, threatens our well-being.

The practical usefulness of the national forest reserves to the mining, grazing, irrigation, and other interests of the regions in which the reserves lie has led to a wide-spread demand by the people of the West for their protection and extension. The forest reserves will inevitably be of still greater use in the future than in the past. Additions should be made to them whenever practicable, and their usefulness should be increased by a thoroughly businesslike management.

At present the protection of the forest reserves rests with the General Land Office, the mapping and description of their timber with the United States Geological Survey, and the preparation of plans for their conservative use with the Bureau of Forestry, which is also charged with the general advancement of practical forestry in the United States. These various functions should be united in the Bureau of Forestry, to which they properly belong. The present diffusion of responsibility is bad from every standpoint. It prevents that effective co-operation between the Government and the men who utilize the resources of the reserves, without which the interests of both must suffer. The scientific bureaus generally should be put under the Department of Agriculture. The President should have by law the power of transferring lands for use as forest reserves to the Department of Agriculture. He already has such power in the case of lands needed by the Departments of War and the Navy.

The wise administration of the forest reserves will be not less helpful to the interests which depend on water than to those which depend on wood and grass. The water supply itself depends upon the forest. In the arid region it is water, not land, which measures production. The western half of the United States would sustain a population greater than that of our whole country to-day if the waters that now run to waste were saved and used for irrigation. The forest and water problems are perhaps the most vital internal questions of the United States at the present time.

Certain of the forest reserves should also be made preserves for the wild forest creatures. All of the reserves should be better protected from fires. Many of them need special protection because of the great injury done by live stock, above all by sheep. The increase in deer, elk, and other animals in the Yellowstone Park shows what may be expected when other mountain forests are properly protected by law and properly guarded. Some of these areas have been so denuded of surface vegetation by overgrazing that the ground breeding birds, including grouse and quail, and many mammals, including deer, have been exterminated or driven away. At the same time the water-storing capacity of the surface has been decreased or destroyed, thus promoting floods in times of rain and diminishing the flow of streams between rains.

The reclamation and settlement of the arid lands will enrich every portion of our country, just as the settlement of the Ohio and Mississippi valleys brought prosperity to the Atlantic States.

—Theodore Roosevelt

In cases where natural conditions have been restored for a few years, vegetation has again carpeted the ground, birds and deer are coming back, and hundreds of persons, especially from the immediate neighborhood, come each summer to enjoy the privilege of camping. Some at least of the forest reserves should afford perpetual protection to the native fauna and flora, safe havens of refuge to our rapidly diminishing wild animals of the larger kinds, and free camping grounds for the ever-increasing numbers of men and women who have learned to find rest, health, and recreation in the splendid forests and flower-clad meadows of our mountains. The forest reserves should be set apart forever for the use and benefit of our people as a whole and not sacrificed to the shortsighted greed of a few.

The forests are natural reservoirs. By restraining the streams in flood and replenishing them in drought they make possible the use of waters otherwise wasted. They prevent the soil from washing, and so protect the storage-reservoirs from filling up with silt. Forest conservation is therefore an essential condition of water conservation.

The forests alone cannot, however, fully regulate and conserve the waters of the arid region. Great storage-works are necessary to equalize the flow of streams and to save the flood waters. Their construction has been conclusively shown to be an undertaking too vast for private effort. Nor can it be best accomplished by the individual States acting alone. Far-reaching interstate problems are involved; and the resources of single States would often be inadequate. It is properly a national function, at least in some of its features. It is as right for the National Government to make the streams and rivers of the arid region useful by engineering works for water storage as to make useful the rivers and harbors of the humid region by engineering works of another kind. The storing of the floods in reservoirs at the headwaters of our rivers is but an enlargement of our present policy of river control, under which levees are built on the lower reaches of the same streams.

The Government should construct and maintain these reservoirs as it does other public works. Where their purpose is to regulate the flow of streams, the water should be turned freely into the channels in the dry season to take the same course under the same laws as the natural flow.

The reclamation of the unsettled arid public lands presents a different problem. Here it is not enough to regulate the flow of streams. The object of the Government is to dispose of the land to settlers who will build homes upon it. To accomplish this object water must be brought within their reach.

The pioneer settlers on the arid public domain chose their homes along streams from which they could themselves divert the water to reclaim their holdings. Such opportunities are practically gone. There remain, however, vast areas of public land which can be made available for homestead settlement, but only by reservoirs and main-line canals impracticable for private enterprise. These irrigation works should be built by the National Government. The lands reclaimed by them should be reserved by the Government for actual settlers, and the cost of construction should so far as possible be repaid by the land reclaimed. The distribution of the water, the division of the streams among irrigators, should be left to the settlers themselves in conformity with State laws and without interference with those laws or with vested fights. The policy of the National Government should be to aid irrigation in the several States and Territories in such manner as will enable the people in the local communities to help themselves, and as will stimulate needed reforms in the State laws and regulations governing irrigation.

The reclamation and settlement of the arid lands will enrich every portion of our country, just as the settlement of the Ohio and Mississippi valleys brought prosperity to the Atlantic States. The increased demand for manufactured articles will stimulate industrial production, while wider home markets and the trade of Asia will consume the larger food supplies and effectually prevent Western competition with Eastern agriculture. Indeed, the products of irrigation will be consumed chiefly in upbuilding local centers of mining and other industries, which would otherwise not come into existence at all. Our people as a whole will profit, for successful home-making is but another name for the upbuilding of the nation.

The necessary foundation has already been laid for the inauguration of the policy just described. It would be unwise to begin by doing too much, for a great deal will doubtless be learned, both as to what can and what cannot be safely attempted, by the early efforts, which must of necessity be partly experimental in character. At the very beginning the Government should make clear, beyond shadow of doubt, its intention to pursue this policy on lines of the broadest public interest. No reservoir or canal should ever be built to satisfy selfish personal or local interests; but only in accordance with the advice of trained experts, after long investigation has shown the locality where all the conditions combine to make the work most needed and fraught with the greatest usefulness to the community as a whole. There should be no extravagance, and the believers in the need of irrigation will most benefit their cause by seeing to it that it is free from the least taint of excessive or reckless expenditure of the public moneys.

Whatever the nation does for the extension of irrigation should harmonize with, and tend to improve, the condition of those now living on irrigated land. We are not at the starting point of this development. Over $200,000,000 of private capital has already been expended in the construction of irrigation works, and many million acres of arid land reclaimed. A high degree of enterprise and ability has been shown in the work itself; but as much cannot be said in reference to the laws relating thereto. The security and value of the homes created depend largely on the stability of titles to water; but the majority of these rest on the uncertain foundation of court decisions rendered in ordinary suits at law. With a few creditable exceptions, the arid States have failed to provide for the certain and just division of streams in times of scarcity. Lax and uncertain laws have made it possible to establish rights to water in excess of actual uses or necessities, and many streams have already passed into private ownership, or a control equivalent to ownership.

Whoever controls a stream practically controls the land it renders productive, and the doctrine of private ownership of water apart from land cannot prevail without causing enduring wrong. The recognition of such ownership, which has been permitted to grow up in the arid regions, should give way to a more enlightened and larger recognition of the rights of the public in the control and disposal of the public water supplies. Laws founded upon conditions obtaining in humid regions, where water is too abundant to justify hoarding it, have no proper application in a dry country.

In the arid States the only right to water which should be recognized is that of use. In irrigation this right should attach to the land reclaimed and be inseparable therefrom. Granting perpetual water rights to others than users, without compensation to the public, is open to all the objections which apply to giving away perpetual franchises to the public utilities of cities. A few of the Western States have already recognized this, and have incorporated in their constitutions the doctrine of perpetual State ownership of water.

The benefits which have followed the unaided development of the past justify the nation's aid and co-operation in the more difficult and important work yet to be accomplished. Laws so vitally affecting homes as those which control the water supply will only be effective when they have the sanction of the irrigators; reforms can only be final and satisfactory when they come through the enlightenment of the people most concerned. The larger development which national aid insures should, however, awaken in every arid State the determination to make its irrigation system equal in justice and effectiveness that of any country in the civilized world. Nothing could be more unwise than for isolated communities to continue to learn everything experimentally, instead of profiting by what is already known elsewhere. We are dealing with a new and momentous question, in the pregnant years while institutions are forming, and what we do will affect not only the present but future generations.

Our aim should be not simply to reclaim the largest area of land and provide homes for the largest number of people, but to create for this new industry the best possible social and industrial conditions; and this requires that we not only understand the existing situation, but avail ourselves of the best experience of the time in the solution of its problems. A careful study should be made, both by the Nation and the States, of the irrigation laws and conditions here and abroad. Ultimately it will probably be necessary for the Nation to co-operate with the several arid States in proportion as these States by their legislation and administration show themselves fit to receive it. . . .

Source: Roosevelt, Theodore. First Annual Message to Congress, December 3, 1901. Available at The American Presidency Project, www.presidency.ucsb.edu/ws/?pid=29542.

The National Reclamation Act

"For the Reclamation of Arid and Semiarid Lands" in the West

June 17, 1902

The National Reclamation Act of 1902, also known as the Newlands Act for its chief author, Congressman and irrigation advocate Francis G. Newlands of Nevada, was one of the most important pieces of "internal improvement" legislation to come out of the Theodore Roosevelt Administration. The Reclamation Act, which was approved on June 17, authorized the federal government to undertake major irrigation projects in the West from the proceeds of land sales. In giving broad discretion to the secretary of the interior and his agency employees in the selection and shaping of these projects, the act "marked the first statutory affirmation of the Progressive idea that environmental assets should be managed not by elected representatives, but by technical professionals and politically neutral administrators working toward the efficient realization of an overall public interest."[1]

To implement the act, President Theodore Roosevelt and his first secretary of the interior, Ethan A. Hitchcock, created a new branch of the U.S. Geological Survey called the Reclamation Service in July 1902. In 1907 the Reclamation Service became a separate agency within the Interior Department, and in 1923 it became the Bureau of Reclamation. From the 1920s through the 1960s this agency became virtually synonymous with significant water engineering projects all across the American West, including hydroelectric and irrigation dams, storage reservoirs, canals, and sophisticated irrigation delivery systems, for cities, towns, and agricultural enterprises throughout the region. Many of these projects have been praised for making the arid West a place where millions of people could live and prosper—and condemned as despoilers of wild rivers and canyonlands and contributors to unsustainable resource use across the region. Following is the full text of the National Reclamation Act that made the Bureau of Reclamation possible:

Be it enacted by the Senate and House of Representatives of the United States of America in Congress assembled, That all moneys received from the sale and disposal of public lands in Arizona, California, Colorado, Idaho, Kansas, Montana, Nebraska, Nevada, New Mexico, North Dakota, Oklahoma, Oregon, South Dakota, Utah, Washington, and Wyoming, beginning with the fiscal year ending June thirtieth, nineteen hundred and one, including the surplus of fees and commissions in excess of allowances to registers and receivers, and excepting the five per centum of the proceeds of the sales of public lands in the above States set aside by law for educational and other purposes, shall be, and the same are hereby, reserved set aside, and appropriated as a special fund in the Treasury to be known as the "reclamation fund," to be used in the examination and survey for and the construction and maintenance of irrigation works for the storage, diversion, and development of waters for the reclamation of arid and semiarid lands in the said States and Territories, and for the payment of all other expenditures provided for in this Act: *Provided,* That in case the receipts from the sale and disposal of public lands other than those realized from the sale and disposal of lands referred to in this section are insufficient to meet the requirements for the support of agricultural colleges in the several States and Territories, under the Act of August thirtieth, eighteen hundred and ninety, entitled "An Act to apply a portion of the proceeds of the public lands to the more complete endowment and support of the colleges for the benefit of agriculture and the mechanic arts, established under the provisions of an Act of Congress approved July second, eighteen hundred and sixty-two," the deficiency, if any, in the sum necessary for the support of the said colleges shall be provided for from any moneys in the Treasury not otherwise appropriated.

[U]pon the determination by the Secretary of the Interior that any irrigation project is practicable, he may cause to be let contracts for the construction of the same, in such portions or sections are available in the reclamation fund.

—The National Reclamation Act

SEC. 2. That the Secretary of the Interior is hereby authorized and directed to make examinations and surveys for, and to locate and construct, as herein provided, irrigation works for the storage, diversion, and development of waters, including artesian wells, and to report to Congress at the beginning of each regular session as to the results of such examinations and surveys, giving estimates of cost of all contemplated works, the quantity and location of the lands which can be irrigated therefrom, and all facts relative to the practicability of each irrigation project; also the cost of works in process of construction as well as of those which have been completed.

SEC. 3. That the Secretary of the Interior shall, before giving the public notice provided for in section four of this Act, withdraw from public entry the lands required for any irrigation works contemplated under the provisions of this Act, and shall restore to public entry any of the lands so withdrawn when, in his judgment, such lands are not required for the purposes of this Act; and the Secretary of the Interior is hereby authorized, at or immediately prior to the time of beginning the surveys for any contemplated irrigation works, to withdraw from entry, except under the homestead laws, any public lands believed to be susceptible of irrigation from said works: *Provided,* That all lands entered and entries made under the homestead laws within areas so withdrawn during such withdrawal shall be subject to all the provisions, limitations, charges, terms, and conditions of this Act; that said surveys shall be prosecuted diligently to completion, and upon the completion thereof, and of the necessary maps, plans, and estimates of cost, the Secretary of Interior shall determine whether or not said project is practicable and advisable, and if determined to be impracticable or unadvisable he shall thereupon restore said lands to entry; that public lands which it is proposed to irrigate by means of any contemplated works shall be subject to entry only under the provisions of the homestead laws in tracts of not less than forty nor more than one hundred and sixty acres, and shall be subject to the limitations, charges, terms, and conditions herein provided: *Provided,* That the commutation provisions of the homestead laws shall not apply to entries made under this Act.

SEC 4. That upon the determination by the Secretary of the Interior that any irrigation project is practicable, he may cause to be let contracts for the construction of the same, in such portions or sections are available in the reclamation fund, and irrigable under such project, and limit of area per entry which limit shall represent the acreage which, in the opinion of the Secretary, may be reasonably required for the support of a family upon the lands in question; also of the charges which shall be made per acre upon the said entries, and upon lands in private ownership which may be irrigated by the waters of the said irrigation project, and the number of annual installments, not exceeding ten, in which such charges shall be paid and the time when such payments shall commence. The said charges shall be determined with a view of returning to the reclamation fund the estimated cost of construction of the project, and shall be apportioned equitably: *Provided,* That in all construction work eight hours shall constitute a day's work, and no Mongolian labor shall be employed thereon.

SEC 5. That the entryman upon lands to be irrigated by such works shall, in addition to compliance with the homestead laws, reclaim at least one-half of the total irrigable area of his entry for agricultural purposes, and before receiving patent for the lands covered by his entry shall pay to the Government the charges apportioned against such tract, as provided in section 4. No right to the use of water for land in private ownership shall be sold for a tract exceeding one hundred and sixty acres to any one landowner, and no such sale shall be made to any landowner unless he be an actual *bona fide* resident on such land, or occupant thereof residing in the neighborhood of said land, and no such right shall permanently attach until all payments therefor are made. The annual installments shall be paid to the receiver of the local land office of the district in which the land is situated, and a failure to make any two payments when due shall render the entry subject to cancellation, with the forfeiture of all rights under this Act, as well as of any moneys already paid thereon. All moneys received from the above sources shall be paid into the reclamation fund. Registers and receivers shall be allowed the usual commissions on all moneys paid for lands entered under this act.

SEC 6. That the Secretary of the Interior is hereby authorized and directed to use the reclamation fund for the operation and maintenance of all reservoirs and irrigation works constructed under the provisions of this act: *Provided,* That when the payments required by this act are made for the major portion of the lands irrigated from the waters of any of the works herein provided for, then the management and operation of such irrigation works shall pass to the owners of the lands irrigated thereby, to be maintained at their expense under such form of organization and under such rules and regulations as may be acceptable to the Secretary of the Interior: *Provided,* That the title to and the management and operation of the reservoirs and the works necessary for their protection and operation shall remain in the Government until otherwise provided by Congress.

SEC 7. That where in carrying out the provisions of this Act it becomes necessary to acquire any rights or property, the Secretary of the Interior is hereby authorized to acquire the same for the United States by purchase or by condemnation under judicial process, and to pay from the reclamation fund the sums which may be needed for that purpose, and it shall be the duty of the Attorney-General of the United States upon every application of the Secretary of the Interior, under this Act, to cause proceedings to be commenced for condemnation within thirty days from the receipt of the application at the Department of Justice.

SEC 8. That nothing in this Act shall be construed as affecting or intended to affect or to in any way interfere with the laws of any State or Territory relating to the control, appropriation, use, or distribution of water used in irrigation, or any vested right acquired thereunder, and the Secretary of the Interior, in carrying out the provisions of this Act, shall proceed in conformity with such laws, and nothing herein shall in any way affect any right of any State or of the Federal Government or of any landowner, appropriator, or user of water in, to, or from any interstate stream or the waters thereof: *Provided,* That the right of the use of water acquired under the provisions of this Act shall be appurtenant to the land irrigated, and beneficial use shall be the basis, the measure, and the limit of the right.

SEC 9. That it is hereby declared to be the duty of the Secretary of the Interior in carrying out the provisions of this Act, so far as the same may be practicable and subject to the existence of feasible irrigation projects, to expend the major portion of the funds arising from the sale of public lands within each State and Territory hereinbefore named for the benefit of arid and semiarid lands within the limits of such State or Territory; *Provided,* That the Secretary may temporarily use such portion of said funds for the benefit of arid or semiarid lands in any particular State or Territory herein before named as he may deem advisable, but when so used the excess shall be restored to the fund as soon as practicable, to the end that ultimately, and in any event, within each ten-year period after the passage of this Act, the expenditures for the benefit of the said States and Territories shall be equalized according to the proportions and subject to the conditions as to practicability and feasibility aforesaid.

SEC 10. That the Secretary of the Interior is hereby authorized to perform any and all acts and to make such rules and regulations as may be necessary and proper for the purpose of carrying the provisions of this Act into full force and effect.

Source: *United States Statutes at Large,* Vol. 32, Part 1. Washington, D.C.: Government Printing Office, 1903, p. 388.

NOTE

1. Richard N. L. Andrews, *Managing the Environment, Managing Ourselves: A History of American Environmental Policy* (New Haven, Conn.: Yale University Press, 1999), 141–142.

DOCUMENT
4.3

The Antiquities Act

"An Act for the Preservation of American Antiquities"

June 8, 1906

President Theodore Roosevelt viewed the Antiquities Act, which he signed into law on June 8, 1906, as one of his greatest conservation victories. The legislation authorized Roosevelt and future presidents to protect "historic landmarks, historic and prehistoric structures, and other objects of historic or scientific interest" in the public domain as national monuments (these national monuments remained under the jurisdiction of the federal agency that otherwise administered the lands in question). From 1906 to 1910 alone, Roosevelt and his successor William H. Taft used the Antiquities Act on twenty-three occasions, most notably to provide the first federal protection to the Grand Canyon in Arizona.

Roosevelt used the Antiquities Act on several occasions to bypass Congress and provide swift protection to areas of archaeological, historic, or natural interest that were vulnerable to development or exploitation. Several of these monuments became the core lands for future national parks, including Grand Canyon, Death Valley in California, and Glacier Bay in Alaska. Since then, many other presidents, most notably Jimmy Carter and Bill Clinton, also have used the act to preserve scenic and historic public lands. But ever since Roosevelt's day, the use of the Antiquities Act has also prompted cries of protest from congressional delegations and local communities who view such designations as federal "land grabs."

An Act for the Preservation of American Antiquities

Be it enacted by the Senate and House of Representatives of the United States of America in Congress assembled, That any person who shall appropriate, excavate, injure, or destroy any historic or prehistoric ruin or monument, or any object of antiquity, situated on lands owned or controlled by the Government of the United States, without the permission of the Secretary of the department of the government having jurisdiction over the lands on which said antiquities are situated, shall, upon conviction, be fined in a sum of not more than $500 or be imprisoned for a period of not more than ninety days, or shall suffer both fine and imprisonment, the discretion of the court.

SEC 2. That the President of the United States is hereby authorized, in his discretion, to declare by public proclamation historic landmarks, historic and prehistoric structures, and other objects of historic or scientific interest that are situated upon the lands owned or controlled by the Government of the United States to be national monuments, and may reserve as a part thereof parcels of land, the limits of which in all cases shall be confined to the smallest area compatible with the proper care and management of the objects to the protected: *Provided,* That when such objects are situated upon tract covered by a bona fide unperfected claim or held in private ownership, the tracts, or so much thereof as may be necessary for the proper care and management of the object, may be relinquished the Government, and the Secretary of the Interior is hereby authorized to accept the relinquishment of such tracts in behalf of the Government of the United States.

SEC. 3. That permits for the examination of ruins, the excavation of archaeological sites, and the gathering of objects of antiquity upon the lands under their respective jurisdictions may be granted by the Secretaries of the Interior, Agriculture, and War to institutions which they may deem properly qualified to conduct such examination, excavation, or gathering, subject to such rules and regulations as they may prescribe: *Provided,* That the examinations, excavations, and gatherings are undertaken for the benefit of reputable museums, universities, colleges, or other recognized scientific or educational institutions, with a view to increasing the knowledge of such objects, and that the gatherings shall be made for permanent preservation in public museums.

SEC. 4. That the Secretaries of the departments aforesaid shall make and publish from time to time uniform rules and regulations for the purpose of carrying out the provisions of this act.

Source: "An Act for the Preservation of American Antiquities." *Antiquities Act, 1906–2006.* National Park Service Archeology Program. www.nps.gov/history/local-law/anti1906.htm.

President Roosevelt's Address at a Conservation Conference of Governors

"The Natural Resources of Our Country Are in Danger of Exhaustion"

May 13, 1908

During his seven and a half years in the Oval Office, President Theodore Roosevelt engineered decisive changes in federal management of America's natural resources. His conservation policies extended major new protections to forests, water and soil resources, and wildlife, and his frequent use of the White House "bully pulpit" in defense of his environmental policies helped generate increased public support for conservation efforts.

By the spring of 1908, however, Roosevelt's tenure in the White House was nearing its end. Back in 1904 Roosevelt had pledged to retire at the close of his single full term, and he intended to make good on that vow. But as his months as chief executive dwindled to a few, he was determined to keep the pro-conservation momentum going well beyond the end of his administration. To this end, Roosevelt and Forest Chief Gifford Pinchot, the president's right-hand man on conservation issues, organized a high-profile White House conference to further publicize the importance of sustainable resource management at the federal, state, and local levels. Attendees at this Conference of Governors, which ran from May 13–15, included virtually all of the nation's governors in addition to hundreds of congressmen, representatives from conservation organizations, scientific experts, and resource agency administrators. The conference, which Pinchot described as "a turning point in human history,"[1] led directly to the creation of the National Conservation Commission. One year later, this commission published the nation's first-ever inventory of natural resources. The following are excerpts from Roosevelt's opening address to the Conference of Governors.

. . . This conference on the conservation of natural resources is in effect a meeting of the representatives of all the people of the United States called to consider the weightiest problem now before the Nation; and the occasion for the meeting lies in the fact that the natural resources of our country are in danger of exhaustion if we permit the old wasteful methods of exploiting them longer to continue.

With the rise of peoples from savagery to civilization, and with the consequent growth in the extent and variety of the needs of the average man, there comes a steadily increasing growth of the amount demanded by this average man from the actual resources of the country. And yet, rather curiously, at the same time that there comes that increase in what the average man demands from the resources, he is apt to grow to lose the sense of his dependence upon nature. He lives in big cities. He deals in industries that do not bring him in close touch with nature. He does not realize the demands he is making upon nature. For instance, he finds, as he has found before in many parts of this country, that it is cheaper to build his house of concrete than of wood, learning in this way only that he has allowed the woods to become exhausted. That is happening, as you know, in parts of this country at this very time. . . .

Every step of the progress of mankind is marked by the discovery and use of natural resources previously unused. Without such progressive knowledge and utilization of natural resources population could not grow, nor industries multiply, nor the hidden wealth of the earth be developed for the benefit of mankind.

From the first beginnings of civilization, on the banks of the Nile and the Euphrates, the industrial progress of the world has gone on slowly, with occasional set-backs, but on the whole steadily, through tens of centuries to the present day.

It never does advance by jumps, gentlemen. It always goes slowly. There are occasional set-backs, but on the whole it goes steadily.

But of late the rapidity of the process has increased at such a rate that more space has been actually covered during the century and a quarter occupied by our national life than during the preceding six thousand years that take us back to the earliest monuments of Egypt, to the earliest cities of the Babylonian plain.

Now, I ask you to think what that means; and I am speaking with historic literalness. In the development, the use, and therefore the exhaustion of certain of the natural resources, the progress has been more rapid in the past century and a quarter than during all preceding time of which we have record. . . .

We have become great in a material sense because of the lavish use of our resources, and we have just reason to be proud of our growth. But the time has come to inquire seriously what will happen when our forests are gone, when the coal, the iron, the oil, and the gas are exhausted.

—Theodore Roosevelt

In 1776 the wares of the merchants of Boston, of Charleston, like the wares of the merchants of Nineveh and Sidon, if they went by water, were carried by boats propelled by sails or oars; if they went by land were carried in wagons drawn by beasts of draft or in packs on the backs of beasts of burden. The ships that crossed the high seas were better than the ships that three thousand years before crossed the Egean, but they were of the same type, after all— they were wooden ships propelled by sails. . . .

In Washington's time anthracite coal was known only as a useless black stone; and the great fields of bituminous coal were undiscovered. As steam was unknown, the use of coal for power production was undreamed of. Water was practically the only source of power, save the labor of men and animals; and this power was used only in the most primitive fashion. But a few small iron deposits had been found in this country, and the use of iron by our countrymen was very small. Wood was practically the only fuel, and what lumber was sawed was consumed locally, while the forests were regarded chiefly as obstructions to settlement and cultivation. The man who cut down a tree was held to have conferred a service upon his fellows.

Such was the degree of progress to which civilized mankind had attained when this nation began its career. It is almost impossible for us in this day to realize how little our Revolutionary ancestors knew of the great store of natural resources whose discovery and use have been such vital factors in the growth and greatness of this Nation, and how little they required to take from this store in order to satisfy their needs.

Since then our knowledge and use of the resources of the present territory of the United States have increased a hundred-fold. Indeed, the growth of this Nation by leaps and bounds makes one of the most striking and important chapters in the history of the world. Its growth has been due to the rapid development, and alas that it should be said! to the rapid destruction, of our natural resources. Nature has supplied to us in the United States, and still supplies to us, more kinds of resources in a more lavish degree than has ever been the case at any other time with any other people. Our position in the world has been attained by the extent and thoroughness of the control we have achieved over nature; but we are more, and not less, dependent upon what she furnishes than at any previous time of history since the days of primitive man.

Yet our fathers, though they knew so little of the resources of the country, exercised a wise forethought in reference thereto. Washington clearly saw that the perpetuity of the States could only be secured by union, and that the only feasible basis of union was an economic one; in other words, that it must be based on the development and use of their natural resources. Accordingly, he helped to outline a scheme of commercial development, and by his influence an interstate waterways commission was appointed by Virginia and Maryland.

It met near where we are now meeting, in Alexandria, adjourned to Mount Vernon, and took up the consideration of interstate commerce by the only means then available, that of water; and the trouble we have since had with the railways has been mainly due to the fact that naturally our forefathers could not divine that the iron road would become the interstate and international highway, instead of the old route by water. Further conferences were arranged, first at Annapolis, and then at Philadelphia. It was in Philadelphia that the representatives of all the States met for what was in its original conception merely a waterways conference; but when they had closed their deliberations the outcome was the Constitution which made the States into a Nation. [Applause]

The Constitution of the United States thus grew in large part out of the necessity for united action in the wise use of one of our natural resources. The wise use of all of our natural resources, which are our national resources as well, is the great material question of today. I have asked you to come together now because the enormous consumption of these resources, and the threat of imminent exhaustion of some of them, due to reckless and wasteful use, once more calls for common effort, common action.

We want to take action that will prevent the advent of a woodless age, and defer as long as possible the advent of an ironless age. [Applause]

Since the days when the Constitution was adopted, steam and electricity have revolutionized the industrial world. Nowhere has the revolution been so great as in our own country. The discovery and utilization of mineral fuels and alloys have given us the lead over all other nations in the production of steel. The discovery and utilization of coal and iron have given us our railways, and have led to such industrial development as has never before been seen. The vast wealth of lumber in our forests, the riches of our soils and mines, the discovery of gold and mineral oils, combined with the efficiency of our transportation, have made the conditions of our life unparalleled in comfort and convenience.

A great many of these things are truisms. Much of what I say is so familiar to us that it seems commonplace to repeat it; but familiar though it is, I do not think as a nation we understand what its real bearing is. It is so familiar that we disregard it. [Applause]

The steadily increasing drain on these natural resources has promoted to an extraordinary degree the complexity of our industrial and social life. Moreover, this unexampled development has had a determining effect upon the character and opinions of our people. The demand for efficiency in the great task has given us vigor, effectiveness, decision, and power, and a capacity for achievement which in its own lines has never yet been matched. [Applause] So great and so rapid has been our material growth that there has been a tendency to lag behind in spiritual and moral growth [laughter and applause]; but that is not the subject upon which I speak to you today.

Disregarding for the moment the question of moral purpose, it is safe to say that the prosperity of our people depends directly on the energy and intelligence with which our natural resources are used. It is equally clear that these resources are the final basis of national power and perpetuity. Finally, it is ominously evident that these resources are in the course of rapid exhaustion.

This Nation began with the belief that its landed possessions were illimitable and capable of supporting all the people who might care to make our country their home; but already the limit of unsettled land is in sight, and indeed but little land fitted for agriculture now remains unoccupied save what can be reclaimed by irrigation and drainage a subject with which this Conference is partly to deal. We began with an unapproached heritage of forests; more than half of the timber is gone. We began with coal fields more extensive than those of any other nation and with iron ores regarded as inexhaustible, and many experts now declare that the end of both iron and coal is in sight.

The mere increase in our consumption of coal during 1907 over 1906 exceeded the total consumption in 1876, the Centennial year. This is a striking fact: Thirty years went by, and the mere surplus of use of one year over the preceding year exceeded all that was used in 1876 and we thought we were pretty busy people even then. The enormous stores of mineral oil and gas are largely gone; and those Governors who have in their States cities built up by natural gas, where the natural gas has since been exhausted, can tell us something of what that means. Our natural waterways are not gone, but they have been so injured by neglect, and by the division of responsibility and utter lack of system in dealing with them, that there is less navigation on them now than there was fifty years ago. Finally, we began with soils of unexampled fertility, and we have so impoverished them by injudicious use and by failing to check erosion that their crop-producing power is diminishing instead of increasing. In a word, we have thoughtlessly, and to a large degree unnecessarily, diminished the resources upon which not only our prosperity but the prosperity of our children and our children's children must always depend.

We have become great in a material sense because of the lavish use of our resources, and we have just reason to be proud of our growth. But the time has come to inquire seriously what will happen when our forests are gone, when the coal, the iron, the oil, and the gas are exhausted, when the soils shall have been still further impoverished and washed into the streams, polluting the rivers, denuding the fields, and obstructing navigation. These questions do not relate only to the next century or to the next generation. One distinguishing characteristic of really civilized men is foresight; we have to, as a nation, exercise foresight for this nation in the future; and if we do not exercise that foresight, dark will be the future! [Applause] We should exercise foresight now, as the ordinarily prudent man exercises foresight in conserving and wisely using the property which contains the assurance of well-being for himself and his children. We want to see a man own his farm rather than rent it, because we want to see it an object to him to transfer it in better order to his children. We want to see him exercise fore-thought for the next generation. We need to exercise it in some fashion ourselves as a nation for the next generation. . . .

Neither the primitive man nor the pioneer was aware of any duty to posterity in dealing with the renewable resources. When the American settler felled the forests, he felt that there was plenty of forest left for the sons who came after him. When he exhausted the soil of his farm, he felt that his son could go West and take up another. The Kentuckian or the Ohioan felled the forest and expected his son to move west and fell other forests on the banks of the Mississippi; the Georgian exhausted his farm and moved into Alabama or to the mouth of the Yazoo to take another. So it was with his immediate successors. When the soil-wash from the farmer's field choked the neighboring river, the only thought was to use the railway rather than the boats to move produce and supplies. That was so up to the generation that preceded ours.

Now all this is changed. On the average the son of the farmer of today must make his living on his father's farm. There is no difficulty in doing this if the father will exercise wisdom. No wise use of a farm exhausts its fertility. So with the forests. We are over the verge of a timber famine in this country, and it is unpardonable for the Nation or the States to permit any further cutting of our timber save in accordance with a system which will provide that the next generation shall see the timber increased instead of diminished. [Applause]

Just let me interject one word as to a particular type of folly of which it ought not to be necessary to speak. We stop wasteful cutting of timber; that of course makes a slight shortage at the moment. To avoid that slight shortage at the moment, there are certain people so foolish that they will incur absolute shortage in the future, and they are willing to stop all attempts to conserve the forests, because of course by wastefully using them at the moment we can for a year or two provide against any lack of wood. That is like providing for the farmer's family to live sumptuously on the flesh of the milch cow. [Laughter.] Any farmer can live pretty well for a year if he is content not to live at all the year after. [Laughter and applause]

We can, moreover, add enormous tracts of the most valuable possible agricultural land to the national domain by irrigation in the arid and semi-arid regions, and by drainage of great tracts of swamp land in the humid regions. We can enormously increase our transportation facilities by the canalization of our rivers so as to complete a great system of waterways on the Pacific, Atlantic, and Gulf coasts and in the Mississippi Valley, from the Great Plains to the Alleghenies, and from the northern lakes to the mouth of the mighty Father of Waters. But all these various uses of our natural resources are so closely connected that they should be coordinated, and should be treated as part of one coherent plan and not in haphazard and piecemeal fashion. . . .

We are coming to recognize as never before the right of the Nation to guard its own future in the essential matter of natural resources. In the past we have admitted the right of the individual to injure the future of the Republic for his own present profit. In fact there has been a good deal of a demand for unrestricted individualism, for the right of the individual to injure the future of all of us for his own temporary and immediate profit. The time has come for a change. As a people, we have the right and the duty, second to none other but the right and duty of obeying the moral law, of requiring and doing justice, to protect ourselves and our children against the wasteful development of our natural resources, whether that waste is caused by the actual destruction of such resources or by making them impossible of development hereafter.

Any right thinking father earnestly desires and strives to leave his son both an untarnished name and a reasonable equipment for the struggle of life. So this Nation as a whole should earnestly desire and strive to leave to the next generation the national honor unstained and the national resources unexhausted. . . .

Finally, let us remember that the conservation of our natural resources, though the gravest problem of today, is yet but part of another and greater problem to which this Nation is not yet awake, but to which it will awake in time, and with which it must hereafter grapple if it is to live the problem of national efficiency, the patriotic duty of insuring the safety and continuance of the Nation. [Applause.] When the People of the United States consciously undertake to raise themselves as citizens, and the Nation and the

States in their several spheres, to the highest pitch of excellence in private, State, and national life, and to do this because it is the first of all the duties of true patriotism, then and not till then the future of this Nation, in quality and in time, will be assured. [Great applause]

Source: Roosevelt, Theodore. "Opening Address by the President." *Proceedings of a Conference of Governors in the White House, May 13–15, 1908*, edited by Newton C. Blanchard. Washington, D.C.: Government Printing Office, 1909, p. 3–12.

NOTE

1. Quoted in Roderick Frazier Nash, *American Environmentalism: Readings in Conservation History,* 3rd ed. (New York: McGraw-Hill, 1990), 84.

DOCUMENT 4.5   Pennsylvania Bars Immigrants from Hunting Wild Game

"An Act . . . Prohibiting Hunting . . . by Unnaturalized Foreign-born Residents"

May 8, 1909

New laws designed to protect wildlife proliferated during the Progressive Era, but in many cases these measures reflected—and exacerbated—profound differences between socioeconomic classes in America. Many of the most prominent defenders of game laws were affluent, educated sportsmen and conservationists. The most frequent violators of the new laws, meanwhile, were poor rural farmers or immigrants who engaged in subsistence hunting. Members of the latter communities deeply resented resource-use limitations imposed by condescending "outsiders" or wealthier brethren and often skirted or ignored the laws. In other cases, ethnic groups endured false charges that they were all wildlife and timber "thieves."

Antagonism between these two camps intensified from the 1880s through the 1920s, when many native-born Americans voiced deep unhappiness with the influx of immigrants from Southern Europe. Conservationists continued to identify immigrants as a leading source of poaching and other illegal activity. This belief became so widespread in Pennsylvania that state legislators actually passed a 1909 law that effectively barred "aliens"—immigrants—from hunting wild game anywhere in the state. This law, excerpted here, was upheld in Commonwealth v. Patsone. In finding for the state, the trial judge declared that "Wild animals and game of all sorts have from time immemorial been the property of the sovereign, and in Pennsylvania the property of the state. Its power to regulate and prohibit the hunting and killing of game has always been conceded." In 1914 this judgment was upheld by the U.S. Supreme Court, which based its finding partly on the fact that the law applied to all immigrant groups.

An Act to Give Additional Protection to Wild Birds and Animals and Game, within the Commonwealth of Pennsylvania; Prohibiting the Hunting for, or Capture or Killing of Such Wild Birds or Animals or Game by Unnaturalized Foreign-born Residents, Forbidding the Ownership or Possession of Shotgun or Rifle by Any Unnaturalized Foreign-born Resident, within the Commonwealth, and Prescribing Penalties for Violation of Its Provisions.

SEC. 1. It shall be unlawful for any unnaturalized foreign-born resident to hunt for or capture or kill, in this commonwealth, any wild bird or animal, either game or otherwise of any description, excepting in defense of person or property; and to that end, it shall be unlawful for any unnaturalized foreign-born resident within this Commonwealth to either own or be possessed of a shotgun or rifle of any make. Each and every person violating any provision of this section shall upon conviction thereof, be sentenced to pay a penalty of twenty-five dollars for each offense, or undergo imprisonment in the common jail of the county for the period of one day for each dollar of penalty imposed: *Provided,* that in addition to the above-named penalty, all guns of the before-mentioned kinds found in the possession or under control of an unnaturalized foreign-born resident shall, upon conviction of such person, or upon his signing a declaration of guilt as prescribed by this act, be declared forfeited to the Commonwealth of Pennsylvania, and shall be sold by the Board of Game Commissioners as hereinafter directed. . . .

SEC. 3. That the possession of a shotgun or rifle at any place outside of buildings within this Commonwealth, by an unnaturalized foreign-born resident, shall be conclusive proof of a violation of the provisions of section one of this act, and shall render any person convicted thereof liable to the penalty as fixed by said section.

SEC. 4. That the presence of a shotgun or rifle in a room or house, or building or tent, or camp of any description, within this Commonwealth, occupied or controlled by an unnaturalized foreign-born resident, shall be prima facie evidence that such gun is owned or controlled by the person occupying or controlling the property in which such gun is found, and shall render such person liable to the penalty imposed by section one of this act.

May 8, 1909

Source: *Pennsylvania State Reports, Vol. 231, Containing Cases Decided by the Supreme Court of Pennsylvania, January Term 1911.* Reported by William I. Schaffer. New York: Banks Law Publishing, 1911, p. 47–49.

DOCUMENT 4.6

A Western Governor Condemns Federal Conservation Policies

"It Is People We Want in the West, not Game Preserves"

September 1910

The Progressive Era is widely recognized as the period during which the American conservation movement first emerged as a major force in U.S. politics. But with the advent of conservationism came new regional and philosophical schisms. Western policymakers, business interests, and residents became bitter critics of some federal conservation policies, which they saw as "eastern" in origin, unduly restrictive to their extraction-based economies, and insufficiently deferential on the issue of states' rights. By the midpoint of William H. Taft's presidency, many prominent western governors, congressmen, industry executives, and newspaper editors were heatedly calling for greater state control over natural resources and less "interference" in their internal affairs from federal authorities.

One such critic was Marion E. Hay, the Republican governor of Washington State from 1909 to 1913. In the following excerpt from a 1910 speech delivered at the Second National Conservation Congress in St. Paul, Minnesota, Hay touches on many of the complaints leveled by western lawmakers and business owners against the national government's role in the management of the region's natural resources. Many of these same concerns about federal regulation of natural resources continue to be voiced by westerners one century later. Hay, however, also acknowledges some of the more pro-development positions adopted by the Taft Administration, which by 1911 had become entangled in a fierce battle with so-called "Roosevelt conservationists" over U.S. natural resource policies.

. . . All that is needed to solve the problem of conserving our natural resources is common sense and the application of the square deal. It is because of a departure from these two essential elements in the consideration of Conservation, that an unsound, unjust, and impracticable policy has been advanced in this country. Common sense has given place to humbug and fairness to intolerance. Instead of calm, dispassionate, logical discussion of the subject, we hear and read on every hand exaggerated statements, misrepresentation, false accusation, dire prophecy, and passionate appeals to prejudice, avarice, and lawlessness. This has given rise to a wholly perverted notion of true Conservation, and has brought about a condition hurtful to the West, and one that, if persisted in, is bound to prove injurious to the Nation.

The only sane and sensible kind of Conservation is that which permits the fullest and freest development of our natural resources under provisions that will perpetuate those resources that can be renewed, and that will obtain the greatest economic good from those that cannot be replaced. But to many of us of the Pacific Coast and Rocky Mountain States, Conservation, as practiced, means to tie up and not to utilize. It signifies to us the letting of our waters run unfettered to the sea for fear some one might develop their power and turn their energy to the benefit of mankind in this generation. To us it means the locking up of our vast forests that they may go to decay or become the prey of the fire king. It means that, to please some bureaucrat, the people of our section are held up to allow the timber trust to secure a profit of a few extra millions each year. It means that our vast coal areas must go undeveloped, and that we be compelled to spend our money with foreign mine owners for fuel, importing the coal at no small expense for the item of transportation alone. It means that the State of Washington is robbed of the use of 500,000 acres of land that the Federal Government granted to it for educational purposes at the time it was admitted to the Union. Conservation as practiced in the past developed into a vast profit-making scheme for certain southern land grant railroads, which under it were given scrip in place of worthless desert land included in forest reservations, treeless since time began and bound to remain treeless to the end of time. And we have seen this scrip brought north and placed upon our timber lands that will cruise from 5,000,000 to 50,000,000 feet per section, and are worth from $20 to $100 per acre. This brand of Conservation means to us that 27 ¼% of the total area of the State of Washington paid a paltry $16,000 into the public coffers in 1909. It means we are called upon to expend large sums each year for policing these Federal reserves, which contribute practically nothing to the cost of State government, while at each session our State Legislature is compelled to appropriate large sums to build roads through Federal reserves. Last year we appropriated $205,000 for this purpose. To us, Conservation means that settlers within forest reserves who have taken up homesteads in good faith are harassed, browbeaten, and often forced to abandon their claims and lose the fruits of the labor of years. . . .

The West is not here to fight Conservation, for, properly directed, it is one of the greatest movements inaugurated in this country since the abolishment of slavery. Our former President instituted many reform movements that, properly directed, mean happiness and prosperity for our people; and of all the movements started by him, in my opinion none means more to the financial welfare of ourselves and our children than Conservation, as vouched for by President Roosevelt.

The complaint we have is not against the principle of Conservation, but against the prostitution of that great movement to the impractical ends of certain men out of sympathy with our institutions. They would disregard the rights of the people of the Western States to regulate affairs within their borders; they would retard development of the younger States; they would compel the citizens of the Western States to contribute annually large sums of money to the timber, coal and power companies operating in those sections. While these bureaucrats claim to be working in the interest of the people, they could not better serve the Special Interests if they were employed by them. In the past they laid unusual burdens upon the Western States, and have ruthlessly crushed and brushed aside the honest homesteader who did not have funds to fight

> *An element composed of fadists, dreamers, and enthusiasts is striving to bend popular sentiment to certain impractical and unfair policies of applying Conservation, and it is against this element that the West has taken arms.*
>
> —Marion E. Hay

or carry his case to the highest court. They are attempting to bottle up and make useless the natural resources of our Western States, and have our local affairs administered through an irresponsible bureau located 3,000 miles away.

All the people of the West ask is a chance with the older communities and an honest shuffle—a square deal above the table—and a show to develop our resources and build up prosperous communities made up of innumerable happy homes. I believe the people of the West are as good citizens, and are just as true and loyal to the interests of the Nation as are the citizens of any other locality. As States we do not like to be looked upon as provinces or colonial possessions to be exploited for the benefit of the other sections of this Nation. I have faith enough in the fairness of the citizens of the other sections of this Nation to believe that they do not covet or desire to rob us of what rightfully belongs to us. We believe the profit arising from the development or exploitation of the natural resources of each State should be applied to the benefit of and to the cost of government of that State.

Let me get this fact set in your minds: 95 ½% of the national reserves are located within the eleven Pacific Coast and Rocky Mountain States, and 27 ¼% of the total area of the State I have the honor to represent is taken up by forest reserves, an area in which could be placed the States of Maryland, Rhode Island, Delaware, Connecticut, and the District of Columbia, with room enough to spare to accommodate another Rhode Island. The extreme Conservationist argues that the people of the Western States are not competent or qualified to manage the natural resources within their borders and that a guardian in the shape of a Federal bureau should be appointed to handle them for us. This is a gratuitous insult to the intelligence and integrity of the people of the West. Almost the worst kind of government that can be placed upon a people is a bureaucracy. Let me call your attention to the fact that practically all of the land, mineral, coal, timber, and power-site steals perpetrated upon the people were made when these titles were vested in the Federal Government.

Now, let us deal a little with common-sense Conservation: The people of the State of Washington started a practical system of Conservation long before Conservation became a national issue. . . . One of the great natural assets of our State is our fisheries. Because of over-fishing it became evident to our people some years ago that, unless proper steps were taken, our fishing industry would be ruined. Laws were passed regulating the taking of fish, and numerous hatcheries were established throughout the State. We are now putting more salmon fry into salt water than is the Federal Government, and today the State of Washington stands first in the Union in the value of the products of its fisheries, all because our people a few years ago started a practical system of Conservation. The expense of enforcing our laws regulating fisheries and the cost of maintaining and operating hatcheries is assessed against that industry. We cannot bring ourselves to consent to turn over the management of this industry to the Federal Government. In fact, so opposed are the fisher-folk of Puget Sound to Federal control of the fishing industry, which is threatened because of the proposed treaty with Great Britain, that they are fighting the ratification of the treaty by the United States Senate.

Let us now take up the question of the national forest reserves as administered in the western States. I doubt that there is a thinking man who does not love the trees, the deep woods and vast forests of our land; but a tree, like everything else that grows, has its youth, its maturity, its old age and death. A tree not used at maturity decays, falls, and becomes a fire-trap and is a serious menace to standing timber. I believe that when a tree reaches its maturity it should be used and not allowed to go to decay. Failure to make use of our natural resources which are going to waste is the antithesis of Conservation. I believe that all non-forested lands adapted for agricultural purposes should be opened to settlement and homesteaders allowed to file upon them. Within the national forest reserves are vast areas with not a stick of timber on them, and on which timber can never be made to grow profitably. These tracts should be thrown open to settlement. It is people we want in the West, not game preserves; it is happy, prosperous communities, not idle wastes. I would not advise the acceptance of homestead filings upon timbered areas until after the timber is removed and it is found the land is suitable for agriculture. If it is valuable only for timber raising, then the land should be turned over to the State for reforestation. It is the duty of the State to all the States to start a system of reforestation. At the last session of our Legislature, an appropriation was made to start a survey and have maps made showing the areas of our State better adapted for timber-growing than for any other purpose. This work is now well under way. A commission composed of twelve of our leading citizens, interested in forestry, have been appointed to draft a forestry bill to be submitted to the coming Legislature, when, without doubt, the State will start in upon a plan of reforestation; something which every State of the Union should take up. It is the duty of the States to attend to the growing of forests within their borders, and not the duty of the Federal Government. I am not in favor of abolishing the Federal forestry department. This department should stand in the same relation to the State forests as the Department of Agriculture stands to the farming interests of the Nation. We would hardly expect Secretary Wilson to go around the country, preparing the ground, planting and harvesting our crops, and collecting the revenue therefrom, and we do not expect the Federal Government to go inside of the State and start a system of reforestation where it is absolutely the duty of the State itself to undertake that work.

The greatest infringement upon the rights of the State to handle their own internal affairs is the attempt on the part of the Federal Government to gain control by indirection of our water-power for the purpose of supervising and deriving the revenue from any possible development of the powers. This, by the way, is a policy particularly waged by the National Conservation Association, an organization which is making of this Conservation question a cult, which has practically set up a dogma, and whose members are now quarreling over their claims to orthodoxy. So far about all it has done has been to play into the hands of the power monopoly, which the first apostles of Conservation claim to fear so greatly.

Of all the lame arguments I have heard, the one that the people of the country have not the brains or authority to regulate the charges of any public service corporation, is the worst. We have two means of reaching them: by regulating the rates, and by taxation. No State in the Union was probably ever more troubled than was the State of Washington a few years ago with a railway lobby. In the year 1905 the Legislature of the State of Washington passed a railway commission law, and placed the regulation and control of railroads under this commission. Three years this commission studied the conditions in the State. It was one of the first States in the Union to make a physical valuation to determine the cost of these plants. In 1909 the railway commission of Washington placed an order into effect that saved to the farmers of the State, in the hauling of wheat and other grains alone, $750,000. At the same time they placed an order reducing the general distance tariffs of the railroads, which cost the railroads of the State $75,000, and the railroads have never appealed from its decision and those rates are in effect today. In 1909 the railway commission traveled over every mile of road in our State, visited every station, held hearings, and as a result of that trip they made 250 orders ordering new stations, enlargement of waiting-rooms and train facilities; all those things that the people complained about they remedied, and of the 250 orders put into effect—which cost the railroads hundreds of thousands of dollars—they never have appealed from but 16, and 234 have gone into effect; so the argument that the States cannot control affairs within their own borders, it seems to me, is very fallacious. If we are not competent to handle affairs within our own borders, if we are not competent to regulate corporations, then let us surrender our Constitution and go back to territorial days and let the Federal Government administer our affairs for us.

Now, with reference to the water-power bill: The bill before Congress introduced by Senator Smoot, of Utah, and a similar bill introduced by Senator Jones, of Washington, are perfectly satisfactory to the people of the Coast, so far as I know. Governor Norris has explained to you that the beds and banks of all streams, up to the limit of medium high tide and medium high water, belong to the States; they do not belong to the Federal Government. That property is just as much ours as is the jack-knife in our pockets. Senator Smoot's bill provides that all the interest the Federal Government has in this is that it owns the sites. We own the water, we own the power. There is no question about that. The Supreme Court has passed upon it time and time again. The Government owns the sites. The Smoot bill provides that the sites in the Federal reserves shall be turned over to the State government, but that in no instance shall the State pass the fee-simple title to the land, and no lease shall be longer than fifty years. This is perfectly satisfactory, and the people of the State of Washington have no objections to that form of relinquishment to the State.

The high-handed manner in which a Federal bureau attempted to hold up the development of the western States was the result of a false conception of the principles upon which the Government is founded, and a dangerous assumption that honor and efficiency existed nowhere but in one self-appointed guide, philosopher, and so-called friend of the people. I believe it is the intention of those now in authority to administer the natural resources of the West according to law and with some respect for the welfare of the State in which the resources are located. But outside of governmental and administrative circles, an element composed of fadists, dreamers, and enthusiasts is striving to bend popular sentiment to certain impractical and unfair policies of applying Conservation, and it is against this element that the West has taken arms. We want Conservation that benefits all the people, not a Conservation that plays into the hands of a few. Conservation that does not make use of resources rapidly going to waste is Conservation gone daffy. I have noticed that there are some States down here shouting loud for Federal control of our natural resources. I want to say that those Governors who are here shouting the loudest for Federal control are from the States that have the least amount of natural resources. It is the desire of these people that the revenue received from these natural resources shall be surrendered to the Federal treasury. That is what the western States certainly object to. Some people and papers here are charging that "the interests," whatever you may call them, are favoring State control of the natural resources. I want to say to you that "the interests" are always against local control in any case, and always prefer that monopoly of all kinds shall be placed in the Federal Government and as far away from the people as it is possible to get it.

The address made here by President Taft this morning is in line with the western idea of Conservation as I understand it, and I believe those of us from the West who look at this question as I do endorse the same safe statement that has been made by our great President. Let western men, using up-to-date western methods and familiar with western conditions, deal with and manage western matters. I thank you.

Source: Address by Governor Marion Hay. *Proceedings of the Second National Conservation Congress at St. Paul, September 5–8, 1910.* Washington, D.C.: National Conservation Congress, 1911, pp. 64–71.

A U.S. Forest Service Chief Defends Federal Forest Reserves

"The Movement for State Ownership Is [an] Attack upon the Integrity of the Forests"

December 28, 1912

The efforts of western states during the 1910s to wrest back control of public lands from federal authorities and "unlock" their water, mineral, and grazing resources met with some success. But campaigns to reduce forest protection and increase timber exploitation generally fizzled out, due in no small measure to Henry S. Graves, the second chief in the history of the U.S. Forest Service. After succeeding Gifford Pinchot in 1910, Graves shielded federal forestlands from states wanting to reclaim ownership and timber companies lobbying for more permissive logging contracts. He also oversaw the expansion of America's national forest system into eastern states after the passage of the 1911 Weeks Act. In the following article from 1912, Graves defends federal ownership of forestlands and touts the economic and ecological benefits of federal forest reserves for western states and communities. He also attacks the capabilities and motives of some of the loudest advocates of state control of forest reserves.

During the last three years the proposal to turn over the national forests to the States has been urged with increasing insistence. It has been advocated at frequent gatherings in the West, by a portion of the press, and by various members of Congress. Legislative measures proposing such a transfer have been framed. Debate on one of these measures clearly showed an astonishing amount of support to the idea that transfer to the States would be the ultimate disposition of the remaining public lands, the national forests included.

Whether the State or Nation should own and administer these public resources is a question thus definitely presented to the American people.

The national forests have been repeatedly charged with blocking the development of the West. Nothing could be further from the facts. Lands chiefly valuable for agriculture are available for settlement. Approximately 1,250,000 acres of such lands have been classified and listed for entry by the Forest Service, to the benefit of 12,000 settlers. Prospecting and bona-fide mining on the national forests are unrestricted. Sales of mature timber are encouraged by every possible means consistent with businesslike administration. Over fifty-six hundred timber sales are made yearly, ninety-five per cent of them of small amounts for local use. Free timber is granted annually to over forty thousand settlers and prospectors for developing homes or mines. Water power development is encouraged as far as practicable under the present inadequate laws. Some two hundred power companies are now using or developing sites within the national forests. The only restrictions imposed upon this widespread use of the national forests are those required to maintain the permanency and value of the resources and to prevent monopoly.

> *The States cannot resist the influence of great business interests, either in making or executing laws, as effectively as the Central Government. The difficulty of even the strongest States in withstanding the constant pressure of such interests through long periods of years has been demonstrated over and over again.*
>
> —Henry S. Graves

The national forests are the most significant and concrete expression of the principle of conservation. That principle has been very commonly misrepresented as a policy of present non-use for the sake of future generations. Its true purpose is twofold—to prevent monopoly of public resources, and to secure their greatest use, both present and future, by scientific development. The stewardship of the Forest Service seeks, as to the national forests, first, use of present resources; second, permanency of such resources; and, third, greater and more valuable resources for the future.

The States have many legitimate interests in the national forests. The administration of the national forests recognizes fully all of these interests. As a matter of fact, the greatest direct benefits of public control are received by the communities nearest to them. The Forest Service is committed to the settlement of lands in the forests chiefly valuable for agriculture. The timber needs of local residents, communities, and industries are amply provided for by free use privileges and local sales. No timber is sold for shipment to the general markets of the country unless there is more than enough to supply both present and future local needs. A similar policy governs the distribution of grazing privileges and the use of forest lands for water development. Charges for any of these resources are made only when the use is distinctly commercial in character.

As rapidly as it can the Forest Service is opening up the inaccessible mountainous regions which make up the bulk of the national forests. Many settlements have been helped to secure an outlet to town, railway, or market by trails, roads, bridges, and ferries built by the Forest Service. Much of this work has been done in co-operation with counties or communities, of settlers. The appropriation act this year made available ten per cent of the gross receipts from the national forests for building roads and trails needed for the development of the country. This is aside from the regular appropriation for permanent improvements needed primarily for the protection and administration of the forests. Under the new clause, $200,000 is available for the current year.

The Forest Service recognized at the start that its local personnel must not only be familiar with the regions in which they worked, but must also be in sympathy with the problems and interests of the people. An early provision of law required the selection of supervisors for the respective forests from residents of the States concerned as far as practicable. This has been scrupulously followed. Furthermore, the regulations governing the national forests provide for the adaptation of administrative measures to the varying needs in different localities.

Loss of local taxes to State and county has been met by legislation giving the county road and school funds twenty-five per cent of the national forest gross receipts. This is entirely distinct from the ten per cent already mentioned. On the more inaccessible and undeveloped forests the returns to the State under this provision are not yet great. From other forests the amounts now received by the counties form no inconsiderable part of their revenue. During the year ending June 30, 1911, the Bitter Root National Forest, Montana, paid $15,000 into the county treasury; the Deer Lodge National Forest, in the same State, $19,400; and the Coconino National Forest, Arizona, $12,800. The revenue derived from the Deer Lodge by Montana is greater than if the entire area were taxable and assessed as timberland of the first class under the Montana laws—a class which, in fact, would include less than a third of the area. The returns in these instances indicate what is approaching on all of the forests as the demand for their resources becomes more general.

Of still greater moment to the national forest communities, however, is the development and maintenance of stable industries. The national forests are capable of producing indefinitely over six billion feet of timber each year. This may be increased to eight or ten billion. Every thousand feet of such timber which is cut pays to the community at least $8 in wages and $2 or more for merchandise. When market conditions make it possible to utilize the full annual yield of these areas, the industries which it will support will distribute at least sixty million dollars every year for labor and supplies in the communities in and near the national forests. Furthermore, this industrial development will be permanent.

Oftentimes local communities are practically the sole beneficiaries of this policy. The sparsely timbered forests of southern California are maintained almost exclusively for the protection of streams used for local irrigation and power development. This protection is known to the people of that region to be vital to the maintenance of the water upon which practically their entire agriculture and horticulture depend. Many areas are held in the national forests, at the request of local communities, primarily to protect municipal water supplies. On some of them the sparse forest growth is being extended by artificial planting. The broad principle of public control of resources to accomplish objects which could not be accomplished under private control is being applied.

It would seem, therefore, that all of the legitimate needs of the western communities are provided for, and that the transfer of ownership of the forests from the Government to the several States cannot be justified on the ground of discrimination against the latter or injury to their interests.

The various grants of public land to the States total nearly 185,000,000 acres. The largest grants have been made to promote education, as vital to the maintenance of democratic government and free institutions. Other grants have been made for public buildings and penitentiaries, still others to promote military training and the construction of post roads. The eleven States west of the one hundredth meridian, which contain most of the national forests, have received nearly 77,000,000 acres. The average grant to the national forest States is therefore 6,985,000 acres, against 2,920,000 acres to each of the other States. The western most States have received sixty per cent of the land granted for education, maintenance of public institutions, and other special purposes, and all of the land granted under the Carey Act for the promotion of irrigation. Aside from the swamp land grants, which benefited particularly the southern States, the national forest States have received, State for State, nearly six times as much public land as their eastern sisters.

Without begrudging this liberal use of public resources to aid the development of the western States, it must be emphasized that the aim of every grant has been to promote the public welfare, judged not only from a local but also from a National standpoint. The transfer of the national forests would be a further gift of 187,000,000 acres, chiefly to the same States.

The protection, administration, and development of the national forests involve financial burdens which the individual States cannot carry. The regular expenditures on the forests during the fiscal year 1911 were over $3,400,000. The receipts for the same year were about $2,000,000. Few, if any, of the national forest States would have been willing to appropriate the amounts necessary to cover the regular expenditures. To meet the additional burden of emergency fire protection would have been impossible. In Montana the emergency expenditure was over $400,000, in Idaho $350,000, and in Oregon over $100,000. If the amounts needed had not been available at the time of critical danger, a vast part of the public wealth in the forests would have been lost.

The foregoing does not include any overhead charges. The national forest States are grouped in six districts, each with a supervising and inspecting staff. The splitting of the six administrative units into twenty would double, if not treble, the overhead charge. In the same way there would be waste and ineffectiveness in the conduct of scientific work. Good forestry, like good farming, must apply scientific knowledge. This knowledge the Government is now gathering in connection with national forest administration. In developing American forestry it has built up a strong technical staff and instituted far-reaching studies and experiments. That the States would sufficiently provide for the cost of such work is improbable. If they did, the cost would be greater, the results smaller, and poorer forestry would result.

Moreover, the forests are still largely undeveloped wilderness. Although nearly 10,000 miles of trail, 7,000 miles of telephone lines, and over 1,000 cabins and other structures have been built, 80,000 miles of trail and 40,000 miles of telephone line are still needed to complete the primary fire protective system. These improvements will cost not less than $8,000,000.

These expenditures are not excessive for an area equivalent to the New England States, New York, New Jersey, Delaware, Pennsylvania, Virginia, West Virginia, and Ohio, in the most rugged and inaccessible parts of the West. The present cost of administering and protecting the forests, supervision included, amounts to little more than two cents an acre annually; or, as insurance on the property protected, two mills on the dollar. It is less than a number of lumber companies are now expending solely for protecting their lands from fire. It is less than one-third the cost of the public forests of British India, which are administered far more cheaply than those of any other foreign nation. But the States are not ready to assume such financial burdens. If they attempted it, the forests would either be inadequately protected and administered or they would be managed with a view to greater immediate money returns. Destruction of the forests by fire or trespass or unrestricted and unscientific methods of cutting, rapid depletion of their timber by overcutting, and private exploitation of their resources at much less than their actual value would be the inevitable results. Few of the States have as yet met their responsibilities in the protection of forest lands now owned by them or their citizens.

Administration by the Federal Government means greater stability of policy. Stability in the policies governing the use of the national forests is a necessity of axiomatic character. Their waterpowers can be developed only under plans made for long periods. Much of their timber can be utilized only under contracts for cutting and removal extending over fifteen or twenty years. Sudden shifts or changes in the policy or methods of administration would be fatal. In the administration of the national forests a clear-cut, uniform policy has been developed and applied by the Nation. Its results are known. It has been in force for years. Transfer the forests to the States, and twenty separate and distinct policies must be developed, tested, and tried out.

It must be conceded, furthermore, that the Federal Government has higher and more stable standards of civil service. The management of the national forests under its direction has been free from political consideration. Every position on the rolls is under the Civil Service Law. It is fair to raise the question whether similar standards of civil service and similar freedom from political considerations could be expected under twenty different State Governments. The people of one of the great eastern States have so distrusted its governmental machinery and have been so fearful of political manipulations that fifteen years ago they for bade the cutting of any timber in the State forests. The more far-sighted citizens and officials of many western States have been sorely handicapped in their efforts to bring about conservative, businesslike handling of the lands which those States now own. Political considerations are openly of controlling weight in the organization of the land and forestry departments of a number of the States. Few of them have stable civil service regulations governing their employees. The temptation to use patronage for political purposes is the dead weight to-day on the administration of the game laws in very many of the States. With its broader responsibility, its more stable civil service regulations, and its openness to more searching public scrutiny, the Federal Government is a far safer custodian of the public interests involved than would be provided by a large number of individual States.

The States cannot resist the influence of great business interests, either in making or executing laws, as effectively as the Central Government. The difficulty of even the strongest States in withstanding the constant pressure of such interests through long periods of years has been demonstrated over and over again. Many States have been absolutely dominated by them. Monopolies of National scope have been developed or are in the making through the opportunities which such interests formerly had to acquire public resources. Each additional foothold obtained by them in the national forests of a single

State would strengthen such monopolies. But its effect upon the prosperity and happiness of the people would not be confined to the State immediately concerned.

After everything else has been said, the fundamental fact remains that public control of the resources contained in the national forests can be assured only under Federal owner ship. The transfer to State ownership is now, in purpose, and would prove in effect, the breaking up of public control of any kind.

The amendment offered to the last Agricultural Appropriation Bill provided that, after the national forests are acquired by the States, "thereafter the lands so conveyed shall be the property of such State, and shall be held, administered, settled, and disposed of by such State in accordance with the laws of such State." And, further, "that after the transfer of such lands to the State, they shall be opened to settlement and sale under the laws of said State." In plain terms, the abandonment of public control altogether and opening the forests to acquisition by individuals is proposed. And the significant fact is that this disposition of the forests appeared to have the support of a majority of the Senators who discussed the bill.

The history of the movement for State ownership supports this belief. Its most earnest advocates are the very interests whose unrestrained exploitation of public resources was stopped by the creation of the forests. The water power corporations have been its foremost champions. Their acknowledged representative spoke in its behalf at the Conservation Congress at St. Paul in 1910. The Public Lands Convention, which met at Denver in October, 1911, composed of the elements in the West which have always fought the reservation of these areas from private acquisition, went on record in support of State control. The forces which opposed the national forests at their inception now attack by this means, not any given agency of administration or any theoretical usurpation of local rights by the Central Government, but the fundamental principle of public control in any form.

A number of the western States themselves, by official acts, have shown the same purpose toward the resources contained in the national forests. The Legislature of the State of Washington passed a resolution in 1903 requesting that 58,240 acres of very heavily timbered land, set aside for forest reservation purposes, be thrown open to entry. In February, 1911, the Legislature of that State, by joint resolution, requested Congress and the President to open to entry 114,000 acres in the Columbia National Forest unfit for agriculture. On February 15, 1911, the Legislature of Idaho requested the President to eliminate 46,000 acres from the Coeur d'Alene National Forest in that State, which contained scarcely one hundred acres of agricultural land. The same State requested on March 3, 1911, the elimination of portions of three townships containing similar land in the Pend Oreille National Forest.

The movement for State ownership is thus largely, if not wholly, a movement for the abandonment of public control. It is a thinly disguised attack upon the integrity of the forests, and, through them, upon the whole conservation policy. Whether private acquisition of these resources is proposed by all advocates of State ownership or not, such would be its practical effect. It is believed that the people have not changed their conviction that public control is necessary. The question becomes, then, simply, What governmental agency is best equipped to exercise this control for them? There can be but one answer to this question. For the strongest, most stable, and most effective administration of these resources for their own good the people must continue to look to the Federal Government.

Source: Graves, Henry S. "Shall the States Own the Forests?" *Outlook*, no. 102, December 28, 1912, pp. 935–944. Reprinted in *The Debaters' Handbook Series: Conservation of Natural Resources*. Compiled by C.E. Fanning. Minneapolis: The H.W. Wilson Company, 1913, pp. 84–92.

The New York Times Covers the Ballinger-Pinchot Feud

"The Pinchot Brand of . . . Conservationists . . . Have Gone to Seed on Conservation"

January 8, and May 28, 1910

When William H. Taft succeeded Theodore Roosevelt as president in March 1909, he kept Roosevelt's long-time ally Gifford Pinchot at the head of the U.S. Forest Service. But Pinchot soon fell into a ferocious power struggle with Richard Ballinger, a former Seattle mayor who Taft had selected to replace James R. Garfield as head of his Interior Department.

The Ballinger-Pinchot feud was a complex one with many facets, but the root causes of the political conflagration included: Pinchot's difficulty in accepting his reduced influence in the White House after Roosevelt's departure; Taft's cautious and pragmatic governing style, which put him at loggerheads with the activist "Roosevelt brand" of conservation; Ballinger's antipathy for the conservation movement and his repeated efforts to open public lands protected by Roosevelt to commercial exploitation; and a strong backlash in the West against federal conservation policies perceived to be hostile to the region's economic interests.

The battle between Ballinger and Pinchot began in earnest in 1909 when a General Land Office investigator named Louis R. Glavis publicly accused the interior secretary of being in league with corporate interests that wanted to seize control of the so-called "Cunningham claims"—a cluster of coal fields in the public domain in Alaska. After Pinchot publicly allied himself with Glavis, the public focus shifted to the hostilities between the forester and the interior secretary, who received a vote of confidence from Taft. Over the next few months, the Ballinger and Pinchot camps continued to trade rhetorical body blows as Taft ineffectually tried to act as peacemaker. The president finally fired Pinchot for insubordination on January 7, 1910. A congressional investigation subsequently exonerated Ballinger, but many people dismissed the judgment as a whitewash. Mortally wounded in the political world, Ballinger resigned from the Department of Interior in March 1911. Pinchot, meanwhile, remained one of the nation's most famous advocates of the "wise use" school of conservation, and he later served two terms as governor of Pennsylvania (1923–1927 and 1931–1935).

Today, the Ballinger-Pinchot feud ranks as one of the most famous controversies in American conservation history. It also did enormous damage to the Taft presidency because it opened up an enduring chasm between the conservative (Taft) and progressive (Roosevelt) wings of the Republican Party. This schism is frequently cited as a pivotal factor in Taft's loss in the 1912 presidential election. Press coverage of the affair, meanwhile, showed that natural resource policy had arrived as one of the hot-button issues in American politics. Following are excerpts from The New York Times' extensive coverage of the famous political battle. The first piece covers Taft's dismissal of Pinchot. The second article offers a glimpse of the bitter recriminations that flew back and forth throughout the joint congressional committee investigation.

—From *The New York Times*

PINCHOT OUSTED; PARTY WAR ON

President Dismisses Forester, Censuring Him in Letter—Two Others in Bureau Dropped.

REPUBLICANS BADLY SPLIT

Fight Between the Roosevelt Radicals and the Conservatives May Make Serious Breach

---

January 8, 1910

WASHINGTON, Jan. 7—President Taft has dismissed Gifford Pinchot, Chief of the Forestry Bureau, and the fight between the Roosevelt radicals and the conservative wing of the Republican Party is on in deadly earnest. The President's action came after a Cabinet session that lasted practically all day. When it broke up, just after dinner time this evening, there was issued at the White House a copy of a letter sent by the President to Mr. Pinchot. In this letter, after summing up the acts of the forester that led him to take such action, Mr. Taft said:

"By your conduct you have destroyed your usefulness as a helpful subordinate of the Government, and it therefore becomes my duty to direct the Secretary of Agriculture to remove you from your office as the Forester."

Secretary Wilson was swift in carrying out the decision of the President. He addressed to Mr. Pinchot, to Overton W. Price, Associate Forester, and Albert C. Shaw, assistant law officer of the Forestry Bureau, letters substantially identical. That to Mr. Pinchot reads:

> Sir: By direction of the President you are hereby removed from your office as Forester. You will deliver possession of your office affairs belonging to the Government to Mr. Albert F. Potter, Assistant Forester.
>
> Respectfully,
> James Wilson,
> Secretary of Agriculture

Mr. Price and Mr. Shaw were charged with being especially active in the anti-Ballinger propaganda. . . .

BLOW FALLS ON BALLINGER, TOO.

Thus the axe falls heavily upon the Forestry Bureau, which was the chief centre of Roosevelt radicalism in the Administration, and, for that matter, in the country. But the blow will also affect Secretary Ballinger not a little. It was pointed out among his friends this evening that it was about the most serious thing that could happen to him in this stage of the controversy. For the general expectation now is that the Pinchot partisans will take the field at once and will raise the cry that the dismissal of the forester is proof positive that the investigation of Mr. Ballinger about to be undertaken by Congress can be nothing but an attempt to whitewash the Secretary of the Interior.

How far such a cry will carry weight with those who follow affairs intelligently remains to be seen, but it is certain now that there will be a hysterical outcry from the Roosevelt radicals which will be taken up pretty generally, and especially in the insurgent West and Northwest. It is doubtful under such circumstances if any Congressional investigating committee can be selected now whose verdict will be accepted as final in that section of the country.

That phase of the situation is clearly recognized by the friends of Mr. Ballinger, who charge that Mr. Pinchot understood it also, and for that reason deliberately sought to forestall a thorough and impartial investigation by the publication of his letter to Senator Dolliver.

As the letter of the President shows, it was Mr. Pinchot's letter to Senator [Jonathan] Dolliver [of Iowa], read yesterday in the Senate, that precipitated the action of this evening. The President had maintained an unruffled exterior in the face of a good many unsatisfactory incidents, which he believed to have been caused by Mr. Pinchot or his subordinates.

TRIED TO END CONTROVERSY.

When the controversy over the administration of the Interior Department under Mr. Ballinger first arose the President gave directions aimed at bottling everything up tight, in the hope that the affair would quiet down. Under those directions the Interior Department maintained silence, although it is known that there is a large amount of material in its possession which could have been used at least in the effort to divide public opinion. But, although there was nothing open from the Forestry Bureau there was plenty of evidence to show that the continued campaign against Mr. Ballinger was receiving very great aid and comfort from the foresters. The efforts of the President to put an end to such tactics were utterly futile.

Finally, Mr. Pinchot himself wrote the letter to Senator Dolliver, in flat violation of the executive order forbidding just that sort of thing. As soon as the President learned what had been done he summoned several members of the Cabinet to the White House, where yesterday evening they discussed the matter for some time. This morning it came up again at the regular Cabinet meeting, but not for settlement The regular Cabinet meeting broke up soon after 1 o'clock. At 3 o'clock a special meeting began, attended by every member of the Cabinet in the city except Mr. Ballinger. Secretaries Dickinson and Nagel are not in Washington, but Secretaries Knox, Wilson, MacVeagh, and Meyer, Attorney General Wickersham, and Postmaster General Hitchcock were present.

This meeting continued until nearly 7 o'clock this evening. When the Cabinet members left the White House none of them would discuss what had occurred at their meeting. Nor was any information forthcoming from the President except such as is contained in the letter to Pinchot.

WILLING TO OVERLOOK ALL.

It is known, however, that the President feels that his patience and good nature have been imposed upon by Mr. Pinchot and that his desire to do justice and see fair play has been abused. Despite his deep sense of outrage, however, he was willing even yet to pass over the action of the Forestry Bureau and regard it, as he said, as merely a personal affront, if he could have felt assured that such a course would put a stop to the irregularities that have been going on and insure a fair and full investigation of the whole controversy by the Congressional committee. There was much discussion of this phase of the affair by the Cabinet, but no one could offer any assurance that further forbearance on the part of the President would promise such a result. And it was felt that such forbearance would put the President in a humiliating position before the country that could not be endured.

There are a good many political observers in Washington who regard the affair as the first definite movement in the splitting up of the Republican Party. There is no doubt in Administration circles that the ultra-Roosevelt men have been playing for such a break for a long time, and that now it has come they will take the field at once, with brass bands and banners, charging the President with being recreant to his pledges and an apostate from the Roosevelt policies. It is a case, in Republican politics, of "after this the deluge." . . .

Mr. Pinchot to-night seemed not a bit disturbed by the action of the President. He received his callers smiling and good-humoredly, and said that he had nothing to say. He refused to discuss his plans or to indicate in any way what he intended to do.

"All I can say," said Mr. Pinchot, "is that to-morrow I shall go to the bureau and surrender my office." . . .

[In the following excerpt, the attorneys for Pinchot, Glavis, and Ballinger occupy center stage. Glavis's attorney in the case was Louis Brandeis, who later served as a U.S. Supreme Court Justice from 1916 to 1939. Legal representation for Pinchot was provided by George Wharton Pepper, who later (1922–1927) represented Pennsylvania in the U.S. Senate. Ballinger's lead attorney was John J. Vertrees, a close personal friend to Taft.]

—From *The New York Times*

PRAISE AND BLAME LAID ON BALLINGER

Charged with Being Unworthy of Trust and a False Friend to Taft.

LAUDED AS A CONSERVATOR

Not One Like Pinchot, Who Has Run to Seed, Declares Secretary's Counsel—Inquiry May End To-day.

May 28, 1910

WASHINGTON, May 27—With the attorneys on one side scoring Secretary Ballinger as a man unfit to be at the head of the Interior Department and with the leading attorney on the other side defending him and denouncing his accusers, whom he termed the "Glavis-Garfield-Gifford group," the Ballinger-Pinchot Investigating Committee listened to summing up arguments by counsel to-day. The argument probably will be concluded to-morrow.

Attorneys Brandeis and Pepper told the committee they had produced evidence which they said established that Ballinger was not "vigilant" and "resolute" in resisting the aggressions of special interests, and that his course had been characterized by a lack of fidelity to the public interest.

Attorney Vertrees's reply was that Mr. Ballinger was as much of a "conservationist" as any one "in a proper sense," but that he did not belong to the "Pinchot brand of thirty-three degree conservationists who have gone to seed on conservation."

Ballinger "Yielded Under Pressure."

"His constant yielding under pressure makes him unfit for the office of Secretary of the Interior," explained Attorney Brandeis, counsel for L. R. Glavis, who addressed the committee for two hours in the forenoon. Mr. Brandeis said that Mr. Ballinger lacked that quality of resoluteness which was so essential for a man in his office, and that the only time there was ever any doubt as to what action he would take was when there was "pressure from both sides."

After criticizing Mr. Ballinger's actions in the Cunningham coal cases Mr. Brandeis asked the committee "if such a man is a safe trustee for the people's property." He said it had been established conclusively that Ballinger was not a man so devoted to the interests of the people and so resolute in resisting the aggressions of special interests that he might be relied upon safely to carry on the broad policy of the conservation of our natural resources.

He denounced the discharge of Glavis without an opportunity to be heard on the charges preferred against him, and said that but for this investigation Glavis, "the ideal public servant, would have been permanently condemned and held up to public disgrace without even knowing that charges had been preferred against him."

Mr. Pepper, counsel for former Forester Pinchot, charged that the course pursued by Secretary Ballinger had been characterized by a lack of fidelity to the public interest, that Ballinger was actually responsible for the "entire series of unhappy events," and that the President had been deceived as to the real significance of what was happening in the department.

"There has been no administration of the Interior Department worthy of the name since Ballinger became Secretary," declared Mr. Pepper, "but only a series of acts unwise in themselves, referable to no sound principle of action, and the cause of embarrassment to the President and of injury to the public.

"You took the measure of the Secretary when he was on the stand. There is not a man who does not know in his heart of hearts that the Secretary has demonstrated his unfitness for the office he holds, and that he is the kind of friend from whom the President ought mercifully to be delivered."

Referring to the testimony which had been adduced before the committee, Mr. Pepper said it had conclusively established three points:

First, that the course pursued in the Interior Department had been characterized by a lack of fidelity to the public interest; second, that Mr. Ballinger was not merely officially but actually responsible for the entire series of unhappy events; and third, that the President would never have found himself irrevocably committed to an indorsement of the Secretary had he not been at critical points successfully deceived of what was happening in the department.

Mr. Pepper said these points were in harmony with Mr. Pinchot's opening statement that Mr. Ballinger had "proved unfaithful to the public, whose property he had endangered, and to the President, whom he had deceived."

"Unfaithfulness to the public interest in dealing with the people's power sites, the people's coal, the people's forests, and the people's land," was charged against Mr. Ballinger. His action in restoring the power sites reveals him as the inspirer of a movement hostile to the policy of the preceding Administration of his own party and of his own friends. His attitude toward the reclamation service has made the year 1909 disastrous to the effectiveness and prestige of this great and important governmental agency." . . .

Mr. Vertrees in his reply to counsel on the other side said:

"I cannot but admire the sublimity of his faith," referring to the statement just made by Mr. Pepper. Then referring to the remarks of both Mr. Brandeis and Mr. Pepper he continued:

"One of these gentlemen tells us what an irresolute and wishy-washy man Secretary Ballinger was. That was the argument of Mr. Brandeis. Now the other gentleman, Mr. Pepper, finds hi a resolute man, absolutely dominating and controlling every man around him. So you see the difficulty I am in in endeavoring to answer arguments like this." . . .

Former Secretary Garfield and former Forester Pinchot came in for most severe castigation from Attorney Vertrees, who did not hesitate to denounce them as disappointed men who sought revenge upon the new Secretary. He declared that Garfield and Pinchot used the water power sites question as a mere pretext and sham, and practiced duplicity in the course they had adopted.

CITES PRESIDENT'S POLICIES.

Reading from letters of President Taft respecting the legality of the water power site withdrawals, Mr. Vertrees undertook to show that Secretary Ballinger had merely carried out the policies of the President. His voice quivering with emotion, Mr. Vertrees said:

"Right or wrong, a Cabinet officer who carries out the policies of his chief is not to be censured before the Nation. Do not misunderstand me as merely insisting that you shall deal with this matter solely because Mr. Ballinger was carrying out the judgment of the President. Not that. I say that his construction of the law was correct, and he is fortified and reinforced by the opinion of the law officers of the Government."

At no inconsiderable length Mr. Vertrees discussed the subject of conservation. "In a just and proper sense," he said, "we are all conservationists, and as such there is none more sound than Mr. Ballinger. Now, I am not talking about these men who gone to seed on conservation—men of the Pinchot brand—thirty third degree conservationists—like some people running off with a fad and a fancy." . . .

Source: "Pinchot Ousted; Party War On," *The New York Times,* January 8, 1910, p. 1; "Praise and Blame Laid on Ballinger," *The New York Times,* May 28, 1910, p. 6.

Gifford Pinchot's Principles of Conservation

"The Greatest Good to the Greatest Number for the Longest Time"

1910

At the same time that Washington was reeling from the fallout from the Ballinger-Pinchot controversy, Gifford Pinchot released The Fight for Conservation *(1910), a defense of conservation principles and Progressive ideals that was written for a general audience. In this book, the famous forester and guardian of Roosevelt policies pitches his vision of conservation with evangelical zeal. He emphasizes his belief that natural resources should be harnessed and used in service to goals of economic development and societal advancement—a position that put him at odds with the growing wilderness preservation movement personified by John Muir and the Sierra Club. But Pinchot also explains his staunch opposition to corporate control of land and resource development, which he sees as anathema to sustainable resource use. The following excerpt is from a chapter in* The Fight for Conservation *titled "Principles of Conservation."*

The principles which the word Conservation has come to embody are not many, and they are exceedingly simple. I have had occasion to say a good many times that no other great movement has ever achieved such progress in so short a time, or made itself felt in so many directions with such vigor and effectiveness, as the movement for the conservation of natural resources.

Forestry made good its position in the United States before the conservation movement was born. As a forester I am glad to believe that conservation began with forestry, and that the principles which govern the Forest Service in particular and forestry in general are also the ideas that control conservation.

The first idea of real foresight in connection with natural resources arose in connection with the forest. From it sprang the movement which gathered impetus until it culminated in the great Convention of Governors at Washington in May, 1908. Then came the second official meeting of the National Conservation movement, December, 1908, in Washington. Afterward came the various gatherings of citizens in convention, come together to express their judgment on what ought to be done, and to contribute, as only such meetings can, to the formation of effective public opinion.

The movement so begun and so prosecuted has gathered immense swing and impetus. In 1907 few knew what Conservation meant. Now it has become a household word. While at first Conservation was supposed to apply only to forests, we see now that its sweep extends even beyond the natural resources.

The principles which govern the conservation movement, like all great and effective things, are simple and easily understood. Yet it is often hard to make the simple, easy, and direct facts about a movement of this kind known to the people generally.

The first great fact about conservation is that it stands for development. There has been a fundamental misconception that conservation means nothing but the husbanding of resources for future generations. There could be no more serious mistake.

Conservation does mean provision for the future, but it means also and first of all the recognition of the right of the present generation to the fullest necessary use of all the resources with which this country is so abundantly blessed. Conservation demands the welfare of this generation first, and afterward the welfare of the generations to follow.

The first principle of conservation is development, the use of the natural resources now existing on this continent for the benefit of the people who live here now. There may be just as much waste in neglecting the development and use of certain natural resources as there is in their destruction. We have a limited supply of coal, and only a limited supply. Whether it is to last for a hundred or a hundred and fifty or a thousand years, the coal is limited in amount, unless through geological changes which we shall not live to see, there will never be any more of it than there is now. But coal is in a sense the vital essence of our civilization. If it can be preserved, if the life of the mines can be extended, if by preventing waste there can be more coal left in this country after we of this generation have made every needed use of this source of power, then we shall have deserved well of our descendants.

Conservation stands emphatically for the development and use of water-power now, without delay. It stands for the immediate construction of navigable waterways under a broad and comprehensive plan as assistants to the railroads. More coal and more iron are required to move a ton of freight by rail than by water, three to one. In every case and in every direction the conservation movement has development for its first principle, and at the very beginning of its work. The development of our natural resources and the fullest use of them for the present generation is the first duty of this generation. So much for development.

In the second place conservation stands for the prevention of waste. There has come gradually in this country an understanding that waste is not a good thing and that the attack on waste is an industrial necessity. I recall very well indeed how, in the early days of forest fires, they were considered simply and solely as acts of God, against which any opposition was hopeless and any attempt to control them not merely hopeless but childish. It was assumed that they came in the natural order of things, as inevitably as the seasons or the rising and setting of the sun. To-day we understand that forest fires are wholly within the control of men. So we are coming in like manner to understand that the prevention of waste in all other directions is a simple matter of good business. The first duty of the human race is to control the earth it lives upon.

> *To-day we understand that forest fires are wholly within the control of men. So we are coming in like manner to understand that the prevention of waste in all other directions is a simple matter of good business. The first duty of the human race is to control the earth it lives upon.*
>
> —Gifford Pinchot

We are in a position more and more completely to say how far the waste and destruction of natural resources are to be allowed to go on and where they are to stop. It is curious that the effort to stop waste, like the effort to stop forest fires, has often been considered as a matter controlled wholly by economic law. I think there could be no greater mistake. Forest fires were allowed to burn long after the people had means to stop them. The idea that men were helpless in the face of them held long after the time had passed when the means of control were fully within our reach. It was the old story that "as a man thinketh, so is he"; we came to see that we could stop forest fires, and we found that the means had long been at hand. When at length we came to see that the control of logging in certain directions was profitable, we found it had long been possible. In all these matters of waste of natural resources, the education of the people to understand that they can stop the leakage comes before the actual stopping and after the means of stopping it have long been ready at our hands.

In addition to the principles of development and preservation of our resources there is a third principle. It is this: The natural resources must be developed and preserved for the benefit of the many, and not merely for the profit of a few. We are coming to understand in this country that public action for public benefit has a very much wider field to cover and a much larger part to play than was the case when there were resources enough for every one, and before certain constitutional provisions had given so tremendously strong a position to vested rights and property in general.

A few years ago President Hadley, of Yale, wrote an article which has not attracted the attention it should. The point of it was that by reason of the XIVth amendment to the Constitution, property rights in the United States occupy a stronger position than in any other country in the civilized world. It becomes then a matter of multiplied importance, since property rights once granted are so strongly entrenched, to see that they shall be so granted that the people shall get their fair share of the benefit which comes from the development of the resources which belong to us all. The time to do that is now. By so doing we shall avoid the difficulties and conflicts which will surely arise if we allow vested rights to accrue outside the possibility of governmental and popular control.

The conservation idea covers a wider range than the field of natural resources alone. Conservation means the greatest good to the greatest number for the longest time. One of its great contributions is just this, that it has added to the worn and well-known phrase, "the greatest good to the greatest number," the additional words "for the longest time," thus recognizing that this nation of ours must be made to endure as the best possible home for all its people.

Conservation advocates the use of foresight, prudence, thrift, and intelligence in dealing with public matters, for the same reasons and in the same way that we each use foresight, prudence, thrift, and intelligence in dealing with our own private affairs. It proclaims the right and duty of the people to act for the benefit of the people. Conservation demands the application of common-sense to the common problems for the common good.

The principles of conservation thus described—development, preservation, the common good—have a general application which is growing rapidly wider. The development of resources and the prevention of waste and loss, the protection of the public interests, by foresight, prudence, and the ordinary business and home-making virtues, all these apply to other things as well as to the natural resources. There is, in fact, no interest of the people to which the principles of conservation do not apply.

The conservation point of view is valuable in the education of our people as well as in forestry; it applies to the body politic as well as to the earth and its minerals. A municipal franchise is as properly within its sphere as a franchise for water-power. The same point of view governs in both. It applies as much to the subject of good roads as to waterways, and the training of our people in citizenship is as germane to it as the productiveness of the earth. The application of common-sense to any problem for the Nation's good will lead directly to national efficiency wherever applied. In other words, and that is the burden of the message, we are coming to see the logical and inevitable outcome that these principles, which arose in forestry and have their bloom in the conservation of natural resources, will have their fruit in the increase and promotion of national efficiency along other lines of national life.

The outgrowth of conservation, the inevitable result, is national efficiency. In the great commercial struggle between nations which is eventually to determine the welfare of all, national efficiency will be the deciding factor. So from every point of view conservation is a good thing for the American people.

The National Forest Service, one of the chief agencies of the conservation movement, is trying to be useful to the people of this nation. The Service recognizes, and recognizes it more and more strongly all the time, that whatever it has done or is doing has just one object, and that object is the welfare of the plain American citizen. Unless the Forest Service has served the people, and is able to contribute to their welfare it has failed in its work and should be abolished. But just so far as by cooperation, by intelligence, by attention to the work laid upon it, it contributes to the welfare of our citizens, it is a good thing and should be allowed to go on with its work.

The Natural Forests are in the West. Headquarters of the Service have been established throughout the Western country, because its work cannot be done effectively and properly without the closest contact and the most hearty cooperation with the Western people. It is the duty of the Forest Service to see to it that the timber, water-powers, mines, and every other resource of the forests is used for the benefit of the people who live in the neighborhood or who may have a share in the welfare of each locality. It is equally its duty to cooperate with all our people in every section of our land to conserve a fundamental resource, without which this Nation cannot prosper.

Source: Pinchot, Gifford. *The Fight for Conservation.* Seattle: University of Washington Press, 1910, pp. 40–52.

DOCUMENT 4.10

Secretary Garfield Defends the Plan to Dam Hetch Hetchy Valley

"The Beauties of the Park . . . Might Have to Give Way to the Higher Public Use"

January 9 and 12, 1909

As the first decade of the twentieth century was drawing to a close, the United States was still processing the economic, ecological, and cultural implications of its Roosevelt-led embrace of conservation. Some constituencies—timber and mining companies, pro-development lawmakers (especially in the West), individuals philosophically allegiant to the idea of limited government—denounced the direction in which the country seemed to be heading. But the prevailing wisdom seemed to be that the conservation movement had come along just in time. To many Americans, the movement's emphasis on "wise use" of the nation's forests, rivers, minerals, and soil struck a sensible middle ground. In addition, the ambitious steps taken by the Roosevelt Administration to protect jewels of wilderness scenery (through national parks and national monuments) and rich biodiversity (through federal bird and game preserves) received broad support from a public that had come to view these resources as a valuable source of aesthetic pleasure and spiritual renewal.

Even as concern for the environment blossomed in the fertile soil of the Progressive Era, signs of division were proliferating within the conservation movement. The leaders of conservation within the Roosevelt Administration—Forest Chief Gifford Pinchot, Interior Secretary James R. Garfield, and the president himself—had all been unyielding advocates of sustainable use, not outright preservation, of most public lands and resources. Sierra Club founder John Muir and others, however, were staking out positions of wide-scale wilderness preservation. This simmering conflict exploded with the Battle for Hetch Hetchy Valley, one of the most famous conflicts in the history of American environmental policy–making.

The battle for the valley was sparked in the early 1900s by city leaders in the San Francisco Bay area seeking inexpensive new water and electricity sources for the city. To this end, the mayors of Oakland and San Francisco called for the damming of the Tuolumne River in the newly minted Yosemite National Park. The Sierra Club responded by launching the nation's first grassroots political campaign on behalf of wilderness preservation. The fight soon expanded to the halls of legislative power in Washington, D.C., where the pro-damming crowd ultimately prevailed. The 1913 passage of the Raker Act granted San Francisco the right to flood the Hetch Hetchy Valley. A decade later the O'Shaughnessy Dam was completed, and the resulting reservoir continues to provide drinking water and hydroelectric power to the San Francisco Bay area.

The following excerpt is from the January 1909 congressional testimony of James Rudolph Garfield, Roosevelt's secretary of the interior, in favor of the dam-building proposal. Oakland Mayor Warren Olney later wrote that "Garfield was its most earnest advocate before the committees of Congress" and "made the best argument" of anyone for the passage of the bill.[1] The congressmen quoted in this excerpt are Andrew John Volstead (R-Minn.), Herbert Parsons (R-N.Y.), John W. Gaines (D-Tenn.), Scott Ferris (D-Okla.), and John M. Reynolds (R-Penn.).

. . . Mr. VOLSTEAD: Here is the proposition that I understand is at the bottom of this; you are required by the special act [the creation of Yosemite National Park], as I call it, to pre-serve any natural beauties there, natural wonders. You may grant rights of way; you may grant provisions for flooding land, and still not destroy those things, because that is a mat-ter of judgment, as to whether you are destroying natural beauties. Now here is a case where it must necessarily destroy natural beauty. It is a question whether you are not limited by the original act, whether it is broad enough to sweep away the original provision that you must preserve the natural beauties. I do not care anything about this discussion, because we are not discussing the question whether it is a legal power or not. I do not think that has any-thing to do with the question before us, because it seems to me the question before us is whether we shall grant it, not whether the Secretary has rightly granted it; that is not of any consequence at all. I am satisfied the Secretary acted in good faith, acted upon the advice of the law officers and upon his own investigation, and I am not going to criticise him a bit because he does not agree with me. What I am anxious to know is, shall we grant it?

Secretary GARFIELD: Let me, in further answer to this question about the law, say that when you consider the last clause there, the definition of public use, it is clear in my mind that Congress recognized that, for the purposes of this act, and upon finding that the same is not incompatible with the public interest that there might be occasions when the beauties of the park or of the reservation might have to give way to the higher public use. In so far as those two things could be called incompatible, yes, there might be that repeal, as you may call it, of so much of the original act as was not compatible with the use Congress directed here. Let us see what you mean by the question of public use.

Domestic supply is definitely stated; the use of water for domestic supply—that is a public use. It has been suggested that in the conclusion reached by the Secretary in regard to this matter the public interest would be limited to the special interests within the park itself. That I hold to be untenable. If the act means anything it means that upon these great reserves—if there was need of the use of the water for domestic purposes on those reserves—that the Secretary could, under that act, grant such a permit so that the water could be stored and then carried away for domestic use outside. . . .

. . . Now, what are the public interests? And that is the proposition that appeared before the Interior Department. What are the public interests to be considered in acting upon this application? Now, for a moment, in dealing with that, the public interests are manifold. There is the original purpose for the creation of this park. There is no need of our discussing the wonderful beauty of the spot. It is a most wonderful place, a most beautiful place; that is one great public interest to be considered. The other public interests are these, the irrigation districts below, the further development of irrigation along the line of that river. Then the public interests of the city of San Francisco and those of adjoining cities nearby in that neighborhood. Those are the three great public interests that the Secretary must consider in acting upon a permit of this sort. They are necessarily relative, and must be considered in their relative importance.

As I stated before the committee at my first hearing, my personal feeling is with the very highest public interest, and the highest use to which the water can be put is the domestic water supply for a great city. Some of these gentlemen are urging the first public interest, namely, that of natural beauty, the desire to keep this open as the playgrounds and parks for the people for camping. I say that those interests ought always to give way to the highest interests of domestic use. Of what importance is it, gentlemen, that 100, 200, 3,000, or 10,000 men who are able to spend their vacations camping should have this water supply if it is needed for the hundreds and thousands and the millions of men, women, and children who are in the great cities in and about San Francisco, who have no opportunity to take vacations, who have no opportunity to get out into the country and enjoy the privileges of camping and seeing these natural beauties? . . .

Mr. VOLSTEAD: Let me ask you this question: Did you investigate the question of whether the city could obtain water from some other source?

Secretary GARFIELD: Without a doubt the city can obtain water from half a dozen other sources which are now owned by private interests—by the interests which I suggested are trying to sell their supply to the city—and those same private interests have seriously opposed the Government giving the city the right, because it would preclude their selling their interests to the city.

Mr. PARSONS: You said something at the start about the attitude of criticism. You do not question but what Mr. John Muir and other people who are opposed to this thing are acting in good faith for what they consider the best interests of the public?

Secretary GARFIELD: I did not mean to imply that. What I meant was this, that a great many gentlemen like Mr. Muir and like Mr. McFarland, and those who have written here, I feel very clear take the wrong view of public interests. They are so interested in the proposition of conserving this as a park and keeping out every other use, or every use that is incompatible with retaining the park in its present condition, that they have failed to understand the tremendous importance of the public interest to which I have referred as the domestic use of water. I think it is simply the question of the point of view from which we approach this proposition. If we look at it from the point of view of those gentlemen, then everything should be made subservient to their single desire to retain the park as it is. . . .

Mr. FERRIS: Just one thing. How serious damage will that do to the park from the standpoint of those who believe that that park should be conserved on account of its natural beauty and on account of the interest that the entire citizenship feels in it?

Secretary GARFIELD: It will change this beautiful meadow with these great trees, there is no doubt about that; it will change it from a meadow to a lake. That is the only change that is made, so far as the scenic effect is concerned. It will make this further difference, of course, that there must be, in years to come, greater care exercised, so that there may not be any unnecessary pollution of the water. As to that, from the information I have I think there is but very little danger. It is a tremendous watershed. It is very inaccessible now. Even those who go there would be so few in number as to practically not interfere with the purity of the water by the time the supply reaches San Francisco. . . .

Mr. REYNOLDS: Is there any pressing need of this legislation at this time?

Secretary GARFIELD: I think that Congress should take action on it now. The city is in the position where it must know whether it has the opportunity to use this water supply or not. I can not see that any further information could be obtained on the questions that have been considered by the committee and by the department, except in so far as personal examination by any of us might give us a view of the land itself.

Mr. REYNOLDS: What are the obstacles in the way of getting a water supply from other sources to the city of San Francisco?

Secretary GARFIELD: That is a matter that the representatives of the city could much better answer than I. It is simply a question of which of the various sources of supply is the best one for the city of San Francisco to have. Their citizens, by their actions thus far, have indicated that they believe that this is the source of supply which they desire to use. . . .

Source: Testimony of James Rudolph Garfield. *Hetch Hetchy Reservoir Hearings Held before the Committee on the Public Lands of the House of Representatives. January 9 and 12, 1909.* 60th Cong., 2d sess., Washington, D.C.: Government Printing Office, pp. 26–39.

NOTE

1. Warren Olney, "Water Supply for the Cities about the Bay of San Francisco." *Out West,* July 1909, 599–605.

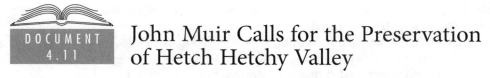

DOCUMENT
4.11

John Muir Calls for the Preservation of Hetch Hetchy Valley

"That Anyone Would Try to Destroy Such a Place Seems Incredible"

1912

The controversy over whether Yosemite National Park's Hetch Hetchy Valley should be sacrificed for a reservoir for water- and electricity-hungry San Francisco pitted the utilitarian-minded "Roosevelt conservationists" against a growing clan of conservationists who subscribed to the idea of preserving wilderness for its own sake. The undisputed leader of this latter group was John Muir, the nomadic hiker, prolific writer, and nature lover who had founded the Sierra Club in 1892.

Muir organized a trailblazing grassroots campaign against the plan to flood Hetch Hetchy. He also sought to solicit public and congressional support for its preservation by writing about the valley's many splendors; a representative paean to Hetch Hetchy from Muir's 1912 book The Yosemite *is excerpted here. Muir's efforts ultimately failed; Congress approved the controversial dam building project in 1913. But Muir's campaign on behalf of Hetch Hetchy nonetheless marked the dawn of a new age in American politics. From this point forward, enlisting grassroots support from the American public for pro-environment policies became a prominent part of the strategic playbook for conservation and environmental organizations.*

Yosemite is so wonderful that we are apt to regard it as an exceptional creation, the only valley of its kind in the world; but Nature is not so poor as to have only one of anything. Several other yosemites have been discovered in the Sierra that occupy the same relative positions on the Range and were formed by the same forces in the same kind of granite. One of these, the Hetch Hetchy Valley, is in the Yosemite National Park about twenty miles from Yosemite and is easily accessible to all sorts of travelers by a road and trail. . . .

After my first visit to it in the autumn of 1871, I have always called it the "Tuolumne Yosemite," for it is a wonderfully exact counterpart of the Merced Yosemite, not only in its sublime rocks and waterfalls but in the gardens, groves and meadows of its flowery park-like floor. The floor of Yosemite is about 4000 feet above the sea; the Hetch Hetchy floor about 3700 feet. And as the Merced River flows through Yosemite, so does the Tuolumne through Hetch Hetchy. The walls of both are of gray granite, rise abruptly from the floor, are sculptured in the same style and in both every rock is a glacier monument.

Standing boldly out from the south wall is a strikingly picturesque rock called by the Indians, Kolana, the outermost of a group 2300 feet high, corresponding with the Cathedral Bocks of Yosemite both in relative position and form. On the opposite side of the Valley, facing Kolana, there is a counterpart of the El Capitan that rises sheer and plain to a height of 1800 feet, and over its massive brow flows a stream which makes the most graceful fall I have ever seen. From the edge of the cliff to the top of an earthquake talus it is perfectly free in the air for a thousand feet before it is broken into cascades among talus boulders. It is in all its glory in June, when the snow is melting fast, but fades and vanishes toward the end of summer. The only fall I know with which it may fairly be compared is the Yosemite Bridal Veil; but it excels even that favorite fall both in height and airy-fairy beauty and behavior. Lowlanders are apt to suppose that mountain streams in their wild career over cliffs lose control of themselves and tumble in a noisy chaos of mist and spray. On the contrary, on no part of their travels are they more harmonious and self-controlled. Imagine yourself in Hetch Hetchy on a sunny day in June, standing waist-deep in grass and flowers (as I have often stood), while the great pines sway dreamily with scarcely perceptible motion. Looking northward across the Valley you see a plain, gray granite cliff rising abruptly out of the gardens and groves to a height of 1800 feet, and in front of it Tueeulala's silvery scarf burning with irised sun-fire. In the first white outburst at the head there is abundance of visible energy, but it is speedily hushed and concealed in divine repose, and its tranquil progress to the base of the cliff is like that of a downy feather in a still room. Now observe the fineness and marvelous distinctness of the various sun-illumined fabrics into which the water is woven; they sift and float from form to form down the face of that grand gray rock in so leisurely and unconfused a manner that you can examine their texture, and patterns and tones of color as you would a piece of embroidery held in the hand. Toward the top of the fall you see groups of booming, comet-like masses, their solid, white heads separate, their tails like combed silk interlacing among delicate gray and purple shadows, ever forming and dissolving, worn out by friction in their rush through the air. Most of these vanish a few hundred feet below the summit, changing to varied forms of cloud-like drapery. Near the bottom the width of the fall has increased from about twenty-five feet to a hundred feet. Here it is composed of yet finer tissues, and is still without a trace of disorder—air, water and sunlight woven into stuff that spirits might wear.

So fine a fall might well seem sufficient to glorify any valley; but here, as in Yosemite, Nature seems in nowise moderate, for a short distance to the eastward of Tueeulala booms and thunders the great Hetch Hetchy Fall, Wapama, so near that you have both of them in full view from the same standpoint. It is the counterpart of the Yosemite Fall, but has a much greater volume of water, is about 1700 feet in height, and appears to be nearly vertical, though considerably inclined, and is dashed into huge outbounding bosses of foam on projecting shelves and knobs. No two falls could be more unlike—Tueeulala out in the open sunshine descending like thistledown; Wapama in a jagged, shadowy gorge roaring and thundering, pounding its way like an earthquake avalanche. . . .

The floor of the Valley is about three and a half miles long, and from a fourth to half a mile wide. The lower portion is mostly a level meadow about a mile long, with the trees restricted to the sides and the river banks, and partially separated from the main, upper, forested portion by a low bar of glacier-polished granite across which the river breaks in rapids.

The principal trees are the yellow and sugar pines, digger pine, incense cedar, Douglas spruce, silver fir, the California and golden-cup oaks, balsam cottonwood, Nuttall's flowering dogwood, alder, maple, laurel, tumion, etc. The most abundant and influential are the great yellow or silver pines like those of Yosemite, the tallest over two hundred feet in height, and the oaks assembled in magnificent groves with massive rugged trunks four to six feet in diameter, and broad, shady, wide-spreading heads. The shrubs forming conspicuous flowery clumps and tangles are manzanita, azalea, spiraea, brier-rose, several species of ceanothus, calycanthus, philadelphus, wild cherry, etc.; with abundance of showy and fragrant herbaceous plants growing about them or out in the open in beds by themselves. . . .

It appears, therefore, that Hetch Hetchy Valley, far from being a plain, common, rock-bound meadow, as many who have not seen it seem to suppose, is a grand landscape garden, one of Nature's rarest and most precious mountain temples. As in Yosemite, the sublime rocks of its walls seem to glow with life, whether leaning back in repose or standing erect in thoughtful attitudes, giving welcome to storms and calms alike, their brows in the sky, their feet set in the groves and gay flowery meadows, while birds, bees, and butterflies help the river and waterfalls to stir all the air into music—things frail and fleeting and types of permanence meeting here and blending, just as they do in Yosemite, to draw her lovers into close and confiding communion with her.

Sad to say, this most precious and sublime feature of the Yosemite National Park, one of the greatest of all our natural resources for the uplifting joy and peace and health of the people, is in danger of being dammed and made into a reservoir to help supply San Francisco with water and light, thus flooding it from wall to wall and burying its gardens and groves one or two hundred feet deep. This grossly destructive commercial scheme has long been planned and urged (though water as pure and abundant can be got from sources outside of the people's park, in a dozen different places), because of the comparative cheapness of the dam and of the territory which it is sought to divert from the great uses to which it was dedicated in the Act of 1890 establishing the Yosemite National Park.

The making of gardens and parks goes on with civilization all over the world, and they increase both in size and number as their value is recognized. Everybody needs beauty as well as bread, places to play in and pray in, where Nature may heal and cheer and give strength to body and soul alike. This natural beauty-hunger is made manifest in the little window-sill gardens of the poor, though perhaps only a geranium slip in a broken cup, as well as in the carefully tended rose and lily gardens of the rich, the thousands of spacious city parks and botanical gardens, and in our magnificent National parks—the Yellowstone, Yosemite, Sequoia, etc.—Nature's sublime wonderlands, the admiration and joy of the world. Nevertheless, like anything else worth while, from the very beginning, however well guarded, they have always been subject to attack by despoiling gain-seekers and mischief-makers of every degree from Satan to Senators, eagerly trying to make everything immediately and selfishly commercial, with schemes disguised in smug-smiling philanthropy, industriously, shampiously crying, "Conservation, conservation, panutilization," that man and beast may be fed and the dear Nation made great. Thus long ago a few enterprising merchants utilized the Jerusalem temple as a place of business instead of a place of prayer, changing money, buying and selling cattle and sheep and doves; and earlier still, the first forest reservation, including only one tree, was likewise despoiled. Ever since the establishment of the Yosemite National Park, strife has been going on around its borders and I suppose this will go on as part of the universal battle between right and wrong, however much its boundaries may be shorn, or its wild beauty destroyed. . . .

The most delightful and wonderful camp grounds in the Park are its three great valleys—Yosemite, Hetch Hetchy, and Upper Tuolumne; and they are also the most important places with reference to their positions relative to the other great features—the Merced and Tuolumne Canons, and the High Sierra peaks and glaciers, etc., at the head of the rivers. The main part of the Tuolumne Valley is a spacious flowery lawn four or five miles long, surrounded by magnificent snowy mountains, slightly separated from other beautiful meadows, which together make a series about twelve miles in length, the highest reaching to the feet of Mount Dana, Mount Gibbs, Mount Lyell and Mount McClure. It is about 8500 feet above the sea, and forms the grand central High Sierra camp ground from which excursions are made to the noble mountains, domes, glaciers, etc.; across the Range to the Mono Lake and volcanoes and down the Tuolumne Canon to Hetch Hetchy. Should Hetch Hetchy be submerged for a reservoir, as proposed, not only would it be utterly destroyed, but the sublime canon way to the heart of the High Sierra would be hopelessly blocked and the great camping ground, as the watershed of a city drinking system, virtually would be closed to the public. So far as I have learned, few of all the thousands who have seen the park and seek rest and peace in it are in favor of this outrageous scheme.

One of my later visits to the Valley was made in the autumn of 1907 with the late William Keith, the artist. The leaf-colors were then ripe, and the great godlike rocks in repose seemed to glow with life. The artist, under their spell, wandered day after day along the river and through the groves and gardens, studying the wonderful scenery; and, after making about forty sketches, declared with enthusiasm that although ts walls were less sublime in height, in picturesque beauty and charm Hetch Hetchy surpassed even Yosemite.

That any one would try to destroy such a place seems incredible; but sad experience shows that there are people good enough and bad enough for anything. The proponents of the dam scheme bring forward a lot of bad arguments to prove that the only righteous thing to do with the people's parks is to destroy them bit by bit as they are able. Their arguments are curiously like those of the devil, devised for the destruction of the first garden—so much of the very best Eden fruit going to waste; so much of the best Tuolumne water and Tuolumne scenery going to waste. Few of their statements are even partly true, and all are misleading. . . .

These temple destroyers, devotees of ravaging commercialism, seem to have a perfect contempt for Nature, and, instead of lifting their eyes to the God of the mountains, lift them to the Almighty Dollar.

Dam Hetch Hetchy! As well dam for water-tanks the people's cathedrals and churches, for no holier temple has ever been consecrated by the heart of man.

Source: Muir, John. *The Yosemite.* New York: The Century Co., 1912, pp. 249–262.

DOCUMENT
4.12

The Weeks Act Paves the Way for National Forests in the East

"For the Purpose of Conserving the Forests and the Water Supply"

March 27, 1911

In March 1911 President William H. Taft signed the Weeks Act, a measure designed to expand federal protection and management of forests beyond the West into the eastern states. The bill was borne out of deep concerns about the impact of deforestation on eastern watersheds, flood control, and wildlife populations, and it enjoyed broad public and legislative support. As far back as 1901, in fact, state legislatures in Virginia, North Carolina, South Carolina, and Tennessee had all passed resolutions approving the creation of federal forest reserves within their borders.[1]

Less than a month after the act (excerpted here) was signed, U.S. Forest Service Chief Henry Graves submitted recommendations to a National Forest Reservation Commission—which had been created by the Weeks Act—for the federal acquisition of large tracts of forestland in the southern Appalachians and White Mountains regions. The Commission eventually approved acquisition of most of these targeted areas, and these became the first eastern units of the nation's National Forest system. In 1924 the Clarke–McNary Act expanded the reach of the Weeks Law by authorizing forest acquisitions explicitly for timber production (unlike the original act, which based acquisition decisions on watershed protection). The passage of the 1924 law ushered in the first great wave of national forest designations in the Great Lakes region. All told, more than 4.7 million forested acres were purchased under the Weeks and Clarke-McNary Acts from 1911 to 1933.[2]

An Act to Enable Any State to Cooperate with Any Other State or States, or with the United States, for the Protection of the Watersheds of Navigable Streams, and to Appoint a Commission for the Acquisition of Lands for the Purpose of Conserving the Navigability of Navigable Rivers.

Be it enacted by the Senate and House of Representatives of the United States of America in Congress assembled, That the consent of the Congress of the United States is hereby given to each of the several States of the Union to enter into any agreement or compact, not in conflict with any law of the United States, with any other State or States for the purpose of conserving the forests and the water supply of the States entering into such agreement or compact.

SEC. 2. That the sum of two hundred thousand dollars is hereby appropriated and made available until expended, out of any moneys in the National Treasury not otherwise appropriated, to enable the Secretary of Agriculture to cooperate with any State or group of States, when requested to do so, in the protection from fire of the forested watersheds of navigable streams; and the Secretary of Agriculture is hereby authorized, and on such conditions as he deems wise, to stipulate and agree with any State or group of States to cooperate in the organization and maintenance of a system of fire protection on any private or state forest lands within such State or States and situated upon the watershed of a navigable river: *Provided,* That no such stipulation or agreement shall be made with any State which has not provided by law for a System of forest-fire protection; *Provided further,* That in no case shall the amount expended in any State exceed in any fiscal year the amount appropriated by that State for the same purpose during the same fiscal year.

SEC. 3. That there is hereby appropriated, for the fiscal year ending June thirtieth, nineteen hundred and ten, the sum of one million dollars, and for each fiscal year thereafter a sum not to exceed two million dollars for use in the examination, survey, and acquirement of lands located on the headwaters of navigable streams or those which are being or which may be developed for navigable purposes; *Provided,* That the provisions of this section shall expire by limitation on the thirtieth day of June, nineteen hundred and fifteen.

SEC. 4. That a commission, to be known as the National Forest Reservation Commission, consisting of the Secretary of War, the Secretary of the Interior, the Secretary of Agriculture, and two members of the Senate, to be selected by the President of the Senate, and two members of the House of Representatives, to be selected by the Speaker, is hereby created and authorized to consider and pass upon such lands as may be recommended for purchase as provided in section six of this Act, and to fix the price or prices at which such lands may be purchased, and no purchases shall be made of any lands until such lands have been duly approved for purchase by said commission; *Provided,* That the members of the commission herein created shall serve as such only during their incumbency in their respective official positions, and any vacancy on the commission shall be filled in the manner of the original appointment. . . .

SEC. 6. That the Secretary of Agriculture is hereby authorized and directed to examine, locate, and recommend for purchase such lands as in his judgment may be necessary to the regulation of the flow of navigable streams, and to report to the National Forest Reservation Commission the results of such examinations: *Provided,* That before any lands are purchased by the National Forest Reservation Commission said lands shall be examined by the Geological Survey and a report made to the Secretary of Agriculture, showing that the control of such lands will promote or protect the navigation of streams on whose watersheds they lie.

SEC. 7. That the Secretary of Agriculture is hereby authorized to purchase, in the name of the United States, such lands as have been approved for purchase by the National Forest Reservation Commission at the price or prices fixed by said commission; *Provided,* That no deed or other instrument of conveyance shall be accepted or approved by the Secretary of Agriculture under this Act until the legislature of the State in which the land lies shall have consented to the acquisition of such land by the United States for the purpose of preserving the navigability of navigable streams. . . .

SEC. 9. That such acquisition may in any case by conditioned upon the exception and reservation to the owner form whom title passes to the United States of the minerals and of the merchantable timber, or either or any part of them, within or upon such lands at the date of the conveyance, but in every case such exception and reservation and the time within which such timber shall be removed and the rules and regulations under which the cutting and removal of such timber and the mining and removal of such minerals shall be done shall be expressed in the written instrument of conveyance, and thereafter the mining, cutting, and removal of the minerals and timber so excerpted and reserved shall be done only under and in obedience to the rules and regulations so expressed. . . .

SEC. 11. That, subject to the provisions of the last preceding section, the lands acquired under this Act shall be permanently reserved, held, and administered as national forest lands. . . . And the Secretary of Agriculture may from time to time divide the lands acquired under this Act into such specific national forests and so designate the same as he may deem best for administrative purposes. . . .

SEC. 13. That five per centum of all moneys received during any fiscal year from each national forest into which the lands acquired under this act may from time to time be divided shall be paid, at the end of such year, by the Secretary of the Treasury to the State in which such national forest is situated, to be expended as the state legislature may prescribe for the benefit of the public schools and public roads of the county or counties in which such national forest is situated: *Provided,* That when any national forest is in more than one State or county the distributive share to each from the proceeds of such forest shall be proportional to its area therein: *Provided further,* That there shall not be paid to any State for any county an amount equal to more than forty per centum of the total income of such county from all other sources.

Source: "Purchase of Lands under the Weeks Law in the Southern Appalachians and White Mountains." U.S. Department of Agriculture, Forest Service. Washington, D.C.: Government Printing Office, March 27, 1911, pp. 7–9.

Notes

1. David A. Adams, *Renewable Resource Policy: The Legal-Institutional Foundations* (Washington, D.C.: Island Press, 1993), 130.
2. *Review of the Work of the National Forest Reservation Commission, 1911–1933* (Washington, D.C.: Government Printing Office, 1933).

The National Park Service Act

"The Service . . . Shall Promote and Regulate the . . . National Parks, Monuments, and Reservations"

August 25, 1916

In 1916 the United States established a National Park Service (NPS) to manage its various national parks, which had previously been administered as wholly separate entities. The creation of the NPS by the National Park Service Act (also known as the 1916 Organic Act) was an essential milestone in the advancement of America's national park system. Under the leadership of its first director, Stephen Mather, the NPS consolidated the individual parks into a unified system dedicated to wilderness preservation and recreational enjoyment above all other considerations. Today, the National Park Service remains the primary steward of the nation's stunning array of national parks, which historian Wallace Stegner described as "the best idea we ever had. . . . They were cooked in the same alembic as other land laws—the Homestead Act, Preemption Act, Timber and Stone Act, Mining Act of 1872—but they came out as something different. Absolutely American, absolutely democratic, they reflect us at our best rather than our worst."[1]

AN ACT TO ESTABLISH A NATIONAL PARK SERVICE, AND FOR OTHER PURPOSES.

Be it enacted by the Senate and House of Representatives of the United States of America in Congress assembled, That there is hereby created in the Department of the Interior a service to be called the National Park Service, which shall be under the charge of a director, who shall be appointed by the Secretary and who shall receive a salary of $4,500 per annum. There shall also be appointed by the Secretary the following assistants and other employees at the salaries designated: One assistant director, at $2,500 per annum; one chief clerk, at $2,000 per annum; one draftsman, at $1,800 per annum; one messenger, at $600 per annum; and, in addition thereto, such other employees as the Secretary of the Interior shall deem necessary: *Provided,* That not more than $8,100 annually shall be expended for salaries of experts, assistants, and employees within the District of Columbia not herein specifically enumerated unless previously authorized by law. The service thus established shall promote and regulate the use of the Federal areas known as national parks, monuments, and reservations hereinafter specified by such means and measures as conform to the fundamental purpose of the said parks, monuments, and reservations, which purpose is to conserve the scenery and the natural and historic objects and the wild life therein and to provide for the enjoyment of the same in such manner and by such means as will leave them unimpaired for the enjoyment of future generations.

SEC. 2. That the director shall, under the direction of the Secretary of the Interior, have the supervision, management, and control of the several national parks and national monuments which are now under the jurisdiction of the Department of the Interior, and of the Hot Springs Reservation in the State of Arkansas, and of such other national parks and reservations of like character as may be hereafter created by Congress: *Provided,* That in the supervision, management, and control of national monuments contiguous to national forests the Secretary of Agriculture may cooperate with said National Park Service to such extent as may be requested by the Secretary of the Interior.

SEC. 3. That the Secretary of the Interior shall make and publish such rules and regulations as he may deem necessary or proper for he use and management of the parks, monuments, and reservations under the jurisdiction of the National Park Service, and any violations of any of the rules and regulations authorized by this Act shall be punished as provided for in section fifty of the Act entitled "An Act to codify and amend the penal laws of the United States," approved March fourth, nineteen hundred and nine, as amended by section six of the Act of June twenty-fifth, nineteen hundred and ten. He may also, upon terms and conditions to be fixed by him, sell or dispose of timber in those cases where in his judgment the cutting of such timber is required in order to control the attacks of insects or diseases or otherwise conserve the scenery or the natural or historic objects in any such park, monument, or reservation. He may also provide in his discretion for the destruction of such animals and of such plant life as may be detrimental to the use of any of said parks, monuments, or reservations. He may also grant privileges, leases, and permits for the use of land for the accommodation of visitors in the various parks, monuments, or other reservations herein provided for, but for periods not exceeding twenty years; and no natural curiosities, wonders, or objects of interest shall be leased, rented, or granted to anyone on such terms as to interfere with free access to them by the public: Provided, however, That the Secretary of the Interior may, under such rules and regulations and on such terms as he may prescribe, grant the privilege to graze live stock within any national park, monument, or reservation herein referred to when in his judgment such use is not detrimental to the primary purpose for which such park, monument, or reservation was created, except that this provision shall not apply to the Yellowstone National Park. . . .

SEC. 4. That nothing in this Act contained shall affect or modify the provisions of the Act approved February fifteenth, nineteen hundred and one, entitled "An Act relating to rights of way through certain parks, reservations, and other public lands."

Approved August 25, 1916

Source: Reports of the Department of the Interior, for the Fiscal Year ended June 1916. Vol. 1. Washington, D.C.: Government Printing Office, 1917, p. 829.

NOTE

1. Wallace Stegner, "The Best Idea We Ever Had," in *Marking the Sparrow's Fall: The Making of the American West* (New York: Macmillan, 1999), 135.

CHAPTER 5

Environmental Health in the Industrial City

1800-1920

The twin forces of industrialization and mass immigration revolutionized life in American cities during the nineteenth and early twentieth centuries. Sleepy towns blossomed into thriving cities, and some urban centers—New York, Boston, Chicago, Pittsburgh, Detroit, San Francisco, New Orleans, and others—became sprawling metropolises. This transformation of American city life had many salutary aspects. Urbanization served as an engine of breathtaking commercial and industrial growth, provided new opportunities for personal and economic fulfillment to native-born and immigrant alike, galvanized the nation's geographic expansion to the shores of the Pacific, and vaulted America to a position of global economic and military prominence. But the rise of the industrial city also brought new and virulent forms of environmental pollution that exacted a particularly heavy toll on urban residents without the financial or educational resources to protect themselves. "The experience of environmental degradation," wrote environmental activist Robert Gottlieb, "took on a class dimension. On the one hand, the industrial city became a source of great wealth and a symbol of progress for those directly benefiting from the industrial and urban expansion of the period. On the other hand, this very same expansion, with its belching factories, polluted waterways, and untreated and sometimes uncollected wastes, became, for many poor and industrial workers, an environmental nightmare that seemed impossible to escape."[1]

Efforts to address the steady environmental deterioration within America's cities were intermittent and mostly ineffectual for much of the nineteenth century. In the latter stages of the century, however, calls for more effective sanitation measures and public health reforms began to be taken more seriously. And as the perceptions of policymakers, medical professionals, factory workers, and other city residents further shifted in favor of industrial regulation during the Progressive Era, the first major laws to curb the worst abuses of the nation's factories, slaughterhouses, and slumlords were drafted and passed.

PUBLIC HEALTH IN AMERICA'S EARLY YEARS

During America's first half-century of life, the nation had virtually no legal or institutional public health infrastructure. Few regulations governing the handling or disposition of toxic materials, sewage, and garbage existed in urban centers. Public health institutions and agencies, meanwhile, were present in only a few pockets of the young nation, and these received meager funding. In 1830 only five major American cities had established

Booming American industry fueled incredible economic growth in the late nineteenth and early twentieth centuries but at great human and environmental costs. Industrial expansion during this time produced incredible fortunes but also exposed workers to unregulated industrial hazards and the public to dangerous levels of pollution.

local boards of health, and only Boston's was permanent; the others were largely inactive when their host cities were not in the grip of outbreaks of disease.

The virtual absence of public health regulations and agencies stemmed from a number of factors. The greatest of these was the simple reality that America was a young nation still in its formative stages of legal and institutional development. Another factor was a self-congratulatory attitude about the climatic and environmental "exceptionalism" of North America in comparison to disease-ridden Europe.[2] This dominant perspective led most Americans to conclude that public health agencies and anti-pollution regulations were simply unnecessary. In addition, Americans, like people all around the world, were ignorant of the bacteriological underpinnings of typhoid, cholera, malaria, tuberculosis, and other dreaded diseases and the vectors through which they spread. Political philosophy was another contributor. Most early Americans subscribed to a vision of Jacksonian democracy with strong anti-government and anti-intellectual pillars, so the few physicians and scientists of the era who dared to issue calls for sanitary regulations were regarded with indignant scorn. "The role of the government was to provide minimal services and leave economic matters to individual citizens," summarized scholar John Duffy. "Regulating nuisance industries, requiring private citizens to clean their premises, or ordering them to remove their hogs from the streets were considered infringements upon individual liberty and private property rights."[3]

Early towns and cities, then, relied almost entirely on private funding and voluntary measures for collection of refuse generated by households, disposal of waste from tanneries and mills, and a multitude of other urban pollutants. These arrangements were completely inadequate for the task of dealing with the massive volumes of garbage and other waste material generated in America's fast-growing towns and cities. Livestock—and the manure they produced—were a ubiquitous part of the urban landscape in the early nineteenth century, and the rotting carcasses of horses, pigs, and other animals often lined urban streets or alleys for weeks before they were removed. Human waste went into privies (usually poorly constructed) that often filled to overflowing because of the effort and expense of having them emptied. The contents of privies that were emptied by private refuse collectors, known as scavengers, frequently were dumped into the nearest street gutter or waterway. These same streams, rivers, harbors, and canals also received toxic stews of effluents and other industrial byproducts from waterfront factories and mills. Docks, alleyways, stables, and intersections, meanwhile, became choked with towering masses of garbage and manure that were left to rot. The end result of this unregulated chaos, opined one mid-century ward inspector in New York City, was a nightmarish environmental tableau: "Domestic garbage and filth of every kind is thrown into the streets, covering their surface, filling the gutters, obstructing the sewer culverts and sending forth perennial emanations which must generate pestiferous disease. In winter the filth and garbage, etc. accumulate in the streets to the depths of sometimes two or three feet."[4] The offensive sights and putrid smells of the city were difficult for all residents to endure, but middle-class workers and wealthy businessmen could at least retreat to comfortable offices and homes. Impoverished residents, however, were nearly swallowed up by their squalid surroundings.

One of the few comparative bright spots in public health in early nineteenth-century cities and towns lay in the realm of water supply systems. Potable water was universally recognized as the lifeblood of a city's present and future vitality, so municipal officials approached water supply issues with an intensity and long-term perspective that they rarely displayed toward other city services. In 1801 Philadelphia became the first American city to complete a municipal waterworks system, and several other cities followed suit in the ensuing decades. The construction of these systems involved huge outlays of public funds, but the projects nonetheless enjoyed support from corporate boosters and other influential local interests who saw these monuments to engineering prowess and technological ingenuity as symbols of civic pride and promise. They were also usually publicly regulated and operated—a clear indication that civic leaders saw the systems as integral to their city's future prospects. And once municipal water supply systems were operational, authorities often began looking into developing complementary sewer networks to handle the increased volumes of wastewater they generated. Unfortunately, construction of effective sewage disposal systems lagged badly for much of the century, and wastewater was often dumped into gutters, cesspools, or nearby waterways, with dire consequences for public health and riverine ecosystem integrity.

Improvements in these areas came slowly—and only after wrenching struggles with disease. In the 1830s and 1840s, for example, a succession of fearsome cholera epidemics struck every corner of the nation. "Cholera," stated Rosenberg, "flourished in the great cities, New York, Cincinnati, Chicago; it crossed the continent with the forty-niners; its victims included Iowa dirt farmers and New York longshoremen, Wisconsin lead miners and Negro field hands."[5] In 1854 British scientist John Snow discovered that pure water for drinking and cleaning was key to warding off cholera, a bacterium capable of reaching its victims through a variety of vectors, from unwashed hands and uncooked food to sewage-contaminated water supplies. News of this scientific breakthrough made it much easier for city officials and taxpayers to accept the large capital expenses associated with water delivery systems.

Cholera outbreaks from this era also aided sanitary reformers and public health advocates in their persistent efforts to overcome what one scholar called "centuries of governmental inertia and indifference in regard to problems of public health."[6] The outbreaks spurred the approval of a variety of sanitary reports and surveys in cities all across the country. Many of the recommendations contained in these documents—creation of refuse collection programs and regulations, funding for public health departments, sanitary inspections of new and existing businesses—were cast aside or pursued halfheartedly. These disappointments prompted the Committee on Sanitary Improvement of the American Medical Association to declare in 1848 that "the United States may be considered as a country in which no legislation exists regulating its sanitary condition."[7] But while the situation remained grim for sanitary reformers in most cities, it was not as unrelentingly bleak as the committee's statement would suggest. Some of their recommendations *were* implemented by far-sighted civic leaders in the 1840s and 1850s. And a few of these reports, such as Lemuel Shattuck's 1850 *Report for the Promotion of Public Health,* ultimately became formative documents in the development of American public health policies **(see Document 5.1)**.

THE INDUSTRIAL CITY

As sanitary reformers prosecuted their sometimes-lonely campaigns to make public health an issue of ongoing concern—rather than one that waxed and waned in response to disease outbreaks—America's urban centers continued to evolve in ways that made their task more daunting.

The Industrial Revolution, which began in England in the late eighteenth century with the harnessing of steam power and then exploded onto American shores in the early nineteenth century, completely changed the nature of American life. This relentless march of technological innovation, scientific ingenuity, and manufacturing prowess crashed over American society in successive waves for the next century, bestowing numerous enduring benefits along the way. "Many of the technical and scientific achievements of the century would eventually make everyday life safer, cleaner, healthier, and more convenient," summarized environmental journalist Philip Shabecoff. "Machinery and new sources of energy eased the burden of work and provided leisure for the creation and enjoyment of arts. . . . Transportation and communications shrank distances and eased the loneliness of human existence."[8]

Civic leaders, business owners, and opinion makers of all political stripes heralded this new industrial age. "The world is now entering upon the mechanical epoch," declared engineering historian Robert H. Thurston in 1878. "There is nothing in the future more sure than the great triumphs which that epoch is to achieve. It has already advanced to some glorious conquests. What miracles of invention new crowd upon us! Look abroad, and contemplate the infinite achievements of the steam power."[9]

In reality, however, the new economic behemoths that roared to life during this era—railroads, steamship companies, steel foundries, oil refineries, pulp and paper mills, makers of industrial chemicals and solvents, slaughterhouse operations, and more—carried both peril and promise for the American public. Industrialization fueled an enormous upsurge in extraction and consumption of the nation's natural resources, which were seen almost exclusively as raw material for economic expansion. By the latter part of the century, recalled famed forester Gifford Pinchot, "the Nation was obsessed . . . by a flurry of development. The American Colossus was fiercely intent on appropriating and exploiting the riches of the richest of all continents—grasping with both hands, reaping where he had not sown, wasting what he thought would last forever."[10] And as the commodification of forests, rivers, and plains (and the minerals and animals contained within) escalated, the industrial city—home of cheap and plentiful labor, huge numbers of potential consumers, and convenient transportation and communication networks—supplanted the rural countryside as the nation's economic and cultural cornerstone.

Not surprisingly, these rapid changes to the nation's culture and economy elicited profound feelings of disorientation and anxiety among many members of the poor and working class. After all, this transformation was being engineered by politicians, inventors, investors, and captains of industry, not foundry workers, seamstresses, and miners. For the latter Americans, industrialization had a dark and fearsome current that they felt helpless to resist. And the environmental conditions that arose in the industrial city did nothing to assuage their feelings of vulnerability. "The environmental effect of the *massing* of industries," observed one study, was devastating:

> A single factory chimney, a single blast furnace, a single dye works may easily have its effluvia absorbed by the surrounding landscape: twenty of them in a narrow area effectively pollute the air or water beyond remedy. So that the unavoidably dirty industries became through urban concentration far more formidable than they were when they had existed on a smaller scale and were more widely dispersed about the countryside.[11]

Some American workers and their families were able to escape the factory-pocked inner city by taking advantage of steam ferries, commuter railroads, elevated railroads, cable cars, and other manifestations of the "transportation revolution" taking place within the larger Industrial Revolution. These mass transit options enabled millions of urban workers to commute to their jobs from peaceful neighborhoods located far from the industrial din. As early as the 1840s, writer Walt Whitman—then a Brooklyn newspaperman—was marveling at the evolving commuter culture taking hold in New York City. "In the morning there is one incessant stream of people—employed in New York on business—tending toward the ferry," he said. "It is highly edifying to see the phrenzy exhibited by certain portions of the younger gentlemen, a few rods from the landing, when the bell strikes . . . they rush forward as if for dear life, and woe to the fat woman or unwieldy person of any kind, who stands in their way."[12] By the 1880s American railways were carrying nearly 190 million passengers a year, many of them on commuter rail lines that held throngs of downtown office workers and factory managers. But the costs of commuting, combined with the higher price tags of homes and rental properties in suburban and finer urban enclaves, kept most poor and working-class residents living in the shadows of factories and warehouses.

Many of the politically marginalized and economically powerless men and women trapped in those grim surroundings adopted attitudes of resignation toward their lot in life, even as urban reformers raged against the corporate interests and political corruption that kept them there (see Document 5.2). Exhausted and defeated, they dismissed the sanitarians' calls for a public health revolution as a fantasy that would never come to pass.

SHIFTING ATTITUDES BRING HOPE

Their skepticism was understandable. Rapid increases in urban populations and industrial activity at mid-century further overwhelmed city services that were already grossly inadequate. To many observers, housing conditions, water and sewer systems, garbage and manure collection, anti-dumping enforcement, and other public health measures seemed even flimsier in the 1850s and 1860s than they had been a few decades earlier. "As a rule," wrote a ward inspector in New York City in 1864,

> The streets are extremely dirty and offensive, and the gutters obstructed with filth. The filth of the streets is composed of house-slops, refuse vegetables, decayed fruit, store and shop sweepings, ashes, dead animals, and even human excrements. These putrefying organic substances are ground together by the constantly passing vehicles. When dried by the summer's heat they are driven by the wind in every direction in the form of dust. When remaining moist of liquid in the form of "slush," they emit deleterious and very offensive exhalations. The reeking stench of the gutters, the street filth, and domestic garbage of this quarter of the city, constantly imperil the health of its inhabitants.[13]

Sewage disposal remained an especially harrowing problem because of the continued reliance on unregulated privies. "The unspeakable filthiness and neglect of the privies pertaining to the tenant-houses demand attention," insisted one group of sanitation advocates in New York. "These necessaries of every domicile are so neglected and filthy in all the crowded districts of the city as to have become prolific sources of obstinate and fatal maladies of a diarrhoeal and febril character, and they must be reckoned among the most active of localizing causes of prevailing diseases among the poor."[14]

The contents of sewer systems and privies that did receive regular attention, meanwhile, were typically directed into rivers, streams, and coastal waters, which were also clotted with stunning amounts of industrial detritus. In Philadelphia, for example, the chief of the city's water bureau described the factory-lined Schuylkill River as a "natural sewer" carrying pollution "as diversified as the occupation of the people: sewerage, chemical, wool-washing, dye stuff, butcher and brewery refuse—there is almost nothing lacking."[15]

The task of improving environmental conditions in American cities thus assumed ever more Herculean dimensions under the new industrial regime. But advocates for public health reform and industrial regulation refused to give up, and in the 1860s and 1870s they finally began to make some meaningful, albeit modest, headway. One asset in this fight was the performance of the U.S. Sanitary Commission during the Civil War. The commission enforced regulations on proper disposal of human wastes and sanitary treatment of food and water by Union soldiers, and it enforced garbage collection, privy cleaning, and sanitary slaughterhouse and stable operations in New Orleans, Memphis, and other southern cities under Union occupation. The health benefits of these regulations were widely recognized. "By the end of military action," wrote Duffy, "the Sanitary Commission had affected the lives of millions of Americans and had given a strong impetus to the movement for sanitary reform."[16]

Another important milestone was the development and acceptance of the germ theory of disease. Led by Louis Pasteur in France and Robert Koch in Germany, scientists of the 1870s and 1880s identified the microbes that were responsible for notorious killers such as cholera, tuberculosis, diphtheria, typhoid fever, and gonorrhea. Researchers then made important advances in identifying vectors of bacteriological transmission such as contaminated municipal water supplies and in the creation of antitoxins and vaccines to combat the spread of these deadly diseases. Of note, these breakthroughs also convinced the public that the rosters of state and municipal health boards should perhaps be populated with doctors and scientists rather than the businessmen and civic leaders who had traditionally dominated such boards.

Advances in medical knowledge also helped erode some of the middle- and upper-class attitudes toward disease that had stymied reform efforts. For much of the nineteenth century, industrial and civic leaders framed environmental degradation as unfortunate but necessary collateral damage in America's march to the capitalist mountaintop, and they insisted that captains of industry had no legal or moral duty to check such negative impacts. In addition, affluent Americans frequently perceived disease "as an affliction of those who lacked virtue, piety, and morality" and regarded the "working poor [as] harbingers of disease, lacking the moral and intellectual fortitude to take care of themselves."[17] But as middle-class and wealthy people gained a greater understanding of the links between public health and water protection and waste disposal—and experienced epiphanies about their own increasing physical and economic vulnerability to urban pollutants—they became more willing to support public health reforms and agencies.

Community-based advocacy groups sensed that public attitudes were shifting in their direction, and they seized the moment. These groups were organized around a cornucopia of distinct causes—teaching basic hygiene to new immigrants, ending child labor, eliminating hookworm from southern mill towns, monitoring the purity of dairy milk, enforcing refuse dumping restrictions—but they all shared a belief in a public health reform approach that focused on environmental improvement.[18]

THE SANITARY REVOLUTION

Legislators in New York played a pioneering role in crafting and supporting new public health policies that would address environmental problems within the cities in a meaningful way. Prodded by a dedicated alliance of physicians and citizens' groups, New York lawmakers passed the New York Metropolitan Health Act in 1866 (see Document 5.3). This legislation established the first bona fide municipal health department in a major American city. It also laid out terms that gave public health professionals real authority and resources to create, monitor, and enforce public health regulations.

Within a few years, the act became a model for legislation creating other urban health departments across the country. Local sanitary associations grew in numbers as well. In 1872 the American Public Health Association was founded, and in 1879 Congress authorized the creation of the National Board of Health, the first federal health agency. Acceptance of a legitimate government role in public health continued to expand in the 1880s and 1890s, when several states established health boards. Worker safety also became a policy issue. In 1877 Massachusetts passed the nation's first factory inspection law, and nearly two dozen other states followed suit by the close of the nineteenth century. Several municipalities with a large industrial sector also passed factory inspection measures, and city health departments received new infusions of funding—and authority—to curb pollution from privies, livestock, and other perennial public health hazards (see Document 5.6).

These agencies were greatly aided in their efforts by major advances in sanitary engineering. New technological advances in water and waste distribution enabled towns and cities to build sophisticated new sanitation and water systems and other pollution-control technologies and regulations—although many of these regulations were difficult to enforce because most municipal plumbing was hidden underground.[19] Around this same time, garbage and refuse collection and street cleaning increasingly became the responsibility of city departments rather than private contractors. "The sanitary revolution in America was in full swing, and health and sanitation were virtually synonymous," summarized Duffy. "Possibly the key factor in all this was a rising standard of living, without which municipalities could not have afforded the enormous capital costs of the sewer and water systems nor the steadily increasing operating costs of health and sanitary programs."[20]

This surge in public works programs for water and sewage disposal came at a crucial time because many civic leaders were feeling growing apprehension about their cities' water supplies in the closing years of the nineteenth century. Urban populations were continuing to grow at a dizzying pace, in part because water system engineers had become so adept at providing water to city businesses and residents far and wide. But the resulting explosion in consumption sorely taxed the traditional water sources that towns and cities had used. This situation was made even worse by the fact that most urban centers had been treating nearby rivers and harbors as dumping grounds for sewage and industrial chemicals for decades. Cities thus began looking far afield for new water supplies. Many of them constructed massive dams, impoundments, and aqueducts to draw water from more pristine rivers and lakes located miles away. This strategic policy shift addressed urban needs for safer water for washing and drinking, but it inflicted major ecological changes on the surrounding countryside. It also sparked a series of early twentieth-century confrontations between thirsty cities and wilderness conservationists. The most famous of these was the epic clash in the early 1900s between San Francisco Bay officials and the Sierra Club over a proposal to dam Yosemite National Park's Hetch Hetchy Valley.

Increased access to distant water resources also led some legislators and municipal officials to look on polluted urban rivers as lost causes that did not need to be redeemed. Factory owners and other urban property owners in some cities were thus given even freer rein to discharge all sorts of pollutants into local waterways without penalty. The shocking environmental degradation of these rivers and streams would have been even worse had it not been for the complaints of public health officials, public advocacy groups, and businesses dependent on water transport for their livelihoods. In 1899, for example, Congress responded to their complaints with the Rivers and Harbors Appropriations Act, which gave the federal government sweeping new authority over the use of all navigable waterways in the United States **(see Document 5.4)**.

The Rivers and Harbors Act of 1899 outlawed several forms of water pollution, but it was silent on the issue of liquid sewage pollution. As a result, cities continued to legally discharge incredible volumes of raw sewage into adjacent rivers and harbors for years. As late as 1914, for example, untreated sewage produced by six million New York City residents was still being dumped into the city's harbor on an annual basis.[21]

THE CITY BEAUTIFUL MOVEMENT

As public health programs proliferated and city officials became more aggressive in combating garbage, livestock manure, smoke from coal burning, and other urban scourges, a corps of influential urban planners joined the urban improvement crusade. Late nineteenth century city planners and architects such as Daniel Hudson Burnham, Frederick Law Olmsted Jr., and Charles Mulford Robinson championed new visions of the American city that would include broad swaths of what we now call "green space"—parks and tree-lined avenues and large, landscaped private yards—and classic architecture. They also advocated moving away from the traditional grid configuration of urban street layouts in favor of winding street designs that complemented rather than obliterated rolling hills, streams, and other natural topography. Their idea was to use the tools of science to combine the works of man and nature into a seamless and complementary whole that would uplift and inspire city residents. Also, they argued, a healthier urban environment would have the practical benefits of boosting property values and worker productivity and reducing public health costs. As Burnham asserted early in the twentieth century, "Fifty years ago, before population had become dense in certain portions of the city, people could live without parks; but we of to-day cannot. We now regard the promotion of robust health of body and mind as necessary public duties, in order that the individual may be benefited, and that the community at large may possess a higher average degree of good citizenship. And after all has been said, good citizenship is the prime object of good city planning."[22]

The ideas propelling this burgeoning movement did not go unchallenged. Some city officials and business interests voiced outrage at the idea of cordoning off valuable city real estate for green space. Other citizens simply dismissed the new breed of city planners as unrealistic dreamers. These doubters recognized that the "advancing commercial and industrial areas, as well as many residential tracts, were neither natural nor friendly to humans. Could something so natural, so filled with life as a park, be sutured into such an unreceptive environment?"[23]

But the movement to create more aesthetically attractive American cities found fertile ground with many sectors of the American public, especially after the 1893 Chicago World's Columbian Exposition. The centerpiece of this grand fair was a breathtaking "White City" of classically inspired buildings and ornate landscaping that was created by Olmsted and Burnham on a nearly 700-acre tract of undeveloped Chicago shoreline. The spectacle of the White City dazzled middle-class and wealthy Americans and inspired an outburst of editorials and speeches exhorting Americans to demand beauty and cleanliness in addition to jobs and markets from their cities.

By the close of the nineteenth century, this campaign had a name—the City Beautiful Movement—and broad popular support in many areas of the country. The City Beautiful banner was then seized by a new wave of urban critics and city planners in the opening decades of the new century. These men—Clarence Stein, Henry Wright, Lewis Mumford, J. Horace McFarland, Benton MacKaye (who was also a major figure in the creation of the Appalachian Trail), and others—often joined forces with settlement house leaders, environmental health advocates, and other civic organizations to advance their cause (see Document 5.8). They also sought to boost support for urban green space and other aesthetic improvements by framing them as an element of the wider conservation movement that, under President Theodore Roosevelt, was sweeping across the nation during that time.

The City Beautiful Movement enjoyed numerous triumphs in the first two decades of the twentieth century. Ambitious urban beautification and "green space" park projects were carried out in Chicago, Cleveland, Columbus, Denver, Detroit, Kansas City, Minneapolis-St. Paul, Philadelphia, Pittsburgh, Washington, D.C., Wilmington, and other cities across the country. But its influence gradually waned with the emergence of a competing city planning philosophy that came to be known as the City Practical Movement. This latter faction of city planners and engineers shared some of the concerns of City Beautiful adherents, such as prompt and effective garbage collection and investment in efficient water and sewage systems. But to members of the City Practical tribe, these sorts of basic public services were paramount considerations, not just part of a broader agenda of aesthetic improvement. They were far more concerned about improving the reliability and usefulness of urban rail lines, for example, than they were about whether rail commuters passed through leafy parks. Yet as historian William Wilson observed, the fight between the two groups "was less over two distinct approaches to planning—the aesthetic and the practical—and more about vocational and professional dominance, appeals to the taxpayer's pocketbook, and bureaucratic control. To simplify somewhat, the architects, engineers, and others fighting for the city practical beat the landscape architects and architects representing the City Beautiful."[24]

ENVIRONMENTAL HEALTH AND THE PROGRESSIVES

Public health reform made additional substantial gains during the Progressive Era, a two-decade span at the beginning of the twentieth century during which numerous social, economic, and political reforms took place. Progressives believed in the power and legitimacy of government as an instrument of economic and social justice, and they were sympathetic to the causes of the urban reformers. Indeed, the problems of the industrial city became a major focus of the progressive movement, and urban activists such as Jane Addams and Alice Hamilton emerged as some of the era's most influential figures.

Progressive-era urban reformers were greatly aided in their efforts by high levels of public dissatisfaction with the perceived excesses of the nation's Gilded Age "robber barons"—wealthy industrialists and bankers who were the subject of much vilification in the nation's union halls and factory floors. This public anger was further stoked by muckraking journalists such as Ida Tarbell, Lincoln Steffens, Charles Edward Russell, and Upton Sinclair, all of whom filed explosive exposés of corporate greed and political corruption—and the urban corrosion and decay that resulted from the combination of the two (see Document 5.7). The muckraking movement of the early 1900s, declared the famous progressive Senator Robert M. La Follette, "strode like a young giant into the arena of public service. Filled with this spirit, quickened with human interest, it assailed social and political evils in high places and low."[25]

The crusading sanitarians and settlement house leaders battling pollution, disease, and other horrors of the inner city were also aided by America's steadily growing faith in science and professional expertise. Mindful of this shift, public health advocates, progressive officials, and professionals in a variety of scientific and technical fields joined with their allies in the press and Congress to mount a two-pronged attack on public apathy. On the one hand, they continued to touch hearts by issuing dramatic accounts of the dehumanizing, dangerous, and soul-crushing working conditions in which millions of Americans—and especially children—labored. But they increasingly supplemented these efforts by appealing to Americans' pragmatic side. Using cogent scientific analysis of the environmental dangers swirling around the nation's urban centers, they asserted that degraded public health posed a mortal threat to the economic and cultural foundations of the United States.

As the Progressive Era unfolded, scientific investigations proliferated into all manner of urban problems. Abatement of smoke pollution from coal consumption became a favorite cause of advocates for cleaner cities (see Document 5.5). City engineers, meanwhile, criticized heedless coal burning from both public health and economy efficiency perspectives. One study of coal burning in St. Louis, for example, declared that smoke abatement is "a source of profit to the smoke maker as well as to the community. . . . With proper installations and operation there should be an efficiency of 60 percent or a savings of 20 percent over present conditions. This means that we are practically throwing away between 1,500,000 and 2,000,000 tons of coal a year. . . . Add to this waste the cost of removing the effects of the smoke and you have an enormous sum which goes into the production of nothing of economic value."[26] Infectious disease in the city also became the subject of intensive scientific research. "It is only along the line of patient investigation of each disease and practical deductions from ascertained facts that public health work can succeed," stated a presenter at the 1902 conference of the American Public Health Association.[27] This activism produced a smattering of smoke abatement ordinances and the like but failed to generate major changes to industrial practices in most cities.

Progressive reformers had greater success in improving other living and working conditions in the industrial city. Social reformers became proficient at using research studies and government reports to highlight public and occupational health issues, especially as progressive political advances gained them greater access to municipal, state, and federal levels of power. Jane Addams and her lieutenants at Hull House, the Chicago settlement house that became the flagship of a movement of more than 500 settlements by 1920, were particularly adept at convincing local officials and state legislatures to address urban ills. Soon after its founding in 1889, Hull House recognized the potential impact of official reports and surveys. In the early 1890s, for example, Hull House stalwart Florence Kelley conducted an exhaustive survey of environmental conditions in inner-city Chicago, paying special attention to the grim conditions in tenement "sweat shops." This research helped pave the way for legislation establishing state factory inspection systems; sanitary standards for some tenement-based industries; and provisions for the eight-hour workday for women, teenage girls, and children.[28] Over the next few decades, Addams and her cohorts repeatedly sponsored or carried out similar research efforts in support of public health and social service legislation that would aid poor families in the city (**see Document 5.9**).

Still, industries continued to enjoy fairly broad latitude in carrying out their daily operations. Regulations restricting environmentally damaging industrial practices remained extremely modest in cities and states long wedded to the idea that unfettered capitalism was the engine driving America's explosive growth. Cozy relationships among powerful business executives, legislators, and public officials further insulated industrial operations from the reach of fledgling departments of public health and conservation. Frequently, municipal or state agencies charged with protecting public safety and environmental assets were reduced to virtual supplication in their interactions with big and small businesses alike (**see Document 5.11**).

ALICE HAMILTON AND THE DANGEROUS TRADES

Occupational health was another special focus of urban reformers—and for good reason. American industries were awash in unregulated toxic chemicals and heavy metals by the early twentieth century. Paper and steel mills, tanneries and slaughterhouses, mining operations, cloth and dye manufacturers, breweries, and bathtub makers all exposed workers to dangerous levels of toxic liquids, fumes, and/or dust, and industries made little or no effort to protect workers from—or educate them about—the dangers of exposure to lead, arsenic, mercury, benzene, and other commonly used industrial materials.

In some cases, this deafening silence was a result of the ignorance of employers themselves. Few studies of occupational diseases had been carried out prior to 1910. Those that were carried out were quickly forgotten because governmental channels to effectively disseminate such findings were either nonexistent or neutralized by industrial interests and their congressional allies.

But this environment changed with the rise of the progressives, and public health advocates jumped on the opportunity. Their methodically documented reports on hazards in the industrial workplace helped pave the way for the passage of numerous industrial safety and health measures during this period. To take but one example, sleuthing by John Andrews of the American Association for Labor Legislation was instrumental in uncovering the linkage between the match industry's use of white phosphorus and phossy jaw, a horrible disfigurement that afflicted match makers. His report on the subject led directly to the 1912 passage of laws that effectively regulated and taxed white phosphorus out of existence in factories.[29]

The most celebrated of America's early investigators of the industrial workplace environment was Hull House resident Alice Hamilton. In many respects, Hamilton was the Progressive Era's version of Rachel Carson. Tenacious, compassionate, and enormously talented, Hamilton began her trailblazing career as an investigator of industrial chemicals and their impact on environmental health in the early 1900s—a period, she later dryly observed, when workplace safety remained a subject stubbornly "tainted with Socialism or with feminine sentimentality for the poor."[30]

After several years of treating immigrants and other poor Chicagoans for diseases triggered by workplace conditions, Hamilton was appointed in December 1908 to be managing director of the Illinois Commission on Occupational Diseases, a state commission organized to investigate incidences of industrial poisoning from lead and other materials. From there she took a position with the Bureau of Labor within the U.S. Department of Commerce, where she issued a series of groundbreaking reports on industrial poisons in the "dangerous trades." The gauntlet of challenges Hamilton faced in these assignments was daunting, from industry stonewalling to workers who refused to cooperate because of fears that they would lose their jobs. But she persevered, and her efforts were essential in establishing industrial toxicology as a legitimate discipline and in the eventual passage of state and federal workplace safety legislation **(see Document 5.10)**. The mild-mannered Hamilton also conducted successful one-woman lobbying campaigns to convince some manufacturers and the industrial physicians in their employ to change their operating practices to better protect workers. "Let me beg the industrial physician not to let the atmosphere of the factory befog his view of his special problem," she said. "His duty is to the [worker], not to the product."[31]

Hamilton believed that World War I played an important part in changing attitudes about workplace safety. Her research uncovered many toxic dangers in the war industries and led to the adoption of many workplace safety procedures and increased government oversight of industrial activity. "The war did have a beneficial influence on industrial hygiene," she noted:

> If it increased the dangers in American industry, it also aroused the interest of physicians in industrial poisons. And that interest has never died down, on the contrary it has increased with the increasing complexity of methods of manufacture. A change took place also in the attitude of employers for a large labor turnover was found to be not only wasteful but an unsatisfactory method of dealing with dangerous processes in industry. The Public Health Service had entered this field during the war and the medical journals had published articles discussing the action of the new poisons and various methods of preventing danger from the old ones. Industrial medicine had at last become respectable.[32]

CREATION OF THE U.S. PUBLIC HEALTH SERVICE

Hamilton's findings and message also resonated with members of the professional class who had moved into positions of increased influence during the Progressive Era. These industrial physicians, civil engineers, and public health officials prized knowledge and efficiency, and they were receptive to the idea of reforming industrial processes to better protect workers and the public interest. In the realm of water quality, for instance, civil engineers in municipal water departments collaborated with scientists in the 1910s to introduce new water treatments like filtration and chlorine disinfection that dramatically reduced public vulnerability to bacterial agents of infectious disease. Professionalization of municipal health departments also expanded greatly in the 1900s and 1910s. This in turn enabled city agencies to establish distinct divisions devoted to various elements of sanitation and public health, from inspection of meatpackers to sewer system care and maintenance.

In addition, the growing body of knowledge about industrial poisons and urban pollutants provided a major impetus for national health legislation and the establishment of a federal health agency to carry out public health laws. Advocates such as Irving Fisher and J. Pease Norton played a prominent role in this effort, and they were joined by such influential organizations as the American Association for the Advancement of Science as well as Florence Kelley's National Consumers League and other social reform and public health advocacy organizations.

By 1910 more than a dozen bills had been introduced in Congress that would have created a national health department or expanded the regulatory authority of the Public Health and Marine Hospital Service (PHMHS). The PHMHS was an association of hospitals whose operational mandate had expanded from treatment of sick merchant seamen at the beginning of the nineteenth century, when it was first established, to include authority to impose quarantines to control outbreaks of infectious diseases. The most significant of these congressional bills was one introduced by Oklahoma Senator Robert L. Owen that would have established a truly national department of health in the federal government. It was fiercely opposed by an odd alliance that included antivaccinationists, lobbyists for the patent medicine industry, and PHMHS Surgeon General Walter Wyman, who wanted his own agency to fill the role.

Wyman orchestrated a series of legislative moves that stymied Owen's bill for several months. But Wyman's death in November 1911 removed the single biggest obstacle in the path of the bill's passage, and in 1912 a revised version of Owen's proposed legislation became law. The act actually kept the foundations of the Marine Hospital Service, but it dramatically increased its reach and responsibilities. Renamed the U.S. Public Health Service, the agency was given explicit authority to "investigate the diseases of man and conditions influencing the propagation and spread thereof, including sanitation and sewage and the pollution either directly or indirectly of the navigable streams and lakes of the Unites States." The federal government thus planted itself firmly at the intersection of public and environmental health for the first time in its history.

NOTES

1. Robert Gottlieb, *Forcing the Spring: The Transformation of the American Environmental Movement* (Washington, D.C.: Island Press, 1993), 54.

2. John Harley Warner, *Major Problems in the History of American Medicine and Public Health: Documents and Essays*, ed. John Harley Warner and Janet A. Tighe (Boston: Houghton Mifflin, 2001), 159.

3. John Duffy, *The Sanitarians: A History of American Public Health* (Chicago: University of Illinois Press, 1992), 84.

4. Quoted in Stephen Smith, *The City That Was* (New York: Frank Allaben, 1911), 65.

5. Charles E. Rosenberg, *The Cholera Years: The United States in 1832, 1849, and 1866,* rev ed. (Chicago: University of Chicago Press, 1987), 1.

6. Ibid., 2.

7. Quoted in Dona Schneider, and David A. Lilienfeld *Public Health: The Development of a Discipline: From the Age of Hippocrates to the Progressive Era* (Piscataway, NJ: Rutgers University Press, 2008), 143.

8. Philip Shabecoff, *A Fierce Green Fire: The American Environmental Movement* (New York: Hill and Wang, 1993), 40–41.

9. Robert H. Thurston, *The History of the Growth of the Steam Engine* (New York: D. Appleton and Co., 1878), 79.

10. Gifford Pinchot, *Breaking New Ground* (New York: Harcourt Brace 1947), 23.

11. Lewis Mumford and Bryan S. Turner. *The Culture of Cities* (New York: Routledge, 1997), 162.

12. Quoted in K.T. Jackson, *Crabgrass Frontier: The Suburbanization of the United States* (New York: Oxford University Press, 1985), 28.

13. Quoted in G.H. Brieger, *Medical America in the Nineteenth Century: Readings from the Literature* (Baltimore: Johns Hopkins University Press, 1972), 268.

14. *Report of the Council of Hygiene and Public Health of the Citizen's Association of New York upon the Sanitary Condition of the City,* (New York: Appleton, 1865), xci.

15. Howard Frumkin, Lawrence Frank, and Richard Jackson, *Urban Sprawl and Public Health: Designing, Planning and Building for Healthy Communities* (Washington, D.C.: Island Press, 2004), 59.

16. Duffy, *Sanitarians,* 113.

17. William and Mary Center for Archaeological Research. "Millworker Life: Health and Sanitation." In *Fabric of Life in a Southern Mill Town: Archaeology of Mill House Lots Near the Main Street Bridge in Danville, Virginia,* http://web.wm.edu/wmcar/Danvilledig/millworkerhealth.htm.

18. Gottlieb, *Forcing the Spring,* 56.

19. Duffy, *Sanitarians,* 178.

20. Duffy, *Sanitarians,* 139.

21. John Duffy, *A History of Public Health in New York City, 1866–1966* (New York: Russell Sage Foundation, 1974), 519–520.

22. Daniel Hudson Burnham and Edward H. Bennett, *Plan of Chicago* (Chicago: Commercial Club, 1909), 123.

23. William H. Wilson, *The City Beautiful Movement* (Baltimore: Johns Hopkins University Press, 1994), 48.

24. Wilson, *The City Beautiful Movement,* 3.

25. Robert Marion L. La Follette, Speech delivered at the Annual Banquet of the Periodical Publishers' Association, Philadelphia, February 2, 1912. In *Autobiography: A Personal Narrative of Political Experiences* (New York: New York Public Library, 1913), 795.

26. Ernest L. Ohle, From *Association of Engineering Societies* 55, November 1915. Reprinted in David Stradling, ed. *Conservation in the Progressive Era: Classic Texts* (Seattle: University of Washington Press, 2004), 82.

27. Charles V. Chaplin, "Dirt, Disease and the Health Officer." *Public Health Papers and Reports Presented at the Thirtieth Annual Meeting of the American Public Health Association (1902),* 28, 1903, p. 296–299.

28. Gottlieb, *Forcing the Spring,* 63.

29. Gottlieb, *Forcing the Spring,* 48.

30. Alice Hamilton, *Exploring the Dangerous Trades: The Autobiography of Alice Hamilton, M.D.* (Boston: Little, Brown, 1943), 115.

31. Quoted in Marcus M. Key, ed. *Occupational Diseases: A Guide to Their Recognition.* (Washington, D.C.: U.S. Department of Health, Education, and Welfare, 1977).

32. Hamilton, *Exploring the Dangerous Trades,* 198.

Shattuck Report for the Promotion of Public Health

"We Recommend That the Laws . . . Relating to Public Health Be Thoroughly Revised"

1850

By the mid-nineteenth century, escalating anxiety about outbreaks of disease and polluted urban conditions led to the creation of several local sanitary surveys. The most influential of these surveys was carried out in Massachusetts under the direction of statistician Lemuel Shattuck. His final report, sponsored by the Massachusetts Sanitary Commission, provided in-depth statistical analysis of morbidity and mortality rates across the state and detailed recommendations for bolstering the state's public health and sanitation laws in population centers. Shattuck's report also asserted that shortcomings in the morality and knowledge base of the residents made state regulation of refuse collection, water and sewage systems, and other public health influences imperative.

Little attention was paid to the Shattuck Report upon its initial release, which occurred at a time when lawmakers and newspaper publishers were increasingly preoccupied with rising sectional tensions between the nation's northern and southern blocs of states. But legislators and public health officials rediscovered the report in the post–Civil War era. Its recommendations helped shape the establishment of Massachusetts' first state board of health in 1869, and other states drew on Shattuck's recommendations to create their own public health boards during the last three decades of the nineteenth century. "Shattuck's report has come to be seen as one of the most farsighted and influential documents in the history of the American public health system," summarized one government study of public health in the United States. "Many of the principles and activities he proposed later came to be considered fundamental to public health."[1] The following excerpt details some of Shattuck's specific public health recommendations:

I. STATE AND MUNICIPAL MEASURES RECOMMENDED

Under this class of recommendations are to be included such measures as require, for their sanction, regulation and control, the legislative authority of the State, or the municipal authority of cities and towns. They may be called the legal measures—the *Sanitary Police* of the State,

I. WE RECOMMEND *that the laws of the State relating to Public Health be thoroughly revised, and that a new and improved act be passed in their stead. . . .*

II. WE RECOMMEND *that a* GENERAL BOARD OF HEALTH *be established, which shall be charged with the general execution of the laws of the State, relating to the enumeration, the vital statistics, and the public health of the inhabitants. . . .*

V. WE RECOMMEND *that a* LOCAL BOARD OF HEALTH *be appointed in every city and town, who shall be charged with the particular execution of the laws of the State, and the municipal ordinances and regulations, relating to public health, within their respective jurisdictions. . . .*

VII. WE RECOMMEND *that local Boards of Health endeavor to ascertain, with as much exactness as possible, the circumstances of the cities and towns, and of the inhabitants under their jurisdictions; and that they issue such local sanitary orders and make such regulations as are best adapted to these circumstances. . . .*

XVI. WE RECOMMEND *that, as far as practicable, there be used in all sanitary investigations and regulations, a uniform nomenclature for the causes of death, and for the causes of disease. . . .*

XVII. WE RECOMMEND *that, in laying out new towns and villages, and in extending those already laid out, ample provision be made for a supply, in purity and abundance, of light, air, and water; for drainage and sewerage; for paving and for cleanliness. . . .*

XIX. WE RECOMMEND *that, before erecting any new dwelling-house, manufactory, or other building, for personal accommodation, either as a lodging-house or place of business, the owner or builder be required to give notice to the local Board of Health, of his intention and of the sanitary arrangements he proposes to adopt. . . .*

XX. WE RECOMMEND *that local Boards of Health endeavor to prevent or mitigate the sanitary evils arising from overcrowded lodging-houses and cellar-dwellings. . . .*

XXI. WE RECOMMEND *that open spaces be reserved, in cities and villages for public walks; that wide streets be laid out; and that both be ornamented with trees. . . .*

XXIII. WE RECOMMEND *that local Boards of Health, and other persons interested, endeavor to ascertain, by exact observation, the effect of mill-ponds, and other collections or streams of water, and of their rise and fall, upon the health of the neighboring inhabitants. . . .*

XXIV. WE RECOMMEND *that the local Boards of Health provide for periodical house-to-house visitation, for the prevention of epidemic diseases, and for other sanitary purposes. . . .*

XXV. WE RECOMMEND *that measures be taken to ascertain the amount of sickness suffered in different localities; and among persons of different classes, professions, and occupations. . . .*

XXIX. WE RECOMMEND *that nuisances endangering human life or health, be prevented, destroyed, or mitigated. . . .*

XXX. WE RECOMMEND *that measures be taken to prevent or mitigate the sanitary evils arising from the use of intoxicating drinks, and from haunts of dissipation. . . .*

XXXIV. WE RECOMMEND *that measures be taken to preserve the lives and the health of passengers at sea, and of seamen engaged in the merchant service. . . .*

XXXV. WE RECOMMEND *that the authority to make regulations for the quarantine of vessels be intrusted to the local Boards of Health. . . .*

XXXVI. WE RECOMMEND *that measures be adopted for preventing or mitigating the sanitary evils arising from foreign emigration. . . .*

II. Social and Personal Measures Recommended

Most of these recommendations may be carried into effect without any special legislative authority, State or municipal. . . .

XXXVIII. WE RECOMMEND *that tenements for the better accommodation of the poor, be erected in cities and villages. . . .*

XL. WE RECOMMEND *that, whenever practicable, the refuse and sewage of cities and towns be collected, and applied to the purposes of agriculture. . . .*

XLI. WE RECOMMEND *that measures be taken to prevent, as far as practicable, the smoke nuisance. . . .*

XLII. WE RECOMMEND *that the sanitary effects of patent medicines and other nostrums, and secret remedies, be observed; that physicians in their prescriptions and names of medicines, and apothecaries in their compounds, use great caution and care; and that medical compounds advertised for sale be avoided, unless the material of which they are composed be known, or unless manufactured and sold by a person of known honesty and integrity. . . .*

XLIII. WE RECOMMEND *that local Boards of Health, and others interested, endeavor to prevent the sale and use of unwholesome, spurious, and adulterated articles, dangerous to the public health designed for food, drink, or medicine. . . .*

XLV. WE RECOMMEND *that persons be specially educated in sanitary science, as preventive advisors as well as curative advisors. . . .*

Source: Shattuck, Lemuel, and the Sanitary Commission of Massachusetts. *Report of a General Plan for the Promotion of Public and Personal Health.* Boston: Dutton and Wentworth, 1850, pp. 109, 111, 115, 121, 149, 153, 164, 166, 168, 171, 183, 198, 200, 206, 207, 212, 218, 220, 228.

NOTE

1. Institute of Medicine (U.S.) Committee for the Study of the Future of Public Health, *The Future of Public Health* (Washington, D.C.: National Academy Press, 1988), 61.

DOCUMENT 5.2   John Griscom Comments on Sanitary Legislation, Past and Future

"Man's Inhumanity to Man Makes Countless Thousands Mourn"

October 3, and November 14, 1861

One of America's most persistent early voices for sanitary reform was John H. Griscom, a physician turned social reformer who served briefly as city inspector for New York City in the early 1840s. Upon being named city inspector in 1842, Griscom launched a crusade against the city's filthy tenements, contaminated water supplies, and overwhelmed refuse and sewage removal systems. But as Griscom observed in the introduction to his 1845 report The Sanitary Condition of the Laboring Population of New York, *his complaints merely got him removed from office. Undaunted by this setback, he continued to lobby for major public health reforms until his death in 1874. The following is an excerpt from an 1861 address in which Griscom urges fellow reformers to keep the faith—and blames official corruption for derailing desperately needed measures to improve environmental health and other social conditions in America's overcrowded cities.*

SANITARY LEGISLATION—PAST AND FUTURE.

Mr. President, and Members of the New York Sanitary Association:
    The period is again approaching when it behooves the friends of Sanitary Reform—a phrase synonymous with saving the lives of the people—to be about the noble work which

they have set out to accomplish. Though seven times defeated in their efforts to stay the progress of disease and death, their hearts fail not, nor is their determination abated. Nor though seventy times seven should the enemies of this holy cause succeed, by bribery and corruption, in postponing the day for the inauguration of the most valuable of all the reforms known amongst men, will its votaries lay aside their armor, or cease to contend for the faith which animates them with the assurance of final success.

Though, like the disciples of Him who went about healing all manner of disease, and unlike them who have thus far betrayed the people to their destruction, they carry neither purse nor scrip, the friends of Sanitary Reform in this city will never cease to show the public their true interests in this matter, and demand of their legislators the abolition of the official nuisances which are the only obstacles to the removal of those physical nuisances, under whose foul influences so many thousands find untimely graves.

One of the most surprising phenomena in the political economy of this state and city, is the indifference of the people to their own death records. They either refuse to listen to, or, if they hear, they heed not, the facts concerning the dealings of death among themselves. There is no denial that the mortality of this city is much greater than that of many others of far inferior advantages for salubrity and longevity, and yet the trump of the archangel sounds in their ears in vain. Their well-cushioned officials drain them of their fat salaries, but do literally nothing in return to raise the standard of health, or check the march of pestilence. Their legislators listen year after year to the appeals in behalf of the thousands of dying infants, and when apparently moved to comply with the urgent cry for relief from the threatenings of disease and death, the demon of bribery drops a golden curtain between them and the pictures of desolate misery which have so moved them, and suddenly all assumes a rose color, and thenceforth, while their pockets are filled with sinful wealth, the cemeteries of the metropolis become populated in an increased ratio. . . .

Lest any one should regard this as too strong language, let me present the facts upon which it is based:

In 1859, a Health Bill, which would have been the means of saving thousands of lives in this city, passed the State Senate, almost unanimously, and went down to the Assembly, where there was every indication that it would soon become a law. It passed readily through all the preliminary stages of legislation, until it reached its third reading, when, on his name being called, a member from this city, who had been its avowed friend, and its acknowledged and accredited advocate before the House, and who had pledged himself, in the face of the Assembly, to the honorable fulfillment of the trust which the friends of the bill had reposed in him—that member rose in his place, and declined to vote, but said if his vote became necessary to carry the bill, he would, in that case, vote in the affirmative—an alternative which he himself could have rendered unnecessary. The withdrawal of his vote and influence, at this juncture, killed the bill, and as a consequence, destroyed the lives of we know not how many of his constituents, and all, as he himself afterward declared, because by the success of the very measure of which he himself was the putative father, three of his friends would be legislated out of office—offices which, of course, they were incompetent to fill.

Dismayed, but not disheartened, by this treachery, justice to the betrayed and down-trodden poor, and the claims of Sanitary Science, demanded a renewal of the efforts the next year. Accordingly the Legislature was approached with a bill, with details improved by experience and a better knowledge of the health laws of other cities, both foreign and domestic. It was presented favorably to the Assembly by the appropriate Standing Committee, with an elaborate report, fully setting forth its merits, and the urgent necessity of the measure. It was, in fact, a measure of life or death to thousands of both city and State.

But, alas! its friends reckoned again without a sufficient knowledge of the character of many of our law-makers. It was the year of gridiron railroad scheming, and Susquehanna bonuses; and again the office-holders of this city, one of whom, from the City Inspector's Department itself, was a member of Assembly, so wrought upon the fears and pockets of the friends of those measures, that the Health Bill was again defeated, even two of the signers of the report voting against it.

The crying of the helpless, nevertheless, ceased not to fill our ears, and the demands of Science, so far from yielding to these base betrayals of her rights, grew louder and stronger. The subject was again presented to the Legislature of the present year, and from the character of many members of the Assembly, there was every prospect that in that branch it would meet with success, with a reasonable hope in the upper house. The vast importance of the measure was appreciated by a majority of the assemblymen, in all its fullness, and though opposed, both covertly with money, and openly by speeches, it passed that body by a vote of exactly two to one. But the seats of the senate chamber were occupied by the same individuals as in the year before, and though there were, among them, many above reproach or suspicion, to a too large number the last chance had come for a pecuniary addition to the unholy gains of legislation.

It is averred that about $30,000 was raised in this city, among the office-holders, and expended to defeat the Health Bill of last winter. To the exactness of this statement, we cannot, of course, affirm, but this we do know: that on the Saturday previous to the Wednesday of adjournment, the vote for a third reading stood 19 to 12, while just on the eve of adjournment, when the bill was put upon its passage, the hopes of a suffering community were dashed to the ground by a reversal of this vote, and some thousands of new-made graves stand as monuments of the wickedness of men whose names are known as partakers of those thirty pieces—the price of innocent blood. Then it was that the enemies of the people's dearest interests triumphed; thus have their selfishness and wickedness stood against the demands of humanity, and opposed the progress of scientific reform.

The recent revelations of a famous libel suit but dimly shadow forth proceedings similar to those attendant upon the defeat of the Health Bill of last winter, the realities of which are well known.

The dying eagle saw on the arrow whose barb had pierced its vitals, feathers plucked from its own wing; so, through the salaries of its officials, the tax-payers of this city supplied the motive power of the machinery which did this death-dealing work among themselves.

Thus were we furnished with another proof that

> "Man's inhumanity to man
>
> Makes countless thousands mourn."

* * *

Principles for the Attainment of Sanitary Reform.

There are two principles which lie at the foundation of all true Sanitary arrangements, and which cannot properly be overlooked in the construction of any system, whose object is the most thorough and efficient protection of the people against diseases of every kind.

The first of these principles is, that it is the *whole* people who are to be thus protected—not merely one ward, one section, one city, or even one State—and if it is designed to do the whole work of Sanitary protection, the whole country should be embraced within the sphere of its operations. For we must remember that while there are many disorders which afflict humanity, of purely local origin, and circumscribed in the extent of their action, and hence removable or preventable at their immediate source, there are others which know no limits, spreading over large areas of country, and communicable from person to person, by clothing, by merchandise, by vehicles, or by atmospheric currents. On this and other accounts, the scope of operations of a Sanitary system should be coextensive with the population; the political and Sanitary government should progress side by side, and hand in hand.

If therefore it were possible, our *National* Government should establish a Sanitary Board, like that now in operation in Great Britain, whose protecting arm is spread over every section, with one central head. The close intimacy and free intercourse which characterize us as a social and commercial people (I speak of what was, and what, I trust and believe, will be restored), bringing together in daily and hourly intercourse the inhabitants of widely diverse climates and susceptibilities, demand that there should be some common regulator of that intercourse, for the protection of all alike. But it has been decided by high authority, that the matter of Health Police is a reserved State right, and that national laws governing the commercial intercourse of the people, must yield to those of the several States in this particular.

To the State, then, we turn, for the next most effective general arrangement; and whether we regard the source of power, or the unity of the people's interest, it is clear that any system of Sanitary protection, to be full and complete, should cover the entire area of the State, from Montauk to Niagara.

Local subordinate agencies, or Boards of Health, are of course necessary for the immediate care of the separate localities, but there should be an authority, superior and independent, for the systematic government of the whole; for action in those cases in which two or more localities are interested, as in the draining of extensive marshes, the regulation of intercourse between infected places, the influence of building dams, railroads, and public institutions, &c., and for appeal in cases of dispute between conflicting interests. . . .

The *second principle* which we claim as essential is, *the proper education of every Sanitary officer.* No intelligent person, who reflects a moment upon the vast variety of subjects included in the idea of Sanitary regulation, but must admit that there is scarcely another branch of public service demanding so varied a knowledge.

"The Officer of Health must himself be thoroughly informed of *all* the circumstances which affect the health of man, not only in his isolated condition as an individual, but in his social condition, and in his state of aggregation.

"Preventive medicine, while it constitutes a special, is itself the highest and most useful, branch of medicine, and requires in its missionaries a correspondingly long and special study, to become useful promulgators of its doctrines, and workers in its cause."

Source: Griscom, John. *Sanitary Legislation, Past and Future: The Value of Sanitary Reform, and the True Principles for Its Attainment. Parts of Two Essays Read Before the New York Sanitary Association, October 3rd and November 14th, 1861.* New York: Edmund Jones, 1861, pp. 3–7, 32–34, 35.

A Grim Assessment of Sanitary Conditions in New York City

"Wisely Administered Sanitary Regulations Would Altogether Remove . . . Nearly Every Source of Public Nuisance"

June 1865

During the course of the 1860s and 1870s, several states haltingly moved to address pressing urban environmental issues such as sewage disposal, water supply protection, refuse removal, and sequestration of industrial activity from residential areas. The state of New York was a pioneer in this movement, resulting in no small part from mounting public pressure. One particularly important source of pressure on legislators in Albany was the Citizens' Association, a group of wealthy business leaders. In June 1865 a committee of the association called the Council of Hygiene and Public Health issued a 500-page report on public health conditions in New York City. This report, which was the result of months of painstaking research and firsthand observation carried out under the supervision of Dr. Elisha Harris, painted a dire environmental picture of life in New York.

The report attracted wide attention from opinion-makers who felt that the city's rising squalor, filth, and struggles with disease had become both an embarrassment and a threat to its long-term future. The New York Times, for example, described the report as "an aggregation of statements and a digest of facts and conclusions, such as no legislature or government has been able to produce" and concluded that it was an epic work of "philosophic spirit, practical illustration, and humanitarian purpose."[1] Health reformers such as John Griscom, meanwhile, added the book's findings to their arguments about the necessity of passing new public health regulations and policies.

The report's publication, combined with an 1865 Asiatic cholera scare, finally broke through the defenses of the industries and entrenched political interests who opposed sanitary reform. In February 1866 the New York Metropolitan Health Act was passed, creating the first municipal health department in a major U.S. city and giving the state broad new regulatory authority in the protection of public health. The New York agency created by the act became a model for Chicago, Cincinnati, St. Louis, and other cities when they finally began to take action to address the challenging public health issues they had allowed to fester and grow for so many decades. The following is an excerpt from the Council of Hygiene report that helped pave the way for the landmark 1866 act; it is from a chapter devoted to the city's "Neglected Privies and Dark Places."

NEGLECTED PRIVIES AND DARK PLACES.

The unspeakable filthiness and neglect of the privies pertaining to the tenant-houses demand attention. These necessaries of every domicile are so neglected and filthy in all the crowded districts of the city as to have become prolific sources of obstinate and fatal maladies of a diarrhœal and febrile character, and they must be reckoned among the most active of localizing causes of prevailing diseases among the poor. The miserable economy that has attached to every tenant-house, court, or cellar a series of *midden* sinks, frequently without any sewer connection, and seldom with sufficient drainage of any kind, should be superseded by suitable water-closet arrangements for constant "flushing" and cleanliness. Reform in these matters is vitally important to the health of tenant-houses. . . .

SPECIAL NUISANCES.

Civilization and refinement, in a city like New York, encounters the same elements of debasement that stand in the way of effectual sanitary reforms; but all the laws of health and all sanitary works are justly counted among the most valued agencies of social elevation and refinement, and were there not abundant force in the sanitary reasons for the abatement of needless nuisances, and for the special management of all the necessarily offensive materials and operations which are incident to civic life, we might leave to the pleadings of an offended and refined community, and to the aggrieved senses of a million of people, the argument and the effort to procure the abatement of the gross nuisances that abound in various districts of the city. It is safe to say that wisely administered sanitary regulations would altogether remove and prohibit nearly every source of public nuisance in this city. It is not our purpose to present unnecessary details upon this subject, but simply to state what nuisances are to be regarded as injurious to public health and to individual welfare in our city. They may be enumerated as follows: (1) filthy streets; (2) neglected garbage and domestic refuse; (3) obstructed and faulty sewers and drains; (4) neglected privies and stables; (5) cattle pens and large stables in the more populous districts; (6) neglected and filthy markets; (7) slaughter-houses and hide and fat depots in close proximity to populous streets; (8) droves of cattle and swine in crowded streets; (9) swill-milk stables and their products; (10) bone-boiling, fat-melting, and their accompaniments within the city limits; (11) the sulphuretted, ammoniacal, and carburetted gases and offensive exhalations that are needlessly liberated and widely diffused in gas manufacture and purification; (12) the accumulations of dumping-grounds and manure-yards in vicinity of populous streets; (13) the present management of refuse and junk materials in the city; (14) the unreasonable overcrowding of the city railway cars, and the absence of all sanitary authority, permitting the unguarded transit and public exposure of persons with small-pox and other loathsome maladies in the public conveyances and otherwise in the streets; (15) the neglect of dead animals in the streets and gutters of the city.

The gross filthiness of the streets, courts, and alleys, the putrefying masses of animal and vegetable matter, together with dead animals, obstructed sewerage and drainage, and poisonous exhalations from manufactories of various kinds, combine to pollute the atmosphere of the entire city.

—Council of Hygiene and Public Health

No section of the city has any security against the encroachment or actual presence of these nuisances. A chart of nuisances as they actually existed, and were described by the Sanitary Inspectors, in the autumn of 1864, is presented here, for the purpose of illustrating the fact that even the *most favored* and wealthy districts of the city are seriously encroached upon by the most removable offensive nuisances. It should be sufficient cause to insure the proper effort to effect the removal and prevention of such nuisances that the Sanitary Inspectors report that all the nuisances we have here mentioned are positive sources of disease, and that they have been and are efficient causes in localizing the prevalence of fatal diseases. The particular character, extent, and insalubrious influence of the nuisances here mapped out, will be found more fully described in the SECOND PART of this volume.

The relation of some of these nuisances to the origin and localization of diarrhœal and typhoid diseases in their neighborhood appears to have been well established by careful observation and medical inquiry; and there is indubitable evidence that certain unseen sources of the most fatal kinds of disease lurk in the unflushed and uncleaned sewers and house drains, when obstructed or neglected, and that there is great danger that the filthy condition, faulty construction and bad management of privy vaults in the crowded districts will not only continue to be among the most distinct and offensive sources of obstinate disease, but that ere long they will become associated with the active and localizing causes of fatal epidemics. Putrescible organic matter, whether of animal or vegetable origin, when left to decay in the midst of a populous neighborhood, will very certainly induce diseases of some sort. It is particularly on this account that the medical and hygienic adviser is compelled to enter a protest against all needless herding and stabling of animals in the midst of densely populated streets; and with yet greater force is this objection urged against all the slaughter-pens and their adjunct nuisances, wherever located in the thickly inhabited portion of the city.

The 173 slaughter houses in this city are too offensive to health and decency to be longer permitted in their present localities. These establishments are now thrust into the midst of the most crowded districts, and it is to be observed that a loathsome train of dependent nuisances is found grouped in the same neighborhoods. We need not comment upon the offensive and debasing influence of the scenes and processes of the slaughter-pen. The intelligence and refined tastes of the people should enforce the demands of hygiene, and at once devise a practical scheme of *abattoirs* that shall be adapted to the wants of this populous and growing metropolis.* That there is a growing necessity for a faithful inspection of slaughtered animals and other food articles previous to their being offered in market, is testified by the best butchers and market-men in our city. It is known that a large proportion of the animals slaughtered in the city have to endure for days such treatment as seriously deteriorates the quality and healthfulness of their flesh; and that animals variously diseased and injured are daily crowded upon the markets of the city. These circumstances, together with the offensiveness of the nuisances that are incident to

---

*The great *abattoir* system of Paris is in effect one of its *sanitary institutions*. There we see the business of slaughtering animals not only rendered inoffensive to health and decency, but the process itself so managed as to insure the proper inspection and care of the animals at the time of slaughter, with reference to the protection of the public health. At the time of Sir Francis Head's visit to the Parisian *abattoir,* he states there were 66 *boucheries* in the *abattoir de Montmartre* alone, and that the number of fat-melting houses within its walls was 48; the number of beef cattle slaughtered every week, 1,300; the number of calves, 650; the number of sheep, 3,500.

The importance of providing by law for the proper sanitary care and supervision of butcheries and shambles is understood by intelligent market-men, and it needs to be understood by the municipal and health authorities. Self-protection will ere long compel the people to ask the intervention of the State to regulate the butcheries and the market system of this city, if municipal authority and private enterprise do not soon remedy the existing evils.

slaughter-pens in the populous streets, render it desirable that there should be a thorough reform of the whole system of supplying animal food for our shambles.[†]

It is not necessary to dwell upon the description or the remedy of the various other nuisances that endanger the public health in this city.[*] The gross filthiness of the streets, courts, and alleys, the putrefying masses of animal and vegetable matter, together with dead animals, obstructed sewerage and drainage, and poisonous exhalations from manufactories of various kinds, combine to pollute the atmosphere of the entire city. Yet all of these sources of insalubrity and increased mortality are of the most preventable character, and it is the unanimous opinion of this Council, that no system of Sanitary Government which fails to comprehend and control such evils can be adequate to the demands of an advancing civilization, or equal to the present wants of this city.

[†] The Council of Hygiene, as a voluntary organization, is not called upon to give the details relating to the gross impositions and the sources of evil that are inflicted by the existing system of butcheries and markets, or rather the absence of control of the sanitary condition of slaughtered animals and food articles; nor is this the occasion to describe and recommend the specific improvements that are required. It is known that very important improvements have been made in the methods of slaughter, as well as in the treatment of butcheries, and all that pertains thereto; and it is well known, moreover, that animals variously diseased, and meats variously injured for use as food, are sold daily to the unsuspecting multitudes who purchase in the established markets of the city, and to still greater numbers who depend upon the thousand minor shambles that are found in all populous districts. . . .

[*]What is known as the *gas nuisance* throughout the city of New York, is caused mainly by a defect in the means that are employed in the purification of the gas at the gas factories. Upon the causes and the remedy of this gross evil, the Professors of Chemistry in this Council have made a final report, explaining the causes of the nuisance, and showing the feasibility of its prevention.

The sewer-gas nuisance, and the abominable exhalations from various manufactories, all admit of being remedied. There is abundant evidence that the gaseous emanations from sewers, privies, decaying garbage, and neglected stables, stagnant water, etc., are always productive of diseases which are particularly fatal to infantile life, and that all great epidemics of fever, cholera, etc. are localized and rendered peculiarly fatal in places where such nuisances abound.

Source: *Report of the Council of Hygiene and Public Health of the Citizens' Association of New York upon the Sanitary Condition of the City.* New York: D. Appleton, 1865, pp. xci–xcvi.

NOTE

1. "New Books," *The New York Times,* June 19, 1865, p. 2.

DOCUMENT
5.4

Rivers and Harbors Appropriation Act

"It Shall Not Be Lawful to Throw, Discharge, or Deposit . . . Refuse . . . into Any Navigable Water of the United States"

March 3, 1899

As the nineteenth century drew to a close, Congress acted to provide greater measures of protection to the nation's navigable rivers, harbors, and canals. The Rivers and Harbors Appropriation Act severely restricted the dumping of a wide range of refuse—although not liquid sewage—into waterways and tributaries. It also imposed a new body of regulatory laws on construction activities adjacent to and within navigable waterways. Much of the impetus for the creation of this law was to keep waterways open and navigable for commercial activity—in fact, the dumping prohibitions did not extend to operations for the improvement of navigation and the construction of public works—but even so, the law had the salutary effect of reducing pollution discharges into rivers on which cities and towns depended for drinking water. The three most important sections of the 1899 law are reprinted here.

An Act Making Appropriations for the Construction, Repair, and Preservation of Certain Public Works on Rivers and Harbors, and for Other Purposes.

Sec. 9. It shall not be lawful to construct or commence the construction of any bridge, causeway, dam, or dike over or in any port, roadstead, haven, harbor, canal, navigable river, or other navigable water of the United States until the consent of Congress to the building of such structures shall have been obtained and until the plans for (1) the bridge or causeway shall have been submitted to and approved by the Secretary of Transportation, or (2) the dam or dike shall have been submitted to and approved by the Chief of Engineers and Secretary of the Army. However, such structures may be built under authority of the legislature of a State across rivers and other waterways the navigable portions of which lie wholly within the limits of a single State, provided the location and plans thereof are submitted to and approved by the Secretary of Transportation or by the Chief of Engineers and Secretary of the Army before construction is commenced. When plans for any bridge or other structure have been approved by the Secretary of Transportation or by the Chief of Engineers and Secretary of the Army, it shall not be lawful to deviate from such plans either before or after completion of the structure unless modification of said plans have previously been submitted to and received the approval of the Secretary of Transportation or the Chief of Engineers and the Secretary of the Army. The approval required by this section of the location and plans or any modification of plans of any bridge or causeway does not apply to any bridge or causeway over waters that are not subject to the ebb and flow of the tide and that are not used and are not susceptible to use in their natural condition or by reasonable improvement as a means to transport interstate or foreign commerce.

Sec. 10. That the creation of any obstruction not affirmatively authorized by Congress, to the navigable capacity of any of the waters of the United States is hereby prohibited; and it shall not be lawful to build or commence the building of any wharf, pier, dolphin, boom, weir, breakwater, bulkhead, jetty, or other structures in any port, roadstead, haven, harbor, canal, navigable river, or other water of the United States, outside established harbor lines, or where no harbor lines have been established, except on plans recommended by the Chief of Engineers and authorized by the Secretary of War; and it shall not be lawful to excavate or fill, or in any manner to alter or modify the course, location, condition, or capacity of, any port, roadstead, haven, harbor, canal, lake, harbor of refuge, or inclosure within the limits of any breakwater, or of the channel of any navigable water of the United States, unless the work has been recommended by the Chief of Engineers and authorized by the Secretary of War prior to beginning the same. . . .

Sec. 13. That it shall not be lawful to throw, discharge, or deposit, or cause, suffer, or procure to be thrown, discharged, or deposited either from or out of any ship, barge, or other floating craft of any kind, or from the shore, wharf, manufacturing establishment, or mill of any kind, and refuse matter of any kind or description whatever other than that flowing from streets and sewers and passing therefrom in a liquid state, into any navigable water of the United States, or into any tributary of any navigable water from which the same shall float or be washed into such navigable water; and it shall not be lawful to deposit, or cause, suffer, or procure to be deposited material of any kind in any place on the bank of any navigable water, or on the bank of any tributary of any navigable water, where the same shall be liable to be washed into such navigable water, either by ordinary or high tides, or by storms or floods, or otherwise, whereby navigation shall or may be impeded or obstructed: *Provided,* That nothing herein contained shall extend to, apply to, or prohibit the operations in connection with the improvement of navigable waters or construction of public works, considered necessary and proper by the United States officers supervising such improvement or public work: *And provided further,* That the Secretary of War, whenever in the judgment of the Chief of Engineers anchorage and navigation will not be injured thereby, may permit the deposit of any material above mentioned in navigable waters, within limits to be defined and under conditions to be prescribed by him, provided application is made to him prior to depositing such material; and whenever any permit is so granted the conditions thereof shall be strictly complied with, and any violation thereof shall be unlawful.

Source: Rivers and Harbors Appropriation Act of March 3, 1899. Available at U.S. Senate Committee on Environment and Public Works, www.epw.senate.gov/rivers.pdf.

DOCUMENT
5.5

A Reformer Condemns Air Pollution in American Cities

"The Health of Women and of Children Is Not a Factor in the Calculations of the Corporation"

April 7, 1905

One of the many targets of Progressive Era reform in the first two decades of the twentieth century was urban air quality. Industrial factories and households alike used huge quantities of coal, and the smoke that resulted from coal consumption cast a pall over cities from coast to coast. But the so-called smoke abatement movement did not arise merely out of aesthetic concerns; it was also grounded in the research of scientists, engineers, and doctors who saw the "smoke problem" as a significant environmental health problem in the nation's growing cities. In fact, heavy discharges of sulfur and particulates in industrial areas had been identified as a contributor to increasing rates of lung disease and nasal, throat, and bronchial problems.

Cincinnati physician Charles A. L. Reed was one of the Midwest's more prominent crusaders against the befouled air afflicting urban areas. On April 7, 1905, Reed delivered a speech on the subject, entitled "The Smoke Question Viewed from a National Standpoint," to a local women's club active in progressive causes (as were many such women's groups of the era). In his address, Reed touches on several themes that foreshadow the environmental justice movement that would emerge in American cities nearly a century later. Reed also explains the widely held belief among reformers that the nation's urban air quality issues can only be effectively addressed through federal, rather than local or state, action.

The smoke problem is in no sense local, but, on the contrary, presents questions of distinctly national interests. It is, in fact, a practical problem that presses for solution upon every class of people in every manufacturing city in the country. But it is a singularly pertinent theme for serious consideration by Women's Clubs, if for no other reason than that women, over and above all others, are martyrs to this existing and unfortunately growing order of things. Their rights never seem to be considered by the manufacturer of that class who fancies that in the assumed interest of his business he has a right to manufacture smoke without let or hindrance. The extra drudgery in house-keeping thus imposed upon women is never taken into account by the company whose factories fill the air with soot that filters alike into the parlor and bed-room. The health of women and of children is not a factor in the calculations of the corporation whose power plants load the atmosphere with irritating and otherwise deleterious vapors. A woman's cherished privilege to wear clean clothing, to say nothing of light becoming gowns, and to keep them clean is not regarded by the municipality that permits its streets to become defiled with the grim of its furnaces. For these and for other equally pertinent reasons it is but natural, indeed it is high time that women individually and through their organizations should voice their sentiment by entering a vigorous protest against conditions that, as applied to them, not only violate their sense of decency but that outrage everybody's convictions of justice.

INTERESTS DAMAGED BY SMOKE

But martyrs as are women to the smoke nuisance, there are other interests that are equally violated by its existence and perpetuation. Thus it would be interesting to know if it were possible to ascertain how many thousands of dollars worth of merchandise is annually lost by our dry goods merchants, solely through the ravages of smoke and soot. Clothiers, milliners, dressmakers, tailors, outfitters, grocers, druggists are singularly subject to damage from the same cause. Jewelers are put to extra labor and expense to protect their wares, especially silverplate against the influence of corroding gases that impregnate the atmosphere as the result of imperfect combustion in numerous manufacturing establishments. The damage that has been done and is being done to residence property in Cincinnati and other cities similarly enshrouded with smoke is beyond computation. And the worst of it is that the inhabitants who have fled from their homes, many of them elegant and even palatial establishments, leaving them at a great loss to the ravages of smoke, are followed by the same pest that presumably in the interest of the manufacturer, now threatens to make our suburbs as untenantable as our down-town districts. There is, in fact, not a single branch of the mercantile business, there is no private property interest that is not forced in this way to pay tribute to what I am convinced are totally unnecessary conditions imposed upon our great urban communities by the manufacturing interests that are, in fact, not in the least advanced by those same conditions. I am reliably informed that quite to the contrary, these same manufacturers who thus insist upon defiling our cities, sacrifice from 15% to 25% of their fuel to accomplish the purpose—not deliberately, perhaps—not maliciously, certainly—but ignorantly, or at least thoughtlessly. For, as Dr. Ohage, the able health commissioner of St. Paul, recently remarked, "smoke is not a mark of industrial activity, but of industrial stupidity."

Sanitary and Moral Aspects of the Question

. . . The sanitary, moral, aesthetic and ethical aspects of the subject have possibly a still further-reaching influence—an influence which if reduced to its final analysis, if carried to its ultimate calculation may tell even more seriously on the wrong side of the ledger.

"The Cincinnati lung," black and pigmented in contrast with the lungs of those who live and die in the country, was a proverb among physicians until other cities became as smoky and thus deprived Cincinnati of the questionable distinction. The slight morning cough with the equally slight expectoration of black mucus, is an experience familiar to the denizens of smoky towns, but an experience which, to the medical mind, suggests a persistent, although slight irritation of the upper air passages that are thus made hospitable avenues for tuberculous infection. Physicians of smoke-ridden cities testify to the greater frequency there of catarrhal or other disorders of the upper air passages induced by the irritating products of incomplete combustion. But the trouble is not alone physical. It is not, on the face of it, a good thing for any community to become too tolerant of dirt. Physical dirt is close akin to moral dirt and both combined lead to degeneracy. It is precisely against these influences, against this combination of influences, that practical philanthropy is today directing its most strenuous efforts in the crowded centers of London, New York, Chicago and other large cities. It is too much to expect the best results from public schools that exist beneath the somber shade of smoke. A dingy atmosphere is not conducive to a clear intellect. It is difficult to imbue the young with a sense of the beautiful when the beauty itself is bedaubed with soot. It is likewise difficult to instil a sense of justice in the minds of youths who are brought up in a community that permits one interest needlessly, but flagrantly and with impunity, to violate the equal rights of other interests. Ministers of the gospel would find it an easier task to teach the religion of a clean life and a happy eternity in a material atmosphere less suggestive of a gloomy present and a cheerless hereafter.

The Ethics of the Air

Then, too, there is something to be said about the ethics of the air. Air is necessary to existence. This being true, to breathe pure air, must be reckoned among man's inalienable rights. No man has any more right to contaminate the air we breathe than he has to defile the water we drink. No man has any more moral right to throw soot into our parlors than he has to dump ashes into our bed-rooms. No man has any more right to vitiate the air that sustains us than he has to adulterate the food that nourishes us. Poison taken into the body through the lungs is just as much a poison as is some other poison swallowed into the stomach. Poisonous air is probably more disastrous to infants than is adulterated milk. A man's proprietorship extends as distinctly into the air above him as into the earth beneath him. . . . . .

Public-spirited citizens of smoke-ridden cities all over the country are at least becoming enlightened on the subject, and, having failed to take preventive steps, are now formulating curative measures. They have come finally to realize that their rights have been encroached upon and they are at last moving vigorously to protect them. . . .

Examples of Successful Municipal Regulation of Smoke

There are, however, cities which have mastered this problem. I have already alluded to New York, which in spite of the adverse decision of its courts has carried on the work by sheer force of public opinion. Philadelphia is practically equally as successful. St. Paul stands as a conspicuous example of an effected reform. Our most hopeful examples, however, are to be found in Europe, where, in many instances, they have successfully overcome precisely the conditions with which we are now contending. In each instance they have solved the problems without sacrificing their industries. Paris, with manufacturing industries vastly more extensive than those of our own city, with domestic chimneys nearly 10 times as numerous, is probably the most conspicuous example of successful smoke regulation, and visitors to the French metropolis, especially visitors from our smoky American cities, will recall the inspiration derived from its clear, buoyant atmosphere. Dresden, remembered by Cincinnatians as being, 40 years ago, one of the smokiest of cities, is today probably the clearest, and one of the most attractive places in Europe. . . .

SOME DEFECTS OF THE ANTISMOKE CAMPAIGN

But, as I have already stated, many of our municipal ordinances to control the smoke situation, seem, on careful examination, to be immature efforts at legislation. Some of them seem to lack the essential elements of law. In instances they fail to define specifically, and upon a scientific basis, what comprises objectionable smoke. Some of them fail to place the execution of the law in the hands of the proper departments of the city government. They nearly all contain a mistaken provision for their enforcement by an elective officer—a fatal defect in the absence of a dominant public sentiment on the side of the law. . . . [R]egardless of outraged feelings, public thought is possibly not as mature on the question as it ought to be to formulate an efficient policy for the regulation of the evil. The example of Cincinnati is, however, enough of itself to convince us that one public-spirited manufacturer, or even a goodly group of them, cannot change the smoke conditions in an entire city.

NECESSITY FOR A NATIONAL MOVEMENT

It is equally impossible for one city, such, for instance, as St. Paul, or New York, or Philadelphia, to change conditions that are essentially national in their extent and influence. One city is afraid to move in the matter for fear that it will drive away some industry to some rival city. This is shown by the letter of a health commissioner of one of our largest interior cities, who among other things says: "Our attitude toward industrial enterprises of the manufacturing kind has been one of encouragement, and we have been reluctant to deal seemingly harshly with them, and I fancy that this attitude has something to do with the non-enforcement of the smoke ordinances."

It is, therefore, important for this movement, if it is to move, that there should be co-operation between different cities looking to the regulation of the evil. For this reason, it seems that cooperation, to be effective, must be national in extent, and must have several distinct objects in view, such, for instance, as:

1. The development of an enlightened and quickened public sentiment on the subject.
2. A careful determination of all economic facts and an equitable adjustment of all conflicting interests involved in the controversy.
3. The determination and demonstration of all principles, practices, plans, and appliances for practical smoke prevention.
4. The formulation of a standard law which, with modifications to meet local conditions, can be adopted by all cities, and which will, therefore, result in the practically uniform regulation of the evil all over the country. . . .

Source: Reed, Charles A. L. "The Smoke Question viewed from a National Standpoint." *American Medicine* 9, no. 17 (April 29, 1905): 703–705.

New Regulations Bring Incremental Change to City Life

DOCUMENT 5.6

"Improvements in the Tenements"

1905

During the last decades of the nineteenth century and the opening years of the twentieth, municipal ordinances seeking to regulate urban pollution and living conditions became more commonplace in many American cities. These new regulations were often modest in scope and fitfully enforced. Over time, however, these incremental advances started to chip away at some of the greatest "evils" of the tenements. In the following excerpt from a 1905 study of New York's clothing industry and the social condition of its workforce, author Jesse Eliphalet Pope extols the salutary effect of several sanitary regulations passed by officials in New York City.

The great evil of the old tenement house was due to the fact that it occupied too great a percentage of the area of the lot. By the law of 1879 the amount of space to be occupied by the building was specifically provided for and a new class of structure, known as the "dumb-bell" or "double-decker" was devised to meet these requirements. The chief innovation was the provision for an inner court. This was little better than an enlarged air shaft, and as it had no opening on street or yard, the rubbish and garbage which naturally collected in it was seldom removed, so that it became a flue for the dissemination of noisome odors. The yard of the house was placed at its extreme rear. While this form of structure was an improvement upon the old, yet it failed to supply sufficient light and ventilation, as the open space was too narrow to permit the entrance of light and air into rooms in any but the upper stories.

On those lots on which former private dwellings stood there was a large unoccupied space in the rear; on this space tenement houses were erected which had no connection with the street except through the buildings in front. It was not alone on lots occupied by remodeled dwelling houses, however, that we find this class of tenements, for they were often constructed in connection with newly erected tenement houses.

The amount of space between the two buildings was so small that very little sunlight reached the lower stories. The first law regulating the distance between these buildings was passed in 1867, but owing to a faulty wording which provided only for those cases in which the rear tenement was built first, it was practically without force until 1879 when a provision was made by which this defect was remedied. The distances provided for in this and succeeding laws, however, are too small. The evils of this kind of tenement are recognized in a letter from the Tenth Ward Sanitary Union, written in 1894, an extract from which follows: "We believe that the rear tenements should be wholly destroyed, and the space reserved for open courts and playgrounds for the children. Even such as are not in an unsanitary condition overshadow the lower stories of the front house and are in turn overshadowed by them, to the exclusion of light and air." In spite of the protests against this form of dwelling, the rear tenement still exists. Lawrence Veiller in a recent investigation found 2124 of them in the borough of Manhattan.

In practically all the early tenements no provision was made for water on the separate floors and all the tenants were obliged to use the same pump or hydrant in the yard below, but in some few cases water was provided on the first floor. In 1887, however, a law was passed making it compulsory for the landlord to furnish water in each story. This law was not generally enforced until the beginning of the Low administration in 1901. The present law provides that in the houses hereafter constructed there shall be a sink with running water in each apartment.

While the law of 1887 remains the same for old tenement houses the actual working out of the laws in regard to other regulations has brought it about that even in the old tenements water in each apartment is becoming the rule. In none of the tenements was provision made for water closets on the various floors and all the occupants of the building were obliged to use common closets situated in the yard. Previous to 1887 vaults were common, and even where sewers were available, connections were often not made. In that year, however, a law was passed abolishing vaults, where possible, and providing that there should be not less than one water closet for every two families. The school sinks which took the place of the vaults were contrivances of unspeakable filth. Despite attempts at regulation these toilets situated in the yard have always been the foulest kind of nuisance. In 1900 a law was passed providing that close accommodations shall be attached to each apartment of tenements hereafter erected. The school sinks connected with the old buildings were made illegal and their places were supplied by water closets either in the yard or on each floor. Most of the owners who have made the changes so far have placed them on each floor, as they find this a distinct improvement to the property. . . .

External surroundings have kept pace with the improvements in the tenements. The great reform wrought by Colonel Waring in the cleaning of the streets and the removal of garbage has revolutionized conditions in this respect. The rude cobble stone has been replaced by asphalt pavements which can be easily flooded and many old buildings have been torn down and the area gave over to small parks. Many narrow streets have been widened and new ones opened. While the tenements of to-day are by no means ideal, yet their condition is immeasurably better than at the beginning of this period. . . .

Source: Pope, Jesse Eliphalet. *The Clothing Industry in New York.* Columbia, Mo.: E.W. Stephens, 1905, pp. 151–155.

DOCUMENT
5.7

Upton Sinclair's *The Jungle*

"The Filth Stays There Forever and a Day"

1906

The 1906 publication of Upton Sinclair's muckraking novel The Jungle *resounded like a thunderclap across America. In this thinly fictionalized account of Chicago's meatpacking industry, Sinclair painted a bleak picture of a world characterized by brutalized and exploited workers, heedless environmental pollution, and routine packaging of diseased and filthy meat for public consumption.*

Sinclair wrote the book in an effort to bring public attention to the plight of the immigrant workers trapped in the slaughterhouses and to the ways in which urban factories and tenement slums and corrupt political machines fed off one another. Instead, most of the public became fixated on the author's gruesome descriptions of sausages spiced with rat feces, workers disintegrating in vats of lard, and chemical injections of diseased and spoiled beef and pork. The outrage over Sinclair's compelling account of impure food processing extended from American living rooms to Congress. Progressive Era reformers harnessed this outrage to pass new food inspection and certification measures, most notably the Meat Inspection Act and the Pure Food and Drug Act of 1906, which established the Food and Drug Administration. The Jungle *thus became a milestone in the improvement of public health and environmental conditions in the workplace—even if Sinclair did later lament that he had aimed for the public's heart and instead hit its stomach. The following is an excerpt from this famous muckraking work.*

And now in the union Jurgis met men who explained all this mystery to him; and he learned that America differed from Russia in that its government existed under the form of a democracy. The officials who ruled it, and got all the graft, had to be elected first; and so there were two rival sets of grafters, known as political parties, and the one got the office which bought the most votes. Now and then, the election was very close, and that was the time the poor man came in. In the stockyards this was only in national and state elections, for in local elections the democratic party always carried everything. The ruler of the district was therefore the democratic boss, a little Irishman named Mike Scully. Scully held an important party office in the state, and bossed even the mayor of the city, it was said; it was his boast that he carried the stockyards in his pocket. He was an enormously rich man—he had a hand in all the big graft in the neighborhood. It was Scully, for instance, who owned that dump which Jurgis and Ona had seen the first day of their arrival. Not only did he own the dump, but he owned the brick-factory as well; and first he took out the clay and made it into bricks, and then he had the city bring garbage to fill up the hole, so that he could build houses to sell to the people. Then, too, he sold the bricks to the city, at his own price, and the city came and got them in its own wagons. And also he owned the other hole near by, where the stagnant water was; and it was he who cut the ice and sold it; and what was more, if the men told truth, he had not had to pay any taxes for the water, and he had built the ice-house out of city lumber, and had not had to pay anything for that. The newspapers had got hold of that story, and there had been a scandal; but Scully had hired somebody to confess and take all the blame, and then skip the country. It was said, too, that he had built his brick-kiln in the same way, and that the workmen were on the city pay-roll while they did it; however, one had to press closely to get these things out of the men, for it was not their business, and Mike Scully was a good man to stand in with. A note signed by him was equal to a job any time at the packing houses; and also he employed a good many men himself, and worked them only eight hours a day, and paid them the highest wages. . . .

Even the packers were in awe of him, so the men said. It gave them pleasure to believe this, for Scully stood as the people's man, and boasted of it boldly when election day came. The packers had wanted a bridge at Ashland Avenue, but they had not been able to get it till they had seen Scully; and it was the same with "Bubbly Creek," which the city had threatened to make the packers cover over, till Scully had come to their aid. "Bubbly Creek" is an arm of the Chicago River, and forms the southern boundary of the yards; all the drainage of the square mile of packing-houses empties into it, so that it is really a great open sewer a hundred or two feet wide. One long arm of it is blind, and the filth stays there forever and a day. The grease and chemicals that are poured into it undergo all sorts of strange transformations, which are the cause of its name; it is constantly in motion, as if huge fish were feeding in it, or great leviathans disporting themselves in its depths. Bubbles of carbonic acid gas will rise to the surface and burst, and make rings two or three feet wide. Here and there the grease and filth have caked solid, and the creek looks like a bed of lava; chickens walk about on it, feeding, and many times an unwary stranger has started to stroll across, and vanished temporarily. The packers used to leave the creek that way, till every now and then the surface would catch on fire and burn furiously, and the fire department would have to come and put it out. Once, however, an ingenious stranger came and started to gather this filth in scows, to make lard out of; then the packers took the cue, and got out an injunction to stop him, and afterward gathered it themselves. The banks of "Bubbly Creek" are plastered thick with hairs, and this also the packers gather and clean.

And there were things even stranger than this, according to the gossip of the men. The packers had secret mains, through which they stole billions of gallons of the city's water. The newspapers had been full of this scandal—once there had even been an investigation, and an actual uncovering of the pipes; but nobody had been punished, and the thing went right on. And then there was the condemned meat industry, with its endless horrors. The people of Chicago saw the government inspectors in Packingtown, and they all took that to mean that they were protected from diseased meat; they did not understand that these hundred and sixty-three inspectors had been appointed at the request of the packers, and that they were paid by the United States government to certify that all the diseased meat was kept in the state. They had no authority beyond that; for the inspection of meat to be sold in the city and state the whole force in Packingtown consisted of three henchmen of the local political machine!*

And shortly afterward one of these, a physician, made the discovery that the carcasses of steers which had been condemned as tubercular by the government inspectors, and which therefore contained ptomaines, which are deadly poisons, were left upon an open platform and carted away to be sold in the city; and so he insisted that these

> *"Bubbly Creek" is an arm of the Chicago River, and . . . it is really a great open sewer a hundred or two feet wide. . . . The grease and chemicals that are poured into it undergo all sorts of strange transformations, which are the cause of its name; it is constantly in motion, as if huge fish were feeding in it, or great leviathans disporting themselves in its depths.*
>
> —Upton Sinclair

---

*"Rules and Regulations for the Inspection of Livestock and Their Products." United States Department of Agriculture, Bureau of Animal Industries, Order No. 125:—

SECTION 1. Proprietors of slaughterhouses, canning, salting, packing, or rendering establishments engaged in the slaughtering of cattle, sheep, or swine, or the packing of any of their products, the carcasses or products of which are to become subjects of interstate or foreign commerce, shall make application to the Secretary of Agriculture for inspection of said animals and their products. . . .

SECTION 15. Such rejected or condemned animals shall at once be removed by the owners from the pens containing animals which have been inspected and found to be free from disease and fit for human food, and *shall be disposed of in accordance with the laws, ordinances, and regulations of the state and municipality in which said rejected or condemned animals are located.* . . .

SECTION 25. A microscopic examination for trichinæ shall be made of all swine products exported to countries requiring such examination. *No microscopic examination will be made of hogs slaughtered for interstate trade, but this examination shall be confined to those intended for the export trade.*

carcasses be treated with an injection of kerosene—and was ordered to resign the same week! So indignant were the packers that they went farther, and compelled the mayor to abolish the whole bureau of inspection; so that since then there has not been even a pretense of any interference with the graft. There was said to be two thousand dollars a week hush money from the tubercular steers alone; and as much again from the hogs which had died of cholera on the trains, and which you might see any day being loaded into box-cars and hauled away to a place called Globe, in Indiana, where they made a fancy grade of lard. . . .

Then one Sunday evening, Jurgis sat puffing his pipe by the kitchen stove, and talking with an old fellow whom Jonas had introduced, and who worked in the canning rooms at Durham's; and so Jurgis learned a few things about the great and only Durham canned goods, which had become a national institution. They were regular alchemists at Durham's; they advertised a mushroom-catsup, and the men who made it did not know what a mushroom looked like. They advertised "potted chicken,"—and it was like the boardinghouse soup of the comic papers, through which a chicken had walked with rubbers on. Perhaps they had a secret process for making chickens chemically—who knows? said Jurgis's friend; the things that went into the mixture were tripe, and the fat of pork, and beef suet, and hearts of beef, and finally the waste ends of veal, when they had any. They put these up in several grades, and sold them at several prices; but the contents of the cans all came out of the same hopper. And then there was "potted game" and "potted grouse," "potted ham," and "devilled ham"—de-vyled, as the men called it. "De-vyled" ham was made out of the waste ends of smoked beef that were too small to be sliced by the machines; and also tripe, dyed with chemicals so that it would not show white; and trimmings of hams and corned beef; and potatoes, skins and all; and finally the hard cartilaginous gullets of beef, after the tongues had been cut out. All this ingenious mixture was ground up and flavored with spices to make it taste like something. . . .

There was another interesting set of statistics that a person might have gathered in Packingtown—those of the various afflictions of the workers. When Jurgis had first inspected the packing-plants with Szedvilas, he had marveled while he listened to the tale of all the things that were made out of the carcasses of animals, and of all the lesser industries that were maintained there; now he found that each one of these lesser industries was a separate little inferno, in its way as horrible as the killing-beds, the source and fountain of them all. The workers in each of them had their own peculiar diseases. And the wandering visitor might be skeptical about all the swindles, but he could not be sceptical [sic] about these, for the worker bore the evidence of them about on his own person—generally he had only to hold out his hand.

There were the men in the pickle-rooms, for instance, where old Antanas had gotten his death; scarce a one of these that had not some spot of horror on his person. Let a man so much as scrape his finger pushing a truck in the pickle-rooms, and he might have a sore that would put him out of the world; all the joints in his fingers might be eaten by the acid, one by one. Of the butchers and floorsmen, the beef-boners and trimmers, and all those who used knives, you could scarcely find a person who had the use of his thumb; time and time again the base of it had been slashed, till it was a mere lump of flesh against which the man pressed the knife to hold it. The hands of these men would be criss-crossed with cuts, until you could no longer pretend to count them or to trace them. They would have no nails,—they had worn them off pulling hides; their knuckles were swollen so that their fingers spread out like a fan. There were men who worked in the cooking-rooms, in the midst of steam and sickening odors, by artificial light; in these rooms the germs of tuberculosis might live for two years, but the supply was renewed every hour. There were the beef-luggers, who carried two-hundred-pound quarters into the refrigerator-cars; a fearful kind of work, that began at four o'clock in the morning, and that wore out the most powerful men in a few years. There were those who worked in the chilling-rooms, and whose special disease was rheumatism; the time limit that a man could work in the chilling-rooms was said to be five years. There were the wool-pluckers, whose hands went to pieces even sooner than the hands of the pickle-men; for the pelts of the sheep had to be painted with acid to loosen the wool, and then the pluckers had to pull out this wool with their bare hands, till the acid had eaten their fingers off. There were those who made the tins for the canned-meat; and their hands, too, were a maze of cuts, and each cut represented a chance for blood-poisoning. Some worked at the stamping-machines, and it was very seldom that one could work long there at the pace that was set, and not give out and forget himself and have a part of his hand chopped off. There were the "hoisters," as they were called, whose task it was to press the lever which lifted the dead cattle off the floor. They ran along upon a rafter, peering down through the damp and the steam; and as old Durham's architects had not built the killing-room for the convenience of the hoisters, at every few feet they would have to stoop under a beam, say four feet above the one they ran on; which got them into the habit of stooping, so that in a few years they would be walking like chimpanzees. Worst of any, however, were the fertilizer-men, and those who served in the cooking-rooms. These people could not be shown to the visitor,—for the odor of a fertilizer-man would scare any ordinary visitor at a hundred yards, and as for the other men, who worked in tank-rooms full of steam, and in some of which there were open vats near the level of the floor, their peculiar trouble was that they fell into the vats; and when they were fished out, there was never enough of them left to be worth exhibiting,—sometimes they would be overlooked for days, till all but the bones of them had gone out to the world as Durham's Pure Leaf Lard! . . .

Source: Sinclair, Upton. *The Jungle.* New York: The Jungle Publishing Co., 1906, pp. 110–117.

DOCUMENT 5.8   A Call for Green Space in American Cities

"The City Plan Is a Slowly Materializing Dream in America"

February 1, 1908

Progressive Era reforms brought about major changes in the daily lives of millions of residents of American cities, including new workplace regulations and refuse disposal measures. Around 1900, the sanitarians and public health advocates who spearheaded this charge were joined by reformers who believed that aesthetic improvements to the urban environment were also worth pursuing. They asserted that parks and tree-lined boulevards and other natural features that we now term "green space" were just as important to the emotional and physical well-being of city residents—and the self-image of the nation as a whole—as clean water and efficient garbage collection systems.

This crusade to reshape the American city by re-introducing stands of trees, natural open spaces, and graceful public buildings was sparked by the 1893 Chicago World's Columbian Exposition, for which Daniel Burnham and Frederick Law Olmsted built their famed "White City." The opulence of the White City inspired the emergence of the City Beautiful Movement, which reached its greatest heights of influence between 1900 and 1910. During this time, major American cities, including Cleveland, Detroit, Denver, Minneapolis-St. Paul, and Washington, D.C., all embarked on significant urban beautification project. Adherents of this philosophy of urban planning believed that soot-choked cities could experience rebirth and reinvigoration through the introduction and careful stewardship of spacious parks, leafy avenues, and grand public buildings. They asserted that by using radial grid designs, encouraging investment in open space and works of classic architecture, and incorporating civic development with natural features like rivers and hillsides, enlightened city planners could transform the American city into a more aesthetically pleasing and spiritually fulfilling place.

J. Horace McFarland was one of the most prominent proponents of the City Beautiful cause. He used his position as president of the American Civic Association to deliver a "crusade against ugliness" lecture to audiences from coast to coast. By 1911, in fact, he had delivered this stump speech in 250 cities across the United States.[1] Following is an excerpt from a 1908 article on city planning by McFarland, which touches on many of the philosophical foundations of the City Beautiful Movement.

Sitting at one of the inquiry desks of the American Civic Association to which come daily earnest questions from all over this broad land, I can testify with knowledge of the relatively restricted general interest in city planning. Occasionally some acute inquirer wants information as to grouping plans or civic centers or the like, but not once to five hundred requests for help along more primary lines. How to get waste paper off the streets, how to have good street trees, what to do about poles and wires and smoke, something about children's gardens and playgrounds, a wail by reason of danger to the Grand Canyon of the Colorado, a plea to "save the White Mountains," and latterly a stream of indignant, earnest inquiries as to means for stemming the flood of billboard ugliness that is pouring out over the whole beautiful country from the planless, hideous, gridironed cities—these keep us wishing our scanty resources were larger and our workers with ten heads and twenty hands each, to cope with the desires of those who are seeking aid to make a "better and more beautiful America." Yet when the occasional and usually acute inquiry as to concrete planning movements is received, we respond with delight; and it is worthy of remark that we were able, recently, to more than double the information at the command of a great city planner, at his request.

Again, city planning is almost incomprehensible to the average city dweller, to whom even yet the city means but highways and houses, to whom taxes are merely an exaction and parks entirely a luxury, to whom civic beauty is only civic wastefulness. . . .

But there is the occasional inquirer after all, and as I have hinted he is sure to be an acute and far-seeing man, who dreams of cities that shall be conveniently attractive, harmoniously complete in essentials for comfort, and free from outbreaking private or public ugliness. He has trouble in having his ideals respected in the free and presumably enlightened United States; for has not every citizen here been constitutionally guaranteed a right to do as he pleases with his own, however his "pleasure" may destroy the comfort or annoy the eyes and the aesthetic sense of his neighbor? Our occasional city planner must face a storm of protest at his ideas of "centralized government," of "paternalism," his wastefulness in attempting to provide beauty in the place of ugliness.

But the stuff of which the city planner is made is that of the old pioneers of liberty, and he persists. Thus it has come to pass that while the great majority of those interested in civic advance look with faint interest upon movements for civic beauty in streets and structures, the truly greater and wonderfully efficient minority have succeeded in forcing attention to some ideals and in having those ideals given the sanction of interested effort. The city plan is a slowly materializing dream in America, and this dream, as I shall briefly show, has recurred in many cities. . . .

As in olden time it was said that "all roads lead to Rome," so now it may be said that all city plans refer to the Columbian Exposition. Until Mr. Burnham's dream of the White City assumed its form of marvelous beauty beside the lake, dazing the world which thought of Chicago only in terms of pork and progress, expositions in America had taken no particular thought for beauty, either of building or environment. When the Centennial exposition in 1876 showed us our material progress and taught us our powers and our resources, Washington was not the open book of accomplishment in city planning she now is. The great buildings in Fairmount Park reflected nothing but hugeness, save for the Memorial Hall, and there was no planned general beauty—nor was it missed, it must be confessed.

It remained for Chicago, then, to awaken our dormant sense of form and appropriateness in architecture and environment, and to show what planning could accomplish. From the White City, I insist, have radiated all the lines of urban elegance and beauty that we are now coming to recognize as desirable. Succeeding expositions have not at all surpassed the impression created by the Chicago fair, though Buffalo, St. Louis and Jamestown, each in order, have undoubtedly deepened and strengthened the desire for that orderly civic beauty which was born in proximity to the "midway."

Chicago herself has been slow to take to her smoky heart the lesson she so strongly enforced upon all the country fifteen years ago, but has now, through her Merchants' Association, undertaken planning of the city beautiful. Mr. Burnham is to suggest plans for her encircling outer parkway, for making sightly the river fronts through the city, for beautifying the lake front, for building great railroad stations, for cleaning the streets of poles, signs and obstructions, for planting trees and introducing refreshing greenery wherever practicable, and for generally turning from careless ugliness to considered sightliness. Who doubts Chicago's ability, or her willingness, to do these things, great though the cost may be? No one, at least, who has cognizance of her humanitarian work for health and citizenship as well as for beauty in the South Side neighborhood centers so recently and broadly established. These centers are part of a planning for a city's service to its people that makes for health, happiness, prosperity and good order, and their successful experience is a most acute endorsement of the whole movement for making over our American cities.

St. Louis, a long-time rival of Chicago, is acutely awake to the defects in the development of her city plan, as evidenced by a notable report, prepared and issued by the active Civic League of St. Louis. This report canvasses the whole field of city planning, and proposes, with complete consideration of the ways and means, a far-reaching and admirable scheme for improvement. I have faith in the future of the people, the city and this plan.

To materially modify the old Knickerbocker plan for New York, with its interesting cowpath reminders toward the point of Manhattan Island, would suggest a staggering expense. Yet no one can overlook the changes, quietly proceeding, which tend toward a city of wonderful beauty. This I say as one willing to stifle his prejudice against the pre-dominance of "sky-scrapers," when he sees those same towers of commerce creating not only a new sky-line, but a general modelling of new city lines that grows into majestic beauty. To realize the danger, the candid observer must divest himself of prejudice, as he views the great city from the Hudson river, or looks up and down Broadway at various happy intersections. And if the observer be alive to beauty in the concrete, he will keenly enjoy a ride up Fifth avenue toward sunset, or a walk from 42nd street to Union square on a bright morning.

But the civic part of this change is impressive. New York city has paid millions for spotting green upon its city plan below City Hall Park, and has, along the Bronx, as well as north and east, added great areas of park territory with connecting boulevards. North of 125th street there is but a reminiscence of the rectangular square plan of the lower city.

The noble use of the bank of the Hudson in Riverside Park may in the expensive future be complemented by a proper water-front development lower down on both of the great river fronts. An official New York City Improvement Commission has projected a comprehensive plan, and who shall say it cannot be carried out!

One of the separated tendencies toward harmonious civic beauty in New York is found in the beneficent operations of the Municipal Art Commission, which has final and complete authority to pass upon the designs for all structures wholly or in part upon public property. The erection of many architectural horrors has been prevented by this unpaid, non-partisan, well entrenched commission, which controls even the design of a letterbox in a public building, as well as the building itself.

Thus, it will be seen, the great metropolis is slowly and almost unconsciously revis-ing its city plan, through these various forces for betterment.

Many other centers of population in which some of the restlessly persistent minor-ity of civic planners live, are doing or proposing great things for improvement in city lines. Baltimore, for instance, secured out of its conflagration a Burnt Districts Commission, which has modified and improved streets. . . . The Municipal Art Society of Baltimore has proposed, under the guidance of Frederick Law Olmsted, Jr., a superb outer park system, adding, when completed, an element of incalculable value to the city plan.

San Francisco, as all know, had been considering her plan deficiencies before the great catastrophe. For a time it appeared possible that Mr. Burnham's revision of her map might be carried out in the burnt district at least; but the forces of graft and greed were too strong. Yet there are now lively hopes for a better city plan near the Golden Gate.

Boston is admirably parked, and her State House suggests a civic center, yet there is now proceeding education for the adoption of a plan involving designed and splendid avenues, to add convenience, dignity and beauty to "the Hub."

The slumbers of good William Penn must be disturbed by what is occurring in his checkerboard city of Philadelphia; for actually a great parkway is being cut diagonally from Logan square to Fairmount park! There is hope, therefore, that the Quaker city may some time endeavor to mitigate the incongruity of its civic center at the city hall by dras-tically cutting out the great buildings she has unfortunately permitted to be erected so as to hide and dwarf her twenty-million dollar city home. An active combination of organi-zation is working periodically to correct park deficiencies in Philadelphia.

Minneapolis and St. Paul have joined in an admirable park provision which modi-fies and adorns the plans of both cities. With thirty-four miles of connecting parkways, the twin cities are girdled in green. It is to be hoped that St. Paul's plan for securing adequate approaches to the fine new capitol building may be concretely realized. . . .

Southern cities are waking to their needs and their possibilities. Columbia, the capital of South Carolina, has secured a report on the work necessary to enable proper advantage to be taken of the hundred-foot avenues provided in the original city plan, as well as to obtain needed parks, and parkways. Mr. Kelsey, who prepared the Columbia plan, has also submitted to the local Municipal League an admirable proposition for the improvement of Greenville, South Carolina. . . .

But what need is there of further examples to prove the splendid activity of the planning minority? These people, philanthropists all, whether individual or corporate, will have it that their philanthropy is mere business. Just so; but what fine business to be engaged in—the business of making this earth most serviceable and heaven-like to the people who cannot—or will not—do it for themselves! . . .

There is a vast deal yet to do, before our American cities can be considered as serving reasonably well the needs and the lives of the congestion of population they represent; that it will be expensive doing, is obvious; but that is our American preponderating "hindsight" way. . . .

So I would urge the doing, whatever the expense, certain that it will never be less than at present, and that even now, it will "pay" a city to make itself convenient, sanitary, serviceable and beautiful, in terms of dollars as well as in the higher, finer terms of human lives.

Source: McFarland, J. Horace. "The Growth of City Planning in America." *Charities and the Commons,* February 1, 1908, pp. 1522–1528.

NOTE

1. William H. Wilson, *The City Beautiful Movement* (Baltimore: Johns Hopkins University Press, 1994), 51, 75.

DOCUMENT
5.9

Jane Addams Fights for Clean Streets and Alleyways

"We Began a Systematic Investigation of the City System of Garbage Collection"

1910

As the nineteenth century drew to a close, America's growing sanitary movement was further bolstered by a general upsurge in public and political support for significant social, industrial, and political reforms. Public health advocates and urban reformers exulted as the dismal state of many American cities became a subject of considerable progressive attention. To their eyes, the roaring factories and squalid tenements that dominated the urban environment fairly cried out for the cleansing powers of reform. After all, as historian J.W. Leavitt summarized, "the urban environment fostered the spread of diseases with crowded, dark, unventilated housing; unpaved streets mired in horse manure and littered with refuse; inadequate or nonexistent water supplies; privy vaults unemptied from one year to the next; stagnant pools of water; ill-functioning open sewers; stench beyond the twentieth-century imagination; and noises from clacking horse hooves, wooden wagon wheels, street railways, and unmuffled industrial machinery."[1]

Each of these sights and sounds constituted a great offense to the sensibilities of many Progressive Era reformers; collectively, they were seen as a mockery of America's professed ideals of nobility, strength, and democracy. Yet the calls issued by voluntary associations and public health advocates for new ordinances and regulations to address troublesome urban conditions often became mired in the political skirmishing that typified turn-of-the-century industrial cities. As a result, reformers dedicated to improving inner-city conditions, such as the famed settlement house icon Jane Addams, often had to content themselves with incremental victories. In the following excerpt from her memoir Twenty Years at Hull-House, *Addams reflects on some of these modest triumphs.*

The policy of the public authorities of never taking an initiative, and always waiting to be urged to do their duty, is obviously fatal in a neighborhood where there is little initiative among the citizens. The idea underlying our self-government breaks down in such a ward. The streets are inexpressibly dirty, the number of schools inadequate, sanitary legislation unenforced, the street lighting bad, the paving miserable and altogether lacking in the alleys and smaller streets, and the stables foul beyond description. Hundreds of houses are unconnected with the street sewer. The older and richer inhabitants seem anxious to move away as rapidly as they can afford it. They make room for newly arrived immigrants who are densely ignorant of civic duties. This substitution of the older inhabitants is accomplished industrially also, in the south and east quarters of the ward. The Jews and Italians do the finishing for the great clothing manufacturers, formerly done by Americans, Irish and Germans, who refused to submit to the extremely low prices to which the sweating system has reduced their successors. As the design of the sweating system is the elimination of rent from the manufacture of clothing, the "outside work" is begun after the clothing leaves the cutter. An unscrupulous contractor regards no basement as too dark, no stable loft too foul, no rear shanty too provisional, no tenement room too small for his workroom, as these conditions imply low rental. Hence these shops abound in the worst of the foreign districts where the sweater easily finds his cheap basement and his home finishers.

The houses of the ward, for the most part wooden, were originally built for one family and are now occupied by several. They are after the type of the inconvenient frame cottages found in the poorer suburbs twenty years ago. Many of them were built where they now stand; others were brought thither on rollers, because their previous sites had been taken for factories. The fewer brick tenement buildings which are three or four stories high are comparatively new, and there are few large tenements. The little wooden houses have a temporary aspect, and for this reason, perhaps, the tenement-house legislation in Chicago is totally inadequate. Rear tenements flourish; many houses have no-water supply save the faucet in the back yard, there are no fire escapes, the garbage and ashes are placed in wooden boxes which are fastened to the street pavements. One of the most discouraging features about the present system of tenement houses is that many are owned by sordid and ignorant immigrants. The theory that wealth brings responsibility, that possession entails at length education and refinement, in these cases fails utterly. The children of an Italian immigrant owner may "shine" shoes in the street, and his wife may pick rags from the street gutter, laboriously sorting them in a dingy court. Wealth may do something for her self-complacency and feeling of consequence; it certainly does nothing for her comfort or her children's improvement nor for the cleanliness of any one concerned. Another thing that prevents better houses in Chicago is the tentative attitude of the real estate men. Many unsavory conditions are allowed to continue which would be regarded with horror if they were considered permanent. Meanwhile, the wretched conditions persist until at least two generations of children have been born and reared in them. . . .

One of the striking features of our neighborhood twenty years ago, and one to which we never became reconciled, was the presence of huge wooden garbage boxes fastened to the street pavement in which the undisturbed refuse accumulated day by day. The system of garbage collecting was inadequate throughout the city but it became the greatest menace in a ward such as ours, where the normal amount of waste was much increased by the decayed fruit and vegetables discarded by the Italian and Greek fruit peddlers, and by the residuum left over from the piles of filthy rags which were fished out of the city dumps and brought to the homes of the rag pickers for further sorting and washing.

The children of our neighborhood twenty years ago played their games in and around these huge garbage boxes. They were the first objects that the toddling child learned to climb; their bulk afforded a barricade and their contents provided missiles in all the battles of the older boys; and finally they became the seats upon which absorbed lovers held enchanted converse. We are obliged to remember that all children eat everything which they find and that odors have a curious and intimate power of entwining themselves into our tenderest memories, before even the residents of Hull-House can understand their own early enthusiasm for the removal of these boxes and the establishment of a better system of refuse collection.

> *Many unsavory conditions are allowed to continue which would be regarded with horror if they were considered permanent. Meanwhile, the wretched conditions persist until at least two generations of children have been born and reared in them.*
>
> —Jane Addams

It is easy for even the most conscientious citizen of Chicago to forget the foul smells of the stockyards and the garbage dumps, when he is living so far from them that he is only occasionally made conscious of their existence but the residents of a Settlement are perforce constantly surrounded by them. During our first three years on Halsted Street, we had established a small incinerator at Hull-House and we had many times reported the untoward conditions of the ward to the city hall. We had also arranged many talks for the immigrants, pointing out that although a woman may sweep her own doorway in her native village and allow the refuse to innocently decay in the open air and sunshine, in a crowded city quarter, if the garbage is not properly collected and destroyed, a tenement-house mother may see her children sicken and die, and that the immigrants must therefore, not only keep their own houses clean, but must also help the authorities to keep the city clean.

Possibly our efforts slightly modified the worst conditions but they still remained intolerable, and the fourth summer the situation became for me absolutely desperate when I realized in a moment of panic that my delicate little nephew for whom I was guardian, could not be with me at Hull-House at all unless the sickening odors were reduced. I may well be ashamed that other delicate children who were torn from their families, not into boarding school but into eternity, had not long before driven me to effective action. Under the direction of the first man who came as a resident to Hull-House we began a systematic investigation of the city system of garbage collection, both as to its efficiency in other wards and its possible connection with the death rate in the various wards of the city.

The Hull-House Woman's Club had been organized the year before by the resident kindergartner who had first inaugurated a mothers' meeting. The members came together, however, in quite a new way that summer when we discussed with them the high death rate so persistent in our ward. After several club meetings devoted to the subject, despite the fact that the death rate rose highest in the congested foreign colonies and not in the streets in which most of the Irish American club women lived, twelve of their number undertook in connection with the residents, to carefully investigate the condition of the alleys. During August and September the substantiated reports of violations of the law sent in from Hull-House to the health department were one thousand and thirty-seven. For the club woman who had finished a long day's work of washing or ironing followed by the cooking of a hot supper, it would have been much easier to sit on her doorstep during a summer evening than to go up and down ill-kept alleys and get into trouble with her neighbors over the condition of their garbage boxes. It required both civic enterprise and moral conviction to be willing to do this three evenings a week during the hottest and most uncomfortable months of the year. Nevertheless, a certain number of women persisted, as did the residents and three city inspectors in succession were transferred from the ward because of unsatisfactory services. Still the death rate remained high and the condition seemed little improved throughout the next winter. In sheer desperation, the following spring when the city contracts were awarded for the removal of garbage, with the backing of two well-known business men, I put in a bid for the garbage removal of the nineteenth ward. My paper was thrown out on a technicality but the incident induced the mayor to appoint me the garbage inspector of the ward.

The salary was a thousand dollars a year, and the loss of that political "plum" made a great stir among the politicians. The position was no sinecure whether regarded from the point of view of getting up at six in the morning to see that the men were early at work; or of following the loaded wagons, uneasily dropping their contents at intervals, to their dreary destination at the dump; or of insisting that the contractor must increase the number of his wagons from nine to thirteen and from thirteen to seventeen, although he assured me that he lost money on every one and that the former inspector had let him off with seven; or of taking careless landlords into court because they would not provide the proper garbage receptacles; or of arresting the tenant who tried to make the garbage wagons carry away the contents of his stable.

With the two or three residents who nobly stood by, we set up six of those doleful incinerators which are supposed to burn garbage with the fuel collected in the alley itself. The one factory in town which could utilize old tin cans was a window weight factory, and we deluged that with ten times as many tin cans as it could use—much less would pay for. We made desperate attempts to have the dead animals removed by the contractor who was paid most liberally by the city for that purpose but who, we slowly discovered, always made the police ambulances do the work, delivering the carcasses upon freight cars for shipment to a soap factory in Indiana where they were sold for a good price although the contractor himself was the largest stockholder in the concern. Perhaps our greatest achievement was the discovery of a pavement eighteen inches under the surface in a narrow street, although after it was found we triumphantly discovered a record of its existence in the city archives. The Italians living on the street were much interested but displayed little astonishment, perhaps because they were accustomed to see buried cities exhumed. This pavement became the *casus belli* between myself and the street commissioner when I insisted that its restoration belonged to him, after I had removed the first eight inches of garbage. The matter was finally settled by the mayor himself, who permitted me to drive him to the entrance of the street in what the children called my "garbage phaeton" and who took my side of the controversy. . . .

Source: Addams, Jane. *Twenty Years at Hull-House, with Autobiographical Notes.* New York: MacMillan, 1910, pp. 98–101, 281–287.

NOTE

1. J.W. Leavitt, *The Healthiest City: Milwaukee and the Politics of Health Reform* (Princeton, N.J.: Princeton University Press, 1982), 22.

DOCUMENT
5.10

Health Hazards in the Chemical Trade

"Workers Were Found Eating Their Lunch with Hands . . . Covered . . . with Poisonous Dusts"

January 15, 1913

On March 25, 1911, a fire at the Triangle Waist Company shirt factory in New York City claimed the lives of 145 employees, most of them women and girls. A subsequent investigation of the tragedy revealed that fire safety and other measures to protect workers were almost completely absent at the facility and in most other New York factories. Public outrage over these findings—and the lingering anger about the Triangle fire itself—led the state legislature to approve a full-scale investigation of industrial health and safety. The Factory Investigating Commission was chaired by Robert F. Wagner, and one of its lead investigators was Alice Hamilton, who was fast becoming recognized as one of the country's leading experts on industrial poisons and other environmental hazards in the workplace.

Like other public health advocates of the Progressive Era, Hamilton recognized that unregulated industrialization had wreaked havoc on environmental conditions in the workplace and wider urban settings. Her undisputed expertise on the subject, gained through years of tireless sleuthing, made her one of the most prominent of the reformers calling for the establishment of municipal and statewide boards of health and other municipal and national public health and environment agencies in the opening decades of the twentieth century. Hamilton's insight and research skills are on full display in the following excerpt from her report for the New York Factory Investigating Commission on working conditions in the state's chemical manufacturing industry. Her incisive report anticipates several themes of the later "environmental justice" movement, including the disproportionate impact of dangerous industrial conditions on immigrants, the poor, and the uneducated.

IV. GENERAL SANITARY CONDITIONS.

Buildings:

There are a number of special reasons why this industry is conspicuous for deplorable conditions under which work is carried on.

In the first place, most chemical establishments are located at some distance from the congested city districts, in special factory buildings of a very inferior type. A large number of them are one-story wooden, ramshackle structures, either hastily built for the industry or converted to its use. On account of the rapid evolution of processes accompanied by changing conditions generally in this trade, it seems to be the tendency among most of the owners not to build permanent structures, but to house the manufacture in temporary frame buildings. In most cases there are a number of separate buildings, to which additions are made from time to time with the growth of production.

Fire Hazard:

In matters of fire protection, the buildings themselves are seldom provided with sprinklers or with other modern fire protecting devices. But the danger from fire is probably the least of the dangers in the trade. Here and there, especially among the very large establishments, modern structures were found amply equipped with all modern improvements, including necessary fire protection. At Niagara Falls most of the buildings housing the chemical industry were of recent construction, and many of them were equipped with all the modern fire preventive devices and improvements.

Machinery Protection:

There is some machinery in nearly every chemical plant, but so far as we could discover very little attention is paid in the majority of plants to the proper protection and safeguarding of the dangerous parts.

Lighting:

Very little close work demanding strong light is done in the average chemical establishment, but the dangerous materials employed and processes demand good light. According to our investigators, however, the lighting was found inadequate in 232, or 64.4 per cent, of the factories inspected.

In going through chemical establishments, one often passes through dimly lighted passages where numbers of workers are engaged either in shoveling dangerous mixtures into wheelbarrows or packing various toxic products into barrels, or working around vats, caldrons and tanks filled with dangerous liquids amid clouds of steam or chemical fumes. Any carelessness on the part of these workers, resulting in a spurt of these liquids, might mean a permanent injury. In one of the electrolytic plants at Niagara Falls a worker was observed in a dark corner passing under an iron trough clumsily supported on wooden blocks and filled with hot liquid caustic soda, every drop of which, coming in contact with the body, would produce a painful and permanent injury. The only light was an incandescent bulb held by the workers to illuminate the running of the caustic in the trough and the filling up of the iron drums with the liquid.

Ventilation:

Mechanical ventilation was found in but forty-one out of the 359 chemical plants. This implies great negligence on the part of the owners of these establishments and heads of the establishments, especially when we take into consideration that there is no industry where mechanical ventilation is so imperatively needed as in chemical works. The poisonous materials, the dangerous fumes and gases, the dusty processes and the excessive temperatures which are so common in this industry cannot otherwise be rendered harmless, and the workers cannot otherwise be protected than by proper systems of mechanical ventilation. Windows and skylights have as a rule been found tightly closed, and the special devices installed in 30.6 percent of the shops were in a large number of cases inoperative, inadequate and useless.

Washing Facilities:

In but very few of the establishments was hot water provided for washing, and even after the new law went into effect in October, making the provision of hot water and towels compulsory, our inspectors found that there were many employers who had not heard of the law and others who, having knowledge of it, made no provision for its fulfillment. Wherever facilities were adequate they were often located in separate buildings at some distance from the main factory buildings, so that considerable time was required to reach them.

In none of the establishments inspected was provision made for the compulsory use of the washing facilities. Hand washing before eating was left to the discretion of the workers, with the result that in most of the establishments inspected workers were found eating their lunch with hands unwashed and covered often with poisonous dusts, etc.

Separate lunch rooms were found in only twelve of the establishments; in all others the workers were compelled to eat their food at their place of work, often in the midst of the dust and gases of the workroom. There were but few places, only thirteen, in which separate dressing rooms were found, and in 23 per cent of the above toilets were outside the factory and usually in a very filthy condition. In a chemical factory at Buffalo the toilet consisted of a ramshackle shed over the Buffalo creek, at a distance of 100 to 150 feet from the various parts of the factory; the distance, according to the workers, was often covered during the winter with deep snow, making it very difficult of access. Such toilet accommodations are in many cases found in chemical plants.

Bathrooms were found in but two or three of the establishments. In one of the establishments at Buffalo shower baths were provided, but these were for the use of what the superintendent called the "white" workmen," which classification included only the more skilled American workers, of whom there were but few. Several hundred workers, assumed to be *not white*, were excluded from the use of these baths. In another of the establishments the bathing facilities consisted of three tanks built in the floor of a shed and filled with water of doubtful purity. Each of these tanks was intended for the use of a separate gang of workers. They were provided for the simple reason—as the superintendent explained—that the workers at their day's work became so dirty and covered with dust, colors, etc., that they were not allowed to ride in the street cars.

V. The Specific Dangers of the Chemical Industry

The conditions just described are not peculiar to the nature of the chemical trade, although the general sanitation is worse in this industry than in many others. The importance and extent, however, of the occupational dangers of an industry cannot be measured by the prevailing sanitary conditions, but rather by the specific risks and hazards of the industry itself. The chief dangers to the workers found in the chemical trade may be summed up as follows: gases and fumes, poisons, dusts, and accidental injuries.

All of the more than fifty poisons on the list prepared by Professors Fischer and Sommerfeld and published in the Bulletin of the Bureau of Labor, No. 100, Department of Commerce and Labor, may be found in the various branches of the chemical trade. Where, in other trades, a poisonous ingredient is used occasionally, and dangerous gases and fumes are generated at intervals, in the chemical trade they are regularly present in most of the working processes.

In no other industry is a knowledge of the poisonous products which are handled so necessary to the worker, and yet, surprising as it may seem, in no industry is the ignorance of the worker as to the deadly nature of the substances with which he works so complete. This may be accounted for by the large number of unskilled, densely ignorant foreign laborers who are employed in extremely dangerous processes. Taking advantage of this ignorance of the worker and subjecting him to conditions fraught with fearful danger to his life, may be characterized as the peculiar reproach of the chemical trade. . . .

We find the presence of gases and fumes and various poisons in the manufacture of aniline dyes, in the manufacture of various arsenical colors; in the distilling of benzine; in lacquer, varnish, and India rubber industries; in the manufacture of benzol; in sugar mills; in the refining of tallow, stearin, paraffin and wax; in the production of industrial gas; in lime and brick kilns; in the manufacture of chloride of lime, chlorine and organic chlorine products; in the manufacture of chromium preparations and chrome colors; in potteries and enameling works; in glass factories; in the manufacture of hydrofluoric and other chemical acids; in the manufacture of lead carbonates and other lead colors; in the manufacture of thermometers, barometers, incandescent electric lamps, etc.; in the manufacture of coal-tar colors and explosives; in the production and refining of oil; in anthracite coal-tar distillation; in the manufacture of phosgene, phosphorus, sulphur, sulphuric acid, sulphide of soda and other sodium preparations; and in the manufacture of tar, turpentine oils, etc., etc.

Although this list of industries is a formidable one, it includes but a very small part of those branches of the chemical industry wherein gases and fumes are evolved or poisons produced and handled in manufacture.

As is to be expected, the constant contact with dangerous elements in the trade and the daily familiarity with them breeds a natural contempt on the part of the employers and workers, and a recklessness and carelessness which would be deemed criminal in any other industry. Over and over again during my inspection of chemical plants, I have seen men handling poisonous materials such as carbonate of lead, Paris green, chrome powder, and various caustic products with less thought than if these dangerous substances were sand or flour. In some of the factories visited the face and clothes of the worker and all exposed parts of his body were thickly covered with poisonous dusts or colors without his taking the least precaution against ingesting or inhaling these materials. . . .

Source: George M. Price and Factory Investigating Commission. *Second Report of the State of New York Factory Investigating Commission, Transmitted to the Legislature, January 15, 1913.* Vol. II. Albany: J.B. Lyone Co., 1913, pp. 464–468.

DOCUMENT
5.11

States Rely on Voluntary Industrial Pollution Abatement

"Manufacturers . . . Nearly Always Show a Willingness to Cooperate"

1920

Even in an age of progressive reforms, municipal and state officials responsible for protecting public health and natural resources usually had limited regulatory authority to stop environmentally destructive industrial practices. In many parts of the country, conservation and public health agencies had no other choice but to seek voluntary cooperation from powerful industrial interests in their pollution-reduction efforts. This reality is evident in this excerpt from a report issued by the Department of Conservation of the State of Louisiana in 1920. In this section devoted to stream pollution in the state, the agency seeks to put the best possible face on its virtual powerlessness by noting that big polluters in the state have exhibited a "disposition" to reduce their emissions of pollutants "when it can be done at a reasonable cost."

STREAM POLLUTION

The main damage along these lines in Louisiana comes from sugar house waste, apparently caused by its fermentation and decomposition which is intensified by the decomposition of the fish and other organism[s] killed by it. However, oil refineries, paper factories, alcohol plants, etc., each add its share to our water pollution troubles in this State.

The management of nearly all such plants have exhibited a disposition to treat polluting wastes when it can be done at a reasonable cost. To attain this end, this department has given a great deal of study, and numerous experiments have been made, at our suggestion, by manufacturers who nearly always show a willingness to cooperate with us.

In most cases the shortage of fish food, good spawning beds, natural breeding conditions, etc., etc., is shown to be principally the result of water pollution. Therefore, these problems should be given cost consideration and study by public officials, and in these our Department should cooperate to the full extent of its power, especially where the conservation of fish and game are concerned. When the question of a menace to the health and comfort of our people, and the well being of domestic animals are involved, they should, we think, be left to the consideration of Municipal and State Health Boards.

The National Coast Anti-Pollution League proposes to institute a national clearing house of information on water pollution problems for the service of State departments interested in these matters, and it is the intention of this Department to assist in every way possible.

Source: Louisiana State Department of Conservation. *Fourth Biennial Report, April 1, 1918 to April 1, 1920.* 1920, pp. 96–97.

CHAPTER 6

Environmental Policy–making during the New Deal

1920–1940

During the Roaring Twenties environmental policy–making went into a period of relative slumber. Conservative politicians and judges rolled back the government's already limited regulatory presence in some industries and economic activities, and the American public gave off signals that government activism and civic reform—the hallmarks of the Progressive Era—were no longer top priorities. Eager to put their memories of a brutal world war behind them, Americans identified economic prosperity and material comfort as their goals. The onset of the Great Depression and its stormy economic seas, however, brought activist government back into vogue again. And the man at the tiller of the ship of state, Franklin D. Roosevelt, ushered in a host of "New Deal" policies and programs that had enormous consequences for America and its natural resources. In fact, Roosevelt's New Deal reflected a heartfelt belief that sound environmental policies were integral to any blueprint for a lasting and sustainable economic recovery.

ENVIRONMENTAL POLICY TRENDS IN POSTWAR AMERICA

During World War I, American resources were funneled toward one overriding goal: military victory. To that end, funding and staffing for Progressive environmental programs was reduced or extinguished altogether, and other resources were diverted for military needs. Some national parks, for example, were used as military training grounds and troop bases, and timbering and mining on public lands intensified to meet wartime demands for raw materials.

After the war concluded, American voters elected three presidents in succession—Warren G. Harding, Calvin Coolidge, and Herbert Hoover—who preached an anti-regulatory, pro-business mantra that was at odds with the Progressive faith in legislation and activist government as tools of social engineering and improvement. The governing philosophy of these men was to reduce federal involvement in America's economic affairs and give industrialists, entrepreneurs, and investors an open field in which to operate. As Coolidge himself famously summarized, "[T]he chief business of America is business." This attitude manifested itself in an abiding faith in the free market and a sympathetic ear for industries that framed increased natural resource exploitation as a necessity of economic expansion.

A variety of stakeholders—labor groups, struggling farmers, conservationists—objected to these trends, but their complaints had little impact on a wider American public that was thirsty for a measure of domestic peace, prosperity, and stability. In March 1924, for instance, the president of the Izaak Walton League, a sportsmen's organization dedicated to protecting fish and their habitat, expressed frustration to the Coolidge administration when an anti-pollution bill was tabled. "Official Washington has no knowledge that the American people give a damn about pollution," responded Herbert Hoover, who was Coolidge's secretary of commerce at the time. "And until they do care and let their State governments and Federal government know that they do care, there will be no great advance as to pollution."[1]

American courts followed much the same pattern, issuing rulings that struck down or limited Progressive Era laws and regulations that had been crafted as instruments of social change and environmental protection. For example, judges redefined "reasonable use" and "reasonable practices"—admittedly amorphous measuring sticks for monitoring industrial activity—to give factories greater leeway to engage in polluting activities. Reluctant to classify pollution as a health hazard or community nuisance that necessitated government regulation, they adopted a de facto "cost-benefit" equation in considering these cases. Judges weighed the damage of pollution to individuals, communities, and affected businesses against the economic burden to the industry—or the larger community or society—of abating its pollution. In most cases, the courts sided with industrial interests.[2] Courts of the 1920s also rolled back federal and state authority to regulate activities on private property. They sided with mining and timber companies, who asserted that some government regulations amounted to a "taking" of their property rights under the Fifth Amendment, and they repeatedly found for private citizens and corporations arguing for the primacy of private property rights over government regulation.[3]

The one notable exception to this trend could be found in the U.S. Supreme Court case of *Euclid v. Ambler Realty*. This momentous 1926 ruling gave municipalities the legal authority to impose zoning laws and regulate land use in the public interest (see Document 6.3). Zoning laws, defined by one scholar as the "practice of allocating different areas of cities for different uses, much as rooms in a house serve different functions,"[4] thus emerged as a common tool used by city planners to segregate polluting industries, refuse dumps, and other potential public health hazards from residential populations.

The timing of this ruling was important because it came during a period when American suburbs were exploding in size and population. Some of these suburbs followed the streetcar and railroad lines that radiated out of city centers like the spokes of a bicycle tire. Streetcar lines were especially popular during the first two decades of the century—by 1915 Los Angeles alone had developed 1,200 miles of street car lines[5]—and became economic lifelines for satellite communities of commuters. Other suburbs crystallized into being all along the periphery of urban metropolises, creating a pattern of annual outward growth akin to the rings of a tree.

Both patterns of suburbanization of the countryside—or sprawl, as it would later come to be known—were greatly influenced by the arrival of the automobile age. During the late nineteenth and early twentieth centuries, the development of the gasoline-powered internal combustion engine sparked the ascension of oil companies and automobile manufacturers into the upper echelons of American industry. In 1900 the entire U.S. auto industry produced only 4,000 automobiles; twenty-nine years later, annual unit sales of cars, buses, and trucks in the United States reached 5.33 million, as mass production, mass advertising, and credit and installment payment plans all became part of the commercial landscape. The ratio of automobiles to Americans during this same period surged from 1 automobile for every 265 people to 1 for every 5.[6] General Motors, Ford

Motor Company, and other automakers also became leading clients for other industries during this time, consuming huge percentages of the nation's rubber (85 percent), aluminum (25 percent), iron and steel (25 percent), and hardwood (10 percent). Escalating demand for gasoline, meanwhile, helped lift American oil production from 46 million barrels annually in 1890 to more than one billion barrels a year by 1930.[7]

By the 1920s, the spectacular popularity of the automobile was sounding the death knell for passenger rail trains and trolley cars and fueling the creation of a vast new automobile service regime of hotels, restaurants, and gas stations. "As [the automobile] came, it changed the face of America," summarized journalist Frederick Lewis Allen in 1931. "In thousands of towns, at the beginning of the [1920s] a single traffic officer at the junction of Main Street and Central Street had been sufficient for the control of traffic. By the end of the decade, what a difference!—red and green lights, blinkers, one-way streets, boulevard stops, stringent and yet more stringent parking ordinances—and still a shining flow of traffic that backed up for blocks along Main Street every Saturday and Sunday afternoon."[8] Railroads and other commercial carriers also suffered mightily from this transportation revolution because freight trucks possessed an agility and flexibility that they simply could not match.

The rise of automobiles and trucks also sparked a veritable frenzy of road building in the United States during the 1920s. Automobile-owning commuters, business owners, farm families, and vacationers all clamored for new roadways to improve connections to home, work, school, church, and recreational destinations. In regard to the latter, the automobile sparked a particularly large surge of popular interest in outdoor recreation activities in parks and national forests. The environmental impact of the roadways themselves, meanwhile, attracted virtually no notice from policymakers or the general public.

These legions of private auto and truck owners were joined by a coalition of automobile, oil, tire, land development, homebuilding, and road-construction interests, all of whom saw the potential profits that could accrue from new roads and highways. Lawmakers were quick to respond to these pressures, crafting a wealth of publicly financed road construction bills. These ranged from state-level bills that approved the construction of specific roadways to broad national legislation such as the 1921 Federal Highway Act, which provided generous federal subsidies to states for new roads, including interstate routes. And with each new automobile sold, gas station opened, and highway mile surveyed, development pressures increased on rural hinterlands, which were subject to virtually no land use regulations or restrictions. States scrambled to accommodate these changes by adopting new allocation plans for water and other natural resources. But in many cases, unrelenting surges in demand would eventually overwhelm these hurriedly constructed schemes (see Document 6.1).

ENVIRONMENTAL HEALTH IN THE WORKPLACE

The laissez faire governing temperament of the Harding, Coolidge, and Hoover administrations also extended to the realm of industrial pollution and safety. All three administrations maintained existing federal programs and regulations in areas of public health, such as food and drug inspection, sanitation and waste disposal, and infectious disease control, but these institutions were of limited scope and authority. The prime responsibility for monitoring industrial activity lay with state and municipal public health agencies that had been created or strengthened from the 1890s through the 1910s as part of larger campaigns of progressive reform.

Businesses probably received the widest latitude from local, state, and federal authorities in the realm of industrial hygiene and occupational health. The Public Health Service (PHS) and other federal agencies concerned with worker health in the 1920s had little authority to regulate the use of toxic materials or otherwise intervene on factory floors on behalf of workers. As a result, much of the control of workplace hazards was left to voluntary industry safety programs, which were frequently nonexistent or indifferently pursued. Authorities at the local and state levels had greater regulatory power than their federal counterparts, but they were often reluctant to exercise it for fear that it would prompt an exodus of industry to neighboring cities or states with less "intrusive" environmental and workplace regulations. Fears of slashed budget appropriations or other forms of retribution from political allies of targeted industries also served to reduce the zeal of regulators.

In the 1920s, then, research into industrial poisons and disposal of toxins fell mostly to private advocacy groups such as the National Consumers League and the Workers' Health Bureau, who were in turn aided by prominent public health researchers such as Alice Hamilton and C. E. A. Winslow. These organizations carried out important research into the environmental and health hazards of benzol, lead, radium, silica dust, and other industrial chemicals and byproducts, often releasing findings that sharply contrasted with the reassuring reports of industry-sponsored scientists. The Workers' Health Bureau, in fact, explicitly defined itself as a "research adjunct to the union movement for health and safety."[9]

The scientists and researchers recruited by the Bureau and other groups examined environmental conditions faced by employees in the coal, glass, textile, petrochemical, automobile, and other industries. Their painstaking research became a valuable tool in political lobbying for new workplace regulations, and it helped individual unions negotiate important safety provisions in labor contracts. Yet throughout the 1920s, the onus remained on public health activists and government agencies to prove that some industrial practices and chemicals were dangerous to workers or the public, rather than on businesses to prove that they were safe.

The main instance in which this seemingly unalterable dynamic was threatened came in the mid-1920s, when the introduction of tetraethyl leaded gasoline quickly metastasized into a public relations nightmare for the automobile and petroleum industries. Government scientists and independent researchers alike warned that the product could result in higher levels of lead poisoning and environmental pollution on an epic scale **(see Document 6.2)**. But federal authorities ultimately did nothing to restrict the sale of leaded gasoline, which became standard automotive fuel for the next half-century. Continued government inaction in the face of clear evidence of environmental danger was a source of enormous frustration to researchers such as Hamilton. As she wrote in 1925, however, she remained stubbornly hopeful "that the day is not far off when we shall take the next step and investigate a new danger in industry before it is put into use, before any fatal harm has been done to workmen, and the question will be treated as one belonging to the public health from the very outset, not after its importance has been demonstrated on the bodies of workmen."[10]

Hamilton's patience was rewarded in the 1930s, when Roosevelt installed his New Deal vision of government activism in service to ordinary Americans. Admittedly, the philosophical orientation of the Public Health Service did not change appreciably during this time. It continued to see scientific research into infectious disease and other public health threats as its primary mission, and it maintained its longtime preference for assisting and advising—rather than regulating—industry and state and municipal health departments. But New Deal agencies such as the Federal Emergency Relief Administration (FERA), Works Progress Administration (WPA), and Public Works Administration (PWA) all provided funding, assistance, and resources (such as new hospitals and laboratories) to the PHS. These new assets enabled the PHS to expand existing operations and roll out new programs.[11]

Much bigger changes were in the offing at the U.S. Department of Labor, which transformed itself into a powerful overseer and regulator of industrial practices and worker safety under the New Deal administration of Secretary of Labor Frances Perkins. The first woman in U.S. history to hold a Cabinet post, Perkins left no doubt as to her views on the importance of monitoring and enforcing environmental safety measures in industrial America. "It seems the cart has always been before the horse in industrial hygiene in this country," Perkins observed early in her tenure. "In the past few years, a considerable amount of groundwork has been done in the way of valuable research and scientific study. I am anxious to see this translated into action. . . . The need for stimulating action in controlling and preventing harmful exposure in a wide range of industrial operations can hardly be overemphasized."[12]

COMPETING VISIONS AND AGENCY RIVALRIES

The divergent philosophies and roles of the PHS and Labor Departments in the 1930s were not crippling in and of themselves, but the agencies did suffer at times from poor interagency coordination of resources and efforts. "Because of their lack of involvement in regulation, Public Health could not develop an adequate program of industrial hygiene," explained historians David Rosner and Gerald Markowitz. "Similarly, the Department of Labor would suffer from a lack of technical expertise at a time when production processes, especially in the sophisticated petrochemical industry that blossomed in the postwar years, would increasingly limit their ability to control or regulate the workplace. Thus one agency had the expertise while the other agency had the ideology and the ability to act on it."[13]

The jockeying for advantage that took place between PHS and Labor was not an isolated incident. Turf battles between federal natural resource management agencies also erupted during the interwar years, and this made environmental policy–making a much more difficult and hazardous undertaking than ever before. The reasons for the escalating interagency tensions were threefold. First, federal environmental agencies that had blossomed into being during the Progressive Era enjoyed significant day-to-day autonomy and jurisdictional authority to manage the natural resources in their kingdoms as they saw fit. This relative freedom conditioned some managers and other personnel to resist compromise when working with other arms of the federal government. Second, the administrators who ran these agencies naturally wanted to increase the size, influence, and responsibilities of the departments they led, partly for career reasons but also out of a sense of personal pride or genuine belief in the agency's mission. Because public domain lands and resources were finite, this growth could sometimes take place only at the expense of other land management agencies. Third, resource management agencies recognized that their future vitality hinged on the cultivation of allies and benefactors. These interest groups ranged from politically connected industrial developers of environmental commodities (stockmen, timber companies, water and land developers, railroads, petrochemical and mining interests, and so on) to sportsmen's groups, wildlife conservation organizations, and wilderness advocates, who seemed to be growing in public stature and political influence with each passing year (**see Document 6.4**). "These constituencies thus came to have as much influence over the agencies as the agencies had over them: the agencies controlled resource use rights, but the resource user groups could mobilize either congressional support or opposition to the agencies themselves," explained historian Richard N. L. Andrews. "The environmental management agencies as a group . . . evolved from expert organizations serving a common public interest to fragmented subgovernments closely allied with their primary political constituencies."[14] This dynamic, born during the 1920s and 1930s, continues to cast a long shadow over American environmental policy–making in the twenty-first century.

A few of the rivalries born during this time, such as the one between the U.S. Corps of Engineers and the Bureau of Reclamation over "ownership" of the nation's rivers and associated water projects, simmered for decades without ever reaching full boil. And others, such as clashes between the Departments of Agriculture and Interior over the 1934 Taylor Grazing Act and placement of the Soil Conservation Service, did not leave lasting legacies of distrust or acrimony. But one feud—between the Interior Department's National Park Service (NPS) and the Agriculture Department's U.S. Forest Service—became "the most celebrated interbureau rivalry in all government."[15] In fact, this intense competition for control of vast tracts of the public domain greatly influenced the historical development of both agencies—and the course of American conservation policy.

THE FOREST SERVICE–PARK SERVICE RIVALRY

The contentious relationship between the two agencies actually dates back to the 1916 formation of the National Park Service, which legendary forester Gifford Pinchot and other Forest Service administrators actively opposed. Once the National Park Service was up and running over their objections, tensions between the two bureaus became almost inevitable. New national parks were likely to be created at least in part by transfers of national forest land to the Park Service, a source of significant apprehension to Forest Service officials and rank and file alike. Moreover, the work of the two agencies was grounded in strikingly different management philosophies. Whereas the Forest Service advocated sensible commercial use of lands based on scientific research, "the Park Service anchored itself in nineteenth-century transcendental views of nature as a place of spiritual encounter," explained scholar Edward R. Grumbine. "The political feuding between the two agencies [was] born of their different approaches to the instrumental use of wild nature."[16]

The rivalry developed slowly, however. During the 1920s, the Forest Service skillfully trimmed its sails to float atop the anti-regulation, pro-business waves rolling across the nation's capital at that time. Administrators devoted their energies to forestry research programs that were popular with timber companies and other private land owners; joint initiatives with state forestry agencies; and maintenance of policies to keep stock grazers, mining firms, and other politically powerful constituencies satisfied. The National Park Service, meanwhile, spent most of its first decade and a half of existence defining its policies, establishing its administrative infrastructure, and conducting studies of potential areas for inclusion in the fledgling system. Perhaps most important, early park directors such as Stephen Mather spent this time honing an operating model bristling with elements that would appeal to both the general public and congressmen, including wilderness conservation, recreation opportunities, and easy road and rail access. "Our national parks are practically lying fallow, and only await proper development to bring them into their own," declared Mather.[17]

Mather's hopes for the agency were realized during the New Deal, which dramatically changed the operating and funding environments in which both the Park Service and the Forest Service worked. Indeed, the arrival of Franklin D. Roosevelt and his New Dealers in 1933 radically altered the framework of existence for *all* federal resource management agencies. Conservation program directors who had once been starved for funding suddenly found themselves with ample financial and personnel resources to carry out their projects. At the same time, the New Deal also unleashed resource *development* projects of previously undreamed of scale, such as great dam and aqueduct projects that tamed the rivers of the West.

These exciting new opportunities also brought daunting challenges, however. "Interagency rivalries increased after 1933," confirmed historian Donald Pisani. "The growth of old programs and the advent of new ones, the personal ambitions of strong bureau chiefs, and the tension between conservation and work relief intensified traditional fears and suspicions."[18] Some agencies prospered more than others during this period. For example, the National Park Service under director Horace Albright took full advantage of its accrued political and popular support to expand its holdings and influence. But this growth often occurred at the expense of the Forest Service, just as Pinchot and others had feared. Again and again during this decade, national parks were carved out of national forest lands. Iconic parks such as Grand Teton, Great Smoky Mountains, Olympic, Kings Canyon, and Shenandoah were all created through these transfers. In 1935, meanwhile, Congress passed legislation enabling the Park Service to expand its holdings to include all national recreation areas and national historic sites, responsibility for which had previously been scattered among an assortment of federal departments. These developments were politically popular with everyone but industrial commodity users, their legislative allies, and the Forest Service itself. From the perspective of Forest Service personnel, these transfers were nothing more than brazen raids on a venerable, proven bureau by an upstart agency.

By the late 1930s the National Park Service was basking in the glow of its own ascendance. Not only was it steadily expanding the national park system, it was also overseeing the development of virtually every state park system in the union. The Forest Service, meanwhile, felt besieged, despite the fact that it was actually gaining land in the eastern United States thanks to various New Deal initiatives to acquire private forest land. It lost numerous big parcels of forestland to the Park Service outright and became trapped in a perpetually defensive political posture on other fronts. The Forest Service, for example, had to fend off proposals from Mather to establish Park Service jurisdiction over recreational programs on *national forest lands.* And in 1937 the Forest Service and the wider Agriculture Department barely beat back a proposal by Interior Secretary Harold Ickes to unite all major federal, soil, water, and forest conservation programs under an expanded Interior Department that would be renamed the Department of Conservation.

Forest Service officials tried to minimize Park Service advances by expanding their own long-neglected wilderness preservation and recreational programs, both of which were proving enormously popular with the ascendant generation of automobile-loving Americans. They had little choice in the matter because, as analyst Jesse Steiner explained in the 1933 government survey *Americans at Play,* "the improvement in means of travel [has created an] increasing demand for great open spaces set apart for the enjoyment of those outdoor diversions which have become so eagerly sought as a means of escape from the noise and confusion of urban life."[19] In addition, the Forest Service rallied its traditional clients—the timber, grazing, and mining industries and their allies in Washington, D.C.—to help defend its territorial parapets from the land-acquisition maneuverings of the NPS. These longstanding constituencies needed little convincing to take up arms, given that lands designated as wilderness or national parks were in most cases padlocked against the commercial extractive activities upon which they relied (see Document 6.11).

These efforts to ward off further Park Service incursions through increased preservation, however, were greeted with dismay by industrial clients who did not want to see commercially valuable forest lands cordoned off from development. The Forest Service thus found itself in the impossible position of trying to placate client groups who had diametrically opposed views on what constituted wise and appropriate forest management policy. To be sure, they were not alone in this regard. Similar conundrums were emerging for other state and federal land and resource management bureaus as well during the first half of the twentieth century. All across the country, in fact, the rising tide of interest in outdoor recreation, wildlife protection, and wilderness preservation posed a formidable threat to the traditional hegemony of commercial considerations in land and resource management. Nonetheless, the sheer size, majesty, and economic value of the Forest Service's holdings ensured that the glare of the spotlight would remain squarely trained on that agency above virtually all others.

The rivalry between the Forest Service and the Park Service has undergone many further permutations since the New Deal era. There have even been periods of relative cordiality between the two agencies, especially with the advent of environmental management plans that emphasize the advantages of treating adjacent park and national forest lands as a single ecologically interdependent entity. But tensions have always persisted. As one Park Service historian observed, "the long history of competing and conflicting objectives . . . developed in each agency a keen but wary respect for the ability of the other to stir up mischief."[20] And the reality is that the rapid mid-century expansion of America's national park system *did* pivot to a significant extent on the transfer of national forest lands to the Park Service—by 1960, 30 percent of the national parklands had been created from tracts once under the supervision of the Forest Service.

New Deal Conservation and the Civilian Conservation Corps

Environmental politics and policies changed in other far-reaching ways during the New Deal. When Roosevelt left the governor's mansion in Albany, New York, for the White House in early 1933, he was already known as one of the country's most conservation-minded politicians. So as he confronted the staggering challenges of the Great Depression, he looked for ways in which environmental policy initiatives could help revitalize and stabilize the floundering economy. And in keeping with their overarching "all hands on deck" approach to fighting the Depression, Roosevelt and his New Deal lieutenants displayed a willingness to enact a variety of resource policy initiatives in this realm. If the proposal seemed at all likely to create jobs, stimulate economic activity, and improve natural resources—either through restoration or reengineering—then Roosevelt was willing to give it a try. And he was blessed with talented cabinet heads, such as Agriculture Secretary Henry A. Wallace and Interior Secretary Harold Ickes, who shared his environmental policy vision and his sense of urgency.

The environmental programs that sprang out of this fertile institutional soil were of a magnitude explicitly designed to match the scale of the task. New Deal policies and agencies were crafted to heal Great Lakes forests and rivers shattered by the excesses of turn-of-the-century timbering; reverse the deterioration of farmland and grazing pastures in the South and West; harness the power of the nation's mighty rivers for electricity, irrigation, and drinking water; install wastewater treatment plants and other pollution abatement technologies in urban centers; and expand outdoor recreation opportunities for all Americans.

In many cases, the grim Depression-era landscape actually eased implementation of these conservation initiatives. For example, one New Deal goal was to expand national and state forest systems. Tax-reverted lands became a cornerstone of these efforts. Twenty-six new national forests were established in the East during the 1930s,[21] and abandoned, purchased, and condemned lands were cobbled together to make numerous state forests. In Michigan alone, more than 2.2 million acres of tax-reverted lands were bestowed on the state's conservation department in the 1930s and early 1940s. The agency sold or leased some of this land to bolster the state treasury, but it also used this windfall to create new state forests, wildlife refuges, and game areas.[22]

Other New Deal measures to yoke together conservation priorities and economic goals were even more sweeping. Of these, the Civilian Conservation Corps (CCC) had perhaps the most wide-reaching and enduring impact. The brainchild of Roosevelt and his fellow New Dealers, the CCC was envisioned as a program that would put America's unemployed young men to work preserving and restoring the nation's natural resources. Within weeks of Roosevelt's inauguration, Congress passed a bill laying out conditions for "Emergency Conservation Work" that reflected the president's desires, and on April 5, 1933, Roosevelt used the authority of this act to issue an executive order ushering the CCC into existence (**see Document 6.6**).

Almost three million young men passed through the CCC program, which was headed first by Robert Fechner and then by James McEntee, during its nine-year existence. In return for modest paychecks, housing in rough tents and barracks, and working environments that bore more than a passing resemblance to military units, enrollees spent long but rewarding days restoring the forests, rivers, lakes, and rangelands of America. They carried out this work under the supervision of two Agriculture Department bureaus—the Forest Service and Soil Conservation Service—and Interior's National Park Service. All told, 71 percent of CCC camps were affiliated with the Department of Agriculture, whereas another 26.5 percent were assigned to the Department of the Interior; the remaining 2.5 percent were under the supervision of the War Department.[23]

The environmental legacy of these CCC camps remains a source of wonderment to historians. All told, the Corps planted more than 2 billion trees on public and private lands; executed anti-erosion measures on 40 million acres of rangelands and fields; built 800 new state parks and 10,000 reservoirs; created more than 3,000 beaches; planted millions of hatchery fish in rivers and lakes; installed an estimated 13,000 miles of hiking trails; built hundreds of state forest, national forest, and national park campgrounds; helped expand the nation's systems of wildlife refuges and sanctuaries; and implemented forestry programs to combat the "Three Horsemen" of fire, insects, and disease. "The billions of trees planted or protected, the millions of acres saved from the ravages of soil erosion or the depredations of flooded rivers, the hundreds of parks and recreation areas which were developed, are a permanent testimony to the success of Corps work," wrote

CCC historian John Salmond. "They constitute a legitimate contribution to the heritage of every American."[24]

Corps camps were eventually established in every state and U.S. territory, in part because the 1933 legislation laying the groundwork for the CCC included provisions explicitly authorizing the Roosevelt administration to acquire private land "by purchase, donation, condemnation, or otherwise." Federal authorities recognized that this authority was not really needed in the West, where vast tracts of federal property already existed, but it was wielded with zeal east of the Mississippi, where public land was scarce—and where the bulk of the nation's unemployed lived. Roosevelt and the New Dealers used the law as a launching board for a sustained campaign of land acquisition. In the end, more than 20 million acres of private land, almost all of it in the East, were purchased. These acquisitions, used to create a plethora of new national parks and refuges, enlarged the federal government's total land holdings by 15 percent during the New Deal era.[25]

By all accounts, the Civilian Conservation Corps held a special place in Roosevelt's heart. He called the CCC "the greatest peacetime movement this country has ever seen," adding that "it is my belief that what is being accomplished [through the program] will conserve our natural resources, create future national wealth and prove of moral and spiritual value not only to those of you who are taking part, but to the rest of the country as well."[26] Many other Americans agreed. In fact, the CCC—or "Roosevelt's Tree Army," as newspapers liked to call it—was in many ways the crown jewel of the New Deal. Even vehement critics of other New Deal programs praised the CCC camps for boosting local economies and demanding hard work in exchange for federal assistance.

WATER PROJECTS OF THE NEW DEAL ERA

Other New Deal programs and initiatives focused on America's natural resources were more concerned with environmental *transformation* than with conservation or restoration. Agencies such as the Works Progress Administration greatly altered urban centers and surrounding landscapes through the construction of metropolitan sewage treatment and water supply systems; hundreds of viaducts and bridges; and an estimated 600,000 miles of highways, streets, and roads.[27] The Agricultural Adjustment Act (AAA), passed in May 1933, tried to reshape the face of American farming through increased regulation of crop cultivation and livestock production. Elsewhere, the Tennessee Valley Authority (TVA) used hydroelectric dams and new soil conservation methods to transform the economic, social, and ecological character of the entire seven-state Tennessee River basin.

But the most enduring symbols of the New Deal era of public works projects were the monumental multi-purpose dams built by the Bureau of Reclamation and U.S. Army Corps of Engineers in the 1930s. These early dams—Hoover, Grand Coulee, Bonneville, Shasta, Fort Peck, and others—owed their existence to a constellation of factors that converged in their favor. One cause was a broad and longstanding public perception that outfitting rivers with locks, levees, dams, and other machinery for economic reasons was legitimate—even desirable—even when negative consequences such as declining fish populations were taken into account. Another factor was the growing enthusiasm for cheap hydroelectric power to light up the urban apartment buildings, farmhouses, and factory floors of the West. A third factor was the development of technology providing for long-distance transmission of electric power. A fourth factor was the onset of the Great Depression, which became the catalyst for a dramatic escalation in dam building and other public works endorsed by Roosevelt (see Document 6.8). Population growth and

A spate of major public works projects during the New Deal included such significant water reclamation projects as the Grand Coulee Dam in Washington which was completed in 1941. Today it is the largest producer of hydroelectric power in the United States.

attendant increases in demand for water for drinking and irrigation also played significant roles. A final major contributor was the 1933 establishment of the Public Works Administration, the New Deal agency that provided the funding for many of the nation's most ambitious water development projects (although not Hoover Dam, which was actually authorized by President Coolidge in 1928 and built from 1931 to 1935).

The groundwork for many of the New Deal water projects was actually laid back in the 1920s, when a succession of economically damaging floods raked the eastern United States and devastated riparian communities. In 1927 these flood events, which had become ever more frequent as a result of decades of counterproductive tinkering with river channels and flood plains by the U.S. Army Corps of Engineers, prompted Congress to ask the Corps to take a fresh look at the navigation, hydropower, flood control, and irrigation potential of the country's major river basins. They returned in the early 1930s with the exhaustive "308 Reports," which became the basis for many of the water development schemes that were set in motion during the 1930s and 1940s.

Prior to the Depression, the Bureau of Reclamation had been a relatively low-profile agency primarily oriented to irrigation works in the West, whereas the politically connected Corps of Engineers had focused its efforts on bolstering navigation and shipping, predominantly in the East. The disparity in power and influence between the two agencies diminished considerably in the 1930s, however. Most of the big rivers targeted for hydroelectric dams and large-scale diversions were located in the Reclamation-friendly West. In addition, western politicians worked their way into influential positions on committees responsible for water project authorizations. These factors leveled the playing field between the two agencies, setting the stage for epic bouts of political wrangling for bureaucratic control of water projects on the Missouri and other river systems with high development potential. These struggles were further complicated by private electric power utilities that fought bitterly against expanding federal ownership of hydroelectric power plants.

In the final analysis, however, both the Bureau and the Corps embraced the Herculean task of reengineering the plumbing of America's mightiest river basins, and there was plenty of work to go around. "Putting people to work and dispersing money into the economy became a goal into itself," noted one study. "At times, construction on New Deal dam projects actually began even before engineers had completed detailed planning and design."[28] Indeed, titanic water projects such as California's Central Valley Project and Grand Coulee Dam (carried out by the Bureau of Reclamation) and Bonneville Dam and Fort Peck Dam (built by the U.S. Army Corps of Engineers) came to be seen by citizens and politicians alike as essential tools in the struggle to resurrect the American economy. "Where the whitecaps toss on the [Columbia River's] expanse of green," wrote one journalist in 1939, "enough horsepower goes to waste to move a thousand trains and light a million homes." The Grand Coulee Dam, he asserted, would finally put that mighty flood to work on mankind's behalf:

> About Grand Coulee there is a universality of appeal which no one can resist. The biggest structure on the planet; making the desert bloom; orchards where now sagebrush grows; power on the last frontier; the final wilderness reclaimed. These are phrases and objectives and aspirations which find acceptance among men of widely conflicting faiths.[29]

The zeal for dam building received even greater momentum with the passage of the Flood Control Act of 1936, which declared flood control to be a function of the federal government and guaranteed that future "flood control projects" (i.e., multipurpose dams and associated infrastructure) would be paid for in their entirety by the U.S. Treasury (**see Document 6.9**). Congressmen rushed to take advantage of this new opportunity to curry favor with their constituents, inserting pork-barrel projects for their districts wherever possible. In the ensuing four decades, the U.S. Army Corps of Engineers built more than 400 dams across the country, and the Bureau of Reclamation contributed another 300.[30] Some of these projects paid enormous economic dividends and became pillars of regional development, but others displaced political powerless Native Americans and other rural residents, and several were little more than testaments to political corruption and opportunism. Even the worthiest projects took a toll on the natural environment. Riparian woodlands were sacrificed for reservoirs; salmon populations plunged on dammed-up rivers; and untold numbers of grizzly, elk, cougars, and migratory waterfowl were destroyed by the transformation of wild valleys and plains into what one critic called "banal palatinate[s] of industrial agriculture."[31] Discussion of these negative impacts was minimal during the New Deal and post–World War II eras. By the 1960s, however, the ecological consequences of four successive decades of intensive dam building and water re-engineering would become a subject of intense public debate.

RESPONDING TO THE DUST BOWL

Yet another front in the New Deal campaign to reinvent the American landscape in the name of economic recovery was found out on the Great Plains. For decades farmers, ranchers, lawmakers, government bureaucrats, and boosters had mistreated this vast land—albeit sometimes unknowingly—in their quest for higher crop yields, fatter cattle,

Land-use practices combined with a multi-year drought in the mid-1930s produced devastating results in the Great Plains. Hundreds of millions of tons of top soil eroded away in powerful dust storms that shocked the nation and prompted swift action by President Roosevelt and Congress.

and larger communities. Millions of acres of grasslands had been sacrificed to plant wheat and other cash crops or to feed sheep, cattle, and horses. Fields and rangelands were used so intensively that soil quality plummeted in many parts of the Plains, and wind and water erosion became serious problems **(see Document 6.10)**.

So when a multi-year drought descended on the Great Plains in the mid-1930s, the region and its inhabitants suffered mightily. Rivers and lakes withered, entire crops failed, and towering dust storms rolled across the landscape with apocalyptic regularity. Some of these "dusters," as they were known, removed hundreds of millions of tons of topsoil from the Plains in a single day and carried them all the way to the Atlantic, where they dusted the decks of oceangoing vessels. "The area seems doomed to become in dreary reality the Great American Desert shown on early maps," wrote one Kansas wheat farmer who became trapped in this epic environmental disaster. "This was something new and different from anything I had ever experienced before—a destroying force beyond my wildest imagination."[32]

Many Americans shared the Kansas wheat farmer's fear that careless stewardship had ruined the Great Plains forever. And some saw it as an omen of future ecological peril for all Americans. Economist Stuart Chase, who first coined the term "New Deal," was thunderstruck by the malignant black lesion that had materialized in the nation's midsection. "North America before the coming of the white man was rich with growing things, incredibly beautiful to look upon, wild and tempestuous in its storm and climatic changes, and perhaps the most bountifully endowed by nature of all the world's continents," he wrote in 1935. "Today, after three centuries of occupation, the old forest, the old grass lands have almost completely disappeared. Desert lands have broadened. A dust desert is forming east of the Rockies on the Great Plains where firm grass once stood."[33]

But Roosevelt and Congress acted decisively to try to reverse the shattered environment and economies of the affected states. In 1934 the first meaningful federal efforts to "stop injury to the public grazing lands" were imposed with the passage of the Taylor Grazing Act. This legislation established a federal Grazing Service (which merged with the General Land Office in 1946 to create the Bureau of Land Management) to administer eighty million acres of federal rangeland. As it turned out, the legislation was flawed in several important respects. The act and subsequent amendments, for instance, established advisory boards that became dominated by powerful ranching interests. These influential boards, backed by advocates in Congress, placed a much higher priority on industry production than conservation, and this prioritization came to be reflected in Grazing Service policies. In essence, the agency became subservient to the very interests it was created to control.

A far more effective federal response to the Dust Bowl came in the form of the Soil Conservation Service (SCS) and its indomitable director, Hugh Hammond Bennett (**see Document 6.7**). Under Bennett's direction, the Soil Conservation Service established local "conservancy districts" that ultimately encompassed virtually every acre of American farmland—more than 200 million acres in all. Under SCS guidance, these districts implemented more environmentally sustainable farming practices, such as crop rotation, terracing, and irrigation methods, which minimized erosion.

Bennett was further aided in these yeoman efforts by huge infusions of workers from the Civilian Conservation Corps and the Soil Conservation and Domestic Allotment Act of 1936, which created the Agricultural Conservation Program (ACP). This program gave farmers financial incentives to shift their emphasis from soil-depleting crops such as corn and cotton to soil-conserving crops and grasses. It also empowered the SCS to initiate numerous small water projects on behalf of struggling farm communities. Finally, the SCS took some exhausted farmlands out of circulation and supplemented others with greenbelts of native trees and grasses that could help keep topsoil in place. Together, these programs became the leading edge of a sustained federal response that not only restored millions of acres of agricultural land to commercial viability, but also instilled in rural America a greater awareness that long-term resource conservation was in its own self-interest.

CHANGING PERSPECTIVES ON WILDLIFE

Perceptions changed from 1920 to 1940 in the realm of wildlife conservation as well. During the opening decades of the twentieth century, federal agencies charged with stewardship of America's environmental treasures became virtual wildlife extermination services for ranchers, sportsmen, and other politically powerful constituencies. The prime focus of these extermination efforts was predator species such as wolves, coyotes, and mountain lions, which ranchers loathed for their depredations on livestock and sportsmen hated for their diet of elk, moose, deer, and other prized game. Policies and regulations of the National Park Service, the National Forest Service, and other departments all supported predator eradication, and the Agriculture Department's Bureau of Biological Survey shifted much of its orientation and resources from wildlife study and bird protection to predatory animal extermination. By 1928 the Bureau of Biological Survey was deploying 500 employees in its predator control programs, and its own reports were proudly trumpeting its goal of "absolute extermination" of the wolf.[34] State resource agencies also contributed to the eradication mission.

The tools used to vanquish targeted species included bullets, steel traps, and huge outlays of poison, and they were spectacularly effective. In Wyoming alone, officials with the Biological Survey reported that from 1916 to 1927, hunters under the direction of state and federal authorities destroyed more than 63,000 wolves, coyotes, bobcats, bears, mountain lions, and lynxes and poisoned hundreds of thousands more predators whose bodies were never found.[35]

In the 1920s, however, a growing number of wildlife conservationists, scientists, and public officials condemned the officially sanctioned annihilation of the country's big predators. Some opined that wolves, bears, and cougars were glorious creatures in their own right, whereas others cautioned that the wholesale slaughter of predators was having unintended and dire consequences for natural resources that were universally valued. They warned, for example, that surging deer populations—which predators had histori-cally kept in check—were severely overgrazing fragile land areas. "It has not been appreci-ated," asserted former Yellowstone ranger Milton P. Skinner in 1924, "that we need these predatory and fur-bearing animals alive and living their normal lives, and . . . that we are slowly losing a valuable possession."[36]

A reassessment of federal policies toward predators was thus undertaken by some agencies. In 1931, for example, the National Park Service announced major changes in its predator policies (see Document 6.5). The greatest laggard in this realm was probably the Biological Survey, which had enormous difficulty breaking out of its longstanding role as executioner for ranching and farming interests. Buffeted by the demands of traditional clients on one side and the criticisms of wildlife biologists and conservation groups on the other, the Bureau was listing badly by the mid-1930s.

Roosevelt could see that organizational changes had to be made. He appointed an editorial cartoonist and respected wildlife conservationist named Jay N. "Ding" Darling to head the Biological Survey. Darling took prompt action to reduce the agency's depen-dence on congressional support for funding, which was often predicated on slavish adher-ence to the wishes of politically connected stockmen and farming interests. Working with conservation-minded lawmakers, he helped steer the Duck Stamp Act of 1934 through Congress. This important legislation established hunting licensing fees that went a long way toward fulfilling the Survey's budgetary needs. Three years later, the Pittman–Robertson Act extended licensing fees to sporting goods and ammunition, with the pro-ceeds explicitly earmarked for various federal and state wildlife research and management agencies. In addition, these fees and licenses had the effect of broadening the constituency for wildlife conservation because they gave participants an "ownership" stake in land and game management issues. "It is pertinent to remind you here," declared Roosevelt in 1936, "that seven million of our citizens take out fishing licenses each year and that six million more take out annual hunting licenses, a total of thirteen million—a veritable army to uphold the banner of conservation."[37]

In 1936 Darling left the Biological Survey to return to newspaper work and help establish the National Wildlife Federation, which became one of the most powerful con-servation groups in the country during the 1950s and 1960s. In 1939 the Roosevelt administration combined the Survey with the Commerce Department's Bureau of Fisher-ies to form the U.S. Fish and Wildlife Service. Thanks to the funding legislation passed by Congress in the 1930s, this agency was much better equipped to manage America's wild-life resources without debilitating interference from business interests and their advocates in Congress. "The effect of these laws was to create not only a dedicated revenue source outside the annual budget struggle," observed one historian, "but also a powerful set of client constituencies to support the agency: hunters, fishermen, and state fish and wildlife agencies."[38]

In return for this support, the U.S. Fish and Wildlife Service implemented policies that greatly bolstered national and regional populations of deer, pheasant, waterfowl, game fish, and other species popular with these groups. The Civilian Conservation Corps and other agencies, meanwhile, helped expand the size of the national wildlife refuge system from 1.8 to 13.6 million acres during the New Deal. By the close of the 1930s, habitat protection and wildlife conservation had become more popular political causes than ever before. The onset of World War II, however, relegated wildlife protection—and nearly every conservation cause—to a virtual afterthought among policymakers.

Notes

1. Quoted in Douglas C. Drake, "Herbert Hoover, Ecologist: The Politics of Oil Pollution Control, 1921–1926," *Mid America,* July 1973, 207–228.

2. R. Dale Grinder, "The Battle for Clean Air: The Smoke Problem in Post-Civil War America," in *Pollution and Reform in American Cities, 1870–1930,* ed. Martin V. Melosi (Austin: University of Texas Press, 1980), 90–93.

3. J. William Futrell, "The History of Environmental Law," in *Sustainable Environmental Law,* ed. Celia Campbell-Mohn, et al. (St. Paul, Minn.: West, 1993), 30.

4. Edward Relph, *The Modern Urban Landscape: 1880 to the Present* (Baltimore: Johns Hopkins University Press, 1987), 67–68.

5. Dolores Hayden, *Building Suburbia: Green Fields and Urban Growth, 1820–2000* (New York: Pantheon Books, 2003), 98.

6. *Historical Statistics of the United States, Colonial Times to 1970,* part 2 (Washington, D.C.: Government Printing Office, 1970), 716.

7. George S. May, *The Automobile Industry, 1920–1980* (New York: Facts on File, 1990).

8. Frederick Lewis Allen, *Only Yesterday: An Informal History of the 1920s* (1931; New York: Harper Perennial, 2000), 142.

9. Robert Gottlieb, *Forcing the Spring: The Transformation of the American Environmental Movement* (Washington, D.C.: Island Press, 1993), 69.

10. Alice Hamilton, "What Price Safety? Tetra-ethyl Lead Reveals a Flaw in Our Defenses," *The Survey Midmonthly,* June 15, 1925, 333.

11. John Duffy, *The Sanitarians: A History of American Public Health* (Chicago: University of Illinois Press, 1992), 258.

12. Quoted in David Rosner and Gerald Markowitz, eds., *Dying for Work: Workers' Safety and Health in Twentieth-Century America* (Bloomington: Indian University Press, 1987), 88, 95.

13. Ibid., 99.

14. Richard N.L. Andrews, *Managing the Environment, Managing Ourselves: A History of American Environmental Policy* (New Haven, Conn.: Yale University Press, 1999), 155–156, 178.

15. William C. Everhart, *The National Park Service* (New York: Praeger, 1972).

16. R. Edward Grumbine, *Ghost Bears: Exploring the Biodiversity Crisis* (Washington, D.C.: Island Press, 1993), 140.

17. Stephen T. Mather, "The National Parks on a Business Basis," *American Review of Reviews,* April 1915, 429–430.

18. Donald J. Pisani, "The Many Faces of Conservation: Natural Resources and the American State, 1900–1940," in *Taking Stock: American Government in the Twentieth Century,* ed. Morton Keller and R. Shep Melnick (New York: Cambridge University Press, 1999), 145.

19. Quoted in Paul S. Sutter, *Driven Wild: How the Fight Against Automobiles Launched the Modern Wilderness Movement* (Seattle: University of Washington Press, 2005), 19.

20. Everhart, *The National Park Service,* 110.

21. David A. Adams, *Renewable Resource Policy: The Legal-Institutional Foundations* (Washington, D.C.: Island Press, 1993), 135.

22. Dave Dempsey, *Ruin and Recovery: Michigan's Rise as a Conservation Leader* (Ann Arbor: University of Michigan Press, 2001), 112.

23. Ibid., 49.

24. John A. Salmond, Chap. 13 in *The Civilian Conservation Corps, 1933–1942: A New Deal Case Study* (Durham, N.C.: Duke University Press), 1967. Available at www.nps.gov/history/history/online_books/ccc/salmond/chap13.htm

25. Neil M. Maher, *Nature's New Deal: The Civilian Conservation Corps and the Roots of the American Environmental Movement* (Cambridge, Mass.: Oxford University Press, 2008), 44.

26. Franklin D. Roosevelt, *The Public Papers and Addresses of Franklin D. Roosevelt* (1933; New York: Random House, 1938), 2:271.

27. Donald S. Howard, *The W.P.A. and Federal Relief Policy* (New York: Russell Sage Foundation, 1943), 125–128.

28. David P. Billington and Donald C. Jackson, *Big Dams of the New Deal Era* (Norman: University of Oklahoma Press, 2008), 8.

29. Neuberger, Richard L. "The Columbia Flows to the Land." *Survey Graphic,* July 1939, p. 440.

30. Andrews, *Managing the Environment, Managing Ourselves,* 165.

31. Marc Reisner, *Cadillac Desert: The American West and Its Disappearing Water,* rev. ed. (1986; repr., New York: Penguin, 1993), 241.

32. Lawrence Svobida, *Farming the Dust Bowl: A First-Hand Account from Kansas.* Originally published as *An Empire of Dust* (1940; repr., Lawrence: University Press of Kansas, 1986), 59, 195.

33. Stuart Chase, "Behind the Drought," *Harper's Magazine* 173 (September 1935): 368–377.

34. Quoted in *War Against the Wolf: America's Campaign to Exterminate the Wolf,* ed, Rick McIntyre (Stillwater, Minn.: Voyageur Press, 1995), 161.

35. Albert M. Day and Almer P. Nelson, *Cooperative Wild Life Conservation and Control in Wyoming Under the Leadership of the United States Biological Survey* (Washington, D.C.: Predatory Animal and Rodent Control Office, U.S Biological Survey, 1928).

36. Milton P. Skinner, "The Predatory and Fur-Bearing Animals of the Yellowstone National Park," *Roosevelt Wildlife Bulletin* 4, no. 2 (1927): 163.

37. Quoted in Edgar B. Nixon, ed., *Franklin D. Roosevelt and Conservation, 1911–1945* (New York, 1957), 1:586.

38. Andrews, *Managing the Environment, Managing Ourselves,* 173.

DOCUMENT 6.1

The Colorado River Compact

"To Provide for the Equitable Division . . . of the Waters of the Colorado River"

November 24, 1922

In 1921 the U.S. Congress authorized the seven states of the Colorado River Basin—California, Arizona, Nevada, New Mexico, Utah, Colorado, and Wyoming—to carry out negotiations for the allocation of the Colorado River's water. The negotiations were extraordinarily tense because all parties recognized that economic development and population expansion in their states was dependent on adequate water supplies. On

November 24, 1922, the states' representatives finally signed an agreement. The Colorado River Compact was promptly approved by Congress, but as one historian noted, "for the time spent debating and drafting it—about eleven months—and its reputation as a western equivalent of the Constitution, the compact didn't settle much."[1]

The terms of the compact divided the seven states into "upper basin" states (Wyoming, Colorado, Utah, and New Mexico) and "lower basin" states (Nevada, Arizona, and California, which had already become by far the most populous and economically powerful state in the West). Each of these arbitrarily defined basins was given 7.5 million annual acre-feet of water for their use, thus laying a claim on 15 million of the total 17.5 million acre-feet of water that flowed down the Colorado on an annual basis (this estimate was provided by the Reclamation Service). An additional 1 million acre-feet were bestowed on California and its fellow lower-basin states, mostly in recognition of California's status as the region's economic powerhouse. The last 1.5 million acre-feet was reserved for Mexico.

The terms of the compact were wildly controversial from the outset. State ratification efforts floundered as various water-hungry constituencies demanded revisions to the agreement. The future of the compact remained uncertain until 1928, when Congress dangled ratification incentives to the states in the form of big new federal water projects, including Boulder (Hoover) Dam. The construction of these projects would go forward only if six of the seven states ratified the compact. All states promptly fell in line with the exception of Arizona, which complained that California was taking too much of the lower basin allotment. Arizona did not ratify the agreement until 1944.

Once the compact came into force, major water development projects sprouted all across the West. Armed with clear information about their allotments of precious water, state and federal engineers, agricultural districts, and city planners all proceeded with expansive development schemes. Over time, however, it became clear that the Reclamation Service had badly misread the average annual flow of the Colorado. The average flow is actually much less than 17.5 million acre-feet, a reality which inevitably led to new water disputes between Compact members. Heady regional growth in state populations and economic activity in the second half of the twentieth century has put additional strain on the Colorado River Compact and sparked a multitude of ugly "water grabs," intra-state squabbling, and other political wars in the West. As one historian observed, the Colorado thus became "the most legislated, most debated, and most litigated river in the entire world."[2] To many environmentalists, meanwhile, the besieged river has also become a tragic symbol of heedless resource consumption and development in the West.

COLORADO RIVER COMPACT, 1922

The States of Arizona, California, Colorado, Nevada, New Mexico, Utah, and Wyoming, having resolved to enter into a compact under the act of the Congress of the United States of America approved August 19, 1921, and the Acts of the Legislatures of the said States, have through their Governors appointed as their Commissioners: W. S. Norviel for the State of Arizona, W. F. McClure for the State of California, Delph E. Carpenter for the State of Colorado, J. G. Scrugham for the State of Nevada, Stephen B. Davis, Jr. for the State of New Mexico, R. E. Caldwell for the State of Utah, Frank C. Emerson for the State of Wyoming, who, after negotiations participated in by Herbert Hoover, appointed by the President as the representative of the United States of America, have agreed upon the following articles:

ARTICLE I

The major purposes of this compact are to provide for the equitable division and apportionment of the use of the waters of the Colorado River System, to establish the relative importance of different beneficial uses of water, to promote interstate comity, to remove causes of present and future controversies and to secure the expeditious agricultural and industrial development of the Colorado River Basin, the storage of its waters, and the protection of life and property from floods. To these ends the Colorado River Basin is divided into two Basins, and an apportionment of the use of part of the water of the Colorado River System is made to each of them with the provision that further equitable apportionment may be made.

ARTICLE II

As used in this compact:

(a) The term "Colorado River System" means that portion of the Colorado River and its tributaries within the United States of America.

(b) The term "Colorado River Basin" means all of the drainage area of the Colorado River System and all other territory within the United States of America to which the waters of the Colorado River System shall be beneficially applied.

(c) The term "States of the Upper Division" means the States of Colorado, New Mexico, Utah, and Wyoming.

(d) The term "States of the Lower Division" means the States of Arizona, California, and Nevada.

(e) The term "Lee Ferry" means a point in the main stream of the Colorado River 1 mile below the mouth of the Paria River.

(f) The term "Upper Basin" means those parts of the States of Arizona, Colorado, New Mexico, Utah, and Wyoming within and from which waters naturally drain into the Colorado River System above Lee Ferry, and also all parts of said States located without the drainage area of the Colorado River System which are now or shall hereafter be beneficially served by waters diverted from the system above Lee Ferry.

(g) The term "Lower Basin" means those parts of the States of Arizona, California, Nevada, New Mexico, and Utah within and from which waters naturally drain into the Colorado River System below Lee Ferry, and also all parts of said States located without the drainage area of the Colorado River System which are now or shall hereafter be beneficially served by waters diverted from the System below Lee Ferry.

(h) The term "domestic use" shall include the use of water for household, stock, municipal, mining, milling, industrial, and other like purposes, but shall exclude the generation of electrical power.

ARTICLE III

(a) There is hereby apportioned from the Colorado River System in perpetuity to the Upper Basin and to the Lower Basin, respectively, the exclusive beneficial consumptive use of 7,500,000 acre-feet of water per annum, which shall include all water necessary for the supply of any rights which may now exist.

(b) In addition to the apportionment in paragraph (a) the Lower Basin is hereby given the right to increase its beneficial consumptive use of such waters by one million acre-feet per annum.

(c) If, as a matter of international comity, the United States of America shall hereafter recognize in the United States of Mexico any right to the use of any waters of the

Colorado River System, such waters shall be supplied first from the waters which are surplus over and above the aggregate of the quantities specified in paragraphs (a) and (b); and if such surplus shall prove insufficient for this purpose, then the burden of such deficiency shall be equally borne by the Upper Basin and the Lower Basin, and whenever necessary the States of the upper division shall deliver at Lee Ferry water to supply one-half of the deficiency so recognized in addition to that provided in paragraph (d).

(d) The States of the Upper Division will not cause the flow of the river at Lee Ferry to be depleted below an aggregate of 75,000,000 acre-feet for any period of 10 consecutive years reckoned in continuing progressive series beginning with the 1st day of October next succeeding the ratification of this compact.

(e) The States of the Upper Division shall not withhold water, and the States of the Lower Division shall not require the delivery of water, which can not reasonably be applied to domestic and agricultural uses.

(f) Further equitable apportionment of the beneficial uses of the waters of the Colorado River System unapportioned by paragraphs (a), (b), and (c) may be made in the manner provided in paragraph (g) at any time after October first, 1963, if and when either Basin shall have reached its total beneficial consumptive use as set out in paragraphs (a) and (b).

(g) In the event of a desire for further apportionment as provided in paragraph (f) any two signatory States, acting through their Governors, may give joint notice of such desire to the Governors of the other signatory States and to the President of the United States of America, and it shall be the duty of the Governors of the signatory States and of the President of the United States of America forthwith to appoint representatives, whose duty it shall be to divide and apportion equitably between the Upper Basin and Lower Basin the beneficial use of the unapportioned water of the Colorado River System as mentioned in paragraph (f), subject to the legislative ratification of the signatory States and the Congress of the United States of America.

Article IV

(a) Inasmuch as the Colorado River has ceased to be navigable for commerce and the reservation of its waters for navigation would seriously limit the development of its Basin, the use of its waters for purposes of navigation shall be subservient to the uses of such waters for domestic, agricultural, and power purposes. If the Congress shall not consent to this paragraph, the other provisions of this compact shall nevertheless remain binding.

(b) Subject to the provisions of this compact, water of the Colorado River System may be impounded and used for the generation of electrical power, but such impounding and use shall be subservient to the use and consumption of such water for agricultural and domestic purposes and shall not interfere with or prevent use for such dominant purposes.

(c) The provisions of this article shall not apply to or interfere with the regulation and control by any State within its boundaries of the appropriation, use, and distribution of water.

Article V

The chief official of each signatory State charged with the administration of water rights, together with the Director of the United States Reclamation Service and the Director of the United States Geological Survey, shall cooperate, ex officio:

(a) To promote the systematic determination and coordination of the facts as to flow, appropriation, consumption, and use of water in the Colorado River Basin, and the interchange of available information in such matters.

(b) To secure the ascertainment and publication of the annual flow of the Colorado River at Lee Ferry.

(c) To perform such other duties as may be assigned by mutual consent of the signatories from time to time.

Article VI

Should any claim or controversy arise between any two or more of the signatory States: (a) with respect to the waters of the Colorado River System not covered by the terms of this compact; (b) over the meaning or performance of any of the terms of this compact; (c) as to the allocation of the burdens incident to the performance of any article of this compact or the delivery of waters as herein provided; (d) as to the construction or operation of works within the Colorado River Basin to be situated in two or more States, or to be constructed in one State for the benefit of another State; or (e) as to the diversion of water in one State for the benefit of another State, the Governors of the States affected upon the request of one of them, shall forthwith appoint Commissioners with power to consider and adjust such claim or controversy, subject to ratification by the legislatures of the States so affected.

Nothing herein contained shall prevent the adjustment of any such claim or controversy by any present method or by direct future legislative action of the interested States.

Article VII

Nothing in this compact shall be construed as affecting the obligations of the United States of America to Indian tribes.

Article VIII

Present perfected rights to the beneficial use of waters of the Colorado River System are unimpaired by this compact. Whenever storage capacity of 5,000,000 acre-feet shall have been provided on the main Colorado River within or for the benefit of the Lower Basin, then claims of such rights, if any, by appropriators or users of water in the Lower Basin against appropriators or users of water in the Upper Basin shall attach to and be satisfied from water that may be stored not in conflict with Article III.

All other rights to beneficial use of waters of the Colorado River System shall be satisfied solely from the water apportioned to that Basin in which they are situated.

Article IX

Nothing in this compact shall be construed to limit or prevent any State from instituting or maintaining any action or proceeding, legal or equitable, for the protection of any right under this compact or the enforcement of any of its provisions.

Article X

This compact may be terminated at any time by the unanimous agreement of the signatory States. In the event of such termination, all rights established under it shall continue unimpaired.

Article XI

This compact shall become binding and obligatory when it shall have been approved by the Legislatures of each of the signatory States and by the Congress of the United States. Notice of approval by the Legislatures shall be given by the Governor of each signatory State to the Governors of the other signatory States and to the President of the United States, and the President of the United States is requested to give notice to the Governors of the signatory States of approval by the Congress of the United States.

Source: "Colorado River Compact, 1922." U.S. Bureau of Reclamation. www.usbr.gov/lc/region/pao/pdfiles/crcompct.pdf.

Notes

1. Marc Reisner, *Cadillac Desert: The American West and Its Disappearing Water* (1986; rev. ed. New York: Penguin, 1993), 124.
2. Ibid., 120.

DOCUMENT 6.2

An Ethyl Industry Consultant Tries to Relieve Fears about Lead Poisoning

"The Apparent Complete Harmlessness of 'Ethyl Gasoline' Exhaust Fumes"

March 1925

The debate over government oversight and regulation of industrial processes in the 1920s reached a crescendo in a heated controversy over ethyl gasoline. In 1922 researchers at General Motors had discovered that when tetraethyl lead was introduced into gasoline it eliminated "knock" and improved engine performance. The automobile company quickly contracted with DuPont Chemical Company and Standard Oil to produce tetraethyl lead, and in early 1924 General Motors and DuPont created the Ethyl Corporation to market and produce leaded gasoline.

These developments alarmed public health advocates and industrial hygienists such as Alice Hamilton, who emphasized that lead was a known industrial toxin. They warned that wide-scale use of leaded gasoline could result in lead poisoning in workers and environmental pollution on an epic scale. The resulting public anxiety led General Motors and DuPont to arrange a study of tetraethyl lead by the U.S. Bureau of Mines. But the terms of this investigation, which was to be funded and monitored by General Motors, aroused suspicion on the part of many opponents of leaded gas. When public health physiologist Yandell Henderson was offered a role in the investigation, for example, he angrily rejected the offer: "It seems to me extremely unfortunate that the experts of the United States Government should be carrying out this investigation on a grant from General Motors."[1]

As the Bureau of Mines launched its program of tetraethyl lead testing on animals, Ethyl Corporation began producing commercial quantities of leaded gasoline. But in late October 1924 most of the 49 workers at a lead processing plant in Elizabeth, New Jersey, were diagnosed with signs of severe lead poisoning. Five of the workers went violently insane and died. This revelation prompted a new wave of unwelcome publicity for tetraethyl lead and led several cities and states to impose a ban on the sale of leaded gasoline.

The deaths also triggered an industrial counteroffensive. The corporations involved trumpeted the preliminary findings of the Bureau of Mines, which stated that leaded gasoline was safe. When the Bureau report—which was released the day after the fifth person from the Elizabeth plant died—failed to allay public fears, Ethyl Corporation infiltrated the pages of the influential American Journal of Public Health. *This strategy was carried out by Emery Hayhurst, an advisor to the Workers Health Bureau who was also a secret consultant to the Ethyl Corporation. Hayhurst used his contacts at the* Journal *to insert an unsigned editorial, written by himself, that praised the Bureau of Mines' investigation and dismissed concerns about the lead threat. An excerpt from Hayhurst's editorial is reprinted here.*

The controversy refused to die, however, and in May 1925 the U.S. Surgeon General of the Public Health Service held a conference on tetraethyl lead use in gasoline. As the conference proceeded, corporate executives and industry scientists faulted worker carelessness for the deaths in New Jersey, described leaded gasoline as an "apparent gift of God," and insisted that "our continued development of motor fuels is essential in our civilization."[2] Opponents testified to the environmental and public health threats posed by lead; denounced industry efforts to paint the dead workers as scapegoats; and, as one historian put it, "argued that the burden of proof should be on the companies to prove tetraethyl lead was safe, rather than on opponents to prove it was dangerous."[3]

In the aftermath of the conference, the Public Health Service announced that it was organizing a special committee of experts to further study the safety of tetraethyl lead. Champions of occupational and public health rejoiced because they believed that the committee would recommend prohibitions on the use of leaded gas and greater federal regulation of industrial processes. But when the committee returned with a limited, cautious report, leaded gas supporters were free to proceed with production. Leaded gasoline became the automotive fuel of choice for the next five decades—an oft-cited factor in the elevated levels of lead present in the bloodstream of people around the world. The United States finally phased out leaded gasoline in the 1970s in response to continued environmental concerns and the incompatibility of leaded gas with catalytic converters, which became a standard part of engine design during that decade.

ETHYL GASOLINE

The public health aspect of "anti-knock" compounds added to gasoline for motor use has been editorially mentioned in this Journal in connection with "ethyl gasoline" and lead poisoning.

The first report from the United States Bureau of Mines on the study of "Exhaust Gases from Engines Using Ethyl Gasoline" is now before us. This covers the first 8 months' investigations of the possible toxic effects of "ethyl gasoline" from the exhaust of a motor. The writer has had the opportunity at intervals of watching the progress of these investigations at the Experiment Station at Pittsburg. "Ethyl gasoline" contains 1/10 per cent of "ethyl fluid" which in itself contains 3 parts of "tetra-ethyl lead" and 2 parts of a halogen carrier (ethylene dibromide or trichloroethylene). Neither "ethyl fluid" nor "tetra-ethyl lead" is a motor fuel.

The gist of the report is the apparent complete harmlessness of "ethyl gasoline" exhaust fumes from the automobile motor so far as lead poisoning is concerned.

It is said that lead tetra-ethyl was discovered in 1854 by a German chemist and that its extreme toxicity has been known almost since that time. It is peculiar and different from other known forms of lead in that it is able to cause poisoning by absorption through the skin, apparently because the ethyl radical is a fat solvent. As Dr. J. H. Shrader points out in his article in this issue of the Journal, the substance was investigated by order of Brigadier General Fries of the Chemical Warfare Service, and found to be only 1/25 as toxic as mustard gas and therefore of no value as a war gas.

The Bureau also conducted an experiment upon men to determine the amount of lead retention from an exhaust containing lead from "ethylized gasoline" and found that, on the average, 85 percent of the lead inhaled was again exhaled (the maximum retention on triply ethylizing the gasoline being 27 per cent). Hence, if one may amuse himself with theorizing, the "in-take retention" of lead by a human being breathing the exhaust gas of regularly ethylized gasoline becomes reduced to something like this: 2/3 of the molecular weight of tetra-ethyl lead is lead which is diluted 6/10 times in "ethyl fluid" which is again diluted 1,000 times in "ethyl gasoline" with retention of 60 to 80 percent of the lead portion in the motor and an average retention by the person of only 15 percent of that escaping (if inhaled) a dilution so great as to appear "homeopathic" indeed and, undoubtedly explaining why the animals were not poisoned. We must not forget also the tendency to form flakes or scale rather than fine dust and that some capacity for handling minute amounts of lead physiologically (Telecky estimates 1.0 mg. daily) so that the amount inhaled and absorbed in the hazard under discussion is evidently far below the "threshold" of toxicity.

Lead is ordinarily found in street dust from automobile tires, other parts of vehicles and things transported, "tin" (lead) foil, etc. It is said that automobile tires themselves often contain lead to the extent of 15–25 per cent of their weight. But there is probably much more oil, water and "drippings" added to the streets on the part of automobiles than the wear-off from tires and the deposits from mufflers, which "drippings" hold or congest dusts very materially, while rains and flushings remove most of it.

These considerations, however, do not detract whatever from the necessity of guarding employees very carefully in the manufacture of tetra-ethyl lead and the handling of "ethyl fluid." President Irenee du Pont of the E. I. Du Pont de Nemours & Company states that the company's tetra-ethyl lead plant, at first, had much trouble, which was finally overcome so that in the past three months there has been no trouble while running at virtually full capacity. A. M. Maxwell, Vice-President and sales manager of the Ethyl Gasoline Corporation, states that further sales of "ethyl fluid" will be made only to refineries where the gasoline will be "ethylized" before distribution to service stations, thus removing the hazard of careless handling there.

Under date of November 12, 1924 (and after), the Ethyl Gasoline Corporation placed an advertisement in many of the newspapers throughout the country to the effect that "ethylized gasoline has been on sale for one year and nine months in about 20,000 filling stations covering one-third of the territory of the United States," and that "about 200,000,000 gallons have been used by more than 1,000,000 motorists with complete safety and satisfaction." Observation evidence and reports to various health officials over the country, previous to and following the above advertisements have, so far as we have been able to find out, corroborated the statement of "complete safety" so far as the public health has been concerned. Press statements that a ban has been placed on its sale in the State of New Jersey are incorrect and evidently confused with the dismantling of the Bay-way Plant where the unfortunate mishap occurred in October, 1924. The extensive plant of the du Pont Co. at Carney's Point, New Jersey, is running as usual.

We understand that the Bureau of Mines is continuing its investigations in order to determine the "threshold concentration" of "ethyl gasoline" necessary to produce symptoms of lead poisoning through breathing exhaust gases, by running up the concentration of "ethyl fluid" until effects *are* produced. The present report, which is in the nature of a preliminary one, concludes with the statement as follows:

"In summing up the investigation, it can be stated that there has been no indication of plumbism in any of the animals used, though they were exposed for 188 days during a period of approximately 8 months to exhaust gases from ethyl gasoline in concentrations with respect to lead content that are several times that allowable from the standpoint of the carbon monoxide."

Source: "Ethyl Gasoline" editorial. *American Journal of Public Health,* March 1925, pp. 239–240. Copyright © 1925 by the American Public Health Association. Used by permission.

Notes

1. Quoted in David Rosner, and Gerald Markowitz, eds., *Dying for Work: Workers' Safety and Health in Twentieth-Century America* (Bloomington: Indian University Press, 1987), 123.

2. United States Public Health Service, "Proceedings of a Conference to Determine Whether or Not there is a Public Health Question in the Manufacture, Distribution, or Use of Tetraethyl Lead Gasoline," *Public Health Bulletin* 158 (Washington D.C.: Government Printing Office, 1925): 62.

3. Rosner, *Dying for Work,* 131.

DOCUMENT 6.3 — *Euclid v. Ambler Realty* Bolsters Zoning Laws

"The Ordinance . . . Is a Valid Exercise of Authority"

November 22, 1926

In the first two decades of the twentieth century, U.S. cities and towns increasingly turned to zoning ordinances to impose order on growth; shield residents from toxic emissions and other pollutants associated with industrial manufacturing operations; and preserve wetlands, woodlands, and other ecologically sensitive areas. Some property owners, however, vociferously objected to zoning measures because they sometimes had the effect of diminishing the value of their investment properties. Opponents decided to seek redress for their grievances in the courts by framing zoning regulations as unconstitutional violations of Fourteenth Amendment guarantees of due process and equal protection under the law.

Conflicting court decisions proliferated for several years, but in 1926 the legal battle over zoning culminated with the landmark case of Village of Euclid v. Ambler Realty Company. *Euclid was a small community outside of Cleveland, Ohio, that had adopted zoning codes in 1922. Under the town's plan, six distinct zoning districts were created: single-family, two-family, apartment house, retail-wholesale stores, commercial, and industrial. The residential district laid out by Euclid, however, included nearly half of a large parcel of land owned by Ambler Realty, a Cleveland-based company that had planned to sell the land for industrial use. Ambler filed legal challenges to the town's zoning ordinances, and in January 1924 a federal court in Ohio sided with the company. The court ruled that Euclid's zoning laws were unconstitutional, and it issued an injunction forbidding the town's building inspector from enforcing the codes. But attorneys for Euclid appealed, and the case made its way to the U.S. Supreme Court. In a 6-3 decision announced on November 22, 1926, the Court overturned the lower court decision and found in favor of Euclid. The majority decision validated the authority of communities to impose zoning laws and regulate land use in the public interest—even in cases where zoning might have a negative economic impact on some individuals. Zoning became a standard tool in urban and town planning in the years following this decision, and it continues to play a major role in shaping land and natural resource use in populated areas across the country. Following are excerpts from the Supreme Court's decision.*

. . . It is specifically averred that the ordinance attempts to restrict and control the lawful uses of appellee's land, so as to confiscate and destroy a great part of its value; that it is being enforced in accordance with its terms; that prospective buyers of land for industrial, commercial, and residential uses in the metropolitan district of Cleveland are deterred from buying any part of this land because of the existence of the ordinance and the necessity thereby entailed of conducting burdensome and expensive litigation in order to vindicate the right to use the land for lawful and legitimate purposes; that the ordinance constitutes a cloud upon the land, reduces and destroys its value, and has the effect of diverting the normal industrial, commercial, and residential development thereof to other and less favorable locations. . . .

It is not necessary to set forth the provisions of the Ohio Constitution which are thought to be infringed. The question is the same under both Constitutions, namely, as stated by appellee: Is the ordinance invalid, in that it violates the constitutional protection "to the right of property in the appellee by attempted regulations under the guise of the police power, which are unreasonable and confiscatory?"

Building zone laws are of modern origin. They began in this country about 25 years ago. Until recent years, urban life was comparatively simple; but, with the great increase and concentration of population, problems have developed, and constantly are developing, which require, and will continue to require, additional restrictions in respect of the use and occupation of private lands in urban communities. Regulations, the wisdom, necessity, and validity of which, as applied to existing conditions, are so apparent that they are now uniformly sustained, a century ago, or even half a century ago, probably would have been rejected as arbitrary and oppressive. Such regulations are sustained, under the complex conditions of our day, for reasons analogous to those which justify traffic regulations, which, before the advent of automobiles and rapid transit street railways, would have been condemned as fatally arbitrary and unreasonable. And in this there is no inconsistency, for, while the meaning of constitutional guaranties never varies, the scope of their application must expand or contract to meet the new and different conditions which are constantly coming within the field of their operation. In a changing world it is impossible that it should be otherwise. But although a degree of elasticity is thus imparted, not to the meaning, but to the application of constitutional principles, statutes and ordinances, which, after giving due weight to the new conditions, are found clearly not to conform to the Constitution, of course, must fall.

The ordinance now under review, and all similar laws and regulations, must find their justification in some aspect of the police power, asserted for the public welfare. The line which in this field separates the legitimate from the illegitimate assumption of power is not capable of precise delimitation. It varies with circumstances and conditions. A regulatory zoning ordinance, which would be clearly valid as applied to the great cities, might be clearly invalid as applied to rural communities. In solving doubts, the maxim '*sic utere tuo ut alienum non laedas* ["one should use his own property in such a manner as not to injure that of another"],' which lies at the foundation of so much of the common low of nuisances, ordinarily will furnish a fairly helpful clew. And the law of nuisances, likewise, may be consulted, not for the purpose of controlling, but for the helpful aid of its analogies in the process of ascertaining the scope of, the power. Thus the question whether the power exists to forbid the erection of a building of a particular kind or for a particular use, like the question whether a particular thing is a nuisance, is to be determined, not by an abstract consideration of the building or of the thing considered apart, but by considering it in connection with the circumstances and the locality. A nuisance may be merely a right thing in the wrong place, like a pig in the parlor instead of the barnyard. If the validity of the legislative classification for zoning purposes be fairly debatable, the legislative judgment must be allowed to control.

There is no serious difference of opinion in respect of the validity of laws and regulations fixing the height of buildings within reasonable limits, the character of materials and methods of construction, and the adjoining area which must be left open, in order to minimize the danger of fire or collapse, the evils of overcrowding and the like, and excluding from residential sections offensive trades, industries and structures likely to create nuisances.

Here, however, the exclusion is in general terms of all industrial establishments, and it may thereby happen that not only offensive or dangerous industries will be excluded, but those which are neither offensive nor dangerous will share the same fate. But this is no more than happens in respect of many practice-forbidding laws which this court has upheld, although drawn in general terms so as to include individual cases that may turn out to be innocuous in themselves. The inclusion of a reasonable margin, to insure effective enforcement, will not put upon a law, otherwise valid, the stamp of invalidity. Such laws may also find their justification in the fact that, in some fields, the bad fades into the good by such insensible degrees that the two are not capable of being readily distinguished and separated in terms of legislation. In the light of these considerations, we are not prepared to say that the end in view was not sufficient to justify the general rule of the ordinance, although some industries of an innocent character might fall within the proscribed class. . . .

It is said that the village of Eucleland is a mere suburb of the city of Cleveland; that the industrial development of that city has now reached and in some degree extended into the village, and in the obvious course of things will soon absorb the entire area for industrial enterprises; that the effect of the ordinance is to divert this natural development elsewhere, with the consequent loss of increased values to the owners of the lands within the village borders. But the village, though physically a suburb of Cleveland, is politically a separate municipality, with powers of its own and authority to govern itself as it sees fit, within the limits of the organic law of its creation and the state and federal Constitutions. Its governing authorities, presumably representing a majority of its inhabitants and voicing their will, have determined, not that industrial development shall cease at its boundaries, but that the course of such development shall proceed within definitely fixed lines. If it be a proper exercise of the police power to relegate industrial establishments to localities separated from residential sections, it is not easy to find a sufficient reason for denying the power because the effect of its exercise is to divert an industrial flow from the course which it would follow, to the injury of the residential public, if left alone, to another course where such injury will be obviated. . . .

We find no difficulty in sustaining restrictions of the kind thus far reviewed. The serious question in the case arises over the provisions of the ordinance excluding from residential districts apartment houses, business houses, retail stores and shops, and other like establishments. This question involves the validity of what is really the crux of the more recent zoning legislation, namely, the creation and maintenance of residential districts, from which business and trade of every sort, including hotels and apartment houses, are excluded. Upon that question this court has not thus far spoken. The decisions of the state courts are numerous and conflicting; but those which broadly sustain the power greatly outnumber those which deny it altogether or narrowly limit it, and it is very apparent that there is a constantly increasing tendency in the direction of the broader view. . . .

It is true that when, if ever, the provisions set forth in the ordinance in tedious and minute detail, come to be concretely applied to particular premises, including those of the appellee, or to particular conditions, or to be considered in connection with specific complaints, some of them, or even many of them, may be found to be clearly arbitrary and unreasonable. But where the equitable remedy of injunction is sought, as it is here, not upon the ground of a present infringement or denial of a specific right, or of a particular injury in process of actual execution, but upon the broad ground that the mere existence and threatened enforcement of the ordinance, by materially and adversely affecting values and curtailing the opportunities of the market, constitute a present and irreparable injury, the court will not scrutinize its provisions, sentence by sentence, to ascertain by a process of piecemeal dissection whether there may be, here and there, provisions of a minor character, or relating to matters of administration, or not shown to contribute to the injury complained of, which, if attacked separately, might not withstand the test of constitutionality. . . .

The relief sought here is of the same character, namely, an injunction against the enforcement of any of the restrictions, limitations, or conditions of the ordinance. And the gravamen of the complaint is that a portion of the land of the appellee cannot be sold for certain enumerated uses because of the general and broad restraints of the ordinance. What would be the effect of a restraint imposed by one or more or the innumerable provisions of the ordinance, considered apart, upon the value or marketability of the lands, is neither disclosed by the bill nor by the evidence, and we are afforded no basis, apart from mere speculation, upon which to rest a conclusion that it or they would have any appreciable effect upon those matters. Under these circumstances, therefore, it is enough for us to determine, as we do, that the ordinance in its general scope and dominant features, so far as its provisions are here involved, is a valid exercise of authority, leaving other provisions to be dealt with as cases arise directly involving them. . . .

Decree reversed.

Source: *Euclid v. Ambler Realty,* 272 U.S. 365 (1926). *United States Reports,* Vol. 272. Washington, D.C.: Government Printing Office, 1927.

Bob Marshall Calls for a New Era of Wilderness Advocacy

"All Friends of the Wilderness Ideal Should Unite"

February 1930

American public support for wilderness conservation increased dramatically during the years between the two world wars, as disastrous floods and bleak Dust Bowl years provided stark evidence of the need for better environmental stewardship. This support brought new levels of constituent pressure on lawmakers to pass wildlife and wilderness protection measures, and it made it much easier for President Franklin D. Roosevelt's administration to carry out further expansion of America's national forest, refuge, and park systems. But unlike many other Depression-era shifts in public sentiment, the call for wilderness preservation was not based on economic considerations. Rather, it hearkened back to Sierra Club founder John Muir and his message, delivered with evangelical zeal at the turn of the century, of the spiritual and aesthetic value of wilderness.

One of the most formidable voices for wilderness preservation during this period was Robert "Bob" Marshall, a top forestry official whose favorite pastimes included long backpacking excursions in the Adirondacks, the Rockies, northern Alaska's Brooks Range, and other wild spots on the American map. In 1930 Marshall wrote one of the most seminal documents in the history of U.S. wilderness preservation. Called "The Problem of the Wilderness," it celebrated pristine wilderness areas as places of spiritual renewal and adventure. But the essay was also a call to arms, challenging wilderness lovers to make their voices heard in statehouses, the halls of Congress, and the White House. The full text of Marshall's essay, which first appeared in the February 1930 issue of The Scientific Monthly, *is reprinted here. Five years after this publication, Marshall helped co-found the Wilderness Society, a pioneering environmental advocacy organization that helped craft and support legislation to protect undeveloped wilderness areas from development. The landmark 1964 Wilderness Act, in fact, was written by Wilderness Society Executive Director Howard Zahniser.*

The seemingly indefatigable Marshall died of a heart attack in 1939 at the age of thirty-eight, only four years after the Wilderness Society was born. But he continues to be remembered as one of the giants of American wilderness conservation. Western Montana's one-million-acre Bob Marshall Wilderness, which was established by the 1964 Wilderness Act, was named in honor of the maverick conservationist.

I

It is appalling to reflect how much useless energy has been expended in arguments which would have been inconceivable had the terminology been defined. In order to avoid such futile controversy I shall undertake at the start to delimit the meaning of the principal term with which this paper is concerned. According to Dr. Johnson a *wilderness* is "a tract of solitude and savageness," a definition more poetic than explicit. Modern lexicographers do better with "a tract of land, whether a forest or a wide barren plain, uncultivated and uninhabited by human beings."[1] This definition gives a rather good foundation, but it still leaves a penumbra of partially shaded connotation.

For the ensuing discussion I shall use the word *wilderness* to denote a region which contains no permanent inhabitants, possesses no possibility of conveyance by any mechanical means and is sufficiently spacious that a person in crossing it must have the experience of sleeping out. The dominant attributes of such an area are: first, that it requires any one who exists in it to depend exclusively on his own effort for survival; and second, that it preserves as nearly as possible the primitive environment. This means that all roads, power transportation and settlements are barred. But trails and temporary shelters, which were common long before the advent of the white race, are entirely permissible.

When Columbus effected his immortal debarkation, he touched upon a wilderness which embraced virtually a hemisphere. The philosophy that progress is proportional to the amount of alteration imposed upon nature never seemed to have occurred to the Indians. Even such tribes as the Incas, Aztecs and Pueblos made few changes in the environment in which they were born. "The land and all that it bore they treated with consideration; not attempting to improve it, they never desecrated it."[2] Consequently, over billions of acres the aboriginal wanderers still spun out their peripatetic careers, the wild animals still browsed in unmolested meadows and the forests still grew and moldered and grew again precisely as they had done for undeterminable centuries.

It was not until the settlement of Jamestown in 1607 that there appeared the germ for that unabated disruption of natural conditions which has characterized all subsequent American history. At first expansion was very slow. The most intrepid seldom advanced further from their neighbors than the next drainage. At the time of the Revolution the zone of civilization was still practically confined to a narrow belt lying between the Atlantic Ocean and the Appalachian valleys. But a quarter of a century later, when the Louisiana Purchase was consummated, the outposts of civilization had reached the Mississippi, and there were foci of colonization in half a dozen localities west of the Appalachians, though the unbroken line of the frontier was east of the mountains.[3]

It was yet possible as recently as 1804 and 1805 for the Lewis and Clark Expedition to cross two thirds of a continent without seeing any culture more advanced than that of the Middle Stone Age. The only routes of travel were the uncharted rivers and the almost impassable Indian trails. And continually the expedition was breaking upon some "truly magnificent and sublimely grand object, which has from the commencement of time been concealed from the view of civilized man."[4]

This exploration inaugurated a century of constantly accelerating emigration such as the world had never known. Throughout this frenzied period the only serious thought ever devoted to the wilderness was how it might be demolished. To the pioneers pushing westward it was an enemy of diabolical cruelty and danger, standing as the great obstacle to industry and development. Since these seemed to constitute the essentials for felicity, the obvious step was to excoriate the devil which interfered. And so the path of empire proceeded to substitute for the undisturbed seclusion of nature the conquering accomplishments of man. Highways wound up valleys which had known only the footsteps of the wild animals; neatly planted gardens and orchards replaced the tangled confusion of

> *Highways wound up valleys which had known only the footsteps of the wild animals; neatly planted gardens and orchards replaced the tangled confusion of the primeval forest; factories belched up great clouds of smoke where for centuries trees had transpired toward the sky.*
>
> —Robert Marshall

the primeval forest; factories belched up great clouds of smoke where for centuries trees had transpired toward the sky, and the ground-cover of fresh sorrel and twin-flower was transformed to asphalt spotted with chewing-gum, coal dust and gasoline.

To-day there remain less than twenty wilderness areas of a million acres, and annually even these shrunken remnants of an undefiled continent are being despoiled. Aldo Leopold has truly said:

> "The day is almost upon us when canoe travel will consist in paddling up the noisy wake of a motor launch and portaging through the back yard of a summer cottage. When that day comes canoe travel will be dead, and dead too will be a part of our Americanism. . . . The day is almost upon us when a pack train must wind its way up a graveled highway and turn out its bell mare in the pasture of a summer hotel. When that day comes the pack train will be dead, the diamond hitch will be merely a rope and Kit Carson and Jim Bridger will be names in a history lesson."[5]

Within the next few years the fate of the wilderness must be decided. This is a problem to be settled by deliberate rationality and not by personal prejudice. Fundamentally, the question is one of balancing the total happiness which will be obtainable if the few undesecrated areas are perpetuated against that which will prevail if they are destroyed. For this purpose it will be necessary: first, to consider the extra-ordinary benefits of the wilderness; second, to enumerate the drawbacks to undeveloped areas; third, to evaluate the relative importance of these conflicting factors, and finally, to formulate a plan of action.

II

The benefits which accrue from the wilderness may be separated into three broad divisions: the physical, the mental and the esthetic.

Most obvious in the first category is the contribution which the wilderness makes to health. This involves something more than pure air and quiet, which are also attainable in almost any rural situation. But toting a fifty-pound pack over an abominable trail, snowshoeing across a blizzard-swept plateau or scaling some jagged pinnacle which juts far above timber all develop a body distinguished by a soundness, stamina and élan unknown amid normal surroundings.

More than mere heartiness is the character of physical independence which can be nurtured only away from the coddling of civilization. In a true wilderness if a person is not qualified to satisfy all the requirements of existence, then he is bound to perish. As long as we prize individuality and competence it is imperative to provide the opportunity for complete self-sufficiency. This is inconceivable under the effete superstructure of urbanity; it demands the harsh environment of untrammeled expanses.

Closely allied is the longing for physical exploration which bursts through all the chains with which society fetters it. Thus we find Lindbergh, Amundsen, Byrd gaily daring the unknown, partly to increase knowledge, but largely to satisfy the craving for adventure. Adventure, whether physical or mental, implies breaking into unpenetrated ground, venturing beyond the boundary of normal aptitude, extending oneself to the limit of capacity, courageously facing peril. Life without the chance for such exertions would be for many persons a dreary game, scarcely bearable in its horrible banality.

It is true that certain people of great erudition "come inevitably to feel that if life has any value at all, then that value comes in thought,"[6] and so they regard mere physical pleasures as puerile inconsequences. But there are others, perfectly capable of comprehending relativity and the quantum theory, who find equal ecstasy in non-intellectual adventure. It is entirely irrelevant which view-point is correct; each is applicable to whoever entertains it. The important consideration is that both groups are entitled to indulge their penchant, and in the second instance this is scarcely possible without the freedom of the wilderness.

III

One of the greatest advantages of the wilderness is its incentive to independent cogitation. This is partly a reflection of physical stimulation, but more inherently due to the fact that original ideas require an objectivity and perspective seldom possible in the distracting propinquity of one's fellow men. It is necessary to "have gone behind the world of humanity, seen its institutions like toadstools by the waydside."[7] This theorizing is justified empirically by the number of America's most virile minds, including Thomas Jefferson, Henry Thoreau, Louis Agassiz, Herman Melville, Mark Twain, John Muir and William James, who have felt the compulsion of periodical retirements into the solitudes. Withdrawn from the contaminating notions of their neighbors, these thinkers have been able to meditate, unprejudiced by the immuring civilization.

Another mental value of an opposite sort is concerned not with incitement but with repose. In a civilization which requires most lives to be passed amid inordinate dissonance, pressure and intrusion, the chance of retiring now and then to the quietude and privacy of sylvan haunts becomes for some people a psychic necessity. It is only the possibility of convalescing in the wilderness which saves them from being destroyed by the terrible neural tension of modern existence.

There is also a psychological bearing of the wilderness which affects, in contrast to the minority who find it indispensable for relaxation, the whole of human kind. One of the most profound discoveries of psychology has been the demonstration of the terrific harm caused by suppressed desires. To most of mankind a very powerful desire is the appetite for adventure. But in an age of machinery only the extremely fortunate have any occasion to satiate this hankering, except vicariously. As a result people become so choked by the monotony of their lives that they are readily amenable to the suggestion of any lurid diversion. Especially in battle, they imagine, will be found the glorious romance of futile dreams. And so they endorse war with enthusiasm and march away to stirring music, only to find their adventure a chimera, and the whole world miserable. It is all tragically ridiculous, and yet there is a passion there which can not be dismissed with a contemptuous reference to childish quixotism. William James has said that "militarism is the great preserver of ideals of hardihood, and human life with no use for hardihood would be contemptible."[8] The problem, as he points, out, is to find a "moral equivalent of war," a peaceful stimulation for the hardihood and competence instigated in bloodshed. This equivalent may be realized if we make available to every one the harmless excitement of the wilderness. Bertrand Russell has skillfully amplified this idea in his essay on "Machines and the Emotions." He expresses the significant conclusion that "many men would cease to desire war if they had opportunities to risk their lives in Alpine climbing."[9]

IV

In examining the esthetic importance of the wilderness I will not engage in the unprofitable task of evaluating the preciousness of different sorts of beauty, as, for instance,

whether an acronical view over the Grand Canyon is worth more than the Apollo of Prax-
iteles. For such a rating would always have to be based on a subjective standard, whereas
the essential for any measure is impersonality. Instead of such useless metaphysics I shall
call attention to several respects in which the undisputed beauty of the primeval, whatever
its relative merit, is distinctly unique.

Of the myriad manifestations of beauty, only natural phenomena like the wilderness
are detached from all temporal relationship. All the beauties in the creation of alteration
of which man has played even the slightest role are firmly anchored in the historic stream.
They are temples of Egypt, oratory of Rome, painting of the Renaissance or music of the
Classicists. But in the wild places nothing is moored more closely than to geologic ages.
The silent wanderer crawling up the rocky shore of the turbulent river could be a savage
from some prehistoric epoch or a fugitive from twentieth century mechanization.

The sheer stupendousness of the wilderness gives it a quality of intangibility which
is unknown in ordinary manifestations of ocular beauty. These are always very definite
two or three dimensional objects which can be physically grasped and circumscribed in
a few moments. But "the beauty that shimmers in the yellow afternoons of October, who
ever could clutch it."[10] Any one who has looked across a ghostly valley at midnight, when
moonlight makes a formless silver unity out of the drifting fog, knows how impossible it
often is in nature to distinguish mass from hallucination. Any one who has stood upon a
lofty summit and gazed over an inchoate tangle of deep canyons and cragged mountains,
of sunlit lakelets and black expanses of forest, has become aware of a certain giddy sensation that there are no distances, no measures, simply unrelated matter rising and falling
without any analogy to the banal geometry of breadth, thickness and height. A fourth
dimension of immensity is added which makes the location of some dim elevation
outlined against the sunset as incommensurable to the figures of the topographer as
life itself is to the quantitative table of elements which the analytic chemist proclaims to
constitute vitality.

Because of its size the wilderness also has a physical ambiency about it which most
forms of beauty lack. One looks from outside at works of art and architecture, listens from
outside to music or poetry. But when one looks at and listens to the wilderness he is
encompassed by his experience of beauty, lives in the midst of his esthetic universe.

A fourth peculiarity about the wilderness is that it exhibits a dynamic beauty. A
Beethoven symphony or a Shakespearean drama, a landscape by Corot or a Gothic cathedral, once they are finished become virtually static. But the wilderness is in constant flux.
A seed germinates, and a stunted seedling battles for decades against the dense shade of
the virgin forest. Then some ancient tree blows down and the long-suppressed plant suddenly enters into the full vigor of delayed youth, grows rapidly from sapling to maturity,
declines into the conky senility of many centuries, dropping millions of seed to start a new
forest upon the rotting débris of its own ancestors, and eventually topples over to admit
the sunlight which ripens another woodland generation.

Another singular aspect of the wilderness is that it gratifies every one of the senses.
There is unanimity in venerating the sights and sounds of the forest. But what are generally esteemed to be the minor senses should not be slighted. No one who has ever strolled
in springtime through seas of blooming violets, or lain at night on boughs of fresh balsam,
or walked across dank holms in early morning can omit odor from the joys of the primor-
dial environment. No one who has felt the stiff wind of mountaintops or the softness of
untrodden sphagnum will forget the exhilaration experienced through touch. "Nothing
ever tastes as good as when it's cooked in the woods" is a trite tribute to another sense.

Even equilibrium causes a blithe exultation during many a river crossing on tenuous foot log and many a perilous conquest of precipice.

Finally, it is well to reflect that the wilderness furnishes perhaps the best opportunity for pure esthetic enjoyment. This requires that beauty be observed as a unity, and that for the brief duration of any pure esthetic experience the cognition of the observed object must completely fill the spectator's cosmos. There can be no extraneous thoughts—no question about the creator of the phenomenon, its structure, what it resembles or what vanity in the beholder it gratifies. "The purely esthetic observer has for the moment forgotten his own soul";[11] he has only one sensation left and that is exquisiteness. In the wilderness, with its entire freedom from the manifestations of human will, that perfect objectivity which is essential for pure esthetic rapture can probably be achieved more readily than among any other forms of beauty.

V

But the problem is not all one-sided. Having discussed the tremendous benefits of the wilderness, it is now proper to ponder upon the disadvantages which uninhabited territory entails.

In the first place, there is the immoderate danger that a wilderness without developments for fire protection will sooner or later go up in smoke and down in ashes.

A second drawback is concerned with the direct economic loss. By locking up wilderness areas we as much as remove from the earth all the lumber, minerals, range land, water-power and agricultural possibilities which they contain. In the face of the tremendous demand for these resources it seems unpardonable to many to render nugatory this potential material wealth.

A third difficulty inherent in undeveloped districts is that they automatically preclude the bulk of the population from enjoying them. For it is admitted that at present only a minority of the genus *Homo* cares for wilderness recreation, and only a fraction of this minority possesses the requisite virility for the indulgence of this desire. Far more people can enjoy the woods by automobile. Far more would prefer to spend their vacations in luxurious summer hotels set on well-groomed lawns than in leaky, fly-infested shelters bundled away in the brush. Why then should this majority have to give up its rights?

VI

As a result of these last considerations the irreplaceable values of the wilderness are generally ignored, and a fatalistic attitude is adopted in regard to the ultimate disappearance of all unmolested localities. It is my contention that this outlook is entirely unjustified, and that almost all the disadvantages of the wilderness can be minimized by forethought and some compromise.

The problem of protection dictates the elimination of undeveloped areas of great fire hazard. Furthermore, certain infringements on the concept of an unsullied wilderness will be unavoidable in almost all instances. Trails, telephone lines and lookout cabins will have to be constructed, for without such precaution most forests in the west would be gutted. But even with these improvements the basic primitive quality still exists: dependence on personal effort for survival.

Economic loss could be greatly reduced by reserving inaccessible and unproductive terrain. Inasmuch as most of the highly valuable lands have already been exploited, it should be easy to confine a great share of the wilderness tracts to those lofty mountain regions where the possibility of material profit is unimportant. Under these circumstances it seems like the grossest illogicality for any one to object to the withdrawal of a few million acres of low-grade timber for recreational purposes when one hundred million acres of potential forest lie devastated.[12] If one tenth portion of this denuded land were put to its maximum productivity, it could grow more wood than all the proposed wilderness areas put together. Or if our forests, instead of attaining only 22 per cent of their possible production,[13] were made to yield up to capacity, we could refrain from using three quarters of the timber in the country and still be better off than we are to-day. The way to meet our commercial demands is not to thwart legitimate divertisement, but to eliminate the unmitigated evils of fire and destructive logging. It is time we appreciated that the real economic problem is to see how little land need be employed for timber production, so that the remainder of the forest may be devoted to those other vital uses incompatible with industrial exploitation.

Even if there should be an underproduction of timber, it is well to recall that it is much cheaper to import lumber for industry than to export people for pastime. The freight rate from Siberia is not nearly as high as the passenger rate to Switzerland.

What small financial loss ultimately results from the establishment of wilderness areas must be accepted as a fair price to pay for their unassessable preciousness. We spend about twenty-one billion dollars a year for entertainment of all sorts.[14] Compared with this there is no significance to the forfeiture of a couple of million dollars of annual income, which is all that our maximum wilderness requirements would involve. Think what an enormously greater sum New York City alone sacrifices in the maintenance of Central Park.

But the automobilists argue that a wilderness domain precludes the huge majority of recreation-seekers from deriving any amusement whatever from it. This is almost as irrational as contending that because more people enjoy bathing than art exhibits therefore we should change our picture galleries into swimming pools. It is undeniable that the automobilist has more roads than he can cover in a lifetime. There are upward of 3,000,000[15] miles of public highways in the United States, traversing many of the finest scenic features in the nation. Nor would the votaries of the wilderness object to the construction of as many more miles in the vicinity of the old roads, where they would not be molesting the few remaining vestiges of the primeval. But when the motorists also demand for their particular diversion the insignificant wilderness residue, it makes even a Midas appear philanthropic.

> Such are the differences among human beings in their sources of pleasure, that unless there is a corresponding diversity in their modes of life, they neither obtain their fair share of happiness, nor grow up to the mental, moral and esthetic stature of which their nature is capable. Why then should tolerance extend only to tastes and modes of life which extort acquiescence by the multitude of their adherents?[16]

It is of the utmost importance to concede the right of happiness also to people who find their delight in unaccustomed ways. This prerogative is valid even though its exercise may encroach slightly on the fun of the majority, for there is a point where an increase in the joy of the many causes a decrease in the joy of the few out of all proportion to the gain of the former. This has been fully recognized not only by such philosophers of democracy as Paine, Jefferson and Mill, but also in the practical administration of governments which spend prodigious sums of money to satisfy the expensive wants of only a fragment of the community. Public funds which could bring small additional happiness to the majority are diverted to support museums, art galleries, concerts, botanical gardens, menageries and golf-links. While these, like wilderness areas, are open to the use of every one, they are vital to only a fraction of the entire population. Nevertheless, they are almost universally approved, and the appropriations to maintain them are growing phenomenally.

VII

These steps of reasoning lead up to the conclusion that the preservation of a few samples of undeveloped territory is one of the most clamant issues before us today. Just a few years more of hesitation and the only trace of that wilderness which has exerted such a fundamental influence in molding American character will lie in the musty pages of pioneer books and the mumbled memories of tottering antiquarians. To avoid this catastrophe demands immediate action.

A step in the right direction has already been initiated by the National Conference on Outdoor Recreation,[17] which has proposed twenty-one possible wilderness areas. Several of these have already been set aside in a tentative way by the Forest Service; others are undergoing more careful scrutiny. But this only represents the incipiency of what ought to be done.

A thorough study should forthwith be undertaken to determine the probable wilderness needs of the country. Of course, no precise reckoning could be attempted, but a radical calculation would be feasible. It ought to be radical for three reasons: because it is easy to convert a natural area to industrial or motor usage, impossible to do the reverse; because the population which covets wilderness recreation is rapidly enlarging and because the higher standard of living which may be anticipated should give millions the economic power to gratify what is today merely a pathetic yearning. Once the estimate is formulated, immediate steps should be taken to establish enough tracts to insure every one who hungers for it a generous opportunity of enjoying wilderness isolation.

To carry out this program it is exigent that all friends of the wilderness ideal should unite. If they do not present the urgency of their view-point the other side will certainly capture popular support. Then it will only be a few years until the last escape from society will be barricaded. If that day arrives there will be countless souls born to live in strangulation, countless human beings who will be crushed under the artificial edifice raised by man. There is just one hope of repulsing the tyrannical ambition of civilization to conquer every niche on the whole earth. That hope is the organization of spirited people who will fight for the freedom of the wilderness.

Notes:

1. Webster's New International Dictionary.
2. Willa Cather, "Death Comes for the Archbishop."
3. Frederic L. Paxson, "History of the American Frontier."
4. Reuben G. Thwaites, "Original Journals of the Lewis and Clark Expedition, 1804–1806," June 13, 1805.
5. Aldo Leopold, "The Last Stand of the Wilderness," *American Forests and Forest Life*, October, 1925.
6. Joseph Wood Krutch, "The Modern Temper."
7. Henry David Thoreau, "Journals," April 2, 1852.

8. William James, "The Moral Equivalent of War."
9. Bertrand Russell, "Essays in Scepticism."
10. Ralph Waldo Emerson, "Nature."
11. Irwin Edman, "The World, the Arts and the Artist."
12. George P. Ahern, "Deforested America," Washington, D.C.
13. U.S. Department of Agriculture, "Timber, Mine or Crop?"
14. Stuart Chase, "Whither Mankind?"
15. "The World Almanac," 1929.
16. John Stuart Mill, "On Liberty."
17. National Conference on Outdoor Recreation, "Recreation Resources of Federal Lands," Washington, D.C.

Source: Marshall, Bob. "The Problem of the Wilderness." *Scientific Monthly* 30, no. 2 (February 1930) pp. 141–148. Reprinted with permission from AAAS.

DOCUMENT 6.5 — The National Park Service Changes Its Policies on Predators

"Predatory Animals Have a Real Place in Nature"

May 1931

Recognition of the intrinsic value and ecological importance of big predators such as wolves, mountain lions, bears, and lynxes increased dramatically during the 1920s and early 1930s. This changing perspective, which was set in motion by the work of a broad coalition of conservationists, wildlife biologists, and agency administrators, resulted in major policy changes within the National Park Service, the National Forest Service, and other federal departments and in many state wildlife management bureaus. Policies of extermination were discarded and replaced by official regulations that encouraged preservation and protection of big predators and their habitats.

The National Park Service was one of the first agencies to announce major changes in its predator policies. In 1931 Park Director Horace Albright published a note in the Journal of Mammalogy, *reprinted in full here, that explained the reasoning for the agency's change of heart. This important change in policy was followed five years later by a Park Service initiative that explicitly called for the reintroduction of "any native species which had been exterminated" from a national park—including big predators.*

The National Park Service is attempting to put the parks to their highest use. Every policy developed is an attempt to meet the purposes for which the parks were formed; First, the national parks must be maintained in absolutely unimpaired form for the use of future generations as well as those of our own time; second, they are set apart for the use, observation, health, pleasure, and inspiration of the people; and third, the national interest must dictate all decisions affecting public or private enterprise in the parks.

Certainly, one of the great contributions to the welfare of the Nation that national parks may make is that of wild life protection. It is one of the understood functions of the parks to give total protection to animal life. A definite policy of wild life protection is being developed with the result that fine herds of game are furnished as a spectacle for the benefit of the public, and those same herds furnish the best of opportunity for scientific study. Many disappearing species are to be found within park areas, so that in some instances we may speak of the parks as providing "last stands."

Of late there has been much discussion by the American Mammalogical Society and other scientific organizations relative to predatory animals and their control. The inroads of the fur trapper and widespread campaigns of destruction have caused the great reduction of some and the near disappearance of several American carnivores. The question naturally arises as to whether there is any place where they may be expected to survive and be available for scientific study in the future.

The National Park Service believes that predatory animals have a real place in nature, and that all animal life should be kept inviolate within the parks. As a consequence, the general policies relative to predatory animals are as follows:

1. Predatory animals are to be considered an integral part of the wild life protected within national parks and no widespread campaigns of destruction are to be countenanced. The only control practiced is that of shooting of coyotes or other predators when they are actually found making serious inroads upon herds of game or other mammals needing special protection.

2. No permits for trapping within the borders of a park are allowed. A resolution opposing the use of steel traps within a park was passed several years ago by the superintendents at their annual meeting.

3. Poison is believed to be a non-selective form of control and is banned from the national parks except where used by Park Service officials in warfare against rodents in settled portions of a park, or in case of emergency.

Though provision is made for the handling of special problems which may arise, it is the intention of the Service to hold definitely to these general policies. It can be seen, therefore, that within the national park system definite attention is given to that group of animals which elsewhere are not tolerated. It is the duty of the National Park Service to maintain examples of the various interesting North American mammals under natural conditions for the pleasure and education of the visitors and for the purpose of scientific study, and to this task it pledges itself.

HORACE M. ALBRIGHT,
Director, National Park Service

Source: Albright, Horace M. "National Park Service Policy on Predatory Mammals." *Journal of Mammalogy* 12, no. 2 (May 1931) pp. 185–186. Copyright © 1931 American Society of Mammalogists. Reprinted by permission of the American Society of Mammalogists/American Allen Press Publishing Services.

DOCUMENT
6.6

President Roosevelt Explains the Purpose of the Civilian Conservation Corps

"This Enterprise . . . Will Pay Dividends to the Present and Future Generations"

March 21, 1933

The Civilian Conservation Corps (CCC) was one of the most successful of President Franklin D. Roosevelt's slate of New Deal economic stimulus and employment programs. It combined the twin goals of employment relief and natural resource improvement and conservation by putting young American men to work restoring degraded forests and other wildlife habitat, restocking depleted fisheries, building trails and roads and campgrounds, and carrying out soil erosion control programs. Roosevelt ushered the CCC into existence by Executive Order 6101 on April 5, 1933, and over the next nine years nearly three million young men passed through the program, serving stints of six months to a year. By the end of 1935 CCC camps existed in every state in the union and in the territories of Alaska, Hawaii, the Virgin Islands, and Puerto Rico.

Unlike many other New Deal programs and entities, the Civilian Conservation Corps was popular across the political spectrum. In fact, state governments jockeyed with each other to claim CCC camps and programs, and the Corps inspired numerous conservation programs at the state level. By the time the CCC program ended in 1942, it had "left as its legacy the most effective eight-year record of conservation work in U.S. history," according to one scholar. "It advanced the nation's forest and conservation programs immeasurably and increased the value of the nation's environmental assets by hundreds of millions of dollars. Perhaps equally significant, it introduced hundreds of thousands of young men to the knowledge and appreciation of nature, the principles of conservation, and the pleasures of outdoor life."[1]

The following is the full text of Roosevelt's March 21, 1933, message to Congress on unemployment relief, in which he first discussed his vision of what the Civilian Conservation Corps could accomplish.

To the Congress:

It is essential to our recovery program that measures immediately be enacted aimed at unemployment relief. A direct attack in this problem suggests three types of legislation. The first is the enrollment of workers now by the Federal Government for such public employment as can be quickly started and will not interfere with the demand for or the proper standards of normal employment. The second is grants to States for relief work.

The third extends to a broad public works labor-creating program.

With reference to the latter I am now studying the many projects suggested and the financial questions involved. I shall make recommendations to the Congress presently.

In regard to grants to States for relief work, I advise you that the remainder of the appropriation of last year will last until May. Therefore, and because a continuance of Federal aid is still a definite necessity for many States, a further appropriation must be made before the end of this special session.

I find a clear need for some simple Federal machinery to coordinate and check these grants of aid. I am, therefore, asking that you establish the office of Federal Relief Administrator, whose duty it will be to scan requests for grants and to check the efficiency and wisdom of their use.

The first of these measures which I have enumerated, however, can and should be immediately enacted. I propose to create a civilian conservation corps to be used in simple work, not interfering with normal employment, and confining itself to forestry, the prevention of soil erosion, flood control and similar projects. I call your attention to the fact that this type of work is of definite, practical value, not only through the prevention of great present financial loss, but also as a means of creating future national wealth. This is brought home by the news we are receiving today of vast damage caused by floods on the Ohio and other rivers.

Control and direction of such work can be carried on by existing machinery of the departments of Labor, Agriculture, War and Interior.

I estimate that 250,000 men can be given temporary employment by early summer if you give me authority to proceed within the next two weeks.

I ask no new funds at this time. The use of unobligated funds, now appropriated for public works, will be sufficient for several months.

This enterprise is an established part of our national policy. It will conserve our precious natural resources. It will pay dividends to the present and future generations. It will make improvements in national and state domains which have been largely forgotten in the past few years of industrial development.

More important, however, than the material gains will be the moral and spiritual value of such work. The overwhelming majority of unemployed Americans, who are now walking the streets and receiving private or public relief, would infinitely prefer to work. We can take a vast army of these unemployed out into healthful surroundings. We can eliminate to some extent at least the threat that enforced idleness brings to spiritual and moral stability. It is not a panacea for all the unemployment but it is an essential step in this emergency. I ask its adoption.

Source: Roosevelt, Franklin D. Address on Unemployment Relief, March 21, 1933. *The Public Papers and Addresses of Franklin D. Roosevelt: Volume 2, The Year of Crisis*. New York: Random House, 1938, pp. 80–81. Available at The American Presidency Project, www.presidency.ucsb.edu/ws/index.php?pid=14596&st=civilian+conservation+corps&st1=.

NOTE

1. Richard N. L. Andrews, *Managing the Environment, Managing Ourselves: A History of American Environmental Policy* (New Haven, Conn.: Yale University Press, 1999), 164.

Hugh Bennett Describes Erosion as a "Costly Farm Evil"

"Most of Us Have Been Blind and Soundly Asleep with Respect to the Real Meaning of Erosion"

January 31, 1933

By the early 1930s evidence was mounting that unsound farming and grazing practices were contributing heavily to the environmental and economic deterioration of the Great Plains and other parts of the country. Manifestations of this decline ranged from eastern farm fields disfigured by gullies and exposed bedrock to raging dust storms that roared across the Plains.

The point man in the Roosevelt Administration's efforts to address the horrors of the Dust Bowl and other weakened farming areas was Hugh Hammond Bennett, a longtime soil expert with the Agriculture Department. During the 1920s Bennett had repeatedly warned that soil erosion needed greater federal attention. In 1928, for example, Bennett and W.R. Chapline co-authored a study called Soil Erosion: A National Menace. *In this report, Bennett bluntly predicted that "an era of land wreckage destined to weigh heavily upon the welfare of the next generation is at hand."[1] Bennett's prophetic voice was finally heeded in the early 1930s, a period when Great Plains dust storms were escalating in size and intensity. He was selected to lead a new agency within the Department of the Interior dedicated to addressing the wind and water erosion issue. This bureau was first called the Soil Erosion Service, but in 1935 it was transferred to the Department of Agriculture and renamed the Soil Conservation Service (the agency was renamed the Natural Resource Conservation Service in the 1990s).*

Under the leadership of Bennett and Agriculture Secretary Henry Wallace, the Soil Conservation Service established more than 2,000 local "conservancy districts" across the country. Using these districts, Bennett ushered in new soil conservation and water engineering policies that ultimately affected more than 200 million acres of farmland. The service's educational programs and policies, which emphasized environmentally sound methods of plowing, planting, and irrigating, helped save the American farm and point it into a more sustainable direction. The following are excerpts from a 1933 speech by Bennett in which he discussed the threat of soil erosion to America's future.

Land impoverishment and land destruction by excessive erosion, the washing of the soil by uncontrolled rains, have recently come to be recognized as farm and ranch problems of sinister and wide-spread importance. The agricultural authorities of a number of states have declared that this form of wastage is the most serious problem confronting the users of land, pointing to vast areas which have been and continue to be seriously impoverished and to others which have been essentially destroyed by this process that never stops of its own accord. Now we have, also, the evil of low prices; but low prices are subject to change for the better, while soil impoverishment by erosion always grows worse, usually increasingly worse, wherever it is unopposed.

In considering the relation of this problem to the rolling farm lands of the United States, it should be pointed out in the beginning that the evil is much more wide-spread and far more vicious than generally has been supposed. A few years ago, before we knew very much about the enormity of losses due to this malignant process, it was estimated that erosion was washing out of the fields and pastures of this country not less than 1,500,000,000 tons of soil annually. This estimate astounded a good many people. Now, on the basis of measurements at one of the recently established soil erosion experiment stations, it is indicated that in 1930, which was about an average year with respect to regional rainfall, 16,534,800 acres in the rolling Red Plains of Texas and Oklahoma lost 440 million tons of soil. On the 10th of May, 1930, a single rain in the Black Belt of central Texas washed off the rich topsoil from slopes of only 4 per cent at the rate of 23 tons per acre. This one rain, according to a survey made at the time, took a toll of not less than 100 million tons of soil from the sloping part of this famous cotton area. Measurements made at the Blackland Erosion Station indicate that in 1930, 300 million tons of soil were washed out of the 11 million acres comprised in this black prairie belt.

In other words, with the quantitative measurements now being made, it is seen that the preliminary estimate referred to was considerably too small. Now, we are beginning to awaken to the realization that here is a problem whose destructiveness not only greatly exceeds all previous conceptions regarding it, but comes close to exceeding the possibilities of human comprehension.

EROSION A CONTINUING PROCESS

Erosion steals part of the soil every time it rains hard enough for water to run downhill, taking, successively, thin layers from the surface of the ground, the richest part of the land. It should be made perfectly clear at the outstart that we are discussing man-induced erosion, the excessive washing following (a) the removal of nature's stabilizing cover of trees, shrubs, grasses and decaying vegetable matter, and (b) the weakening of the ground structure by plowing and by excessive trampling of livestock. Probably it would be not far from correct to assert that not one person in this audience has ever seen or ever will see clear rainwater flowing off cultivated slopes in summertime; but most of you undoubtedly have seen clear water running out of woodlands and grass-covered areas at all seasons of the year. The one is discolored with soil picked up from the bare surface of the ground; the other is clear because the ground was protected with the instruments nature employs to prevent rapid scouring away of the earth's surface.

In this connection, please remember that erosion has modified the surface of the earth more than the combined activities of volcanoes, earthquakes, tidal waves, tornadoes and all the excavations of mankind

We have gravely pointed fingers of warning in the direction of China as a country whose land practices should be anathema to the farmers of our own youthful country. This would seem amusing, if it were not so tragic. The probability is that of all the countries of the world, we of the United States have been most wasteful of our land resources.

—Hugh Hammond Bennett

since the beginning of history. That it proceeds slowly, usually taking a thin layer at a time, does not in the least alter the significance of the impoverishing effects of the agency, speeded up by man's activities and operating through long periods of time. Unfortunately, this fact of slow procedure does seem to blind the eyes of mankind. The mental processes of the average person never seem to focus sharply upon the accumulative effects of sheet

erosion. For some peculiar cause the average man, although seeing the actual performance during every rain, really fails to comprehend its meaning. He views it unconsciously; or, forgetting the principle of mathematics, the progress seems too slow to be
impressive. At any rate, few are concerned about the matter until raw, unproductive clay,
even bedrock, begins to appear in sloping fields, at which stage it usually is too late to do
very much about it. Even now, having forgotten the original condition of the fields, many
believe the soil was always yellow or red like the erosion-exposed subsoil, or that the rocks
were "heaved up" by frost or invaded the fields by some indefinite process not worth the
trouble of looking into.

Erosion an Old Process

Not all men have been so blind to the effects of erosion. The process is an old one. It began
in the dim past, probably in the first sloping field cultivated by man. In various parts of
the world the evil has been strenuously opposed for many centuries. There are terraces in
the Mediterranean basin on which olive trees a thousand years old are still growing. Some
of these ancient walled benches were constructed before the time of Christ, built to hold
the land in place for continuing agricultural use. . . .

In 1813 Thomas Jefferson, writing about his farm in Albemarle County, Virginia,
said:

"Our country is hilly and we have been in the habit of plowing in straight rows,
whether up or down hill, in oblique lines, or however they lead, and our soil was all rapidly running into the rivers. We now plow horizontally following the curvature of the hills
and hollows on dead level, however crooked the lines may be. Every furrow thus acts as a
reservoir to receive and retain the waters, all of which go to the benefit of the growing
plant instead of running off into the streams."

Many of Jefferson's fields are still in good shape, but those of some of the farms
adjacent to his estate are terribly gullied. The contrast is enough to suggest that some of
his neighbors were not convinced of his assertion that the soil in that part of the country
was rapidly running off into the rivers. There still are among us a few who will insist that
some of our assertions with respect to erosion are not true. I am inclined to the view that
these are men who feel such things should not be true, and, therefore, are not true, as they
see it. . . .

The United States the Most Wasteful Nation

When I speak of many farmers having failed to see these things, I do not want to be
understood as meaning that only farmers have been guilty. Most of us have been blind
and soundly asleep with respect to the real meaning of erosion. Some of our classical
volumes have described practically every process relating to the agricultural use of land,
save this one. Some of them do not so much as mention the problem, which more than
any other single agency having to do with man's activities, or combination of such agencies, is impoverishing the agricultural lands of this country. We have gravely pointed
fingers of warning in the direction of China as a country whose land practices should be
anathema to the farmers of our own youthful country. This would seem amusing, if it
were not so tragic. The probability is that of all the countries of the world, we of the
United States have been most wasteful of our land resources. I am familiar with the
greater part of the agricultural area of this continent and most of that over the northern

half of South America. Within that great area not one country has even remotely approximated the conditions with respect to impoverishing erosion that we have in great abundance here in the United States. This is due partly to the peculiar characteristics of our soils and rainfall and partly to our farm practices. It is also due in part to our stupendous ignorance with respect to the gouging effects of rainwater running across unprotected slopes. We are 75 to a hundred years behind with our studies relating to these processes and to methods of controlling them. We have diligently studied almost every other agricultural subject but this one, the one which should have been studied first. Vast areas of land have been destroyed in other countries, to be sure, but the destroying process took thousands of years. The headway we have made in this direction, which I am going to discuss more specifically in a moment, has largely been achieved within the brief period of less than two centuries, most of it within the past 30 to 50 years. . . .

Cost of Erosion

The potential value of the plant food contained in the soil washed out of the fields of America every year, based on the average chemical analysis of the soils of the country and the cheapest form of commercial fertilizers, amounts to about $2,000,000,000. The indications are that in normal times the actual annual cost caused by erosion is in the neighborhood of $400,000,000.

The debit side of the process does not end with the direct impoverishment and destruction of upland fields, and the consequent increased cost of cultivating, fertilizing, liming and the growing of soil-improving crops on stiff erosion-exposed clay. Much of the material washed out of fields and pastures is deposited over lower slopes and productive bottom lands where it usually is not needed because of the original productivity of these lands. Unfortunately, much of this overwash is poorer than the soil it covers, as in the instance of relatively unproductive sand and gravel laid down over rich loam or clay; or of poor, raw, humus-deficient clay washed out of gullies down over good loam, mellowed with humus. Moreover, with stream channels choked, overflows become more frequent, causing the abandonment of land that once was high-grade farm land. Reservoirs are filled with mud, as well as irrigation and drainage ditches, harbors and fish ponds. Highways are covered and culverts are filled with outwash material; even the streets of some cities and towns have to be cleared of the products of erosion following spring rains, i.e., they have to be de-mudded. . . .

National Program of Soil Conservation

Realizing the enormous cost of soil erosion, and the fact that with tens of thousands of hard-working farmers, operating on severely eroded lands, it is impossible to make a real living even when prices are good, Congress, four years ago, provided funds for getting under way a national program of soil conservation. The primary purpose of this program is to devise practical measures for saving the soil yet remaining on the sloping farm land of the country, and to determine the best use for those lands which have been largely stripped of their productive surface soil. Eleven erosion experiment stations have been established in as many major soil and climatic regions, where erosion is known to be a very grave problem.

For the first time in history this problem is being studied in a really scientific manner. The information which we should have had 50 or 75 years ago is just now being acquired. We are finding out how rapidly soil is being lost from different soils, occupying different slopes, devoted to various crops, cultivated in different ways, and the manner by which these losses occur. We are learning, also, how the losses can be reduced or controlled. Every promising practical method is being tried out as rapidly as it can be put under experimentation. Already we have learned that we really have known very little about erosion processes. But we are making headway, we are getting our hands on some of the fundamental facts that long have been acutely needed as a basis for correct procedure. We have learned, also, that the job is one of immense proportions. The difficulties are legion. Obviously, we ere going to need all the help we can get. If any of you have any suggestions to give us, any worth while results based on actual farm experience, please tell us about them, remembering that if this is to be a permanent nation we must save this most indispensable of all our God-given assets—the soil, from which comes our food and raiment. If we fail in this, remember that much sooner than we have expected this will be a nation of subsoil farmers. For lack of foresight and willingness to look to the future, our children will condemn us, as already I have heard the children condemn the practices of their forebears in a number of American communities where erosion has turned back the hands of progress by laying waste the very productive substance of the country.

We can not afford to admit the possibility of failure in this fight. The penalty is too inconceivably severe. We must, in this combat, insist, as some one has said, that "There is no failure except ceasing to try."

Source: Bennett, Hugh H. "Soil Erosion a Costly Farm Evil." Address to Farmers' Week Program, Ohio State University, January 31, 1933. *Speeches of Hugh Hammond Bennett.* Natural Resources Conservation Service, U.S. Department of Agriculture. www.nrcs.usda.gov/about/history/speeches/19330131.html.

NOTE

1. Hugh Hammon Bennett and W.R. Chapline, *Soil Erosion: A National Menace.* U.S. Department of Agriculture Circular No. 33 (Washington, D.C.: U.S. Government Printing Office, 1928), 22.

| DOCUMENT 6.8 | # President Roosevelt Dedicates Hoover Dam |

"The Mighty Waters of the Colorado Were Running Unused to the Sea"

September 3, 1935

The twin goals of economic recovery and environmental transformation were firmly yoked together during the New Deal era. President Franklin D. Roosevelt and his fellow New Dealers understood that poor environmental stewardship was one of the chief corrosive agents responsible for the crumbling of America's economic foundations. They believed that if they could reverse destructive environmental policies—and introduce new policies that harnessed the nation's natural resources for economic advancement in more sensible and sustainable ways—they would be well on their way to bringing the Great Depression to an end.

The belief that natural resource development and economic revitalization went hand in hand was especially evident in the realm of water policy. Massive hydroelectric dams, aqueducts, irrigation systems, and other water development projects sprouted all across the United States during the 1930s and 1940s. These initiatives were especially important in the West, where water and energy were in enormous demand. Engineers, architects, and laborers with the Bureau of Reclamation and other federal agencies were thus given sanction to wrench the waters of the Colorado, Columbia, and other major rivers of the West into submission for the purposes of irrigation, flood control, and electricity.

Today, these re-engineered rivers of the West are mourned by some environmentalists and sportsmen as tragic shadows of their formerly wild and ecologically vibrant selves. But when they were first built, these creations of steel and concrete were almost universally applauded by Depression-devastated Americans as heralds of a brighter economic future. Certainly, that was how Roosevelt viewed these projects, as evidenced by his remarks at the dedication of Boulder Dam—now known as Hoover Dam—on September 3, 1935, excerpted here.

Senator Pittman, Secretary Ickes, Governors of the Colorado's States, and you especially who have built Boulder Dam:

This morning I came, I saw and I was conquered, as everyone would be who sees for the first time this great feat of mankind.

Ten years ago the place where we are gathered was an unpeopled, forbidding desert. In the bottom of a gloomy canyon, whose precipitous walls rose to a height of more than a thousand feet, flowed a turbulent, dangerous river. The mountains on either side of the canyon were difficult of access with neither road nor trail, and their rocks were protected by neither trees nor grass from the blazing heat of the sun. The site of Boulder City was a cactus-covered waste. The transformation wrought here in these years is a twentieth-century marvel.

We are here to celebrate the completion of the greatest dam in the world, rising 726 feet above the bed-rock of the river and altering the geography of a whole region; we are here to see the creation of the largest artificial lake in the world—115 miles long, holding enough water, for example, to cover the State of Connecticut to a depth of ten feet; and we are here to see nearing completion a power house which will contain the largest generators and turbines yet installed in this country, machinery that can continuously supply nearly two million horsepower of electric energy.

> *We know that, as an unregulated river, the Colorado added little of value to the region this dam serves. When in flood the river was a threatening torrent. In the dry months of the year it shrank to a trickling stream.*
>
> —Franklin D. Roosevelt

All these dimensions are superlative. They represent and embody the accumulated engineering knowledge and experience of centuries; and when we behold them it is fitting that we pay tribute to the genius of their designers. We recognize also the energy, resourcefulness and zeal of the builders, who, under the greatest physical obstacles, have pushed this work forward to completion two years in advance of the contract requirements. But especially, we express our gratitude to the thousands of workers who gave brain and brawn to this great work of construction.

Beautiful and great as this structure is, it must also be considered in its relationship to the agricultural and industrial development and in its contribution to the health and comfort of the people of America who live in the Southwest.

To divert and distribute the waters of an arid region, so that there shall be security of rights and efficiency in service, is one of the greatest problems of law and of administration to be found in any Government. The farms, the cities, the people who live along the many thousands of miles of this river and its tributaries—all of them depend upon the conservation, the regulation, and the equitable division of its ever-changing water supply. What has been accomplished on the Colorado in working out such a scheme of distribution is inspiring to the whole country. Through the cooperation of the States whose people depend upon this river, and of the Federal Government which is concerned in the general welfare, there is being constructed a system of distributive works and of laws and practices which will insure to the millions of people who now dwell in this basin, and the millions of others who will come to dwell here in future generations, a just, safe and permanent system of water rights. In devising these policies and the means for putting them into practice the Bureau of Reclamation of the Federal Government has taken, and is destined to take in the future, a leading and helpful part. The Bureau has been the instrument which gave effect to the legislation introduced in Congress by Senator Hiram Johnson and Congressman Phil Swing.

We know that, as an unregulated river, the Colorado added little of value to the region this dam serves. When in flood the river was a threatening torrent. In the dry months of the year it shrank to a trickling stream. For a generation the people of Imperial Valley had lived in the shadow of disaster from this river which provided their livelihood, and which is the foundation of their hopes for themselves and their children. Every spring they awaited with dread the coming of a flood, and at the end of nearly every summer they feared a shortage of water would destroy their crops.

The gates of these great diversion tunnels were closed here at Boulder Dam last February. In June a great flood came down the river. It came roaring down the canyons of the Colorado, through Grand Canyon, Iceberg and Boulder Canyons, but it was caught and safely held behind Boulder Dam.

Last year a drought of unprecedented severity was visited upon the West. The watershed of this Colorado River did not escape. In July the canals of the Imperial Valley went dry. Crop losses in that Valley alone totaled $10,000,000 that summer. Had Boulder Dam been completed one year earlier, this loss would have been prevented, because the spring flood would have been stored to furnish a steady water supply for the long dry summer and fall.

Across the San Jacinto Mountains southwest of Boulder Dam, the cities of Southern California are constructing an aqueduct to cost $220,000,000, which they have raised, for the purpose of carrying the regulated waters of the Colorado River to the Pacific Coast 259 miles away.

Across the desert and mountains to the west and south run great electric transmission lines by which factory motors, street and household lights and irrigation pumps will be operated in Southern Arizona and California. Part of this power will be used in pumping the water through the aqueduct to supplement the domestic supplies of Los Angeles and surrounding cities.

Navigation of the river from Boulder Dam to the Grand Canyon has been made possible, a 115-mile stretch that has been traversed less than half a dozen times in history. An immense new park has been created for the enjoyment of all our people.

At what cost was this done? Boulder Dam and the power houses together cost a total of $108,000,000, all of which will be repaid with interest in fifty years under the contracts for sale of the power. Under these contracts, already completed, not only will the cost be repaid, but the way is opened for the provision of needed light and power to the consumer at reduced rates. In the expenditure of the price of Boulder Dam during the depression years work was provided for 4,000 men, most of them heads of families, and many thousands more were enabled to earn a livelihood through manufacture of materials and machinery.

And this picture is true on different scales in regard to the thousands of projects undertaken by the Federal Government, by the States and by the counties and municipalities in recent years. The overwhelming majority of them are of definite and permanent usefulness.

Throughout our national history we have had a great program of public improvements, and in these past two years all that we have done has been to accelerate that program. We know, too, that the reason for this speeding up was the need of giving relief to several million men and women whose earning capacity had been destroyed by the complexities and lack of thought of the economic system of the past generation.

No sensible person is foolish enough to draw hard and fast classifications as to usefulness or need. Obviously, for instance, this great Boulder Dam warrants universal approval because it will prevent floods and flood damage, because it will irrigate thousands of acres of tillable land and because it will generate electricity to turn the wheels of many factories and illuminate countless homes. But can we say that a five-foot brushwood dam across the head waters of an arroyo, and costing only a millionth part of Boulder Dam, is an undesirable project or a waste of money? Can we say that the great brick high school, costing $2,000,000, is a useful expenditure but that a little wooden school house project, costing five or ten thousand dollars, is a wasteful extravagance? Is it fair to approve a huge city boulevard and, at the same time, disapprove the improvement of a muddy farm-to-market road?

While we do all of this, we give actual work to the unemployed and at the same time we add to the wealth and assets of the Nation. These efforts meet with the approval of the people of the Nation.

In a little over two years this great national work has accomplished much. We have helped mankind by the works themselves and, at the same time, we have created the necessary purchasing power to throw in the clutch to start the wheels of what we call private industry. Such expenditures on all of these works, great and small, flow out to many beneficiaries; they revive other and more remote industries and businesses. Money is put in circulation. Credit is expanded and the financial and industrial mechanism of America is stimulated to more and more activity. Labor makes wealth. The use of materials makes wealth. To employ workers and materials when private employment has failed is to translate into great national possessions the energy that otherwise would be wasted. Boulder Dam is a splendid symbol of that principle. The mighty waters of the Colorado were running unused to the sea. Today we translate them into a great national possession.

I might go further and suggest to you that use begets use. Such works as this serve as a means of making useful other national possessions. Vast deposits of precious metals are scattered within a short distance of where we stand today. They await the development of cheap power.

These great Government power projects will affect not only the development of agriculture and industry and mining in the sections that they serve, but they will also prove useful yardsticks to measure the cost of power throughout the United States. It is my belief that the Government should proceed to lay down the first yardstick from this great power plant in the form of a State power line, assisted in its financing by the Government, and tapping the wonderful natural resources of Southern Nevada. Doubtless the same policy of financial assistance to State authorities can be followed in the development of Nevada's sister State, Arizona, on the other side of the River.

With it all, with work proceeding in every one of the more than three thousand counties in the United States, and of a vastly greater number of local divisions of Government, the actual credit of Government agencies is on a stronger and safer basis than at any time in the past six years. Many States have actually improved their financial position in the past two years. Municipal tax receipts are being paid when the taxes fall due, and tax arrearages are steadily declining.

It is a simple fact that Government spending is already beginning to show definite signs of its effect on consumer spending; that the putting of people to work by the Government has put other people to work through private employment, and that in two years and a half we have come to the point today where private industry must bear the principal responsibility of keeping the processes of greater employment moving forward with accelerated speed.

The people of the United States are proud of Boulder Dam. With the exception of the few who are narrow visioned, people everywhere on the Atlantic Seaboard, people in the Middle West and the Northwest, people in the South, must surely recognize that the national benefits which will be derived from the completion of this project will make themselves felt in every one of the forty-eight States. They know that poverty or distress in a community two thousand miles away may affect them, and equally that prosperity and higher standards of living across a whole continent will help them back home.

Today marks the official completion and dedication of Boulder Dam, the first of four great Government regional units. This is an engineering victory of the first order—another great achievement of American resourcefulness, American skill and determination.

That is why I have the right once more to congratulate you who have built Boulder Dam and on behalf of the Nation to say to you, "Well done."

Source: Roosevelt, Franklin D. Dedication of Boulder Dam. *Franklin D. Roosevelt and Conservation, 1911–1945*, edited by Edgar B. Nixon. 2 vols. New York, 1957. vol. 1, pp. 430–441.

DOCUMENT
6.9

The Flood Control Act

"Improvements of Rivers . . . Are in the Interest of the General Welfare"

June 22, 1936

The Flood Control Act of 1936 was crafted and passed in response to a series of damaging floods that rocked Depression-era America in the early 1930s. Under the terms of this legislation, the federal government was given permanent authority to sponsor major flood control projects across the United States, from the Mississippi and Tennessee valleys of the East to the Missouri and other major river systems of the West. These projects included levee construction, river channelization, dam and related hydropower construction, large-scale pumping systems, and coastal protection measures, and in many locales they succeeded in reducing levels of vulnerability to flooding. The act, however, was passed in a Depression-era political environment that was already disposed to look favorably on any dam, lock, or canal that promised construction jobs, cheap energy, protection from catastrophic floods and drought, improved commercial navigation, and other forms of economic stimulus. In addition, the language of the Flood Control Act stipulated that the federal government would shoulder 100 percent of the costs for these projects.

This wrinkle, which remained entrenched in subsequent renewals and incarnations of the Flood Control Act, laid the groundwork for one of the most ambitious and sustained public works campaigns in the nation's history. Hundreds of major water development projects were undertaken across the country over the ensuing years, and collectively these projects are frequently described as a testament to our nation's "technical skill and humane spirit."[1] But the funding terms of the 1936 act also made water development projects a major source of pork-barrel spending in twentieth-century American politics. Legions of congressmen, backed by local economic interests, maneuvered to insert federally financed projects into appropriations bills for the benefit of their districts. In the meantime, water development agencies such as the U.S. Corps of Engineers and the Bureau of Reclamation thrived on this unleashed political dynamic, receiving annual boosts to their budgets that were the envy of most other federal agencies. In return, officials and engineers sought out all manner of water development projects to justify their generous funding, ensure the continued vitality of their particular bureaucratic kingdoms, and score points in their ongoing competition with other federal water agencies for prestige and primacy. This escalating cycle of development ultimately resulted in major upheavals to vast areas of the American landscape, including the damming of nearly every major U.S. river at virtually any point along its length where it was 1) technically feasible and 2) profitable for politically connected local stakeholders. The following is an excerpt from the 1936 act, which President Franklin D. Roosevelt signed into law on June 22.

Be it enacted by the Senate and House of Representatives of the United States of America in Congress assembled.

DECLARATION OF POLICY

Section 1. It is hereby recognized that destructive floods upon the rivers of the United States, upsetting orderly processes and causing loss of life and property, including the erosion of lands and impairing and obstructing navigation, highways, railroads, and other channels of commerce between the States, constitute a menace to national welfare; that it is the sense of Congress that flood control on navigational waters or their tributaries is a proper activity of the Federal Government in cooperation with States, their political sub-divisions and localities thereof; that investigations and improvements of rivers and other waterways, including watersheds thereof, for flood-control purposes are in the interest of the general welfare; that the Federal Government should improve or participate in the improvement of navigable waters or their tributaries including watersheds thereof, for flood-control purposes if the benefits to whomsoever they may accrue are in excess of the estimated costs, and if the lives and social security of people are otherwise adversely affected.

Sec 2. That, hereafter, Federal investigations and improvements of rivers and other waterways for flood control and allied purposes shall be under the jurisdiction of and shall be prosecuted by the War Department under the direction of the Secretary of War and supervision of the Chief of Engineers, and Federal investigations of watersheds and measures for runoff and waterflow retardation and soil erosion prevention on watersheds shall be wider the jurisdiction of and shall be prosecuted by the Department of Agriculture under the direction of the Secretary of Agriculture, except as otherwise provided by Act of Congress; and that in their reports upon examinations and surveys, the Secretary of War and the Secretary of Agriculture shall be guided as to flood-control measures by the principles set forth in section 1 in the determination of the Federal interests involved: *Provided,* That the foregoing grants of authority shall not interfere with investigations and river improvements incident to reclamation projects that may now be in progress or may be hereafter undertaken by the Bureau of Reclamation of the Interior Department pursuant to any general or specific authorization of law.

Sec. 3. That hereafter no money appropriated under authority of this Act shall be expended on the construction of any project until States, political sub-divisions of, or other responsible local agencies have given assurances satisfactory to the Secretary of War that they will (a) provide without cost to the United States all lands, easements, and rights of way necessary for the construction of the project except as otherwise provided herein; (b) hold and save the United States free from damages due to the constructed works; (c) maintain and operate all the works after completion in accordance with regulations prescribed by the Secretary of War: *Provided,* That the construction of any dam authorized herein may be undertaken without delay when the dam site has been acquired and the assurances prescribed herein have been furnished, without awaiting the acquisition of the easements, and rights-of-way required for the reservoir area: *And provided further,* That whenever expenditures for lands, easements, and rights-of-way by States political sub-divisions thereof, or responsible local agencies for any individual project or useful part thereof shall have exceeded the present estimated construction cost therefor, the local agency concerned may be reimbursed one-half of its excess expenditures over said estimated construction cost: *And provided further:* That when benefits of any project or useful part thereof accrue to lands and property outside of the State in which said project or part thereof is located, the Secretary of War with the consent of the State wherein the same are located may acquire the necessary lands, easements, and rights-of-way for said project or part thereof after he has received from the States, political subdivisions thereof, or responsible local agencies benefited the present estimated cost of said lands, easements, and rights-of-way, less one-half the amount by which the estimated cost of these lands, easements, and rights-of-way exceeds the estimated cost of construction cost corresponding thereto: And providing further, That the Secretary of War shall determine the proportion of the present estimated cost of said lands, easements, and rights-of-way that each State in which said project or part thereof is located, provision (c) of this section shall not apply thereto; nothing herein shall impair or abridge the powers now existing in the Department of War with respect to navigable streams: *And provided further,* That nothing herein shall be construed to interfere with the completion at any reservoir or flood control work authorized by the Congress and now under way.

Sec. 4. The consent of Congress is hereby given to any two or more States to enter into compacts or agreements in connection with any project or operation authorized by this Act for flood control or the prevention of damage to life or property by reason of floods upon any stream or streams and their tributaries which lie in two or more such States approved by the Secretary of War, funds for construction and maintenance, for the payment of damages, and for the purchase of rights-of-way, lands, and easements in connection with such project or operation. No such compact or agreement shall become effective without the further consent or ratification of Congress, except a compact or agreement which provides that all money to be expended pursuant thereto and all work to be performed thereunder shall be expended and performed by the Department of War, with the exception of such reasonable sums as may be reserved by the States entering into the compact or agreement for the purpose of collecting taxes and maintaining the necessary State organizations for carrying out the compact or agreement.

Source: Flood Control Act of 1936. Center for Columbia River History. www.ccrh.org/comm/cottage/primary/1936.htm.

NOTE

1. Joseph L. Arnold, *The Evolution of the Flood Control Act* (Fort Belvoir, Va.: Office of History, U.S. Army Corps of Engineers), 1988.

DOCUMENT 6.10

Report of the Great Plains Drought Area Committee

"This Destruction Has Been Caused Partly by Over grazing, Partly by Excessive Plowing"

August 27, 1936

The stunning specter of the Dust Bowl and its millions of refugees prompted President Franklin D. Roosevelt to request a study of the past, present, and possible futures of the Great Plains. "Before spending any more money, the president wanted to know if the plains could be saved, and if so, how," summarized one historian. In addition, he wanted to know "whether the arid flatlands should have been settled. Had it been a colossal mistake to allow homesteading on the land? Was the Jeffersonian small farmer, small town, agri-citizen model a horrible fit for the grasslands? Had this environmental catastrophe—the worst in American history—been aided by government?"[1]

Responsibility for responding to these questions was put at the feet of seven federal officials affiliated with various resource agencies, including Hugh Hammond Bennett, Soil Conservation Service chief; John C. Page of the Bureau of Reclamation;, Secretary of Agriculture Henry A. Wallace; and Morris L. Cooke, director of the Rural Electrification Administration. Cooke served as chairman of this group, called the Great Plains Drought Committee. The committee spent months analyzing Great Plains data and studies from various corners of the federal government then issued a "personal and confidential" report to the president on August 27, 1936. This committee report—in addition to a second one released at the end of the year called Future of the Great Plains*—affixed blame for the Dust Bowl on a wide range of players, from ignorant settlers to shortsighted policymakers to avaricious speculators. In fact, these remarkable documents comprised a stunning "denunciation of the pioneering ethos"[2] that was so integral to America's self-image, and they offered no easy and painless solutions for Great Plains restoration. But the committee* *did lay out a path for gradual recovery based on federally mandated strategies of soil conservation, sustainable water use, and regional cooperation among stakeholders. The committee members also emphasized that failure in these efforts was not an option. Following are excerpts from the first report, which had a major impact on the Roosevelt Administration's subsequent approach to Great Plains restoration.*

. . . A trip through the drought area, supplementing data already on record, makes it evident that we are not confronted merely with a short term problem of relief, already being dealt with by several agencies of the Federal Government, but with a long term problem of readjustment and reorganization.

The agricultural economy of the Great Plains will become increasingly unstable and unsafe, in view of the impossibility of permanent increase in the amount of rainfall, unless over cropping, over grazing and improper farm methods are prevented. There is no reason to believe that the primary factors of climate temperature, precipitation and winds in the Great Plains region have undergone any fundamental change. The future of the region must depend, therefore, on the degree to which farming practices conform to natural conditions. Because the situation has now passed out of the individual farmer's control, the reorganization of farming practices demands the cooperation of many agencies, including the local, State and Federal governments.

We wish to make it plain that nothing we here propose is expected or intended to impair the independence of the individual farmer in the Great Plains area. Our proposals will look toward the greatest possible degree of stabilization of the region's economy, a higher and more secure income for each family, the spreading of the shock of inevitable droughts so that they will not be crushing in their effects, the conservation of land and water, a steadily diminishing dependence on public grants and subsidies, the restoration of the credit of individuals and of local and State governments, and a thorough going consideration of how great a population, and in what areas, the Great Plains can support. . . .

> *The Homestead Act of 1862, limiting an individual holding to 160 acres, was on the western plains a stimulus to over cultivation, and, for that matter, almost an obligatory vow of poverty.*
>
> —Great Plains Drought Committee

These objectives are not now attainable by individual action, but we believe they will restore an individual independence which has been lost. Mistaken public policies have been largely responsible for the situation now existing. That responsibility must be liquidated by new policies. The Federal Government must do its full share in remedying the damage caused by a mistaken homesteading policy, by the stimulation of war time demands which led to over cropping and over grazing, and by encouragement of a system of agriculture which could not be both permanent and prosperous.

In many measures the Federal Government must take the initiative, particularly in furnishing leadership and guidance, and in participating to a substantial extent in the construction or financing of the needed public works. . . . There need not be, and should not be, conflict of interest or jurisdiction between State and local agencies on the one hand and Federal agencies on the other, There need not be, and should not be, impairment of local and individual initiative.

There must be, on the other hand, continuous and sustained joint efforts on the part of all agencies concerned. The problem of the Great Plains is not the product of a single act of nature, of a single year or even of a series of exceptionally bad years. It has come into being over a considerable period of time, and time will be required to deal with it.

The steps taken must be continuous, non intermittent and patiently followed. A reasonably stable agricultural economy must be established, maintained and handed on to the children of this generation.

CAUSES OF THE PRESENT SITUATION

We must analyze causes before we can prescribe remedies. The basic cause of the present Great Plains situation is an attempt to impose upon the region a system of agriculture to which the Plains are not adapted to bring into a semi arid region methods which, on the whole, are suitable only for a humid region.

The Great Plains area has climatic attributes which cannot be altered by any act of man, although they may slowly become changed, for better or worse, by natural weather cycles which we cannot yet predict.

With respect to plant growth, however, the stripping off of the mellow top soil, by unrestrained erosion, down to less absorptive, less tractable sub soil, is the equivalent of an unfavorable soil climate change. Adoption of soil conserving farm practices based on increased use of the rainfall by increase of its absorption, results in conservation not only of the soil but also of the water without which the soil cannot be utilized with maximum efficiency.

By the Great Plains is meant, in general, an area stretching from west central Texas to the border of Canada, definitely bounded on the west by the Rocky Mountains, more irregularly delimited on the east near the 100th meridian, where, before settlement by the white man, the "short grass" country merged gradually with the "tall grass," or prairie, country. The critical area now under discussion excludes southwestern Texas but includes the Texas Panhandle, the Oklahoma Panhandle, northeastern New Mexico, and all the northern portion of the Plains. The area may again be divided, by a line run midway east and west across Kansas and eastern Colorado, into the Northern Plains and the Southern Plains.

The entire region is marked by a low annual rainfall, often concentrated in storms of short duration and great intensity, by wide fluctuations of temperature, and by prevailing winds not equaled in average strength anywhere in the United States except along the sea coasts. The soil is derived mainly from old water transported material, with some areas of drifting sand. In the North the Bad Lands of South Dakota are evidence of extensive prehistoric erosion, but the longer winters, protecting the ground by frost and snow, have made wind erosion a somewhat less serious danger in the North than in the South. In the South much sandy soil is naturally unstable and the finer grained soil becomes loose and unstable with exhaustion of the humus supply by continuous cultivation. These lands have been held in place chiefly by such natural growths as buffalo grass and grama grass.

One primary source of disaster has been the destruction of millions of acres of this natural cover, an act which in such a series of dry years as that through which we are now passing left the loose soil exposed to the winds. This destruction has been caused partly by over grazing, partly by excessive plowing. It has been an accompaniment of settlement, intensified in operation and effect since the World War. . . . As the ranges were enclosed feed crops were raised to fatten stock, requiring intensive cultivation, and the ranges themselves were overstocked. Thus there was not only a progressive breaking up of the native sod but a thinning out of the grass cover on lands not yet plowed.

The settlers lacked both the knowledge and the incentive necessary to avoid these mistakes. They were misled by those who should have been their natural guides. The

Federal homestead policy, which kept land allotments low and required that a portion of each should be plowed, is now seen to have caused immeasurable harm. The Homestead Act of 1862, limiting an individual holding to 160 acres, was on the western plains a stimulus to over cultivation, and, for that matter, almost an obligatory vow of poverty.

Subsequent enlargement of the allowable individual holding did not solve the problem. A study of homestead holdings in North Dakota and Montana shows that whereas in eastern North Dakota a 160 acre tract was sufficient to support a family, tracts of two and three times this size were inadequate in western North Dakota and Montana. In the latter area tracts of several times the homesteads actually granted would have been necessary. . . .

> *We are certain that under any conceivable climatic conditions the practices which have destroyed the sod and desiccated the soil are harmful and must, for the good of all concerned, be changed or abandoned.*
>
> —Great Plains Drought Committee

Fortunately or unfortunately, the settlement of the Western Plains occurred at the end of what appears to have been a forty year dry period and at the beginning of a wet period which has apparently terminated. Thus the brief and occasional droughts which descended during the latter part of the nineteenth end early years of the twentieth century were assumed to be exceptional and were not taken as warnings. On the contrary, speculation continued and harmful methods of farming persisted.

As the twentieth century advanced higher powered plowing, planting and harvesting machinery made possible the cultivation of larger areas without increased labor. The World War, with its high prices for food crops during years of abundant rains, stimulated production to new heights, and after the war farmers were forced to expand their acreage in order to sustain their cash income during a period of falling prices. In the Texas Panhandle alone wheat planting increased from 876,000 acres in 1924 to 2,458,000 in 1929.

Nature and the market combined to make wheat farming highly speculative. Extreme instances can be found in which more than 90 per cent of the entire net income of a wheat farm over a period of twenty years was concentrated in a single year. Yet each year some or all of the wheat land was plowed and the soil exposed to the destructive forces of sun and wind.

The economic results have been general insecurity, bankruptcy, tax delinquencies, absentee ownership, and an increase in tenancy. In eight Great Plains states the percentage of tenant farmers rose from 15.5 in 1880 to 38.9 in 1930. Since 1930 it has risen again, standing at 41.1 in 1935. Notwithstanding heroic efforts of their occupants, many farms have been abandoned. About 150,000 persons moved out of the Great Plains region between 1930 and 1935. The "suit case farmer" has made his appearance, visiting his land only a few weeks a year to plant and harvest his crop, making no permanent improvements and abandoning his crop in drought years.

The economic deterioration of communities, with loss of public credit, suspension of schools, neglect of roads and a general decline of community activities, is more difficult to measure, but its reality is apparent to any one who studies or even visits the region.

The physical results of a mistaken agricultural policy are now being experienced under the blistering winds of the droughts. With the destruction of the natural grass cover the soil has been exposed to the drying influence of the summer winds, to blowing, and to washing by the rains. Water has not been adequately conserved. In many parts of the area there has been a decline in the ground water level, though. How much of this effect is due to excessive use and how much to the decline in rainfall is not yet certain.

The dust storms of 1934 and 1935 have been visible evidence to nearly every American living east of the Rocky Mountains that something is seriously wrong. The extent of erosion on the Great Plains has not yet been accurately measured. It is safe to say that 80 per cent is now in some stage of erosion. As much as 15 per cent may already have been seriously and permanently injured.

This is a situation that will not by any possibility cure itself. A series of wet years might postpone the destructive process, yet in the end, by raising false hopes and by encouraging renewal of mistaken agricultural practices, might accelerate it. . . .

We should adapt our policies to promote the welfare of the present inhabitants of the Plains under the conditions we can reasonably foresee, We are certain that under any conceivable climatic conditions the practices which have destroyed the sod and desiccated the soil are harmful and must, for the good of all concerned, be changed or abandoned. . . .

LINES OF ACTION

. . . The necessary steps are clearly indicated. The region should be divided into sub-areas according to the types of use to which each portion of it may be best and most safely devoted; and, in addition, to determine the kinds of agricultural practice and engineering treatment required to fit each portion to its indicated use. Certain sub-marginal lands should be taken permanently out of commercial production. On arable farms such soil conserving practices as re-grassing, contour plowing, listing, terracing, strip cropping and the planting of shelter trees should be followed. Grasses of demonstrated fitness to local conditions should be developed and used.

In a land of little rain it is imperative that water should never be allowed needlessly to go to waste. The farming practices described will help to reduce run-off and to hold water in the soil. Dams may be of use not only in checking water erosion but in holding back water for use during dry periods. In some cases they may produce power for pumping and other local uses. Thousands of stock reservoirs and wells should be developed to provide a more adequate supply for stock. Small irrigation systems for groups of families will be found useful, and construction of large irrigation projects to supply families already in the region should be considered.

Some readjustment of water rights appears essential. It is contrary to the basic principles of conservation to allow water to be diverted to poor lands when there is not enough to supply neighboring lands of better quality.

Some of these projects may be carried out as a part of a work relief program, others as major public works, still others by the farmers themselves, either individually or in cooperating groups. In the case of works by the farmers the necessity for credit will immediately be felt of a kind available to a capital structure already burdened with its maximum load of ordinary commercial credit.

Measures of this sort will improve the conditions and practices on individual farms, but they cannot be expected to effect the change which is urgently needed in the land use pattern of the region. We believe that public acquisition of lands should be continued.

Some types of land within the area, we believe, should be leased or optioned, with the stipulation that the owners shall carry on an approved program of restoration to grass or forest, other lands, too seriously injured to warrant restoration by private enterprise, should be taken over by county, State or Federal governments and put permanently under grass or forest.

It may be found advisable to extend the grazing range by taking some arable farm lands under public ownership. In some cases abandoned farms or farms reverting to public ownership under tax forfeiture may be acquired in this way, with proper compensation to owners for such equities as exist.

Obviously no permanency of the agricultural system or of the land itself is possible if the individual owner is allowed to put his holdings to uses which will ultimately destroy them and endanger the property of his neighbors. We suggest that the possibilities of restraining such owners, within the limits of laws now existing or which may be constitutionally enacted, be fully explored. The States affected are already keenly aware of this problem. . . .

Wherever possible the cooperative principle should be invoked and encouraged, as particularly adapted to the needs and problems of the region. The Taylor Grazing Act and the grazing regulations in the National Forests and on State lands should be administered with the definite aim of stimulating the formation of cooperative grazing associations. Cooperative grazing districts should be assisted to prevent the over stocking of their lands, and should be aided by a program of public land acquisition to block up their ranges. Citizens of several States and the Pueblo Indians of New Mexico have taken cooperative action to prevent overgrazing. Other farmers may well follow the example they have set.

Local committees, informally selected; have played an important role under the Agricultural Adjustment Administration and the Resettlement Administration. By such committees the interests and wishes of the people may receive adequate expression. The formation of such committees should be encouraged and all governmental agencies should consult and cooperate with them in order to make sure that what is done will have the support of local public opinion.

An educational campaign should be undertaken without delay by the Agricultural Extension Service and the Rehabilitation supervisors, supplemented by suitable curricula in the schools. Churches, farmers' organizations, civic bodies and fraternal orders should be urged to take a part in this campaign, and community discussions of the problem should be stimulated. The results of research carried out by State and Federal agencies should be disseminated. Particular attention should be directed to the demonstrations of the Resettlement Administration and the Soil Conservation Service. The government agencies should be ready at all times to pool their experience and information with that of local agencies and of individuals, in order that there may be the greatest attainable degree of mutual confidence.

A Coordinated Program of Cooperation

It is clear that none of the activities proposed will be of the greatest possible use unless they are coordinated parts of a well-devised project envisaging the entire region. There is no reason why such a project should not exist, nor why it should not be carried through without friction between local and State agencies on the one hand and Federal agencies on the other. The emergency is a test of the democratic system, which we believe can be met without any exercise of arbitrary power by any agency. . . .

The situation is so serious that the Nation, for its own sake, cannot afford to allow the farmer to fail. The future of the Great Plains involves the future not only of the more than 2,500,000 people now living there, and of their descendants; it involves also the future of the nearly 10,000,000 in the states affected, and more remotely but yet substantially the more than 120,000,000 people of the Nation. It is bound up with the development of a sound national farming policy, upon which, in turn, depends our ability to provide both opportunities for and the requirements of a reasonable standard of living for all our people. We endanger our democracy if we allow the Great Plains, or any other section of the country, to become an economic desert.

The Nation has profited by the courage and endurance of the people of the Plains. We have all had large responsibility for the direction of settlement and for the development of agricultural conditions in the area. We cannot discharge ourselves of the obligation thus incurred until we have helped them to create, within the natural and climatic conditions which can be prepared against but cannot be controlled, a secure and prosperous agriculture.

Source: Cooke, Morris, et al. "Report of the Great Plains Drought Area Committee, Aug., 1936." Franklin D. Roosevelt Library, Hopkins Papers. Available at The New Deal Network, http://newdeal.feri.org/hopkins/hop27.htm.

Notes

1. Timothy Egan, *The Worst Hard Time* (Boston: Houghton Mifflin, 2006), 266.
2. Sarah T. Phillips, *This Land, This Nation: Conservation, Rural America, and the New Deal* (New York: Cambridge University Press, 2007), 130.

DOCUMENT
6.11

Interior Secretary Ickes and the Publisher of *Mining World* Clash over Parks

"The People of the West Have No Faith in [Your] Pledges"

August 7 and 20, 1940

During the 1920s and 1930s the U.S. national park system underwent significant expansion, adding iconic parks such as Shenandoah, Great Smoky Mountains, Olympic, Isle Royale, and Bryce Canyon to its fold. In addition, New Deal legislation expanded the authority of the National Park Service to include management of historic sites, national monuments, and national recreational areas—the latter of which represented America's growing interest in tourism and rugged outdoor activities such as hiking, camping, and canoeing, which were viewed as spiritual balms for the everyday pressures of urban-industrial society.

But the growth in the power and influence of the National Park Service (NPS) was controversial in some quarters. In the Pacific Northwest, for example, a federal proposal to establish a huge national park or recreation area in Washington's North Cascades mountain range aroused a storm of condemnation from a wide range of opponents. The dispute began in earnest in 1937, when an NPS study of the region led by Owen A. Tomlinson, superintendent of Mount Rainier National Park, declared that the range's stately forests, wild rivers, and glacier-skirted mountains were "unquestionably of national park caliber."[1] In response, a coalition of local communities, timber and mining interests, pro-development lawmakers, and U.S. Forest Service officials united to shut the park proposal down. The leading representative of industry and local communities in this fight was the Washington State Planning Council, which warned that a national park or recreational area would "lock up" the potential timber and mineral resources in the North Cascades from economic development. This was a potent line of argument in the West at any time but especially during the Depression. The Council declared that public lands in the North Cascades should remain with the Forest Service, which was rightly perceived as more accommodating of mining, timber, and other commercial interests in its management policies. Officials within the Forest Service, meanwhile, worked behind the scenes to torpedo the national park proposal. Their hostility stemmed from the fact that five national forests in the Cascades would have to be handed over to the Department of Interior if the proposed park came to pass.

The battle over the North Cascades eventually drew in Interior Secretary Harold L. Ickes, who was determined to carve a sprawling national recreation area out of the region. In August 1940 Ickes exchanged blistering letters with Miller Freeman, a founder of the Planning Council and publisher of the industry periodical Mining World. *The venom-tipped letters written by these two men alluded to many of the controversies that swirled around federal land policies in the twentieth-century West, including fears that wilderness preservation spelled economic hardship for local towns and industries; rivalries between federal land management agencies; the growing importance of scenic and recreational factors in public land assessments; appropriate allocation of resource stewardship responsibilities between state and federal governments; and heated debates about what constituted "wise use" of natural resources. The August correspondence between Ickes and Freeman is reprinted here.*

After responding to Ickes, Freeman also sent an August 22 letter to Roosevelt in which he urged the president to rebuke his interior secretary for his "vilification" of the Council. He also challenged Roosevelt directly: "After you have examined the matter, I would be glad to hear your present view in the light of these developments by which it seems plain that the Secretary of the Interior entirely ignores State interests, and is attempting to arbitrarily enforce Federal Dictatorship. Do you support his position?"[2]

Roosevelt responded to Freeman a month later with a note that strongly defended Ickes, his administration's record on national park creation, and his efforts to strike an appropriate balance between wilderness conservation and commercial exploitation of America's natural resources. Roosevelt also offered a wry commentary on Freeman's hostile stance:

> *In replying to Secretary Ickes, you, as the founder and a charter member of the Washington State Planning council, state that you ignored his pledges because, you state, the people of the West have no faith in his word, and, moreover, that they prefer that the public lands be administered by some other agency.*

> *Perhaps the Secretary had these actions and expressions of attitude in mind when he called to your attention the fact that the study had not been objective.[3]*

Questions of objectivity aside, the Washington State Planning Council and its allies in the Forest Service and elsewhere stirred up so much public opposition to the creation of a national park or recreation area in the North Cascades that NPS officials reluctantly abandoned the scheme in the early 1940s. But the victory was relatively short-lived. By the early 1960s, public disenchantment with the U.S. Forest Service's pro-industry orientation, combined with the growing political clout of environmental groups such as the Sierra Club and Wilderness Society, triggered a reassessment of the North Cascades national park idea. The battle between wilderness preservationists and politically powerful extractive industries was joined anew in the Pacific Northwest, but this time the preservationists won. On October 2, 1968, President Lyndon B. Johnson signed a law creating the more than 1,000-square-mile North Cascades National Park Complex, which includes North Cascades National Park, Lake Chelan National Recreation Area, and Ross Lake National Recreation Area.

Letter from Harold L. Ickes, Secretary of the Interior, to *The Mining World,* Seattle

August 7, 1940

Washington, *Aug. 7th, 1940*

GENTLEMEN: I have received a copy of the July issue of *Mining World.*

On page one of this issue I note that *Mining World* devotes itself to its field "without sectionalism, without sensationalism, and with scrupulous regard for accuracy." Thirty pages later I come to an article entitled "Conservation—Should it Serve—or Only Save?" which is composed chiefly of sectionalism, sensationalism, and inaccuracy.

I suggest that before you printed this obviously biased attack upon the Department of the Interior you might have attempted to ascertain the facts from any authorized representative of the Department. You might have asked the Washington State Planning Council to let you read the material presented by the National Park Service, which the Council buried in its files while giving publicity to a theme to which it was already committed. If you had made the inquiry you would have found newsworthy facts.

You would have found that in the early stages of the study the Planning Council held seven public mass meetings to pass public judgment on a park proposal which had not been made, and in the light of facts which had not been ascertained. You would have found that after this park proposal had served its purpose in arousing public apprehension, the Council then broadened the scope of its study to include a general inventory of the resources and potentialities of five national forests in the Cascade Range, and concluded that since those five national forests, as a whole, had extensive resources and potentialities no area therein could be considered for national park status. The Council now cites the sentiment of the seven mass meetings as evidence of the soundness of its position.

Had you made inquiry, you would have found that the Planning Council asked the National Park Service for policy statements, which statements were supplied by Superintendent Tomlinson of Mount Rainier National Park and by the Director of the Service. The Council ignored these official statements of policy and used instead its own statement of National Park Service policies, even after the Park Service had notified the council that the Council's statement was inadequate. The Council included in its report a national forest policy statement which was largely prepared by the Forest Service. Your readers would have been interested in knowing that I authorized the Park Service to state that if the study should result in recommending an area for park status that included important mineralized zones, I would be willing to recommend to the Congress that prospecting and mining be continued. That assurance was given in complete candor. How could it possibly be construed as a threat to mining? Yet, both the Council and your magazine played down my statement, and you informed your readers that this Department's "ambitions threaten to close important areas to prospecting and mining."

You also did your readers a disservice when you further elaborated the Planning Council's fantastic statements about H.R. 9351, a bill to amend the Antiquities Act. That bill contains no new authority for the President; it actually restricts existing authority. If the bill were passed, the reservations that the President would be authorized to establish under it would be less restrictive than the national monuments that he can now establish under the Antiquities Act. If the bill were passed, the President would no longer have authority to establish national monuments, which are closed to mining, closed to water conservation projects, and to hunting; under the amended act, he would have authority only to establish recreational areas, in which prospecting and mining, water conservation projects, hunting and grazing would be permitted. The purpose of the bill is to permit the recognition and to integration the development of outstanding recreational resources with the development and use of certain other resources in the same areas. The bill rightly provides no authority for logging in such areas, because the management of timber producing lands is already the responsibility of established Federal agencies.

The authority that the President has to eliminate lands from national forests, and that you view with such alarm in connection with this bill, he has had for forty-three years. He has had, also, authority under the Antiquities Act to remove lands from national forests and to establish them as national monuments since 1906, or for thirty-four years. Those powers of the President exist whether this bill is enacted or not. The real question involved in the bill is a very simple one: do you want recreational reservations set up by Executive Order that are closed to prospecting and mining, water conservation projects, hunting, and grazing, or do you want them open to these activities?

There are undoubtedly areas in the High Cascades that are primarily recreational, and that cannot justifiably be classified as timber producing lands. Even the State Planning Council admits this in a modest statement tucked away on page fourteen of its report, where it says:

"In addition to its national parks, comprising more than 1,140,000 acres, Washington has 1,207,694 acres within the national forests of the Cascade Mountains dedicated by executive order primarily to recreational uses."

The purpose of the study, of course, was to determine how these and similar lands might best be used, but at no time could the Council bring itself to the collection and analysis of facts pertaining to the point because it was so captivated by its symphonic development of the multiple-use theme.

If you had taken the trouble to analyze for your readers the meaning of this term "multiple use," you would have found that it is a meaningless expression. It is definitive of nothing. Its conflicting promises are as subject to question as are the promises of any patent medicine that claims to cure all ills. What conflicts will be resolved by repeating multiple-use platitudes? Any land use may be said to be a multiple use or a single use, depending upon one's point of view, but whether land use is called multiple or single is of no consequence. The main problem in land planning is to determine the most profitable use or combination of uses to which an area may be put. If there is to be profitable management, the area must be devoted to its dominant use or uses, and the extent and kind of subordinate uses must be gauged accordingly.

How best can the great scenic areas of the Cascade Range be used? That is the problem that the Washington State Planning Council had before it when it undertook the Cascade Mountain Study, but its final report throws no light on the question. The broad generalities and fine-sounding assumptions between the report's imposing covers have very little to do with the case. We may as well face the unpleasant fact that the "study" was not a study at all. It was merely a smoke screen to cover a dilatory maneuver. It produced fifty-six pages of nothing new.

Mount Baker, Glacier Peak, Mount Adams, Mount Saint Helens, Mount Hood, and the scenic wilderness areas of the High Cascades are national recreational resources. They cannot profitably be considered as timber producing, or forestry, lands. They should in fact be established as National Recreational Areas, to be administered like Boulder Dam National Recreational Area, by the one authorized recreational agency of the Federal Government. In this liberal type of recreational reservation, prospecting and mining, water conservation projects, and grazing should be permitted, and hunting in accordance with State and Federal laws.

For years the scenic resources of the Cascade Mountains have been subordinated under a land management system that did not dare to recognize one resource above another. Establishment of National Recreational Areas will liberate these outstanding resources, to the benefit of both the State and the Nation.

Sincerely yours,

(Signed) Harold L. Ickes

Letter from Miller Freeman, Publisher, *The Mining World,* to Harold L. Ickes

August 20, 1940

Aug. 20th, 1940

DEAR MR. SECRETARY: We have your letter of August 7th in which you comment at some length upon the article headed "Conservation—Should it Serve, or Only Save?" in the July issue of *Mining World.*

We shall not reply to, nor resent, the charge of "sectionalism, sensationalism and inaccuracy" which you lay against this journal, but we do resent and resist your castigation of the Washington State Planning Council and the special advisory committee for its Cascade Mountains Study.

You typically attribute roguery to those who have the temerity honestly to disagree with you.

The writer of this letter has served as a member of the Washington State Planning Council from the time of its creation six years ago. It is a non-partisan, non-salaried body, composed of men of high character and intelligence—men far above the petty lack of principle which you imply.

You accuse the Council of having ignored an official statement of National Park Service policy which it requested. I wonder if you know this official statement of policy was received by the State Planning Council in exactly nine days less than six months after it had been formally requested. Moreover, the National Park Service statement omitted any reference to "national recreational areas," an element of its program to which you point in your letter.

For these reasons, the Council and its committee rejected the official statement of policy as inadequate and used its own well considered statement.

People of the West know that National Park Service policies are better expressed by present evidence and the record of historic fact than by statements composed to conform to current expediency.

You point out in your letter that you had given a pledge, hedged by conditions, that you would recommend to Congress that prospecting and mining be permitted in Cascade lands given national park status.

Frankly, the people of the West have no faith in such pledges, whether they be made by yourself or the National Park Service.

Still fresh in memory is such a pledge, given at the time that Rainier National Park was created, only to be rescinded later by obscure and unheralded legislation.

You quibble about portions of the Cascade Mountains national forests which "cannot justifiably be classed as timber producing lands" and overlook the evident desire of the National Park Service to escheat to itself vast regions which cannot justifiably be classed as possessing the unique characteristics for which national park treatment is desirable.

The Western states prefer that the enormous areas of the public domain within their borders be administered by the Forest Service rather than the National Park Service because the former has shown willingness to permit true public use of the public domain; to permit people to work, as well as play on it; to permit men to earn, as well as spend on it.

You say the term "multiple use" is a "meaningless expression . . . definitive of nothing." Perhaps that is true in Chicagoanese, but to us in the West, as applied to the public lands it means employment of those lands for the benefit of Americans just as fully as is consistent with sound conservation for their resources.

Conservation has been defined as meaning "wise use." We conceive wise use of the public lands to include logging of ripe timber on a sustained basis; prospecting and mining of mineral deposits; grazing in such manner as to preserve the pastures; utilization of water for power and irrigation; enjoyment of their recreational aspects in full measure.

To the West, wise use of the public domain does not mean its dedication solely to recreation, save for those rare portions whose character specially recommends such treatment.

We will stand on the conclusions of the Washington State Planning Council that the Cascade Mountains do not come within this category.

Mr. Ickes, we wonder if since becoming Secretary of the Interior you have read the Parable of the Talents and have considered Christ's view of hoarding, compared with utilization, expressed in this Parable?

You may remember that the "wicked and slothful servant" only saved the talent with which he had been entrusted; but the "good and Faithful servant" employed his talents and increased them—put them to "multiple use," if you will.

It seems to us that this parable applies to public servants and the public domain with singular directness.

Very truly yours,

Miller Freeman

Source: Correspondence between Interior Secretary Harold L. Ickes and Miller Freeman, Aug. 7 and Aug. 20, 1940. In *Franklin D. Roosevelt and Conservation, 1911–1945*, edited by Edgar B. Nixon. 2 vols. New York, 1957. vol. 2, pp. 462–466.

Notes

1. National Park Service, "North Cascades Area Report," November 1937, 3.
2. Miller Freeman, letter to President Roosevelt, Aug. 22, 1940, in *Franklin D. Roosevelt and Conservation, 1911–1945*, ed. Edgar B. Nixon (New York, 1957), 2:461.
3. Franklin D. Roosevelt, letter to Miller Freeman, September 19, 1940, in *Franklin D. Roosevelt and Conservation, 1911–1945*, ed. Edgar B. Nixon (New York, 1957), 2:475.

CHAPTER 7

Environmental Politics in the Age of Suburbanization

1940–1960

During World War II and the decade of heady economic expansion that followed, issues of environmental protection and wilderness conservation were not high priorities for the American people or their representatives in state legislatures and Washington, D.C. Instead, governmental policies were first crafted to bring America's industrial might to bear against the Axis powers, then funneled into efforts to nurture postwar America to new heights of economic prosperity and growth. These policies succeeded spectacularly, but the rise of middle-class affluence and suburban settlement patterns also brought tremendous new pressures on the nation's environmental resources. By the close of the 1950s, public concern about the state of America's environmental heritage was once again on the rise and infiltrating the chambers of Congress and statehouses across the land.

THE ARSENAL OF DEMOCRACY

When World War II erupted in Europe in 1939, the administration of President Franklin D. Roosevelt scrambled to put America's industrial might to work making armaments and other supplies for the Allies. But it was not until two years later, when the attack on Pearl Harbor triggered the United States' entrance into the war, that American industry fully threw off its Depression-era enfeeblement and sprung back to full-throated life. Manufacturers and providers of raw materials alike were able to greatly expand their operations in response to wartime demands, and jobs sprouted in numerous industrial sectors and every geographic region.

The impact of the war mobilization effort on the American economy was electrifying. The U.S. gross national product expanded from $100 billion in 1940 to more than $210 billion in 1945, energy consumption nearly doubled, and a wide assortment of long-standing economic problems were finally solved. Industry-driven metropolitan areas experienced heady growth in wages, better employment options, and increased savings for down payments on homes and automobiles, while rural Americans lifted by thriving agricultural markets and rural electrification policies realized that their postwar world could be one of refrigeration, radio, and other modern conveniences. "World War II was the juggernaut that ran over American society," summarized historian Anthony Badger.[1]

War mobilization, however, reduced some federal agencies to shadows of their prewar selves. Departments and programs that were not explicit parts of the war effort suffered significant budgetary and staffing cutbacks, and state and federal conservation

During the 1940s and 1950s, economic prosperity, surging consumerism, and rising enthusiasm for outdoor recreation all created concerns that America's wildlife and other natural resources were being "loved to death."

and natural resource management agencies were no exception. The Civilian Conservation Corps, which had been the most wildly popular conservation initiative of the entire New Deal era, was disbanded entirely and replaced by the military draft. Recreation programs in national forests and state parks were suspended. The National Park Service (NPS) saw its annual appropriation steadily drop (from $35 million in 1940 to $5 million by 1945), so it radically scaled down its operations for the duration of the war. "Stress of war has compelled the National Park Service to take stock of its functions and responsibilities," explained Park Director Newton B. Drury in 1943. "Travel to the parks has declined to the point where it is only 27 percent of the peak figure of 22,000,000 visitors in 1941, and it is obvious that increasing transportation restrictions will result in still further decreases. Appropriations and personnel have been curtailed and activities of many sorts have been suspended. Until after the war, the main task of the Service is one of protection and maintenance."[2]

In numerous instances, natural resource agencies and the lands they managed were recruited to help in the war effort. Mining activity on public lands soared, and logging rates in the national forests doubled, from two to four billion board feet (BBF) per year.[3] The NPS issued hundreds of permits to the Army, Navy, Coast Guard, and other war agencies for the utilization of lands and facilities within the park system, and wartime exceptions were approved for mining of copper in the Grand Canyon, tungsten in Yosemite, and manganese in Shenandoah.[4] Not all such proposals to increase extraction on public lands were approved, however. In the Pacific Northwest, for example, timber interests and advocates launched an aggressive wartime campaign to open Olympic National Park to commercial logging. But this bid, which was heavily cloaked in patriotic rhetoric, was beaten back by conservation officials in the Roosevelt Administration who expressed great alarm at the precedent that such a move would set (**see Document 7.1**).

As aircraft, tanks, jeeps, ships, rifles, helmets, blankets, clothing, torpedoes, and mess kits poured out of the nation's factories, extraction industries labored to keep pace with demand. This sustained and government-sanctioned expansion of coal, uranium, and iron mining; oil drilling; steel and aluminum production; food production; and timber cutting had significant ecological consequences for both public and private landholdings. "With the tremendous lumber demands which have characterized World War II, destructive cutting has increased," warned Secretary of Agriculture Claude R. Wickard in an October 1942 note to Roosevelt. "I am appalled at the reports which are reaching me of its extent and severity. . . . Probably not over 20 percent of present private land cutting is with any conscious intent to maintain forest productivity. More than at any time in the past the land is being skinned of everything big enough to make a 2 × 4 or a piece of car blocking."[5] Other members of the Roosevelt Administration shared Wickard's dismay at the shortsighted extraction practices of some industries. But federal authorities made little effort to curb such behavior. There was a war to be won, and all other considerations—environmental or otherwise—were secondary.

The Postwar Suburbanization Boom

When the war ended with an Allied victory in 1945, the United States was poised for years of continued economic growth. The onset of the Cold War ensured a continuation of heavy federal spending on defense-related areas, the end of wartime rationing released pent-up demand for a wide array of consumer items, veterans' benefits lifted new home construction and other bellwethers of economic expansion, technological advances increased industrial efficiency and profitability, and postwar confidence and euphoria helped millions of Americans to abandon their Depression-era caution about money and spend more freely on everything from automobiles and furniture to vacuum cleaners and waffle irons. A new era of middle-class affluence was at hand, and it unleashed transformative changes on the country's natural resources and patterns of land usage.

The rate of suburbanization, for example, accelerated greatly during this period. Between 1950 and 1970 alone, the suburban population in America doubled from about 35 million to nearly 75 million. This phenomenon was fed by several factors, including the "baby boom" (birthrates jumped by almost 25 percent from 1946 to 1957 over prewar levels) and New Deal–era federal housing policies such as the National Housing Act of 1934, which made single-family residential home construction and ownership more affordable. By the mid-1950s, in fact, loan programs available through the Veterans' Administration and Federal Housing Administration had become the foundation for more than 1.5 million new housing starts a year.[6]

On average, these single-family homes were built on significantly larger lots than those of the suburbs of yesteryear, which further intensified their ecological impact. Larger and more numerous suburban lawns, for example, prompted a mind-boggling jump in annual sales of gasoline-powered lawnmowers, from 139,000 in 1946 to 3.8 million by 1960.[7] In addition, the high tax base of these communities enabled municipal and state officials to cradle suburbanites in newly minted schools and streets, state-of-the-art sewers and water treatment facilities, and other infrastructure that increased real estate values and promoted further low-density development—thus creating a seemingly endless loop of land development deeper and deeper into the nation's hinterlands. As one scholar dryly asserted, "[S]prawl became the national housing policy."[8]

Another major factor contributing to mid-century suburbanization was the automobile, which gave Americans a greater variety of places in which to live, work, shop, and play than ever before. By 1956 Americans owned two-thirds of the world's cars, despite accounting for only 6 percent of the global population, and they were using these vehicles to bridge ever greater distances on a daily basis. But automobile use was limited by the nation's road system, which had not kept pace with increasing rates of suburbanization and automobile ownership. Increased traffic congestion prompted outcries for new and better road systems from commuters and local businesses. Their calls were supplemented by furious lobbying from politically influential industries that stood to benefit from increased road construction and highway use. Automakers, car dealers, labor unions, banks, bus and truck operations, asphalt and rubber and oil companies—all of these constituencies and more worked together to push for new state and federal expenditures on road transportation infrastructure. Military leaders added their voices, characterizing new road systems as a strategic necessity in evacuation and armed forces mobilization scenarios.

State legislatures and the U.S. Congress responded with alacrity to this massive wave of political pressure. Generous allocations of state and federal dollars for new roads, sewers, bridges, and other infrastructure poured forth, and more than 20,000 miles of new highways were completed annually from 1952 to 1962.[9] The centerpiece of this explosion of road construction came in 1956, when President Dwight D. Eisenhower signed the Federal-Aid Interstate Highway Act. His signature launched one of the greatest public works projects in the nation's history—a 41,000-mile interstate highway system that became the heartbeat of the nation's transportation grid over the next several decades (**see Document 7.6**).

The suburbanization movement was not universally praised, however. Some critics saw creeping social conformity, xenophobia, and estrangement from the natural world as underlying factors in the growth of suburbs. Historian and social critic Lewis Mumford provided some of the most cutting arguments along these lines. "Whilst the suburb served only a favored minority, it neither spoiled the countryside nor threatened the city," he wrote in his 1961 work *The City in History:*

> But now that the drift to the outer ring has become a mass movement, it tends to destroy the value of both environments without producing anything but a dreary substitute, devoid of form and even more devoid of the original suburban values. . . . [The new suburbs are] a multitude of uniform unidentifiable houses, lined up inflexibly, at uniform distances, on uniform roads, in a treeless communal waste, inhabited by people of the same class, the same income, the same age group, witnessing the same television performances, eating the same tasteless prefabricated foods, from the same freezers, conforming in every respect to a common mold.[10]

Of course, residents of America's fast-spreading suburbs took strong exception to such characterizations of their motivations and their communities. They saw the new subdivisions as refuges from crime, pollution, overcrowding, and other problems of the inner cities. In addition, they accurately perceived the suburbs to be focal points of economic opportunity and prosperity in the postwar era.

GROWING PRESSURE ON ENVIRONMENTAL RESOURCES

The new era of affluence was understandably intoxicating to American families and businesses that had spent almost two decades struggling in the shadow of the Depression or engaged in a global war for survival. But lawmakers, government officials, and ordinary Americans were all slow to comprehend the new pressures that this exciting new age of mass consumption and suburbanization was placing on the natural resources of the nation—and the world. And the few efforts to take stock of America's prodigious postwar appetite for natural resources failed to gain entrance into the bloodstream of national policymaking. In 1952, for example, a President's Materials Policy Commission appointed by President Harry S. Truman submitted a five-volume report called *Resources for Freedom* that bluntly warned that U.S. consumption rates for oil, timber, minerals, and other resources were outstripping its domestic reserves. The study, also known as the Paley Report, noted, for example, that in 1900 the United States produced 15 percent more materials than it consumed, but by 1950, it was consuming 9 percent more materials than it produced.[11] But these and other cautionary notes were mostly drowned out by the din of humming factories, rumbling bulldozers, and ringing cash registers in all corners of the country.

Meanwhile, the environmental consequences of the postwar economic boom were deepening at both ends of the consumption process—from the swallowing or transformation of land and resources to feed economic growth to the pollution and waste materials generated during and after ingestion of those materials. Of these two areas, the impact of converting existing environmental assets for economic use was initially much more visible than the impact of waste and pollution generated by that use.

Rural farmlands, fields, and woodlands on the periphery of metropolitan centers ranked at the top of the resources that were developed in service to growth. The conversion of farmland for new subdivisions, shopping centers, manufacturing facilities, and roadways left no part of the nation untouched, but its effects were particularly dramatic in places such as the Northeast, the Ohio Valley, the upper Great Lakes region, the Piedmont plateau, and California. Ohio, for example, lost 12 percent of its farmland between 1950 and 1960. Oregon lost 85,000 acres of pastureland and field annually during this same period, and the number of farms in New Jersey plunged from 26,900 in 1950 to 15,800 at the close of the decade. In addition, the forces unleashed during this period continued unabated through the remainder of the century, resulting in an overall 17 percent loss of farmland in the United States from 1945 to 1990.[12]

Ecologically fragile wetlands and floodplains emerged as favored locales for many of the big suburban developments of this era. State and federal regulations protecting marshlands, swamps, and coastal estuaries were virtually nonexistent at this time. As a result, nearly a million acres of these lands, which had long served as buffer zones against flooding and provided vital habitat for a wide array of fish and wildlife species, were destroyed to make way for new development between the mid-1950s and mid-1970s.[13]

Publicly owned forests also experienced higher rates of exploitation, both at the state and federal levels. "Getting out the cut"—whether by sanctioning of clear cutting, "salvage sales," or other means—became the dominant mantra of industry and agency alike. This jump in intensive commercial logging would never have been possible without the active support of the Truman and Eisenhower Administrations, which regularly approved healthy increases in annual cut allotments on public lands. In addition, both administrations increased appropriations to the Forest Service for road construction, which was essential for commercial loggers wishing to reach otherwise inaccessible areas. "Millions of acres of wild forest land must await an adequate road system before they will return their full worth in forest products and growing capacity," asserted U.S. Forest Service Chief Richard E. McArdle in 1952.[14]

All told, road mileage in the national forests doubled between 1940 and 1960, from 80,000 to 160,000 miles.[15] This de facto federal subsidy of timber operations, as along with numerous other pro-logging policies, lifted logging on public lands to new heights. Annual timber production from national forests surged from 3.5 BBF to 9.3 BBF during the 1950s alone. Virtually all national forests in the system experienced increases in timber activity, with the valuable old-growth forests of the Pacific Northwest shouldering the greatest share of the burden. Whereas these forests accounted for only 21 percent of the total national forest cut at the beginning of the decade, they accounted for 35 percent by the close of the 1950s.[16] Overall, twice as much timber was cut in the national forests between 1950 and 1966 as had been cut in the entire previous forty-five years that the national forest system had been in existence.[17]

This increase in logging on public land was a result, in no small measure, of the continuation of abusive and shortsighted practices on private timber reserves. A few companies, such as Weyerhaeuser, carried out reforestation and watershed protection plans on their properties during the 1940s and 1950s, but most mid-century logging companies clear cut vast swaths of their private lands, then abandoned or sold off the shattered, slash-strewn remains without engaging in even the most cursory restoration efforts. They paid no economic penalty for this behavior, however, because of the aforementioned Forest Service road building program, which allowed them to shift their operations onto the public domain without a backward glance.

Pressures on other environmental "raw materials" also soared. This trend alarmed perceptive conservationists and scientists such as Aldo Leopold, whose 1949 book *A Sand County Almanac* made the case for a more holistic concept of land and ecosystem stewardship (**see Document 7.3**). But it would be another generation before these messages penetrated the public consciousness. In the meantime, authorities approved new oil drilling and mining operations on public lands to feed America's growing energy needs and product wants. Harvests of commercial fisheries surged. Soaring public demand for beef put new pressure on rangelands. And entire watersheds were reengineered to meet escalating demands for hydroelectricity; flood control; navigational improvements; and water for irrigation, drinking, and waste disposal.

WATER RESOURCE POLITICS IN THE POSTWAR ERA

The postwar era comprised the heart of a four-decade span in which virtually all of America's major river systems were subjugated for human use by titanic water engineering projects carried out by the U.S. Army Corps of Engineers and the Bureau of Reclamation. These projects ranged from massive hydroelectric dams to complex systems of locks and canals for navigation and commercial trade. The first great wave of water projects of the 1930s and early 1940s—projects such as Hoover Dam, Grand Coulee Dam, and Bonneville Dam—were initially seen as New Deal symbols of American grit and economic rejuvenation. But when World War II arrived and these great dams poured cheap and plentiful electricity into shipyards and airplane factories up and down the West Coast, they also came to be regarded as linchpins of national security. By the end of the war, the Bureau of Reclamation had largely completed its metamorphosis from ally of the western family farm to titan of electric power and urban water use. At the war's close, in fact, the Bureau of Reclamation ranked as the single largest producer of power on the planet.[18]

It is not surprising that schemes for grand new federally subsidized water projects proliferated in the postwar era. Politicians, industries, and workers alike were mesmerized by the multipurpose New Deal dam, which combined flood control, electricity generation, and irrigation capabilities in a single magnificent edifice, and they clamored for similar dams of their own. In the West especially, federal dam projects came to be regarded as nearly essential elements in any regional economic development plan. As a result, formidable political alliances developed among industries, unions, community boosters, giant agricultural enterprises, and their elected representatives in Washington. They found sympathetic ears at the Bureau of Reclamation and the U.S. Army Corps of Engineers, which remained the two main federal bureaucracies responsible for making water project dreams become realities. Working together, these disparate but mutually dependent entities established a stranglehold over federal water policies that did not diminish until the 1960s.

They were able to do so because the advent of federally financed water projects—described by one observer as "an engineering regime that aimed taxpayer-funded technology at wild water"[19]—created an ideal environment for the practice of "pork barrel" politics. Members of Congress had strong incentives to support virtually every Bureau and Corps project proposal that came up for a vote. "Almost every project [was] economically viable *at the local level*," explained policy historian David A. Adams:

> Politicians are elected and remain in office because of votes from their local areas. If they support a project that is locally popular but is not in the best interests of the larger area, they may lose a few friends there, but they will win votes from the local area benefited. If, on the other hand, they fail to support a local project that is adverse to the state or national interest, they may win a few friends outside their district but lose the next election. When elected officials consider proposals for projects in others' districts, it is a matter of "you scratch my back and I'll scratch yours"—a difficult system to beat.[20]

The Bureau of Reclamation and the U.S. Army Corps of Engineers were delighted with this state of affairs because each new public work project increased their power and budget. Moreover, administrators and engineers within these agencies took personal satisfaction in the work itself. In their view, the process of putting wild rivers to work for the American people was an imminently worthy one. Finally, building these majestic multipurpose dams was "terrifically exhilarating work," acknowledged one critic of the dam-building era. "Stopping a wild river was a straightforward job, subjugable to logic, and the result was concrete, heroic, real: a dam."[21]

Both the Roosevelt and Truman Administrations expressed reservations about the political power wielded by the Corps and the Bureau and their benefactors in Congress, but their efforts to restrain the runaway water project appropriations process came to naught. "Franklin D. Roosevelt, generally regarded as a strong president, lost every round he fought with the Corps," declared one 1949 report. "Although the Champ swung angrily and often, he never laid a glove on the Army Engineers."[22] The Truman White House had no better luck. In 1949 a presidential commission charged with reorganizing the executive branch criticized Congress's incestuous relationship with the Bureau and the Corps, and it urged the administration to combine the two federal agencies into a single Water Development and Use Service in the Department of the Interior. But defenders of the status quo easily beat back these and other reform initiatives, and the re-engineering of America's river systems marched on.

By the 1950s, observers such as former Interior Secretary Harold L. Ickes were calling the Corps "the most powerful and most pervasive lobby in Washington. The aristocrats who constitute it are our highest ruling class. . . . Within the fields that they have elected to occupy, they are the law—and therefore above the law. . . . Their record shows that they not only regard themselves as independent of the Secretary of the Army and the Secretary of Defense, but even of the President."[23] The Bureau of Reclamation, meanwhile, had become what historian John McPhee called the "patron agency of the American West, dispenser of light, life, and water to thirty million people whose gardens would otherwise be dust."[24]

Historians today marvel at the sheer number of public water resource projects undertaken during this era. Between 1936 and 1976 the U.S. Army Corps of Engineers built more than 400 multipurpose dams in forty-two states, and it retooled the entire Great Lakes–St. Lawrence River system for commercial purposes (see Document 7.5). The West-based Bureau of Reclamation added another 300 dams—including 31 dams alone on the Columbia River and its major tributaries. Other federal agencies were sanctioned to erect dam-reservoir systems as well. The Tennessee Valley Authority built 33 multipurpose dams within the Tennessee River system, and the 1954 Small Watersheds Act gave the Soil Conservation Service (SCS) authority to launch its own program of dam building and rechannelization for irrigation purposes. Nearly 1,100 water projects were ultimately carried out by the SCS.[25]

Many of the water development projects carried out by Reclamation, the Corps, and other agencies during the 1940s and 1950s, such as the St. Lawrence Seaway project, were widely viewed as projects of considerable economic merit. Objections raised by conservation groups to the "choking" of rivers and "drowning" of canyons by dam projects were heard occasionally, but these were largely ineffectual. By the late 1950s, however, most of the obvious water development projects had been completed, and the task of justifying the next generation of multipurpose dams and river engineering projects became more daunting. In the 1960s and 1970s, federal water development proposals received much greater levels of scrutiny, especially from conservation groups who by that time were wielding far greater levels of political clout than their predecessors of the 1930s and 1940s.

A Cautionary Tragedy in Donora

As noted earlier, the postwar consumption of environmental assets in furtherance of economic and lifestyle goals also brought dramatic increases in the volume of toxic emissions, garbage, and other effluents. Everywhere one turned in the "affluent society" of the 1950s, statistics pointed to a rising tide of pollution and waste. Surges in the use of pesticides and herbicides contaminated entire ecosystems and threatened birds and other wildlife. Use of fertilizers for suburban lawns and agricultural fields also soared, exacerbating problems of groundwater contamination and waterway eutrophication. Deposits in landfills of everything from lawn clippings to appliances escalated at dizzying speed, as did discharges of pollutants into air and water from automobiles, trucks, buses, airplanes, recreational boats, and other elements of the nation's transportation system. Millions of haphazardly installed suburban septic tanks leaked or failed, contaminating drinking water and threatening nearby populations of fish and other wildlife. Overreliance on wells in new subdivisions also caused problems by diverting replenishing water from local streams and rivers. Utilities, meanwhile, "generated radioactive waste, poured sulfur into the air, and sent fish-killing streams of hot water into rivers"[26] to meet the galloping demand for electricity from homeowners armed with the latest appliance models.

Many of these corrosive but gradual changes to the environment escaped the notice of the general public, lawmakers, and government officials whose responsibilities did not extend to issues of public or environmental health. But one environmental issue that attracted widespread attention in the postwar era was air pollution. Prior to the 1940s, urban air pollution was recognized as a hazard to public health, but regulatory efforts to address the problem were mostly limited to municipal zoning laws and other local smoke-control ordinances. Federal agencies charged with protecting public health and environmental resources were kept on the sidelines by successive pro-business administrations, and states feared that even modest air pollution regulations would trigger the relocation of important industries to more "business-friendly" states. In addition, many public officials at the state and federal levels were wary of angering pro-business lawmakers who controlled the purse strings of their agencies. Finally, a variety of mid-century technological advances—most notably a switch from high-polluting coal to natural gas for home heating needs—blunted calls for regulation of air emissions. Opponents of clean air campaigns insisted that these sorts of technological breakthroughs—fruits blossoming out of the fertile soil of free-market capitalism, as it were—provided a better path to the mitigation of air pollution. As a result of these various obstacles, efforts to establish air pollution regulations at the national level foundered, and only one state in the entire union—California—had a statewide air pollution control law in place by the end of the 1940s.

During the late 1940s and early 1950s, however, several notorious air pollution events in the United States and Europe decisively changed the political landscape. The worst of these events on American soil was a nightmarish "killer smog" that beset the town of Donora, Pennsylvania, in 1948. Over the space of a single late October weekend, a stationary weather front trapped emissions from area steel, wire, and zinc plating mills over the shops and homes of Donora, a town with a population of about 14,000 residents about twenty miles south of Pittsburgh. Thousands of townspeople were sickened by the toxic brew they inhaled that weekend, and twenty residents died. "The source of the poison in Donora was never identified," wrote one historian, "[but] whatever killed these people slipped deeply and directly into the body, making a bloody, swollen mess of the lower lungs, much like phosgene, a nerve gas used in World Wars I and II."[27]

The Public Health Service launched an investigation into the Donora disaster, but its final report offered little more than tepid calls for voluntary reductions in factory emissions and further research into the causes and effects of air pollution. Public health advocates called for far stronger government intervention. "Let us hope that the Donora disaster will awaken people everywhere to the dangers they face from pollution of the air they must breathe to live," wrote physician Clarence A. Mills in a 1950 editorial for *Science Magazine*. "These 20 suffered only briefly, but many of the 6,000 made ill that night will face continuing difficulties in breathing for the remainder of their lives. Herein lies the greatest health danger from polluted air—continuing damage to the respiratory system through years of nonkilling exposure."[28]

As Mills hoped, air pollution became a much more important policy issue in the wake of the Donora tragedy and other similar events—most notably a killer smog that claimed the lives of 4,000 Londoners in December 1952. The Donora incident underscored the inadequacy of the smoke abatement campaigns that had come before it and forced Americans to take a closer look at the ecological costs of unregulated industrialization. "The smoke-filled skies of Pittsburgh" that had been "regarded as a sign of economic progress in the 1930s," wrote scholar Christopher Bailey, came to be seen as a "harbinger of death and illness a generation later."[29]

More than a dozen states enacted statewide air pollution laws by the early 1960s, despite enduring fears about the impact of these regulations on their ability to keep existing industries and attract new ones. The federal government even took its first tentative steps to address the issue after years of inaction. In 1955 Congress passed and Eisenhower signed the Air Pollution Control Act of 1955 (**see Document 7.7**). This law was exceptionally modest in scope; it reaffirmed that air pollution regulation and control were the responsibility of states and municipalities—*not* the federal government—and it earmarked only a small amount of federal tax dollars for research into air pollution. Nonetheless, the act is regarded by environmental historians as a significant milestone. It signaled recognition among federal policymakers that the national government could not wholly ignore the issue, and it paved the way for more far-reaching federal initiatives on pollution issues in the 1960s and 1970s.

CLEAN ENERGY THROUGH NUCLEAR TECHNOLOGY

The arrival of air pollution on the national policy agenda also gave a boost to the young nuclear power industry. The quest to harness atomic power as a clean and inexpensive energy source began in earnest in 1946, when the Atomic Energy Commission (AEC) was established under the terms of that year's Atomic Energy Act. From the outset, the AEC's mandate was to promote the commercialization of nuclear power across the United States. "We look to the Commission to foster the development of atomic energy for industrial use and scientific and medical research," stated Truman in his January 1947 State of the Union address. "In the vigorous and effective development of peaceful uses of atomic energy rests our hope that this new force may ultimately be turned into a blessing for all nations."

Under the guidance of the Atomic Energy Commission, the United States government launched a major new initiative to make nuclear energy a reality. Government laboratories and private industries worked in concert—and in secret—to adapt nuclear technology for electric power production. In the meantime, Truman, Eisenhower, and other proponents painted nuclear power both as a pathway to the eradication of air pollution and as a vehicle for the realization of energy independence. In a famous "Atoms for Peace" speech before the United Nations in December 1953, Eisenhower also framed nuclear technology as a tool for international peace (**see Document 7.4**). Some conservationists, meanwhile, saw nuclear power as an attractive alternative to power generated by fossil fuels and hydroelectric dams. "If we learn to use [nuclear power] properly," declared a writer in the *Sierra Club Bulletin* in 1948, "we won't need to harness all the rivers of the land. . . . At least we might wait a little while and see what happens before we drown our greatest canyons and destroy forever so much natural beauty."[30]

In 1954 the Civilian Nuclear Power Act formally called on the AEC to develop nuclear power as a clean alternative to fossil fuels such as coal and oil—and to put this new industry in civilian hands. The AEC did so by licensing private corporations to build and operate nuclear-fueled power plants. This licensing process proceeded slowly, in large measure because of skepticism from U.S. utilities, which were already generating huge profits with *proven* energy sources and *existing* facilities. But the federal government subsidized the nascent industry by underwriting reactor construction costs, bestowing free fuel for reactors, providing generous research and development funding, limiting the liability of nuclear reactor owners in cases of accident, and promising that it would take responsibility for nuclear waste disposal.[31]

The first civilian nuclear reactors were up and running by the close of the 1950s, and investments in nuclear energy surged well into the 1960s. By 1975 there were fifty-five electricity-generating nuclear reactors up and running across the United States, with more than 150 more under construction or on order.[32]

This new industry, however, was dogged by safety concerns from the outset. Even as the Eisenhower Administration touted the peaceful applications of atomic energy, revelations about the dangers of radioactive waste trickled into the public consciousness. Most of these early revelations did not concern the significant volumes of toxic waste generated by civilian reactors. Instead, they focused on the impact of radioactive fallout from years of above-ground nuclear weapons testing. The nuclear fallout controversy ultimately led to a 1958 moratorium and a 1963 treaty banning above-ground testing of nuclear weapons, but it also spurred the creation of citizens' groups vehemently opposed to nuclear power. Finally, the fallout controversy planted seeds of public distrust about the truthfulness and honor of private and governmental proponents of nuclear energy. The conservative *Saturday Evening Post,* for instance, published a scathing August 1959 editorial about the nuclear fallout issue: "The public, paying out its tax billions for the bomb tests and the study of their troublesome debris, deserves more understandable answers than it has received," wrote the editors. "For its picture of fallout the public has had to rely upon the interpretation of fragmentary data by authorities with different viewpoints and policies. They can make the picture dark or light, depending on how they mix emphasis and adjectives with facts that are, at best, incomplete. They can even omit a detail here and there, by accident or for the sake of over-all effect."[33]

HARBINGERS OF AN EXPANDED FEDERAL ROLE

Although neither the Truman nor Eisenhower Administrations made environmental policy a high priority, they did respond to certain areas of ecological concern. Among the most visible of these was the state of world fisheries. During the course of the 1940s and 1950s, world fishing fleets expanded dramatically, both in size and harvesting capacity. Many of the vessels in these fleets were of such immense scale that they amounted to virtual fish-processing factories, and thousands of boats were outfitted with technological gear that would have dumbfounded trawling captains of the prewar era. Many fishing grounds began to experience unprecedented levels of pressure.

As concerns about unsustainable fishing levels mounted, the Truman Administration took action in several ways. First and foremost, it unilaterally claimed full ownership of the North American continental shelf extending from its territories. This declaration of ownership, which extended to the natural resources contained in the seabed and waters of the shelf, cordoned off large expanses of the Pacific and Atlantic oceans but refrained from proclaiming exclusive rights of extraction for the U.S. fleet (see Document 7.2). Around this same time, Truman issued an executive order in which he reserved the right of federal authorities to proclaim conservation zones in America's coastal waters if deemed necessary.

Over the next several years, the Truman White House participated in a number of international initiatives to protect fish and wildlife on the high seas. These negotiations marked some of the United States' first forays into international treatymaking on environmental issues. Milestones in this area included the 1946 International Whaling Convention, the 1950 Convention on Northwest Atlantic Fisheries, and several multi-country agreements to expand scientific study and management of fishery resources.

When the Eisenhower Administration took up the reins of power in 1953, it made no major changes to U.S. ocean policies. To the contrary, the United States was an active participant in the 1958 Geneva Convention, which sparked the eventual creation of a number of important international accords governing future uses of the world's high seas, including the Convention on Fishing and Conservation of Living Resources of the High Seas and the Convention on the Continental Shelf. The Eisenhower Administration also signed on to several international agreements to reduce ocean pollution from oil and other hazardous substances.

In most other areas of environmental policy–making from 1945 to 1960—especially in the realm of air and water pollution—federal officials and lawmakers proceeded with caution. Most were philosophically resistant to the idea of federal environmental regulation anyway, but there were also practical considerations. Essentially, they were reluctant to intervene out of fears that 1) federal regulations might actually gum up the gears of the humming economy or 2) federal regulations could be *portrayed* as onerous and unfair by political adversaries. Moreover, empirical scientific research into environmental conditions during this era was limited, so obtaining a clear and accurate picture of environmental problems—and their potential solutions—was a challenge at both the state and federal level.

All of these considerations convinced Washington to keep pollution control and many other environmental matters within the bailiwick of state and local authorities. The Water Quality Act of 1948, for example, provided federal grants to states for water pollution control but explicitly avoided placing federal authorities in any regulatory role. Eight years later, Congress approved funding to cities for new sewage treatment plants but again avoided any federal mandates regarding the operation of these plants.

Still, federal authorities and legislators recognized that they could not wholly ignore events like the Donora tragedy, which aroused nationwide concern about air-quality issues. They also found it increasingly difficult to disregard the proliferating reports of environmental stress and degradation that were being issued by environmental advocacy groups, newspaper publishers, and other advocates of federal intervention in the 1950s. Federal authorities responded by attempting a balancing act in which they reasserted the responsibility of state and local governments for addressing environmental issues but also stepped forward with big increases in federal funding for scientific research into pollution and other emerging environmental problems. Many of the reports generated by these allocations, however, put Congress and federal agencies in a difficult position because they emphasized that air and water pollutants did not respect municipal or state boundaries. As the body of scientific research into environmental issues expanded, observed one analysis, "the premise that the federal role in pollution control should be a non-regulatory one became increasingly tenuous."[34]

RESPONDING TO THE SURGE IN OUTDOOR RECREATION

At the same time that all this reassessment was going on, U.S. politicians and government officials were trimming their rhetorical, legislative, and operational sails in response to a remarkable evolution in American perceptions of the great outdoors. The United States had long included men and women who loved spending time hunting, fishing, hiking, canoeing, and camping in the country's forested valleys and rocky canyons. But in post-war America, public enthusiasm for outdoor recreation reached heights never before seen. Greater quantities of leisure time, rising economic prosperity, and new and improved transportation networks all played major roles in the country's growing love affair with nature, but perhaps the biggest factor of all was less quantifiable—a thirst for a respite from the cacophony of modern urban and suburban life. This idea of the "wilderness as sanctuary" also was seized on by the mass media, which produced a flood of books, magazines, television shows, films, and other works that portrayed America's wild places and wild creatures as some of the nation's most priceless treasures.

State and federal natural resource agencies scrambled to accommodate these new throngs of visitors. The most prominent of these agencies was the National Park Service, which was responsible for safeguarding the country's most majestic, famous, and popular natural areas. For the first decade after the war, the NPS was saddled with a budget that was completely inadequate to withstand middle-class America's newfound craving for tent pads, park roads, and scenic vistas. By 1955 the national parks were receiving 56 million visitors annually, more than three times the number that they welcomed in 1940. In addition, the land included in the national park system had grown by more than two million acres during that same period. Yet the annual budget for the NPS in 1955 was actually $1 million *less* than it had been in 1940.[35]

This inattention took a heavy toll on the park system and aroused the ire of a rising chorus of critics. One particularly influential broadside on the problem of woeful park funding was penned by conservationist Bernard De Voto. Writing in *Harper's* in 1953, he declared that

> the deterioration of roads and plants [within the parks and national monuments] that began with the war years, when proper maintenance was impossible, has been accelerated by the enormous increase in visitors, by the shrinkage of staffs, and by miserly appropriations that have prevented both repair and expansion of facilities. The Service is like a favorite figure of American legendry, the widow who scrapes and patches and ekes out, who by desperate expedients succeeds in bringing up her children to be a credit to our culture. . . . So much of the priceless heritage which the Service must safeguard for the United States is beginning to go to hell.[36]

In 1955 NPS Director Conrad Wirth mounted a public relations blitz to rouse Congress out of its parsimonious stance toward the parks. The centerpiece of this offensive was Mission 66, which sought to modernize crumbling and inadequate park infrastructure through a massive wave of capital improvements **(see Document 7.8)**. Wirth's gambit worked. The Mission 66 proposal garnered the enthusiastic support of Eisenhower, who vowed in his 1956 State of the Union address to "provide more adequate facilities to keep abreast of the increasing interest of our people in the great outdoors." Congress belatedly took note of the voting public's warm sentiments toward the parks as well, and it approved significant boosts in Park Service funding throughout the late 1950s and 1960s.

In terms of fulfilling its intended purpose, the Mission 66 program was a spectacular success. It turned America's national parks into the country's wilderness playgrounds, bristling with amenities and attractions that appealed to a wide cross-section of American (and international) tourists. But as the Mission 66 campaign proceeded, it also exposed fault lines between park administrators and longstanding allies in the environmental community. Wilderness conservationists contended that "Mission 66 was the essence of those things which they detested; it was the sacrifice of preservation to mass use. It was catering to the lowest common denominator of park taste."[37] These criticisms were roundly rejected as elitist by Wirth, the NPS, and other supporters of Mission 66. But the charge prompted considerable institutional soul-searching within the NPS over subsequent years, and the struggle to strike an appropriate—and politically popular—balance between wilderness protection and public use and enjoyment of resources remains a difficult one for Park Service managers **(see Document 7.9)**.

THE FOREST SERVICE BEDEVILED ON ALL SIDES

The U.S. Forest Service was another prominent federal resource agency whose practices and operations underwent dramatic change as a result of the outdoor recreation boom. But whereas the National Park Service had seen opportunity in the rising public enthusiasm for nature and outdoor recreation, the Forest Service saw this trend as unsettling. By the 1950s the Forest Service had well-entrenched policies that emphasized large-scale commercial timber production over recreational offerings. This state of affairs suited many Forest Service managers and employees; they saw the emphasis on timber harvesting not only as vital to the agency's own prosperity, but also as an important asset in the nation's economic expansion.

The reality behind the Forest Service's reassuring euphemisms about "sustained yields" and "multiple uses" of its holdings, however, could not be hidden from postwar America. National forests offered eye-catching patches of green on American roadmaps, and millions of automobiles stuffed with camping gear and other outdoor equipment descended on these lands in the 1950s. In fact, total recreational visits to national forests soared from less than 10 million in 1948 to 190 million in 1976.[38] Many of the visitors who descended on these public forestlands in the late 1940s and 1950s, however, were aghast at what they found. The prevalence of clear-cut hillsides, erosion-choked streams, and other signs of destructive logging practices aroused great public indignation that gradually filtered up to their legislative representatives, who in turn exerted political pressure on the Forest Service to adopt more recreation- and environment-friendly policies.

As it turned out, however, the Forest Service struggled mightily to wean itself off its close relationship to the commercial timber industry and its allies in Congress. "The forestry profession did not seem to be able to accept the new values," observed historian Samuel Hays. "The Forest Service was never able to 'get on top' of the wilderness movement to incorporate it in 'leading edge' fashion into its own strategies. As the movement evolved from stage to stage the Service seemed to be trapped by its own internal value commitments and hence relegated to playing a rear-guard role to protect wood production."[39]

The Forest Service's commitment to genuine conservation of America's national forests was cast in further doubt in the late 1950s, when the agency approved commercial logging contracts on a number of high-profile areas in Oregon and New Mexico that had previously been protected from commercial logging. As late as 1958, only 7 percent of the 188 million acres contained in the national forest system were designated as "primitive" or "wilderness," and most of this protected land consisted of grasslands or mountains—tracts that had little timber value anyway.

Buoyed by widespread public support, wilderness preservation groups began lobbying Congress to establish new "wilderness areas" in the national forests that would be forever protected from commercial exploitation or intensive recreation development (the latter was a direct response to conservationists' unhappiness with the perceived excesses of the National Park Service's Mission 66 program). These proposals were strongly opposed by representatives of western states and other rural areas with close ties to resource extraction industries. But the threat from the conservationists did not subside, and Forest Service administrators grudgingly indicated their willingness to consider expanded wilderness protection schemes. These tentative steps, however, brought down storms of protest from commercial interests and local communities who relied on timbering for jobs and school funding.

Finally, even as it was trying to navigate its way through this thicket of thorny political problems, the Forest Service found itself battling once again with an old nemesis: the National Park Service. By the late 1950s the NPS was riding high on surging public interest in scenic recreation lands and Mission 66–inspired upturns in its budget. Park Service leadership talked openly about further expanding the park system, and just as it had done in the 1920s and 1930s, it openly coveted national forest parcels. National forest managers and other U.S. Forest Service personnel reacted furiously to the suggestion of transferring national forest land to the Park Service, and things got so heated that Forest Service Chief Richard McArdle felt obligated to issue a memo on February 12, 1960, warning employees to tone down their rhetoric. "I regret this situation has arisen," he stated. "The Forest Service seeks no quarrel with the National Park Service and has only the highest regard for that agency and its competent personnel as a sister agency in conservation. From time to time, as is to be expected, differences in policy viewpoints arise where the two agencies have mutual interests. But these differences are generally resolved in a judicious and dispassionate manner without name-calling."[40]

Bedeviled on all sides, the U.S. Forest Service in 1960 floated a proposal that it hoped would at least partially mollify the warring constituencies while at the same time address the looming threat of another round of NPS encroachment. The proposed Multiple-Use Sustained Yield Act (MUSYA) of 1960 explicitly placed recreation on an equal footing with timbering and watershed management as a national forest management principle—but also gave local forest managers considerable autonomy. Despite reservations from western legislators, Congress passed MUSYA into law later that year (see Document 7.10).

Echo Park—A Turning Point

The most vocal critics of the Multiple-Use Sustained Yield Act were conservation groups, such as the Sierra Club and Wilderness Society, who believed that MUSYA's wilderness protection provisions were inadequate. Immediately after MUSYA's passage, they defiantly announced their intention to continue lobbying Congress for more substantive wilderness legislation.

This declaration was not inconsequential; in the late 1950s America's conservation movement had had an epiphany of sorts about its capacity to influence environmental politics and policymaking in Washington, D.C. And the spark for this epiphany was a remote section of Utah canyon land known as Echo Park.

Echo Park began its rise from obscurity in the early 1950s, when the five states of the upper Colorado River basin, in league with the powerful Bureau of Reclamation, pressed for federal approval of an Upper Colorado Storage Project (UCSP). The cornerstone of this grand economic development proposal was a series of high multipurpose dams that would be built at various strategic points in the Rockies. One of the proposed dam sites was Echo Park, a section of gorgeous canyons tucked into Dinosaur National Monument. Both the Truman and Eisenhower Administrations supported the UCSP, and they turned aside conservationist complaints about the loss of Echo Park and its local wildlife.

But America's wilderness preservationist groups did not go quietly. They instead reminded each other about the loss of the fabled Hetch Hetchy Valley to California dam builders nearly a half-century earlier. This time, they vowed, the outcome would be different. The Council of Conservationists—a wilderness preservation coalition that included the Sierra Club, the Audubon Society, the Wilderness Society, the Izaak Walton League, and others—mounted a massive and sustained public relations campaign to arouse public opposition to the Echo Park Dam. These efforts, spearheaded by environmental legends such as David Brower and Howard Zahniser, were enormously effective. Bombarded by editorials, books, and films about the wonders of Dinosaur National Monument, many Americans came to see the proposed Echo Park Dam as a symbol of needless wilderness destruction. As the debate over Echo Park intensified, advocates of the UCSP gradually realized that the entire proposal was being tainted by the controversy.

The Bureau of Reclamation and its legislative and business allies blinked first, revising their plans so that Dinosaur National Monument would be spared. This retreat triggered a spate of grousing about the conservationists from supporters of the proposed dam, including Eisenhower himself. Speaking at a February 29, 1956, news conference, he acknowledged that the conservationist crusade for the preservation of Echo Park had slowed approval of the UCSP. "I think their fears were groundless," he said, "but [the Echo Park Dam] has been eliminated and removed that particular bone of contention."[41]

Once the Echo Park Dam was removed, the Sierra Club withdrew its opposition to the UCSP and the project went forward. Some of the dams built as part of the project—most notably Glen Canyon Dam—are today viewed by many environmentalists as blights on the western landscape. But the successful battle to spare Dinosaur's Echo Park canyons from submersion still ranks as a significant landmark in the evolution of America's environmental movement. "The movement came of age during Echo Park," wrote one historian. "The conservationists, perhaps to their own surprise, beat down federal bureaus and private commercial interests. They even influenced the cabinet politics of an unfriendly administration."[42] Indeed, the Echo Park showdown gave America's environmental and wilderness advocates an infusion of confidence that they could take on even bigger political challenges in the future **(see Document 7.11)**. And as the 1960s and 1970s would prove, their confidence was well-placed.

NOTES

1. Anthony J. Badger, *The New Deal: The Depression Years, 1933–1940* (Chicago: Ivan R. Dee, 2002), 310.

2. Newton B. Drury, "The National Parks in Wartime," *American Forests*, August 1943.

3. Richard N.L. Andrews, *Managing the Environment, Managing Ourselves: A History of American Environmental Policy* (New Haven, Conn.: Yale University Press, 1999), 181.

4. Dyan Zaslowsky and T.H. Watkins, *These American Lands: Parks, Wilderness, and the Public Lands*, rev. ed. (Washington, D.C.: Island Press, 1994), 34.

5. Quoted in Edgar B. Nixon, ed., *Franklin D. Roosevelt and Conservation, 1911–1945* (Hyde Park, NY: General Services Administration, 1957), 2:562.

6. Kenneth T. Jackson, *Crabgrass Frontier: The Suburbanization of the United States* (New York: Oxford University Press, 1985), 233.

7. Adam Rome, "Building on the Land: Toward an Environmental History of Residential Development in American Cities and Suburbs, 1870–1990." *Journal of Urban History* 20, no. 3 (May 1994): 408.

8. Dolores Hayden, *Building Suburbia: Green Fields and Urban Growth, 1820-2000* (New York: Pantheon Books, 2003), 151.

9. Andrews, *Managing the Environment, Managing Ourselves,* 198.

10. Lewis Mumford, *The City in History: Its Origins, Its Metamorphoses, and Its Prospects* (New York: Harcourt, Brace Jovanovich, 1961), 506.

11. *Resources for Freedom: A Report to the President by the President's Materials Policy Commission,* 5 vols (Washington, D.C.: Government Printing Office, 1952).

12. Thomas L. Daniels and Deborah Bowers, *Holding Our Ground: Protecting America's Farms and Farmlands* (Washington, D.C.: Island Press, 1997), 10.

13. Rome, "Building on the Land," 408.

14. Quoted in Charles Wilkinson, *Crossing the Next Meridian: Land, Water, and the Future of the West* (Washington, D.C.: Island Press, 1993), 136.

15. Ibid., 137.

16. Paul W. Hirt, *A Conspiracy of Optimism: Management of the National Forests since World War II* (Lincoln: University of Nebraska Press, 1996), 130.

17. Wilkinson, *Crossing the Next Meridian,* 137.

18. Donald C. Swain, "The Bureau of Reclamation and the New Deal, 1933–1940," *Pacific Northwest Quarterly,* July 1970, 146.

19. Chip Ward, *Hope's Horizon* (Washington, D.C.: Island Press, 2004), 139.

20. David A. Adams, *Renewable Resource Policy: The Legal-Institutional Foundations* (Washington, D.C.: Island Press, 1993), 358.

21. Marc Reisner, *Cadillac Desert: The American West and Its Disappearing Water,* 1986, rev. ed. (New York: Penguin, 1993), 118.

22. Robert de Roos and Arthur A. Maass, "The Lobby That Can't be Licked: Congress and the Army Engineers," *Harper's,* August 1949, 21–30.

23. Harold L. Ickes, foreword to *Muddy Waters: The Army Engineers and the Nation's Rivers,* by Arthur Maas (Cambridge, Mass.: Harvard University Press), ix–xiv.

24. John McPhee, *Encounters with the Archdruid* (1971; repr., New York: Noonday, 1990), 162.

25. Andrews, *Managing the Environment, Managing Ourselves,* 165, 189–190.

26. Rome, "Building on the Land," 408.

27. Devra Davis, *When Smoke Ran Like Water: Tales of Environmental Deception and the Battle against Pollution* (New York: Basic Books, 2002), 24.

28. Quoted in Davis, *When Smoke Ran Like Water,* 25.

29. Christopher J. Bailey, *Congress and Air Pollution: Environmental Policies in the USA* (New York and Manchester: Manchester University Press, 1998), 15.

30. Quoted in Donald J. Pisani, "A Tale of Two Commissioners: Frederick H. Newell and Floyd Dominy." Presented at *History of the Bureau of Reclamation: A Symposium,* Las Vegas, Nev., June 18, 2002. Available at www.waterhistory.org.

31. Bruce Podobnik, *Global Energy Shifts: Fostering Sustainability in a Turbulent Age* (Philadelphia: Temple University Press, 2006), 105.

32. Ellis C. Armstrong, Michael Robinson, and Suellen Hoy, eds., *History of Public Works in the United States, 1776–1976* (Chicago: American Public Works Association, 1976), 393.

33. Quoted in Louis S. Warren, ed., *American Environmental History* (Malden, Mass.: Blackwell, 2003), 259–260.

34. Robert V. Percival et al., *Environmental Regulation: Law, Science, and Policy* (Boston: Little, Brown, 1992), 105.

35. Conrad L. Wirth, *Parks, Politics, and the People* (Norman: University of Oklahoma Press, 1980), 238.

36. Bernard De Voto, "Let's Close the National Parks," *Harper's,* October 1953, 49.

37. Ronald A. Foresta, *America's National Parks and Their Keepers* (Washington, D.C.: Resources for the Future, 1984).

38. Wilkinson, *Crossing the Next Meridian,* 137.

39. Samuel P. Hays, "From Conservation to Environment: Environmental Politics in the United States since World War II," in *Out of the Woods: Essays in Environmental History* ed. Char Miller and Hal Rothman (Pittsburgh: University of Pittsburgh Press, 1997), 106.

40. Quoted in "National Forests vs. National Parks, 1959–1960." Available at www.foresthistory.org/ASPNET/Policy/Recreation/USFSvNPS2.aspx.

41. Dwight D. Eisenhower, "President's News Conference of February 29, 1956," in *Public Papers of the Presidents of the United States: Dwight D. Eisenhower, 1956* (Washington, D.C.: Government Printing Office, 1959).

42. Stephen Fox, *The American Conservation Movement: John Muir and His Legacy* (Madison: University of Wisconsin Press, 1985), 286.

**DOCUMENT
7.1**

Irving Brant Comments on Wartime Proposals to Cut Timber in National Parks

"An Elimination . . . Would Set All the Hounds of the Northwest Converging on Washington"

July 7, 1943

During World War II, domestic mobilization of resources for the war effort became a prime focus of the Roosevelt Administration. This escalation took many forms, including increased extraction from public lands of raw materials such as timber, coal, and uranium for wartime manufacturing needs. The American public and federal natural resource agencies accepted the higher rate of industrial activity in national forests and other public lands as a necessary patriotic sacrifice for the greater good of the world. But when a coalition of timber interests, government officials, and congressmen cited wartime needs in an attempt to pry open the gates of Washington State's Olympic National Park for commercial logging, the bid prompted an outcry of protest.

The target of the logging proposal was the park's large stands of Sitka spruce, a species of timber prized for airplane construction because of its high strength-to-weight ratio. In the early 1940s Pacific Northwest timber companies—which had bitterly opposed the creation of Olympic National Park in 1938—joined forces with the federal War Production Board and called on the Roosevelt Administration to grant a "waiver" or "temporary elimination" of the ban on logging in national parks. They framed logging in Olympic as both patriotic and a strategic necessity. And because the War Production Board was the federal agency responsible for making sure that America's producers of warplanes, tanks, artillery shells, and other war materials received adequate supplies, its recommendation could not be taken lightly.

But Roosevelt's inner circle of conservation advisors urged the president to keep loggers out of Olympic. They argued that the roster of the War Production Board was dotted with former Forest Service officials who disliked the National Park Service, and they ridiculed pro-logging assertions that Olympic was the only place where necessary quantities of Sitka spruce could be obtained. Interior Secretary Harold Ickes, for example, icily pointed out that neighboring British Columbia had large forests of Sitka spruce open for logging and that other stands of Sitka spruce could be found in privately owned and national forests. National Park Service Director Newton Drury made the same point in asking "whether, in view of the national importance of these last remnants of the once vast virgin forests of the Olympic Peninsula, the alternatives should not be exhausted before, rather than after, these forests are destroyed and an outstanding natural spectacle is lost to America forever."[1]

In the view of Ickes and other conservationist foes of the Olympic logging proposal, any erosion of the ban would pose a potentially deadly threat to the entire national park system. The purpose of the timber industry campaign, according to noted mid-century conservationist Bernard De Voto, "was to make a breach in the national parks policy with the aid of war emotions, and to create a precedent. Once that precedent should be set, the rest would follow. Lumber companies could log the parks. Cattle and sheep associations could graze them. Mining companies could get at their mineral deposits. Power companies could build dams in them, water companies could use their lakes and rivers. Each of those objectives had been repeatedly attempted in the past and the sun never sets on the West's efforts to achieve them."[2]

Another influential voice opposed to the Olympic logging proposal was Irving Brant, a journalist who served as a semi-official counsel, advisor, and speechwriter to the president on environmental issues. Brant had even served as lead author of a Department of Interior report on Olympic's worthiness for national park status back in the mid-1930s; this survey played an important role in Roosevelt's decision to establish the park in 1938. In July 1943, at the height of a heated congressional debate over whether to open Olympic for commercial logging, Brant wrote a letter to Ickes in which he urged the administration to reject the bid. In addition to rebutting industry assertions about the necessity of opening Olympic's forests to their saws and axes, Brant offered an assortment of policy alternatives. The full text of the letter is reprinted here. Ickes promptly passed the letter on to Roosevelt with a reminder to the president that Brant "knows more about the lumber situation in Olympic National Park than anyone in my acquaintance."[3]

Roosevelt did not formally reject the Olympic logging proposal, but he never showed any inclination to support it either. As it turned out, he did not need to take any action. The whole issue faded away in November 1943 when the War Production Board, sensing that the political winds were not in its favor, abruptly told Congress that new innovations in aircraft assembly relieved airplane manufacturers of the need for the wood contained in Olympic's Sitka spruce forests.

Letter from Irving Brant to Harold L. Ickes

Chicago, Illinois, July 7, 1943

Dear Mr. Secretary: Newton Drury has shown me his proposed report on Sitka spruce in the Olympic National Park. While I understand from him that they outline concessions to which he is opposed, but which he fears may become necessary later, I can't help feeling that this is a time for an "offensive defensive" rather than the charting of a line of retreat. Also, I feel that the matter involves some new dangers to the entire park and monument system.

The only reason assigned for opening the park to lumbering is a shortage of man-power in the lumber camps. It is therefore argued that available lumberjacks should be used in the timber easiest of access, which is said to be in the park. There is no actual shortage of timber outside, and a call for bids for some state-owned timber actually produced not one bidder.

Why is there a shortage of lumberjacks? Because they have been lured into shipyards and airplane factories by higher wages, or have been drafted. The argument for opening the national park to lumbering therefore comes down to this: That all future generations, as well as we ourselves, should be deprived of the scenic and recreational and scientific values of these big trees and rain forests, because we haven't sense enough to send a few hundred men back into the work for which they are trained. That's about as monstrous a failure of democracy as I ever heard of.

You and I both know, of course, that the real drive behind this call for lumbering is the desire of timber interests at Gray's Harbor and elsewhere to exploit and despoil; also that the lumber decisions of the War Production Board are being made by people who have never been sympathetic toward the park. . . . Neither the War Department nor the Manpower Commission, left to itself, will lift a finger to send lumberjacks back into the woods, for the purpose of saving this park from ruin. They will act only if the President orders them to, and probably only if he issues the orders two or three times. I don't see how he can refrain from acting if he understands that the cutting is absolutely needless, and that the area threatened with destruction is the portion of the park which he has always been most anxious to preserve—the Hoh, Bogachiel, and Queets River Valleys. The unhappy results of the cutting in the Queets corridor is enough to show what the devastation will be, even under the most carefully supervised cutting.

I note what Mr. Drury says about eliminating these river valleys from the park if they are to be lumbered, and agree with him in theory but would go somewhat farther than he did (in conversation) in pointing to the danger found in any method of elimination. He is unquestionably right in saying that Congress should not be asked to make an elimination—that would set all the hounds of the Northwest converging on Washington. I think it would be a great misfortune to have even a legal ruling that the President has power to make such an elimination by proclamation. Based, as it apparently would be, on a distinction between the status of land placed in a park by Congress, and by the President under authority derived from Congress, it would not be limited to war power (which would be equal in relation to both classes of land), but would unsettle all the national monuments in the country. The Wallgren Bill [the Olympic National Park Act of 1938] was worded so that it would not give sanction to the action of President Wilson in cutting down the Mt. Olympus National Monument during the first World War. It would be far better, in my opinion, to leave a despoiled area in the park than to open other areas to despoliation by the influence of pressure groups upon future Presidents.

But it will be a crime and a dereliction if a manpower shortage which can be remedied by one positive order is allowed to ruin these last scenic forests of the Northwest. It is not a case of putting these forests ahead of the lives of soldiers. If any soldiers die because of a shortage of lumber, the fault will lie upon those who drafted the lumberjacks out of the woods, or allowed them to shift to higher paid war jobs which could be done by men and women without their training.

Sincerely yours,

Irving Brant

Source: Brant, Irving. Letter to Interior Secretary Harold L. Ickes. In *Franklin D. Roosevelt and Conservation, 1911–1945*, edited by Edgar B. Nixon. 2 vols. New York, 1957. vol. 2, pp. 578–579.

NOTES

1. Newton B. Drury, "The National Parks in Wartime," *American Forests*, August 1943.

2. Bernard De Voto, "The West against Itself," *Harper's*, January 1947.

3. Quoted in *Franklin D. Roosevelt and Conservation, 1911–1945*, ed. Edgar B. Nixon (New York, 1957), 2:578.

DOCUMENT 7.2

The Truman Proclamation on the Continental Shelf

"The United States Regards the . . . [Continental Shelf as] Subject to Its Jurisdiction and Control"

September 28, 1945

In September 1945 President Harry S. Truman issued a momentous presidential proclamation stipulating that the United States owned and controlled the continental shelf—and the natural resources contained therein—off its coastal territories. As a result of this unilateral declaration, seabed areas beyond territorial sea limits were no longer to be treated as a part of the wider "high seas" beyond the sovereignty of any one nation. Truman's proclamation was prompted by several factors, including concern about pressure on North American fisheries from foreign fleets and growing recognition that technological advances were opening the doors to expanded offshore oil and mineral resource exploitation.

The "Truman Proclamation," as it was known, did not ignite any diplomatic rows, however. To the contrary, the U.S. assertion of "jurisdiction and control" over the continental shelf adjacent to its land mass quickly became the template for other nations to declare sovereignty over their own respective continental shelves. Some of these declarations were even more expansive than the one issued by Truman. In 1947, for example, Chile declared its complete and total "sovereignty over the sea adjacent to its coasts, whatever their depth may be, to the full extent necessary to reserve, protect, conserve, and utilize the natural resources and wealth of whatever nature, found on, in, or under said seas."[1] By 1958 nearly two dozen states and affiliated dependent territories had established claims similar to those first laid out by the United States, and the right to exploit seabed resources beyond territorial seas was widely accepted by international law.

In retrospect, the flurry of proclamations prompted by Truman marked the beginning of a new age of international concern and diplomatic maneuvering regarding ownership of the oceans and its contents. Conventions and treaties regulating the conservation and exploitation of marine resources proliferated in the ensuing years. The most notable of these milestones in ocean conservation during the Truman–Eisenhower years was the 1958 United Nations Convention of the Law of the Sea, which established a wide range of international guidelines for continental shelf ownership and protection of maritime resources from overharvesting. Following is the full text of Truman's historic proclamation.

Presidential Proclamation No. 2667

28th September, 1945

Policy of the United States with Respect to the Natural Resources of the Subsoil and Sea Bed of the Continental Shelf.

By the President of the United States of America a Proclamation:

WHEREAS the Government of the United States of America, aware of the long range world-wide need for new sources of petroleum and other minerals, holds the view that efforts to discover and make available new supplies of these resources should be encouraged; and

WHEREAS its competent experts are of the opinion that such resources underlie many parts of the continental shelf off the coasts of the United States of America, and that with modern technological progress their utilization is already practicable or will become so at any early date; and

WHEREAS recognized jurisdiction over these resources is required in the interest of their conservation and prudent utilization when and as development is undertaken; and

WHEREAS it is the view of the Government of the United States that the exercise of jurisdiction over the natural resources of the subsoil and sea bed of the continental shelf by the contiguous nation is reasonable and just, since the effectiveness of measures to utilize or conserve these resources would be contingent upon cooperation and protection from the shore, since the continental shelf may be regarded as an extension of the land-mass of the coastal nation and thus naturally appurtenant to it, since these resources frequently form a seaward extension of a pool or deposit lying within the territory, and since self-protection compels the coastal nation to keep close watch over activities off its shores which are of their nature necessary for utilization of these resources;

NOW THEREFORE I, HARRY S. TRUMAN, President of the United States of America, do hereby proclaim the following policy of the United States of America with respect to the natural resources of the subsoil and sea bed of the continental shelf.

Having concern for the urgency of conserving and prudently utilizing its natural resources, the Government of the United States regards the natural resources of the subsoil and sea bed of the continental shelf beneath the high seas but contiguous to the coasts of the United States as appertaining to the United states, subject to its jurisdiction and control. In cases where the continental shelf extends to the shores of another State, or is shared with an adjacent State, the boundary shall be determined by the United States and the State concerned in accordance with equitable principles. The character as high seas of the waters above the continental shelf and the right to their free and unimpeded navigation are in no way thus affected. . . .

Source: Truman Proclamation of September 28, 1945. *Digest of International Law,* edited by Marjorie Whiteman. Vol. 4. Washington, D.C.: U.S. Government Printing Office, 1965, pp. 756–757. Available at http://oceancommission.gov/documents/gov_oceans/truman.pdf.

Note

1. Quoted in Ram Prakash Anand, *Local Regime of the Sea-Bed and the Developing Countries* (1975; repr., Brill Archive, 1976), 33–34.

Aldo Leopold Calls for a New Land Ethic

"Thinking Like a Mountain"

1949

Aldo Leopold ranks among the leading shapers of American conservation thought and, by extension, environmental policy–making. Leopold spent most of the first half of the twentieth century as a noted forester, game manager, and conservationist, and in 1936 he helped found the Wilderness Society. By the time World War II drew to a close in 1945, Leopold was convinced that Americans needed to make fundamental changes to their relationship with the natural world around them. His manifesto for a new land ethic—the 1949 essay collection A Sand County Almanac—*was published posthumously, one year after he suffered a fatal heart attack while helping a neighbor extinguish a brushfire.*

In Sand County Almanac, *Leopold asserted that American land use and wildlife policies need to display greater awareness of the interconnected quality of ecosystems. He identified mechanization, industrialization, hubris, and selfishness as particularly formidable—but not insurmountable—obstacles to the achievement of greater harmony between humankind and the natural world. The following is a famous section from the* Almanac *called "Thinking Like a Mountain," in which the author explores the ecological strands connecting wolves, deer, and their habitat as a way of advancing his arguments for a more humble and holistic—and less anthropocentric—approach to natural resource management. These ideas would become bedrock tenets of ecological thought in the 1960s and 1970s, when many of America's most enduring environmental laws came into existence.*

A deep chesty bawl echoes from rimrock to rimrock, rolls down the mountain, and fades into the far blackness of the night. It is an outburst of wild defiant sorrow, and of contempt for all the adversities of the world.

Every living thing (and perhaps many a dead one as well) pays heed to that call. To the deer it is a reminder of the way of all flesh, to the pine a forecast of midnight scuffles and of blood upon the snow, to the coyote a promise of gleanings to come, to the cowman a threat of red ink at the bank, to the hunter a challenge of fang against bullet. Yet behind these obvious and immediate hopes and fears there lies a deeper meaning, known only to the mountain itself. Only the mountain has lived long enough to listen objectively to the howl of a wolf.

Those unable to decipher the hidden meaning know nevertheless that it is there, for it is felt in all wolf country, and distinguishes that country from all other land. It tingles in the spine of all who hear wolves by night, or who scan their tracks by day. Even without sight or sound of wolf, it is implicit in a hundred small events: the midnight whinny of a pack horse, the rattle of rolling rocks, the bound of a fleeing deer, the way shadows lie under the spruces. Only the ineducable tyro can fail to sense the presence or absence of wolves, or the fact that mountains have a secret opinion about them.

My own conviction on this score dates from the day I saw a wolf die. We were eating lunch on a high rimrock, at the foot of which a turbulent river elbowed its way. We saw what we thought was a doe fording the torrent, her breast awash in white water. When she climbed the bank toward us and shook out her tail, we realized our error: it was a wolf. A half-dozen others, evidently grown pups, sprang from the willows and all joined in a welcoming mêlée of wagging tails and playful maulings. What was literally a pile of wolves writhed and tumbled in the center of an open flat at the foot of our rimrock.

In those days we had never heard of passing up a chance to kill a wolf. In a second we were pumping lead into the pack, but with more excitement than accuracy: how to aim a steep downhill shot is always confusing. When our rifles were empty, the old wolf was down, and a pup was dragging a leg into impassable slide-rocks.

We reached the old wolf in time to watch a fierce green fire dying in her eyes. I realized then, and have known ever since, that there was something new to me in those eyes—something known only to her and to the mountain. I was young then, and full of trigger-itch; I thought that because fewer wolves meant more deer, that no wolves would mean hunters' paradise. But after seeing the green fire die, I sensed that neither the wolf nor the mountain agreed with such a view.

* * *

Since then I have lived to see state after state extirpate its wolves. I have watched the face of many a newly wolfless mountain, and seen the south-facing slopes wrinkle with a maze of new deer trails. I have seen every edible bush and seedling browsed, first to anaemic desuetude, and then to death. I have seen every edible tree defoliated to the height of a saddlehorn. Such a mountain looks as if someone had given God a new pruning shears, and forbidden Him all other exercise. In the end the starved bones of the hoped-for deer herd, dead of its own too-much, bleach with the bones of the dead sage, or molder under the high-lined junipers.

I now suspect that just as a deer herd lives in mortal fear of its wolves, so does a mountain live in mortal fear of its deer. And perhaps with better cause, for while a buck pulled down by wolves can be replaced in two or three years, a range pulled down by too many deer may fail of replacement in as many decades.

So also with cows. The cowman who cleans his range of wolves does not realize that he is taking over the wolf's job of trimming the herd to fit the range. He has not learned to think like a mountain. Hence we have dustbowls, and rivers washing the future into the sea.

> *Since then I have lived to see state after state extirpate its wolves. I have watched the face of many a newly wolfless mountain, and seen the south-facing slopes wrinkle with a maze of new deer trails. . . . I now suspect that just as a deer herd lives in mortal fear of its wolves, so does a mountain live in mortal fear of its deer.*
>
> —Aldo Leopold

* * *

We all strive for safety, prosperity, comfort, long life, and dullness. The deer strives with his supple legs, the cowman with trap and poison, the statesman with pen, the most of us with machines, votes, and dollars, but it all comes to the same thing: peace in our time. A measure of success in this is all well enough, and perhaps is a requisite to objective thinking, but too much safety seems to yield only danger in the long run. Perhaps this is behind Thoreau's dictum: In wildness is the salvation of the world. Perhaps this is the hidden meaning in the howl of the wolf, long known among mountains, but seldom perceived among men.

Source: Leopold, Aldo. *A Sand County Almanac: And Sketches Here and There.* 1949. Reprint. New York: Oxford University Press, 1989, pp. 129–133. Copyright © 1949 by Oxford University Press, Inc. Used by permission of Oxford University Press, Inc.

| DOCUMENT 7.4 | President Eisenhower's "Atoms for Peace" Speech |

"Peaceful Power from Atomic Energy Is No Dream of the Future"

December 8, 1953

On December 8, 1953, President Dwight D. Eisenhower appeared before the General Assembly of the United Nations in New York City and delivered an historic address on potential peaceful applications for nuclear power. His "Atoms for Peace" speech, excerpted here, was a decisive event in the history of the nuclear energy industry.

Eisenhower spent the first half of his speech recounting nuclear power's capacity for wreaking death and destruction and his hopes for defusing Cold War tensions with the Soviet Union through treaties of disarmament. He then moved on to deliver an earnest defense of nuclear technology's capacity for providing clean and abundant electricity along with a proposal for advancing this goal under the aegis of the United Nations. In addition, the address reflected the Eisenhower Administration's interest in controlling proliferation of nuclear arms around the globe by implementing guidelines and rules that distinguished civilian uses of nuclear technology from military uses. The "Atoms for Peace" speech also signaled to the world that the United States itself intended to move swiftly in developing non-military applications for nuclear power. This message was further underscored less than one year later by the passage of the 1954 Atomic Energy Act, which authorized private U.S. companies to own nuclear reactor facilities and expanded federal research programs on nuclear power. By the close of the 1950s, America's first civilian nuclear power reactors were up and running.

Madame President, Members of the General Assembly:

When Secretary General Hammarskjold's invitation to address this General Assembly reached me in Bermuda, I was just beginning a series of conferences with the Prime Ministers and Foreign Ministers of Great Britain and of France. Our subject was some of the problems that beset our world.

During the remainder of the Bermuda Conference, I had constantly in mind that ahead of me lay a great honor. That honor is mine today as I stand here, privileged to address the General Assembly of the United Nations.

At the same time that I appreciate the distinction of addressing you, I have a sense of exhilaration as I look upon this Assembly.

Never before in history has so much hope for so many people been gathered together in a single organization. Your deliberations and decisions during these somber years have already realized part of those hopes.

But the great tests and the great accomplishments still lie ahead. And in the confident expectation of those accomplishments, I would use the office which, for the time being, I hold, to assure you that the Government of the United States will remain steadfast in its support of this body. This we shall do in the conviction that you will provide a great share of the wisdom, the courage, and the faith which can bring to this world lasting peace for all nations, and happiness and well-being for all men. . . .

I therefore decided that this occasion warranted my saying to you some of the things that have been on the minds and hearts of my legislative and executive associates and on mine for a great many months—thoughts I had originally planned to say primarily to the American people.

I know that the American people share my deep belief that if a danger exists in the world, it is a danger shared by all—and equally, that if hope exists in the mind of one nation, that hope should be shared by all.

Finally, if there is to be advanced any proposal designed to ease even by the smallest measure the tensions of today's world, what more appropriate audience could there be than the members of the General Assembly of the United Nations?

I feel impelled to speak today in a language that in a sense is new—one which I, who have spent so much of my life in the military profession, would have preferred never to use.

That new language is the language of atomic warfare.

The atomic age has moved forward at such a pace that every citizen of the world should have some comprehension, at least in comparative terms, of the extent of this development of the utmost significance to every one of us. Clearly, if the peoples of the world are to conduct an intelligent search for peace, they must be armed with the significant facts of today's existence.

My recital of atomic danger and power is necessarily stated in United States terms, for these are the only incontrovertible facts that I know. I need hardly point out to this Assembly, however, that this subject is global, not merely national in character.

On July 16, 1945, the United States set off the world's first atomic explosion. Since that date in 1945, the United States of America has conducted 42 test explosions.

Atomic bombs today are more than 25 times as powerful as the weapons with which the atomic age dawned, while hydrogen weapons are in the ranges of millions of tons of TNT equivalent.

Today, the United States' stockpile of atomic weapons, which, of course, increases daily, exceeds by many times the explosive equivalent of the total of all bombs and all shells that came from every plane and every gun in every theatre of war in all of the years of World War II.

A single air group, whether afloat or land-based, can now deliver to any reachable target a destructive cargo exceeding in power all the bombs that fell on Britain in all of World War II.

In size and variety, the development of atomic weapons has been no less remarkable. The development has been such that atomic weapons have virtually achieved conventional status within our armed services. In the United States, the Army, the Navy, the Air Force, and the Marine Corps are all capable of putting this weapon to military use.

But the dread secret, and the fearful engines of atomic might, are not ours alone.

In the first place, the secret is possessed by our friends and allies, Great Britain and Canada, whose scientific genius made a tremendous contribution to our original discoveries, and the designs of atomic bombs.

The secret is also known by the Soviet Union.

The Soviet Union has informed us that, over recent years, it has devoted extensive resources to atomic weapons. During this period, the Soviet Union has exploded a series of atomic devices, including at least one involving thermo-nuclear reactions.

If at one time the United States possessed what might have been called a monopoly of atomic power, that monopoly ceased to exist several years ago. Therefore, although our earlier start has permitted us to accumulate what is today a great quantitative advantage, the atomic realities of today comprehend two facts of even greater significance.

First, the knowledge now possessed by several nations will eventually be shared by others—possibly all others.

Second, even a vast superiority in numbers of weapons, and a consequent capability of devastating retaliation, is no preventive, of itself, against the fearful material damage and toll of human lives that would be inflicted by surprise aggression.

The free world, at least dimly aware of these facts, has naturally embarked on a large program of warning and defense systems. That program will be accelerated and expanded.

But let no one think that the expenditure of vast sums for weapons and systems of defense can guarantee absolute safety for the cities and citizens of any nation. The awful arithmetic of the atomic bomb does not permit of any such easy solution. Even against the most powerful defense, an aggressor in possession of the effective minimum number of atomic bombs for a surprise attack could probably place a sufficient number of his bombs on the chosen targets to cause hideous damage.

Should such an atomic attack be launched against the United States, our reactions would be swift and resolute. But for me to say that the defense capabilities of the United States are such that they could inflict terrible losses upon an aggressor—for me to say that the retaliation capabilities of the United States are so great that such an aggressor's land would be laid waste—all this, while fact, is not the true expression of the purpose and the hope of the United States.

To pause there would be to confirm the hopeless finality of a belief that two atomic colossi are doomed malevolently to eye each other indefinitely across a trembling world. To stop there would be to accept helplessly the probability of civilization destroyed-the annihilation of the irreplaceable heritage of mankind handed down to us generation from generation—and the condemnation of mankind to begin all over again the age-old struggle upward from savagery toward decency, and right, and justice.

Surely no sane member of the human race could discover victory in such desolation. Could anyone wish his name to be coupled by history with such human degradation and destruction.

Occasional pages of history do record the faces of the "Great Destroyers" but the whole book of history reveals mankind's never-ending quest for peace, and mankind's God-given capacity to build.

It is with the book of history, and not with isolated pages, that the United States will ever wish to be identified. My country wants to be constructive, not destructive. It wants agreements, not wars, among nations. It wants itself to live in freedom, and in the confidence that the people of every other nation enjoy equally the right of choosing their own way of life.

So my country's purpose is to help us move out of the dark chamber of horrors into the light, to find a way by which the minds of men, the hopes of men, the souls of men everywhere, can move forward toward peace and happiness and well being.

In this quest, I know that we must not lack patience.

I know that in a world divided, such as ours today, salvation cannot be attained by one dramatic act.

I know that many steps will have to be taken over many months before the world can look at itself one day and truly realize that a new climate of mutually peaceful confidence is abroad in the world.

But I know, above all else, that we must start to take these steps—now.

The United States and its allies, Great Britain and France, have over the past months tried to take some of these steps. Let no one say that we shun the conference table.

On the record has long stood the request of the United States, Great Britain, and France to negotiate with the Soviet Union the problems of a divided Germany.

On that record has long stood the request of the same three nations to negotiate an Austrian Peace Treaty.

On the same record still stands the request of the United Nations to negotiate the problems of Korea.

Most recently, we have received from the Soviet Union what is in effect an expression of willingness to hold a Four Power Meeting. Along with our allies, Great Britain and France, we were pleased to see that this note did not contain the unacceptable preconditions previously put forward.

As you already know from our joint Bermuda communique, the United States, Great Britain, and France have agreed promptly to meet with the Soviet Union.

The Government of the United States approaches this conference with hopeful sincerity. We will bend every effort of our minds to the single purpose of emerging from that conference with tangible results toward peace—the only true way of lessening international tension.

We never have, we never will, propose or suggest that the Soviet Union surrender what is rightfully theirs.

We will never say that the peoples of Russia are an enemy with whom we have no desire ever to deal or mingle in friendly and fruitful relationship.

On the contrary, we hope that this coming Conference may initiate a relationship with the Soviet Union which will eventually bring about a free intermingling of the peoples of the East and of the West—the one sure, human way of developing the understanding required for confident and peaceful relations.

Instead of the discontent which is now settling upon Eastern Germany, occupied Austria, and the countries of Eastern Europe, we seek a harmonious family of free European nations, with none a threat to the other, and least of all a threat to the peoples of Russia.

Beyond the turmoil and strife and misery of Asia, we seek peaceful opportunity for these peoples to develop their natural resources and to elevate their lives.

These are not idle words or shallow visions. Behind them lies a story of nations lately come to independence, not as a result of war, but through free grant or peaceful negotiation. There is a record, already written, of assistance gladly given by nations of the West to needy peoples, and to those suffering the temporary effects of famine, drought, and natural disaster.

These are deeds of peace. They speak more loudly than promises or protestations of peaceful intent.

But I do not wish to rest either upon the reiteration of past proposals or the restatement of past deeds. The gravity of the time is such that every new avenue of peace, no matter how dimly discernible, should be explored.

There is at least one new avenue of peace which has not yet been well explored—an avenue now laid out by the General Assembly of the United Nations.

In its resolution of November 18th, 1953, this General Assembly suggested—and I quoted—"that the Disarmament Commission study the desirability of establishing a sub-committee consisting of representatives of the Powers principally involved, which should seek in private an acceptable solution . . . and report on such a solution to the General Assembly and to the Security Council not later than 1 September 1954."

The United States, heeding the suggestion of the General Assembly of the United Nations, is instantly prepared to meet privately with such other countries as may be "principally involved," to seek "an acceptable solution" to the atomic armaments race which overshadows not only the peace, but the very life, of the world.

We shall carry into these private or diplomatic talks a new conception.

The United States would seek more than the mere reduction or elimination of atomic materials for military purposes.

It is not enough to take this weapon out of the hands of the soldiers. It must be put into the hands of those who will know how to strip its military casing and adapt it to the arts of peace.

The United States knows that if the fearful trend of atomic military buildup can be reversed, this greatest of destructive forces can be developed into a great boon, for the benefit of all mankind.

The United States knows that peaceful power from atomic energy is no dream of the future. That capability, already proved, is here—now—today. Who can doubt, if the entire body of the world's scientists and engineers had adequate amounts of fissionable material with which to test and develop their ideas, that this capability would rapidly be transformed into universal, efficient, and economic usage.

To hasten the day when fear of the atom will begin to disappear from the minds of people, and the governments of the East and West, there are certain steps that can be taken now.

I therefore make the following proposals:

The Governments principally involved, to the extent permitted by elementary prudence, to begin now and continue to make joint contributions from their stockpiles of normal uranium and fissionable materials to an International Atomic Energy Agency. We would expect that such an agency would be set up under the aegis of the United Nations.

The ratios of contributions, the procedures and other details would properly be within the scope of the "private conversations" I have referred to earlier.

The United States is prepared to undertake these explorations in good faith. Any partner of the United States acting in the same good faith will find the United States a not unreasonable or ungenerous associate.

Undoubtedly initial and early contributions to this plan would be small in quantity. However, the proposal has the great virtue that it can be undertaken without the irritations and mutual suspicions incident to any attempt to set up a completely acceptable system of world-wide inspection and control.

The Atomic Energy Agency could be made responsible for the impounding, storage, and protection of the contributed fissionable and other materials. The ingenuity of our scientists will provide special safe conditions under which such a bank of fissionable material can be made essentially immune to surprise seizure.

The more important responsibility of this Atomic Energy Agency would be to devise methods whereby this fissionable material would be allocated to serve the peaceful pursuits of mankind. Experts would be mobilized to apply atomic energy to the needs of agriculture, medicine, and other peaceful activities. A special purpose would be to provide abundant electrical energy in the power-starved areas of the world. Thus the contributing powers would be dedicating some of their strength to serve the needs rather than the fears of mankind.

The United States would be more than willing—it would be proud to take up with others "principally involved" the development of plans whereby such peaceful use of atomic energy would be expedited.

Of those "principally involved" the Soviet Union must, of course, be one.

I would be prepared to submit to the Congress of the United States, and with every expectation of approval, any such plan that would:

First—encourage world-wide investigation into the most effective peacetime uses of fissionable material, and with the certainty that they had all the material needed for the conduct of all experiments that were appropriate;

Second—begin to diminish the potential destructive power of the world's atomic stockpiles;

Third—allow all peoples of all nations to see that, in this enlightened age, the great powers of the earth, both of the East and of the West, are interested in human aspirations first, rather than in building up the armaments of war;

Fourth—open up a new channel for peaceful discussion, and initiate at least a new approach to the many difficult problems that must be solved in both private and public conversations, if the world is to shake off the inertia imposed by fear, and is to make positive progress toward peace.

Against the dark background of the atomic bomb, the United States does not wish merely to present strength, but also the desire and the hope for peace.

The coming months will be fraught with fateful decisions. In this Assembly; in the capitals and military headquarters of the world; in the hearts of men everywhere, be they governors or governed, may they be the decisions which will lead this world out of fear and into peace.

To the making of these fateful decisions, the United States pledges before you—and therefore before the world—its determination to help solve the fearful atomic dilemma—to devote its entire heart and mind to find the way by which the miraculous inventiveness of man shall not be dedicated to his death, but consecrated to his life.

I again thank the delegates for the great honor they have done me, in inviting me to appear before them, and in listening to me so courteously. Thank you.

Source: Eisenhower, Dwight. Address Before the General Assembly of the United Nations, December 8, 1953. *Congressional Record.* 83rd Cong., 2d sess., vol. 100, January 7, 1954, pp. 61–63. Available at The American Presidency Project, www.presidency.ucsb.edu/ws/index.php?pid=9774.

A Report on the Proposed St. Lawrence Seaway

"Interior Heartily Agrees with the Objectives of Developing the St. Lawrence for Both Navigation and Power"

April 16, 1953

Of the great public works programs undertaken by the United States in the 1950s, the individual project that perhaps most closely rivaled the massive Interstate Highway System—as a feat of civil engineering, as an instrument of economic growth, and as an agent of wrenching environmental transformation—was the St. Lawrence Seaway.

The Seaway was an epic exercise in river alteration undertaken by a partnership of the U.S. and Canadian governments in furtherance of commercial navigation and hydroelectric power goals. The river in question was the 800-mile-long St. Lawrence River, which extends from the eastern shores of Lake Ontario—the easternmost of the five Great Lakes—to the Atlantic Ocean. For many years, both Canadian and American lawmakers, officials, engineers, and business interests had pondered the river's potential as a commercial artery. But the river's rapids and its overall gradient—it dropped 226 feet between Lake Ontario and Montreal—made any development schemes extremely daunting. In addition, railroad interests and eastern ports saw the proposed marine highway as competition for freight business, so they mobilized their advocates in Congress against these schemes.

In 1951, however, Canadian authorities announced their intention to undertake the project, with or without U.S. participation. This move galvanized American supporters, including members of Congress allied with the powerful U.S. Army Corps of Engineers, to press for a U.S. commitment to the Seaway. "The prospect of turning the Great Lakes into an American Mediterranean with ocean vessels traveling 2,000 miles into the heart of the continent—'every lakeport a seaport'—was a powerful lure to midwest farmers, shippers, and chambers of commerce," explained historian D.W. Meinig.[1] In 1953 President Eisenhower formally endorsed a U.S.–Canada partnership after receiving positive reviews of the proposal from key federal agencies. One such report, filed by the National Security Council with input from Interior, State, Defense, and other cabinet departments, is excerpted here. The contribution from the Department of Interior makes it clear that on this particular issue, the agency interpreted the Great Lakes and St. Lawrence River primarily as natural resource commodities to be developed for economic expansion and prosperity.

One year later, in 1954, Congress passed the Wiley-Dondero Act (also known as the Seaway Act), which cleared the way for a U.S.–Canada partnership in building the Seaway. The U.S. Army Corps of Engineers went to work on the project, and in 1959 this ambitious joint engineering effort to connect America's freshwater seas to the Atlantic's salty depths was completed. The Seaway—which became a term used for all programs of navigational/hydropower development along the river—quickly made its presence felt. The city of Duluth, strategically perched both on Lake Superior's far western shores and in the shadows of Minnesota's famous Mesabi Iron Range, became America's second-leading seaport as a steady stream of freighters departed its docks, their holds filled with iron ore for steelmakers in the East. Seaway use peaked in 1977, when 57 million tons of freight passed through its network of locks and canals, but its annual freight tonnage now ranges from 30 to 40 million tons—about half what Seaway advocates envisioned. The environmental impact of the Seaway, meanwhile, was significant. Its creation brought about a cascade of shifting land use patterns along the St. Lawrence Valley and the Great Lakes region. In addition, invasive marine species such as Atlantic sea lampreys and zebra mussels from the Caspian Sea became a nightmare for U.S. and Canadian resource agencies. These and other alien species entered Great Lakes waters from the released ballast water of oceangoing vessels, and since their arrival they have thoroughly disrupted marine ecosystems throughout the Great Lakes. Efforts to outlaw such ballast releases have intensified in recent years.

Environmental concerns have also complicated proposals to modernize the Seaway so that it can better accommodate the huge container ships that dominate today's shipping industry. Environmentalists contend that proposals to deepen channels and rework locks for bigger ships will further disrupt fish and wildlife populations, increase ecosystem vulnerability to oil and chemical spills and exposure, and worsen problems with invasive species. Proponents of modernization insist that all of these fears are overblown and that these measures are vital to keep the Seaway viable.

SUMMARY OF DEPARTMENT AND AGENCY VIEWS ON ST. LAWRENCE SEAWAY PROJECT AND BILLS RELATING THERETO.

State (March 20)—State favors U.S. participation in the Seaway project. It also notes that (1) Canada attaches urgency to the development of power which it considers vitally urgent for the industrial and defense economy of Ontario, and (2) Canada also desires that completion of the seaway not be delayed.

Defense (pending)—Defense states that the Department has consistently and vigorously supported the navigation and power phases of the St. Lawrence Seaway project as important to the national defense from both a long and a short-term point of view. It states that the Department's statements made in 1952 to this effect are even more timely now than last year, since Canada has indicated its desire to proceed unilaterally on construction of the St. Lawrence Seaway if the United States does not decide to participate. Defense states that if Canada proceeds unilaterally, the United States would be precluded from exercising an equal voice in the control of traffic through the Seaway, not only in time of peace but also when the United States is at war; and that only by United States participation now in construction of the Seaway can the United States be assured of active participation in its future operation and control. In summary, Defense strongly favors participation by the United States at this time in the construction of the St. Lawrence Seaway. While Defense offers no comment on the use of a government corporation to implement United States participation, it does suggest that the Congress give consideration to an amendment which would assign construction to the Army Corps of Engineers. The Department recommends early enactment of one of the bills or resolutions pending before the Senate Foreign Relations Committee. . . .

Interior (pending)—Interior heartily agrees with the objectives of developing the St. Lawrence for both navigation and power. Interior states that: (1) the domestic supply of high grade iron ore is limited and is already insufficient to supply our needs; (2) our blast furnaces are concentrated in Ohio and western Pennsylvania, removed from the eastern seaboard and served by Great Lakes traffic routes; (3) these furnaces must soon be supplied with large tonnages of ore from new sources. These new sources are primarily Quebec-Labrador and Venezuela. Interior notes that the record shipments of ore from

Mesabi and other Lake Superior ranges to blast furnaces in the lower lakes steel centers was made possible by the navigation works in the upper Great Lakes as improved before and during the early part of World War II. The Department states that unless improved by deep waterway, as proposed, the international rapids section of the St. Lawrence would constitute a bottleneck in the transportation of iron ore in substantial quantities from Seven Islands [a location on the Quebec north shore] to the blast furnaces in the lower lakes area. It notes that the emergency measures taken in 1950 to ship iron ore all-rail from the Lakes Superior mines resulted in moving by all-rail only 8 percent of the total shipped. It notes also that the Seaway would not result in the surrender of iron ore rail traffic to navigation. The Department states that the greatest need for iron ore obtains during times of war and it is then that open sea transportation is most hazardous and the St. Lawrence Seaway would afford a supply relatively inexpensive and safe from submarine attack. Moreover, early construction would relieve the current heavy drain on open-pit and direct-shipping ores of the Mesabi range and thereby preserve the maximum degree of rapid production expansibility for future emergencies. This expansibility constitutes a most urgent reason for immediate increases of imported ore. The Department notes the Canadian intention to proceed unilaterally, if necessary, and states that it would be highly undesirable to leave any part of the welfare of our great industries to the sole determination of a foreign power no matter how friendly our relations have been, are, and will continue to be. The Department observes with respect to the power development in the international rapids section that this lower cost power would find an ample market in New York and New England as soon as it can be made available.

Commerce (April 3)—Commerce states that there are substantial arguments for, as well as substantial arguments against, the St. Lawrence waterway project, but that on the assumption that Canada is prepared to proceed forthwith with its part of the program and on balance, after considering pro and con viewpoints, it is prepared to recommend that the United States join in completing the waterway project subject to one proviso. Its proviso is that the project should be set up on a self-liquidating basis and that this Government's involvement should not exceed a known or fixed amount. The Department adds that under all the circumstances, its position would naturally be influenced by this amount, whatever it may be. . . .

Justice (April 1)—Justice has advised the Senate Committee that whether the bills on St. Lawrence should be enacted involves a question of policy concerning which the Department prefers to make no recommendation. Notwithstanding this public position, the Attorney General has, in a memorandum to Sherman Adams, stated that in summary and on the basis of a limited acquaintanceship with the problem, S. 589, (Wiley Bill) and the position taken by the Great Lakes-St. Lawrence Association seem deserving of support by the Administration. . . .

Source: *A Report to the National Security Council by the NSC Planning Board on National Security Interests in the St. Lawrence-Great Lakes Seaway Project,* April 16, 1953, pp. 6–8. www.eisenhower .archives.gov/Research/Digital_Documents/StLawrenceSeaway/New%20PDFs/1953%2004%2016%20 Report%20to%20NSC.pdf.

NOTE

1. D.W. Meinig, *The Shaping of America: A Geographical Perspective on 500 Years of History* (New Haven, Conn.: Yale University Press, 2004), 84.

President Eisenhower Urges the Creation of a "National Highway Program"

"The Highway System . . . Is Inadequate for the Nation's Growing Needs"

February 22, 1955

In the early 1950s President Dwight D. Eisenhower and administration officials decided that economic expansion, soaring levels of automobile use, and national defense concerns all pointed to the need for a major upgrade of the U.S. interstate road system. In Eisenhower's view, the overarching goals were to modernize and expand the nation's existing road transportation infrastructure into a grand system of "speedy, safe, transcontinental travel" that would generate new economic opportunities, relieve traffic congestion, and eliminate the "appalling inadequacies to meet the demands of catastrophe or defense should an atomic war come."[1]

Honoring a personal request from Eisenhower, retired U.S. Army general Lucius D. Clay took the reins of a special committee organized to study how the federal government could best proceed in making the president's vision of a vastly expanded highway system a reality. In January 1955 the Clay Committee returned with a "Ten-Year Plan for a National Highway Program." This report became the basis for the infrastructure investment program Eisenhower sent to Congress for consideration. Eisenhower also relied heavily on the Committee's findings in preparing a special address to Congress on the need for federal investment in a national highway program. This address, which Eisenhower delivered on February 22, 1955, is reprinted here.

Months of congressional debate and maneuvering ensued in subsequent months, but sixteen months after Eisenhower's pitch to Congress, the 1956 Federal-Aid Highway Act was sent to the president for his signature. This legislation contained most of Eisenhower's long-sought highway expansion goals, and it ultimately added 41,000 miles of roads, 16,000 entrance and exit ramps, and more than 50,000 bridges and overpasses to America's sprawling roadway system.

These interstate highways became integral hubs in the distribution of virtually all U.S. goods and services, and they continue to support a sizable proportion of America's business and recreational travel. But the environmental and social consequences of this ambitious expansion effort have been subjects of intense debate for the past half-century. Critics assert that the interstates have also exacerbated America's air pollution and land loss problems, created an unhealthy addiction to foreign oil, and devoured billions in federal funding that would have otherwise gone to urban improvements.

To the Congress of the United States:

Our unity as a nation is sustained by free communication of thought and by easy transportation of people and goods. The ceaseless flow of information throughout the Republic is matched by individual and commercial movement over a vast system of interconnected highways criss-crossing the Country and joining at our national borders with friendly neighbors to the north and south.

Together, the uniting forces of our communication and transportation systems are dynamic elements in the very name we bear—United States. Without them, we would be a mere alliance of many separate parts.

The Nation's highway system is a gigantic enterprise, one of our largest items of capital investment. Generations have gone into its building. Three million, three hundred and sixty-six thousand miles of road, travelled by 58 million motor vehicles, comprise it. The replacement cost of its drainage and bridge and tunnel works is incalculable. One in every seven Americans gains his livelihood and supports his family out of it. But, in large part, the network is inadequate for the nation's growing needs.

In recognition of this, the Governors in July of last year at my request began a study of both the problem and methods by which the Federal Government might assist the States in its solution. I appointed in September the President's Advisory Committee on a National Highway Program, headed by Lucius D. Clay, to work with the Governors and to propose a plan of action for submission to the Congress. At the same time, a committee representing departments and agencies of the national Government was organized to conduct studies coordinated with the other two groups. All three were confronted with inescapable evidence that action, comprehensive and quick and forward-looking, is needed.

First: Each year, more than 36 thousand people are killed and more than a million injured on the highways. To the home where the tragic aftermath of an accident on an unsafe road is a gap in the family circle, the monetary worth of preventing that death cannot be reckoned. But reliable estimates place the measurable economic cost of the highway accident toll to the Nation at more than $4.3 billion a year.

Second: The physical condition of the present road net increases the cost of vehicle operation, according to many estimates, by as much as one cent per mile of vehicle travel. At the present rate of travel, this totals more than $5 billion a year. The cost is not borne by the individual vehicle operator alone. It pyramids into higher expense of doing the nation's business. Increased highway transportation costs, passed on through each step in the distribution of goods, are paid ultimately by the individual consumer.

Third: In case of an atomic attack on our key cities, the road net must permit quick evacuation of target areas, mobilization of defense forces and maintenance of every essential economic function. But the present system in critical areas would be the breeder of a deadly congestion within hours of an attack.

Fourth: Our Gross National Product, about $357 billion in 1954, is estimated to reach over $500 billion in 1965 when our population will exceed 180 million and, according to other estimates, will travel in 81 million vehicles 814 billion vehicle miles that year. Unless the present rate of highway improvement and development is increased, existing traffic jams only faintly foreshadow those of ten years hence.

To correct these deficiencies is an obligation of Government at every level. The highway system is a public enterprise. As the owner and operator, the various levels of Government have a responsibility for management that promotes the economy of the nation and properly serves the individual user. In the case of the Federal Government, moreover, expenditures on a highway program are a return to the highway user of the taxes which he pays in connection with his use of the highways.

Congress has recognized the national interest in the principal roads by authorizing two Federal-aid systems, selected cooperatively by the States, local units and the Bureau of Public Roads.

The Federal-aid primary system as of July 1, 1954, consisted of 234,407 miles, connecting all the principal cities, county seats, ports, manufacturing areas and other traffic generating centers.

In 1944 the Congress approved the Federal-aid secondary system, which on July 1, 1954, totalled 482,972 miles, referred to as farm-to-market roads—important feeders linking farms, factories, distribution outlets and smaller communities with the primary system.

Because some sections of the primary system, from the viewpoint of national interest are more important than others, the Congress in 1944 authorized the selection of a special network, not to exceed 40,000 miles in length, which would connect by routes, as direct as practicable, the principal metropolitan areas, cities and industrial centers, serve the national defense, and connect with routes of continental importance in the Dominion of Canada and the Republic of Mexico.

This National System of Interstate Highways, although it embraces only 1.2 percent of total road mileage, joins 42 State capital cities and 90 percent of all cities over 50,000 population. It carries more than a seventh of all traffic, a fifth of the rural traffic, serves 65 percent of the urban and 45 percent of the rural population. Approximately 37,600 miles have been designated to date. This system and its mileage are presently included within the Federal-aid primary system.

In addition to these systems, the Federal Government has the principal, and in many cases the sole, responsibility for roads that cross or provide access to Federally owned land—more than one-fifth the nation's area.

Of all these, the Interstate System must be given top priority in construction planning. But at the current rate of development, the Interstate network would not reach even a reasonable level of extent and efficiency in half a century. State highway departments cannot effectively meet the need. Adequate right-of-way to assure control of access; grade separation structures; relocation and realignment of present highways; all these, done on the necessary scale within an integrated system, exceed their collective capacity.

If we have a congested and unsafe and inadequate system, how then can we improve it so that ten years from now it will be fitted to the nation's requirements?

A realistic answer must be based on a study of all phases of highway financing, including a study of the costs of completing the several systems of highways, made by the Bureau of Public Roads in cooperation with the State highway departments and local units of government. This study, made at the direction of the 83rd Congress in the 1954 Federal-aid Highway Act, is the most comprehensive of its kind ever undertaken.

Its estimates of need show that a 10-year construction program to modernize all our roads and streets will require expenditure of $ 101 billion by all levels of Government.

The preliminary 10-year totals of needs by road systems are:

Interstate—urban $11 billion, rural $12 billion, total $23 billion

Federal-aid Primary—urban $10 billion, rural $20 billion, total $30 billion

Federal-aid Secondary—entirely rural, $15 billion

Sub-total of Federal-aid Systems—urban $21 billion, rural $47 billion, total $68 billion

Other roads and streets—urban $16 billion, rural $17 billion, total $33 billion

TOTAL OF NEEDS—urban $37 billion, rural $64 billion, total $101 billion

The Governors' Conference and the President's Advisory Committee are agreed that the Federal share of the needed construction program should be about 30 percent of the total, leaving to State and local units responsibility to finance the remainder.

The obvious responsibility to be accepted by the Federal Government, in addition to the existing Federal interest in our 3,366,000-mile network of highways, is the development of the Interstate System with its most essential urban arterial connections. In its report, the Advisory Committee recommends:

1. That the Federal Government assume principal responsibility for the cost of a modern Interstate Network to be completed by 1964 to include the most essential urban arterial connections; at an annual average cost of $2.5 billion for the ten year period.

2. That Federal contributions to primary and secondary road systems, now at the rate authorized by the 1954 Act of approximately $525 million annually, be continued.

3. That Federal funds for that portion of the Federal-aid systems in urban areas not on the Interstate System, now approximately $75 million annually, be continued.

4. That Federal funds for Forest Highways be continued at the present $22.5 million per year rate.

Under these proposals, the total Federal expenditures through the ten year period would be:

Interstate System—$25.000 billion

Federal-aid Primary and Secondary—$5.250 billion

Federal-aid Urban—$.750 billion

Forest Highways—$.225 billion

TOTAL—$31.225 billion

The extension of necessary highways in the Territories and highway maintenance and improvement in National Parks, on Indian lands and on other public lands of the United States will continue to be treated in the budget for these particular subjects. . . .

Source: Eisenhower, Dwight D. "Special Message to the Congress Regarding a National Highway Program, February 22, 1955." In *Public Papers of the Presidents of the United States: Dwight D. Eisenhower, 1955.* Washington, D.C.: Government Printing Office, 1958, p. 39. Available at The American Presidency Project, www.presidency.ucsb.edu/ws/index.php?pid=10415&st=&st1=.

NOTE

1. Quoted in Richard F. Weingroff, "Essential to the National Interest," *Public Roads* 69, no. 5, March–April 2006. U.S. Department of Transportation, Federal Highway Administration, www.tfhrc.gov/pubrds/06mar/07.htm.

The Air Pollution Control Act

"In Recognition of the Dangers to the Public Health and Welfare"

July 14, 1955

American policymakers of the post–World War II era were largely disinclined to take regulatory actions that could be seen as unfriendly to business and industry. But harrowing incidents such as a 1948 "killer smog" that descended on Donora, Pennsylvania, killing 20 residents and debilitating another 3,000, convinced Congress that rising air pollution levels from industrial activity, automobiles and other transportation sources, and other elements of modern American society had to be confronted.

The result was the Air Pollution Control Act of 1955, the first federal air pollution law in U.S. history. This law was of extremely limited scope, however, so it encountered far less political opposition than subsequent air pollution control legislation from the 1970s forward. It aimed only to provide federal research assistance to states and cities grappling with air-quality issues. Specifically, the legislation granted $5 million annually for five years to the Public Health Service (PHS) to provide technical assistance and training to local and state agencies in air pollution abatement and to carry out new research on air pollution. It imposed no federal regulations on industrial emissions or other sources of air pollution, and, in fact, explicitly signaled Congress's belief—despite growing evidence to the contrary—that municipalities and states possessed the financial resources and regulatory authority to adequately address this threat.

The bill sailed through the Senate in June 1955 with minimal debate, then passed the House of Representatives by voice vote in early July. The Senate promptly agreed to accept the House version without any revisions, so the Air Pollution Control Act went to the White House, where it was signed by President Dwight Eisenhower on July 14, 1955. Today, the Act is seen as a milestone in American environmental policy. Despite the act's timid approach and limited language, it did lay the groundwork for much more substantive air pollution legislation in later decades, such as the Clean Air Acts of 1963 and 1970 because it established air pollution control as a legitimate concern of the federal government.

AN ACT TO PROVIDE RESEARCH AND TECHNICAL ASSISTANCE RELATING TO AIR POLLUTION CONTROL

Be it enacted by the Senate and House of Representatives of the United States of America in Congress assembled, That in recognition of the dangers to the public health and welfare, injury to agricultural crops and livestock, damage to and deterioration of property, and hazards to air and ground transportation, from air pollution, it is hereby declared to be the policy of Congress to preserve and protect the primary responsibilities and rights of the States and local governments in controlling air pollution, to support and aid technical research to devise and develop methods of abating such pollution, and to provide

Federal technical services and financial aid to State and local government air pollution control agencies and other public or private agencies and institutions in the formulation and execution of their air pollution abatement research programs. To this end, the Secretary of Health, Education, and Welfare and the Surgeon General of the Public Health Service (under the supervision and direction of the Secretary of Health, Education, and Welfare) shall have the authority relating to air pollution control vested in them respectively by this Act.

Sec. 2. (a) The Surgeon General is authorized, after careful investigation and in cooperation with other Federal agencies, with State and local government air pollution control agencies, with other public and private agencies and institutions, and with the industries involved, to prepare or recommend research programs for devising and developing methods for eliminating or reducing air pollution. For the purpose of this subsection the Surgeon General is authorized to make joint investigations with any such agencies or institutions.

(b) The Surgeon General may (1) encourage cooperative activities by State and local governments for the prevention and abatement of air pollution; (2) collect and disseminate information relating to air pollution and the prevention and abatement thereof; (3) conduct in the Public Health Service, and support and aid the conduct by State and local government air pollution control agencies, and other public and private agencies and institutions of, technical research to devise and develop methods of preventing and abating air pollution; and (4) make available to State and local government air pollution control agencies, other public and private agencies and institutions, and industries, the results of surveys, studies, investigations, research, and experiments relating to air pollution and the prevention and abatement thereof.

Sec. 3. The Surgeon General may, upon request of any State or local government air pollution control agency, conduct investigations and research and make surveys concerning any specific problem of air pollution confronting such State and local government air pollution control agency with a view to recommending a solution of such problem.

Sec. 4. The Surgeon General shall prepare and publish from time to time reports of such surveys, studies, investigations, research, and experiments made under the authority of this Act as he may consider desirable, together with appropriate recommendations with regard to the control of air pollution.

Sec. 5. (a) There is hereby authorized to be appropriated to the Department of Health, Education, and Welfare for each of the five fiscal years during the period beginning July 1, 1955, and ending June 30, 1960, not to exceed $5,000,000 to enable it to carry out its functions under this Act and, in furtherance of the policy declared in the first section of this Act, to (1) make grants-in-aid to State and local government air pollution control agencies, and other public and private agencies and institutions, and to individuals, for research, training, and demonstration projects, and (2) enter into contracts with public and private agencies and institutions and individuals for research, training, and demonstration projects. . . .

Source: Air Pollution Control Act of 1955. In *Legal Compilation: Statutes and Legislative History, Executive Orders, Regulations, Guidelines and Reports.* Washington, D.C.: The Environmental Protection Agency. January 1973, pp. 81–82. Available at http://nepis.epa.gov.

The National Park Service Unveils Mission 66

"The Parks Are Being Loved to Death"

January 27, 1956

America's national parks were favorite tourism destinations during the post–World War II economic boom. The numbers of American families making pilgrimages to the parks increased dramatically during this era, rising from 17 million visits in 1940 to 56 million visits in 1955. The soaring popularity of the national parks, however, was a double-edged sword. It increased the American public's sense of ownership and connection to the parks specifically and the world of nature in general, which paid enormous dividends for conservation-oriented groups and policymakers in the 1960s and beyond. But it also exposed years of fiscal neglect of the parks themselves. Facilities and staff levels in many of the parks were woefully inadequate to accommodate the rising tide of automotive visitors, and the public's experience of the parks suffered correspondingly. By the mid-1950s prominent press outlets were filing reports that depicted the U.S. government as being almost criminally derelict in its stewardship of the parks. Reader's Digest, for example, published a damning article entitled "The Shocking Truth about Our National Parks" that warned potential national park tourists that their visit was "likely to be fraught with discomfort, disappointment, even danger."[1] A growing chorus of voices asserted that "quantities of both ideas and money were needed if the parks were to remain cultural icons, revered by the same public that now threatened their viability."[2]

National Park Service Director Conrad Wirth recognized the truth of these charges, but he also sensed opportunity amid the rising swirl of censure. Determined to take advantage of the heightened debate over the parks, Wirth mobilized park service staff to prepare a proposal for a ten-year program of capital improvements that would modernize and expand the national park system for a new generation of tourists. He named the overall program Mission 66, in reference to the goal of completing the program by 1966, the fiftieth anniversary of the founding of the National Park Service.

Wirth presented the plan in January 1956 to President Dwight Eisenhower, who had been stung by the criticism of the parks—and its potential political impact. The full text of Wirth's presentation is reprinted here. The political benefits of Wirth's proposal, meanwhile, were also touted at the presentation by officials such as Assistant Interior Secretary Wesley A. D'Ewart, who described Mission 66 as a "program in the very best tradition of Teddy Roosevelt. It is sound, saleable, economical, and a good political horse to ride. It can be a lasting credit to this Administration, to the Department of the Interior, and to the National Park Service. Here is an opportunity to assure from 50 to 80 million Americans that the Republican Party recognizes the problems of increased use of our national parks and that we are going to do something about it. MISSION 66 will pay good political dividends."[3]

An impressed Eisenhower promptly gave his endorsement of Mission 66, and a few months later Congress signaled that it was also on board with the plan. Mindful of the estimated $700 million price tag for the entire program, Congress regularly approved higher appropriations for the park service over the next several years. By 1962 the park service's *budget had jumped to more than $100 million annually (from $32 million in 1955), and by 1966 Congress had spent approximately $1 billion on the Mission 66 program.[4]*

The results of these expenditures were impressive. Three thousand miles of new roads were built or repaired in existing parks, and seventy newly minted national park units (parks, preserves, recreation areas, monuments and historic sites) were added to the system. Private landholdings within park boundaries were purchased and became sites for some of the nearly 600 campgrounds developed under Mission 66. Water, sewer, and electric services were introduced in hundreds of parks, and new administration buildings, park residences, picnic shelters, and visitors' centers—the latter often constructed in accordance with contemporary architectural trends—appeared in parklands all across the country. Staffing levels also were increased, especially at the more popular parks. By the time the Mission 66 program was completed, the national park system was far better equipped to absorb the projected 80 million visitors it would receive on an annual basis.

Mission 66, however, triggered a deep schism between the National Park Service and some conservationists that had long been among its staunchest allies. Wilderness advocates became convinced that the recasting of the parks into dramatically more user-friendly forms signified a worrisome shift in agency priorities. Convinced that wilderness protection was being sacrificed to the gods of tourism, mass consumption, and the service's own aggrandizement, leading environmentalists such as Wilderness Society Director Olaus Murie condemned Mission 66. "There is a decided cleavage in the [Park] Service over the question of quality" of the program, he wrote in an October 1956 letter to fellow conservationists Sigurd Olson and Howard Zahniser. "But the opinion of those humble devoted people, employees of the service, do not reach to the surface of high officialdom. Several employees have told me that the famous Mission 66 is really an appropriation drive, to spend a lot of money; to enhance the status of a bureau."[5]

For his part, Wirth firmly denied all charges that "Mission 66 is somehow damaging the parks or that it is inimical to the purpose for which the Parks were created." To the contrary, he defended the modernization effort with unyielding vigor and conviction throughout the life of the program. "I make no apology for the construction included in Mission 66. It's the people's right to visit their parks, and they do so in large numbers."[6]

[Note: The original speech text has been marked up by hand. Text in the original speech marked as omitted has been omitted in the following document.]

MISSION 66 SPECIAL PRESENTATION

Mr. President and Members of the Cabinet: thank you for giving us this opportunity to report on the National Parks, and to discuss plans for their future.

As you know, these are the areas where the Nation preserves its irreplaceable treasures in lands, scenery—and its historic sites—to be used for the benefit and enjoyment of the people, and passed on unimpaired to future generations. The areas of the National Park System are among the most important vacation lands of the American people. Today, people flock to the parks in such numbers that it is increasingly difficult for them to get the benefits which parks ought to provide, or for us to preserve these benefits for Americans of tomorrow.

This is why the Department of the Interior and the National Park Service have surveyed the parks and their problems, and propose to embark upon MISSION 66—a program designed to place the national parks in condition to serve America and Americans, today and in the future.

National Parks are an American idea—Yellowstone became the first national park in the world when it was established during the administration of President U.S. Grant. Other parks, monuments, and historic sites have been added—each located for you on this map—until today there are 181 areas, widely scattered throughout the States and Territories. The national parks have become a real part of the American way of life, as attested by the phenomenal increase in their popularity.

But the intangible benefits of refreshment, understanding, and inspiration are not the only dividends. The national parks contribute substantially to the economic life of the Nation. With working hours going down and leisure time going up, vacation travel and vacation spending are, in fact, among the three biggest industries in the States pictured on this map. National park travel—as Estes Park Village—Gateway to Rocky Mountain National Park—suggests—benefits innumerable large and small enterprises throughout the Nation. The more the parks are used for their inherent, cultural, and recreational values, the more they contribute to the economy of the Nation. Here is one resource that earns its greatest human and economic profits the less it is used up.

The problem of today is simply that the parks are being loved to death. They are neither equipped nor staffed to protect their irreplaceable resources, nor to take care of their increasing millions of visitors.

Here is the attendance picture—358 thousand visitors in 1916—21 million in 1941—50 million last year—and by 1966, the parks will have at least 80 million visitors.

Are all of these 50 million people finding, as this family group is, the unspoiled refreshment they seek and deserve?

[MOTION PICTURES OF SUMMER 1955]

What we have just seen is a plant operating at 200 percent capacity. How long would a business concern continue to operate its plant at a 100% overload? If it is to stay in business, it must plan and develop for the demand ahead.

We must design to meet the needs of today and tomorrow. That is exactly what MISSION 66 will do. Fortunately, the problems of today can be solved without undue difficulty, without prolonged disruption of public use, and at surprising low cost, if handled on a long-range, one-package basis. By a one-package program I mean simply bringing each part of the program along together, so that when we build a road, the lodges, campgrounds, public use buildings, utility systems and the other things the road leads to will be ready for use at the same time, and, so that the parks will be staffed to meet their responsibilities to the visitor.

Now, specifically, what are the needs today, and how will MISSION 66 meet these needs? There is no point cataloguing every project, but let me give you enough examples to give you the broad picture of the things which MISSION 66 will accomplish:

The most obvious is: modern accommodations so that the park visitor can be assured—as this couple was not—of a comfortable place to stay. Much of what we have is out-worn and outmoded, and will be replaced as we double total capacity.

We will encourage private business to build more accommodations in the gateway communities near the parks.

Within the parks, we shall encourage greater participation by private enterprise, as illustrated by the new Jackson Lake Lodge in the Tetons. This encouragement will take two forms:

Loan guarantees, such as now given to other enterprises through the Small Business Administration, should be extended to some of the smaller concessioners.

But, the best encouragement the National Park Service can give is to go forward with its own part of the park development. For example, the Yellowstone Park Company is now ready to build 12 million dollars worth of new accommodations, but must wait until the Government installs utilities at a cost of 4 ½ million dollars. We have to do our part before the park concessioners can go ahead.

Not all park visitors sleep under a roof. Americans heading for the wide-open spaces are justifiably frustrated when they find themselves intruded upon by the very crowds they intended to leave behind. Campground capacity will be doubled, so that this will be the typical camping picture. Picnic areas will be expanded.

But places to eat and to sleep comprise only a part of what it takes to run a park—many of the other necessary facilities are pitifully inadequate. Public use buildings, ranger stations, fire lookouts, and repair and storage buildings, and other facilities necessary for a complete park operation will be provided.

Many of our employees live in shacks—eyesores that shame the Government, mar the scenery, and sap employee morale.

Adequate employee housing will be supplied—its upkeep and replacement paid back through rentals. Narrow and dangerous roads must be modernized for safety, and to improve the flow of traffic; trails improved, and the presently authorized National Parkways—essentially completed.

MISSION 66 will give us an adequate staff, to protect the parks against forest fire and other dangers, to maintain the roads and buildings, operate the utility systems, and to serve the visiting public. This is a very important need, for while park attendance has increased from 21 million in 1941 to 50 million today, our field staff has actually decreased in term of man-years of employment.

Today some parks are checkerboarded with unsightly private inholdings—land parcels standing in the way of planned development and use. These should be acquired.

Right along with our own improvement, one of our major goals is the parallel development of County and State parks, Wildlife Refuges, Indian Reservations, National and State Forests, Public lands and Recreation Areas, so that each level of Government and private enterprise, will share its appropriate part of the expanding recreational use load.

These are the pressing needs today—the things MISSION 66 will accomplish—so that the American people can enjoy, in the best sense, their national parks.

To put the National Parks in shape is an investment in the physical, mental, and spiritual well-being of Americans as individuals. It is a gainful investment contributing substantially to the national economy, as I have mentioned. It is an investment in good citizenship.

Where else do so many Americans under the most pleasant circumstances come face to face with their Government?

Where else but on historic ground can they better renew the idealism that prompted the patriots to their deeds of valor?

Where else but in the great out-of-doors as God made it can we better recapture the spirit and something of the qualities of the pioneers?

Pride in their Government, love of the land, and faith in the American Tradition—these are the real products of our national parks.

[LIGHTS ON]

And here, gentlemen, are the costs outlined on this chart. As it now stands, the authorized budget for the National Park System for Fiscal Year 1957 totals 62 million, 888 thousand dollars. If we continue to operate at the present scale, the national parks will cost 628 million, 880 thousand dollars over the next ten year period—represented on this chart by the area in green.

The yellow represents what MISSION 66 adds to present costs—154 million, 315 thousand, 6 hundred dollars in ten years—the entire one-package 10 year program.

In total new money, gentlemen, MISSION 66 represents a 10 year investment of less than ¼ the cost of the Grand Coulee Dam. It seems a small amount to devote to the preservation of this national heritage for the use of the people. This is a program pared down to the essentials, and to the essentials only.

If adequately financed, most of the MISSION 66—starting this year—can be carried out under present authority.

As the program goes forward, additional legislation may be needed. This will be submitted for normal clearance through the Bureau of the Budget, as the need arises.

Source: Mission 66 Presentation, January 27, 1956. United States Department of Interior Archives, Harpers Ferry Center.

NOTES

1. Charles Stevenson, "The Shocking Truth about Our National Parks," *Reader's Digest*, January 1955, 45.

2. Ethan Carr, *Mission 66: Modernism and the National Park Dilemma* (Amherst: University of Massachusetts Press, 2007), 6.

3. Mission 66 Special Presentation, January 27, 1956. National Park Service History Collection, Harpers Ferry Center, West Virginia.

4. Carr, *Mission 66*, 10.

5. Quoted in David Backes, *A Wilderness Within: The Life of Sigurd F. Olson* (Minneapolis: University of Minnesota Press, 1997), 262.

6. Quoted in Carr, *Mission 66*, 281, 282.

DOCUMENT 7.9

Preserving Wilderness in the National Parks

"The Back Country Is Becoming the Front Country"

1960

As the 1950s drew to a close, state and federal natural resource management agencies were grappling with rapidly rising pressures from recreation-minded Americans. The National Park Service sought to accommodate increasing visitor levels through its Mission 66 development program. But even as this ambitious project got under way, individual park managers faced the task of keeping "back country" wilderness areas from being overrun.

The following back country management plan for California's Sequoia and Kings Canyon National Parks, originally written in 1960, discusses some of the challenges involved in maintaining wilderness tracts for ecological health and scientific research in an era of automobile-fueled tourism.

[Note: Parenthetical references have been removed from the text.]

A BACK COUNTRY MANAGEMENT PLAN FOR SEQUOIA AND KINGS CANYON NATIONAL PARKS

Part I—General Principles and Guidelines

Wilderness Defined

To avoid misunderstanding, the definition of wilderness as used in this report has been taken from *The National Park Wilderness*. It can be summed up thus: A wilderness is a large, undeveloped, wild area extending beyond roads and developments for permanent occupancy, in which one can experience solitude, quiet, beauty, a sense of adventure, and feelings of remoteness from modern civilization, including mechanized transportation—and in which the drama of natural forces is permitted to unfold without interference except for such management practices as may be required to counteract major destructive influences.

The Needs of Science

The value of wilderness for scientific research used to be largely ignored, or at least not mentioned in reports such as this one. But the dates and titles of hundreds of research publications show that for many years the national parks have been recognized by scientists from all over the world as areas uniquely qualified for basic research, by virtue of their unmodified wilderness characteristics. A landmark along the route toward the growing appreciation of wilderness as a scientific resource was reached with the publication, in 1960, of "The Meaning of Wilderness to Science," a book on which the National Park Service collaborated with distinguished representatives of other conservation and research organizations and institutions.

Since that time, a growing awareness of the unique contributions that unmodified park environments can make to basic research has been reflected in increasingly adequate budgets in support of research programs in the parks. This trend is adding a new dimension to the concept of wilderness protection, and the responsibilities of the National Park Service in that connection.

The Ultimate Aim of Conservation

The ultimate aim of conservation is to leave our earth as rich and productive as we found it. William Dean Howells said, "A nation is great not because it mines coal, cuts timber or builds railways, but rather because it has learned how to produce, build and grow without destroying the bases of its future existence."

The National Park System wilderness is a culmination of processes and events that have been unfolding since the beginning of time. It presents the story of the evolution of the American land, and of the development of life upon it. It is a never-ending story that will continue to unfold, for the inspiration and general welfare of mankind and the advancement of science, so long as the integrity of these "islands of nature" is maintained. . . .

As our society continues to increase in complexity and in population, such an understanding of natural, balanced environments will become increasingly essential for developing ways of living harmoniously, rather than destructively, on our Nation's lands, which are *not* increasing in area.

Science needs these environments as a point of reference and as a yardstick with which to measure man's success or failure in the countless land-management programs that he carries out in the rest of his environment.

Gaining worldwide recognition and acceptance is the belief that National Parks, preserved as natural ecological entities, can supply man with a more complete understanding of the natural laws that may govern his future—and possibly his ultimate survival—in lands and environments everywhere.

We Are the Custodians

"The Nation's most treasured wilderness lands are set apart and dedicated as National Parks and Monuments." By these words are we reminded, in *The National Park Wilderness,* of our responsibilities.

The custodians of a library are obligated to preserve the qualities and atmosphere of a library. In like degree, are we as one of the acknowledged national custodians of wilderness, obligated to preserve and manage the back country—as back country—for the enjoyment, education, physical and spiritual refreshment of our people, for basic scientific research, for an understanding of the natural laws that govern man's existence. Recognition of this obligation is the basis for the present report.

Population Trends and Wilderness Use

. . . Recreation and land use planners are faced with the fact that a U.S. population of 100 million in 1920 grew to 180 million in 1960, is expected to reach 230 million in 1975, and 350 million by the year 2000.

Along with this anticipated quadrupling of the population in a period of about a century, there has already taken place an average increase in travel per person from 1500 miles in 1920 to 4700 miles in 1960. During this 40-year period, leisure time increased by nearly 40 percent, while use of state and national parks showed a more than sixfold increase, jumping from 50 million to over 331 million visits per year. The rate of leisure-time increase can be expected to accelerate under the influence of automation.

Visitor use of the wilderness areas of Sequoia and Kings Canyon National Parks has nearly doubled since 1950. The current and anticipated population growth in the State of California over the next 20 years precludes any thought that there will be a slackening off in the numbers of persons who visit the National Park wilderness of the Sierra.

The Back Country Is Becoming the Front Country

The gradual deterioration of Sierra meadows through overgrazing has been of serious concern as far back as 1940, when the first report was written concerning this problem in Sequoia and Kings Canyon National Parks.

Increasing visitor use has made serious inroads on the fish population of many of the high lakes and streams. Most of the fish habitat in the parks is limited by various physical factors. In earlier times of light fishing pressure it was a fisherman's paradise, but its accessibility threatens to bring its own doom. In several places this has already occurred. As county and state roads push ever closer to the exterior boundaries of the parks, mass invasions of visitors will extend the heavy fishing pressure almost the entire length of the fertile zone of fish habitat.

In 1958, over three tons of litter were removed from just one of the more popular back-country areas. In 1960, a full-scale Service-sponsored program was launched to begin initial cleanup work; and at season's end over 20 tons had been hauled out.

The litter problem will always necessitate a program for backcountry cleanup in much the same manner as litter is removed from front-country campgrounds, though it is hoped that wilderness users will show a greater sense of social responsibility in this regard than do the more predominantly urban users of park highways and other heavily developed facilities for motorists.

A review of these trends serves as a potent reminder that important areas of the parks that in an earlier day were wilderness or back country, now that they are easily accessible and serve heavy concentrations of visitors, are considered front country. The loss of the primeval wilderness qualities that appealed to an earlier generation of users has been gradual; some pockets of unchanged back country remain today, but they will suffer the same fate unless the trend is controlled soon. This report suggests ways to accomplish such control.

Carrying Capacity Determinations

Many deteriorating wilderness situations can be checked by appropriate management measures. But no management plan can be effective if it ignores the practical limitations of the natural environment. . . .

This concept has long been applied with precision to the management of domestic livestock. Likewise, since the thirties, it has been standard procedure to base wildlife management programs on careful studies of the wildlife ranges to determine, and operate within, their carrying capacities. As human use of wilderness ranges begins to approach a saturation point, management has the responsibility of identifying basic factors that limit the carrying capacities of each area, and of tailoring the respective management programs to conform to these natural limitations.

When the present Committee determined from observation the minimum distance required for wilderness-type privacy between high country campsites, it was, in effect, determining the camper-carrying capacities of these areas. Similar carrying-capacity determinations and judgments were called for in preparing other phases of the management plan. Precedents and techniques for measuring wilderness carrying capacities are few; but present use trends clearly indicate the need for further application and refinement of known techniques, and the development of new ones.

Wilderness Protection vs Personal Freedom

Oldtime use of wilderness was completely free of restrictions. Wilderness explorers could hunt and fish without limit, cut down trees at will, camp, make fires and graze their stock anywhere. The tradition of personal freedom in wilderness dies hard, and one of the foremost endeavors of the National Park Service is to respect and preserve the personal freedom of the wilderness user to the fullest extent possible within the framework of each area's carrying capacity.

But when human populations expand they become subject to the biological limitations that govern other dense populations: The greater the number of individuals the greater the loss of individual freedom of action. An illustration of this in the daily lives of all of us is afforded the congestion, delays, and complicated regulations on today's crowded highways.

Wilderness users may with justice complain that they seek wilderness to escape the regimentation of daily life. But the time is past, for example, when a Boy Scout can use his axe to cut fresh pine branches for his bed in the old tradition. . . .

The Committee recognizes a major responsibility to preserve all possible freedom in wilderness, but feels that the answer to complaints over present day restrictions is not "bureaucracy" but "Born too late."

Source: "A Back Country Management Plan for Sequoia and Kings Canyon National Parks," Office of the Chief of Resources Management, Sequoia and Kings Canyon National Parks, National Park Service. Washington, D.C.: Government Printing Office, 1963, pp. 3–9, 104–106. Reprinted in *America's National Park System: The Critical Documents,* edited by Lary M. Dilsaver. Lanham, Md.: Rowman and Littlefield, 1994. www.nps.gov/history/history/online_books/anps/anps_5b.htm.

DOCUMENT
7.10

The Multiple-Use Sustained Yield Act

"Management . . . That Will Best Meet the Needs of the American People"

June 12, 1960

In 1960 Congress explicitly redefined the purpose of America's national forests to include recreation, wildlife, fishing, hunting, and soil concerns in addition to their longstanding timber and watershed management uses. It did this through the Multiple-Use Sustained Yield Act (MUSYA), which codified "multiple use" as the official land management policy of the U.S. Forest Service. This law was in part a response to the American public's enthusiasm for outdoor recreation and its interest in wilderness protection. But the legislation also gave the Forest Service and its parent agency, the Department of Agriculture, a stronger hand in dealing with national forest commodity users, from sportsmen to timber companies, and their advocates in Congress.

Conservation and sportsmen's groups approved of the law's formal recognition of the validity of recreation and wildlife maintenance in national forest management policies. But these groups expressed deep reservations about the Act's ambiguous language, which gave the Forest Service wide latitude to define what constituted "sustainable yield" of resources. They openly worried that the Forest Service's historically close relationship with the timber industry would serve to keep timber production as the agency's top priority, despite the act's professed intention to make timber no more and no less important than the national forests' other "uses." Following is the full text of the act.

An Act to Authorize and Direct that the National Forests Be Managed under Principles of Multiple Use and to Produce a Sustained Yield of Products and Services, and for Other Purposes

Be it enacted by the Senate and House of Representatives of the United States of America in Congress assembled, That it is the policy of the Congress that the national forests are established and shall be administered for outdoor recreation, range, timber, watershed, and wildlife and fish purposes. The purposes of this Act are declared to be supplemental to, but not in derogation of, the purposes for which the national forests were established as set forth in the Act of June 4, 1897. Nothing herein shall be construed as affecting the jurisdiction or responsibilities of the several States with respect to wildlife and fish on the national forests. Nothing herein shall be construed so as to affect the use of [sic] administration of the mineral resources of national forest lands or to affect the use or administration of Federal lands not within national forests.

SEC. 2. The Secretary of Agriculture is authorized and directed to develop and administer the renewable surface resources of the national forests for multiple use and sustained yield of the several products and services obtained therefrom. In the administration of the national forests due consideration shall be given to the relative values of the various resources in particular areas. The establishment and maintenance of areas of wilderness are consistent with the purposes and provisions of this Act.

SEC. 3. In the effectuation of this Act the Secretary of Agriculture is authorized to cooperate with interested State and local governmental agencies and others in the development and management of the national forests.

SEC. 4. As used in this Act, the following terms shall have the following meanings:

(a) "Multiple use" means: The management of all the various renewable surface resources of the national forests so that they are utilized in the combination that will best meet the needs of the American people; making the most judicious use of the land for some or all of these resources or related services over areas large enough to provide sufficient latitude for periodic adjustments in use to conform to changing needs and conditions; that some land will be used for less than all of the resources; and harmonious and coordinated management of the various resources, each with the other, without impairment of the productivity of the land, with consideration being given to the relative values of the various resources, and not necessarily the combination of uses that will give the greatest dollar return or the greatest unit output.

(b) "Sustained yield of the several products and services" means the achievement and maintenance in perpetuity of a high-level annual or regular periodic output of the various renewable resources of the national forests without impairment of the productivity of the land.

SEC. 5. This Act may be cited as the "Multiple-Use Sustained-Yield Act of 1960."

Source: Multiple-Use Sustained Yield Act of 1960. www.fs.fed.us/emc/nfma/includes/musya60.pdf.

DOCUMENT
7.11

Wallace Stegner's "Wilderness Letter"

"These Are Some of the Things Wilderness Can Do for Us"

December 3, 1960

After the American conservation movement defeated the Echo Park Dam proposal in 1956, it charted a much more ambitious path for wilderness protection going forward. Conservationists now realized that they were capable of galvanizing formidable levels of political and public support to defend wild tracts of public land from development. They also recognized that with the American public's surging interest in outdoor recreation, the political climate for the passage of more far-reaching pro-wilderness federal legislation was as hospitable as it had ever been.

With these considerations in mind, conservation organizations led by the Wilderness Society and the Sierra Club joined with sympathetic government scientists and officials to press for sweeping new wilderness preservation laws. One of their strategies was to ensure that pro-wilderness views were included in reports issued by federal agencies and committees such as the Outdoor Recreation Resources Review Commission (ORRRC), which had been established in 1958 to assess national outdoor recreation issues and problems.

On December 3, 1960, conservationist and writer Wallace Stegner, who had been deeply involved in the Echo Park battle, sent a letter to David E. Pesonen at the University of California Wildland Research Center. Pesonen was part of the ORRRC effort, and Stegner wanted to make certain that the forthcoming ORRRC report reflected his views on the value of wilderness. Stegner's eloquent note quickly found its way to Secretary of the Interior Stewart Udall, who was in the midst of preparing a speech at a major wilderness conference in San Francisco when he received it. After reading Stegner's words, Udall discarded his own prepared remarks and instead read the letter to the assembled conservationists.

Stegner's "Wilderness Letter," as it became known, became one of the philosophical touchstones of the burgeoning environmental movement. Environmental historian Roderick Nash described the letter, which was one of the anchors of the final 1962 ORRRC report, as the "classic statement of the relationship of wilderness to man's spirit."[1] The report, meanwhile, has been cited as a key contributor to some of the greatest wilderness protection legislation of the 1960s, including the establishment of the Land and Water Conservation Fund (LWCF) in 1965 and the passage of the Wilderness Act (1964) and the Wild and Scenic Rivers Act (1968).

In 1969 Stegner included his "Wilderness Letter" in his essay collection The Sound of Mountain Water. *The letter is reprinted in its entirety here.*

Dear Mr. Pesonen:

I believe that you are working on the wilderness portion of the Outdoor Recreation Resources Review Commission's report. If I may, I should like to urge some arguments for wilderness preservation that involve recreation, as it is ordinarily conceived, hardly at all. Hunting, fishing, hiking, mountain-climbing, camping, photography, and the enjoyment of natural scenery will all, surely, figure in your report. So will the wilderness as a genetic reserve, a scientific yardstick by which we may measure the world in its natural balance against the world in its man-made imbalance. What I want to speak for is not so much the wilderness uses, valuable as those are, but the wilderness *idea,* which is a resource in itself. Being an intangible and spiritual resource, it will seem mystical to the practical minded—but then anything that cannot be moved by a bulldozer is likely to seem mystical to them.

I want to speak for the wilderness idea as something that has helped form our character and that has certainly shaped our history as a people. It has no more to do with recreation than churches have to do with recreation, or than the strenuousness and optimism and expansiveness of what the historians call the "American Dream" have to do with recreation. Nevertheless, since it is only in this recreation survey that the values of wilderness are being compiled, I hope you will permit me to insert this idea between the leaves, as it were, of the recreation report.

Something will have gone out of us as a people if we ever let the remaining wilderness be destroyed; if we permit the last virgin forests to be turned into comic books and plastic cigarette cases; if we drive the few remaining members of the wild species into zoos or to extinction; if we pollute the last clear air and dirty the last clean streams and push our paved roads through the last of the silence, so that never again will Americans be free in their own country from the noise, the exhausts, the stinks of human and automotive waste. And so that never again can we have the chance to see ourselves single, separate, vertical and individual in the world, part of the environment of trees and rocks and soil, brother to the other animals, part of the natural world and competent to belong in it. Without any remaining wilderness we are committed wholly, without chance for even momentary reflection and rest, to a headlong drive into our technological termite-life, the Brave New World of a completely man-controlled environment. We need wilderness preserved—as much of it as is still left, and as many kinds—because it was the challenge against which our character as a people was formed. The reminder and the reassurance that it is still there is good for our spiritual health even if we never once in ten years set foot in it. It is good for us when we are young, because of the incomparable sanity it can bring briefly, as vacation and rest, into our insane lives. It is important to us when we are old simply because it is there—important, that is, simply as an idea.

Even when I can't get to the back country, the thought of the colored deserts of southern Utah, or the reassurance that there are still stretches of prairies where the world can be instantaneously perceived as disk and bowl, and where the little but intensely important human being is exposed to the five directions of the thirty-six winds, is a positive consolation. The idea alone can sustain me.

—Wallace Stegner

We are a wild species, as Darwin pointed out. Nobody ever tamed or domesticated or scientifically bred us. But for at least three millennia we have been engaged in a cumulative and ambitious race to modify and gain control of our environment, and in the process we have come close to domesticating ourselves. Not many people are likely, any more, to look upon what we call "progress" as an unmixed blessing. Just as surely as it has brought us increased comfort and more material goods, it has brought us spiritual losses, and it threatens now to become the Frankenstein that will destroy us. One means of sanity is to retain a hold on the natural world, to remain, insofar as we can, good animals. Americans still have that chance, more than many peoples; for while we were demonstrating ourselves the most efficient and ruthless environment-busters in history, and slashing and burning and cutting our way through a wilderness continent, the wilderness was working on us. It remains in us as surely as Indian names remain on the land. If the abstract dream of human liberty and human dignity became, in America, something more than an abstract dream, mark it down at least partially to the fact that we were in subdued ways subdued by what we conquered.

The Connecticut Yankee, sending likely candidates from King Arthur's unjust kingdom to his Man Factory for rehabilitation, was over-optimistic, as he later admitted. These things cannot be forced, they have to grow. To make such a man, such a democrat, such a believer in human individual dignity as Mark Twain himself, the frontier was necessary, Hannibal and the Mississippi and Virginia City, and reaching out from those the wilderness; the wilderness as opportunity and idea, the thing that has helped to make an American different from and, until we forget it in the roar of our industrial cities, more fortunate than other men. For an American, insofar as he is new and different at all, is a civilized man who has renewed himself in the wild. The American experience has been the confrontation by old peoples and cultures of a world as new as if it had just risen from the sea. That gave us our hope and our excitement, and the hope and excitement can be passed on to newer Americans, Americans who never saw any phase of the frontier. But only so long as we keep the remainder of our wild as a reserve and a promise—a sort of wilderness bank.

As a novelist, I may perhaps be forgiven for taking literature as a reflection, indirect but profoundly true, of our national consciousness. And our literature, as perhaps you are aware, is sick, embittered, losing its mind, losing its faith. Our novelists are the declared enemies of their society. There has hardly been a serious or important novel in this century that did not repudiate in part or in whole American technological culture for its commercialism, its vulgarity, and the way in which it has dirtied a clean continent and a clean dream. I do not expect that the preservation of our remaining wilderness is going to cure this condition. But the mere example that we can as a nation apply some other criteria than commercial and exploitative considerations would be heartening to many Americans, novelists or otherwise. We need to demonstrate our acceptance of the natural world, including ourselves; we need the spiritual refreshment that being natural can produce. And one of the best places for us to get that is in the wilderness where the fun houses, the bulldozers, and the pavement of our civilization are shut out.

Sherwood Anderson, in a letter to Waldo Frank in the 1920's, said it better than I can. "Is it not likely that when the country was new and men were often alone in the fields and the forest they got a sense of bigness outside themselves that has now in some way been lost. . . . Mystery whispered in the grass, played in the branches of trees overhead, was caught up and blown across the American line in clouds of dust at evening on the prairies. . . . I am old enough to remember tales that strengthen my belief in a deep semi-religious influence that was formerly at work among our people. The flavor of it hangs over the best work of Mark Twain. . . . I can remember old fellows in my home town speaking feelingly of an evening spent on the big empty plains. It had taken the shrillness out of them. They had learned the trick of quiet. . . ."

We could learn it too, even yet; even our children and grandchildren could learn it. But only if we save, for just such absolutely non-recreational, impractical, and mystical uses as this, all the wild that still remains to us.

It seems to me significant that the distinct downturn in our literature from hope to bitterness took place almost at the precise time when the frontier officially came to an end, in 1890, and when the American way of life had begun to turn strongly urban and industrial. The more urban it has become, and the more frantic with technological change, the sicker and more embittered our literature, and I believe our people, have become. For myself, I grew up on the empty plains of Saskatchewan and Montana and in the mountains of Utah, and I put a very high valuation on what those places gave me. And if I had not been able periodically to renew myself in the mountains and deserts of western America I would be very nearly bughouse. Even when I can't get to the back country, the thought of the colored deserts of southern Utah, or the reassurance that there are still stretches of prairies where the world can be instantaneously perceived as disk and bowl, and where the little but intensely important human being is exposed to the five directions of the thirty-six winds, is a positive consolation. The idea alone can sustain me. But as the wilderness areas are progressively exploited or "improved," as the jeeps and bulldozers of uranium prospectors scar up the deserts and the roads are cut into the alpine timberlands, and as the remnants of the unspoiled and natural world are progressively eroded, every such loss is a little death in me. In us.

I am not moved by the argument that those wilderness areas which have already been exposed to grazing or mining are already deflowered, and so might as well be "harvested." For mining I cannot say much good except that its operations are generally short-lived. The extractable wealth is taken and the shafts, the tailings, and the ruins left, and in a dry country such as the American West the wounds men make in the earth do not quickly heal. Still, they are only wounds; they aren't absolutely mortal. Better a wounded wilderness than none at all. And as for grazing, if it is strictly controlled so that it does not destroy the ground cover, damage the ecology, or compete with the wildlife it is in itself nothing that need conflict with the wilderness feeling or the validity of the wilderness experience. I have known enough range cattle to recognize them as wild animals; and the people who herd them have, in the wilderness context, the dignity of rareness; they belong on the frontier, moreover, and have a look of rightness. The invasion they make on the virgin country is a sort of invasion that is as old as Neolithic man, and they can, in moderation, even emphasize a man's feeling of belonging to the natural world. Under surveillance, they can belong; under control, they need not deface or mar. I do not believe that in wilderness areas where grazing has never been permitted, it should be permitted; but I do not believe either that an otherwise untouched wilderness should be eliminated from the preservation plan because of limited existing uses such as grazing which are in consonance with the frontier condition and image.

Let me say something on the subject of the kinds of wilderness worth preserving. Most of those areas contemplated are in the national forests and in high mountain country. For all the usual recreational purposes, the alpine and the forest wildernesses are obviously the most important, both as genetic banks and as beauty spots. But for the spiritual renewal, the recognition of identity, the birth of awe, other kinds will serve every bit as well. Perhaps, because they are less friendly to life, more abstractly nonhuman, they will serve even better. On our Saskatchewan prairie, the nearest neighbor was four miles away, and at night we saw only two lights on all the dark rounding earth. The earth was full of animals—field mice, ground squirrels, weasels, ferrets, badgers, coyotes, burrowing owls, snakes. I knew them as my little brothers, as fellow creatures, and I have never been able to look upon animals in any other way since. The sky in that country came clear down to the ground on every side, and it was full of great weathers, and clouds, and winds, and hawks. I hope I learned something from looking a long way, from looking up, from being much alone. A prairie like that, one big enough to carry the eye clear to the sinking, rounding horizon, can be as lonely and grand and simple in its forms as the sea. It is as good a place as any for the wilderness experience to happen; the vanishing prairie is as worth preserving for the wilderness idea as the alpine forests.

So are great reaches of our western deserts, scarred somewhat by prospectors but otherwise open, beautiful, waiting, close to whatever God you want to see in them. Just as a sample, let me suggest the Robbers' Roost country in Wayne County, Utah, near the Capitol Reef National Monument. In that desert climate the dozer and jeep tracks will not soon melt back into the earth, but the country has a way of making the scars insignificant. It is a lovely and terrible wilderness, such a wilderness as Christ and the prophets went out into; harshly and beautifully colored, broken and worn until its bones are exposed, its great sky without a smudge of taint from Technocracy, and in hidden corners and pockets under its cliffs the sudden poetry of springs. Save a piece of country like that intact, and it does not matter in the slightest that only a few people every year will go into it. That is precisely its value. Roads would be a desecration, crowds would ruin it. But those who haven't the strength or youth to go into it and live can simply sit and look. They can look two hundred miles, clear into Colorado; and looking down over the cliffs and canyons of the San Rafael Swell and the Robbers' Roost they can also look as deeply into themselves as anywhere I know. And if they can't even get to the places on the Aquarius Plateau where the present roads will carry them, they can simply contemplate the *idea,* take pleasure in the fact that such a timeless and uncontrolled part of earth is still there.

These are some of the things wilderness can do for us. That is the reason we need to put into effect, for its preservation, some other principle than the principles of exploitation or "usefulness" or even recreation. We simply need that wild country available to us, even if we never do more than drive to its edge and look in. For it can be a means of reassuring ourselves of our sanity as creatures, a part of the geography of hope.

Very sincerely yours,
Wallace Stegner

Source: Stegner, Wallace. "Wilderness Letter." From *The Sound of Mountain Water.* Garden City, N.Y., Doubleday, 1969. © 1969 by Wallace Stegner. Used by permission of Doubleday, a division of Random House, Inc.

NOTE

1. Roderick Nash, *Wilderness and the American Mind,* rev. ed. (New Haven, Conn.: Yale University Press, 1973), 250.

CHAPTER 8

The "Golden Age" of Environmental Legislation

1960–1980

The 1960s and 1970s are universally recognized as decades of unprecedented environmental policy–making in the United States. At the outset of this twenty-year span, Rachel Carson's *Silent Spring* triggered new public awareness and governmental policies on the issue of toxic chemical pollution. At the conclusion of this era, President Jimmy Carter signed a momentous act that doubled the size of America's national park, wildlife refuge, and wild and scenic rivers systems. And in between these two events, a host of important and politically popular federal agencies and laws came into being to address all sorts of environmental problems and challenges. The arrival of these agencies and regulations, in turn, brought about major changes in the ways that the federal government and private businesses operated. Some of these changes were generally recognized as necessary and beneficial when they were first implemented. By the close of the 1970s, however, many of the newly minted environmental regulations and policy priorities that had been created during America's "golden age" of environmentalism had become the targets of a raucous—and politically potent—backlash.

RACHEL CARSON AND *SILENT SPRING*

Ecologist Rachel Carson published *Silent Spring,* her groundbreaking exposé of the threat of toxic pollutants on public and environmental health, at a fortuitous crossroads in American history. The post–World War II era had bestowed dizzying new levels of economic opportunity, material comfort, and recreational options on Americans. But citizens and policymakers alike recognized that troubling undercurrents existed beneath the placid surface of everyday life. Concerns about air and water pollution were on the rise, as were anxieties about the potential health hazards of new chemicals, downturns in wildlife populations, and erosion of ecosystem integrity. And for some Americans, at least, continued assurances from federal authorities and industries that the environment was both safe and sound came to have a tinny quality to them.

Silent Spring, then, arrived like a thunderclap across the American political landscape. First serialized in the *New Yorker* in June 1962, it was also published in book form that year. Carson's carefully researched, methodically organized, and accessibly written book condemned DDT and other widely popular pesticides for killing wildlife and poisoning soil and water. Marshalling a wide array of scientific evidence to her side, she described DDT's deleterious impact on the health of birds, animals, and human beings

Rachel Carson's landmark Silent Spring, *published in 1962, detailed the far-ranging ecological dangers of pesticide use, most notably DDT, which would later be banned from use in the United States.*

and the implications of this impact on wider ecosystems. She warned that unquestioning public faith in technological progress and corporate benevolence had to stop if the Earth and the life contained thereon—including human life—were to be saved from the escalating toxicity of the natural environment (**see Document 8.1**).

Carson's book created a media firestorm. It became a huge bestseller, and its findings were seized on by public health and conservation advocates. But *Silent Spring* and its author were subjected to a barrage of condemnation from the chemical industry. "If man were to faithfully follow the teachings of Miss Carson," declared one executive of the American Cyanamid Company, "we would return to the Dark Ages, and the insects and diseases and vermin would once again inherit the earth."[1] *Chemical and Engineering News,* meanwhile, issued a review of *Silent Spring* that alternated between excoriations of Carson as a pseudo-scientific fearmonger and reassurances about the safety of pesticides and other products churned out by the chemical industry. "The responsible scientist," sneered the reviewer, "should read this book to understand the ignorance of those writing on the subject and the education task which lies ahead."[2]

The invective unleashed against Carson failed to marginalize her and her findings, however. Many Americans were freshly skeptical of the infallibility of industry authorities in the wake of the "thalidomide baby" tragedy in Europe. In this horrifying event of the late 1950s and early 1960s, thousands of newborns were born with serious birth defects, including blindness, deafness, missing limbs, and flipper-like appendages, after their mothers were given thalidomide prescriptions to treat insomnia and morning sickness. In addition, many eminent scientists rushed to Carson's defense, and President John F. Kennedy took her warnings seriously. Subsequent governmental and industry research confirmed her findings about the hazards of DDT and other toxic chemicals on the environment. Within a decade, DDT itself had been banned in the United States. Moreover, the wider public debate shifted in the wake of *Silent Spring* "from *whether* pesticides were dangerous to *which* pesticides were dangerous, and the burden of proof shifted from the opponents of unrestrained pesticide use to the chemicals' manufacturers."[3]

Increased awareness of environmental problems produced a wide variety of policy and public responses in the 1960s and 1970s. These ranged from new federal anti-pollution laws to events like the 1970 Earth Day celebration (pictured here), which drew the participation of millions of Americans.

Today, many historians trace the beginnings of the modern environmental movement to the investigative work and deep sense of mission that informed *Silent Spring,* and they credit Carson as a seminal figure in advancing the belief that government had an integral and legitimate role to play in regulating the activities and outputs of industry. As biographer Linda Lear wrote at the close of the twentieth century, "[T]he magnitude of Carson's impact on the public's understanding of such issues as ecology and environmental change still astonishes."[4]

New Milestones in Wilderness Conservation

At the same time that *Silent Spring* was shepherding Americans toward a more sophisticated understanding of the potential ecological perils of runaway technology, wilderness preservationists were continuing their long-running battle to protect pristine wildlands from commodity extraction and other forms of development. These advocates entered the 1960s with the political winds firmly at their backs. Conservation victories in the late 1950s—most notably the successful campaign to stop a proposed dam in Utah's Dinosaur National Monument—had infused the wilderness movement with a renewed sense of purpose and confidence. Moreover, they sensed that public opinion on the issue of wilderness preservation had shifted decisively in their favor. Signs of America's growing appreciation for nature were everywhere, from the public outcry in response to *Silent Spring* to the surge in recreational visits to wilderness areas across the United States— from three to seven million visitor days between 1960 and 1970 alone. Organizations devoted to wilderness protection saw a pronounced upturn in their fortunes—and their political clout. Membership in the Sierra Club, one of the organizations at the forefront of the Dinosaur fight, exploded from 15,000 members in 1960 to more than 100,000 members by the beginning of the following decade.[5]

These groups were led by people such as David Brower (Sierra Club) and Howard Zahniser (Wilderness Society), who were intensely dedicated to their cause. They were determined to secure meaningful statutory protection for what Brower called "real wilderness, big wilderness—country big enough to have a beyond to it and an inside. With space enough to separate you from the buzz, bang, screech, ring, yammer, and roar of the 24-hour commercial you wish hard your life wouldn't be."[6] They were equally dedicated to the idea of moving beyond piecemeal protection to a truly national program of preservation. "Let us be done with a wilderness preservation program made up of a sequence of overlapping emergencies, threats, and defense campaigns," Zahniser said.[7]

The first Wilderness Act bill was crafted by Zahniser himself and introduced into Congress by congressional allies in the spring of 1956. It called for the establishment of a national wilderness system that would permanently safeguard designated wilderness on public lands. Zahniser's proposal extended strong new legal protections to existing wild or wilderness areas and set up a process to review potential other primitive areas in national parks, national forests, and federal wildlife refuges for eventual inclusion in the system.

The bill was roundly condemned by resource extraction industries and pro-development congressmen. It was viewed with ambivalence by the National Park Service and U.S. Forest Service, both of which thought it would reduce their institutional autonomy and flexibility. But the bill's advocates insisted that a federal statute was essential for long-term wilderness preservation. As things currently stood, contended one conservation group, "our rare, irreplaceable samples of wilderness can be diminished at the will of the administrator, without the sanction of Congress. . . . Under the bill Congress would protect the wilderness interior as well as the boundaries of all dedicated wilderness. This would strengthen the hand of the good administrator [and] steady the hand of the weak one."[8]

Wilderness supporters also initiated savvy public relations campaigns to rally public support for the bill—and to challenge the bill's detractors. Brower, for example, declared that if the value of wilderness

> could somehow be reflected on the financial pages as part of the nation's capital, rising in value fast enough to warrant a two-for-one split, if it could only be advertised in four color ads, as if it were a private asset and not a public resource, if it related to the Dow-Jones average and not just to survival, if it fitted better the materialists' mores, if the developers could only speculate in its real estate and make a killing, if it meant ulcers and not just a chance for a better life—if all these things were true, maybe the chambers of commercialism and the rough riders of range and forest would stop stalling the WB [Wilderness Bill]. . . . Nobody wants it but the people.[9]

The campaign for the Wilderness Act was a long and arduous one, spanning eight years and four Congresses. During that period Zahniser's bill went through sixty-six drafts and eighteen separate congressional hearings, and it was bruised and battered by seemingly endless legislative maneuvering and political gamesmanship. But the Sierra Club, Wilderness Society, and other advocacy groups never relented in their quest to establish a federally protected wilderness preservation system, and public support for the measure remained strong throughout. In addition, the bill benefited from steadfast support from congressional champions such as Senator Clinton P. Anderson (D-N.M.), who stated that "wilderness is an anchor to windward. Knowing it is there, we can also know that we are still a rich nation, tending our resources as we should—not a people in despair searching every last nook and cranny of our land for a board of lumber, a barrel of oil, a blade of grass, or a tank of water."[10] In September 1964 the Wilderness Act finally became law, and a new era of wilderness preservation in America began (**see Document 8.2**).

DAMS AND RIVERS IN THE WEST

Shifting public sentiments about the intrinsic value of undeveloped natural areas also played a major role in water politics in the American West. For decades, the Bureau of Reclamation and the U.S. Army Corps of Engineers had received virtual rubber stamp approval of multi-purpose dams and other major water projects from Congresses eager to reap the political benefits that accrued from such spending. But as public interest in environmental issues rose in the 1950s and 1960s, the value of federal water projects and other schemes of land alteration (such as clear cutting) became a subject of greater and greater debate. Resource agencies were increasingly characterized by conservationists and fiscal responsibility watchdogs as "powerful and self-interested subgovernments, each acting as a mouthpiece of powerful client constituencies and as a vehicle for its own staff's ideologies and ambitions," in the words of scholar Richard N. L. Andrews. "In reality what had happened was not only that the agencies had formed supportive alliances with powerful constituencies, but also that public consensus on their policy goals had itself unraveled, opening a new era of rising conflict between extractive and protective uses of the environment."[11]

As the 1960s unfolded, the Bureau of Reclamation and its powerful commissioner, Floyd Dominy, occupied center stage in this clash. Dominy was a famously colorful administrator who headed the Bureau from 1959 to 1969. Arrogant, ambitious, and charismatic, he energetically championed the dambuilding ethos that had played such an important part in the development of both the West and the Bureau itself. "His vision—of a West where every river was tapped and plumbed—was heroic, not humble," wrote one observer. "His projects were technologically daring and politically compelling because they provided contracts, profits and power."[12]

During the first few years of Dominy's tenure, the Bureau's fearsome political muscle remained undiminished. "This is the stage I like to describe as having no naysayers," Dominy recalled years later. "If we proposed a project, it was endorsed, and it got built."[13] But as time went on, soaring public enthusiasm for outdoor recreation and concern with wilderness preservation shaped political calculations in Washington to a greater and greater degree. A movement to shield America's remaining undammed rivers from development began to coalesce in the late 1950s and early 1960s under the guidance of conservationists such as John and Frank Craighead, Paul Bruce Dowling, Joseph Penfold, and Sigurd Olson. And these activists adroitly hitched their star to the wider wilderness preservation movement. "Today it is still possible to challenge and to enjoy a wild river, but already they are a rarity," wrote John Craighead in *Naturalist* magazine in 1965.

> Only a few such rivers exist and these are threatened by an expanding, groping civilization, public indifference and bureaucratic sluggishness. In spite of the durability of rock-walled canyons and the surging power of cataracting water, the wild river is a fragile thing—the most fragile portion of wilderness country. A dam can still its turbulent flow, a road eternally change the river bend, and a logging operation completely alter the watershed.[14]

These would-be saviors of America's remaining wild rivers decried the mindset of the Bureau of Reclamation and its fiery commissioner. Their perspective was identical to that of historian Marc Reisner, who held that in Dominy's view, "[N]othing in nature was worthwhile unless it was visited by a lot of people. If it was a pristine river, accessible only by floatplane or jeep or on foot, navigable only by whitewater raft or kayak or canoe, populated by wily fish such as steelhead that were difficult to catch, then it was no good. But if the river was transformed into a big flatwater reservoir off an interstate highway, with marinas and houseboats for rent—then it was worth something after all."[15] Advocates of free-flowing rivers also attacked new dam projects in the West on financial grounds, arguing that American taxpayers in the East and Midwest were in effect subsidizing the growth of cities and states in the West.

Dominy and the Bureau responded with vigor to the arguments of the preservationists. "Let's *use* our environment," Dominy declared in an interview with journalist John McPhee.

> Nature changes the environment every day of our lives—why shouldn't *we* change it? We're part of nature. Just to give you a for-instance, we're cloud-seeding the Rockies to increase the snowpack. We've built a tunnel under the Continental Divide to send water toward the Pacific that would have gone to the Atlantic. The challenge to man is to do and save what is good but to permit man to progress in civilization. Hydroelectric power doesn't pollute water and it doesn't pollute air. You don't get any pollution out of my dams. The unregulated Colorado was a son of a bitch. It wasn't any good. It was either in flood or in trickle.[16]

As the battles over water development intensified, the Bureau of Reclamation and U.S. Army Corps of Engineers repeatedly cited the agricultural and energy benefits of federal water projects and their role in attracting business to communities eager to expand their tax bases. In addition, Bureau and Corps representatives took note of the shifting political landscape by emphasizing the outdoor recreation opportunities created by their projects. In 1965 testimony before Congress, for instance, Dominy pointed out that the ten most-visited Bureau of Reclamation reservoirs attracted more visitors on an annual basis than the country's ten most heavily used national parks.[17] By the mid-1960s the recreational benefits of Bureau projects had become the centerpiece of many of Dominy's speeches (see Document 8.3).

But the political momentum continued to shift away from the water developers, in part because the most economically justifiable water projects in the United States had long since been built. Even Interior Secretary Stewart Udall, a lifelong westerner and early backer of Dominy's pro-development philosophy, was swayed by the conservationist crusade. "My thinking gradually changed in the early sixties at the same time that I was testifying for dams," Udall later admitted.[18] A turning point for Udall came in 1964, when he joined conservationists in a failed attempt to block the construction of new dams on the Clearwater River in Idaho. "I got involved, and it dramatized for me the flaws and misconceptions in the dam-building philosophy of the New Deal. The values were changing, and if that dam were considered in 1964 it never would have been authorized."[19]

Advocates for wild rivers scored several significant political victories in the mid-1960s. The Water Resources Planning Act of 1965 created a Federal Water Resources Council to coordinate national water resource development and preservation issues—and to provide an independent body to review proposed water development projects. Proposed hydroelectric dams were halted on the Yukon, Trinity, and Cumberland rivers by a mix of grassroots organizing and congressional arm-twisting. And in 1968 the National Wild and Scenic Rivers Act was passed, giving Congress the authority to preserve "free-flowing rivers with outstanding natural, cultural, and recreational values" for future generations of Americans **(see Document 8.5)**. This momentous law exemplified the seismic philosophical and emotional shift that was taking place in America in the realms of river preservation and land protection.

A NEW GENERATION OF ENVIRONMENTAL GROUPS

Laws such as the Wilderness Act and the Wild and Scenic Rivers Act also heralded the surging influence of conservation organizations on electoral politics. But even as veteran groups such as the Sierra Club, Wilderness Society, Audubon Society, and National Wildlife Federation made their presence felt in Washington on a host of natural resource management fronts, a new crop of environmental organizations entered the fray. These groups—the Environmental Defense Fund (EDF; founded in 1967), the Natural Resources Defense Council (NRDC; 1970), and many others—left the protection of redwood stands and pristine mountain rivers to the older groups. They instead focused much of their time and resources on "hot" ecological issues such as toxic waste contamination, overpopulation, and pollution. Their manifestos were works such as Carson's *Silent Spring*, Paul Ehrlich's *The Population Bomb* (1968), Garrett Hardin's "Tragedy of the Commons" (1968), and Barry Commoner's *The Closing Circle* (1970), not the essays of Henry Thoreau and John Muir. As James Gustave "Gus" Speth, one of the co-founders of NRDC recalled, "[U]nregulated discharge pipes, fish kills, urban air pollution, all kinds of industrial pollution—those were the issues that originally turned my head. It was not establishing wilderness areas in Montana."[20]

The policy priorities of the traditional conservation groups and the new breed of environmental organizations differed significantly during the late 1960s and 1970s, and only a few of them (such as the Sierra Club) ever expanded their parameters of activism to the point where they became a force in multiple realms of public policymaking. But whether these national, state, and local groups were primarily concerned with energy conservation, wilderness preservation, population control, public health reform, pollution abatement, agricultural practices, or sprawl issues, they all came to see themselves as part of a wider, unified "environmental" movement.[21] And despite their divergent passions and strategic approaches, virtually all of these organizations shared an abiding faith in the power of public opinion, the need to professionalize operations, and the ascendant role of the courts as an instrument of policymaking.

These considerations profoundly shaped the next phase of development in the environmental movement. Groups scrambled to create staff positions dedicated solely to membership drives, fundraising, lobbying, or scientific research. Task specialization also became more commonplace. For example, the Environmental Policy Institute (EPI), founded in 1972, became known for its backroom huddles with congressional committees, monitoring of resource agencies, and strategic alliances with a wide variety of stakeholders inside and outside of government.[22] The League of Conservation Voters (1970), meanwhile, established admirably comprehensive operations to track the voting records of administrations and congressmen and galvanize public support for "pro-environment" candidates. The Natural Resources Defense Council eschewed the "tactics and strategies of mobilization" and instead carved out a niche for itself as experts in drafting legislation and crafting authoritative reports on pressing environmental issues.[23]

Whatever their orientation, however, all effective environmental groups at local, state, and national levels learned to use the courts to challenge industry's influence over legislation, shape the practices of regulatory agencies, and contest governmental decisions that were seen as environmentally problematic or destructive.[24] Citizens' groups became particularly adept at taking advantage of provisions and regulations contained in new laws, such as the Endangered Species Act (ESA), which was passed by Congress and signed into law by Nixon in 1973 **(see Document 8.11)**. The ESA issued a firm mandate to federal agencies to make sure that their actions did not jeopardize endangered or threatened species (or the habitat on which they depended). In addition, the Endangered Species Act contained provisions that gave the public strong legal rights to ensure that the Act's wildlife preservation measures were carried out faithfully. The overall practical effect of the ESA was to elevate endangered species protection to the highest priority level in federal offices.

In addition to the ESA, environmental groups also took advantage of newly minted laws including the National Environmental Policy Act (NEPA) of 1969 **(see Document 8.6)**, the Clean Water Act of 1972, the Resource Conservation and Recovery Act of 1976, and the Toxic Substances Control Act of 1976. The citizen suit provisions contained in these and other federal environmental laws of this era generated a stunning upsurge in environmental litigation, and the federal courts frequently issued rulings favorable to the plaintiffs. Several of these judgments, in fact, are now regarded as landmarks in the evolution of American environmental law. In the case of *Scenic Hudson Preservation Conference v. Federal Power Commission*, a federal court affirmed that a group of environmentalists had legal standing to oppose a proposed power plant at the Hudson River's Storm King Mountain on aesthetic rather than economic grounds. In *West Virginia Isaak Walton League v. Butz* a contract to clear cut national forest land was canceled by a federal judge who agreed with environmentalists' contentions that it violated the language of the Forest Service Organic Administration Act. And in the 1972 case of *Sierra Club v. Butz* the Sierra Club Legal Defense Fund succeeded in forcing the U.S. Forest Service to incorporate NEPA-mandated environmental impact statements into its assessments of potential wilderness areas (the agency capitulated before the judge made a final ruling on the lawsuit). "Environmentalism," summarized David Sive, one of the co-founders of NRDC, "used litigation as no other social movement has before or since."[25]

POLITICIANS RUSH TO CLAIM THE "ENVIRONMENTALIST" MANTLE

By the mid-1960s Republicans and Democrats alike were tacking strongly toward pro-environment stances. They could read the polls, which showed widespread support for pollution abatement, wildlife protection, habitat preservation, and other efforts to improve environmental conditions, and they recognized that legislators who were seen as advocates of clean air and water would reap benefits on election day. Indeed, public opinion polls regularly ranked pollution as among the nation's most serious problems in the late 1960s and early 1970s.[26]

The inaugural celebration of Earth Day on April 22, 1970, further underscored the broad public concern for the environment. An estimated 20 million Americans participated in one fashion or another in the event, which was the masterstroke of the conservationist Senator Gaylord Nelson (D-Wis.) **(see Document 8.7)**. In its aftermath, countless participants vowed to remain vigilant defenders of the nation's land, air, and water. "Many Americans responded to the rallying cry of Earth Day not because of any aesthetic or mystical affinity for nature, to fight for social justice, or to search for new consumer amenities or a more pleasant lifestyle, but out of fear—fear of cancer or other disease caused by toxic substances, fear for the future of their children, and fear that the value of their property would be diminished by pollution or inappropriate development," wrote environmental journalist Philip Shabecoff. "Americans who worried about PCBs in mother's milk, about polybrominated biphenyls in Michigan cattle, about poisons leaking from rusty drums in their backyards, or about strontium 90 from atmospheric testing of nuclear weapons . . . were expressing outrage and demanding change."[27]

Catastrophic and highly publicized pollution events kept the pressure on lawmakers. In January 1969 an oil spill from a rig off the coast of southern California dumped three million gallons of crude oil into Santa Barbara Channel. Eight hundred square miles of ocean were affected by the disaster, and 35 miles of coastline were coated with oil. Six months later, a small debris-clogged section of Cleveland's Cuyahoga River caught fire, and the river immediately became a national symbol of industrial pollution run amok. The public and media attention given to these sorts of events made it difficult for congressmen from all but the most conservative, anti-regulatory parts of the country to oppose environmental legislation. Presidents were not exempt from this pressure, either. All the presidents of this era—John F. Kennedy, Lyndon B. Johnson, Richard M. Nixon, Gerald Ford, and Jimmy Carter—worked hard to frame their administrations as dedicated to the cause of environmental stewardship and restoration (see Document 8.12).

This political landscape nurtured a veritable flood of new environmental laws and initiatives from the mid-1960s through the mid-1970s. In 1964, for example, three air pollution bills were introduced in Congress; in 1970 the number increased to ninety-seven. Similarly, fourteen different congressional panels held a total of thirty-three hearings on air pollution in 1970; six years earlier a lone panel held three hearings on the same subject.[28] The Democratic-controlled Congress played a dominant role in the move toward stronger protections, but Republicans also voted for strong environmental policy provisions. "Divided government," explained one scholar, "produced bidding wars as each party tried to show it was at least as 'green' as the other."[29] In addition to landmarks such as the Wilderness Act, the Clean Air and Clean Water Acts, the Endangered Species Act, and the 1970 establishment of the Environmental Protection Agency (EPA) and Occupational Safety and Health Administration (OSHA), other major environmental legislation included the Land and Water Conservation Fund Act (1964); the Water Quality Act (1965); the Highway Beautification Act (1965) (see Document 8.4); the Clean Water Restoration Act (1966); the Wild and Scenic Rivers Act (1968); the National Environmental Policy Act (1969); the Environmental Quality Improvement Act (1970); the Federal Environmental Pesticide Control Act (1972); the Noise Control Act (1972); the Coastal Zone Management Act (1972); the Marine Mammals Protection Act (1972); the Safe Drinking Water Act (1974); the Toxic Substances Control Act (1976); the Resource Conservation and Recovery Act (1976); the Federal Land Management Act, also known as the BLM Organic Act (1976); and the National Forest Management Act (1976).

Many of these new laws and policies were not of the incremental variety; to the contrary, they brought sweeping changes to the mandates of existing federal agencies and created entirely new agencies and departments to enforce ambitious new environmental and public health regulations. In addition, they mandated the creation of new departments, agencies, and boards at the local and state levels because many of the freshly minted environmental laws still gave state governments the chief responsibility for regulatory enforcement.

Of all these institutional changes and creations, the EPA merits special mention. When it was first established by the Nixon Administration in a 1970 government reorganization, the agency was widely seen on both sides of the political aisle as an appropriate and necessary response to 1) the nation's environmental problems, and 2) the public's demands for action on those problems (**see Document 8.8**).

The EPA benefited immensely in its early years from the able leadership of its first two directors, William Ruckelshaus and Russell Train. These administrators oversaw the development of vital local and regional offices and shaped the agency's infrastructure to better shoulder the new regulatory responsibilities that Congress continuously shoveled onto its plate in the 1970s. They also have been credited with recruiting idealistic staff, establishing high professional standards, actively soliciting both public and industry voices on regulatory matters, and effectively rolling out new regulations contained in the Clean Air Act and other major legislation of the decade.

Still, the agency often struggled to fulfill its envisioned role as the "federal government's watchdog, police officer, and chief weapon against all forms of pollution."[30] By the close of the 1970s, the EPA's status as the nation's foremost pollution fighter was undisputed and its funding had seen a corresponding increase in its first decade of existence. But it also came to be seen by some industry sectors, municipal governments, and pro-development lawmakers and agencies as an inflexible adversary. Ironically, by this time it was also being criticized by members of the environmental community as an ineffective and underfunded bureaucracy that was all too vulnerable to political pressure from big business and its allies.

THE QUEST FOR CLEANER AIR

After the EPA was created, enforcement of clean air and water regulations immediately became its most pressing policy obligations. In fact, air and water pollution were the focus of more far-reaching laws during the 1960s and 1970s than any other environmental problem. The proliferation of this legislation was driven in part by lawmakers' desire to curry favor with voters, but it also stemmed from genuine anxiety about the growing body of scientific evidence that identified air and water pollution as a serious ecological, economic, and public health threat.

The first federal statute that had addressed air pollution was the Clean Air Act or Air Pollution Control Act of 1955. But this was essentially a research funding measure that left air quality regulation in the hands of states. Federal authorities stayed mostly on the regulatory sidelines for the next ten years, despite studies confirming that air quality was steadily worsening as a result of rising industrial and vehicle emissions. The federal government finally stepped in more decisively in 1963 with the first federal legislation authorizing air pollution *control* (via a program within the U.S. Public Health Service created by the Clean Air Act of 1963) and then again in 1965 with the Motor Vehicle Air Pollution Control Act. This act, which was strongly supported by the Johnson Administration, provided for the establishment of national exhaust emission standards for all new automobiles and other motor vehicles. It also authorized new research into domestic and international air quality issues.

In February 1966 Johnson applauded Congress for its work on air pollution up to that point but added that further legislation was needed "to improve and increase federal research, financing, and technical assistance to help states and local governments take the measures needed to control air pollution."[31] One year later, the Air Quality Act of 1967 was passed by overwhelming margins. Provisions of this act required states to develop implementation plans for air pollution control—and held out the threat of federal intervention if states failed to follow through. Keeping regulatory enforcement at the state level pleased some industries but caused anxiety within others, who feared that it would create a crazy quilt of different standards that would be impossible to navigate. Automakers and other companies subsequently began lobbying for "sensible" federal pre-emption of state authority on the issue. Meanwhile, Senator Edmund Muskie (D-Maine) and other major actors in the legislation's passage offered subdued takes on the act's likely long-term influence. The 1967 Act was "not a magic wand," agreed Johnson. "It is a law whose ultimate effectiveness rests out there with the people of this land—on our seeing damnation that awaits us if the people do not act responsibly."[32]

By 1970 every state had passed some manner of air pollution control law. But their limited resources made it difficult for them to carry out both standard-setting and enforcement requirements, and environmental groups and federal officials expressed concern that some states were so skittish about losing industry that their air quality provisions were paper tigers. In February 1970 President Nixon bluntly told a joint session of Congress that air pollution remained the most serious environmental problem facing the country. He then publicly sided with many Democrats in Congress who had been pushing legislation that would nationalize air quality standards, tighten automobile emissions, and impose new emission regulations on industrial factories, refineries, and other stationary/point source pollution sources.

The proposal to dramatically expand federal regulatory authority over air quality sparked tremendous opposition from industry and business groups. But popular support for air pollution legislation gave Congress the necessary cover to proceed, especially after Muskie and others crafted language that emphasized public health. "I was convinced that strict federal air pollution regulation would require a legally defensible premise," said Muskie. "Protection of public health seemed the strongest and most appropriate such premise."[33] The Clean Air Act Amendments of 1970, which was signed into law by Nixon on New Year's Eve of that year, mandated the establishment of national air quality standards and gave the EPA the authority to regulate automobile and other emissions. It remains one of the landmark laws in U.S. environmental history (**see Document 8.9**).

Congress and Nixon Battle over the Clean Water Act

The political complexion of the maneuvering for federal water pollution legislation took on a decidedly different hue. Congress had passed modest water pollution control legislation in 1948 (the Federal Water Pollution Control Act) and 1956, but it took its first major swing at clean water legislation in 1965 with the Water Quality Act. Unlike earlier efforts, this law emphasized pollution prevention and the setting of water quality standards. It also codified water pollution as an environmental concern *and* a public health issue. One year later, the Clean Water Restoration Act imposed small fines for regulatory violations, and the Water Quality Improvement Act of 1970 gave the executive branch new authority to combat oil pollution and other forms of pollution in rivers, lakes, and coastal areas. These laws helped, but environmental groups, public health organizations, government scientists, and lawmakers all contended that they merely nibbled around the edges of the essential problem. They argued for a much more comprehensive program that would tackle the deteriorating state of America's water resources head on.

Congress responded with the 1972 Clean Water Act, also known as the Federal Water Pollution Control Act. This law was shaped by statesmen such as Muskie and Howard Baker (R-Tenn.), who wanted to create a "pollution control program whose implementation produced tangible results, avoided crippling legal challenges, sustained public confidence, and allowed for continuous advances."[34] It established a stringent permit system and other measures to regulate discharges of pollutants into the waters of the United States, and it also set regulations for monitoring and enforcing quality standards for surface waters across the country. The uncompromising regulatory requirements and expensive provisions contained in the final Senate version of the bill, however, dismayed both the White House and industry. The action quickly shifted to the House of Representatives, where an intense political war was waged between pro-business and pro-regulatory factions. The House ultimately passed a less ambitious bill, but it still contained pollution reduction goals that struck opponents as both exorbitantly expensive and wildly unrealistic.

In May 1972 a House–Senate conference committee was convened to reconcile the two versions of the bill. The committee convened almost forty times over the next four months—during which time the rhetorical war remained at full throttle. "Blind pursuit of absolutely pure water quality is a form of economic brinkmanship," went one representative lament from a lobbyist for the National Association of Manufacturers.[35]

"You have to spend money" to clean and protect rivers and lakes, countered Muskie:

> Can we afford clean water? Can we afford rivers and lakes and streams and oceans which continue to make possible life on this planet? Can we afford life itself? Those questions were never asked as we destroyed the waters of our Nation, and they deserve no answers as we finally move to restore and renew them. These questions answer themselves. And those who say that raising the amounts of money called for in this legislation may require higher taxes, or that spending this much money may contribute to inflation simply do not understand the language of this crisis.[36]

In September 1972 the House–Senate conference committee finally completed its work and returned a reconciled bill to Congress. The Federal Water Pollution Control Act Amendments of 1972 was approved by a 74-0 vote in the Senate and 366-11 in the House, despite Nixon's declaration that he would veto the legislation. Nixon kept his promise, but Congress easily overrode his veto and on October 18, 1972, the act became law (**see Document 8.10**). Nearly four decades later, the Clean Water Act remains one of the landmark environmental laws in U.S. history. As EPA Director Carol Browner stated on the twenty-fifth anniversary of the law's passage, the 1972 act marked the point at which "America finally got serious about addressing the pollution threat and restoring the quality of the nation's waters."

A CHANGING POLITICAL ENVIRONMENT

The Clean Water Act of 1972 was actually one of the last landmark pieces of environmental legislation of the "golden age" of environmentalism. When the Watergate scandal prompted Nixon's resignation from office in August 1974, the incoming administration of Gerald Ford relegated environmental policy to the back burner. Ford did sign the Toxic Substances Control Act and the Resource Conservation and Recovery Act and some federal land management policies underwent substantial overhaul, but the administration and Congress were generally reactive rather than proactive on the environment in the mid-1970s. Most of their attention was focused on economic policy, a mushrooming energy crisis, and efforts to restore the public's shaken post-Watergate faith in government institutions.

When Jimmy Carter took office in January 1977, the environmental community hoped that their causes would assume greater prominence. And the Carter Administration did take steps in that direction. It negotiated an agreement with Canada to address environmental problems in the Great Lakes, and it willingly enlisted in international efforts to combat acid rain (see Document 8.15). The Carter White House also supported greater investments in alternative energy, set aside new wilderness areas, and signed 1977 Amendments to the Clean Air and Clean Water Acts.

Other environmental initiatives floundered, however, as cascading crises at home and overseas (especially the Iran hostage crisis) sapped the popularity and resources of the administration. In 1978, for example, Carter lost a bruising battle with Congress—which was controlled by his own Democratic Party—over several major water development projects in the West. The administration targeted dozens of these projects as "pork barrel" and tried to kill them. But Congress, egged on by political pressure from industry, federal water development agencies, and other pro-development constituencies, fought back and prevailed. Numerous water projects of questionable economic value and detrimental environmental impact went forward. "[Carter] had a great big chip on his shoulder about water projects, that was his problem," asserted Guy Martin, who served as assistant Interior secretary in the Carter Administration. "It made him focus way too much on the environmental issue, when the only way he could win was with the economic one. Most Congressmen don't really care about wild rivers. . . . Carter loved wild rivers, and in the end they thought he was just plain kooky."[37]

Around the same time that Carter had his showdown with Congress, "Love Canal" became a household term across America. In the fall of 1978 Americans learned that the state authorities in New York had ordered the evacuation of 240 families from Love Canal, a small working-class community in Niagara Falls, New York. The order was given after citizen activists documented that the families were being exposed to toxins from an abandoned industrial chemical waste dump in the area. Over the ensuing months, news reports and congressional hearings detailed shocking levels of ineptitude and callous behavior on the part of state public health agencies toward the Love Canal residents (see Document 8.16). Simultaneously, explosive revelations about deformed newborns and poisoned children vaulted pollution back to the forefront of public policy. "Toxic contamination alone had not destroyed families in Love Canal," summarized scholar Eileen Maura McGurty. "The debacle demonstrated that the government was culpable in contamination from disposal of industrial waste and that the response was inadequate and inept. As the drama unfolded before the television audience, empathy for the Love Canal residents transformed the entire landscape of toxic policy."[38]

As the flickering images from Love Canal and congressional committee hearings fanned the flames of public outrage, lawmakers in Washington scrambled to respond. The result was the Comprehensive Environmental Response, Compensation, and Liability Act of 1980 (CERCLA), commonly known as Superfund. This law gave the federal government the statutory authority and financial means to clean up polluted industrial sites that had been abandoned. "[Superfund] fills a major gap in the existing laws of our country," declared Carter when he signed the act on December 11, 1980. "It provides adequate funding, coming primarily from industry, but also from government, and it establishes certain standards for liability if toxic chemicals are damaging to people or to property."[39]

THE SAGEBRUSH REBELLION

Even as public demands for decisive state and federal intervention on toxic pollution were increasing, complaints about intrusive federal land management policies were also on the upswing, especially in the rural West. America's western states had been repositories of robust anti-regulatory, pro-resource extraction political sentiments ever since their territorial days. Decade after decade, business interests and politicians regularly issued calls for the transfer of the West's vast public lands into private ownership. In times of general prosperity, these calls became more infrequent and muted. But in the late 1970s, a series of federal land management policies were enacted that inflamed these perennially simmering views. The conflagration that erupted came to be known as the Sagebrush Rebellion, and it permanently changed the complexion of environmental politics in the West.

The backlash against federal authority that surged across the West in the late 1970s was primarily a result of three pieces of legislation. The first of these was the National Forest Management Act (NFMA) of 1976, which sought to curb environmentally destructive logging practices in national forests. Specifically, this act instructed the U.S. Forest Service to impose regulations that would restrict annual cut rates and curb clear cutting, demand better reforestation programs from timber companies, and extend greater protections to streams and rivers in logging areas. "The days have ended when the forest may be viewed only as trees and trees viewed only as timber," proclaimed Senator Hubert Humphrey (D-Minn.) after the NFMA became law. "The soil and the water, the grasses and the shrubs, the fish and the wildlife, and the beauty of the forest must become integral parts of the resource manager's thinking and actions."[40] Timber companies and rural communities that depended on logging revenue, however, bitterly opposed these provisions as job and profit killers.

A second source of discontent was the U.S. Forest Service's Roadless Area Review and Evaluation (RARE II). This was a national inventory of federal forestlands carried out in the late 1970s. Its primary goal was to identify roadless areas within the system that warranted protection as designated "wilderness." The final report on RARE II, which began in 1977 and ended in early 1979, laid out Forest Service findings for more than 60 million acres scattered across more than 3,000 roadless areas within the national forest system. It called for official "wilderness" protection for 15.4 million of these acres (including 5 million acres in Alaska's Tongass National Forest), recommended further study of another 11 million acres, and greenlighted commercial logging and other development on the remaining 36 million acres. The RARE II review was condemned by a wide array of western constituencies who saw the proposed wilderness designations as a "lock up" of commodity resources that the region had a right to develop (ironically, RARE II also was scorned by wilderness conservationists, who thought that much more land should have been given protection). RARE II quickly became mired in such a political and legal quagmire that its recommendations were never implemented.

The greatest factor in the rise of the Sagebrush Rebellion, however, was probably the 1976 Federal Land Policy and Management Act (FLPMA), also known as the BLM Organic Act (see Document 8.13). This act explicitly affirmed that the federal government was the rightful owner and manager of public lands in the West, it confirmed the government's intention to *retain* ownership of these lands, and it instructed the Bureau of Land Management (BLM)—which managed more land than any other federal resource agency—to place environmental values on an equal footing with economic considerations in crafting and carrying out its policies.

Extraction-based industries and their benefactors in public office immediately cried foul. Nevada state senator Richard Blakemore complained that federal acts designed to protect the environment were cordoning off great parts of the public domain from ranching, mining, and other "traditional" uses: "Westerners see these restrictions in the use of the public lands as a portent of things to come—that eventually most of today's public lands will be locked up in wilderness or other restrictive uses."[41] In Utah, San Juan County commissioner Calvin Black denounced FLPMA as "the worst piece of legislation ever passed against the people of the West."[42]

These charges spurred the creation of a movement dedicated to the cause of transferring federal lands into private and state ownership—where they could be used more freely and extensively. This Sagebrush Rebellion, as it came to be known, first flared in Nevada, then spread like wildfire across the interior West (see Document 8.14). It was organized and directed by powerful ranching, mining, and timber interests and their political allies. But it also included other constituencies, including rural communities dependent on resource extraction industries for jobs and economic sustenance and individual citizens committed to the banners of states' rights and free markets. Whatever their background, members framed the movement as consistent with traditional western tenets of rugged individualism, freedom, and regional solidarity. As the Select Committee on Public Lands of the Nevada Legislature stated in 1979, the Rebellion arose out of a belief that "federal policies affecting the West . . . are made in ignorance of conditions and concerns in the West, that those policies are made for a so-called national constituency without regard for western problems, and that this 'colonial' treatment is going to get worse."[43]

The environmental community had a different perspective. Activists regarded the Sagebrush Rebels as selfish profiteers cynically exploiting western mythology to enrich themselves and despoil the country's natural heritage. Conservationist and wildlife biologist Bernard Shanks, for example, wrote that the Sagebrush Rebellion was built on a foundation of "hysteria and slander supported neither by history nor by facts, but by a thin tissue of lies. It was fueled by greed. Every 'rebel' leader was tied to public-land exploitation."[44]

As these charges and countercharges flew back and forth in the West, another long-running battle between wilderness development and preservation forces was drawing to a close in Washington. Back in 1971 the Alaska Native Claims Settlement Act (ANCSA), which bestowed $963 million and 44 million acres of federal land on native tribes to settle longstanding aboriginal land claims, had included provisions that gave Congress the option of reserving up to 80 million acres of Alaskan land as federal land. These so-called "d-2" lands could then be designated by Congress as national parks, wildlife refuges, wild and scenic rivers, or national forests.

Under the terms of ANCSA, however, Congress had only five years to make such claims. Any lands not selected for federal protection by that time could be claimed by the state of Alaska, native tribes, or industry for development. Congress voted to extend this deadline for itself, but by the late 1970s the negotiations in Washington had become a tangle of bitter partisanship and acrimonious salvos between pro-conservation and pro-development camps. As the deadline drew near without any breakthrough, many observers began to doubt whether any "d-2" lands would ever be designated. In 1978, however, the Carter Administration broke the impasse by circumventing Congress altogether. It designated more than 100 million acres for federal protection—more than 40 million acres under the authority of Secretary of the Interior Cecil Andrus and the rest by Carter, who used his executive powers to give national monument status to about 60 million acres.

This bold maneuver broke the logjam. Members of the Alaskan congressional delegation, which had anchored the "d-2" opposition, decided that an Alaska lands bill that they had a hand in shaping was better than the alternative unfurled by Carter—especially because the administration agreed to rescind the withdrawals by Andrus if it received a bill the president could sign. Negotiations thus resumed on the "d-2" issue. Agreements to keep some targeted lands open to drilling, mining, and logging gave a small measure of comfort to pro-development forces, and in November 1980 Congress finally passed an Alaska National Interest Lands Conservation Act (ANILCA) and sent it to Carter for his signature. On December 2, 1980, Carter signed the measure into law—and in one fell swoop doubled the size of America's national park and wildlife refuge system and tripled the size of its wilderness system **(see Document 8.17)**.

After leaving office, Carter repeatedly described his signing of ANILCA as one of the greatest moments of his presidency. But to some Americans, it marked yet another sign of federal land and resource policies gone awry. They believed that economic development and personal freedoms were being needlessly—and often senselessly—sacrificed on the altar of environmentalism. Over the next several years, these Americans would become well-represented in Washington.

Notes

1. Quoted from "The Story of Silent Spring," Natural Resources Defense Council Web site, www.nrdc .org/health/pesticides/hcarson.asp.

2. William J. Darby, "Silence, Miss Carson," *Chemical and Engineering News,* October 1, 1962, 63.

3. Quoted from "The Story of Silent Spring," www.nrdc.org/health/pesticides/hcarson.asp.

4. Quoted in Rachel Carson, *Lost Woods: The Discovered Writing of Rachel Carson,* ed. Linda Lear (Boston: Beacon Press, 1998), ix.

5. James Morton Turner, "The Politics of Modern Wilderness," in *American Wilderness: A New History,* ed. Michael Lewis (New York: Oxford University Press, 2007), 245.

6. David Brower, "Wilderness—Conflict and Conscience," *Sierra Club Bulletin* 42, June 1957.

7. Quoted in *The Wilderness Act Handbook* (Washington, D.C.: Wilderness Society, 2004), 7.

8. Quoted in Doug Scott, *The Enduring Wilderness* (Golden, CO: Fulcrum Publishing, 2004), 51.

9. Quoted in Douglas Hillman Strong, *Dreamers and Defenders: American Conservationists* (Lincoln: University of Nebraska Press, 1988), 205–206.

10. Quoted in *American Forests,* July 1963.

11. Richard N.L. Andrews, *Managing the Environment, Managing Ourselves: A History of American Environmental Policy* (New Haven, Conn.: Yale University Press, 1999), 179–180.

12. Chip Ward, *Hope's Horizon* (Washington, D.C.: Island Press, 2004), 143.

13. Floyd Dominy, "Floyd Dominy: An Encounter with the West's Undaunted Dam-Builder," interview with Ed Marston, *High Country News,* August 28, 2000.

14. Quoted in Tim Palmer, *Endangered Rivers and the Conservation Movement,* rev. ed. (1986; Lanham, MD: Rowman and Littlefield, 2004), 156.

15. Marc Reisner, *Cadillac Desert: The American West and Its Disappearing Water.* 1986, rev. ed. (New York: Penguin, 1993), 245–246.

16. John McPhee, *Encounters with the Archdruid* (New York: Farrar, Strous and Giroux, 1971), 173.

17. Donald J. Pisani, "A Tale of Two Commissioners: Frederick H. Newell and Floyd Dominy." Presented at *History of the Bureau of Reclamation: A Symposium.* Las Vegas, Nev., June 18, 2002. www .waterhistory.org.

18. Quoted in Tim Palmer, *Wild and Scenic Rivers of America* (Washington, D.C.: Island Press, 1993), 18.

19. Ibid., 19.

20. Quoted in Philip Shabecoff, *A Fierce Green Fire: The American Environmental Movement* (New York: Hill and Wang, 1993), 117.

21. Mark Dowie, Losing Ground: American Environmentalism at the Close of the Twentieth Century (Cambridge, Mass.: MIT Press, 1995), 24.

22. Robert Gottlieb, *Forcing the Spring: The Transformation of the American Environmental Movement* (Washington, D.C.: Island Press, 1993), 198.

23. Ibid., 196.

24. Shabecoff, 123.

25. Quoted in Tom Turner, "Legal Eagles," in *Crossroads: Environmental Priorities for the Future,* ed. Peter Borelli (Washington, D.C.: Island Press, 1988), 52.

26. Charles O. Jones, *Clean Air: The Policies and Politics of Pollution Control* (Pittsburgh: University of Pittsburgh Press), 1975.

27. Shabecoff, 118.

28. Christopher J. Bailey, *Congress and Air Pollution: Environmental Policies in the United States* (Manchester, UK: Manchester University Press, 1998), 117.

29. R. Shep Melnick, "Risky Business: Government and the Environment after Earth Day" in *Taking Stock: American Government in the Twentieth Century,* ed. Morton Keller and R. Shep Melnick (New York: Woodrow Wilson Center Press and Cambridge University Press, 1999), 167.

30. Shabecoff, 130.

31. Lyndon B. Johnson, "Special Message to Congress, 23 February 1966," *Public Papers of the Presidents of the United States: Lyndon B. Johnson, 1966* (Washington, D.C.: Government Printing Office, 1967).

32. Lyndon B. Johnson, "Remarks Upon Signing the Air Quality Act 1967," November 21, 1967, *Public Papers of the Presidents of the United States: Lyndon B. Johnson, 1967* (Washington, D.C.: Government Printing Office, 1968).

33. Edmund S. Muskie, "The Clean Air Act: A Commitment to Public Health," *Environmental Forum* 12 (1990): 14.

34. Paul Charles Milazzo, *Unlikely Environmentalists: Congress and Clean Water, 1945–1972* (Lawrence: University Press of Kansas, 2006), 221.

35. Ibid., 228.

36. Amendment of Federal Water Pollution Control Act, *Congressional Record-Senate,* 92nd Cong., 2d sess. October 4, 1972, page 33692, available at the Edmund S. Muskie Archives and Special Collections Library Web site, http://abacus.bates.edu/Library/aboutladd/departments/special/ajcr/1972/CWA%20Conference%20opening.shtml#33692-72-T.

37. Quoted in Reisner, *Cadillac Desert,* 330.

38. Eileen Maura McGurty, *Transforming Environmentalism: Warren County, PCBs and the Origins of Environmental Justice* (Brunswick, NJ: Rutgers University Press, 2007), 40–41.

39. Jimmy Carter, "Remarks upon Signing the Comprehensive Environmental Response, Compensation, and Liability Act," December 11, 1980, *Public Papers of the Presidents of the United States: Jimmy Carter, 1980* (Washington, D.C.: Government Printing Office, 1981).

40. Quoted in Charles F. Wilkinson and H. Michael Anderson, *Land and Resource Planning in the National Forests* (Washington, D.C.: Island Press, 1987), 292.

41. Richard Blakemore, "Sagebrush Rebellion: Nevada's View," *State Government News,* November 1979, 3.

42. Quoted in Daniel Kemmis, *This Sovereign Land: A New Vision for Governing the West* (Washington, D.C.: Island Press, 2001), 56.

43. Quoted in R. McGreggor Cawley, *Federal Land, Western Anger: The Sagebrush Rebellion and Environmental Politics* (Lawrence: University Press of Kansas, 1993), 68.

44. Bernard Shank, *This Land Is Your Land: The Struggle to Save America's Public Lands* (San Francisco: Sierra Club Books, 1984), 265.

Rachel Carson's *Silent Spring*

"The Chemical War Is Never Won, and All Life Is Caught in Its Violent Crossfire"

1962

Rachel Carson's emergence as a seminal figure in the history of American environmentalism and environmental policy–making began in the late 1950s, when she received a letter from a friend describing the devastating ecological impact of DDT use on a private bird sanctuary in Massachusetts. The correspondence prompted Carson to undertake a detailed study of the environmental impact of pesticides—especially DDT—and other toxic pollutants.

Carson published her findings in the 1962 book Silent Spring, *which has been cited as one of the most politically explosive and influential books in U.S. history. Blending layman-friendly language with painstaking scientific research, Carson charged that pesticides, nuclear fallout, and other toxic pollutants posed a major threat to the planet and its inhabitants. The counterattack from industry was fierce. "It was probably as bitter and unscrupulous as anything of the sort since the publication of Charles Darwin's* Origin of Species *a century before," commented Paul Brooks, Carson's book editor. "Hundreds of thousands of dollars were spent by the chemical industry in an attempt to discredit the book and malign the author."[1]*

Over the ensuing months, however, governmental and independent scientists endorsed Carson's research and findings. Meanwhile, the book soared to the top of bestseller lists around the country. By 1963 Silent Spring *had triggered a series of congressional hearings and the appointment of a Presidential Commission to study the dangers posed by pesticides, herbicides, and other industrial chemicals. The reports that came out of these investigations confirmed the dangers Carson had outlined.*

In May 1964—one month after Carson's death from cancer—President Lyndon B. Johnson signed an amendment to the Federal Insecticide, Fungicide, and Rodenticide Act placing significant new regulations on the use of pesticides. Numerous state legislatures followed suit. In 1972 the Environmental Protection Agency placed an outright ban on DDT, an insecticide on which Carson devoted particular attention in Silent Spring. *Following are excerpts from the opening chapter of the book, which remains a touchstone of the environmental movement.*

A FABLE FOR TOMORROW

There was once a town in the heart of America where all life seemed to live in harmony with its surroundings. The town lay in the midst of a checkerboard of prosperous farms, with fields of grain and hillsides of orchards where, in spring, white clouds of bloom drifted above the green fields. In autumn, oak and maple and birch set up a blaze of color that flamed and flickered across a backdrop of pines. Then foxes barked in the hills and deer silently crossed the fields, half hidden in the mists of the fall mornings.

Along the roads, laurel, viburnum and alder, great ferns and wildflowers delighted the traveler's eye through much of the year. Even in winter the roadsides were places of beauty, where countless birds came to feed on the berries and on the seed heads of the dried weeds rising above the snow. The countryside was, in fact, famous for the abundance and variety of its bird life, and when the flood of migrants was pouring through in spring and fall people traveled from great distances to observe them. Others came to fish the streams, which flowed clear and cold out of the hills and contained shady pools where trout lay. So it had been from the days many years ago when the first settlers raised their houses, sank their wells, and built their barns.

Then a strange blight crept over the area and everything began to change. Some evil spell had settled on the community: mysterious maladies swept the flocks of chickens; the cattle and sheep sickened and died. Everywhere was a shadow of death. The farmers spoke of much illness among their families. In the town the doctors had become more and more puzzled by new kinds of sickness appearing among their patients. There had been several sudden and unexplained deaths, not only among adults but even among children, who would be stricken suddenly while at play and die within a few hours.

It was a spring without voices. On the mornings that had once throbbed with the dawn chorus of robins, catbirds, doves, jays, wrens, and scores of other bird voices there was now no sound; only silence lay over the fields and woods and marsh.

—Rachel Carson

There was a strange stillness. The birds, for example—where had they gone? Many people spoke of them, puzzled and disturbed. The feeding stations in the backyards were deserted. The few birds seen anywhere were moribund; they trembled violently and could not fly. It was a spring without voices. On the mornings that had once throbbed with the dawn chorus of robins, catbirds, doves, jays, wrens, and scores of other bird voices there was now no sound; only silence lay over the fields and woods and marsh.

On the farms the hens brooded, but no chicks hatched. The farmers complained that they were unable to raise any pigs—the litters were small and the young survived only a few days. The apple trees were coming into bloom but no bees droned among the blossoms, so there was no pollination and there would be no fruit.

The roadsides, once so attractive, were now lined with browned and withered vegetation as though swept by fire. These, too, were silent, deserted by all living things. Even the streams were now lifeless. Anglers no longer visited them, for all the fish had died.

In the gutters under the eaves and between the shingles of the roofs, a white granular powder still showed a few patches; some weeks before it had fallen like snow upon the roofs and the lawns, the fields and streams.

No witchcraft, no enemy action had silenced the rebirth of new life in this stricken world. The people had done it to themselves.

This town does not actually exist, but it might easily have a thousand counterparts in America or elsewhere in the world. I know of no community that has experienced all the misfortunes I describe. Yet every one of these disasters has actually happened somewhere, and many real communities have already suffered a substantial number of them. A grim specter has crept upon us almost unnoticed, and this imagined tragedy may easily become a stark reality we all shall know.

What has already silenced the voices of spring in countless towns in America? This book is an attempt to explain. . . .

The Obligation to Endure

The history of life on earth has been a history of interaction between living things and their surroundings. To a large extent, the physical form and the habits of the earth's vegetation and its animal life have been molded by the environment. Considering the whole span of earthly time, the opposite effect, in which life actually modifies its surroundings, has been relatively slight. Only within the moment of time represented by the present century has one species—man—acquired significant power to alter the nature of his world.

During the past quarter century this power has not only increased to one of disturbing magnitude but it has changed in character. The most alarming of all man's assaults upon the environment is the contamination of air, earth, rivers, and sea with dangerous and even lethal materials. This pollution is for the most part irrecoverable; the chain of evil it initiates not only in the world that must support life but in living tissues is for the most part irreversible. In this now universal contamination of the environment, chemicals are the sinister and little-recognized partners of radiation in changing the very nature of the world—the very nature of its life. Strontium 90, released through nuclear explosions into the air, comes to earth in rain or drifts down as fallout, lodges in soil, enters into the grass or corn or wheat grown there, and in time takes up its abode in the bones of a human being, there to remain until his death. Similarly, chemicals sprayed on croplands or forests or gardens lie long in soil, entering into living organisms, passing from one to another in a chain of poisoning and death. Or they pass mysteriously by underground streams until they emerge and, through the alchemy of air and sunlight, combine into new forms that kill vegetation, sicken cattle, and work unknown harm on those who drink from once pure wells. As Albert Schweitzer has said, "Man can hardly even recognize the devils of his own creation."

It took hundreds of millions of years to produce the life that now inhabits the earth—eons of time in which that developing and evolving and diversifying life reached a state of adjustment and balance with its surroundings. The environment, rigorously shaping and directing the life it supported, contained elements that were hostile as well as supporting. Certain rocks gave out dangerous radiation; even within the light of the sun, from which all life draws its energy, there were short-wave radiations with power to injure. Given time—time not in years but in millennia—life adjusts, and a balance has been reached. For time is the essential ingredient; but in the modern world there is no time.

The rapidity of change and the speed with which new situations are created follow the impetuous and heedless pace of man rather than the deliberate pace of nature. Radiation is no longer merely the background radiation of rocks, the bombardment of cosmic rays, the ultraviolet of the sun that have existed before there was any life on earth; radiation is now the unnatural creation of man's tampering with the atom. The chemicals to which life is asked to make its adjustment are no longer merely the calcium and silica and copper and all the rest of the minerals washed out of the rocks and carried in rivers to the sea; they are the synthetic creations of man's inventive mind, brewed in his laboratories, and having no counterparts in nature.

To adjust to these chemicals would require time on the scale that is nature's; it would require not merely the years of a man's life but the life of generations. And even this, were it by some miracle possible, would be futile, for the new chemicals come from our laboratories in an endless stream; almost five hundred annually find their way into actual use in the United States alone. The figure is staggering and its implications are not easily grasped—500 new chemicals to which the bodies of men and animals are required somehow to adapt each year, chemicals totally outside the limits of biologic experience.

Among them are many that are used in man's war against nature. Since the mid-1940's over 200 basic chemicals have been created for use in killing insects, weeds, rodents, and other organisms described in the modern vernacular as "pests"; and they are sold under several thousand different brand names.

These sprays, dusts, and aerosols are now applied almost universally to farms, gardens, forests, and homes—nonselective chemicals that have the power to kill every insect, the "good and the "bad," to still the song of birds and the leaping of fish in the streams, to coat the leaves with a deadly film, and to linger on in soil—all this though the intended target may be only a few weeds or insects. Can anyone believe it is possible to lay down such a barrage of poisons on the surface of the earth without making if unfit for all life? They should not be called "insecticides," but "biocides."

The whole process of spraying seems caught up in an endless spiral. Since DDT was released for civilian use, a process of escalation has been going on in which ever more toxic materials must be found. This has happened because insects, in a triumphant vindication of Darwin's principle of the survival of the fittest, have evolved super races immune to the particular insecticide used, hence a deadlier one has always to be developed—and then a deadlier one than that. It has happened also because, for reasons to be described later, destructive insects often undergo a "flareback," or resurgence, after spraying, in numbers greater than before. Thus the chemical war is never won, and all life is caught in its violent crossfire.

Along with the possibility of the extinction of mankind by nuclear war, the central problem of our age has therefore become the contamination of man's total environment with such substances of incredible potential for harm—substances that accumulate in the tissues of plants and animals and even penetrate the germ cells to shatter or alter the very material of heredity upon which the shape of the future depends.

Some would-be architects of our future look toward a time when it will be possible to alter the human germ plasm by design. But we may easily be doing so now by inadvertence, for many chemicals, like radiation, bring about gene mutations. It is ironic to think that man might determine his own future by something so seemingly trivial as the choice of an insect spray.

All this has been risked—for what? Future historians may well be amazed by our distorted sense of proportion. How could intelligent beings seek to control a few unwanted species by a method that contaminated the entire environment and brought the threat of disease and death even to their own kind? Yet this is precisely what we have done. We have done it, moreover, for reasons that collapse the moment we examine them. We are told that the enormous and expanding use of pesticides is necessary to maintain farm production. Yet is our real problem not one of *overproduction?* Our farms, despite measures to remove acreages from production and to pay farmers *not* to produce, have yielded such a staggering excess of crops that the American taxpayer in 1962 is paying out more than one billion dollars a year as the total carrying cost of the surplus-food storage program. And is the situation helped when one branch of the Agriculture Department tries to reduce production while another states, as it did in 1958, "It is believed generally that reduction of crop acreages under provisions of the Soil Bank will stimulate interest in use of chemicals to obtain maximum production on the land retained in crops."

All this is not to say there is no insect problem and no need of control. I am saying, rather, that control must be geared to realities, not to mythical situations, and that the methods employed must be such that they do not destroy us along with the insects. . . .

Much of the necessary knowledge [to control insect populations in an environmentally responsible way] is now available but we do not use it. We train ecologists in our universities and even employ them in our governmental agencies but we seldom take their advice. We allow the chemical death rain to fall as though there were no alternative, whereas in fact there are many, and our ingenuity could soon discover many more if given opportunity.

Have we fallen into a mesmerized state that makes us accept as inevitable that which is inferior or detrimental, as though having lost the will or the vision to demand that which is good? Such thinking, in the words of the ecologist Paul Shepard, "idealizes life with only its head out of the water, inches above the limits of toleration of the corruption of its own environment. Why should we tolerate a diet of weak poisons, a home in insipid surroundings, a circle of acquaintances who are not quite our enemies, the noise of motors with just enough relief to prevent insanity? Who would want to live in a world which is just not quite fatal?"

Yet such a world is pressed upon us. The crusade to create a chemically sterile, insect-free world seems to have engendered a fanatic zeal on the part of many specialists and most of the so-called control agencies. On every hand there is evidence that those engaged in spraying operations exercise a ruthless power. "The regulatory entomologists . . . function as prosecutor, judge and jury, tax assessor and collector and sheriff to enforce their own orders," said Connecticut entomologist Neely Turner. The most flagrant abuses go unchecked in both state and federal agencies.

It is not my contention that chemical insecticides must never be used. I do contend that we have put poisonous and biologically potent chemicals indiscriminately into the hands of persons largely or wholly ignorant of their potentials for harm. We have subjected enormous numbers of people to contact with these poisons, without their consent and often without their knowledge. If the Bill of Rights contains no guarantee that a citizen shall be secure against lethal poisons distributed either by private individuals or by public officials, it is surely only because our forefathers, despite their considerable wisdom and foresight, could conceive of no such problem.

I contend, furthermore, that we have allowed these chemicals to be used with little or no advance investigation of their effect on soil, water, wildlife, and man himself. Future generations are unlikely to condone our lack of prudent concern for the integrity of the natural world that supports all life.

There is still very limited awareness of the nature of the threat. This is an era of specialists, each of whom sees his own problem and is unaware of or intolerant of the larger frame into which it fits. It is also an era dominated by industry, in which the right to make a dollar at whatever cost is seldom challenged. When the public protests, confronted with some obvious evidence of damaging results of pesticide applications, it is fed little tranquilizing pills of half truth. We urgently need an end to these false assurances, to the sugar coating of unpalatable facts. It is the public that is being asked to assume the risks that the insect controllers calculate. The public must decide whether it wishes to continue on the present road, and it can do so only when in full possession of the facts. In the words of Jean Rostand, "The obligation to endure gives us the right to know."

Source: Carson, Rachel. *Silent Spring.* 1962. Reprint. New York: Houghton Mifflin Harcourt, 2002, pp. 1–3, 5–9, 11–13. Copyright © 1962 by Rachel L. Carson. Used by permission of Frances Collin, Trustee. Any electronic copying or distribution of this text is expressly forbidden.

NOTE

1. Quoted in Rachel Carson, *Silent Spring,* ed. Paul Brooks (Boston: Houghton Mifflin, 1994), xii.

DOCUMENT 8.2

Stewart Udall Recalls the Fight for Passage of the Wilderness Act of 1964

"This Was a Great Moment for the Country"

September 19, 2004

The Wilderness Act of 1964 marked the first major triumph in a decade-long barrage of landmark environmental legislation in the United States. This bill was championed by conservation groups including the Wilderness Society, Sierra Club, and Audubon Society, all of which were determined to take full advantage of their newfound political influence in Washington. The initial proposal for a "wilderness system" that would protect millions of acres of undeveloped public land in America's national parks and forest reserves was made, in fact, by Wilderness Society Executive Director Howard Zahniser in 1956. Zahniser's proposed legislation was first introduced into Congress the following year by Democratic senator Hubert H. Humphrey of Minnesota and Republican congressman John Saylor of Pennsylvania.

Zahniser's wilderness bill became the subject of protracted political battle in Washington between conservation-minded legislators and advocates of resource extraction industries and rural communities that opposed the bill. The National Park Service and U.S. Forest Service also worked behind the scenes to block the bill, which they viewed as a threat to their administrative judgment and independence (the U.S. Fish and Wildlife Service, however, strongly supported the proposal).

Time and again, Zahniser revised the bill's language to advance it past various procedural roadblocks. It was an exhausting effort, and Zahniser and his allies were forced to jettison some prized provisions to keep the bill alive. The support of the sportsman-oriented National Wildlife Federation, for instance, was secured only after Zahniser agreed to change the bill's language to preserve hunting rights in wilderness areas. But the perseverance of Wilderness Act supporters eventually paid off. In 1960 John F. Kennedy endorsed the bill as part of his presidential election campaign, and when he entered the White House in 1961 he appointed Stewart Udall as Interior secretary and Orville Freeman as agriculture secretary. Both Udall and Freeman supported the proposed Wilderness Act, and their stance went a long way toward muting the earlier opposition of the Forest Service and Park Service.[1]

Nonetheless, the Wilderness Act bill continued to be buffeted by political winds. Time and again, its path to the White House for presidential signature was blocked by procedural machinations by Representative Wayne Aspinall (D-Colo.) and other foes. But Zahniser and his many allies in Congress kept the bill alive through a mix of compromise and relentless grassroots lobbying, and in April 1963 the Senate passed the wilderness bill by a 73-12 vote. Fifteen months later, the House of Representatives approved it by a 373-1 vote. The measure was signed into law by President Lyndon B. Johnson on September 3, 1964—four months after Zahniser died in his sleep.

The Wilderness Act was welcomed by Udall, who served as secretary of the Interior from 1961 to 1969. Armed with a strong pro-conservation orientation, Udall recognized that the 1964 Wilderness Act was a milestone in environmental stewardship and protection. In 2004 Udall attended a special commemorative dinner organized to celebrate the fortieth anniversary of the passage of the Wilderness Act. In his remarks, Udall recalled several of the conservationists and legislators who battled for and against the act, including Zahniser, Humphrey, Saylor, Tom Kuchel (R-Calif.), Morris Udall (D-Ariz. and Stewart Udall's younger brother), John Dingell (D-Mich.), Clinton Anderson (D-N.M.), and Wayne Aspinall (D-Colo.). Following are excerpts from Udall's remarks.

I am honored and delighted to be here tonight with John Dingell and Gaylord Nelson and Bob Byrd. I was running for Congress 50 years ago right now, and I came in the door with John Dingell and Bob Byrd had been there two years, and they considered him a "hick,"—he played the fiddle, he loved the folk music of his people and now he is the conscience of the Senate. . . .

John Dingell, you were given too little credit tonight. The National Environmental Policy Act would probably not have been passed if it had not been for John Dingell. What you don't know is Wayne Aspinall thought it was a crazy idea, and John Dingell said "if he doesn't want it, then I will pick it up." And he carried the mail through the House. So I want to say something—I'm on a "lecture tour" this evening. There was something about that time, and John Dingell and I discussed it—the 60s into the 70s was called a golden age of sorts. One of the things that comes to my mind as I go back there is the way you saw young Congressmen and Senators who were pretty raw in the beginning, but they had open minds and they grew and they developed new convictions and they developed new horizons. One example was John and Robert Kennedy—changing before your eyes. And John Dingell and Bob Byrd are examples of this, and my brother—yes, my brother. It did not take him long to enlarge his mind and encompass it. And that is a great gift—to be open minded and have the capacity to grow. It's a very great gift. And can we see members of Congress now, too many of them that come in with fixed ideologies and fixed views, and they will stay for 10 or 25 years, and when they leave they have the very same views. They haven't changed a damn thing. It's pathetic. . . .

> **What happened was the citizens all over the country—in the West and the East, the Congressmen and the Senators got behind wilderness bills, and that is why we have the 110 million acres today.**
>
> —Stewart Udall

One person left out [in earlier commemorative remarks about contributors to the passage of the Wilderness Act] was Humphrey. John Saylor—what a great man he was. Thomas Kuchel, Republican from California was one. And he shortly became the deputy leader—the whip to Everett Dirksen, and the reason we got an overwhelming bipartisan vote, in the Senate, was Tom Kuchel. Tom Kuchel, so give him credit for it. What a great, great man he was. To show you the spirit of bipartisanship, we worked on Point Reyes [National Seashore] together. When I went to his office, he'd say, "Hi Stewie, what do you want today?" And that's the way it was in that period. But the Wilderness Bill—Howard Zahniser—Mr. Zahniser—the man was a saint. He rewrote and touched up that bill 60 times over a period of 8 years. Every time Aspinall raised a new argument, he'd work on a little language and tried to offset it. He was truly a saintly person—a poet, a lover of Thoreau, a wonderful man.

But when the wilderness bill got off the ground, and too much we, all of us, when it's all over, like to take credit. I have been given more than my share tonight. Two persons I would single out are President John F. Kennedy and Senator Clinton Anderson of New Mexico. Clint Anderson had been as a young insurance man, a personal friend of Aldo

Leopold in Albuquerque, and when he became chairman of the Committee [on Interior and Insular Affairs] after the 1960 election, and Kennedy was president. I didn't tell Kennedy what to do. Clint Anderson went to the White House and said, "Kennedy didn't campaign on wilderness, I can't find anything in the campaign." He said put in your message to Congress on conservation—Presidents used to send up such messages, if they had a conservation program—a call for the enactment of a wilderness bill along the lines of Senate bill five—his bill. Kennedy put it in, and that electrified the country—to have a call like that. And in July the bill went to the floor of the Senate, and I'll tell you I was startled. I was startled, Senator Byrd. The vote was 78 to 12, and people all over the country—the conservationists—suddenly began to arouse and see how much power they have.

We give too much credit in my view—I was a Congressman—to members of Congress. Lyndon Johnson was great at that—"the Congress, they did it." They enact laws, yes. But there was an upsurge, an uplifting of people. Conservation had been put on the shelf after Pearl Harbor and then there was a Cold War and Kennedy issued a call for national seashores and we got started on 14 of them. Some of them passed later on, but I have to say what made it all possible was a bipartisanship and affection between the members of the old generation—my generation. We were Depression kids, we fought the war, we believed in mutual respect. That was what made it so wonderful in those days. And that spirit carried forward. Richard Nixon was a damn good conservation president.

I like metaphors, and I have likened what happened—we just saw the Olympics—to a relay race, because the work and conservation in those days was never finished. There was a pipeline. Heavens, it took Gaylord Nelson—because he wanted the people to accept it—12 years to do the Apostle Islands National Seashore. It took Bill Hart 10 years to do Sleeping Bear Dunes [National Lakeshore] in Michigan. And this meant that when we came, and a different party won the White House, you carried the baton. I am not sure Nixon understood in the beginning, but they took it and they ran with it. . . . And Gerald Ford carried it on, and Jimmy Carter. And then—no names mentioned—but a Secretary of the Interior when 1981 began, refused. In fact, he said—and I never understood where he was coming from—we've been going in the wrong direction for the last 20 years, so he wouldn't take the baton. And it has been on the floor ever since.

The bipartisanship by these five presidents was ended, and I want to say because there is so much doublespeak these days—don't let a president or his people say because he signed a wilderness bill that he is for wilderness. Does he issue a call for more wilderness? That's the test. That's the test. The Land and Water Conservation Fund—oh I can take some credit on that, but I won't—too long. Do you know, 10 billion dollars in 1960 dollars, Senator Byrd, went into that program and half of it went to the states and they matched it, and almost 40 thousand projects—cities, counties, open space, playgrounds— boy, do we need playgrounds with this plague of obesity that is claiming this country. We ought to go back to that program.

Well that's enough, I guess, and you know how strongly I feel. The fight is not over, as everyone has said tonight. And we may have gaps and we have an ebb and flow. I'd like to believe, I am a troubled optimist, but there will be a flow again in terms of wilderness preservation. And I like to end, and my vision is gone so I have to memorize things. I can't use notes, I just blabber away. Congressman Aspinall—from Colorado—was an honorable man, as John Dingell and I have discussed. He was strong-headed, but an honorable man. Very stubborn and he could be dictatorial. He wouldn't even let his committee consider the bill—no hearings—no bill reported. John Saylor would say, "Wayne, you cannot get away with this forever," and we tried to persuade him. Where was he? He said to me once, Stuart—I was one of his boys, I trained under him, he taught you a lot of things—and he said people that don't understand me, don't understand that my congressional district is a mining district. It had been a mining district. He was a great champion of the American Mining Congress. He regarded a wilderness bill as a lock up. That was the argument that Howard Zahniser had to work against all the time. He said, "Stuart, you may get a bill from out of my committee, but you might not recognize it." And so it came to a compromise. And he and Clinton Anderson were two old bulls that ended up hating and distrusting each other. And Anderson's bill had all of the elements, the framework, and the language about how you identified a wilderness bill and how you passed a wilderness bill. And Anderson put in 50 million acres of lands that the Forest Service largely had already identified. Aspinall cut it back to nine. And they made the compromise because Anderson had to give in if he wanted to get a wilderness bill. So it was cut way back. Aspinall thought it might be true today—but not in the next 20 or 30 years—that if every bill had to pass individually through the Senate and House, that Congressmen who held the views that he did, would not want a wilderness in their area because it was locking up very valuable resources. And so that is the way it played out. And the wilderness bill—the essential elements of the wilderness bill—were there when the bill was passed. And this was a great moment for the country. What happened was the citizens all over the country—in the West and the East, the Congressmen and the Senators got behind wilderness bills, and that is why we have the 110 million acres today. . . .

Don't give out—the fight goes on. I'm finally going to end, I'm sorry, I got carried away. The case for wilderness was made against the lock up argument by Clinton Anderson, who said "wilderness is an anchor to windward." Knowing it is there, we can go about our business of managing our resources wisely and not be a people in despair, ransacking our public lands for the last barrel of oil, the last board of timber, the last blade of grass, the last tank of water. That was Clint Anderson's answer to the lock up argument.

Wallace Stegner, as usual, caught the spirit in that wonderful essay he wrote in 1960. He said, "We need this wild country even if we do no more than go to the edge and look in. We need it as a symbol of our sanity as creatures as part of the geography of hope." And Ansel Adams, the great photographer said it in a different way, and I once said, "Ansel, can I apply your statement to the Grand Canyon and Yosemite?" "Of course," he said. Ansel was writing home after his first trip to New Mexico and he used these words: "All is very beautiful and magical here." He is talking about the landscape. "All is beautiful and magical here." A quality one cannot describe. He said, "The sky and the land is so enormous and that the detail is so precise and exquisite," the eye of the photographer—"that wherever you are, there is a golden glow and everything is sideways under you and over you, and the clocks stopped long ago."

Keep up the fight, and good night.

Source: "Remarks of Former Interior Secretary Stewart Udall, Wilderness Act Commemorative Dinner, Washington, D.C., September 19, 2004." *Congressional Record—Senate*, 108th Cong., 2d sess., September 29, 2004. Washington, D.C.: Government Printing Office, 2004, pp. S9928–S9929.

NOTE

1. Doug Scott, *The Enduring Wilderness* (Golden, Colo.: Fulcrum Publishing, 2004), 51.

Floyd Dominy Defends Reclamation Projects in the West

"What Good Is Beauty if There Is No One to Enjoy It?"

April 1, 1965

During his twelve years as head of the Bureau of Reclamation from 1959 to 1971, Floyd Dominy enthusiastically waded into numerous conflicts between pro-wilderness conservationists, who decried dams and other federal water projects as despoilers of nature, and pro-development businesses and communities, who embraced the economic and recreational benefits of such projects. The bombastic but canny Dominy was firmly in the pro-development camp. He believed that the Bureau of Reclamation had transformed vast territories of the arid West into productive and hospitable land on which millions of Americans could live and work, and he saw no reason to apologize for the agency's works.

Dominy exerted enormous power in Washington, D.C., during the 1960s. He cultivated close relationships with powerful politicians such as Congressman Wayne Aspinall (D-Colo.) and Senator Carl Hayden (D-Ariz.), who served as chairs of the House Interior Committee and the Senate Appropriations Committee, respectively. "With their support, Dominy could defy the presidency itself if he had to," wrote historian Chip Ward. "Presidents come and go, Dominy realized, but plutocrats live on. And the language of Western plutocrats was water, in which Dominy was fluent."[1]

During Dominy's tenure, however, the rising environmental movement cast doubt on the wisdom of many water projects undertaken by the Bureau and the U.S. Army Corps of Engineers. "By the 1960s," observed policy scholar Richard N. L. Andrews, "publicity campaigns by the Sierra Club and fish and wildlife protection groups against water projects had redefined the water resource agencies from Progressive heroes to environmental villains, mindlessly destroying the landscape for short-term economic, political, and bureaucratic purposes."[2]

Dominy ridiculed conservationists as irrational people who "want to lock away our scenic wonders and keep people out." But he also recognized that their arguments about wilderness preservation were gaining traction with an American public that was increasingly devoted to outdoor recreation and environmental protection. Dominy responded by fashioning defenses of the Bureau's record that emphasized the recreational benefits of agency projects to nature-loving Americans. His best-known address on this topic, titled "Open Space for All Americans," was delivered to the Outdoor Recreation Congress for the Greater Pacific Northwest, in Wenatchee, Washington, on April 1, 1965.

Dominy's speech, which is excerpted here, is also notable because it discusses at some length a proposed Bureau project in the area of Grand Canyon National Park. Despite the Reclamation commissioner's best efforts, this proposal was ultimately torpedoed by a masterful—and duplicitous, in Dominy's view—public relations campaign carried out by the Sierra Club and other influential conservation groups.

[Note: Handwritten additions and deletions to the original typed manuscript have been included in the following document.]

OPEN SPACE FOR ALL AMERICANS

The President has called on us to cooperate in building a Great Society, where all Americans will share in the inherent material and spiritual richness of this country.

One of the most important aspects of the Great Society is the preservation of open spaces and to make them readily accessible to our citizens. Programs have been initiated to supply the fundamental necessities of decent food and shelter to those of our countrymen who still lack them, but this is not enough for a Great Society of free men. . . .

A Great Society, where, to quote the President, "The meaning of our lives matches the marvelous products of our labor," involves much more than material welfare. Man lives not by bread alone. Besides sustenance for his body, he needs inspiration and stimulation for his spirit.

These await him along quiet streams, on the shores of sparkling lakes, in the solitude of the mountains, and at outdoor playgrounds. In recent years Americans in ever-increasing numbers have been seeking spiritual fulfillment and physical well-being in the great outdoors.

With the burgeoning population, increased leisure and higher income, and constantly improving transportation, these numbers can be expected to skyrocket in the next several years. And the development of recreation opportunities is lagging behind the rising demand.

The President is keenly aware of man's need for the spiritual refreshment afforded by nature. In his special message to Congress on natural beauty he stressed the need for establishing outdoor recreation areas in all sections of the United States—national parks, seashores, lakeshores, and recreation areas, as well as smaller open spaces in centers of population. His national beautification program requires not only the setting aside of open spaces in urban areas wherever possible, but also the improvement of the natural beauty of these precious precincts. . . .

As I am sure you know, the Bureau of Reclamation has long been doing all in its legal power to provide outdoor recreation for the people of the western States and those who visit the West. Reclamation multiple-purpose development has provided public access and has brought the satisfying and invigorating pleasures of the outdoors to millions.

> *I bow to no one in the wish to conserve our natural resources compatible with wise use to meet the Nation's needs. But I want to conserve them for the good and enjoyment of the people. I cannot accept the brand of conservation that advocates locking them up.*
>
> —Floyd Dominy

Nevertheless, because this authority was limited, recreation on Reclamation projects, up until recent years, was like Topsy. It "jes growed." In the early days of our program little financing was available to develop the aesthetic values of Reclamation development or to anticipate the needs of the visiting public. We built a dam to regulate riverflow and to provide irrigation water for growing crops on arid land. The idea of anyone's traveling to the usually inaccessible damsite in pursuit of pleasure simply did not register.

However, once a river was plugged by a dam and water began to fill the valley behind it, the public literally beat a path through the wilderness to the rim, to look at the expanse of impounded water and the works of the dam itself. Before long, [ever increasing numbers?] were using the water and the shoreline for fishing, swimming, camping, and other recreational activities, whether there were any planned facilities for their use or not.

Thus what was an incidental by-product of Reclamation, ripened, after a singularly inauspicious start, into a major benefit of the program. This valuable asset of water-oriented recreational facilities may well turn out to be one of Reclamation's greatest contributions to the enrichment of the Great Society.

The trickle of visitors who made their way across rough terrain to view the dams and enjoy the water impoundment quickly grew to a steady stream of nature and sports buffs, who, by 1964, numbered some 35 million. Inevitably, these visitors required transportation, accommodations, sports equipment, and various services. They have been a leading factor in sparking a new industry—tourism—which has brought great economic development to the western States, as well as bestowing untold benefits of happiness, health, and relaxation from the rapid pace of today's world.

Not long ago, I spent several days at one of our new recreation areas, this one at Lake Powell, the reservoir that has been impounded by Glen Canyon Dam on the Colorado River at the Arizona-Utah border. A main feature of the Colorado River Storage Project, Glen Canyon Dam and Powerplant are in themselves worth a trip to the site. They comprise one of the engineering wonders of the world. The dam was honored by the American Society of Civil Engineering as the outstanding civil engineering achievement of 1964.

But this great dam—710 feet high, with a base 340 feet thick, that tapers to a 1,550-foot-long crest, 25 feet wide—is much more than a monument to modern engineering skill.

It is food for growing America, drinking water for dwellers in an arid country, electric energy to provide the comforts of life and to turn the wheels of industry. It is jobs and paychecks—in the West and across the Nation—and it is also taxes for the United States Treasury.

Most significant of all, however, it is health and fun and the contentment of contemplating Nature's beauty for thousands who might never experience these thrills of the outdoors if engineers had not inserted between the steep walls of Glen Canyon a mammoth concrete slab to control and clear the erratic river that used to be known as the "Big Red."

Last summer Secretary of the Interior Stewart L. Udall, who took a 5-day boating and camping trip on the new lake, described it as "without question the most beautiful and scenic man-made lake in the world."

When filled, this reservoir will extend 186 miles upstream from the dam, will have a surface of 162,700 acres, and a shoreline of almost 1,900 miles. The fishing, boating, and swimming in the lake itself, and the camping and picnicking nearby provide some of the best recreation potential on the North American continent.

The superb scenery itself is breathtaking. I feasted my eyes—and the lens of my camera—on sights seldom before seen by man. Of course, the scenery was always there, but until Glen Canyon Project was built, only a handful of hardy, adventurous boatmen ever viewed it.

Now that Lake Powell is stretching far upstream and is reaching venturesome fingers into little canyons and pockets along its sides, the visitor is privileged not only to enjoy the sports provided on the lake, but also to probe into virtually virgin territory hidden beyond every turn in the hundreds of side canyons.

There is no doubt that Lake Powell is well on its way to becoming one of the most popular attractions in the country. We in the Bureau of Reclamation are very proud of it and of the enthusiasm shown by visitors to the Recreation Area, which is administered by the National Park Service.

However, developing this project was by no means clear sailing. It was, in fact, fraught with headaches and controversy.

Let me say here that I bow to no one in the wish to conserve our natural resources compatible with wise use to meet the Nation's needs. But I want to conserve them for the good and enjoyment of the people. I cannot accept the brand of conservation that advocates locking them up.

When conservation first emerged into the national consciousness shortly after the turn of this century, the theme of the conservationists was, simply, the preservation of our resources. They had seen some grim results in other lands and in our own country, of the waste and destruction of natural resources. It was logical that their tendency was to cherish and husband America's natural treasures that they be not dissipated and destroyed, to put a fence around them to save them for the future.

Today our concept of conservation is quite different. As the late President Kennedy explained in a speech on September 25, 1963, "Our primary task now is to increase our understanding of our environment to a point where we can enjoy it without defacing it, use its bounty without detracting permanently from its value, and, above all, maintain a living balance between man's actions and nature's reactions, for this Nation's great resource is as elastic and productive as our ingenuity can make it."

Last fall, out here in your own Northwest, President Johnson defined conservation as "the cooperation of all in the development of our resources for the benefit of all."

But many of our professed conservationists close their eyes to this interpretation of conservation; they still want to lock away our scenic wonders and keep people out. They appear to want only the real adventurers to invade the wilderness. What good is beauty if there is no one to enjoy it? When President Johnson urges the doctrine of open spaces, he means open spaces that can enrich men's lives by bringing them into contact with the majesty and age-old freshness of nature.

Despite their former opposition, I believe that even the dedicated diehards among the "status quo" conservationists would be unable to sustain their argument that the Glen Canyon development has "destroyed" the beauty of Glen Canyon. Lake Powell has changed the environment. But I will not accept the premise that change in scenic values is always negative. The famed Glen Canyon and its environs, including Rainbow Bridge National Monument, have not been destroyed. Quite the contrary—the area has been enhanced for public use and enjoyment. . . .

And, even more important perhaps, is the fact that the lake has made it all accessible to thousands who would have been denied the opportunity to see its splendors if those who criticized the project had had their way.

Well, Glen Canyon is an accomplished fact. But we are now getting more of the same frantic flak from the same groups. Their new targets are Bridge and Marble Canyon Dams on the Lower Colorado. I do not believe they will be successful in their attempts to prevent construction of these structures, which are necessary to the multipurpose development of the Colorado River. But, doubtless, we shall have to combat their propaganda, which seems aimed at keeping much of the remote areas of Grand Canyon a private preserve for the exclusive benefit of a few river runners.

The Lower Colorado River Basin is at the same time the fastest growing and the driest area in the United States. Since the water shortage is already critical and promises to worsen, early development of additional water is essential to the area's very survival. Extensive studies are being made to determine how to increase the water supply and protect that now available.

To this end, a bill has been introduced in Congress which would authorize the initial phase of a comprehensive Lower Colorado River Project. Main features of the plan are: the diversion of Colorado River water from Lake Havasu behind Park Dam to the Central Arizona area; the Southern Nevada Water Supply Unit; salvage operations to conserve river water presently wasted by phreatophytes and other water-gorging plants; and building the two dams on the Colorado.

The area is borrowing a leaf from basin development patterns elsewhere and calling on hydroelectric power to pay most of the bill. It is for this reason that Marble and Bridge Canyon Dams must be built if the Southwest is to reach its ultimate development—or even to maintain its present level of development.

Power revenues from these projects, together with those from established Federal dams on the Lower Colorado River will be pooled in a basin fund, from which monies will be used to repay project costs that are beyond the ability of the water users to carry.

This follows the repeatedly endorsed—by the Congress—classic Reclamation formula whereby 90 percent of the Federal investment is being repaid into the Federal Treasury over a long term period of amortization. Repayment is a cornerstone of Reclamation operations and the Lower Colorado River Basin Project is no exception.

As soon as Marble and Bridge Canyon Dams were proposed, a great cry went up that they would "flood out" Grand Canyon National Park. There is no basis for such accusations.

Site of the proposed Marble Canyon Dam is in the Marble gorge of the Colorado River, well above the boundaries of Grand Canyon National Park; it will back water through the Marble and Glen Canyons to the tailrace of presently existing Glen Canyon Dam.

It will in no way affect the Colorado River through the Grand Canyon, other than to take out such silt as washes into the river below Glen Canyon Dam, except from the Little Colorado River, which joins the Colorado below the proposed damsite. Glen Canyon Dam already has evened out the flow of the river so that the springtime highwater floods are controlled and minimum flows of late fall and winter are augmented, thus providing much more uniform flows through the Grand Canyon stretch of the river.

Bridge Canyon Dam will be constructed near the headwaters of Lake Mead and within the boundaries of the Lake Mead National Recreation Area. The Bridge Canyon Reservoir will back water through the Grand Canyon National Monument and for 13 miles along the Colorado River where the river marks the Park boundary. The reservoir, throughout its length, will be within the deep inner gorge of the canyon. The plateau of the canyon rim towers as much as a mile above the riverbed so it is plain that by no stretch of the imagination will the reservoir "flood out" the canyon. At the down-river park boundary the canyon wall is 2,100 feet above the river. The water in a full Bridge Canyon Reservoir would be only 90 feet above the present river level, and this added depth would taper to zero 13 miles upstream.

Three other facts need to be borne in mind. One is a reservation in the Act creating Grand Canyon National Park which authorizes the Secretary of the Interior to permit Reclamation development within the Park under certain circumstances. The same reservation exists in the proclamation creating the Grand Canyon National Monument. Secretary Udall has found that these circumstances now exist and has recommended the construction of Bridge Canyon Dam.

A second fact is that there will be 105 miles of white water between the headwaters of Bridge Canyon Reservoir and Marble Canyon Dam which will not be disturbed. Ninety-two miles of this untouched river will be within the confines of Grand Canyon National Park.

The third fact is that when Bridge Canyon Dam is constructed, there will be created another extraordinary man-made lake which I expect will rival the beauty of Lake Powell. Here you will have in the depth of the inner gorge of the canyon a waterway which will take boaters 93 miles upstream into some of the most spectacular scenery in America.

Heretofore, 99.9 percent of the travelers and seekers after recreation have been able to view the lower reaches of Grand Canyon only from the rim within the National Park. None of the inundated area is visible from these viewpoints. The only entry into the downstream section of the canyon at the present time is the horseback trail down Havasu Creek to the Havasupai Indian Reservation, and a foot trail from there down to the inner gorge overlooking the river.

When the dam is built there will be an access road from the plateau down to the structure, a launching area for boats, and then a clear, cool, lake of deepest blue which can accommodate thousands of visitors annually without destroying the feeling of solitude and isolation with which the area abounds today.

When this development becomes reality and when Flaming Gorge Recreation Area is added to that at Glen Canyon, the entire 1,270-mile length of the Colorado River within the boundaries of the United States will be the spine of a spectacular American playground for millions of sun-worshippers, nature lovers, fishermen, and water sports enthusiasts.

Here in the Northwest, Nature has been exceptionally lavish with all substances required for man's needs and pleasures. At the beginning of the century when far-sighted men were seeking ways to develop the area, they turned to that vigorous river which is the lifeline of this country, the Columbia. And it has fulfilled its promise, bringing wealth and good living to modern Astorians.

The Columbia Basin Project of the Bureau of Reclamation has brought pyramiding prosperity to a large section, at the same time enhancing the natural beauty of the area. More than 137,000 acres of water surface have been created there, where once were only sagebrush and desert. Now, besides rich crops and herds of cattle, hydroelectricity, and municipal and industrial water supplies, there are also lakes and streams for swimming, fishing, and boating—and beauty wherever one looks.

Other Federal projects in the Northwest have also contributed not only to the economy, but also to the beauty of this already beautiful land. These include the nearby Corps of Engineers' Chief Joseph Dam, by which Bureau of Reclamation development has brought into being some of the loveliest orchards in the country. And completion of the Whitestone-Coulee Unit of the Okanogan-Silmilkameen Division will provide conservation and development of fish and wildlife resources, as well as improvement of public recreation facilities. The two reservoirs on the Bureau's Okanogan Project are always heavily used by outdoorsmen for boating, fishing, and camping.

Scattered over the Northwest, as features of the Yakima, Deschutes, Crooked River, and Owyhee Reclamation projects, are dozens of reservoirs. These furnish countless hours of healthful, happy, recreation for Americans.

I think that the people of the Northwest have been especially cognizant of the recreation potentials in their natural wonderland. But here, as elsewhere, more remains to be done than has been accomplished. The snowballing demand for recreation exceeds the supply, and the gap will widen unless steps are taken immediately to develop more recreation. . . .

The Bureau of Reclamation welcomes this challenge and stands ready to develop recreation on its own projects wherever possible, and to offer cooperation and assistance to other government agencies and to individuals and private groups who join in this important aspect of building our Great Society. . . .

Source: Dominy, Floyd E. "Open Spaces for All Americans," Remarks before the Outdoor Recreation Congress for the Greater Pacific Northwest, Wenatchee, Washington, April 1, 1965. Floyd F. Dominy Papers, Collection No. 02129, American Heritage Center, University of Wyoming.

NOTES

1. Chip Ward, *Hope's Horizon: Three Visions for Healing the American Land* (Washington, D.C.: Island Press, 2004), 143.

2. Richard N. L. Andrews, *Managing the Environment, Managing Ourselves: A History of American Environmental Policy* (New Haven, Conn.: Yale University Press, 1999), 166.

DOCUMENT
8.4

President Johnson Praises the Highway Beautification Act of 1965

"This Bill Will Bring the Wonders of Nature Back into Our Daily Lives"

October 22, 1965

As the environmental movement gained strength and momentum in the 1960s, it cast a critical eye on a wide array of perceived social ills and ecological problems. Besides obvious targets such as air and water pollution, environmentalists mounted public relations and legislative campaigns against littering and other "blights" on natural scenery. One of the most high profile of these campaigns focused on highway billboards, which were sprouting along high-traffic thoroughfares throughout the country.

This cause was taken up with particular vigor by Lady Bird Johnson, the wife of President Lyndon B. Johnson. The First Lady believed that billboards and junkyards were ruining the scenic value of America's roadways, and she became an outspoken advocate for highway "beautification," which she saw as related to many other quality-of-life issues of the 1960s. "Getting on the subject of beautification is like picking up a tangled skein of wool," wrote Johnson in her diary in January 1965. "All the threads are interwoven— recreation and pollution and mental health, and the crime rate, and rapid transit, and highway beautification, and the war on poverty, and parks—national, state, and local. It is hard to hitch the conversation into one straight line, because everything leads to something else."[1]

Johnson's husband willingly took up her cause, but proposals to ban most highway billboards triggered a fierce lobbying response from the Outdoor Advertising Association of America and its powerful membership. The final law came after months of political wrangling, and it contained significant compromises with business interests. To the First Lady's relief, the final bill forbade billboards from encroaching on the federal interstate system except in clearly defined commercial zones. But the bill also allowed for continued billboard advertising on a wide range of other urban, suburban, and rural roadways, and it provided "just compensation" to businesses that lost billboard space under the law.

Following are excerpts from President Lyndon B. Johnson's remarks on signing the Highway Beautification Act on October 22, 1965. He characterized the legislation as a triumph for "lovers of beauty" but also vaguely acknowledged that it was an imperfect bill. Those imperfections have become more evident over the years. Today, many environmental advocates and urban reformers regard the Highway Beautification Act as a failure—and a cautionary example of how lobbyists and their legislative allies can reduce the impact of regulatory legislation. According to Scenic America, a national organization with a self-described mission to fight roadway blight, more than 450,000 billboards girded America's highways in 2008—100,000 more than existed in 1965.

. . . America likes to think of itself as a strong and stalwart and expanding Nation. It identifies itself gladly with the products of its own hands. We frequently point with pride and with confidence to the products of our great free enterprise system—management and labor.

These are and these should be a source of pride to every American. They are certainly the source of American strength. They are truly the fountainhead of American wealth. They are actually a part of America's soul.

But there is more to America than raw industrial might. And when you go through what I have gone through the last two weeks you constantly think of things like that. You no longer get your computers in and try to count your riches.

There is a part of America which was here long before we arrived, and will be here, if we preserve it, long after we depart: the forests and the flowers, the open prairies and the slope of the hills, the tall mountains, the granite, the limestone, the caliche, the unmarked trails, the winding little streams—well, this is the America that no amount of science or skill can ever recreate or actually ever duplicate. . . .

Well, in recent years I think America has sadly neglected this part of America's national heritage. We have placed a wall of civilization between us and between the beauty of our land and of our countryside. In our eagerness to expand and to improve, we have relegated nature to a weekend role, and we have banished it from our daily lives.

Well, I think that we are a poorer Nation because of it, and it is something I am not proud of. And it is something I am going to do something about. Because as long as I am your President, by choice of your people, I do not choose to preside over the destiny of this country and to hide from view what God has gladly given it.

And that is why today there is a great deal of real joy within me, and within my family, as we meet here in this historic East Room to sign the Highway Beautification Act of 1965.

Now, this bill does more than control advertising and junkyards along the billions of dollars of highways that the people have built with their money—public money, not private money. It does more than give us the tools just to landscape some of those highways.

This bill will bring the wonders of nature back into our daily lives.

This bill will enrich our spirits and restore a small measure of our national greatness.

As I rode the George Washington Memorial Parkway back to the White House only yesterday afternoon, I saw nature at its purest. And I thought of the honor roll of names—a good many of you are sitting here in the front row today—that made this possible. And as I thought of you who had helped and stood up against private greed for public good,

I looked at those dogwoods that had turned red, and the maple trees that were scarlet and gold. In a pattern of brown and yellow, God's finery was at its finest. And not one single foot of it was marred by a single, unsightly, man-made construction or obstruction—no advertising signs, no old, dilapidated trucks, no junkyards. Well, doctors could prescribe no better medicine for me, and that is what I said to my surgeon as we drove along.

This bill does not represent everything that we wanted. It does not represent what we need. It does not represent what the national interest requires. But it is a first step, and there will be other steps. For though we must crawl before we walk, we are going to walk.

I remember the fierce resolve of a man that I admired greatly, a great leader of a great people, Franklin D. Roosevelt. He fought a pitched battle in 1936 with private interests whose target was private gain. And I shall long remember the words that I believe he echoed at Madison Square Garden, when he declared to the Nation that the forces of selfishness had not only met their match, but these forces had met their master.

Well, I have not asked you to come here today to tell you that I have a desire to master anyone. But until the clock strikes the last hour of the time allotted to me as President by vote of all the people of this country, I will never turn away from the duty that my office demands or the vigilance that my oath of office requires.

And this administration has no desire to punish or to penalize any private industry, or any private company, or any group, or any organization of complex associations in this Nation. But we are not going to allow them to intrude their own specialized private objective on the larger public trust. Beauty belongs to all the people. And so long as I am President, what has been divinely given to nature will not be taken recklessly away by man. . . .

Source: Johnson, Lyndon B. "Remarks at the Signing of the Highway Beautification Act of 1965." *Public Papers of the Presidents of the United States: Lyndon B. Johnson, 1965.* Volume II. Washington, D.C.: Government Printing Office, 1966, pp. 1072–1075. Available at The American Presidency Project, www.presidency.ucsb.edu/ws/print.php?pid=27325.

NOTE

1. Quoted in "Lady Bird Johnson: The First Lady's Beautification Campaign," in *Lady Bird: The Biography of First Lady Lady Bird Johnson,* PBS, 2001, www.pbs.org/ladybird/shattereddreams/shattereddreams_report.html.

DOCUMENT
8.5

President Johnson Signs Four Major Conservation Bills in One Day

"An Unspoiled River Is a Very Rare Thing in This Nation Today"

October 2, 1968

One of the most symbolic events in the history of the American environmental movement took place on October 2, 1968. On this date, President Lyndon B. Johnson presided over a momentous signing ceremony at the White House in which four major conservation acts became law. Each of these acts—the Wild and Scenic Rivers Act, the National Trails System Act, an act establishing Redwood National Park in California, and an act establishing North Cascades National Park and Ross Lake and Lake Chelan National Recreation Areas in Washington State—were significant in their own right. But by passing them into law together, the Johnson Administration underscored its recognition that a new era of conservation and environmental protection in America was truly at hand.

The following is a transcript of Johnson's remarks at the signing ceremony. He refers to several people who played roles in the passage of the various bills, including Chief Justice Earl Warren, Secretary of the Interior Stewart L. Udall, Secretary of Agriculture Orville Freeman, Senator Mike Mansfield (D-Mont.), Senator Thomas Kuchel (R-Calif.), Senator Clinton P. Anderson (D-N.M.), Representative John P. Saylor (R-Pa.), Representative Wayne N. Aspinall (D-Colo.), Representative Roy A. Taylor (D-N.C.), Senator Henry M. Jackson (D-Wash.), Senator Alan Bible (D-Nev.), and Melville Bell Grosvenor (editor in chief of National Geographic *magazine).*

Most of Johnson's remarks, however, are concerned with explaining why the nation should embrace the new laws. And in this regard, Johnson not only describes the merits of each of the individual bills, but also rebukes earlier generations of Americans for their careless environmental stewardship. Most notably, the president implicitly frames the Wild and Scenic Rivers Act as a long-overdue corrective to the pro-development guiding philosophy of the Bureau of Reclamation and U.S. Army Corps of Engineers, which had spent the previous half-century "harnessing" free-flowing rivers through dam building and other water projects. Certainly, the Wild and Scenic Rivers System created by that act has been of enduring popularity; as of 2008, the system protected more than 11,000 miles of 166 rivers in 38 states and Puerto Rico.

Mr. Chief Justice, Secretary Udall, Senator Mansfield, Senator Kuchel, Senator Anderson, Congressman Saylor, distinguished Members of Congress, ladies and gentlemen:

This is the fourth time this week that we have met here in the White House to further the cause of conservation.

I believe that all of us who have served in the Government, and particularly in the Congress, during this decade of the sixties will always be proud of this great treasure that together we have conserved.

There are now 24 million acres in our National Park System. Out of 24 million acres, 2,400,000 acres—or at least 10 percent of the total acreage that the Nation has—has been put into that park system since 1961. That compares with fewer than 30,000 acres that were acquired in the entire previous decade.

The 1960's, therefore, have been truly an era of conservation in this country. But no achievement of these past 8 years can surpass what we are about to achieve this afternoon. I speak of saving the great redwoods of California.

Half a century ago, a great conservationist said, "The forests of America, however slighted by man, must have been a great delight to God, for they were the best that He ever planted."

In the past 50 years, we have learned—all too slowly, I think—to prize and to protect God's precious gifts. Because we have, our own children and grandchildren will come to know and come to love the great forests and the wild rivers that we have protected and left to them.

I believe this act establishing the Redwood National Park in California will stand for all time as a monument to the wisdom of our generation. It will surely be remembered, I think, as one of the great conservation achievements of the 90th Congress.

It is a great victory for every American in every State, because we have rescued a magnificent and a meaningful treasure from the chain saw. For once we have spared what is enduring and ennobling from the hungry and hasty and selfish act of destruction.

The redwoods will stand because the men and women of vision and courage made their stand—refusing to suffer any further exploitation of our national wealth, any greater damage to our environment, or any larger debasement of that quality and beauty without which life itself is quite barren.

Yes, the redwoods will stand. So long as they do, they will give delight. They will give instruction of God's work as well as nature's miracles. They will declare for all to hear, when other great conservation battles are being fought: "We stand because a nation found its greatest profit in preserving for its heritage its greatest resource, and that is the beauty and the splendor of its land."

The Redwood National Park will contain some 58,000 acres. Its boundaries will surround three State parks. With the approval of the California Legislature, these may some day become part of this great National Park System.

So today we are also approving an act of Congress that sets aside another 1,200,000 acres for parks and recreation in the State of Washington. The North Cascades National Park and its adjoining acres in what have been called the "American Alps" [are] next door to the Pacific Northwest's most populous communities.

We are preserving for the pleasure of these people one of the most beautiful regions on God's earth. I also have before me the first Federal legislation providing a national system of both urban and rural trails.

The simplest pleasures—and healthful exercise—of walking in an outdoor setting have been almost impossible for the millions of Americans who live in the cities. And where natural areas exist within the cities, they are usually not connected by walkways. In many cities, there are simply just no footpaths that lead out of the city into the countryside.

Our history of wise management of America's national forests has assisted us in designating the initial elements of the National Trails System. Two National Scenic Trails, one in the East and one in the West, are being set aside as the first components of the Trails System: the Appalachian Trail and the Pacific Crest Trail. The legislation also calls for study of 14 additional routes for possible inclusion in the Trails System.

A few summers ago, after Secretary Udall took his lovely family on a float trip of high adventure down the turbulent Colorado River, he returned to Washington and said that every individual and every family should get to know at least one river.

So today we are initiating a new national policy which will enable more Americans to get to know more rivers. I have been informed as recently as this morning that I am going to have the rather novel experience of getting to know the Pedernales a good deal better after January. I played on it as a child. I roamed it as a college student and I visited it frequently as President. But my wife has some more specific plans for me to go back and walk it with her—both sides, I think.

I am signing an act today which preserves sections of selected rivers that possess outstanding conservation values. An unspoiled river is a very rare thing in this Nation today. Their flow and vitality have been harnessed by dams and too often they have been turned into open sewers by communities and by industries. It makes us all very fearful that all rivers will go this way unless somebody acts now to try to balance our river development.

So we are establishing a National Wild and Scenic Rivers System which will complement our river development with a policy to preserve sections of selected rivers in their free-flowing conditions and to protect their water quality and other vital conservation values.

The National Wild and Scenic Rivers System Act will give immediate protection to portions of eight rivers and a ribbon of land along each river bank. Five of the eight wild and scenic rivers are located in the National Forest System. Our opportunity to designate these scenic streams depends in large measure on the bold efforts of Secretary Freeman and his Forest Service in preserving their very special qualities. The act further names 27 rivers as potential additions to the Wild and Scenic Rivers System sometime in the future.

I wish we could find the time—or, if we need to—the courage, to tell our American people more about some of these things than what they are having to listen to.

So, today I want to pay a very special tribute to the leaders in Congress who have made some of these things possible—these men who were all fearless and who were skilled and forceful and whose vitality has given us these magnificent options for conservation. I want to thank Congressman Aspinall, Congressman Saylor, Congressman Taylor, Senator Jackson, and Senator Anderson. This must be a proud day for our beloved friend Senator Kuchel and Senator Bible, who is not with us.

Above all, I want to pay my very special thanks to our beloved Chief Justice who stands for all that is good in this country, and to Mr. Grosvenor of the National Geographic, who has given me inspiration when I needed it most and has given me courage when I thought I needed some more.

Finally, to Mrs. Johnson, who has been an ardent, enthusiastic, pertinacious advocate—long before she ever dreamed that she would be in this house, but every minute that she has been in it—for the complete cause of conservation.

I hope that I may be able to visit some of the locations that you all have helped us to preserve for the American people.

To the business people, to the labor people, to all of you, we say thank you. We are very grateful. The American people should say to you, "Well done." This is really a monument to you, Secretary Udall. Our children will remember your great adventures and pioneering.

Now it gives me great pleasure to approve these bills which I think will add still more to the scenic wealth of our country which I think is going to mean so much to my little grandson and all the others like him who will live in a beautiful America during their lives.

Thank you.

Source: Johnson, Lyndon B. "Remarks upon Signing Four Bills Relating to Conservation and Outdoor Recreation." *Public Papers of the Presidents of the United States: Lyndon B. Johnson, 1968–1969.* Washington, D.C.: Government Printing Office, 1969.

DOCUMENT
8.6

The National Environmental Policy Act

"To Create and Maintain Conditions under Which Man and Nature Can Exist in Productive Harmony"

January 1, 1970

Of all the environmental legislation that became law in the 1960s and 1970s, few bills would have as great and enduring an impact on American politics and policymaking as the National Environmental Policy Act (NEPA) of 1969. This act, which was actually signed into law by President Richard M. Nixon on January 1, 1970, established the White House Council on Environmental Quality. It also explicitly mandated that all federal agencies and departments "monitor, evaluate, and control" their activities to protect and enhance the nation's environmental assets. In addition, it required federal agencies to incorporate NEPA standards of assessment into all of these decision-making processes. Finally, NEPA granted private citizens and organizations much greater legal standing than ever before to 1) influence the crafting of environmental policy and 2) challenge developmental projects on environmental grounds.

The impact of these NEPA provisions was immediately felt on projects such as the proposed Trans-Alaska Pipeline System (TAPS). Construction of the pipeline was blocked for two years in the early 1970s by lawsuits from environmental groups charging that TAPS violated the National Environmental Policy Act because it did not include NEPA-mandated studies of the environmental impacts of the proposed pipeline and alternative ways of getting the oil to market. "Every citizen, no matter where he or she lived, had the legal right under NEPA to demand a valid environmental impact statement on any project under federal jurisdiction," explained one account of the lawsuit. "[Friends of the Earth Director] David Brower didn't have to own land in Alaska, or live in Alaska, or ever go to Alaska, to demand a legally adequate environment analysis of the pipeline project."[1]

Construction of the Trans-Alaska Pipeline eventually went forward after the Interior Department produced and released the necessary EIS documents, and TAPS was completed in 1977. But the debate over the wisdom and necessity of NAPA's "environmental impact statement," or EIS, intensified in subsequent years. Business interests excoriated the EIS as an onerous example of regulatory overkill. Environmental organizations and other citizens' groups, meanwhile, strongly defended the ecological and societal value of environmental impact statements. And they have applauded the many states who passed their own equivalent of NEPA following the passage of the federal law. But environmental groups have frequently accused state and federal agencies of indifferent fulfillment of EIS requirements and other regulations contained in these laws. In the first two decades after NEPA's passage, in fact, environmental groups and other complainants filed more than 2,000 lawsuits against federal agencies for flawed execution of environmental impact studies and other NEPA requirements. Many of these lawsuits forced alteration—or even blocked in their entirety—projects that would have had an adverse impact on the environment.

Following are excerpts from the National Environmental Policy Act, which remains a major point of contention between environmental advocates and business interests in the twenty-first century.

An Act to Establish a National Policy for the Environment, to Provide for the Establishment of a Council on Environmental Quality, and for Other Purposes, 1969

Be it enacted by the Senate and House of Representatives of the United States of America in Congress assembled. That this Act may be cited as the "National Environmental Policy Act of 1969."

SEC. 2. The purposes of this Act are: To declare a national policy which will encourage productive and enjoyable harmony between man and his environment; to promote efforts which will prevent or eliminate damage to the environment and biosphere and stimulate the health and welfare of man; to enrich the understanding of the ecological systems and natural resources important to the Nation; and to establish a Council on Environmental Quality.

Title I

Declaration of National Environmental Policy

SEC. 101. (a) The Congress, recognizing the profound impact of man's activity on the interrelations of all components of the natural environment, particularly the profound influences of population growth, high-density urbanization, industrial expansion, resource exploitation, and new and expanding technological advances and recognizing further the critical importance of restoring and maintaining environmental quality to the overall welfare and development of man, declares that it is the continuing policy of the Federal Government, in cooperation with State and local governments, and other concerned public and private organizations, to use all practicable means and measures, including financial and technical assistance, in a manner calculated to foster and promote the general welfare, to create and maintain conditions under which man and nature can exist in productive harmony, and fulfill the social, economic, and other requirements of present and future generations of Americans.

(b) In order to carry out the policy set forth in this Act, it is the continuing responsibility of the Federal Government to use all practicable means, consistent with other essential considerations of national policy, to improve and coordinate Federal plans, functions, programs, and resources to the end that the Nation may—

(1) fulfill the responsibilities of each generation as trustee of the environment for succeeding generations;

(2) assure for all Americans safe, healthful, productive, and esthetically and culturally pleasing surroundings;

(3) attain the widest range of beneficial uses of the environment without degradation, risk to health or safety, or other undesirable and unintended consequences;

(4) preserve important historic, cultural, and natural aspects of our national heritage, and maintain, wherever possible, an environment which supports diversity and variety of individual choice;

(5) achieve a balance between population and resource use which will permit high standards of living and a wide sharing of life's amenities; and

(6) enhance the quality of renewable resources and approach the maximum attainable recycling of depletable resources.

(c) The Congress recognizes that each person should enjoy a healthful environment and that each person has a responsibility to contribute to the preservation and enhancement of the environment.

SEC. 102. The Congress authorizes and directs that, to the fullest extent possible:

(1) the policies, regulations, and public laws of the United States shall be interpreted and administered in accordance with the policies set forth in this Act, and

(2) all agencies of the Federal Government shall—

(A) utilize a systematic, interdisciplinary approach which will insure the integrated use of the natural and social sciences and the environmental design arts in planning and in decisionmaking which may have an impact on man's environment;

(B) identify and develop methods and procedures, in consultation with the Council on Environmental Quality established by Section 202 of this Act, which will insure that presently unquantified environmental amenities and values may be given appropriate consideration in decisionmaking along with economic and technical considerations;

(C) include in every recommendation or report on proposals for legislation and other major Federal actions significantly affecting the quality of the human environment, a detailed statement by the responsible official on—

(i) the environmental impact of the proposed action,

(ii) any adverse environmental effects which cannot be avoided should the proposal be implemented,

(iii) alternatives to the proposed action,

(iv) the relationship between local short-term uses of man's environment and the maintenance and enhancement of long-term productivity, and,

(v) any irreversible and irretrievable commitments of resources which would be involved in the proposed action should it be implemented.

Prior to making any detailed statement, the responsible Federal official shall consult with and obtain the comments of any Federal agency which has jurisdiction by law or special expertise with respect to any environmental impact involved. Copies of such statement and the comments and views of the appropriate Federal, State, and local agencies, which are authorized to develop and enforce environmental standards, shall be made available to the President, the Council on Environmental Quality and to the public... and shall accompany the proposal through the existing agency review process;

(Remainder of section 102(D) omitted)

(E) study, develop, and describe appropriate alternatives to recommended courses of action in any proposal which involves unresolved conflicts concerning alternative uses of available resources;

(F) recognize the worldwide and long-range character of environmental problems and, where consistent with the foreign policy of the United States, lend appropriate support to initiatives, resolutions, and programs designed to maximize international cooperation in anticipating and preventing a decline in the quality of mankind's world environment;

(G) makes available to States, counties, municipalities, institutions, and individuals, advice and information useful in restoring, maintaining, and enhancing the quality of the environment;

(H) initiate and utilize ecological information in the planning and development of resource-oriented projects;

(Remainder of paragraph omitted)

SEC. 103. All agencies of the Federal Government shall review their present statutory authority, administrative regulations, and current policies and procedures for the purpose of determining whether there are any deficiencies or inconsistencies therein which prohibit full compliance with the purpose and provisions of this Act and shall propose to the President not later than July 1, 1971, such measures as may be necessary to bring their authority and policies into conformity with the intent, purposes, and procedures set forth in this Act.

SEC. 104. Nothing in Section 102 or 103 shall in any way affect the specific statutory obligations of any Federal agency (1) to comply with criteria or standards of environmental quality, (2) to coordinate or consult with any other Federal or State agency, or (3) to act, or refrain from acting contingent upon the recommendations or certification of any other Federal or State agency.

SEC. 105. The policies and goals set forth in this Act are supplementary to those set forth in existing authorizations of Federal agencies.

Title II

Council On Environmental Quality

SEC. 201. The President shall transmit to the Congress annually beginning July 1, 1970, an Environmental Quality Report (hereinafter referred to as the "report") which shall set forth (1) the status and condition of the major natural, manmade, or altered environmental classes of the Nation, including, but not limited to, the air, the aquatic, including marine, estuarine, and fresh water, and the terrestrial environment, including, but not limited to, the forest, dryland, wetland, range, urban, suburban, and rural environment; (2) current and foreseeable trends in the quality, management and utilization of such environments and the effects of those trends on the social, economic, and other requirements of the Nation; (3) the adequacy of available natural resources for fulfilling human and economic requirements of the Nation in the light of expected population pressures; (4) a review of the programs and activities (including regulatory activities) of the Federal Government, the State and local governments, and nongovernmental entities or individuals, with particular reference to their effect on the environment and on the conservation, development and utilization of natural resources; and (5) a program for remedying the deficiencies of existing programs and activities, together with recommendations for legislation.

SEC. 202. There is created in the Executive Office of the President a Council on Environmental Quality (hereinafter referred to as the "Council"). The Council shall be composed of three members who shall be appointed by the President to serve at his pleasure, by and with the advice and consent of the Senate. The President shall designate one of the members of the Council to serve as Chairman. Each member shall be a person who, as a result of his training, experience, and attainments, is exceptionally well qualified to analyze and interpret environmental trends and information of all kinds; to appraise programs and activities of the Federal Government in the light of the policy set forth in title I of this Act; to be conscious of and responsive to the scientific, economic, social, esthetic, and cultural needs and interests of the Nation; and to formulate and recommend national policies to promote the improvement of the quality of the environment. . . .

SEC. 204. It shall be the duty and function of the Council—

(1) to assist and advise the President in the preparation of the Environmental Quality Report required by section 201;

(2) to gather timely and authoritative information concerning the conditions and trends in the quality of the environment both current and prospective, to analyze and interpret such information for the purpose of determining whether such conditions and trends are interfering, or are likely to interfere, with the achievement of the policy set forth in title I of this Act, and to compile and submit to the President studies relating to such conditions and trends;

(3) to review and appraise the various programs and activities of the Federal Government in the light of the policy set forth in title I of this Act for the purpose of determining the extent to which such programs and activities are contributing to the achievement of such policy, and to make recommendations to the President with respect thereto;

(4) to develop and recommend to the President national policies to foster and promote the improvement of environmental quality to meet the conservation, social, economic, health, and other requirements and goals of the Nation;

(5) to conduct investigations, studies, surveys, research, and analyses relating to ecological systems and environmental quality;

(6) to document and define changes in the natural environment, including the plant and animal systems, and to accumulate necessary data and other information for a continuing analysis of these changes or trends and an interpretation of their underlying causes;

(7) to report at least once each year to the President on the state and condition of the environment; and;

(8) to make and furnish such studies, reports thereon, and recommendations with respect to matters of policy and legislation as the President may request. . . .

Source: National Environmental Policy Act of 1969. www.nps.gov/history/local-law/fhpl_ntlenvirn polcy.pdf.

NOTE

1. Marc Mowrey and Tim Redmond, *Not in Our Backyard: The People and Events that Shaped America's Modern Environmental Movement* (New York: William Morrow, 1993), 54.

DOCUMENT
8.7

Senator Gaylord Nelson Inaugurates Earth Day

"Our Goal Is a New American Ethic"

April 22, 1970

On April 22, 1970, an estimated 20 million Americans participated in rallies, protests, teach-ins, and other events for "Earth Day," a public demonstration of ecological concern that was the brainchild of Democratic senator Gaylord Nelson of Wisconsin. "I was satisfied that if we could tap into the environmental concerns of the general public and infuse the student anti-war energy into the environmental cause, we could generate a demonstration that would force this issue onto the political agenda," recalled Nelson. "It was a big gamble, but worth a try."1

Nelson's Earth Day event—which is still celebrated in American schoolrooms and communities every April 22—changed the complexion of the environmental movement. Earth Day united traditional conservation groups and newer anti-pollution advocates under a single "environmental movement" banner for the first time. "When the children of the sixties tentatively pulled the two strands of old-style wilderness conservation and populist polluting fighting together on April 22, 1970, they created what is now considered the contemporary environmental movement," wrote one environmental historian. "Both the environmental agenda and its constituency had broadened."2

Indeed, Earth Day fundamentally altered the political calculus undergirding environmental policy–making. In the weeks leading up to April 22, 1970, congressional offices were deluged with reports of new rallies and events that were being organized in their districts or states for Earth Day. Members of Congress knew that public anxiety about pollution and wilderness protection was on the rise, but these reports made it clear that the environment had arrived as a priority issue for American voters. When droves of lawmakers responded by scheduling appearances at Earth Day events, Congress went into recess. Governors in Maryland, New Jersey, Ohio, and other states, meanwhile, used the symbolic occasion to sign environmental legislation. And after Earth Day was over, senators and representatives returned to Washington with clear marching orders from their constituents: Protect our land, air, and water. Earth Day, it was widely recognized, had become "the most visible manifestation of a groundswell of feeling that was already propelling far-reaching legislation through Congress,"3 including the Clean Air and Clean Water Acts.

As unofficial master of ceremonies for Earth Day, Nelson spent April 20 through 24 crisscrossing the country to speak at various rallies and give interviews with local and national media. The following excerpt is from a speech he delivered at an Earth Day rally in Denver, Colorado, on April 22, 1970. In his remarks, Nelson explicitly places environmentalism within the framework of wider social reforms.

I congratulate you, who by your presence here today demonstrate your concern and commitment to an issue that is more than just a matter of survival. *How* we survive is the critical question.

Earth Day is dramatic evidence of a broad new national concern that cuts across generations and ideologies. It may be symbolic of a new communication between young and old about our values and priorities.

Take advantage of this broad new agreement. Don't drop out of it. Pull together a new national coalition whose objective is to put Gross National Quality on a par with Gross National Product.

Campaign nationwide to elect an "Ecology Congress" as the 92nd Congress—a Congress that will build bridges between our citizens and between man and nature's systems, instead of building more highways and dams and new weapons systems that escalate the arms race.

Earth Day can—and it must—lend a new urgency and a new support to solving the problems that still threaten to tear the fabric of this society . . . the problems of race, of war, of poverty, of modern-day institutions.

Ecology is a big science, a big concept—not a copout. It is concerned with the total eco-system—not just with how we dispose of our tin cans, bottles, and sewage.

Environment is all of America and its problems. It is rats in the ghetto. It is a hungry child in a land of affluence. It is housing that is not worthy of the name; neighborhoods not fit to inhabit.

Environment is a problem perpetuated by the expenditure of tens of billions of dollars a year on the Vietnam War, instead of on our decaying, crowded, congested, polluted urban areas that are inhuman traps for millions of people.

If our cities don't work, America won't work. And the battle to save them and end the divisiveness that still splits this country won't be won in Vietnam.

Winning the environmental war is a whole lot tougher challenge by far than winning any other war in the history of Man. It will take $20 to $25 billion more a year in Federal money than we are spending or asking for now.

Our goal is not just an environment of clean air and water and scenic beauty. The objective is an environment of decency, quality, and mutual respect for all other human beings and all other living creatures.

Our goal is a new American ethic that sets new standards for progress, emphasizing human dignity and well being rather than an endless parade of technology that produces more gadgets, more waste, more pollution.

Are we able to meet the challenge? Yes. We have the technology and the resources. Are we willing? That is the unanswered question.

Establishing quality on a par with quantity is going to require new national policies that quite frankly will interfere with what many have considered their right to use and abuse the air, the water, the land, just because that is what we have always done. . . .

Source: Nelson, Gaylord. Earth Day Speech in Denver, Colorado, April 22, 1970. From "Speeches and Other Documents on Earth Day, 1970," Wisconsin Historical Society Digital Collection, http://content .wisconsinhistory.org/cdm4/document.php?CISOROOT=/tp&CISOPTR=29697&CISOSHOW=29642.

NOTES

1. Gaylord Nelson, *Beyond Earth Day: Fulfilling the Promise* (Madison: University of Wisconsin Press, 2002), 7.
2. Susan Zakin, *Earth First! And the Environmental Movement* (New York: Viking Penguin, 1993), 36.
3. Ibid., 37.

President Nixon Submits a Plan for Creating an Environmental Protection Agency

DOCUMENT
8.8

"A Profound Commitment to the Rescue of Our Natural Environment"

July 9, 1970

As the environment rose in prominence on America's political agenda, the Nixon Administration responded with a plan to create a new federal department to oversee environmental protection and pollution control efforts across the country. This agency—the Environmental Protection Agency (EPA)—would be grafted together out of various existing federal departments, offices, and programs, most notably the Federal Water Quality Administration from the Department of Interior and the National Air Pollution Control Administration of the Public Health Service. Reporting directly to the president, it would absorb environmental responsibilities that had previously been scattered throughout the federal government.

Rather than seek legislative authority from Congress for the new Environmental Protection Agency, however, President Nixon decided to submit the proposal as an executive branch reorganization plan. By taking this approach, the EPA could begin operations in sixty days barring a formal objection from Congress. The Nixon White House submitted Reorganization Plan No. 3 (which also laid the groundwork for the establishment of the National Oceanic and Atmospheric Administration, or NOAA) on July 9, 1970. This plan, excerpted here, lays out the rationale for the creation of a new regulatory agency dedicated to environmental protection. Congress was amenable to the idea of the EPA, and in September subcommittees from both houses signaled their approval of the plan. The reorganization was ratified by Congress a few months later, and on December 2, 1970, the Environmental Protection Agency came into existence, with William D. Ruckelshaus at the helm.

Special Message from the President to the Congress about Reorganization Plans to Establish the Environmental Protection Agency and the National Oceanic and Atmospheric Administration

To the Congress of the United States:

As concern with the condition of our physical environment has intensified, it has become increasingly clear that we need to know more about the total environment—land, water, and air. It also has become increasingly clear that only by reorganizing our Federal efforts can we develop that knowledge, and effectively ensure the protection, development and enhancement of the total environment itself.

The Government's environmentally-related activities have grown up piecemeal over the years. The time has come to organize them rationally and systematically. As a major step in this direction, I am transmitting today two reorganization plans: one to establish an Environmental Protection Agency, and one to establish, with the Department of Commerce, a National Oceanic and Atmospheric Administration.

Environmental Protection Agency (EPA)

Our national government today is not structured to make a coordinated attack on the pollutants which debase the air we breathe, the water we drink, and the land that grows our food. Indeed, the present governmental structure for dealing with environmental pollution often defies effective and concerted action.

Despite its complexity, for pollution control purposes the environment must be perceived as a single, interrelated system. Present assignments of departmental responsibilities do not reflect this interrelatedness.

Many agency missions, for example, are designed primarily along media lines—air, water, and land. Yet the sources of air, water, and land pollution are interrelated and often interchangeable. A single source may pollute the air with smoke and chemicals, the land with solid wastes, and a river or lake with chemical and other wastes. Control of the air pollution may produce more solid wastes, which then pollute the land or water. Control of the water-polluting effluent may convert it into solid wastes, which must be disposed of on land.

Similarly, some pollutants—chemicals, radiation, pesticides—appear in all media. Successful control of them at present requires the coordinated efforts of a variety of separate agencies and departments. The results are not always successful.

A far more effective approach to pollution control would:

Identify pollutants.

Trace them through the entire ecological chain, observing and recording changes in form as they occur.

Determine the total exposure of man and his environment.

Examine interactions among forms of pollution.

Identify where in the ecological chain interdiction would be most appropriate.

In organizational terms, this requires pulling together into one agency a variety of research, monitoring, standard-setting and enforcement activities now scattered through several departments and agencies. It also requires that the new agency include sufficient support elements—in research and in aids to State and local anti-pollution programs, for example—to give it the needed strength and potential for carrying out its mission. The new agency would also, of course, draw upon the results of research conducted by other agencies.

Components of the EPA

Under the terms of Reorganization Plan N0.3, the following would be moved to the new Environmental Protection Agency:

The functions carried out by the Federal Water Quality Administration (from the Department of the Interior).

Functions with respect to pesticides studies now vested in the Department of the Interior.

The functions carried out by the National Air Pollution Control Administration (from the Department of Health, Education, and Welfare).

The functions carried out by the Bureau of Solid Waste Management and the Bureau of Water Hygiene, and portions of the functions carried out by the Bureau of Radiological Health of the Environmental Control Administration (from the Department of Health, Education, and Welfare).

Certain functions with respect to pesticides carried out by the Food and Drug Administration (from the Department of Health, Education, and Welfare).

Authority to perform studies relating to ecological systems now vested in the Council on Environmental Quality.

Certain functions respecting radiation criteria and standards now vested in the Atomic Energy Commission and the Federal Radiation Council.

Functions respecting pesticides registration and related activities now carried out by the Agricultural Research Service (from the Department of Agriculture).

With its broad mandate, EPA would also develop competence in areas of environmental protection that have not previously been given enough attention, such, for example, as the problem of noise, and it would provide an organization to which new programs in these areas could be added. . . .

Advantages of Reorganization

This reorganization would permit response to environmental problems in a manner beyond the previous capability of our pollution control programs. The EPA would have the capacity to do research on important pollutants irrespective of the media in which they appear, and on the impact of these pollutants on the total environment. Both by itself and together with other agencies, the EPA would monitor the condition of the environment—biological as well as physical. With these data, the EPA would be able to establish quantitative "environmental baselines"—critical if we are to measure adequately the success or failure of our pollution abatement efforts.

As no disjointed array of separate programs can, the EPA would be able—in concert with the States—to set and enforce standards for air and water quality and for individual pollutants. This consolidation of pollution control authorities would help assure that we do not create new environmental problems in the process of controlling existing ones. Industries seeking to minimize the adverse impact of their activities on the environment would be assured of consistent standards covering the full range of their waste disposal problems. As the States develop and expand their own pollution control programs, they would be able to look to one agency to support their efforts with financial and technical assistance and training.

In proposing that the Environmental Protection Agency be set up as a separate new agency, I am making an exception to one of my own principles: that, as a matter of effective and orderly administration, additional new independent agencies normally should not be created. In this case, however, the arguments against placing environmental protection activities under the jurisdiction of one or another of the existing departments and agencies are compelling.

In the first place, almost every part of government is concerned with the environment in some way, and affects it in some way. Yet each department also has its own primary mission—such as resource development, transportation, health, defense, urban growth or agriculture—which necessarily affects its own view of environmental questions.

In the second place, if the critical standard-setting functions were centralized within any one existing department, it would require that department constantly to make decisions affecting other departments—in which, whether fairly or unfairly, its own objectivity as an impartial arbiter could be called into question.

Because environmental protection cuts across so many jurisdictions, and because arresting environmental deterioration is of great importance to the quality of life in our country and the world, I believe that in this case a strong, independent agency is needed. That agency would, of course, work closely with and draw upon the expertise and assistance of other agencies having experience in the environmental area.

Roles and Functions of the EPA

The principal roles and functions of the EPA would include:

The establishment and enforcement of environmental protection standards consistent with national environmental goals.

The conduct of research on the adverse effects of pollution and on methods and equipment for controlling it, the gathering of information on pollution, and the use of this information in strengthening environmental protection programs and recommending policy changes.

Assisting others, through grants, technical assistance and other means in arresting pollution of the environment.

Assisting the Council on Environmental Quality in developing and recommending to the President new policies for the protection of the environment.

One natural question concerns the relationship between the EPA and the Council on Environmental Quality, recently established by Act of Congress.

It is my intention and expectation that the two will work in close harmony, reinforcing each other's mission. Essentially, the council is a top-level advisory group (which might be compared with the Council of Economic Advisers), while the EPA would be an operating, "line" organization. The Council will continue to be a part of the Executive Office of the President and will perform its overall coordinating and advisory roles with respect to all Federal programs related to environmental quality.

The Council, then, is concerned with all aspects of environmental quality—wildlife preservation, parklands, land use, and population growth, as well as pollution. The EPA would be charged with protecting the environment by abating pollution. In short, the Council focuses on what our broad policies in the environmental field should be; the EPA would focus on setting and enforcing pollution control standards. The two are not competing, but complementary—and taken together, they should give us, for the first time, the means to mount an effectively coordinated campaign against environmental degradation in all of its many forms. . . .

Ultimately, our objective should be to insure that the nation's environmental and resource protection activities are so organized as to maximize both the effective coordination of all and the effective functioning of each.

The Congress, the Administration and the public all share a profound commitment to the rescue of our natural environment, and the preservation of the Earth as a place both habitable by and hospitable to man. With its acceptance of the reorganization plans, the Congress will help us fulfill that commitment.

Source: Nixon, Richard M. "Special Message to Congress transmitting Reorganization Plan No. 3 of 1970," July, 9, 1970. *Public Papers of the Presidents of the United States: Richard Nixon, 1970.* Washington, D.C.: Government Printing Office, 1971, pp. 578–586.

DOCUMENT 8.9 · A Congressman Remembers the Battle for the Clean Air Act of 1970

"It Was Necessary to Get the Attention of Industry and the American People"

January/February 1990

In 1970 a pitched battle was waged in Washington over the Clean Air Act Amendments of 1970. One of the most important advocates of this legislation in the House of Representatives was Paul G. Rogers, a conservative Democrat from Florida. During his twenty-four years (1955–1979) in Congress, Rogers compiled a deeply conservative record in the areas of economics, civil rights, and foreign policy. But he often voted with more liberal members on health and environmental issues. In fact, he acquired the sobriquet

"Mr. Health" in recognition of his deep and abiding interest in advancing federal health care and environmental legislation.

Because of his position as chairman of the House Subcommittee on Health and the Environment, Rogers was a key supporter of the Clean Air Act Amendments of 1970. He guided the bill skillfully past legislative hurdles and repeatedly spoke out on its behalf during deliberations, declaring that "we know what can be done, and we should do it."[1] Twenty years after the Clean Air Act of 1970 became law, Rogers recalled the political factors that contributed to that bill's passage—and gave advice to a new generation of lawmakers grappling with the issue of air pollution.

Historians of the environmental movement are likely to peg Earth Day 1970 as a key turning point in the American public's consciousness about environmental problems. I believe that Congress' enactment of the 1970 amendments to the Clean Air Act a few months later was an equally significant landmark. For the 1970 amendments moved environmental protection concerns to a prominent position on Capitol Hill, where they by and large have remained ever since. . . .

The juxtaposition of Earth Day and the 1970 amendments was no accident. As a representative body, Congress was responding to the heightened public concern about the environmental pollution that was symbolized by the Earth Day demonstrations. Some have said that Congress reacted to public pressure too quickly and rushed through clean-air legislation that was not up to the task of responding to real air-pollution concerns. I disagree.

While the 1970 amendments may have been the first time that pollution-control efforts obtained such a high profile in Congress, they were not Congress' first effort to address air pollution problems. On the contrary, we drafted those amendments to correct previous pollution control strategies that had failed. With the passage of the 1970 amendments, Congress adopted new approaches to regulation such as national air quality standards and statutory deadlines for compliance that are commonplace today, but represented a significant turning point in 1970.

To put the 1970 amendments in proper context, one needs to look back at Congress' prior efforts to control air pollution, particularly the Air Quality Act of 1967. That statute authorized the Secretary of Health, Education, and Welfare (who then had chief responsibility for federal environmental protection programs) to designate so-called air quality regions throughout the country; the states were given primary responsibility for adopting and enforcing pollution control standards within those regions.

Some of us involved in the enactment of the 1967 statute had significant doubts as to the viability of the regional approach to air pollution control; after all, air contamination does not stop at neatly defined regional boundaries. Nevertheless, Congress as a whole and American industry were not yet convinced of the need for a national strategy for pollution control; therefore, as a first step, the 1967 statute's regional approach became the law of the land.

The approach was a notable failure. By 1970, fewer than three dozen air quality regions had been designated, as compared to an anticipated number in excess of 100. Moreover, not a single state had developed a full pollution control program.

This unsatisfactory record, coupled with the public pressures created by the Earth Day movement, provided the necessary impetus to convince Congress that national air quality standards were the only practical way to rectify the United States' air pollution problems. Similarly, the record of inaction under the 1967 law led Congress to impose statutory deadlines for compliance with the emissions standards authorized under the 1970 statute, in the hope that those deadlines would spur action.

Thus, the two key provisions in the 1970 act were not a frenzied reaction to public pressure, but instead were a deliberate response aimed at correcting the demonstrated failures of previous regulatory efforts.

Of course, no one would argue that the 1970 statute achieved all of its objectives; the deadlines were extended, and for the most part, the national standards were not attained. Yet I believe that history, on balance, should judge the 1970 amendments as a major and positive turning point in the national environmental protection effort. The 1977 Clean Air Act amendments confirm this judgment.

For just as important as its deadlines and innovative nationwide standard-setting approach was the 1970 statute's underlying purpose: to raise the consciousness of the American public and American business regarding the importance of pollution control. In enacting the 1970 statute, Congress knew that a central element in any successful approach to air pollution control (and, indeed, environmental protection generally) would have to be a change in attitude about the value of environmental protection.

During the House floor debate on the amendments, one of my colleagues quoted a small town mayor, who (in expressing the previous conventional wisdom that environmental protection and economic growth were not compatible) is reported to have said: "If you want this town to grow, it has got to stink." Before 1970, there were still many persons and companies throughout the United States who agreed with the mayor that pollution was the inevitable price of progress. In the 1970 amendments, however, Congress signaled its firm belief that economic growth and a clean environment are not mutually exclusive goals.

In order to change these previously entrenched attitudes, it was necessary to get the attention of industry and the American people. By taking the then-bold step of making air pollution control a national responsibility, with strict deadlines for compliance, Congress accomplished that purpose in the 1970 statute. Even though the deadlines originally imposed in the 1970 amendments ultimately were not met, the amendments unquestionably succeeded in fostering a profound attitude shift in this country.

A consensus has emerged from the experiences gleaned under the 1970 amendments that environmental protection and economic growth can, and must, be accomplished hand-in-hand. Indeed, I suspect that if the mayor quoted by my colleague were to seek election today, he or she would be soundly rejected at the polls. This attitudinal change in American society is itself a significant achievement for which the 1970 Clean Air Act amendments deserve a share of the credit.

But a positive change in attitude and assumptions about environmental protection does not in itself clean up dirty air. Congress is still struggling with the difficult question of how to achieve that goal. Thus it is fair to ask what lessons the 1970 amendments might hold for Congress as it sets about revising the Clean Air Act once again. I believe several lessons may be drawn.

Strike while the iron is hot. While the 1970 amendments gradually evolved to correct previous statutory initiatives that had failed, their actual enactment by the full Congress was accomplished with unaccustomed speed. This was made possible because of the high priority assigned to environmental issues on the public agenda following Earth Day.

Today's political climate is similar. Rising public concerns over well-reported environmental problems such as acid rain, global warming, and fouled beaches, coupled with the high profile that environmental issues took in the 1988 presidential elections, provide this Congress with one of the most promising opportunities for legislative initiatives on clean air in recent years. Since this positive combination of events is likely to have a somewhat limited life span, Congress should seize the opportunity—as it did in 1970—and act now to revise the statute.

Avoid artificial limits on pollution control efforts. Just as the 1970 amendments demonstrated Congress' acknowledgment that air pollution could not be effectively addressed on a regional level, the current effort to amend the statute should take into account the increasing emphasis on the international nature of air pollution problems. The recent Montreal Protocol on reducing use of chlorofluorocarbons and our ongoing dialogue with Canada regarding acid rain are but two examples of the growing recognition that air pollution does not stop at state or regional boundaries; it crosses national boundaries as well.

Just as in 1970 Congress took the ground-breaking step of making air pollution control a national effort, Congress today should not hesitate to lay the groundwork for international approaches to environmental issues.

Take advantage of improved knowledge. Striking developments since the 1970 amendments have been the explosion of knowledge about the nature of air pollution, and the advanced new technologies available to control that pollution. The study of pollution and the design of pollution control techniques were in their infancies in 1970. Congress did not have the benefit of the wealth of additional knowledge at society's disposal today. This expanded knowledge base should permit Congress to adopt compliance deadlines that are better pegged to technical feasibility than in 1970.

Follow through with oversight and enforcement. One of the reasons the 1967 Air Quality Act failed and thus spurred Congress to enact a tough national air quality program in 1970 was the almost complete lack of enforcement of the earlier statute. A similar fate befell the 1970 amendments and has continued to plague implementation of the Clean Air Act ever since (although the enforcement activity has increased somewhat in recent years).

Congress, of course, can only pass laws; it is up to the Executive Branch to enforce them. It is imperative that Congress follow through on the upcoming amendments to the Clean Air Act with a stringent oversight role. It will be critical to keep the pressure on in order to see to it that those who are covered by the statute obey it—or pay the requisite penalties for violations.

Overall, the concepts set forth in the 1970 Clean Air Act amendments and revised and strengthened in the 1977 amendments are still valid. A national approach to air pollution control remains the only practical way to respond to this problem. Indeed, as I mentioned earlier, the real question today is not so much whether more efforts should be ceded to more localized governments, but the extent to which international cooperation is needed to fight air pollution.

Similarly, the use of statutory deadlines to force compliance with air quality standards is, if anything, more appropriate today, given our greater information base and technological capabilities upon which to base such deadlines. What is needed is not so much a change in approach from the framework of the 1970 amendments, but a reinvigorated commitment on the part of government, industry, and the population at large to meet the new compliance deadlines that are likely to be part of the Clean Air Act expected to pass later this year.

As our environmental problems accumulate, and as our concerns about air pollution grow broader and more complex, we cannot afford to let the current opportunity to amend the Clean Air Act go by without success. The 1970 Clean Air Act amendments were a watershed that paved the way for the widespread consensus in our country today that air pollution control must be a top priority of the federal government. Those of us who had a hand in drafting the 1970 amendments therefore can take satisfaction because that legislation has had a positive impact on our nation's environmental protection efforts. It is now up to our successors to build on that foundation and make further progress in improving air quality in the United States.

Source: Rogers, Paul G. "The Clean Air Act of 1970." *EPA Journal,* January/February 1990. www.epa .gov/history/topics/caa70/11.htm.

NOTE

1. Dennis Hevesi, "Paul G. Rogers, 'Mr. Health' in Congress, is Dead at 87," *New York Times,* October 15, 2008.

DOCUMENT 8.10

Senators Baker and Muskie Attack Nixon's Veto of the Clean Water Act

"If We Cannot Swim in Our Lakes and Rivers . . . What Other Comforts Can Life Offer Us?"

October 17, 1972

During the early 1970s Washington once again took up the politically explosive issue of water pollution. Both the Senate and House of Representatives crafted new Clean Water Act proposals that attracted broad bipartisan support, but the Nixon White House strongly objected to the bills. Citing assessments from the Council on Environmental Quality, Environmental Protection Agency, and Office of Management and Budget, the Nixon Administration argued that some provisions in the bills, such as federal grants for municipal water treatment facilities and imposition of federal emissions standards, would "precipitate marginal plant closures, increase unemployment, promote an unfavorable balance of trade, drive consumer prices and taxes higher, and drain funds away from other vital public services."[1]

Nixon himself utilized the bully pulpit in an effort to sidetrack the legislation—or at least convince Congress to water down some of its more objectionable provisions. "It is vitally important that more attention be given to the cost factor," he told the Detroit Economic Club in 1971. "We are committed to cleaning up the air and water. But we are also committed to a strong economy, and we are not going to allow the environmental issue to be used sometimes falsely and sometimes in a demagogic way basically to destroy the system—the industrial system that made this the great country that it is."[2]

Nixon's warnings of impending calamity came to naught, however. In November 1971 the Senate approved its water pollution bill (S. 2770) by a 72-0 vote. A few months later, the House approved H.R. 11896, their version of the bill, by a 380-14 vote. A joint

House–Senate conference was established to hammer out a compromise bill. It convened nearly forty times during the summer and early fall of 1972 before finishing its work. The resulting bill—the Clean Water Act of 1972, also known as the Federal Water Pollution Control Amendments of 1972—was whisked back to Congress. The Senate approved the legislation by a 74-0 vote and the House followed suit with a 366-11 margin.

Nixon fulfilled his vow to veto the measure. "Legislation which would continue our efforts to raise water quality, but which would do so through extreme and needless overspending, does not serve the public interest," he asserted in his veto remarks. "For this reason, I am compelled to withhold my approval from S. 2770, the Federal Water Pollution Control Act Amendments of 1972—a bill whose laudable intent is outweighed by its unconscionable $24 billion price tag."³

Wary of the political fallout of vetoing an environmental measure that enjoyed broad public support, Nixon had initially hoped to derail the bill through a "pocket veto"—a maneuver whereby the president can kill legislation by not taking action on it during a period of congressional adjournment. But congressional leaders eliminated this option by sending the bill to Nixon in early October, early enough to keep Nixon from running out the clock on the bill (presidents have only ten days to act on a bill when Congress is in session, or it automatically becomes law). Nixon finally vetoed the bill on October 17, the last day before the House was scheduled to adjourn for the year. But Congress stayed in session and scheduled override votes. The following are excerpts from the pre-vote statements of Senator Edward Muskie (D-Maine) and Senator Howard Baker (R-Tenn.), who had played pivotal roles in crafting the legislation. Both men challenged Nixon's assertions about the economic impact of the bill's water pollution control measures, framed the legislation as essential to the nation's future vitality, and urged their colleagues to override the president's veto.

The sentiments expressed by Baker and Muskie proved widespread in Congress, which overrode Nixon's veto by overwhelming margins—52-12 in the Senate and 247-23 in the House. The Federal Water Pollution Control Amendments of 1972 were thus enacted on October 18, 1972.

STATEMENT BY SENATOR BAKER

Mr. President [the Vice President, who also serves as president of the Senate], I am deeply disappointed that President Nixon has chosen to veto the Federal Water Pollution Control Act Amendments of 1972. I hope that my colleagues will vote to override the President's veto.

I am as eager as anyone to see Federal spending held to responsible limits. I am as eager as anyone to see a tax increase avoided. Nonetheless, the Congress has gone out of its way to make it clear to the President that the funds authorized by the water pollution bill did not have to be spent in their entirety. If the President received legal advice to the contrary, I believe that such legal advice was misguided.

There are many, many Federal programs that are wasteful, and many American tax dollars are idly spent on programs that do no produce commensurate results. But that is not true of the Federal pollution effort. I have spent more time, as an individual Senator, on environmental legislation than on any other field of endeavor since coming to the Congress in 1967.

I believe that the Federal Water Pollution Control Act Amendments of 1972 is far and away the most significant and promising piece of environmental legislation ever enacted by the Congress.

The goal of the legislation is to eliminate the discharge of pollutants into the waters of the United States by 1985. Of course such an ambitious program will cost money—public money and private money. The bill vetoed by the President strikes a fair and reasonable balance between financial investment and environmental quality. Study after study, public opinion poll after public opinion poll have revealed that the economy of this Nation can absorb the costs of cleaning up pollution without inflation or without a loss in economic productivity. As I have talked with thousands of Tennesseans, I have found that the kind of natural environment we bequeath to our children and grandchildren is of paramount importance. If we cannot swim in our lakes and rivers, if we cannot breathe the air God has given us, what other comforts can life offer us?

I have not yet read the veto message of the President. I both hope and expect that the President's veto is not based on any lack of commitment to the quality of the human environment but, rather, solely on fiscal grounds. I believe that this Administration has an excellent record in protecting the environment. William D. Ruckelshaus, the Administrator of the Environmental Protection Agency, is among the finest appointments made by President Nixon, and I cannot imagine a more dedicated champion of the public interest. The President's Council on Environmental Quality has the potential of becoming a major force for progressive environmental improvement.

> *Those who say that raising the amounts of money called for in this legislation may require higher taxes, or that spending this much money may contribute to inflation, simply do not understand the language of this crisis.*
>
> —Edward Muskie

Mr. President, the Federal Water Pollution Control Act Amendments of 1972 have twice been approved unanimously by the Senate. They are genuinely a bipartisan product. I am proud to have worked with members of both parties in the evolution of this legislation. I hope that the vote to override the President's veto will, again, be both bipartisan and unanimous. . . .

EXCERPT FROM SENATOR MUSKIE'S REMARKS

Mr. President, I am at a loss to explain the President's veto of the Federal Water Pollution Control Act Amendments of 1972.

To accept the argument that the regulatory and enforcement provisions of the bill are too strict presumes that the President has not meant what he has said in the past.

To accept the argument that the money authorizations of the bill are inflationary implies that the President thinks that we cannot afford to support life on this planet.

And I find it difficult, Mr. President, to put into words my reaction to the veto. To call the President's decision "dangerous" falls short of adequately describing the risk it asks us to take with our rivers, lakes, and streams.

To call the President's decision "false economy" does not describe in strong enough terms either the President's bad judgment or the effect of his mistake.

The House of Representatives approved this legislation by a vote of 366 to 11. The Senate concurred with a unanimous vote of 74 to zero. I cannot imagine a congressional statement of public policy that could be more clear or more definite. I think that both Houses responded to a deeply felt determination on the part of our constituents to do what we must, and to pay the price for water that will support life. Now the President has told us to ignore that resolve. . . .

Since the President has told us that the price tag on this legislation is too high, let us compare the funding levels of the bill with his own administration's figures. Since the legislation requires Federal participation in all funded projects at a rate of 75 percent of the project's total cost, we should look at the difference between the $18 billion authorized in the bill for fiscal years 1973 through 1975, and 75 percent of the $14.5 billion in EPA's estimated needs for fiscal years 1972 through 1974, or approximately $11 billion; $11 billion is also the amount authorized in the bill for fiscal year 1973–74.

The difference of $7 billion between what the bill provides and what the EPA estimates indicated were required is identical to the bill's 1975 authorization, a year not anticipated by the EPA study of cost. There were added factors that forced the conferees to reach the $18 billion figure:

First. As I indicated earlier, the EPA estimate was based on existing standards and requirements. The new act will make those requirements more stringent and make meeting them more expensive.

Second. The old estimates did not take into account the statutory deadlines established by the new act. Those deadlines will accelerate the construction timetables in many jurisdictions, and thus require more money in less time.

Third. The EPA estimates did not include the costs of constructing and reconstructing collection systems and dealing with the problem of combined storm sewers. In order to meet the new requirements set forth in this act, municipalities will have to cope with these problems and will need more money to do so. The new act, therefore, makes these projects eligible for Federal construction grants.

Fourth. The EPA estimates did not anticipate wide, special use of joint municipal and industrial waste treatment; the new act encourages this course as more efficient and more economical. Even though one-half of this industrial share of the Federal grant will be repaid to the Treasury, initial capital construction costs will be higher, and the municipalities will need more money.

Thus, Mr. President, the conferees decided that $18 billion was the required level of funding for Federal grants. None of us were pleased that the price tag is that high, but none of us are prepared—as the President is—to back off from the challenge by claiming we cannot afford to pay that price.

Mr. President, the question of adequate funding for the construction of waste treatment facilities has been a source of almost constant frustration for this Senator, members of the Public Works Committee, and the Senate since the grant program was expanded in 1966. It has been frustrating because in the face of facts which could not be more stark, in the face of a threat to life that could not be more real, in the face of all these things, there are still those in high places who question whether we can afford to spend this money.

At the time the Senate approved the conference report on the bill, I asked these questions: "Can we afford clean water? Can we afford rivers and lakes and streams and oceans which continue to make life possible on this planet? Can we afford life itself?" The answers are the same. Those questions were never asked as we destroyed the waters of our Nation, and they deserve no answers as we finally move to restore and renew them. These questions answer themselves. And those who say that raising the amounts of money called for in this legislation may require higher taxes, or that spending this much money may contribute to inflation, simply do not understand the language of this crisis. . . .

If we entertain any serious hopes of preserving life on this planet, the water pollution bill will have to be paid—soon. And it is not going to get any cheaper or less inflationary as time goes by.

Conclusion

It seems to me, Mr. President, and I think most Members will agree, that we have reached a point in our struggle against water pollution where—as we say in New England—we must either "fish or cut bait." If we are serious about restoring the quality of our Nation's waters to a level that will support life in the future, then we ought to be prepared to make some sacrifices in that effort now. If we are not serious, then let us bury our heads in the sand, sustain the President's veto, and count on some unlikely providence to save us from ourselves.

This bill does not discriminate against Republicans or Democrats, industrial or municipal polluters, small businesses or conglomerates, private citizens or public officials. It simply says to everybody: We have no choice. Water pollution must stop. And here is a uniform, effective law to make sure that it does.

Let us close ranks, Mr. President, override this veto, and approve this bill one last time—so that we can take home to our constituents this week the realistic hope for a clean environment; so that we can leave to our children rivers and lakes and streams that are at least as clean as we found them, and so that we can begin to repay the debt we owe to the water that has sustained our Nation.

Source: U.S. Senate Debate on Federal Water Pollution Control Act Amendments of 1972, Veto Message. *Congressional Record—Senate,* 92nd Cong., 2d sess., October 17, 1972, Washington, D.C.: Government Printing Office, 1972, pp. 36871–36875. Available at the Muskie Archives and Special Collection Archives, Bates College, http://abacus.bates.edu/muskie-archives/ajcr/1972/CWA%20Override.shtml.

NOTES

1. Paul Charles Milazzo, *Unlikely Environmentalists: Congress and Clean Water, 1945–1972* (Lawrence: University Press of Kansas, 2006), 228.

2. Quoted in Tom Wicker, *One of Us: Richard Nixon and the American Dream* (New York: Random House, 1991), 514.

3. Richard M. Nixon, "Veto of the Federal Water Pollution Control Act Amendments of 1972," October 17, 1972, *Public Papers of the Presidents of the United States: Richard M. Nixon, 1972* (Washington, D.C.: Government Printing Office, 1973).

DOCUMENT
8.11

The Endangered Species Act

"To Provide a Program for the Conservation of . . . Endangered Species"

December 28, 1973

One of the most far-reaching laws to emerge out of the "golden age" of environmental legislation of the 1960s and 1970s was the Endangered Species Act (ESA). This law, enacted in 1973, was designed to identify and protect animal and plant species threatened by extinction. Pillars of the act included regulations that required federal agencies to make sure that their actions did not jeopardize endangered or threatened species (or the habitat on which they depended); and provisions that gave the public strong legal rights to ensure that the act's various mandates were carried out faithfully. The overall practical effect of the ESA was to elevate endangered species protection to the highest priority level in federal offices. The importance of the issue was further underscored one year later, when the United States became the first nation to ratify a major wildlife conservation treaty known as the Convention on Trade in Endangered Species of Wild Fauna and Flora (CITES).

In the years since its passage, the Endangered Species Act has become a major flashpoint of environmental debate. Supporters believe that the wildlife conservation law has saved numerous species from extinction and preserved entire ecosystems from ruin. Critics, however, assert that the ESA restrictions on land and water development projects have stifled economic growth, unnecessarily impeded job creation, and trampled on private property rights.

When the act first made its way through Congress in the halcyon days of bipartisan environmentalism, however, the Endangered Species Act was not controversial. Rather, it was hailed across much of the political spectrum for providing much-needed safeguards for vulnerable fish, wildlife, and plant species. The law enjoyed broad support from both Democrats and Republicans—it passed the Senate unanimously and received only four nay votes in the House—and President Richard M. Nixon enthusiastically signed the bill into law on December 28, 1973. "Nothing is more priceless and more worthy of preservation than the rich array of animal life with which our country has been blessed," Nixon said in his signing statement. "I congratulate the 93d Congress for taking this important step toward protecting a heritage which we hold in trust to countless future generations of our fellow citizens." Following are excerpts from this historic act.

AN ACT TO PROVIDE FOR THE CONSERVATION OF ENDANGERED AND THREATENED SPECIES OF FISH, WILDLIFE, AND PLANTS, AND FOR OTHER PURPOSES.

Be it enacted by the Senate and House of Representatives of the United States of America in Congress assembled, That this Act may be cited as the "Endangered Species Act of 1973." . . .

Findings, Purposes, and Policy

SEC. 2 (a) FINDINGS.—The Congress finds and declares that—

(1) various species of fish, wildlife, and plants in the United States have been rendered extinct as a consequence of economic growth and development, untempered by adequate concern and conservation;

(2) other species of fish, wildlife, and plants have been so depleted in numbers that they are in danger of or threatened with extinction;

(3) these species of fish, wildlife, and plants are of esthetic, ecological, educational, historical, recreational, and scientific value to the Nation and its people;

(4) the United States has pledged itself as a sovereign state in the international community to conserve to the extent practicable the various species of fish or wildlife and plants facing extinction, pursuant to—

(A) migratory bird treaties with Canada and Mexico;

(B) the Migratory and Endangered Bird Treaty with Japan;

(C) the Convention on Nature Protection and Wildlife Preservation in the Western Hemisphere;

(D) the International Convention for the Northwest Atlantic Fisheries;

(E) the International Convention for the High Seas Fisheries of the North Pacific Ocean;

(F) the Convention on International Trade in Endangered Species of Wild Fauna and Flora; and

(G) other international agreements; and

(5) encouraging the States and other interested parties, through Federal financial assistance and a system of incentives, to develop and maintain conservation programs which meet national and international standards is a key to meeting the Nation's international commitments and to better safeguarding, for the benefit of all citizens, the Nation's heritage in fish, wildlife, and plants.

(b) PURPOSES.—The purposes of this Act are to provide a means whereby the ecosystems upon which endangered species and threatened species depend may be conserved, to provide a program for the conservation of such endangered species and threatened species, and to take such steps as may be appropriate to achieve the purposes of the treaties and conventions set forth in subsection (a) of this section.

(c) POLICY.—(1) It is further declared to be the policy of Congress that all Federal departments and agencies shall seek to conserve endangered species and threatened species and shall utilize their authorities in furtherance of the purposes of this Act.

(2) It is further declared to be the policy of Congress that Federal agencies shall cooperate with State and local agencies to resolve water resource issues in concert with conservation of endangered species. . . .

Determination of Endangered Species and Threatened Species

SEC. 4. (a) GENERAL.—(1) The Secretary [of Interior, Commerce, or Agriculture, as appropriate under the Act's stipulations] shall by regulation promulgated in accordance with subsection (b) determine whether any species is an endangered species or a threatened species because of any of the following factors:

(A) the present or threatened destruction, modification, or curtailment of its habitat or range;

(B) overutilization for commercial, recreational, scientific, or educational purposes;

(C) disease or predation;

(D) the inadequacy of existing regulatory mechanisms; or

(E) other natural or manmade factors affecting its continued existence. . . .

(3) The Secretary, by regulation promulgated in accordance with subsection (b) and to the maximum extent prudent and determinable—

(A) shall, concurrently with making a determination under paragraph (1) that a species is an endangered species or a threatened species, designate any habitat of such species which is then considered to be critical habitat; and

(B) may, from time-to-time thereafter as appropriate, revise such designation.

(b) BASIS FOR DETERMINATIONS.—(1)(A) The Secretary shall make determinations required by subsection (a)(1) solely on the basis of the best scientific and commercial data available to him after conducting a review of the status of the species and after taking into account those efforts, if any, being made by any State or foreign nation, or any political subdivision of a State or foreign nation, to protect such species, whether by predator control, protection of habitat and food supply, or other conservation practices, within any area under its jurisdiction, or on the high seas. . . .

(c) LISTS.—(1) The Secretary of the Interior shall publish in the Federal Register a list of all species determined by him or the Secretary of Commerce to be endangered species and a list of all species determined by him or the Secretary of Commerce to be threatened species. Each list shall refer to the species contained therein by scientific and common name or names, if any, specify with respect to such species over what portion of its range it is endangered or threatened, and specify any critical habitat within such range. The Secretary shall from time to time revise each list published under the authority of this subsection to reflect recent determinations, designations, and revisions. . . .

(d) PROTECTIVE REGULATIONS.—Whenever any species is listed as a threatened species pursuant to subsection (c) of this section, the Secretary shall issue such regulations as he deems necessary and advisable to provide for the conservation of such species. . . .

(f)(1) RECOVERY PLANS.—The Secretary shall develop and implement plans . . . for the conservation and survival of endangered species and threatened species listed pursuant to this section, unless he finds that such a plan will not promote the conservation of the species. . . .

Source: Endangered Species Act of 1973. Available at U.S. Senate Committee on Environment and Public Works Web site, http://epw.senate.gov/esa73.pdf.

President Nixon Addresses Congress on Natural Resources and the Environment

"[A]n Opportunity for Unprecedented Progress"

February 15, 1973

The record of Republican President Richard M. Nixon and his administration on the environment has been a subject of considerable debate and speculation over the years. On the one hand, Nixon played an integral role in advancing many of America's most famous environmental policy milestones, including the passage of the National Environmental Policy Act of 1969, the 1970 creation of the Environmental Protection Agency, the enactment of the Clean Air Act of 1970, and the establishment of the Endangered Species Act in 1973. He also spoke out publicly on the need for strong environmental protections on numerous occasions. For these reasons, Nixon's environmental record has been praised by people such as Stewart Udall, who was widely regarded as an ally of the environmental movement during his eight-year tenure (1961–1969) as Interior Secretary.

Historians and members of Nixon's inner circle of White House advisors, however, frequently assert that Nixon's pro-environment initiatives stemmed from political pragmatism. In their view, Nixon pursued environmental legislation not out of sympathy for the environmental cause, but because it was politically popular—especially in the weeks and months following Earth Day—and because it distracted public attention from the unpopular Vietnam War.[1]

To be sure, Nixon had a very low opinion of the environmental groups that had descended on Washington, and he frequently lumped them in with other political enemies. In one Oval Office meeting with auto industry executives in April 1971, Nixon described environmentalists and consumer advocates as "people that aren't one really damn bit interested in safety or clean air. What they're interested in is destroying the system. They're enemies of the system."[2] *And later in his tenure, Nixon expressed profound anxiety about the new regulatory age he had helped build. "We have gone overboard on the environment," he wrote to advisor John Ehrlichman, "and are going to reap the whirlwind for our excesses."*[3] *Indeed, when public interest in environmental issues flagged somewhat in the last two years of Nixon's presidency, so too did the administration's dedication to robust environmental protection.*

Whatever the purity of Nixon's motives, the federal government's role in safeguarding the environment was undeniably strengthened and expanded under his watch. "Nixon never demonstrated that he had a deep personal commitment to the environment," acknowledged historian Charles S. Warren. "[But] he obviously heard the public outcry for stronger laws and reacted to that spur. He also surrounded himself with strong environmental leaders such as [EPA Directors] Russell Train and William Ruckelshaus, who were able to advance the cause quite significantly in those early years."[4]

The following excerpt is from one of Nixon's many environmental speeches during his presidency. In this February 15, 1973, State of the Union message to Congress devoted exclusively to "Natural Resources and the Environment," Nixon claims credit for many of the environmental laws and policies implemented over the previous few years, takes the Democrat-controlled Ninety-second Congress to task for various "failures" of environmental stewardship, and lays out a wide array of environmental priorities for the coming year.

YEARS OF PROGRESS

While I am disappointed that the 92nd Congress failed to act upon 19 of my key natural resources and environment proposals, I am pleased to have signed many of the proposals I supported into law during the past four years. They have included air quality legislation, strengthened water quality and pesticide control legislation, new authorities to control noise and ocean dumping, regulations to prevent oil and other spills in our ports and waterways, and legislation establishing major national recreation areas at America's Atlantic and Pacific gateways, New York and San Francisco.

On the organizational front, the National Environmental Policy Act of 1969 has reformed programs and decision-making processes in our Federal agencies and has given citizens a greater opportunity to contribute as decisions are made. In 1970 I appointed the first Council on Environmental Quality—a group which has provided active leadership in environmental policies. In the same year, I established the Environmental Protection Agency and the National Oceanic and Atmospheric Administration to provide more coordinated and vigorous environmental management. Our natural resource programs still need to be consolidated, however, and I will again submit legislation to the Congress to meet this need.

The results of these efforts are tangible and measurable. Day by day, our air is getting cleaner; in virtually every one of our major cities the levels of air pollution are declining. Month by month, our water pollution problems are also being conquered, our noise and pesticide problems are coming under control, our parklands and protected wilderness areas are increasing. . . .

PRINCIPLES TO GUIDE US

A record is not something to stand on; it is something to build on. And in this field of natural resources and the environment, we intend to build diligently and well.

As we strive to transform our concern into action, our efforts will be guided by five basic principles:

The first principle is that we must strike a balance so that the protection of our irreplaceable heritage becomes as important as its use. The price of economic growth need not and will not be deterioration in the quality of our lives and our surroundings.

Second, because there are no local or State boundaries to the problems of our environment, the Federal Government must play an active, positive role. We can and will set standards and exercise leadership. We are providing necessary funding support. And we will provide encouragement and incentive for others to help with the job. But Washington must not displace State and local initiative, and we shall expect the State and local governments-along with the private sector—to play the central role in making the difficult, particular decisions which lie ahead.

Third, the costs of pollution should be more fully met in the free marketplace, not in the Federal budget. For example, the price of pollution control devices for automobiles should be borne by the owner and the user and not by the general taxpayer. The costs of eliminating pollution should be reflected in the costs of goods and services.

Fourth, we must realize that each individual must take the responsibility for looking after his own home and workplace. These daily surroundings are the environment where most Americans spend most of their time. They reflect people's pride in themselves and their consideration for their communities. A person's backyard is not the domain of the Federal Government.

Finally, we must remain confident that America's technological and economic ingenuity will be equal to our environmental challenges. We will not look upon these challenges as insurmountable obstacles.

Instead, we shall convert the so-called crisis of the environment into an opportunity for unprecedented progress.

CONTROLLING POLLUTION

We have made great progress in developing the laws and institutions to clean up pollution. We now have formidable new tools to protect against air, water and noise pollution and the special problem of pesticides. But to protect ourselves fully from harmful contaminants, we must still close several gaps in governmental authority.

I was keenly disappointed when the last Congress failed to take action on many of my legislative requests related to our natural resources and environment. In the coming weeks I shall once again send these urgently needed proposals to the Congress so that the unfinished environmental business of the 92nd Congress can become the environmental achievements of the 93rd.

Among these 19 proposals are eight whose passage would give us much greater control over the sources of pollution:

—Toxic Substances. Many new chemicals can pose hazards to humans and the environment and are not well regulated. Authority is now needed to provide adequate testing standards for chemical substances and to restrict or prevent their distribution if testing confirms a hazard.

—Hazardous Wastes. Land disposal of hazardous wastes has always been widely practiced but is now becoming more prevalent because of strict air and water pollution control programs. The disposal of the extremely hazardous wastes which endanger the health of humans and other organisms is a problem requiring direct Federal regulation. For other hazardous wastes, Federal standards should be established with guidelines for State regulatory programs to carry them out.

—Safe Drinking Water. Federal action is also needed to stimulate greater State and local action to ensure high standards for our drinking water. We should establish national drinking water standards, with primary enforcement and monitoring powers retained by the State and local agencies, as well as a Federal requirement that suppliers notify their customers of the quality of their water.

—Sulfur Oxides Emissions Charge. We now have national standards to help curtail sulfur emitted into the atmosphere from combustion, refining, smelting and other processes, but sulfur oxides continue to be among our most harmful air pollutants. For that reason, I favor legislation which would allow the Federal Government to impose a special financial charge on those who produce sulfur oxide emissions. This legislation would also help to ensure that low-sulfur fuels are allocated to areas where they are most urgently needed to protect the public health.

—Sediment Control. Sediment from soil erosion and runoff continues to be a pervasive pollutant of our waters. Legislation is needed to ensure that the States make the control of sediment from new construction a vital part of their water quality programs.

—Controlling Environmental Impacts of Transportation. As we have learned in recent years, we urgently need a mass transportation system not only to relieve urban congestion but also to reduce the concentrations of pollution that are too often the result of our present methods of transportation. Thus I will continue to place high priority upon my request to permit use of the Highway Trust Fund for mass transit purposes and to help State and local governments achieve air quality, conserve energy, and meet other environmental objectives.

—United Nations Environmental Fund. Last year the United Nations adopted my proposal to establish a fund to coordinate and support international environmental programs. My 1974 budget includes a request for $10 million as our initial contribution toward the Fund's five-year goal of $100 million, and I recommend authorizing legislation for this purpose.

—Ocean Dumping Convention. Along with 91 other nations, the United States recently concluded an international convention calling for regulation of ocean dumping. I am most anxious to obtain the advice and consent of the Senate for this convention as soon as possible. Congressional action is also needed on several other international conventions and amendments to control oil pollution from ships in the oceans.

Managing the Land

As we steadily bring our pollution problems under control, more effective and sensible use of our land is rapidly emerging as among the highest of our priorities. The land is our Nation's basic natural resource, and our stewardship of this resource today will affect generations to come.

America's land once seemed inexhaustible. There was always more of it beyond the horizon. Until the twentieth century we displayed a carelessness about our land, born of our youthful innocence and desire to expand. But our land is no longer an open frontier.

Americans not only need, but also very much want to preserve diverse and beautiful landscapes, to maintain essential farm lands, to save wetlands and wildlife habitats, to keep open recreational space near crowded population centers, and to protect our shorelines and beaches. Our goal is to harmonize development with environmental quality and to add creatively to the beauty and long-term worth of land already being used.

Land use policy is a basic responsibility of State and local governments. They are closer to the problems and closer to the people. Some localities are already reforming land use regulation—a trend I hope will accelerate. But because land is a national heritage, the Federal Government must exercise leadership in land use decision processes, and I am today again proposing that we provide it. In the coming weeks, I will ask the Congress to enact a number of legislative initiatives which will help us achieve this goal:

—National Land Use Policy. Our greatest need is for comprehensive new legislation to stimulate State land use controls. We especially need a National Land Use Policy Act authorizing Federal assistance to encourage the States, in cooperation with local governments, to protect lands of critical environmental concern and to regulate the siting of key facilities such as airports, highways and major private developments. Appropriate Federal funds should be withheld from States that fail to act.

—Power Plant Siting. An open, long-range planning process is needed to help meet our power needs while also protecting the environment. We can avoid unnecessary delays with a power plant siting law which assures that electric power facilities are constructed on a timely basis, but with early and thorough review of long-range plans and specific provisions to protect the environment.

—Protection of Wetlands. Our coastal wetlands are increasingly threatened by residential and commercial development. To increase their protection, I believe we should use the Federal tax laws to discourage unwise development in wetlands.

—Historic Preservation and Rehabilitation. An important part of our national heritage are those historic structures in our urban areas which should be rehabilitated and preserved, not demolished. To help meet this goal, our tax laws should be revised to encourage rehabilitation of older buildings, and we should provide Federal insurance of loans to restore historic buildings for residential purposes.

—Management of Public Lands. Approximately one-fifth of the Nation's land is considered "public domain," and lacks the protection of an overall management policy with environmental safeguards. Legislation is required to enable the Secretary of the Interior to protect our environmental interest on those lands.

—Legacy of Parks. Under the Legacy of Parks program which I initiated in 1971, 257 separate parcels of parklands and underused Federal lands in all 50 States have been turned over to local control for park and recreational purposes. Most of these parcels are near congested urban areas, so that millions of citizens can now have easy access to parklands. I am pleased to announce today that 16 more parcels of Federal land will soon be made available under this same program. . . .

—Mining on Public Lands. Under a statute now over a century old, public lands must be transferred to private ownership at the request of any person who discovers minerals on them. We thus have no effective control over mining on these properties. Because the public lands belong to all Americans, this 1872 Mining Act should be repealed and replaced with new legislation which I shall send to the Congress.

—Mined Area Protection. Surface and underground mining can too often cause serious air and water pollution as well as unnecessary destruction of wildlife habitats and aesthetic and recreational areas. New legislation with stringent performance standards is required to regulate abuses of surface and underground mining in a manner compatible with the environment. . . .

PROTECTING OUR NATURAL HERITAGE

An important measure of our true commitment to environmental quality is our dedication to protecting the wilderness and its inhabitants. We must recognize their ecological significance and preserve them as sources of inspiration and education. And we need them as places of quiet refuge and reflection.

Important progress has been made in recent years, but still further action is needed in the Congress. Specifically, I will ask the 93rd Congress to direct its attention to the following areas of concern:

—Endangered Species. The limited scope of existing laws requires new authority to identify and protect endangered species before they are so depleted that it is too late. New legislation must also make the taking of an endangered animal a Federal offense.

—Predator Control. The widespread use of highly toxic poisons to kill coyotes and other predatory animals has spread persistent poisons to range and forest lands without adequate foresight of environmental effects. I believe Federal assistance is now required so that we can find better means of controlling predators without endangering other wildlife.

—Wilderness Areas. Historically, Americans have always looked westward to enjoy wilderness areas. Today we realize that we must also preserve the remaining areas of wilderness in the East, if the majority of our people are to have the full benefit of our natural glories. Therefore I will ask the Congress to amend the legislation that established the Wilderness Preservation System so that more of our Eastern lands can be included.

—Wild and Scenic Rivers. New legislation is also needed to continue our expansion of the national system of wild and scenic rivers. Funding authorization must be increased by $20 million to complete acquisitions in seven areas, and we must extend the moratorium on Federal licensing for water resource projects on those rivers being considered for inclusion in the system.

—Big Cypress National Fresh Water Preserve. It is our great hope that we can create a reserve of Florida's Big Cypress Swamp in order to protect the outstanding wildlife in that area, preserve the water supply of Everglades National Park and provide the Nation with an outstanding recreation area. Prompt passage of Federal legislation would allow the Interior Department to forestall private or commercial development and inflationary pressures that will build if we delay.

—Protecting Marine Fisheries. Current regulation of fisheries off U.S. coasts is inadequate to conserve and manage these resources. Legislation is needed to authorize U.S. regulation of foreign fishing off U.S. coasts to the fullest extent authorized by international agreements. In addition, domestic fishing should be regulated in the U.S. fisheries zone and in the high seas beyond that zone.

—World Heritage Trust. The United States has endorsed an international convention for a World Heritage Trust embodying our proposals to accord special recognition and protection to areas of the world which are of such unique natural, historical, or cultural value that they are a part of the heritage of all mankind. I am hopeful that this convention will be ratified early in 1973.

—Weather Modification. Our capacity to affect the weather has grown considerably in sophistication and predictability, but with this advancement has also come a new potential for endangering lives and property and causing adverse environmental effects. With additional Federal regulations, I believe that we can minimize these dangers. . . .

GOING FORWARD IN CONFIDENCE

The environmental awakening of recent years has triggered substantial progress in the fight to preserve and renew the great legacies of nature. Unfortunately, it has also triggered a certain tendency to despair. Some people have moved from complacency to the opposite extreme of alarmism, suggesting that our pollution problems were hopeless and predicting impending ecological disaster. Some have suggested that we could never reconcile environmental protection with continued economic growth.

I reject this doomsday mentality—and I hope the Congress will also reject it. I believe that we can meet our environmental challenges without turning our back on progress. What we must do is to stop the hand-wringing, roll up our sleeves and get on with the job. . . .

Source: Nixon, Richard M. "State of the Union Message to Congress on Natural Resources and the Environment," February 15, 1973. *Public Papers of the Presidents of the United States: Richard Nixon, 1973.* Washington, D.C.: Government Printing Office, 1974.

NOTES

1. Samuel Hays, *Beauty, Health, and Permanence: Environmental Politics in the United States, 1955–1985* (New York and Cambridge: Cambridge University Press, 1987), 58.

2. Quoted in Tom Wicker, *One of Us: Richard Nixon and the American Dream* (New York: Random House, 1991), 516.

3. Quoted in Stephen E. Ambrose, *Nixon, V2: The Triumph of a Politician, 1962–1972* (New York: Simon and Schuster, 1989), 460.

4. Charles S. Warren, "The Nixon Environmental Record," in *Richard M. Nixon, Politician, President, Administrator,* ed. Leon Friedman and William F. Levantrosser (Westport, Conn.: Greenwood, 1991), 194.

DOCUMENT
8.13

Federal Land Policy and Management Act

"Management . . . on the Basis of Multiple Use and Sustained Yield"

1976

For much of America's history, public lands outside of the national park, forest, or wildlife refuge systems were managed inconsistently and fitfully. In addition, the welter of outdated and conflicting land management laws and regulations that accumulated over the decades made the task of managing homesteading, grazing, timber and mineral harvesting, hunting, and other activities on these lands an extremely challenging and vexing one.

By the 1960s management responsibility for most of these public lands lay squarely with the Bureau of Land Management (BLM), an agency within the Department of the Interior that had been created by a 1946 merger of the Grazing Service and the General Land Office. But the BLM continued to suffer from fragmented authority; conflicting instructions from the executive, legislative, and judicial branches; and periodic threats from Congress to sell off most of the lands under their care into private ownership.

Washington finally took action to help the Bureau of Land Management in 1964, when Congress established a Public Land Law Review Commission to study how America's public lands should be managed. Six years later, the Commission released a report, titled One Third of the Nation's Land, *that recommended sweeping changes to the BLM's operations and mission. However, it rejected calls to sell off the federal land to private or state ownership. Instead, it recommended "retaining [land] in Federal ownership whose values must be preserved so that they may be used and enjoyed by all Americans."[1]*

For the next six years, congressional leaders labored to craft the Commission's recommendations into workable law under intense lobbying pressure from ranchers, mining companies, environmental organizations, hunting and fishing groups, and other constituencies with a vested interest in the management of the nation's public lands.

The final result of these deliberations was the Federal Land Policy and Management Act (FLPMA) of 1976, which is excerpted here. Under the terms of this legislation, Congress explicitly asserted its intention to keep public domain lands "retained in federal ownership" unless it was determined that "disposal of a particular parcel will serve the national interest." FLPMA also gave the Bureau of Land Management much-needed guidance in terms of its responsibilities. In fact, the law is sometimes called the BLM Organic Act because of its far-reaching impact. It established the general organization and administrative responsibilities of the Bureau, and it finally articulated a clear mandate for the agency—to manage the natural resources under its care on the basis of "multiple use" and "sustained yield" principles.

FLPMA marked a decisive turning point in the history of the Bureau of Land Management, which remains the custodian of more public land than any other agency in the federal government. But the law's formal declaration that BLM land would not be transferred to private or state ownership but instead remain under federal control was poorly received in many parts of the rural West. In fact, the passage of the Federal Land Policy and Management Act was a major factor in the growth of the "Sagebrush Rebellion," a regional movement that demanded the return of federal lands to individual states.

Declaration of Policy

Sec. 102. The Congress declares that it is the policy of the United States that—

1. the public lands be retained in Federal ownership, unless as a result of the land use planning procedure provided for in this Act, it is determined that disposal of a particular parcel will serve the national interest;

2. the national interest will be best realized if the public lands and their resources are periodically and systematically inventoried and their present and future use is projected through a land use planning process coordinated with other Federal and State planning efforts;

3. public lands not previously designated for any specific use and all existing classifications of public lands that were effected by executive action or statute before the date of enactment of this Act be reviewed in accordance with the provisions of this Act;

4. the Congress exercise its constitutional authority to withdraw or otherwise designate or dedicate Federal lands for specified purposes and that Congress delineate the extent to which the Executive may withdraw lands without legislative action;

5. in administering public land statutes and exercising discretionary authority granted by them, the Secretary be required to establish comprehensive rules and regulations after considering the views of the general public; and to structure adjudication procedures to assure adequate third party participation, objective administrative review of initial decisions, and expeditious decision making;

6. judicial review of public land adjudication decisions be provided by law;

7. goals and objectives be established by law as guidelines for public land use planning, and that management be on the basis of multiple use and sustained yield unless otherwise specified by law;

8. the public lands be managed in a manner that will protect the quality of scientific, scenic, historical, ecological, environmental, air and atmospheric, water resource, and archeological values; that, where appropriate, will preserve and protect certain public lands in their natural condition; that will provide food and habitat for fish and wildlife and domestic animals; and that will provide for outdoor recreation and human occupancy and use;

9. the United States receive fair market value of the use of the public lands and their resources unless otherwise provided for by statute;

10. uniform procedures for any disposal of public land, acquisition of non-Federal land for public purposes, and the exchange of such lands be established by statute, requiring each disposal, acquisition, and exchange to be consistent with the prescribed mission of the department or agency involved, and reserving to the Congress review of disposals in excess of a specified acreage;

11. regulations and plans for the protection of public land areas of critical environmental concern be promptly developed;

12. the public lands be managed in a manner which recognizes the Nation's need for domestic sources of minerals, food, timber, and fiber from the public lands including implementation of the Mining and Minerals Policy Act of 1970 as it pertains to the public lands; and

13. the Federal Government should, on a basis equitable to both the Federal and local taxpayer, provide for payments to compensate States and local governments for burdens created as a result of the immunity of Federal lands from State and local taxation.

(b) The policies of this Act shall become effective only as specific statutory authority for their implementation is enacted by this Act or by subsequent legislation and shall then be construed as supplemental to and not in derogation of the purposes for which public lands are administered under other provisions of law.

Source: The Federal Land Policy and Management Act of 1976. U.S. Department of the Interior, Bureau of Land Management, and Office of the Solicitor. Washington, D.C.: Bureau of Land Management Office of Public Affairs, 2001, pp. 1–2. www.blm.gov/flpma/FLPMA.pdf.

NOTE

1. Susan Searcy, "A Guide to the Records of the Sagebrush Rebellion Collection No. 85–04," July 20, 1999, University of Nevada, Reno Libraries, Special Collections. www.library.unr.edu/specoll/mss/85–04.html.

DOCUMENT
8.14

The Sagebrush Rebellion Bill

"Nevada Has a Legal Claim to the Public Land Retained by the Federal Government"

June 2, 1979

By the late 1970s, the Sagebrush Rebellion had become a major force in the political environment of the interior West. "Sagebrush Rebels" dotted the ranks of local and state governments throughout the Rocky Mountain region, and in 1978 the Western Regional Council of State Governments and the Western Interstate Region of the National Association of Counties joined forces to found the Western Coalition on Public Lands. This organization energetically pressed the denationalization cause in Washington and in national media outlets.

The birth of the Sagebrush Rebellion is often traced to Nevada, which had more land managed and controlled by federal authorities (87 percent of its land area) than any other state in the Union. Angered by the 1976 Federal Land Policy and Management Act and other federal policies that "locked up" public lands from grazing, oil exploration, and other purposes, Nevada state senators Richard Blakemore and Norman D. Glaser introduced a bill—Senate Bill 398—that explicitly demanded the transfer of public lands in Nevada to state control. This bill died in committee, but two years later an almost identical bill was introduced into the 1979 legislature by state assemblyman Dean Rhoads, a Republican from Elko County. Assembly Bill 413 was wildly popular, and it was approved by the Assembly with almost universal support. A state Senate version—Senate Bill 240—also passed easily. The bill, which was dubbed the Sagebrush Rebellion bill, was then signed into law by Republican governor Robert List on June 2, 1979, with an effective date of July 1, 1979.[1]

This symbolic legislative act had no practical effect on the disposition of federal land in Nevada. But as one western historian observed, AB 413 faithfully embodied the sentiments of the larger Sagebrush Rebellion, "in which Western businessmen lamented their victimization at the hands of the federal government and pleaded for the release of the public domain from its federal captivity. Ceded to the states, the land that once belonged to all the people of the United States would at last be at the disposal of those whom the Sagebrush Rebels considered to be the right people—namely, themselves."²

Following are excerpts from two documents. The first is a statement issued by Glaser in support of AB 413/SB 240 at a legislative hearing in April 1979. The second document is AB 413 as it was first introduced in the state assembly in February 1979.

Presentation on S.B. 240/A.B. 413, Senator Norman D. Glaser

April 1979

. . . I would like to offer some brief background on the public lands situation in Nevada as an introduction to the reasons for this legislation. First, there are basically two categories of federal land. The first type is federally *owned* land which includes land for federal buildings, national parks and defense establishments. The second type is federally *controlled* land. From the beginning of this nation until October 1976, the theory as to the second type of federal lands—the public domain controlled by the federal government—was that such land was to be disposed of into private ownership. This policy was formally established in 1785 with the passage of the Northwest Ordinance and continued through the Public Land Act of 1796, the Homestead Act of 1862 on through the Desert Land Entry Act and the Carey Act. Indeed, disposition of the public lands into private ownership was almost total westward to the Rockies.

From the Rockies west to the Sierras, very little land was suitable for homesteading and not much more was suitable for disposal under the laws designed for the Great Basin. The land was useful only for open grazing and was used for this until 1934 when the Taylor Grazing Act was passed. That act instituted leases and set up grazing fees. This closed the open range.

Even though the public lands area suffered badly from a lack of clear direction and clear policy up to 1976, the official policy of the federal government remained one of custodial management of the lands under a multiple use concept with disposal into private ownership whenever feasible. In fact, over the past 20 years or so, disposal of any kind has become progressively more rare.

In October 1976, Congress passed the Federal Land Policy Management Act, commonly called the BLM Organic Act. It did many things but most significantly, it said that the policy of the federal government was now to retain the public domain in federal ownership in perpetuity. Certain limited exceptions are provided but basically, the public domain is to remain under federal control, period.

The Organic Act woke a lot of people up—all across the West. Public lands, after all, are a Western phenomenon. Of all the land west of the Rockies, 63 percent is federal. It was subsequent to the passage of the Organic Act that Senator [Rick] Blakemore and I introduced S.B. 398 last session. That was much the same bill as those you have before you.

We decided in 1977 that we should first try for a political solution to the problem so we created the Select Committee on Public Lands. . . . At this point, let me say that while political solutions still offer some possibilities, we think it's time for opening another front in this battle. That brings me to the specific intent and context of these bills.

We believe that there is no constitutional basis for the perpetual retention of the public lands by the federal government. In fact, we believe the contrary to be the case. . . . The passage of one of these bills will result in the adjudication of this issue. The courts will not adjudicate the issue in the abstract and the federal government is not likely to consent to be sued. This means that we must create a situation in which the state poses a challenge to the federal government which will lead to a Supreme Court test of the right of the federal government to hold the public domain indefinitely. . . .

A frequent and entirely proper question is whether the state could manage the public domain. In the first place, the record of the Bureau of Land Management in managing the land is hardly a source of inspiration. In fact, they don't even claim to be proud of their effort. They claim things are getting better. Perhaps. . . . The state can manage the lands at least at the current level with little additional state cost. . . .

I have not attempted to provide a section by section explanation of the bills at this point. We thought that the concept needs to be considered and discussed first. After that, we can get into the specifics and the mechanics of the bill.

Admittedly, these bills are a bold and innovative approach to a problem that promises only to get worse. Those of us who've been closely involved in public lands issues feel strongly that the time is here for bold action to assert our rights as an equal state in the Union. . . .

Assembly Bill 413

February 1979

AN ACT relating to public lands; creating a board of review; providing for state control of certain lands within the state boundaries; providing penalties; making an appropriation; and providing other matters properly relating thereto.

The People of the State of Nevada, represented in Senate and Assembly, do enact as follows:

SECTION 1. Chapter 321 of NRS is hereby amended by adding thereto the provisions set forth as sections 2 to 9, inclusive, of this act.

SEC. 2. The legislature finds that:

1. The State of Nevada has a strong moral claim upon the public land retained by the Federal Government within Nevada's borders because:

(a) On October 31, 1864, the Territory of Nevada was admitted to statehood on the condition that it forever disclaim all right and title to unappropriated public land within its boundaries;

(b) From 1850 to 1894, newly admitted states received 2 sections of each township for the benefit of common schools, which in Nevada amounted to 3.9 million acres;

(c) In 1880 Nevada agreed to exchange its 3.9-million-acre school grant for 2 million acres of its own selection from public land in Nevada held by the Federal Government;

(d) At the time the exchange was deemed necessary because of an immediate need for public school revenues and because the majority of the original federal land grant for common schools remained unsurveyed and unsold;

(e) Unlike certain other states, such as New Mexico, Nevada received no land grants from the Federal Government when Nevada was a territory;

(f) Nevada received no land grants for insane asylums, schools of mines, schools for the blind and deaf and dumb, normal schools, miner's hospitals or a governor's residence as did states such as New Mexico; and

(g) Nevada thus received the least amount of land, 2,572,478 acres, and the smallest percentage of its total area, 3.9 percent, of the land grant states in the far west admitted after 1864, while states of comparable location and soil, namely Arizona, New Mexico, and Utah, received approximately 11 percent of their total area in federal land grants.

2. The State of Nevada has a legal claim to the public land retained by the Federal Government within Nevada's borders because:

(a) In the case of the State of Alabama, a renunciation of any claim to unappropriated lands similar to that contained in the ordinance adopted by the Nevada constitutional convention was held by the Supreme Court of the United States to be "void and inoperative" because it denied to Alabama "an equal footing with the original states" in *Pollard v. Hagan* (1845);

(b) the State of Texas, when admitted to the Union in 1845, retained ownership of all unappropriated land within its borders, setting a further precedent which inured to the benefit of all states admitted later "on an equal footing"; and

(c) The Northwest Ordinance of 1787, adopted into the Constitution of the United States by the reference of Article VI to prior engagements of the Confederation, first proclaimed the "equal footing" doctrine, and the treaty of Guadelupe Hidalgo, by which the territory including Nevada was acquired from Mexico and which is "the supreme law of the land" by virtue of Article VI, affirms it expressly as to the new states to be organized therein.

3. The exercise of broader control by the State of Nevada over the public lands within its borders would be of great public benefit because:

(a) Federal holdings in the State of Nevada constitute 86.7 percent of the area of the state, and in Esmeralda, Lincoln, Mineral, Nye and White Pine counties the Federal Government controls from 97 to 99 percent of the land;

(b) Federal jurisdiction over the public domain is shared among 17 federal agencies or departments which adds to problems of proper management of land and disrupts the normal relationship between a state, its residents and its property;

(c) None of the federal lands in Nevada are taxable and Federal Government activities are extensive and create a tax burden for the private property owners of Nevada who must meet the needs of children of Federal Government employees, as well as provide other public services;

(d) Under general land laws only 2.1 percent of federal lands in Nevada have moved from federal control to private ownership;

(e) Federal administration of the retained public lands, which are vital to the livestock and mining industries of the state and essential to meet the recreational and other various uses of its citizens, has been of uneven and sometimes arbitrary and capricious; and

(f) Federal administration of the retained public lands has not been consistent with the public interest of the people of Nevada because the Federal Government has used those lands for armament and nuclear testing thereby rendering many parts of the land unusable and unsuited for other uses and endangering the public health and welfare.

4. The intent of the framers of the Constitution of the United States was to guarantee to each of the states sovereignty over all matters within its boundaries except for those powers specifically granted to the United States as agent of the states.

5. The attempted imposition upon the State of Nevada by the Congress of the United States of a requirement in the enabling act that Nevada "disclaim all right and title to the unappropriated public lands lying within said territory," as a condition precedent to acceptance of Nevada into the Union, was an act beyond the power of the Congress of the United States and is thus void.

6. The purported right of ownership and control of the public lands within the State of Nevada by the United States is without foundation and violates the clear intent of the Constitution of the United States.

7. The exercise of such dominion and control of the public lands within the State of Nevada by the United States works a severe, continuous and debilitating hardship upon the people of the State of Nevada. . . .

SEC. 4. 1. The division [of state lands of the state department of conservation and natural resources] shall hold the public lands of the state in trust for the benefit of the people of the state and shall manage them in an orderly and beneficial manner consistent with the public policy declared in Section 6 of this act. . . .

SEC. 5. 1. Subject to existing rights, all public lands in Nevada and all minerals not previously appropriated are the property of the State of Nevada and subject to its jurisdiction and control. . . .

SEC. 6. The public lands of Nevada must be administered in such a manner as to conserve and preserve natural resources, wildlife habitat, wilderness areas, historical sites and artifacts, and to permit the development of compatible public uses for recreation, agriculture, ranching, mining and timber production and the development, production and transmission of energy and other public utility services under principles of multiple use which provide the greatest benefit to the people of Nevada. . . .

SEC. 10. 1. The department of conservation and natural resources shall conduct an inventory and a study of the public lands of Nevada to determine, in conjunction with the respective boards of country commissioners and the planning commissions of the several counties, the methods of management that will best satisfy the requirements of Section 6 of this act and establish a basis for determining the best uses of the land. . . .

Source: "Assembly Bill 413" and "Presentation on S.B. 240/A.B. 413, Senator Norman D. Glaser." In *Statutes of the State of Nevada Passed at the Sixtieth Session of the Legislature, 1979,* Vol. 1. Carson City, Nev.: SPO, 1980. www.leg.state.nv.us/lcb/research/library/1979/AB413,1979.pdf.

NOTES

1. Author correspondence with Susan Searcy, Archivist in the Nevada State Archives, March 2009.

2. Patricia Nelson Limerick, *The Legacy of Conquest: The Unbroken Past of the American West* (New York: W.W. Norton, 1988), 46–47.

The Convention on Long-Range Transboundary Air Pollution

"The Contracting Parties . . . Are Determined to Protect Man and His Environment against Air Pollution"

1979

During the 1960s and 1970s, scientific research brought increased global awareness of acid rain and other ecological threats stemming from transboundary air pollution. The issue of acid rain became a matter of particular concern in the United States, Canada, and Scandinavian states as evidence mounted that industrial emissions of sulfur dioxide and nitrogen oxides were destroying prized forest, lake, and river ecosystems when they returned to earth in rain, fog, snow, and gas form.

As the 1970s progressed, the United States, Canada, and other nations worked to develop policies that would reduce the emissions that lead to acid rain and fund new research programs to investigate the problem. The negotiations carried out in Geneva, Switzerland, were often arduous, but in 1979 the parties announced the Convention on Long-Range Transboundary Air Pollution. This international environmental agreement was modest in scope, but it established a framework for international cooperation, information exchange, and monitoring. It was the world's first multilateral convention in the realm of air pollution control and was hailed by supporters as a sign that a new era of international cooperation and communication on global environmental issues was at hand. This convention, excerpted here, has since been supplemented by several Protocols that lay down more specific commitments.

The Parties to the present Convention,

Determined to promote relations and cooperation in the field of environmental protection,

Aware of the significance of the activities of the United Nations Economic Commission for Europe in strengthening such relations and co-operation, particularly in the field of air pollution including long-range transport of air pollutants,

Recognizing the contribution of the Economic Commission for Europe to the multilateral implementation of the pertinent provisions of the Final Act of the Conference on Security and Co-operation in Europe,

Cognizant of the references in the chapter on environment of the Final Act of the Conference on Security and Co-operation in Europe calling for cooperation to control air pollution and its effects, including long-range transport of air pollutants, and to the development through international cooperation of an extensive programme for the monitoring and evaluation of long-range transport of air pollutants, starting with sulphur dioxide and with possible extension to other pollutants,

Considering the pertinent provisions of the Declaration of the United Nations Conference on the Human Environment, and in particular principle 21, which expresses the common conviction that States have, in accordance with the Charter of the United Nations and the principles of international law, the sovereign right to exploit their own resources pursuant to their own environmental policies, and the responsibility to ensure that activities within their jurisdiction or control do not cause damage to the environment of other States or of areas beyond the limits of national jurisdiction,

Recognizing the existence of possible adverse effects, in the short and long term, of air pollution including transboundary air pollution,

Concerned that a rise in the level of emissions of air pollutants within the region as forecast may increase such adverse effects,

Recognizing the need to study the implications of the long-range transport of air pollutants and the need to seek solutions for the problems identified,

Affirming their willingness to reinforce active international cooperation to develop appropriate national policies and by means of exchange of information, consultation, research and monitoring, to coordinate national action for combating air pollution including long-range transboundary air pollution,

Have agreed as follows:

ARTICLE 1: DEFINITIONS

For the purposes of the present Convention:

(a) *"air pollution"* means the introduction by man, directly or indirectly, of substances or energy into the air resulting in deleterious effects of such a nature as to endanger human health, harm living resources and ecosystems and material property and impair or interfere with amenities and other legitimate uses of the environment, and "air pollutants" shall be construed accordingly;

(b) *"long-range transboundary air pollution"* means air pollution whose physical origin is situated wholly or in part within the area under the national jurisdiction of one State and which has adverse effects in the area under the jurisdiction of another State at such a distance that it is not generally possible to distinguish the contribution of individual emission sources or groups of sources.

ARTICLE 2: FUNDAMENTAL PRINCIPLES

The Contracting Parties, taking due account of the facts and problems involved, are determined to protect man and his environment against air pollution and shall endeavour to limit and, as far as possible, gradually reduce and prevent air pollution including long-range transboundary air pollution.

ARTICLE 3

The Contracting Parties, within the framework of the present Convention, shall by means of exchanges of information, consultation, research and monitoring, develop without undue delay policies and strategies which shall serve as a means of combating the discharge of air pollutants, taking into account efforts already made at national and international levels.

ARTICLE 4

The Contracting Parties shall exchange information on and review their policies, scientific activities and technical measures aimed at combating, as far as possible, the discharge of air pollutants which may have adverse effects, thereby contributing to the reduction of air pollution including long-range transboundary air pollution.

ARTICLE 5

Consultations shall be held, upon request, at an early stage between, on the one hand, Contracting Parties which are actually affected by or exposed to a significant risk of long-range transboundary air pollution and, on the other hand, Contracting Parties within which and subject to whose jurisdiction a significant contribution to long-range transboundary air pollution originates, or could originate, in connection with activities carried on or contemplated therein.

ARTICLE 6: AIR QUALITY MANAGEMENT

Taking into account articles 2 to 5, the ongoing research, exchange of information and monitoring and the results thereof, the cost and effectiveness of local and other remedies and, in order to combat air pollution, in particular that originating from new or rebuilt installations, each Contracting Party undertakes to develop the best policies and strategies including air quality management systems and, as part of them, control measures compatible with balanced development, in particular by using the best available technology which is economically feasible and low- and non-waste technology.

ARTICLE 7: RESEARCH AND DEVELOPMENT

The Contracting Parties, as appropriate to their needs, shall initiate and cooperate in the conduct of research into and/or development of:

(a) Existing and proposed technologies for reducing emissions of sulphur compounds and other major air pollutants, including technical and economic feasibility, and environmental consequences;

(b) Instrumentation and other techniques for monitoring and measuring emission rates and ambient concentrations of air pollutants;

(c) Improved models for a better understanding of the transmission of long-range transboundary air pollutants;

(d) The effects of sulphur compounds and other major air pollutants on human health and the environment, including agriculture, forestry, materials, aquatic and other natural ecosystems and visibility, with a view to establishing a scientific basis for dose-effect relationships designed to protect the environment;

(e) The economic, social and environmental assessment of alternative measures for attaining environmental objectives including the reduction of long-range transboundary air pollution;

(f) Education and training programmes related to the environmental aspects of pollution by sulphur compounds and other major air pollutants. . . .

Source: 1979 Convention on Long-Range Transboundary Air Pollution. www.unece.org/env/lrtap/full%20text/1979.CLRTAP.e.pdf.

DOCUMENT
8.16

Lois Gibbs Testifies about the Government Response to Love Canal

"No Authorities or Agencies Are Willing to Take a Stand and Help Us"

March 21, 1979

In the late 1970s the American public learned that hundreds of residents of Love Canal, a community in New York State, had been exposed for years to dangerous levels of toxic chemicals buried in the area. The alarming revelations about Love Canal triggered new heights of public anxiety about America's vulnerability to industrial poisons. These concerns became even more acute after they learned about the abysmal governmental response to the public health dangers uncovered at Love Canal.

The person most responsible for exposing the deplorable environmental conditions at Love Canal—and the woeful response of environmental and public health agencies to the crisis—was Lois Gibbs, an unassuming Love Canal housewife who emerged as a forceful advocate for her community. She also became a dedicated crusader for new industrial and governmental reforms that would establish new public protections against toxic chemicals. Her efforts helped elevate the previously underreported issues of toxic contamination and hazardous waste disposal into the public policy spotlight, which in turn led to the 1980 passage of the Comprehensive Environmental Response Compensation and Liability Act (CERCLA), better known as Superfund.

The following are excerpts from testimony Gibbs gave to the U.S. House of Representatives Subcommittee on Oversight and Investigation on March 21, 1979. In her remarks, Gibbs recounts the inept response of federal and state agencies to the Love Canal crisis and makes recommendations for various policy reforms.

My name is Lois Gibbs and I am president of the Love Canal Homeowners Association (L.C.H.A.). The L.C.H.A. is a citizens group consisting of over 1,000 families representing more than 90% of the residents in the area. L.C.H.A. was formed to deal with the problem of living near the Love Canal chemical dumpsite. I became involved in this situation after discovering that toxic chemicals were buried two blocks from my home and that these chemicals could be aggravating my children's health problems, one of whom attended the 99th Street School located in the center of the dump. I started by canvassing the neighborhood to find if other residents had similar problems. I discovered that the majority of residents had what seemed to me an unusually high amount of illnesses. I then worked with residents to form an organization to identify their problems and to help them find solutions.

The L.C.H.A. was formed to voice the opinion of residents on the decisions made by State authorities which would affect our lives. We wanted to work with the Health Department in identifying problems and suggesting solutions to improve the neighborhood. This organization wanted to work with the different agencies by openly communicating and sharing information with them.

At the start I would like to say that upon learning of the situation at Love Canal, the State moved very quickly to begin health and environmental studies. They also put into effect a remedial construction plan which would attempt to reduce chemical migration from the canal.

Although there are many problems which I could discuss, I will limit my testimony to the experiences I have had dealing with the different State agencies involved at Love Canal. . . .

(1) *Problems of being a precedent*

Probably the most difficult obstacle to relieving the problems at Love Canal has been "being the first." Neither the State nor the Federal agencies who could help were responsible for the situation. And neither wanted to take financial responsibility for cleaning it up. Arguing between State and Federal authorities over who should pay for what expenses has continued since the first discovery of contamination. In fact, the remedial work for the middle section of the canal which was supposed to start in mid-March has just been postponed under mid-summer. The reasons given are that the construction contract is going from emergency status to an open-bidding process and that the EPA [Environmental Protection Agency], who was partially funding the work, refuses to review the construction plans until they know who is paying for what proportions. This is especially alarming since on Friday, March 9th, thick, black, oily leachate was found running off the north section of the canal onto the street and into the storm sewers. Remedial work on this section of the canal, which has not begun at all, must now await the decisions of the bureaucrats while residents remain in a contaminated area which is not being remedied.

(2) *Lack of objectivity of the scientific studies underway*

The State is conducting major studies to define the health problems and the chemical contamination in the area. The outcome of these studies will be the basis of any decision to relocate families because of chemical contamination resulting in health effects. Twice, it has been necessary to relocate people living in different areas around the canal. In each instance,

> [C]onfidence in this plan was greatly shaken by a statement made by a State spokesman who, when asked to comment on what he would do if toxic vapors were released through the neighborhood, replied: "I wouldn't wait for the bus, I'd run like hell."
>
> —Lois Gibbs

the State had to absorb most of the cost to buy homes or temporarily relocate these families. However, many people with health problems remain, and many questions about the extent of contamination are still being resolved. Meanwhile, the State is conducting a scientific study, the results of which may end up costing the State many millions of dollars if the results indicate further contamination. This is especially alarming since continued announcements by State officials have been made that they do not intend to relocate any more families because of the lack of a cause and effect linkage between contamination from Love Canal and health effects found in the area. The political and bureaucratic pressures to be "absolutely certain" of the results place great constraints on the objectivity of the scientists working on these studies. The very nature of the uncertainties of determining or establishing the significance of low-level contamination to many chemicals preclude obvious conclusions of cause and effect. Therefore, the Health Department, in an obvious conflict of interest, must make subjective recommendations to the politicians who will decide what must be done. I want to stress that the objectivity necessary for good science would be near impossible in these circumstances.

(3) *Lack of resources that the State and local authorities had at their disposal for handling an emergency situation of the magnitude of the Love Canal crisis*

The means and capabilities of the State and local resources were—and still are—simply not sufficient to protect the public health and welfare of the residents during such an emergency situation. In fact, the ability of a governmental body to react to public needs is limited by both the laws defining its responsibilities and the appropriations limiting its ability to function. For example, it was necessary to pass special legislation to give the Commissioner of Health authority and financing to investigate the problems and determine actions to solve them. $500,000 was provided but it has been estimated that total costs will be at least $22 million. The following comments provide examples of necessary actions taken by the State which are very much out of the ordinary:

1. Thousands of blood samples were taken from residents within a matter of a few weeks. The Department of Health does not as a general matter perform laboratory tests on people except for communicable diseases or reference work.

2. The large scale environmental sampling which was undertaken is not a matter of normal operating conditions especially testing for soil and sump contamination. The identification of unknown chemicals complicate this limitation even more. When dioxin, one of the most toxic chemicals known, was found in the canal, the State was not able to determine with any degree of certainty just what areas are contaminated with dioxin. This is because of the expense and difficulty in measuring this chemical.

3. Very little is known about low level contamination of many chemicals. The Health Department made its best estimate of what the levels found in the homes may suggest. However, the best minds in the country should have been called in to evaluate what these levels of contamination mean.

4. A large scale epidemiological effort was implemented to describe the nature of the health problems of the residents. This has only been duplicated in similar major disasters and is not part of the prior experience of the Health Department.

Although the State reacted to the circumstances as best they could, they were not able to provide the kinds of assistance needed in an emergency situation to protect the health of its residents.

(5) *The lack of a single scientific director in charge of coordinating and organizing the epidemiological and environmental studies*

Because of the nature of the problems at Love Canal, it was necessary to bring together different professionals to determine how best to solve the problems. Appropriate State professionals were placed in charge of the individual studies; however, a scientific director was not selected to oversee the entire program. Such a director would ensure that similar goals were followed and that each study group received the advantage of the efforts of the other groups.

A political appointee is presently in charge. This is not surprising, since the State selected people from within their different departments. This has created a great many uncertainties as to who is in charge of what studies, who is doing what work, and who is responsible for planning and follow-up. This has made our communication with the State especially difficult. The major problem that resulted was that no coordinated plan of action which could systematically define the problems and then select the best available solutions, was established. I certainly understand the constraints of urgency the authorities were under, but this offers little comfort.

(6) Insensitivity of State authorities

In the situation where people are exposed to a threat, the magnitude of which no one understands, there are going to be many anxious moments. The residents have been very scared and emotional. And at the first, the Health Department was unsure of how great a problem they were facing. Because they had never dealt with such an emergency crisis before, they had no easy method through which to communicate with the residents. Because of the fear of panic, the State did not know how far to involve the residents in the decisions and findings that were made. And officials often did not inspire confidence in the residents, which made matters worse. For example, prior to starting the remedial construction work on the south portion of the canal, I received a draft safety plan for the construction. Although it included precautions for the workers, no considerations were provided to protect residents from possible dangers as a result of the construction. I was told at the time that "a good on-site plan was a good off-site plan." Many of the chemicals in the canal were unknown as was the boundary of the canal. As a result, it was unclear if during construction the workers would disrupt the barrels of chemicals. These uncertainties frightened the residents and we demanded a safety plan and an on-site monitor to help provide protection for the residents in the event of an accident. What resulted was a meeting held by the Office of Disaster Preparedness during which a "total" safety plan was prepared and later presented to the residents at a public meeting. However, the confidence in this plan was greatly shaken by a statement made by a State spokesman who, when asked to comment on what he would do if toxic vapors were released through the neighborhood, replied: "I wouldn't wait for the bus, I'd run like hell."

Another problem was the flow of information to the residents. A lot of data and information was given to residents without any explanation of what the data meant. Air values of chemicals found in each home were given to the resident without any interpretation of what the values represented. A need to understand the significance of these values was a major concern of the people. Many residents were also given results of blood tests and liver function tests without any idea of the meaning of the results. In some instances, residents were asked to go for repeated tests without any explanation of why. With so many people afraid that their health was at risk, it would have greatly alleviated the fear of the unknown to have someone accessible to the residents who could answer their many questions. All that was really available was a "hot-line" to Albany.

There were also many instances where neither the residents nor our representatives were invited to meetings held by State officials during which decisions that were affecting the future of the residents were being decided. We were often told that we were not "professionals" and that we would disrupt the ability of people to speak freely. These closed-door meetings fostered mistrust, confusion, and gossip about the concern of the Health Department for the residents. These feelings were further perpetuated when information on the health and environmental studies was held back from the homeowners and our representatives. This situation has improved; although the homeowners association does not receive any routine communications from the State regarding the status of ongoing health and environmental studies. In fact, the only communications that I receive are to announce public meetings or in direct response to a memo or request that I have made. This general insensitivity has greatly polarized the homeowners from the State. It is unfortunate that this situation has developed because it could have been mostly avoided by better communication and the involvement of people who have had some experience working with people during difficult times. . . .

I have tried to limit my comments because the stories could go on forever as even today is part of still another story. I will now finish my testimony by making several suggestions and recommendations. First of all it is apparent that a means for responding to environmental incidents such as Love Canal must be provided by the Federal government. A group analogous to the infectious disease response unit of the Center for Disease Control should be set up to respond to environmental emergencies that require immediate action and special expertise. Specialists in the effects of chemicals on skin disease, kidney disorders, urinary infections, and so on could be alerted and called in as needed. This did not happen at Love Canal. We are the first but we are not likely to be the last. Something must be done.

Such an agency would provide an agency responsible to pick up the costs of the studies needed and possibly for the remedial construction. It would also provide a mechanism for ensuring that a State agency with limited resources would not be faced with the difficult task of responding to such an emergency. It would also ensure that an "outside" group of experts, who would not be involved in the situation and who would have no real or vested interest in any outcome of the studies, would be involved. This outside group could thus conduct an objective scientific study of existing health problems.

If necessary a special "Blue Ribbon Panel" of experts could be collected and asked to further review the data. However, the identity of such an advisory group should be publicly announced and its findings and recommendations made available immediately if urgency is required. At Love Canal such a Blue Ribbon Panel has been involved but its members and recommendations have been kept secret. If urgency is not needed, then interim reports should be available, as should minutes of the meetings. In either case, sufficient time should be provided for such a committee to properly complete its task.

We have made many requests for such an outside group to come to Love Canal and review the existing data or even conduct a new study which would include a control population. No Federal agency has responded to our requests claiming they have no authority to do so.

Finally, I would like to say that we have faced many problems at Love Canal, some of which have been solved. Yet many others remain. I hope the Congressman [sic] and women who are here today have grasped a sense of the awfulness of our situation. Not only has our neighborhood become a test site for scientists, but no authorities or agencies are willing to take a stand and help us. I ask that you do what you can for us and do what you *must* to prevent what has happened at Love Canal from ever happening again.

Source: Gibbs, Lois. Testimony Presented to the House Sub-committee on Oversight and Investigation, U.S. Congress. House. 96th Cong., 1st sess., March 21, 1979. Available at *Love Canal Online Documents,* State University of New York at Buffalo Web site, http://library.buffalo.edu/specialcollections/lovecanal/documents/pdfs/gibbs.pdf.

President Carter Signs the Alaska National Interest Lands Conservation Act

DOCUMENT
8.17

"We Are Setting Aside for Conservation an Area . . . Larger than the State of California"

December 2, 1980

When the Alaska National Interest Lands Conservation Act (ANILCA) was signed into law by President Jimmy Carter on December 2, 1980, public reaction was strikingly divided. The great majority of Americans welcomed this unprecedented expansion of the nation's wilderness system, interpreting it as a tangible manifestation of the country's respect and appreciation for its natural heritage. Wilderness conservation and environmental organizations—many of which had played important roles in cajoling and pressuring Congress into making the act a reality—also hailed the measure. After all, the ANILCA extended wilderness protection to more than 55 million acres of Alaskan wildlands, including 32 million acres in eight new and existing national park units, 18 million acres in thirteen new and existing national wildlife refuges, and 5 million acres in fourteen national forest areas. In addition, it established twenty-five new wild and scenic rivers and extended conservation restrictions to another 50 million acres of lakes, forests, meadows, and mountains across the state. All told, more than 107 million acres of Alaskan wilderness were affected by the act. The scope of ANILCA—and the majesty of the lands it protected—led environmental historian Roderick Nash to describe it as "the greatest single instance of wilderness preservation in world history."[1]

ANILCA was not universally praised, however. Industry and business groups across the country, and most of Alaska's elected officials, decried the act as a federal "land grab" that unfairly limited their access to valuable oil, timber, and mineral resources. Many Alaskan citizens also condemned the conservation measure as an outrageous violation of state and individual sovereignty. And on the other side of the political divide, some environmental advocates expressed disappointment with the bill, asserting that eleventh-hour legislative concessions to pro-development interests robbed it of some of its full potential.

Despite these criticisms, however, ANILCA continues to rank as one of the pivotal moments in the history of American wilderness preservation. And Carter has repeatedly pointed to his signing of the Alaska National Interest Lands Conservation Act as one of the proudest moments of his presidency. Following are excerpts from Carter's signing remarks on December 2, 1980.

This is indeed a proud day for me and for the Congress and for all of you who've worked so hard to help create and enact this legislation. To Mo Udall, to John Seiberling, to Senator Jackson, to Phil Burton, Paul Tsongas—who can't be here today because of the death of his father—Alan Cranston, Ted Stevens, to the Alaska coalition, not to be confused with the entire Alaska delegation—[laughter] both of which deserve credit for the passage of the legislation, and for Secretary Andrus and others, I am deeply grateful.

For nearly a quarter of a century, really, since even before 1958 [when Alaska achieved statehood], thousands of dedicated Americans have worked for this historic moment. The bill before me now, the Alaska National Interest Lands Conservation Act, without a doubt is one of the most important pieces of conservation legislation ever passed in this Nation. I was going over this morning early the comparison between what this bill is and the original administration proposal that we submitted to the Congress, and they are remarkably similar. Never before have we seized the opportunity to preserve so much of America's natural and cultural heritage on so grand a scale.

We are setting aside for conservation an area of land larger than the State of California. By designating more than 97 million acres for new parks and refuges, we are doubling the size of our National Park and Wildlife Refuge System. By protecting 25 free-flowing Alaskan rivers in their natural state, we are almost doubling the size of our Wild and Scenic Rivers System. By classifying 56 million acres of some of the most magnificent land in our Federal estate as wilderness, we are tripling the size of our Wilderness System.

We've preserved the unparalleled beauty of areas like the Misty Fiords and Admiralty Island National Monuments in southeast Alaska. And we've ensured that Alaska's Eskimos and Indians and Aleuts can continue their traditional way of life. And we've given the State of Alaska, finally, the opportunity to choose the land which will be theirs through eternity.

I've been fortunate. I've seen firsthand some of the splendors of Alaska. But many Americans have not. Now, whenever they or their children or their grandchildren choose to visit Alaska, they'll have the opportunity to see much of its splendid beauty undiminished and its majesty untarnished.

This act of Congress reaffirms our commitment to the environment. It strikes a balance between protecting areas of great beauty and value and allowing development of Alaska's vital oil and gas and mineral and timber resources. A hundred percent of the offshore areas and 95 percent of the potentially productive oil and mineral areas will be available for exploration or for drilling. With this bill we are acknowledging that Alaska's wilderness areas are truly this country's crown jewels and that Alaska's resources are treasures of another sort. How to tap these resources is a challenge that we can now face in the decade ahead.

As a nation, we have been blessed with an abundance of natural resources. We've also been blessed with an abundance of natural wonders—from the Grand Canyon to the Gates of the Arctic, from the Everglades to Yellowstone—we're only just now learning how to use the one without abusing the other. We must not let the pressures of the day interfere with these efforts to enhance the quality of our lives. We cannot let our eagerness for progress in energy and in technology outstrip our care for our land, for our water and for air, and for the plants and animals that share all of these precious vital resources with us. Every time we dig out minerals or drill wells, every time we ignore erosion or destroy a sand dune or dam a wild river or dump garbage or create pollution, we're changing the living Earth.

Sometimes this change might be beneficial, but we should always change the world in which we live with great care. We are affecting the air we breathe and the water we drink. We have nothing more precious than life itself, nothing more valuable to us than health. We must not forfeit these in the pursuit of progress. . . .

Years ago, Americans used to feel secure surrounded by wide oceans, but today, we have a different world view and different kinds of oceans to contemplate. Today, we know that all of us, the globe over, belong to the same, very small world, adrift in the vast areas of space. We see more clearly that we have a duty—to ourselves and to our descendants, to the environment and to the world itself—to conserve, to preserve, to use, but to think before we act, and always to care.

We Americans have a history of viewing the environment as wilderness and wilderness as something that must be conquered. But we must never forget that as vast and dark and forbidding as the forests may seem, they are very fragile; and as wide and as boundless as the oceans may seem, they're quite vulnerable. For all that the Earth has given us, we owe it our respect and, more importantly, our understanding. We're the stewards of an irreplaceable environment. That's an awesome task as well as a precious gift.

In the decade past we've worked hard to build strong programs to protect the environment and, where there was damage, to clean our skies and waterways. We have made some progress. It has not been easy. Human greed is not an easy foe to conquer. As Governor and as President, this has been one of my most difficult political challenges, and throughout my life in the future, it's a challenge that I will continue to meet.

In the last four years, we've strengthened the Clean Air and Clean Water Acts and the Coastal Zone Management Act. We've established strict Federal environmental standards for coal mining, provided for better control of pesticides and toxic chemicals. We have at least continued our protection of endangered species. Outside of Alaska, we've made vast additions to our National Park System. We've created new wilderness areas and designated new Wild and Scenic Rivers. We cannot afford to retreat from these efforts now. We cannot afford to look at the immediate financial profits and ignore the long-term costs of misusing the environment.

Protecting our environment also brings immediate results to our health and to the development of new technology, new areas of understanding, new knowledge that benefits us all. It brings us some financial costs as well, but these costs, compared to the benefits, are very modest indeed. The price of not protecting the environment would be far greater and far more lasting. Much of the damage cannot possibly be repaired at any price. We protect it today, or we lose it for all time.

In tackling our challenges—the problems of hazardous waste disposal and eroding beaches, extinction of plant and animal species, and human overpopulation—we have our forebears to emulate. When they came to these shores they faced challenges beyond any they had known previously, and they had to think and they had to fight their way through: Their success is our legacy now. Their triumphs and their mistakes have much to teach us.

We've learned the hard way, in some cases, that we cannot, without consequence, take from the land without giving. We've learned, too, that what we need as we enter the 1980's is the same thing the pioneers had when they first entered the wilderness of this country—determination, courage, daring.

We were determined to preserve portions of Alaska. Fifty-six million acres of that State can now stand pristine. We dared to act with foresight, instead of hindsight, and with an understanding that Alaska will help keep our Nation both energy-strong and environmentally rich.

As our descendants look back on the 1980s, I hope it will be said by them that we kept our commitment to the restoration of environmental quality; that we protected the public health from the continuing dangers of toxic chemicals, from pollution, from hazardous and radioactive wastes; that we put this Nation on a path to a sustainable energy future, one based increasingly on renewable resources and on the elimination of waste.

Let it be said that we moved to protect America's countryside, that this year, the Year of the Coast, was perhaps the turning point in protecting, finally, our coastland from mismanagement; that we redirected the management of the Nation's water resources toward water conservation and environmental protection; that we've faced squarely such worldwide problems as deforestation, acid rain, toxic waste disposal, carbon dioxide buildup, and nuclear proliferation.

That all of us have won so much in Alaska is all the more reason to continue our fight for our other environmental concerns. That we've struck a balance between Alaska's economic interests and its natural beauty, its industry and its ecology, is all the more reason to try now to strike similar balances elsewhere in our Nation. This act of Congress gives us both the knowledge and the impetus and inspiration.

For today, in closing, let me say, let us celebrate. The mountains that rim the Misty Fjords and rise above Admiralty Island, the tracks of man's past along the Bering Strait, the rivers and lakes that harbor salmon and trout, the game trails of caribou and grizzly in the Brooks Range, the marshes where our waterfowl summer—all these are now preserved, now and, I pray, for all time to come. I thank God that you have helped to make it possible for me to sign this bill.

Source: Carter, Jimmy. "Remarks upon Signing the Alaska National Interest Lands Conservation Act," December 2, 1980. *Public Papers of the Presidents of the United States: Jimmy Carter, 1980.* Washington, D.C.: Government Printing Office, 1981.

NOTE

1. Roderick Nash, *Wilderness and the American Mind,* 3rd ed. (New Haven, Conn: Yale University Press, 1982), x.

CHAPTER 9

Public Health and
Environmental Regulation

1980–Present

Since the curtain was drawn on the so-called "golden age" of environmentalism at the close of the 1970s, environmental policy in the United States has become a polarizing subject in Washington and statehouses across the country. The relative amity that had existed between the nation's political parties on environmental issues disintegrated in the 1980s and 1990s. The chief cause of this spectacular buckling of bipartisanship was the advent of new environmental regulations that energized—and in some cases radicalized—political constituencies to heightened levels of involvement in the policymaking process. This phenomenon was particularly evident within conservative Republican circles, where concern about the economic toll of environmental regulations on business, traditional allegiance to federalist philosophy and private property rights, skepticism about "alarmist" environmental rhetoric, and doubts about the efficacy of so-called command-and-control regulation all became prominent tenets of party orthodoxy. The end result was a formidable backlash against what was perceived to be environmental regulation run amok.

The most dramatic rejection of the precepts of 1970s-era environmental regulation came during Ronald Reagan's two-term presidency in the 1980s. Many of the "regulatory relief" efforts of the Reagan White House were staved off by Democratic policymakers and their allies within the environmental movement. But the battle inaugurated a policy-making stalemate that endured through three subsequent presidencies. To be sure, both Democrats (and their environmentalist constituency) and Republicans (and their pro-business, pro–property-rights supporters) enjoyed moments of triumph during the presidencies of George H. W. Bush, Bill Clinton, and George W. Bush. But neither side was able to sustain its momentum over the long haul, so federal and state agencies responsible for pollution control, public health, and other environmental policy areas have been periodically whipsawed back and forth between diametrically opposite philosophies of governance and environmental stewardship. Historically, no agency has experienced these dizzying shifts in philosophical direction more acutely than the Environmental Protection Agency (EPA).

REAGAN AND THE ENVIRONMENTAL PROTECTION AGENCY

The 1980s got off to an auspicious start for the environmental movement. Major environmental and public health initiatives and laws passed during the 1970s were fast becoming

Since the 1980s, America has been plunged into divisive and seemingly insoluble debates over the efficacy of environmental protection laws—such as ones regulating activity on waterways that are repositories of wildlife—and the impact of those laws on economic growth and individual rights.

part of the fabric of American society, thanks in large measure to the yeoman efforts of the EPA, the Food and Drug Administration (FDA), and other federal agencies charged with crafting and implementing the environmental policies and regulations that had been mandated by Congress during the Johnson, Nixon, Ford, and Carter administrations. In addition, environmentalists were heartened by the passage of the landmark toxic waste clean-up program popularly known as Superfund (officially called CERCLA—the Comprehensive Environmental Response, Compensation and Liability Act). This measure, which was signed into law in December 1980 by President Jimmy Carter, gave the EPA the authority to respond quickly and decisively to public health emergencies caused by abandoned waste dumps **(see Document 9.1)**. In addition, Superfund's main funding provision was a five-year, $1.6 billion trust fund financed primarily by a tax on industrial chemical manufacturers. Such a funding mechanism would have been unimaginable a mere two decades earlier.

In November 1980, however, Republican presidential candidate and former California governor Ronald Reagan routed Carter in the presidential election. The electoral landslide gave Reagan considerable political momentum when he entered the White House in January 1981, and the genial Republican moved decisively to imprint his pro-business, anti-regulatory philosophy on Washington. The Environmental Protection Agency was a prominent focus of this overarching effort because, although it was barely a decade old at the time, the EPA had already come to be seen by some movers and shakers in the world of American business and finance as a bloated, vitality-sapping bureaucracy squatting on the chest of American industry.

Ironically, this negative view of the EPA stemmed in part from the unrealistically high expectations of the agency held by some of Washington's most ardent environmentalist lawmakers. From its inception in 1970, the EPA had become the designated agency for carrying out all manner of pollution control and public health measures. By the mid-1970s, the agency was being deluged with new laws for which it had primary responsibility, and EPA employees were engaged in a perpetual scramble to create, roll out, maintain, and enforce all sorts of compliance guidelines and standards in accordance with extremely ambitious deadlines. "Most of us thought we would take care of the big problems in short order, and then it would be a matter of maintenance," recalled one top administrator. "We began to see this wasn't the case in the later 1970s when we were missing all the deadlines in the new programs. We thought then that the deadlines were tough, but now we see they were laughable."[1]

Despite this daunting administrative overload, the EPA managed to make significant—and sometimes startling—inroads against air and water pollution levels during its first decade of existence. Among the myriad success stories was a reduction in the emissions of soot and dust particulates in Massachusetts from 29,000 tons in 1972 to 790 tons in 1979. On the Gulf of Mexico, meanwhile, EPA enforcement of Clean Water Act provisions ended massive corporate dumping of toxic wastes into gulf waters.[2] These and other notable achievements are often attributed to the able leadership of the agency's first three directors: William D. Ruckelshaus (1970–1973), Russell Train (1973–1977), and Doug Costle (1977–1981).

When Reagan assumed the reins in the Oval Office, however, the EPA's increasing size and influence attracted far more attention than its successes in combating America's pollution problems. The Reagan Administration viewed the agency's rapidly growing body of rules and regulations as a major obstacle to revitalization of the moribund American economy. This perspective was greatly shaped by people such as Congressman David Stockman (R-Mich.), who was tapped to be Reagan's first director of the Office of Management and Budget (OMB) in no small measure because of a November 1980 memorandum he wrote about the economic terrain that Reagan would face after inauguration. In this memorandum, famously titled "Avoiding a GOP Economic Dunkirk," Stockman warned that federal regulations imposed during the 1970s will "sweep through the industrial economy with near gale force" unless the new administration carries out "a series of unilateral administrative actions to reduce the regulatory burden. . . . If bold policies are not swiftly, deftly and courageously implemented in the first six months, Washington will quickly become engulfed in political disorder commensurate with the surrounding economic disarray. A golden opportunity for permanent conservative policy revision and political realignment could be thoroughly dissipated before the Reagan administration is even up to speed."[3]

The Reagan Administration was determined not to let Stockman's prophecy come to pass. Less than a month after taking the oath of office, Reagan issued Executive Order 12291, which greatly extended the role of economic analysis in the formation of regulatory policy. The order mandated that any new regulation issued by the EPA or other federal agencies first be approved by the OMB, which would put all proposed regulations through a vigorous cost-benefit analysis. This requirement was praised by industry and some economists who said that the "real world" economic impact of environmental and other regulations had to be given greater weight. Opponents asserted that there were inevitable uncertainties associated with estimating dollar benefits and costs of many environmental policies. "The order took a useful tool of economic inquiry—cost-benefit analysis—and made it an imperative of federal decision making," wrote Philip Shabecoff, a critic of Reagan's environmental policies. "In the hands of the administration's political appointees, the order served as a meat cleaver with a keen edge to be wielded against regulations that cost industry money, particularly environmental regulations."[4] During this same period, the Reagan Administration unveiled a Task Force on Regulatory Relief chaired by Vice President George H. W. Bush that placed special emphasis on scrutinizing environmental regulations (see Document 9.2).

EPA during the Gorsuch Years

Reagan also tapped Colorado state legislator Anne Gorsuch, a staunch anti-regulatory conservative, to be his first EPA director. The appointment would soon provide striking confirmation of how the nominally independent operations of the EPA are, in actuality, often closely guided by White House priorities. Gorsuch and her inner circle of administrators—many of whom were plucked from the industries they were charged with overseeing—immediately set about reducing the EPA's regulatory presence. During Gorsuch's twenty-two months at the EPA, enforcement referrals to the Justice Department were cut in half, the agency's budget was cut by more than 20 percent, and the morale of rank-and-file staff plummeted. Gorsuch made no attempt to disguise her satisfaction with these cuts or her general anti-regulatory zeal. She openly boasted, for example, that she reduced the thickness of the EPA's manual of clean water regulations from six inches to a half-inch during her tenure.[5] Major staffing cuts were also imposed at other regulatory agencies such as the Occupational Safety and Health Administration (OSHA) (11 percent), Consumer Product Safety Commission (20 percent), and the Department of Interior's Office of Surface Mining (40 percent).[6]

The U.S. business community responded enthusiastically to these changes at the EPA and other federal agencies. Other observers, however, were apoplectic at what they saw as an outrageous evisceration of the nation's anti-pollution laws. They claimed that because Reagan and the Republican-controlled Senate knew they could not get their regulatory relief initiatives through the Democrat-controlled House, they were bypassing Congress altogether and seeking to accomplish their goals by starving federal regulatory agencies of the staffing and funding they needed to fulfill their duties. William Drayton, who served as an assistant administrator for the EPA in the Carter Administration, offered a representative assessment of the Reagan White House: "Knowing that the public will never stand for the repeal of these environmental laws, Reagan is gutting them through the personnel and budgetary back doors," he complained. "With only the shattered shell of an EPA left, our environmental statutes will be largely meaningless."[7]

Gorsuch's EPA came under greater fire in the summer of 1982, when congressional investigators launched an inquiry into the agency's disposition of Superfund money. As the investigation into allegations of misuse of the funds deepened, EPA administrator Rita Lavelle, who was in charge of the Superfund program, became a particular focus of scrutiny. When Reagan's Justice Department instructed the EPA to withhold requested Superfund documents from Congress in the fall, the Democratic leadership promptly issued subpoenas for the records and for Gorsuch's testimony. The controversy further escalated on November 30, when the Reagan Administration asserted executive privilege in withholding the documents and further stated that Gorsuch would not comply with the subpoena. Both Democratic and Republican members of Congress reacted angrily to this rebuke of their authority, and Congress voted Gorsuch in contempt by a wide margin just before Christmas. The Justice Department promptly filed suit to halt the contempt proceedings, but by this point the Reagan White House sensed that public opinion was shifting away from them on what newspapers had begun dubbing "Sewergate." Administration anxiety about political fallout from the fast-metastasizing Superfund scandal was further exacerbated by the December 1982 evacuation of Times Beach, Missouri, in the wake of findings of widespread PCB contamination. This event underscored the importance of a robust and well-managed Superfund program to many Americans, and it further sowed public doubts about the health of the country's environmental protection infrastructure under Reagan.

As charges of obstructionism, illegal destruction of records, and improper manipulation of the Superfund process for corporate profit grew louder, the Reagan Administration began seeking a way out. Reagan publicly defended Gorsuch's performance in early 1983, but Lavelle was fired on February 4 (she was eventually convicted of felony perjury charges) and the EPA issued a succession of press releases trumpeting various reorganization measures it was taking to alleviate problems (**see Document 9.3**). These steps failed to stem the political bleeding, however. Gorsuch resigned under enormous pressure in early March, and more than thirty other senior EPA appointees were shown the door at about the same time.

Gorsuch's replacement was William Ruckelshaus, the EPA's first-ever director (1970–1973) and a figure known and respected by environmentalists and industry executives alike. Reagan's choice of Ruckelshaus had the desired effect of quieting the political storms swirling around the EPA, but it came at a price: Ruckelshaus stated that he would return to EPA only if the agency was unshackled from OMB oversight. The White House glumly acceded to this condition, and Ruckelshaus took up the EPA reins once again.

Ruckelshaus's belief in the legitimacy of environmental regulation and his ability to reverse the EPA's budgetary freefall helped restore a measure of the agency's internal morale, organizational efficiency, and public credibility. But historians such as Joel Mintz believe that the agency never fully recovered from the trauma of the Gorsuch era: "The approach of the EPA's early Reagan administration managers . . . led to an almost complete politicization of the enforcement process."[8] Historian Richard N. L. Andrews offered a similar assessment. "In both its substance and its tactics, Reagan's deregulatory initiative caused deep and lasting damage to EPA, and to the evolution of U.S. environmental policy more generally," he wrote. "It eroded the agency's expertise, and tainted it for the first time with corruption and scandal. More broadly, it fractured the public consensus that had been emerging in support of regulatory reform, and triggered instead a more bitter and far more partisan period of distrust and ideological trench warfare over environmental protection policy."[9]

PARTISAN DIVIDE ON ENVIRONMENTAL REGULATION

After Ruckelshaus's return to the EPA, the agency ceased to be a major target of the Reagan White House's deregulation initiatives. The administration still regularly opined that environmental and other regulations were far too burdensome to American business. But the lingering effects of the Gorsuch debacle—combined with the similarly disastrous tenure of Reagan's first Interior secretary, James Watt, who resigned his post in November 1983—made Reagan officials gun-shy about launching any further systematic attempts to reform federal environmental policy. In addition, Democrats—who controlled the House for all eight years of Reagan's presidency (as well as the Senate for the last two)—continued to thwart or water down those regulatory relief initiatives that did emerge from the White House, Republican policymakers, and Reaganites within the federal government.

This evolving political environment, in fact, enabled the EPA to implement sweeping new regulations in a number of areas during Reagan's second term. The agency moved to phase out the usage of the carcinogenic pesticide ethylene dibromide; banned asbestos; and executed significant amendments to the Safe Drinking Water Act, Resource Conservation and Recovery Act, Federal Environmental Pesticide Control Act, and Superfund. EPA director Lee Thomas, who succeeded Ruckelshaus for Reagan's second term, also helped gain passage of the 1987 Montreal Protocol on Substances that Deplete the Ozone Layer, a major international initiative to address the damaging effects of chlorofluorocarbons (CFCs) on the earth's upper atmosphere (**see Document 9.5**).

By the mid-1980s, some parties were asserting that Reagan's first-term attempts to rein in the EPA's regulatory presence had actually backfired in spectacular fashion. "Ronald Reagan has motivated far more people to join the [Sierra] Club and other environmental organizations than all of his predecessors combined," declared Sierra Club political director (later executive director) Carl Pope. "He has done so with appointments and policy initiatives that have offended and alarmed the American people—efforts consistent with the President's general hostility toward activist government and his unlimited faith in private economic institutions. But it is one thing to promise to get the government off the taxpayers' backs. It is an altogether different proposition—and an unacceptable one to most Americans—to relieve polluting industries of the burden of complying with environmental laws."[10]

Other opponents of Reagan's anti-regulatory initiatives pointed out that many of the administration's major deregulatory decisions were eventually struck down by U.S. courts, which had the effect of strengthening the institutional authority of major environmental laws and the command-and-control mechanisms of enforcement they typically used ("command-and-control" is a term often used to refer to programs of environmental regulation in which agencies mandate specific, detailed rules of compliance to affected parties, then ensure their adherence to those rules through detailed inspections and other monitoring systems). In addition, some state governments responded to reduced federal enforcement of environmental regulations by increasing investment in their own environmental protection agencies and programs.

Whatever the shortcomings and failures of Reagan's first-term efforts to reduce the regulatory burden on businesses and private property owners, his reform efforts did halt—and in some cases roll back—the growth of federal involvement in business affairs and operations. Moreover, he severed the bipartisan political consensus on environmental issues that had existed in the 1960s and 1970s. In the eight years that Reagan stood atop the national political stage, he altered the dominant Republican perspective on environmental regulation to a remarkable degree. Republicans came to speak with near unity about the sanctity of private property rights and the dubious effectiveness of "zero risk" pollution-fighting approaches favored by some environmental organizations, and they increasingly questioned whether some alleged environmental "problems" actually posed a genuine and substantial risk to public health. "Initially, environmental regulation did prove to be cost-effective," acknowledged the prominent conservative physicist and environmental analyst S. Fred Singer in the early 1990s.

Removing the first large increment of pollutants from water and air probably produced more benefits than it cost. In the last 20 years there have indeed been tremendous improvements in the quality of the air, and of streams and lakes. But removing the last few percent of pollution is enormously expensive and often not even within the reach of technology. Science tells us that there is little if any additional return from the complete elimination of "hazards" such as pesticides, asbestos, dioxin, radon, and various air pollutants. Most gains come from eliminating the initial 90 percent—which is generally simple and cheap—rather than from eliminating the last 1 percent—which is frightfully difficult, in many cases virtually impossible, and in almost all instances extremely costly. The goal of zero risk is not only unrealistic, but unattainable and infinitely costly.[11]

This perspective, which was also widely trumpeted by business and industry groups traditionally aligned with the Republican Party, had become thoroughly integrated into mainstream conservative political thought by the close of Reagan's presidency. Meanwhile—and at least partly in response to the rightward drift of the Republicans on environmental issues—the Democratic Party's ties to the environmental movement and allegiance to environmental regulation schemes deepened even further. These irreconcilable policy goals would prove daunting for Reagan's successors to surmount.

PASSING THE 1990 CLEAN AIR ACT AMENDMENTS

When Republican President George H. W. Bush took over at the White House in early 1989, he shared many of the standard Republican concerns about environmental over-regulation. But he also recognized that federal environmental protection efforts still enjoyed broad support from the voting public at large. To that end, he was determined to fulfill a campaign pledge to beef up the 1970 Clean Air Act, the provisions of which had not kept pace with the nation's evolving air quality challenges. Bush thus took a hands-on role in pushing proposed Clean Air Act amendments through Congress. He was greatly aided in these efforts by new Senate majority leader George Mitchell (D-Maine), who was far more open to the legislation than had been his predecessor, Robert Byrd (D-W.Va.), who hailed from the coal state of West Virginia. Their partnership, combined with the efforts of congressmen such as John Dingell (D-Mich.) and Henry Waxman (D-Calif.), produced a major restructuring of the Clean Air Act that actually received broad bipartisan support. The bill passed by a 401-21 vote in the House and 89-11 vote in the Senate, and Bush signed the 1990 Clean Air Act Amendments into law on November 15, 1990[12] (see Document 9.6).

This law did not contain everything that environmentalists wanted. It failed, for example, to provide for any regulation of carbon dioxide at a time when most other industrialized nations were passing major legislation to rein in emissions of the greenhouse gas. But in other ways the 1990 bill expanded on the original Clean Air Act. It established a cap-and-trade regulatory scheme for combating "acid rain"—rain and snowfall saturated with lake-killing sulfur dioxide and nitrogen oxides from coal-burning power plants—and it significantly toughened EPA regulation of nearly 200 toxic air pollutants. The legislation also laid out an ambitious plan to bring all urban areas into compliance with national air quality standards over a twenty-year period.

The 1990 Clean Air Act was the high-water mark of the Bush presidency in terms of environmental policy–making. In fact, it was integral in continuing and even increasing the progress that America had made in combating air pollution since the first major Clean Air Act was passed in 1970. The EPA has estimated, for example, that between 1970 and 2004, total emissions of the six principal air pollutants regulated by the Clean Air Act decreased by 54 percent—even though the nation's population grew by 39 percent, the gross domestic product increased by 187 percent, and vehicle miles traveled increased by 171 percent during that same period.[13] These stunning gains would never have been possible without the 1990 Clean Air bill signed by Bush.

In most other areas, however, the Bush Administration followed a path more pleasing to business and private property advocates than to environmentalists. The Bush White House generally resisted new proposals for environmental regulation from Democrats and environmental groups, and it showed little inclination to meaningfully engage with the international community on global environmental issues such as species loss and climate change. The Bush Administration also sided with the biotechnology industry when it approved major changes to FDA policy on genetically modified (GM) foods in mid-1992. In essence, the new rules removed almost all regulatory distinctions—including labeling and monitoring—between bioengineered foods and those derived by conventional farming methods. This shift was praised by many scientists and analysts who heralded GM foods as a safe way to increase agricultural production and thus alleviate world hunger and reduce development pressure on vulnerable natural areas. But it was condemned by others who cited uncertainty about the long-term environmental and public health impact of GM foods **(see Document 9.8)**.

As the 1992 election season approached and Bush sought to reassure Republican voters of his conservative bona fides, the environment further faded as a focus of the Bush White House. But it re-emerged in the administration of his successor, Democratic governor Bill Clinton from Arkansas. The election of Clinton, in fact, sparked expressions of outright joy from environmental leaders who predicted that pressing environmental issues would, after twelve years of Reagan and Bush, no longer be consigned to the political wilderness.

ESCALATING POLITICAL WARFARE

Environmental groups were openly enthused about the prospects of a Clinton Administration during the post-1992 election transition and the opening months of Clinton's presidency. They approved of many of the agency appointments made by Clinton, gloried in the ascension of environmentalist Al Gore to the vice presidency, and applauded the administration's tone-setting moves in its opening days. These moves included further distancing of environmental regulations from OMB cost-benefit analyses, increased funding for renewable energy and endangered species programs, and expressions of support for the goals of the burgeoning environmental justice movement.

In the mid-term elections of 1994, however, Republicans won control of both houses of Congress and the political environment in Washington changed decisively. The election results, which were widely characterized as a public referendum on the Clinton White House, emboldened conservative leaders within and without Congress to challenge Clinton on a multitude of fronts, including the realm of environmental policy. Indeed, the mid-1990s saw Republican leaders such as House Speaker Newt Gingrich (R-Ga.) take up the Reagan-era banner of regulatory relief with crusading zeal.

As in the 1980s, the EPA became a primary target of these reform efforts. The agency's place in the crosshairs of Republican rhetoric about innovation-choking federal bureaucracy was in part the inevitable consequence of its role as the agency responsible for carrying out the requirements of the nation's major pollution control statutes. But it also resulted from widely acknowledged and persistent problems with EPA operations. By the mid-1990s the administrative burden imposed on the EPA by years of accumulating congressional laws and administration mandates had reached an unparalleled level. The EPA had become responsible for regulating 40,000 major sources of air pollution; 68,000 point sources of water pollution; 650,000 generators of hazardous waste; 27,000 abandoned hazardous waste dumps; 79,000 public water systems; and millions of cars, trucks, motorcycles, planes, and motorboats.[14] And as one analyst noted, setting compliance and monitoring standards for many of these pollution sources is often an extremely difficult task:

> The EPA must set health standards for thousands of substances. In doing so, agency officials inevitably encounter a high degree of scientific uncertainty. Not only is the evidence produced by scientific research spotty and shifting, but there is substantial disagreement about how one extrapolates from what is known (for example, the effects of extraordinarily high doses of a potential carcinogen on a rodent) to what one needs to know to set a standard intelligently (the long term effect of very low doses on humans). . . . A second problem is that frequently no technology currently exists to achieve the desired environmental goal at a reasonable cost. Many statutory provisions are designed to be "technology forcing"—far enough beyond what can currently be accomplished to induce the development of innovative technologies. For technology forcing to work, of course, business firms must believe that the government will stand behind its strict standards and tight deadlines. That the government seldom does so is one reason why technology forcing has worked poorly. Yet hope—or at least political posturing—springs eternal.[15]

Congress bears major culpability for many of these regulatory problems, as several scathing studies attest. "The EPA lacks focus, in part, because Congress has passed more than a dozen environmental statutes that drive the agency in a dozen directions, discouraging rational priority-setting or a coherent approach to environmental management," charged the National Academy of Public Administration in a 1995 report. "The EPA is sometimes ineffective because . . . Congress has set impossible deadlines and unrealistic expectations, given the Agency's budget."[16] Moreover, the agency's involvement in so many different aspects of American society, from the energy and transportation sectors to agriculture and construction, means that various facets of its operations are under the jurisdiction and scrutiny of numerous congressional committees. One 1995 study, for example, found that 13 committees and 31 subcommittees in Congress had a meaningful level of jurisdiction over EPA activities.[17] With so many masters to serve, it is little wonder that the EPA has to spend considerable time and resources defending its performance and digesting and implementing new directives.

Another extraordinary fact of life in the EPA is that it retains a unique place within the federal government. The agency's high-profile place within the firmament of the executive branch of government—and its history as the spear point of many modern White House policy priorities—inevitably makes it a lightning rod for criticism from partisan political opponents. And the fact of the matter is that the Oval Office *does*, as a consequence of this reporting relationship, wield enormous influence in setting the nation's environmental agenda. As former EPA administrator Christine Todd Whitman flatly stated in 2003, "[T]he President sets overall environmental policy"[18] for the country.

Finally, the EPA and its regulatory brethren have weathered heavy criticism for periodically "moving the regulatory goalposts." EPA history, for example, is punctuated with instances in which the agency has tightened its standards for emissions of various pollutants and toxins. Industry groups and sympathetic congressmen have complained loudly about such revisions, contending that they make it much more difficult for industrial corporations to plan and invest in future operations. But EPA officials and environmental groups respond to these criticisms by pointing out that ongoing scientific research sometimes reveals environmental risks that were simply unknowable when the initial standards were handed down. To do nothing when confronted with these new data, they assert, would be a betrayal both of the American public and of the agency's central mandate of environmental stewardship.

THE REPUBLICAN REVOLUTION AND ENVIRONMENTAL LAW

Environmental organizations and likeminded policymakers asserted that many complaints about EPA performance and responsiveness stemmed from inadequate funding and institutional support rather than over-regulation. After the electoral "Republican Revolution" of 1994, however, influential party leaders such as House Speaker Newt Gingrich , House Whip Tom DeLay (R-Texas), Senate Majority Leaders Robert Dole and Trent Lott (R-Miss.), and conservative radio personality Rush Limbaugh agitated for major reductions in regulatory oversight of American business by the EPA, FDA, and other federal agencies. Republicans and their allies in industry and conservative think tanks also insisted that responsibility for many federal anti-pollution statutes and resource conservation programs more properly belonged to individual states (**see Document 9.10**). They asserted that once the regulators in the federal bureaucracy were tamed, long-suffering industries and entrepreneurs could lift the United States to new heights of economic growth and prosperity. And they further claimed that these regulatory reforms would return America's tarnished promises of economic and personal liberty for its citizenry to their full luster.

Four subjects of longstanding conservative ire came into particular focus during this time—regulatory "takings," unfunded mandates, legal standing doctrine, and the regulatory threshold for "acceptable" environmental risk. All of these policy elements had become integrated into environmental law during the 1960s and 1970s, and all were anathema to conservative Republicans by the mid-1990s. Advocates of the "takings" agenda held that regulations that curbed private uses of personal property without fully compensating property owners violated the Takings Clause of the Fifth Amendment to the U.S. Constitution. Republicans used this argument to assert that many regulations limiting the potential value of land and other property—up to and including zoning regulations, historic landmark laws, wetlands permitting requirements, and habitat protection measures—were illegal.[19] Unfunded mandates, meanwhile, are regulations and statutes handed down by federal authorities to states or local governments without accompanying federal funds to fulfill those requirements. Critics argued, correctly, that these mandates—contained in laws ranging from the Clean Water Act to the Americans with Disabilities Act—put additional fiscal pressure on state and municipal budgets. The legal standing controversy, meanwhile, stemmed from the fact that American citizens and environmental groups were making extensive use of provisions within the Endangered Species Act, Clean Air Act, and other major environmental laws that gave them legal standing to sue violators of these laws. These "citizen suit" provisions authorized ordinary Americans to act as "private attorneys general" to help enforce anti-pollution and resource conservation laws,[20] but Republicans argued that they were being used frivolously as part of an overall strategy of green obstructionism by environmental zealots. Finally, conservatives pushed for legislation that would mothball the discretionary "acceptable risk" criterion that had long governed regulation of environmental contaminants and replace it with a more business-friendly risk-assessment/cost-benefit analysis model for environmental regulations.

These efforts were mostly neutralized by the joint efforts of the Clinton White House and environmental groups—the latter of which worked furiously to portray the Republican leadership as legislative water carriers for modern-day robber barons in the corporate world. But as the assault went on and on, Republicans did succeed in breaching the barricades in several significant areas of environmental policy–making. As with the Reagan years, these triumphs generally came not from striking down or rolling back major environmental laws, but from cutting funding for agencies and programs. After 1995, for example, the Republican-controlled Congress declined to renew the fees levied on chemical and oil companies that had supported the Superfund trust fund since its inception in 1980. This produced a marked decline in Superfund cleanups and a shifting of the financial burden for Superfund remediation to the general public (where it remained as of 2009).

In numerous instances, the U.S. judiciary system ended up as the final arbiter of these clashes **(see Document 9.11)**. Indeed, all parties involved in these disputes over environmental regulation came to see the courts as essential to advancing or defending their interests. The EPA also came to recognize that the courts had evolved into entities capable of exerting profound influence over its daily operations. In fact, some observers say that compliance with court orders has become a bigger priority for the EPA and other regulatory agencies than following congressional mandates.[21] "In the first years of a new regulatory program, an agency can expect virtually every major decision to be challenged through litigation, usually by an interest alleging the agency has failed to interpret properly its statutory responsibilities," wrote environmental policy scholar Walter A. Rosenbaum. "An agency sometimes invites such litigation because it can work to its advantage. By interpreting the manner in which risk determinations should be made by agencies, judges often dissipate the fog of uncertainty about congressional intent and provide agencies with firm guidelines for future determinations."[22]

Still, the growing influence of the court system over environmental policy has also had adverse consequences. The ideologies and policy preferences of individual judges, who have wide latitude in their decisions, have been drawn into the gravitational pull of politics like never before. As a result, partisan tensions over nominees to fill vacant seats in the court system escalated markedly during the 1990s and 2000s, with environmental groups, business interests, and their respective standard bearers in Congress all clamoring for and against assorted nominees for federal judgeships.

CLINTON'S BID TO "REINVENT" ENVIRONMENTAL REGULATION

The Clinton White House responded to the highly charged political landscape surrounding environmental policy–making with a balancing act. On the one hand, it tried to stay in the good graces of the environmental community—a key political constituency—by tapping respected individuals for key environmental posts and rebuffing what it saw as the most brazen and irresponsible Republican gambits to roll back or otherwise neuter important environmental and resource conservation laws and regulations. In addition, regulatory agencies of the Clinton years stepped up enforcement actions on a wide range of laws protecting land, water, air, and wildlife resources from polluters. Clinton also signed the Safe Drinking Water Act Amendments of 1996 and the Transportation Equity Act for the 21st Century, which greatly increased federal funding for investment in water systems and mass transit, respectively. Another notable bill signed by Clinton was the Food Quality Protection Act of 1996, which replaced the Delaney Act's longstanding blanket ban on even trace amounts of carcinogens in pesticides with standards that focused on children's health risks. Clinton also showed much greater interest in international cooperation on environmental issues than had his Republican predecessors. He signed both the Biodiversity Convention and the Law of the Sea Treaty (although both required Senate ratification that, as of early 2009, had not yet occurred), and he publicly supported the emission-reduction schemes contained in the 1997 Kyoto Protocol, a United Nations Convention on Climate Change.

During these same years, the Clinton Administration also made highly publicized attempts to "reinvent" environmental regulations so that they would be more efficient, navigable, and responsive to business needs while simultaneously fulfilling their core environmental protection purposes. These reform efforts included Project XL, which gave businesses increased flexibility to meet EPA regulatory requirements, extensive EPA reorganization of processes and responsibilities, and the introduction of more collaborative environmental protection schemes with industry and other stakeholders. Like many observers, former EPA administrator Eric Schaeffer gave these efforts a mixed grade. The Clinton-era approach at the EPA, he wrote, "frequently suffered from incoherent objectives, haphazard leadership, and a decentralized structure that made managing anything like herding cats. But as messy and inefficient as it sometimes was, this . . . approach led to some real creative tension. For example, we were able to move quickly to eliminate penalties for companies that voluntarily discovered, reported, and corrected all but the most serious violations, which allowed us to concentrate our resources on major investigations."[23]

Other actions by Clinton divided the environmental movement, most notably his successful shepherding of the North American Free Trade Agreement (NAFTA) and the General Agreement on Tariffs and Trade (GATT) through Congress and into law. Some environmentalists thought that some provisions in these pacts could spur better governmental responses to pollution in developing countries, but others worried that member nations would be tempted to slash existing environmental regulations and rebuff new environmental protection measures to attract and keep manufacturers. Major environmental groups split so bitterly (both internally and with one another) on the merits of these agreements—and especially on their likely environmental repercussions—that environmental journalist Mark Dowie called the NAFTA rift "perhaps the nastiest internecine squabble in the movement's hundred-year history."[24]

Other aspects of the Clinton record on environmental and natural resource protection issues received more universal disapproval from environmental groups, ranging from his infamous (in environmental circles) 1995 signing of a "salvage rider" that opened new tracts of national forestlands for logging to his inaction in the face of calls for higher fuel-efficiency standards for automobiles and his prevarication on the Kyoto Protocol. By the close of his presidency, many environmental groups felt that Clinton's overall record on environmental and public health issues was one of temporization and equivocation rather than decisive leadership. Others, however, asserted that the administration performed as well as could be reasonably expected, given the challenges of dealing with a pugnacious Republican-controlled Congress. Sierra Club national conservation director Bruce Hamilton summarized the Clinton environmental record as a generally strong one, albeit one that had pronounced peaks and valleys. "It all depends [on] when you decide to take your snapshot," he said.[25]

Advocates of regulatory relief, meanwhile, offered similarly mixed reviews of the Clinton White House. "The legislative record of the Clinton administration is consistent with its own rhetoric," declared William Niskanen of the libertarian Cato Institute. "It is neither pro-regulation nor anti-regulation." An official with the conservative think tank The Heritage Foundation was more dismissive, characterizing Clinton's regulatory reforms as "repackaging the same old regulatory system and passing it off as something new."[26]

George W. Bush and "Smart" Environmental Regulation

Clinton's successor was George W. Bush, a conservative Republican governor from Texas who was also the eldest son of the forty-first president. Like his father and Reagan before him, Bush spent his early tenure issuing statements of support for resource conservation and environmental protection. But Bush's basic policy orientation was an anti-regulatory one, and during his two terms in office his administration worked energetically to provide regulatory relief to industrial corporations and to expand the business opportunities of the timber, mining, oil, and agriculture industries, all of which were core Republican constituencies. As part of this effort, the Bush White House filled many key positions at the EPA, Department of the Interior, Department of Energy, and elsewhere with executives from those industries. It also launched a sustained campaign to re-shape the regulatory environment in America, pushing a variety of programs and initiatives that promised "smarter" regulation and a bigger role for states in environmental law enforcement. Corporate interests and conservative think tanks applauded this approach, whereas environmental groups decried it as a nightmarish return to the priorities of Reagan's first term.

The Bush Administration was unperturbed by such accusations, in part because it recognized that dissatisfaction with the performance of the EPA, OSHA, Department of Health and Human Services, and other agencies responsible for public health and environmental protection was not limited to industry and free-market conservatives in the early 2000s. State and local government officials, environmental and public interest organizations, and environmental policy analysts of widely differing ideologies all expressed dissatisfaction with the administrators of the nation's environmental programs.[27] Many of the complaints leveled against the EPA and other agencies naturally varied from stakeholder to stakeholder, but there were also areas of almost universal agreement. Business groups and environmental organizations, for example, have both excoriated EPA cost-benefit analyses of environmental regulations as inaccurate and unreliable over the years.

These swirling debates about the competence, character, and necessity of federal environmental protection programs provided the Bush White House with fertile soil to sow its seeds of "smart" regulation. Bush officials implicitly—and sometimes explicitly—framed this campaign as a sensible successor to Clinton's flexible regulatory approach, which sought to get agencies and industries working collaboratively rather than at cross purposes to develop and maintain effective and efficient environmental programs that did not unfairly burden businesses (see Document 9.14).

As the administration's environmental agenda unfurled, however, it garnered scalding reactions from environmental groups and their allies on Capitol Hill. By the end of Bush's first term, environmental groups were calling him the worst president in U.S. history. They lambasted Bush for his blanket rejection of the Kyoto Protocol on global climate change and for a series of administration moves to expand logging, mining, drilling, and other resource extraction and development activities on public lands. Considerable anger was also directed at the Bush White House's regulatory relief efforts, which included new strategies to restrict or eliminate regulatory takings, reduce citizen lawsuits against alleged violations of environmental laws, and transfer environmental stewardship responsibilities from federal agencies to states.

Environmental and public interest groups and Democratic members of Congress also leveled pointed accusations that the Bush Administration systematically disregarded, suppressed, and altered scientific findings on the environment to further its pro-business agenda and that it further sought to neutralize independent scientific analysis of environmental issues through restructuring of the federal bureaucracy (see Document 9.18). "There is a well established pattern of suppression and distortion of scientific findings by high-ranking Bush administration political appointees across numerous federal agencies," summarized the nonprofit Union of Concerned Scientists in a 2004 report that included twenty Nobel Laureates as signatories. "These actions have consequences for human health, public safety, and community well-being."[28]

During the course of Bush's two terms, the litany of alleged environmental abuses and outrages laid at his doorstep reached truly monumental levels[29]—as did the counterattacks from exasperated Bush officials and anti-regulatory, pro-development constituencies who depicted the memberships of the Sierra Club, Natural Resources Defense Council, Public Citizen, and other supporters of robust environmental regulation as left-wing communes of hysterical Luddites. The EPA was buffeted to and fro by this sustained political storm, and every decision it made on the regulation of toxic chemicals and other pollutants became more closely scrutinized than ever. Controversies over pro-industry EPA rulings on the regulation of dioxin, arsenic, lead, mercury, diisononyl phthalate (DINP), and other dangerous chemicals flared up throughout the Bush years. On each of these occasions, lawmakers and spokespeople from the opposing camps wearily returned to the rhetorical front lines to lambaste each other in print and on television, while lawyers for the two sides dueled in the nation's courtrooms over various fine points of regulatory law (see Document 9.15).

This incessant partisan bickering over environmental policy left many ordinary American citizens in a state of dazed uncertainty about the true condition of the environment and the severity of alleged threats to public health. This atmosphere of doubt and confusion also extended into state legislative chambers and Capitol Hill, where liberal and conservative stakeholders—nongovernmental groups, businesses, think tanks, and the like—bombard lawmakers with reports, studies, and polls buttressing their own positions. As scholar Walter A. Rosenbaum noted, even "wonky" subjects such as risk assessment draw "contending battalions of experts—garlanded with degrees and publications and primed to dispute each other's judgment—[to] congressional and administrative hearings. . . . Policy makers are often left to judge not only the wisdom of policies but also the quality of the science supporting the policies."[30]

THE ENVIRONMENTAL JUSTICE MOVEMENT

The haze of uncertainty and controversy that swirls around many contemporary environmental issues also extends to the claims of the "environmental justice" movement, which has exerted significant influence over the direction and tenor of environmental policy–making—and perhaps even greater influence over the focus and tenor of modern environmental activism—since the early 1980s. This crusade, inspired and still led by African American, Latino, Native American, Asian, and other minority groups, is dedicated to shining a spotlight on—and ultimately alleviating—the disproportionate impact that pollution and other environmental ills have on minority and poor families and communities in the United States.

The movement was born in Warren County, North Carolina, a poor, rural outpost of the state with a mostly black population. In the early 1980s state officials decided to make the county the site for a new landfill that would house large quantities of toxic PCB-laced soil. But local residents mounted a vigorous and well-coordinated campaign against the proposed landfill and its PCB contents, which they viewed as a potentially serious threat to their drinking water. Utilizing marches and other nonviolent protest methods that had once been used in the struggle for civil rights, Warren County residents and supporters from around the country delayed the delivery of PCB-contaminated materials to the landfill for several weeks, despite hundreds of arrests. The struggle eventually moved into the courts, where the residents of Warren County were ultimately defeated. But their defiant struggle awakened minority activists and communities across the country. Convinced that American communities of color and poverty lived in more polluted environments than their wealthier white counterparts, minority grassroots organizations sprung up from coast to coast to document this problem and demand policy changes that would address it.

The so-called environmental justice movement spread so rapidly that the federal government began undertaking studies of the issue within months of the Warren County showdown. These studies gave further credence to the claims of environmental justice activists. In 1983 the General Accounting Office (GAO) issued a report documenting that three of the four offsite hazardous waste disposal sites in the American South were located in predominantly poor and African American communities (see Document 9.4). Three years later, a report prepared by the GAO for the Congressional Black Caucus confirmed that hazardous waste disposal facilities were frequently placed in communities with high percentages of poor people or minorities. In 1987 the Commission for Racial Justice of the United Church of Christ issued a famous report, *Toxic Wastes and Race in the United States,* which found that the United States systemically exposed communities of color to greater levels of toxins and other pollutants than white communities. In 1988 a *Los Angeles Times* investigation revealed that the California Waste Management Board had, during the mid-1980s, repeatedly advised officials and companies looking to site hazardous waste facilities to focus their efforts on low-income and rural communities with low levels of education and political influence.[31] And in 1992, the *National Law Journal* reported that "white communities see faster action, better results and stiffer penalties than communities where blacks, Hispanics and other minorities live. This unequal protection often occurs whether the community is wealthy or poor."[32] These findings gave new strength and legitimacy to established public health advocacy groups such as the National Toxics Campaign Fund and the Citizens Clearinghouse for Hazardous Waste (now the Center for Health, Environment, and Justice), led by Love Canal activist Lois Gibbs. It also helped spawn hundreds of smaller grassroots organizations in rural and urban communities across the nation.

The issues and policy priorities of these groups, however, were in many cases distinct from those of the established (and overwhelmingly white) mainstream environmental organizations of the 1980s and early 1990s **(see Document 9.7)**. As journalist Mark Dowie observed, "[T]he central concern of the new movement is human health. Its adherents consider wilderness preservation and environmental aesthetics worthy but overemphasized values."[33] In fact, many of the activists within the environmental justice movement were openly dismissive of the Sierra Club, Friends of the Earth, Wilderness Society, Audubon Society, National Wildlife Federation, and other environmental groups that had played such important roles in building the nation's existing arsenal of environmental laws. They asserted that these organizations had historically displayed little interest in urban pollution and other environmental problems that disproportionately affect poor and minority people.

Some members of the wider environmental movement agreed that these criticisms were not without merit. In 1992, for example, Sierra Club executive director Michael Fisher issued a direct challenge to the group's membership: "Will we remain a middle-class group of backpackers, overwhelmingly white in membership, program, and agenda—and thus condemn ourselves to losing influence in an increasingly multicultural country? Or will we be of service to, of relevance to people of color, combine forces, and strengthen our efforts at our chapter and group level, especially in the localities where the environmental and civil rights battles are going to be lost or won?"[34] By the mid-1990s, many national environmental organizations had crafted new programs to address environmental justice issues and create more ethnically diverse memberships and leadership.

State and federal governments also responded to the demands of environmental justice advocates. In 1994 President Clinton issued Executive Order 12898, which required the EPA and all other federal agencies to integrate environmental justice principles into programs and policies **(see Document 9.9)**. A variety of local, state, and federal regulations were also implemented to address environmental concerns in inner-city neighborhoods and rural locales. These ranged from the landmark 2001 Brownfields Revitalization Act—a rare example of bipartisan agreement on an environmental bill during the George W. Bush years—to a 2004 executive order by New Jersey's governor mandating that the state develop a strategy to reduce pollution exposure in minority and low-income communities **(see Document 9.13)**.[35]

The basic tents of environmental justice are now widely accepted by mainstream environmental organizations and civil rights groups. But as the ability of environmental justice advocates to influence public policy has grown, criticism of the movement's goals and the scientific basis of its claims have also increased. Industry groups have blasted the research methodologies used by environmental justice advocates as fundamentally flawed, and conservative Republicans have expressed growing alarm that alleged incidents of environmental injustice have eroded private property rights to an unacceptable degree. These critics have also bristled at the rhetoric of some environmental justice advocates who have used words such as "genocidal" to describe the conditions in inner-city communities. Even some observers who are sympathetic to the poor living conditions that exist in impoverished minority neighborhoods have registered objections to the scientific basis for some claims of environmental racism. "To be sure, poor communities have long been subjected to more pollution than wealthier ones, and communities of color have been subjected to more pollution than white ones," wrote the authors of one dissent.

> But these communities have not been targeted for pollution because of the race of their inhabitants. Corporate executives locate their facilities in neighborhoods for a variety of reasons having to do with zoning regulations, easy access to transportation, low land prices, the likelihood of residents to effectively resist in a not-in-my-backyard (NIMBY) campaign, and historic development, which was, indeed, often discriminatory. But executives and government officials are not siting facilities in those neighborhoods out of racism. Labeling the disproportionate impact of pollution on Americans of color as either racist or genocidal serves only to distort the community's understanding of the problem and alienate potential allies.[36]

These critics argue that the problem of environmental racism has been overstated by advocacy studies that do not sufficiently account for factors such as the decision of the people who are economically disadvantaged to move *into* the vicinity of hazardous waste sites because of low housing prices or family connections (**see Document 9.12**). Other detractors insist that environmental justice concerns have been knowingly utilized by activists as a sort of Trojan horse to mobilize minorities to act on a wide range of other historical grievances. "The amalgam of politicized civil rights groups and politicized environmentalists often summons the worst reflexes of both movements, combining frivolous charges of racism along with unfounded environmental scares," charged Steven F. Hayward, an analyst of environmental and other public policy issues for the pro-business American Enterprise Institute. "For much of the civil rights movement, it is always the Edmund Pettis Bridge in Selma; for much of the environmental movement, the Cuyahoga River is always burning."[37]

Supporters of the environmental justice movement reject these assertions. They maintain, in fact, that as scientific studies on the issue have grown more sophisticated and complete, the evidence that minorities and poor people are disproportionately exposed to health risks from environmental pollutants has become even more damning (**see Document 9.16**). And they are quick to highlight specific events and locales where evidence of environmental injustice seems overwhelming (**see Document 9.17**). Federal authorities, meanwhile, acknowledge that environmental injustice is a genuine problem that has, in too many instances, not yet been adequately confronted. In both 2004 and 2006, for example, the EPA's inspector general issued reports excoriating the agency for its lack of progress in implementing the terms of Clinton's 1994 executive order on environmental justice into its day-to-day operations.[38]

NOTES

1. Quoted in *The Environmental Protection Agency: A Retrospective,* EPA press release, Nov. 29, 1990. www.epa.gov/history/topics/epa/20a.htm.
2. "This Ice Queen Does Not Melt," *Time Magazine,* January 18, 1982.
3. Quoted in William Grieder, *The Education of David Stockman* (New York: Dutton, 1982), 137.
4. Philip Shabecoff, *A Fierce Green Fire: The American Environmental Movement* (New York: Hill and Wang, 1993), 218.

5. Patricia Sullivan, "Anne Gorsuch Burford, 62, Dies; Reagan EPA Director," *Washington Post,* July 22, 2004, B6.

6. Robert Bartlett, "The Budgetary Process and Environmental Policy," in *Environmental Policy in the 1980s: Reagan's New Agenda,* ed. Norman Vig and Michael Kraft (Washington, D.C.: CQ Press, 1984), 127–131.

7. "This Ice Queen Does Not Melt," *Time Magazine,* January 18, 1982.

8. Joel A. Mintz, *Enforcement at the EPA: High Stakes and Hard Choices* (Austin: University of Texas Press, 1995), 57.

9. Richard N. L. Andrews, *Managing the Environment, Managing Ourselves: A History of American Environmental Policy* (New Haven, Conn.: Yale University Press, 1999), 259.

10. Carl Pope, "The Politics of Plunder," in *Reagan as President: Contemporary Views of the Man, His Politics, and His Policies,* ed. Paul Boyer (Chicago: Ivan R. Dee, 1990).

11. S. Fred Singer, "The Costs of Environmental Overregulation," *Human Events,* August 7, 1993.

12. Mark Andrew Kelso and Glen Sussman, "Environmental Priorities and the President as Legislative Leader," in *The Environmental Presidency,* ed. Dennis L. Soden (Albany: State University of New York Press, 1999), 123.

13. Michael E. Kraft, and Scott R. Furlong, *Public Policy: Politics, Analysis, and Alternatives* (Washington, D.C.: CQ Press, 2007), 342.

14. R. Shep Melnick, "Risky Business: Government and the Environment after Earth Day," in *Taking Stock: American Government in the Twentieth Century,* ed. Morton Keller and R. Shep Melnick (New York: Woodrow Wilson Center Press and Cambridge University Press, 1999), 182.

15. Ibid., 181.

16. National Academy of Public Administration (NAPA), *Setting Priorities, Getting Results: A New Direction for the Environmental Protection Agency* (Washington, D.C.: NAPA, 1995), 8.

17. Ibid., 124–125.

18. Quoted in "Clearing the Air: Christine Todd Whitman on Life in and Outside the EPA," *NOW with Bill Moyers,* September 19, 2003. Transcript available at www.pbs.org/now/transcript/transcript_clearingtheair.html.

19. "Regulatory Takings." Georgetown Environmental Law and Policy Institute, n.d. www.law.georgetown.edu/gelpi/current_research/regulatory_takings/.

20. Ibid.

21. Rosemary O'Leary, "Environmental Policy in the Courts," in *Environmental Policy: New Directions for the Twenty-First Century,* 6th ed., ed. Norman J. Vig and Michael E. Kraft (Washington, D.C.: CQ Press, 2006).

22. Walter A. Rosenbaum, *Environmental Politics and Policy* (Washington, D.C.: CQ Press, 2008), 128.

23. Eric Schaeffer, "Clearing the Air: Why I Quit the EPA," *Washington Monthly,* July/August 2002.

24. Mark Dowie, *Losing Ground: American Environmentalism at the Close of the Twentieth Century* (Cambridge, Mass.: MIT Press, 1995), 187.

25. "Environmentalists Run Hot and Cold on Clinton Environmental Record," Newsmax.com, January 4, 2001. archive.newsmax.com/archives/articles/2001/1/4/104858.shtml.

26. Quoted in Cindy Skrzycki, *The Regulators: Anonymous Power Brokers in American Politics* (Lanham, Md.: Rowman and Littlefield, 2003), 163.

27. Michael E. Kraft, and Norman J. Vig, "Environmental Policy from the 1970s to the Twenty-First Century," in *Environmental Policy: New Directions for the Twenty-First Century,* ed. Norman J. Vig and Michael E. Kraft (Washington, D.C.: CQ Press, 2006), 1.

28. Union of Concerned Scientists, *Scientific Integrity in Policymaking: An Investigation into the Bush Administration's Misuse of Science,* February 2004, 9.

29. Natural Resources Defense Council (NRDC), *The Bush Administration's Dirty Legacy,* n.d. www.nrdc.org/BushRecord/.

30. Rosenbaum, *Environmental Politics and Policy,* 119.

31. Renee Skelton and Vernice Miller, "The Environmental Justice Movement," Natural Resources Defense Council, n.d. www.nrdc.org/ej/history/hej.asp.

32. Marianne Lavelle and Marcia Coyle, "Unequal Protection," *National Law Journal,* September 21, 1992, S1-S2.

33. Mark Dowie, *Losing Ground: American Environmentalism at the Close of the Twentieth Century* (Cambridge, Mass.: MIT Press, 1995), 127.

34. Quoted in Dowie, *Losing Ground,* 289–290.

35. Rosenbaum, *Environmental Politics and Policy,* 135.

36. Ted Nordhaus and Michael Shellenberger, *Breakthrough: From the Death of Environmentalism to the Politics of Possibility* (New York: Houghton Mifflin Harcourt, 2007), 72.

37. Steven F. Hayward, "Environmental Justice: Where Selma and the Cuyahoga River Fire Meet," *Environmental Policy Outlook,* November-December 2003. Washington, D.C.: American Enterprise Institute for Public Policy Research, November 1, 2003. www.aei.org/publications/pubID.19581/pub_detail.asp.

38. Office of EPA Inspector General. EPA Needs to Consistently Implement the Intent of the Executive Order on Environmental Justice. Washington, D.C.: General Accounting Office, 2004; Office of EPA Inspector General. EPA Needs to Conduct Environmental Justice Reviews of Its Programs, Policies, and Activities. Washington, D.C.: General Accounting Office, 2006.

DOCUMENT 9.1

President Carter Signs Superfund into Law

"It Fills a Major Gap in the Existing Laws of Our Country"

December 11, 1980

In the late 1970s the waters of U.S. environmental policy were roiled by horror stories of public exposure to industrial toxins and careless disposal of hazardous waste materials— and by the hapless governmental response to these emerging public health problems. As grim reports documenting public health threats from abandoned industrial and chemical operations cascaded out of places such as Love Canal in upstate New York and the so-called Valley of the Drums outside Louisville, Kentucky, hazardous waste disposal became a major public policy issue.

In 1979 and 1980 Congress and the administration of President Jimmy Carter labored to put together a law capable of cleaning up the thousands of hazardous waste dump sites scattered across the country. The effort was complicated enormously by lobbying pressure from a wide assortment of stakeholders, from public health groups and environmental organizations to various business and industry constituencies, but in late 1980 the Comprehensive Environmental Response Compensation and Liability Act (CERCLA), better known as Superfund, was passed into law. This legislation gave the federal government broad authority to clean up hazardous waste sites and other toxic releases that are deemed to be a threat to public health or the environment. It also gave federal officials the authority to exact payment from polluters or to establish a trust fund to pay for cleanup when the responsible parties could not be found. Three decades after its passage, Superfund remains America's primary tool for cleaning up toxic sites.

The following document covers the signing ceremony for CERCLA on December 11, 1980. Speakers at the ceremony in addition to President Carter include Senator Jennings Randolph (D-W.Va.), Senator Robert Stafford (R-Vt.), Congressman Jim Florio (D-N.J.), EPA administrator Doug Costle, and Congressman (later vice president) Al Gore (D-Tenn). Their remarks reflect unmistakable relief that Superfund passed and satisfaction that CERCLA was able to garner a measure of bipartisan support.

The President: . . . Almost 1 ½ years ago I sent to the Congress the original proposal for this landmark legislation, landmark in its scope and in its impact on preserving the environmental quality of our country. It was known as a superfund bill, which began a massive and a needed cleanup of hazardous wastes in our country, a problem that had been neglected for decades or even generations. It fills a major gap in the existing laws of our country and also will tend to focus the attention of the public on this very crucial problem that must be resolved. It provides adequate funding, coming primarily from industry, but also from government, and it establishes certain standards for liability if toxic chemicals are damaging to people or to property.

We responded directly and quickly to some of the highly publicized problems with toxic wastes that are just representative of many similar challenges and problems throughout the country. Love Canal and Valley of the Drums come to my memory right this moment. They are stark reminders of the neglect in our society to deal with a growing problem.

We've created in this country great prosperity and a leadership in the entire world with our chemical industry and with the energy industries, but we had neglected to pay part of the cost of that development. And now, of course, we must face that responsibility. The result here is a bill that substantially meets the criteria that I set out in the original proposal that I made to the Congress a year and a half ago. Most important, it enables the Government to recover from responsible parties the costs of their actions in the disposal of toxic wastes. While it does not deal with oil pollution in the way that I did propose, I understand that the Congress intends to act on a comprehensive oil pollution superfund similar to this in scope next year.

In my four years as President I think everyone who knows me understands that one of my greatest pleasures has been to strengthen the protection of our environment. Along with the Alaska lands bill and other major legislation, this superfund bill represents a fine achievement for the Congress and for my own administration and for the whole Nation.

I now take great pleasure in signing into law H.R. 7020, and I'm proud that the Congress and my administration have come together to produce this timely and urgently needed response. Following the signature I'd like to ask Congressman Florio to speak first, and I'll call on a few others to follow him.

[At this point, the President signed the bill.]

Senator Randolph: Why don't we cheer you, Mr. President, while you sign? [Applause]

Representative Florio: I appreciate that applause. [Laughter]

Let me just say that I and the other Members of the Congress, as well as the President and this administration, I think can all be very proud of what we've done in this very crucial area, not just this legislation but really to address the whole problem of the inappropriate disposal of toxic materials. Really, that's a two-part problem. Prospectively we have a new regulatory system which is just going into effect now, the Resource Conservation and Recovery Act, and therefore we should have no new Love Canals being created.

And this bill, of course, is the second part, which is to go back and clean up what, unfortunately, has been done over the last number of years.

So, this is a very important piece of legislation. The administration should be very proud—and I know they are—of what they've done to bring to the public's attention this problem and the remedial actions that we're taking. I'm very pleased to be part of it as well.

The President: Thank you, Jim. Senator Randolph?

I'd like to say just a word before Senator Randolph speaks, not because he led the applause for me but [laughter]. Over a four-year period, the term of any President, there is a series of achievements of which a President and a nation can be proud. And it's an extraordinary thing for me, as I look back on my own administration here, to recall the unbelievably large number of times when basic legislation like this has been sponsored by and supported by and husbanded through the Congress by Jennings Randolph.

A lot of these problems that arose, he very early—long before I got involved in politics at all—could see the threat to our country, and to see the culmination of his longstanding effort is indeed an inspiration to a President and also an inspiration to all those who admire you.

Senator Randolph.

Senator Randolph: Thank you very much, Mr. President.

You have been innovative, you've been creative, you've been well reasoned in what you have done so many times as President of the United States. You were very supportive; in fact you brought in a sense this legislation to the Hill. I will say for our committee—and I mention not by name but all members of our committee on Environment and Public Works—I thank them all, many who are here today, because we have never permitted in that committee the so-called mere partisanship and politics to surface. We've had our differences, to be sure, but we have worked together, and we believe that that's necessary.

So, I thank Bob Stafford, I thank all of the members, and Bob, of course, is moving up. [Laughter]

The President: Because of that I want him to speak in a minute. [Laughter]

Senator Randolph: I don't have this opportunity often enough—captive audiences. [Laughter] But I want to thank all the Members on the Hill and Doug Costle—here's Doug—and all of the people who are here that have been so helpful as individuals and through their organizations to bringing this good day. It is a good day.

I wish to add this, that for a long time we've been at this in our committee. We started three years ago, and we began to work and churn our way through the many problems that seemed unsolvable, at least in part. Now what you, Mr. President, and others have done is to bring to fruition not the final conclusion, but certainly a bold step forward in this effort to clean up the waste materials, the hazardous waste materials of this country that have afflicted the body politic and made our life less than the quality we hope will sometime come into being.

And so, I'd like to add this: We've been very haphazard over the years, as the American people, in handling and in the disposition of these hazardous wastes. So, again, I'm just so grateful for your words and for the opportunity to have worked with you and all others, all in this room, working towards something that calls for the best from the American people.

The President: Well, I'd like to call now on the man who helped to resurrect this bill when we thought it might be doomed after the election returns came in, but, Senator Stafford, if you would say a few words.

Senator Stafford: Thank you very much, Mr. President.

A few months ago I didn't really think that we could achieve this moment, and getting this bill passed reminded me often of something like the "Perils of Pauline" as we tried to steer it from one crisis to another. But thanks to your help and everybody on the committees on both sides of the aisle, we now, I think, have an effective way of coping with the toxic releases in this country. And I'm just elated, as all of us are, that we've been able together to reach this point. Thank you, sir.

The President: Thank you. There are many others on the various committees that I should designate for deserved recognition, but I'd like to call on Al Gore, who I think as far as the leadership in the House, really came to the forefront in the last few days, and on Rules Committee influence and others he performed a very notable function. Would you say a word, Congressman Gore?

Representative Gore: Thank you very much, Mr. President.

Just briefly I'd like to personally thank you for those who worked hard on this legislation. It was of invaluable assistance to have the President of the United States on the telephone personally calling Members of the House and Senate, bending their ear on a regular basis, saying, "Vote for this legislation." It wouldn't have been passed without your help. I'd also like to thank the enthusiastic men and women that you brought to this city who worked tirelessly to get this legislation enacted, and they're in the Justice Department and in the EPA and on the White House staff. We couldn't have done it without them either.

Thank you, Mr. President.

The President: Thank you. And finally, I rarely call on any of my own Cabinet officers or agency heads to make a comment, but I would particularly like for Doug Costle to say a word or two. He doesn't know I'm going to call on him but—

Mr. Costle: Thank you, Mr. President.

I think this bill is, in fact, very strong testimony to what has been a truly bipartisan effort in the last year, and I feel really undeserving to be here. The people who've done the work at EPA and on the Hill, the Members of the Congress, who have, in the face of a lot of pressures to go a different direction, who've stuck with it, it just takes an enormous amount of effort and energy to get something like this to happen, and I just feel very moved this morning that it finally came to pass. Thank you, Mr. President.

The President: I'd like to say one other word before I leave, and that is that I've noticed some analyses in the press and otherwise that the so-called lameduck Congress has not been productive. The legislation that has been passed in this last month has been truly extraordinary.

When I went down the list of key bills that I wanted to see put into law before I leave this office, back early in November, the list included things that we thought were highly doubtful: The reconciliation legislation, that not only saves more than $8 billion in deficits but also sets a precedent for the future, the paperwork bill, that I signed a few minutes ago, the Alaska lands bill, this bill on superfund, and others is a real testimony to a dynamic, hardworking, and very effective 96th Congress. And on behalf of my administration and the entire Nation, I want to express both my admiration for you and my appreciation to all the Members of the Congress for a superb achievement.

Thank you very much.

Source: Carter, Jimmy. "Remarks at the Signing of the Comprehensive Environmental Response, Compensation, and Liability Act of 1980 (H.R. 7020) into Law," December 11, 1980. *Public Papers of the Presidents of the United States: Jimmy Carter, 1980–81. Book 3: September 29, 1980 to January 20, 1981.* Washington, D.C.: Government Printing Office, 1982.

The Reagan Administration Inaugurates a New Era of Environmental Deregulation

DOCUMENT
9.2

"Excessive Regulation Is a Very Significant Factor in Our Current Economic Difficulties"

February 18, 1981

During the presidency of Ronald Reagan, sweeping policy changes were introduced and carried out in the realm of environmental regulation. The Reagan Administration believed that America's economic health and free-market capitalism traditions were in jeopardy from excessive business regulation, high taxes, and other flawed policies of the 1960s and 1970s. From the conservative perspective of Reagan and his allies in Congress and the business community, the burdens and costs of regulations issuing forth from the Environmental Protection Agency, the Food and Drug Administration, and other warrens of the federal bureaucracy were onerous and self-defeating.

Reagan vowed throughout the 1980 presidential campaign to correct this perceived imbalance in government–business relations. Dismissing the federal government as "too large, too bureaucratic, too wasteful, too unresponsive,"[1] he declared his intention to free American industry from the shackles of bureaucracy by rolling back the regulatory regime that had been put in place during the previous two decades. And when Reagan took the reins of the Oval Office, he immediately took action to fulfill his campaign pledge. The White House report excerpted here was released less than a month after Reagan's inauguration. Within its pages, the White House frames Reagan's plan to reduce environmental and other regulations as a crucial element in its overall "program for economic recovery."

. . . We have forgotten some important lessons in America. High taxes are not the remedy for inflation. Excessively rapid monetary growth cannot lower interest rates. Well-intentioned government regulations do not contribute to economic vitality. In fact, government spending has become so extensive that it contributes to the economic problems it was designed to cure. More government intervention in the economy cannot possibly be a solution to our economic problems.

We must remember a simple truth. The creativity and ambition of the American people are the vital forces of economic growth. The motivation and incentive of our people—to supply new goods and services and earn additional income for their families—are the most precious resources of our Nation's economy. The goal of this Administration is to nurture the strength and vitality of the American people by reducing the burdensome, intrusive role of the Federal Government; by lowering tax rates and cutting spending; and by providing incentives for individuals to work, to save, and to invest. It is our basic belief that only by reducing the growth of government can we increase the growth of the economy.

The U.S. economy faces no insurmountable barriers to sustained growth. It confronts no permanently disabling tradeoffs between inflation and unemployment, between high interest rates and high taxes, or between recession and hyperinflation. We can revive the incentives to work and save. We can restore the willingness to invest in the private capital required to achieve a steadily rising standard of living. Most important, we can regain our faith in the future.

The plan consists of four parts: (1) a substantial reduction in the growth of Federal expenditures; (2) a significant reduction in Federal tax rates; (3) prudent relief of Federal regulatory burdens; and (4) a monetary policy on the part of the independent Federal Reserve System which is consistent with those policies. These four complementary policies form an integrated and comprehensive program. . . .

V. Providing Regulatory Relief

The rapid growth in Federal regulation has retarded economic growth and contributed to inflationary pressures. While there is widespread agreement on the legitimate role of government in protecting the environment, promoting health and safety, safeguarding workers and consumers, and guaranteeing equal opportunity, there is also growing realization that excessive regulation is a very significant factor in our current economic difficulties.

The costs of regulation arise in several ways. First, there are the outlays for the Federal bureaucracy which administers and enforces the regulations. Second, there are the costs to business, nonprofit institutions, and State and local governments of complying with regulations. Finally, there are the longer run and indirect effects of regulation on economic growth and productivity.

The most readily identifiable of the costs are the administrative outlays of the regulatory agencies, since they appear in the Federal budget. These costs are passed on to individuals and businesses directly in the form of higher Federal taxes. Much larger than the administrative expenses are the costs of compliance, which add $100 billion per year to the costs of the goods and services we buy. The most important effects of regulation, however, are the adverse impacts on economic growth. These arise because regulations may discourage innovative research and development, reduce investment in new plant and equipment, raise unemployment by increasing labor costs, and reduce competition. Taken together, these longer run effects contribute significantly to our current economic dilemma of high unemployment and inflation.

In many cases the costs of regulation can be substantially reduced without significantly affecting worthwhile regulatory goals. Unnecessarily stringent rules, intrusive means of enforcement, extensive reporting and record-keeping requirements, and other regulatory excesses are all too common.

During this Administration's first month in office, five major steps have been taken to address the problem of excessive and inefficient regulation. Specifically, we have:

- Established a Task Force on Regulatory Relief chaired by Vice President George Bush,
- Abolished the Council on Wage and Price Stability's ineffective program to control wage and price increases,
- Postponed the effective dates of pending regulations until the end of March,
- Issued an Executive order to strengthen Presidential oversight of the regulatory process, and
- Accelerated the decontrol of domestic oil.

Presidential Task Force on Regulatory Relief

Previous efforts to manage the proliferation of Federal regulation failed to establish central regulatory oversight at the highest level. On January 22, the President announced the creation of a Task Force on Regulatory Relief to be chaired by the Vice President. The membership is to include the Secretary of the Treasury, the Attorney General, the Secretary of Commerce, the Secretary of Labor, the Director of the Office of Management and Budget, the Assistant to the President for Policy Development, and the Chairman of the Council of Economic Advisers.

The Task Force's charter is to:

- Review major regulatory proposals by executive branch agencies, especially those that appear to have major policy significance or involve overlapping jurisdiction among agencies.
- Assess executive branch regulations already on the books, concentrating on those that are particularly burdensome to the national economy or to key industrial sectors.
- Oversee the development of legislative proposals designed to balance and coordinate the roles and objectives of regulatory agencies.

Termination of CWPS's Wage-Price Standards Program

The Council on Wage and Price Stability (CWPS) was created in 1974, and like many government agencies, rapidly grew in size and scope. But the CWPS program of wage price standards proved to be totally ineffective in halting the rising rate of inflation.

On January 29, the President rescinded the CWPS's wage-price standards program. As a result, taxpayers will save about $1.5 million, employment in the Executive Office of the President will decline by about 135 people, and Federal requirements that businesses submit voluminous reports will end.

Postponing Pending Regulations

On January 29, the President also sent a memorandum to cabinet officers and the head of the Environmental Protection Agency (EPA), requesting that, to the extent permitted by law, they postpone the effective dates of those regulations that would have become effective before March 29 and that they refrain from issuing any new final regulations during this 60-day period.

This suspension of new regulations has three purposes: First, it allows the new Administration to review the "midnight" regulations issued during the last days of the previous Administration to assure that they are cost-effective. Second, the Administration's appointees now can become familiar with the details of the various programs for which they are responsible before the regulations become final. Lastly, the suspension allows time for the Administration, through the Presidential Task Force, to develop improved procedures for management and oversight of the regulatory process.

The Executive Order on Federal Regulation

The President has signed a new Executive order designed to improve management of the Federal regulatory process. It provides reassurance to the American people of the government's ability to control its regulatory activities. The Office of Management and Budget is charged with administering the new order, subject to the overall direction of the Presidential Task Force on Regulatory Relief.

The order emphasizes that regulatory decisions should be based on adequate information. Actions should not be undertaken unless the potential benefits to society outweigh the potential costs, and regulatory priorities should be set on the basis of net benefits to society. The order requires agencies to determine the most cost-effective approach for meeting any given regulatory objective, taking into account such factors as the economic condition of industry, the national economy, and other prospective regulations.

As part of the development of any important regulation, the order also requires that each agency prepare a Regulatory Impact Analysis to evaluate potential benefits and costs. The Task Force will oversee this process; OMB will make comments on regulatory analyses, help determine which new and existing regulations should be reviewed, and direct the publication of semiannual agendas of the regulations that agencies plan to issue or review.

Source: "White House Report on the Program for Economic Recovery." In *America's New Beginning: A Program for Economic Recovery—February 18, 1981.* Washington, D.C.: Government Printing Office, 1981.

NOTE

1. Quoted in Hendrick Smith, *Reagan: The Man, the President* (New York: Macmillan, 1980), 154.

DOCUMENT 9.3

President Reagan Defends Ann Gorsuch's Stewardship of the EPA

"The Splendid Record [of] . . . EPA in These Last Two Years Is Being Overlooked"

February 16, 1983

The swirling controversy over Ann Gorsuch's performance as director of the EPA was one of the principal topics of a press conference that President Ronald Reagan held on February 16, 1983. The issue was raised by James Gerstenzang, a reporter with the Associated Press. Reagan responded to the query by signaling his interest in defusing a showdown between his administration and Congress over access to various EPA Superfund records. But he also defended the EPA's overall record during his administration. Making no mention of the steep cuts that had been made to the EPA's budget and personnel during Gorsuch's tenure, Reagan insisted that Superfund was being managed effectively. He also dismissed accusations of malfeasance or incompetence on the part of Gorsuch or her staff, giving her a public vote of confidence. The full exchange between Gerstenzang and Reagan is reprinted here.

The imbroglio surrounding Gorsuch and Reagan's EPA did not subside, however. Environmental groups and their Democratic allies in Congress remained on the offensive, and Gorsuch resigned scarcely two weeks after Reagan's mid-February press conference.

The president steadfastly denied that he pressured Gorsuch to resign, but many historians believe that her departure was engineered by White House officials concerned that the EPA's tarnished public image was becoming a political albatross for Reagan. Around the same time as Gorsuch's resignation, the White House abandoned its claim of executive privilege over the disputed Superfund documents and furnished them to Congress.

Q: Mr. President, in the controversy over the Environmental Protection Agency, there have been suggestions of protection of private interests, of mismanagement, of manipulation, all of this creating the impression of an agency in cahoots with business. What's the proper relationship between the EPA, business, and the rest of the nation? Is the agency living up to your standards, and do you have complete confidence in its director?

The President: I certainly do, and I think that the splendid record that has been accomplished by EPA in these last two years is being overlooked in the flurry of accusations that have been made now.

First of all was, we know, about a month before I arrived here, the Superfund was created. That was a billion six hundred million dollars of government money to help in the locating and cleaning up of chemical dumps or waste dumps that have taken place over the years. And so this particular fund is to provide money if there is no one else that can be held responsible for some of these dumps, for the government to fund clearing them up. But the law also provides for EPA to bring suit, to make out-of-court settlements to try and get those responsible, where they can be located, to fund or help fund in these cleanups. So far, they have named 418 such dumps in the country—there must be thousands—but they've named those as high priority because of the risk associated with them.

Now, there have been 23 settlements so far that I know of. There's been one conviction, criminal conviction, and I have to tell you that I believe that the relationship is what it should be, working together with the concerns that are involved to try and get these cleaned up and, where there is responsibility, to get the private sector paying for it. So far, they've used up about $220 million of the Superfund, but they've also gotten about—somewhere in the neighborhood of another $150 million from private concerns in these cleanups.

Now, let me point out one thing, because this ties into the whole matter of whether the executive privilege that was invoked over something less than a hundred documents has played some part in what's going on now.

We made available to the Congress some 800,000 documents, and less than a hundred were held out as actually being involved in cases and litigation—cases involved cleanup and private concerns. And traditionally this makes them eligible for executive privilege, because it would be disastrous to law enforcement, to our own efforts, and to the cleanup of these places if some of the information in these investigative reports was made public.

However, we offered to the congressional committees that they could come and go over these reports themselves to make sure that they were what we said they were, and they refused. But now with this thing that has come up suggesting that there might be wrongdoing, we will never invoke executive privilege to cover up wrongdoing. And so I have ordered complete investigation by the Justice Department into every charge that is made. I hope we're not getting back to a place where accusation is once again going to be taken as proof of guilt.

And we have been negotiating, because the judge that ruled the other day on the executive privilege idea, he really ruled that we and Congress had not done enough to seek a compromise and to get together. So, all afternoon we've been up on the Hill working with the Congress to work out some compromise whereby we can meet this problem, because I can no longer insist on executive privilege if there's a suspicion in the minds of the people that maybe it is being used to cover some wrongdoing. And that, we will never stand for.

Q: So, as far as the suggestions, though, of mismanagement of the Superfund and manipulation, you seem to be saying you don't buy that.

The President: This is what I've told the Department of Justice to look into on all of these. I have been confident of the management by Anne Gorsuch at the department, and we are talking about getting someone to be of help and to counsel with regard to the congressional relationships in the future so that she can devote her time to managing the agency.

Source: Reagan, Ronald. "Excerpts from Presidential News Conference," February 16, 1983. *Public Papers of the President of the United States: Ronald Reagan, 1983. Book 1: January 1 to July 1, 1983*. Washington, D.C.: Government Printing Office, 1984.

DOCUMENT
9.4

A Landmark Government Report on the Siting of Hazardous Waste Landfills

"The Landfill Is Located in Area A Which Has a 90-Percent Black Population"

June 1, 1983

Concerns about environmental pollution in the inner cities and other population centers with large numbers of low-income and minority residents simmered during the "environmental decade" of the 1970s. Activism about the issue during this period, however, was mostly limited to neighborhood groups and civil rights organizations because the mainstream environmental groups continued to focus primarily on wilderness conservation, habitat and wildlife preservation, and natural aesthetics.

This state of affairs did not measurably change until the early 1980s, when the subject of "environmental racism" ascended to a much more prominent place in public policymaking. The impetus for this change came from grassroots community groups and national civil rights leaders who opposed the siting of a PCB-contaminated hazardous waste site in a poor, overwhelmingly African American area of Warren County, North Carolina. Mass protests, lawsuits, and acts of civil disobedience failed to stop the establishment of the site, but the showdown gave environmental justice advocates a forum to publicize their cause. It also moved District of Columbia delegate Walter Fauntroy of the Congressional Black Congress to commission a General Accounting Office (GAO) study of hazardous waste landfill siting in EPA region 4—essentially the American South.

GAO investigators conducted the study from December 1982 to April 1983. Their final report, excerpted here, permanently changed America's environmental policy–making terrain. It forced policymakers to acknowledge evidence of environmental inequities in minority communities, started the gradual migration of environmental justice issues into the wider environmental movement, and became an enduring touchstone for the work of important figures such as Leon White of the United Church of Christ's Commission for Racial Justice, Benjamin Chavis of the Southern Christian Leadership Conference (and later the NAACP), and environmental justice scholar Robert Bullard.

The Honorable James J. Florio
Chairman, Subcommittee on Commerce, Transportation and Tourism
Committee on Energy and Commerce
House of Representatives

The Honorable Walter E. Fauntroy
House of Representatives

By letter dated December 16, 1982, you requested us to determine the correlation between the location of hazardous waste landfills and the racial and economic status of the surrounding communities. As agreed with your offices, we focused our review on offsite landfills—those not part of or contiguous to an industrial facility—found in the eight southeastern States comprising the Environmental Protection Agency's (EPA's) Region IV. You also asked for information on site location standards, public participation requirements for siting offsite hazardous waste landfills, and EPA's class permit proposal which addresses the permitting, as a group, less complex waste management facilities such as storage tanks.

We found that:

—There are four offsite hazardous waste landfills in Region IV's eight States. Blacks make up the majority of the population in three of the four communities where the land-fills are located. At least 26 percent of the population in all four communities have income below the poverty level and most of this population is black.

—The determination of where a hazardous waste landfill will be located is currently a State responsibility. Federal regulations, effective in January 1983, require that selected sites meet minimal location standards. EPA has just begun its review process to determine if sites meet these standards.

—Federal legislation requires public participation in the hazardous waste landfill per-mit process except for the approval of disposal for polychlorinated biphenyls (PCBs), which are regulated under separate legislation that does not provide for public participation. Because of delays in issuing final regulations three of the four landfills in Region IV have not yet undergone the final permit process where public participation is required. The fourth is a PCB landfill and even though not subject to Federal requirements, has under-gone this process. Only one site in the Nation (in Region VI) has been granted a final haz-ardous waste landfill permit and had been subjected to the public participation process.

—EPA's class permit proposal for regulating facilities, such as tanks or containers that use proven technology, would change public participation at the local level by limit-ing the issues to be discussed. However, class permits would not apply to landfills.

Objective, Scope, and Methodology

Our objective was to determine the correlation between the location of hazardous waste landfills and the racial and economic status of surrounding communities. As agreed with your office, we reviewed offsite hazardous waste landfills in EPA's Region IV (consisting of Alabama, Florida, Georgia, Kentucky, Mississippi, North Carolina, South Carolina, and Tennessee).

We reviewed files and interviewed responsible officials at EPA and the Bureau of the Census headquarters in Washington, D.C. . . . .

To obtain information on communities surrounding these landfills, Bureau of the Census, Department of Commerce, officials located the sites on maps that delineated census areas and provided 1980 racial and economic data for census areas in which the landfills are located and other census areas that have borders within about 4 miles. Bureau of the Census officials also provided similar data for the county and State where the landfills are located.

As agreed with your office we did not verify Bureau of the Census supplied data nor determine why the sites were selected, the population-mix of the area when the site was established, the distribution of the population around the landfill, nor how the communities' racial and economic status compared to others in the State. Also, we did not determine whether any of these sites pose a risk to the surrounding communities.

We also reviewed the landfill siting and public participation requirements of the Resources Conservation and Recovery Act of 1976 and the Toxic Substances Control Act of 1976. . . . .

RACIAL AND ECONOMIC DATA

Based on 1980 census data at three of the four sites—Chemical Waste Management, Industrial Chemical Company, and the Warren County PCB Landfill—the majority of the population in census areas (areas within a county such as a township or subdivision) where the landfills are located is Black. Also, at all four sites the Black population in the surrounding census areas has a lower mean income than the mean income for all races combined and represents the majority of those below poverty level (the poverty level was $7,412 for a family of four in the 1980 census).

Table 1: 1980 Census Population, Income, and Poverty Data for Census Areas Where Landfills Are Located

Landfill	Population		Mean family income ($)		Population below poverty level		
	Number	*% Black*	*All races*	*Black*	*Number*	*%*	*% Black*
Chemical Waste Management	626	90	11,198	10,752	265	42	100
SCA Services	849	38	16,371	6,781	260	31	100
Industrial Chemical Co.	728	52	18,996	12,941	188	26	92
Warren County PCB Landfill	804	66	10,367	9,285	256	32	90

Appendix I

Racial and Economic Data on Four Hazardous Waste Sites

Chemical Waste Management

In 1977 Chemical Waste Management established a commercial hazardous waste treatment, storage, and disposal facility. The facility is located in western Alabama on State Highway 17 in Sumter County. The landfill has RCRA interim status and is approved by EPA for PCB disposal.

As shown [in Table 2], the landfill is located in area A which has a 90-percent Black population. Also, Blacks represent 100 percent of the population that is below the poverty level.

Areas that have borders within 4 miles of the site are area B, still in Sumter County, which is 84 percent Black and area C, in Mississippi, which is 69 percent Black. In these areas, Blacks make up over 93 percent of those below the poverty level.

Table 2: Chemical Waste Management 1980 Census Data

Landfill	Population		Mean family income ($)		Population below poverty level		
Location	Number	% Black	All races	Blacks	Number	%	% Black
Alabama	3,893,888	26	19,199	12,655	719,905	19	52
Sumter Co.	16,908	69	16,573	11,015	5,508	33	93
Area A	626	90	11,198	10,752	265	42	100
Area B	1,335	84	12,025	9,375	620	46	96
Mississippi	2,520,638	35	17,772	11,424	587,217	24	65
Kemper Co.	10,148	54	13,418	9,428	3,757	37	80
Area C	1,060	69	14,257	9,041	532	50	93

SCA Services

In 1977 SCA Services established a commercial hazardous waste treatment, storage, and disposal facility. The facility is located in Sumter County near Lake Marion and close to Clarendon and Calhoun Counties, South Carolina. The facility has RCRA interim status.

As shown [in Table 3], the landfill is located in area A with a 38-percent Black population. However, in areas that have borders within 4 miles—B,C, and D—Blacks make up the majority of the population. In all four areas Blacks represent 84 percent or more of those below the poverty level.

Industrial Chemical Company

In 1972 the Industrial Chemical Company established an offsite landfill to dispose of its own hazardous waste. The site is located in Chester county on U.S. Highway 21 near York and Lancaster Counties, South Carolina. In 1982 the State prohibited the company from disposing of any more waste in the landfill. During our review the site, however, still had interim status under RCRA.

Table 3:   SCA Services, Inc., 1980 Census Data

Landfill	Population		Mean family income ($)		Population below poverty level		
Location	Number	% Black	All races	Blacks	Number	%	% Black
South Carolina	3,121,820	30	19,582	13,508	500,363	16	61
Sumter Co.	88,243	44	16,424	10,978	20,029	23	81
Area A	849	38	16,371	6,781	260	31	100
Claredon Co.	27,464	57	15,202	11,219	7,985	29	81
Area B	607	92	11,203	11,814	244	40	84
Area C	484	74	12,192	11,385	167	35	96
Calhoun Co.	12,206	55	16,991	12,510	2,683	22	85
Area D	724	69	19,282	11,066	216	30	91

As shown [in Table 4], the landfill is located in area A, which has a 52-percent Black population, and Blacks represent 92 percent of those below the poverty level. Areas that have borders within 4 miles show that the Black population ranges from 30 percent to 56 percent. The number of Blacks below the poverty level range from 24 percent in area E to 100 percent in area B.

Table 4:   Industrial Chemical Co., 1980 Census Data

Landfill	Population		Mean family income ($)		Population below poverty level		
Location	Number	% Black	All races	Blacks	Number	%	% Black
South Carolina	3,121,820	30	19,582	13,508	500,363	16	61
Chester Co.	30,148	39	18,153	14,221	4,840	16	70
Area A	728	52	18,996	12,941	188	26	92
Area B	922	30	21,430	17,988	35	4	100
York Co.	106,720	22	21,530	15,383	11,407	11	50
Area C	420	41	18,946	13,200	35	8	Not avail.
Lancaster Co.	53,361	24	19,372	14,880	5,930	11	49
Area D	923	56	18,307	15,945	148	16	79
Area E	1,125	30	17,535	17,240	136	12	24

Warren County PCB Landfill

The Warren County landfill was established to dispose of PCBs that were illegally dumped during 1978 along 241 miles of North Carolina roads. The site is located in Shocco Township in Warren County, N.C. In 1979 EPA approved the site for PCB disposal.

As shown [in Table 5], Shocco Township and three of the five areas that have borders within 4 miles—Sandy Creek, Warrenton, and Fork Townships—have a majority Black population and Blacks make up the majority of those below the poverty level. The population of Judkins Township is 48 percent Black and Fishing Creek Township is 44 percent Black and 47 percent American Indian. The American Indians make up 49 percent of those below poverty level.

Table 5: PCB Landfill 1980 Census Data

Landfill	Population		Mean family income ($)		Population below poverty level		
Location	Number	% Black	All races	Blacks	Number	%	% Black
North Carolina	5,881,766	22	19,513	13,648	839,950	14	46
Warren Co.	16,232	60	15,053	11,463	4,880	30	80
Shocco Township	804	66	10,367	9,285	256	32	90
Sandy Creek Township	1,331	70	14,009	11,806	545	41	91
Warrenton Township	4,596	61	15,812	11,746	1,360	30	90
Fishing Creek Township	1,285	44	11,454	10,296	425	33	39
Fork Township	556	81	10,897	10,378	179	32	81
Judkins Township	850	48	35,329	Not avail.	259	31	Not avail.

. . . The State considered several options for disposing of the PCB-contaminated soil including incineration, transportation to an existing landfill in Alabama, treatment along the roads, or development of a landfill within North Carolina. However, EPA had not approved the incineration and treatment-in-place processes, and the State had determined that transportation to Alabama was too costly. Therefore, the State chose the development of a landfill in North Carolina as the best available alternative.

After the state evaluated over 90 locations, it determined that Warren County was the best available site. The State considered available tracts of State-owned land and those offered by private individuals, corporations, and county governments. The State used the TSCA landfill requirements for PCBs and its own siting criteria to screen and evaluate possible locations. The PCB regulations require that a landfill be in an area of low to moderate relief, with silt and clay soils, and above the historic groundwater table. The State wanted the landfill to be in an area of low to moderate relief, with silt and clay soils, and above the historical groundwater table. The State wanted the landfill to be in an area (1) bounded by the counties where the PCB spills had occurred, (2) with a minimum area of 16 acres, (3) isolated from highly populated areas, and (4) accessible by road with a deeded right-of-way.

Most of the 90 proposed sites were eliminated, according to a State-prepared Environmental Impact Statement (EIS), because they did not meet one or a combination of the evaluation standards. Although 11 of the remaining sites were considered to have a high probability for meeting the PCB landfill criteria, 9 were rejected after the State performed detailed subsurface investigations. The remaining two sites were in Chatham and Warren Counties.

The State evaluated Chatham and Warren County sites essentially equivalent. However, the Chatham site was publicly owned and the county would not sell it, and according to the State Attorney General, the State did not have the power of eminent domain to take over the land. The Warren County site was selected for the landfill because it met the evaluative criteria and was available.

The Warren County landfill is located on 5 acres in the middle of a 142-acre area. The acreage around the landfill serves as a buffer zone. According to the EIS, the landfill site met PCB landfill requirements for topography, hydrology, and soil conditions and the additional State criteria including size, isolation from population centers, access, and location in an area of the PCB spill.

At the State's initiative, a public hearing was held in Warren County on January 4, 1979, to inform the public of the site's selection and to discuss public concerns. Although EPA approved the site in June 1979, construction was delayed for 3 years because of two court suits brought against the State to prevent the site from being used as a PCB landfill. Both suits were settled in favor of the State, and construction of the landfill began on June 26, 1982.

A final attempt to stop the landfill occurred on July 2, 1982. At that time, the local chapter of the National Association for the Advancement of Colored People requested, on the basis of racial discrimination, a preliminary injunction in a Federal district court to prohibit the placement of PCBs in Warren County. The court denied the request and stated in its decision that race was not an issue because throughout all the Federal and State hearings and private party suits, it was never suggested that race was a motivating factor in the location of the landfill. The court went on to state that various criteria and standards were used in selecting the sites, and Warren County was chosen mainly because of site availability.

Source: U.S. General Accounting Office (GAO). *Siting of Hazardous Waste Landfills and Their Correlation with Racial and Economic Status of Surrounding Communities.* Washington, D.C.: GAO, June 1, 1983.

DOCUMENT 9.5

President Reagan Signs the Montreal Protocol on Ozone-depleting Substances

"Ozone Depletion Is a Global Problem"

April 5, 1988

For much of the twentieth century manufacturers around the world relied on a family of industrial compounds known as chlorofluorocarbons (CFCs) in the manufacture of a multitude of consumer products. CFCs were used, among other things, as cooling agents in household and automotive refrigeration and air conditioning, as propellants for dispensing aerosol sprays, and as ingredients in insulation and foam packaging. In the 1970s, however, scientists discovered that the cumulative release of CFCs into the atmosphere was wreaking havoc on the ozone layer, the thin membrane of ozone in the stratosphere that protects all life on earth from dangerous ultraviolet radiation. Researchers and policymakers spent the next several years debating the scope of the problem and various proposals to address ozone depletion.

This debate took on added urgency in the mid-1980s, when British scientists documented an annually appearing "ozone hole" above Antarctica. These grim tidings, coupled with increased recognition of the greenhouse gas properties of CFCs, prompted international calls for a ban on CFC production. Indeed, the transboundary nature of ozone depletion made a global response essential. Fortunately, the international community had by the mid-1980s already established a modest but real track record of cooperation on ocean protection, wildlife conservation, and other pressing environmental issues, and it responded to the ozone threat with alacrity. A 1985 gathering in Vienna produced the Vienna Convention for the Protection of the Ozone Layer, which committed twenty industrialized nations (including most of the main CFC producers) to negotiating new international regulations to halt CFC production and emissions. Subsequent negotiations produced the Montreal Protocol on Substances that Deplete the Ozone Layer, which phased out production of CFCs and other ozone-depleting chemicals (by 1996 for developed countries and 2006 for other nations). Fifty-seven industrial nations signed the Montreal Protocol after it was opened for signature in September 1987. President Ronald Reagan formally signed the Protocol on April 5, 1988; following are his signing statement remarks.

The Montreal Protocol, which entered into force on January 1, 1989, has been credited with effectively addressing the ozone depletion threat. Tracking data indicate that the Antarctic ozone hole is shrinking and that CFC levels in the atmosphere have declined dramatically since its regulations went into effect. In addition, this decisive and effective international response to a clear environmental danger has been cited by people as evidence that another worldwide ecological and economic threat—global warming—can also be effectively combated through international efforts.

I am pleased to sign the instrument of ratification for the Montreal protocol on substances that deplete the ozone layer. The protocol marks an important milestone for the future quality of the global environment and for the health and well-being of all peoples of the world. Unanimous approval of the protocol by the Senate on March 14th demonstrated to the world community this country's willingness to act promptly and decisively in carrying out its commitments to protect the stratospheric ozone layer from the damaging effects of chlorofluorocarbons and halons, but our action alone is not enough. The protocol enters into force next January only if at least 11 nations representing two-thirds of worldwide consumption of chlorofluorocarbons and halons ratify the agreement. Our immediate challenge, having come this far, is to promote prompt ratification by every signatory nation.

I believe the Montreal protocol, negotiated under the auspices of the United Nations Environment Programme, is an extremely important environmental agreement. It provides for internationally coordinated control of ozone-depleting substances in order to protect a vital global resource. It requires countries that are parties to reduce production and consumption of major ozone-depleting chemicals by 50 percent by 1999. It creates incentives for new technologies—chemical producers are already working to develop and market safer substitutes—and establishes an ongoing process for review of new scientific data and of technical and economic developments. A mechanism for adjustment of the protocol is established to allow for changes based upon the review process. The wisdom of this unique provision is already being realized.

Data made available only during the last few weeks demonstrate that our knowledge of ozone depletion is rapidly expanding. For our part, the United States will give the highest priority to analyzing and assessing the latest research findings to assure that the review process moves expeditiously.

The Montreal protocol is a model of cooperation. It is a product of the recognition and international consensus that ozone depletion is a global problem, both in terms of its causes and its effects. The protocol is the result of an extraordinary process of scientific study, negotiations among representatives of the business and environmental communities, and international diplomacy. It is a monumental achievement.

Source: Reagan, Ronald. Statement on signing the Montreal Protocol of Ozone-depleting Substances, April 5, 1988. *The Public Papers of President Ronald W. Reagan.* Ronald Reagan Presidential Library. www.reagan.utexas.edu/archives/speeches/1988/040588a.htm.

DOCUMENT
9.6

President Bush Signs the Clean Air Act Amendments

"This Bill Will Cut Emissions That Cause Acid Rain in Half"

November 15, 1990

When George H. W. Bush succeeded Ronald Reagan as president in 1989, he proposed legislation to reauthorize and strengthen the original Clean Air Act of 1970 and its 1977 amendments, which had been mired in partisan warfare for years. Bush had pledged to push for measures to control acid rain, urban smog, and other worsening air quality problems during his 1988 presidential campaign, and after his inauguration Bush Administration officials became actively involved in the ongoing debate over clean air policies.

Significant new air pollution control legislation was finally passed by Congress with broad bipartisan support in the fall of 1990, after months of haggling, lobbying, and legislative maneuvering by environmental groups, industry representatives, and other stakeholders with influence in Washington—and repeated prodding from the Bush White House. The final bill was assailed by some business leaders for imposing unreasonable new financial burdens on the private sector. Some activists and researchers criticized it for making too many compromises in the areas of public health and being silent on the issue of carbon dioxide emissions, a key greenhouse gas. But the Clean Air Act Amendments also won high praise from many quarters—including spokespersons from environmental groups such as the Sierra Club and the National Clean Air Coalition—for taking aggressive but pragmatic steps to reduce air pollution in America without alienating industry.

Today the 1990 reauthorization of the Clean Air Act is widely touted as the most momentous environmental policy event of George H. W. Bush's presidency. Its various mandates resulted in cleaner air in urban areas, lower emissions of pollutants from motor vehicles, a dramatic downturn in emissions of all major sources of toxic or hazardous air pollutants, and a complete phase out of the use of ozone-depleting chlorofluorocarbons.

Yet of all these accomplishments, the bill's acid rain provisions offered perhaps the most startling results. The "cap and trade" Acid Rain Program included in the 1990 legislation imposed a cap on total acid rain emissions permissible in the United States and set in place mechanisms whereby companies that exceeded their emissions allowance could purchase credits or allowances from low-polluting companies—a transaction known as a trade. This program greatly reduced acid rain emissions in the United States during the 1990s and 2000s. In 2007, in fact, total U.S. sulfur dioxide emissions fell below the Acid Rain Program's long-term emission cap of 9.5 million tons a full three years before the 2010 statutory deadline. And one year later, EPA reported that the Acid Rain Program had reduced sulphur dioxide emissions by more than 50 percent since 1990.[1] These triumphs have helped resuscitate thousands of lakes and rivers in the United States and Canada that had been poisoned by acid deposition.

Following are excerpts from the president's remarks at the signing ceremony for the Clean Air Act Amendments on November 15, 1990.

Thanksgiving is still a week away, but I believe this really is a true red-letter day for all Americans. Today we add a long-awaited and long-needed chapter in our environmental history, and we begin a new era for clean air.

This last weekend, I spent some pleasant hours up at Camp David. Saturday and Sunday really were fantastic—clear and crisp and beautiful, bright sunshine and those magnificent fall colors. And it was great to get out in the woods. But no American should have to drive out of town to breath clean air. Every city in America should have clean air. And with this legislation, I firmly believe we will.

I first made a commitment to comprehensive clean air legislation when I was running for this job, and soon after coming into office, we developed a comprehensive clean air proposal. I think we did have consultation in the best spirit with the Democratic leadership and with the Republican leadership in the Congress, with environmentalists and with representatives of industry, because I believed, and I think we all felt, that it was time for a new approach. It was time to break the logjam that hindered progress on clean air for 13 years. And so, I told our best minds, assembled that morning a year and a half ago, every American expects and deserves to breathe clean air. And as President, it is my mission to guarantee it for this generation and for the generations to come.

Well, as we used to say in the Navy: Mission defined, mission accomplished. Today I am very proud on behalf of everyone here to sign this clean air bill—Clean Air Act of 1990.

This landmark legislation will reduce air pollution each year by 56 billion pounds—that's 224 pounds for every man, woman, and child in America. It will go after the three main types of air pollution: acid rain, smog, and toxic air pollutants. This bill will cut emissions that cause acid rain in half and permanently cap them at these new levels. It will reduce pollutants that cause smog in our cities by 40 percent, so that by the year 2000, over 100 major American cities with poor air quality will have safer, healthier air. And it will cut dangerous air toxics emissions by over 75 percent, using new technologies. And by the next decade, its alternative fuel provisions will help reduce our dependence on foreign oil. This bill means cleaner cars, cleaner power plants, cleaner factories, and cleaner fuels; and it means a cleaner America. Virtually every person in every city and every town will enjoy its benefits.

This legislation isn't just the centerpiece of our environmental agenda. It is simply the most significant air pollution legislation in our nation's history, and it restores America's place as the global leader in environmental protection.

Nineteen ninety is now a milestone year for the environment. I also hope that it will be remembered as an important year for environmental cooperation. There were several members of my administration who saw to it, through thick and thin, that this bill got to my desk: Bill Reilly, the EPA Administrator; Jim Watkins, the Secretary of Energy. From my own staff, our Chief of Staff worked tirelessly—John Sununu. Roger Porter did an outstanding job, working day in and day out with the Members of Congress. Boyden Gray—the same thing. Bob Grady and so many others. And they did a great job on this.

And I also want to thank once again the Senators and Members of Congress from both sides of the aisle. Many of you are with us today, and as I mentioned earlier, others couldn't be with us today. But it isn't because of lack of interest. Congress is out; many are scattered to the winds. But the list is too long to single out everybody from the Hill that worked on this. But again, I just want to thank you that are here today and the others who couldn't be with us for your commitment and dedication—as well as the governors, the governors and the experts from local governments who were also instrumental in building true bipartisan support for this legislation.

We met with business leaders who saw stewardship to the environment as a key to long-term economic growth. And we met with academics and innovative problem-solvers from every side who have helped build the foundation for this approach.

I want to commend the environmental groups that we've met with, like the Environmental Defense Fund, under the leadership of Fred Krupp, for bringing creativity to the table to end what could have been a hopeless stalemate.

We all had tough choices to make. Some said we went too far; others said we didn't go far enough. But despite our differences, we all agreed on the goal: clean air for all Americans. We agreed on the means: a new Clean Air Act.

And we all agreed it was time to take a new approach. This bill is both ambitious in its goals and innovative in its methods. For the first time, we've moved away from the red tape bureaucratic approach of the past. The old tradition of command and control regulation is not the answer. By relying on the marketplace, we can achieve the ambitious environmental goals we have as a country in the most efficient and cost-effective way possible. We'll have to take advantage of the innovation, energy, and ingenuity of every American, drawing local communities and the private sector into the cause. It's time for a new kind of environmentalism, driven by the knowledge that a sound ecology and a strong economy can coexist.

The approach in this bill balances economic growth and environmental protection. The approach is comprehensive, cost-effective; and most of all, it will work. The first major pollution reductions are where we need them most. It offers incentives, choice, and flexibility for industry to find the best solutions, all in the context of continued economic growth. The bill is balanced: It will stimulate the use of natural gas from the wells of Texas and Louisiana; and fuels made from the farms of Iowa, Illinois, the great Midwest; and cleaner, low-sulfur coal from the hills of West Virginia to the Rocky Mountain States. This bill can make America the global leader in developing a new generation of environmental technologies to which the world is now turning.

But it does more. The legislation sets reasonable deadlines for those who must comply; but once deadlines go by, once they pass, the penalties are severe. American heritage is precious. We will not turn our backs or look the other way. That means polluters must pay. And so, there is a new breeze blowing, a new current of concern for the environment. Today marks a great victory for the environment, a day when we have strengthened our clean air statutes, already the world's toughest. This legislation is not only in America's interest; like so many of the environmental issues that we are working on, this bill is in the interest of people all over the world.

And the new environmental ethos is growing. We see it in community efforts and in school involvement across America, and we're seeing it in the innovative response of private industry—in alternative fuel service stations, electric vehicles. These companies understand we must pioneer new technology, find new solutions, envision new horizons if we're to build a bright future and a better America for our children.

There's an old saying: "We don't inherit the Earth from our parents. We borrow it from our children." We have succeeded today because of a common sense of global stewardship, a sense that it is the Earth that endures and that all of us are simply holding a sacred trust left for future generations. For the sake of future generations, I again thank each and every one of you for your commitment to our precious environment. I am now honored to sign this clean air bill into law.

Thank you all who have worked so hard for this day to become possible. Thank you, and God bless all of you.

Source: Bush, George H. W. "Remarks on Signing the Bill Amending the Clean Air Act," November 15, 1990. *Public Papers of the Presidents of the United States: George H.W. Bush, 1990.* Washington, D.C.: Government Printing Office, 1991.

Note

1. Acid Rain Program 2008 Progress Report: Emission, Compliance and Market Data. Available at www.epa.gov/airmarkt/progress/ARP_1.html.

**DOCUMENT
9.7**

Activists Release "Principles of Environmental Justice"

"Environmental Justice Demands That Public Policy Be Based on Mutual Respect and Justice for All Peoples"

October 24–27, 1991

In October 1991 the United Church of Christ, led by Benjamin Chavis, spearheaded the organization of the First National People of Color Environmental Leadership Summit in Washington, D.C. This summit, which ran from October 24 to October 27, reaffirmed the importance of environmental justice issues to the civil rights community and heralded the arrival of minorities as equals in the wider environmental movement (even as some grassroots activists explicitly rejected the notion that they were part of the environmental movement).

Extensive media coverage of the summit also contributed to a belated effort by mainstream environmentalism to do some soul searching about their past history. Several leading environmental groups that had always been overwhelmingly white, middle class, and conservation oriented in their demographic makeup subsequently acknowledged paternalistic and exclusionary elements in their histories. They also admitted to histories of neglect of urban pollution issues.

At the opening of the summit, the 500 or so activists who attended the event passed a resolution detailing seventeen distinct "Principles of Environmental Justice" that they viewed as pillars of their cause. This set of principles, reprinted here, remains a touchstone for environmental justice advocates seeking to influence public policy in the United States.

WE THE PEOPLE OF COLOR, gathered together at this multinational People of Color Environmental Leadership Summit, to begin to build a national and international movement of all peoples of color to fight the destruction and taking of our lands and communities, do hereby re-establish our spiritual interdependence to the sacredness of our Mother Earth; to respect and celebrate each of our cultures, languages and beliefs about the natural world and our roles in healing ourselves; to insure environmental justice; to promote economic alternatives which would contribute to the development of environmentally safe livelihoods; and, to secure our political, economic and cultural liberation that has been denied for over 500 years of colonization and oppression, resulting in the poisoning of our communities and land and the genocide of our peoples, do affirm and adopt these Principles of Environmental Justice:

1. *Environmental Justice* affirms the sacredness of Mother Earth, ecological unity and the interdependence of all species, and the right to be free from ecological destruction.

2. *Environmental Justice* demands that public policy be based on mutual respect and justice for all peoples, free from any form of discrimination or bias.

3. *Environmental Justice* mandates the right to ethical, balanced and responsible uses of land and renewable resources in the interest of a sustainable planet for humans and other living things.

4. *Environmental Justice* calls for universal protection from nuclear testing, extraction, production and disposal of toxic/hazardous wastes and poisons and nuclear testing that threaten the fundamental right to clean air, land, water, and food.

5. *Environmental Justice* affirms the fundamental right to political, economic, cultural and environmental self-determination of all peoples.

6. *Environmental Justice* demands the cessation of the production of all toxins, hazardous wastes, and radioactive materials, and that all past and current producers be held strictly accountable to the people for detoxification and the containment at the point of production.

7. *Environmental Justice* demands the right to participate as equal partners at every level of decision-making, including needs assessment, planning, implementation, enforcement and evaluation.

8. *Environmental Justice* affirms the right of all workers to a safe and healthy work environment without being forced to choose between an unsafe livelihood and unemployment. It also affirms the right of those who work at home to be free from environmental hazards.

9. *Environmental Justice* protects the right of victims of environmental injustice to receive full compensation and reparations for damages as well as quality health care.

10. *Environmental Justice* considers governmental acts of environmental injustice a violation of international law, the Universal Declaration On Human Rights, and the United Nations Convention on Genocide.

11. *Environmental Justice* must recognize a special legal and natural relationship of Native Peoples to the U.S. government through treaties, agreements, compacts, and covenants affirming sovereignty and self-determination.

12. *Environmental Justice* affirms the need for urban and rural ecological policies to clean up and rebuild our cities and rural areas in balance with nature, honoring the cultural integrity of all our communities, and provided fair access for all to the full range of resources.

13. *Environmental Justice* calls for the strict enforcement of principles of informed consent, and a halt to the testing of experimental reproductive and medical procedures and vaccinations on people of color.

14. *Environmental Justice* opposes the destructive operations of multi-national corporations.

15. *Environmental Justice* opposes military occupation, repression and exploitation of lands, peoples and cultures, and other life forms.

16. *Environmental Justice* calls for the education of present and future generations which emphasizes social and environmental issues, based on our experience and an appreciation of our diverse cultural perspectives.

17. *Environmental Justice* requires that we, as individuals, make personal and consumer choices to consume as little of Mother Earth's resources and to produce as little waste as possible; and make the conscious decision to challenge and reprioritize our lifestyles to insure the health of the natural world for present and future generations.

Source: "Principles of Environmental Justice." Charles Lee, ed. Proceedings: The First National People of Color Environmental Leadership Summit, October 24–27, 1991, Washington, D.C. Copyright © 1991 by United Church of Christ Commission for Racial Justice: New York (now Justice and Witness Ministries, a Covenanted Ministry of the United Church of Christ, Cleveland, Ohio). Reprinted by permission.

DOCUMENT
9.8

The FDA Blurs Distinctions between GM and Non-GM Foods

"This Action . . . Does Not Individually or Cumulatively Have a Significant Effect on the Human Environment"

May 28, 1992

During much of the 1980s, Monsanto and other companies heavily involved in developing genetically modified (GM) crops embraced an incremental GM food rollout strategy. They believed that careful scientific review and voluntary acceptance of government regulation (albeit regulation that they influenced) would alleviate public anxiety about bioengineered foods and lay the groundwork for decades of commercial success.

In the early 1990s, however, the industry's growing confidence about the safety and potential profitability of GM foods led them to discard their incremental, measured approach. Instead, industry spokespeople called on federal authorities to immediately loosen the regulatory reins on bioengineered food products. The George H. W. Bush Administration was receptive to these calls. On May 26, 1992, Vice President Dan Quayle, chairman of the president's Council on Competitiveness, and Health and Human Services secretary Louis Sullivan announced a major overhaul of Food and Drug Administration policy on genetically modified foods. In essence, the new FDA policy made virtually no distinctions in labeling, inspections, and other regulatory sectors between GM foods and those derived by conventional farming methods. From this point forward, bioengineered foods and conventional foods would be treated the same by FDA regulators in virtually all cases.

The basic premise of this new policy—that genetically engineered crops are no different than those created through traditional methods—was hotly contested by environmental and consumer groups and their allies in Congress. They asserted that the long-term safety of bioengineered food was unproven and that the full environmental implications of genetically modified crops had not been adequately researched. U.S. biotech firms and critics of "burdensome and unnecessary regulation" praised the decision, however, and the first biotechnology-based agri-food products entered the marketplace two years after this policy change was announced. Today, GM production of corn, cotton, soybeans, and many other agricultural products is widespread across the United States. Following are excerpts from the FDA policy announcement (footnotes removed).

I. Background and Overview of Policy

New methods of genetically modifying plants are being used to develop new varieties that will be sources of foods. These methods, including recombinant DNA techniques and cell fusion techniques, enable developers to make genetic modifications in plants, including some modifications that would not be possible with traditional plant breeding methods. This policy discusses the safety and regulatory status of foods derived from new plant varieties, including plants developed by the newer methods of genetic modification.

FDA has received numerous inquiries from industry, government agencies, academia, and the public requesting clarification of the regulatory status of foods, such as fruits, vegetables, grains and their byproducts, derived from new plant varieties developed using recombinant DNA techniques. The questions that FDA has received center on issues such as whether the agency will conduct premarket review of these new foods, whether such foods introduced into interstate commerce would be challenged by FDA on legal grounds, which new plant varieties might come under the jurisdiction of FDA, what scientific information may be necessary to satisfy FDA that such foods are safe and comply with the law, whether petitions would be required by the agency, and whether special labeling would be required.

Representatives of the food biotechnology industry have expressed to FDA the need for strong but appropriate oversight by Federal agencies to ensure public confidence in foods produced by the new techniques. FDA has received several specific comments and suggestions from the industry and from the public concerning Federal oversight of foods developed through new methods of genetically modifying plants. The agency has considered these and other documents, including scientific research papers, in developing this notice, and is setting forth this policy statement to clarify its interpretation of the act with respect to human foods and animal feeds derived from new plant varieties, including but not limited to plants developed by new methods of genetic modification.

Under this policy, foods, such as fruits, vegetables, grains, and their byproducts, derived from plant varieties developed by the new methods of genetic modification are regulated within the existing framework of the act, FDA's implementing regulations, and current practice, utilizing an approach identical in principle to that applied to foods developed by traditional plant breeding. The regulatory status of a food, irrespective of the method by which it is developed, is dependent upon objective characteristics of the food and the intended use of the food (or its components). The method by which food is produced or developed may in some cases help to understand the safety or nutritional characteristics of the finished food. However, the key factors in reviewing safety concerns should be the characteristics of the food product, rather than the fact that the new methods are used.

The safety of a food is regulated primarily under FDA's postmarket authority of section 402(a)(1) of the act (21 U.S.C. 342(a)(1)). Unintended occurrences of unsafe levels of toxicants in food are regulated under this section. Substances that are expected to become components of food as result of genetic modification of a plant and whose composition such or has been altered such that the substance is not generally recognized as safe (CRAS) or otherwise exempt are subject to regulation as "food additives" under section 409 of the act (21 U.S.C. 348). Under the act, substances that are food additives may be used in food only in accordance with an authorizing regulation.

In most cases, the substances expected to become components of food as a result of genetic modification of a plant will be the same as or substantially similar to substances commonly found in food, such as proteins, fats and oils, and carbohydrates. . . . FDA has determined that such substances should be subject to regulation under section 409 of the act in those cases when the objective characteristics of the substance raise questions of safety sufficient to warrant formal premarket review and approval by FDA. The objective characteristics that will trigger regulation of substances as food additives are described in the guidance section of this notice. . . .

The guidance section also describes scientific considerations that are important in evaluating the safety and nutritional value of foods for consumption by humans or animals, regardless of whether the food is regulated under section 402(a)(1) or section 409 of the act. The guidance section outlines a "decision tree" approach to safety assessment of foods derived from new plant varieties that FDA believes is compatible with current practice among scientists knowledgeable in this area. The guidance section also identifies certain scientific questions that may raise sufficient safety concern to warrant consultation with FDA.

Finally, this notice addresses FDA's responsibility under the National Environmental Policy Act (NEPA) and the food labeling provisions of the act as such provisions affect labeling of foods derived from new plant varieties.

This policy statement reflects FDA's current judgment based on the new plant varieties now under development in agricultural research. FDA invites comments on this document. Because scientific developments in this field are occurring rapidly, FDA will refine its policy, if circumstances warrant, in a future *Federal Register* notice. . . .

VIII. Environmental Consideration: Applicability of NEPA

NEPA requires FDA to consider in its decisionmaking the environmental impact of its major Federal actions that significantly affect the quality of the human environment. The promulgation of a food additive regulation is an agency action that ordinarily triggers the NEPA requirement for development of an environmental assessment. . . .

FDA does not consider that the activities it may undertake with respect to foods from new plant varieties other than promulgation of food additive regulations, such as consultation with producers on safety issues and providing advice on the regulatory status of foods from new plant varieties, will constitute agency action under NEPA. . . .

X. ENVIRONMENTAL IMPACT

The agency has determined under 21 CFR 25.24(a)(8) that this action is of a type that does not individually or cumulatively have a significant effect on the human environment. Therefore, neither an environmental assessment nor an environmental impact statement is required. . . .

Source: "Statement of Policy: Foods Derived from New Plant Varieties; Notice." *Federal Register.* Part IX: Department of Health and Human Services, Food and Drug Administration. Vol. 57, No. 104. Washington, D.C.: Government Printing Office, May 29, 1992, pp. 22984–22985, 23005.

DOCUMENT 9.9 — President Clinton Issues an Executive Order on Environmental Justice

"Each Federal Agency Shall Make Achieving Environmental Justice Part of Its Mission"

February 11, 1994

The growing influence of the environmental justice movement on national policy was made manifest with the decision by President Bill Clinton to sign and issue Executive Order No. 12898 on February 11, 1994. This executive order, titled Federal Actions To Address Environmental Justice in Minority Populations and Low-Income Populations, required every federal agency to adhere to various environmental justice practices and goals in their programs, policies, and activities. In addition, most federal agencies were explicitly directed to design and implement environmental justice plans. Following is the full text of Clinton's executive order.

By the authority vested in me as President by the Constitution and the laws of the United States of America, it is hereby ordered as follows:

SECTION 1–1. IMPLEMENTATION.

1–101. Agency Responsibilities. To the greatest extent practicable and permitted by law, and consistent with the principles set forth in the report on the National Performance Review, each Federal agency shall make achieving environmental justice part of its mission by identifying and addressing, as appropriate, disproportionately high and adverse human health or environmental effects of its programs, policies, and activities on minority populations and low-income populations in the United States and its territories and possessions, the District of Columbia, the Commonwealth of Puerto Rico, and the Commonwealth of the Mariana Islands.

1–102. Creation of an Interagency Working Group on Environmental Justice. (a) Within 3 months of the date of this order, the Administrator of the Environmental Protection Agency ("Administrator") or the Administrator's designee shall convene an interagency Federal Working Group on Environmental Justice ("Working Group"). The Working Group shall comprise the heads of the following executive agencies and offices, or their designees: (a) Department of Defense; (b) Department of Health and Human Services; (c) Department of Housing and Urban Development; (d) Department of Labor; (e) Department of Agriculture; (f) Department of Transportation; (g) Department of Justice; (h) Department of the Interior; (i) Department of Commerce; (j) Department of Energy; (k) Environmental Protection Agency; (l) Office of Management and Budget; (m) Office of Science and Technology Policy; (n) Office of the Deputy Assistant to the President for Environmental Policy; (o) Office of the Assistant to the President for Domestic Policy; (p) National Economic Council; (q) Council of Economic Advisers; and (r) such other Government officials as the President may designate. The Working Group shall report to the President through the Deputy Assistant to the President for Environmental Policy and the Assistant to the President for Domestic Policy.

(b) The Working Group shall: (1) provide guidance to Federal agencies on criteria for identifying disproportionately high and adverse human health or environmental effects on minority populations and low-income populations;

(2) coordinate with, provide guidance to, and serve as a clearinghouse for, each Federal agency as it develops an environmental justice strategy as required by section 1–103 of this order, in order to ensure that the administration, interpretation and enforcement of programs, activities and policies are undertaken in a consistent manner;

(3) assist in coordinating research by, and stimulating cooperation among, the Environmental Protection Agency, the Department of Health and Human Services, the Department of Housing and Urban Development, and other agencies conducting research or other activities in accordance with section 3–3 of this order;

(4) assist in coordinating data collection, required by this order;

(5) examine existing data and studies on environmental justice;

(6) hold public meetings as required in section 5–502(d) of this order; and

(7) develop interagency model projects on environmental justice that evidence cooperation among Federal agencies.

1–103. Development of Agency Strategies. (a) Except as provided in section 6–605 of this order, each Federal agency shall develop an agency-wide environmental justice strategy, as set forth in subsections (b)-(e) of this section that identifies and addresses disproportionately high and adverse human health or environmental effects of its programs, policies, and activities on minority populations and low-income populations. The environmental justice strategy shall list programs, policies, planning and public participation processes, enforcement, and/or rulemakings related to human health or the environment that should be revised to, at a minimum: (1) promote enforcement of all health and environmental statutes in areas with minority populations and low-income populations; (2) ensure greater public participation; (3) improve research and data collection relating to the health of and environment of minority populations and low-income populations; and (4) identify differential patterns of consumption of natural resources among minority populations and low-income populations. In addition, the environmental justice strategy shall include, where appropriate, a timetable for undertaking identified revisions and consideration of economic and social implications of the revisions.

(b) Within 4 months of the date of this order, each Federal agency shall identify an internal administrative process for developing its environmental justice strategy, and shall inform the Working Group of the process.

(c) Within 6 months of the date of this order, each Federal agency shall provide the Working Group with an outline of its proposed environmental justice strategy.

(d) Within 10 months of the date of this order, each Federal agency shall provide the Working Group with its proposed environmental justice strategy.

(e) Within 12 months of the date of this order, each Federal agency shall finalize its environmental justice strategy and provide a copy and written description of its strategy to the Working Group. During the 12 month period from the date of this order, each Federal agency, as part of its environmental justice strategy, shall identify several specific projects that can be promptly undertaken to address particular concerns identified during the development of the proposed environmental justice strategy, and a schedule for implementing those projects.

(f) Within 24 months of the date of this order, each Federal agency shall report to the Working Group on its progress in implementing its agency-wide environmental justice strategy.

(g) Federal agencies shall provide additional periodic reports to the Working Group as requested by the Working Group.

1–104. Reports to the President. Within 14 months of the date of this order, the Working Group shall submit to the President, through the Office of the Deputy Assistant to the President for Environmental Policy and the Office of the Assistant to the President for Domestic Policy, a report that describes the implementation of this order, and includes the final environmental justice strategies described in section 1–103(e) of this order.

Sec. 2–2. Federal Agency Responsibilities for Federal Programs. Each Federal agency shall conduct its programs, policies, and activities that substantially affect human health or the environment, in a manner that ensures that such programs, policies, and activities do not have the effect of excluding persons (including populations) from participation in, denying persons (including populations) the benefits of, or subjecting persons (including populations) to discrimination under, such programs, policies, and activities, because of their race, color, or national origin.

Sec. 3–3. Research, Data Collection, and Analysis.

3–301. Human Health and Environmental Research and Analysis. (a) Environmental human health research, whenever practicable and appropriate, shall include diverse segments of the population in epidemiological and clinical studies, including segments at high risk from environmental hazards, such as minority populations, low-income populations and workers who may be exposed to substantial environmental hazards.

(b) Environmental human health analyses, whenever practicable and appropriate, shall identify multiple and cumulative exposures.

(c) Federal agencies shall provide minority populations and low-income populations the opportunity to comment on the development and design of research strategies undertaken pursuant to this order.

3–302. Human Health and Environmental Data Collection and Analysis. To the extent permitted by existing law, including the Privacy Act, as amended (5 U.S.C. section 552a): (a) each Federal agency, whenever practicable and appropriate, shall collect, maintain, and analyze information assessing and comparing environmental and human health risks borne by populations identified by race, national origin, or income. To the extent practical and appropriate, Federal agencies shall use this information to determine whether their programs, policies, and activities have disproportionately high and adverse human health or environmental effects on minority populations and low-income populations;

(b) In connection with the development and implementation of agency strategies in section 1–103 of this order, each Federal agency, whenever practicable and appropriate, shall collect, maintain and analyze information on the race, national origin, income level, and other readily accessible and appropriate information for areas surrounding facilities or sites expected to have a substantial environmental, human health, or economic effect on the surrounding populations, when such facilities or sites become the subject of a substantial Federal environmental administrative or judicial action. Such information shall be made available to the public, unless prohibited by law; and

(c) Each Federal agency, whenever practicable and appropriate, shall collect, maintain, and analyze information on the race, national origin, income level, and other readily accessible and appropriate information for areas surrounding Federal facilities that are: (1) subject to the reporting requirements under the Emergency Planning and Community Right-to-Know Act, 42 U.S.C. section 11001–11050 as mandated in Executive Order No. 12856; and (2) expected to have a substantial environmental, human health, or economic effect on surrounding populations. Such information shall be made available to the public, unless prohibited by law.

(d) In carrying out the responsibilities in this section, each Federal agency, whenever practicable and appropriate, shall share information and eliminate unnecessary duplication of efforts through the use of existing data systems and cooperative agreements among Federal agencies and with State, local, and tribal governments.

Sec. 4–4. Subsistence Consumption of Fish and Wildlife.

4–401. Consumption Patterns. In order to assist in identifying the need for ensuring protection of populations with differential patterns of subsistence consumption of fish and wildlife, Federal agencies, whenever practicable and appropriate, shall collect, maintain, and analyze information on the consumption patterns of populations who principally rely on fish and/or wildlife for subsistence. Federal agencies shall communicate to the public the risks of those consumption patterns.

4–402. Guidance. Federal agencies, whenever practicable and appropriate, shall work in a coordinated manner to publish guidance reflecting the latest scientific information available concerning methods for evaluating the human health risks associated with the consumption of pollutant-bearing fish or wildlife. Agencies shall consider such guidance in developing their policies and rules.

Sec. 5–5. Public Participation and Access to Information. (a) The public may submit recommendations to Federal agencies relating to the incorporation of environmental justice principles into Federal agency programs or policies. Each Federal agency shall convey such recommendations to the Working Group.

(b) Each Federal agency may, whenever practicable and appropriate, translate crucial public documents, notices, and hearings relating to human health or the environment for limited English speaking populations.

(c) Each Federal agency shall work to ensure that public documents, notices, and hearings relating to human health or the environment are concise, understandable, and readily accessible to the public.

(d) The Working Group shall hold public meetings, as appropriate, for the purpose of fact-finding, receiving public comments, and conducting inquiries concerning environmental justice. The Working Group shall prepare for public review a summary of the comments and recommendations discussed at the public meetings.

Sec. 6–6. General Provisions.

6–601. Responsibility for Agency Implementation. The head of each Federal agency shall be responsible for ensuring compliance with this order. Each Federal agency shall conduct internal reviews and take such other steps as may be necessary to monitor compliance with this order.

6–602. Executive Order No. 12250. This Executive order is intended to supplement but not supersede Executive Order No. 12250, which requires consistent and effective implementation of various laws prohibiting discriminatory practices in programs receiving Federal financial assistance. Nothing herein shall limit the effect or mandate of Executive Order No. 12250.

6–603. Executive Order No. 12875. This Executive order is not intended to limit the effect or mandate of Executive Order No. 12875.

6–604. Scope. For purposes of this order, Federal agency means any agency on the Working Group, and such other agencies as may be designated by the President, that conducts any Federal program or activity that substantially affects human health or the environment. Independent agencies are requested to comply with the provisions of this order.

6–605. Petitions for Exemptions. The head of a Federal agency may petition the President for an exemption from the requirements of this order on the grounds that all or some of the petitioning agency's programs or activities should not be subject to the requirements of this order.

6–606. Native American Programs. Each Federal agency responsibility set forth under this order shall apply equally to Native American programs. In addition, the Department of the Interior, in coordination with the Working Group, and, after consultation with tribal leaders, shall coordinate steps to be taken pursuant to this order that address Federally-recognized Indian Tribes.

6–607. Costs. Unless otherwise provided by law, Federal agencies shall assume the financial costs of complying with this order.

6–608. General. Federal agencies shall implement this order consistent with, and to the extent permitted by, existing law.

6–609. Judicial Review. This order is intended only to improve the internal management of the executive branch and is not intended to, nor does it create any right, benefit, or trust responsibility, substantive or procedural, enforceable at law or equity by a party against the United States, its agencies, its officers, or any person. This order shall not be construed to create any right to judicial review involving the compliance or noncompliance of the United States, its agencies, its officers, or any other person with this order.

William J. Clinton
THE WHITE HOUSE,
February 11, 1994.

Source: Clinton, William J. Federal Actions To Address Environmental Justice in Minority Populations and Low-Income Populations. Executive Order 12898 of February 11, 1994. *Federal Register,* Vol. 59, No. 32, February 16, 1994, p. 7629.

The EPA Inspector General Details Problems with State Environmental Programs

"States and Even EPA Regions Disregarded Agency Requirements"

September 1998

The distribution of responsibility for environmental regulation and protection between federal and state authorities has been a recurring source of debate and acrimony in the United States since the 1970s, when most of the country's major environmental laws first came on the books. Since that time, California, Minnesota, New Jersey, Oregon, Vermont, Wisconsin, and other states have been credited with implementing some of the nation's most progressive environmental policies and laws—and in some cases with crafting regulations that became models for federal regulatory efforts. Many of these advances have been products of direct democracy—initiatives, referendums, and other ballot measures that are not possible at the federal level. These avenues of lawmaking have even produced new environmental regulations in traditionally anti-regulatory states such as Montana, which in 2004 passed ballot initiatives establishing a state fund to control noxious weeds and imposing a ban on the use of cyanide in gold and silver mining operations.[1] Finally, many states have taken federal agencies to court in an effort to rouse them to more vigorous enforcement of environmental laws governing air and water quality, hazardous waste disposal, and wilderness protection.

It is also widely recognized that states shoulder the primary burden for environmental monitoring and enforcement in many policy areas, including waste management, groundwater protection, transportation, and electricity regulation. Collectively, it is estimated that they are responsible for the issuance of more than 90 percent of environmental permits and 75 percent of environmental enforcement actions across the country. They fulfill these duties—many of which are federally mandated—even though they receive less than half (and in some cases as little as a quarter) of their total funding in the resource protection and environmental arenas from the Environmental Protection Agency and other federal government sources.[2]

These factors, combined with federalism's longstanding currency in American political dialogue, have led many policymakers and assorted political constituencies (especially business and industry groups) to argue for increased state oversight of environmental policy—and a correspondingly diminishing role for the Environmental Protection Agency and other federal agencies with resource protection and environmental health responsibilities.

Opponents of these proposals contend, however, that states are ill-equipped to exercise responsible environmental stewardship without federal oversight. Members of this camp, which include national environmental organizations and many state and grassroots groups, say that without federal oversight, the competition between states for jobs and economic development would further exacerbate an already vexing problem with lax state enforcement of environmental regulations. They further charge that some states, especially in the nation's western and southern regions, are simply too philosophically hostile to environmental law and resource conservation to manage such affairs without a federal *presence. State officials in those regions, charged one former EPA official, are invariably hostile "when EPA steps in to take enforcement action against one of 'their' businesses. Some of this is jurisdictional . . . but the constant and petty turf battles with state political managers were one of my most dispiriting experiences."[3]*

To support their arguments against proposed rollbacks of federal oversight, environmental activists and other opponents frequently cite reports such as this 1998 report of the EPA Office of the Inspector General (OIG). In the following excerpts, the OIG excoriates various states for their failure to uphold basic clean air and water oversight responsibilities, and it delivers a particularly stinging rebuke to the environmental monitoring programs in Idaho, one of the "reddest" of western states.

EPA's Oversight of Regional and State Air Enforcement Programs Is Inadequate

Programs

The Inspector General Act requires the OIG to initiate reviews and other activities to promote economy and efficiency and to detect and prevent fraud, waste, and mismanagement in EPA programs and operations. Internal and performance audits and reviews are conducted to accomplish these objectives largely by evaluating the economy, efficiency, and effectiveness of operations. The OIG conducted a number of major reviews of EPA programs. The following are the most significant internal audit, performance audit, and special review findings and recommendations resulting from our efforts.

EPA sets national standards for the more serious toxic air pollutants that threaten human health and the environment. Section 105 of the Clean Air Act (Act) authorizes federal grants to help state and local agencies prevent and control air pollution by ensuring that facilities meet EPA standards. In fiscal year 1996, EPA awarded $160 million in grants to states to carry out the Agency's priorities for air enforcement. The OIG performed six audits on EPA's oversight of the states' air enforcement data. National issues surfaced during these audits which formed the basis for this consolidated report.

We Found That

The six air enforcement audits disclosed fundamental weaknesses with state identification and reporting of significant violators of the Act. Despite performing more than 3,300 inspections during the fiscal year reviewed, the six states we audited reported a total of only 18 significant violators to EPA. In contrast, we reviewed state enforcement files for 430, or 13 percent of the major facilities in these states and identified an additional 103 significant violators that the states did not report to EPA. In response to these audits, states and EPA regions agreed to corrective actions to improve enforcement, and EPA should ensure that they fulfill these commitments. Numerous significant air pollution violators went undetected, and many of those identified were not reported to EPA. This occurred because states either did not want to report violators or the quality of state inspections of facilities were inadequate to detect the violations. Without information about significant violators, EPA could neither assess the adequacy of the states' enforcement programs, nor take action when a state did not enforce the Act. Moreover, because violators were not always reported, EPA's information systems were unable to communicate accurate information to the general public.

States and even EPA regions disregarded Agency requirements. The effectiveness of air enforcement programs suffered, in large part, because EPA and the states did not adhere to EPA's Timely and Appropriate Enforcement requirement (TAE) and its Compliance Monitoring Strategy (CMS).

For EPA's oversight system to work properly, the Office of Enforcement and Compliance Assurance (OECA) should oversee EPA regions, which are responsible for working with state agencies to promote an effective enforcement program. OECA had not assigned internal responsibility for the oversight and implementation of CMS. EPA regions did not always know who to contact in OECA for clarification of enforcement issues. OECA did not routinely analyze enforcement data to detect trends and problem areas, and its regional reviews did not always assess the adequacy of regional oversight to identify violators. Air grants did not include specific amounts for enforcement, which resulted in EPA's loss of leverage to ensure state compliance.

We Recommended That

The Assistant Administrator for Enforcement and Compliance Assurance:

- Continually reinforce EPA regional compliance with the TAE and CMS.
- Assign oversight responsibility for the CMS.
- Work with the Office of Air and Radiation to earmark Section 105 grant funds for enforcement.
- Perform quality assurance of enforcement data.
- Evaluate regional air enforcement programs that assess regional compliance with the TAE and CMS.
- Improve communications with the EPA regions.
- Establish focal points within OECA so that states and EPA regions can obtain clarification of Agency enforcement directives.

What Action Was Taken

The final report (8100244) was issued to the Assistant Administrator for Enforcement and Compliance Assurance on September 25, 1998. In response to the draft report, the Assistant Administrator agreed with the findings and recommendations, and stated OECA formed a workgroup to streamline and clarify guidance. OECA met several times with state and local air enforcement officials and have tentatively agreed to a new definition of significant violator. Further workgroup discussion on the timely and appropriate aspects of the TAE guidance will follow. To improve communications with states and regions, OECA has designated two focal points, one each for TAE and CMS oversight. Also, OECA stated it will work with the Office of Air and Radiation to modify grant guidance to incorporate enforcement priorities. A response to the final report is due by December 24, 1998.

Idaho's Air Enforcement Program Did Not Prevent Threats to Human Health and the Environment

The Clean Air Act (CAA) authorizes EPA to set and enforce national standards for emissions that pollute the air to protect human health and the environment. The CAA assigns primary responsibility to the states for ensuring adequate air quality. Although Region 10 granted authority to Idaho to implement and enforce the stationary source air program, it still has oversight responsibilities to ensure that the program complies with federal laws and regulations.

We Found That

Idaho's stationary source air enforcement program for significant violators (SVs) did not ensure compliance with laws and regulations and did not prevent threats to human health and the environment. A stationary source is a permanently fixed facility. Enforcement actions were either not taken or were not escalated against 18 of the 24 SVs we reviewed. In many instances, the sources had a history of repeated and continuous air quality violations of permit conditions that lasted for years.

Of the few penalties that Idaho had assessed, none included amounts for the economic benefit gained from noncompliance. Penalties were not large enough to credibly deter major air polluters. This happened because Idaho focused more on compliance assistance rather than enforcement. A lack of enforcement, and small or no penalties, gave SVs a financial incentive to continue polluting rather than returning their facilities to compliance. Further, the Compliance Assurance Agreement between Region 10 and Idaho did not require Idaho to follow EPA's enforcement guidance.

Region 10's lack of oversight contributed to Idaho's ineffective enforcement program. Specifically, the Region did not: (1) have a plan for assessing the State's program; (2) review any of the State's programs in the past five years; and (3) use its enforcement authority at all, and did not take enforcement actions when the State failed to do so. In addition, the Region did not recognize Idaho's air enforcement program as a weakness in its Federal Managers' Financial Integrity Act (FMFIA) assurance letter to the Administrator.

We Recommended That

The Regional Administrator, Region 10:

- Require the State to develop and implement policies and procedures that are consistent with EPA enforcement and inspection frequency guidance.
- Report the weaknesses in Idaho's stationary air enforcement program as a management control deficiency in the next FMFIA assurance letter to the EPA Administrator.
- Assume responsibility for enforcement of the stationary source program if the State is unable or unwilling to implement an enforcement program that is consistent with the Clean Air Act and EPA guidance.

What Action Was Taken

The final report (8100249) was issued to the Regional Administrator on September 30, 1998. In responding to the draft report, the Regional Administrator concurred with the recommendations and described corrective actions that have been or will be taken. These actions included discussions at the highest levels of management in both the Region and the State to work jointly through the steps to improve Idaho's air enforcement program. A response to the final report is due by December 29, 1998.

Source: U.S. Environmental Protection Agency (EPA). *Office of Inspector General Semiannual Report to Congress*. Washington, D.C.: EPA, September 1998. www.epa.gov/oig/reports/1998/998semi.htm#Section %201%20%E2%80%94%20ffice%20f%20Audit%20%E2%80%94%20Significant%20Findings.

NOTES

1. Barry G. Rabe, "Power to the States: The Promise and Pitfalls of Decentralization," in *Environmental Policy: New Directions for the Twenty-First Century*, 6th ed., eds. Norman J. Vig and Michael E. Kraft (Washington, D.C.: CQ Press, 2006), 35, 37.

2. Ibid., 36, 45.

3. Eric Schaeffer, "Clearing the Air: Why I Quit the EPA," *Washington Monthly*, July/August 2002.

DOCUMENT 9.11

A Landmark Supreme Court Ruling in *Friends of the Earth v. Laidlaw*

"The Relevant Showing . . . Is Not Injury to the Environment But Injury to the Plaintiff"

January 12, 2000

During the 1980s and 1990s America's courts became prominent battlegrounds in the bitter partisan struggle to shape the character and direction of federal environmental policy. Environmental groups and public health advocates turned to the courts to stop alleged violations of environmental law by government, industry, and private individuals. Similarly, champions of private property rights and the free market regularly used litigation to challenge the viability—and often the constitutionality—of various environmental and public health rules and regulations.

One recurring bone of legal contention between these warring parties concerned the "legal standing" doctrine—essentially the question of whether a prospective plaintiff has the legal right to prosecute a claim in court. Several major federal environmental laws, including the Clean Water Act, the Clean Air Act, and the Endangered Species Act, contained language explicitly giving private citizens the right to sue violators of their provisions. Individuals and environmental groups made extensive use of this legal weapon in the 1970s and 1980s to stop violations of environmental law and levy fines on transgressors. Conservative lawmakers and business interests responded to this perceived threat to economic expansion and free enterprise with legal sorties designed to curb or even eliminate this right.

The crux of the legal standing debate lies with U.S. Supreme Court interpretations of Article III, section 2 of the Constitution, which grants the judiciary the power to hear "cases" and "controversies." But according to the Court, a plaintiff must meet three requirements to have Article III standing. First, the plaintiff must show that he or she has suffered an "injury in fact." Second, the plaintiff must show that the "injury in fact" can be reasonably traced to the challenged action of the defendant. Third, the plaintiff must show that the injury "is likely to be redressed by a favorable decision" of the court.

During the 1970s and 1980s—and especially after the arrival of conservative Justice Antonin Scalia in 1987—the standing requirements laid out by the U.S. Supreme Court gradually tightened. This pattern intensified in the 1990s, when the Court issued a series of opinions that made it more difficult for citizens and environmental organizations to establish that they met all the Article III requirements for standing. In 2000, however, the Supreme Court issued a landmark decision that decisively changed the legal landscape in favor of the environmentalists.

The Friends of the Earth v. Laidlaw *case had its roots in the late 1980s, when Laidlaw Environmental Services began dumping illegal levels of mercury and other pollutants from one of its hazardous waste incinerator facilities in Roebuck, South Carolina, into a local waterway, the North Tyger River. Laidlaw violated the terms of its discharge permit numerous times over the next several years, and the company did not curb its rampant pollution dumping until a consortium of environmental groups including Friends of the Earth, Sierra Club, and Citizens Local Environmental Action Network threatened the company with a lawsuit in April 1992.*

In June 1992 the citizens' consortium officially filed a lawsuit against Laidlaw, but the company responded by claiming that the environmental consortium had no standing to sue because no "injury in fact" to the environmentalists from the dumping had been proven. In 1997 a federal district court judge found in favor of the environmentalists, but in July 1998 the U.S. Court of Appeals for the Fourth Circuit reversed the lower court ruling and found in favor of Laidlaw. The court explained that because Laidlaw eventually came into compliance with the terms of its discharge permit in the early 1990s, the case became moot and the environmentalists did not have standing to sue. The Fourth Circuit's rationale was ridiculed by the environmental community. "As a practical matter, this ruling significantly undermines effective enforcement of the Clean Water Act," said one critic. "Even if a company is flagrantly violating the law when the suit is filed, the company can escape liability so long as it comes into compliance during the (sometimes protracted) course of the litigation. This obviously undermines polluters' willingness to comply with the Clean Water Act, and creates a perverse incentive for polluters to prolong litigation."[1]

The environmental consortium promptly appealed the Fourth Circuit's ruling to the U.S. Supreme Court, which agreed to hear the case of Friends of the Earth v. Laidlaw *in 1999. In January 2000 the Court returned a ruling that firmly sided with the environmentalists. The Court ruled 7-2 (Justices Scalia and Clarence Thomas dissented) that citizens had the clear right to sue to enforce environmental laws if they had a reasonable basis to claim that ongoing or projected activities by the defendant could adversely affect environmental resources they use and enjoy. This ruling displayed in vivid fashion just how much influence the judiciary exerts on the shape of environmental policy in America. "Without the citizen suit provision of the Clean Water Act," observed one analysis, "the environmentalists most likely would not have sued Laidlaw and the violations of the statute most likely would have continued. Without a finding by the Supreme Court that the environmentalists had standing, they would not have had the legal authority to sue. This combined citizen suit-standing decision delivered a one-two punch that strengthened the role of citizens and environmentalists in environmental policy."[2]*

Following is the section of the majority opinion in Friends of the Earth v. Laidlaw, *written by Justice Ruth Bader Ginsburg, that explicitly tackles the "standing" issue (footnotes removed).*

. . . Laidlaw contends first that FOE lacked standing from the outset even to seek injunctive relief, because the plaintiff organizations failed to show that any of their members had sustained or faced the threat of any "injury in fact" from Laidlaw's activities. In support of this contention Laidlaw points to the District Court's finding, made in the course of setting the penalty amount, that there had been "no demonstrated proof of harm to the environment" from Laidlaw's mercury discharge violations. 956 F. Supp., at 602; see also ibid. ("[T]he NPDES permit violations at issue in this citizen suit did not result in any health risk or environmental harm.").

The relevant showing for purposes of Article III standing, however, is not injury to the environment but injury to the plaintiff. To insist upon the former rather than the latter as part of the standing inquiry (as the dissent in essence does, post, at 2—3) is to raise the standing hurdle higher than the necessary showing for success on the merits in an action alleging noncompliance with an NPDES permit. Focusing properly on injury to the plaintiff, the District Court found that FOE had demonstrated sufficient injury to establish standing. . . . For example, FOE member Kenneth Lee Curtis averred in affidavits that he lived a half-mile from Laidlaw's facility; that he occasionally drove over the North Tyger River, and that it looked and smelled polluted; and that he would like to fish, camp, swim, and picnic in and near the river between 3 and 15 miles downstream from the facility, as he did when he was a teenager, but would not do so because he was concerned that the water was polluted by Laidlaw's discharges. reaffirmed these statements in extensive deposition testimony. For example, he testified that he would like to fish in the river at a specific spot he used as a boy, but that he would not do so now because of his concerns about Laidlaw's discharges.

Other members presented evidence to similar effect. CLEAN member Angela Patterson attested that she lived two miles from the facility; that before Laidlaw operated the facility, she picnicked, walked, birdwatched, and waded in and along the North Tyger River because of the natural beauty of the area; that she no longer engaged in these activities in or near the river because she was concerned about harmful effects from discharged pollutants; and that she and her husband would like to purchase a home near the river but did not intend to do so, in part because of Laidlaw's discharges. CLEAN member Judy Pruitt averred that she lived one-quarter mile from Laidlaw's facility and would like to fish, hike, and picnic along the North Tyger River, but has refrained from those activities because of the discharges. FOE member Linda Moore attested that she lived 20 miles from Roebuck, and would use the North Tyger River south of Roebuck and the land surrounding it for recreational purposes were she not concerned that the water contained harmful pollutants. In her deposition, Moore testified at length that she would hike, picnic, camp, swim, boat, and drive near or in the river were it not for her concerns about illegal discharges. CLEAN member Gail Lee attested that her home, which is near Laidlaw's facility, had a lower value than similar homes located further from the facility, and that she believed the pollutant discharges accounted for some of the discrepancy. Sierra Club member Norman Sharp averred that he had canoed approximately 40 miles downstream of the Laidlaw facility and would like to canoe in the North Tyger River closer to Laidlaw's discharge point, but did not do so because he was concerned that the water contained harmful pollutants. Ibid.

These sworn statements, as the District Court determined, adequately documented injury in fact. We have held that environmental plaintiffs adequately allege injury in fact when they aver that they use the affected area and are persons "for whom the aesthetic and recreational values of the area will be lessened" by the challenged activity. . . .

Our decision in *Lujan v. National Wildlife Federation,* 497 U.S. 871 (1990), is not to the contrary. In that case an environmental organization assailed the Bureau of Land

Management's "land withdrawal review program," a program covering millions of acres, alleging that the program illegally opened up public lands to mining activities. The defendants moved for summary judgment, challenging the plaintiff organization's standing to initiate the action under the Administrative Procedure Act, 5 U.S.C. § 702. We held that the plaintiff could not survive the summary judgment motion merely by offering "averments which state only that one of [the organization's] members uses unspecified portions of an immense tract of territory, on some portions of which mining activity has occurred or probably will occur by virtue of the governmental action."

In contrast, the affidavits and testimony presented by FOE in this case assert that Laidlaw's discharges, and the affiant members' reasonable concerns about the effects of those discharges, directly affected those affiants' recreational, aesthetic, and economic interests. These submissions present dispositively more than the mere "general averments" and "conclusory allegations" found inadequate in *National Wildlife Federation*. Nor can the affiants' conditional statements—that they would use the nearby North Tyger River for recreation if Laidlaw were not discharging pollutants into it—be equated with the speculative "'some day' intentions" to visit endangered species halfway around the world that we held insufficient to show injury in fact in *Defenders of Wildlife*.

. . . [I]t is undisputed that Laidlaw's unlawful conduct—discharging pollutants in excess of permit limits—was occurring at the time the complaint was filed. Under Lyons, then, the only "subjective" issue here is "[t]he reasonableness of [the] fear" that led the affiants to respond to that concededly ongoing conduct by refraining from use of the North Tyger River and surrounding areas. Unlike the dissent, post, at 200, we see nothing "improbable" about the proposition that a company's continuous and pervasive illegal discharges of pollutants into a river would cause nearby residents to curtail their recreational use of that waterway and would subject them to other economic and aesthetic harms. The proposition is entirely reasonable, the District Court found it was true in this case, and that is enough for injury in fact.

Laidlaw argues next that even if FOE had standing to seek injunctive relief, it lacked standing to seek civil penalties. Here the asserted defect is not injury but redressability. Civil penalties offer no redress to private plaintiffs, Laidlaw argues, because they are paid to the government, and therefore a citizen plaintiff can never have standing to seek them.

Laidlaw is right to insist that a plaintiff must demonstrate standing separately for each form of relief sought. . . . But it is wrong to maintain that citizen plaintiffs facing ongoing violations never have standing to seek civil penalties.

We have recognized on numerous occasions that "all civil penalties have some deterrent effect." *Hudson v. United States*, 522 U.S. 93, 102 (1997); see also, e.g., *Department of Revenue of Mont. v. Kurth Ranch*, 511 U.S. 767, 778 (1994). More specifically, Congress has found that civil penalties in Clean Water Act cases do more than promote immediate compliance by limiting the defendant's economic incentive to delay its attainment of permit limits; they also deter future violations. This congressional determination warrants judicial attention and respect. . . .

It can scarcely be doubted that, for a plaintiff who is injured or faces the threat of future injury due to illegal conduct ongoing at the time of suit, a sanction that effectively abates that conduct and prevents its recurrence provides a form of redress. Civil penalties can fit that description. To the extent that they encourage defendants to discontinue current violations and deter them from committing future ones, they afford redress to citizen plaintiffs who are injured or threatened with injury as a consequence of ongoing unlawful conduct.

The dissent argues that it is the availability rather than the imposition of civil penalties that deters any particular polluter from continuing to pollute. This argument misses the mark in two ways. First, it overlooks the interdependence of the availability and the imposition; a threat has no deterrent value unless it is credible that it will be carried out. Second, it is reasonable for Congress to conclude that an actual award of civil penalties does in fact bring with it a significant quantum of deterrence over and above what is achieved by the mere prospect of such penalties. A would-be polluter may or may not be dissuaded by the existence of a remedy on the books, but a defendant once hit in its pocketbook will surely think twice before polluting again.

We recognize that there may be a point at which the deterrent effect of a claim for civil penalties becomes so insubstantial or so remote that it cannot support citizen standing. The fact that this vanishing point is not easy to ascertain does not detract from the deterrent power of such penalties in the ordinary case. Justice Frankfurter's observations for the Court, made in a different context nearly 60 years ago, hold true here as well:

> "How to effectuate policy—the adaptation of means to legitimately sought ends—is one of the most intractable of legislative problems. Whether proscribed conduct is to be deterred by qui tam action or triple damages or injunction, or by criminal prosecution, or merely by defense to actions in contract, or by some, or all, of these remedies in combination, is a matter within the legislature's range of choice. Judgment on the deterrent effect of the various weapons in the armory of the law can lay little claim to scientific basis." *Tigner v. Texas,* 310 U.S. 141, 148 (1940).

In this case we need not explore the outer limits of the principle that civil penalties provide sufficient deterrence to support redressability. Here, the civil penalties sought by FOE carried with them a deterrent effect that made it likely, as opposed to merely speculative, that the penalties would redress FOE's injuries by abating current violations and preventing future ones—as the District Court reasonably found when it assessed a penalty of $405,800.

Laidlaw contends that the reasoning of our decision in *Steel Co.* directs the conclusion that citizen plaintiffs have no standing to seek civil penalties under the Act. We disagree. . . .

Source: *Friends of Earth, Inc. V. Laidlaw Environmental Services (TOC), Inc.* (98–822) 528 U.S. 167 (2000) 149 F.3d 303, reversed and remanded (January 12, 2000). Available at http://supreme.justia.com/us/528/167/case.html.

Notes

1. John D. Echeverria, "Standing Up for the Environment: Justices Should Welcome Green Groups into Court," *Washington Legal Times,* October 11, 1999. Available at www.law.georgetown.edu/gelpi/research_archive/standing/StandingUpWelcomeGreen.pdf.
2. Rosemary O'Leary, "Environmental Policy in the Courts," in *Environmental Policy: New Directions for the Twenty-First Century.* 6th ed., eds. Norman J. Vig and Michael E. Kraft (Washington, D.C.: CQ Press, 2006), 155.

Environmental Justice Advocacy from the Perspective of a Critic

"The Lens of Environmental Justice Can Blind One to the Big Picture"

2000

Since its birth in the late 1970s, the environmental justice movement has grown to the point that it has become a significant influence on public policy agendas at the federal and state levels (and frequently at the county and municipal levels). This growing clout has been hailed by a wide array of organizations, activists, and officials with strong interests in environmental, consumer, civil rights, and urban issues. But the goals, methods, and rhetoric of the environmental justice movement have also aroused alarm from business interests, free-market advocates, and even some urban revitalization and public health advocates. These critics assert that much of the movement is based on exaggeration, flawed research, unrealistic demands, and a mentality of victimization. Some critics even assert that these alleged flaws actually work to the detriment of minority and low-income communities because they detract attention away from more salient economic and public health issues.[1]

The following critical assessment of the environmental justice movement was written by Christopher H. Foreman Jr., director of the social policy program at the University of Maryland, a fellow at the Brookings Institution, and the author of The Promise and Peril of Environmental Justice *(1998) and numerous other works on environmental justice issues. Foreman's work has attracted wide attention in part because his orientation as a self-described progressive public policy analyst (he served, for example, on the board of governors of the Nature Conservancy from 1999 to 2005) differentiates him politically from many other critics of the "EJ" movement. However, Foreman's work is frequently cited by conservative opponents of regulations crafted in response to environmental justice concerns.*

Ensuring that authorities effectively address any disproportionate risks borne by low-income and minority communities has been a central theme of advocates for "environmental justice" (Foreman, 1998; Bullard, 1994b). Since the early 1980s the environmental justice movement, a diverse coalition of grassroots activists and groups, has insisted that communities of color are too often the "invisible man" of environmentalism—underrepresented in environmental organizations and policy processes. The result, say activists and their sympathizers, is that communities of color have been unfairly victimized by polluted sites and inadequate environmental law enforcement, a claim bolstered by some widely trumpeted empirical research findings (Lavelle and Coyle, 1992; United Church of Christ/Commission for Racial Justice, 1987). Some have suggested that such communities have been routinely targeted for environmental poisons, perhaps leading to higher rates of chronic illness such as cancer. "Environmental racism" is the incendiary label often applied to such claims. More broadly, according to one leading interpreter, environmental racism refers "to any environmental policy, practice, or directive that differentially affects or disadvantages . . . individuals, groups, or communities based on race or color" (Bullard, 1994a).

Do low-income and minority persons in fact bear a disproportionate share of society's environmental risk? Do they develop pollution-related illnesses more often than other persons? We are far from answering either question, much farther regarding the latter. Perhaps more interestingly, a close examination of environmental justice activism makes abundantly clear that, despite persistent rhetoric to the contrary, the movement is not fundamentally risk-driven. And anyone hoping for the day when U.S. EPA and state environmental authorities have a reliable analytic handle on disproportionate risk borne by environmental justice constituencies should receive fair warning: don't hold your breath.

To be sure, we are more likely to find certain environmental risks in closer proximity to poor people than to wealthier ones. An EPA task force on environmental equity, created in July 1990 by administrator William Reilly in the wake of activist prodding, determined that one problem—lead exposure—stood out in the data as a particular threat among low-income black youngsters (USEPA, 1992). There probably are other industrial substances having a greater cumulative adverse impact on minorities than on whites—toxic residues ingested via fish consumption is often mentioned (Wright, Bryant and Bullard, 1994)—but any resulting disproportionate disease incidence has so far eluded science. Moreover, scaring consumers away from fish only makes sense in health terms if the replacement food does not prove even riskier (Anderson and Wiener, 1995).

The lens of environmental justice can blind one to the big picture. For one thing, environmental risks are very widely distributed. Many low-income persons and persons-of-color reside and work (alongside a great many whites) in and near cities. Anyone who does is almost certainly breathing dirtier air than more rural folk. No one disputes that a fair amount of what migrates into urban airsheds would ideally not be there, especially the ozone that, as a significant respiratory irritant, can help trigger asthma attacks (Lave, 1997). African Americans, young and old, suffer disproportionately from asthma, as reflected by rates of asthma-associated mortality and hospitalization (U.S. Centers for Disease Control, 1995). But even in urban areas both indoor and outdoor environments may be implicated in asthma incidence (Rosenstreich et al, 1997). In any case, environmental justice enthusiasts have yet to present a compelling rationale for making race *per se* a driving factor in clean air policy.

> [T]he mythical "Cancer Alley" endures in movement rhetoric, and it is not hard to understand why. A connection between petrochemical plants—or, for that matter, between any source of fearsome and unwanted material—and disease has powerful intuitive appeal for citizens even though science may identify no causal linkage.
> —Christopher H. Foreman Jr.

At a purely impressionistic level it is hard to discern any inkling of racial distinctiveness among the headline environmental controversies of our time. New Jersey has long been renowned for its abundance of hazardous waste, including the nation's top-ranked Superfund site, Lipari (Mazmanian and Morell, 1992). Would anyone claim that the size of the state's minority population in any way explains this? One might pose the same question about the Hanford nuclear waste site in Washington state, or even the infamous Love Canal and Times Beach episodes of years ago (Wildavsky, 1995). The huge Fresh Kills landfill on State Island, the sole facility of its kind in New York City, has endured since the 1940s for many reasons but, even in a city with a large minority population, race is surely not among them (Martin and Revkin, 1999). More convincingly, however, recent empirical studies do little to bear out the claim of regular or systematic ethnic bias either in facility siting or in cleanup decisionmaking (Foreman, 1998).

Any risk management professional who has closely watched the environmental justice movement has probably noticed two phrases being repeated with an almost mantra-like regularity. One is "cancer alley." The other is "multiple, cumulative and synergistic risk." In movement lore, "cancer alley" endures as perhaps the signal example of environmental harm disproportionately borne by communities of color (Wright, Bryant and Bullard, 1994). In 1993 congressional testimony Pat Bryant, representative of the Gulf Coast Tenants Association, proclaimed:

> " 'Cancer Alley' . . . remains one of the most poisoned areas anyplace. One hundred and thirty-eight petro-chemical facilities have made home in large plantations, most of the time as close as possible to African-American communities. . . .
>
> "Despite denials of the petro-chemical industry financed studies, we know that cancer incidence in this corridor is higher than the national average. Cancer is so commonplace in "Cancer Alley" that almost every family is touched.
>
> " . . . This area has become a zone of national sacrifice. This is genocide at its finest, and it is a national disgrace." (U.S. House of Representatives, 1993).

The trouble is, careful research does not sustain the allegation that the petrochemical industrial corridor extending from Baton Rouge to New Orleans promotes excess cancer incidence (Groves et al, 1996).

Actually it is not surprising that black Louisianans have been seeing a lot of cancer since everyone else is too. Science writer Michael Fumento (1993) observers that "one fourth of us will contract cancer and one fifth of us will die of it. Indeed, as the population ages and fewer and fewer people die of other causes, more and more will die of cancer." But have black Louisianans been seeing more cancer than other Americans? In 1990 the respective cancer incidence rates among blacks and whites nationally stood at 423 and 393 per 100,000 (Fisher, Worth and Mayer, 1995). Differences in behavior and health care access are clearly part of the explanation. Behavior (and some occupational) factors have been associated with cancer incidence in Louisiana but there appears to be no overall "cancer epidemic" in that state or in the so-called "Cancer Alley."

But the mythical "Cancer Alley" endures in movement rhetoric, and it is not hard to understand why. A connection between petrochemical plants—or, for that matter, between any source of fearsome and unwanted material—and disease has powerful intuitive appeal for citizens even though science may identify no causal linkage. As Margolis (1996) argues, a divergence between expert and citizen perception of risk remains one of the more treacherous fault lines in environmental politics, precisely because of the profound grip that intuition wields over citizen perceptions. And since one cannot prove a negative—that is, prove beyond all doubt that factories and dumpsites could *never* cause cancer—uncertainty prevails.

That uncertainty also provides powerful leverage for mobilizing citizens, and for holding the Establishment's feet to the fire. In the end, this is the real game that environmental justice activists are playing. These activists (especially those more or less full-time advocates who champion a broad agenda transcending specific site-level grievances) are best perceived as social justice proponents who happen to specialize in environmental themes. Employing such themes, they try to win a larger voice, and more resources, for disadvantaged communities, broadly defined. Their specific targets are many and varied, their overarching motivation strongly egalitarian. On behalf of their redistributive ends, they wish to arouse and unify citizens in order to make and enforce demands on business and government. The environmental justice movement is, of necessity, highly opportunistic and improvisational. Because the movement's main thrust is toward the "empowerment" of a diverse citizen constituency, scientific findings that blunt or conflict with that goal are a decided inconvenience, and are therefore either ignored or ridiculed.

Formal analysis, including risk assessment, is thus largely irrelevant to the underlying objectives and gratifications that stir activist and community enthusiasm under the environmental justice rubric. The cry of "multiple, cumulative and synergistic risk" bundles a partly disingenuous plea for more research along with an intuitively appealing presumption that minority and low-income communities face substantial environmental risks that remain unrecognized and unassessed. But the plea is disingenuous because activists have no intention of using risk assessment, however careful, to guide their advocacy priorities. Indeed, much of their rhetoric betrays the tone of hostility toward "establishment science" common in grassroots environmentalism as a whole.

Sympathetic accounts of the movement's rise often highlight studies published by the U.S. General Accounting Office (1983) and by the United Church of Christ/Commission for Racial Justice (1987). These studied purported to show that commercial hazardous waste facilities were more likely to be found near minority communities. What is most important to grasp about these studies is not just that they were crude and woefully misleading—though they were—but rather that they were always merely agenda-setting instruments of the movement, not its cause. Although more refined risk analyses may have some uses in the environmental justice context, it would be naïve to imagine that their conclusions will matter much to communities unless bonded to a gratifying practical politics anchored within those communities. And analytic conclusions cannot achieve this effect unless they demonstrate what activists want shown, that minority and low-income people are disproportionately victimized.

The environmental justice perspective is powerful not because it speaks honestly to technical questions of harm or risk—it often does not—but because it appears to promise something larger, more uplifting, more viscerally engaging than mere careful calculation can offer. It effectively speaks to the fear and anger among local communities feeling overwhelmed by forces beyond their control, and outraged by what they perceive to be assaults on their collective quality of life. In this context, "multiple, cumulative and synergistic risk" must be seen as representing a kind of technically-grounded rhetoric rather than an authentic commitment to a technical perspective. Such language seems to its users to be the price of admission to the policy process, but it most certainly is *not* what the ticket buyers are really all about.

"Multiple, cumulative and synergistic" is useful to the environmental justice movement in yet another way: it is virtually impossible that environmental authorities can, in the foreseeable future at least, successfully study and attack it. In December 1996 EPA staff from the Office of Policy Planning and Evaluation (OPPE) came before EPA's National Environmental Justice Advisory Council (NEJAC) to brief members on the cumulative exposure project under way. NEJAC learned that the project was using existing data to independently estimate cumulative concentrations/exposures from three pathways (*i.e.,* outdoor air, drinking water, food) in an attempt to lay the groundwork for consideration of multi-pathway cumulative exposure. But that last word—exposure—bears emphasis, for it remains a long way indeed from "risk." For the moment, let us assume that one can have full faith in the data being assembled, and that the inevitable gaps and uncertainties don't too badly afflict those substances (such as dioxin, PCBs, pesticides, and lead) ranking highest in the activist pantheon of environmental horrors. Even so, can one expect EPA reliably to gauge the various interactive and cumulative effects of these (often very low) doses and exposures, and to do so in a way that would win the confidence of activists? The simple answer is no (unless, again, the results happen to provide a convenient platform for activist claims). To hope otherwise is to yearn for a pot of gold at the end of an analytic rainbow. Yet EPA's all but certain failure on this score will help activists in one potent way: it offers grounds for additional rhetorical leverage over the agency.

There are serious environmental problems afflicting low-income and minority communities. But they are overwhelmingly quality-of-life problems: odors, noise, unsightly construction or destruction, traffic congestion—as well as the economic fragility that often brings people into unhappy proximity with such things. Truth be told, activist carping about "risk and racism" is really a cover for trying to crank up collateral attention to these other issues. There are serious health problems disproportionately affecting low-income persons and persons of color, but the potential leverage offered by pollution control over most of them ranges from slim to none.

But at the end of the day, one should not be too hard on environmental justice activists. Their manifest limitation as analysts stems from their commitment to a non-analytic enterprise that is deeply democratic in aspiration. And up to a point their strategy of racialized NIMBY ("Not In My Backyard!") advocacy is compelling. It effectively blends civil rights and environmentalism, two of the great domestic policy progressive causes of the last 40 years, into a politically potent brew. From the White House to the county court house, the environmental policy milieu has been dramatically transformed as a result. And, like grassroots environmentalism generally, environmental justice advocacy has proved remarkably adept at one crucial task: just saying no (to dumps, incinerators, and facilities of many kinds). Advocacy is driven to an important extent not by risk or health *per se* but by the deeper political imperative to find new language and alternative policy vehicles with which to drive egalitarian social change. For better or worse (and to the enduring frustration of risk analysts) this often means also "saying no" to the premises, methods, and results of risk assessment.

References

Anderson, P. and Wiener, J. 1995. Eating fish. In: Graham, J.D. and Wiener, J.B., Eds. *Risk vs. Risk: Tradeoffs in Protecting Health and the Environment.* Cambridge, MA and London, Harvard University Press, pp. 104–123.

Bullard, R. 1994a. *Dumping in Dixie: Race, Class and Environmental Quality.* Boulder, San Francisco and Oxford, Westview Press.

Bullard, R. 1994b. *Unequal Protection: Environmental Justice and Communities of Color.* San Francisco, Sierra Club Books.

Fisher, A., Worth, W., and Mayer, D. 1995. *Update: Is There a Cancer Epidemic in the United States?* New York, American Council on Science and Health.

Foreman, C. 1998. *The Promise and Peril of Environmental Justice.* Washington, DC, Brookings Institution Press.

Fumento, M. 1993. *Science Under Siege: Balancing Technology and the Environment.* New York, William Morrow and Company.

Groves, F., et al. 1996. "Is there a 'cancer corridor' in Louisiana?" *Journal of the Louisiana State Medical Society,* 143, 155–165.

Lave, I. 1997. "Clean air sense," *Brookings Review* 15 (Summer).

Lavelle, M. and Coyle, M. 1992. "Unequal protection: the racial divide in environmental law." *National Law Journal,* September 21, S1-S6.

Margolis, H. 1996. *Dealing with Risk: Why the Public and the Experts Disagree on Environmental Issues.* Chicago and London: University of Chicago Press.

Martin, D. and Revkin, A. 1999. "As deadline looms for dump, alternative plan proves elusive." *New York Times,* August 30: A1.

Mazmanian, D. and Morell, D. 1992. *Beyond Superfailure: America's Toxics Policy for the 1990s.* Boulder, San Francisco, and Oxford, Westview Press.

Rosenstreich, D., et al. 1997. "The role of cockroach allergy and exposure to cockroach allergen in causing morbidity among inner-city children with asthma." *New England Journal of Medicine,* 336, May 8, 1356–1363.

United Church of Christ/Commission for Racial Justice. 1987. *Toxic Wastes and Race in the United States: A National Report on Racial and Socio-Economic Characteristics of Communities with Hazardous Waste Sites.* New York.

USEPA (U.S. Environmental Protection Agency). 1992. *Environmental Equity: Reducing Risks for All Communities.* Office of Policy, Planning and Evaluation, Washington, D.C. 20460 EPA230-R-92–08. Report to the Administrator from the EPA Environmental Equity Workgroup, June 1992.

U.S. Centers for Disease Control. 1995. "Children at risk from ozone air pollution—United States, 1991–1993." *Morbidity and Mortality Weekly Report* 44, April 28, pp. 309–312.

U.S. General Accounting Office. 1983. *Siting of Hazardous Waste Landfills and Their Correlation with Racial and Economic Status of Surrounding Communities.* Washington, DC GAO/RCED-83–168, June 1, 1983.

U.S. House of Representatives. Committee on the Judiciary. 1993. *Environmental Justice* (hearings before the subcommittee on civil and constitutional rights) 103d Con., 1st sess., March 3–4.

Wildavsky, A. 1995. *But Is It True? A Citizen's Guide to Environmental Health and Safety Issues.* Cambridge, Massachusetts and London, Harvard University Press.

Wright, B., Bryant P., and Bullard, R. 1994. Coping with poisons in cancer alley. In: Bullard R., Ed. *Unequal Protection: Environmental Justice and Communities of Color.* San Francisco: Sierra Club Books.

Source: Foreman, Christopher H., Jr. "Environmental Justice and Risk Assessment: The Uneasy Relationship." *Human and Ecological Risk Assessment,* vol. 6, no. 4, 2000, pp. 549–554. Used by permission of the Taylor & Francis Group, www.informaworld.com.

NOTE

1. Ted Nordhaus and Michael Shellenberger, *Breakthrough: From the Death of Environmentalism to the Politics of Possibility* (New York: Houghton Mifflin Harcourt, 2007), 83.

Bipartisan Support for a Brownfields Revitalization Act

"The Bill Is a Carefully Crafted Compromise"

February 27, 2001

Beginning with the administration of Ronald Reagan and continuing through the presidencies of George H. W. Bush, Bill Clinton, and George W. Bush, Republicans and Democrats have found little common ground on environmental policy–making. To the contrary, the two parties have generally glared at each other across an ideological abyss that has sometimes seemed to widen with each new administration. This general state of affairs made the passage of the Small Business Liability Relief and Brownfields Revitalization Act of 2002 with broad bipartisan support a particularly noteworthy event.

This act built on the 1980 Superfund law and various EPA programs instituted during the Clinton years to clean up abandoned industrial properties saddled with hazardous waste problems. It incorporated elements of both H.R. 1831 (the Small Business Liability Protection Act), which passed the House of Representatives in May 2001 by a 419-0 vote, and S. 350 (the Brownfields Revitalization and Environmental Restoration Act), which passed the Senate in April 2001 by a vote of 99-0. The final bill, H.R. 2869, passed the House by voice vote on December 19 and the Senate by unanimous consent on December 20 and was signed into law by George W. Bush on January 11, 2002.

The Small Business Liability Relief and Brownfields Revitalization Act was designed as a sort of parallel program to Superfund. It provided new federal grants and other tools to both public and private sectors to promote the environmental restoration and sustainable reuse of brownfields—abandoned urban industrial and commercial sites with low-level environmental contamination. Some environmental, consumer, and taxpayer groups and analysts complained that the measure unfairly shifted the financial burden of cleaning up toxic sites from polluters to the taxpaying public. And once the program got under way, environmental and civil rights groups charged that the sites were not always sufficiently cleaned up or monitored. But other organizations touted the beneficial environmental health impact of the legislation on inner-city communities. The brownfields program also appealed to many other constituencies. As one journalist noted, "[C]orporations that buy Brownfield sites are freed of liability for the pollution; businesses and nonprofit organizations receive tax breaks and grant money; and cities get their contaminated sites cleaned up without the stigma of Superfund."[1]

The following statements by Republican Senator Lincoln Chafee (R.I.) and Democratic Senator Barbara Boxer (Calif.) are taken from a February 2001 Senate hearing on the brownfields issue. Their comments provide a fairly representative sampling of the reasons why both Republicans and Democrats ultimately supported the legislation.

Statement of Hon. Lincoln D. Chafee,
U.S. Senator from the State of Rhode Island

February 27, 2001

Good morning. Today, the subcommittee will receive testimony on S. 350, the Brown-fields Revitalization and Environmental Restoration Act of 2001. Together with Senators [Bob] Smith, [Harry] Reid, and Boxer, and other members of the committee, I introduced this legislation on February 15. This bill is the same bipartisan legislation that was introduced in the 106th Congress and amassed 67 cosponsors. This landmark, bipartisan bill which is pro-environment and pro-economic development has attracted broad support from Senators and stakeholder groups.

The nation's laws governing abandoned hazardous waste sites date back to the late 1970s and the discovery of thousand of barrels of toxic waste buried illegally in a New York community outside of Buffalo. Congress responded to Love Canal and other sites by enacting Superfund. This law was intended to clean up the nation's worst sites and ensure that the parties responsible for the pollution cleaned it up. Litigation ensued throughout the 1980s, which slowed down the pace of clean-ups. By the 1990s, Superfund clean-ups increased. But the fear of prolonged entanglements in Superfund liability became an impediment to the clean-up of lightly contaminated sites, today known as brownfields.

> *By enacting this legislation, we can recycle our nation's contaminated land, reinvigorate our urban cores, stimulate economic development, revitalize blighted communities, abate environmental health risks, and reduce the pressure to develop pristine land.*
>
> —Lincoln D. Chafee

While all parties agreed that we should remove the barriers to redeveloping brownfields, those reforms were always considered as part of broader comprehensive Superfund reform. Based on a multitude of letters and phone calls from various stakeholders, the sponsors of this legislation decided to move brownfields legislation separately and in a bipartisan manner. This is not to say that there is not merit to broader Superfund proposals. Issues such as natural resource damages need to be examined and we will look at those issues later. But it is important that we move this legislation, with broad bipartisan support, first.

As the chairman of the Senate Superfund Subcommittee, I have made brownfields reform my top environmental priority. As one of six former mayors in the Senate, I understand the environmental, economic, and social benefits that can be realized in our communities from revitalizing brownfields. Estimates show there to be between 450,000 and 600,000 brownfield sites in the United States. Why do we have so many of these abandoned sites? The shift away from an industrialized economy, the migration of land use from urban areas to suburban and rural areas, and our nation's strict liability contamination statutes have all contributed. By enacting this legislation, we can recycle our nation's contaminated land, reinvigorate our urban cores, stimulate economic development, revitalize blighted communities, abate environmental health risks, and reduce the pressure to develop pristine land.

People may legitimately question the necessity of enacting Federal brownfields legislation. Given the frequent touting of brownfield success stories, is Federal legislation necessary? The short answer is "yes." While many States have implemented innovative and effective brownfield programs, they cannot remove the Federal barriers to brownfield redevelopment. By providing Federal funding, eliminating Federal liability for developers, and reducing the role of the Federal Government at brownfield sites, we will allow State and local governments to improve upon what they are already doing well.

I would like to briefly describe the highlights of our legislation. The bill authorizes $150 million per year to State and local governments to perform assessments and clean up at brownfield sites. In addition, that money will allow EPA to issue grants for clean-up of sites to be converted into parks or open space. It also authorizes $50 million per year to establish and enhance State brownfield programs.

The bill clarifies that prospective purchasers, innocent landowners, and contiguous property owners, that act appropriately, are not responsible for paying clean-up costs. Finally, this legislation offers finality by precluding EPA from taking an action at a site being addressed under a State clean-up program unless there is an "imminent and substantial endangerment" to public health or the environment, and additional work needs to be done.

Enactment of this legislation and the accompanying redevelopment will provide a building block for the revitalization of our communities. Communities whose fortunes sank along with the decline of mills and factories will once again attract new residents and well-paying jobs. We will bring vibrant industry back to the brownfield sites that currently host crime, mischief and contamination. There will be parks at sites that now contain more rubble than grass. City tax rolls will burgeon; schools will be invigorated; new homes will be built, and community character will be restored. This vision for our communities can be realized with enactment of this legislation.

As with all legislation, we must reach across the aisle and work with bipartisan cooperation to be successful. While no compromise legislation makes everyone one hundred percent happy, this bill enjoys strong support from the real estate community, local government officials, State officials, business groups, and environmental groups.

I look forward to its quick consideration in the Senate.

Statement of Hon. Barbara Boxer, U.S. Senator from the State of California

February 27, 2001

I am pleased to be here today in my new role as Ranking Member of the Subcommittee on Superfund, Waste Control, and Risk Assessment. The issues that will come before this subcommittee are very important and I look forward to working closely with the chairman on these matters.

I am also pleased to welcome two witnesses from California: Mayor Myrtle Walker of East Palo Alto, and Alan Front from the Trust for Public Land, which is based in San Francisco.

I expect that both of these witnesses will highlight how important and relevant brownfields clean-up is to my State. I am particularly interested to hear from the Mayor about the role that the Federal Government has played in assisting with the clean-up efforts in Palo Alto. The question of the appropriate Federal role is likely to provoke vigorous debate in this committee.

I am sorry to say that some of California's industries have left the State with a frightening legacy of contamination. In my State, there are estimated to be hundreds of sites. While the State has struggled to address these, a Federal role is clearly needed and that is one reason I am a strong supporter of S. 350 (the Brownfields Revitalization and Environmental Restoration Act).

In California, many of these sites are located in low-income, minority communities in places like Los Angeles, Oakland, San Diego, and Sacramento. The result is that this toxic legacy disproportionately impacts our most vulnerable and disempowered citizens.

But these are not the only communities at risk. A recent report by the U.S. Conference of Mayors highlighted the fact that brownfields sites are found throughout the Nation and are a concern for nearly every community.

The bill that we are discussing today fills an important need in the efforts to address our past mistakes.

Currently, Superfund directs the Environmental Protection Agency to give priority to our Nation's most toxic sites. While EPA is struggling to keep up with the over 1,400 so-called "Superfund" sites that it has on its National Priorities List, tens of thousands of other less polluted sites are left unattended.

These so called "brownfields" sites are left unused, or only partially used. The result is that these sites become pockets of blight. The worst case scenario is that these brownfields pose a serious hazard to human health and the environment.

At best, these sites represent a missed opportunity to "recycle" the land for better uses. Failure to reclaim brownfields often means that clean undeveloped areas are used instead, contributing further to the sprawl that afflicts many parts of the country. Neglect of brownfields also means that the land is not put to productive use, either for economic redevelopment or as parkland and green space.

To its credit, EPA has tried to fill this gap through the development of its Brownfields Initiative. California has been the site of two of EPA's leading brownfields initiatives. The mayor will tell us about East Palo Alto's experiences as a brownfields "Showcase Community." These communities are at the cutting edge of the brownfields effort; their experiences will help us learn how to bring together Federal, State, local, and non-governmental interests to address the brownfields problem. They will serve as a model for the rest of the Nation.

I know that Californians believe that the program has been fairly successful; however, it has been operating with one hand tied behind its back. It lacks adequate funding and would benefit from clear statutory authority that enables it to confidently move forward and expand.

This bill will help EPA take the next step with this important program. By authorizing increased funding for this program, clarifying some of the liability questions, and directing the program to the areas of greatest need, this legislation will help expand the scope of this program and elevate its visibility in the eyes of the American public.

As Senator Chafee stated, the bill is a carefully crafted compromise—one that has succeeded in bringing together diverse interests who come from divergent political viewpoints. That matters. Because it means that we might finally be successful in improving our management of the brownfields problem that now plagues our communities.

Nevertheless, I expect that some of our witnesses today will provide detailed criticism of this bill. I look forward to hearing their concerns and hope they can offer us constructive solutions. At the same time, we must not lose site of the end game. The status quo is not acceptable and thoughtful legislation is needed.

I believe that we owe it to our children to leave them an environment that is cleaner and healthier than the one we have inherited. And, I believe that the promotion of redevelopment will bring with it a multitude of benefits that are both environmental and economic in nature. This bill will help take us in that direction.

Source: Hearing on a Bill to Amend the Comprehensive Environmental Response, Compensation, and Liability Act of 1980 to Promote the Cleanup and Reuse of Brownfields, to Provide Financial Assistance for Brownfields Revitalization, to Enhance State Response Programs, and for Other Purposes. Committee on Environment and Public Works, U.S. Senate, 107th Congress, First Session, February 27, 2001. Washington, D.C.: Government Printing Office, 2001.

NOTE

1. Laura Paskus, "Brownfields Program Makes Cleanup Profitable," *High Country News*, December 9, 2002.

An OMB Administrator Touts a "Smart-Regulation" Agenda

"We Are . . . Working to Streamline the Sea of Existing Federal Regulations"

May 19, 2004

One of the central articles of faith of the administration of President George W. Bush was that the totality of business regulations crafted and enforced by the Environmental Protection Agency and other federal agencies during the final decades of the twentieth century had become an onerous burden on America's free enterprise system. During the Bush Administration's eight years in power, it frequently utilized cost-benefit analyses— weighing the costs of regulations against their benefit to society—to gauge the efficacy of various existing and proposed federal regulations. In the administration's calculations, these regulations were frequently found wanting; in many such cases, the regulations in question were revised or removed.

One of the key Bush Administration officials involved in these efforts to scale back regulation was John D. Graham, administrator of the Office of Information and Regulatory Affairs (OIRA), an obscure but powerful agency within the Office of Management and Budget. Graham had entered the public sector from the industry-supported Harvard Center for Risk Analysis, where he served as founding director from 1989 to 2001. Environmental organizations, consumer groups, and others had been aghast at Graham's selection for the post. "[Graham] has undermined regulatory efforts by understating many of the potential benefits of health, safety and environmental regulation and overstating their costs," charged a group of fifty-three academic scholars who opposed his nomination. "Graham's work has . . . demonstrated a remarkable congruency with the interests of regulated industries [and] . . . shows that he is unlikely to serve as an honest broker as OIRA director."[1]

Graham's selection for the OIRA post was widely praised, however, by the business community and many other supporters of regulation reform. "Dr. Graham's nomination presents us with the question of the value of cost-benefit analysis and risk assessment in agency rule making once again," said Democratic senator Carl Levin of Michigan. "That's because Dr. Graham's career has been founded on these principles. He believes in them. So do I. And, Dr. Graham sees cost-benefit analysis not as the be-all and end-all in regulatory decisionmaking; rather, like many of us, he sees it as an important factor to consider."[2] *Graham was eventually confirmed by a 61-37 vote in the U.S. Senate.*

Once ensconced at OIRA, Graham became a point person in pursuing the regulatory changes sought by the Bush White House. He promoted and oversaw the development of an OIRA that took on a much more active role in regulatory policymaking than it had in previous administrations. OIRA became well-known for using cost-benefit analyses, risk assessments, and other tools to block, delay, or demand revisions of regulatory proposals from the EPA, OSHA, and other federal agencies.

The following 2004 statement by Graham at a hearing of the Small Business Committee of the U.S. House of Representatives provides insights into the philosophy that informed OIRA operations and "smart regulation" initiatives throughout the Bush era.

First, I would like to briefly describe to the Committee the origins of our manufacturing reform initiative. Streamlining regulation is a key plank in the President's Six-Point Plan for the Economy. The last twenty years have witnessed an explosion of new federal rules and paperwork requirements that burden consumers, businesses, taxpayers and State and local governments. Many of these regulations undoubtedly are essential to protect consumers, workers and the environment; however, their cumulative burden is onerous, especially for small businesses and others trying to create new jobs. Recent studies show that regulations have significantly raised the cost of doing business in the United States, especially for manufacturers.

The Administration is moving on several fronts to facilitate the streamlining of regulation. First, we have insisted that new federal regulations be supported by good science and economics to ensure that they are necessary and cost effective, and have worked closely with the Congress to limit the number of new laws that would spawn unnecessary regulatory burdens. We are happy to report significant success in this regard: even by conservative estimates, this Administration has slowed the growth of burdensome new rules by at least 75 percent when compared to the previous Administration, while still moving forward with crucial safeguards for homeland security, human health, and environmental protection.

We are also working to streamline the sea of existing federal regulations, which is a humbling and difficult task. As with the federal budget, actually shrinking the absolute burden of imposed regulatory cost is much more difficult than slowing its growth. Our primary approach to date has been a series of solicitations for reform nominations. As a result of our first two reform solicitations in 2001 and 2002, the Administration is working on reforms to over 100 rules, guidance documents, and paperwork requirements.

In OMB's 2004 Draft Report on the Congress on the Costs and Benefits of Federal Regulation on February 13, 2004, we included an expanded review of the impacts of regulations on small business, and an expanded review of the impact of regulation on the manufacturing sector.

In short, our Report confirms once again the relatively large burden that regulation imposes on small businesses, and demonstrates the need for an effective voice for small business during the regulatory review process. We also found that the cumulative regulatory burdens on the manufacturing sector are larger than the costs imposed on other sectors of the economy—and disproportionately large for small and medium-sized manufacturers. One study found that manufacturing firms face a regulatory burden approximately 5 times greater than the average firm, and even when adjusted by the number of employees, manufacturing firms face a regulatory burden per employee approximately 1.7 times greater than the average firm. Environmental regulations impose the largest burden; followed by economic regulations, which include direct controls on the structure of certain markets; tax compliance; and workplace rules; which include categories such as employee benefits, occupational safety and health, and labor standards.

In addition to our work on this issue, the President's Council of Economic Advisors recently reported that, while manufacturing is beginning to share in the economic recovery, the rebound in manufacturing employment has not been as rapid as in other sectors. A recent Commerce Department report included a broad-based review of manufacturing policy and also recommended that federal regulations be re-examined for reform.

Because of these findings, we decided to launch this Administration's 3rd solicitation of reform nominations, and for this reform initiative we decided to solicit reforms relevant to the manufacturing sector. We encouraged commenters to suggest specific reforms to regulations, guidance documents or paperwork requirements that would improve manufacturing regulation by reducing unnecessary costs, increasing effectiveness, enhancing competitiveness, reducing uncertainty and increasing flexibility. We are particularly interested in reforms that address burdens on small and medium-sized small manufacturers, where burdens tend to be relatively large. In addition, because studies have found that tax compliance was particularly burdensome for small businesses, we solicited nominations on ways to simplify IRS paperwork requirements.

In the report, we requested that commenters concentrate on presenting us, to the extent possible, a quantitative or qualitative benefit-cost case that can be made for the reform. We must approach regulatory reform with care because many rules governing this sector may produce substantial benefits for workers, consumers and the environment. Even where the benefits of rules are substantial, it makes sense to search for more cost-effective ways of achieving those benefits; for example, replacing outdated command and control regulations with market-based policy instruments. Whenever the costs of rules are substantial, the search for cost-effective reforms is critical.

We also requested that commenters focus on reforms that the agency or multiple agencies have statutory authority to make. Even nominations that agencies have the authority to pursue often require notice and comment rulemaking, thus it is likely to require a bit of time to enact a substantial number of reforms.

Reform nominations are due at OMB by May 20, 2004, and we will release those nominations as soon as possible. In consultation with the relevant departments and agencies, we will then identify a group of promising reform nominations. Our 2004 Final Report to Congress on the Costs and Benefits of Federal Regulation will report in detail on the progress on this initiative.

In closing, let me assure you that this Administration understands the needs for regulatory reform of the manufacturing sector. The progress we have made so far is a direct result of the President's leadership. Reining-in regulatory costs is a critical part of the

President's six-point plan to stimulate the economy, create jobs and foster economic prosperity for all Americans. We also acknowledge that we have a considerable way to go.

Thank you very much for the opportunity to appear today. I am willing to answer any questions you may have.

Source: Graham, John D., Administrator, Office of Information and Regulatory Affairs. Statement before the Small Business Committee, U.S. Congress. House. 108th Cong., 2d sess., May 19, 2004. www .whitehouse.gov/omb/legislative/testimony/graham/040519_graham_reg_reform.html.

NOTES

1. Letter from 53 Academics to Senate Governmental Affairs Committee, May 9, 2001. Available at www.citizen.org/congress/regulations/graham/academics.html.
2. Office of Carl Levin, Statement on the Nomination of John D. Graham of Massachusetts to be Administrator of the Office of Information and Regulatory Affairs. July 19, 2001. http://levin.senate .gov/newsroom/release.cfm?id=211298.

DOCUMENT
9.15

Environmental Groups Attack the EPA's "Clean Air Mercury Rule"

"EPA's Arguments Are Unlawful and Arbitrary and Capricious"

January 12, 2007

In 2005 the Environmental Protection Agency unveiled a "Clean Air Mercury Rule," which it said would bring about reductions in emissions of mercury, a toxic heavy metal released by power plants that has been identified as a dangerous threat to public health and lake and river ecosystems. The rule, however, was challenged in court by seventeen states, dozens of American Indian tribes, and numerous environmental and public health groups. These opponents contended that the Clean Air Mercury Rule was a cynical Orwellian term for a weak emissions-reduction scheme that would have actually excluded coal- and oil-fired power plants from making mandatory cuts in emissions of mercury and other toxic air pollutants. The following excerpts from a court brief filed in the case by a coalition of environmental groups including the Natural Resources Defense Council, Waterkeeper Alliance, Chesapeake Bay Foundation, EarthJustice, and Clean Air Task Force (Natural Resources Council of Maine, Ohio Environmental Council, and United States PIRG [the federation of state public interest research groups]) provide a good overview of the main objections to the Clean Air Mercury Rule (footnotes in the brief have been deleted).

On February 8, 2008, the U.S. Court of Appeals ruled in favor of the plaintiffs, declaring that the EPA's Clean Air Mercury Rule illegally removed coal- and oil-fired power plants from the Clean Air Act list of sources of hazardous air pollutants. A coalition of utilities backed by the Bush Administration promptly asked the U.S. Supreme Court to hear their appeal. Their hope was that the Court would reverse the federal court decision vacating the mercury rule.

In January 2009, however, a changing of the guard at the White House dramatically changed the complexion of the struggle. Bush was succeeded by Democrat Barack Obama, who had condemned Bush Administration environmental policies throughout his 2008 presidential campaign. On February 6, 2009, Department of Justice officials in the Obama Administration formally asked the Supreme Court to remove the EPA from the appeal. Less than three weeks later, on February 23, the U.S. Supreme Court announced that it would not hear the case. This decision, which effectively killed the Bush-era Clean Air Mercury Rule, prompted expressions of satisfaction from plaintiffs such as New Jersey Attorney General Anne Milgram, who said that "as of today, the protracted legal battle that has delayed proper regulation of mercury emissions from power plants is over, and the practice of allowing those plants to spew harmful quantities of a dangerous neurotoxin into our air in violation of federal law is at an end."[1] The Obama Administration also welcomed the decision, and officials such as EPA administrator Lisa Jackson pledged to move quickly to develop stringent new mercury emission standards for coal- and oil-fired power plants.

Statement of the Case. These petitions seek vacatur of three final agency actions that remove power plants from the list under CAA Section 112(c) requiring the maximum achievable reductions of toxic air emissions from listed industries, and substitute an illegal cap-and-trade program for mercury alone.

I. Factual and Procedural Background

The electric power industry is among the nation's largest domestic emitters of toxic air pollution and the single largest industrial emitter of mercury air pollution. Nationwide, approximately 1,100 coal-fired units at more than 450 existing power plants emit 48 tons of mercury into the air each year. Power plants also emit tens of thousands of tons of other air toxics, including hydrogen chloride, arsenic and lead.

Mercury contamination of air and watersheds imposes devastating impacts on environmental and human health. According to EPA, over 40 states had issued mercury fish consumption advisories in 2003 urging certain citizens—including children and women who are pregnant, may become so, or are nursing—to avoid or limit specific kinds of fish. In 21 of these states the mercury warnings apply statewide. Mercury advisories blanket significant segments of our recreational waterways. Some 13,068,900 lake acres and 766,872 river miles (approximately 32 percent and 24 percent of nationwide totals, respectively) were subject to advisories for mercury contamination in 2003.

The threats posed by toxic chemicals in power plant air emissions are both serious and long-lasting. Mercury is deposited on soil and in water, where it persists and transforms chemically into a highly toxic form (methylmercury) that bio-accumulates in fish. Human exposure to mercury most commonly occurs through the consumption of contaminated fish. Mercury is particularly toxic to developing fetuses and young infants exposed during periods of rapid brain development. Hundreds of thousands of children born in the U.S. each year are at risk of serious harm from exposure to high maternal blood-mercury levels resulting from contaminated fish consumption. Mercury's risks include delayed developmental milestones, reduced neurological test scores and, at high doses, cerebral palsy. Significant evidence also links methylmercury exposure to cardiovascular disease in adults. A large body of scientific literature exists documenting numerous risks to wildlife.

The economic impact of this mercury contamination is significant: total costs of lost U.S. population IQ points due to *in utero* exposure to methylmercury from all sources has been estimated at $3.1 billion to $19.9 billion per year. By contrast, estimated benefits from $86 million to $4.9 billion per year could accrue from the avoided cardiovascular events and premature mortality from even a modest 70 percent cut in power planet mercury. . . .

The 1990 Clean Air Act Amendments.

Frustrated by EPA's decades-long failure to control air toxics, Congress amended the Clean Air Act in 1990. Abandoning its earlier approach, Congress listed more than 180 hazardous air pollutants in the text of the statute . . . and required EPA to list all industrial categories with "major" sources of HAPs [hazardous air pollutants] by November 1991. Congress said EPA "shall" regulate all listed major and "area" source categories under Section 112(d) and must establish emission standards for each HAP emitted.

For each category of major sources, such as power plants, EPA's standards must require at each major source in the category the "maximum" degree of reduction in each emitted HAP that is "achievable" for the category—an approach known as "Maximum Achievable Control Technology" or "MACT." Section 112 also establishes strict schedules for EPA to issue MACT standards for listed categories and for source compliance. New major sources of HAPs generally must comply with MACT standards immediately, and existing sources must comply with MACT standards "as expeditiously as practicable, but in no event later than 3 years after the effective date of such standard."

Congress required EPA within 3 years of November 1990 to "perform a study of the hazards to public health reasonably anticipated to occur as a result of emissions by electric utility steam generating units of pollutants listed under subsection (b) of this section after impositions of the requirements of this chapter," and to report the results of that study to Congress. Congress further declared that EPA "shall regulate electric utility steam generating units under this section, if the Administrator finds such regulation is appropriate and necessary after considering the results of the study."

EPA failed to include power plants on the initial list of source categories containing major sources and missed statutory deadlines for issuing the required studies; by the late 1990s EPA had largely refused to deal with this very large hazardous pollution source. In 1998, EPA produced its utility study. Noting the neurotoxicity and bioaccumulative nature of mercury and referencing its "complete assessment of the health effects, exposures, risks, ecological effects, sources, and control technologies," EPA concluded that there was "a plausible link between anthropogenic releases of mercury from industrial and combustion sources in the United States and methylmercury in fish" and that "mercury emissions from utility units may add to the existing environmental burden."

The EPA Listing Decision.

On December 20, 2000, EPA belatedly made its regulatory determination concerning HAP emissions from power plants. EPA concluded, *inter alia,* that coal-fired power plants emit a significant number of HAPs on the Section 112(b) list and that these toxic air emissions would increase with projected growth in the coal-fired utility industry. EPA confirmed that utility units are the largest source of anthropogenic mercury in the country, that mercury can have serious toxicological effects on both wildlife and humans, and that serious public health impacts could result from HAPs (such as nickel) emitted by oil-fired units. EPA concluded that it was "appropriate and necessary" to regulate coal- and oil-fired power plants under Section 112(n)(1)(A). The agency found that "[t]here are a number of alternative control strategies that are effective in controlling some of the HAP emitted from electric utility steam generating units," and EPA added coal- and oil-fired power plants to the Section 112(c) list of major source categories of HAPs for which the agency must develop Section 112(d) control standards.

EPA was required by settlement agreement to propose MACT standards by 2003 and adopt final standards by 2004, later modified to early 2005. Existing power plants were to be subject to protective MACT standards covering all listed HAP emissions by no later than 2008.

EPA 2004/2005 Rulemaking Process.

EPA initially assembled a Working Group of governmental representatives, scientists, environmental groups, and industry officials to begin the process of crafting the required Section 112 MACT standards. After holding 14 meetings between August 2001 and March 2003, EPA abruptly disbanded the task force without explanation. "It was a huge decision that demonstrated that [EPA's] desire wasn't to regulate mercury in the way that Congress and a federal advisory committee and other stakeholders had anticipated," said the executive director of a nonpartisan association of state air quality officials.

Nine months later, EPA proposed to abandon Section 112 MACT protections in favor of a mercury pollution trading scheme under a different statutory provision, CAA Section 111. This scheme, later the "Clean Air Mercury Rule" ("CAMR"), authorizes individual sources to trade pollution allowances in order to meet an aggregate target. The initial phase of the two-phase program proposed by EPA was expressly tied to the amount of mercury that EPA expected would be emitted by coal-fired power plants after a separate non-mercury control program, the so-called "Clean Air Interstate Rule" ("CAIR"), went into effect. Although EPA also nominally proposed a MACT standard, EPA's Inspector General found that "EPA senior management instructed EPA staff to develop a standard for mercury that would achieve the same results as CAIR—emissions of 34 tons annually—instead of basing the standard on an unbiased determination of what the top performing units were achieving in practice." In other words, EPA decided as a policy matter it did not want MACT limits for power plants, but instead would base standards on the estimated mercury reductions coincident to a different, non-mercury related program effective only in 28 eastern states.

Investigations further revealed that EPA's "proposal to regulate mercury emissions from coal-burning power plants was written using key language provided by utility lobbyists," including virtually verbatim text from a memo prepared by lawyers for Latham & Watkins, the former employer of key EPA political officials developing the rule.

In 2005, EPA finalized two rules, one removing power plants from the Section 112(c) list of MACT-regulated sources (the "Delisting Rule"), and the other establishing CAMR. In its Delisting Rule, EPA reversed its 2000 determination that Section 112 regulation was "appropriate and necessary," and on that basis alone removed coal-fired power plants from the Section 112 list. By doing so, EPA opened the door for CAMR, which in final form establishes a two-phase, nationwide pollution target of 38 tons in 2010 and 15 tons in 2018, and permits sources to bank pollution credits in order to avoid making later reductions—delaying ultimate attainment of the 15-ton target until many years after

2018. The final rule claimed that CAMR—this Section 111 mercury trading program—rendered regulation under Section 112 no longer "necessary."

EPA also justified the final rule—for the first time, without notice or opportunity for public comment—with an argument that Section 112 regulation is not "appropriate" either, because of the incidental mercury reductions due to CAIR (the separate regulatory program that established state budgets for nitrogen oxides and sulfur dioxide reductions in the eastern U.S.) or, separately, those due to CAMR. EPA based this decision on its estimate that the remaining mercury pollution from power plants would not—if one ignored all other mercury pollution—cause public health problems.

CAMR and the Delisting Rule closely tracked legislation to amend the Act that the administration attempted to steer through Congress between 2002 and 2005, which would have repealed the MACT program for power plants and substituted a mercury trading scheme nearly identical to CAMR. The bill failed to pass either body of Congress, however, suffering an unsuccessful Senate Environment Committee vote on March 9, 2005, with no vote ever scheduled in the House. EPA signed CAMR and the Delisting Rule six days after the bill failed to pass out of the Senate committee. . . .

II. Summary of Argument

EPA's delisting unlawfully avoids Section 112 MACT standards by circumventing the clear requirements of CAA Section 112(c)(9), which became applicable to coal- and oil-fired utilities from the moment EPA added the industry to the Section 112(c) list in 2000. It is uncontested that EPA failed to make either of the Section 112(c)(9) determinations. Instead EPA advances several different theories claiming authority to "revisit" the regulatory determination it made in December 2000, and then undo the listing decision without satisfying Section 112(c)(9). In this fashion, EPA evades its obligation to issue a MACT standard for the industry. EPA's arguments are unlawful and arbitrary and capricious.

Other statutory requirements bar EPA from unmaking its prior listing decision. Section 111—one of the provisions EPA relies on to address mercury pollution (but only mercury, and only weakly)—is not a lawful mechanism to control power plant HAPs. EPA's Section 111 rule contravenes the statute both because it regulates HAP emissions and because it does so through an emissions trading approach that fails to achieve the "continuous emission reductions" from all covered source and states as required by the Act.

Nor may EPA undo its regulatory determination or listing decision in reliance on far later and uncertain mercury reductions resulting from other pollution programs, because this reliance upsets Congress's expeditious schedule for securing public health protections against power plant HAP emissions. . . .

IV. Argument

A. EPA's Removal of Coal- and Oil-Burning Power Plants from the CAA Section 112(c) List Contravenes the Statute.

1. The Clean Air Act's Plain Text Demonstrates that EPA May Not Delist an Industry Without First Making the Determinations Required by Section 112(c)(9). . . .

4. EPA Cannot Delist Categories by Just Declaring that the Original Listing Decision Was a Mistake. . . .

B. EPA Has Illegally Undone Its Regulatory Determination.

EPA posits that it can simply undo its earlier listing decision and Section 112(n)(1) (A) regulatory determination by now asserting that Section 112 regulation of the utility industry is neither "appropriate" nor "necessary." Specifically, EPA argues that CAMR (enacted under Section 111(d)) or, alternatively, CAIR (enacted under Section 110(a)(2) (D)) can lawfully supplant Section 112 regulation of utility mercury emissions and thereby obviate the need for Section 112 regulation. EPA's reliance on CAMR and CAIR as surrogates for Section 112 regulation is unlawful and arbitrary. Moreover, the Section 111(d) CAMR approach is itself unlawful.

1. The Plain Language of Section 111(d) Precludes Regulation of Power Plant HAPs.

The CAA Amendments of 1990 contain two provisions prohibiting HAP regulation under Section 111(d)—one originating in the House and one in the Senate. The Statutes at Large, which EPA admits control here, reflect these twin provisions in parentheses: Section 111(d) applies to "any air pollutant . . . which is not included on a list published under section 7408(a) *(or emitted from a source category which is regulated under section 112) [House amendment] (or 112(b) [Senate amendment])*." Thus, the text of Section 111(d)(1)(A) makes clear that EPA may not set standards for a pollutant that is "emitted from a source category which is regulated under section 112" or included on the Section 112(b) list of hazardous air pollutants. Mercury is a HAP emitted by source categories regulated under Section 112 and is on the 112(b) list. Therefore, EPA may not set Section 111 standards for mercury. . . .

2. CAMR's Trading is Unlawful.

Even if EPA were permitted to regulate utility HAPs under Section 111, its rule violates the Act by allowing inter-source, intra-state and interstate mercury emissions trading. While the delisting action and Section 111 rule are unlawful for the reasons set forth above and the Court need not reach the trading question, CAMR's trading scheme—in which individual sources and even entire states experience mercury *increases* for over twenty years—is independently unlawful and arbitrary and capricious.

a. Plain statutory language prohibits CAMR trading.

Section 111(d)(1) instructs States to "establish[] standards of performance for any existing source" for relevant air pollutants . . . EPA has long recognized that Section 111 performance standards are governed by Section 302(1)'s definition of "standard of performance" as well as by Section 111(a)'s definition. In sum, the statute mandates that each State plan apply the best system of emission reduction "to *any* existing source"—on a source-specific basis—and that each source subject to this standard demonstrate "continuous emission reduction[s]."

Attempting to evade these plain requirements, EPA first protests that "'continuous' is not defined" in the statute; but EPA does not and cannot argue that "continuous emission reduction" is ambiguous. Moreover, the lack of a statutory definition does not render a term ambiguous. EPA then absurdly proceeds to equate Section 302(1)'s mandate for "continuous emission *reduction*" with a mandate authorizing emission *increases* (including increases in one year and reductions in other years). EPA concedes that *each source* must achieve continuous emission reductions under Sections 302(1) and 111(d) (1) "standards of performance" (arguing that CAMR satisfies the "requirement of 'continuous' emissions reductions because all of a source's emissions must be covered by allowances"). But EPA fails to note that the possession of "allowances" is actually a term of art for the right *not to reduce* emissions. Moreover, Section 302(1) plainly does not speak in terms of "continuous allowance possession," nor does EPA justify its interpretations severing "continuous" from "emission reductions" and abandoning the need for reductions from *particular* sources.

Indeed, as a result of EPA's rule, 432 utility units out of approximately 1,100 nationwide are projected to *increase* mercury emissions above current levels between now and 2018, and 129 units are expected to do so thereafter. This result—which directly contravenes the statutory mandates for source-specific, continuous reductions—illustrates the unlawfulness of EPA's rule.

CAMR also flouts the statutory mandate that each State plan include "the best system of reduction" for "*any* existing source." That is, each State plan must reduce emissions from any and all existing sources covered by its plan. In defiance of these requirements, EPA authorizes and expects many states to actually *increase* their mercury emissions under EPA's new rule. Indeed, EPA admits that compared to 1999 mercury levels, 19 states will *increase* mercury emissions over the course of the rule's first phase, and five states will continue experiencing emission increases indefinitely after 2018.

EPA tries to sidestep the plain statutory language of Sections 111(a) and 302 by proffering two irrelevant points: (1) that CAMR will achieve "reductions in nationwide Hg [mercury] emissions"; and (2) that standards of performance must be "achievable." EPA never does explain how achieving "reductions in nationwide Hg emissions" discharges the plain statutory obligation in Section 111(d)(1) that "each State" plan the "best system of emission reduction" standard from "any existing source." Similarly, while standards of performance must be "achievable," the statute provides no authority to skirt the mandate that continuous emission reductions be achieved at any existing source subject to the standards. Nor does EPA explain why additional source-specific reductions are not achievable given available controls.

Finally, EPA's convoluted interpretation of Sections 111(a) and (d)(1) leads to a topsy-turvy outcome where "reduction" can actually mean "increase." EPA admits that CAMR is designed *not* to require mercury-specific emission reductions until 2018, and that any earlier mercury reductions are merely coincidental, occurring under CAIR caps on other non-HAP pollutants. . . . Yet EPA pretends that this approach—even during CAMR's Phase I *itself*—satisfies Section 111(d)'s "best system of emission reduction" for *mercury* (arguing conclusorily that "[a] Phase I cap based on 'co-benefits' fulfills EPA's obligation to set a standard of performance based on the best system of emissions reduction that has been adequately demonstrated."). Completely missing is any attempt to determine the degree to which utilities can secure achievable HAP reductions now. Accordingly, EPA's rule allowing emissions increases until 2018 and beyond from numerous power plants (and entire states) violates the plain language of Section 111(a), Section 111(d), and Section 302(1). . . .

3. EPA's Reliance on CAIR to Supplant Section 112 Regulation is Equally Unlawful.

EPA also argues that CAIR by itself, without CAMR, is sufficient justification to evade Section 112 regulation of power plants, even while conceding that it estimates CAIR will only reduce mercury emissions 29 percent by 2020. EPA's reliance on CAIR is unlawful and arbitrary and capricious. . . .

Source: Opening Brief of Environmental Petitioners in *State of New Jersey et al v. U.S. Environmental Protection Agency,* January 12, 2007. No. 05–1162, U.S. Court of Appeals, District of Columbia Circuit. Available at www.earthjustice.org/library/legal_docs/opening-brief-in-challenge-to-weak-epa-mercury-reduction-plan.pdf.

NOTE

1. "Attorney General Welcomes U.S. Supreme Court Denial of Appeal by Utility Group on Regulation of Harmful Mercury Emissions," Office of the Attorney General, State of New Jersey, March 23, 2009. www.nj.gov/oag/newsreleases09/pr20090223a.html.

DOCUMENT
9.16

Toxic Wastes and Race at Twenty, 1987–2007

"Race Maps Closely with the Geography of Pollution"

2007

In 1987 the Commission for Racial Justice of the United Church of Christ issued a famous report called Toxic Wastes and Race in the United States: A National Report on the Racial and Socio-economic Characteristics of Communities with Hazardous Waste Sites. *According to the Commission's findings, toxic waste sites in the United States were disproportionately sited in communities of color. The publication of the study, which was carried out under the direction of the Commission's executive director, Benjamin Chavis, increased public recognition of the environmental justice issue and served as a rallying point for environmental justice advocates demanding policy changes. As the report itself declared, "[T]he magnitude of the problem of hazardous wastes in racial and ethnic communities demands that an aggressive action plan be implemented, combining the best efforts of environmental agencies, corporations, environmental organizations, legislators, churches, civil rights, and community-based organizations."[1]*

Twenty years later, the United Church of Christ published a follow-up report, Toxic Wastes and Race at Twenty, 1987–2007, *to mark the twentieth anniversary of the publication of that landmark report. The 2007 publication reported that communities of color and/or poverty continued to serve as the primary hosts for toxic waste facilities in the United States. The report, which was authored by Robert D. Bullard (a legendary figure in the environmental justice movement), Paul Mohai, Robin Saha, and Beverly Wright, also laid out a variety of public policy recommendations for Congress, the executive branch, and state and local governments. Following is an excerpt.*

CONCLUSIONS

Twenty years after the release of *Toxic Wastes and Race,* significant racial and socioeconomic disparities persist in the distribution of the nation's commercial hazardous waste facilities. Although the current assessment uses newer methods that better match where people and hazardous waste facilities are located, the conclusions are very much the same as they were in 1987. In fact, people of color are found to be more concentrated around hazardous waste facilities than previously shown.

Race matters. People of color and persons of low socioeconomic status are still disproportionately impacted and are particularly concentrated in neighborhoods and communities with the greatest number of facilities. Race continues to be an independent predictor of where hazardous wastes are located, and it is a stronger predictor than income, education and other socioeconomic indicators. Indeed, a watershed moment has occurred in the last decade. People of color now comprise a majority in neighborhoods with commercial hazardous waste facilities, and much larger (more than two-thirds) majorities can be found in neighborhoods with clustered facilities. People of color in 2007 are more concentrated in areas with commercial hazardous sites than in 1987. African Americans, Hispanics/Latinos and Asian Americans/Pacific Islanders alike are disproportionately burdened by hazardous wastes in the U.S.

Race maps closely with the geography of pollution. The findings in our new report are consistent with a September 2005 Associated Press (AP) study showing African Americans were more than twice as likely as white Americans to live in neighborhoods where air pollution seems to pose the greatest health danger. Hispanics and Asian also were more likely to breathe dirty air in some regions of the United States. However, toxic chemical assaults are not new for many people of color who are forced to live next to and often on the fence line with chemical industries that spew their poisons into the air, water and ground.

Place matters. People of color are particularly concentrated in neighborhoods and communities with the greatest number of hazardous waste facilities, a finding that directly parallels that of the original UCC report. This current appraisal also reveals that racial disparities are widespread throughout the country—whether one examines EPA regions, states or metropolitan areas, where the lion's share of facilities is located. Significant racial and socioeconomic disparities exist today despite the considerable societal attention to the problem noted in previous chapters.

> *The impetus for changing the dominant environmental protection paradigm did not come from within regulatory agencies, the polluting industry, academia or the "industry" that has been built around risk management. The impetus for change came from grassroots mobilization that views environmental protection as a basic right, not a privilege.*
>
> —Toxic Wastes and
> Race at Twenty, 1987–2007

These findings raise serious questions about the ability of current policies and institutions to adequately protect people of color and the poor from toxic threats.

Unequal protection places communities of color at special risk. Not only are people of color differentially impacted by toxic wastes and contamination, they can expect different responses from the government when it comes to remediation—as clearly seen in the two case studies in Post-Katrina New Orleans and in Dickson County, Tennessee. Thus, it does not appear that existing environmental, health, and civil rights laws and local land use controls have been adequately applied or adapted to reducing health risks or mitigating various adverse impacts to families living in or near toxic "hot spots."

Polluting industries still follow the path of least resistance. For many industries, it is a "race to the bottom," where land, labor, and lives are cheap. It's about profits and the "bottom line." Environmental "sacrifice zones" are seen as the price of doing business. Vulnerable communities, populations and individuals often fall between the regulatory cracks. They are in many ways "invisible" communities. The environmental justice movement served to make these disenfranchised communities visible and vocal.

The current environmental protection apparatus is "broken" and needs to be "fixed." The current environmental protection system fails to provide equal protection to people of color and low-income communities. Various levels of government have been slow to respond to environmental health threats from toxic waste in communities of color. The mission of the U.S. EPA was never designed to address environmental policies and practices that result in unfair, unjust and inequitable outcomes. The impetus for changing the dominant environmental protection paradigm did not come from within regulatory agencies, the polluting industry, academia or the "industry" that has been built around risk management. The impetus for change came from grassroots mobilization that views environmental protection as a basic right, not a privilege reserved for a few who can "vote with their feet" and escape from or fend off locally undesirable land uses or LULUs—such as landfills, incinerators, chemical plants, refineries and other polluting facilities.

Slow government response to environmental contamination and toxic threats unnecessarily endangers the health of the most vulnerable populations in our society. Government officials have knowingly allowed people of color families near Superfund sites and other contaminated waste sites to be poisoned with lead, arsenic, dioxin, TCE, DDT, PCBs and a host of other deadly chemicals. Having the facts and failing to respond is tantamount to an immoral "human experiment."

Clearly, the environmental justice movement over the last two decades has made a difference in the lives of people of color and low-income communities that are overburdened with environmental pollution. After years of intense study, targeted research, public hearings, grassroots organizing, networking and movement building, environmental justice struggles have taken center stage. Yet, all communities are still *not* created equal. People of color neighborhoods are still the dumping grounds for all kinds of toxins. Federal agencies such as the EPA have dropped the ball in implementing environmental justice and civil rights policies and programs that could truly make a difference to affected communities.

Community leaders who have been on the front line for justice for decades know that the lethargic, and too often antagonistic, government response to environmental emergencies in their communities is not the exception, but the general rule. They have come to understand that waiting for the government to respond can be hazardous to their health and the health of their communities. Many of these leaders are not waiting, but are mobilizing to force all levels of government to do the right thing—and do it in a timely manner before disaster strikes.

While communities all across the nation celebrate the twentieth anniversary of *Toxic Wastes and Race* and the new report, they know all too well that there is still much work to be done before we achieve the goal of environmental justice for all. While much progress has been made in mainstreaming environmental protection as a civil rights, human rights and social justice issue, the key is getting government to enforce the laws and regulations equally across the board—without regard to race, color or national origin.

Getting government to respond to the needs of low-income and people of color communities has not been easy, especially in recent years when the United States Environmental Protection Agency, the governmental agency millions of Americans look to for protection, has mounted an all-out attack on environmental justice and environmental justice principles established in the early 1990s. It has not been easy fending off attacks and proposals from the EPA that would dismantle or weaken the hard-fought gains made by individuals and groups that put their lives on the front line. Moreover, the agency has failed to implement the Environmental Justice Executive Order 12898 signed by President Bill Clinton in 1994 or apply Title VI of the Civil Rights Act.

RECOMMENDATIONS

Many of the environmental injustice problems that disproportionately and adversely affect low-income and people of color communities could be eliminated if current environmental, health, housing, land use, and civil rights laws were vigorously enforced in a nondiscriminatory way. Many of the environmental problems facing low-income persons and people of color are systemic and will require institutional change, including new legislation. We also recognize that government alone cannot solve these problems but need the support and assistance of concerned individuals, groups and organizations from various walks of life. The following recommendations are offered:

Congressional Actions

Codify Environmental Justice Executive Order 12898. In order to strengthen compliance and enforcement of environmental justice objectives at the federal level, ensure that discriminatory agency decisions and actions are addressed, and to provide clear leadership to the states, Congress should codify into law Executive Order 12898 "Federal Actions to Address Environmental Justice in Minority Populations and Low-Income Populations." By codifying the Executive Order, Congress will establish an unequivocal legal mandate and impose federal responsibility in ways that advance equal protection under law in communities of color and low-income communities. Executive Order 12898 provides significant impetus at the federal level and in the states. However, arguably the power of the Executive Branch alone is limited. Enacting a law which codifies the government's role in achieving environmental justice, expands the original list of seventeen agencies required to comply and establishes annual reports to Congress that would pave the way to government-wide action and provide a means of accountability.

Provide Legislative "Fix" for Title VI of the Civil Rights Act of 1964. Work toward a legislative "fix" of Title VI of the Civil Rights Act of 1964 that was gutted by the 2001 *Alexander v. Sandoval* U.S. Supreme Court decision that requires intent, rather than disparate impact, to prove discrimination. Congress should act to restore the status quo that existed prior to *Sandoval* by passing legislation to reestablish that there is a private right of action for disparate impact discrimination under the Title VI regulation. The failure to restore the private right of action will mean that private advocacy organizations will have to fight many discrimination battles with one hand tied behind their backs.

Re-instate the Superfund Tax. The new Congress needs to act immediately to re-instate the Superfund Tax, re-examine the National Priorities List (NPL) hazardous site ranking system and reinvigorate Federal Relocation Policy implementation in communities of color to move those communities that are directly in harm's way.

Hold Congressional Hearings on EPA Response to Contamination in EJ Communities. We urge the U.S. congress to hold hearings on the U.S. Environmental Protection Agency's (EPA's) response to toxic contamination in EJ communities, including post-Katrina New Orleans, the Dickson County (Tennessee) Landfill water contamination problems, and similar toxic contamination problems found in low-income and people of color communities throughout the United States.

Convene Congressional Black Caucus and Congressional Hispanic Caucus Policy Briefings. We urge the Congressional Black Caucus and the Congressional Hispanic Caucus to convene policy briefings on the findings of *Toxic Wastes and Race at Twenty* to explore possible legislative and policy remedies.

Enact Legislation Promoting Clean Production and Waste Reduction. Require industry to use clean production technologies and support necessary R&D for toxic use reduction and closed loop production systems. Create incentives and buy back programs to achieve full recovery, reuse, recycling of waste and product design that enhances waste material recovery and reduction. Policies must include material restrictions for highly toxic and carcinogenic materials.

Require Comprehensive Safety Data for all Chemicals. Chemical manufacturing companies must provide publicly available safety information about a chemical for it to remain on or be added to the market. The information must allow for reasonable evaluation of the safety of the chemical for human health and the environment and must include hazard, use and exposure information. This is referred to as the "No Data, No Market" principle.

Executive Branch Actions

Implement EPA Office of Inspector General's Recommendations. Even the EPA's own Inspector General (IG) agrees that the agency has not developed a clear vision or a comprehensive strategic plan, and has not established values, goals, expectations and performance measurements for integrating environmental justice into its day-to-day operations. The EPA should implement the EJ recommendations of the IG's 2004 and 2006 reports for addressing Executive Order 12898.

Fully Implement Environmental Justice Executive Order 12898. The U.S. EPA, FEMA, Army Corps of Engineers, Department of Labor, HUD and other federal agencies need to fully implement the Environmental Justice Executive Order 12898 in the cleanup and rebuilding in the hurricane-ravaged Gulf Coast region.

Protect Community Right-to-Known. Reinstate reporting emissions to the Toxic Release Inventory (TRI) database on an annual basis to protect communities' right to know. Reinstate reporting lower emission thresholds to the TRI.

End EPA Rollback of Environmental Justice Initiatives. Environmental justice leaders are demanding that the U.S. EPA end its attempts to roll back environmental justice and take aggressive steps to implement EJ Executive Order 12898 and provide targeted enforcement where the needs are the greatest, and where unequal protection places low-income and people of color populations at special risk.

Require Cumulative Risk Assessments in Facility Permitting. EPA should require assessments of multiple, cumulative and synergistic exposures, unique exposure pathways and impacts to sensitive populations in issuing environmental permits and promulgating regulations under the Resource Conservation and Recovery Act (RCRA), Clean Air Act (CAA), Clean Water Act (CWA) and other federal laws. Similar considerations should be made in establishing site-specific clean-up standards under Superfund and Brownfields programs.

Require Safety Buffers in Facility Permitting and Fenceline Community Performance Bonds for Variances. The EPA and states should adopt site location standards requiring a safe distance between a residential population and an industrial facility so that the population is not located within the area where deaths or serious injury to health or property would result in the event that a toxic or flammable substance stored, processed or generated by the facility would be released to the environment through explosion, fire or spill. If safety buffer exemptions are granted, require a locally administered Fenceline Community Performance bond to provide recovery resources for residents impacted by chemical accidents.

State and Local Actions

Require State-by-State Assessments (Report Cards) on Environmental Justice. Require states to evaluate and report their progress made on environmental justice. From 1993 to present, nearly three dozen states have expressly addressed environmental justice, demonstrating increased attention to the issue at a political level by passing legislation. However, little is known about the efficacy of these laws and if in fact they are being enforced.

Require Brownfields Community Revitalization Analysis (CRA). Parties seeking to benefit from government subsidies should be required to conduct a Community Revitalization Analysis (CRA) and take steps to address the most serious impacts identified in the analysis.

Develop Brownfields Partnerships with Academic Institutions. Residents in neighborhoods with brownfield sites must be an integral part of the redevelopment process. Many brownfields are located in or near low-income and people of color communities and historically black colleges and universities (HBCUs), Hispanic Serving Institutions (HSIs), and American Indian Tribally Controlled Colleges and Universities.

Establish Tax Increment Finance (TIF) Funds to Promote Environmental Justice-Driven Community Development. Environmental justice organizations should become involved in redevelopment processes in their neighborhoods in order to integrate brownfields priorities into long-range neighborhood redevelopment plans. This will allow for the use of Tax Increment Finance (TIF) funds accrued by the redevelopment process to fund the cleanup and redevelopment of brownfields sites for community-determined uses. It is imperative that EJ groups and other community-based organizations are provided resources to drive the development process, as investment in an area increases and as real-estate values rise—to minimize gentrification and displacement of incumbent residents.

Establish Community Land Trusts. The establishment of Community Land Trusts (CLTs) could allow communities to purchase or obtain brownfields from local governments at below-market rates, and then redevelop them for a variety of community needs including limited-equity housing. CLTs are community-governed nonprofits, with development priorities that are determined by local residents.

Adopt Green Procurement Policies and Clean Production Tax Policies. State and local governments can show leadership in reducing the demand for products produced using unsustainable technologies that harm human health and the environment. Government must use its buying power and tax dollars ethically by supporting clean production systems. Ecological tax reform can assure that public money goes to safer materials and promotes pollution prevention. . . .

Source: Bullard, Robert D., Paul Mohai, Robin Saha, and Beverly Wright. "Chapter 8: Conclusions and Recommendations." *Toxic Wastes and Race at Twenty, 1987–2007.* A Report Prepared for the United Church of Christ Justice & Witness Ministries. Copyright © March 2007 by the United Church of Christ. www.ucc.org/environmental-ministries/environment/toxic-waste-20.html.

NOTE

1. Commission for Racial Justice, United Church of Christ, *Toxic Wastes and Race in the United States: A National Report on the Racial and Socio-Economic Characteristics of Communities with Hazardous Waste Sites* (New York: Public Data Access, 1987).

Assessing the Impact of Uranium Poisoning in the Navajo Nation

"This Pitiful Response to an Obvious Disaster Must End"

October 23, 2007

Between the 1940s and the 1980s an estimated 3.9 million tons of uranium ore were extracted out of 27,000 square miles of Navajo reservation land in Arizona, New Mexico, and Utah. The Navajo nation cooperated with this mining activity, which was undertaken first as part of a World War II effort and then to increase Cold War nuclear stockpiles. The U.S. government's framing of the mining as both patriotic and as a source of jobs resonated with Navajo leaders, who were also reassured by contractual language that assured them that the mining companies would leave the land "in as good condition as received." But when the companies that leased the lands ended their mining activities and departed, they left thousands of radioactive wounds to fester on the land. These sites—abandoned mines; mounds of heavy metal tailings; and water-filled pits with high concentrations of uranium, lead, arsenic, and cadmium that Navajo families used for drinking water and to water their herds—became part of the landscape for the 180,000 or so people who live in scattered communities across the reservation.

During the 1970s and 1980s evidence rapidly accumulated that this detritus from the Cold War nuclear arms race posed a deadly threat to the Navajo people. Cancer rates soared, as did birth defects and other serious health problems. A spate of investigations carried out by Navajo inspectors and government scientists with the Environmental Protection Agency, Indian Health Service, and other federal agencies revealed spectacularly high levels of radiation and heavy metal contamination in numerous homes and yards. No comprehensive plan for addressing these problems was ever produced, however, in part because the Navajo people had no political influence in Washington and in part because scattered distribution, impoverishment, and internal squabbling kept the Navajo nation from ever mobilizing on its own behalf.

The federal government did take some measures to respond to the crisis. In mid-1984, for example, the Department of Energy embarked on a ten-year program to cover tailing piles left over at the reservation's abandoned uranium mills. And in 1990 Congress passed the Radiation Exposure Compensation Act, which offered former uranium miners in the West financial compensation (and a formal apology) for their years of exposure. But efforts to obtain Superfund status for the abandoned mines and pits foundered amid bureaucratic sniping and maneuvering, and individual agencies ruled out comprehensive remediation programs as unattainable because of funding limitations. This state of affairs endured into the first decade of the twenty-first century to the despair of people such as Navajo president Joe Shirley Jr. "It's an emergency that is not being treated like an emergency," he said. "Where is our guardian?"[1]

In 2006 the Los Angeles Times published a four-part investigative series detailing the nightmarish conditions that existed on the Navajo reservation in addition to the federal government's history of fitful and half-hearted clean-up efforts. The revelations contained in the series so scandalized Henry Waxman (D-Calif.), chair of the House

Committee on Oversight and Government Reform, that he called a hearing to review the issue. Officials from five federal agencies with varying levels of responsibility for protecting Navajo health and the environment—the Environmental Protection Agency, the Department of Energy, the Nuclear Regulatory Commission, the Bureau of Indian Affairs, and the Indian Health Service—testified at the hearing, which was held on October 23, 2007.

Waxman served notice in his opening statement that the hearing would be an uncomfortable one for the agency representatives. "If a fraction of the deadly contamination the Navajos live with every day had been in Beverly Hills or any wealthy community, it would have been cleaned up immediately," he asserted. "But a different standard applied to Navajo lands. Half-measures or outright neglect has been the official response. It's hard to review this record and not feel ashamed. What's happened just isn't right."[2] As the hearing continued, some committee members voiced clear displeasure with the testimony they received from some federal agency representatives. When Representative Tom Udall (D-N.M.) asked Bureau of Indian Affairs director Jerry Gidner whether he believed that the United States government had carried out its pledge to protect the welfare of the Navajo people, Gidner responded, "That's hard to say." Udall responded with disbelief. "Hard to say?" he said. "I would think that you'd be outraged."[3]

The hearing also featured testimony from a wide range of Navajo citizens and public health experts (following are excerpts from two of the hearing's witnesses: Stephen Etsitty, the executive director of the Navajo Nation EPA, and Doug Brugge, a public health scholar and expert on uranium contamination on Navajo land). Their litany of horror stories and tales of unfulfilled promises further angered the committee members. By the close of the hearing, all five agencies had been explicitly directed to put together a list of steps and funding needs to conduct detailed health surveys and clean up the reservation once and for all. On June 16, 2008, the five agencies jointly submitted to the committee a five-year plan to clean up the contaminated uranium mining sites on and around the Navajo reservation.

Testimony of Stephen Etsitty

October 23, 2007

My name is Stephen Etsitty. I am a member of the Navajo Nation and the Executive Director of the Navajo Nation Environmental Protection Agency. It is my privilege to be here this morning representing the Navajo people and the Navajo Environmental Protection Agency. The "legacy" of past uranium mining and processing blankets the Navajo Nation from the Eastern Agency communities of Smith Lake and Ambrosia Lake, to Church Rock, near Gallup, on up to the northern region near the four corners area that includes the Navajo communities of Shiprock, New Mexico, and Cove, Arizona, across the beautiful Chuska mountains to my home area of Lukachukai and from there westward to Tuba City and Cameron, only a few miles from the Grand Canyon. All of those areas, all are a part of what we refer to as Diné Bikeyeah, and all have suffered and continue to suffer the health and environmental impacts from past uranium mining and processing.

This unfortunate legacy resulted from several past activities—uranium exploration, the mining of uranium, either underground or open pit mining, and the processing of the mined uranium done at facilities producing yellow-cake for the United States nuclear weapons arsenal. The legacy lingers due to the current slow pace of cleanup of known contaminated sites.

There are four former uranium processing sites spread across the Navajo Nation at Church Rock, Shiprock, Mexican Hat, and Tuba City. All of these sites were decommissioned by the United States government, meaning that the radioactive mill tailings were capped with clay and rock and left in place at or adjacent to the former mill site. None of the sites were lined, meaning that there was nothing placed underneath the radioactive materials to keep the radioactive waste from leaching into the groundwater, and we believe that is exactly what is happening today. We know there is radioactive and chemical groundwater contamination under all of these sites and that in Tuba City and Shiprock the contamination is moving towards municipal drinking water wells. We know the federal government is working on that contamination and claims that things will be better in twenty or thirty years. We also know that it would be extremely difficult, if not impossible, to construct a solid waste, not to mention a hazardous waste, landfill in your home state today in accordance with current environmental laws and regulations unless that landfill was built with a liner to protect the underlying groundwater. Yet in my homeland, the Navajo Nation, we have what amounts to four unlined radioactive waste dumps threatening our groundwater.

Not one of the four mill sites have been properly remediated with contaminants removed from the living areas of the Navajo. As we gather mounting evidence that these unlined landfills seep uranium waste into our groundwater, we watch the federal government dig up and properly remediate a similar site located near Moab, Utah, which is outside the borders of the Navajo Nation. Why is this not happening on the Navajo reservation? Are we seeing environmental injustice in action once again?

With reference to former uranium mining we know that there are over 600 former uranium mining sites either on or within one mile of Navajo lands and that there are over 1200 site features, such as contaminated waste piles, associated with these sites. Although many of these site features have been reclaimed, meaning that mine shafts have been sealed and other physical site dangers addressed, only one of the abandoned mine sites has been thoroughly assessed in accordance with U.S. EPA Superfund program protocols and that assessment has only been completed within the past year.

Waste from the mines and mills found their way over the years throughout the Navajo Nation. Radioactive building materials have been found in Navajo homes. Grazing animals sip water from contaminated ponds. A public highway, state road 566, became contaminated with radioactive materials spilling from mining trucks. A Geiger counter held while driving that highway today will click and scream, revealing a radioactive public transportation corridor. . . .

I'm here today not only as a spokesperson of the Navajo government, but also as an individual Navajo who has walked across these sites, come to know these families, felt their anger, heard their stories of unexplained cancers, kidney failures, birth defects, and sores that don't heal. This pitiful response to an obvious disaster must end. Please accept that the Navajo Nation has proven that it is capable of being a true and equal partner with the United States in restoring the Navajo land and people to *hozho* (harmony). But we can't do it with our current woefully underfunded budget and diminishing resources. We can't continue to have to beg the U.S. government for help only to be rejected and have to prove time and time again that we know our land better than the federal authorities.

We opened the borders of our land for uranium mining in an act of patriotism during the Cold War Era. Now we are left with a legacy of uranium contamination without substantial federal monetary help. Navajo patriotism and Navajo per capita contributions to American armed forces are now, and always have been, unsurpassed. It's time for America to support the people who support America. We are a people who have a treaty with the government of the United States. The treaty of 1868 is sacred to my people. We have always honored our obligations under that treaty. The presence of unpermitted, unlawful hazardous waste dumps on our land amounts to a taking of our land in violation of this treaty. We now look to the government we have faithfully served to honor its obligations.

Testimony of Doug Brugge

October 23, 2007

. . . Appearing before this congressional hearing today reminds me of the long history of such hearings, beginning in the 1960s and continuing through the 1970s, 80s, and 90s, that sought and eventually achieved a semblance of compensation for Navajo and other uranium miners. I am deeply saddened by the fact that so little has been accomplished over those decades to eliminate the health hazards faced by the enormous quantities of uranium waste on the Navajo reservation. There has been too little research on the health impacts of uranium mining in Navajo communities. The one study underway, for example, will mostly address kidney disease and not birth defects or cancer. Today as we begin the public process of addressing community exposures, I can only hope that the path is far shorter than the one traveled by the uranium miners and their families.

I will now spend a few moments describing the hazards faced by the Navajos today. Clearly, uranium ore is a toxic brew of numerous nasty hazardous materials. Uranium, itself highly toxic, gives rise to a series of other radioactive decay elements that are found in raw, natural ore. Most significant among these are radium and thorium, both of which are highly radioactive. When radium decays it produces radon gas, a potent toxicant. Because it is a gas that becomes airborne, when radon decays it transforms into a series of highly radioactive "radon daughters" that can lodge in the lungs.

The primary heavy metal toxicants in uranium ore include uranium itself and arsenic, as well as vanadium and manganese. During the first phase of processing uranium, most of the uranium is removed, leaving behind mill tailings which retain most of the other toxic contaminants from the ore. The milling of uranium is an industrial process that involves crushing and grinding of the rock and the addition of acids and organic solvents to facilitate concentration and removal of the uranium. Hence, uranium mill tailings and mill tailings effluent are not only highly radioactive, but they are acutely hazardous.

The health effects of uranium and its associated radioactive decay products and heavy metals that rise to the level of proven or near-proven causal links include:

1. Radon, which causes lung cancer and . . . is the primary source of lung cancer among Navajo uranium miners;
2. Uranium, which as a heavy metal causes damage to the kidneys and birth defects;
3. Radium, which causes bone cancer, cancer of the nasal sinuses and mastoid air cells and leukemia; and
4. Arsenic, which causes lung and skin cancer, as well as neurotoxicity, hyperpigmentation, and hyperkeratosis of the skin.

There are [also] . . . many other negative health effects from exposure to uranium and its byproducts. In short, there is a clear causal link between uranium exposure and human health. The Navajos continually exposed to uranium and its byproducts even today face grave threats to their health.

I would like to conclude with some observations about the Navajo community of Church Rock, both historical and present day. Church Rock is located outside of Gallup, New Mexico, in the Navajo Nation. The Church Rock tailings spill remains the largest industrial release of radioactive wastes in the history of the United States. In 1979, only months after the Three Mile Island release, a dam holding back a tailings lagoon maintained by United Nuclear Corporation failed, sending 94 million gallons of radioactive and acidic wastewater and 1,100 tons of toxic and radioactive mill waste into the Puerco River. This release, which was substantially larger than the release at TMI, flowed into a low-income, largely Native American community. This incident has been virtually ignored in the press and scientific literature.

For the people in Church Rock and other Navajo communities contaminated for decades with uranium ore tailings there are no "good" options, too much harm has already been done. But there are ways that we can gradually make things better so that maybe the children and the grandchildren of the Navajo uranium miners are not still grappling with this toxic legacy. A good start would be to provide sufficient resources to secure or remove contamination at these hazardous waste sites and to do so in a manner that prevents additional exposure to nearby residents. And Congress must fund the Navajo Nation and federal health agencies to provide resources for health studies among the tens of thousands of Navajo community members who still live next to abandoned mines and-or who were exposed to uranium from the contaminated dusts brought home by their working relatives.

I leave you to ponder a simple observation about this egregious situation: As terrible as the health effects that we know arise from toxins in uranium tailings, there are almost certainly additional ways that the health of Navajo people living near uranium mill and mine waste has been affected. If we are to understand the full extent of this injustice, we will also need additional health studies. . . .

Source: Testimony of Stephen Etsitty and Doug Brugge. Hearing on the Health and Environmental Impacts of Uranium Contamination in the Navajo Nation. U.S. Congress. House. Committee of Oversight and Government Reform, 110th Cong., 1st sess., October 23, 2007. http://oversight.house .gov/story.asp?ID=1560.

NOTES

1. Quoted in Judy Pasternak, "Blighted Homeland: A Peril that Dwelt Among the Navajos," *Los Angeles Times,* November 19, 2006. www.latimes.com/news/la-na-navaj019nov19,0,5351917.story.

2. Opening statement of Chairman Waxman. Hearing on the Health and Environmental Impacts of Uranium Contamination in the Navajo Nation. U.S. House of Representatives, Committee of Oversight and Government Reform, October 23, 2007. http://oversight.house.gov/story.asp? ID=1560.

3. Quoted in Judy Pasternak, "Navajos Seek Funds to Clear Uranium Contamination," *Los Angeles Times,* October 24, 2007. www.latimes.com/features/health/la-na-navaj024oct24,0,1848950.story.

DOCUMENT
9.18

A Critique of Bush Administration Regulatory Reforms

"[OIRA Has] an Unwarranted Choke-hold over Regulatory Decisions"

April 30, 2009

During the eight years in which George W. Bush occupied the Oval Office, relations between his administration and the environmental movement devolved from one of mutual suspicion and wariness to one of outright loathing. Bush officials saw most of the policy priorities of environmental groups and their congressional allies as unreasonable and needlessly injurious to job creation and economic expansion. For their part, opponents decried the Bush Administration's public land policies on logging, mining, and drilling activities as rapacious and irresponsible, and they described Bush's "smart regulation" agenda as a transparent scheme to gut environmental protections by gumming up the government's regulatory works.

One particular focal point of environmentalists' anger was the Office of Information and Regulatory Affairs, an influential office within the Office of Management and Budget responsible for monitoring the development and introduction of federal regulations. During most of Bush's two terms OIRA was headed by John D. Graham, a risk-analysis expert who made the agency a much bigger player in regulatory policymaking than it had been in previous administrations. OIRA became well-known for using cost-benefit analyses, risk assessments, and other tools to block, delay, or demand revisions of regulatory proposals from the EPA, OSHA, and other federal agencies.

These actions triggered condemnation from environmental and public health activists who accused Graham of waging a relentless campaign against vital environmental and public health safeguards. Environmentalist Robert F. Kennedy Jr., for example, described him as the "engine-room mechanic of the Bush stealth strategy"[1] to eviscerate American environmental law. But Graham was also widely praised by groups who believed that the government needed to reduce its regulatory presence in American business. William Kovacs, vice president of the U.S. Chamber of Commerce, marveled in 2002 that Graham had transformed OIRA into a "real, live regulatory-review agency" capable of getting "agencies to respond to real problems instead of political problems."[2] Susan E. Dudley of the free market-oriented Mercatus Center at George Mason University, meanwhile, wrote approvingly that "OIRA, headed by John D. Graham, has reinvigorated the [regulatory] review process, sending back to the agencies more rules during the first year of the Bush administration than were returned during the entire eight years of the Clinton administration. This level of activity contrasts sharply with the previous administration, in which OIRA rarely challenged an agency initiative on any grounds."[3]

One OIRA announcement in 2003—that it intended to funnel all of the government's peer-review processes, which assess the scientific validity of research used in the crafting of regulations and programs, into its office—struck a particular nerve with Graham's critics. Opponents warned that with this scheme, hand-picked peer-review panels chosen by OIRA would be able to delay or weaken federal responses to environmental and public health *problems by calling for additional rounds of research to resolve lingering "uncertainties" about the severity of those threats. Legitimate scientific studies would thus be trapped in a limbo of endless study—and industry would avoid being saddled with new regulations.[4]*

Graham defended the proposal, stating that "a more uniform peer review policy promises to make regulatory science more competent and credible, thereby advancing the Administration's 'smart regulation' agenda. The goal is fewer lawsuits and a more consistent regulatory environment, which is good for consumers and business." In this case, however, the sustained outcry against the agency's peer review changes from public advocacy groups, policy analysts, and members of the scientific community convinced the Bush Administration to relent. OIRA was forced to cut back considerably on the scope and reach of its peer review plan.

One of Graham's most prominent critics was the Center for Progressive Reform (CPR), an organization dedicated to the study of federal regulations "to protect public health, natural resources, and worker safety." In April 2009 CPR president Rena Steinzor was invited to testify on Capitol Hill about the need to reform OIRA operations in the new presidential administration of Barack Obama. Her comments, excerpted here, provide a good overview of the environmental community's perspective on "regulatory czar" John Graham and OIRA during the Bush era, its view of the aborted peer review changes, and its concerns about cost-benefit analysis in the regulatory process.

This hearing could not be more timely because the Senate hearing for Cass Sunstein, President Obama's choice to serve as "regulatory czar," will be held very soon and because the president has directed the Office of Management and Budget's (OMB) Office of Information and Regulatory Affairs (ORA) to rewrite Executive Order 12,866, which governs the structure of regulatory review. Mr. Sunstein's predecessor, John Graham, used OIRA to expand control over regulatory policy to an unprecedented extent, delivering a body blow to the effectiveness of the nation's regulatory system in the name of "reforming" it. Consistent with President Obama's strong plurality in what the pundits call a "change election," Mr. Graham's discredited and destructive approach must be rejected and the role of regulatory czar must be fundamentally redefined.

My testimony today makes three crucial points:

1. The Obama Administration and Congress should define a new mission for the regulatory czar. The term "regulatory reform" has become a shorthand reference to the assertion that regulatory agencies—especially in the health and safety arena and most especially with respect to the Environmental Protection Agency (EPA)—must have a heavy net thrown over them to contain their excessive rules and overzealous staff. This approach was never a good idea and, in any event, is outmoded. *The American people need more, not less regulation on every front, from mortgage lending to workplace hazards. The regulatory czar's mission should be to rescue struggling regulatory agencies by helping them to obtain more resources and stronger legal authority.*

2. OIRA should stop reviewing individual regulatory proposals. Empirical studies reveal that OIRA has served for well over 30 years as a killing ground for protective regulations. Except during the Clinton Administration, OIRA's threat to target any given regulatory proposal has chilled the development of strong and effective legislation. *OIRA has plenty of work to do formulating regulatory policy and should leave the drafting of individual rule regulatory impact analyses and the making of final decisions to agency experts, supervised by Obama political appointees.*

3. OIRA must stay out of science policy. OIRA is a small office, comprised of approximately 40–50 professionals, the vast majority of whom are economists. During the Graham era of kingdom-building, five or six of these positions were set aside to hire scientists, who proceeded to propose radical changes in the way research would be used to make regulatory policy. *OIRA is not competent to propose science policy in the regulatory arena and should abandon this role.*

A New Mission for the Regulatory Czar and OIRA

Regulatory Killing Ground

The Reagan Administration introduced the requirement—continued by all subsequent presidents—that agencies must produce a cost-benefit analysis for every "significant rule," a term of art meaning requirements imposing more than $100 million in compliance costs. President Reagan and his successors also prohibited agencies from proposing or adopting rules until they are approved by economists at OIRA. This requirement gives this small office an unwarranted choke-hold over regulatory decisions.

Cost-benefit analyses are designed to provide a *quantified*—or numerical—estimate of both the potential costs and benefits of a proposed rule. Potential costs include whatever money companies will be compelled to spend to implement the remedies proposed in the rule, such as installation of pollution control equipment or obtaining and enforcing the use of hardhats and respirators for workers dealing with hazardous conditions or materials. When a rule requires the use of an emerging technology, prices fall as the market expands, lowering compliance costs. But these dynamics are ignored and compliance costs are routinely overstated by industries opposing the new rules, and agencies do a poor job of critically evaluating such claims.

> *[R]egulatory agencies covering the full spectrum of safety, health, environmental and financial protection of Americans are in a frighteningly dysfunctional state that threatens the well-being of every American.*
>
> —Rena Steinzor

Potential benefits of a regulatory proposal include the harm that will be avoided if the regulation is implemented. Economists also insist on quantifying these benefits in monetary terms, an ostensibly straightforward approach that causes huge problems in practice. "Monetizing" human suffering or the irrevocable loss of natural resources is controversial from an ethical perspective. And much of the harm addressed by health and safety regulation is very difficult to reduce to numbers. An equally important problem is that the economists also insist on treating these figures as if they were any other kind of financial investments. People expect to receive a "return" on investments of money that increase the value of the initial amount over time. In essence, people get paid for allowing others—the banks or the government—to use their money. The economists argue that if someone who is exposed to a hazardous chemical today will not die of cancer for 25 more years, the value of the life saved by a regulatory intervention should be quantified as if it was such an investment. So the question becomes how much money would we need to invest today, at a rate of return of either three or seven percent (numbers specified by OIRA), to come up with $6.8 million (a common estimate of the value of saving one life) in 30 years. This practice is known as "discounting."

Because cost-benefit number-crunching deals with such uncertainty, these analyses can run to hundreds of pages of complex, dense, and highly technical data, projections, modeling, and mathematical formulas that deter any but the most determined stakeholders from challenging these analytical bottom lines. As troubling, distilling the series of arbitrary assumptions that underlie such calculations into a small set of numbers leaves a misleading impression of objectivity when, in fact, such analyses are notoriously susceptible to manipulation, making them ideal useful political cover for decisions to weaken regulations.

Although this point is rejected by cost-benefit enthusiasts, retrospective examinations of regulatory decisionmaking shows that the primary impact of such analyses is to weaken the protection of health, safety, and the environment, not strengthen it. . . .

Acute Regulatory Dysfunction

. . . Beginning with the first Reagan Administration, OIRA has served mainly to suppress and delay regulation thought to be excessive. This focus is hardly appropriate for the challenges confronting today's regulatory system. The allegation that these agencies have run amok, and are galloping across the tundra regulating without common sense and at an unaffordable cost to industry is no more credible than the argument made shortly before the current economic crisis an overweening Securities and Exchange Commission was thwarting financial institutions from bringing prosperity to the world. Instead, like the SEC, regulatory agencies covering the full spectrum of safety, health, environmental and financial protection of Americans are in a frighteningly dysfunctional state that threatens the well-being of every American.

The place to start in rescuing this failed system is to announce a fundamental re-orientation of the OIRA. Rather than chiding regulators for their alleged excesses, the OIRA should be helping agencies like the Consumer Products Safety Commission (CPSC), the Environmental Protection Agency (EPA), the Food and Drug Administration (FDA), the National Highway Traffic Safety Administration (NHTSA), and the Occupational Safety and Health Administration (OSHA) to producer smarter, better government. Rescuing these agencies by giving them adequate resources to fulfill their statutory mandates, helping them to develop strong, proactive agendas, and ensuring that they receive enhanced legal authority to take decisive action should be the top priorities for the regulatory czar and his OIRA staff.

This reorientation of rules is urgent, as illustrated by the acute and dangerous regulatory dysfunction that makes headlines every day. These incidents inflict real injury. They occur because these five agencies lack the resources and the political will to carry out their vitally important statutory missions effectively. The ranks of the civil service are decimated. The agencies are overburdened by mischievous Bush Administration "midnight regulations" and illegal regulatory decisions now under challenge in the courts. Congress has not reviewed or refreshed many of their authorizing statues in at least two decades. Their budget resources are a fraction of what they need to fulfill mandates made infinitely more complex by the importation of foreign products, food, and pollution. . . .

Solutions

OMB should revamp its Performance Assessment and Ratings Tool to focus on funding gaps.

Rather than view the primary job of a "regulatory czar" as stopping excessive regulation, Cass Sunstein and his OIRA staff should define [it] as revamping the regulatory system to ensure that agencies are able to fulfill their regulatory missions in a vigorous, timely, effective, and wise manner. One crucial place to start is for OMB to revamp its Performance Assessment Rating Tool (PART) used to audit the effectiveness of individual government programs to serve a much more crucial function: undertaking an analysis of the resource gap between how much it would cost to implement all of an agency's statutory mandates and the agency's individual budgets. . . .

The President should suspend OIRA review of individual rules.

A second crucial reform is to terminate OIRA's responsibility for spot-checking individual regulatory impact analyses. As explained above, this review is far from comprehensive because OIRA has such a small staff. Instead, under Republican presidents, the historical purpose of such reviews was to intimidate agencies into reducing the protectiveness of their own rules in anticipation of potential OIRA disapproval. Apparently, these administrations did not have confidence that their appointees to head the agencies could exert enough control over career staffs to accomplish presidential goals. Ironically, this fear that agency administrators would "go native" did not really materialize, especially under the Bush II Administration. Furthermore, all of the agencies have ample expertise to prepare such documents, under the supervision of political appointees who have expertise in the matter, and OIRA review is duplicative.

Instead of bogging itself down in the micromanagement of specific rulemaking, OIRA should spend its time doing work that no other unit of government is set up to accomplish:

• Resolving interagency disputes over cross-cutting policies. OIRA should play a central role in convening the principles of warring agencies to resolve disputes over regulatory policy. In this role, OIRA must avoid the pitfall of hauling one agency (e.g., EPA) before a panel of other agencies and departments that it is assigned to regulate (e.g., the military) to answer for its sins. Instead, OIRA should serve as a neutral broker, well-informed on the legal constraints, especially the requirements of agency statutory mandates that affect the resolution of the dispute, obtaining the assistance of Justice Department experts as necessary.

• Conducting original research on cross-cutting regulatory issues. OIRA should spend a significant part of its time exploring important research topics of broad application. For example, as I mentioned earlier, limited research by academics shows that regulatory costs are chronically over-estimated by industries attempting to avoid or weaken regulatory proposals. OIRA's economists, who have at their disposal considerable retrospective data on the government's experience with regulation, could assist greatly in the development of more reliable methodologies for such estimates. Other cross-cutting issues include the efficacy of deterrence-based enforcement, as opposed to compliance counseling and the development of more meaningful "accountability metrics" to ensure that agencies are performing their statutory missions effectively.

OIRA and Science

At various bitter moments in the past, the present, and—I fear—the future, the legal profession is subjected to impassioned attacks for attempting to dominate the nation's civic affairs. More than once, we have heard the accusation that a piece of legislation is a "lawyers' full employment act" drafted for the primary purpose of making sure that we attorneys always have jobs meddling in other people's affairs. Yet I am afraid that as appropriate as this taunt may be in certain contexts, another profession—namely, economists—has provided the legal profession with serious competition on the power-grabbing front.

Under John Graham, OIRA embarked on two fundamentally misguided projects to change the way regulatory science is analyzed and used. The first involved the peer review of studies used by federal agencies to make such decisions. The second purported to announce a "one-size-fits-all" risk assessment policy for the entire government. These proposals were drafted by a tiny group of scientists hired by Graham to expand his reach into science policy. The documents were so poorly informed and extreme that they provoked a backlash of opposition from the scientific community, the public interest community, and this Committee. A panel convened by the National Research Council condemned the risk assessment bulletin in no uncertain terms. In the end, OIRA was compelled to drastically revise the peer review bulleting, cutting back severely on its scope. It withdrew the risk assessment guidance. . . .

Given this unfortunate track record, it is vitally important that OIRA under the Obama Administration confine its supervision of government to areas within its expertise, leaving to experts such as White House science policy advisor John Holdren the difficult job of restoring the independence and integrity of regulatory and other science policy issues throughout the government. . . .

Source: Steinzor, Rena. "The Role of Science in Regulatory Reform." Testimony before the U.S. House of Representatives Subcommittee on Investigations and Oversight Committee on Science and Technology, U.S. Congress. House. 111th Cong., 1st sess., April 30, 2009. Available at http://democrats.science.house .gov/Media/file/Commdocs/hearings/2009/Oversight/30apr/Steinzor_Testimony.pdf.

Notes

1. Robert F. Kennedy Jr., "Crimes against Nature," *Rolling Stone,* December 11, 2003. www.rollingstone .com/politics/story/5939345/crimes_against_nature.

2. Alex Fryer, "Bush's Gatekeeper Weighs Costs, Benefits of New Regulations," *Seattle Times,* September 29, 2004. http://seattletimes.nwsource.com/html/nationworld/2002049154_graham29m.html.

3. Susan E. Dudley, "The Bush Administration Regulatory Record," *Regulation,* Winter 2004/2005. www.cato.org/pubs/regulation/regv27n4/v27n4-mercreport.pdf.

4. David Kohn, "Foes Say Bush Plan Would Create 'Debating Society over Science,'" *Baltimore Sun,* December 19, 2003. Available at www.commondreams.org/headlines03/1219–03.htm.

CHAPTER 10

Conservation and Land Use

1980–Present

During the eight-year tenure of Ronald Reagan in the White House, the relative amity that had existed between Republicans and Democrats during the 1960s and early 1970s on land use and conservation issues disappeared. At the same time, political tensions between resource development–based communities in the rural West and South and "big city" environmental organizations increased exponentially. These polarizing events were in large measure the product of mounting anxiety from conservative political constituencies about the accumulating impact of 1970s-era environmental regulation rollouts on property rights and economic health. But they were also fed from the left, where activists and lawmakers, finally armed with potent regulatory weaponry to advance their causes, pressed for new and more stringent land-use regulations and wilderness protections.

These opposing armies waged some of their fiercest battles during the Reagan years, but they did not lay down their arms after his retirement and return to California. To the contrary, battles between land, water, and wildlife conservation advocates and proponents of natural resource development were joined on a daily basis during the administrations of George H. W. Bush, Bill Clinton, and George W. Bush, and there is little reason to think that hostilities will subside during Barack Obama's presidency. This reality has made it difficult for American policymakers to find common ground on endangered species protection, forest and wetland conservation, urban sprawl mitigation, escalating freshwater shortages, and other pressing resource stewardship issues.

SAGEBRUSHERS AND "WISE USERS"

American resource management and development policies had taken a decided turn toward conservation in the 1960s and 1970s, in large part because of steadily rising public concern about environmental pollution and degradation. But federal conservation laws of the 1970s such as the Federal Land Policy and Management Act (also known as the BLM Organic Act) and the National Forest Management Act, both of which shifted the framework of public land management toward preservation and away from unfettered development, galvanized political opponents. This was especially true in the West, where the vast majority of America's 635 million acres of federal public lands were located. Indeed, public lands constitute one-fourth to one-half of the acreage in Arizona, California, Colorado, Montana, New Mexico, and Washington—and more than half of the land in Alaska, Idaho, Nevada, Oregon, Utah, and Wyoming.

Given this state of affairs, the policies of the guardians of these public lands—primarily the U.S. Forest Service (USFS), the National Park Service, and the Bureau of Land Management—exerted enormous influence over everyday life in the West. As the policies of these agencies trended toward conservation over commercial development, however, constituencies that had long depended on easy access to the pasturelands, rivers, minerals, and timber in the public domain became increasingly uneasy.

To some degree, this uneasiness transcended political parties. When President Jimmy Carter tried to cut funding for eighteen major water projects in the West in the late 1970s, for example, he was defeated by a determined coalition of Democratic and Republican officials and lawmakers. "The outrage of western officialdom, from the Right to the Left, demonstrated the extent to which these giant water-reclamation projects had become the lodestone of regional politics, regardless of ideology or partisan ties," observed historians Michael P. Malone and F. Ross Peterson.[1]

Broadly speaking, however, conservative Republican-leaning activists and lawmakers spearheaded the backlash against new land, water, and resource conservation programs and regulations in the West. And by the late 1970s, their opposition had coalesced into a "Sagebrush Rebellion" that transformed the political zeitgeist in many regions of the Intermountain West. These self-proclaimed rebels, nurtured and organized in some instances by the region's ranching, timber, and mining industries, demanded unrestricted rights to graze, drill, and mine on public lands. They also called for a sweeping transfer of western lands from federal ownership to private and state control. Proponents of these reforms insisted that only through such steps could the pernicious influence of the federal government be reduced and the health and vitality of the rural West be saved. Supporters of continued federal ownership of western lands—and the resources contained therein—countered by stating that the parks and forests of the West belonged to *all* Americans, not just those who lived next door to them. They also asserted that western states had a long track record of supporting shortsighted and environmentally destructive resource policies, and they charged that resource-hungry corporations were the authors of much of the Sagebrushers' populist rhetoric and legal strategies.

In 1981 the Sagebrushers received a tremendous boost with the inauguration of Ronald Reagan as president. The Reagan Administration's natural resources policymaking rested on two firm pillars: a determination to expand industrial and other economic activity on public lands, and a belief in the sanctity of private property rights. As part of his efforts to accomplish the former, Reagan selected James Watt, a well-known advocate of commercial use of public lands and expansive private property rights, to be his secretary of the Interior. From this perch, Watt exercised tremendous influence over the policies and practices of the Bureau of Land Management (BLM), the U.S. Fish and Wildlife Service, the Bureau of Reclamation, the National Park Service, and other agencies charged with overseeing federal lands (see Document 10.1). Watt was so accommodating to private and state demands for commercial access to public lands, in fact, that calls for transfers of federal land to state control actually subsided under his watch.[2]

The second pillar—defending and expanding private property rights—focused in large part on the "takings clause" of the Fifth Amendment to the Constitution, which states that private property cannot "be taken for public use, without just compensation." The Reagan Administration's position was that state and federal regulations—including land and resource conservation statutes—that reduce the actual or potential value of private property constitute clear violations of this clause. "The [administration's] grand plan," explained Charles Fried, who served as Reagan's solicitor general from 1985 to 1989, "was to make government pay compensation as for a taking of property every time its regulations impinged too severely on a property right—limiting the possible uses for a parcel of land or restricting or tying up a business in regulatory red tape. If the government labored under so severe an obligation, there would be, to say the least, much less regulation."[3]

By the time Reagan's two terms in office came to a close, the Sagebrush cause had evolved into a wider and even more ambitious Wise Use movement. This movement, which cannily took its name from the utilitarian "wise use" management philosophy of Gifford Pinchot, Teddy Roosevelt's famous forest chief, pursued the goal of public land privatization and preached the hegemony of private property rights with evangelical zeal. Groups such as the Mountain States Legal Foundation—which cemented its reputation as the primary litigation arm of the Wise Use movement under president William Perry Pendley—and Ron Arnold's Center for the Defense of Free Enterprise became major players in western politics during this time. By the early 1990s, in fact, their criticisms of city-bred environmental extremists and feckless government bureaucrats were being echoed not only by westerners, but also by Wisconsin loggers, West Virginia coal miners, and Alabama entrepreneurs. Property rights and Wise Use groups also helped elect sympathetic conservative legislators at the local, state, and federal levels.

Environmental groups and pro-conservation lawmakers responded to the Wise Use threat by highlighting the leading roles that real estate developers, agri-business, oil and mining companies, and other corporate interests were playing in many Wise Use campaigns. They also attacked the philosophical underpinnings of the movement. The beliefs of property rights activists, charged analyst Tarso Ramos of the Western States Center, an advocacy organization for progressive causes in the West, would be "more accurately termed 'property primacy' for its subordination of the public good to private financial interests."[4]

But even conservationists who found the Wise Use movement to be a fundamentally sinister corporate creation had to grapple with the fact that Wise Use themes resonated in many parts of America. Journalist Blain Harden, for example, described widespread public misgivings about government efforts to restore dam-decimated salmon runs in the Pacific Northwest's Columbia River system in the early 1990s. Harden wrote:

> [Along the Columbia] I heard countless variations on [the] theme of the resource-using westerner as endangered species. Utility executives and farm wives, dam operators and river dredgers complained of a conspiracy to destroy the "working river," ruin their livelihoods, and sabotage what was good and godly about life in the West. Most of these people sounded furious and seemed afraid. Everywhere they looked they saw the dark hand of the federal government and the arrogant, interfering ways of high-salaried yuppies. They believed city people were trying to turn the Columbia River—along with the forests, mountains, and deserts of the entire West—into a theme park where the only jobs would be menial and minimum wage. They blamed salmon as co-conspirators.[5]

LAND-USE POLICIES SPUR CONTROVERSY AND GALVANIZE OPPOSITION

Reagan Administration efforts to increase commercial activity on public lands, transfer management of public domain lands to states, and bolster private property rights enjoyed mixed success. On the one hand, many of Reagan's political appointees—who were frequently plucked from the industries they were assigned to regulate—labored mightily to turn Wise Use dreams into policy realities. Robert Burford, a rancher turned BLM director, for example, turned some public land management responsibilities— including environmental protection programs—over to ranchers who held grazing permits, and he worked hard to streamline the dispensation of mineral leases on BLM lands. And Watt himself proved to be an energetic facilitator of the transfer of control of public lands and resources into private hands. Time after time, he shifted Interior funds that had previously been allocated to land, water, and wildlife conservation and research programs into freshly minted initiatives to increase drilling, mining, grazing, and logging activities on federal lands within his purview. These types of administrative actions dramatically changed the conservation terrain in the West, both literally and figuratively. By 1986, for example, fully 80 percent of the land in the Greater Yellowstone Ecosystem—essentially Yellowstone National Park and the eight national forests that surround it—had been leased for oil and gas development.[6] Meanwhile, Watt imposed a moratorium on acquiring more land for national parks and preserves—although he also increased funding for the operation and maintenance of parks and preserves already in existence.

Not all of the administration's public land development desires came to fruition, however. For example, White House proposals to sell off "surplus" public lands to private interests as a way of reducing the national debt and spurring economic rejuvenation were blocked by Democrats and moderate Republicans in Congress, and environmental and public interest groups used the courts to slow or halt many land management proposals that they felt were damaging to wildlife or wilderness. An administration proposal to lease the entire Outer Continental Shelf to oil and gas companies also ran afoul of Congress and was soundly rejected, as was a Watt proposal to permit mining and drilling in designated wilderness areas. And when Assistant Secretary of Agriculture John Crowell, a former timber industry lobbyist, pressured the U.S. Forest Service to increase the volume of logging in national forests by as much as 50 percent, agency professionals refused to accede to his demands.[7]

A public backlash against Reagan's land management policies also became evident by the latter part of his first term. This shift stemmed at least in part from uneasiness about Watt, who struck many observers as excessively gleeful about the pro-development mandate he had been given. But public perceptions of the administration's stewardship of public lands and resources were also tainted by the Environmental Protection Agency (EPA), which had become mired in scandal under another anti-regulatory Reagan appointee, Anne M. Gorsuch. By the time Gorsuch resigned under pressure in early 1983 (mere weeks after marrying BLM director Burford) conservation groups were actively working to establish Watt as an anti-environmental zealot cut from the same ideological cloth as the disgraced EPA administrator. Watt weathered these attacks, only to end his controversial run at the Interior Department a few months later with a crude public assessment of the gender and ethnic make-up of members of an advisory panel. Unable to recover from this self-inflicted wound, Watt resigned on November 8, 1983. Negative public perceptions of Reagan's environmental record persisted, however—a worrisome trend that likely contributed to Reagan's decision to attach wilderness protections to eight million acres of public land in the months leading up to the 1984 election.

The resignation of Watt was widely welcomed by environmental groups, despite the fact that it deprived them of one of their staple subjects of direct mail fundraising appeals and membership drives. By the time of his departure from the administration, in fact, the Sierra Club, Audubon Society, Natural Resources Defense Council, Environmental Defense Fund, and other organizations had already parlayed public anxiety about Reagan's environmental policies and appointees into new levels of relevance and power in Washington. And this resurgence continued throughout Reagan's remaining five years in office, even as the administration modified or abandoned some of its more unpopular bids to reform environmental regulations and public land policies. "In the late 1980s, every conservation group in the United States fattened off the Reagan Administration's black hole of an environmental policy," wrote journalist Susan Zakin, a strong critic of Reagan's conservation record. "With each new Reagan perfidy, membership in environmental organizations went through the roof."[8]

The Reagan Administration's efforts to roll back "burdensome" environmental regulations and public land policies that "locked up" valuable timber, grass, and minerals also spawned a radicalized new generation of environmental activists and wilderness champions. These groups—Greenpeace, Earth First!, and others—were modest in terms of membership, but they shook up mainstream environmentalists and industry groups alike. "To many loggers and miners [of the West]," wrote conservationist G. Jon Roush in 1992, "[John] Muir's descendent Sierra Club is a symbol of everything that is dangerously radical and vaguely socialistic about environmentalists. Yet some truly radical environmentalists see it as an overgrown relic that doesn't go nearly far enough."[9] The arrival of these militant groups, which were perfectly willing to engage in brazenly confrontational tactics and acts of civil disobedience, convinced some mainstream environmentalists that they needed to step up their own games. But the aggressive tactics of groups such as Earth First! also exacerbated tensions with resource-dependent communities and corporate interests, both of which became adept at framing radical environmentalists as representative of the entire movement. The term "environmentalist," in fact, became freighted with unsavory meaning among right-leaning people in the so-called "culture wars" of the 1980s and 1990s.

All of this sound and fury over federal policymaking, meanwhile, obscured notable evolutions in state regulation of land management practices on privately owned farms and woodlands. During the late 1970s and 1980s, for example, concerns over the environmental impact of timber harvesting on private land (whether held by individuals or corporations) on wildlife and water quality prompted numerous states to implement regulatory programs governing private forestry practices. These regulations built on modest but precedent-setting state laws of the 1940s and 1950s that required private forest landowners to promptly reseed cut-over lands and engage in other soil and watershed protection measures. Some of the new regulations were very limited in scope, but others—such as the comprehensive regulations for private forestry practices that were passed in California, Oregon, Washington, and Massachusetts in the late 1970s and early 1980s—were wide-reaching.[10] By the early 2000s, thirty-eight states had established laws or regulatory programs governing private forestry practices. In earlier eras, this trend toward increased state involvement in private forest stewardship might have prompted a backlash, but it came at a time when more ecologically sensitive, sustainable timber-cutting practices were being voluntarily implemented on many corporate-owned lands.[11]

The toxic levels of distrust between federal authorities and conservationists that accumulated during the Reagan years subsided somewhat during the one-term presidency of George H. W. Bush. To be sure, environmental groups criticized Bush and his Interior secretary, Manuel Lujan Jr., for perceived fealty to industry groups and other pro-development constituencies in the crafting of western land policies. But many environmentalists were pleasantly surprised by Bush's active involvement in drafting and passing the 1990 Clean Air Act Amendments, and administration rhetoric about the need for smarter and less intrusive regulation of activities by industry and private landowners was more pragmatic and less ideological than the language that had been used by Reagan-era agencies.

In addition, industry officials and free market advocates in Congress muted their calls for deregulation in the wake of the March 1989 Exxon Valdez oil tanker disaster, which wreaked ecological devastation on Alaska's Prince William Sound. Indeed, this event aroused such widespread anger and condemnation among American voters that a new slate of federal regulations designed to mitigate marine pollution from oil transport was passed into law with broad bipartisan support (**see Document 10.2**).

LAND AND WILDLIFE CONSERVATION POLICY DURING THE CLINTON YEARS

Disputes over public land and resource use that had simmered throughout Bush's four years in the Oval Office boiled over once again with the election of Democrat Bill Clinton to the presidency. Clinton carried the burden of high expectations from environmental groups and pro-conservation lawmakers when he took office, and in some respects his administration's eight-year record on wilderness conservation and public land stewardship affirmed their faith in him. But the same Clinton policies that won plaudits from environmentalists—on endangered species protections, land conservation, river restoration, and other issues—received failing grades from resource extraction industries, property rights advocates, and rural westerners who believed that the policies killed jobs, flouted constitutional rights, and strangled economic development. Clinton did anger environmentalists—a key political constituency for him and the wider Democratic Party—on several occasions, especially in the aftermath of the 1994 Republican takeover of Congress. But in general, the playing field tilted toward pro-conservation forces during the Clinton years.

Some of the Clinton Administration's conservation and land management policy initiatives were widely popular or uncontroversial and did not arouse sustained opposition outside of Wise Use circles. These steps included the 1993 creation of a National Biological Service within the Interior Department to better integrate biological science research into mining, grazing, and logging policymaking; the 1995 establishment of new livestock grazing restrictions to relieve pressure on degraded public grasslands; and the implementation in 1996 of new federal incentives for farmland conservation. Under the enthusiastic direction of Interior secretary Bruce Babbitt, the Clinton Administration also inaugurated a new era of dam removals and associated river restoration projects that garnered effusive praise from conservationists, commercial and sport fishermen, and taxpayer watchdog groups alike (**see Document 10.7**).

The Clinton Administration received far greater blowback from conservative Republicans and other pro-development parties, however, when it came to its support for the Endangered Species Act (ESA) and other wildlife restoration and protection efforts. When the ESA was first signed into law in 1973, it had received broad bipartisan support. But as the number of species protected under the act expanded—the Clinton

Administration added 521 species of flora and fauna to the program in eight years—the legislation became much more controversial. State and federal environmental impact statements (EISs) forced revisions or outright cancellation of some private and public land development proposals because of concerns that the development threatened listed species. In addition, highly publicized clashes over government protection and restoration strategies for the endangered spotted owl (in the old-growth forests of the Pacific Northwest), the snail darter (in the Tennessee Valley), the gray wolf (in the northern Rockies), and other species ignited emotional debates not only about appropriate government responses to species and habitat protection, but also about fundamental American values and priorities (see Documents 10.3 and 10.4).

A good portion of the criticisms of ESA policies and programs under the Clinton Administration were clearly partisan in nature. But many conservatives expressed genuine concern that the act was metastasizing from a well-intentioned but flawed law into a vexing, inflexible obstacle to economic growth, job creation, and private enterprise. Opponents expressed particular anger about an Interior Department decision early in Clinton's first term to expand the statute's prohibition on direct "taking" of endangered or threatened species (by hunting, trapping, etc.) to include "significant habitat modification or degradation where it actually kills or injures wildlife." This decision was quickly challenged in court, but in 1995 the U.S. Supreme Court responded to the case of *Babbitt v. Sweet Home Chapter of Communities for a Great Oregon* with a 6-3 ruling that upheld the legitimacy of the Interior Department's habitat protection regulation.

This ruling greatly intensified conservative unhappiness with the ESA and guaranteed that regulatory takings would remain a prominent issue for right-leaning voters, activists, and legislators. "When Congress adopted the law in 1973, almost everyone voted for it," recounted William Perry Pendley of the Mountain States Legal Foundation in the late 1990s. "But, at that time, they all thought there would be about 100 species—bears, birds, and manatees, for example. Today there are some 10,000 listed species and we are headed for 20,000 or even 30,000. At the time of enactment, the intention was that species would be protected on federal or public land and not on private land. At the time of enactment, there was no intention to cause local economic dislocation."[12] Pendley also voiced another common western meme about the Endangered Species Act—that it had become a deadly weapon for litigation in the hands of unscrupulous environmental groups. "The purpose of the Endangered Species Act has become the stopping of all activities of which environmental extremists disapprove," he charged in his 1995 book *War on the West: Government Tyranny on America's Great Frontier*. "Westerners are losing jobs and property not just to owls and grizzly bears, but to snails and flies."[13]

ESA supporters within the Clinton Administration, Congress, and the environmental community acknowledged that the act's habitat protection provisions had negative economic repercussions in some cases. But they rejected contentions that ESA enforcement represented regulatory takings on an epic scale, pointing out that state and federal agencies still approved the vast majority of public and private development proposals that came before them. ESA advocates also emphasized that wildlife conservation had long been recognized as a legitimate responsibility of both federal and state governments, and that wildlife regulations at the state level had—like those at the federal level—evolved over time in response to changing environmental conditions (see Document 10.11). Defenders also noted that the Clinton Administration introduced federal grants and other voluntary, incentive-based programs to encourage endangered species habitat protection on private land and cushion landowners from economic loss. Finally, advocates insisted that endangered species protection was of paramount importance not only as a vehicle for preserving fragile ecosystems—which have momentous economic benefits in their own right—but also as an expression of moral resource stewardship that would benefit future generations.

CLINTON AND FEDERAL LOGGING POLICIES

The wide-reaching ESA also had a major impact on the Clinton Administration's federal forest management policies, which elicited an amazing range of both vituperation and praise from conservationists over the years. Indeed, the administration's management of U.S. forestlands became a hot-button issue from the moment Clinton was sworn in, and it remained so for the next eight years.

When Clinton took office, he inherited a combustible situation in the forests of the Pacific Northwest. In 1988 environmental organizations had filed suit against the U.S. Fish and Wildlife Service to force the agency to give the northern spotted owl ESA protection and to halt logging of spotted owl habitat: old-growth stands of timber in the national forests of the Pacific Northwest. The USFS responded to the litigation by designating the spotted owl as a threatened species, and in May 1991 a U.S. district court judge ruled that the USFS and other federal agencies had violated federal environmental laws by treating the forests as timber reserves rather than ecosystems. The judge also banned logging on some twenty-four million acres of spotted owl habitat in seventeen national forests until the Forest Service came up with a regional logging program that incorporated necessary ESA protections for the spotted owl.

This decision virtually shut down logging operations in Pacific Northwest national forests. From 1988 to 1997, in fact, the amount of federal timber cut in Oregon and Washington decreased by 87 percent.[14] Local communities that had long depended on logging and sawmill operations suffered economic dislocation and spikes in unemployment as a result. They also experienced a marked decrease in funding for schools and road building as a result of a nearly century-old law that predicated such funding on local timber operations. Back in 1908, Congress had approved a pro-logging agreement whereby local communities received 25 cents for every dollar the Forest Service garnered in timber sales of nearby tracts. But with the court-ordered prohibitions on logging in Pacific Northwest national forests, this revenue stream dried up.

Timber lobbyists, logging families, proponents of deregulation, and conservative lawmakers all excoriated these developments—and condemned the environmental litigants as radicals who valued birds and moss-encrusted trees more than good-paying jobs and community stability. Pro-conservation legislators and conservation groups countered by noting that logging jobs were being lost to mechanization and timber exports anyway and that many western communities transitioning away from longtime dependence on logging, ranching, mining, and other forms of natural resource exploitation were actually enjoying economic renaissances. By embracing land and water preservation measures, these communities were providing welcoming environments both for tourists—kayakers, backpackers, mountain bikers, and other affluent outdoor recreation enthusiasts—and for businesses that incorporated "quality of life" considerations into their siting decisions. Conservationists also cited studies documenting that Oregon and Washington both experienced robust economic *growth* during the logging ban—including a combined 21 percent surge in per capita income—to support their contention that the Pacific Northwest was far less reliant on resource-extraction industries than it had once been.[15]

As the debate raged on over the merits of the Pacific Northwest logging ban, the Clinton Administration tried to settle the issue—and get the court-ordered ban lifted—with its Option 9 or Northwest Forest Plan. This scheme, which set aside more than twenty-four million acres of national forestland in Oregon, Washington, and California from logging, preserved critical habitat for northern spotted owls, salmon, steelhead trout, marbled murrelets, and other threatened species. But it also proposed "a sustainable timber harvest of 1.2 billion board feet annually on the spotted owl forests," including national forests west of the Cascade crest and BLM lands in western Oregon, and increased federal aid to logging communities affected by the ban.[16] This compromise did not satisfy conservationists, who did not want to see *any* resumption of commercial logging in the region's old-growth forests, or pro-logging constituencies, who decried the Option 9 set-aside as a typical federal land-grab.

The Clinton Administration's efforts to transcend the deep political polarization swirling around federal forest policies and find a moderate middle ground suffered another blow in November 1994, when mid-term election gains enabled Republicans to claim control of both houses of Congress. This constituted a major alteration of the political terrain in numerous realms, including governance of national forests and other public lands. Sensitive to the desires of pro-resource extraction and anti-regulatory constituencies within their party's coalition of supporters, Speaker of the House Newt Gingrich (R-Ga.), Senate Majority Leader Robert Dole (R-Kan.), and Republican committee chairmen sponsored or approved a host of bills designed to loosen federal regulations and restrictions of mining, logging, drilling, and grazing activities on BLM, Forest Service, and other public domain lands.

The Clinton Administration beat back many of these bills, despite its politically weakened state. But it blinked in July 1995, when Republicans attached a "salvage timber" legislative rider to a budget bill that also contained funds for surviving family members of the Oklahoma City bombing. The salvage rider was described by supporters as a badly needed forest management program that would remove heavy "fuel loads" of diseased and insect-riddled timber responsible for catastrophic wildfires. Critics such as journalist Paul Roberts noted, however, that "the bill authorized the agency to sell not just dead or dying trees but any 'associated' green trees, a wonderfully ambiguous term that effectively permitted *any* tree to qualify as 'salvage.'"[17] In addition, the rider suspended virtually all public, administrative, and judicial oversight of federal timber sales, and it also mandated big increases in timber harvest volumes.

Cognizant of the political benefit that Republicans could reap from the veto of any bill that provided benefits to mourning families in Oklahoma City, Clinton signed the bill despite misgivings about the salvage rider. "On balance I am very pleased with this bill," he said. "The timber provisions are not exactly what I wanted, but they are better than they were, and I believe we can and should carry out the timber salvage plans and that we can do it consistent with our forest plan and existing environmental laws."[18]

Clinton's decision to approve the salvage timber rider, however, threatened to open a permanent schism between the administration and conservationists, who had been among the president's stoutest supporters. Sierra Club president J. Robert Cox, for example, stated that the organization had not felt such a "depth of disappointment, disbelief, and anger over a President's action on the environment in many, many years."[19] This feeling of betrayal only intensified over the eighteen-month life of the rider, as massive "salvage" operations were launched in ecologically rich national forests in Alaska, the Pacific Northwest, the Intermountain West, and other parts of the country (see Document 10.5).

A Second-Term Push for Wilderness Conservation

Republicans, however, overreached in their efforts to roll back environmental regulations and wilderness protections. Republican-sponsored bills to repeal the Clean Air Act and approve major oil and drilling operations in designated wilderness areas were unpopular with large majorities of Americans. Seizing on these missteps, the Clinton White House used the executive powers of the presidency to withdraw public lands for a proposed mine near Yellowstone National Park and establish 1.7-million-acre Grand Staircase-Escalante National Monument in southern Utah. These moves—whether borne out of political calculus, a genuine conservationist sensibility, or some combination of the two—brought about a rapprochement of sorts between the Clinton White House and conservation groups in the run-up to the November 1996 election. Conversely, these same actions— and the creation of Grand Staircase-Escalante National Monument in particular— outraged many westerners. U.S. senator Orrin Hatch (R-Utah) aptly summarized their feeling about the national monument designation when he declared: "In all my 20 years in the U.S. Senate, I have never seen a clearer example of the arrogance of federal power. Indeed, this is the mother of all land grabs"[20] **(see Document 10.6)**.

During Clinton's second term, his administration generally sided with wilderness preservationists and wildlife advocates on issues of public land management. The administration warded off Republican bids to open the Alaska National Wildlife Refuge (ANWR) for drilling. Clinton also proclaimed twenty-one new or expanded national monuments in addition to Grand Staircase-Escalante,[21] and in a break from historical practice, it kept most of these protected lands under the authority of the Bureau of Land Management (BLM) instead of transferring them over to the National Park Service.

This decision was part of a conscious effort by Clinton's Interior Department to change the culture and image of the BLM, an agency that had long been derided by some environmentalists as a pro-tenantholder "Bureau of Livestock and Mining." Scholars such as Richard N. L. Andrews have called this an unfair characterization that does not adequately account for basic realities under which the BLM operated. "The BLM was responsible for four times the land area managed by the Forest Service," wrote Andrews, "but had only one-third the budget and one-seventh the staff. Until 1976 it lacked even a basic statute authorizing it to manage these lands. . . . While the Forest Service operated with clear statutory authority and through decentralized expertise in individual forest units, therefore, the BLM's far thinner staff could only hope to work cooperatively with state and local governments and with local ranchers, mining companies, and other public-land users."[22]

The Roadless Rule

The Clinton Administration's most ambitious wilderness conservation effort was a late-term effort to permanently ban road building in fifty-eight million acres of roadless wilderness in the national forest system. Forest Service chief Michael Dombeck framed this effort—which stunned both environmentalists and supporters of expansive commercial use of public lands, albeit in dramatically different ways—as both a milestone in American wilderness and wildlife protection and an exercise in fiscal responsibility. Regarding the former, Dombeck said that the "Roadless Rule," as it came to be known to friend and foe alike, would protect vital watersheds, preserve some of the continent's most ancient forests, and prevent fragmentation of vital habitat for charismatic "megafauna" such as wolves, grizzly bears, lynx, and bull trout. In terms of the latter, Dombeck and other supporters of the proposed ban pointed out that the rule would help the Forest Service deal with an $8.4 billion road reconstruction and maintenance backlog for the 380,000 miles of roads already located in the national forest system. They also asserted that the ban would have virtually no impact on national timber supplies, emphasizing that only 5 percent of the country's timber came from national forests in any given year anyway. Finally, proponents dismissed complaints about the economic impact of the ban on western communities as hoary leftovers from yesteryear. "The benefits of cutting timber in roadless areas would be quite narrow," declared Wilderness Society economist Spencer Phillips. "By and large the economies out west have become far more complex than 'trees equal jobs,' but the folk economics of the timber industry die hard."[23]

Clinton signed the Roadless Area Conservation Policy into law on January 5, 2001 (**see Document 10.8**). As it turned out, however, the signing marked only the beginning of a long political and legal battle over implementation of the rule. When George W. Bush took the oath of office on January 20, 2001—a mere fifteen days after the Roadless Rule signing ceremony—one of his administration's top environmental policy priorities was to keep the law from being rolled out. This touched off a bitter legal war between the Bush Administration and conservation groups (and their respective allies in the media and Congress) that lasted for all eight years of Bush's tenure. Some of the court rulings and political maneuverings that took place during this protracted battle heartened Bush and fellow opponents of the Roadless Rule (**see Document 10.10**). But final victory remained elusive, and the issue remained unsettled when Bush departed the White House. It is widely believed that his successor, Democrat Barack Obama, will fully implement the Clinton-era Roadless Rule.

PUBLIC LAND AND RESOURCE MANAGEMENT IN THE BUSH YEARS

The Roadless Rule was one of numerous clashes between the Bush Administration and pro-conservation advocates and lawmakers. Bush and leading land management officials in his administration—people such as Interior secretary Gale Norton, whose résumé included stints at the Mountain States Legal Foundation and as Attorney General of Colorado; James Connaughton, a Washington attorney and industry lobbyist who chaired Bush's White House Council on Environmental Quality; and Mark Rey, a former timber industry lobbyist who headed the U.S. Forest Service and Natural Resources Conservation Service as Undersecretary for Natural Resources and the Environment—espoused models of federal land management that would be responsive to legitimate environmental concerns but also partner with private enterprise to boost regional economic health and bolster national energy security. Democrats and conservation organizations argued, however, that the administration prioritized mining leases, grazing permits, drilling rights, and timber sales over all other considerations. This perspective was shared by some scientists and other professionals within the leading land management agencies.

Bush-era mining policies, for example, elicited heavy criticism from environmental groups (the stance of Democratic members of Congress toward these policies frequently hinged on whether they represented districts that were heavily reliant on mining industry jobs and profits). Bush officials repealed Clinton-era regulations crafted to give the government the authority to reject proposed mines that would cause "substantial irreparable harm" to watersheds or habitat, choosing instead to return to a regulatory landscape that actively promoted mining and drilling on federal lands.[24] As a result, the number of drilling permits issued for development on public lands increased 361 percent between 1999 and 2007, and the BLM formalized policies that relaxed corporate cleanup responsibilities and restricted public input into energy development decisions on public land.[25] In mid-2008, Bush officials in the BLM also issued rules designed to eventually pave the way for extraction of an estimated 800 billion barrels of oil trapped in sedimentary rock in Colorado, Utah, and Wyoming. This move was framed by the Bush White House, western Republican congressmen, and oil companies as a vital step toward eventual energy independence. Environmental groups and many Democratic lawmakers, however, argued that if such operations come to pass, they will destroy valuable wildlife habitat, increase air pollution, exacerbate regional water shortages, and require massive amounts of energy in their own right.

Other elements of the Bush Administration's pro-mining orientation also aroused the ire of environmental groups. The Bush Administration resisted calls to revisit and reform the venerable 1872 Mining Law, a pillar of the aforementioned pro-mining regulatory landscape (see Document 10.14). And in the Appalachians, the longtime epicenter of U.S. coal mining, Bush officials loosened several significant industrial mining regulations. These reforms included weakening of "buffer zone" rules that banned coal mining operations within 100 feet of a stream, acceptance of industry proposals to mitigate the ecological impact of destroyed natural streams through the creation of man-made stream channels, and exemption of so-called "mountaintop removal" mining practices from Clean Water Act regulations (see Document 10.9). "These changes were unequivocally helpful," said a representative of the West Virginia Coal Association. "By revising certain ambiguous regulations and contorted legal interpretations of the Clean Water Act, the administration has improved regulatory stability and predictability."[26]

Environmental groups blasted these changes as irresponsible, however, and they turned to the courts for redress. In March 2007 a U.S. district judge rescinded four Appalachian mountaintop mining permits granted by the U.S. Army Corps of Engineers, citing violations of the Clean Water Act, ecological damage to regional aquatic resources, and the inadequacy of the Bush Administration's "stream creation" rules. Bush officials responded to this setback by codifying new compensatory mitigation rules, and in February 2009 a federal appeals court ruled that the Corps of Engineers had the legal authority to issue Clean Water Act permits for mountaintop removal operations without insisting on environmental impact statements. One month later, however, the two-month old Obama Administration issued a clear signal that the political tides had turned against the coal mining industry. EPA director Lisa Jackson announced that the agency intended to review as many as 200 mountaintop coal-mining permit applications for their potential impacts on streams and wetlands. She also publicly urged the Corps of Engineers to withhold permits for two new mountaintop mining projects in West Virginia and Kentucky unless the operators dramatically reduced the ecological impact of their proposed operations.

Rhetorical firefights also broke out between the Bush Administration and natural resource conservation groups on a host of other fronts during Bush's eight years in office. Flashpoints included administration proposals to expand off-road vehicle access to national forests and wilderness study areas; the administration's allegedly diffident efforts to combat the spread of ecologically and economically destructive invasive species; continued loose environmental regulation of agribusiness, including confined animal feeding operations (CAFOs) (see Document 10.15); significant cuts in funding for the Land and Water Conservation Fund; soaring maintenance backlogs in the National Park System; and rule changes that sought to remove the "population viability rule" and other mandatory protections for wildlife and habitat contained in the 1976 National Forest Management Act, the primary statute governing the administration of the national forest system.

The Bush Administration also engaged in memorable clashes with conservation groups over sweeping laws such as the Healthy Forest Restoration Act of 2003. Supporters of this bill, which enjoyed considerable Democratic support (it passed the Senate by an 80-14 vote), claimed that it would reduce the severity of catastrophic wildfires by reducing the fuel loads in western forests. "Too many are looking at this as a zero-sum game," said Senator Mike Crapo (R-Idaho). "We need to get beyond that fallacious argument and realize that what is important is restoring a healthy ecosystem: an ecosystem that allows for a natural fire regime to exist without threatening our communities and lives."[27] Bush himself hailed provisions in the legislation that he said would remove unnecessary environmental regulations that delay forest thinning projects. "We do not want our intentions bogged down by regulations," he said.

In 2004 Greenpeace activists attached themselves to trees near Petersburg, Alaska, to protest a George W. Bush Administration proposal that would allow governors to decide whether to seek protection of roadless national forest land.

"When we see a problem, this government needs to be able to move."[28] Conservation groups, however, were critical of the act. Many of these opponents acknowledged that excess fuel loads were a problem, but they asserted that the fuel reduction plans contained in the Healthy Forest Restoration Act frequently targeted remote but commercially valuable timber areas rather than forested areas near vulnerable communities.[29]

ENDANGERED SPECIES PROTECTION DURING THE BUSH YEARS

Bush's two terms in office were also marked by a renewal of political hostilities over the Endangered Species Act. The Bush Administration supported significant revisions to the ESA, as did Republicans who controlled both houses of Congress for the first six years of Bush's presidency. Many of their complaints about the shortcomings of the ESA were familiar, such as the assertion that the ESA leveled unfair economic penalties on private landholders who owned endangered species habitat. But in the opening years of the twenty-first century, critics increasingly questioned whether the ESA even fulfilled its stated reason for being. Administration officials, state and national Republicans, and advocates of strong private property rights all observed that of the 1,300 domestic species afforded ESA protection since the act's passage in 1973, only 17 species had been delisted because of recovery as of 2006.[30] One possible solution to this alleged poor performance, they suggested, was to narrow the ESA's listing parameters so that the Fish and Wildlife Service, the Department of the Interior agency primarily responsible for the program, could focus its limited resources on protecting only the most charismatic and ecologically vital endangered species. "It's like we're checking [patients] in willy-nilly but we're not checking them out," charged a spokesman for the Republican-controlled House Resources Committee in 2004. "It's totally dysfunctional. We're heading toward an implosion in the [ESA] system."[31] Supporters of this type of program modification also predicted that reining in and narrowing the focus of the ESA would provide badly needed and long overdue regulatory relief to private landowners and commercial users of public lands.[32]

Environmental groups and most Democratic legislators at the state and national levels rejected this characterization of the ESA as a failed program, however. Defenders of the ESA pointed out that most species are not designated as endangered or threatened species until their numbers are extremely depleted, which makes recovery a long process. Supporters also noted that more than 40 percent of all listed species had experienced population stabilization or improvement since listing and that still-endangered species such as red wolves and California condors almost certainly owed their continued existence to ESA protections.[33] Some devoted ESA defenders expressed concern, however, that some litigation from environmental groups might actually contribute to negative perceptions of the program's efficacy. "Spooked by the prospect of endless, grossly expensive litigation, the department [of Interior] has a long record of not delisting recovered species when it gets pressured by groups committed to permanent protection of all species and all individuals of all species," wrote conservationist Ted Williams. "The court battles bleed away limited resources, thereby denying effective protection to creatures that really might vanish from our planet."[34]

Congressional attempts to overhaul the Endangered Species Act were derailed before they could reach Bush's desk for his signature, although a GOP-sponsored House bill did pass in 2005 (a similar bill failed in the Senate). Although the legislative avenue for ESA modifications was sealed off by the program's defenders, the Bush Administration managed to make several ESA policy and administrative changes over the years that, according to a *Washington Post* report, "made it substantially more difficult to designate domestic animals and plants for protection under the Endangered Species Act."[35] Most galling to conservation groups was the Fish and Wildlife Service's practice of preemptively identifying species as "candidates" for ESA protection. This policy, which was kept in place by the Bush Administration for more than two years until it was overturned in court, prevented private citizens from filing their own petitions for species protection. Since the U.S. Fire and Wildlife Service was legally bound to rule on citizen petitions by firm deadlines stipulated in the ESA—but faced no such deadlines for determining the status of species on its "candidate list"—this maneuver enabled officials to indefinitely delay extending ESA protections to imperiled species. The practical result of this stratagem, charged Kieran Suckling of the Center for Biological Diversity, was to create "endangered species purgatory."[36] Critics allege that these maneuvers were a big reason why only 61 species received ESA protection during Bush's eight years in office, compared to 521 species under the Clinton Administration and 231 during George H. W. Bush's single term in office.

Other aspects of the Bush Administration's oversight of the endangered species program also drew harsh condemnation from conservation groups, wildlife biologists, and Democratic politicians. A prime example was a December 2008 Interior rule that gave government agencies the green light to decide whether proposed projects would harm endangered or threatened animals or plants without consulting with the Fish and Wildlife Service or the National Marine Fisheries Service of the National Oceanic and Atmospheric Administration (NOAA), which has ESA jurisdiction over sixty-eight marine and anadromous species (the Obama Administration rescinded this rule in early 2009).

Finally, conservation groups and Democratic lawmakers asserted that the federal endangered species program became horribly politicized during the Bush years. These critics leveled numerous allegations that taxpayer-funded species recovery plans and listing decisions were unduly influenced by industry representatives and anti-regulatory ideologues within the Department of Interior. Bush officials, agency spokespeople, congressional Republicans, and industry groups initially rejected these accusations, but in 2007 and 2008 both the Department of Interior inspector general and the Government Accountability Office issued scathing reports documenting widespread political meddling within the endangered species program (see Document 10.16).

Even the most vehement critics of Bush-era species protection and habitat conservation policies, however, applauded a bold conservation move by Bush during the closing days of his presidency. In January 2009 Bush used the powers of the Antiquities Act of 1906 to create three huge marine national monuments in the Pacific Ocean. Under the provisions of Bush's order, commercial fishing and oil and gas exploration were sharply limited in the ecologically valuable waters around numerous U.S.-owned islands in the central and western Pacific. The total ocean area protected by these new monuments amounted to more than 195,000 square miles. Environmental organizations and scientists agree that these designations, coupled with Bush's 2006 creation of 138,000-square-mile Papahanaumokuakea Marine National Monument in the Hawaiian Islands, make marine conservation the brightest aspect of his environmental legacy.

WATER MANAGEMENT IN AN ERA OF SHORTAGES

Water management policy represented another rare area in which the Bush Administration and environmental critics could find at least some common ground. To be sure, the two sides still differed on appropriate policy prescriptions for many water management controversies. Bush-era agencies, for example, sided with agribusiness and dam operators when conservationists sought to remove dams that were injurious to salmon runs. But from the opening days of Bush's presidency, officials within the Department of Interior, Department of Agriculture, and U.S. Army Corps of Engineers acknowledged that drought conditions and associated freshwater shortages were serious areas of concern, and some of these departments rolled out meaningful water conservation programs in response. Meanwhile, local municipalities and state governments, whether headed by Republicans or Democrats, became increasingly proactive in mandating water conservation programs for their residents.

All of these policy responses—and especially those in the West—reflected a sometimes halting but clear turn away from the once-dominant water policy approach described by conservationist Wallace Stegner as "engineering [aridity] out of existence"[37] through the construction of massive reservoirs and aqueducts. To be sure, these marvels of engineering remained an important part of America's water distribution and supply systems, but their operation could not mask the fact that population growth, drought cycles, diminishing rainfall and snowfall as a result of climate change, and long-entrenched water use schemes have resulted in unsustainable rates of withdrawal from groundwater aquifers (most notably in the Great Plains) and rivers (especially in the Southwest and heavily populated regions of the South).

A wide array of stakeholders from across the political spectrum has warned about the devastating ecological and economic consequences if unsustainable freshwater consumption patterns are not effectively addressed. Yet reversing—or even slowing—the steady declines in water tables and river volumes is a daunting prospect for water managers at all levels of government. Obstacles to meaningful reform include the political clout of users who have become dependent on existing water allocation systems and rates of consumption, such as growers in California, wheat farmers in Kansas, and suburbanites in Atlanta; pricing systems for water consumption that have historically given Americans little economic motivation to conserve; and water allocation agreements that provide perverse incentives to consume all freshwater to which one is legally entitled. These problems are particularly acute for newer cities in the West that do not have the ironclad surface water rights that older cities secured a century or more earlier.[38] (In contrast to the "first in time, first in right" maxim that governs water allocations across the West, the riparian water rights doctrine that prevails in eastern states spreads the burden of shortages more evenly across all holders of land claims overlying or adjoining the freshwater source in question.[39])

The steadily widening gap between water supply and water demand has placed an increased strain on relations among neighboring states—and even among different regions of the country (it has also given rise to all-too-credible predictions of future "water wars" between thirsty nations). For people who live and work in the West such squabbling has long been a familiar fact of life, given the perpetual wrangling that western states have engaged in over the Colorado River and other major waterways over the decades (see Document 10.12). "Nothing is more emotional and nothing is more political than water in the West," confirmed Patricia Mulroy, general manager of the Southern Nevada Water Authority and a leading force in shaping twenty-first century water policies in the West.[40] But many observers believe that even in the West, regional conflicts over water use have sharpened in intensity in recent years. This escalation in tensions is attributable not only to declines in existing conditions, but also to proliferating scientific studies that predict potentially dire water shortages in the future. In 2008, for example, scientists at the Scripps Institute of Oceanography released a highly publicized study that estimated that the Lake Mead reservoir—the primary source of water for Las Vegas, Arizona, and southern California—has a 50 percent chance of going dry by 2021.[41]

Regions of the country that once believed that water shortages would never bedevil them also have been forced to address the issue. Alarmed by musings from western lawmakers about the possibility of relieving their region's mounting thirst with massive amounts of water from the Great Lakes, Republican and Democratic governors of the eight states bordering the Great Lakes joined together to craft a preemptive water management pact that expressly forbids any large-scale diversions of Great Lakes water out of the region. Further south, meanwhile, North Carolina and Virginia have repeatedly locked horns over access to Roanoke River water, whereas the states of Alabama, Florida, and Georgia have been entangled in a bitter two-decade-long war over the allocation of water contained in transboundary river basins (see Document 10.18).

Lawmakers and water managers have also responded to the evolving crisis with a variety of water conservation policies. At municipal and state levels, policy prescriptions to address water shortages have included new restrictions on homeowner and business water use; new investments in "gray water" recycling (re-using water from showers, dishwashing, laundry washing, and other domestic activities) and other forms of waste-water treatment; programs to reduce watershed contamination from agricultural runoff; investments in desalination technology (removing salt from ocean water to make it suitable for drinking); and "water banks" which are mechanisms that facilitate the temporary lease of water from holders of water rights with surplus water (irrigation districts, for example) to cities or farming operations in need of additional water.[42]

The centerpiece of the Bush Administration's federal water conservation efforts, meanwhile, was the Department of Interior's "Water 2025" proposal. This sweeping initiative, which was first unveiled by Secretary Norton in 2003, contained a variety of grant programs and other measures aimed at supporting water conservation and efficiency practices; cultivating the creation of long-term watershed management plans; reducing expensive and time-consuming litigation over water rights; and removing institutional barriers to cooperation among various stakeholders, including local, state, and federal water management authorities, tribal groups, and private industry and individuals.

Some conservation groups gave the Water 2025 proposal generally high marks. These organizations acknowledged that they would have preferred more muscular regulation of water use in the initiative, and many complained that funding for the initiative was inadequate. But they credited the Bush Administration for supporting meaningful conservation steps to address the problem of chronic and worsening water shortages. "Secretary Norton's Water 2025 report is actually quite remarkable, given the Bush administration's political base in the interior West," stated Thomas Graff, a water specialist at Environmental Defense. "It promises almost nothing in the way of funding traditional dam and canal projects, and it supports most of the reform agenda that environmentalists, libertarians, and hard-nosed economists of both parties have traditionally espoused."[43] In 2008 the Water 2025 program was folded into the administration's Water for America initiative, which set aside $23 million to help western communities invest in voluntary, incentive-based collaborative projects and water conservation technologies. In 2009 the Obama Administration announced the creation of a Water Conservation Initiative, managed by the Bureau of Reclamation, that was devoted to encouraging expanded use of some of the same tools—voluntary water banks, wastewater treatment programs, and market-based water conservation measures—that were prominent features of Water 2025.

BACKLASH AGAINST SMART GROWTH

So-called "smart growth" strategies for limiting urban sprawl stand as yet another sector of land management policymaking that has become mired in controversy. Smart growth regulations proliferated in the 1970s and 1980s in response to the rapid "sprawl" of commercial development—residential subdivisions, industrial parks, shops, roads, and schools—deeper and deeper into the countryside. The negative consequences of this phenomenon, wrote scholar Donald D. Chen, included, "worse congestion, escalating tax rates, disinvestment in older communities, and the devouring of open space," including ecologically rich wetlands and woodlands that also served as natural filters and absorbers of regional water supplies.[44]

The state of Oregon—and particularly the city of Portland—adopted a variety of smart growth regulations during the 1970s, and these schemes became models for other states and metropolitan areas. Still, cities armed with robust smart growth laws remained the exception rather than the rule. In the mid-1990s an average of 3.2 million acres of forest, wetland, farmland, and open space were converted to more urban uses on an annual basis.[45] The limited application—and local origins—of these blueprints for controlled, environmentally sensitive growth nonetheless ran afoul of the Wise Use wave of the 1980s, and by the mid-1990s "regulatory takings" bills of varying stripes had passed in fifteen states, mostly in the West.

The most dramatic evidence of this backlash came in Oregon, which had long been touted as a pioneer in—and beneficiary of—smart growth regulations. In 2004 Oregon voters passed Measure 37, a public referendum bankrolled by real estate developers and timber companies and supported by property rights advocates. This measure removed most of the land-use regulations that had been in place in Portland and elsewhere over the previous three decades. A mere three years later, however, Oregon voters reversed course and passed Measure 49, a referendum crafted by local conservation groups that established a new set of state land-use regulations **(see Document 10.13)**. These dramatic swings suggest that designing policy prescriptions that strike the "right" balance between private rights and conservation imperatives—ones that are accepted by a broad majority of the public and special interest stakeholders—remain exceedingly elusive for both Republican and Democratic politicians and officials.

WILDERNESS CONSERVATION IN A PARTISAN ERA

Partisan battle lines have also hindered conservationist efforts to establish new parks and wilderness areas for the protection of forests, rivers, wetlands, coastal areas, and other ecologically and economically valuable tracts of land. This oft-poisonous political environment has been attributed to a wide range of factors, from controversies over appropriate government oversight of public and private land use to the dwindling presence of moderates in both the Democratic and Republican parties (a trend that has been traced to the cumulative impacts of gerrymandering, primary tests of ideological purity, and corrosive rhetoric from prominent media personalities).

The 1980s and 1990s were particularly difficult decades for conservation campaigns. It was during that time that conservative Republicans used their pro-development, anti-regulation positions to establish a political stranglehold over the interior West. As a result, proposals to establish new parks, monuments, refuges, and designated wilderness areas in the West—still home to the vast majority of lands in the public domain—were received with skepticism or outright hostility by western Republican lawmakers. And because many of these same Congress members chaired important committees governing public land use, they were able to let some of these proposals quietly languish (national monuments created by presidents under the authority of the 1906 Antiquities Act were a notable exception to this rule).

Since 2000, however, some political analysts have asserted that attitudes about conservation and resource stewardship have shifted markedly in some parts of the West. This evolution in thought stems partly from practical economic considerations because residents recognize that the region's increasingly tourist-oriented economies depend on attractive parks, forests, and rivers to draw visitors. But mounting environmental concerns about overdevelopment have also been cited as a factor. "Voters have reacted to the oil and gas rush in the Rockies, and to other threats posed by development, population growth and climate change, by taking on a greenish hue,"[46] wrote *High Country News* editor Ray Ring in 2008.

Evidence of a shift toward "greenish" conservation attitudes across the interior West is considerable. From 2000 to 2008 Democratic candidates who were publicly backed by environmental organizations won three Senate seats and four House seats from Republicans. During this same time, Democrats claimed governor's offices in seven of eleven states across the West.[47] Moreover, a growing number of Republican officials and legislators made notable displays of independence from longstanding party orthodoxy on conservation and regulation issues. In 2006, for example, the all-Republican membership of the Arizona Corporation Commission imposed significant mandates on renewable power use on state utilities, and one year later Republican state legislators in Colorado joined with Democrats to pass new restrictions on drilling to protect wildlife habitat.[48]

Signs of this shifting political terrain have also been seen at the national level, most notably with the congressional passage and signing by President Obama of the landmark Omnibus Public Land Management Act of 2009. This act, which set aside more than two million acres of public land as designated wilderness, received near-unanimous support from Democrats, as widely expected. But Republican legislators championed the inclusion of several important tracts of wilderness in the bill, and twenty-one Senate Republicans (including all six Republican senators from Idaho, Utah, and Wyoming) and thirty-eight House Republicans ultimately voted in favor of the Act (**see Document 10.17**). The passage of the act, declared the conservation group Republicans for Environmental Protection, constituted "a powerful demonstration of the good that can be accomplished for our country when Republicans return to their roots as the party of conservation."[49]

NOTES

1. Michael P. Malone and F. Ross Peterson, "Politics and Protests," in *The Oxford History of the American West,* ed. Clyde A. Milner II, Carol A. O'Connor, and Martha A. Sandweiss (New York: Oxford University Press, 1994), 530.

2. Scott Lehmann, *Privatizing Public Land* (New York: Oxford University Press, 1995), 7.

3. Charles Fried, *Order and Law: Arguing the Reagan Revolution, A Firsthand Account* (New York: Simon and Schuster, 1991), 183.

4. Tarso Ramos, "Regulatory Takings and Private Property Rights," *PublicEye.org,* 1995, www.publiceye .org/eyes/privprop.html.

5. Blain Harden, *A River Lost: The Life and Death of the Columbia* (New York: W.W. Norton, 1996), 43.

6. Susan Zakin, *Coyotes and Town Dogs: Earth First! And the Environmental Movement* (New York: Penguin, 1993), 214.

7. Harold K. Steen, *The U.S. Forest Service: A History,* 4th ed (Seattle: University of Washington Press, 2004), xxix.

8. Ibid., 200.

9. G. Jon Roush in *Voices from the Environmental Movement: Perspectives for a new Era,* ed. Donald Snow (Washington, D.C.: Island Press, 1992), 11.

10. V. Alaric Sample and Antony S. Cheng. *Forest Conservation Policy* (Santa Barbara, Calif.): ABC-CLIO, 2004), 62–73.

11. Frederick W. Cubbage and David H. Newman, "Forest Policy Reformed: A United States Perspective," *Forest Policy and Economics,* December 1, 2006, 261–273.

12. William Perry Pendley, "Remarks before the Wyoming Water Association's Annual Meeting and Educational Seminar," 1999. Available at www.mountainstateslegal.org/articles_speeches.cfm? articleid=15.

13. William Perry Pendley, *War on the West: Government Tyranny on America's Great Frontier* (New York: Regnery, 1995), 89.

14. Ernie Niemi, Ed Whitelaw, and Elizabeth Grossman, "Bird of Doom . . . Or Was It?" *Amicus Journal,* Fall 2000, 20.

15. Ibid., 21.

16. Ross W. Gorte, *The Clinton Administration's Forest Plan for the Pacific Northwest,* Washington, D.C.: Congressional Research Service (CRS) Report for Congress, July 16, 1993, http://ncseonline.org/ NLE/CRSreports/Forests/for-3.cfm.

17. Paul Roberts, "The Federal Chain-Saw Massacre," *Harper's Magazine,* June 1997, www.harpers.org/ archive/1997/06/0059189.

18. Bill Clinton, Remarks on Signing Emergency Supplemental Appropriations and Rescissions Legislation," *Weekly Compilation of Presidential Documents* 31, no. 30, July 23, 1995, 1310.

19. J. Robert Cox, "The (Re)making of the 'Environmental President,'" in *Green Talk in the White House: The Rhetorical Presidency Encounters Ecology,* ed. Tarla Rai Peterson (College Station: Texas A&M University Press, 2004), 157.

20. Orrin Hatch, "The Mother of All Land Grabs," *High Country News,* September 30, 1996. Reprinted in *Give and Take: How the Clinton Administration's Public Lands Offensive Transformed the American West,* ed. Paul Larmer (Paonia, Colo.: High Country News Books, 2004), 17.

21. National Park Service, "The Monumental Legacy of the Antiquities Act of 1906," NPS Archaeology and Ethnography Program, n.d., www.nps.gov/history/aad/pubs/Georgia/georgia_1.htm.

22. Richard N. L. Andrews, *Managing the Environment, Managing Ourselves: A History of American Environmental Policy* (New Haven, Conn.: Yale University Press, 1999), 313–314.

23. Quoted in Ned Daly, "The Roadless Trammeled," *Multinational Monitor,* May 2001. www.multi nationalmonitor.org/mm2001/052001/daly.html.

24. Robert McClure and Andrew Schneider, "The General Mining Act of 1872 Has Left a Legacy of Riches and Ruin," *Seattle Post-Intelligencer,* June 11, 2001.

25. Raúl Grijalva, Chairman, Subcommittee on National Parks, Forests, and Public Lands, *A Report on the Bush Administration Assaults on Our National Parks, Forests, and Public Lands,* October 22, 2008, http://grijalva.house.gov/uploads/Grijalva_Public_Lands_Report_10_22_2008.pdf.

26. Quoted in Joby Warrick, "Appalachia is Paying Price for White House Rule Change," *Washington Post,* August 17, 2004, A1.

27. Mike Crapo, "Crapo Includes Fallen Firefighters," Press Release, Office of U.S. Senator Mike Crapo, July 23, 2003, http://crapo.senate.gov/media/newsreleases/release_full.cfm?id=233031.

28. George W. Bush, "Remarks on Signing the Healthy Forests Restoration Act of 2003," December 3, 2003. *Public Papers of the Presidents of the United States: George W. Bush, 2003* (Washington, D.C.: Government Printing Office, 2004), 1669.

29. Michael Peterson, "Testimony on Healthy Forests Restoration Act before the Senate Agriculture, Nutrition, and Forestry Committee," June 26, 2003, http://agriculture.senate.gov/Hearings/testimony .cfm?id=824&wit_id=2258.

30. Government Accountability Office (GAO), *Endangered Species: Time and Costs Required to Recover Species are Largely Unknown* (Washington, D.C.: Government Accountability Office, April 26, 2006).

31. Amanda Griscom Little, "Kick the Habitat: GOP Has Set its Sights on Revamping the Endangered Species Act," *Grist Magazine,* Nov 17, 2004, www.grist.org/article/little-species/.

32. Alexander Annett, "Reforming the Endangered Species Act to Protect Species and Property Rights," *Heritage Foundation Backgrounder,* November 13, 1998, www.heritage.org/research/energyan denvironment/bg1234.cfm.

33. Eugene H. Buck and M. Lynne Corn, "Endangered Species: Difficult Choices," *CRS Issue Brief for Congress,* June 5, 2001, (Washington, D.C.: Congressional Research Service, June 5, 2001), 3.

34. Ted Williams, "Living with Wolves," *Audubon,* November-December 2000, http://audubonmagazine .org/features0011/livingwithwolves.html.

35. Juliet Eilperin, "Since '01, Guarding Species is Harder," *Washington Post,* March 23, 2008, A1.

36. Ibid.

37. Wallace Stegner, *The American West as Living Space* (Ann Arbor: University of Michigan Press, 1987), 27.

38. Jon Gertner, "The Future Is Drying Up," *New York Times Magazine,* October 21, 2007, www .nytimes.com/2007/10/21/magazine/21water-t.html?_r=1.

39. Megan Mullin, *Governing the Tap: Special District Governance and the New Local Politics of Water* (Cambridge, Mass.: MIT Press, 2009), 13.

40. Quoted in Robert Jerome Glennon, *Unquenchable: America's Water Crisis and What to Do About It* (Washington, D.C.: Island Press, 2009), 12.

41. Tim P. Barnett and David W. Pierce, "When Will Lake Mead Go Dry?" *Water Resources Research,* March 29, 2008.

42. Matt Jenkins, "Liquid Assets: 'Water Banks' Help Cities Weather Drought," *High Country News,* October 27, 2008, www.hcn.org/issues/40.19/liquid-assets.

43. John Tierney, "Trying for Balance at Interior Dept.," *New York Times,* June 9, 2003, www.nytimes .com/2003/06/09/politics/09NORT.html?tntemai10=&pagewanted=all.

44. Donald D. T. Chen, "Science of Smart Growth," *Scientific American,* December 2000, 86.

45. Michael Dombeck, "History of the Public Lands of the U.S. and Conservation Policy." Address at Williams College, Williamstown, Mass., October 7, 2004, www.uwsp.edu/cnr/gem/Dombeck/ MDSpeeches/2004/2004%20October%207%20Williamstown,%20Massachusetts.pdf.

46. Ray Ring, "A Fractured Party," *High Country News,* July 21, 2008, www.hcn.org/issues/40.13/ a-fractured-party.

47. Ibid.

48. Ibid.

49. Republicans for Environmental Protection, "Passage of Omnibus Lands Bill a Great Step Forward for Conservation." Press release, March 25, 2009, www.rep.org/opinions/press_releases/release09–3-25.html.

DOCUMENT 10.1

James Watt Describes His Conservation Philosophy

"On All Fronts We Will Be Removing Unneeded Regulations and Policies"

March 23, 1981

Interior Secretary James Watt was one of President Ronald Reagan's most controversial appointments. A Wyoming native and long-time public official, Watt had in 1976 founded the Mountain States Legal Foundation, a powerful law firm dedicated to the cause of "individual liberties," including free market and property rights. After taking the reins at Reagan's Department of the Interior, he happily set about reshaping the agency to help the administration advance its goal of making greater commercial use of America's public lands. Despite his abbreviated tenure—the pugnacious Watt's stormy reign ended after two years—he made significant progress in this effort. He steered the Department of Interior down a markedly more business-friendly path than it had trod in the previous few decades, and he did so without benefit of major changes in environmental and resource law. His tools, observed Time, *"were budgetary finesse, regulatory manipulation, and personnel shifts."*[1]

The following speech, delivered to the North American Wildlife and Natural Resources Conference on March 23, 1981, was Watt's first major address as Reagan's Interior secretary. Given that the attendees included many conservation-oriented professionals and advocates, his remarks constitute a remarkably candid overview of his plans to radically retool the agency—and public land policy—in ways that will advance the Reagan Administration's wider policy agenda.

Thank you for providing this excellent forum for my first speaking engagement as Secretary of the Interior. I am happy for the opportunity to address this gathering of North America's leading conservationists and authorities on fish and wildlife.

Two months ago today I was confirmed by the Senate and sworn in at the White House. Since that time I have been immersed in the intricacies of reshaping the Department and enmeshed in discussions with congressional committees. During these two months I have made some major changes in the policies of the Department.

These actions have caused tremors in some segments of the conservation community. But let there be no mistaken views, this Administration will be in the mainstream of the conservation-environmental movement of America. Our management will be made up of real professionals.

The top two officials in the fish and wildlife areas of the Reagan Administration will be professional wildlife managers with experience as the chief executive officers of State fish and wildlife programs. In addition, we of the Reagan Administration have a proven and highly respected professional to head the National Park Service.

Today I want to share with you some of my views on conservation. I want to give you some of the reasoning for the actions which I have taken and will be taking.

There are four solid cornerstones in this Administration's conservation policy:

1. America must have a sound economy if it is to be a good steward of its fish and wildlife, its parks, and all of its natural resources.
2. America must have orderly development of its vast energy resources to avert a crisis development which could be catastrophic to the environment.
3. America's resources were put here for the enjoyment and use of people, now and in the future, and should not be denied to the people by elitist groups.
4. America has the expertise to manage and use resources wisely, and much of that expertise is in State Government and in the private sector.

All the actions which President Reagan or I have taken which impact upon conservation grow out of these principles.

This administration *is* conservative.

Conservatives *believe* in conservation—it's basic to our philosophy.

We all want our children and grandchildren—all who come after us—to have the opportunity to experience nature—to exult in the beauty of this country.

We will use the resources of the earth, but we will do so with the knowledge that mankind has been sustained by this earth for thousands of years and will be dependent upon it for generations to come.

When I became Secretary of the Interior I took an oath to uphold the law of the Nation which calls for the preservation of some lands and the development of other lands. This means finding a balance between competing uses. It also means finding that balance between how much we can use today without depriving future generations of Americans of the resources they too will need.

This is what I swore to when I took the oath of office; this is what I believe in. This is what the President believes in.

Let's look at the four principles a little closer.

First, rebuilding the American economy as a prerequisite to continued strong conservation.

In November the American people demonstrated that they agree our Nation is in grave economic peril. They gave an overwhelming mandate for an end to inflationary overspending and suffocating overregulation by the Federal Government.

Those of us in the Reagan Administration are committed to fulfilling this mandate.

I have responded by cutting more than one and one-quarter billion dollars from the Department's current budget and proposed budget for 1982.

Some of these cuts are being accomplished through consolidation of redundant functions. In one instance we are shifting essential functions of the Heritage Conservation and Recreation Service to the National Park Service. In another, we propose replacing the Water Resources Council and Office of Water Research and Technology with a more efficient Office of Water Policy.

We are cutting out all State grants under the Land and Water Conservation Fund and limiting Federal acquisition expenditures to $45 million—and only for emergencies. We believe a good steward learns to take care of what he has before he takes on additional responsibilities. Where park expansion is critically needed, we will seek to work out exchanges of land with existing owners.

Throughout the Department there has been a severe belt tightening.

We have looked at all programs; we have put many on the shelf.

Some of these programs will come off the shelf in better economic times.

We believe we have used wisdom in making these decisions. Congress has the final responsibility.

Moving on to the second cornerstone of conservation policy—the need for accelerated economic development on the public lands, especially for energy and strategic minerals.

America is desperately in need of a national minerals policy which enables us to develop our own resources so that we will not be dependent upon imports from nations which could cut off supplies at any time or which could bankrupt us. Our national security and our economic well-being are both at stake because we have neglected the development of a meaningful minerals policy. This Administration will take action to safeguard the Nation.

I am making adjustments in policy to see that we have orderly exploration and development of needed energy and other mineral resources. We will do this in consultation with the States, with local governments, and with private landowners who would be impacted. And we will do it with full regard for the fish, wildlife, and other natural values.

If orderly development of our energy resources with proper environmental safeguards is not allowed, economic, political, or social pressures could force the Federal Government to order a crash program under crisis conditions to develop the energy resources. If this were to occur, the destruction of our fragile ecological system could be experienced—particularly in my native West.

The third principle I listed at the outset is an orientation toward people.

This Administration will be a good neighbor to the users of public lands and to the States. On all fronts we will be removing unneeded regulations and policies which have irritated people not only in the West but all over this country.

Our public lands, our forests, our parks, our refuges, our wilderness, our wild and scenic rivers—all should be managed in ways which directly or ultimately serve the needs of people.

Our wildlife and fishery management programs, including our endangered species programs—these exist because it is in the interest of mankind to maintain a balanced and healthy natural world.

Some areas must be set aside primarily for wildlife and fish.

Other areas should be more intensively used. People make these decisions.

Look at our national park system. This was created so that people could forever share and enjoy the greatest natural treasures. It was not created to lock the treasures away from the people.

In recent years the National Park Service has been pressured to grab for more and more lands. It has been pushed into recreation areas which might more properly be the domain of the cities, the counties or the States.

Our parks and facilities have been deteriorating.

The public's access to the parks is being eroded.

Our National Park Service has been fighting a valiant but losing battle.

It's time to retarget our efforts and our money.

It's time to round out the Federal estate.

That's why I propose a halt to expansion of the park system.

That's why we need to look at what we have to make sure that it consists only of that which is truly unique and of national significance. We should not squander national tax dollars on non-national lands.

That's why we are asking Congress to allocate $105 million from the Land and Water Conservation Fund for park maintenance and restoration.

We want to see the truly national parks improved so that they can be used by the people.

We do not believe that the parks nor any of our resources should be held for the exclusive enjoyment of the elite.

At the same time, we understand fully that there must be management which will assure that our use and enjoyment of parks, refuges, seashores and other areas does not in itself destroy them. We will not throw the gates open and say "Here they are, folks, help yourself." We will manage the lands.

This Administration has the confidence that our country has the expertise and the self-discipline to manage our resources properly.

We believe that the key to conservation is management.

Conservation is not the blind locking away of huge areas and their resources because of emotional appeals.

Man has altered nature. He must now provide a balance in the use of Nature's provisions. It is an awesome responsibility and one we cannot shirk.

Wildlife and resources managers must be allowed to manage by the best scientific knowledge available and not be deterred from their task by emotionalism.

In this Administration we will be looking more and more to user groups to help pay the bill for this management. The Pittman-Robertson and the Dingell-Johnson programs have been great. Now there is some sentiment for expansion, and I applaud that possibility.

On the international front, we will be careful not to make agreements which are detrimental to State and Federal fish and wildlife programs.

In our conservation programs, we will be targeting our dollars to get the most management out of our investment. We're going to channel the available funds "to the ground"—the refuges, wildlife ranges, parks and public lands.

We are retargeting our effort in the Endangered Species Program so that we can try to help species recover rather than compiling endless lists of those which are endangered or threatened. The Endangered Species Program will be managed for scientific purposes not for political or philosophical objectives.

These are some of the actions which we have taken in these past two months, and some of the thinking behind our actions.

My job is not an easy job, but it has its satisfactions. It is a pleasure to work with a President who understands natural resource issues. When I talk about BLM or the U.S. Fish and Wildlife Service or some other important resource managing agency, the President understands immediately. As Governor of our most populated State, with 50 percent of its land Federally owned, he learned about wildlife and about natural resources and he learned well. He is a man who has a great love for the outdoors, but who loves his country so much that he now finds himself able to enjoy the outdoors only on very limited occasions.

Let me close by reading a brief message from the President which pretty well summarizes and emphasizes what I have said:

"Our natural resources are a precious heritage which provide the basis for our national wealth and well-being. We have a sacred responsibility to manage them wisely.

"This 46th Annual North American Wildlife and Natural Resources Conference comes at a time when we are working to devise new approaches to achieving these vital conservation goals in the face of necessary fiscal self-discipline. Our country will be relying upon you and your colleagues to help us carry out the planned, orderly and scientific management of our wonderful wildlife resources as economically and as efficiently as possible.

"In your theme, 'Resources Management for the Eighties,' I perceive a dedication to a new beginning. May you have a most productive conference and every success in your conservation endeavors which lie ahead."

Source: Watt, James. Address to the 46th North American Wildlife and Natural Resources Conference, Washington, D.C., March 23, 1981. Washington, D.C.: Department of the Interior, March 23, 1981.

NOTE

1. "The Legacy of James Watt," *Time,* October 24, 1983.

| DOCUMENT 10.2 | President Bush Signs the Oil Pollution Act |

"The Threat of Oil Pollution Is a Global Challenge"

August 18, 1990

During the last quarter of the twentieth century, several environmental disaster events suddenly and dramatically changed the complexion of environmental policy-making in the United States. These "game-changing" events included both domestic incidents, such as the

Love Canal scandal of the late 1970s and the 1979 Three Mile Island incident in
Pennsylvania, and international events, including the deadly 1984 gas release at a Union
Carbide facility in Bhopal, India, and the Soviet nuclear disaster at Chernobyl in 1986.
Another epic tragedy that had enduring environmental policy repercussions occurred on
March 24, 1989 in Alaska's Prince William Sound. That night, the Exxon Valdez oil tanker
hit a reef and spilled an estimated 10.8 million gallons of crude oil into the sound's
ecologically rich waters.

The incident sparked widespread public outrage and a full-blown media scrum to
assign blame. Environmentalists, lawmakers, Exxon spokespeople, industry officials, and
Alaskan fishermen all weighed in with pointed charges and countercharges. (The Exxon
Corporation was ultimately found liable for the disaster, but a fine of $2.5 billion in
punitive damages was vacated in 2008 by the U.S. Supreme Court, which remanded the
case back to a lower court.) This finger pointing further intensified as the full dimensions
of the environmental disaster came into focus. The spill killed half a million seabirds, more
than 1,000 otters and seals, 22 killer whales, and billions of salmon and herring.[1] Winds
and tides eventually spread the contamination over 11,000 square miles of ocean. A 2007
study estimated that 21,000 gallons of crude oil still poison the sound's coastline.[2]

This tragedy also radically altered the political terrain in Washington, D.C. Prior to
the Valdez spill, Republicans had been pushing hard to expand oil exploration and drilling
activities into offshore sites and the Alaska National Wildlife Refuge (ANWR). Meanwhile,
efforts to bolster anemic and outdated federal oil pollution regulations through new
legislation had repeatedly been turned aside by industry allies in Congress. But the Exxon
Valdez decisively turned the momentum on both of these issues. Public anger about events
in Alaska forced advocates of expanded drilling not only to suspend those activities, but
also to find tangible ways of showing their concern about marine pollution from oil spills.
The final result of this sudden stampede of environmental concern was the Oil Pollution
Act of 1990.

This law imposed a wide array of new restrictions on oil tanker operations and
included significant measures to improve government and industry response times to oil
spills. It also affirmed state authority to establish stringent laws governing oil spill
prevention and response. The act also included a provision—inserted by anti-drilling
members of Congress—that placed a moratorium on oil and natural gas exploration off
the Atlantic coastline. The act did not include ratification of a major international
convention that had already been crafted to compensate victims of oil spills because
opponents in Congress preferred a system of unlimited liability for spill incidents.[3]
President George H. W. Bush felt that both the drilling moratorium and the rejection of
the 1984 Protocol to the International Convention on Civil Liability for Oil Pollution
Damage constituted significant flaws in an otherwise "responsible" piece of legislation.
Bush made these sentiments clear in his signing remarks, reprinted here.

I am today signing into law H.R. 1465, the "Oil Pollution Act of 1990." In May 1989 the
Administration sent its comprehensive oil pollution liability and compensation legislation to the Congress in the wake of the worst marine environmental disaster this Nation
has ever experienced. During this disaster 11 million gallons of oil spilled into the
waters of Prince William Sound, Alaska. Since then, California, the Gulf of Mexico, the
Mid-Atlantic, and New England have suffered serious oil spills.

In most respects, the Oil Pollution Act of 1990 is a responsible piece of legislation.
Most important, the prevention, response, liability, and compensation components fit

together into a compatible and workable system that strengthens the protection of our environment.

The Act addresses the wide-ranging problems associated with preventing, responding to, and paying for oil spills. It does so by creating a comprehensive regime for dealing with vessel and facility-caused oil pollution. It provides for greater environmental safeguards in oil transportation by: setting new standards for vessel construction, crew licensing, and manning; providing for contingency planning; enhancing Federal response capability; broadening enforcement authority; increasing penalties; and authorizing multi-agency research and development. A one billion dollar trust fund will be available to cover cleanup costs and damages not compensated by the spiller, whose financial responsibility requirements are significantly increased.

Although I am approving this legislation, I deeply regret the Act's inclusion of an unrelated provision that would place a moratorium on exploration for oil and natural gas off the coast of North Carolina. This area, located over 38 miles offshore, is the largest potential natural gas field east of the Mississippi and could be used to offset our dependence on foreign energy sources. Much work has been done to address my environmental concerns related to exploration in this area—and it should be noted that exploration for gas this far offshore carries little environmental risk. It is shortsighted to restrict exploration for this relatively clean energy source, especially in light of our recent efforts to accommodate national and State concerns regarding the environmental effects of energy exploration and development. Such a moratorium is ill-advised in view of recent events in the Persian Gulf, where I have found it necessary to deploy American soldiers 7,000 miles from home to protect our vital national interests. The moratorium contained in H.R. 1465 is highly objectionable, and my Administration will seek to repeal it.

In addition, H.R. 1465 does not implement the 1984 Protocols to the 1969 Civil Liability Convention and the 1971 Fund Convention. These oil spill treaties, if ratified, would provide our Nation with swift and assured compensation for foreign tanker oil spills and access to up to $260 million per spill from an international fund. Our failure to ratify the Protocols may weaken long-standing U.S. leadership in the development of international maritime standards.

Ultimately, the threat of oil pollution is a global challenge, and the solutions we devise must be broad enough to address the needs of all nations. Therefore, I urge the Senate to give immediate consideration to the international Protocols and give its advice and consent to ratification of these treaties.

I am concerned about another consequence of the failure to ratify the Protocols. We must work to ensure that, in response to the provisions of this Act, a situation is not created in which larger oil shippers seeking to avoid risk are replaced by smaller companies with limited assets and a reduced ability to pay for the cleanup of oil spills. We will need to monitor developments in order to protect against such undesirable consequences.

The oil industry faces many new requirements as a result of this legislation. These requirements include substantially increased financial responsibility; preparation of contingency plans; and the replacement of fleets with safer oil tankers. A balance has been sought to give the industry the flexibility to meet the requirements of the Act without incurring excessive costs.

Finally, I note that section 3004 of the bill could be construed to infringe on my constitutional authority over the conduct of diplomacy by requiring me to take certain actions with respect to international organizations. I shall construe this section consistently with the Constitution and therefore shall regard it as advisory.

In signing this landmark Act, I pledge the support of the Administration for the Oil Pollution Act of 1990, notwithstanding the concerns that I have addressed. This represents a continuation of my Administration's efforts to work with the Congress and other nations to protect the Earth's environment.

George Bush
The White House,
August 18, 1990.

Source: Bush, George. "Remarks upon Signing the Oil Pollution Act of 1990." *Public Papers of the Presidents of the United States: George Bush.* Washington, D.C.: U.S. Government Printing Office, 1991. http://bushlibrary.tamu.edu/research/public_papers.php?id=2169&year=1990&month=8.

Notes

1. Tony Long, "March 24, 1989: *Valdez* Spill Causes Environmental Catastrophe," *Wired.com,* March 24, 2009, www.wired.com/science/discoveries/news/2009/03/dayintech_0324.

2. Exxon Valdez Oil Spill Trustee Council, "Oil Remains: The Persistence, Toxicity, and Impact of Exxon Valdez Oil," 2007, www.evostc.state.ak.us/recovery/lingeringoil.cfm.

3. "International Convention on Civil Liability for Oil Pollution Damage (CLC), 1969," International Maritime Organization., n.d., www.imo.org/Conventions/contents.asp?doc_id=660&topic_id=256.

DOCUMENT 10.3

Opposing Wolf Reintroduction in the West

"A Wolf Release Program that Flouts the Endangered Species Act and Established Science"

January 26, 1995

The Endangered Species Act (ESA) has ranked as one of the cornerstones of American environmental policy ever since its passage in 1973. But it has also become one of the most controversial federal laws in existence because of its power to influence land use (both public and private) and prioritize wildlife protection over economic development. Indeed, federal wildlife preservation efforts became one of the most explosive flashpoints of conflict between environmental groups and private property/free market/states' rights advocates during the Reagan years, and these clashes erupted again and again in subsequent administrations.

One of the most acrimonious and highly publicized of these battles was a mid-1990s clash over a U.S. Fish and Wildlife Service (USFS) plan to place endangered gray wolves into Montana, Wyoming, and Idaho. Specifically, the USFS's Northern Rocky Mountain Gray Wolf Recovery Plan was designed to establish a viable population of gray wolves, which had been listed as an endangered species since 1973, in Yellowstone National Park and central Idaho. Under this Recovery Plan, and in accordance with section 10(j) of the Endangered Species Act, federal authorities captured fourteen Canadian gray wolves and delivered them to the park in January 1995 (fifteen other wolves were released directly into the Idaho wilderness). As wildlife officials began acclimating the wolves to the Yellowstone area prior to their scheduled release in March, however, the Republican-controlled House Committee on Resources hurriedly convened hearings on the Recovery Plan. The hearing featured angry statements from politicians such as Helen Chenoweth (R-Idaho), who told Interior secretary Bruce Babbitt that "I strongly believe that not only have your wolves trespassed on to the lands of the State of Idaho, your agencies have trespassed onto the Constitution of the United States of America, the supreme law of the land."[1] Heartfelt testimony for and against the wolf introduction plan was also presented at the hearing. One of the strongest of the latter statements was presented by Larry J. Bourret, executive vice president of the Wyoming Farm Bureau Federation. In his testimony, which is excerpted here, Bourret asserted that the recovery plan blatantly violated section 10(j) of the ESA, and he demanded that the wolf reintroduction plan be halted (see document 10.4 for testimony from a pro-wolf reintroduction advocate).

Despite the opposition voiced by western Republican congress members, ranching interests, and Wise Use activists, the release went ahead as planned in March 1995. One year later, four more small packs of Canadian gray wolves were released in Yellowstone. In 1997 a legal challenge to the recovery plan filed by the American Farm Bureau Federation was upheld by a U.S. district court in Wyoming. The court ruled that the newly introduced wolves from Canada illegally reduced the protection granted to naturally expanding wolf populations. Under this finding, all of the introduced wolves would have to be removed. The Clinton Administration appealed the ruling, however, and on January 13, 2000, the Tenth Circuit Court of Appeals ruled that the Recovery Plan had been carried out in full compliance with section 10(j) and that the reintroduced wolves should be allowed to stay in the recovery areas.[2]

By 2009 the Fish and Wildlife Service estimated that the gray wolf population in Montana, Wyoming, and Idaho had reached 1,500—a number that prompted the agency to recommend delisting western gray wolf populations from the Endangered Species Act. In March 2009 the Department of the Interior upheld that recommendation to delist wolf populations in the northern Rockies but noted that wolves in Wyoming will continue to be protected under the act as a result of that state's "inadequate" wolf management plan. After this delisting, wolves within Yellowstone boundaries will remain protected, but those that stray outside the park can be killed once affected states establish hunting regulations. In September 2009 both Idaho and Montana carried out limited hunting seasons for gray wolves. In addition, Interior officials have announced the agency's intention to remove ESA protections from gray wolf populations in the western Great Lakes states of Michigan, Minnesota, and Wisconsin, but that decision has been delayed by legal challenges (ESA status for endangered gray wolf populations in the Southwest remained unchanged).

STATEMENT OF LARRY J. BOURRET, EXECUTIVE VICE PRESIDENT, WYOMING FARM BUREAU FEDERATION

In its haste to turn loose a major predator into Wyoming, Montana, and Idaho, the U.S. Fish & Wildlife Service has ignored the concerns of the farmers, ranchers, hunters, and others who actually live in the experimental areas and will be affected by the release, and has also ignored the concerns of the state governments into whose jurisdictions these wolves are released and who are supposed to be partners with the Fish & Wildlife Service in this project. The Service has also played fast and loose with the dictates of the Endangered Species Act and its own regulations, creating a wolf release program that flouts the

Endangered Species Act and established science, and shortcuts the procedural requirements of its own regulations.

As an initial proposition, it is important to remember that the gray wolf is not in danger of becoming extinct, nor is it threatened with becoming endangered. There are more than 60,000 gray wolves in Canada, with another 6,000 in Alaska and 2,000 more in Minnesota, Michigan and Wisconsin. Releasing wolves into the Rocky Mountain area is not necessary to save the gray wolf.

Also, wolves will not stay in Yellowstone Park or in Central Idaho. According to the Final Environmental Impact Statement, wolves can travel up to one thousand miles. Instead, the program encompasses vast areas and affect a significant number of people. For example, the entire state of Wyoming is within the experimental population area for the planned introduction into the Yellowstone area. Similarly, approximately 90% of the State of Idaho and more than 60% of the State of Montana are in the experimental population areas. Such areas are entirely too large to allow such a significant predator as the wolf to roam at large with virtually no restrictions.

> *The experimental population rules give considerable responsibilities to the states and "state management plans" for the management of released wolves. Yet, the federal agencies did not even wait for the states to adopt these management plans before they began releasing wolves.*
>
> — Larry J. Bourret

The extremely large experimental population area gives the federal government virtual control over three entire states, and the potential for federal land use control in the name of wolf protection is awesome. The government has already reneged on its pledge that the introduction will not cause any land use restrictions by stating in the final EIS that some restrictions might be necessary, without saying what those restrictions might be. References in the final rules—the provisions allowing FWS to capture problem wolves and relocating them anywhere within the "experimental population area," or the provision allowing FWS to relocate wolves anywhere in the experimental area to "enhance recovery," creates the potential for land use restrictions anywhere within this vast area, and makes the entire State of Wyoming the private game reserve of the gray wolf. Such a result should be avoided at all cost. . . .

1. The Wolf Introduction Program Does Not Adequately Allow Ranchers to Protect Their Livestock from Wolf Depredation.

. . . The Service has attempted to sell the program on the basis that it adequately protects landowners from any pet, livestock or other type of losses that wolves will inflict. But if there is one point upon which all sides agree, it is that the proposed protective measures are a sham. . . . In the first place, any nonessential experimental population designation does not apply in "areas within the National Wildlife Refuge System or the National Park System." [Section 10(j)(C)(1)] Livestock are permitted to graze in several of the wildlife refuges within the experimental population areas. Full section 7 consultation will be required in all of these areas, which could result in the loss of grazing permits due to possible impacts on wolf introduction. Producers who rely on these lands for grazing operations could face severe consequences as a result of this introduction.

Conditions are hardly any better for lands outside the boundaries of the wildlife refuges and the national parks.

The program would allow a landowner to kill or injure a wolf on his private property but only if certain very restrictive conditions are met.

First, the landowner must actually catch the wolf "in the act of killing, wounding, or biting livestock." . . . In fact, it is an extremely rare occurrence to actually catch a wolf in the act of killing, wounding or biting livestock.

Second, livestock freshly wounded or killed (less than 24 hours in most cases) must be evident, and the Service must make a determination that the cause of death was the wolf.

Combined, these conditions make it very difficult to protect livestock and pets.

The situation is even worse for permittees on federal lands to protect their livestock. In addition to the requirements described above, they must first obtain a permit from the Service. In addition, there must be at least 6 breeding pairs of wolves in the experimental population area, there must be documented and verified wolf kills, and the Service must have unsuccessfully attempted to have resolved the problem. In addition, subsequent livestock losses must be documented. . . .

2. The "Experimental Population" Designation Is Likely to be Overturned by a Court of Law.

Inadequate as the "protective measures" described above may be, they are better than the alternative—having the wolves be fully protected under the Endangered Species Act and leaving farmers and ranchers completely powerless to protect themselves or their livestock from wolf predation.

The protective measures come only as a result of the introduced wolf populations being designated as "nonessential experimental populations" pursuant to section 10j of the Endangered Species Act. Unfortunately, circumstances in both of the introduction areas make both of those designations vulnerable to legal challenges as violating the Endangered Species Act. In fact, the "experimental population" designations have been challenged in court by both the Farm Bureau and the Sierra Club Legal Defense Fund in separate suits. Farm Bureau and the Sierra Club represent completely different sides of the spectrum on this issue, but they both make the same argument in their suits (the only difference is the remedy they seek).

Section 10j of the Endangered Species Act defines an experimental population as any which "is wholly separate geographically from nonexperimental populations of the same species." Implementing regulations make it clear that "[w]here part of an experimental population overlaps with natural populations of the same species . . . specimens of the experimental population will not be recognized as such while in the area of overlap." [50 CFR 17.80(a)]. The Act makes it clear, therefore, that whenever any members of a designated experimental population overlap with any naturally occurring members of the same species, they are all treated as if they were naturally occurring, and given full protection under the Endangered Species Act.

Section 10j also includes as members of the experimental population any offspring, but only "arising solely therefrom"—in other words, only if both parents are members of the experimental population.

The final rules for both the Yellowstone and central Idaho introductions provide the opposite result. They both state that any gray wolf found in either of the experimental areas—whether naturally occurring or introduced—will be treated as a member of the experimental population under the rules. Likewise, any offspring will be treated as members of the experimental population, whether both parents were introduced wolves, or whether one or even none of the parents were introduced. Both of these results are clearly and directly contrary to the law and implementing regulations, which control in such situations. . . .

3. The Introduction Program Does Not Provide Compensation for Damages or Losses Occasioned by Released Wolves.

While the wolf introduction program was developed with the full knowledge and expectation that wolves would cause damages to private property and losses to privately owned livestock, the rules acknowledge no governmental responsibility for such losses or damages. The government has in the past acknowledged the existence of a private Wolf Fund, but the government cannot guarantee that compensation would be provided for wolf losses out of that fund. Once again, the government has directly placed the burden of feeding and sheltering listed species on the farmers and ranchers unfortunate enough to have such species thrust upon them, rather than having the costs paid by the general public as they properly should. . . .

The argument against government responsibility for damages caused by wild animals does not extend to cases where the animals have been controlled "by skillful capture." Since any introduced wolves would necessarily have been live-trapped in Canada and transported to the introduction sites and actually released in those sites, there can be no doubt that such animals have been subject to "skillful capture," and the government is liable for damages caused by these animals.

Likewise, because the federal government is the entity that is capturing the wolves and releasing them, and it is the federal Endangered Species Act that applies, the onus of responsibility cannot be pawned off to the states in this case.

These circumstances raise serious Fifth Amendment Just Compensation issues that are not addressed in the proposal. The Takings analysis prepared in accordance with Executive Order No. 12630 (Appendix 6 in the FEIS) refers to the private compensation fund, but fails to acknowledge any federal responsibilities if the private fund fails to compensate. In this respect, the federal proposal runs afoul of the Just Compensation Clause.

4. The Federal Government Has Failed to Take into Account the Interests of Affected State Governments.

State governments are traditionally responsible for plants and wildlife within their borders. The importation of a major predator from a foreign country thus has large impacts on the discharge of those state responsibilities. This is especially true where, as here, the introduced species is expected to use state and private lands. . . .

The FWS has failed to fully involve the affected state governments to the extent that they should be involved. State governments have been told that they had no authority to independently test imported wolves for disease or other conditions, but rather had to take the verification provided by the federal authorities. In addition, states have been told that there is little or nothing that they could do to alter the programs developed by the federal authorities.

One of the primary purposes behind enactment of section 10j of the Endangered Species Act was to make reintroduction proposals more acceptable to both the host state and to any private landowners who might have necessary habitat. As a result, FWS promulgated regulations that require the FWS to "consult with appropriate State fish and wildlife agencies, local government entities, affected Federal agencies, and affected private landowners in developing and implementing experimental population rules." [50 CFR 17.81(d)]. The same regulation requires "[a]ny regulation promulgated pursuant to this section shall, to the maximum extent practicable, represent an agreement between the Fish and Wildlife Service, the affected state and federal agencies, and persons holding any interest in land which may be affected by the establishment of an experimental population."

That the required partnership between State and Federal agencies has not been formed becomes more evident with each passing day. The experimental population rules give considerable responsibilities to the states and "state management plans" for the management of released wolves. Yet, the federal agencies did not even wait for the states to adopt these management plans before they began releasing wolves, thus giving states responsibilities for wolf management without allowing them the opportunity to formulate plans for such management. An Idaho state permit authorizing the federal government to release wolves into the state was expressly conditioned upon compliance with a state management plan, and yet those wolves were released prior to that management plan being in place. According to recent news accounts, when that plan was finally adopted by the State it was rejected by the federal authorities because it contained items that they did not like.

There is little doubt that this program is not a state-federal partnership as contemplated by section 10j of the Act. Despite considerable state interests being affected, they have little or no input into how wolves dumped in their states and left to their management will actually be managed. That decision is made by bureaucrats in Washington, D.C. This program is an unfunded mandate of the purest form. . . .

5. Prospects for Future De-Listing of the Gray Wolf.

The object of any program taken under the Endangered Species Act is the eventual de-listing of the species. To answer the question at what point the Northern Rocky Mountain gray wolf will be considered recovered, the issue must be examined from both a biological and a political standpoint.

From a biological standpoint, the final rules say that 10 breeding packs in each of the three recovery areas is sufficient to downlist and de-list the species. The FWS gives the number at approximately 300 wolves.

From a political standpoint, however, de-listing will not be that simple. Experience shows that once a species is listed, it is almost impossible to obtain its de-listing, even if recovery "goals" have been accomplished. For example, the Eastern Timber Wolf Recovery Plan from Minnesota indicates wolves may be considered recovered when they reach 125–1500 in numbers. Today estimates are close to 2,000 wolves in Minnesota, Wisconsin and Michigan, yet there is no move by FWS to begin de-listing.

Closer to home, the grizzly bear recovery "goals" for the Northern Continental Divide area and for the Yellowstone Park area have both been exceeded since 1900. Instead of beginning the process of de-listing, FWS instead has changed the numbers and criteria for recovery. When the same circumstances occurred in 1992 with those two populations, the FWS once again changed the criteria. The upshot is that such animals, once placed on the endangered list, stay there. . . .

Conclusion

The proposals to introduce wolves into Yellowstone and Central Idaho are good examples of questionable science being used to implement political decisions. But in this case it is easy to look behind the "science" to unmask the real motives behind introduction. No one can seriously argue that gray wolves are in danger of extinction, with more than 70,000 wolves in Canada and another 7,000–8,000 in Alaska and Minnesota. Nor can anyone seriously argue that they are "returning" an animal to his historic habitat, because the wolf being introduced is not native to the areas of introduction. Nor can anyone seriously argue that the proposed rules would allow farmers and ranchers to protect their livestock, pets and other private property from destruction by the introduced wolves. . . .

That leaves us with the conclusion that the real reason for the proposal is that the Fish & Wildlife Service thinks it would be "nice" if wolves were returned to Yellowstone Park and to Central Idaho. That is not a valid reason. Farmers, ranchers and area landowners (including the entire state of Wyoming) are being asked to support the introduction of these animals into their midst, while at the same time they will alone be compelled to bear the costs of feeding and sheltering these animals.

Source: Statement of Larry J. Bourret, Executive Vice President, Wyoming Farm Bureau Federation. *Introducing Gray Wolves in Yellowstone and Idaho: Oversight Hearing before the Committee on Resources, House of Representatives, One Hundred Fourth Congress, First Session, on Federal Efforts to Introduce Canadian Gray Wolves into Yellowstone National Park and the Central Idaho Wilderness, January 26, 1995.* Washington, D.C.: Government Printing Office, pp. 115–123.

NOTES

1. Quoted in *Introducing Gray Wolves in Yellowstone and Idaho: Oversight Hearing before the Committee on Resources, House of Representatives, One Hundred Fourth Congress, First Session, on Federal Efforts to Introduce Canadian Gray Wolves into Yellowstone National Park and the Central Idaho Wilderness, January 26, 1995* (Washington, D.C.: Government Printing Office, 1995), 6.

2. Martin A. Nie, *Beyond Wolves: The Politics of Wolf Recovery and Management,* (Minneapolis: University of Minnesota Press, 2003), 99–100.

DOCUMENT
10.4

A Proponent of Wolves in Yellowstone

"We Made a Grave Error in Exterminating Them"

January 26, 1995

Many political battles have been waged over the Endangered Species Act (ESA) since its passage in 1973. But few reached the fever pitch that surrounded the U.S. Fish and Wildlife Service's (USFS) 1995 release of endangered gray wolves into Montana, Wyoming, and Idaho.

The USFS's Northern Rocky Mountain Gray Wolf Recovery Plan was to re-introduce a viable population of gray wolves, which had been listed as an endangered species since 1973, in Yellowstone National Park and central Idaho. Under the Yellowstone plan, federal authorities captured fourteen Canadian gray wolves and delivered them to the park in January 1995. As wildlife officials began acclimating the wolves to the Yellowstone area prior to their scheduled release in March, however, the Republican-controlled House Committee on Resources hurriedly convened hearings on the Recovery Plan. The hearing featured testimony from numerous opponents of the wolf introduction plan, but it also included statements from dedicated supporters of the scheme. One such advocate was Reneé Askins, founder of the Wolf Fund, a grassroots organization dedicated to returning wolves to the Yellowstone ecosystem. Her testimony at the hearing is excerpted here. (See document 10.3 for testimony from an opponent of wolf reintroduction and further information on government protection efforts for gray wolves in Yellowstone and other parts of the United States.)

STATEMENT OF RENEÉ ASKINS, WOLF FUND

If I were a rancher I probably would not want wolves returned to the West. If I had significant numbers of sheep or cattle killed each year by predators I would dread and fight the addition of another predator. If I faced the conditions that ranchers face in the West—falling stock prices, rising taxes, prolonged drought, and a nation that is eating less and less beef and wearing more and more synchilla—I would not want to add wolves to my woes. If I were a rancher in Montana, Idaho, or Wyoming in 1995, watching my neighbors give up and my way of life fade away, I would be afraid. If everything I believed in and worked for and prayed for was disappearing, I would be afraid and I would be angry. I would want to blame something, to fight something, even kill something because Westerners are not, on the whole, a helpless lot.

Ranchers can't change the weather, or make people eat beef or wear wool, the tax thing is hopeless, but they can fight to stop those wolves, they could even kill those wolves. Ranchers know, and the people in this room know, that the wolves aren't the cause of western woes or the changes that are causing those woes, any more than the rooster crowing is the cause for the sun rising.

Almost every rancher I know in the West right now is afraid and angry. I have lived in the West for fifteen years. I spent a good part of two of those years on the road talking to people in rural Wyoming, Montana, and Idaho, mostly ranchers, mostly about wolves. When you talk to ranchers (the ones on the ground, the ones running stock, not lobbying organizations) they say, "you know it's not the wolves we're worried about, it's what the wolves represent. It's not what they'll do, it's what they mean." Wolves mean changes. Wolves mean challenges to the old way of doing things. Wolves mean loss of control.

> *The livestock industry has been very effective in promoting the concept that having wolves in Yellowstone is some sort of environmental luxury, some romantic nonsense that only urbanites and rich easterners advocate, at the costs of the poor beleaguered western livestock industry. Having wolves in Yellowstone is not a luxury but a right.*
>
> —Reneé Askins

Ranchers deserve our compassion and our concern. Whether the threat of wolves is perceived or actual, their fear and anger are real. I honor that. It is my job, however, as a scientist and an advocate to distinguish the fact from the fiction, and the purpose from the perceived. It is the job of the members of this committee, as representatives of a democratic public, to create laws and, in creating them, inform your decision-making with the most accurate information, and it is Secretary Babbitt's job to implement and enforce those laws.

Democracy must be more than laws expressing exemplary ideals. For [Thomas] Jefferson it was, above all, an active process whereby an informed and passionate public shaped their own history. It is through our participation and our representation that we are rendered accountable to the ideas of our legislation. It is easy to pass visionary laws; it is often difficult to live by their mandates.

When Congress passed The Endangered Species Act it expressed the nation's willingness to sacrifice some economic advantage for the protection and restoration of species. The creation of Yellowstone National Park expressed our desire to preserve our natural heritage. The Wilderness Act expressed our commitment to wild places and their wild inhabitants. All were recognized, by the world, as visionary legislation. Now we face the difficult task of living up to our visions.

To possess a fine recipe is one thing, to prepare a fine meal requires more—some thought and effort and care. The Endangered Species Act is like a fine recipe, but it needs to be enacted to be meaningful to America. The northern Rocky Mountain wolf was classified as an Endangered Species in 1973. This classification required the return of wolves to Yellowstone. The wolves are not yet running free in Yellowstone, and—so far—our legislation has proved unequal to its mission. After twenty years of stalling and sabotage by special interest groups, Jefferson's original vision of democracy, laws made of the people, by the people, and for the people is itself endangered.

The Endangered Species Act was passed by an overwhelming majority in Congress in 1973 and it enjoyed tremendous support among the general public. Our laws, however, are only as good as our ability to live up to them. Americans want clean air, clean water, wild places, wild creatures, and are willing to sacrifice to have those things, but because of pressure from special interest groups, usually industry-driven special interests, our laws are not always observed, and what Americans sought to protect is bartered away in nickels and dimes . . . one acre at a time, one species at a time. . . .

The wolf is a prime victim of industry's "barter" methods. For over twenty years special interests have undermined national law by intentionally dragging out the legal process of wolf recovery and driving up the costs. Ironically, the wolf issue has recently been depicted as a "hurried and autocratic" effort by the federal government, forced upon the states of Wyoming, Idaho, and Montana, that has ignored the concerns and interest of the local public. The foundation of this plan was forged under the Reagan and Bush administrations with an emphasis on deriving a solution from the West, rather than imposing one on the West. In 1991 Wyoming GOP Senators Malcolm Wallop and Alan Simpson, working with former U.S. Fish and Wildlife Service Director John Turner (who was also a former Republican state senator and a third generation western rancher), established a wolf management committee bringing together federal and state agencies, conservationists and ranchers to find a solution that carried out the law and considered people. Their work provided the foundation for today's plan, a hard won, middle of the road position.

Assertions have also been made that the states have not been involved, and that the public, particularly the ranchers, have not had the opportunity to comment. This is simply untrue. Since 1973, when the wolf was placed on the Endangered Species list, the livestock industry has participated on the Wolf Recovery Team in the production of two wolf recovery plans. Four volumes (1,314 pages) of research on the economic, biological and social impact of wolf reintroduction were produced principally to respond to their concerns. (More research had been done on wolves than on any animal that lives here!) Ranchers and hunters were represented on the Wolf Management Committee, and participated extensively at hearing associated with the Committee.

Ranchers, hunters, and representatives from the state government also participated extensively in the two-year EIS [environmental impact statement] process. . . . Opponents of wolf recovery have participated in this planning process every step of the way, and their concerns have indeed been addressed, although not necessarily acceded to, in both the EIS and the Rulemaking.

Additionally, the Game and Fish Departments of all three states have already been paid $7,000 a year to participate in the planning and implementation of the EIS and each state received $30,000 in 1993 to develop their wolf management plans. Objections have been raised about the U.S. Fish and Wildlife Service proceeding with reintroduction before state plans are in place. The time frame of the reintroduction has been known for several years [and] the preparation and completion of these plans is of course the responsibility of the state game and fish departments and not the federal government.

Opponents of this project have also asserted that residents in the region are opposed to this, but numerous regional surveys have shown majorities of the residents in Wyoming, Montana, and Idaho support the presence of wolves. A 1991 survey in Wyoming, commissioned by the Wyoming Game and Fish Department (which at the time was on record against reintroduction) indicated that Wyoming residents favored reintroduction by a margin of 44% to 34.5%. . . . Bath and Phillips (1990) and Bath (1991) . . . found that 43.7% of Montanans, 48.5% of Wyomingites and 56% of Idahoans favored wolf reintroduction into Yellowstone National Park. 40.3% of Montanans, 34.5% of Wyomingites, and 27% of Idahoans were opposed. No opinion on wolf reintroduction was held by 16% of Montanans, 17% of Wyomingites and 17% of Idahoans. . . . National surveys indicate an overwhelming majority of the national public support Yellowstone wolf reintroduction.

Reintroduction opponents claim that wolves will devastate the livestock industry in the West, and yet all the science, the studies, the experts, and the facts show that wolves kill less than 1/10 of 1 percent of the livestock available to them. . . .

According to the *Bozeman Chronicle,* even if federal specialists have wildly underestimated the number of cows and sheep that wolves would kill in the Yellowstone and Central Idaho areas, the total would be much smaller than the number that die each year in the state of Montana alone because of storms, dogs, and ovine ineptitude. In fact, the number of wolf-caused sheep deaths would have to be almost 30 times higher than predicted before it would match the number of Montana sheep that died in 1993 because they rolled over onto their backs and were unable to get up and starved. . . .

Opponents claim that reintroducing wolves is a waste of taxpayer dollars. Let's take a closer look at the projected 6.7 million dollars it would take to reintroduce wolves. One man's "cost" is another man's "income," as we have learned with defense spending cuts. Whatever money is spent on wolf reintroduction largely flows into the regional economy, as will money for the ongoing management of a recovered population. The cost of not doing anything, that is allowing natural recolonization to occur, would be higher due to the prolonged time it would take for natural recovery to occur and due to the increased restrictions that accompany the presence of a fully endangered species.

It is projected that wolf reintroduction will cost approximately $900,000 a year. Of those costs the federal government anticipates earmarking approximately $100,000 to $150,000/year for each of the three states or a total of $300,000 to $450,000/year to support state involvement in management of wolves. Because wolf management is not a full time proposition the equipment (trucks, snowmobiles, telemetry receivers etc.), salaries, etc. would most likely be used for other projects as well. . . .

Let's also take a look at the expenditure of 6.7 million dollars in relationship to other expenditures. For the first 17 years of the Endangered Species Act (1973–1990), the federal government spent a total of approximately $700 million to implement the Act, including land acquisition and grants to the states. The appropriation to the Fish and Wildlife Service for implementing the Act in 1992 was $35.7 million. By comparison, a single mile of interstate highway costs, on average, $39 million. For less than the price of a mile of four-lane highway, the U.S. Fish and Wildlife Service ran its entire endangered species program nationwide for a year. To say that we cannot afford to protect endangered species is absurd.

Here is another way to look at it. The significant number of timber sales on the national forests of this country have lost money. By subsidizing timber sales we over harvested our national forests and, in many places, ruined opportunities for sustainable forests. Every year we—the taxpayers—subsidize the logging of federal forests at the rate of over $250 million. At this rate, the total costs of the entire 18 years of Endangered Species Act could be recovered in a little more than 2 years if below-cost timber sales were eliminated. Applied to wolf reintroduction: we could recover the entire cost of wolf recovery ($12.7 million) by eliminating below-cost timber sales on public lands for nineteen days. . . . Can we afford to reintroduce wolves? Relative to other federal projects, it's a bargain.

Let's take a look at one direct subsidy ranchers receive. (I am a supporter of controlling wolves that kill livestock, and the funding that is allocated in the FEIS budget for ADC). Taxpayers pay approximately 36 million a year to support Animal Damage Control which clearly benefits just a few special interests. . . .

The livestock industry has successfully transferred one of their most basic operational costs to the general public—prevention of predator losses. If you raise Christmas trees, part of the cost, and risk of doing business is losing a few to gypsy moths and ice storms; inherent in the cost of ranching, particularly on public lands, should be the cost and risk of losing livestock to predators. Instead, every year 36 million tax dollars go to kill native wildlife on our public lands so that private industry can make a profit. We shouldn't bar wolves from Yellowstone because of the possibility that a livestock depredation might occur anymore than we should close highways because a cow could get hit by a motorist.

The livestock industry has been very effective in promoting the concept that having wolves in Yellowstone is some sort of environmental luxury, some romantic nonsense that only urbanites and rich easterners advocate, at the costs of the poor beleaguered western livestock industry. Having wolves in Yellowstone is not a luxury but a right, a right of the people in the Yellowstone region and the people of this nation who own Yellowstone and the public lands surrounding it. . . .

Wolves are missing from the Yellowstone region because we eliminated them. They didn't disappear in response to a loss of prey or the lack of habitat; they didn't die out in response to a natural disease or catastrophic event; we didn't just remove wolves that killed livestock. We systematically, intentionally, consciously killed every wolf we could find. And we found them all. Yellowstone has been without wolves for sixty years. We came to accept the absence of wolves as normal. That is the tragedy. Wolves were an integral part of the Yellowstone ecosystem for thousands of years. We made a grave error in exterminating them and their current absence is an ecologically perverse and abnormal situation.

Opponents falsely assume that because there are no wolves, there should be no wolves, and over the last two decades they have very effectively framed the wolf recovery arguments around that assumption. In fact, they have promoted the idea that the return of wolves is somehow radical or extreme. The costs to the general public of not having wolves have virtually been eclipsed by the livestock industry's cry of economic loss or burden. In the West we now live in a "wolf-free" environment. Or is it "wolf-deprived"? Who has gained and who has lost? How do we assign a value to the importance of a predator in an ecosystem? How do we determine the cost of removing one note from a Mozart symphony or one brush stroke from a Rembrandt? How do we quantify the loss to the millions of people who have visited Yellowstone and never had the opportunity to experience the wild, hair-raising chill of a wolf howl or see the real drama of life enacted as elk or antelope streak across sage plains pursued by the predator responsible for their swiftness and agility. Who should be compensating whom?

Because of the passion and the emotion and the politics it is very easy to try to diminish this debate to one of black or white. Opponents of reintroduction want to use wolves as the proverbial "line in the sand" that divides the old West from the new. They want us to see this issue as a distillation of all Endangered Species conflicts, as simply a question of "either/or": Don't touch a tree vs. clear-cut all trees; no wolves vs. fully protected, untouchable wolves; unrestricted grazing vs. no grazing. But these issues, like wolves, come in many different shades.

Both sides have tried to use the wolf as a principle weapon in what I call the crush and conquer warfare. Both sides have used exaggerated rhetoric to alarm and frighten constituents. The tragedy is that while the crush and conquer armies fight their wars, the rest of America stands by, confused, uncertain, and unaware that something they care about might be at stake. I believe this "us against them" rhetoric is simply a construct to enable not the war on the West, but the war from the West. There is no us against them, it is us against us. We are all in it together. Chief Seattle said,

> If all the beasts were gone, we would die from a great loneliness of spirit, for whatever happens to the beast, happens to us. All things are connected. Whatever befalls the earth, befalls the children of the earth.

We have to give up this notion of who is winning and who is losing—we need to return to the things that we care about—the trees, the range, the wildlife, our livelihood, our families, our homes. The real issue is one of making room—for there is still a little room in the West—for hunters, for environmentalists, for ranchers, and for wolves.

Source: Statement of Reneé Askins, Executive Director, Wolf Fund. *Introducing Gray Wolves in Yellowstone and Idaho: Oversight Hearing before the Committee on Resources, House of Representatives, One Hundred Fourth Congress, First Session, on Federal Efforts to Introduce Canadian Gray Wolves into Yellowstone National Park and the Central Idaho Wilderness, January 26, 1995.* Washington, D.C.: U.S. Government Printing Office, pp. 109–114.

DOCUMENT
10.5

President Clinton and the Salvage Rider

"There Is No Choice But to Comply with the Court's Decision"

August 1, and October 28, 1995

During Bill Clinton's eight years in the Oval Office, relations between his administration and wilderness conservationists hit their nadir in 1995. That year, Clinton signed a congressional rescission bill for the FY 1995 budget that included a deeply controversial timber salvage "rider," or amendment. This rider, which was described by sponsors as a vital step in reducing destructive wildfires on federal lands in the West, expedited logging in national forests by mandating increased harvesting of dead and dying trees and suspending or loosening several environmental review regulations. The rider's most controversial elements were 1) provisions that ordered the preparation for sale of timber in the Pacific Northwest that had been covered under Clinton's 1994 "Option 9" or Northwest Forest Plan and 2) language that paved the way, in September 1995, for a district court to order release of so-called Section 318 sales—timber sales dating back to 1990 in Oregon and Washington state that had been suspended for assorted environmental reasons. The court ruled that these Section 318 tracts, which included significant expanses of healthy old-growth forest and totaled an estimated 250 million board feet of timber, could no longer be blocked from development in light of the timber salvage rider.[1]

Environmental groups and their congressional allies in Washington were horrified by Clinton's decision from the outset, as were members of the Pacific Northwest fishing industry who predicted disastrous consequences for salmon and other migrating fish species. Many of these critics, who had always seen the rider as a cynical ploy to increase timber cutting on ecologically valuable public lands, cast Clinton's decision to sign the rider as a shameless betrayal of some of his administration's most stalwart political allies. Their anger was greatly intensified by the September 1995 court decision regarding the Section 318 tracts. The White House, however, insisted that it was blindsided by the court ruling and the eventual full environmental impact of the rider's passage. "Exactly who knew what depended on who was talking, and the ambiguity left considerable space for reinvention," summarized historian Mark P. Moore. "Clinton, who began as an active opponent of the rider (and its exemptions to environmental laws), endorsed the bill with what Republicans called full knowledge of the implications, only to oppose it again with a claim of ignorance soon after logging began. Whether Clinton knew or not, the timber industry would get their logs."[2]

In late 1995 and 1996, congressional Democrats introduced bills that would repeal all or part of the salvage rider, but these were narrowly defeated. Meanwhile, salvage rider timber sales such as one in Montana's Kootenai National Forest, which allowed clear cuts of hundreds of acres of previously protected grizzly bear habitat, brought new waves of condemnation from environmentalists.[3] *In July 1996 Agriculture secretary Dan Glickman issued strict new restrictions for the criteria under which sales could be classified as salvage. Senator Elizabeth Furse (D-Ore.) spoke for many when she said that Glickman's announcement showed that "the White House sees there's been real political trouble with the rider, and it's trying to contain the damage."*[4] *One month later, Glickman told Congress that 157 salvage sales covering 653 million board feet of timber had been canceled as a result of his July directive.*[5] *These developments infuriated the forest products industry and Republican lawmakers.*

Seventeen months after its contentious birth, the salvage rider expired on December 1, 1996. Two months later, the General Accounting Office (GAO) issued a report on the emergency salvage rider program. It found that the U.S. Forest Service offered a total of 4.6 billion board feet of salvage timber during the program's operation, about 1.2 billion board feet more than it had originally planned to offer before the rider's passage. But the GAO also found that fourteen salvage sales contested by environmental groups were handled appropriately by the Forest Service and met the agency's definition of a genuine "salvage sale," and it further stipulated that "the volume of salvage timber offered for sale under the salvage rider could have been significantly greater."[6]

The GAO findings did little to assuage the bitterness felt by all sides of this policy dispute. To the contrary, claims of betrayal and double dealing continued to fly fast and furious from all involved stakeholders. As one analysis observed, "[T]he 1995 salvage rider poisoned relations between the Forest Service, the forest products industry, and the environmental community. Any future attempt to expedite forest health treatment on the

National Forests, regardless of its scientific basis, will have to withstand the challenge that it is not 'just another salvage rider.'"[7]

The following two documents from President Clinton were released at two pivotal points in the salvage rider saga. The first is a memorandum Clinton wrote to administration officials after he first signed the bill. The second is a statement he issued in the aftermath of the 1995 court order that opened Section 318 forestlands to salvage logging operations.

Memorandum on Timber Salvage Legislation

August 1, 1995

Memorandum for the Secretary of the Interior; the Secretary of Agriculture; the Secretary of Commerce; the Administrator, Environmental Protection Agency

   Subject: Implementing Timber-Related Provisions to Public Law 104–19

On July 27th, I signed the rescission bill (Public Law 104–19), which provides much-needed supplemental funds for disaster relief and other programs. It also makes necessary cuts in spending, important to the overall balanced budget plan, while protecting key investments in education and training, the environment, and other priorities.

While I am pleased that we were able to work with the Congress to produce this piece of legislation, I do not support every provision, most particularly the provision concerning timber salvage. In fact, I am concerned that the timber salvage provisions may even lead to litigation that could slow down our forest management program. Nonetheless, changes made prior to enactment of Public Law 104–19 preserve our ability to implement the current forest plans' standards and guidelines, and provides sufficient discretion for the Administration to protect other resources such as clean water and fisheries.

With these changes, I intend to carry out the objectives of the relevant timber-related activities authorized by Public Law 104–19. I am also firmly committed to doing so in ways that, to the maximum extent allowed, follow our current environmental laws and programs. Public Law 104–19 gives us the discretion to apply current environmental standards to the timber salvage program, and we will do so. With this in mind, I am directing each of you, and the heads of other appropriate agencies, to move forward expeditiously to implement these timber-related provisions in an environmentally sound manner, in accordance with my Pacific Northwest Forest Plan, other existing forest and land management policies and plans, and existing environmental laws, except those procedural actions expressly prohibited by Public Law 104–19.

I am optimistic that our actions will be effective, in large part, due to the progress the agencies have already made to accelerate dramatically the process for complying with our existing legal responsibilities to protect the environment. To ensure this effective coordination, I am directing that you enter into a Memorandum of Agreement by August 7, 1995, to make explicit the new streamlining procedures, coordination, and consultation actions that I have previously directed you to develop and that you have implemented under existing environmental laws. I expect that you will continue to adhere to these procedures and actions as we fulfill the objectives of Public Law 104–19.

   William J. Clinton

* * *

Statement on the Court Decision on Timber Sales

October 28, 1995

I am deeply disappointed in the court's decision to force the Forest Service and the Bureau of Land Management to release these sales of healthy ancient timber.

My administration's agreement with the Congress on this issue was significantly different from the interpretation upheld this week by the courts. We agreed that the administration would not have to violate our standards and guidelines for our forest plan and for forest management in general, but only speed up sales that met those standards. We do not believe that this extreme expansion of ancient timber sales was authorized by the 1995 rescission act. My administration will actively pursue a legislative remedy to correct this extreme result.

At this time, however, there is no choice but to comply with the court's decision. The decision forces the release of timber that may lead to grave environmental injury to chinook salmon and other wildlife and damage our rivers and streams. This could jeopardize the livelihoods of thousands of people who depend on the Pacific Northwest's vibrant commercial and sport fisheries.

I have directed the Secretaries of Agriculture and the Interior to work with the companies awarded contracts to seek changes to mitigate any harm to salmon and other species and water quality.

In signing the rescission legislation and in subsequent directives to my Cabinet, I pledged to uphold existing environmental laws and standards. I will continue to fight for those laws and standards.

Source: Clinton, Bill. "Memorandum on Timber Salvage Legislation," August 1, 1995, and "Statement on the Court Decision on Timber Sales," October 28, 1995. *Public Papers of the Presidents of the United States: William J. Clinton, July 1–December 31, 1995.* Washington, D.C.: Government Printing Office, pp. 1192, 1693.

Notes

1. Mark P. Moore, "Colliding Ironies and Clinton's Salvage Rider Rhetoric in the Northwest Timber Controversy," in *Green Talk in the White House: The Rhetorical Presidency Encounters Ecology,* ed. Tarla Rai Peterson (College Station: Texas A&M University Press, 2004), 196.

2. Ibid., 197.

3. Susan Elderkin, "What a Difference a Year Makes," *High Country News,* September 2, 1996, www.hcn .org/issues/89/2748.

4. Quoted in Moore, "Colliding Ironies," 198.

5. Elerkin, "What a Difference a Year Makes."

6. General Accounting Office (GAO), *Emergency Salvage Sale Program: Forest Service Met Its Target, But More Timber Could Have Been Offered for Sale* (Washington, D.C.: General Accounting Office, February 1997).

7. R. N. Sampson and L. A. DeCoster, "The 1995 Salvage Rider," in *Forest Health in the United States* (Washington, D.C.: American Forests, 1998). Available at www.idahoforests.org/health2e.htm.

A Utah Senator Blasts Clinton's Establishment of a National Monument

"President Clinton Is Violating the Spirit of . . . American Democracy Itself"

September 18, 1996

When President Bill Clinton used the venerable Antiquities Act of 1906 to establish 1.7-million-acre Grand Staircase-Escalante National Monument in southern Utah on September 1, 1996, public reaction in the West was decidedly mixed. Environmental groups such as the Southern Utah Wilderness Alliance, which had spearheaded the drive to establish the monument, applauded the move, as did many citizens and politicians from western metropolitan areas. As far as proponents of the designation were concerned, the main subject of debate was not whether Clinton's actions were correct, but whether they were sullied by political opportunism or insufficient regard for local feelings. In High Country News, *for example, one writer opined that "one can applaud the results of the Grand Staircase-Escalante designation and still retain some qualms about the way it was done. It was, by any definition, a sweeping, if legal, exercise of executive power, always a cause for concern in a republic." Another* High Country News *contributor, however, declared that "some [environmentalists] are so cynical about President Clinton's motives and timing that they can't get the bad taste out of their mouths. That doesn't bother me in the slightest. Even Lincoln signed the Emancipation Proclamation with politics in mind. The main thing is, he signed it."[1]*

Clinton's designation of Grand Staircase-Escalante was much less popular in the hamlets of southern Utah and other rural western communities that have traditionally depended on natural resource development on public lands for jobs and economic sustenance. It was also deeply resented by conservative western lawmakers. The same day that Clinton signed the monument into law, U.S. Senator Orrin Hatch (R-Utah) lambasted the decision on the Senate floor. His speech, which is reprinted here, detailed specific grievances of local communities directly affected by the national monument designation and more general objections to the president's action.

In the months following the creation of Grand Staircase-Escalante, some of the local grievances mentioned by Hatch were squarely addressed. In May 1997, for instance, Interior secretary Bruce Babbitt and Utah governor Mike Leavitt announced that the state agency responsible for managing all school trust lands in Utah was transferring ownership of all of the widely dispersed school trust holdings within Utah's parks, monuments, Indian reservations, and most national forests to the federal government in exchange for 139,000 acres of federal land with promising commercial potential elsewhere in Utah and a $50 million cash payment.[2]

Although these efforts reduced tensions somewhat, they failed to appease Hatch and other states' rights advocates. In fact, the Republican-led House twice (in 1999 and 2002) passed bills that would have curtailed the president's authority to create national monuments through the Antiquities Act. The Senate failed to pass similar legislation, however, and with Clinton's retirement in early 2001, the issue faded in urgency.

SENATOR HATCH: Mr. President, for my colleagues who may have missed it, today President Clinton used executive power under the 1906 Antiquities Act to designate nearly 2 million acres in southern Utah as a national monument.

A national monument, as my colleagues know, effectively locks up land within its boundaries preventing any kind of responsible development and limiting existing rights, including water rights, in the second driest State in this Union.

Utah is already home to five national parks, two national monuments, two national recreation areas, seven national forests, one national wildlife refuge, and 800,000 acres of wilderness.

We prize our land in Utah. We believe we ought to preserve as much of it as we can, and we would like to continue working on legislation to designate more wilderness in Utah.

But the process the President is using is flawed and inherently unfair. I just say, the unilateral action taken by the President today is out of bounds. Members from Utah's congressional delegation and our State Governor had to read about this proposal in the *Washington Post*. That is the first time we heard about it. There has been no consultation whatsoever in the development of the proposal. We have seen no maps; no boundaries; there have been no phone conversations; no TV or radio discussion shows; no public hearings; absolutely nothing from this President.

None of the procedures for review and comment that are built into our environmental laws, such as the National Environmental Policy Act or FLPMA have been followed. These procedures are a part of our law precisely to guard against the Federal Government from usurping State or local prerogatives without public knowledge or comment.

While the 1906 Antiquities Act may, indeed, give the President the literal authority to take this action, it is quite clear to me that in using this authority, President Clinton is violating the spirit of U.S. environmental laws and, indeed, of American democracy itself.

It was no doubt inconceivable before today that any President of the United States would take such dramatic action—action that so dramatically affects any State—without due diligence. And it is plain to this Senator that the White House either flunks the test of due diligence or takes this action deliberately without regard to its negative impact on our State.

What should be especially relevant, and alarming, to every Senator is that this disregard for established public law requiring public input, let alone the disregard of established traditions of democracy, can be applied elsewhere other than Utah. Today, Utah; tomorrow, your State.

I hope my colleagues will not brush off the precedent this Executive action creates. There are numerous negative consequences to this President's action today. Among the most serious is the effect on education in Utah.

Many States in the West depend on school trust lands to help finance their educational systems. In fact, 22 States, most of the States west of the Mississippi River, have trust lands.

Utah relies heavily on the income produced by these trust lands to help finance our schools. The national monument proclaimed by President Clinton will capture approximately 200,000 acres of Utah school trust lands and render them useless to Utah schoolchildren. I say to my colleagues, and to President Clinton if he is listening, this is a potential loss of $1 billion to Utah schools, and these environmental extremists are already talking that it is only $36,000 a year. That is how ridiculous they are.

There is not a single State in America that can afford to lose that kind of money for education—that is $1 billion worth—let alone Utah, which, because we have so much public nontaxable land, is always straining to fund education.

What is even more appalling is the fact that the resources President Clinton is taking away from Utah kids, in effect, is their own land. These school trust lands were deeded to Utah to be held in trust for our children's education, and with one stroke of the pen, these 200,000 acres will be gone.

The Utah Public Education Coalition, which includes professional educators, State and local administrators, the PTA and school employees, have come out strongly against this arbitrary action by the President.

I ask unanimous consent that their letter to President Clinton, position statement and resolution, be printed in the Record at the conclusion of my remarks.

The PRESIDING OFFICER: Without objection, it is so ordered.

SEN. HATCH: Mr. President, another adverse ramification of the President's action today is inability to responsibly extract the high-quality, clean-burning, low-sulfur coal that lies in the Kaiparowits coal basin. Please note, the coal is in the basin, not on the Kaiparowits Plateau. This is not a strip mine. This is a mine right in the side that will not even show.

The basin has been called the "Saudi Arabia of coal." There are about 62 billion tons of coal here, about 16 billion tons of which can be mined with existing technologies. That is enough coal to fulfill Utah's energy needs for the next 1,000 years, and, I might add, the energy needs of this country. That is environmentally sound coal that could be blended with the dirty coal from the East, and it would be in the best interest of the environment of this country.

I find it a little ironic that the President wants to prevent the mining of this clean, environmentally beneficial coal while we are still paying billions of dollars to clean our dirty air from burning high-sulfur, dirty coal.

These coal reserves, in addition to being a financial asset to our State, are a critical energy resource for our entire country. We are being extremely shortsighted if we forget this fact.

How can we justify sending U.S. troops to keep the Middle East stable and to keep the oil flowing when President Clinton refuses to develop energy resources right here in our own country? We have to do both. We have to act in the best interest of the energy needs of this country. What the President did today is not in the best interest.

Mr. President, we should not forget the impact the restrictions on water rights will have, not only on Utah, but also on Colorado, New Mexico, Nevada, Arizona, and California.

Utah is the second driest state in the union. This action by President Clinton would deny our state the right to develop its water in southern Utah.

Finally, Mr. President, I wonder how the Administration plans to pay for the operations and maintenance of what would be the largest national monument in the United States.

Already, the National Park Service is stretched to the limit. Adding nearly 2 million acres to their inventory—almost the size of Yellowstone—raises real questions about our stewardship of this land. We want to preserve land in southern Utah. There is no question that Utahans want to protect as much land as we can. We would support a well thought out proposal for additional national park or wilderness areas in southern Utah.

We also recognize that there are differences of opinion concerning the number of acres and management prerogatives. We believe those are matters for negotiation and compromise, not for making political hay with important special interest groups.

We would like to work with President Clinton to develop a sound preservation plan. And, the offer is still open to work together on this.

But, frankly, I say to my colleagues, real damage has been done here—both to Utah and to the tradition of open debate. The failure even to consult prior to making this decision should be considered devastating to representative democracy.

Source: Hatch, Orrin. Floor Statement on President Clinton's Designation of Grand Staircase-Escalante National Monument, September 18, 1996. Available at http://thomas.loc.gov/home/r104query.html.

NOTES

1. Quoted *in Give and Take: How the Clinton Administration's Public Lands Offensive Transformed the American West,* ed. Paul Larmer (Paonia, Colo.: High Country News Books, 2004), 20, 69.

2. Michelle Nijhuis, "Monumental Deal over Utah's Trust Lands," *High Country News,* May 25, 1998, www.hcn.org/issues/131/4199?searchterm=Monumental+Deal+Over+.

DOCUMENT 10.7

Interior Secretary Babbitt Defends Dam Removal

"America Overshot the Mark in Our Dam Building Frenzy"

August 4, 1998

During the 1990s a clear shift in federal policy toward dam removal and river restoration became evident in many parts of the country. The Clinton Administration oversaw the removal of several longstanding dams that were determined to be ecologically destructive, and officials announced that federal agencies intended to assess the continued need for other dams that had been challenged on grounds of safety, economic viability, and their impact on river ecosystems. Clinton's Interior secretary, Bruce Babbitt, was a vocal champion of this shift toward a new era of river management, in part because he was able to call on a rapidly growing body of environmental and scientific studies that touted the ecological and economic benefits of dam removal. "Americans are finding promise, not peril, in the unleashing of rivers," Babbitt stated. "By removing dams, they are diversifying their economies, healing watersheds, reducing Endangered Species Act headaches, and restoring beauty, vigor, and recreation to their downtown centers."[1]

During Babbitt's eight-year tenure at the Department of Interior, twenty-two major dams were removed from American rivers and dozens of smaller dams were dismantled. This trend continued after Clinton's departure from the White House. From 1999 to 2009 an estimated 600 outdated dams were removed across the country, according to the conservation group American Rivers.[2]

In the following speech from 1998, Babbitt explains the various reasons why he views dam removal and the adoption of more environmentally friendly dam operation regimens as beneficial not only to river ecosystems, but also to the public interest.

In keeping with the theme of this year's conference, I would like to briefly revisit some aquatic ecosystems I have toured since we last met. Usually my trips to rivers involve a canoe and paddle, or flyfishing rod and reel. More recently I arrive with sledgehammer in hand, to celebrate destruction of dams.

I suspect this breaks with tradition. Six decades ago, President Franklin Delano Roosevelt and his Interior Secretary Harold Ickes toured the country to dedicate dams, new dams, powerful dams, including four of the largest dams in the history of civilization. They built dams for barge traffic, for electricity, for irrigation, for drinking water, for flood control. For most of this century, politicians have eagerly rushed in, amidst cheering crowds, to claim credit for the construction of 75,000 dams all across America. Think about that number. That means we have been building, on average, one large dam a day, every single day, since the Declaration of Independence. Many of these dams have become monuments, expected to last forever.

You could say forever just got a lot shorter.

Starting last June 17: I hoisted a sledgehammer to mark the removal of four dams, opening 160 miles of the Menominee River flowing between Wisconsin and Michigan.

September 23: I visited the Olympic Peninsula to see two Elwha River dams which the Administration plans to remove to restore one of the fabled Chinook salmon runs of the river.

December 17: I took my sledgehammer to punch open the 55 year old, 260-foot Quaker Neck Dam on the Neuse River, opening 925 miles of fish spawning habitat.

May 26: Beside the Kennebec River, in the heart of Augusta, Maine, I signed documents clearing the way for the removal of the 160-year-old 917-foot Edwards Hydro Dam.

July 14: On Butte Creek, in the heart of California's agricultural Central Valley, I took the first crack at breaking up McPherrin Dam to restore Chinook Salmon in that Sacramento river tributary.

July 15: One day later, in downtown Medford, Oregon, I unpacked the sledgehammer to breach Bear Creek dam, the first dam removed in the Pacific Northwest, for Coho salmon.

Every stop on this dam-busting tour attracts enormous local, regional and national attention. In fact, a lot more attention than we earned with our paddle and canoe during the National Heritage Tours in 1995 and 1996. Even more than we got with our fly rod during the rare native fishing tours last year.

So what is it about the clang of sledgehammer on concrete that evokes such a response?

I believe that huge public interest reflects a deep, widespread understanding that America overshot the mark in our dam building frenzy. In the Nineteenth Century, construction of the Erie Canal triggered a spasm of canal building that went on and on, beyond any realistic expectation of economic return. Having a canal became the symbol of a progressive community. Everyone just had to have one, irrespective of its utility.

In this century, dam building has moved on a similar trajectory—dams that were clearly justified for their economic value gradually gave way to projects built with excessive taxpayer subsidies, then justified by dubious cost/benefit projections.

The public is now learning that we have paid a steadily accumulating price for these projects in the form of: fish spawning runs destroyed, downstream rivers altered by changes in temperature, unnatural nutrient load and seasonal flows, wedges of sediment piling up behind structures, and delta wetlands degraded by lack of fresh water and saltwater intrusion. Rivers are always on the move and their inhabitants know no boundaries; salmon and shad do not read maps, only streams.

The clang of the sledge hammer is one of the oldest sounds known to man. Yet now, at the end of the twentieth century, we are using it to ring in an entirely new era of conservation history, moving beyond preservation or protection towards a deeper, more complex movement, the affirmative act of restoration.

Restoration grows out of the same stewardship impulse as preservation, but pushes beyond, as one might renovate an old, neglected farm to inhabit once again. Perhaps Aldo Leopold pointed the way with his sand county shack. Yet he was only one man, and his focus was more on land than the nearby river. The coming age of restoration requires the active involvement of the citizens who live on the entire watershed. Most of all it requires a creative act; we must see not only what is, but envision what can be. It requires us to reach back into our history in order to grasp the future in which we might live.

Restoration invites us to understand how the natural world—with its complex storms, fires, forests, watersheds and wildlife—functions as a whole. And the best unit to measure that whole, how it is more than the sum of its parts, is the river that runs through us. For that river reflects the condition of every single acre of the whole, integrated watershed. Thirty six centuries ago, Emperor Yu of China advised "To protect your rivers, protect your mountains." That same rule applies today. To restore our aquatic ecosystems, look beyond the water's edge out onto the land that borders it. For the two are inseparable. What happens on that land inevitably is reflected in our rivers.

But even protecting mountains, we discover, goes only so far. I doubt that Emperor Yu, for all his wisdom, could foresee the construction of Three Gorges Dam or what it would do to the life of that river. And lest we condemn China too quickly, I should point out that we in America have been slow to recognize the ecological costs of dams. And slower still to envision watershed restoration through dam removal.

I began to reflect on these issues over the course of many days and nights spent in the Grand Canyon over the last half century. I hiked and boated and camped beside the Colorado River before Glen Canyon was built in the 1960s. In those years it was a wild, unpredictable, brown, sediment-laden stream flooding into the early summer, then settling down in the winter. The gates of Glen Canyon were closed in 1963. Today, you see an ice cold, Jell-O-green river, manipulated up and down, rising and falling on a daily cycle, flushed with the regularity, and predictability, of a giant toilet.

Over time, as I floated down the river, I saw trees on talus slopes wither and die for lack of water. I saw sandbars—once covered with arrow, willow and cottonwood—disappear, the banks scoured down to granite boulders. I saw once plentiful native fish—unlike those anywhere on earth—driven back to the brink of survival in only a few isolated tributaries.

It may seem hard to comprehend now that, at the time, no one even considered the possibility of these dramatic changes in a National Park located just ten miles downstream. At the time Glen Canyon was built, we were still thinking of dams as stand alone projects that, lamentably, flooded out nice scenery upstream. But without consequences for the entire river system. And the Grand Canyon is only one of thousands of examples.

Nowhere has the impact of dams been more visible than on aquatic life. We once believed that freshwater flowing to the sea was "wasted." By trying to hold it back as long as possible, we blocked out anadromous fisheries from their ancient spawning grounds. In the 19th century, from Maine to the Chesapeake on down to Florida, in the course of damming rivers, we virtually destroyed the rich Atlantic salmon, shad, striped bass, herring and sturgeon as they made their way inland from the Atlantic.

And in this century, with our massive projects up and down the Pacific-bound rivers, we have repeated this process of destruction, virtually decimating the great salmon and steelhead runs of the northwest, by continuing to build dams clear up into the 1970s. This year, we learn that roughly one third of all fish, two thirds of all crayfish, and three quarters of the bivalve freshwater mussels in America are rare or threatened with extinction.

Let's give the economists their due: We seem to value something only when it becomes rare. The loss of fisheries that we once took for granted has led to a new urgency demanding ways we can replenish them. Every single dam to which I brought my sledge-hammer was removed for the benefit of one or more endangered aquatic species.

Yet despite this progress there are still—if we use established figures—74,993 dams in America, blocking 600,000 miles of what had once been free flowing rivers. That's about 17 percent of all rivers in the nation. If one wanted to unleash every one of those rivers—something I clearly don't advocate as policy—and restore those watersheds, it would take a lot more than one person swinging a sledgehammer every few months.

But as we contemplate future ceremonies involving dams, here are some considerations:

1. Dams are not America's answer to the pyramids of Egypt. We did not build them for religious purposes and they do not consecrate our values (even if some are named after Presidents). Dams do, in fact, outlive their function. When they do, some should go. There is a dam in Pawtucket, Rhode Island, spanning the Blackstone River. It powered the first mechanical mill in America, birthplace of our Industrial Revolution. Today, even as we move centuries beyond the water powered mills, we have chosen to preserve that dam as a historic marker of where we once were as a nation. As such, it is the exception that proves this rule.

2. There also comes a point in the life of a dam where we can get the same benefits in other ways. On Butte Creek, the Sacramento River tributary, irrigation farmers could replace McPherrin Dam and three others with an irrigation pump and siphon. Quaker Neck Dam, which stored water for power generators, could be replaced with a different cooling system.

3. Moreover, in some cases the price for the benefits is simply too high; the dam has grown too expensive relative to the loss of fish. On the Kennebec River, the age, location (close to the river's mouth), huge environmental costs and low generation at Edwards made it a relatively easy call for removal. Owners of dams coming out on the Menominee found that taking a holistic approach to the entire watershed would save them time, money and energy. Some could be phased out, while others reoperated with screens, fish passage and drawdowns.

But all these conditions rest on the values and the scientific understanding of the larger community. Who, besides nature, decides whether a dam stands or falls?

One recent column made a reference to "Babbitt, the nation's dam-remover-in-chief" as if I were some Roman emperor giving thumbs up or down. The truth is I have not brought my sledgehammer to a single dam that was not approved for removal by consensus of the inhabitants of the watershed. Each community made a thoughtful, deliberative choice in how they could restore their river, whether as part of a downtown restoration—as Medford, Oregon, and Augusta, Maine—or to open miles of spawning in rural areas, from North Carolina to California. Many of these consensus based decisions are brought about by democratic, voluntary watershed councils that are cropping up all over the country.

Larger dams pose more complex issues, for there are more, and bigger, economic stakeholders. Entire industries, the price of electricity for millions of people, water storage for cities. We are rapidly reaching a consensus with Congress to remove the dams at Elwha and Glines Canyon. The debate over four dams on the Snake River will surely continue for years, beyond my time in this office. Yet even when a community decides that a dam should remain, it may discover progressive new ways to operate it that restore some of the ecological damage. That explains the public interest in the artificial flood that we released at Glen Canyon to restore Colorado River beaches downstream in the Grand Canyon.

So what can you do as citizens and scientists to shape this restoration movement? What you can do as ecologists is research and examine and document the benefits that might be accrued by restoration of the aquatic ecosystem by removal or reoperation of a given dam in the watershed you may be involved in. We have plenty of powerful stakeholders willing to reassert the known, traditional benefits of dams—irrigation, hydropower, urban water authorities, engineers. But the process of putting a value on the native life intrinsic to watersheds and ecosystems is something new, and the degree to which you can do so goes a long way.

There is another way of expressing this: My parents' generation gloried in the construction of dams across America's rivers. My generation saw how those rivers were changed, deformed, killed by dams. Your generation must help decide if, how and where those dams stand or fall.

I am reminded of Ecclesiastes:

> One generation passeth away,
>
> and another generation cometh:
>
> but the earth abideth always. . . .
>
> All the rivers runneth to the sea,
>
> yet the sea is not full;
>
> to the place where the rivers flow,
>
> there they flow again. . . .

A beautiful passage, but now haunting, for it is no longer true due to changes in my lifetime. I think back to my beloved Colorado River, which I hiked and rafted and saw change before my eyes. Once one of the mightiest rivers in America, it no longer makes it to the sea. That is a shame. As our generation passes, the toughest decisions rest firmly in your hands.

Thank you.

Source: Babbitt, Bruce. "Dams are Not Forever." Remarks of the Secretary of the United States Department of Interior to the Ecological Society of America Annual Meeting, August 4, 1998.

NOTES

1. Bruce Babbitt, "Unleashing the Power of Rivers," *Living in the Runaway West: Partisan Views from Writers on the Range* (Golden, Colo: Fulcrum Publishing, 2000), 129.

2. "The 10th Anniversary of the Removal of Maine's Edwards Dam." American Rivers, 2009, www.americanrivers.org/our-work/restoring-rivers/dams/projects/edwards-anniversary.html.

DOCUMENT
10.8

President Clinton Unveils the Roadless Area Conservation Rule

"Nearly 60 Million Acres of Pristine Forest Land for Future Generations"

January 5, 2001

In October 1999 President Bill Clinton astounded political allies and foes alike when he announced ambitious plans to permanently preserve as much as forty million acres of roadless national forests as wilderness. This announcement, which came in the form of a speech at George Washington National Forest in Virginia, was followed later the same day with a presidential directive to Agriculture secretary Daniel Glickman to develop "regulations to provide appropriate long-term protection for most or all . . . currently inventoried 'roadless' areas, and to determine whether such protection is warranted for any smaller 'roadless' areas not yet inventoried."[1] This directive was universally seen as a strategic decision to bypass a recalcitrant Republican-led Congress and rely instead on the broad rulemaking authority of the administration.

Clinton's proposal elicited a storm of protest from Republicans, timber and mining interests, states' rights advocates, and assorted other opponents who decried it as a brazen federal land grab, but environmental groups and Democratic allies in Congress expressed elation and described the bid as one of the most significant environmental policy initiatives in U.S. history. Over the ensuing year, the Forest Service held more than 600 public meetings nationwide on Clinton's "Roadless Rule" and studied the potential scientific and economic ramifications. The Forest Service received a record total of 1.6 million public comments on the measure, with expressions of support for the Roadless Rule winning the day by twenty to one (this lopsided response was due in no small measure to the U.S. Public Interest Research Group, the Sierra Club, the Heritage Forests Campaign, and other organizations that mobilized members and canvassed neighborhoods in support of the initiative).[2]

One week after the disputed 2000 presidential election took place, the U.S. Forest Service released its Final Environmental Impact Statement (FEIS) on the wilderness preservation plan. It proclaimed that Clinton's Roadless Area Conservation Rule—as it was officially called—would apply to all fifty-eight million acres of roadless wilderness in all national forests. As a result of sustained pressure from conservation groups and support from important players such as U.S. Forest Service chief Michael Dombeck, the final rule even applied to roadless areas in Alaska's sixteen-million-acre Tongass National Forest, long regarded as the single most valuable timber prize in the country by logging companies and their benefactors in Washington.[3]

On January 5, 2001, Clinton, Glickman, and Dombeck all appeared at a ceremony to mark the administration's adoption of the Roadless Area Conservation Rule. Clinton's statement following Glickman's signing of the order is excerpted here. Ken Rait, director of the Heritage Forests Campaign, offered a representative expression of conservationist sentiment when he described the signing as "a great moment in history, and it is something for which our children will express gratitude."[4]

On January 12, the rule was published in the Federal Register; *once a rule has been published in the* Register *it automatically takes effect after sixty days—after which time it can only be overturned by Congress or an official new rulemaking initiative. Eight days later, however, George W. Bush began his presidency. Mindful of opposition to the Roadless Rule from western states, resource industries, and other political constituencies, the Bush Administration immediately moved to block implementation of the order. This move marked the opening salvo in a titanic, decade-long, legal and political struggle between conservation and development stakeholders over the future of the Roadless Rule.*

. . . In one way or another, all of us have come here, and I now have come to know many of you in this audience. And I know we come from different backgrounds and have traveled different paths through life, but somehow or another, we have in common our view that nature is a priceless but fragile gift, an important part of the fabric of our lives, and a major part of our responsibility to our children and our children's children.

I grew up in a State where more than half the land is covered by forest. I grew up in a town surrounded by a national park. Most of the people who enjoy our public lands are like the people I grew up with—hard-working families who very often could afford no other kind of vacation and can afford nature's bounty because our forebears made sure that it belongs to them, and it belongs to us all.

I am grateful that we can stand here today because of the work done by Theodore Roosevelt, Gifford Pinchot, and John Muir. I am grateful for all those who have walked in their footsteps for a hundred years. I am grateful that for the last eight years I had a Vice President who spoke out strongly for these values and these policies and helped us to do what we have done to be good stewards of the land.

We have saved and restored some of our most glorious natural wonders, from Florida's Everglades to Hawaii's coral reefs, from the redwoods of California to the red rock canyons of Utah. We have helped hundreds of communities, under the Vice President's leadership, to protect parks and farms and other green spaces. We've built new partnerships with landowners to restore and preserve the natural values of our private land.

We've modernized the management of our national forests to strengthen protections for water quality, wildlife, and recreation, while ensuring a steady and sustainable supply of timber. We have greatly expanded our cooperation with other nations to protect endangered species and threatened areas, like tropical forests.

In a larger sense, I hope and believe we have helped to put to rest the old debate between economic growth and environmental protection. We have the strongest economy in a generation and the cleanest environment in a generation. And I might say, parenthetically, that as we come to grips—as inevitably we must—with the challenge of climate change . . . those of you who are here today will have to be in the vanguard reminding people that we can break the iron chain between more greenhouse gas emissions and economic growth. It is not necessary any longer, but we have to be smarter about what we're doing.

Today we take, as Secretary Glickman said, a truly historic lead on the path of environmental progress. Throughout our national forest system there are millions of acres of land that do not have and, in most cases, have never had roads cut through them. These areas represent some of the last, best unprotected wild lands anywhere in America.

These uniquely American landscapes are sanctuaries to hike and hunt and ski and fish. They're a source of clean water for millions of our fellow citizens. They are havens for wildlife and home to about one quarter of all threatened or endangered species in our Nation.

On a beautiful fall afternoon more than a year ago now, Secretary Glickman and many of you joined me at Virginia's Washington and Jefferson National Forest to launch a process to safeguard these lands. As Secretary Glickman just described, we reached out to the American people to help us develop the plan. More than a million and a half responded.

I'm told that more Americans were involved in shaping this policy than any land preservation initiative in the history of the Republic. Thanks to their extraordinary support, the process is now complete.

Sometimes, progress comes by expanding frontiers, but sometimes, it's measured by preserving frontiers for our children. Today we preserve the final frontiers of America's national forests for our children.

I am proud to announce that we will protect nearly 60 million acres of pristine forest land for future generations. That is an area greater in size than all our national parks combined. From the Appalachian Mountains to the Sierra Nevada, forest land in 39 States will be preserved in all its splendor, off limits to road-building and logging that would destroy its timeless beauty.

This will include protection for the last great temperate rain forest in America, Alaska's Tongass National Forest. This initiative will provide strong, long-term protection for the Tongass, while honoring our commitment to address the economic concerns of local communities. We will work with them to ensure a smooth transition and to build a sound, sustainable economic base for the future.

Indeed, our entire approach to managing our national forests has been based on striking the right balance. For example, under this rule, the Forest Service still will be able to build a road or fight a fire or thin an area in an environmentally sensitive way, if it is essential to reducing the risk of future fires. And even as we strengthen protections, the majority of our forests will continue to be responsibly managed for timber production and other activities.

Bear in mind, as has already been said, only about 4 or 5 percent of our country's timber comes from our national forests. And less than 5 percent of that is now being cut in roadless areas. Surely we can adjust the Federal program to replace 5 percent of 5 percent. But we can never replace what we might destroy if we don't protect those 58 million acres.

Ultimately, this is about preserving the land which the American people own for the American people that are not around yet, about safeguarding our magnificent open spaces, because not everyone can travel to the great palaces of the world, but everyone can enjoy the majesty of our great forests. Today we free the lands so that they will remain unspoiled by bulldozers, undisturbed by chainsaws, and untouched for our children. Preserving roadless areas puts America on the right road for the future, the responsible path of sustainable development.

The great conservationist Aldo Leopold, who pioneered the protection of wild forest roadless areas, said, "When we see the land as a community to which we belong, we may begin to use it with love and respect." If there is one thing that should always unite us as a community, across the generations, across parties, across time, it is love for the land. We keep faith with that tradition today, and we must keep faith with it in all the tomorrows to come.

This is a great day for America. I thank all of you who made it happen. It is your achievement, but it is a gift that you give to all future generations, to walk in the woods, fish in the streams, breathe the air. The beauty of our wild lands will now be there for our children, and all our children, for all time to come. And I hope you will always be very proud that you were a part of it.

Source: Clinton, Bill. "Remarks on Signing the Roadless Area Conservation Policy," January 5, 2001. *Public Papers of the Presidents of the United States: Bill Clinton, 2000–2001.* Vol. 3, pp. 2827–2829. Washington, D.C.: U.S. Government Printing Office, 2001. www.gpoaccess.gov/pubpapers/search.html.

NOTES

1. Bill Clinton, "Protection of Forest 'Roadless' Areas: Memorandum for the Secretary of Agriculture," October 13, 1999. White House Council on Environmental Quality, October 13, 1999, http://clinton4.nara.gov/CEQ/forest.html.
2. Tom Turner, *Roadless Rules: The Struggle for the Last Wild Forests,* (Washington, D.C.: Island Press, 2009), 46.
3. Ibid., 32–33, 43–46.
4. Douglas Jehl, "Road Ban Set for One-Third of U.S. Forests," *New York Times,* January 5, 2001, www.nytimes.com/2001/01/05/us/road-ban-set-for-one-third-of-us-forests.html.

DOCUMENT
10.9

The Mountaintop Mining Rule

"The Regulation Will . . . Remove Ambiguity from Clean Water Act's Regulations"

May 3, 2002

During the late 1980s and 1990s coal operators in the Appalachian region increasingly utilized a controversial mining method wherein mountaintops containing coal deposits were sheared off with machinery and explosive charges so miners could get at the coal beneath. This practice of "mountaintop removal" elicited outraged protests from environmental and other public interest groups. They objected to these practices not only because of the impact they had on mountaintop scenery and wildlife habitat, but also because the operations were dumping thousands of tons of rocky debris into surrounding valleys, where they smothered hundreds of miles of streams. The latter damage was seen as a clear and blatant violation of the Clean Water Act, so opponents went to court to block the practice, with considerable success.

Bombarded by legal challenges and adverse court rulings, Appalachian coal companies reduced their use of mountaintop mining in the late 1990s. In 2002, however, the Bush Administration removed the single greatest legal impediment to mountaintop removal when it approved a small but momentous change in wording to the Clean Water Act. Essentially, Bush officials reclassified the rocks and rubble that were being dumped in Appalachian streams as "fill material" rather than "waste." This alteration breathed new life into mountaintop removal mining.

The following document is the press release that the Army Corps of Engineers and Environmental Protection Agency issued on May 3, 2002, to explain the rule change. The press release frames the change as a sensible step to reduce legal confusion about Clean Water Act provisions and thus improve environmental protection of fragile waterways. Indeed, much of the press release is devoted to reassuring the public about the administration's dedication to responsible environmental stewardship. Opponents of mountaintop mining in Congress and the environmental movement, however, described the change as a death sentence for Appalachian streams. They also characterized the rule change as further evidence of the Bush Administration's predilection for weakening environmental regulations through backdoor manipulations rather than high-profile legislative proposals.

The U.S. Environmental Protection Agency and the U.S. Army Corps of Engineers today announced that they are taking action to better coordinate federal programs affecting protection of wetlands and streams. Completing a regulation proposed by the Clinton Administration in 2000, the Army Corps of Engineers is adopting EPA's approach to the Clean Water Act's definition of "fill material," which has been in place since 1977. The regulation will not only remove ambiguity from Clean Water Act's regulations, but also enhance environmental protection of our wetlands and streams by prohibiting the dumping of trash or garbage in them.

In addition, the agencies will apply new conditions to permits issued to regulate the placement of dirt and rock from mountaintop mining in streams. The Department of Interior is also developing regulations intended to improve environmental protection by reducing the volume of mining discharges in streams. EPA and the Corps, working with the Department of Interior's Office of Surface Mining and Fish and Wildlife Service and the State of West Virginia, are preparing an Environmental Impact Statement evaluating the impacts of mountaintop removal mining in Appalachia and developing recommendations for further improvements in the agencies programs regulating this practice.

"We are committed to working with the affected States to reduce mining-related environmental impacts, while providing the nation with the advantages of cleaner burning coal," EPA Administrator Christie Whitman said.

"Mountaintop mining is a long-established practice in Appalachia, and this Administration is committed to working with the affected states to strengthen the environmental safeguards governing this practice. We are working to establish a regulatory environment that is clear, predictable, fair and fosters good environmental stewardship," said Undersecretary of the Army Les Brownlee.

The Corps and EPA will publish in the Federal Register a rule to harmonize differences between existing EPA and Army Corps of Engineers regulations by adopting EPA's effects-based approach to the definition of the term "fill material." The final rule is substantially identical to the rule proposed in 2000, but includes additional environmental protections. For example, under the new rules, garbage or trash will not be permitted in the nation's waters.

As a result of improvements already implemented in West Virginia by the agencies and the State in 1998, there have been 30 percent fewer valley fills and a reduction in the overall stream impact of almost 25 percent from these fills. These improvements are now being applied elsewhere in Appalachia and we anticipate similar reductions in mining related impacts.

The Administration is also undertaking several related actions to further bolster protection of Appalachian watersheds impacted by mining.

The Corps is taking steps now to put tougher new restrictions on mining activities that can be permitted by establishing limits on the size of valley fills that can be built in Appalachian streams. The Corps is also requiring more effective mitigation to compensate for environmental impacts. The Office of Surface Mining will be proposing changes to its regulations intended to ensure that mining discharges in streams are reduced in both size and number. OSM's changes will also require that better information is provided by permit applicants regarding their projects so that adverse environmental impacts can be more effectively addressed.

EPA, the Corps, Office of Surface Mining, the U.S. Fish and Wildlife Service and the State of West Virginia are currently preparing a joint Environmental Impact Statement that evaluates the environmental impacts of mountaintop coal mining and provides recommendations for improving Federal regulatory programs responsible for the review of proposed mining operations. The draft Statement will be released later this summer for public review and comment.

The Office of Surface Mining is responsible for developing the rules that govern mountaintop removal coal mining under the Surface Mining Control and Reclamation Act. Most Appalachian states administer these rules through programs delegated to them by OSM.

EPA is responsible for the development and approval of the standards, criteria, and effluent guidelines that govern impacts to the Nation's waters under the Clean Water Act. EPA approves state water quality standards in accordance with the Act, which are achieved primarily through programs administered by the states. EPA also fosters the development of state wetlands programs, as well as provides environmental standards and oversight for the administration of the wetlands permit program under section 404 of the Act.

The Corps regulates the discharge of rock and dirt into wetlands and streams from mining operations under the section 404 permit program of the Clean Water Act. Discharges under the permit program may only be authorized in compliance with environmental standards that include mitigation for unavoidable impacts to the aquatic environment.

Source: U.S. Army Corps of Engineers. "Corps and EPA Clarify Clean Water Act Definition; New Environmental Improvements Also to Be Made in Appalachian Mining Rules." Press release, May 3, 2002. www.usace.army.mil/CECW/Documents/cecwo/reg/fillrelease.pdf.

Revising the Roadless Rule

"The Rule Allows Governors . . . to Develop Regulations to Manage Roadless Areas"

May 5, 2005

One of the major policy events in the evolution of the "Roadless Rule," a Clinton Administration bid to protect fifty-eight million acres of federal forestlands from road building, logging, and other commercial development, was a 2005 attempt by the Bush Administration to give western states much greater influence over the conservation and management of affected national forests within their boundaries. Under the revised Bush plan, state governors were given an eighteen-month window to petition the federal government to open state forestlands included in the Roadless Rule to logging, mining, and other development or to keep them protected. These petitions would, under the new rules, be subject to approval from Bush's secretary of agriculture, Mike Johanns. The press release announcing this new roadless forest policy is reprinted here.

    Response to the state petition option was swift from industry and environmental groups and their respective supporters in Congress and state legislatures. Pro-conservation governors in Oregon, California, Washington, and New Mexico joined together to challenge the repeal of the Roadless Rule in court. A similar lawsuit against the Bush state petition rule was filed by a coalition of twenty conservation organizations in October 1995.

    As expected, wilderness conservationists assailed the decision as a giveaway to big timber and big mining. "They are going to target roadless areas that have commercial timber that industry is interested in, and the pro-industry governors in Western states are going to help them," asserted Sean Cosgrove, the Sierra Club's national forest specialist. "Today's announcement is just one more lousy proposal from the administration put in the context of the entire assault on the national forests."[1] But the plan also sparked criticism from unexpected quarters such as the libertarian Cato Institute, which supports the idea of privatizing national forests and most other public lands: "We can't help but suspect that the real policy objective behind this new rule is to transfer [logging] fights to political playing fields where environmentalists are typically weaker and industry is politically stronger."[2]

    Many western policymakers, however, expressed strong support for the petition plan. The governors of Alaska and Idaho, for example, declared that it would finally give individual states a legitimate voice in the process. Representatives of the forest products industry and logging-dependent communities also praised the change. "Despite the environmental rhetoric, chain saws, bulldozers and drilling rigs are not gassing up to enter roadless areas," said Chris West of the American Forest Resource Council, an industry group. "But the public ought to be gearing up to participate in a process to manage and protect these important lands."[3]

    On September 20, 2006, Idaho—which holds 9.3 million acres of roadless wilderness, second only to Alaska in terms of total roadless area—became the first state to submit a petition that would allow road building and logging in some of its roadless areas (this petition, later modified and supported by conservation groups such as Trout Unlimited and the Idaho Conservation League, was approved and went into effect in October 2008). That same day, however, a California district court struck down the Bush revision and reinstated the Clinton-era Roadless Rule. This decision was swiftly appealed by the Bush Administration and assorted western states and industry groups, and more legal jousting ensued.

    In January 2009, however, President Barack Obama—who had campaigned in support of Clinton's Roadless Rule—assumed office. Five months later his administration announced a total moratorium on road building in national forest wilderness outside of Idaho. The momentum for permanent wilderness protection for roadless areas became even greater on August 5, 2009, when a federal court formally scuttled Bush's plan and reinstated the Clinton-era rule everywhere but in Idaho and Alaska's Tongass National Forest, which had been exempted in a separate 2003 decision. The court found that the state petition plan violated the Endangered Species Act and the National Environmental Policy Act. It also stated that "[t]he Forest Service's use of a categorical exemption to repeal the nationwide protections of the Roadless Rule and to invite States to pursue varying rules for roadless area management was unreasonable. It was likewise unreasonable for the Forest Service to assert that the environment, listed species, and their critical habitats would be unaffected by this regulatory change."⁴ In the wake of these developments, the Obama Administration is widely expected to press to make the Roadless Rule a permanent and unassailable feature of U.S. forest policy in the twenty-first century.

Agriculture Secretary Mike Johanns today announced a final rule that invites input from state governors in the conservation and management direction for inventoried roadless areas within national forests. This rule will provide environmental benefits and help to ensure that the needs of local communities are considered in roadless area conservation.

"Our actions today advance President Bush's commitment to cooperatively conserve inventoried roadless areas within our national forests," Johanns said. "USDA is committed to working closely with the nation's governors to meet the needs of our local communities while protecting and restoring the health and natural beauty of our national forests."

The new rule was developed after the previous regulation, issued January 12, 2001, was struck down by a U.S. District Court in July 2003 and deemed in violation of both the National Environmental Policy Act and the Wilderness Act.

The rule sets a straightforward, collaborative path toward conserving inventoried roadless areas by working with the states on regulations specific to the needs and requirements of each state. It incorporates the department's five conservation principles for inventoried roadless areas. They are:

- Make informed decisions to ensure that inventoried roadless area management is implemented with reliable information and accurate mapping, including local expertise and experience.
- Work with states, tribes, local communities and the public through a process that is fair, open and responsive to local input and information.
- Protect forests to ensure that the potential negative effects of severe wildfire, insect and disease activity are addressed.
- Protect communities, homes and property from the risk of severe wildfire and other risks on adjacent federal lands.
- Ensure that states, tribes and private citizens who own property within inventoried roadless areas have access to their property as required by existing law.

The rule allows governors to petition the secretary of agriculture to develop regulations to manage roadless areas that meet the specific needs within each state. USDA will accept state petitions from governors for 18 months after the effective date of the final rule. During the state-petitioning process, the Forest Service will continue to maintain interim measures to conserve inventoried roadless areas.

Petitions must identify areas for inclusion and may also include ways to protect public health and safety, reduce wildfire risks to communities and critical wildlife habitat, maintain critical infrastructure (such as dams and utilities), and ensure that citizens have access to private property.

Once a state has submitted its petition and the secretary accepts it, the Forest Service will work with the state to develop and publish a subsequent state-specific rule that addresses the management requirements set forth in the petition. The state-specific rulemaking process will include any required National Environmental Policy Act analysis and invite public input during a notice and comment period. If a state chooses not to file a petition, inventoried roadless areas within that state will continue to be managed in accordance with the direction set forth in each national forest's land and resource management plan.

While 38 states and Puerto Rico have inventoried roadless areas on National Forest System lands within their boundaries, 56.6 million acres, or 97 percent, of all inventoried roadless areas in the country are contained within 12 states. Those states are Alaska, Arizona, California, Colorado, Idaho, Montana, Nevada, New Mexico, Oregon, Utah, Washington and Wyoming.

The department is also announcing the establishment of a national advisory committee to provide advice and recommendations to the secretary on implementing this rule. Members of the committee will represent diverse national organizations interested in the conservation and management of National Forest System inventoried roadless areas.

The final rule and the notice announcing the establishment of the advisory committee will be published in the *Federal Register* this week and are available at http://www .roadless.fs.fed.us.

Source: USDA Forest Service Acts to Conserve Roadless Areas in National Forests: Announces National Advisory Committee to Help Implement New Rule. Press release, U.S. Department of Agriculture, May 5, 2005. www.usda.gov/wps/portal/!ut/p/_s.7_0_A/7_0_10B?contentidonly=true&contentid=2005/05/ 0148.xml.

Notes

1. Bettina Boxall, "Bush Ends Ban on Roads in National Forests," *Los Angeles Times*, May 6, 2005, http:// articles.latimes.com/2005/may/06/nation/na-roadless6.
2. Jerry Taylor and Peter Van Doren. "The Fight Over the Roadless Rule," The Cato Institute, July 21, 2004, www.cato.org/pub_display.php?pub_id=2748.
3. Felicity Barringer, "Bush Administration Rolls Back Rule on Building Forest Roads," *New York Times*, May 6, 2005, www.nytimes.com/2005/05/06/politics/06roadless.html.
4. "Obama Administration Joins Roadless Rule Battle," *OMB Watch*, August 18, 2009, www.ombwatch .org/node/10314.

DOCUMENT
10.11

A Timeline of Michigan Deer Hunting Regulations

"2006: Over 1,160,000 Deer Licenses Total Sold"

1859–2006

Sustainable management of game and wildlife has long ranked as one of the leading responsibilities of state natural resource agencies. This is a tremendously challenging task in many areas of the country, especially in regions that have experienced high rates of population growth, economic expansion, and land development. In the early twentieth century state legislatures began providing wildlife agencies with desperately needed laws and regulatory authority to more effectively carry out these responsibilities. The repertoire of regulatory tools available to departments and agencies have since expanded steadily through the decades, and modern sportsmen are required to heed a much more extensive body of hunting and fishing regulations than did their forefathers. Some sportsmen resent state wildlife departments and their rules as overbearing or capricious, but many others perceive them to be necessary—if imperfect—institutions to ensure the continued health and vitality of game populations and regional ecosystems.

In 2007 the Wildlife Division of the Michigan Department of Natural Resources published a historical chronology of the state's white-tailed deer hunting regulations dating back to 1859, when the state issued its first deer hunting restriction. This document, excerpted here, offers a striking example of how state hunting and fishing regulations have expanded over time.

Year	Description
1859	• Open season: August 1 to December 31 statewide. . . .

1881	• Open season:
	  o UP (Upper Peninsula): August 15 to November 15.
	  o LP (Lower Peninsula): October 1 to December 1
	• Unlawful to take deer with spotted or red coat or while deer is in the water.
	• Unlawful to use pit, pitfall, or traps in the taking of deer.
	• Deer may be taken only for food.
	• Unlawful to ship deer or parts thereof in any form from the state. . . .

1891	• Open season:
	  o UP: September 25 to October 25.
	  o LP: November 5 to November 25.
	• First deer hunting closures to increase deer numbers: Allegan and Van Buren counties closed for three years. . . .

1895	• Open season: November 1 to 25.
	• First deer hunting license required.
	  o Deer license fee: resident $.50, non-resident $25.00.
	  o 14,477 resident licenses sold, 22 non-resident licenses sold.
	• First bag limit: five deer per hunter per year. . . .

1905	• Open season: November 10 to 30 (until 1911) • Deer hunting closures extended and expanded: Bois Blanc Island and Lapeer, Huron, Sanilac, Tuscola, Macomb, Allegan, Ottawa, St. Clair, Lake, Osceola, Clare, Mason, Manistee, Wexford, Missaukee, Newaygo, Mecosta, Isabella, Benzie, Leelanau, Grand Traverse, Oceana, Gladwin counties closed until January 1, 1908. Kalkaska County closed until September 17, 1910. • Bag limit: two deer per hunter. • 14,878 resident licenses sold, 105 non-resident licenses sold. . . .
1915	• Open season: November 10 to 30 • Bag limit: one deer per hunter. • Age restrictions created: individuals under the age of 17 must be accompanied by parent or legal guardian when obtaining license and while hunting. • 21,061 resident licenses sold, 178 non-resident licenses sold. . . .
1926	• Open season: November 15 to 30 (until 1962) • Deer hunting closures extended and expanded: Emmet, Charlevoix and all counties south of the north line of Township 20 North closed to deer hunting for a period of five years by the Conservation Commission. . . .
1936	• Deer hunting closures extended and expanded: Leelanau County and all counties and parts of counties lying south of M-47 and M-46 between Bay City and Muskegon and including the Thumb closed to deer hunting until 1947. . . .

Year	Description

1937
- First archery season and license:
  - o Available for Iosco and Newaygo counties only.
  - o November 1 to 14.
  - o Bears and antlered deer may be harvested.
  - o 186 archery licenses sold.
- Possession of firearms by archery hunter or in archer's vehicle unlawful.
- Sportsmen allowed either archery or firearm license but not both.
- Over 150,000 deer hunters hunted during the regular firearm season. . . .

1939
- Firearm deer season: November 15 to 30
- Archery deer hunting season:
  - o Counties open to archery deer hunting same as during the firearm season.
  - o November 1 to 14.
  - o Antlered deer only may be harvested.
- Age limit: minimum age 14 to hunt deer (firearm or archery)
- Deer harvest reported: 45,148 deer harvested during firearm season, 4 deer harvested during archery season.
- Bag limit: one deer (archery or firearm equipment).
- Bear not included on deer hunting license. . . .

1948
- Regular firearm deer season:
  - o Entire state open to firearm deer hunting for first time since 1891.
  - o Antlered deer only.
  - o November 15 to 30 (statewide through 1961).
- Firearms limited to shotguns in southern Michigan. . . .

1964
- Regular firearm deer seasons:
  - o UP west of M-77: open Saturday on or nearest November 15 (Nov. 14 to 29).
  - o Remainder of the state regular firearm season: November 15 to 30.
- Any-deer firearm permits—legal to harvest any deer in 62 areas with special permit during regular firearm deer seasons.
- Bear license valid with a deer license.
- Bear license fee: $5.00 resident, $25.00 non-resident.
- Over 500,000 deer hunters hunted during the regular firearm season. . . .

1970
- UP (except Bois Blanc Island) closed to antlerless deer hunting with firearms.
- Any-deer firearm permits—legal to harvest any deer in 58 areas with special permit during regular firearm deer seasons.
- Archery age limit created: minimum age 12 to hunt deer with archery equipment.
- Sportsman's license available. Valid for firearm, archery, and muzzleloader hunting in the respective seasons. Included deer licenses, bear, small game, & fishing. Resident fee: $18.50.
- Military license available to servicemen on furlough. Valid for deer and small game hunting during the open seasons; over 3,000 sold. . . .

1977
- Any-deer firearm permits—legal to harvest any deer in 76 areas with special permit.
  - o Areas 106 to 135 open November 15 to November 21.
  - o Areas 2 to 49: November 15 to November 30.
- Hunter orange: deer hunters required to wear a vest, jacket, or cap of a highly visible orange color, variously referred to as hunter, fluorescent, blaze, or fluorescent blaze orange.
- Bag limit: two deer per hunter per year provided one deer is taken with firearm and the other with archery equipment during the appropriate season.

Year	Description

- Landowners not receiving regular Hunter's Choice permits were given the opportunity to obtain Landowners Limited Permits for use on their own property or adjoining private land with permission of the owner, during the hunter's choice season. This was done to increase the harvest of antlerless deer on certain private lands. . . .

1993
- Ground blinds on public land:
  - Unlawful for ground blinds constructed of manufactured materials to be placed on public land prior to seven days before the hunting season.
  - All ground blinds must be removed at the end of hunting season.
  - Label with owner's name and address required.
  - State game and wildlife areas: blinds built of manufactured materials must be removed daily.
- Firearm regulations: firearms must be unloaded, and arrows in a quiver when afield outside hunting hours.
- Private land antlerless drawing:
  - Landowner must have 40 or more acres of huntable land within DMUs open to hunting to apply for drawing.
  - First priority given to guests, lessees, and family members not residing on the property. . . .
- South Fox Island deer hunting:
  - Drawing established for deer hunting permits.
  - Antler restriction established: unlawful to take an antlered deer with less than six antler points.
- Severely disabled hunters may apply for a permit to use crossbows for hunting deer.
- Hunters permitted to use salt to draw deer into shooting range during the hunting season. . . .

1998
- Secondary archery and firearm deer licenses eliminated.
- Combination deer license established: two tags issued with this license.
- Late archery season closed on January 3.
- TB [tuberculosis] regulations created.
  - TB control permits established.
  - TB management area established (Northeast LP north of M-55 and east of I-75).
  - DMU 066 the special restrictions on taking antlerless deer only with an antlerless deer license removed from due to TB management area expansion.
  - Unlawful to bait or feed deer for recreation in TB management area.
  - Core TB management area (DMU [Deer Management Unit] 452):
    - Early firearm deer season on private land established for antlerless deer only: October 17 to October 26.
    - Late firearm deer season on private and public land established for antlerless deer only: December 11 to January 3.
- Antlerless deer hunting regulations:
  - Late firearm antlerless deer season on private land in all but 19 DMUs in the LP: December 19 to January 3.
  - Private land antlerless deer licenses valid with permission on any private land within specific DMU.
  - Acreage requirements to qualify for private land antlerless deer licenses reduced in Southern LP to 5 acres from 10 acres or more of contiguous huntable land.
  - Unlimited antlerless deer license quotas in 63 LP DMUs.

Year	Description

- "No spike" rule on South Fox Island, Drummond Island, and DMU 101 (in Iosco County): antlered deer harvest restricted to deer with at least two or more points on one side, each one or more inches in length.
- DMAPs [Deer Management Assistance Permits] expanded to include areas of serious deer overpopulation as documented by the DNR.
- Hunting from elevated platforms:
  - Firearm deer and bear hunters may hunt from elevated platforms.
  - Treestands and raised platforms cannot be placed on public lands prior to September 1 and must be removed one day after the deer season closes.
  - Screw-in tree steps unlawful on public lands.
- A dog may be used to locate down or mortally wounded deer if the dog is on a leash and no firearm or archery equipment is in possession.
- Bag limit: two antlered deer (one must have at least one antler with four or more antler points one inch or longer).
- Over 835,000 deer hunters hunted during the regular firearm season.
- Over 2,200,000 deer hunting licenses sold (archery, firearm, combination, and antlerless deer licenses). . . .

2006
- Antlerless deer hunting regulations:
  - Application date for private land antlerless licenses changed from July 1 to 31 to July 15 to August 15.
  - Youths allowed to purchase an antlerless license during the application period (no application necessary).
  - A telephone number of a landowner granting permission to hunt is required to purchase a private land antlerless deer license.
  - Permission to hunt a parcel of at least 40 contiguous acres is required to purchase a private land antlerless deer license in Zone 1 and 2 (except within special regulations units).
  - Antler point restrictions in DMUs 152, 155, and 252 removed (remain in effect in DMU 122).
  - Number of private land antlerless deer licenses per hunter limited to three, with no more than two in Zones 1 and 2 combined.
- QDM antler point restrictions removed from DMUs 152, 155, and 252 after survey of landowners and hunters did not meet 66% approval to retain the restrictions. Antler point restrictions remain in effect in DMUs 045 and 122. "No spike" rule remains unchanged from 2001.
- Youth firearm deer season for 10–16 year olds: September 23 and 24. Youth 10 and 11 years restricted to archery equipment.
- Legal age to archery hunt deer lowered to 10; legal age to firearm deer hunt on private land lowered to 12.
- The Managed Deer Hunt permit authority is expanded to include public land requiring an access permit and open to a special firearm deer hunt by lottery.
- Online hunter harvest survey available to report deer harvest.
- Over 690,000 deer hunters hunted during the regular firearm season.
- Over 1,160,000 deer licenses total sold (combined archery, firearm, combination, and antlerless deer licenses). . . .

Source: Michigan Department of Natural Resources, Wildlife Division. "Deer Hunting Regulations." 2007. www.michigan.gov/documents/dnr/DEER_REGULATION_HISTORY_210705_7.pdf.

**DOCUMENT
10.12**

A New Pact for Colorado River Water Use

"You Have Found the Serene Waters of Partnership and Cooperation"

December 13, 2007

In 2007 federal officials at the Department of the Interior reached a long-sought new water allocation pact with western states within the Colorado River basin. The accord, which experts described as the most significant western water policy initiative since the 1922 Colorado River Compact, outlined a new regional agreement for sharing the river's water resources. The agreement included explicit regulations for maintaining water levels in the region's two main reservoirs (Lake Powell and Lake Mead), which have lost nearly half of their water since 1999. It also set triggers in periods of drought for signatory states to implement water conservation measures. In addition, the pact permitted water-hungry Las Vegas to consume a greater share of the river's water; in return, the city agreed to finance a new $172 million reservoir project in California that will enable that state to capture additional water that would otherwise flow into Mexico.

The agreement, which came after two and a half years of tense negotiations—and in the eighth year of a record drought across much of the basin—was hailed by supporters as a pathway to give all seven states the water they need to meet growing needs from business and industry and fast-growing residential populations. "I think for the first time in 85 years we are on the same page," stated Herb Guenther, Arizona's director of water resources.[1] Water managers in the affected states also said that the accord would reduce expensive litigation over Colorado River water allocations and relieve some of the intrastate tension that has bedeviled the region over the previous few decades. Some environmental groups, hydrologists, and climatologists, however, warned that the water conservation and smart growth recommendations contained in the pact failed to squarely confront a basic reality: that the region's limited water supplies cannot accommodate continued economic and population growth. "There is more water on paper than there actually is on the landscape," said John Weisheit of Living Rivers, a Utah-based environmental group.[2]

On December 13, 2007, Interior secretary Dirk Kempthorne delivered a speech to the Colorado River Water Users Association that summarized the benefits of the Colorado River pact and other recent western water agreements from the perspective of the Bush Administration while also touching on some of the daunting water issues that the American West—and the world—still faces. His remarks are excerpted here.

We have had good news and bad news. Fortunately, the good far overshadows the bad.

The bad news is that the historic drought continues in the Colorado River Basin with no sign of ending. The good news is that we have achieved remarkable victories in the basin that chart a course for the future through times of drought and surplus alike. Landmark accomplishments that change for the better the way we manage our water—providing more security, more transparency, and more flexibility to all seven basin states.

Last year, I challenged you to work together to resolve the water issues of the basin, rather than force me as water master to unilaterally intervene or a federal court to decide your future. You rose to the challenge. I applaud you.

This is truly an historic moment. As the Colorado River navigates a 1,500-mile journey down mountains through canyons and across desert landscapes, you have navigated the shoals of history. You have steered around the cataracts and sharp boulders of litigation and acrimony. You have found the serene waters of partnership and cooperation. This is the most important agreement among the seven basin states since the original 1922 Compact. An extraordinary achievement.

It was not easy reaching this day. A couple of times we peered over the edge of the abyss, the white water churning under our keel, threatening to capsize our vessel. But we stayed afloat. We reached the goal. In doing so, we have provided a course for the rest of the country—and other river basins around the world—to follow. . . .

Unfortunately, the drought situation both here in America and around the world threatens to get worse.

Here in the West, for example, runoff in five of the seven Colorado River basin states is projected to decline by more than 15 percent during the 21st century. If the basin warms and evaporation increases, we could face a situation in which the amount of precipitation we are receiving today produces significantly less runoff in the future.

Imagine this happening across the country—and around the world—and you see the challenge ahead.

This is why what we have done together here in the Colorado River basin is so extraordinarily important.

In the past seven years, the management of the Colorado River Basin has been a top priority of this Administration. Together, we have proven that, through cooperation and partnership, we can successfully manage a river that meets the water and power generation needs of millions of people and irrigates one of our most important agricultural breadbaskets. We've done this during a period of sustained and unprecedented drought. Look at the list of accomplishments:

- In 2001, the Interim Surplus Guidelines.
- In 2003, the California 4.4 settlement.
- In 2004, the Arizona Water Settlements Act.
- In 2005, the Lower Colorado River Multi-Species Conservation Plan.
- In 2006, the preliminary agreement on the shortage guidelines and coordinated operations of Lake Powell and Lake Mead.

We had enormous momentum going into 2007 to secure a future of cooperation and partnership in the basin. But we also faced significant risks.

When I spoke to you a year ago, I challenged you to follow four principles.

First, cooperate, don't litigate.

Second, seek creative solutions to the challenges you face.

Third, hope for the best but expect the worse—prepare for continued drought.

Fourth—and most important—don't fumble the ball in the Red Zone. Don't march down the field only to drop the ball on the one-yard line. Punch it across the goal line.

How did we do? Today, I am pleased to say that 2007 has been the best year yet. This is a landmark year.

First and foremost, we reached final agreement on the Coordinated Operations of Lake Powell and Lake Mead and on the Shortage Guidelines. For the first time since 1922, all seven basin states have reached an agreement on the management of the Colorado River. This is a triumph of federalism under our Constitution. It is a victory for both the states and the United States.

This is an agreement to share adversity. It is easier to be gracious when you have surplus. Much tougher in times of scarcity. Sharing adversity is what good neighbors do. You have been good neighbors.

During the process of reaching this agreement, we saw a remarkable consensus emerge in the basin among stakeholders including the representatives of the seven basin States. This consensus had a number of common themes:

- encouraging conservation
- planning for shortages
- implementing closer coordination of the operations of Lake Powell and Lake Mead
- preserving flexibility to deal with further challenges such as climate change and persistent drought
- implementing operational rules for a long—but not permanent—period in order to gain valuable operating experience
- and continuing to have the federal government facilitate—but not dictate— informed decision-making in the Colorado River Basin.

The detailed, technical work by the Bureau of Reclamation to identify options and facilitate solutions during this process also was a key element in our shared success. . . .

When I sign the Record of Decision in a few moments, we will adopt four key elements of river management.

- First, the new guidelines establish rules for shortages—specifying who will take reductions and when they take them. This is essential for prudent water planning in times of drought.
- Second, the new operational rules for Lake Powell and Lake Mead will allow these two massive reservoirs to rise and fall in tandem, thereby better sharing the risk of drought.
- Third, the new guidelines establish rules for surpluses, so that when we are blessed with ample runoff, we will have rules in place to distribute the extra water.
- Fourth, the new rules will address the ongoing drought by encouraging new initiatives for water conservation.

Together, these guidelines put the entire basin in a much better position to deal with the impacts of both wet cycles and dry cycles, droughts and surpluses.

I am particularly impressed by the innovative approaches you have taken to conserve water, especially the construction project known as Drop 2. The project will be located in California, but it is being paid for Nevada. It will create a small—but important—reservoir to conserve additional water for Nevada's use over the next two decades. After that, the additional water will benefit all state users in the lower basin states. This is truly an innovative example of cooperation among states. A win together. It is an idea that may help other states facing shortages meet their needs.

I was impressed with other conservation measures—for example, the agreement allows water users to obtain future credit for conserving water and leaving it in Lake Mead. It also sets up a framework to allow cities to contract with willing farmers to temporarily fallow fields in dry years while respecting the basin's agricultural heritage.

As these conservation initiatives move forward and new ones are developed, we will review them through a transparent process. That means that as we are reviewing them, you will have the opportunity to review them as well.

Perhaps most important for the long term, the Record of Decision activates a legal agreement among the seven basin states that contains a key provision. The states are committing themselves to address future controversies on the Colorado River through consultation and negotiation—as an absolute requirement—before resorting to litigation.

I am convinced that 50 or 100 years from now, the people of the basin will look back on 2007 in the same way they do on 1922. This is why this is truly historic.

I am also convinced that as other states—and other countries—struggle to resolve their water issues in the coming decades, they will look to this agreement as a model. A way to embrace consensus rather than conflict. To conserve and share water rather than fight over water. To ensure that everyone walks away from the table a winner. . . .

The Record of Decision was our most significant accomplishment in 2007, but it was only one.

We resolved all the litigation issues surrounding the All-American Canal. The lining project—a key element of the 2003 California 4.4 Settlement—is now back on track.

We are working with Mexico to resolve cross-border water issues. In August, I met with Mexican Ambassador Arturo Sarukhan and we issued a Joint U.S. Mexico Statement on Colorado River Cooperation. The Joint Statement reflects both nations' commitment to identifying solutions to stretch limited supplies of water, especially during this historic drought.

Before I left Washington yesterday, I signed documents that complete all the requirements necessary to put the Arizona Water Settlements Act into full force and effect.

This is yet another historic milestone.

This Act will provide benefits in Arizona and New Mexico and represents the largest Indian Water Rights Settlement in United States history. It is an extraordinary accomplishment that required enormous effort by the state of Arizona, tribes, local water users and the federal government. I applaud all of you who spent years—decades really—making this a reality.

I don't have to tell you, however, that for all our success in 2007, we must continue to be vigilant. We still have outstanding issues such as the adaptive management of Glen Canyon Dam. No doubt other potentially contentious issues will crop up in the future. We must build on the spirit of partnership that has brought us to this day. To this hour.

We also have to deal with our national water issues. We have a huge information gap. We haven't done a full inventory of our nations' water resources for three decades. We have serious questions about our long-term supplies.

Furthermore, as we have seen the High Plains Aquifer and other subsurface water diminish, we have come to realize we don't fully understand the relationship between the use of surface and subsurface water.

And, of course, there continues to be the elephant in the room: climate change. I am determined not to get ensnared in the politics of this issue. The simple fact is the earth is warming. We have to figure out how this is going to affect our water supplies. We have to come up with an adaptive management approach that will allow us to be good stewards. . . .

Source: Kempthorne, Dirk. Remarks at Signing of the Record of Decision for New Colorado River Management Strategies, December 13, 2007. www.doi.gov/secretary/speeches/121708_speech.html.

NOTES

1. Quoted in Randal C. Archibold, "Federal Pact Would Allocate Colorado River Water to Western States," *New York Times,* November 9, 2007, www.nytimes.com/2007/12/09/world/americas/09iht-10water.8658554.html.

2. Randal C. Archibold, "Federal Pact Would Allocate Colorado River Water to Western States," *New York Times,* November 9, 2007, www.nytimes.com/2007/12/09/world/americas/09iht-10water.8658554.html.

**DOCUMENT
10.13**

Oregon's Ballot Measure 49

"A Workable Land Use Policy That Will Allow Us to Keep Our Precious Oregon Assets"

November 6, 2007

Oregon has long been regarded as a trailblazer in the United States in fighting urban sprawl and preserving open space. In the 1960s and 1970s state lawmakers, led by Republican governor Tom McCall, passed a variety of measures to manage and limit land development statewide. Denouncing "grasping wastrels of the land," McCall framed "sagebrush subdivision, coastal condomania, and the ravenous rampage of suburbia in the Williamette Valley" as dire threats to Oregon's natural beauty and quality of life.[1] During this same period, city planners in Portland, the largest city in the Willamette Valley, implemented an ambitious plan to contain sprawl through an emphasis on mass transit (rather than new highway construction) and, most important, the establishment of a permanent "greenbelt" of undeveloped land around the city's designated "growth boundaries."

These various steps, carried out at municipal and state levels, succeeded in slowing the rate of land development in Portland and many other parts of Oregon. But in Portland and elsewhere, they also triggered a surge in real estate prices, which reduced home affordability. In addition, critics assailed many of the smart growth policies as placing unacceptable—even draconian—limits on individual property rights. Regional planning schemes of the 1990s further affirmed the commitment of the Portland area to building "up not out"—increasing population density and commercial activity in already developed areas so as to preserve green space. The results of these growth-control initiatives provided fodder for both advocates and opponents of anti-sprawl regulations. According to scholar Robert Bruegmann, proponents assert that "the Portland region today remains a highly livable, green metropolis that has managed to control its own destiny by careful planning. They claim that the Portland System has allowed the area to avoid excessive road building, introduce more public transportation, enhance the vitality of downtown, and conserve farmland at the urban periphery." But Bruegmann adds that "critics of the system believe that there has already been considerable pressure in some neighborhoods to accept higher densities than residents want . . . [and] that the process has been highly inequitable because more affluent communities have been able to maintain their low densities and deflect population growth to less affluent neighborhoods."[2]

In 2004 the state's nationally renowned "smart growth" program was rocked to its core by a successful ballot measure championed by property rights advocates. Measure 37, as it was known, was passed by Oregon voters by a whopping 61 percent to 39 percent margin, and it became effective on December 2, 2004. The new law compelled the state to pay restitution to longtime (pre-1973) property owners when land-use restrictions reduce the value of their property or, if payment is not made, allow landowners to develop their property without penalty. The impact of Measure 37 became almost immediately apparent. "Because there is virtually no local or state money to pay landowners," reported the Washington Post, *"Measure 37 is starting to unravel smart growth laws that have defined living patterns, set land prices, and protected open space in this state for more than three decades."*

Oregon's conservation and smart growth contingents, however, were galvanized by the setback. As sales of farmland and other green tracts to land developers exploded across the state, they became convinced that the majority of Oregon residents were having second thoughts about Measure 37. State lawmakers agreed, and they placed a new proposal—Measure 49—on the November 6, 2007, special election ballot. This law, claimed supporters, would rein in the excesses contained in Measure 37 and strike an appropriate "balance" between land conservation and property rights. Measure 49 passed easily, garnering 62 percent of all votes.

Following are excerpts from the official ballot proposal. The first item is a summary of Measure 49, followed by a selection of "Arguments" favoring and opposing the measure (there were a total of 117 paid—$500 for inclusion—Arguments contained in the voter's pamphlet for the election).

Ballot Title 49

Modifies Measure 37; Clarifies Right to Build Homes; Limits Large Developments; Protects Farms, Forests, Groundwater

Result of "Yes" Vote: "Yes" vote modifies Measure 37; clarifies private landowners' rights to build homes; extends rights to surviving spouses, limits large developments; protects farmlands, forestlands, groundwater supplies.

Result of "No" Vote: "No" vote leaves Measure 37 unchanged; allows claims to develop large subdivisions, commercial, industrial projects on lands now reserved for residential, farm and forest uses.

Summary: Modifies Measure 37 (2004) to give landowners with Measure 37 claims the right to build homes as compensation for land use restrictions imposed after they acquired their properties. Claimants may build up to three homes if previously allowed when they acquired their properties, four to 10 homes if they can document reductions in property values that justify additional homes, but may not build more than three homes on high-value farmlands, forestlands and groundwater-restricted lands. Allows claimants to transfer homebuilding rights upon sale or transfer of properties; extends rights to surviving spouses. Authorizes future claims based on regulations that restrict residential uses of property or farm, forest practices. Disallows claims for strip malls, mines, other commercial industrial uses. See Explanatory Statement for more information . . .

Arguments in Favor

A Message from Four Oregon Governors

Dear Fellow Oregonian:

We come from different political parties, different parts of Oregon, different occupations, and we each had the privilege of serving Oregon as Governor during very different times.

For all our differences, however, we share a love of Oregon. We appreciate the legacy we have been given, and understand the tremendous responsibility we have to protect that legacy and pass it long.

Oregon is loveable—and livable—because Oregonians have actively engaged in protecting that legacy. That's why we have the bounty that other states have lost:

- Majestic forests that offer beauty, recreation and a livelihood for many communities.
- Irreplaceable farmland that supports a rich and varied agricultural economy; and
- A balance that protects Oregon's unique assets and the property rights of Oregonians.

That is why we come together to ask you to vote Yes on Measure 49.

Measure 49 will fix the flaws in Measure 37—flaws that threaten the Oregon we love. Measure 37, passed in 2004, has opened the door to massive development that will destroy the farmland, forestland and water resources we have today.

Measure 49 will deliver what Oregonians had in minds when they voted on Measure 37: a balance that protects Oregon's farms, forests, and water and allows individual property owners to build more than one home on their property.

Measure 49 will also deliver something bigger: a workable land use policy that will allow us to keep our precious Oregon assets—the things that make Oregon special—and be fair to property owners.

Please join us in voting Yes on Measure 49.

Governor Vic Atiyeh (1979–1987)

Governor Barbara Roberts (1991–1995)

Governor John Kitzhaber MD (1995–2003)

Governor Ted Kulongoski (2003–present)

(This information furnished by Theodore Kulongoski.)

Polk County Farm Bureau for Measure 49

If you want the "little guy" to get a fair shake, vote "Yes" on Measure 49.

Over 42% of claims for development under Measure 37 seek 1–3 homesites.

Measure 49 gives these claims a green light and transferability.

That is what Oregon voters had in mind in 2004 when they approved Measure 37.

Measure 49's limits are needed. Nearly 58% of Measure 37 development claims are for large housing subdivisions, nearly 3,800 of them right on farm and forest land. The proposed subdivisions average 134 acres each; and over 60% are in the Willamette Valley.

These subdivisions threaten farms. How? Go to Oregon Department of Agriculture's website, http://www.oregon.gov/ODA/NRD/m37.shtml, and see for yourself. ODA's maps show 969 Measure 37 subdivision claims scattered throughout the heart of vibrant farm areas of Marion, Clackamas, and Washington counties alone—Oregon's TOP THREE producing farm counties.

These subdivisions would be an economic and environmental disaster for the Willamette Valley.

Measure 49 gives Oregon voters a chance to say, "Wait a minute! I didn't intend Measure 37 to undermine Willamette Valley agriculture, or to ruin the Valley's beauty."

Measure 49 allows what Oregon voters intended—some development for the little guy, but preserving our farmland:

- 3 homesites if the claim is on high value farm or forest land, or in a restricted groundwater area. These homesites must be clustered at one end of the property and can only be 5 acres each, so they have the least impact on large swaths of farmland;
- 4–10 lots if a claim is on any other type of land, based on proof of loss of property value—backed up by an appraisal.

Under Measure 49, every Measure 37 claim goes forward. But Measure 49 sets limits that we can live with.

Measure 49 fixes the wrongs of Measure 37. Vote "YES" on Measure 49.

Thank you, from the heart of the Willamette Valley.

(This information furnished by Paul Thorp, Polk County Farm Bureau.)

The Association of Oregon Rail and Transit Advocates (AORTA) urges a YES vote on Measure 49.

Measure 49 helps fix problems with Measure 37.

In 2004 voters were told Measure 37 was meant to allow individual property owners to build a few houses on their land. Most voters did not realize they were also allowing "timber" companies and developers to create huge subdivisions and commercial developments on prime farm and forest lands far beyond our urban growth boundaries.

Measure 37 requires local governments to either pay for claimed loss of value or waive current land use regulations on the property. Measure 37 provides no money for strapped local governments to compensate these massive claims. Cut services or raise taxes to pay claims? Not likely! *Without the changes proposed in Measure 49, there is nothing to stop these developments and this will produce the kind of sprawl that Oregonians have consistently opposed.*

Washington County alone has 902 claims totaling over $750 million. 700+ claims involve 55,206 acres, most for urban density subdivisions *well outside* the Urban Growth Boundary!

For scattered, massive subdivisions, far from existing development, the only practical way to travel is by car. Sprawl increases the costs of nearly all services: police, fire, roads, water, sewers, social services, transit, etc. Because development fees will never cover all these costs, *this increases your taxes.* Sprawl forces more people to drive longer distances, creating more traffic.

AORTA is a citizen organization founded in 1976 to encourage balanced, environmentally sound, fiscally responsible, safe transportation. We recognize that our economy and environment suffer from a poorly functioning transportation system. How we manage our growth and land use can positively or negatively affect the travel options we can afford our citizens. Information at: www.aortarail.org.

Fix Measure 37: Fairness without costly sprawl. YES on Measure 49

(This information furnished by Robert Krebs, president, Association of Oregon Rail & Transit Advocates [AORTA].)

Protect Oregon's Hunting Heritage: Vote Yes On 49

In Oregon we are blessed with wildlife habitat that sustains big game like elk, deer, cougar, black bear, and big horn sheep. Unfortunately, poorly-planned development allowed by Measure 37 threatens to destroy and hamper access to much of the critical winter range that this wildlife needs to survive.

Measure 37 claims span 750,000 acres across Oregon—on mostly forest and farmland. *Over 4,000 subdivisions could result from these claims, permanently destroying the habitat that big game needs to survive.*

If we don't act to fix the flaws of Measure 37, we'll lose much of the big game that make Oregon's outdoors so unique. Here are just a few of the claims that Measure 37 loopholes have unleashed:

- A highway rest area, public tourism center, and RV campground with gift shop, convenience store and restaurant on open space conservation in Southern Oregon;
- Subdivisions and commercial development on open space conservation land in Jefferson County;
- Commercial development and subdivisions on over 6,000 acres in Jackson County;
- Loss of protected big game habitat to residential development on over 800 acres in Union County;
- 142 condos, town homes, and houses on open space conservation land in Douglas County.

The Oregon Division of the Izaak Walton League of America supports Measure 49 because it provides the responsible conservation necessary to sustain healthy wildlife populations for future generations. Measure 49 will protect the habitat that sustains our big game and other wildlife from development into housing tracts, strip malls, and big box stores, while protecting Oregon families' rights to build a few homes on their land.

Please Protect Oregon's Hunting Heritage by Voting "YES" on Measure 49

(This information furnished by Dawn A. Olson, Oregon Division, Izaak Walton League of America.)

Arguments in Opposition

We urge you to read Measure 49 *very carefully* before voting.

Measure 49 is not what it appears to be.

Measure 49 passed by a single vote in the Oregon Legislature. It is poorly drafted and will lead to years of litigation and political infighting in Salem.

The Ballot Title Is Intentionally Misleading:

What you read on your ballot for Measure 49 was not written by the Attorney General or Secretary of State. It was not reviewed by the Oregon Supreme Court for neutrality and objectivity. The legislature used a rare political trick to draft the language using public opinion polls—to find the most deceptive "political" language. Why? Because special interest groups don't want you to know what is really in Measure 49.

They Had to Mislead Voters to Hide the True Intent Of Measure 49

Measure 49 will allow state and local government to take your home and property without compensation, wiping out laws that require government to pay fair value for what it takes.

Measure 49 Repeals Your Vote on Measure 37

Section 4 of Measure 49 repeals your vote on Measure 37 and replaces it with a complex process for property owners, which experts say will not work, and opens property owners up [to] lawsuits, fees, and years of frustration. The most offensive part is that Measure 49 was forced through the Legislature without a single public hearing!

Implementing Measure 37

Our job this session was to implement your overwhelming votes supporting Measure 7 and Measure 37 to protect property owners. The Legislature ignored your votes, invented a crisis, and sent you Measure 49—forcing you to vote a third time!

Measure 37 can be fairly implemented without stealing your property—but Measure 49 is not the answer. Please join us in voting No on 49.

Senator Larry George Representative Bill Garrard

(This information furnished by Senator Larry George and Representative Bill Garrard.)

The Oregon Cattlemen's Association Asks You to Vote No on Measure 49

Measure 49 is about one simple issue: Should government be able to take your property without paying for it?

Measure 49 would allow Oregon's state, regional, and local governments to take your private property—and take your property with zero compensation for your loss. And if you demand your property back, you will have to pay the government's lawyers and appraisers to get it back—even if you win!

We believe that if government wants your property, then they must pay you for it. If you agree with us, please join us in voting No on Measure 49.

You will read rather unbelievable statements that Measure 49 will protect farmland, forestland, and groundwater—those statements are used to fool you. Politicians and special interests groups used polling to find out what words to use to best manipulate Oregon voters. Measure 49 is not about protecting those resources, it is about changing the law to allow government to take your property without compensation.

Nobody relies more on the protection of land and water than Oregon's ranchers and cattlemen. We are committed to conserve these resources and ensure that they last for generations—many of us are fourth and fifth generation ranchers.

Measure 49 undermines those efforts—if our property is not safe from government takings, then we cannot make long-term plans for future generations and we wipe out generations of ranchers. Measure 49 is a direct assault on Oregon's family farmers and ranchers and traditional agriculture.

Those that support Measure 49 may think that we can be replaced with mega-corporate farms, but we believe that small-scale, family-based agriculture is best for our state, our natural resources, and our environment.

Please reject the misleading campaign and help us protect Oregon agriculture for future generations. Vote No on Measure 49.

www.orcattle.com

(This information furnished by Kay Teisl, Oregon Cattlemen's Association.)

The Hood River Agriculture, Forestry, and Landowner's Association Asks You to Vote NO on Measure 49

We are all long time agricultural and forest property owners. Together we represent the vast majority of EFU land in Hood River County. We own orchards, vineyards, hay fields, and forest acreage. We raise kids and pears and apples and grapes and cherries and fir trees and cows. We are all farmers with "family farms." The next time you read in the newspaper about agriculture in the Hood River Valley, they are talking about us.

We are also unanimously opposed to Measure 49. Why? Because Measure 49 strips us of our most valuable commodity—the right to control how we operate our farms and use our land.

Today, foreign competition along with state and federal laws are slowly combining to put us out of business. In order for us to compete, we must be able to make changes to the way we use our land based on economics, not how pretty the view is or the soil type.

But Oregon's statewide, centralized land use laws, the only ones of their kind in the nation, prevent us from making changes based on economics.

To them, it is all about protecting "farmland." But no one cares about protecting the "farmer."

Measure 49 strips us of our property rights. It is a cruel blow to an industry that is already struggling to stay alive. If Measure 49 passes, we will be unable to diversify our operations, and to use our unproductive areas for higher economic uses, which allow us to keep farming on the productive parts of our farms.

We are proud to be Americans working in the natural resource industry. It is our hope that our children and grandchildren will continue our heritage. But Measure 49 and Oregon's ridiculous land use laws make that unlikely.

Please vote NO on Measure 49.

(This information furnished by John M. Benton, Sr., Hood River Agriculture, Forestry and Landowner's Association.)

Oregon Employers Oppose Measure 49

As some of Oregon's largest employers, we oppose Ballot Measure 49.

Our companies employ thousands of Oregonians throughout the state at family wages. Each of us has been in business for decades in Oregon.

Our employees serve on the local school board. They coach little league baseball. They sit by you at church. They shop in local stores. Their children go to public schools. They pay taxes.

In short, we are part of your community. Many Oregon communities were formed around our industries.

We believe that a fundamental key to a healthy economy is a respect for the ability of every citizen to own and use property.

Without this ability, our companies would not be successful, we would not have jobs for our employees, and we would be unable to serve our communities.

Measure 49 strikes at the heart of your ability to own and use your property. That is why we vigorously oppose it.

If Measure 49 is approved, the investments we make in our companies and our property are in jeopardy. Measure 49 allows government to take our property and businesses without compensation. If our property is taken, so are the jobs we provide.

What Measure 49 supporters fail to realize is that in a competitive global market, one regulation can wipe out an industry. Measure 49 makes it far more likely that such a regulation will be adopted.

So while Measure 49 supporters call us names and ridicule us for standing up for free enterprise and the right to use our property in the manner we could when we purchased it, we'll continue to do what we can to defend every Oregonian's right to own and use their property.

Please vote No on Measure 49.

Aaron Jones, President, Seneca Sawmill Co.

Michael Fahey, President, Columbia Helicopters

Robert Freres Jr., Freres Lumber Co.

Joan Austin, Executive Vice President, A-dec

Steven Swanson, Swanson Group

(This information furnished by Aaron Jones, President, Seneca Sawmill Co.; Michael Fahey, President, Columbia Helicopters; Robert Freres Jr., Freres Lumber Co.; Joan Austin, Executive Vice President, A-dec; Steven Swanson, Swanson Group.)

Source: Measure 49 "Arguments in Favor" and "Arguments in Opposition." www.sos.state.or.us/elections/nov62007/guide/m49.html.

NOTES

1. Quoted in Robert Bruegmann, *Sprawl: A Compact History* (Chicago: University of Chicago Press, 2006), 203.

2. Bruegmann, 206, 208–209.

DOCUMENT 10.14

Calling for Reform of an "Antiquated" Mining Law

"There Are Few Laws More in Need of an Overhaul than the 1872 Mining Law"

January 24, 2008

The 1872 Mining Law is one of the most venerable—and controversial—laws governing public land use in the United States. The law, which was signed into law by President Ulysses S. Grant as an incentive for settlement of the western frontier, permitted hard rock miners to claim mining rights on public land for $2.50 to $5.00 an acre. The law, which has resulted in virtually unfettered commercial exploitation of millions of acres of public land, remains in effect today.

Since the rise of the environmental movement in the 1970s, periodic attempts to pass laws that would modernize and reform the law's provisions have been beaten back by industry allies in Congress. Proponents of reform, however, continue to press for action, citing a wide array of negative repercussions for taxpayers and the environment from the law. The U.S. Bureau of Mines, for example, has estimated that 12,000 miles of rivers in the West are contaminated with metals from mining operations, and the Environmental Protection Agency reported that it spent about $2.2 billion between 1998 and 2007 to clean up abandoned hard rock mines across the nation.[1] Fiscal watchdog groups, meanwhile, have excoriated the law as one that allows mining companies to extract massive riches from public lands without paying a penny to the U.S. Treasury as a royalty or for environmental cleanup. "For over a century, mining companies have been taking gold, copper, and other minerals worth up to $1 billion a year from our public lands for free and

taxpayers are footing the bill for the cleanup of water and other contamination left behind,"
charged Taxpayers for Common Sense.[2]

Mining interests and free enterprise, anti-regulatory think tanks such as the Cato
Institute, however, claim that problems with the law are overstated. "It is probably best to
leave the 1872 Mining Law alone and press for public land privatization outside the
context of this debate," testified Cato's Richard L. Gordon in 1999 congressional testimony.
"If a consensus is ever reached that the federal government should divest itself of its vast
Western land holdings, there will be more than enough time to then repeal the 1872
Mining Law as an inferior and obsolete tool of land disposal. Any reform aimed specifically
at the law, no matter how well intentioned or theoretically sound, would probably be
corrupted in its execution and prove to be a cure worse than the disease."[3]

Despite such expressions of opposition, efforts to change the 1872 Mining Law
continue. In the following document, Michael Dombeck, who was a director of the Bureau
of Land Management and served as chief of the U.S. Forest Service from 1997 to 2001, lays
out many of the criticisms of the existing law. Within months of this 2008 testimony,
Democratic leaders in both the House and Senate introduced legislation that would impose
royalty fees on hard rock mining operators on public land, to be funneled into the Treasury
and environmental restoration projects.

Mining is a legitimate use of public lands, but there are few laws more in need of an overhaul than the 1872 Mining Law. The 1872 Mining Law, signed into existence 135 years
ago by President Ulysses Grant, is the most outdated natural resource law in the nation.
Under the 1872 law, mining takes precedence over all other public land uses, including
hunting and fishing. The Secretary of the Interior must sell public land to mining companies, often foreign-owned, for as little as $2.50 per acre. Furthermore, mining companies
pay no royalties for hard rock minerals including gold, copper, and zinc that belong to all
citizens. The price of uranium, gold, and other heavy metals continues to drive companies
to stake claims across the West. Mining claims dot millions of acres of public land across
the West. Once claimed, it is nearly impossible to prohibit mining under the current
framework of the 1872 Mining Law, no matter how serious the impacts might be.

The legacy of the 1872 Mining Law is extensive, and the damage from mining is still
ongoing today. For example, the EPA estimates that 40 percent of western headwater
streams are degraded by abandoned mines. The following are some examples of impacts
to water and fish and wildlife habitat caused by specific mines in the recent past as well as
threats from proposed mines.

- A Canadian mining company is pushing to develop a large, open pit, cyanide
leach gold mine at the headwaters of the Boise River. The Boise River is responsible for more than 20 percent of the city's municipal water supply, as well as
supplying critical wildlife and fish habitat, irrigation for agriculture and recreational opportunities. The Mayor of Boise has opposed the mine.
- One of five known grizzly bear populations in the lower 48 states as well as
imperiled bull trout may be eliminated due to a proposed silver mine in the
Cabinet Mountain Wilderness in northwestern Montana.
- In 1992, the Summitville mine in Colorado released a toxic brew including cya-
nide and acid mine drainage, killing all fish and wildlife in a 17 mile stretch of the
Alamosa River. Cleanup costs at the now-Superfund site exceed $150 million.
- Historic placer mining operations have affected Resurrection Creek in the Chugach
National Forest, Alaska, by re-channeling the stream and separating it from its

floodplain. These impacts degraded fish rearing and spawning habitat along the river, as well as adjacent wildlife riparian habitat for species like bears and eagles.

- The Beal Mountain Mine, located in the Beaverhead Deerlodge National Forest and operated from 1989 through 1998, has polluted valuable trout waters with cyanide, selenium, and copper. Using more recent cyanide heap-leach technologies, the mining company promised that there would be no discharge of pollutants into receiving waters. The technologies failed and waters downstream have been contaminated with selenium and other heavy metals. The Forest Service and the Montana Department of Environmental Quality are working to contain the contamination which may have to be treated in perpetuity. With the mining company bankrupt, the taxpayers must pay the bill.

Professional resource managers at the Forest Service and BLM need to have the ability to make science-based decisions about where and when mining on public land should occur. Without this discretion, professional land managers cannot maintain their commitments as stewards of the public trust.

Public lands managed by the BLM and the Forest Service harbor some of the most important fish and wildlife habitat and provide some of the finest hunting and angling opportunities in the country. For example, public lands contain well more than 50 percent of the nation's blue-ribbon trout streams and are strongholds for imperiled trout and salmon in the western United States. More than 80 percent of the most critical habitat for elk is found on lands managed by the Forest Service and the BLM, alone. Pronghorn antelope, sage grouse, mule deer, salmon and steelhead, and countless other fish and wildlife species are similarly dependent on public lands.

The national forests are a major source of water and of particular importance in the West. Forest Service and EPA scientists have determined that the national forests alone provide drinking water to more than 60 million people in 33 states.

Mr. Chairman, in your letter of invitation, you asked that I comment on five very important questions about the types of environmental reforms that may be needed to modernize this law so that its provisions protect fish and wildlife resources, and hunting and fishing. I will summarize my responses by providing you with the five major ways the law needs to be changed.

Any reform of the 1872 Mining Law should contain the following provisions:

A fair royalty from any minerals taken from public lands, a portion of which should be invested in an abandoned mine clean up fund. Since 1977, royalties associated with coal mining have generated $7.4 billion to help clean up abandoned mines and recover lands and waters and communities affected by coal mining. We need a similar fund for hard rock mining. And a sensible reform should include all mining operations, present and future. Almost every commodity developed off public lands—coal, wood fiber, oil, gas, and forage—has dedicated funding for mitigation of impacts and restoration measures. The only commodity that lacks such a dedicated fund is hard rock minerals. As a result, non-profit organizations such as TU, local communities, and state agencies, are dependent on cobbling funding from an array of private, state, and federal sources to get work done on the ground.

Affirm the values of fish and wildlife habitat, water resources, and hunting and fishing, on public lands and make it clear that mining should not be the dominant use of our federal lands. Professional land managers that work for the Forest Service and BLM believe the 1872 Mining Law makes hard rock mining a dominant use of public lands. Mining reform legislation needs to reaffirm the doctrine of multiple-use and recognize the inherent value of public lands for other important uses and values, including hunting and fishing opportunities and fish and wildlife habitat. This is a major priority for sportsmen, land management agencies, and other users of public lands.

Agency managers should be given the discretion to make logical decisions based on land health about where to mine and where not to mine. Special places with important fish and wildlife and water values such as wilderness areas, National Parks, Fish and Wildlife Refuges, and inventoried roadless areas ought to be placed off-limits to mining entirely. Discretion ought to be afforded to managers on other lands to allow for balanced and reasoned decisions about ecological, social, and economic values. And on highly mineralized lands with low fish and wildlife values, and high levels of mining company investment, mining companies ought to have a higher degree of certainty that mining projects can proceed in accordance with other laws and regulations.

Funding and common-sense liability relief must be made available for would-be Good Samaritans and volunteers to clean up abandoned mines. Abandoned mines are one of the single most important, least addressed environmental challenges in the nation. The geographic scope of the problem is staggering. EPA estimates that abandoned hard rock mines degrade nearly 40 percent of all western headwater streams. The enormity and scope of the problem have led to a collective sense of futility that has fostered inactivity in many places. Good Samaritans, who have no connection to the abandoned mine waste or interest in re-mining it for profit, should be provided with reclamation incentives and commonsense liability relief.

Finally, mining reform legislation should prohibit the patenting or sale of public lands. The U.S. Government has practically given away more than three million acres of our public lands to mining companies through the practice of patenting. It is troublesome that anyone can stake a claim on public lands and then buy the land for as little as $2.50 an acre. With the increase in the price of metals, so have the number of claims staked. For example, in Arizona, the number of claims filed in the state has risen 80 percent since 2003. Thousands of these claims are within five miles of the Grand Canyon National Park, a crown jewel of the American public but also prime wildlife habitat for mule deer.

This Committee, and the Senate, have a rare opportunity to improve this law. The House has passed a strong reform bill. Key Senators have expressed their willingness to explore changes to it. We urge you to careful consider our recommendations, draft a good bill, and move it through the Senate as quickly as possible next year. Sportsmen and women around the nation, especially in the West, are counting on you to end the long stalemate and reform the 1872 Mining Law.

Source: Dombeck, Michael. Testimony to the Senate Committee on Energy and Natural Resources on Reform of the Mining Law of 1872, U.S. Congress. Senate. 110th Cong., 2d sess., January 24, 2008. Available at www.uwsp.edu/cnr/gem/Dombeck/MDSpeeches/2008/MDombeck%20mining%20reform %20testimony%201-24-2008%20final.pdf.

NOTES

1. Scott Streater, "Reform of 1872 Mining Law Won't Save Western Splendors," *New York Times,* April 16, 2009, www.nytimes.com/gwire/2009/04/16/16greenwire-reform-of-1872-law-wont-save-western-splendors-10569.html.

2. "Make Sure Mining Companies Pay Their Fair Share," Taxpayers for Common Sense, http://capwiz .com/taxpayer/issues/alert/?alertid=13484181.

3. Quoted in "Reform of 1872 Mining Law Would Probably 'Be a Cure Worse Than the Disease,'" Cato Institute press release, August 3, 1999, www.cato.org/new/catonew-08-99.html.

DOCUMENT
10.15

An Environmental Health Warning about Industrial Animal Feeding Operations

"There Are Unintended Consequences of This Type of Animal Production"

2008

During the last decades of the twentieth century, large farm animal feeding operations—which are also sometimes referred to as industrial farm animal production (IFAP) systems, confined animal feeding operations (CAFOs), or simply factory farms—have become the focus of increased scrutiny from environmental and public health advocacy groups, policymakers, and regulatory agencies. Members of the industry "see their systems as the way of the future," acknowledged agriculture analyst Daryll E. Ray. "They are able to provide a product the customer wants at a price the customer can afford. They have cut the fat not only out of the animal, they have cut it out of the cost of production as well."[1] Critics, however, have assailed industrial farm animal production systems for polluting area waterways and aquifers, endangering the health of workers, inhumane treatment of livestock, crowding out smaller farm operations, and excessive reliance on antibiotics, which in turn creates antibiotic-resistant infections in humans that are costly and difficult to treat.

One of the most high-profile investigations of CAFOs in recent years was the report Putting Meat on the Table, which was released in 2008 by the Pew Commission on Industrial Farm Animal Production. This fifteen-member commission was chaired by former Kansas governor John Carlin and included a wide cross-section of contributors including a former secretary of agriculture (Dan Glickman), a former assistant surgeon general/chief of staff to the surgeon general (Michael Blackwell), a food policy scholar (Marion Nestle), and the former president of the Western Montana Stockgrowers Association (Dan Jackson). The report they produced included special sections dedicated to explaining the deleterious impact of factory farms on public health, environment, animal welfare, and rural America. The report also included numerous "urgent" policy recommendations to reduce these impacts, including new systems for disposing of farm wastes, transference of regulatory responsibilities for agribusiness from state agricultural agencies to state environmental agencies, and the creation of new federal agencies to address public health risks associated with intensive farm animal production. The excerpt featured here is taken from the report's general summary and public health summary, with footnotes removed.

The Commission acknowledged, however, that affecting significant change in factory farm operations will likely be an arduous process, given the entrenched political clout of industrial farming operations in state capitols and Washington, D.C. As Commission executive director Robert P. Martin noted in the report's preface, "the formation of this Commission was greeted by industrial agriculture with responses ranging from open hostility to wary cooperation. In fact, while some industrial agriculture representatives were recommending potential authors for the technical reports to Commission staff, other industrial agriculture representatives were discouraging those same authors from assisting

us by threatening to withhold research funding for their college or university. We found
significant influence by the industry at every turn: in academic research, agriculture policy
development, government regulation, and enforcement."[2]

Executive Summary

. . . Over the past 50 years, the production of farm animals for food has shifted from the traditional, extensive, decentralized family farm system to a more concentrated system with fewer producers, in which large numbers of animals are confined in enormous operations. While we are raising approximately the same number of swine as we did in 1950, for example, we are doing so on significantly fewer, far larger farms, with dramatically fewer farm workers. This production model—sometimes called industrial farm animal production—is characterized by confining large numbers of animals of the same species in relatively small areas, generally in enclosed facilities that restrict movement. In many cases, the waste produced by the animals is eliminated through liquid systems and stored in open pit lagoons.

The IFAP system, as it exists today, too often concentrates economic power in the hands of the large companies that process and sell the animal products, instead of the individuals who raise the animals. In many cases, the "open market" for animal products has completely disappeared, giving the farmer only one buyer to sell to, and one price to be received.

In addition to raising animals in closer proximity, steps were taken to streamline the process of raising animals for food, including standardized feed for rapid weight gain and uniformity; genetic selection to accentuate traits, such as leanness, that create uniform meat products; and mechanization of feeding, watering, and other husbandry activities. This streamlined processing and standardization is typical of the evolution of industrial pursuits, and is intended to be more economical by lowering the amount of input required to achieve a marketable product, as well as to ensure a uniform product. This process in food animal production has resulted in farms that are easier to run, with fewer and often less-highly-skilled employees, and a greater output of uniform animal products. However, there are unintended consequences of this type of animal production.

This transformation, and the associated social, economic, environmental, and public health problems engendered by it, have gone virtually unnoticed by many American citizens. Not long ago, the bulk of the fruit, grain, vegetables, meat, and dairy products consumed by the American people were produced on small family farms. These farms once defined both the physical and the social character of the US countryside. However, the steady urbanization of the US population has resulted in an American populace that is increasingly disassociated from the production system that supplies its food. Despite the dramatic decline in family farms over the past 50 years, many Americans, until very recently, continued to think that their food still came from these small farms.

While increasing the speed of production, the intensive confinement production system creates a number of problems. These include contributing to the increase in the pool of antibiotic-resistant bacteria because of the overuse of antibiotics; air quality problems; the contamination of rivers, streams, and coastal waters with concentrated animal waste; animal welfare problems, mainly as a result of the extremely close quarters in which the animals are housed; and significant shifts in the social structure and economy of many farming regions throughout the country. It was on these areas that the Commission focused its attention.

EXECUTIVE SUMMARY: PUBLIC HEALTH

As previously mentioned, one of the most serious unintended consequences of industrial food animal production (IFAP) is the growing public health threat of these types of facilities. In addition to the contribution of IFAP to the major threat of antimicrobial resistance, IFAP facilities can be harmful to workers, neighbors, and even those living far from the facilities through air and water pollution, and via the spread of disease. Workers in and neighbors of IFAP facilities experience high levels of respiratory problems, including asthma. In addition, workers can serve as a bridging population, transmitting animal-borne diseases to a wider population. A lack of appropriate treatment of enormous amounts of waste may result in contamination of nearby waters with harmful levels of nutrients and toxins, as well as bacteria, fungi, and viruses, all of which can affect the health of people both near and far from IFAP facilities.

Antibiotics are one type of antimicrobial. Antimicrobials are substances that kill bacteria or suppress their multiplication or growth, and include antibiotics, some minerals, metals, and synthetic agents.

The use of antibiotics for growth promotion began with the poultry industry in the 1940s when it discovered that the use of tetracycline-fermentation byproducts resulted in improved growth. Since then, the practice of adding low levels of antibiotics and growth hormones to stimulate growth and improve production and performance parameters has been common among IFAP operations for all species. Because any use of antibiotics results in resistance, this widespread use of low-level antibiotics in animals, along with use in treating humans, contributes to the growing pool of antimicrobial resistance in the environment.

The threat from antimicrobial resistance became more apparent in the 1990s as the number of cases of drug-resistant infections increased in humans. A World Health Organization (WHO) Report on Infectious Diseases published in 2000 expressed alarm at the spread of multi-drug-resistant infectious disease agents, and pointed to food as a major source of antimicrobial-resistant bacteria. Since the discovery of the growth-promoting and disease-fighting capabilities of antibiotics, farmers, fish-farmers, and livestock producers have used antimicrobials. This ongoing and often low-level dosing for disease prevention and growth inevitably results in the development of resistance in bacteria in or near livestock because a selective pressure that does not kill fosters resistance.

While it is difficult to measure what percent of resistant infections in humans are caused by antimicrobial use in agriculture as opposed to other settings, it can be assumed that the wider the use of antimicrobials, the greater the chance for the development of resistance. Reports on the amounts of antibiotics used in animals range from 17.8 to 24.6 million pounds per year. The Union of Concerned Scientists estimates that 70% of the antibiotics used in the United States annually are used in farm animals.

As the amount of antimicrobials present in the general environmental pool becomes greater, so too does the chance of resistance developing within many different bacterial populations. This is due, in part, to the way resistance is spread between capable bacteria. For example, many bacteria live in the human digestive tract or on human skin. These are not normally harmful (and are often helpful). However, these harmless bacteria may still be capable of passing resistance to other bacteria that *are* harmful, or could then *become* harmful.

Feed formulation further influences risks because the feeds supplied to confined animal populations are significantly different from the foraged feeds traditionally available to poultry, swine, or cattle.

IFAP not only causes concerns about the health of the animals present, but the basic production model creates concerns with respect to human health, as well. Health risks are a function of exposure, with those engaged directly in livestock production typically having more frequent and more concentrated exposures to chemical or infectious agents, and others, such as those involved in support services, having lower rates of exposure. Health risks may extend far from the IFAP facility, however. Groundwater contamination, for example, can extend throughout the aquifer, affecting drinking water supplies far from the source of contamination. Infectious agents arising in IFAP facilities may be transmissible from person to person in a community setting and well beyond. An infectious agent that originates at an IFAP facility may persist through meat processing and contaminate a consumer meat product, resulting in a serious disease far from the IFAP facility.

Agricultural workers may serve as a bridging population between their communities and animal confinement facilities. Because it is categorized as an agricultural process, IFAP is largely exempt from state and federal industrial exposure monitoring, inspection, injury-disease reporting, and surveillance. Without monitoring, it is extremely difficult for public health officials to reduce the occupational health risk associated with IFAP.

The toxic gases and organic dusts associated with IFAP facilities have the potential to produce upper respiratory irritation in confinement facility workers. The emissions from confinement facilities, however, may affect communities proximate to those facilities, as well as populations far away from these operations. In particular, the elderly, those with compromised respiratory systems or chronic conditions that limit their mobility, and children are at most risk of asthma and other respiratory illnesses. Depression and other symptoms have also been attributed to emissions from such facilities.

Source: Executive Summary. *Putting Meat on the Table: Industrial Farm Animal Production in America.* Washington, D.C.: Pew Commission on Industrial Farm Animal Production, 2008, pp. 1–3, 5–7.

NOTES

1. Daryll E. Ray, "Are CAFOs and Small Producers Entering a Time of Benign Co-existence?" Agricultural Policy Analysis Center, May 8, 2009, www.agpolicy.org/weekcol/458.html.

2. Robert P. Martin, "Preface," *Putting Meat on the Table: Industrial Farm Animal Production in America* (Washington, D.C.: Pew Commission on Industrial Farm Animal Production, 2008), viii.

DOCUMENT
10.16

Political Interference with the Endangered Species Act

"Her Agenda Has Caused Considerable Harm to the Integrity of the ESA Program"

December 15, 2008

During George W. Bush's eight years in office, officials and administrators within his administration were repeatedly accused of undercutting and distorting federal environmental laws for ideological reasons. One of the most heavily publicized of these cases concerned an Interior Department official, Julie MacDonald, who was accused of improperly influencing decisionmaking within the country's endangered species program.

In May 2007 an investigation of the federal endangered species program conducted by Interior inspector general (IG) Earl Devaney uncovered repeated instances in which MacDonald, who had served as deputy assistant secretary for Fish, Wildlife and Parks in the U.S. Fish and Wildlife Service since 2004, influenced endangered species decisionmaking with politically motivated actions. This report prompted MacDonald's resignation— although she denied all allegations of wrongdoing—and spurred the launch of new investigations to determine the degree to which the endangered species program had been compromised. In May 2008 the Government Accountability Office (GAO) confirmed the Department of Interior IG's findings, documenting numerous cases in which MacDonald and three other high-ranking Department of Interior officials exerted improper pressure on department directives about endangered species management and protection. The report touched off another volley of condemnation from Democratic members of Congress. "A disconcerting picture has emerged of officials working at the highest levels of the Interior Department continuing to tamper with the endangered species program, trumping science with politics," said Representative Nick J. Rahall (Wis.), chair of the House Natural Resources Committee.[1] On December 15, 2008, Devaney delivered the results of a second inquiry into the scandal to Interior secretary Dirk Kempthorne. The following document is a cover letter summary of that report, which also paints a grim picture of the regulatory environment surrounding endangered species decisionmaking over several administrations.

Subject: Report of Investigation: The Endangered Species Act and the Conflict Between Science and Policy

With this memorandum, I am transmitting the Report of Investigation on the Endangered Species Act (ESA) decisions influenced by the former Deputy Assistant Secretary for Fish and Wildlife and Parks (FW), Julie MacDonald. This investigation was initiated by request of Senator Ron Wyden who believed that 18 ESA decisions may have been improperly affected by MacDonald. Our investigation was expanded by requests from Chairman Nick J. Rahall, II, House Committee on Natural Resources, and Congressmen Jay Inslee and Peter DeFazio, who requested that we add two other decisions to those under our review.

As you know, in previous investigations we determined that MacDonald injected herself personally and profoundly in a number of ESA issues. We determined that MacDonald's management style was abrupt and abrasive, if not abusive, and that her conduct demoralized and frustrated her staff as well as her subordinate managers.

Our findings from this investigation are much the same, although we found that the nature and extent of MacDonald's influence varied dramatically from one decision to another. For example, in one instance we found that MacDonald went to extraordinary efforts to influence a particular decision, but her efforts ultimately had no effect on the outcome. In other instances, her involvement clearly caused a particular result. Ironically, in several instances, she played no role in the decision-making process, but because of her reputation, FW personnel believed that she had, in fact, been exerting influence, as did members of Congress and the public.

Overall, however, MacDonald's zeal to advance her agenda has caused considerable harm to the integrity of the ESA program and to the morale and reputation of the FW, as well as potential harm to individual species. Her heavy-handedness has cast doubt on nearly every ESA decision issued during her tenure; of the 20 decisions we reviewed, her influence potentially jeopardized 13 ESA decisions. MacDonald's conduct was backed by the seemingly blind support of former Assistant Secretary for Fish and Wildlife and Parks, Judge Craig Manson. Judge Manson so thoroughly supported MacDonald that even when a known error in a Federal Register notice, which was caused by MacDonald's calculations, was brought to Manson's attention, he directed that the notice be published regardless of the error. MacDonald was also ably abetted in her attempts to interfere with the science by Special Assistant Randal Bowman, Office of the Assistant Secretary for Fish and Wildlife and Parks, who held the position and authority to advance the unwritten policy to exclude as many areas as practicable from Critical Habitat Determinations, as well as Attorney Thomas Graf, Office of the Solicitor, whose remarkable lack of recollection leaves one to speculate whether he was doing MacDonald's bidding or was a rogue actor simply emulating her policy style.

In the end, the cloud of MacDonald's overreaching, and the actions of those who enabled and assisted her, have caused the unnecessary expenditure of hundreds of thousands of dollars to re-issue decisions and litigation costs to defend decisions that, in at least two instances, the courts found to be arbitrary and capricious. (Ironically, in many of the decisions that ended up in litigation, advice from the Office of the Solicitor (SOL) had been ignored, yet the SOL subsequently had to suffer the indignity of defending decisions that it had deemed legally flawed.) These costs are in addition to the monies expended by the OIG on three separate investigations into MacDonald's influence over ESA decisions.

Perhaps most importantly, however, is that our investigation revealed an enormous policy void, which MacDonald was able to readily exploit. While the ESA affords the Secretary great discretion in several areas—exclusions of habitat being one example—the absence of policy in exercising that discretion has resulted, in MacDonald's case, [in] a wholesale lack of consistency, a process built on guess-work, and decisions that could not pass legal muster. This dearth of policy and guidance seems less than coincidental. For many years, through several administrations, this appears to be an area of intentional failure to clarify, in order to maximize the agenda du jour.

The Department owes the public a fair and consistent application of rules in making its ESA decisions. When the career FW staff responsible for building the evidence for an administrative record does not know what the rules are—because they changed, sometimes on a daily basis—surely, the public cannot have confidence in the process.

As it stands, lawsuits are driving nearly everything FW does in the ESA arena. Lawsuits should not be driving regulatory decisions. As Fish and Wildlife Service (FWS) Director Dale Hall has explained, FWS has developed draft regulations that would purportedly address the most problematic areas in implementing the ESA. He also noted that the ESA implementing regulations have not been revised since 1986. Revised regulations, Hall said, would reflect over 20 years of working knowledge of the law and could clearly define what criteria would be evaluated in making ESA decisions.

Short of issuing regulations, FWS should develop policy to lend a sense of consistency, to guide ESA decisions where discretion is allowed, and to provide the public the transparency that is fundamentally lacking in this high-profile program. Whether by regulation or policy, action is necessary to restore the integrity of the ESA program, and the morale and reputation of the FWS in the eyes of the public and of Congress. Seeking direction and support from Congress would certainly bolster the legitimacy of any such effort, and would ensure that FWS is in keeping with Congressional intent.

Recognizing that this comes late in your tenure as Secretary of the Interior, we are providing this report to you for whatever action you deem appropriate; however, it is also my intention to thoroughly brief and refer this report to your successor.

Source: Inspector General's Office, Department of Interior. *Report of Investigation: The Endangered Species Act and the Conflict between Science and Policy.* Washington, D.C.: DOI, December 15, 2008. www .doioig.gov/upload/Endangered%20Species%20FINAL%20REDACTED5%20w_TOC_encryption.pdf.

Note

1. Quoted in "GAO Investigation Uncovers Political Meddling by Four Top Interior Officials," House Committee on Natural Resources press release, May 21, 2008, http://resourcescommittee.house.gov/ index.php?option=com_content&task=view&id=387&Itemid=27.

DOCUMENT 10.17

The Omnibus Public Land Management Act

"A Herculean First Step in President Obama's Agenda for Our Open Lands"

March 30, 2009

In March 2009 the Democrat-controlled Congress passed and President Barack Obama signed the Omnibus Public Land Management Act of 2009, a sweeping law that provided for one of the greatest expansions of wilderness protection in decades. The act, which united almost 170 separate measures, set aside more than two million acres in nine states as protected wilderness, including tracts in California's Sequoia and Kings Canyon National Parks, Michigan's Pictured Rocks National Lakeshore, and Utah's Zion National Park. Other features of the act included the addition of another 1,100 miles of protected waterways to America's National Wild and Scenic Rivers System; prohibition of oil and gas development on another million acres of public land managed by the Bureau of Land Management (BLM) and other federal agencies; establishment of new scientific research programs for the preservation of Great Lakes and ocean resources; and bestowal of new protections on the National Landscape Conservation System, which protects areas of archaeological, cultural, and ecological significance.

The act was not universally hailed in Washington. Many Republicans voiced disappointment with the law, including congressman Tom Price (Ga.), who described it as a "pork-filled package" that would "block millions of acres for energy development, expand federal land holdings, give the government even more control over American land, and trample private property rights."[1] Democrats, however, rejected this interpretation, as did twenty-one Republican senators and thirty-eight Republican House members who voted for the measure and, in some cases, sponsored or co-sponsored key provisions of the final bill.[2] Environmental and conservation groups, meanwhile, expressed elation about most elements of the act. Franz Matzner, acting legislative director of the Natural Resources Defense Council, called it "historic legislation" that provides "yet another reminder that our government has pressed the reset button on its priorities, recognizing that there is more value in preserving these precious resources than destroying them."[3]

The following document provides excerpts from remarks given by Interior secretary Ken Salazar and President Obama at the signing ceremony for the "Omni," as it came to be known in congressional negotiations.

Remarks of Interior Secretary Ken Salazar

March 30, 2009

It is an honor to be here today with all of you who worked so hard, for so many years, to write this new chapter for America's treasured landscapes.

Over the last two centuries, America's best ideas for protecting our vast lands and open spaces have often arrived while our country has faced its greatest trials.

It was in the midst of our nation's bloodiest conflict—the Civil War—that President Abraham Lincoln set aside the lands that are now Yosemite National Park.

It was at the dawn of the 20th century, with our cities and industries growing and our open lands and watersheds disappearing, that President Teddy Roosevelt expanded our national parks and set aside the world's largest system of lands dedicated to wildlife conservation, the national wildlife refuge system.

And it was in the darkest days of the Great Depression that President Franklin Roosevelt put three million young Americans to work in the Civilian Conservation Corps. They built the trails, campgrounds, parks, and conservation projects we enjoy today.

In these moments when our national character is most tested we rightly seek to protect that which fuels our spirit.

For America's national character—our optimism, our dreams, our shared stories—are rooted in our landscapes.

We each have places we love. For me, it is the San Luis Valley in Colorado. It is the lands my family has farmed for five generations. The waters of the San Antonio River. The snows on the Sangre de Cristo Mountains.

As Americans, we are defined most by our people and our places. President Barack Obama is one of those Americans. As a young boy he discovered the beautiful landscapes of America with his grandmother, mother, and sister. They drove from Seattle down the coast to California. They saw the Grand Canyon, the Great Plains, and the Great Lakes. And then: Yellowstone.

Those experiences—those places—bind us together as one people.

Yes, we are in a time of deep uncertainty and economic pain. But for Americans, moments of crisis are opportunities to rebuild, renew, and restore the places we cherish.

We are now at such a moment in our nation's history. A transformational moment. A new beginning, led by a president who tells us it is time once again for America's best ideas.

It is time once again to create for our children, and our grandchildren, a legacy of stewardship on the scale of the challenges we face.

Our population has nearly doubled since President John F. Kennedy created the Land and Water Conservation Fund in 1964. And though we have made progress, our open lands, wetlands, and wildlife are still disappearing.

But in a few minutes, President Obama will sign legislation that represents one of the most significant protections for our treasured landscapes in a generation. He will do so less than 100 days into his presidency.

This legislation will put into law the 26-million acre National Landscape Conservation System within the Bureau of Land Management. It will add 2 million acres of new wilderness across the country. It will preserve 1,000 new miles of wild and scenic rivers. And it will better protect some of America's most special places—from Oregon's Mount Hood to the dinosaur tracks of New Mexico to Virginia's wild forests.

This bill is a Herculean first step in President Obama's agenda for our open lands.

> *This legislation guarantees that we will not take our forests, rivers, oceans, national parks, monuments, and wilderness areas for granted; but rather we will set them aside and guard their sanctity for everyone to share. . . . And that's why so much of this legislation, some of it decades in the making, has the backing of Americans from every walk of life and corner of this country.*
>
> —President Barack Obama

It would not have happened without the patient and tireless efforts of the people in this room and Americans across the country: hard-working citizens who are saving historic sites in their communities so that we never forget our past; tribal leaders who are forging solutions to complex and long-standing natural resource challenges; mayors and county commissioners who are protecting the backcountry for hunting and fishing and hiking; business leaders who know that good stewardship makes good economic sense; and the many members of the House and Senate, Republicans and Democrats—including Senate Majority Leader Harry Reid and Speaker of the House Nancy Pelosi—whose leadership and persistence made this possible.

This historic legislation lays the foundation for the agenda for America's treasured landscapes that President Obama asked me to work on.

I am proud this bill is here today. I am proud of the bipartisan work that went into it. And I am honored to introduce to all of you the President of the United States of America, Barack Obama.

Remarks of President Barack Obama

March 30, 2009

Well, thank you so much, Ken, for that extraordinary introduction and for the work that you and your team are undertaking at the Department of the Interior. We're going to add a little bit to your plate today as a consequence of this extraordinary piece of legislation. . . .

It is fitting that we meet on a day like this. Winter's hardships are slowly giving way to spring and our thoughts naturally tend to turn to the outdoors. We emerge from the shelter offered by home and work and we look around, and we're reminded that the most valuable things in this life are those things that we already possess.

As Americans, we possess few blessings greater than the vast and varied landscapes that stretch the breadth of our continent. Our lands have always provided great bounty: food and shelter for the first Americans—for settlers and pioneers, the raw materials that grew our industry, the energy that powers our economy.

What these gifts require in return is our wise and responsible stewardship. As our greatest conservationist President, Teddy Roosevelt, put it almost a century ago, "I recognize the right and duty of this generation to develop and use the natural resources of our land; but I do not recognize the right to waste them, or to rob, by wasteful use, the generations that come after us." That's the spirit behind the bipartisan legislation I'm signing today, legislation among the most important in decades to protect, preserve, and pass down our Nation's most treasured landscapes to future generations.

Many Senators and Congressmen here deserve enormous credit for making this bill possible. I'm grateful to all their hard work. As I mentioned before, Harry Reid made this a top priority. He made sure this was the first bill the Senate passed this year. This day would not be possible without his tireless dedication to protecting our treasured lands.

This legislation—just to give you a sense of the scope—this legislation guarantees that we will not take our forests, rivers, oceans, national parks, monuments, and wilderness areas for granted; but rather we will set them aside and guard their sanctity for everyone to share. That's something all Americans can support. And that's why so much of this legislation, some of it decades in the making, has the backing of Americans from every walk of life and corner of this country. Ranchers and fishermen, small-business owners, environmentalists, conservative Republicans and liberal Democrats on the local, State, and Federal levels, all united around the idea that there should be places that we must preserve; all doing the hard work of seeking common ground to protect the parks and other places that we cherish.

We're talking about places like Colorado, where this bill will realize a vision 35 years in the making by protecting the wild back country of Rocky Mountain National Park, which attracts 3 million visitors a year. Folks in communities around this park know they don't have to choose between economic and environmental concerns; the tourism that drives their local economy depends on good stewardship of their local environment. And year after year, these communities have worked together with Members of Congress in an attempt to ensure that Rocky Mountain National Park will forever remain as breathtaking as it is today.

And that is what this bill does from coast to coast. It protects treasured places from the Appalachians of Virginia and West Virginia to Michigan's Upper Peninsula; from the canyons of Idaho to the sandstone cliffs of Utah; from the Sierra Nevadas in California to the Badlands of Oregon.

It designates more than 2 million acres across nine States as wilderness, almost as much as was designated over the past 8 years combined. It creates thousands of miles of new scenic, historic, and recreational trails, cares for our historic battlefields, strengthens our National Park System. It safeguards more than 1,000 miles of our rivers, protects watersheds and cleans up polluted groundwater, defends our oceans and Great Lakes, and will revitalize our fisheries, returning fish to rivers that have not seen them in decades.

And it wisely faces our future challenges with regard to water. This bill assesses how growth and climate change will affect our access to water resources, especially in the West and Southwest, and it includes solutions to complex and long-simmering water disputes. It's hard to overstate the real and measurable impact this will have on people's lives, people like Frank Chee Willetto, a Navajo code talker in World War II, who's joined us today. And because of this legislation, Frank, along with 80,000 others in the Navajo Nation, will have access to clean running water for the very first time. That's something worth applauding. [Applause] Thank you for your service.

When coupled with the Recovery Act [the American Recovery and Reinvestment Act], which makes an historic $3 billion investment creating jobs that will restore and protect our landscapes and our ecosystems, preserve our national monuments, retrofit our facilities for energy efficiency and renewable energy—taken together, today's legislation takes another step toward fulfilling Teddy Roosevelt's vision for this land that we love. It's a vision that sees America's great wilderness as a place where what was, and what is, and what will be—all are the same; a place where memories are lived and relived; a place where Americans both young and young at heart can freely experience the spirit of adventure that has always been at the heart of the rugged character of America. . . .

All in all, this legislation is that rare end product of what happens when Americans of all parties and places come together in common purpose to consider something more than the politics of the moment. It's the very idea at the heart of this country: that each generation has a responsibility to secure this Nation's promise for the next. And by signing this bill into law, that's what we're doing today.

Source: Salazar, Ken. Remarks at Presidential Signing of the Omnibus Public Land Management Act of 2009, March 30, 2009. www.doi.gov/news/09_News_Releases/033009.html; Obama, Barack. Remarks upon Signing the Omnibus Public Land Management Act of 2009, March 30, 2009. www.gpoaccess.gov/presdocs/2009/DCPD-200900200.pdf.

NOTES

1. Quoted in "Congress Votes 'Yes' to Sweeping Public Lands Protection Act," *Environmental News Service,* March 25, 2009, www.ens-newswire.com/ens/mar2009/2009–03–25–01.asp.
2. Ray Ring, "Democrats and Republicans Can Work Together," *High Country News,* May 18, 2009, www.hcn.org/wotr/democrats-and-republicans-can-work-together.
3. Quoted in Catharine Livingston, "Go Green: Congress Gone Wild; Omnibus Public Land Management Act Passes," *National Geographic Adventure Blog,* March 26, 2009, http://ngadventure.typepad.com/blog/2009/03/go-green-congress-gone-wildomnibus-public-land-management-act-passed.html.

DOCUMENT 10.18

Southern Governors React to a Momentous Water Ruling

Atlanta's "Massive Illegal Water Grab Will Be Coming to an End"

July 17, 2009

As demand for finite—and in many cases diminishing—freshwater supplies increases, many conservation groups and hydrologists expect that political–legal "water wars" such as the two-decade-long feud of Florida, Georgia, and Alabama over waters of the Apalachicola-Chattahoochee-Flint (ACF) river basin are going to become more commonplace.

The roots of this bitter conflict were first sown in 1945, when the U.S. Congress authorized the construction of Georgia's Lake Sidney Lanier for hydroelectric power generation and flood control of the Chattahoochee River. The reservoir became a reality in 1960, when the U.S. Army Corps of Engineers completed Buford Dam on the

Chattahoochee. Reservoir and dam operations proceeded quietly during their first years of existence, but in the 1970s metropolitan Atlanta became increasingly dependent on Lake Lanier water for its drinking supply. This diversion reduced downstream water allocations to Florida and Alabama, which became increasingly agitated over the damage that these reductions wreaked on farms, Gulf Coast fisheries, municipal water supplies, and wildlife habitat. By the early 1990s the three states were openly battling each other over allocations of water from Lake Lanier and other Corps-operated reservoirs in the Chattahoochee basin. The acrimony became even greater in 2003, when Georgia and the U.S. Army Corps of Engineers announced an agreement that would permit metro Atlanta and its exploding population to increase water withdrawals from Lake Lanier for household and industrial use.

The conflict continued indecisively until 2007–2008, when successive years of severe drought brought matters to a head. As regional reservoir levels dropped to historic lows, the states held a new round of negotiations over a new water-sharing agreement. When these broke down, federal authorities at the Department of the Interior and the Corps of Engineers tried to broker an arrangement. But these efforts also faltered, doomed by the simple reality that the three states wanted more water than was available. By the spring of 2009, all eyes were on U.S. District Judge Paul Magnuson, who had been charged with determining whether Atlanta's massive water withdrawals from Lake Lanier were legal.

On July 17, 2009, Magnuson issued his ruling, which resounded like a thunderclap over the entire Southeast. Magnuson declared that because Congress had authorized Lake Lanier for hydroelectric power, flood control, and recreational purposes—not for drinking water—metropolitan Atlanta's water diversions were illegal. The judge gave Georgia a three-year deadline to 1) obtain congressional approval to use Lake Lanier for drinking water or 2) work out a compromise with the states of Florida and Alabama. If the state failed to solve the problem within that three-year period, Atlanta would have to return to mid-1970s levels of withdrawals from the lake.

Magnuson acknowledged that his deadline, if unmet, would constitute a crippling blow to the Atlanta region, given that the metropolitan area's population has doubled to five million residents since 1980. But he said that the 2003 water diversion agreement made by the Corps of Engineers with Georgia authorities was clearly illegal, and he implied that his ruling amounted to a warning shot across the bow of other water development stakeholders across the United States. "The blame for the current situation [with Lake Lanier] cannot be placed solely on the Corps' shoulders," wrote Magnuson.

> *Too often, state, local, and even national actors do not consider the long-term consequences of their decisions. Local governments allow unchecked growth because it increases tax revenue, but these same governments do not sufficiently plan for the resources such unchecked growth will require. Nor do individual citizens consider frequently enough their consumption of our scarce resources, absent a crisis situation such as that experienced in the ACF basin in the last few years. The problems faced in the ACF basin will continue to be repeated throughout this country, as the population grows and more undeveloped land is developed. Only by cooperating, planning, and conserving can we avoid the situations that gave rise to this litigation.[1]*

Within hours of the District Court ruling, the governors of all three states had issued statements. The tone of the releases from the offices of Florida governor Charlie Crist and

Alabama governor Bob Riley was one of mixed jubilance and relief. By contrast, the grim, terse wording of the release from Georgia governor Sonny Perdue indicated just how potentially grave a blow the ruling was to the people of Georgia in general and Atlanta in particular.

Press Release from the Florida Governor's Office

July 17, 2009

Florida Governor Charlie Crist and Florida Department of Environmental Protection Secretary Michael W. Sole are delighted and satisfied with Federal Court Judge Paul Magnuson's decision today in ongoing litigation over the waters of the Apalachicola-Chattahoochee-Flint (ACF) River Basin.

In the decision, U.S. District Court Judge Paul A. Magnuson ruled that Congress needs to approve use of the water from Lake Lanier for water supply—which currently amounts to nearly one-quarter of the conservation storage. In addition, Judge Magnuson ordered that all water withdrawals be frozen at current levels for the next three years until Congressional authorization is given or if some other resolution is reached. If Congress does not approve a reallocation within that period, then water withdrawals from Lake Lanier will revert to "baseline" operation of the mid-1970s.

"Today's ruling is a monumental milestone in the 18-year battle between Florida, Alabama and Georgia over the waters of the ACF basin, underscoring the importance of the Apalachicola's environment and economy," said Governor Crist. "The Judge's decision allows the governors to come together to reach an agreement outside of the court system. I look forward to working with Governors Riley and Perdue to find a solution that will be beneficial for all of our states."

Florida has long maintained that the United States Army Corps of Engineers and Georgia cannot allocate the water within Lake Lanier for water supply purposes without Congressional approval. Judge Magnuson's ruling reaffirms that position. In addition, through the litigation, Florida has sought protection for the Apalachicola ecosystem and the federally threatened and endangered species within the bay and the entire system.

"The Apalachicola River and Bay are one of the most productive and diverse estuarine systems on the Gulf of Mexico coast," said Secretary Sole. "The Army Corps of Engineers' operation of the system has been harmful and detrimental to the ecosystem. It is my hope through this ruling the states can come to a solution that protects the important natural resources of the region."

Florida, Georgia, Alabama and the United States Army Corps of Engineers have been engaged in litigation over sharing the waters within the basin of the ACF Rivers for nearly two decades. The disputes have focused primarily on the Corps' operation of its four Chattahoochee River dams. The largest is Buford Dam, which forms Lake Lanier located north of Atlanta.

"Florida has always been ready to negotiate, in good faith, a fair equitable sharing of the waters in the basin," stated Governor Crist. "We remain committed to doing so in the future."

* * *

Press Release from the Alabama Governor's Office

July 17, 2009

Governor Bob Riley is praising a major victory the state won today in water wars litigation involving Alabama, Georgia and Florida.

A federal court in Jacksonville ruled that the current water withdrawals from Lake Lanier to provide water supply to the Atlanta area are illegal under federal law.

"The significance of today's ruling for Alabama's economic and environmental future is tremendous," said Governor Riley. "Atlanta has based its growth on the idea that it could take whatever water it wanted whenever it wanted it, and that the downstream states would simply have to make do with less. Following the Court's ruling today, this massive illegal water grab will be coming to an end.

"Now that these critical legal issues have been resolved, I hope this sets the stage for renewed negotiations between the three states so that a fair and equitable agreement to share the water can be reached," said Governor Riley. "Any congressional approval for Atlanta's water supply withdrawals will have to be tied to a comprehensive agreement among the states. Alabama is ready to resume negotiations immediately."

Alabama filed suit in 1990 challenging the operations of the U.S. Army Corps of Engineers. Alabama has always contended that Lake Lanier was built for the purposes of flood control, hydropower generation, and navigation support. Based upon the Water Supply Act of 1958, Alabama argued that Congress had to approve any substantial usage of Lake Lanier for water supply, but no such congressional approval has ever been obtained.

Today Judge Paul Magnuson agreed with Alabama, ruling that only Congress could approve such a massive use of water from Lake Lanier by Atlanta-area entities. Judge Magnuson ordered that all water withdrawals be frozen at current levels for the next three years. If Congress does not approve a reallocation within that period, then water withdrawals from Lake Lanier will revert to the much lower levels of the mid-1970s.

This decision comes on the heels of a 2008 ruling from the federal appellate court in Washington, D.C. that struck down a secret agreement between the Corps and Georgia to dedicate even more of Lake Lanier to Atlanta's water supply in the future.

* * *

Press Release from the Georgia Governor's Office

July 17, 2009

Governor Sonny Perdue issued the following statement today regarding ruling in water litigation:

"Obviously, I am deeply disappointed by Judge Magnuson's decision today. His conclusions rely on decades-old assumptions about the construction of federal reservoirs and the role those reservoirs play in providing water supply for growing states such as Georgia. Our country has changed substantially since the 1940s, when many of these reservoirs were constructed, and I will use this opportunity not only to appeal the judge's decision but, most importantly, to urge Congress to address the realities of modern reservoir usage. The judge's ruling allows a three-year window for either Congressional action or an agreement by the states and we will work diligently with Georgia's delegation and members of Congress to re-establish the proper use of federal reservoirs throughout the country."

Source: "Judge's Ruling Signals End to Tri-State Water Dispute." Office of the Governor, State of Florida, July 17, 2009. www.flgov.com/release/10905; "Alabama Wins Major Water War Victory." Office of the Governor, State of Alabama, July 17, 2009. http://governorpress.alabama.gov/pr/pr-2009-07-17-02-water_wars.asp; "Statement of Governor Perdue Regarding Ruling in Water Litigation." Office of the Governor, State of Georgia, July 17, 2009. http://gov.georgia.gov/00/press/detail/0,2668, 78006749_144947052_146040701,00.html.

NOTE

1. Memorandum and Order, Tri-state Water Rights Litigation, United States District Court, Middle District of Florida, July 17, 2009. Available at http://graphics8.nytimes.com/packages/pdf/us/ 20090816_water_order.pdf.

CHAPTER 11

Energy Policy and Global Climate Change

Before researchers began tying rising global temperatures to fossil fuel consumption and other anthropogenic (human) factors, energy policy in the United States was shaped primarily by concerns about energy security; economic stability; pollution trends; and, to a lesser extent, public land conservation. In the 1990s and 2000s, however, a steady stream of reports from the world's most illustrious scientific research institutions warned—using progressively more urgent language—that the United States and the rest of the world need to immediately and dramatically curtail the use of fossil fuels to stave off catastrophic alterations to the world's climate. The litany of potential blows to the planet from climate change, these reports asserted, includes significantly higher sea levels, widespread desertification, wholesale species extinctions, and heightened vulnerability to virulent diseases and famine. These forecasts have altered the terrain of energy policymaking in the United States, even as the scientific basis for these warnings has become a topic of heated political debate.

ENERGY NEEDS DRIVE EARLY POLICYMAKING

Prior to the 1970s American policymakers saw little need to craft a unified platform of energy policies for the nation. The United States seemingly had plentiful supplies of oil, coal, and natural gas for many of its energy needs, and any shortfalls could be easily imported. Policymakers did involve themselves more directly in the nuclear energy industry, putting together subsidies and legal protections (most notably the 1957 Price-Anderson Act) that would help the industry grow. But the main priority was simply to create and maintain stable market conditions that would keep inexpensive, reliable, and job-creating energy flowing through America's economic veins.

In 1973, however, the oil embargo imposed by the Organization of Petroleum Exporting Countries (OPEC) and an accompanying jump in oil prices jolted U.S. policymakers and pushed concerns about energy independence and energy development to the fore. Presidents Nixon, Ford, and Carter all sought to find common ground with Congress in crafting a genuine national energy policy that would reduce U.S. vulnerability to disruptions in the delivery of fossil fuels from overseas. The main focus of these efforts was expansion of domestic supplies of coal, oil, and natural gas through increased extraction and development, coupled with new policies designed to further boost America's nuclear power capacity. The heightened focus on energy development also prompted the 1977 creation of the Department of Energy, which consolidated policymaking authority on energy issues that had previously been widely dispersed through the federal bureaucracy.

Modest energy conservation and efficiency programs were also implemented for the first time during this period. The most notable early efforts to reduce dependence on fossil fuels included the 1975 passage of the Energy Policy Conservation Act, which mandated the first Corporate Average Fuel Economy (CAFE) standards for passenger cars and light trucks, and the unveiling in the late 1970s of tax credits for investments in renewable energy projects such as solar panels and wind farms. These federal tax incentives inspired California and several other states to offer similar tax credit incentives for citizens who invested in solar and wind industry start-ups.

When Ronald Reagan became president in January 1981, his administration, like those of his immediate predecessors, framed increased domestic drilling and coal mining as essential to America's future prosperity. The Reagan Administration thus pursued—with

America's transition from fossil fuels to renewable energy has been a fitful and tentative one, despite growing concerns about energy independence, oil availability, and global climate change.

a fair amount of success—deregulatory policies that aimed to free oil and gas companies and the coal industry from many of the environmental and safety laws and other operational restraints that had been imposed on them during the 1960s and 1970s.

The Reagan Administration also worked mightily to expand U.S. nuclear energy capacity, but in this area it was less successful **(see Document 11.1)**. Nuclear power had long been touted by proponents as a wonderful source of "clean" energy that produced none of the air pollution associated with coal- and oil-fired power plants, and by 1988 it accounted for almost 7 percent of all U.S. energy used. Nonetheless, the technology was strongly opposed by most environmental groups and viewed with profound skepticism by significant numbers of policymakers, scientists, and members of the general public. This opposition stemmed from intense concerns about the disposal of radioactive waste materials and doubts about the adequacy of government oversight of reactor operations. This latter concern stemmed primarily from the fact that the federal government's designated regulator of the industry, the Atomic Energy Commission (AEC), also was operating under an explicit mandate to *support* commercial development of the technology.[1] Safety fears were further fed by reactor accidents at Browns Ferry in Alabama (in 1975), Three Mile Island in Pennsylvania (in 1979), and the 1986 Chernobyl disaster in the Soviet Union. The notoriety of the Three Mile Island incident was particularly difficult for the nuclear power industry to overcome. In this event, which took place on March 28, 1979, a reactor at the Three Mile Island nuclear power facility near Harrisburg, Pennsylvania, overheated and released radioactive gases. A full reactor meltdown was averted, but the evacuations of area residents and nightmarish meltdown scenarios reported by national news media during the week-long crisis cast a dark pall over the entire industry.

Despite Three Mile Island, the Reagan Administration shepherded many nuclear plants already in the construction pipeline to full operation by the close of his second term. These efforts, combined with increases in reactor capacity, lifted the industry to a 20 percent share of all electricity generation in the United States by the opening years of the twenty-first century. But dozens of other reactor orders were cancelled, and Reagan's pro-nuclear policies failed to spur any orders for new nuclear power plants. By the close of the 1980s the industry was—if not exactly moribund—operating under a cloud of suspicion that its best days were behind it.

Meanwhile, the nascent renewable energy industry that had formed in the late 1970s and early 1980s was shaken to its core by the vagaries of Washington policymaking. By 1985 state and federal tax incentives for investment in wind turbines and other renewable technologies had lifted sales of wind power to $748 million—up from $21 million a mere four years earlier. In fact, the United States boasted 80 percent of the world's wind energy and 90 percent of its solar capacity by 1985. But that same year the Reagan Administration killed the federal investment tax credit that had sparked this heady growth in renewable energy production. The domestic industry withered in response, and private investment in renewable technologies promptly shifted overseas, where European governments provided a much more hospitable environment for clean technology development. As one twenty-first century "clean tech" investment executive put it, the Reagan Administration's decision to end the renewable tax credit "sent the wind and solar industry to Europe for three decades."[2]

GLOBAL WARMING ARRIVES AS A POLICY ISSUE

American energy policies and consumption patterns were still heavily weighted toward fossil fuels in June 1988, when James E. Hansen, the director of the NASA Goddard Institute for Space Studies, delivered a blunt warning to members of the Senate Energy and Natural Resource Committee. In testimony that attracted worldwide attention, Hansen declared that "global warming"—a theory that emissions of carbon dioxide and other heat-trapping gases generated primarily by human activity were causing gradual warming of the planet via a so-called "greenhouse" effect—was a real threat. "It is time to stop waffling so much and say that the evidence is pretty strong that the greenhouse effect is here," he said.[3]

The idea that burning fossil fuels, clearing forests (which when left intact can serve as major "sinks" or depositories of carbon dioxide) for timber and agriculture, and other human activities might be creating an atmospheric blanket of greenhouse gases (GHGs) capable of baking the planet was not a new one. To the contrary, it had been the subject of serious research and speculation for more than a decade. But Hansen's reputation and official status as the top climate scientist at NASA gave his remarks considerable weight, and over the next few years his findings were corroborated by a proliferating number of climate studies.

This wave of scientific research—made possible by a host of complementary factors, including increased collaboration among international scientific organizations, leaps in technological research capacity in various branches of science, increasing support for environmental research and monitoring programs among western governments, and spectacular improvements to communications technology—convinced many policymakers to revise their previously diffident attitudes toward global climate change. Energy efficiency and conservation policies even became an increasing area of focus in the generally pro-oil and coal administration of George H. W. Bush (see Document 11.2).

The growing body of scientific research on climate change made global warming mitigation a central focus of the June 1992 Conference on Environment and Development in Rio de Janeiro, Brazil. This landmark conference, also known as the Earth Summit, attracted delegations from 179 countries. As the summit unfolded, delegates crafted an elaborate "Agenda 21" program of policy goals and initiatives that emphasized environmentally sustainable paths to long-term economic growth and prosperity. Participants paid special attention to global warming in their deliberations, but the U.S. delegation rebuffed repeated calls from nations in Western Europe and elsewhere to commit to explicit greenhouse gas reduction goals. The George H. W. Bush Administration officials tried to minimize the political fallout from this stance by noting that the United States did sign one of the most highly publicized documents to come out of the Earth Summit, the United Nations Framework Convention on Climate Change (UNFCCC). But critics were quick to point out that this convention, which the U.S. Congress ratified in October 1992, set no mandatory limits on greenhouse gas emissions and contained no enforcement provisions.

THE KYOTO PROTOCOL

The George H. W. Bush Administration's stance in Rio opened a global warming policy rift between America and its European allies that has yet to be mended. Republican officials and policymakers, however, remained unapologetic. They argued that studies warning about impending climate change were excessively speculative and flawed, and they insisted that proposed policy prescriptions for mitigating global warming would be injurious to American businesses and workers. These same concerns were also expressed by regulation-wary industry groups and free-market think tanks, Democratic lawmakers of the industrial Midwest, and a small but vocal minority of scientists whose contrarian views were regularly amplified—and in some cases funded—by industry interests.

By contrast, the Clinton Administration signaled from the outset that it viewed global climate change as a proven fact that could not be ignored. On April 22 (Earth Day), 1993 President Bill Clinton announced that his administration aimed to reduce America's emissions of greenhouse gases to 1990 levels by the year 2000, and he directed federal agencies to assemble plans that would meet that goal. Six months later the administration released a "Climate Change Action Plan" to further advance the GHG mitigation cause. Some environmental groups and climatologists criticized the plan as toothless for its emphasis on voluntary measures and market incentives over regulatory intervention, but economists Jeffrey Frankel and Peter Orszag noted that "even if not different in substance, the Clinton administration's Climate Action Plan differed greatly in tone from what had been Bush administration policy."[4] Observers also noted that the Clinton Administration's approach to climate change mitigation reflected certain political realities. Regulation of greenhouse gases remained anathema to the Republican majority in Congress, and it enjoyed only tepid support from an American public that had become dazed by a steady onslaught of contradictory global warming assessments.

As Clinton's first term progressed, his administration embarked on a series of policy initiatives that were 1) designed to reduce American dependence on GHG-generating fossil fuels and 2) did not require approval from Congress. These programs included new restrictions on oil, gas, and coal extraction on public lands and new investments in renewable energy technologies. In 1996 the Clinton Administration decided to test Congress on the global warming issue once again with a new push for GHG regulation. At a follow-up conference or "protocol" to the UNFCCC held in Geneva in July of that year, the U.S. delegation issued an explicit statement of support for mandatory and legally binding timetables and targets for GHG reduction for all industrialized nations. The congressional backlash to this proposal, which excluded China, India, and other still-industrializing countries, was swift and decisive. In July 1997 the U.S. Senate passed by a 95-0 vote the so-called Byrd-Hagel Resolution, which declared that the United States should oppose any international climate agreements that did not impose binding emission reduction targets on *all* nations.

The Clinton Administration responded to this setback with a defiance that surprised and pleased environmental organizations. In December 1997 a U.S. delegation led by Vice President Al Gore traveled to Kyoto, Japan, for a third UNFCCC conference. As the conference progressed, the Americans willingly contributed to the crafting of a much more rigorous and ambitious treaty for combating global climate change than the 1992 Earth Summit had managed. This treaty, which became known as the Kyoto Protocol, laid out explicit and binding GHG emission targets for thirty-seven industrialized nations and the European community (it committed the U.S. to a 7 percent overall emission reduction) and authorized the creation of an international "emissions trading" regime whereby nations could buy and sell GHG emission "allowances" as long as they did not exceed their overall emission ceilings **(see Document 11.3)**.

Under the terms of the Kyoto Protocol, the agreement would enter into force when it was ratified by at least fifty-five countries that collectively accounted for at least 55 percent of the total 1990 carbon dioxide emissions of developed countries. But the Clinton Administration recognized that it did not have the votes in the Senate for ratification, so it refrained from submitting the agreement to a vote. Once this decision was made, the Clinton White House essentially set the Protocol—and the wider global warming issue—aside for the last years of the president's tenure. This political deadlock greatly slowed the implementation of the Protocol because the United States alone accounts for about a quarter of global carbon dioxide emissions. The treaty finally entered into force in February 2005 after Russia's late 2004 ratification put it over the top on the "55 percent" clause. As of September 2009 a total of 184 nations had ratified the Protocol.

ENERGY AND GLOBAL WARMING POLICIES IN THE BUSH WHITE HOUSE

U.S. energy and global warming policies underwent yet another dramatic swing in 2001 with the inauguration of George W. Bush. During his time on the presidential campaign trail, Bush had promised to implement federal regulations that would reduce U.S. production of carbon dioxide and other greenhouse gases. But upon reaching the White House Bush asserted that the Kyoto Protocol was "fatally flawed" because its mandates extended only to the United States and other developed countries. He said that if emerging economic powers such as India and China were not subject to the same emission requirements, American business would be operating at an unacceptable competitive disadvantage. Finally, White House officials and other critics of the Protocol implied that ratifying the agreement would unacceptably compromise U.S. sovereignty. Western European signatories to the Protocol responded to Bush's rejection of Kyoto with a mix of anger and dismay, denouncing it as "irresponsible" and "arrogant." The administration, however, shrugged off these attacks and remained steadfast in its position.[5]

Over the next several years the Bush Administration essentially ignored or discounted the climate change issue, even after its own Environmental Protection Agency (EPA) issued a 2002 "Climate Action Report" describing global warming as a serious threat. White House officials contradicted the EPA analysis by stating that considerable uncertainty still existed regarding the science of climate change, and Bush himself dismissed the report as a product of "the bureaucracy." Other climate studies issued around this time by the Intergovernmental Panel on Climate Change, the U.S. National Academy of Sciences, and other leading scientific institutions also received only cursory acknowledgement from the Bush Administration.

The administration's impassive response to these reports reflected the fact that they were being released at a time when the Bush White House was working mightily to execute an ambitious overhaul of U.S. energy policy that would increase U.S. extraction and consumption of fossil fuels. The administration and its conservative supporters in Congress, industry, and the media described this overhaul as a badly needed effort to boost American energy supplies and increase the nation's energy independence in a post–September 11 world.

This campaign had begun in the opening weeks of the Bush Administration, when the president issued two executive orders designed to "expedite" domestic production of coal, oil, and natural gas. It reached another milestone in May 2001, when a formal energy plan that made major new commitments to fossil fuels and nuclear energy was submitted to Congress for its consideration. And it manifested itself in federal agency directives like the one that Bureau of Land Management (BLM) director Nina Rose Hatfield issued to employees in fall 2001. This memorandum instructed BLM staffers to prepare a "Statement of Adverse Energy Impact" every time "your decisions or actions will have a direct or indirect adverse impact on energy development, production, supply and/or distribution." The meaning of this sort of directive, wrote *High Country News* writer Jon Margolis, was unmistakable to "anyone who understands how bureaucracies work. . . . The burden of argument is on the denier, and the BLMer who wants commendations on his/her personnel file will deny very carefully and quite rarely."[6]

But while federal agencies reworked their day-to-day policies to better reflect the pro-development priorities of the Bush White House, the Bush Energy Plan was derailed repeatedly on Capitol Hill. Majority Democrats in the Senate objected to many elements of the plan, which had been crafted by an industry-oriented "energy task force" led by Vice President Dick Cheney. They decried the bill's emphasis on fossil fuel development as foolish and environmentally irresponsible, criticized the plan's generous subsidies to industry as corporate welfare, and charged that the bill's package of energy conservation measures were too modest. But perhaps no single provision of the Bush Energy Plan attracted as much negative attention from Democrats as a proposal to allow oil exploration and drilling in the Alaska National Wildlife Refuge (ANWR) **(see Documents 11.4 and 11.5)**. The Bush Energy Plan was stalled for four years as a result of this opposition, and when it finally passed as the Energy Policy Act of 2005, several of the provisions most objectionable to Democrats had been revised or—in the case of drilling in ANWR— stripped entirely from the bill. Still, the debate over drilling in ANWR appears to be one that will exist as long as the drilling prohibitions remain in place; in the 2008 presidential election, for example, ANWR became a central point of debate between the pro-drilling Republican ticket of Senator John McCain (Ariz.) and Alaska governor Sarah Palin and the Democratic ticket of Senator Barack Obama (Ill.) and Senator Joe Biden (Del.), who favored continuing the prohibitions on drilling in ANWR.

CITIES AND STATES TAKE ACTION

The Bush Administration's steadfast opposition to the Kyoto Protocol, combined with its reluctance to support mandated emission control programs or to negotiate other binding climate pacts with other countries, frustrated environmental groups, prominent scientific organizations, members of Congress, and citizens who believed that the threat of global warming required a more robust response from the U.S. government. As this political gridlock in Washington deepened state lawmakers and city officials displayed an increasing willingness to take matters into their own hands.

These initiatives took a variety of forms. In 2002 lawmakers in California, the single largest market for automobiles in the union, approved legislation that would force automobile manufacturers to build more fuel-efficient vehicles, which would in turn reduce emissions of carbon dioxide. This measure was immediately challenged by the Bush Administration in court, and their battle over implementation of the new state standards continued throughout Bush's tenure in the White House. But California's policies also provided a blueprint for several other states to pursue similar regulations, and in 2009 the Obama Administration announced plans to set national limits on greenhouse gas emissions from automobiles. This national policy, observed experts, closely followed the contours of the California law.

States in the northeast have also been pioneers in passing meaningful legislation to slash their GHG emissions. In 2008 ten northeastern states agreed to an ambitious pact called the Regional Greenhouse Gas Initiative. Under this scheme, utilities in the region have to pay state treasuries for emission allowances—essentially the right to emit carbon dioxide. The revenue generated by this carbon auction will be used by member states to fund an array of GHG mitigation programs.

California and the states of the northeast have not been alone in crafting GHG mitigation strategies and standards, however. By the mid-2000s, in fact, more than half of the nation's states had taken official steps—usually in the form of an executive order or legislative bill—to reduce their emissions of greenhouse gases. Nineteen states representing more than 45 percent of the total U.S. population had enacted "renewable portfolio standards"—policies that require electricity providers to obtain a minimum percentage of their power from wind, solar, and other renewable energy sources by a certain date. Fifteen states had also implemented "societal benefit charges" on utility use to fund renewable energy and energy efficiency projects. Other state measures included strong legislation to regulate carbon dioxide emissions from power plants operating within their borders and newly minted tax incentives to attract "clean energy" companies and investment.[7] "From wind energy in Texas to carbon dioxide standards in New Hampshire and Oregon, the elements of a bottom-up American approach to climate change are taking shape," wrote environmental policy analyst Barry Rabe. "States have clearly positioned themselves to achieve significant reductions in greenhouse gas emissions."[8]

Of course, some of these state-level efforts to address global climate change were more politically controversial than others. In left-leaning California, for example, ambitious legislation such as the 2006 Global Warming Solutions Act (AB 32), which seeks to reduce the state's GHG emissions by 25 percent by 2020 through a system of mandatory emission caps on everything from cars to power plants, enjoyed relatively broad public support. But in conservative Kansas, Democratic governor Kathleen Sebelius's repeated vetoes of proposals to build two new coal-fired power plants in the state sparked a political firestorm (see Document 11.11).

In addition to this state-level action, hundreds of American towns and cities have adopted GHG mitigation measures and strategies of their own. A key galvanizing event in this regard was the unveiling of the U.S. Mayors Climate Protection Agreement in February 2005. This agreement, which was founded by Seattle mayor Greg Nickels, called on member officials to "strive to meet or exceed Kyoto Protocol targets in their city operations and communities." As expected, it was embraced by the liberal mayors of cities in New England and the West Coast. Within a year of its creation, however, the agreement had also garnered the signatures of the mayors of Norman, Oklahoma; Bellevue, Nebraska; Billings, Montana; Laredo, Texas; and other mid-sized "red state" population centers (see Document 11.6).

Partisan Politics and the Global Warming Debate

Environmental groups and scientists concerned about global warming hailed all of these municipal- and state-level energy conservation and GHG mitigation schemes. But they continued to insist that the necessary national reductions in emissions of carbon dioxide and other gases responsible for climate change could not be achieved without new and stringent federal emission regulations. It was here, however, that political divisions and gamesmanship—and genuine disagreement about the severity of the threat—continued to undercut all efforts at achieving policy consensus.

Indeed, longstanding partisan divisions over global warming yawned wider than ever by the closing months of the Bush Administration. The Republican Party remained adamant that stringent GHG mitigation regulations would strangle the American economy, kill jobs, and allow emerging economic powerhouses such as China and India to eclipse the United States. Many Republican legislators, industry spokespersons, and conservative media figures have also suggested that climate changes might actually be the product of natural weather cycles rather than human activity. And a good many have questioned whether the "global warming threat" is even legitimate or merely the fevered fantasy of unscrupulous "greens" and gullible media (see Document 11.7).

Global warming skeptics have frequently argued that climate science is still in its infancy and that the computer models that weigh heavily in many climate change forecasts are too unreliable. "Some experts have asserted that many computer models are based on inaccurate measures of historical temperature change, that climate warming models fail to describe the long-range physics of climate change, that other historical climate data are misconstrued or misapplied in climate modeling, and much more," summarized policy analyst Walter Rosenbaum.[9] In addition, opponents of GHG regulation have noted that some well-known scientists, such as Massachusetts Institute of Technology atmospheric science professor Richard Lindzen, have vocally rejected the current mainstream scientific consensus on global climate change and the need for decisive regulatory action. "There is no compelling evidence that the warming trend we've seen will amount to anything close to catastrophe," said Lindzen in 2007. "The current alarm rests on the false assumption not only that we live in a perfect world, temperature-wise, but also that our warming forecasts for the year 2040 are somehow more reliable than the weatherman's forecast for next week."[10] Given all of these considerations, Republicans have asserted that the most appropriate and responsible course of action is to support additional research on climate change, encourage voluntary emission reduction efforts by business and industry, and refrain from imposing any unnecessary regulatory regimes hurtful to the U.S. economy.

Most (although not all) Democratic members of Congress, by contrast, have become progressively more supportive of the idea that firm and binding regulations to reduce GHG emissions are necessary to combat global warming. This position has been strongly supported by the environmental movement and all internationally recognized institutions and academies that have undertaken climate change studies, including the Intergovernmental Panel on Climate Change (IPCC), National Oceanic and Atmospheric Administration (NOAA), EPA, Royal Society of the United Kingdom, National Academy of Sciences, American Geophysical Union, and National Center for Atmospheric Research **(see Document 11.10)**.

Unlike their opponents, these parties assert that the scientific verdict on climate change is indisputable **(see Document 11.8)**. And they note that virtually all other industrialized nations in the world have already decisively concluded that anthropogenic climate change is real and that it will require a muscular response with sweeping mitigation and adaptation components. These proponents of regulatory action also insist that the economic costs associated with effective and ambitious regulation of GHG emissions pale compared to the economic Armageddon that would be unleashed on the planet over the course of the twenty-first century by catastrophic climate change. Analysts such as renowned economist Sir Nicholas Stern have even asserted that "tackling climate change is the pro-growth strategy; ignoring it will ultimately undermine economic growth. . . . Mitigation—taking strong action to reduce emissions—must be viewed as an investment, a cost incurred now and in the coming few decades to avoid the risks of very severe consequences in the future. If these investments are made wisely, the costs will be manageable, and there will be a wide range of opportunities for growth and development along the way."[11]

Other pro-regulation commentators have offered similar sentiments about the economic impact of climate change regulations, even as they acknowledge that "green" technology players would fare better than traditional fossil fuel industries in such a world. And it is this reality, they say, that accounts for much of the political resistance to GHG mitigation proposals in the United States. "Responding to climate change with the vigor that the threat deserves would not, contrary to legend, be devastating for the economy as a whole," wrote *New York Times* columnist Paul Krugman. "But it would shuffle the economic deck, hurting some powerful vested interests even as it created new economic opportunities. And the industries of the past have armies of lobbyists in place right now; the industries of the future don't."[12] Indeed, a 2009 study by the Center for Responsive Politics estimated that the number of Washington lobbyists billing clients for hours worked on climate change issues jumped by 300 percent from 2003 to 2008 and that total lobbying expenditures on climate change topped $90 million in 2008 alone.[13] In addition, there have been persistent allegations from Democrats, environmental groups, and climatologists alike that the Bush White House has engaged in systematic efforts to manipulate results of climate change science research and mislead policymakers and the public about the risks and likelihood of global warming.[14]

Oil companies, coal industry groups, and business associations such as the National Association of Manufacturers (NAM) and the U.S. Chamber of Commerce who oppose any government action to mitigate climate change also stand accused of using their political influence with Republican legislators and their vast financial resources to flood the public commons with distortions and half-truths about the trustworthiness of studies that warn about climate change (and many other environmental or public health threats stemming from industry activities). "Industry has learned that debating the *science* is much easier and more effective than debating the *policy*," charged public policy analyst David Michaels, who worked in the Clinton Administration as assistant secretary of energy for environment, safety, and health. "The vilification of any research that might threaten corporate interests as 'junk science' and the sanctification of its own bought-and-paid-for research as 'sound science' is . . . Orwellian—and nothing less than standard operating procedure today."[15] These business groups say that these charges are untrue, but their unyielding stance on the issue of climate change has caused some attrition within their ranks. High-profile companies including Apple Computers, Pacific Gas and Electric, and Exelon, the nation's leading provider of nuclear energy, all resigned from the U.S. Chamber of Commerce in 2009 over climate policy differences.

These charges and countercharges have kept the American people from reaching any sort of real consensus on whether global warming is cause for great concern or the delusion of alarmist scientists and environmentalists. This lack of consensus, combined with the fact that the most serious predictions of ecological and human carnage stemming from climate change would not manifest themselves for decades, has kept the issue from becoming a policy priority to most voters. A Pew Research Center for the People and the Press poll in January 2009, for example, found global warming ranked dead last in a list of twenty priorities for the nation.[16] The partisan overtones of the dispute over global climate change, meanwhile, have also led many Americans—Democrat and Republican alike—to instinctively side with the "tribe" to which they are normally allegiant. A March 2009 Gallup Poll, for example, found that 41 percent of all Americans polled believe that the threat of global warming is "exaggerated"—but that among self-identified Republicans, 66 percent of respondents felt that way.[17]

INCREASED REGULATION OF GREENHOUSE GASES ON THE HORIZON

The partisan warfare over global warming did not derail all energy-related legislation during George W. Bush's two terms in office. In addition to the 2005 Energy Policy Act, Congress managed to pass a modest Energy Independence and Security Act (EISA) in 2007. This bill, which Bush signed into law on December 19, mandated small improvements in CAFE standards, increased support for biofuel development, and implemented new energy efficiency measures in public buildings and lighting. But legislative proposals on climate change, including those with a veneer of bipartisanship, failed to gain any traction in Congress. In 2008, for example, independent but Democrat-leaning Joseph Lieberman (Conn.) and veteran Republican John Warner (Va.) collaborated to put together a so-called "cap and trade" emission reduction proposal. Under the terms of their bill, the United States would cap the total amount of permissible GHG emissions for the nation while simultaneously implementing a system wherein electric utilities, industries, oil refineries, and other producers of GHGs can "trade"—that is, purchase and sell—emission allowances on an emissions "market." But the Lieberman-Warner bill was actively opposed by the Bush Administration, and it fell short of passage when it came up for a Senate vote.

The defeat of the Lieberman-Warner bill actually defied prognostications made by many policy analysts only one year earlier. In 2007 the Supreme Court had ruled in *Massachusetts et al. v. EPA* that the Environmental Protection Agency had both the authority and the legal obligation to regulate greenhouse gases under the Clean Air Act

(see Document 11.9). In the immediate aftermath of that decision, policymakers and stakeholders on both side of the global warming issue had openly speculated that the decision was a game-changing one that would pave the way for the passage of meaningful GHG mitigation legislation in Congress. "Conventional wisdom was that fear of regulation would drive utilities and manufacturers to the bargaining table, changing the dynamic in Congress," explained Grist.org's Dave Roberts. "EPA was supposed to play the role of the big, silent goon in the corner, tapping his baseball bat in his hand."[18]

But the defeat of Lieberman-Warner implied that industry groups and their allies in Washington had determined that global warming regulations enacted by federal agencies might be easier to combat than those contained in congressional legislation. One reason for this gamble is that Republican administrations have kept a loose regulatory hand over industry in recent decades. The other is that "while regulation can be challenged in court if it oversteps precedent, legislation is for keeps," acknowledged a spokesman for Electric Reliability Coordinating Council, a power industry trade group.[19]

When President Barack Obama strode onto this hazy playing field in 2009, his administration adopted a two-tiered strategy to try to fulfill his stated campaign goal of reducing America's emissions of carbon dioxide and other greenhouse gases. On the one hand, the Obama White House expressed support for bills such as the American Clean Energy and Security Act (ACESA), which passed the House in June 2009. This legislation, which was crafted by Democrats Henry Waxman (Calif.) and Edward Markey (Mass.), proposed a cap-and-trade approach to realize major reductions in greenhouse gas emissions by 2020 **(see Document 11.13)**.

Obama Administration officials acknowledged that they would much rather see climate change addressed through something like ACESA than through bureaucracy-generated federal regulations that will inevitably be complex to craft, difficult to roll out and monitor, and subject to extensive litigation. Absent the passage of breakthrough legislation, however, the Obama Administration directed the Environmental Protection Agency to prepare new rules and regulations that will enable the agency to, if necessary, rein in the nation's GHG emissions itself.

In addition, Obama Administration officials and members of Congress convinced of the need for greater action on climate change supported a variety of measures and programs designed to recalibrate how America uses energy and where it gets that energy. These include reforestation and wilderness conservation initiatives designed to sequester carbon, support for increased reliance on nuclear power technology, new national energy efficiency standards for buildings and appliances, further boosts to CAFE standards, and heightened investment in high-speed rail and other mass transit systems that reduce fossil fuel consumption **(see Document 11.12)**. The administration and midwestern members of both parties also remained staunch supporters of corn-based ethanol and other "biofuels"—despite growing evidence that the high levels of energy required for biofuel production in the early twenty-first century actually *increase* overall GHG emissions and concerns that biofuels exacerbate worldwide hunger by reducing the amount of acreage and crops allocated to feeding people. In addition, the Obama Administration received plaudits from environmental and energy efficiency groups for including $167 billion in direct grants, loan guarantees, and tax credits for renewable energy in its February 2009 American Recovery and Reinvestment economic stimulus package. This burst of financial support for wind, solar, and other clean energy projects, combined with firm instructions to the Department of Energy to invest *directly* in promising renewable energy companies, gave desperately needed help to numerous clean-tech start-up companies that had been pushed to the abyss by the loss of access to credit and investment capital that followed the late 2008 financial convulsions on Wall Street. "The stimulus package essentially saved the renewable-energy industry in the United States," stated the managing director of one venture capital firm.[20]

Researchers and environmental activists who believe in anthropogenic climate change praise these steps toward securing a cleaner and more energy independent future for the United States. But they also assert that far more significant federal intervention and international cooperation will be necessary—and soon—if Americans and the rest of the planet's citizenry hope to avoid wrenching, devastating alteration of the environments in which they live and work. This point of view is supported by new reports that indicate that the planet may have already reached a global warming "tipping point" that renders certain environmental changes inevitable in the coming decades. A September 2009 *Climate Change Science Compendium* report by the United Nations Environment Programme (UNEP), for example, predicted that even if the world's leading emitters of GHG immediately fulfilled their most ambitious emission-reduction pledges, the planet would still warm by 6.3°F and experience rising seas of six feet or more by 2100 from emissions that have already been pumped into the atmosphere. "The pace and scale of climate change may now be outstripping even the most sobering predictions of the last [2007] report of the Intergovernmental Panel of Climate Change (IPCC)," reported UNEP. "An analysis of the very latest, peer-reviewed science indicates that many predictions at the upper end of the IPCC's forecasts are becoming ever more likely."[21]

In light of such grim forecasts, policy analysts believe that advocates of strong regulation of GHG emissions actually face a counterintuitive challenge in enlisting the support of the American public against global climate change. They recognize that the harrowing possibilities for ecological and economic carnage delineated in studies carried out by the IPCC and other organizations have the potential to rouse skeptics and fence straddlers to their side, which would in turn increase the pressure on lawmakers to act and corporations to reduce their carbon footprints. But scientists, legislators, officials, and environmental groups supportive of ambitious GHG mitigation strategies also recognize the need to reassure listeners that if America and the rest of the world acts swiftly and decisively, the worst impacts of global climate change can be avoided **(see Document 11.14)**. Otherwise, individuals, corporations, and governments alike may simply throw up their hands and remain on the sidelines, waiting resignedly for the coming surging seas.

NOTES

1. Richard N. L. Andrews, *Managing the Environment, Managing Ourselves: A History of American Environmental Policy* (New Haven, Conn.: Yale University Press, 1999), 186.

2. Joshua Green, "The Elusive Green Economy," *The Atlantic,* July/August 2009. www.theatlantic.com/doc/200907/carter-obama-energy.

3. Quoted in Phillip Shabecoff, "Global Warming Has Begun, Expert Tells Senate," *New York Times,* June 24, 1988. www.nytimes.com/1988/06/24/us/global-warming-has-begun-expert-tells-senate.html?pagewanted=1.

4. Jeffrey A. Frankel, and Peter R. Orszog, *American Economic Policy in the 1990s* (Cambridge, Mass.: MIT Press, 2002), 617.

5. Walter A. Rosenbaum, *Environmental Politics and Policy* (Washington, D.C.: CQ Press, 2008), p. 331.

6. Jon Margolis, "Bush's Energy Push Meets Unintended Consequences," in *Give and Take: How the Clinton Administration's Public Lands Offensive Transformed the American West,* ed. Paul Larmer. (Paonia, Colo.: High Country News Books, 2004), 169–170.

7.   Barry G. Rabe, *Statehouse and Greenhouse: The Emerging Politics of American Climate Change Policy* (Washington, D.C.: Brookings Institution Press, 2004).

8.   Ibid., 109.

9.   Rosenbaum, *Environmental Politics and Policy,* 335.

10. Richard S. Lindzen, "Why So Gloomy?" *Newsweek,* [n.d.] 2007. www.newsweek.com/id/35543/page/1.

11. Nicholas Stern, "Executive Summary," *Stern Review on the Economics of Climate Change* (Great Britain: HM Treasury, 2006). www.hm-treasury.gov.uk/d/Executive_Summary.pdf.

12. Paul Krugman, "Cassandras of Climate," *New York Times,* September 27, 2009. www.nytimes.com/2009/09/28/opinion/28krugman.html.

13. Marianne Lavelle, "The Climate Change Lobby Explosion" (Washington, D.C.: Center for Public Integrity, Feb. 24, 2009). www.publicintegrity.org/investigations/climate_change/articles/entry/1171/.

14. U.S. House of Representatives, Committee on Oversight and Government Reform, *Political Interference with Climate Change Science under the Bush Administration,* December 2007. http://oversight.house.gov/documents/20071210101633.pdf.

15. David Michaels, *Doubt Is Their Product: How Industry's Assault on Science Threatens Your Health* (New York: Oxford University Press, 2008), xii.

16. Pew Research Center for the People and the Press, "Economy, Jobs Trump All Other Policy Priorities in 2009: Overview," January 22, 2009. http://people-press.org/report/485/economy-top-policy-priority.

17. Lydia Saad, "Increased Number Think Global Warming Is 'Exaggerated,'" Gallup Poll, March 11, 2009. www.gallup.com/poll/116590/increased-number-think-global-warming-exaggerated.aspx.

18. David Roberts, "Everything You Always Wanted to Know about EPA Greenhouse Gas Regulations, but Were Afraid to Ask," Grist.org, September 15, 2009. www.grist.org/article/2009–09–15-everything-you-always-wanted-to-know-about-epa-greenhouse-gas-re.

19. "U.S.: Warming Gases Are Health Threat," *MSNBC.com,* April 17, 2009. www.msnbc.msn.com/id/30264214/.

20. Green, "The Elusive Green Economy."

21. "Impacts of Climate Change Coming Faster and Sooner: New Science Report Underlines Urgency for Governments to Seal the Deal in Copenhagen," Press Release, Washington/Nairobi: United Nations Environment Programme, September 24, 2009. www.unep.org/Documents.Multilingual/Default.asp?DocumentID=596&ArticleID=6326&l=en.

DOCUMENT 11.1

President Reagan Seeks to Revitalize the Nuclear Energy Industry

"Safe Commercial Nuclear Power Can Help Meet America's Future Energy Needs"

October 8, 1981

One key element of President Ronald Reagan's overall energy policy was to remove regulatory obstacles to increased investment in nuclear energy. Reagan and many senior officials believed that nuclear power had the potential to fulfill the nation's growing energy needs and boost business productivity and overall economic growth. On October 8, 1981,

Reagan unveiled a series of policy initiatives designed to rejuvenate the nuclear energy industry, which was still grappling with the public relations fallout from the 1979 Three Mile Island scare. His statement about these initiatives is reprinted here.

The Reagan Administration succeeded in clearing the way for full operation of reactors that were already under construction. By the time Reagan left the White House, the Nuclear Regulatory Commission had granted full electric power licenses to more than forty plants across the country, many of which had been under construction since the 1970s. But support for new nuclear plant construction declined among both utilities and the general public during the 1980s as a result of concerns about the technology's cost-competitiveness with other energy options and continued concerns about safety and waste disposal. By the close of the twentieth century, commercial nuclear power was being frequently ignored in policy discussions about twenty-first century energy options—despite the fact that it accounted for about 20 percent of all electricity being generated in the United States.

A more abundant, affordable, and secure energy future for all Americans is a critical element of this administration's economic recovery program. While homeowners and business firms have shown remarkable ingenuity and resourcefulness in meeting their energy needs at lower cost through conservation, it is evident that sustained economic growth over the decades ahead will require additional energy supplies. This is particularly true of electricity, which will supply an increasing share of our energy.

If we are to meet this need for new energy supplies, we must move rapidly to eliminate unnecessary government barriers to efficient utilization of our abundant, economical resources of coal and uranium. It is equally vital that the utilities—investor-owned, public, and co-ops—be able to develop new generating capacity that will permit them to supply their customers at the lowest cost, be it coal, nuclear, hydro, or new technologies such as fuel cells.

One of the best potential sources of new electrical energy supplies in the coming decades is nuclear power. The United States has developed a strong technological base in the production of electricity from nuclear energy. Unfortunately, the Federal Government has created a regulatory environment that is forcing many utilities to rule out nuclear power as a source of new generating capacity, even when their consumers may face unnecessarily high electric rates as a result. Nuclear power has become entangled in a morass of regulations that do not enhance safety but that do cause extensive licensing delays and economic uncertainty. Government has also failed in meeting its responsibility to work with industry to develop an acceptable system for commercial waste disposal, which has further hampered nuclear power development.

To correct present government deficiencies and to enable nuclear power to make its essential contribution to our future energy needs, I am announcing today a series of policy initiatives:

1. I am directing the Secretary of Energy to give immediate priority attention to recommending improvements in the nuclear regulatory and licensing process. I anticipate that the Chairman of the Nuclear Regulatory Commission will take steps to facilitate the licensing of plants under construction and those awaiting licenses. Consistent with public health and safety, we must remove unnecessary obstacles to deployment of the current generation of nuclear power reactors. The time involved to proceed from the planning stage to an operating license for new nuclear power plants has more than doubled since the

mid-1970's and is presently some 10–14 years. This process must be streamlined, with the objective of shortening the time involved to 6–8 years, as is typical in some other countries.

2. I am directing that government agencies proceed with the demonstration of breeder reactor technology, including completion of the Clinch River Breeder Reactor. This is essential to ensure our preparedness for longer-term nuclear power needs.

3. I am lifting the indefinite ban which previous administrations placed on commercial reprocessing activities in the United States. In addition, we will pursue consistent, long-term policies concerning reprocessing of spent fuel from nuclear power reactors and eliminate regulatory impediments to commercial interest in this technology, while ensuring adequate safeguards.

It is important that the private sector take the lead in developing commercial reprocessing services. Thus, I am also requesting the Director of the Office of Science and Technology Policy, working with the Secretary of Energy, to undertake a study of the feasibility of obtaining economical plutonium supplies for the Department of Energy by means of a competitive procurement. By encouraging private firms to supply fuel for the breeder program at a cost that does not exceed that of government-produced plutonium, we may be able to provide a stable market for private sector reprocessing and simultaneously reduce the funding needs of the U.S. breeder demonstration program.

4. I am instructing the Secretary of Energy, working closely with industry and State governments, to proceed swiftly toward deployment of means of storing and disposing of commercial, high-level radioactive waste. We must take steps now to accomplish this objective and demonstrate to the public that problems associated with management of nuclear waste can be resolved.

5. I recognize that some of the problems besetting the nuclear option are of a deep-seated nature and may not be quickly resolved. Therefore, I am directing the Secretary of Energy and the Director of the Office of Science and Technology Policy to meet with representatives from the universities, private industry, and the utilities, and requesting them to report to me on the obstacles which stand in the way of increased use of nuclear energy and the steps needed to overcome them in order to assure the continued availability of nuclear power to meet America's future energy needs, not later than September 30, 1982.

Eliminating the regulatory problems that have burdened nuclear power will be of little use if the utility sector cannot raise the capital necessary to fund construction of new generating facilities. We have already taken significant steps to improve the climate for capital formation with the passage of my program for economic recovery. The tax bill contains substantial incentives designed to attract new capital into industry.

Safe commercial nuclear power can help meet America's future energy needs. The policies and actions that I am announcing today will permit a revitalization of the U.S. industry's efforts to develop nuclear power. In this way, native American genius, not arbitrary Federal policy, will be free to provide for our energy future.

Source: Reagan, Ronald. Statement Announcing a Series of Policy Initiatives on Nuclear Energy, October 8, 1981. www.reagan.utexas.edu/archives/speeches/1981/100881b.htm.

DOCUMENT 11.2

President Bush Extols the Energy Policy Act

"What We're Trying to Do Is Cut through the Regulation"

October 24, 1992

The 1992 Energy Policy Act signed by President George H. W. Bush was the first successful—albeit modest—effort to craft a national energy policy for the United States. President Jimmy Carter had made forays in this direction during his single term, only to be thwarted by economic and political troubles, and President Ronald Reagan's faith in the free market had led him to consciously avoid using government institutions and authority to chart any sort of preordained energy course for the nation.

The Bush Administration followed Reagan's example in some significant respects. It labored to loosen regulatory restraints on domestic exploration and extraction of coal, oil, and natural gas resources, and it championed nuclear energy as a key to long-term American energy security. The 1992 Energy Policy Act reflected those goals. But this legislation also included the first federal energy conservation programs of any consequence, including measures designed to support research into alternative-fuel vehicles, promote energy conservation in buildings and appliances, and encourage renewable energy use by electric utilities.

In publicizing the act, however, the Bush Administration placed far more emphasis on deregulation elements that would be popular with its political base than the legislation's energy conservation features. This political calculation also contributed to the White House's decision to make a Maurice, Louisiana, drilling company the site of the signing ceremony on October 24, 1992—a mere ten days before the 1992 presidential election. Following are Bush's remarks at the ceremony.

President Bush: Please be seated. And I want to thank Jack, Jack Wilson [owner of Jack-Wade Drilling Co.], for making all this possible. He ain't making any money while we're standing here, with that rig waiting for a little more action. But it's very, very nice of him to do this. And I'm grateful to him, to the superintendent, the tool pushers, all the guys here and those from Arco, a company for whom Jack is drilling this rig. And Chip Rimer and Leon Smith, particularly, I want to thank. Also I want to single out Secretary Jim Watkins, our Secretary of Energy, my mate in the Cabinet. He is doing a superb job. And we invited several Members of the United States Congress who have been interested in this, and I don't know that they're here. But I want to thank the Louisiana delegation who worked hard, and all of you have fought hard to strengthen America's energy future. And it's an honor to have you here today and to be with you.

Two years ago our administration proposed a national energy strategy. It was a blueprint to promote economic growth and make the country more secure. And our strategy was based on the simple premise that the greatest single energy resource America possesses is the wisdom and enterprise of its citizens. The last two years have seen much hard work, many hundreds of hours of hard study and negotiation. And we know, and I know especially because I used to be in this business, how rough it's been on those who have been working the oilfields and the drilling business and, yes, in the production business as well. But now our efforts have borne fruit, and this afternoon, right here, and it's fitting it happens in the shadow of a drilling rig, we're going to sign the Energy Policy Act of 1992.

We're in a political year, but I think it's only fitting to say that this bill is a tribute to many, the work of many people. And it's not a Republican accomplishment or a Democratic accomplishment; it's an accomplishment for all America. And the Senate, to be very fair about it—I wish the guy would see the light on the rest of the things, but Bennett Johnston deserves great credit because he's been working closely with Jim Watkins on this. So give credit where credit is due. And I'll talk to him about something else later on, you know what I mean? [Laughter] But I salute him. And I salute Senator Malcolm Wallop, the Senator from Wyoming, who also was very active in all of this. And in the House, the Democratic chairman over there, John Dingell, deserves credit and Phil Sharp and then Republican Carlos Moorhead. So I mean it when I say it's a team effort. Jim can bring that out and talk to you about that. He'll certainly confirm it because he's working with all of them, as well as with his colleagues in the Cabinet.

Another—but this one that I mentioned earlier deserves very special praise—and a man of vision and integrity, and that's Jim Watkins. I'll tell you, he has stayed in this thing from day one, fought against a lot of political odds, changed and worked and given and taken, but we've ended up with good, sound national energy. So once again, I want to thank Jim Watkins for what he's done. For three years he's been fighting this battle, working to strengthen America's energy industry through more than 90 administrative actions so that we may compete in this new world economy. And he's already made great progress, but the bill, in our view, will accelerate progress. And it's a crowning achievement.

The Energy Policy Act will increase domestic energy production, and in the process we all—you know this better than most Americans—that means there will be less reliance on foreign oil, foreign energy. And it will promote conservation and efficiency. And it will create American jobs. The IPA—what was that figure?

Secretary Watkins: Forty-five thousand jobs just next year.

The President: All right, Jim is telling me there's a new estimate by IPAA, which is the Independent Petroleum Association [of America], that will create 45,000 American jobs next year, 7,000 wells. And we're doing this not by resorting to the failed methods of Government control but by unleashing the genius of the private sector; guys like Jack, tool pushers and roughnecks like these guys standing right here.

And the act, now, it's got other facets to it that get across the broad energy spectrum. The act increases competition in the way that electricity is generated and sold. And that will cut prices, reducing the strain on family budgets across the country. By the year 2010, and most of you look young enough to think you'll be around by then, our reforms will save the average household $150 a year in annual electricity bills. The act also improves licensing procedures for new nuclear power plants, safe use of nuclear power, guaranteeing that this safe and clean resource will help meet our needs for the next century. It also encourages the development and use of clean-burning alternative fuels so that the robust production of energy will go hand in hand with a clean environment.

The act provides much needed tax relief for you, our Nation's independents, independent oil and gas producers. By far the most important change that we make as it affects the independents is to reform the alternative minimum tax to better reflect the risk, the risk that it takes to explore for oil. And that will create good jobs, as Jim has pointed out to me just now once again, good jobs all across the oil States. The reform will allow producers to keep more of your hard-earned money to reinvest in the production of some domestic fossil fuels. And the facts are simple: We must work to produce more of our energy here at home and import less from abroad. And our national security demands it. Future generations deserve it. And now we can make sure that it will be done.

I spent much of my life, and Barbara at my side, in the oil business, starting out in west Texas in the supply business and then in the land drilling business, in the offshore drilling business, as well as the production business, doing some wild-catting and producing some oil. And I saw firsthand how the Government can sometimes help. But I also saw firsthand, particularly when I was in the offshore business, how the Government can hinder things with too darn much regulation. And so what we're trying to do is cut through the regulation. And I believe that I do understand the men and women who are out there trying to meet America's energy needs. I believe that this act opens a new era in which Government acts not as a master but as a partner and the servant.

Once again, to the families in south Louisiana and other places who have been hurting, we understand that. And I do think that this act, with the repeal particularly of the alternative minimum tax, offers a much, much brighter future. And I'm proud to be back in this wonderful part of the world.

Thank you all very, very much. Now you're going to see how it works when you sign some of this legislation.

Source: Bush, George. Remarks on Signing the Energy Policy Act of 1992 in Maurice, Louisiana, October 24, 1992. http://bushlibrary.tamu.edu/research/public_papers.php?id=4994&year=1992&month=10.

DOCUMENT 11.3

The Kyoto Protocol

"The Parties . . . Shall Pursue Limitation or Reduction of Emissions of Greenhouse Gases"

December 1997

In December 1997 the United Nations unveiled the Kyoto Protocol to the Framework Convention on Climate Change, an international agreement to fight global warming that was negotiated by representatives from more than 160 countries. The centerpiece of the agreement was a provision that required thirty-eight industrialized countries to reduce the emissions of six major greenhouse gases (GHGs) by 5.2 percent during the 2008 to 2012 period. The Clinton Administration supported the Kyoto Protocol, but the treaty ran aground in Congress. Kyoto never came close to being ratified during the Clinton years because of concerns about the economic impact of its GHG-fighting provisions and public and congressional skepticism about the legitimacy of the global warming phenomenon. When George W. Bush took office, he abandoned the Protocol altogether, describing it as a fatally flawed document. Despite the United States' stance, however, the Kyoto Protocol entered into force in February 2005 after Russia's late 2004 ratification put it over the top on the "55 percent" clause. As of September 2009 a total of 184 nations had ratified the Protocol. Following are excerpts from the opening sections of the Protocol:

The Parties to this Protocol,

Being Parties to the United Nations Framework Convention on Climate Change, hereinafter referred to as "the Convention,"

In pursuit of the ultimate objective of the Convention as stated in its Article 2,

Recalling the provisions of the Convention,

Being guided by Article 3 of the Convention,

Pursuant to the Berlin Mandate adopted by decision 1/CP.1 of the Conference of the Parties to the Convention at its first session,

Have agreed as follows:

ARTICLE 1

For the purposes of this Protocol, the definitions contained in Article 1 of the Convention shall apply. In addition:

1. "Conference of the Parties" means the Conference of the Parties to the Convention.

2. "Convention" means the United Nations Framework Convention on Climate Change, adopted in New York on 9 May 1992.

3. "Intergovernmental Panel on Climate Change" means the Intergovernmental Panel on Climate Change established in 1988 jointly by the World Meteorological Organization and the United Nations Environment Programme.

4. "Montreal Protocol" means the Montreal Protocol on Substances that Deplete the Ozone Layer, adopted in Montreal on 16 September 1987 and as subsequently adjusted and amended.

5. "Parties present and voting" means Parties present and casting an affirmative or negative vote.

6. "Party" means, unless the context otherwise indicates, a Party to this Protocol.

7. "Party included in Annex I" means a Party included in Annex I to the Convention, as may be amended, or a Party which has made a notification under Article 4, paragraph 2(g), of the Convention.

ARTICLE 2

1. Each Party included in Annex I, in achieving its quantified emission limitation and reduction commitments under Article 3, in order to promote sustainable development, shall:

(a) Implement and/or further elaborate policies and measures in accordance with its national circumstances, such as:

(i) Enhancement of energy efficiency in relevant sectors of the national economy;

(ii) Protection and enhancement of sinks and reservoirs of greenhouse gases not controlled by the Montreal Protocol, taking into account its commitments under relevant international environmental agreements; promotion of sustainable forest management practices, afforestation and reforestation;

(iii) Promotion of sustainable forms of agriculture in light of climate change considerations;

(iv) Research on, and promotion, development and increased use of, new and renewable forms of energy, of carbon dioxide sequestration technologies and of advanced and innovative environmentally sound technologies;

(v) Progressive reduction or phasing out of market imperfections, fiscal incentives, tax and duty exemptions and subsidies in all greenhouse gas emitting sectors that run counter to the objective of the Convention and application of market instruments;

(vi) Encouragement of appropriate reforms in relevant sectors aimed at promoting policies and measures which limit or reduce emissions of greenhouse gases not controlled by the Montreal Protocol;

(vii) Measures to limit and/or reduce emissions of greenhouse gases not controlled by the Montreal Protocol in the transport sector;

(viii) Limitation and/or reduction of methane emissions through recovery and use in waste management, as well as in the production, transport and distribution of energy;

(b) Cooperate with other such Parties to enhance the individual and combined effectiveness of their policies and measures adopted under this Article, pursuant to Article 4, paragraph 2(e)(i), of the Convention. To this end, these Parties shall take steps to share their experience and exchange information on such policies and measures, including developing ways of improving their comparability, transparency and effectiveness. The Conference of the Parties serving as the meeting of the Parties to this Protocol shall, at its first session or as soon as practicable thereafter, consider ways to facilitate such cooperation, taking into account all relevant information.

2. The Parties included in Annex I shall pursue limitation or reduction of emissions of greenhouse gases not controlled by the Montreal Protocol from aviation and marine bunker fuels, working through the International Civil Aviation Organization and the International Maritime Organization, respectively.

3. The Parties included in Annex I shall strive to implement policies and measures under this Article in such a way as to minimize adverse effects, including the adverse effects of climate change, effects on international trade, and social, environmental and economic impacts on other Parties, especially developing country Parties and in particular those identified in Article 4, paragraphs 8 and 9, of the Convention, taking into account Article 3 of the Convention. The Conference of the Parties serving as the meeting of the Parties to this Protocol may take further action, as appropriate, to promote the implementation of the provisions of this paragraph.

4. The Conference of the Parties serving as the meeting of the Parties to this Protocol, if it decides that it would be beneficial to coordinate any of the policies and measures in paragraph 1(a) above, taking into account different national circumstances and potential effects, shall consider ways and means to elaborate the coordination of such policies and measures.

ARTICLE 3

1. The Parties included in Annex I shall, individually or jointly, ensure that their aggregate anthropogenic carbon dioxide equivalent emissions of the greenhouse gases listed in Annex A do not exceed their assigned amounts, calculated pursuant to their quantified emission limitation and reduction commitments inscribed in Annex B and in accordance with the provisions of this Article, with a view to reducing their overall emissions of such gases by at least 5 per cent below 1990 levels in the commitment period 2008 to 2012.

2. Each Party included in Annex I shall, by 2005, have made demonstrable progress in achieving its commitments under this Protocol. . . .

Source: Kyoto Protocol to the United Nations Framework Convention on Climate Change. United Nations, 2008. http://unfccc.int/resource/docs/convkp/kpeng.pdf.

DOCUMENT
11.4

A Congressman Makes the Case for Drilling in Alaska National Wildlife Refuge (ANWR)

"[ANWR] Is Potentially the Largest Undiscovered Onshore Oil Field in North America"

March 12, 2003

Proposals to open the Alaska National Wildlife Refuge (ANWR) to oil and gas drilling have been an important and highly publicized element of Republican energy policy schemes since the Reagan Administration. Supporters of these proposals to tap the vast subterranean lakes of oil that lie beneath the refuge's surface argue that ANWR oil will increase American energy independence and reduce domestic energy prices and that it can be obtained in an environmentally sensitive manner. In the following excerpt from a 2003 congressional hearing on an ANWR drilling bill, conservative Republican Richard Pombo (Calif.) laments earlier legislative efforts to open ANWR that have fallen short, then offers a representative summary of pro-drilling arguments and rhetoric. (See document 11.5 for the perspective of an opponent of drilling in ANWR.)

. . . With a few exceptions, H.R. 39 is identical to what was passed in the House in the 107th Congress as part of the comprehensive energy bill. The Senate version of the energy bill did not contain a provision opening ANWR and a conference Committee failed to reconcile the two bills.

H.R. 39 authorizes environmentally sound oil and gas exploration, development, and production on the 1.5 million acre coastal plain of the Arctic National Wildlife Refuge, an area specifically reserved by Congress for its oil and gas potential. Under this bill, the rest of ANWR itself will remain untouched. We are holding a hearing on H.R. 39 because ANWR again will be a cornerstone of the House's comprehensive energy bill.

Many of you must be wondering why there has been continuing interest in ANWR for the last 25 years. What is so special about this flat, treeless, arctic desert?

ANWR's coastal plain is potentially the largest undiscovered onshore oil field in North America. The U.S. Geological Survey estimates that there are 5.7 to 16 billion barrels of recoverable oil there, with a mean of 10.4 billion barrels. Putting this in perspective, 10.4 billion barrels is twice as much as all proven reserves in the State of Texas. It could increase America's reserves by 50 percent. It could be one of the world's largest discoveries of oil in the last 30 years.

As America's dependence on foreign oil approaches 60 percent, it is foolish not to look for oil in a place that could hold resources of this magnitude, especially at a time when a substantial amount of the foreign oil is imported from hostile governments. It defies common sense to buy oil from a dictator who can convert American dollars into weapons of mass destruction that will be used against the American people.

While opening ANWR may not end dependence on foreign oil, it can substantially reduce it. For example, it could replace all Iraqi imports for the next several decades. It can lower our trade deficit, which has an impact on interest rates, the Federal budget, and economic growth.

Oil development in ANWR is locally supported, as we will hear directly from our witnesses today. Over the past several years, the Federal Government has closed off some of the most promising areas from oil and gas exploration on the grounds that such activities lack local support. If this is the government's criteria for oil exploration, then there should be no argument over ANWR.

Unfortunately, I have observed that some of the most aggressive opponents of ANWR are the ones who have declined invitations to the North Slope to view firsthand exactly what they are talking about. Anyone who visits Alaska will immediately see that under the State and local government's rigorous environmental rules, wildlife and their habitat have peacefully coexisted with the production of 14 billion barrels of oil for America's consumers.

For example, the caribou herd using the Prudhoe Bay oil fields has grown from 5,000 to 32,000 since development began a quarter century ago. The fact is, no wildlife species population has been adversely affected by Alaska oil development. But don't just take my word for this. This is the finding in a recent study of the Argonne National Laboratory. This record can and will be replicated in ANWR.

I previously mentioned that it defies common sense to buy oil from our enemies. It also defies logic to purchase oil from nations having little or no regard for environmental protection. Developing resources and creating jobs here in the U.S. under the world's most stringent environmental standards contributes to a cleaner, healthier environment around the world.

I have been to Alaska's North Slope, and I challenge anyone to tell me where else 14 billion barrels can be produced with so little disturbance.

Alaskans treasure their wildlife and their environment as much as we treasure ours. The views of the people who live in Alaska's Arctic Coastal Plain should be this Committee's highest consideration. They have the most at stake in this debate because they depend on the land for their virtual survival. They want to contribute to America's energy security by tapping into ANWR's world class energy resources. Who better to judge whether or not oil exploration can be done safely and properly? . . .

Source: Pombo, Richard. *Statement on H.R. 39, Arctic Coastal Plain Domestic Energy Security Act.* Legislative Hearing before the Committee on Resources, U.S. Congress. House. 108th Cong., 1st sess., March 12, 2003. Washington, D.C.: Government Printing Office, 2003, pp. 1–3.

A Congressman Criticizes ANWR Drilling Proposals

"The Road to Energy Independence Will Never Run through the Arctic Refuge"

March 12, 2003

Beginning in the 1980s, a sustained political battle has been waged over management of the Arctic National Wildlife Refuge (ANWR), an oil-rich expanse of Alaska's remote North Slope. Republican Administrations and members of Congress have repeatedly sought to open ANWR to commercial exploration and development of oil and natural gas, only to be thwarted by largely Democratic opposition, both in the White House and Capitol Hill, and the public relations campaigns of major environmental organizations such as the Sierra Club, World Wildlife Fund, and Natural Resources Defense Council. In the following excerpt from a 2003 congressional hearing on an ANWR drilling bill, liberal Democrat Edward Markey (Mass.) provides an impassioned—and characteristic—analysis of the issue from an anti-drilling perspective. (See document 11.4 for the perspective of a proponent of drilling in ANWR.)

"In our lifetimes, we have few opportunities to shape the very earth on which our descendants will live their lives." So said [Arizona Democratic Congressman] Mo Udall, 23 years ago as the Alaska National Interest Lands Conservation Act neared passage. . . .

We are here to discuss H.R. 39, the Arctic Coastal Plain Domestic Energy Security Act of 2003. This bill would overturn the 23-year Congressional precedent of protecting the coastal plain of the Arctic National Wildlife Refuge from oil development.

Before we take that drastic step, I believe this Committee deserves to debate the full range of policy options for this precious part of America. Unfortunately, we are not having that debate today. I have requested a hearing on H.R. 770, the Morris K. Udall Arctic Wilderness Act of 2003, which would designate the coastal plain as wilderness and permanently protect it from development, because permanent protection is an equally valid policy option for this Committee to consider. But the closest we will come to a full debate today is holding this hearing in the Morris K. Udall Room.

The panels are also missing an important voice, that of the Gwich'in People, whose culture and lives are intimately tied to the porcupine caribou herd that rely on the Arctic's Refuges Coastal Plain for calving.

Lucy Beech, a member of the Gwich'in Steering Committee, joins us in the audience today, and I would ask unanimous consent that a statement from the Gwich'in Steering Committee be included in the record. To quote from their statement, "As Gwich'in this is a human rights issue. We have relied on the caribou for thousands of years and the caribou continues to be a critical element of our culture." . . .

Proponents of this bill have told you why they think we should open the refuge for development. Let me tell you why I think the Arctic Refuge should remain wild.

The wilderness is unparalleled. Nowhere on Earth is the diversity of Arctic habitat and wildlife represented as it is in the Arctic National Wildlife Refuge. According to the Fish and Wildlife Service, this relative compactness of habitats provides for a greater degree of ecological diversity than any other similar sized area in Alaska's North Slope.

Industry isn't interested in drilling there. According to media reports, British Petroleum, the major North Slope player, is looking elsewhere in the world for the next big field and is even considering shutting down their Badami field, the field closest to the Arctic Refuge.

Looking in the Refuge is the wrong place to find energy security. Developing the Arctic Refuge will not make us independent of foreign oil sources. To become energy independent, we should tap American ingenuity to make more efficient buildings and vehicles and design new renewable technologies that our domestic resources can fuel cleanly.

And we don't need Arctic Refuge oil to replace Iraqi oil. From 1991 to 1995, oil imports from Iraq were banned. Oil prices and supplies barely hiccuped, and the period coincided with one of the greatest expansions in United States history.

And damaging precedent would also be set by allowing the oil and gas development in the Arctic Refuge. This would overturn a 35-year history of refuge protection, dating back to the 1966, the National Wildlife Refuge System Administration Act. Nearly 300 refuges in 44 States would be threatened by this precedent.

Ignoring recent National Academy findings that oil development has caused wildlife and their habits harm. We are considering a bill that finds oil exploration and development compatible with the mission of the refuge, that relies on an environmental impact statement from 1987, and that doesn't allow the Secretary of Interior to consider a no-leasing alternative.

Faced with reclamation liabilities that the General Accounting Office estimates could be as high as $6 billion for the current state of development, we are considering allowing the oil industry to invade into the only portion, less than 5 percent of the North Slope, that is currently off limits.

When will we realize that the road to energy independence will never run through the Arctic Refuge? Rational energy policy will begin the day that Congress drops any idea of turning the refuge into a filling station and instead grants this extraordinary area the full Wilderness Act protection it deserves.

The American People sense in their bones that the value of the Arctic Refuge should never be measured in barrels of oil or employee work days or drops in the Federal deficit bucket. They consider it priceless, one of a kind, a national environmental treasure that should not be sacrificed by this Congress or this Committee, not now, not ever. . . .

Source: Markey, Edward J. *Statement on H.R. 39, Arctic Coastal Plain Domestic Energy Security Act.* Legislative Hearing before the Committee on Resources, U.S. Congress. House. 108th Cong, 1st sess., March 12, 2003. Washington, D.C.: Government Printing Office, 2003, pp. 6–7.

DOCUMENT 11.6

U.S. Mayors Climate Protection Agreement

"Reducing Global Warming Pollution . . . in Our Own . . . Communities"

February 16, 2005

The longstanding federal gridlock over policies governing greenhouse gas (GHG) emissions, fossil fuel consumption, and other aspects of energy creation and use has prompted numerous players at the state and local levels to step into the policymaking void and craft their own strategies and policies for combating global warming. Numerous states have turned to the courts to try to reduce greenhouse gas emissions, and several states have approved legislation that mandates significant reductions in emissions of carbon dioxide and other greenhouse gases.

In addition, leaders of many of the nation's metropolitan areas have formally committed to pursuing and implementing policies and programs to reduce their own GHG emissions. The most notable of these efforts is the U.S. Mayors Climate Protection Agreement, which was launched on February 16, 2005—the same day that the Kyoto Protocol became law for ratifying nations. The U.S. Mayors Climate Protection Agreement was the brainchild of Seattle mayor Greg Nickels, who quickly found that his proposal tapped a formidable wellspring of frustration and anger among his fellow mayors regarding federal inaction on global warming issues. City leaders from around the country signed on to the agreement by the score, and in May 2007 Tulsa mayor Kathy Taylor became the 500th mayor to pledge formal support for the pact's goals and guidelines. By November 2008 more than 900 mayors had signed the agreement.[1] Following is the full text of the U.S. Mayors Climate Protection Agreement.

A. We urge the federal government and state governments to enact policies and programs to meet or beat the target of reducing global warming pollution levels to 7 percent below 1990 levels by 2012, including efforts to: reduce the United States' dependence on fossil fuels and accelerate the development of clean, economical energy resources and fuel-efficient technologies such as conservation, methane recovery for energy generation, waste to energy, wind and solar energy, fuel cells, efficient motor vehicles, and biofuels;

B. We urge the U.S. Congress to pass bipartisan greenhouse gas reduction legislation that 1) includes clear timetables and emissions limits and 2) a flexible, market-based system of tradable allowances among emitting industries; and

C. We will strive to meet or exceed Kyoto Protocol targets for reducing global warming pollution by taking actions in our own operations and communities such as:

1. Inventory global warming emissions in City operations and in the community, set reduction targets and create an action plan;
2. Adopt and enforce land-use policies that reduce sprawl, preserve open space, and create compact, walkable urban communities;
3. Promote transportation options such as bicycle trails, commute trip reduction programs, incentives for car pooling and public transit;

4. Increase the use of clean, alternative energy by, for example, investing in "green tags," advocating for the development of renewable energy resources, recovering landfill methane for energy production, and supporting the use of waste to energy technology;

5. Make energy efficiency a priority through building code improvements, retrofitting city facilities with energy efficient lighting and urging employees to conserve energy and save money;

6. Purchase only Energy Star equipment and appliances for City use;

7. Practice and promote sustainable building practices using the U.S. Green Building Council's LEED program or a similar system;

8. Increase the average fuel efficiency of municipal fleet vehicles; reduce the number of vehicles; launch an employee education program including anti-idling messages; convert diesel vehicles to bio-diesel;

9. Evaluate opportunities to increase pump efficiency in water and wastewater systems; recover wastewater treatment methane for energy production;

10. Increase recycling rates in City operations and in the community;

11. Maintain healthy urban forests; promote tree planting to increase shading and to absorb CO_2; and

12. Help educate the public, schools, other jurisdictions, professional associations, business and industry about reducing global warming pollution.

Source: The U.S. Mayors Climate Protection Agreement (as endorsed by the 73rd Annual U.S. Conference of Mayors meeting, Chicago, 2005). http://usmayors.org/climateprotection/documents/mcp Agreement.pdf.

NOTE

1. United States Conference of Mayors, "More than 900 Mayors Join Climate Change Agreement," press release, November 21, 2008. http://usmayors.org/climateprotection/documents/climateagreement 112108.pdf.

DOCUMENT 11.7

A Global Warming Skeptic in the U.S. Senate

"The American People Know When Their Intelligence Is Being Insulted"

September 25, 2006

Since the emergence of global warming as a policy issue, numerous senators and representatives—and especially members of the Republican Party—have expressed profound skepticism about global warming predictions. These critics have questioned the scientific basis for such prognostications, slammed the motivations of environmental organizations that have issued climate change warnings, and decried the "slanted" media coverage of the issue.

Perhaps no Republican congressman has been a more persistent and outspoken
skeptic of global warming than James Inhofe, a Republican senator from Oklahoma.
He has made particularly effective use of his position as the top Republican on the Senate
Committee on Environment and Public Works to denounce climate change "alarmists"
of various stripes on a regular basis. Following are excerpts from a speech that Inhofe
delivered on the Senate floor on September 25, 2006, to coincide with his office's release of
A Skeptic's Guide to Debunking Global Warming Alarmism, *a compilation of speeches,*
op-ed pieces, and other works purporting to refute reports of catastrophic climate change.

I am going to speak today about the most media-hyped environmental issue of all time, global warming. I have spoken more about global warming than any other politician in Washington today. My speech will be a bit different from the previous seven floor speeches, as I focus not only on the science, but on the media's coverage of climate change.

Global Warming—just that term evokes many members in this chamber, the media, Hollywood elites and our pop culture to nod their heads and fret about an impending climate disaster. As the senator who has spent more time speaking about the facts regarding global warming, I want to address some of the recent media coverage of global warming and Hollywood's involvement in the issue. And of course I will also discuss former Vice President Al Gore's movie "An Inconvenient Truth."

Since 1895, the media has alternated between global cooling and warming scares during four separate and sometimes overlapping time periods. From 1895 until the 1930's the media peddled a coming ice age.

From the late 1920's until the 1960's they warned of global warming. From the 1950's until the 1970's they warned us again of a coming ice age. This makes modern global warming the fourth estate's fourth attempt to promote opposing climate change fears during the last 100 years.

Recently, advocates of alarmism have grown increasingly desperate to try to convince the public that global warming is the greatest moral issue of our generation. Last year, the vice president of London's Royal Society sent a chilling letter to the media encouraging them to stifle the voices of scientists skeptical of climate alarmism.

During the past year, the American people have been served up an unprecedented parade of environmental alarmism by the media and entertainment industry, which link every possible weather event to global warming. The year 2006 saw many major organs of the media dismiss any pretense of balance and objectivity on climate change coverage and instead crossed squarely into global warming advocacy. . . .

END OF LITTLE ICE AGE MEANS WARMING

The media have missed the big pieces of the puzzle when it comes to the Earth's temperatures and mankind's carbon dioxide (CO_2) emissions. It is very simplistic to feign horror and say the one degree Fahrenheit temperature increase during the 20th century means we are all doomed. First of all, the one degree Fahrenheit rise coincided with the greatest advancement of living standards, life expectancy, food production and human health in the history of our planet. So it is hard to argue that the global warming we experienced in the 20th century was somehow negative or part of a catastrophic trend.

Second, what the climate alarmists and their advocates in the media have continued to ignore is the fact that the Little Ice Age, which resulted in harsh winters which froze New York Harbor and caused untold deaths, ended about 1850. So trying to prove man-made global warming by comparing the well-known fact that today's temperatures are warmer than during the Little Ice Age is akin to comparing summer to winter to show a catastrophic temperature trend.

In addition, something that the media almost never addresses are the holes in the theory that CO_2 has been the driving force in global warming. Alarmists fail to adequately explain why temperatures began warming at the end of the Little Ice Age in about 1850, long before man-made CO_2 emissions could have impacted the climate. Then about 1940, just as man-made CO_2 emissions rose sharply, the temperatures began a decline that lasted until the 1970's, prompting the media and many scientists to fear a coming ice age.

Let me repeat, temperatures got colder after CO_2 emissions exploded. If CO_2 is the driving force of global climate change, why do so many in the media ignore the many skeptical scientists who cite these rather obvious inconvenient truths?

Sixty Scientists

My skeptical views on man-made catastrophic global warming have only strengthened as new science comes in. There have been recent findings in peer-reviewed literature over the last few years showing that the Antarctic is getting colder and the ice is growing and a new study in Geophysical Research Letters found that the sun was responsible for 50% of 20th century warming.

Recently, many scientists, including a leading member of the Russian Academy of Sciences, predicted long-term global cooling may be on the horizon due to a projected decrease in the sun's output.

A letter sent to the Canadian Prime Minister on April 6 of this year by 60 prominent scientists who question the basis for climate alarmism, clearly explains the current state of scientific knowledge on global warming. The 60 scientists wrote:

> *[A]fter years of hearing about the computer generated scary scenarios about the future of our planet, I now believe that the greatest climate threat we face may be coming from alarmist computer models.*
>
> —James Inhofe

> "If, back in the mid-1990s, we knew what we know today about climate, Kyoto would almost certainly not exist, because we would have concluded it was not necessary."

The letter also noted:

> "'Climate change is real' is a meaningless phrase used repeatedly by activists to convince the public that a climate catastrophe is looming and humanity is the cause. Neither of these fears is justified. Global climate changes occur all the time due to natural causes and the human impact still remains impossible to distinguish from this natural 'noise.'"

Computer Models Threaten Earth

One of the ways alarmists have pounded this mantra of "consensus" on global warming into our pop culture is through the use of computer models which project future calamity. But the science is simply not there to place so much faith in scary computer model scenarios which extrapolate the current and projected buildup of greenhouse gases in the atmosphere and conclude that the planet faces certain doom.

Dr. Vincent Gray, a research scientist and a 2001 reviewer with the UN's Intergovernmental Panel on Climate Change (IPCC) has noted, "The effects of aerosols, and their uncertainties, are such as to nullify completely the reliability of any of the climate models."

Earlier this year, the director of the International Arctic Research Center in Fairbanks Alaska, testified to Congress that highly publicized climate models showing a disappearing Arctic were nothing more than "science fiction."

In fact, after years of hearing about the computer generated scary scenarios about the future of our planet, I now believe that the greatest climate threat we face may be coming from alarmist computer models.

This threat is originating from the software installed on the hard drives of the publicity and grant seeking climate modelers.

It is long past the time for us to separate climate change fact from hysteria.

KYOTO: ECONOMIC PAIN FOR NO CLIMATE GAIN

One final point on the science of climate change: I am approached by many in the media and others who ask, "What if you are wrong to doubt the dire global warming predictions? Will you be able to live with yourself for opposing the Kyoto Protocol?"

My answer is blunt. The history of the modern environmental movement is chock full of predictions of doom that never came true. We have all heard the dire predictions about the threat of overpopulation, resource scarcity, mass starvation, and the projected death of our oceans. None of these predictions came true, yet it never stopped the doomsayers from continuing to predict a dire environmental future.

The more the eco-doomsayers' predictions fail, the more the eco-doomsayers predict.

These failed predictions are just one reason I respect the serious scientists out there today debunking the latest scaremongering on climate change. Scientists like MIT's Richard Lindzen, former Colorado State climatologist Roger Pielke, Sr., the University of Alabama's Roy Spencer and John Christy, Virginia State Climatologist Patrick Michaels, Colorado State University's William Gray, atmospheric physicist S. Fred Singer, Willie Soon of the Harvard-Smithsonian Center for Astrophysics, Oregon State climatologist George Taylor and astrophysicist Sallie Baliunas, to name a few.

But more importantly, it is the global warming alarmists who should be asked the question—"What if they are correct about man-made catastrophic global warming?"—because they have come up with no meaningful solution to their supposed climate crisis in the two decades that they have been hyping this issue.

If the alarmists truly believe that man-made greenhouse gas emissions are dooming the planet, then they must face up to the fact that symbolism does not solve a supposed climate crisis.

The alarmists freely concede that the Kyoto Protocol, even if fully ratified and complied with, would not have any meaningful impact on global temperatures. And keep in mind that Kyoto is not even close to being complied with by many of the nations that ratified it, including 13 of the EU-15 nations that are not going to meet their emission reduction promises.

Many of the nations that ratified Kyoto are now realizing what I have been saying all along: The Kyoto Protocol is a lot of economic pain for no climate gain. . . .

In addition, we now have many environmentalists and Hollywood celebrities, like Laurie David, who have been advocating measures like changing standard light bulbs in your home to fluorescents to help avert global warming. Changing to more energy-efficient light bulbs is a fine thing to do, but to somehow imply we can avert a climate disaster by these actions is absurd.

Once again, symbolism does not solve a climate crisis.

But this symbolism may be hiding a dark side. While greenhouse gas limiting proposals may cost the industrialized West trillions of dollars, it is the effect on the developing world's poor that is being lost in this debate.

The Kyoto Protocol's post 2012 agenda which mandates that the developing world be subjected to restrictions on greenhouse gases could have the potential to severely restrict development in regions of the world like Africa, Asia and South America—where some of the Earth's most energy-deprived people currently reside.

Expanding basic necessities like running water and electricity in the developing world are seen by many in the green movement as a threat to the planet's health that must be avoided.

Energy poverty equals a life of back-breaking poverty and premature death.

If we allow scientifically unfounded fears of global warming to influence policy makers to restrict future energy production and the creation of basic infrastructure in the developing world—billions of people will continue to suffer. . . .

I firmly believe that when the history of our era is written, future generations will look back with puzzlement and wonder why we spent so much time and effort on global warming fears and pointless solutions like the Kyoto Protocol.

French President Jacques Chirac provided the key clue as to why so many in the international community still revere the Kyoto Protocol, who in 2000 said Kyoto represents "the first component of an authentic global governance."

Furthermore, if your goal is to limit CO_2 emissions, the only effective way to go about it is the use of cleaner, more efficient technologies that will meet the energy demands of this century and beyond.

The Bush administration and my Environment and Public Works Committee have been engaged in these efforts as we work to expand nuclear power and promote the Asia-Pacific Partnership. This partnership stresses the sharing of new technology among member nations including three of the world's top 10 emitters—China, India and South Korea—all of whom are exempt from Kyoto.

MEDIA COVERAGE OF CLIMATE CHANGE:

Many in the media, as I noted earlier, have taken it upon themselves to drop all pretense of balance on global warming and instead become committed advocates for the issue.

Here is a quote from *Newsweek* magazine:

> "There are ominous signs that the Earth's weather patterns have begun to change dramatically and that these changes may portend a drastic decline in food production—with serious political implications for just about every nation on Earth."

A headline in the *New York Times* reads: "Climate Changes Endanger World's Food Output." Here is a quote from *Time Magazine*:

> "As they review the bizarre and unpredictable weather pattern of the past several years, a growing number of scientists are beginning to suspect that many seemingly contradictory meteorological fluctuations are actually part of a global climatic upheaval."

All of this sounds very ominous. That is, until you realize that the three quotes I just read were from articles in 1975 editions of *Newsweek Magazine* and *The New York Times,* and *Time Magazine* in 1974.

They weren't referring to global warming; they were warning of a coming ice age.

Let me repeat, all three of those quotes were published in the 1970's and warned of a coming ice age. . . .

[Inhofe proceeds to quote from several newspapers of the 1920s through the 1970s warning of global cooling or warming trends.]

These past predictions of doom have a familiar ring, don't they? They sound strikingly similar to our modern media promotion of former Vice president's brand of climate alarmism.

After more than a century of alternating between global cooling and warming, one would think that this media history would serve a cautionary tale for today's voices in the media and scientific community who are promoting yet another round of eco-doom. . . .

TIME MAGAZINE HYPES ALARMISM

In April of this year, *Time Magazine* devoted an issue to global warming alarmism titled "Be Worried, Be Very Worried."

This is the same *Time Magazine* which first warned of a coming ice age in [the] 1920's before switching to warning about global warming in the 1930's before switching yet again to promoting the 1970's coming ice age scare.

The April 3, 2006 global warming special report of *Time Magazine* was a prime example of the media's shortcomings, as the magazine cited partisan left-wing environmental groups with a vested financial interest in hyping alarmism . . .

To his credit, *New York Times* reporter Revkin saw fit to criticize *Time Magazine* for its embarrassing coverage of climate science.

So in the end, *Time's* cover story title of "Be Worried, Be Very Worried," appears to have been apt. The American people should be worried—very worried—of such shoddy journalism.

AL GORE'S INCONVENIENT TRUTH

In May, our nation was exposed to perhaps one of the slickest science propaganda films of all time: former Vice President Gore's "An Inconvenient Truth." In addition to having the backing of Paramount Pictures to market this film, Gore had the full backing of the media, and leading the cheerleading charge was none other than the Associated Press.

On June 27, the Associated Press ran an article by Seth Borenstein that boldly declared "Scientists give two thumbs up to Gore's movie." The article quoted only five scientists praising Gore's science, despite AP's having contacted over 100 scientists.

The fact that over 80% of the scientists contacted by the AP had not even seen the movie or that many scientists have harshly criticized the science presented by Gore did not dissuade the news outlet one bit from its mission to promote Gore's brand of climate alarmism.

I am almost at a loss as to how to begin to address the series of errors, misleading science and unfounded speculation that appear in the former Vice President's film. Here is what Richard Lindzen, a meteorologist from MIT, has written about "An Inconvenient Truth."

"A general characteristic of Mr. Gore's approach is to assiduously ignore the fact that the earth and its climate are dynamic; they are always changing even without any external forcing. To treat all change as something to fear is bad enough; to do so in order to exploit that fear is much worse." . . .

Alarmism Has Led to Skepticism

It is an inconvenient truth that so far, 2006 has been a year in which major segments of the media have given up on any quest for journalistic balance, fairness and objectivity when it comes to climate change. The global warming alarmists and their friends in the media have attempted to smear scientists who dare question the premise of man-made catastrophic global warming, and as a result some scientists have seen their reputations and research funding dry up.

The media has so relentlessly promoted global warming fears that a British group called the Institute for Public Policy Research—and this from a left leaning group—issued a report in 2006 accusing media outlets of engaging in what they termed "climate porn" in order to attract the public's attention.

Bob Carter, a Paleoclimate geologist from James Cook University in Australia has described how the media promotes climate fear:

"Each such alarmist article is larded with words such as 'if,' 'might,' 'could,' 'probably,' 'perhaps,' 'expected,' 'projected' or 'modeled'—and many involve such deep dreaming, or ignorance of scientific facts and principles, that they are akin to nonsense," professor Carter concluded in an op-ed in April of this year.

Another example of this relentless hype is the reporting on the seemingly endless number of global warming impact studies which do not even address whether global warming is going to happen. They merely project the impact of potential temperature increases.

The media endlessly hypes studies that purportedly show that global warming could increase mosquito populations, malaria, West Nile Virus, heat waves and hurricanes, threaten the oceans, damage coral reefs, boost poison ivy growth, damage vineyards, and global food crops, to name just a few of the global warming linked calamities. Oddly, according to the media reports, warmer temperatures almost never seem to have any positive effects on plant or animal life or food production.

Fortunately, the media's addiction to so-called "climate porn" has failed to seduce many Americans.

According to a July Pew Research Center Poll, the American public is split about evenly between those who say global warming is due to human activity versus those who believe it's from natural factors or not happening at all.

In addition, an August *Los Angeles Times*/Bloomberg poll found that most Americans do not attribute the cause of recent severe weather events to global warming, and the portion of Americans who believe global warming is naturally occurring is on the rise.

Yes—it appears that alarmism has led to skepticism.

The American people know when their intelligence is being insulted. They know when they are being used and when they are being duped by the hysterical left.

The American people deserve better—much better—from our fourth estate. We have a right to expect accuracy and objectivity on climate change coverage. We have a right to expect balance in sourcing and fair analysis from reporters who cover the issue.

Above all, the media must roll back this mantra that there is scientific "consensus" of impending climatic doom as an excuse to ignore recent science. After all, there was a so-called scientific "consensus" that there were nine planets in our solar system until Pluto was recently demoted.

Breaking the cycles of media hysteria will not be easy since hysteria sells—it's very profitable. But I want to challenge the news media to reverse course and report on the objective science of climate change, to stop ignoring legitimate voices this scientific debate and to stop acting as a vehicle for unsubstantiated hype.

Source: Inhofe, James. "Hot and Cold Media Spin: A Challenge to Journalists Who Cover Global Warming." September 25, 2006. http://epw.senate.gov/public/index.cfm?FuseAction=PressRoom.Speeches&Content Record_id=07F23E38-D271-4300-AC40-90C84A49134A.

DOCUMENT 11.8

Al Gore Issues a Call to Action on Global Warming

"Our World Faces a True Planetary Emergency"

March 21, 2007

Former Democratic senator and vice president Al Gore ranks as the United States' most visible and influential advocate of decisive and wide-reaching government measures to address the threat of global climate change. Gore's interest in the issue dated back to the 1980s, when he sponsored congressional hearings about global climate change. He also discussed the issue in his 1992 book Earth in the Balance *and played an important role in the Kyoto Protocol negotiations. After the disputed 2000 presidential election, in which Republican George W. Bush secured the presidency over Gore by virtue of a controversial Supreme Court decision that halted a vote recount in Florida, Gore's activism in the global warming arena increased. He crisscrossed the country delivering lectures on the scientific basis for climate change fears, and in 2006 he produced a highly publicized documentary film on global warming called* An Inconvenient Truth. *One year later Gore and the Intergovernmental Panel on Climate Change (IPCC) shared the Nobel Peace Prize for their efforts to publicize and combat anthropogenic climate change. In bestowing the award on Gore, the Nobel Committee described him as "the single individual who has done most to create greater worldwide understanding of the measures that need to be adopted [against global warming]."[1]*

Gore's March 2007 global warming testimony on Capitol Hill marked his first appearance before Congress since the release of An Inconvenient Truth. *Following are excerpts from his March 21st statement to a joint gathering of two House subcommittees about the importance of governmental action in the face of the growing "climate crisis."*

This is the greatest country on the face of this Earth. And the hopes for freedom and the viability and efficacy of self-government rests with the legislative branch of our government in this day and time.

There have been times in the past when our Nation has been called upon to rise above partisanship, above political calculations, above the pressures that have always been present for two and a quarter centuries from special interests of this, that or the other kind, and reach across the aisle and do what history is calling upon all of us as Americans to do.

America is the natural leader of the world. And our world faces a true planetary emergency. I know the phrase sounds shrill. And I know it is a challenge to the moral imagination to see and feel and understand that the entire relationship between humanity and our planet has been radically altered.

We quadrupled human population in less than one century from 1.6 billion in 1900 to 6.56 billion today. Population is stabilizing of its own accord as girls are educated and women are empowered and family planning that is culturally acceptable in country after country becomes widely available and, most importantly, as child survival rates increase and infant mortality decreases. When those things happen and especially when literacy among women increases around the world, the birth rates come down. The death rates come down, and then the birth rates come down. And it is stabilizing.

But having multiplied by four the number of people on this planet—and we are going from over 6.5 [billion] now to over 9.1 almost certainly within the next 40, 45 years—that in itself causes a big change in the relationship between humanity and the planet.

Second, our technologies are thousands of times more powerful than any our grandparents had at their disposal. And so we are even more skillful and more effective in doing the things we have always done, exploiting the Earth for sustenance and providing for our families and going about productive lives. The side effects of what we are doing sometimes now outstrip the development of extra wisdom to make sure that we handle these new powers in a way that doesn't do unintended harm. And somehow we have also adopted a kind of a short-term way of thinking that is also different from what our grandparents more commonly used. . . .

Were they too blinded and numbed by the business of political life or daily life to take a deep breath and look at the reality of what we are facing? Did they think it was perfectly all right to keep dumping 70 million tons every single day of global warming pollution into this Earth's atmosphere? Did they think all of the scientists were wrong? What were they thinking?

—Al Gore

What we are facing now is a crisis that is by far the most serious we have ever faced. And the way we are going to solve it is by asking you on both sides of the aisle to do what some people have, as you know, begun to fear we don't have the capacity to do any more. I know they are wrong. I know that politics can seem frustratingly slow, like it doesn't move but an inch a year. But when there are enough people who become seized of the gravity of the challenge and talk with you and you yourselves immerse yourselves in it and learn what is at stake, all of a sudden it can move very quickly. . . .

This is building. And it is building in both parties. The faith communities, the evangelical communities, the business leaders, ten of the CEOs of the biggest corporations in America just the day before the State of the Union Address last month, most of them in their personal lives have been supporters of President Bush. That is irrelevant to this issue. They had a press conference the day before the State of the Union Address calling on you to act, adopt legislation that will address this crisis. These are not normal times. . . .

Because I promise you, I say this to each of you as individuals, I promise you, the day will come when our children and grandchildren will look back. And they will ask one of two questions. Either they will ask, what in God's name were they doing? Didn't they see the evidence? Didn't they realize that four times in 15 years, the entire scientific community of this world issued unanimous reports calling upon them to act? What was wrong with them? Were they too blinded and numbed by the business of political life or daily life to take a deep breath and look at the reality of what we are facing? Did they think it was perfectly all right to keep dumping 70 million tons every single day of global warming pollution into this Earth's atmosphere? Did they think all of the scientists were wrong? What were they thinking?

Or they will ask another question. They may look back, and they will say, how did they find the uncommon moral courage to rise above politics and redeem the promise of American democracy and do what some said was impossible and shake things up and tell the special interests, OK, we have heard you and we are going to do the best we can to take your considerations into account, but we are going to do what is right?

I am going to do my part to make sure that you have all the support that I and lots of other folks can muster for you in both parties when you do the right thing. If some of you in tough districts face pressures that just are overwhelming, I would ask you to walk through that fire.

I have got a few specific suggestions that I would like to make and thank you for the courtesy of giving me a longer than normal opening statement. . . .

Here is what I think we should do. Number 1, I think we should immediately freeze CO_2 emissions in the United States of America and then begin a program of sharp reductions to reach at least 90 percent reductions by 2050. All of the complex formulas of how we might start reductions years from now and have a little bit in the first year and a little bit more in the second year, I think we need to freeze it right now, and then start the reductions.

Second, I believe—and I know how difficult this is to contemplate—but I believe that we should start using the Tax Code to reduce taxes on employment and production, and make up the difference with pollution taxes, principally CO_2. Now I fully understand that this is considered politically impossible. But part of our challenge is to expand the limits of what is possible. Right now we are discouraging work and encouraging the destruction of the planet's habitability.

We are also in a new world, Mr. Chairman. We have talked many times about the competitive challenges that America faces in an outsourcing world. And with information-technology empowering these developing countries with large and fast-growing populations and lower wage rates, our biggest disadvantage is in the area of our high wage rates. We don't want to lower our wages, but we shouldn't worsen that disadvantage by stacking on top of the wages the full cost of our health and welfare and social programs. I understand this is a longer-term shift. But we ought to start making that shift. It would make us more competitive. It would also discourage pollution while encouraging work.

I understand how difficult it is, I will say again, but carbon pollution is not presently priced into the marketplace. It does not have a price tag. It is considered an externality. And there are reasons for that. But if you think about the externalities, they include air and water. I internalize air and water, as most of us do. And I think the economic system should, too. And I think that one way to do it is by this revenue-neutral tax shift.

Third, a portion of those revenues must be earmarked for those in lower-income groups who will have a more difficult time making this transition unless you in the Congress make sure that we are giving them the assistance that they need.

Fourth, we need to be part of a strong global treaty. Now, I am in favor of Kyoto, but I fully understand that Kyoto, as a brand if you will, has been demonized. I remember, Mr. Chairman, when I first came to this Congress, one of the issues I worked on was nuclear arms control. Some of the Members here I worked with closely. In those years, Former President Carter had a treaty pending the SALT II treaty. And for a variety of reasons, including the invasion of Afghanistan by the former Soviet Union, it was withdrawn, and the name itself became a political liability.

President Reagan was elected. And I worked across the aisle with President Reagan on arms control. And after only a couple of years in office, he came to a realization, we need nuclear arms control. He had been against it but the realities of the situation made it clear that we needed to move forward.

And he came up with even deeper reductions and a new name called the START Treaty, and people who had been opposed to SALT II all of a sudden were in favor of the START Treaty.

I think that we should work toward de facto compliance with Kyoto. If we can ratify it, fine. But, again, I understand the difficulty. But we should work toward de facto compliance.

And here is my formal proposal. We ought to move forward the starting date of the next treaty now scheduled to begin in 2012, to 2010 so that whoever is elected President and is sworn-in in January 2009 can use his or her political chips, if you will, all of the good will that comes out of that election campaign and the new inauguration, not just on trying to fight a rear guard action in a bitter battle to ratify a treaty that will expire by the time it is ratified, but to work toward de facto compliance and then start an all out sprint to negotiate and ratify a new tougher treaty that will begin in 2010.

And we have to find a creative way to build more confidence that China and India and the developing nations will be a party to that treaty sooner rather than later. Land cover and methane and soot may be opportunities to have provisions that are binding upon them sooner rather than later, but some creative way must be found to make them a part of this effort.

Next, this Congress should enact a moratorium on the construction of any new coal-fired power plant that is not compatible with carbon capture and sequestration. And that means that we should have an all-out push to develop carbon capture and sequestration.

Next, I believe, Mr. Chairman, that just as this committee and the Science and Technology Committee were instrumental in the early years of assisting the scientists and engineers to take what was then known as ARPA-Net and DARPA Net and develop the new switches and the new high-performance computers and assist them in their creation of what became the Internet, that I believe this Congress should develop an ElectroNet, a smart grid. Just as the widely distributed processing of information everywhere in this country and around the world led to the biggest new surge of productivity that we have ever seen in this Nation, we ought to have a law that allows homeowners and small business people, to put up photable generators and small wind mills and any other new sources of widely distributed generation that they can come up with and allow them to sell that electricity into the grid without any artificial caps at a rate that is determined, not by a monopsony—as you know, that is the flip side of a monopoly. You can have the tyranny of a single seller; you can also have the tyranny of a single buyer.

And if a utility sets the price, it will never get off the ground. But if it is a tariff, if it is regulated according to the market for electricity the same way public utility commissions do it now, then you may not ever need another central station generating plant. In the same way that the Internet took off and stimulated the information revolution, we could see a revolution all across this country with small-scale generation of electricity everywhere. And let people sell it. Don't reserve it for the single big seller.

Next, I believe that we should raise the CAFE standards, and I support your initiative, Congressman Markey. But I support your idea, Chairman Dingell, as well, that it ought to be part of a comprehensive package. And I have taken note of your statements and also some of the automobile industry statements that as long as it is part of a comprehensive package that includes the utilities and includes buildings and all the other sources—don't single out cars and trucks and pretend that that is all the problem. It is only a slice of the problem. And it is not even the biggest part of it. But it is a big part of it.

Make it a part of the comprehensive solution. But let's not bring up the rear anymore on these auto standards. Basically, the problem is cars, coal and buildings, so you have got to address all three of them in an intelligent way.

Next, I believe that, along with using the tax system and a cap and trade treaty approach, you should also not shy away from using the regulatory power. And I believe that this Congress should set a date in the future for the ban on incandescent light bulbs, give the industry enough time to make sure they have got all of the socket sizes worked out and all of the different features, like dimmers and the rest that people want and to improve the quality of life. They will do it. You set the date.

Tell them we are not going to be able to sell that old, inefficient, wasteful kind at a set date in the future. They will adjust. As long as everybody plays by the same rules, they will adjust, and they will surprise you.

Next, where buildings are concerned, I would like to see you pass a law that I call Connie Mae, a carbon-neutral mortgage association and here's why. I used to be, in a small way, in the home-building business when I came back from the Army and before I was elected to the Congress. And the selling price of a new house is something the market is very sensitive to. Some of you all know this a lot better than I do because you have been in the business in a bigger way. And so the selling price is what people look at, both the sellers and the buyers. But all of the things that we need to do to cut back down on carbon emissions are things that add to the selling price but don't pay for themselves until a couple or 3 years have passed.

And so the appropriate thing of insulation, the window treatments, the improvements that will sharply reduce the operating costs of that home or building is routinely excluded from the initial purchase price because the market discriminates against it.

We ought to set up a carbon-neutral mortgage association where all of those costs are set aside. They will pay for themselves. But just like Fanny Mae and Freddie Mac, put them in an instrument that is separate from the purchase price, and when you go to closing on a house, you sign the mortgage, and they will say, well, now here is your Connie Mae home improvement package here. You don't have to worry about paying for that because it will pay for itself. The Congress of the United States has made sure of that. I recommend that strongly.

Next, I think . . . the FCC ought to require disclosure of carbon emissions in the corporate reporting. Just the day before yesterday, the largest pension funds in this country, $4 trillion worth of assets managed by them, called upon the FCC and the Congress to require disclosure because it is a material risk. There are lots of companies where investors need to know if there is an exposure to carbon constraints, if they are going to be in real trouble because of some aspect of the climate crisis that they are not disclosing to their investors. Stockholders ought to know that, and those disclosures ought to be required. . . .

I would like to close by referring back to the unprecedented nature of the challenge. As many of you know, the way the Chinese and the Japanese, both of whom use the so-called Kanji characters, express the concept of crisis, they use two symbols together. And the first one means danger, and the second one means opportunity. This is the most dangerous crisis we have ever faced. But it is also the greatest opportunity we have ever been confronted with.

And there are people who look around the world, Mr. Chairman, and look at the genocide in Darfur and the chronic civil wars and, in places like the Congo, fought by child soldiers; and they look at the tens of millions that die of easily preventable diseases and the destruction of the Asian fisheries and the rain forest and these other things; and they say, we just have all of these problems, isn't it terrible?

Well, there were problems back in those days after World War II as well. But when your generation rose to meet them, the vision they acquired in facing down fascism served them well in giving them the ability to see that these other challenges were not political problems; they were moral imperatives. And that is what our opportunity is today, not only to solve this and to say to the future generations, we did our part, this was our Thermopylae, and we defended civilization's gate, and we rose to the challenge; but to also say, in the process, we dug deeply, and we found a capacity we didn't know we had. It is there. We all know that. And that is what will give us the ability to successfully solve these other crises. That is the greatest opportunity of all that comes out of this climate crisis. . . .

Source: Gore, Al. *Testimony at "Perspectives on Climate Change."* Hearing before the House Subcommittee on Energy and Air Quality of the Committee on Energy and Commerce and the House Subcommittee on Energy and the Environment of the Committee on Science and Technology, 110th Cong., 1st sess, March 21, 2007. Washington, D.C.: Government Printing Office, 2007.

NOTE

1. Quoted in Walter Gibbs and Sarah Lyall, "Gore Shares Peace Prize for Climate Work," *New York Times,* October 13, 2007. www.nytimes.com/2007/10/13/world/13nobel.html/.

**DOCUMENT
11.9**

Massachusetts et al. v. EPA

"EPA Has Refused to Comply with This Clear Statutory Command"

April 2, 2007

On April 2, 2007, a long legal battle between the Bush Administration and twelve states over greenhouse gas regulation culminated with a resounding victory for the states. The case of Massachusetts et al. v. EPA *pitted Massachusetts and eleven other states—and a number of local governments and environmental organizations—against Bush's Environmental Protection Agency (EPA), which had refused to regulate the emissions of carbon dioxide (CO$_2$) and other greenhouse gases (GHGs) from the transport sector on various legal grounds. Essentially, the Bush EPA contended that*

Clean Air Act provisions did not give it the authority to regulate GHGs—and that even if it had the regulatory authority, it had discretionary power to hold off on imposing new regulations.

In a 5-4 ruling, the U.S. Supreme Court rejected both of these arguments. It instead ruled that GHGs are pollutants under the Clean Air Act and that the EPA had both the authority and the legal responsibility to regulate these emissions. Following are excerpts from the majority decision, which was written by Justice John Paul Stevens (footnotes removed).

VI

On the merits, the first question is whether §202(a)(1) of the Clean Air Act authorizes EPA to regulate greenhouse gas emissions from new motor vehicles in the event that it forms a "judgment" that such emissions contribute to climate change. We have little trouble concluding that it does. In relevant part, §202(a)(1) provides that EPA "shall by regulation prescribe . . . standards applicable to the emission of any air pollutant from any class or classes of new motor vehicles or new motor vehicle engines, which in [the Administrator's] judgment cause, or contribute to, air pollution which may reasonably be anticipated to endanger public health or welfare." 42 U.S.C. §7521(a)(1). Because EPA believes that Congress did not intend it to regulate substances that contribute to climate change, the agency maintains that carbon dioxide is not an "air pollutant" within the meaning of the provision.

The statutory text forecloses EPA's reading. The Clean Air Act's sweeping definition of "air pollutant" includes "*any* air pollution agent or combination of such agents, including *any* physical, chemical . . . substance or matter which is emitted into or otherwise enters the ambient air. . . ." §7602(g) (emphasis added). On its face, the definition embraces all airborne compounds of whatever stripe, and underscores that intent through the repeated use of the word "any." Carbon dioxide, methane, nitrous oxide, and hydrofluorocarbons are without a doubt "physical [and] chemical . . . substance[s] which [are] emitted into . . . the ambient air." The statute is unambiguous.

Rather than relying on statutory text, EPA invokes postenactment congressional actions and deliberations it views as tantamount to a congressional command to refrain from regulating greenhouse gas emissions. Even if such postenactment legislative history could shed light on the meaning of an otherwise-unambiguous statute, EPA never identifies any action remotely suggesting that Congress meant to curtail its power to treat greenhouse gases as air pollutants. That subsequent Congresses have eschewed enacting binding emissions limitations to combat global warming tells us nothing about what Congress meant when it amended §202(a)(1) in 1970 and 1977. And unlike EPA, we have no difficulty reconciling Congress' various efforts to promote interagency collaboration and research to better understand climate change with the agency's pre-existing mandate to regulate "any air pollutant" that may endanger the public welfare. See 42 U.S.C. §7601(a)(1). Collaboration and research do not conflict with any thoughtful regulatory effort; they complement it.

EPA's reliance on *Brown & Williamson Tobacco Corp.,* 529 U.S. 120, is similarly misplaced. In holding that tobacco products are not "drugs" or "devices" subject to Food and Drug Administration (FDA) regulation pursuant to the Food, Drug and Cosmetic Act (FDCA), see 529 U. S., at 133, we found critical at least two considerations that have no counterpart in this case.

First, we thought it unlikely that Congress meant to ban tobacco products, which the FDCA would have required had such products been classified as "drugs" or "devices." Id., at 135–137. Here, in contrast, EPA jurisdiction would lead to no such extreme measures. EPA would only regulate emissions, and even then, it would have to delay any action "to permit the development and application of the requisite technology, giving appropriate consideration to the cost of compliance," §7521(a)(2). However much a ban on tobacco products clashed with the "common sense" intuition that Congress never meant to remove those products from circulation, *Brown & Williamson,* 529 U. S., at 133, there is nothing counterintuitive to the notion that EPA can curtail the emission of substances that are putting the global climate out of kilter.

Second, in *Brown & Williamson* we pointed to an unbroken series of congressional enactments that made sense only if adopted "against the backdrop of the FDA's consistent and repeated statements that it lacked authority under the FDCA to regulate tobacco." We can point to no such enactments here: EPA has not identified any congressional action that conflicts in any way with the regulation of greenhouse gases from new motor vehicles. Even if it had, Congress could not have acted against a regulatory "backdrop" of disclaimers of regulatory authority. Prior to the order that provoked this litigation, EPA had never disavowed the authority to regulate greenhouse gases, and in 1998 it in fact affirmed that it *had* such authority. See App. 54 (Cannon memorandum). There is no reason, much less a compelling reason, to accept EPA's invitation to read ambiguity into a clear statute.

EPA finally argues that it cannot regulate carbon dioxide emissions from motor vehicles because doing so would require it to tighten mileage standards, a job (according to EPA) that Congress has assigned to DOT. See 68 Fed. Reg. 52929. But that DOT sets mileage standards in no way licenses EPA to shirk its environmental responsibilities. EPA has been charged with protecting the public's "health" and "welfare," 42 U.S.C. §7521(a)(1), a statutory obligation wholly independent of DOT's mandate to promote energy efficiency. See Energy Policy and Conservation Act, §2(5), 89 Stat. 874, 42 U.S.C. §6201(5). The two obligations may overlap, but there is no reason to think the two agencies cannot both administer their obligations and yet avoid inconsistency.

While the Congresses that drafted §202(a)(1) might not have appreciated the possibility that burning fossil fuels could lead to global warming, they did understand that without regulatory flexibility, changing circumstances and scientific developments would soon render the Clean Air Act obsolete. The broad language of §202(a)(1) reflects an intentional effort to confer the flexibility necessary to forestall such obsolescence. See *Pennsylvania Dept. of Corrections v. Yeskey,* 524 U.S. 206, , 212 (1998) ("[T]he fact that a statute can be applied in situations not expressly anticipated by Congress does not demonstrate ambiguity. It demonstrates breadth" (internal quotation marks omitted)). Because greenhouse gases fit well within the Clean Air Act's capacious definition of "air pollutant," we hold that EPA has the statutory authority to regulate the emission of such gases from new motor vehicles.

VII

The alternative basis for EPA's decision—that even if it does have statutory authority to regulate greenhouse gases, it would be unwise to do so at this time—rests on reasoning divorced from the statutory text. While the statute does condition the exercise of EPA's authority on its formation of a "judgment," 42 U.S.C. §7521(a)(1), that judgment must relate to whether an air pollutant "cause[s], or contribute[s] to, air pollution which may reasonably be anticipated to endanger public health or welfare," *ibid.* Put another way, the use of the word "judgment" is not a roving license to ignore the statutory text. It is but a direction to exercise discretion within defined statutory limits.

If EPA makes a finding of endangerment, the Clean Air Act requires the agency to regulate emissions of the deleterious pollutant from new motor vehicles. *Ibid.* (stating that "[EPA] shall by regulation prescribe . . . standards applicable to the emission of any air pollutant from any class of new motor vehicles"). EPA no doubt has significant latitude as to the manner, timing, content, and coordination of its regulations with those of other agencies. But once EPA has responded to a petition for rulemaking, its reasons for action or inaction must conform to the authorizing statute. Under the clear terms of the Clean Air Act, EPA can avoid taking further action only if it determines that greenhouse gases do not contribute to climate change or if it provides some reasonable explanation as to why it cannot or will not exercise its discretion to determine whether they do. *Ibid.* To the extent that this constrains agency discretion to pursue other priorities of the Administrator or the President, this is the congressional design.

EPA has refused to comply with this clear statutory command. Instead, it has offered a laundry list of reasons not to regulate. For example, EPA said that a number of voluntary executive branch programs already provide an effective response to the threat of global warming, 68 Fed. Reg. 52932, that regulating greenhouse gases might impair the President's ability to negotiate with "key developing nations" to reduce emissions, *id.*, at 52931, and that curtailing motor-vehicle emissions would reflect "an inefficient, piece-meal approach to address the climate change issue," *ibid.*

Although we have neither the expertise nor the authority to evaluate these policy judgments, it is evident they have nothing to do with whether greenhouse gas emissions contribute to climate change. Still less do they amount to a reasoned justification for declining to form a scientific judgment. In particular, while the President has broad authority in foreign affairs, that authority does not extend to the refusal to execute domestic laws. In the Global Climate Protection Act of 1987, Congress authorized the State Department—not EPA—to formulate United States foreign policy with reference to environmental matters relating to climate. See §1103(c), 101 Stat. 1409. EPA has made no showing that it issued the ruling in question here after consultation with the State Department. Congress did direct EPA to consult with other agencies in the formulation of its policies and rules, but the State Department is absent from that list. §1103(b).

Nor can EPA avoid its statutory obligation by noting the uncertainty surrounding various features of climate change and concluding that it would therefore be better not to regulate at this time. See 68 Fed. Reg. 52930–52931. If the scientific uncertainty is so profound that it precludes EPA from making a reasoned judgment as to whether greenhouse gases contribute to global warming, EPA must say so. That EPA would prefer not to regulate greenhouse gases because of some residual uncertainty—which, contrary to JUSTICE SCALIA's apparent belief, *post*, at 5–8, is in fact all that it said, see 68 Fed. Reg. 52929 ("We do not believe . . . that it would be either effective or appropriate for EPA *to establish [greenhouse gas] standards for motor vehicles* at this time" (emphasis added))—is irrelevant. The statutory question is whether sufficient information exists to make an endangerment finding.

In short, EPA has offered no reasoned explanation for its refusal to decide whether greenhouse gases cause or contribute to climate change. Its action was therefore "arbitrary, capricious, . . . or otherwise not in accordance with law." 42 U.S.C. §7607(d)(9) (A). We need not and do not reach the question whether on remand EPA must make an endangerment finding, or whether policy concerns can inform EPA's actions in the event that it makes such a finding. *Cf. Chevron U. S. A. Inc. v. Natural Resources Defense Council, Inc.*, 467 U.S. 837, 843–844 (1984) . We hold only that EPA must ground its reasons for action or inaction in the statute.

VIII

The judgment of the Court of Appeals is reversed, and the case is remanded for further proceedings consistent with this opinion.

It is so ordered.

Source: *Massachusetts et al. v. Environmental Protection Agency,* 549 U.S. 497 (April 2, 2007). Washington, D.C.: April 2, 2007. www.supremecourtus.gov/opinions/06pdf/05–1120.pdf.

DOCUMENT 11.10

The IPCC Delivers a Grim Status Report on Global Warming

"Warming of the Climate System Is Unequivocal"

2007

The Intergovernmental Panel on Climate Change (IPCC) is the world's most prominent research organization on the issue of global warming and climate change. Established by the United Nations Environment Program (UNEP) and the World Meteorological Organization (WMO) in 1988, the group's operational mandate since its inception has been to 1) assess new and existing scientific, technical, and socioeconomic information relevant to the understanding of anthropogenic (human-made) climate change; 2) communicate the myriad potential impacts of climate change on human populations and environmental systems; and 3) lay out policy options for mitigation and adaptation strategies.

The IPCC has released four major assessments of scientific findings regarding climate change since its founding. The most recent of these climate reviews was released in 2007, and its grim tidings generated extensive news coverage in the United States and around the world. The report also elicited statements from world leaders, prominent environmental organizations, and other researchers dedicated to climate change science about the vital importance of decisively tackling the threat of global warming. In the months following the release of this summary, however, neither the United States nor the international community made any appreciable progress in hammering out new GHG mitigation schemes or pacts. Following are excerpts from the IPCC's Climate Change 2007 *report for policymakers (figures not included).*

1. Observed Changes in Climate and Their Effects

Warming of the climate system is unequivocal, as is now evident from observations of increases in global average air and ocean temperatures, widespread melting of snow and ice, and rising global average sea level.

Eleven of the last twelve years (1995–2006) rank among the twelve warmest years in the instrumental record of global surface temperature (since 1850). The 100-year linear trend (1906–2005) of 0.74 [0.56 to 0.92] °C is larger[1] than the corresponding trend of 0.6 [0.4 to 0.8] °C (1901–2000) given in the Third Assessment Report (TAR). The temperature increase is widespread over the globe, and is greater at higher northern latitudes. Land regions have warmed faster than the oceans.

Rising sea level is consistent with warming. Global average sea level has risen since 1961 at an average rate of 1.8 [1.3 to 2.3] mm/yr and since 1993 at 3.1 [2.4 to 3.8] mm/yr, with contributions from thermal expansion, melting glaciers and ice caps, and the polar ice sheets. Whether the faster rate for 1993 to 2003 reflects decadal variation or an increase in the longer-term trend is unclear.

Observed decreases in snow and ice extent are also consistent with warming. Satellite data since 1978 show that annual average Arctic sea ice extent has shrunk by 2.7 [2.1 to 3.3] % per decade, with larger decreases in summer of 7.4 [5.0 to 9.8] % per decade. Mountain glaciers and snow coverage on average have declined in both hemispheres.

From 1900 to 2005, precipitation increased significantly in eastern parts of North and South America, northern Europe and northern and central Asia but declined in the Sahel, the Mediterranean, southern Africa and parts of southern Asia. Globally, the area affected by drought has *likely*[2] increased since the 1970s.

It is *very likely* that over the past 50 years: cold days, cold nights and frosts have become less frequent over most land areas, and hot days and hot nights have become more frequent. It is *likely* that: heat waves have become more frequent over most land areas, the frequency of heavy precipitation events has increased over most areas, and since 1975 the incidence of extreme high sea level[3] has increased worldwide.

---

[1] Numbers in square brackets indicate a 90% uncertainty interval around a best estimate, i.e. there is an estimated 5% likelihood that the value could be above the range given in square brackets and 5% likelihood that the value could be below that range. Uncertainty intervals are not necessarily symmetric around the corresponding best estimate.

[2] Words in italics represent calibrated expressions of uncertainty and confidence. Relevant terms are explained in the Box 'Treatment of Uncertainty' in the Introduction of this Synthesis Report. [Author's Note: Following is an explanatory excerpt from the aforementioned 'Treaty of Uncertainty': "Where uncertainty is assessed qualitatively, it is characterized . . . though a series of self-explanatory terms such as: high agreement, much evidence; *high agreement, medium evidence; medium agreement, medium evidence, etc.* Where uncertainty is assessed more quantitatively using expert judgment of the correctness of underlying data, models or analyses, then the following scale of confidence levels is used to express the assessed chance of a finding being correct: *very high confidence* at least 9 out of 10; *high confidence* about 8 out of 10; *medium confidence* about 5 out of 10; *low confidence* about 2 out of 10; and *very low confidence* less than 1 out of 10. Where uncertainty in specific outcomes is assessed using expert judgment and statistical analysis of a body of evidence (e.g. observations or model results), then the following likelihood ranges are used to express the assessed probability of occurrence: *virtually certain* >99%; *extremely likely* >95%; *very likely* >90%; *likely* >66%; *more likely than not* >50%; *about as likely as not* 33% to 66%; *unlikely* <33%; *very unlikely* <10%; *extremely unlikely* <5%; *exceptionally unlikely* <1%."]

[3] Excluding tsunamis, which are not due to climate change. Extreme high sea level depends on average sea level and on regional weather systems. It is defined here as the highest 1% of hourly values of observed sea level at a station for a given reference period.

There is observational evidence of an increase in intense tropical cyclone activity in the North Atlantic since about 1970, with limited evidence of increases elsewhere. There is no clear trend in the annual numbers of tropical cyclones. It is difficult to ascertain longer-term trends in cyclone activity, particularly prior to 1970.

Average Northern Hemisphere temperatures during the second half of the 20th century were *very likely* higher than during any other 50-year period in the last 500 years and *likely* the highest in at least the past 1300 years.

Observational evidence[4] from all continents and most oceans show that many natural systems are being affected by regional climate changes, particularly temperature increases.

Changes in snow, ice and frozen ground have with *high confidence* increased the number and size of glacial lakes, increased ground instability in mountain and other permafrost regions, and led to changes in some Arctic and Antarctic ecosystems.

There is *high confidence* that some hydrological systems have also been affected through increased runoff and earlier spring peak discharge in many glacier- and snow-fed rivers, and effects on thermal structure and water quality of warming rivers and lakes.

In terrestrial ecosystems, earlier timing of spring events and poleward and upward shifts in plant and animal ranges are with *very high* confidence linked to recent warming. In some marine and freshwater systems, shifts in ranges and changes in algal, plankton and fish abundance are with *high confidence* associated with rising water temperatures, as well as related changes in ice cover, salinity, oxygen levels and circulation.

Of the more than 29,000 observational data series, from 75 studies, that show significant change in many physical and biological systems more than 89% are consistent with the direction of change expected as a response to warming. However, there is a notable lack of geographic balance in data and literature on observed changes, with marked scarcity in developing countries.

There is *medium confidence* that other effects of regional climate change on natural and human environments are emerging, although many are difficult to discern due to adaptation and non-climatic drivers.

They include effects of temperature increases on:

- agricultural and forestry management at Northern Hemisphere higher latitudes, such as earlier spring planting of crops, and alterations in disturbance regimes of forests due to fires and pests
- some aspects of human health, such as heat-related mortality in Europe, changes in infectious disease vectors in some areas, and allergenic pollen in Northern Hemisphere high and mid-latitudes.
- some human activities in the Arctic (e.g. hunting and travel over snow and ice) and in lower-elevation alpine areas (such as mountain sports).

2. Causes of Change

Changes in atmospheric concentrations of greenhouse gases (GHGs) and aerosols, land-cover and solar radiation alter the energy balance of the climate system.

---

[4] Based largely on data sets that cover the period since 1970.

Global GHG emissions due to human activities have grown since pre-industrial times, with an increase of 70% between 1970 and 2004.[5]

Carbon dioxide (CO_2) is the most important anthropogenic GHG. Its annual emissions grew by about 80% between 1970 and 2004. The long-term trend of declining CO_2 emissions per unit of energy supplied reversed after 2000.

Global atmospheric concentrations of CO_2, methane (CH_4), and nitrous oxide (N_2O) have increased markedly as a result of human activities since 1750 and now far exceed pre-industrial values determined from ice cores spanning many thousands of years.

Atmospheric concentrations of CO_2 (379ppm) and CH_4 (1774 ppb) in 2005 exceed by far the natural range over the last 650,000 years. Global increases in CO_2 concentrations are due primarily to fossil fuel use, with land-use change providing another significant but smaller contribution. It is *very likely* that the observed increase in CH_4 concentration is predominantly due to agriculture and fossil fuel use. Methane growth rates have declined since the early 1990s, consistent with total emissions (sum of anthropogenic and natural sources) being nearly constant during this period. The increase in N_2O concentration is primarily due to agriculture.

There is *very high confidence* that the net effect of human activities since 1750 has been one of warming.[6]

Most of the observed increase in globally-averaged temperatures since the mid-20th century is *very likely* due to the observed increase in anthropogenic GHG concentrations.[7] . . .

During the past 50 years, the sum of solar and volcanic forcings would *likely* have produced cooling. Observed patterns of warming and their changes are simulated only by models that include anthropogenic forcings. Difficulties remain in simulating and attributing observed temperature changes at smaller than continental scales.

Advances since the TAR show that discernible human influences extend beyond average temperature to other aspects of climate.

Human influences have:

Very likely contributed to sea level rise during the latter half of the 20th century

Likely contributed to changes in wind patterns, affecting extra-tropical storm tracks and temperature patterns

Likely increased temperatures of extreme hot nights, cold nights and cold days

More likely than not increased risk of heat waves, area affected by drought since the 1970s and frequency of heavy precipitation events.

Anthropogenic warming over the last three decades has *likely* had a discernible influence at the global scale on observed changes in many physical and biological systems.

Spatial agreement between regions of significant warming across the globe and locations of significant observed changes in many systems consistent with warming is *very unlikely* to be due solely to natural variability. Several modeling studies have linked some specific responses in physical and biological systems to anthropogenic warming.

---

[5] Includes only CO_2, CH_4, N_2O, HFCs, PFCs and SF_6 whose emissions are covered by the UNFCCC. These GHGs are weighted by their 100-year Global Warming Potentials, using values consistent with reporting under the UNFCCC.

[6] Increases in GHGs tend to warm the surface while the net effect of increases in aerosols tends to cool it. The net effect due to human activities since the pre-industrial era is one of warming. . . . In comparison, changes in solar irradiances are estimated to have caused a small warming effect. . . .

[7] Consideration of remaining uncertainty is based on current methodologies.

More complete attribution of observed natural system responses to anthropogenic warming is currently prevented by the short time scales of many impact studies, greater natural climate variability at regional scales, contributions of non-climate factors and limited spatial coverage of studies.

3. Projected Climate Change and Its Impacts

There is *high agreement* and *much evidence* that with current climate change mitigation policies and related sustainable development practices, global GHG emissions will continue to grow over the next few decades.

The IPCC Special Report on Emission Scenarios (SRES, 2000) projects an increase of global GHG emissions by 25–90% (CO_2-eq) between 2000 and 2030, with fossil fuels maintaining their dominant position in the global energy mix to 2030 and beyond. . . .

Continued GHG emissions at or above current rates would cause further warming and induce many changes in the global climate system during the 21st century that would *very likely* be larger than those observed during the 20th century.

For the next two decades a warming of about 0.2 °C per decade is projected for a range of SRES emissions scenarios. Even if the concentration of all GHGs and aerosols had been kept constant at year 2000 levels, a further warming of about 0.1 °C per decade would be expected. Afterwards, temperature projections increasingly depend on specific emission scenarios. . . .

There is now higher confidence than in the TAR in projected patterns of warming and other regional-scale features, including changes in wind patterns, precipitation, and some aspects of extremes and sea ice.

Regional-scale changes include:

- warming greatest over land and at most high northern latitudes and least over Southern Ocean and parts of the North Atlantic Ocean, continuing recent observed trends
- contraction of snow cover area, increases in thaw depth over most permafrost regions, and decrease in sea ice extent; in some projections using SRES scenarios, Arctic late-summer sea ice disappears almost entirely by the latter part of the 21st century
- *very likely* increase in frequency of hot extremes, heat waves, and heavy precipitation
- *likely* increase in tropical cyclone intensity; less confidence in global decrease of tropical cyclone numbers
- poleward shift of extra-tropical storm tracks with consequent changes in wind, precipitation, and temperature patterns
- *very likely* precipitation increases in high latitudes and *likely* decreases in most subtropical land regions, continuing observed recent trends.

There is *high confidence* that by mid-century, annual river runoff and water availability are projected to increase at high latitudes (and in some tropical wet areas) and decrease in some dry regions in the mid-latitudes and tropics. There is also *high confidence* that many semi-arid areas (e.g. Mediterranean basin, western United States, southern Africa and northeast Brazil) will suffer a decrease in water resources due to climate change. . . .

Some systems, sectors and regions are *likely* to be especially affected by climate change.[8]

Systems and sectors:

- particular ecosystems:
  - o terrestrial: tundra, boreal forest and mountain regions because of sensitivity to warming; Mediterranean-type ecosystems because of reduction in rainfall; and tropical rainforests where precipitation declines
  - o coastal: mangroves and salt marshes, due to multiple stresses
  - o marine: coral reefs due to multiple stresses; the sea ice biome because of sensitivity to warming
- water resources in some dry regions at mid-latitudes[9] and in the dry tropics, due to changes in rainfall and evapotranspiration, and in areas dependent on snow and ice melt
- agriculture in low-latitudes, due to reduced water availability
- low-lying coastal systems, due to threat of sea level rise and increased risk from extreme weather events
- human health in populations with low adaptive capacity.

Regions:

- the Arctic, because of the impacts of high rates of projected warming on natural systems and human communities
- Africa, because of low adaptive capacity and projected climate change impacts
- small islands, where there is high exposure of population and infrastructure to projected climate change impacts
- Asian and African megadeltas, due to large populations and high exposure to sea level rise, storm surges and river flooding.

Within other areas, even those with high incomes, some people (such as the poor, young children, and the elderly) can be particularly at risk, and also some areas and some activities.

Ocean Acidification

The uptake of anthropogenic carbon since 1750 has led to the ocean becoming more acidic with an average decrease in pH of 0.1 units. Increasing atmospheric CO_2 concentrations lead to further acidification. Projections based on SRES scenarios give a reduction in average global surface ocean pH of between 0.14 and 0.35 units over the 21st century. While the effects of observed ocean acidification on the marine biosphere are as yet undocumented, the progressive acidification of oceans is expected to have negative impacts on marine shell-forming organisms (e.g. corals) and their dependent species. . . .

Anthropogenic warming and sea level would continue for centuries due to the time scales associated with climate processes and feedbacks, even if GHG concentrations were to be stabilized.

. . . Contraction of the Greenland ice sheet is projected to continue to contribute to sea level rise after 2100. Current models suggest virtually complete elimination of the Greenland ice sheet and a resulting contribution to sea level rise of about 7 m if global

---

[8] Identified on the basis of expert judgement of the assessed literature and considering the magnitude, timing and projected rate of climate change, sensitivity and adaptive capacity.

[9] Including arid and semi-arid regions.

average warming were sustained for millennia in excess of 1.9 to 4.6°C relative to pre-industrial values. The corresponding future temperatures in Greenland are comparable to those inferred for the last interglacial period 125,000 years ago, when palaeoclimatic information suggests reductions of polar land ice extent and 4 to 6 m of sea level rise.

Current global model studies project that the Antarctic ice sheet will remain too cold for widespread surface melting and gain mass due to increased snowfall. However, net loss of ice mass could occur if dynamical ice discharge dominates the ice sheet mass balance.

Anthropogenic warming could lead to some impacts that are abrupt or irreversible, depending upon the rate and magnitude of the climate change.

Partial loss of ice sheets on polar land could imply metres of sea level rise, major changes in coastlines and inundation of low-lying areas, with greatest effects in river deltas and low-lying islands. Such changes are projected to occur over millennial time scales, but more rapid sea level rise on century time scales cannot be excluded.

Climate change is *likely* to lead to some irreversible impacts. There is *medium confidence* that approximately 20–30% of species assessed so far are *likely* to be at increased risk of extinction if increases in global average warming exceed 1.5–2.5°C (relative to 1980–1999). As global average temperature increase exceeds about 3.5°C, model projections suggest significant extinctions (40–70% of species assessed) around the globe.

Based on current model simulations, the meridional overturning circulation (MOC) of the Atlantic Ocean will *very likely* slow down during the 21st century; nevertheless temperatures over the Atlantic and Europe are projected to increase. The MOC is *very unlikely* to undergo a large abrupt transition during the 21st century. Longer-term MOC changes cannot be assessed with confidence. Impacts of large-scale and persistent changes in the MOC are *likely* to include changes in marine ecosystem productivity, fisheries, ocean CO_2 uptake, oceanic oxygen concentrations and terrestrial vegetation. Changes in terrestrial and ocean CO_2 uptake may feed back on the climate system.

Adaptation and Mitigation Options[10]

A wide array of adaptation options is available, but more extensive adaptation than is currently occurring is required to reduce vulnerability to climate change. There are barriers, limits and costs, which are not fully understood.

Societies have a long record of managing the impacts of weather- and climate-related events. Nevertheless, additional adaptation measures will be required to reduce the adverse impacts of projected climate change and variability, regardless of the scale of mitigation undertaken over the next two to three decades. Moreover, vulnerability to climate change can be exacerbated by other stresses. These arise from, for example, current climate hazards, poverty and unequal access to resources, food insecurity, trends in economic globalization, conflict and incidence of diseases such as HIV/AIDS.

Some planned adaptation to climate change is already occurring on a limited basis. Adaptation can reduce vulnerability especially when it is embedded within broader sectoral initiatives. There is *high confidence* that there are viable adaptation options that can be implemented in some sectors at low cost, and/or with high benefit-cost ratios. However, comprehensive estimates of global costs and benefits of adaptation are limited.

Adaptive capacity is intimately connected to social and economic development but is unevenly distributed across and within societies.

---

[10] While this section deals with adaptation and mitigation separately, these responses can be complementary. . . .

A range of barriers limit both the implementation and effectiveness of adaptation measures. The capacity to adapt is dynamic and is influenced by a society's productive base including: natural and man-made capital assets, social networks and entitlements, human capital and institutions, governance, national income, health and technology. Even societies with high adaptive capacity remain vulnerable to climate change, variability and extremes.

Both bottom-up and top-down studies indicate that there is *high agreement* and *much evidence* of substantial economic potential for the mitigation of global GHG emissions over the coming decades that could offset the projected growth of global emissions or reduce emissions below current levels. . . .

Future energy infrastructure investment decisions, expected to exceed 20 trillion US$ between 2005 and 2030, will have long-term impacts on GHG emissions, because of the long life-times of energy plants and other infrastructure capital stock. The widespread diffusion of low-carbon technologies may take many decades, even if early investments in these technologies are made attractive. Initial estimates show that returning global-energy related CO_2 emissions to 2005 levels by 2030 would require a large shift in investment patterns, although the net additional investment required ranges from negligible to 5–10%.

A wide variety of policies and instruments are available to governments to create the incentives for mitigation action. Their applicability depends on national circumstances and sectoral context.

They include integrating climate policies in wider development policies, regulations and standards, taxes and charges, tradable permits, financial incentives, voluntary agreements, information instruments, and research, development and demonstration (RD&D). . . .

There is *high agreement* and *much evidence* that mitigation actions can result in near-term co-benefits (e.g. improved health due to reduced air pollution) that may offset a substantial fraction of mitigation costs.

There is *high agreement* and *medium evidence* that Annex I countries' [industrialized nations listed in the Kyoto Protocol] actions may affect the global economy and global emissions, although the scale of carbon leakage remains uncertain.

Fossil fuel exporting nations (in both Annex I and non-Annex I countries) may expect, as indicated in the TAR, lower demand and prices and lower GDP growth due to mitigation policies. The extent of this spill over depends strongly on assumptions related to policy decisions and oil market conditions.

There is also *high agreement* and *medium evidence* that changes in lifestyle, behaviour patterns and management practices can contribute to climate change mitigation across all sectors.

Many options for reducing global GHG emissions through international cooperation exist. There is *high agreement* and *much evidence* that notable achievements of the UNFCCC and its Kyoto Protocol are the establishment of a global response to climate change, stimulation of an array of national policies, and the creation of an international carbon market and new institutional mechanisms that may provide the foundation for future mitigation efforts. Progress has also been made in addressing adaptation within the UNFCCC and additional international initiatives have been suggested.

Greater cooperative efforts and expansion of market mechanisms will help to reduce global costs for achieving a given level of mitigation, or will improve environmental effectiveness. Efforts can include diverse elements such as emission targets; sectoral, local, sub-national and regional actions; RD&D programmes; adopting common policies; implementing development oriented actions; or expanding financing instruments. . . .

5. The Long-term Perspective

Determining what constitutes "dangerous anthropogenic interference with the climate system" in relation to Article 2 of the UNFCCC involves value judgements. Science can support informed decisions on this issue, including by providing criteria for judging which vulnerabilities might be labeled "key."

Key vulnerabilities[11] may be associated with many climate sensitive systems including food supply, infrastructure, health, water resources, coastal systems, ecosystems, global biogeochemical cycles, ice sheets, and modes of oceanic and atmospheric circulation.

The five "reasons for concern" identified in the TAR remain a viable framework to consider key vulnerabilities. These "reasons" are assessed here to be stronger than in the TAR. Many risks are identified with higher confidence. Some risks are projected to be larger or to occur at lower increases in temperature. Understanding about the relationship between impacts (the basis for "reasons for concern" in the TAR) and vulnerability (that includes the ability to adapt to impacts) has improved.

This is due to more precise identification of the circumstances that make systems, sectors and regions especially vulnerable, and growing evidence of the risks of very large impacts on multiple century time scales.

- Risks to unique and threatened systems. There is new and stronger evidence of observed impacts of climate change on unique and vulnerable systems (such as polar and high mountain communities and ecosystems), with increasing levels of adverse impacts as temperatures increase further. An increasing risk of species extinction and coral reef damage is projected with higher confidence than in the TAR as warming proceeds. There is *medium confidence* that approximately 20–30% of plant and animal species assessed so far are *likely* to be at increased risk of extinction if increases in global average temperature exceed 1.5–2.5°C over 1980–1999 levels. Confidence has increased that a 1–2°C increase in global mean temperature above 1990 levels (about 1.5–2.5°C above pre-industrial) poses significant risks to many unique and threatened systems including many biodiversity hotspots. Corals are vulnerable to thermal stress and have low adaptive capacity. Increases in sea surface temperature of about 1–3°C are projected to result in more frequent coral bleaching events and widespread mortality, unless there is thermal adaptation or acclimatization by corals. Increasing vulnerability of indigenous communities in the Arctic and small island communities to warming is projected.
- Risks of extreme weather events. Responses to some recent extreme events reveal higher levels of vulnerability than the TAR. There is now higher confidence in the projected increases in droughts, heat waves, and floods as well as their adverse impacts.

---

[11] Key Vulnerabilities can be identified based on a number of criteria in the literature, including magnitude, timing, persistence/reversibility, the potential for adaptation, distributional aspects, likelihood and 'importance' of the impacts.

- Distribution of impacts and vulnerabilities. There are sharp differences across regions and those in the weakest economic position are often the most vulnerable to climate change. There is increasing evidence of greater vulnerability of specific groups such as the poor and elderly in not only developing but also developed countries. Moreover, there is increased evidence that low-latitude and less-developed areas generally face greater risk, for example in dry areas and megadeltas.
- Aggregate impacts. Compared to the TAR, initial net market-based benefits from climate change are projected to peak at a lower magnitude of warming, while damages would be higher for larger magnitudes of warming. The net costs of impacts of increased warming are projected to increase over time.
- Risks of large-scale singularities. There is *high confidence* that global warming over many centuries would lead to a sea level rise contribution from thermal expansion alone which is projected to be much larger than observed over the 20th century, with loss of coastal area and associated impacts. There is better understanding than in the TAR that the risk of additional contributions to sea level rise from both the Greenland and possibly Antarctic ice sheets may be larger than protected by ice sheet models and could occur on century time scales. This is because ice dynamical processes seen in recent observations but not fully included in ice sheet models assessed in AR4 could increase the rate of ice loss.

There is *high confidence* that neither adaptation nor mitigation alone can avoid all climate change impacts; however, they can complement each other and together can significantly reduce the risks of climate change. . . .

Many impacts can be reduced, delayed or avoided by mitigation. Mitigation efforts and investments over the next two to three decades will have a larger impact on opportunities to achieve lower stabilization levels. Delayed emission reductions significantly constrain the opportunities to achieve lower stabilization levels and increase the risk of more severe climate change impacts. . . .

There is *high agreement* and *much evidence* that all stabilization levels assessed can be achieved by deployment of a portfolio of technologies that are either currently available or expected to be commercialized in coming decades, assuming appropriate and effective incentives are in place for their development, acquisition, deployment and diffusion and addressing related barriers.

All assessed stabilization scenarios indicate that 60–80% of the reductions would come from energy supply and use, and industrial processes, with energy efficiency playing a key role in many scenarios. Including non-CO_2 and CO_2 land-use and forestry mitigation options provides greater flexibility and cost-effectiveness. . . .

Responding to climate change involves an iterative risk management process that includes both adaptation and mitigation and takes into account climate change damages, co-benefits, sustainability, equity, and attitudes to risk.

Impacts of climate change are *very likely* to impose net annual costs which will increase over time as global temperatures increase. Peer-reviewed estimates of the social cost of carbon[12] in 2005 average US$12 per tonne of CO_2, but the range from 100 estimates is large (-$3 to $95/t$CO_2$). This is due in large part to differences in assumptions regarding climate sensitivity, response lags, the treatment of risk and equity, economic and non-economic impacts, the inclusion of potentially catastrophic losses, and discount

---

[12] Net economic costs of damages from climate change aggregated across the globe and discounted to the specified year.

rates. Aggregate estimates of costs mask significant differences in impacts across sectors, regions and populations and *very likely* underestimate damage costs because they cannot include many non-quantifiable impacts. . . .

Choices about the scale and timing of GHG mitigation involve balancing the economic costs of more rapid emissions reductions now against the corresponding medium-term and long-term climate risks of delay.

Source: Intergovernmental Panel on Climate Change (IPCC). Contribution of Work Groups I, II and III to the Fourth Assessment Report of the Intergovernmental Panel on Climate Change, SPM. "Climate Change 2007: Synthesis Report." Summary for Policymakers. Geneva, Switzerland: IPCC, 2007. www.ipcc.ch/pdf/assessment-report/ar4/syr/ar4_syr_spm.pdf

DOCUMENT
11.11

Fighting over Coal Plants in Kansas

"The Legislature Is Intent on Darkening Kansas' Energy Future"

April 13, and May 4, 2009

From 2007 through 2009 the Republican-controlled state legislature in Kansas repeatedly clashed with second-term Democratic governor Kathleen Sebelius over the construction of new coal-fired power plants in the state. The political tempest began in earnest in October 2007, when state environmental officials cited concerns about carbon dioxide emissions as the basis for rejecting the Sunflower Electric Corp.'s application to build two 700-megawatt, coal-fired power generators. Sebelius promptly issued statements of support for the decision, citing an array of environmental and economic factors.

This rejection—which marked the first time in U.S. history that global warming concerns had scuttled new coal-powered plant construction—aroused the ire of the state's Republican leadership, Sunflower executives, and the national coal industry. Although the state legislature fought back with four different bills that would have approved construction of the plants (and removed state environmental agencies from the permit-granting process), Sebelius refused to back down. She vetoed all four bills as environmentally irresponsible pieces of legislation, and each time, coal-plant proponents were unable to muster enough votes for an override. Sebelius also used her veto messages to urge lawmakers to pry the state loose from its historic dependence on fossil fuels and make new investments in wind power and other renewable energy assets. The full text of her fourth and final veto statement, issued on April 13, 2009, is reprinted here.

Fewer than three weeks after issuing her fourth coal plant veto, however, Sebelius was confirmed and sworn in as the Obama Administration's first Secretary of Health and Human Services. Her successor as governor of Kansas was Mark Parkinson, a former state Republican Party chairman who in 2006 had switched to the Democratic Party to run as Sebelius's lieutenant governor. Parkinson took up negotiations with Sunflower and Republican lawmakers on the coal plant issue almost immediately after his April 28 swearing-in ceremony. On May 4 Parkinson announced that he had reached an agreement to allow Sunflower to build a single 895-megawatt coal-fired power plant in the state.

The press release from the governor's office announcing this compromise agreement is also reprinted here.

Parkinson emphasized that the agreement he struck with Sunflower required the utility company to generate 15 percent of its power from renewable sources by 2016 (and 20 percent by 2020) and included strong carbon mitigation measures for the new plant, but the agreement was condemned by state and national environmental groups. These critics argued that whatever the pact's renewable energy provisions, the bottom-line reality was that many details in the agreement—including one that allows Sunflower to file for another coal plant permit after April 30, 2011—bound Kansas citizens more tightly to King Coal than ever before. "While the country is moving away from polluting fossil fuels, Kansas has opened the door for outdated, dirty technology other states are rejecting," stated the Sierra Club. "This is not a compromise, but a giveaway to the coal industry Kansans have stood up against."

In July 2009 the political saga took yet another turn when the federal Environmental Protection Agency notified the state of Kansas and Sunflower that construction of the plant can not begin until the Parkinson-approved project—a modification of the original coal plant scheme from the mid-2000s—repeats the permit process to ensure that it meets all Clean Air Act requirements. Plant opponents exulted in this news, but Sunflower executives vowed that re-starting the permit process would not derail the project.

Governor Sebelius's Veto Statement for House Bill 2014

April 13, 2009

Last year, I vetoed legislation that forced the Secretary of the Kansas Department of Health and Environment to issue air quality permits for two new coal fired plants which would produce 11 million tons of carbon dioxide each year. These new plants would generate 1400 megawatts of electricity, most of which would be exported to Colorado and Texas. In fact, Kansas would only get 200 megawatts of electricity, while we would get all of the new pollution.

I vetoed that legislation because while the rest of the country was trying to reduce greenhouse emissions, Kansas would be creating massive new emissions for power we don't need. Additionally, it appeared that federal legislation that would penalize new carbon dioxide emissions was on the horizon leaving Kansans vulnerable for years to come.

The bill before me now attempts to take us down that failed path once again. What was a bad idea last year, is an even worse idea today. Now, we know that according to Sunflower Electric's own reports, their customers will not need additional power until 2018. We also know that President Obama is moving aggressively to regulate new carbon dioxide emissions. These developments reaffirm that now is not the time for new coal plants in Kansas.

Prior to the start of this legislative session, Lieutenant Governor Parkinson and I worked with utility stakeholders to develop a renewable portfolio standard that would have further developed the natural resource we have in wind energy. Our proposed energy legislation contained real net-metering so that Kansans would be fairly compensated for power they generated; we also included energy efficiency measures to reduce our future energy needs.

We presented these proposals to the legislature, with the hope that the legislature would move towards a renewable energy economy creating thousands of jobs right here in Kansas. However, the legislature chose instead to sacrifice real comprehensive energy legislation in the pursuit of more coal-fired power plants.

Despite what supporters of this legislation say, HB 2014 does little to advance clean, renewable energy. In fact, the renewable energy standards established in HB 2014 are less than the voluntary standards we already have today. The net metering provisions in the bill are weaker than any of the 42 states that currently offer net metering to utility consumers.

Kansas needs legislation that will increase development of our renewable energy resources, increase energy efficiency measures and create good-paying jobs. Once again, as the rest of the country moves toward a renewable energy future, the legislature is intent on darkening Kansas' energy future with new coal plants that will provide energy we don't yet need.

I encourage the legislature to abandon its efforts to saddle Kansas with massive new carbon dioxide emissions, and instead adopt a plan that will take advantage of our enormous wind assets and really look at energy efficiency as a way to stretch our power sources well into the future while creating thousands of sustainable Kansas jobs.

Pursuant to Article 2, Section 14 of the Constitution of the State of Kansas, I veto House Bill 2014.

Governor Parkinson and Sunflower Electric Agree to New Energy Plan

May 4, 2009

Governor Mark Parkinson, together with Sunflower Electric Power Corporation President and CEO, Earl Watkins, have announced a comprehensive energy plan to encourage the production of more renewable energy in Kansas.

"We're bringing people together to create hundreds of jobs, increase our renewable energy production and ensure a comprehensive energy plan for our state," said Governor Parkinson. "Prior to this agreement, the Legislature was at an impasse on energy issues. With this agreement, we can start to move forward."

The current agreement will allow Sunflower to construct one 895 megawatt coal plant with an unprecedented level of carbon mitigation. This project is estimated to create more than 1,500 jobs at the peak of its construction.

The agreement between the Governor's Administration and Sunflower Electric is contingent upon the Legislature's passage of the Comprehensive Energy Package proposed by Parkinson and then-Governor Kathleen Sebelius in January.

"We are pleased to work with Governor Parkinson as this proposal meets the base load needs of the region and will promote the development of renewable resources in Kansas. The proposal will allow our out-of-state cooperative partners to participate in the project in a smaller way while preserving the 200 MW needed by Kansas cooperative and municipal utilities. Agreement provisions for wind, biomass and transmission development will promote renewable energy development in western Kansas," said Earl Watkins, president and chief executive officer for Sunflower.

"I want to acknowledge every legislator, stakeholder and environmental advocate who have worked for the past 18 months on comprehensive energy policy for this state," Parkinson continued. "I may not have a full term as Governor, but I do have a full agenda. We will be bringing people together—Republicans and Democrats; labor and business; public and private stakeholders—to move this state forward."

"We appreciate the leadership shown by the Governor to recognize the need for base load power in the Sunflower system. This effort will move the project forward bringing much needed economic activity and jobs to Kansas," said Watkins.

"This agreement meets the goals of our project, but will also address concerns of our coalition partners that the regulatory process is clear and follows the federal clean air act. The legislative proposal will move Kansas toward a comprehensive energy policy that utilizes all forms of generation, encourages the wise use of energy and balances concerns for cost and the environment."

Source: Sebelius, Kathleen. Veto Statement for House Bill 2014, April 13, 2009. www.kslegislature.org/bills/2010/gov_2014.pdf; Office of the Governor, Kansas. "Governor Parkinson and Sunflower Electric Agree to New Energy Plan." Press release, May 4, 2009. www.governor.ks.gov/News/NewsRelease/2009/nr-09–0504a.htm.

DOCUMENT 11.12

President Obama Touts the Benefits of High-speed Rail

"Equal to Removing One Million Cars from Our Roads"

April 16, 2009

Environmental organizations, "green" legislators, climate scientists, municipal planners, and transportation experts have all cited increased investment in mass transit as an essential part of any overarching effort to reduce energy consumption and greenhouse gas emissions in the United States. In some cases, their calls for new spending priorities in the transportation sector have also been supported by researchers who have documented the negative toll that traffic congestion, rampant road building, and automobile dependency have had on economic productivity, energy independence, "quality-of-life" trends, open space preservation, air quality, and other aspects of modern American society.

For many years, however, bills designed to increase federal allocations for high-speed rail and other mass transit systems have been buried under the weight of partisan gamesmanship; lobbying from automotive, road construction, and other groups; and recognition that automobiles and the "open road" are embedded deep in American culture and mythology.

In 2009, however, the United States signaled that it might be altering course in this regard. In February of that year President Barack Obama signed a major economic stimulus package passed by Congress that included $8 billion in funding for new rail corridor networks that would blend revitalized rail lines already in existence with new high-speed lines featuring the latest technology. Two months later, the Obama White House organized a special event to formally unveil the administration's "vision for high-speed rail *in America." Obama used this occasion to frame investment in high-speed rail as a transformational step in the modernization of the nation's wider transportation system. His remarks are excerpted here.*

The $8-billion allocation for high-speed rail was hailed by mass transit advocates, who noted that Obama has also proposed a separate five-year, $5 billion investment in high-speed rail as part of the administration's suggested fiscal year 2010 budget. "Transportation systems have enormous impacts on the lives of the American people— from our pocket books to climate change, from our household expenses to the global economy," stated James Corless, director of Transportation for America. "Americans are increasingly rejecting the status quo in favor of more transportation options that will make our communities more walkable, more energy efficient, more equitable and healthier. The President's commitment to high speed rail is an important piece of what must be a bold new vision for our national transportation program."[1]

You know, I've been speaking a lot lately about what we're doing to break free of our economic crisis so to put people back to work and move this nation from recession to recovery. And one area in which we can make investments with impact both immediate and lasting is in America's infrastructure.

And that's why the Recovery and Reinvestment Plan we passed not two months ago included the most sweeping investment in our infrastructure since President Eisenhower built the Interstate Highway System in the 1950s. And these efforts will save money by untangling gridlock, and saving lives by improving our roads, and save or create 150,000 jobs, mostly in the private sector, by the end of next year. Already, it's put Americans back to work. And so far, we're ahead of schedule, we're under budget, and adhering to the highest standards of transparency and accountability.

But if we want to move from recovery to prosperity, then we have to do a little bit more. We also have to build a new foundation for our future growth. Today, our aging system of highways and byways, air routes and rail lines is hindering that growth. Our highways are clogged with traffic, costing us $80 billion a year in lost productivity and wasted fuel. Our airports are choked with increased loads. Some of you flew down here and you know what that was about. We're at the mercy of fluctuating gas prices all too often; we pump too many greenhouse gases into the air.

What we need, then, is a smart transportation system equal to the needs of the 21st century. A system that reduces travel times and increases mobility. A system that reduces congestion and boosts productivity. A system that reduces destructive emissions and creates jobs.

What we're talking about is a vision for high-speed rail in America. Imagine boarding a train in the center of a city. No racing to an airport and across a terminal, no delays, no sitting on the tarmac, no lost luggage, no taking off your shoes. [Laughter.] Imagine whisking through towns at speeds over 100 miles an hour, walking only a few steps to public transportation, and ending up just blocks from your destination. Imagine what a great project that would be to rebuild America.

Now, all of you know this is not some fanciful, pie-in-the-sky vision of the future. It is now. It is happening right now. It's been happening for decades. The problem is it's been happening elsewhere, not here.

In France, high-speed rail has pulled regions from isolation, ignited growth, remade quiet towns into thriving tourist destinations. In Spain, a high-speed line between Madrid and Seville is so successful that more people travel between those cities by rail than by car and airplane combined. China, where service began just two years ago, may have more miles of high-speed rail service than any other country just five years from now. And Japan, the nation that unveiled the first high-speed rail system, is already at work building the next: a line that will connect Tokyo with Osaka at speeds of over 300 miles per hour. So it's being done; it's just not being done here.

There's no reason why we can't do this. This is America. There's no reason why the future of travel should lie somewhere else beyond our borders. Building a new system of high-speed rail in America will be faster, cheaper and easier than building more freeways or adding to an already overburdened aviation system—and everybody stands to benefit.

And that's why today, with the help of Secretary [Ray] LaHood and Vice President [Joe] Biden, America's number one rail fan, I've been told [laughter]—I'm announcing my administration's efforts to transform travel in America with an historic investment in high-speed rail.

And our strategy has two parts: improving our existing rail lines to make current train service faster . . . but also identifying potential corridors for the creation of world-class high-speed rail. To make this happen, we've already dedicated $8 billion of Recovery and Reinvestment Act funds to this initiative, and I've requested another $5 billion over the next five years.

The Department of Transportation expects to begin awarding funds to ready projects before the end of this summer, well ahead of schedule. And like all funding decisions under the Recovery Act, money will be distributed based on merit—not on politics, not as favors, not for any other consideration—purely on merit.

Now, this plan is realistic. And the first round of funding will focus on projects that can create jobs and benefits in the near term. We're not talking about starting from scratch, we're talking about using existing infrastructure to increase speeds on some routes from 70 miles an hour to over 100 miles per hour—so you're taking existing rail lines, you're upgrading them. And many corridors merit even faster service, but this is the first step that is quickly achievable, and it will create jobs improving tracks, crossings, signal systems.

The next step is investing in high-speed rail that unleashes the economic potential of all our regions by shrinking distances within our regions. There are at least 10 major corridors in the United States of 100 to 600 miles in length with the potential for successful high-speed rail systems. And these areas have explored its potential impact on their long-term growth and competitiveness, and they've already presented sound plans. I want to be clear: No decision about where to allocate funds has yet been made, and any region can step up, present a plan and be considered.

The high-speed rail corridors we've identified so far would connect areas like the cities of the Pacific Northwest; southern and central Florida; the Gulf Coast to the Southeast to our nation's capital; the breadth of Pennsylvania and New York to the cities of New England; and something close to my heart, a central hub network that draws the cities of our industrial heartland closer to Chicago and one another.

Or California, where voters have already chosen to move forward with their own high-speed rail system, a system of new stations and 220 mile-per-hour trains that links big cities to inland towns; that alleviates crippling congestion on highways and at airports; and that makes travel from San Francisco to Los Angeles possible in two and a half hours.

And by making investments across the country, we'll lay a new foundation for our economic competitiveness and contribute to smart urban and rural growth. We'll create highly-skilled construction and operating jobs that can't be outsourced, and generate demand for technology that gives a new generation of innovators and entrepreneurs the opportunity to step up and lead the way in the 21st century. We'll move to cleaner energy and a cleaner environment, we'll reduce our need for foreign oil by millions of barrels a year, and eliminate more than 6 billion pounds of carbon dioxide emissions annually—equal to removing 1 million cars from our roads.

Now, I know that this vision has its critics. There are those who say high-speed rail is a fantasy—but its success around the world says otherwise. I know Americans love their cars, and nobody is talking about replacing the automobile and our highways as critical parts of our transportation system. We are upgrading those in the Recovery Package, as well. But this is something that can be done, has been done, and can provide us enormous benefits.

Now, there are those who argue that if an investment doesn't directly benefit the people of their district, then it shouldn't be made. . . . But if we followed that rationale, we'd have no infrastructure at all.

There are those who say, well, this investment is too small. But this is just a first step. We know that this is going to be a long-term project. But us getting started now, us moving the process forward and getting people to imagine what's possible, and putting resources behind it so that people can start seeing examples of this around the country, that's going to spur all kinds of activity.

Now finally, there are those who say at a time of crisis, we shouldn't be pursuing such a strategy; we've got too many other things to do. But our history teaches us a different lesson.

As Secretary LaHood just mentioned, President Lincoln was committed to a nation connected from East to West, even at the same time he was trying to hold North and South together. He was in the middle of a Civil War. While fighting raged on one side of the continent, tens of thousands of Americans from all walks of life came together on the other. Dreamers and risk-takers willing to invest in America. College-educated engineers and supervisors who learned leadership in war. American workers and immigrants from all over the world. Confederates and Yankees joined on the same side. And eventually, those two sets of tracks met. And with one final blow of a hammer, backed by years of hard work and decades of dreams, the way was laid for a nationwide economy. A telegraph operator sent out a simple message to a waiting nation. It just said, "DONE." [Laughter.] A newspaper proclaimed: "We are the youngest of peoples. But we are teaching the world to march forward."

In retrospect, America's march forward seems inevitable. But time and again, it's only made possible by generations that are willing to work and sacrifice and invest in plans to make tomorrow better than today. That's the vision we can't afford to lose sight of. That's the challenge that's fallen to this generation. And with this strategy for America's transportation future, and our efforts across all fronts to lay a new foundation for our lasting prosperity, that is the challenge we will meet.

"Make no little plans." That's what Daniel Burnham said in Chicago. I believe that about America: Make no little plans. So let's get to work. Thank you, everybody. [Applause.]

Source: Obama, Barack. "Remarks by the President and the Vice President on a Vision for High Speed Rail in America," White House press release, April 16, 2009. www.whitehouse.gov/the_press_office/ Remarks-by-the-President-and-the-Vice-President-on-High-Speed-Rail/.

NOTE

1. James Corless, quoted in "Transportation for America Applauds President Obama and Transportation Department's High-Speed Rail Initiative," Transportation for America press release, April 16, 2009. http://t4america.org/pressers/page/2/.

Debating the Merits of the Waxman-Markey "Cap and Trade" Bill

"An Economic Declaration of War on the Midwest"

April 22, and September 2, 2009

On June 26, 2009, the House of Representatives passed the American Clean Energy and Security Act (HR 2454) by a narrow margin (219-212). This bill, also known as Waxman-Markey in recognition of its two primary architects, Democratic congressmen Henry Waxman (Calif.) and Edward Markey (Mass.), was the first climate change mitigation bill ever passed in either house of Congress.

The Waxman-Markey bill contains many provisions to move the United States toward more efficient energy use and greater use of renewable energy sources, but its controversial cornerstone is a "cap and trade" scheme designed to reduce greenhouse gas (GHG) emissions from major sources by 17 percent by 2020 and 83 percent by 2050 relative to 2005 levels. The act caps the total amount of permissible GHG emissions in the United States and puts in place policy mechanisms whereby electric utilities, industries, oil refineries, and other producers of GHGs can purchase and sell finite emission allowances on the emissions "market."

Opinions on the Waxman-Markey bill ran the gamut. Supporters described it as Congress's first serious attempt to combat global warming, even as they acknowledged that the political compromises needed to secure its passage had weakened it. But some advocates for decisive regulatory steps to address global warming, most prominently NASA climate scientist James Hansen, argued that a carbon tax scheme was preferable. These criticisms of Waxman-Markey were muted, however, compared to those that issued from Republican legislators and conservative free-market think tanks.

The following two documents illustrate the stark differences of opinion that swirled around Waxman-Markey. In the first document, Environmental Protection Agency administrator Lisa Jackson praises the proposed bill as a thoughtfully crafted piece of legislation that will produce meaningful reductions in GHG emissions while simultaneously protecting the American economy. The second document presents a speech that conservative Republican congressman Mike Pence (Ind.) gave after the bill's passage. In his remarks, Pence describes Waxman-Markey as "cap and tax legislation" that will destroy businesses, spark rampant unemployment, and undermine American society if it is ever enacted.

Testimony of EPA Administrator Lisa Jackson before the House Committee on Energy and Commerce

April 22, 2009

Let me begin by commending this Committee for embarking on the serious, difficult, and essential work of crafting comprehensive, detailed energy legislation and moving it through an open, careful process in which representatives hold hearings, make amendments, and cast votes. EPA is grateful for your work.

When President Obama was inaugurated ninety-two days ago, the United States found itself in the worst economic crisis since the Great Depression. So the President worked with Congress to craft the American Recovery and Reinvestment Act, which he signed into law sixty-four days ago. That law is now creating good jobs for Americans. Thanks to the Act, EPA is putting Americans to work overhauling clean-water systems, restoring and redeveloping polluted properties, installing clean-air equipment on diesel engines, and cleaning up leaking underground fuel tanks.

The American Recovery and Reinvestment Act also injected an essential shot of adrenaline into the American clean energy sector. Economic recovery would not have been possible without that immediate relief. But President Obama has leveled with the American people: Lasting economic recovery will come only when the federal government looks beyond the quick fix and invests in building the advanced energy industries that will help restore America's economic health over the long term.

So President Obama has called on Congress to pass forward-looking energy legislation.

That legislation should create, here in America, millions of the clean-energy jobs that cannot be shipped overseas. It should catapult American innovators past the foreign competitors who, due to aggressive investments by their governments, now enjoy a head start in the advanced energy technologies that represent the new Internet revolution, the new biotech wave. It should reduce our dependence on oil and strengthen America's energy security. And it should start, in a real and tangible way, to tackle greenhouse-gas pollution, which threatens to leave to our children and grandchildren a diminished, less prosperous, less secure world.

Twenty-two days ago, Chairmen Waxman and Markey released draft legislation that strives to accomplish those goals.

The American Clean Energy and Security Act would introduce a clean energy requirement for American electric utilities and new energy efficiency programs for American buildings. Those initiatives aim to create good American jobs that cannot be shipped overseas.

The legislation would launch programs to promote electric vehicles and deploy technologies for capturing, pipelining, and geologically storing carbon dioxide produced at coal-fueled power plants. Those incentives aim to help American companies make up for lost time in the advanced energy industries that will be to the 2010s what Internet software was to the 1990s.

The legislation would institute new low-carbon requirements for vehicles and fuels, and programs to help reduce vehicle-miles traveled with increased transportation options and help for communities that want to plan for sustainable growth. Those proposals aim to reduce America's dependence on oil and cut back on the hundreds of billions of dollars that Americans send overseas every year.

And the legislation would put in place a declining cap on greenhouse-gas pollution. That market-based system aims to protect our children and grandchildren from severe environmental and economic harm, and great threats to national-security while further invigorating advanced, American energy industries.

The American Clean Energy and Security Act draws on the thoughtful legislation that Chairman-Emeritus Dingell and Congressman Boucher drafted last October and is a serious effort at constructing comprehensive energy and climate legislation. We look forward to working with Congress as this bill moves forward to ensure that it meets the President's objectives in the areas of an efficient and comprehensive approach that creates jobs, leverages our tremendous capacity for innovation, reduces our dependence on oil, and prevents the worst consequences of climate change.

I would like to note that the Waxman-Markey discussion draft tracks many of the recommendations put forward by the U.S. Climate Action Partnership, a coalition that includes American manufacturers such as Alcoa, John Deere, Caterpillar, Dow, Ford, General Motors, and General Electric. Those employers of American workers recognize, as they declare at the outset of their *Blueprint for Legislative Action,* that:

"The United States faces an urgent need to transform our nation's economy, make the country more energy secure, and take meaningful action to slow, stop, and reverse [greenhouse-gas] emissions to address climate change."

I believe that the leadership of this Committee is stepping up to provide the kind of "new vision and policy direction" that those companies talk about.

Now, the "no, we can't" crowd will spin out doomsday scenarios about runaway costs. But EPA's available economic modeling indicates that the investment Americans would make to implement the cap-and-trade program of the American Clean Energy and Security Act would be modest compared to the benefits that science and plain common sense tell us a comprehensive energy and climate policy will deliver.

I ask the members of this Committee to recall the Acid Rain Trading Program, drafted by this Committee and signed by a Republican President in 1990. Beltway corporate lobbyists insisted that the law would cause "death for businesses across the country." But as the members of this Committee who worked hard on that legislation know well, it ended up delivering annual health and welfare benefits estimated to be over 120 billion dollars at an annual cost of only 3 billion dollars. Our economy grew by 64 percent even as the program cut acid rain pollution by more than 50 percent. And past auto-emissions standards sparked key technological innovations that made cars more appealing to consumers here and abroad.

Achieving energy independence and reducing carbon emissions are not easy challenges. But this Committee has dealt with difficult challenges before. When Chairman Dingell and Chairman Waxman joined together with other Members of the Committee to pass the 1990 Clean Air Act Amendments, they were reported out of this Committee by a 42-to-1 vote. That bill dealt with controversial issues—not just acid rain, but also smog, hazardous air pollutants, and the threat to the ozone layer. But you found consensus, and your legislation has ended up cutting pollution at a fraction of the cost that was predicted at the time.

There may be more than one dissenting vote this time, but that does not mean that the Committee's history cannot be repeated this year. We want to work with you in finding consensus in the coming weeks, so that we can reduce our dependence on oil, create millions of new jobs in innovative energy technologies, and significantly reduce greenhouse-gas emissions.

Remarks of Representative Mike Pence at the Columbus Energy Summit

September 2, 2009

The American Energy Solutions Group is a group of House Republicans working to lower energy prices for American families and small businesses and create energy independence for the American people. As the energy debate has unfolded over the course of this year, the solutions group has worked on two tracks. First, we have gathered the various ideas of House Republicans and crafted them, with the assistance of Leader [John] Boehner, into the aforementioned American Energy Act, which is our "all-of-the-above" solution that offers energy independence, more jobs and a cleaner environment.

Second, the solutions group has been engaged in communicating with the American people about the disastrous effects that the Waxman-Markey cap and trade bill will have on our economy, jobs, and family budgets. This is the fifth energy summit the solutions group has held. We have been in Pittsburgh, PA; Indianapolis, IN; San Luis Obispo, CA; and Washington, DC. We have literally been across the country and back taking this conversation to the American people.

It is particularly appropriate that we are in Ohio today. Ohio is home to a tremendous amount of manufacturing, and states in the Midwest get the majority of their electricity from coal. Eighty-six percent of the power generated in Ohio comes from coal-fired power plants. Energy policy made in Washington will affect each and every citizen of Ohio, and I can commit that this group will take what we hear today back to Washington.

We are honored to have a great panel of academics, industry representatives, and energy experts with us to share their expertise and insight. This summit is intended to be a discussion about not only the economic impacts of the national energy tax proposed in the Waxman-Markey legislation, but also the future of coal and other sources of energy. To set the stage, I want to note that the Waxman-Markey bill (H.R. 2454) passed the House of Representatives, by a narrow margin (219–212), on June 26, 2009. From President Obama to Senate Majority Leader Harry Reid to Speaker Nancy Pelosi, this bill has been set as a top Democrat priority. It is awaiting consideration by the Senate when Congress returns this fall, so time is of the essence.

Our nation is experiencing a very difficult recession. The unemployment rate stands at 9.4% nationally, and 11.2% here in Ohio. We have witnessed the loss of millions of jobs, trillions of dollars of retirement savings, and the closing of thousands of small businesses across our great nation. With this current state of affairs, it is unconscionable to me that Democrats in Washington would impose a new national energy tax on already burdened taxpayers.

There is no doubt that the Democrats' misguided bill will kill jobs, raise taxes and lead to more government intrusion in the lives of Americans. If Waxman-Markey becomes law, estimates suggest that household energy costs could rise by thousands of dollars. And those hardest hit by this massive national energy tax will be the poor—who experts agree spend a greater proportion of their income on energy consumption.

To make matters worse, a devastating consequence of the Democrats' legislation will be fewer jobs. A recent independent study suggests that up to 2.4 million jobs would be lost by 2030, even after any new "green" jobs are factored in. At a time when our nation's economy is suffering, the last thing Congress should do is support legislation that will cause job loss.

This energy tax will not be borne evenly across the United States. According to a study that ranks Congressional districts based on their manufacturing employment and amount of electricity derived from coal, the Midwest and Southeast will suffer the most. In fact, eight of Ohio's Congressional districts rank in the top 20 most negatively affected. I might add that my Congressional district in eastern Indiana is the fifth-most affected.

That's a heavy price to pay for a plan that will do very little to clean up our environment, since manufacturers will likely ship their jobs and plants, and their pollution, to countries with less stringent environmental safeguards.

The reality is the cap and tax legislation offered by the Democrats amounts to an economic declaration of war on the Midwest by liberals on Capitol Hill.

Let me be clear. Republicans want to protect our environment, and believe we can do so while at the same time growing our economy and protecting jobs. Republicans believe we can increase American energy production made by American workers, encourage greater efficiency and conservation, and promote the use of alternative fuels without enacting a national energy tax. We have put forward such solutions in the American Energy Act offered by Leader Boehner and the American Energy Solutions Group.

The American Energy Act is centered on domestic exploration of our natural resources, and a renewed commitment to safe and emissions-free nuclear energy. According to the Department of Energy, the safest and most efficient way for utility companies to control carbon emissions is to increase their supply of nuclear energy. We lay down a national goal of licensing 100 new nuclear reactors over the next twenty years by streamlining a burdensome regulatory process and ensuring the recycling and safe storage of spent nuclear fuel.

We also increase domestic supply by lifting restrictions on the Arctic Coastal Plain, the Outer Continental Shelf, and oil shale in the Mountain West. Revenues generated through domestic exploration will support innovation in renewable and alternative energy sources, like wind and solar technologies. Finally, we include various incentives to spur greater conservation among individuals and businesses. For example, I'm glad we're holding this event in a LEED Silver-certified building, as we take energy efficiency seriously and provide tax incentives for improving the energy efficiency of homes and businesses in our bill.

We look forward to hearing from our witnesses today about the Waxman-Markey bill and the American Energy Act.

Source: Jackson, Lisa. Testimony at Hearing on the American Clean Energy and Security Act of 2009, House Committee on Energy and Commerce, 111th Cong., 1st sess., April 22, 2009. http://energycommerce.house .gov/Press_111/20090422/testimony_jackson.pdf; Pence, Mike. Prepared Remarks for the Columbus Energy Summit, September 2, 2009. www.gop.gov/general/09/09/02/pence-prepared-remarks-for-columbus.

Energy Secretary Chu Issues a "Call to Arms" on Climate Change

"The Task Ahead Is Daunting, but We Can and Will Succeed"

June 12, 2009

Climate scientists, environmental activists, and lawmakers concerned about global warming acknowledge that galvanizing American public and political support for climate protection regulatory regimes is an exceedingly tricky undertaking. On the one hand, they feel that Americans are much more likely to support greenhouse gas mitigation strategies, federal investments in renewable energy technologies, and other efforts to wean the nation off the fossil fuels responsible for climate change if they understand the urgency of the global warming threat. Yet they know that a relentless drumbeat of dire warnings about impending ecological and economic apocalypse can engender feelings of hopelessness that actually reduce public demand for policy solutions. With this reality in mind, advocates of robust national and international policy responses to global climate change labor mightily to strike a rhetorical balance—one that convinces listeners that the threat of climate change is real and immediate, while also assuring them that it can be countered effectively through international cooperation, smart domestic energy policies, and American ingenuity. This blend of cautionary tale and inspirational message is evident in the following excerpt from a commencement address that Department of Energy secretary Steven Chu (a leading voice within the Obama Administration on global warming issues) delivered to the graduating class of the California Institute of Technology on June 12, 2009.

To the Class of 2009, let me congratulate you on your achievement. You should be proud of the fact that you survived many shocks and are here today. The first shock might have been the discovery your freshman year that you are not alone: child prodigies are every-where. Take pride in the fact that you have survived your last "Finals Week." You will never have to listen to the Ride of the Valkyries again . . . unless you want to.

You should also be proud that you now have one of the finest liberal arts educations possible. "How does my Caltech training qualify as a liberal arts education?" you may well ask. The goal of a liberal arts education is to teach you how to think rigorously and criti-cally, and to give you the tools to teach yourself. Your quantitative and intellectually demanding training will allow you to venture wherever your curiosity will take you.

Finally, you should be proud to be graduating from an institution where nerds are welcomed. In the commencement speech I gave at Harvard last week, I noted that J.K. Rowling, the billionaire novelist, who started as a shy classics student, gave last year's address. She was preceded by Bill Gates, the mega-billionaire philanthropist and computer nerd. "Today, sadly," I confessed, "you have me. I am not a billionaire, but at least I am a nerd."

Most of my Harvard speech was devoted to a vitally important issue: the climate change problem and what we could do about it. What made the newspaper headlines was that I had called myself a "nerd." Clearly the talk was too nerdy.

What is a nerd? I looked up the description of the nerd phenotype in that ultimate cyberspace authority, Wikipedia.

"The stereo-typical nerd" the Wiki article intoned, "is intelligent but socially and physically awkward. . . . They typically appear either to lack confidence or to be indifferent or oblivious to the negative perceptions held of them by others. . . . Some nerds show a pronounced interest in subjects which others tend to find dull or complex . . . especially topics related to science, mathematics and technology. On the opposite end of the spectrum, nerds may show an interest in activities that are viewed by their peers as immature for their age, such as . . . being obsessed with Star Trek and Star Wars . . ."

First, I dispute that a fondness for Star Wars is at the opposite end of the intellectual spectrum. Second, I claim that many of my fellow nerds are widely read, socially engaging, talented musicians, and good athletes. You might think, "If a person is athletic, socially graceful, and has broad interests, then they are not nerds." Perhaps so, but I want to celebrate people of intelligence, focus, and technical achievement. The ability to understand details does not mean that you are incapable of forming deep insights. In your future life, it is important that you develop broad interests to help you see the forest as well as the trees. It is also important that you cherish your skill to understand something deeply.

Commencement speeches usually contain unsolicited advice. This advice, worth every penny you paid, is seldom remembered and never followed. While I will not depart from this time honored tradition, I will only give you only one piece of advice. Here it is. Cultivate a generous spirit. In all negotiations, don't bargain for the last, little advantage. Leave the change on the table. In your collaborations, always remember that "credit" is not a conserved quantity. In a successful collaboration, everybody gets 90 percent of the credit. . . .

I now come to the central part of my talk. I begin with a story about an extraordinary scientific discovery and the new dilemma it poses. I will end with a call to arms, and about making a difference. In the spirit of full disclosure, this talk borrows heavily from the Harvard commencement. In my defense, I have learned that in order to be heard, it is important to deliver the same message more than once. The major difference is that this talk will contain more techie details.

In the past several decades, our climate has been changing. Climate change is not new: the Earth went through six ice ages in the past 600,000 years. However, recent measurements show that the climate has begun to change rapidly. The size of the North polar ice cap in the month of September is only half the size it was fifty years ago. The sea level has been rising since direct measurements began in 1870, but the rate since 1990 is five times faster than it was at the beginning of recorded measurements.

Here is the remarkable scientific discovery: For the first time in human history, science has told us that human activity is dramatically altering the destiny of our planet. Our carbon emissions since the beginning of the industrial revolution have caused the climate to change, and science is now projecting how our actions will affect the Earth fifty and a hundred years from now.

If the world continues on a business-as-usual path, a number of studies predict that there is a fifty-fifty chance the temperature will rise somewhere between 4 to 5 degrees by the end of this century. This increase may not sound like much, but let me remind you that during the last ice age, the world was only 6 degrees colder. During this time, most of Canada and the U.S. down to Ohio and Pennsylvania were covered year round by a glacier. A world five degrees warmer will be a very different place. The change will be so rapid that many species, including humans, will have a hard time adapting.

We also face the specter of non-linear "tipping points" that may cause much more severe changes. An example of a tipping point is the thawing of the permafrost. The permafrost contains immense amounts of frozen organic matter that have been accumulating for millennia. If the soil melts, microbes will spring to life and cause this debris to rot.

The difference in biological activity below freezing and above freezing is something we are very familiar with. Frozen food remains edible for a very long time in the freezer, but once thawed, it spoils quickly. How much methane and carbon dioxide might be released from the rotting permafrost? Even if only a fraction of the carbon is released, it could be greater than all the greenhouse gases we have released to date. Once started, a runaway effect could begin.

Here is the dilemma. How much are we willing to invest, as a world society, to mitigate the consequences of climate change that will not be fully realized for at least 100 years? Deeply rooted in all cultures is the notion of generational responsibility. Parents work hard so that their children will have a better life. Climate change will affect the entire world, but our natural focus is on the welfare of our immediate families. Can we, as a world society, meet our responsibility to future generations?

The United States has less than 5 five percent of the world population, but we consume more than 20 percent of the world's energy. We depend on fossil energy to keep our homes warm in the winter, cool in the summer, and lit at night. We use energy to travel across town and across continents. Energy is the fundamental reason for the prosperity we enjoy. By contrast, there are 1.6 billion people who don't have access to electricity. The life we enjoy may not be within the easy reach of many in the developing world, but it is within sight, and they want what we have.

Even if our collective societies accept a global generational responsibility, there are those who believe that it is impossible to transition to a sustainable world of nine billion people where the standard of living of everybody can be substantially elevated.

As a scientist, I refuse to accept this judgment. Scientists, if not optimistic by nature, have to be optimistic by natural selection in order to be successful. Without optimism, we would not have the audacity to believe we can go beyond the discoveries of the giants that went before us. Nor would we be willing to take on challenges where others have failed.

Part of my optimism comes from the fact that science has come to our aid in the past. As an example, I remind you of the agricultural revolution that occurred last century. In his 1898 inaugural speech, Sir William Crookes, President of the Royal Society, began with the warning "England and all civilized nations stand in deadly peril." Crop rotation and manure were not sufficient to replenish the depleted soils, and he predicted that fertilizer based on South American bird guano (guano is the technical term for bird do-do) and Chilean sodium nitrate would soon be exhausted. The solution, Crookes proposed was to create artificial fertilizer. "It is the chemist," he declared, "who must come to the rescue."

In 1909, Fritz Haber demonstrated the catalytic synthesis of ammonia from air and hydrogen, a path unsuccessfully pursued by two distinguished chemists and future Nobel Prize winners, Walther Nerst and Wilhelm Ostwald. For this achievement, Haber was awarded the 1918 Noble Prize for Chemistry. The production of fertilizer was considered so important that the industrialization of ammonia synthesis was recognized by a second Nobel Prize to Carl Bosch in 1931.

The second part of the agricultural revolution was led by Norman Borlaug. He created hybrid strains of wheat that increased the yield per acre four to seven-fold in

Mexico, India and Pakistan. Because of his work, the starvation of hundreds of millions of people was prevented.

Science and technology was the basis of the agricultural revolution, but current agricultural practices are not sustainable. We need a second green revolution that will create perennial plants for food, fiber and energy that fix their own nitrogen, and draw precious nutrients into their roots for the following year.

We also need a second industrial revolution. In this revolution, there will be no single magical discovery [that] will rescue us. We will need a wide assortment of solutions in both the demand and supply side of energy. A price on carbon, energy efficiency standards, and other policy mechanisms are necessary tools to align technology directions with environmental necessities. However, it is science and innovation that will provide the path forward.

As a scientist, I am extremely privileged to be part of the Obama Administration. The message the President delivers is not one of doom and gloom, but of optimism and opportunity. I share this optimism. The task ahead is daunting, but we can and will succeed. If there ever was a time to help steer America and the world towards a path of sustainable energy, now is the time.

America has the opportunity to lead in this new industrial revolution. In the coming decades, we will almost certainly face higher oil prices and be in a carbon constrained economy. We can either recognize this new reality and seize the opportunity, or wish it weren't happening. The great hockey player, Wayne Gretzky, was asked how he positions himself on the ice. He replied, "I skate to where the puck is going to be, not where it's been." America must do the same.

As Secretary of Energy, I have the opportunity to help rev up the remarkable American research and innovation engine that will produce needed solutions. By skating to where the puck is going to be, we will also lay the foundation of a new prosperity.

Energy efficiency and conservation will remain the lowest hanging fruit for the next several decades. The Department of Energy will help America recapture the technological lead in fuel efficient automobiles, and drive the development of advanced batteries needed for the electrification of personal vehicles.

We will nurture a system integration approach to building design, aided by computer tools with embedded energy analysis. It was the system integration of the automobile engine, transmission, brakes and battery that enabled Toyota to create the Prius. With computer control of ignition timing and fuel mix, today's automobile engines operate at 20 percent higher efficiency. With computer monitoring and continuous, real-time control of HVAC systems, lighting, and shading, far more spectacular efficiencies can be realized in buildings. There is a growing realization that we should be able to build buildings that will decrease energy use by 80 percent with investments that will pay for themselves in less than 15 years. Buildings consume 40 percent of the energy in the U.S., so that energy efficient buildings can decrease our carbon emissions by one third.

The Department of Energy will help re-start our dormant nuclear power industry, and seek to develop fourth generation reactors and proliferation-resistant fuel recycling methods to maximize the value of nuclear fuel and minimize its waste. We are collaborating with industry to test existing carbon dioxide capture and sequestration technologies, while we search for out-of-the-box methods that can dramatically lower the cost. We will also begin to invest in research that may allow us to capture and sequester carbon dioxide directly from the atmosphere.

We will invest in nanotechnology and other approaches that will lead to low cost, efficient photovoltaic generation of electricity. In the area of bio-fuels, we support three bio-energy institutes. One of these institutes used synthetic biology methods to reprogram yeast and e-coli to produce gasoline-like and diesel-like fuels. The task is now to convince these organisms that their entire raison d'etre is to produce transportation fuel.

As we begin to lay the foundation for a sustainable energy future, we can frame the challenge, but the real answers will come from you. As our future science and engineering leaders, take the time to learn more about what's at stake, and then act on that knowledge with your considerable intellectual horsepower.

Finally, I appeal to your humanist side, and the humanist side in all of us.

One of the cruelest ironies about climate change is that the ones who will be hurt the most by are the most innocent: the world's poorest and those yet to be born. A quote taken from Martin Luther King when he spoke of ending the war in Vietnam in 1967 seems so fitting for today's climate crisis:

> "This call for a worldwide fellowship that lifts neighborly concern beyond one's tribe, race, class, and nation is in reality a call for an all-embracing and unconditional love for all mankind. This oft misunderstood, this oft misinterpreted concept, so readily dismissed by the Nietzsches of the world as a weak and cowardly force, has now become an absolute necessity for the survival of man. . . . We are now faced with the fact, my friends, that tomorrow is today. We are confronted with the fierce urgency of now. In this unfolding conundrum of life and history, there is such a thing as being too late."

The final quote is from William Faulkner. On December 10th, 1950, in his Nobel Prize banquet speech, he spoke of the role of humanists in a world facing potential nuclear holocaust.

> "I believe that man will not merely endure: he will prevail. He is immortal, not because he alone among creatures has an inexhaustible voice, but because he has a soul, a spirit capable of compassion and sacrifice and endurance. The poet's, the writer's, duty is to write about these things. It is his privilege to help man endure by lifting his heart, by reminding him of the courage and honor and hope and pride and compassion and pity and sacrifice which have been the glory of his past."

Graduates of the class of 2009, you have an extraordinary role to play in our future. As you enter the next phase in you life, you will no doubt follow your intellectual passions. Pursuing your personal passion is important, but it shouldn't be your only goal.

When you are old and gray, and look back on your life, you will want to be proud of what you have done. The source of that pride won't be the things you have acquired or the recognition you have received. It will be the lives you have touched and the difference you have made. I hope you will develop the passion and the voice to help the world in ways both large and small. Nothing will give you greater satisfaction.

Please accept my warmest congratulations. May you live long and prosper. May the Force be with you. May you help save our planet for your children and for all the future children of the world.

Source: Chu, Steven. Commencement Address at California Institute of Technology, June 12, 2009. www.energy.gov/news2009/7457.htm.

Chronology

1607 Jamestown settlement is established in Virginia colony.

1609 Spanish explorers settle modern-day Santa Fe, New Mexico.

1620 Plymouth settlement is founded in modern-day Massachusetts.

1630s British colonies pass the first wildlife and fish conservation laws in North America.

1675 King Philip's War breaks out between Indians and New England colonists.

1682 William Penn signs land treaty with Indians that paves way for the establishment of Pennsylvania.

1691 England issues "Broad Arrow" policies reserving white pine forests in American colonies for exclusive use by the Royal Navy.

1699 French settlers establish early communities in Louisiana and Mississippi.

1730 British authorities and colonial governors issue proclamations reiterating that all forests in the British colonies belong to England.

1739 Ben Franklin leads anti-pollution campaign against Philadelphia tanners.

1754 The French and Indian War begins; by the time it ends nine years later, France has lost huge expanses of territory in Canada and the American Midwest to the British.

1775 The Revolutionary War begins in the American colonies after years of escalating tensions between the British Crown and colonists.

1776 Rebellious American colonies issue a formal "Declaration of Independence" from England.

1783 The Revolutionary War draws to a close and victorious American colonists begin the process of building a new nation.

1787 The Northwest Ordinance, combined with the earlier Land Ordinance of 1785, lays the groundwork for orderly settlement of the western frontier.

1793 Eli Whitney invents the cotton gin.

1801 Philadelphia becomes the first American city to complete a municipal waterworks system.

1803 President Thomas Jefferson executes the Louisiana Purchase, acquiring 523 million acres of North American territory from France.
Lewis and Clark begin their famous three-year exploration of the American West.

1807   Robert Fulton invents a commercially viable steam-powered boat, inaugurating major advances in water resource development and major expansions in commercial activity.

1812   The War of 1812 erupts between American and British forces and their Indian allies.

1813   Francis Cabot Lowell opens his first textile mill in Massachusetts, an early landmark in American industrial development.

1820   Congress approves the Missouri Compromise, which bans slavery west of the Mississippi River and north of 36°30' latitude, with the exception of Missouri.

1825   The Erie Canal opens, linking the Great Lakes to the East Coast.

1830   Andrew Jackson signs the Indian Removal Act.
The Baltimore & Ohio Railroad, America's first major railroad, opens for business.

1838   Cherokee Indians from the Southeast embark on the "Trail of Tears," a forced march to a reservation in Oklahoma.

1845   Newspaperman John O'Sullivan coins the term "manifest destiny" to describe the widespread public sentiment that America is uniquely favored by God and divinely ordained to conquer the entire North American continent.

1846   The Mexican-American War begins; two years later the beaten Mexican government cedes virtually all of the modern American Southwest (334 million acres) to the United States.

1849   The Department of the Interior is created.
The California Gold Rush accelerates western settlement and lays the groundwork for major industrial mining operations in the West.

1850   Congress passes the Swamp and Overflow Act, which authorized states to "reclaim" wetlands rich in biodiversity for agricultural use and flood control.
Lemuel Shattuck issues his landmark *Report for the Promotion of Public Health*, which becomes a blueprint for anti-pollution measures and other public health policies across the country.

1853   The United States acquires 19 million acres in the American Southwest from Mexico in the Gadsden Purchase.

1854   Henry David Thoreau publishes *Walden; or, Life in the Woods*.

1861   The Civil War begins.

1862   The Homestead Act transfers vast quantities of public land into private hands for farming and other forms of development.

1864   George Perkins Marsh publishes *Man and Nature*.
Congress passes the Yosemite Act, which establishes a broad swath of Yosemite Valley as parkland to be administered by the state of California.

1865   The Civil War ends with the surrender of the South, and President Abraham Lincoln is assassinated.

1866   The Mining Law of 1866 makes public lands available for virtually all mining activity.

New York City establishes the first genuine municipal health department in a major American city.

1869   The first Transcontinental Railroad is completed.

1870   John D. Rockefeller and partners formally establish the Standard Oil Company, which dominates the oil industry for the next half century.

1871   For the first time, the United States establishes a federal agency—the U.S. Fish Commission—explicitly to conserve a specific natural resource.

1872   America's first national park—Yellowstone—is created.

The General Mining Act further codifies the mining industry's inexpensive and wide-reaching access to lands in the public domain.

1873   *Forest and Stream,* America's leading pro-conservation outdoor magazine of the nineteenth century, begins publication.

1874   President Ulysses S. Grant decides to leave unsigned a congressional act that would have extended federal protection to fast-dwindling bison populations.

1878   Passage of two pro-logging bills—the Timber and Stone Act and the Free Timber Act—dramatically increases logging pressure on public forests.

John Wesley Powell issues his *Report on the Arid Lands of the United States.*

1879   The U.S. Geological Survey (USGS) is established to survey western land and resources for development purposes.

1891   The General Revision Act imposes a wide array of public land management reforms.

The Forest Reserve Act is passed, empowering the president to create "national forest reserves" from public lands.

1892   The Sierra Club is founded by John Muir and other conservationists.

1893   The Chicago World's Columbian Exposition inspires the emergence of an urban beautification and "green space" movement known as the City Beautiful Movement.

1899   The Rivers and Harbors Appropriation Act extends new federal protections to rivers, harbors, and canals.

1900   The Lacey Bird Law establishes federal penalties for interstate and international commerce in wild game.

1901   Theodore Roosevelt, universally regarded as the greatest conservationist ever to work in the Oval Office, is sworn in as president.

1902   The Reclamation Act expands the federal government's authority to develop and manage water and power resources in the West.

1903   President Theodore Roosevelt establishes the first wildlife refuge—Pelican Island in Florida—in the United States.

1905 The Transfer Act moves management responsibilities for America's national forest system from the Department of the Interior to the Department of Agriculture.

1906 The Antiquities Act is signed into law, and President Theodore Roosevelt uses it to create eighteen national monuments in three years.
Upton Sinclair's novel *The Jungle* exposes shocking inner-city pollution and workplace conditions in Chicago's stockyards.

1908 Henry Ford unveils the Model T, launching America's "automobile age."

1909 Pennsylvania passes a state law forbidding any immigrant from hunting wild game in the state.

1911 President William H. Taft signs the Weeks Act, which greatly expands federal forest conservation and management programs in eastern states.

1913 Congress passes the Raker Bill, which paves the way for the flooding of the Hetch Hetchy Valley in Yosemite National Park.

1914 World War I begins in Europe and ends in 1918, one year after America's entrance into the conflict.

1916 The National Park Service is established.

1922 Seven western states agree to a Colorado River Compact—a regional water distribution scheme that governs Colorado River water use for the remainder of the twentieth century.

1925 Alice Hamilton publishes *Industrial Poisons in the United States*.

1926 A U.S. Supreme Court ruling in *Euclid v. Ambler Realty* gives municipalities the legal authority to impose zoning laws and regulate land use in the public interest.

1931 The National Park Service announces major new protections for predator species within its parks.

1933 The Civilian Conservation Corps (CCC) is launched, setting millions of young Americans to work on projects in national parks, national forests, and other public lands over the nine-year life of the program.
The first wave of massive "New Deal" water and resource development projects begins under the direction of the Works Progress Administration (WPA), the Bureau of Reclamation, the U.S. Army Corps of Engineers, the Tennessee Valley Authority (TVA), and other New Deal agencies.
"Dusters"—towering dust storms—begin raking the Great Plains, the result of years of misuse of fragile farming and grazing lands.

1934 The Taylor Grazing Act is passed.

1935 The Soil Conservation Service is established through the Soil Conservation Act. The Wilderness Society is founded.

1936 Passage of the Flood Control Act unleashes a new era of major water development and river re-engineering projects.

1939   The U.S. Fish and Wildlife Service is established.

1946   The Bureau of Land Management (BLM) is created.

1948   Twenty residents of Donora, Pennsylvania, die from a "killer smog" of air
pollution that envelops the town.

1949   Aldo Leopold's *Sand County Almanac* is published.

1953   President Eisenhower delivers his "Atoms for Peace" speech at the United Nations.

1955   The Air Pollution Control Act of 1955 assigns a federal role for air pollution
mitigation for the first time.

1956   President Eisenhower signs the Federal-Aid Interstate Highway Act, which
sparks increased rates of suburbanization and deepens U.S. dependence
on the automobile.
The National Park Service launches its Mission 66 program to refurbish and
modernize national park amenities and infrastructure.
A sustained campaign of protest from environmentalists convinces federal
authorities to shelve plans to build a dam in Dinosaur National Monument's
Echo Park.

1957   The Price-Anderson Act gives the nuclear power industry unprecedented
levels of legal protection from liability for accidents.

1960   The Multiple-Use Sustained Yield Act (MUSYA) places recreation on an equal
footing with timber extraction and watershed management as a national
forest management priority.

1962   Rachel Carson publishes *Silent Spring*.

1964   The Wilderness Act becomes law.

1968   President Johnson signs the National Wild and Scenic Rivers Act.

1969   The National Environmental Policy Act is signed into law.

1970   Congress passes and President Nixon signs the Clean Air Act.
Wisconsin senator Gaylord Nelson organizes America's first Earth Day
celebration.
The Natural Resources Defense Council (NRDC) is founded, one of several
nationally recognized and politically influential environmental organizations
established during this era.
The Environmental Protection Agency (EPA) is created by executive action.

1972   The Clean Water Act is passed by Congress over President Nixon's veto.

1973   The Endangered Species Act becomes law.
The Organization of Petroleum Exporting Countries (OPEC) imposes an oil
embargo that makes energy a top policy priority for U.S. lawmakers.

1975   The Energy Policy Conservation Act mandates the first Corporate Average Fuel
Economy (CAFE) standards for passenger cars and light trucks.

1976   The Resource Conservation and Recovery Act is passed into law.
Congress passes the Toxic Substances Control Act.

The Federal Land Management Act (also known as the BLM Organic Act) and the National Forest Management Act bring major changes to public land management practices.

1978   The Love Canal tragedy alerts the American public to the dangers of hazardous wastes in their communities.

1979   A "Sagebrush Rebellion" erupts in the American West in response to federal land management actions.

The United States signs the Convention on Long-Range Transboundary Air Pollution, the world's first multilateral convention in the realm of air pollution control.

The nuclear reactor scare at Three Mile Island in Pennsylvania casts a pall over the nuclear energy industry in the United States.

1980   President Carter signs the Alaska National Interest Lands Conservation Act into law, doubling the size of the nation's national park system and tripling the acreage in its wilderness system.

The Comprehensive Environmental Response, Compensation and Liability Act—also known as Superfund—becomes law.

1981   Ronald Reagan becomes president and makes "regulatory relief" a cornerstone of modern Republican political philosophy.

1982   The grassroots-oriented Environmental Justice Movement emerges.

1983   Anne Gorsuch and James Watt resign from leadership positions at the Environmental Protection Agency (EPA) and Department of Interior (DOI), respectively, after two stormy years.

1987   The United States agrees to the Montreal Protocol on Substances that Deplete the Ozone Layer.

The Commission for Racial Justice of the United Church of Christ issues *Toxic Wastes and Race in the United States*.

1988   The Intergovernmental Panel on Climate Change is established.

1989   The *Exxon Valdez* oil tanker runs aground and spills millions of gallons of oil into Alaska's Prince William Sound.

1990   The Clean Air Act Amendments are signed into law.

1991   A U.S. District Court bans logging in seventeen national forests in the Pacific Northwest to protect endangered spotted owl habitats.

1992   The so-called Earth Summit in Rio de Janeiro, Brazil, produces global commitments to engage in more environmentally sustainable practices and combat global warming.

Regulatory changes further integrate genetically modified (GM) foods into the overall U.S. food distribution system.

1994   President Clinton issues an executive order requiring all federal agencies to integrate environmental justice principles into their policies and programs.

1995   President Clinton signs a "timber salvage rider" that alienates even his staunchest supporters in the environmental community.

The U.S. Fish and Wildlife Service oversees the reintroduction of gray wolves into the Yellowstone ecosystem.

1996 President Clinton signs the Safe Drinking Water Act Amendments and the Food and Quality Protection Act.

President Clinton establishes Grand Staircase-Escalante National Monument in Utah.

1997 The United States signs—but fails to ratify—the Kyoto Protocol, a major international climate change agreement.

2001 President Clinton signs the Roadless Area Conservation Law, or Roadless Rule, into law.

The Brownfields Revitalization Act is signed into law.

2002 The Bush Administration loosens regulations for the so-called "mountaintop removal" method of coal mining.

2003 The Bush Administration releases its Water 2025 water conservation program for western communities.

2004 Oregon voters pass Measure 37, which rolls back many "smart growth" regulations.

2005 The Republican-controlled House of Representatives passes a bill to repeal the Endangered Species Act.

The Bush Administration approves controversial revisions to the Roadless Rule that give individual states greater authority to determine logging and other forest management decisions.

The Kyoto Protocol enters into force.

Congress passes the Bush Administration's Energy Policy Act but only after stripping it of provisions that allowed for oil drilling in the Alaska National Wildlife Refuge (ANWR).

Hurricane Katrina and other tropical storms spark debate about the role that global warming might play in intensifying severe weather events.

2007 The U.S. Supreme Court rules in *Massachusetts et al. v. EPA* that the Environmental Protection Agency has both the authority and the legal obligation to regulate greenhouse gases under the Clean Air Act.

Oregon voters pass Measure 49, which restores significant land development restrictions that had been removed with the 2004 passage of Measure 37.

Western states announce a new water allocation pact for Colorado River water.

The Intergovernmental Panel on Climate Change (IPCC) issues its most dire forecasts yet about the likelihood of catastrophic global climate change in the twenty-first century.

2009 The U.S. Fish and Wildlife Service recommends delisting the gray wolf from endangered species protections in most western states.

The Obama Administration announces a one-year moratorium on road building in national forest wilderness areas and expresses support for making the Roadless Rule permanent.

The Omnibus Public Land Management Act is passed, extending wilderness protection to two million acres and doubling the size of the nation's Wild and Scenic Rivers system.

Bibliography

Adams, David A. *Renewable Resource Policy: The Legal-Institutional Foundations.* Washington, D.C.: Island Press, 1993.

Andrews, Richard N. L. *Managing the Environment, Managing Ourselves: A History of American Environmental Policy.* New Haven, Conn.: Yale University Press, 1999.

Axtell, James. *The Invasion Within: The Contest of Cultures in Colonial North America.* New York: Oxford University Press, 1985.

Bailey, Christopher J. *Congress and Air Pollution: Environmental Policies in the United States.* Manchester, UK: Manchester University Press, 1998.

Bakken, Gordon Morris. "American Mining Law and the Environment: The Western Experience." *Western Legal History* 1 (Summer/Fall 1988): 211–236.

Bates, James Leonard. "Fulfilling American Democracy: The Conservation Movement, 1907–1921." *Mississippi Valley Historical Review,* 44 (1957): 29–57.

Benfield, F. Kaid, Donald D. T. Chen, and Matthew D. Raimi. *Once There Were Greenfields: How Urban Sprawl is Undermining America's Environment, Economy and Social Fabric.* Washington, D.C.: Natural Resources Defense Council, 1999.

Bruegmann, Robert. *Sprawl: A Compact History.* Chicago: University of Chicago Press, 2005.

Bryant, Bunyan. *Environmental Justice: Issues, Policies, and Solutions.* Washington, D.C.: Island Press, 1995.

Bullard, Robert. *Dumping in Dixie: Race, Class, and Environmental Quality.* Boulder Colo.: Westview Press, 1990.

Conary, Janet S. "An Emerging Nation: The Early Presidents and the Development of Environmental Policy." In *The Environmental Presidency,* edited by Dennis L. Soden. Albany: State University of New York Press, 1999.

Cronon, William. *Changes in the Land: Indians, Colonists, and the Ecology of New England.* New York: Hill and Wing, 1983.

Cronon, William. *Uncommon Ground: Rethinking the Human Place in Nature.* New York: W.W. Norton, 1996.

Cutright, Paul. *Theodore Roosevelt: The Making of a Conservationist.* Urbana: University of Illinois Press, 1985.

Czech, Brian. "*Ward vs. Race Horse:* Supreme Court as Obviator?" *Journal of the West* 35 (1996): 61–69.

Dana, Samuel T. *Forest and Range Policy.* New York: McGraw-Hill, 1956.

Danz, Harold P. *Of Bison and Man.* Niwot, Colo.: University Press of Colorado, 1997.

Davis, Allen F. *Spearheads for Reform: The Social Settlements and the Progressive Movement, 1890–1914.* New Brunswick, N.J.: Rutgers University Press, 1984.

Dowie, Mark. *Losing Ground: American Environmentalism at the Close of the Twentieth Century.* Cambridge, Mass.: MIT Press, 1995.

Duffy, John. *The Sanitarians: A History of American Public Health.* Chicago: University of Illinois Press, 1992.

Foreman, Christopher, Jr. *The Promise and Peril of Environmental Justice.* Washington, D.C.: Brookings Institution, 1998.

Frumkin, Howard, Lawrence Frank, and Richard Jackson. *Urban Sprawl and Public Health: Designing, Planning and Building for Healthy Communities.* Washington, D.C.: Island Press, 2004.

Fur, Fin and Feather: A Compilation of the Game Laws of the Different States and Provinces of the United States and Canada: To Which is Added a List of Hunting and Fishing Localities, and Other Useful Information for Gunners and Anglers. New York: M.B. Brown and Co., 1871.

Gates, Paul W. *History of Public Land Law Development.* U.S. Public Land Law Review Commission. Washington D.C.: Government Printing Office, 1968.

Gitlin, Jay. "Empires of Trade, Hinterlands of Settlement." In *The Oxford History of the American West,* edited by Clyde A. Milner II, Carol A. O'Connor, and Martha Sandweiss. New York: Oxford University Press, 1994.

Goldmark, Josephine. *Impatient Crusader: Florence Kelley's Life Story.* Urbana: University of Illinois Press, 1953.

Gottlieb, Robert. *Forcing the Spring: The Transformation of the American Environmental Movement.* Washington, D.C.: Island Press, 1993.

Hamilton, Alice. *Exploring the Dangerous Trades: The Autobiography of Alice Hamilton, M.D.* Boston: Little, Brown, 1943.

Hayden, Dolores. *Building Suburbia: Green Fields and Urban Growth, 1820–2000.* New York: Pantheon Books, 2003.

Hays, Samuel. *Conservation and the Gospel of Efficiency.* Cambridge, Mass.: Harvard University Press, 1959.

Hays, Samuel. *Beauty, Health, and Permanence: Environmental Politics in the United States, 1955–1985.* New York and Cambridge: Cambridge University Press, 1987.

Higgs, Robert, and Carl P. Close, eds. *Re-Thinking Green: Alternatives to Environmental Bureaucracy.* Oakland, Calif.: Independent Institute, 2005.

Hirt, Paul W. *A Conspiracy of Optimism: Management of the National Forests Since World War II.* Lincoln: University of Nebraska Press, 1996.

Huber, Peter. *Hard Green: Saving the Environment from Environmentalists, a Conservative Manifesto.* New York: Basic Books, 1999.

Jackson, Kenneth T. *Crabgrass Frontier: The Suburbanization of the United States.* New York: Oxford University Press, 1985.

Jacoby, Karl. *Crimes Against Nature: Squatters, Poachers, Thieves, and the Hidden History of American Conservation.* Berkeley: University of California Press, 2001.

Jennings, Francis. *The Invasion of America: Indians, Colonialism, and the Cant of Conquest.* Chapel Hill: University of North Carolina Press for the Institute of Early American History and Culture, 1975.

Johnson, Benjamin Heber. "Conservation, Subsistence, and Class at the Birth of Superior National Forest." *Environmental History* 4, no. 1 (January 1999): 80–99.

Josephy, Alvin M., Jr. *500 Nations: An Illustrated History of North American Indians.* New York: Gramercy, 1994.

Judd, Richard W. *Common Lands, Common People: The Origins of Conservation in Northern New England.* Cambridge, Mass.: Harvard University Press, 1997.

Keller, Morton. *Regulating a New Society: Public Policy and Social Change in America, 1900-1933.* Cambridge, Mass.: Harvard University Press, 1994.

Kelman, Ari. "Forests and Other River Perils." In *Transforming New Orleans and Its Environs,* edited by Craig E. Colten. Pittsburgh: University of Pittsburgh Press, 2000.

Krech III, Shepard. *The Ecological Indian: Myth and History.* New York: W.W. Norton, 1999.

Lacey, Michael J., ed. *Government and Environmental Politics: Essays on Historical Developments since World War Two.* Baltimore: Johns Hopkins University Press, 1991.

Larmer, Paul, ed. *Give and Take: How the Clinton Administration's Public Lands Offensive Transformed the American West.* Paonia, Colo.: High Country News Books, 2004.

Leuchtenberg, William E. *The FDR Years: On Roosevelt and His Legacy.* New York: Columbia University Press, 1995.

Lewis, Michael, ed. *American Wilderness: A New History.* New York: Oxford University Press, 2007.

Limerick, Patricia Nelson. *The Legacy of Conquest: The Unbroken Past of the American West.* New York: W.W. Norton, 1988.

Lookingbill, Brad D. *Dust Bowl, USA: Depression America and the Ecological Imagination, 1929–1941.* Athens: Ohio University Press, 2001.

Maher, Neil M. *Nature's New Deal: The Civilian Conservation Corps and the Roots of the American Environmental Movement.* Cambridge, Mass.: Oxford University Press, 2008.

McCloskey, Michael. "Twenty Years of Change in the Environmental Movement." *Society and Natural Resources: An International Journal.* 4, no. 3 (1991): 273–284.

McEvoy, Arthur F. *The Fisherman's Problem: Ecology and Law in the California Fisheries, 1850–1980.* New York: Cambridge University Press, 1986.

Melnick, R. Shep. "Risky Business: Government and the Environment after Earth Day." In *Taking Stock: American Government in the Twentieth Century,* edited by Morton Keller and R. Shep Melnick. New York: Woodrow Wilson Center Press and Cambridge University Press, 1999.

Melosi, Martin, ed. *Pollution and Reform in American Cities, 1870–1930.* Austin: University of Texas Press, 1980.

Merchant, Carolyn. *Ecological Revolutions: Nature, Gender, and Science in New England.* Chapel Hill: University of North Carolina Press, 1989.

Merchant, Carolyn. *Major Problems in American Environmental History.* 2nd ed. Boston: Houghton Mifflin, 2005.

Merk, Frederick. *History of the Westward Movement.* New York: Knopf, 1978.

Milazzo, Paul Charles. *Unlikely Environmentalists: Congress and Clean Water, 1945–1972.* Lawrence: University Press of Kansas, 2006.

Mumford, Lewis. *The City in History: Its Origins, Its Transformations, and Its Prospects.* New York: Harcourt, Brace, 1961.

Nixon, Edgar B., ed. *Franklin D. Roosevelt and Conservation, 1911–1945.* 2 vols. Hyde Park, N.Y.: General Services Administration, 1957.

Nobles, Gregory H. *American Frontiers: Cultural Encounters and Continental Conquest.* New York: Hill and Wang, 1997.

Orsi, Richard J. *Sunset Limited: The Southern Pacific Railroad and the Development of the American West 1850–1930.* Berkeley: University of California Press, 2005.

Palmer, Tim. *Endangered Rivers and the Conservation Movement.* 1986. Rev. ed. Lanham, Md.: Rowman and Littlefield, 2004.

Pendley, William Perry. *War on the West: Government Tyranny on America's Great Frontier.* Washington, D.C.: Regnery, 1995.

Penick, James L. *Progressive Politics and Conservation: The Ballinger-Pinchot Controversy of 1910.* Chicago: University of Chicago Press, 1968.

Percival, Robert V., Alan S. Miller, Christopher H. Schroeder, and James P. Leape. *Environmental Regulation: Law, Science, and Policy.* 2nd ed. Boston: Little, Brown, 1996.

Phillips, Sarah T. *This Land, This Nation: Conservation, Rural America, and the New Deal.* New York: Cambridge University Press, 2007.

Pisani, Donald J. *Water, Land and Law in the West: The Limits of Public Policy.* Lawrence: University Press of Kansas, 1996.

Platt, Harold L. *Shock Cities: The Environmental Transformation and Reform of Manchester and Chicago.* Chicago: University of Chicago Press, 2005.

Reiger, John F. *American Sportsmen and the Origins of Conservation.* 3rd ed. Corvallis: Oregon State University Press, 2001.

Reisner, Marc. *Cadillac Desert: The American West and Its Disappearing Water.* 1986. Rev. ed. New York: Penguin, 1993.

Richardson, Elmo. *Dams, Parks and Politics: Resource Development and Preservation in the Truman-Eisenhower Era.* Lexington: University Press of Kentucky, 1973.

Roberts, David. "Everything You Always Wanted to Know about EPA Greenhouse Gas Regulations, but Were Afraid to Ask." *Grist.org,* September 15, 2009.

Rome, Adam. "Building on the Land: Toward an Environmental History of Residential Development in American Cities and Suburbs, 1870–1990." *Journal of Urban History* 20, no. 3 (May 1994): 408–426.

Rome, Adam. *The Bulldozer in the Countryside: Suburban Sprawl and the Rise of American Environmentalism.* New York: Cambridge University Press, 2001.

Rome, Adam. "Nature Wars, Culture Wars: Immigration and Environmental Reform in the Progressive Era." *Environmental History* (July 2008).

Rosenbaum, Walter A. *Environmental Politics and Policy.* Washington, D.C.: CQ Press, 2008.

Rosner, David, and Gerald Markowitz, eds. *Dying for Work: Workers' Safety and Health in Twentieth-Century America.* Bloomington: Indiana University Press, 1987.

Salisbury, Neil. *Manitou and Providence: Indians, Europeans, and the Making of New England.* New York: Oxford University Press, 1982.

Schlosberg, David. *Defining Environmental Justice: Theories, Movements, and Nature.* New York: Oxford University Press, 2009.

Shabecoff, Philip. *A Fierce Green Fire: The American Environmental Movement.* New York: Hill and Wang, 1993.

Shogren, Jason F., and Tschirhart, John. *Protecting Endangered Species in the United States: Biological Needs, Political Realities, Economic Choices.* New York: Cambridge University Press, 2001

Slotkin, Richard. *The Fatal Environment: The Myth of the Frontier in the Age of Industrialization, 1800–1890.* New York: Atheneum, 1985.

Smith, V. Kerry. *Environmental Policy under Reagan's Executive Order: The Role of Benefit-Cost Analysis.* Chapel Hill: University of North Carolina Press, 1984.

Spence, Mark David. *Dispossessing the Wilderness: Indian Removal and the Making of the National Parks.* New York: Oxford University Press, 2000.

Steinberg, Theodore. *Nature Incorporated: Industrialization and the Waters of New England.* New York: Cambridge University Press, 1991.

Stradling, David. *Smokestacks and Progressives: Environmentalists, Engineers, and Air Quality in America, 1881–1951.* Baltimore: Johns Hopkins University Press, 1999.

Sunstein, Cass R. *Risk and Reason: Safety, Law, and the Environment.* Cambridge University Press, 2004.

Swain, Donald. *Federal Conservation Policy, 1921–1933.* Berkeley: University of California Publications in History, 1963.

Taylor, Alan. *American Colonies.* New York: Viking, 2001.

Tober, James. A. *Who Owns the Wildlife? The Political Economy of Conservation in Nineteenth-Century America.* Westport, Conn.: Greenwood Press, 1981.

Turner, James Morton. "The Politics of Modern Wilderness." In *American Wilderness: A New History,* edited by Michael Lewis. New York: Oxford University Press, 2007.

Utley, Robert M., and Barry Mackintosh. *The Department of Everything Else: Highlights of Interior History.* Washington, D.C.: Department of Interior, 1989.

Vig, Norman J., and Michael E. Kraft, eds. *Environmental Policy in the 1980s: Reagan's New Agenda.* Washington, D.C.: CQ Press, 1984.

Vig, Norman J., and Michael E. Kraft, eds. *Environmental Policy: New Directions for the Twenty-First Century.* Washington, D.C.: CQ Press, 2006.

Warren, Louis. *The Hunter's Game: Poachers and Conservationists in Twentieth-Century America.* New Haven, Conn.: Yale University Press, 1997.

White, Richard. *"It's Your Misfortune and None of My Own": A History of the American West.* Norman: University of Oklahoma Press, 1991.

Wilkins, David E. *The Masking of Justice: American Indian Sovereignty and the U.S. Supreme Court.* Austin: University of Texas Press, 1997.

Wilkinson, Charles. *Crossing the Next Meridian: Land, Water, and the Future of the West.* Washington, D.C.: Island Press, 1993.

Williams, Michael. *Americans and Their Forests: A Historical Geography.* Cambridge: Cambridge University Press, 1989.

Williams, Michael. "Thinking about the Forest." In *The Great Lakes Forest: An Environmental and Social History,* edited by Susan Flader and the Forest History Society. Minneapolis: University of Minnesota Press, 1983.

Wilson, James. *The Earth Shall Weep: A History of Native America.* New York: Atlantic Monthly Press, 1999.

Wilson, William H. *The City Beautiful Movement.* Baltimore: Johns Hopkins University Press, 1994.

Worster, Donald. *Rivers of Empire: Water, Aridity, and the Growth of the American West.* New York: Oxford University Press, 1985.

Zakin, Susan. *Coyotes and Town Dogs: Earth First! and the Environmental Movement.* New York: Penguin, 1993.

Illustration Credits

Index